10th Edition

COST ACCOUNTING
PLANNING AND CONTROL

Milton F. Usry, PhD, CPA

Mary Ball Washington
Professor of Accountancy
College of Business
University of West Florida

Lawrence H. Hammer, DBA, CPA

Professor of Accounting
College of Business Administration
Oklahoma State University

Consulting Editor:
William K. Carter, PhD, CPA

Associate Professor of Accounting
McIntire School of Commerce
University of Virginia

COLLEGE DIVISION South-Western Publishing Co.

CINCINNATI   DALLAS   LIVERMORE

AE88JA

Sponsoring Editor: Mark Hubble   Associate Editor: Nancy Watson
Developmental Editor: Sara Bates   Designer: Joseph M. Devine
Production Editor: Mark Sears   Marketing Manager: Skip Wenstrup

Library of Congress Cataloging-in-Publication Data

Usry, Milton F.
    Cost accounting : planning and control / Milton F. Usry, Lawrence
H. Hammer; consulting editor, William K. Carter. -- 10th ed.
        p.   cm.
    Includes bibliographical references and index.
    ISBN 0-538-80925-6
    1. Cost accounting.   I. Hammer, Lawrence H.   II. Carter, William
K., 1951-   .   III. Title.
HF5686.C8M344   1990
657'.42--dc20   90-44820
                                                       CIP

PREFACE

The tenth edition of COST ACCOUNTING: PLANNING AND CONTROL maintains its focus on the twin management functions of planning and control in the context of modern concepts and techniques. The **planning function** is essentially a decision-making process dealing with the establishment of desired results, the deployment of resources, and the creation of a communication system that permits the reporting and controlling of actual results and the comparison of these results with plans. The **control function** is the systematic effort by management to organize and marshal natural forces, human behavior, and material objects into a coordinated unit in order to accomplish plans.

The connecting link between these functions is the cost accounting information system, rightly termed a tool of management. This system permits effective communication, continuous feedback, and managerial flexibility. The processing and reporting of an organization's historical and projected economic data assist management in developing new potentials, improving present opportunities, establishing more aggressive yet flexible control of operations, and enhancing the management process through objective evaluation of feedback.

Although the information and underlying data required for the planning and control functions often are quite different, the cost accounting information system is expected to respond to the needs of both functions. This dual responsibility of the cost accounting information system strongly influenced the authors in structuring the presentation followed in this textbook.

■ HIGHLIGHTS OF CHANGES IN THE TENTH EDITION

The textbook has undergone a significant reorganization and rewrite throughout to enhance clearness and thoroughness of the coverage. The most noticeable changes from the ninth edition are as follows:

Chapter

1	The planning and control discussion is expanded.
1	The discussion of the role of cost accounting is enhanced.
1	The coverage of professional ethics is expanded and cases are included.
2	The discussion of cost objects and cost traceability is expanded, including examples from service businesses.
2	A discussion of nonfinancial performance measures is added.
3	The discussion of distinctions among different cost systems is expanded.
3	A section on backflush costing is added.
4	The coverage of scrap, spoilage, and defectives is moved to the job order costing chapter.
4	The use of predetermined overhead rates based on factors other than direct labor is emphasized.

Chapter	
4	A section on the use of multiple overhead rates in a single department is added.
4	A section on activity costing is added.
4	A section on job order costing in service businesses is added.
6	Process costing is expanded to discuss the effects of lost units on beginning inventory and to include journal entries related to the cost of production report.
7	The theory of accounting for joint and by-products is elaborated upon.
8	A vendor certificates discussion is added.
9	Optimum production runs assuming noninstantaneous receipts is added.
9	The just-in-time inventory control methods discussion is expanded.
10	A new section is added covering organizational gainsharing incentive plans.
10	The theory and application of the learning curve is further developed.
11	Payroll tax rules and regulations are updated to include new provisions.
12	The use of managerial judgment in cost behavior analysis has been added.
13	The transactions base approach to overhead allocation has been added as an application of activity costing and the principal chapter illustration now applies a machine hour base.
14	The concept of multiple cost pools within single departments is developed.
16	A discussion of budgeting and human behavior has been added.
17	The discussion of the elements of the cash budget have been tied together with a fully illustrated cash budget.
17	The flexible budgeting discussion has been expanded, including illustrations of alternative forms of variance reports.
18	The standard cost discussion has been updated to include consideration of automated production systems.
18	A graphic reconciliation of the different factory overhead variance methods has been added.
20	Direct costing and cost-volume-profit analysis have been integrated into one chapter.
21	Illustrations of the make-or-buy decision, the decision to shut down facilities, and the decision to discontinue products have been added.
22	A discussion of ethical considerations peculiar to capital budgeting has been added.
22	A discussion of strategic considerations and the impact of robotics and flexible manufacturing systems on capital budgeting have been added.
23	The discussion of decision making under conditions of uncertainty has been removed from the differential cost chapter, expanded, and integrated into a separate chapter with capital budgeting under uncertainty.
23	Nonuniform cash flows have been introduced into the capital budgeting evaluation methods under uncertainty.

■ ORGANIZATION OF THE BOOK

Parts One and Two of the tenth edition fuse planning and control into a functional whole by first presenting fundamental cost accounting concepts and objectives, followed by a comprehensive illustration depicting the flow of costs in a manufacturing enterprise, including its interface with the balance sheet and income statement. Cost data accumulation procedures using backflush costing and job order and process costing are then developed as a fundamental means of providing reliable cost data.

Part Three deals with the cost elements of materials and labor from both the planning and control phases, followed by consideration of cost behavior analysis which provides the foundation for cost planning and control. The part concludes with an in-depth treatment of factory overhead and responsibility accounting.

Part Four elaborates on the heart of the planning function—budgeting—including the flexible budget. This part also treats standard costing, which is basic to effective cost control.

Part Five, the final section, covers the entire spectrum of analysis of costs and profits, including direct costing; cost-volume-profit analysis; differential cost analysis including linear programming; the planning, evaluating, and control of capital expenditures; decision making under uncertainty; marketing cost and profitability analysis, including gross profit analysis; profit performance measurements; and transfer pricing.

Like many other disciplines, cost accounting has been influenced by the development of quantitative techniques and behavioral science concepts. These tools and their applications are presented in a clear and concise manner throughout the textbook as they relate to particular topics. Also, the appropriate consideration of income tax effects is integrated throughout this edition, as is the relevance of inflation's impact on the management process. The concepts and techniques developed in this textbook are intended to have broad applicability to all phases of business and not-for-profit organizations, both large and small.

■ ORGANIZATION FOR INSTRUCTION

The presentation of the fundamental theoretical and practical aspects of cost accounting provides wide flexibility for classroom usage. In addition to its applicability to the traditional two-semester course sequence, the textbook may be used in a variety of one-semester courses. For these alternative courses, a suggested outline, by chapter numbers, follows:

Course	Textbook Chapters
Cost Accounting (two-semester course)	Chapters 1–15 (first semester)
	Chapters 16–25 (second semester)
Cost Accounting (one-semester course)	Chapters 1–15 and 20
Cost Control (one-semester course)	Chapters 1–4, 8–15, 18–19
Budgetary Control (one-semester course)	Chapter 1–4, 12, 16–20, 22
Cost Analysis (one-semester course)	Chapters 12, 16–25

■ END-OF-CHAPTER MATERIALS

Most of the end-of-chapter materials are new or revised and include discussion questions, exercises, problems, and cases. For each topic, these materials afford coverage of relevant concepts and techniques at progressive levels in the learning process, thereby providing a significant student-learning benefit. Selected items with which the template diskette and/or the tools diskette may be used are designated by the following icons: 🆂🆂 spread sheet template and/or 🅳🅰 decision assistant tool. The end-of-chapter materials include numerous items from the examinations administered by the American Institute of Certified Public Accountants (AICPA adapted), the Institute of Certified Management Accountants of the National Association of Accountants (ICMA adapted), the Institute of Internal Auditors (CIA adapted), the Canadian Institute of Chartered Accountants (CICA adapted), the Certified General Accountants' Association of Canada (CGA-Canada adapted), and the Society of Management Accountants of Canada (SMAC adapted). The authors are indebted to these organizations for permission to use their materials.

■ SUPPLEMENTARY MATERIALS

The materials accompanying the text include a solutions manual, an instructor's manual, transparencies of solutions and illustrations, an examinations booklet, and software. For the student, a study guide, four practice cases, and check figures are available.

For the Instructor

Solutions Manual. This manual contains detailed solutions to the end-of-chapter materials, including the discussion questions, exercises, problems, and cases. A listing of items coded for use with the template diskette and/or the tools diskette is provided.

Instructor's Manual, prepared by William K. Carter of the McIntire School of Commerce, University of Virginia. This manual contains a Summary section, which gives an abbreviated restatement of the contents of each chapter; and a Discussion section, which gives additional material for use in responding to students' questions and in clarifying some of the more difficult points in a chapter. In addition, a schedule of concepts covered by the exercises and problems, and a schedule of estimated time requirements for solving problems are included.

Transparencies. Transparencies of solutions to all exercises, problems, and cases are available. Also included with the transparencies are illustrations from the textbook.

Examinations Booklet, prepared by Edward J. VanDerbeck of Xavier University, Cincinnati. A test bank of multiple choice questions and examination problems, with solutions, is available to adopters. Care has been taken to check these materials which may be readily reproduced by those instructors who wish to construct their own tests. A microcomputer version (MicroSWAT III) of the test bank is available also.

Template Diskette. This data disk is used with Lotus® 1-2-3® [1] for solving selected end-of-chapter exercises and problems. This diskette is copyable and may be ordered, upon adoption, from South-Western Publishing Co.

Tools Diskette. The Decision Assistant software diskette, which is designed for use with the IBM PC[2], contains eight basic procedures that solve the following types of problems: inventory planning models, cost behavior analysis, factory overhead service department allocation, standard cost variance analysis, gross profit analysis, probability analysis, linear programming routines, and capital expenditure analysis.

For the Student

Study Guide, prepared by Edward J. VanDerbeck. This study guide contains a brief summary of each chapter, as well as questions and exercises with answers, thus providing students with immediate feedback on their comprehension of material. This material has been checked for correctness.

---

[1]Lotus 1-2-3 are trademarks of the Lotus Development Corporation. Any reference to Lotus 1-2-3 refers to this footnote.
[2]IBM is a registered trademark of International Business Machines Corporation. Any reference to the IBM Personal Computer refers to this footnote.

Practice Cases, prepared by Lawrence H. Hammer and William K. Carter. Four cases—a job order cost case, a process cost case, a standard cost analysis case, and a budgeting case—are available. Each case acquaints students with basic procedural and analytical characteristics without involving time-consuming details. Also, each case is available in a microcomputer version for use with Lotus 1-2-3. Notes and solutions for the four cases are provided for the instructor.

Check Figures. Instructors may order check figures for distribution to students. These check figures may be used by students in checking their solutions to end-of-chapter problems.

■ ACKNOWLEDGEMENTS

The authors wish to express appreciation to the many users of the previous editions who offered helpful suggestions. Thanks are given to the students and teachers of Oklahoma State University, the University of West Florida, and the University of Virginia who class-tested new materials and made suggestions for improvements.

Colleagues in the teaching profession have been generous in contributing to the ongoing improvement of this text and it ancillary items. Those who devoted time as reviewers include Dr. Thomas Lin, University of Southern California; Dr. Jacob Birnberg, University of Pittsburg; and Dr. Jack Bailes, Oregon State University. For their numerous valuable suggestions we extend special thanks to Professor Ralph Rust of Sinclair Community College, Professor Paul Lewis of Spokane Community College, and to the many other professors who responded to the detailed survey and who have communicated information through South-Western's sales representatives.

We also wish to express our appreciation to our wives, Dona White Usry and Jane Nickelson Hammer, for their assistance and encouragement in the preparation and completion of this as well as earlier editions.

Finally, we wish to express special appreciation to William K. Carter, of the University of Virginia, who reviewed and made contributions to the entire textbook in his position as Consulting Editor.

Milton F. Usry

Lawrence H. Hammer

ABOUT THE AUTHORS

Milton F. Usry is the Mary Ball Washington Professor of Accountancy at the University of West Florida after previously serving on the Oklahoma State University faculty (1961–1986). He earned his BBA from Baylor University, MBA from the University of Houston, PhD from the University of Texas at Austin, and is a CPA. He has written numerous articles, especially in the areas of cost accounting and accounting education. Dr. Usry served as Associate Editor of two American Accounting Association books: *Accounting Education: Problems and Prospects* and *Researching the Accounting Curriculum: Strategies for Change*. He has served on the editorial boards of several national professional journals.

Professor Usry received the Oklahoma State University College of Business Administration Outstanding Teacher Award on three occasions. He has served in numerous professional organizations. Currently his organization service responsibilities include: the American Accounting Association, Accounting Education Advisory Committee; the American Institute of CPAs, Education Executive Committee; and the National Association of Accountants, Committee on Education.

In the area of professional certification, Dr. Usry has been a member of the AICPA Board of Examiners and the Institute of Certified Management Accountants Board of Regents. In the field of government service, he has served on the National Board of the Fund for the Improvement of Postsecondary Education of the U.S. Department of Education.

Lawrence H. Hammer teaches primarily in the areas of cost accounting and income taxation at Oklahoma State University. He earned his BS from Sam Houston State University, MBA from North Texas State University, and DBA from Indiana University at Bloomington, and he is a CPA.

Dr. Hammer is widely published in the tax literature, and he has served on the editorial review boards of *The Accounting Review* and *The Journal of Accounting Education*. He is a member of the American Accounting Association Management Accounting Section, the American Taxation Association, the American Institute of CPAs, and the National Association of Accountants.

William K. Carter teaches cost accounting and managerial accounting at the graduate and undergraduate levels in the McIntire School of Commerce, University of Virginia. He earned BS and MS degrees in accounting from the University of Southern Mississippi and a PhD from Oklahoma State University, and he is a CPA. He has written articles on accounting, accounting education, marketing, and finance, which have appeared in a variety of journals including *The Accounting Review* and the *Journal of Accountancy*. He has published cases on cost accounting and on business policy.

Dr. Carter has served on committees of the American Assembly of Collegiate Schools of Business and the American Accounting Association, and on the editorial boards of *The Journal of Accounting Education* and the Education Section of *The Accounting Review*. He has testified as an expert witness in litigation involving accounting matters and has conducted consulting engagements and executive development programs for clients that include IBM, Babcock & Wilcox, the Institute of Chartered Financial Analysts, the Consumer Bankers Association, and the Administrators of Accounting Programs Group of the American Accounting Association.

Dr. Carter is a member of the National Association of Accountants, the American Institute of CPAs, and the American Accounting Association's Management Accounting Section.

CONTENTS

IN BRIEF

CONTENTS

New sections are shown in green.
Significantly enhanced sections are marked with an asterisk.*

PART 3   PLANNING AND CONTROL OF THE ELEMENTS OF COST

PART 4   BUDGETING AND STANDARD COSTING

▼

PART

1

Costs: Concepts
and Objectives

▼

CHAPTER 1

The Management Concept and the Function of the Controller

The management of a business enterprise is composed of individuals who belong to one of three groups: (1) the operating management group, consisting of supervisors; (2) the middle management group, represented by department heads, division managers, and branch managers; and (3) the executive management group, consisting of the president, the executive vice-presidents, and the executives in charge of the various functions of marketing, purchasing, engineering, manufacturing, finance, and accounting. Executive management is principally concerned with long-range decisions, middle management with decisions of medium-range impact, and operating managers with short-range decisions.

One of management's chief concerns is the effective use of company capital. This capital is invested in productive facilities, such as factory buildings, tools, and equipment, as well as in circulating capital or current assets. The use of this capital is determined by management's short- and long-range plans for the future.

■ THE MANAGEMENT CONCEPT

The management concept may be described by such phrases as "making decisions, giving orders, establishing policies, providing work and rewards, and hiring people to carry out policies." Management sets objectives that may be achieved by integrating its knowledge and skills with the ability and experience of the employees. To be successful, management must effectively perform the basic functions of planning, organizing, and control. Planning and organizing are primarily functions of executive management, while control is principally the duty of operating management. All three functions require appropriate participation of the various levels of the management team.

For theoretical purposes, planning and control are divided. Similarly, time frames are divided into discrete operating periods. However, one must keep in mind that these divisions are artificially designed for the convenience of analysis and for operations management and do not reflect the dynamic manner in which an entity evolves and changes. In the reality of management, planning and control are simultaneous, inseparable, interwoven processes.

Time frames such as short- and long-range periods are not clearly distinguishable. Control of an activity takes place simultaneously with the planning for the next cycle of that same activity, and simultaneously with the planning and control of other activities. Plans are made for the immediate future and for the long term, controlled action takes place, feedback from operations is obtained, plans are adjusted, and the continuum repeats itself.[1]

Planning

Planning refers to the construction of a detailed operating program for all phases of operations. Planning is the process of sensing external opportunities and threats, determining desirable objectives, and employing resources to accomplish these objectives. Planning includes such areas of investigation as the nature of the company's business, its major policies, and the timing of major steps and other factors related to short-range and to long-range plans. Effective planning is based on analyses of collected facts. Such analyses require reflective thinking, imagination, and foresight in order to make rational decisions.

The establishment of an effective plan also requires the participation and coordination of the engineering, manufacturing, marketing, research, finance, and accounting functions. No single group should plan and act independently from other groups. Failure to recognize this fundamental principle may cause unnecessary planning difficulties and may result in financial disaster for the organization.

Closely allied with proper planning is the determination of company objectives. An objective is a measurable target or end result. In stating the objectives of a business enterprise, many people point to the need for realizing a profit. Although profits are the indispensable element in a successful business, profit is a limited concept in today's economic society. Profits cannot remain the sole objective of a business enterprise. The companies best

SERVICE ENTITIES   able to maximize profits are those which produce products or render services at an excellent level of quality and value, in a volume, at a time, at a cost, and at a price that will, in the long run, assure a profit and also win the cooperation of employees, gain the goodwill of customers, and meet social responsibilities. Business logic and changing public expectations suggest that plans should be formulated within a framework of four major parameters—economic, technological, social, and political.

Three kinds of plans are identifiable in business entities. *Strategic plans* are formulated at the highest levels of management, take the broadest view of the company and its environment, are the least quantifiable, and are formulated at irregular intervals by an essentially unsystematic process that begins with identifying an external threat or opportunity. Strategic planning involves fundamental decisions that will determine the future nature of the firm, its products, and its customers, and that have the potential to alter the firm's external

---

[1]*Management Accounting Guidelines*, No. 3, "Framework for Internal Control (exposure draft)" (Hamilton, Ontario: The Society of Management Accountants of Canada, 1984).

environment. *Short-range plans*, often called budgets, are sufficiently detailed and thorough to permit preparation of a budgeted set of financial statements for the entity as of some future date, typically the date corresponding to the end of the budget period. These plans are prepared through a systematized process, are highly quantified, are expressed in financial terms, focus mainly on the organization itself by taking the external environment as a given, and are usually prepared for periods of a quarter or year. In addition to these two very different kinds of plans, there are the long-range plans prepared by some entities. *Long-range plans*, sometimes called long-range budgets, typically extend three to five years into the future. In terms of degree of detail and quantifiability, long-range plans are an intermediate step between short-range plans and strategic plans. For example, a long-range plan may culminate in a highly summarized set of financial statements, or some other set of quantified objectives such as targeted values of important financial ratios (e.g., earnings per share and growth rates) as of a date five years in the future. Ideally, as a long-range plan is revised and refined during the early portions of the planning period, it serves as a starting point for preparing each successive set of short-range plans.

Planning is one of the most complex of all human activities, and is a fruitful and challenging area of study for accountants, business strategists, economists, political scientists, and others.

Organizing

Organizing, essentially, is the establishment of the framework within which required activities are to be performed. The terms "organize" and "organization" refer to the systematization of various interdependent parts into one unit. Organizing requires (1) bringing the many functional units of an enterprise into a well-coordinated structure and (2) assigning authority and responsibility to certain individuals. These organizational efforts include the task of motivating people to work together for the good of the company. Because of the attitudes and ambitions of the many persons involved, the desired organizational structure is developed through instruction and patience.

Creation of an organization involves the establishment of functional divisions, departments, sections, or branches. These units are created for the purpose of dividing tasks, which leads to specialization of labor. A manufacturing enterprise usually consists of at least three large fundamental activities: manufacturing, marketing, and administration. Within these three units, numerous departments are formed according to the nature and the amount of work, the degree of specialization, the number of employees, and the location of the work.

After organizational units have been created, management must assign the work to be done within each unit. The appropriate distribution of work among employees is vital to the attainment of company objectives. Of greater importance to a company's success are the relationships between superiors and subordinates and among managers within the management team.

Control

Control is management's systematic effort to achieve objectives by comparing performance to plans and taking appropriate action to correct important differences. Activities should be continually supervised if management expects to stay within previously defined boundaries. Actual results of each activity classification are compared with plans, and if significant differences are noted, remedial actions may be taken. The following diagram illustrates the control process:

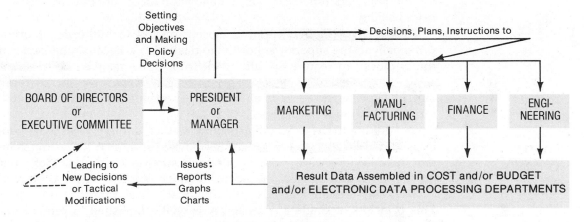

Control Diagram

This concept of control in business differs from that used in engineering, where controls are designed to work continuously, to use physical measures as their information inputs, and to work largely independent of human decision making. Thermostats, fuses, and pressure-release valves are simple examples of engineering controls. In contrast, the control process in business always includes a human decision maker, the information on which control actions are based includes much financial information, and the control activity is continual (periodic) rather than continuous.

The concept of control in business also differs from that of military science and police work, in which the need for coercive force is always possible, although undesirable, in achieving control. In business, control is achieved through others' actions only with their implicit or explicit cooperation.

Authority, Responsibility, and Accountability

In a small company, planning and control activities are generally performed by one person without elaborate analysis. This person probably will be the owner or general manager, who has an intimate knowledge of employees, materials, financing, and customers. In a large company with numerous divisions and a variety of products or services, planning and control of the activities of individual units is complex. For this reason, large firms assign the planning and control functions to more than one person, so that reports and any corrective actions are closer to the activity.

Authority is the power to direct others to perform or not perform activities. Authority is the key to the managerial job and the basis for responsibility. It is the force that binds the organization together.

Authority originates with executive management, which delegates it to the various managerial levels. Such delegation is essential to the existence of an organizational structure. Through delegation, the chief executive's area of operations is extended. However, the chief executive retains overall authority for assigned functions, since delegation does not mean release from responsibility.

Responsibility, or obligation, is closely related to authority. It originates principally in the superior-subordinate relationship because the superior has the authority to require specific work from other people. As these people accept the obligation to perform the work, they create their own responsibility. The superior, however, is ultimately responsible for the subordinates' performance or nonperformance.

In addition to the aspect of achieving results, another facet of responsibility is *accountability*—reporting results to higher authority. Reporting is important because it makes possible the measurement—in terms of quantity, quality, time, and cost—of the extent to which objectives have been reached.

Basically, accountability is an individual rather than a group problem. This principle of single accountability is well established in profit and nonprofit organizations. If the organizational structure permits pooling of judgment, responsibility is diffused and accountability is nullified. Without single accountability, control reports would not only be meaningless, but corrective actions would be delayed or not forthcoming at all.

QUALITY
CONTROL

The Organization Chart

The organization chart sets forth each principal management position and helps to define authority, responsibility, and accountability. An organization chart is essential to the development of a cost accounting system and cost reports which indicate the responsibilities of individuals for implementing management plans. The coordinated development of a company's organization with the cost and budgetary system will lead to an approach to accounting and reporting called *responsibility accounting.*

Generally, an organization chart is based on the line-staff concept. The basic assumption of this concept is that all positions or functional divisions may be categorized into two groups: the line, which makes decisions and performs the true management functions and the staff, which gives advice or performs any technical functions. A line-staff organization chart is illustrated on page 7.

Another type of organization chart is based on the functional-teamwork concept of management, which is structured to emphasize the most important functions of an enterprise: resources, processes, and human interrelations. The *resources function* involves the acquisition, disposal, and prudent

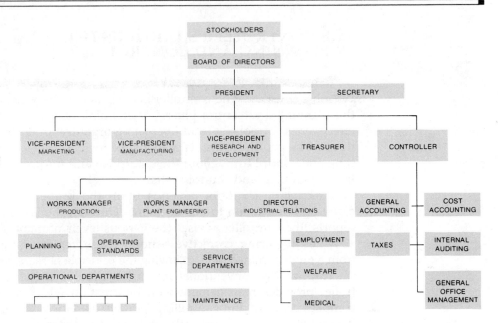

Organization Chart Based on Line-Staff Concept

management of a wide variety of resources—tangible and intangible, human and physical. The *processes function* deals with activities such as product design, research and development, purchasing, manufacturing, advertising, marketing, and billing. The *human interrelations function* directs the company's efforts in relation to the behavior of people inside and outside the company. An organization chart based on the functional-teamwork concept is illustrated as follows:

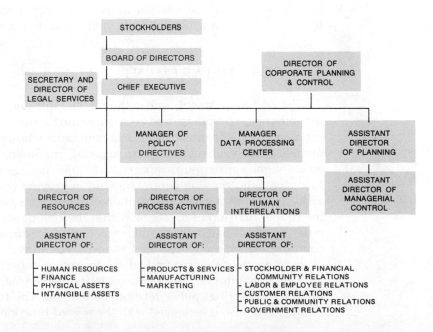

Organization Chart Based on Functional-Teamwork Concept

■ THE CONTROLLER'S PARTICIPATION IN PLANNING AND CONTROL

The controller is the executive manager responsible for a company's accounting function. The controller coordinates management's participation in the planning and control phases of attaining objectives, in determining the effectiveness of policies, and in creating organizational structures and procedures. The controller also is responsible for observing the methods of planning and control throughout the enterprise and for proposing improvements in the planning and control system.

Effective cost control depends upon the proper communication of accounting information to management. Through the issuance of performance reports, the controller advises the various levels of management in regard to activities requiring corrective action. These reports emphasize deviations from a predetermined plan, following the principle of management by exception.

Through the conventional accounting system and other models, the controller provides management with information which it uses in planning a company's future and controlling its daily activities. The models include the balance sheet, the income statement, and the statement of cash flows, which are based on historical dollars. The controller also gathers, compiles, and communicates much information which is beyond the scope of these models, yet is obtainable from the accounting system and other information systems.

External users, including stockholders, future investors, and government agencies, also must receive information by which management's effectiveness may be judged. This information is usually communicated to external users via the company's quarterly and annual reports, which include the basic financial statements of the company. These statements lack the depth of explanatory detail available to internal decision makers, because it is impossible to include all the data which the large variety of external users would find useful.

■ THE COST DEPARTMENT

The cost department, under the direction of the controller, is responsible for gathering, compiling, and communicating a variety of information regarding a company's manufacturing and nonmanufacturing activities. This department also analyzes costs of manufacturing, marketing, and administration. It issues significant control reports and other decision-making data to those managers who assist in controlling and improving costs and operations. The analysis of costs and the preparation of reports are greatly facilitated through the proper division of functions within the cost department. These functions must be coordinated with other accounting functions, such as general accounting, which are closely tied to cost accounting.

In addition to the cost and other accounting departments, a company may have one or more of the following departments: manufacturing, personnel, treasury, marketing, public relations, and legal. The functions of the cost department are also coordinated with the related functions of these departments.

The *manufacturing departments*, under the direction of engineers and factory superintendents, design and control production. In research and design, cost estimates for each type of material, labor, and machine process are used in deciding whether to accept or reject a design. Likewise, the scheduling, producing, and inspecting of jobs and products by the manufacturing departments are measured for efficiency in terms of quantities, quality, and the costs incurred and, to the extent practical, in terms of the benefits provided.

The *personnel department* interviews and selects employees for various job classifications. It maintains personnel records, which include the wage rates and the methods of remuneration for each employee. This information forms the basis for computing payroll costs and for calculating the labor-related components of the cost of any activity, service, or good that is produced.

The *treasury department* is responsible for the financial administration of a company. In scheduling cash requirements and expectations, it relies upon budgets and related reports from the cost department.

The *marketing department* needs a good product at a competitive price in order to attract customers. While prices should not be set merely by adding a predetermined percentage to cost, costs cannot be ignored. Marketing managers use pertinent cost data to determine which products are most profitable and to determine sales policies.

The *public relations department* has the primary function of maintaining good relations between the company and its public, especially its customers and stockholders. Points of friction are most likely to be prices, wages, profits, and dividends. The cost department may be asked to provide basic information for public releases concerning policies in these areas.

The *legal department* uses cost information as an aid in maintaining company affairs according to law. Some of these legal areas include the Equal Pay Act, terms of industry-wide union contracts, the Robinson-Patman Act, social security taxes, unemployment compensation, the Employee Retirement Security Act of 1974, and income tax.

■ THE ROLE OF COST ACCOUNTING

In the past, cost accounting was often regarded as being limited to the calculation of an inventory cost for presentation in a balance sheet and the corresponding cost of goods sold figure for an income statement. This view limits the broad range of information that managers need for decision making to the kinds of inventory costings that satisfy the reporting requirements of tax regulations and generally accepted accounting principles. Such a restrictive definition is inappropriate today, and is certainly inaccurate as a description of the present uses of cost accounting information. Cost accounting

QUALITY CONTROL should furnish management with the necessary accounting tools for planning and controlling activities, improving quality and efficiency, and making both routine and strategic decisions. Specifically, the collection, presentation, and analysis of information regarding costs and benefits helps management accomplish the following tasks:

1. Creating and executing plans and budgets for operating under expected competitive and economic conditions. An important aspect of plans is their potential for motivating people to perform in a way that is consistent with company goals.
2. Establishing costing methods that permit control of activities, reductions of costs, and improvements of quality.
3. Controlling physical quantities of inventory, and determining the cost of each good or service produced for the purpose of pricing and for evaluating the performance of a product, department, or division.
4. Determining company costs and profit for an annual accounting period or a shorter period. This includes determining the cost of inventory and cost of goods sold according to financial reporting and tax reporting requirements.
5. Choosing from among two or more short-run or long-run alternatives which might increase revenues or decrease costs.

SERVICE ENTITIES

Notice the implied distinction between determining the cost of a product in task #3 and the costing of inventory for external reporting in task #4. The distinction is that the cost of a product (task #3) may be calculated for many purposes, including predicting costs and making decisions, while inventory costing for financial statements (task #4) deals with satisfying external reporting rules. In very simple production settings, the two are often the same. For example, if all units produced in a facility are alike, any reasonable way of dividing the total cost equally among the units will suffice for both external reporting and for many decision-making purposes. While the costs incurred in such a setting may be large and complex, the product line is extremely simple—all units are identical—and so the costing of each unit of the product is simple, too. This is the model of manufacturing that is generally assumed in economic theory.

Actual manufacturing settings usually are much more complicated than the economist's model. A firm can produce a diverse product line in a single facility, where an individual machine or some other important component of cost is used in the production of several very different products. In addition to a complicated product line, some actual settings exhibit complicated cost structures, and the combination of the two makes it difficult to predict or even to identify the costs of producing one unit of one product. In these complicated settings, the challenge to cost accounting is to measure the cost of all the things that are used up in making a unit, batch, or lot of one particular product. When precision is needed in such a calculation (for example, in quoting a fiercely competitive price to a customer who wants to buy one million units or batches), then the level of detail needed in calculating cost goes far beyond anything required by external reporting rules.

In sum, the information needs of managers range from simple to complex, depending on a large number of factors that include the diversity of the product line produced in a single facility, the particular decision or prediction to be made, and the current competitive environment. In contrast, the nature of inventory costing required in external reporting is constant through time unless an external reporting rule is changed, and it must satisfy the following: (a) it must be based on actual historical costs, verifiable through documented transactions; (b) it must be consistent from period to period; and (c) it must include all manufacturing costs in the cost calculated for each unit.

Even in a factory that has a complex cost structure, a fiercely competitive market, and a diverse product line, the simplest cost accounting systems can meet these external inventory costing requirements (task #4). There is a dangerous tendency among some executives to support only the amount of cost accounting effort that minimally satisfies external inventory costing rules, ignoring managers' potentially much greater needs for detailed, reliable product cost information (task #3).

Budgeting

The *budget* is the quantified, written expression of management's plans. All levels of management should be involved in creating the budget program and welding it into a homogeneous unit. A workable, realistic budget will not only help promote coordination of people, clarification of policies, and crystallization of plans, but it will also create greater internal harmony and unanimity of purpose among managers and workers.

In recent years, considerable attention has been given to the behavioral implications of providing managers with the data required for planning and control of activities. Cost accounting and budgeting play an important role in influencing individual and group behavior at all stages of the management process, including: (1) setting goals; (2) informing individuals about what they must do to contribute to the accomplishment of these goals; (3) motivating desirable performance; (4) evaluating performance; and (5) suggesting when corrective action should be taken. In short, accountants cannot ignore the behavioral sciences (psychology, social-psychology, and sociology) because the decision-making function of accounting is essentially a behavioral function.

An individual manager's attitude toward the budget will depend greatly upon the existing good relationship within the management group. Guided by the company plan, with an opportunity for increased compensation, greater satisfaction, and eventually promotion, the middle and lower management group might achieve remarkable results. On the other hand, a discordant management group, unwilling to accept the budget's underlying figures, might show such poor performance that the administration would be compelled to defer implementation of the planning and control concept.

The following elements have been suggested as a means for motivating personnel to aim for the goals set forth in the budget:[2]

1. A compensation system that builds and maintains a clearly understood relationship between results and rewards.
2. A system for performance appraisal that employees understand with regard to their individual effectiveness and key results, their tasks and

---

[2]Paul E. Sussman, "Motivating Financial Personnel," *The Journal of Accountancy,* Vol. 141, No. 2, p. 80.

their responsibilities, their degree and span of influence in decision making, as well as the time allowed to judge their results.

3. A system of communication that allows employees to query their superiors with trust and honest communication.
4. A system of promotion that generates and sustains employee faith in its validity and judgment.
5. A system of employee support through coaching, counseling, and career planning.
6. A system that not only considers company objectives, but also employees' skills and capacities.
7. A system that will not settle for mediocrity, but which reaches for realistic and attainable standards, stressing improvement and providing an environment in which the concept of excellence can grow.

Empirical research in this field aids in providing a useful understanding of the interrelationships of budgeting and human behavior. Numerous research projects have been undertaken and more of such research is needed. To illustrate the insights that can be offered by such studies, the results of one research project indicated that budgetary participation and budget goal clarity had positive and significant effects on managers' job-related and budget-related attitudes as well as on their budgetary performance, while excessively high goals that were difficult to attain resulted in adverse effects on attitudes and performance. The study also found that budgetary evaluation and feedback had only weak or insignificant effects on managers' attitudes and performance.[3] Such conclusions, however, must be viewed as tentative until additional research produces similar results. Budgeting is examined in greater depth in Chapters 16 and 17.

Controlling Costs

The responsibility for cost control should be assigned to specific individuals, who are also accountable for budgeting the costs under their control. Each manager's responsibilities generally should be limited to the costs that are controllable by the manager, and performance should be measured by comparing actual costs with budgeted costs. The responsibility for sales revenues and profits should be assigned to those managers as well. Systems designed to achieve these goals are called *responsibility accounting systems*.

To aid the process of controlling costs, the cost accountant may use *standard costs*. These predetermined costs are established by using information accumulated from past experience and from scientific research. When standards are used, they form the foundation for the budget and for cost reports which identify variances between actual and standard costs. The uses of standard costs are examined in Chapters 18 and 19.

---

[3]Izzettin Kenis, "Effects of Budgetary Goal Characteristics on Managerial Attitudes and Performance," *The Accounting Review*, Vol. LIV, No. 4, pp. 707-721.

An aspect of cost control that is receiving increased attention is the careful identification of the costs of different activities, rather than only the costs of different departments and products. In a complex production setting with a number of very different goods or services being produced, it is common to find that only a small fraction of total activity actually adds any value to the final output. Other activities, called *non-value-added activities*, generally result from the complexity that becomes embedded in such production settings, rather than from the production of any particular good or service. Examples of non-value-added activities in a factory are retrieving, handling, moving materials, expediting, holding inventories, and reworking defective units. Highlighting the costs of non-value-added activities is the first step toward their reduction and, ideally, toward their elimination.

Pricing

Management's pricing policy should assure not only the long-run recovery of all costs, but also the securing of a profit, even under adverse conditions. Although supply and demand usually are determining factors in pricing, the establishment of a profitable sales price requires consideration of costs. The need to submit a competitive bid on a proposed job presents a difficult pricing decision, when there may be little or no past experience in producing the particular kind of good or service involved.

Determining Profits

Cost accounting provides for consistent allocation of historical manufacturing costs to units of products in the ending inventory and to units sold during a period. At the end of a fiscal period, the matching of costs with revenues determines the reported profits for the period. These costs and profits may be reported for segments of the firm or for the entire firm, depending upon management's needs, generally accepted accounting principles, and tax reporting requirements.

The matching process requires an identification of short-run and long-run costs and variable and fixed (capacity) costs. Variable manufacturing costs are assigned first to the units manufactured and then matched with revenue when these units are sold. Variable nonmanufacturing costs typically are matched with sales revenues. Fixed costs are arbitrarily matched with revenues by one of the following alternatives:

1. Matching total fixed costs assigned to a period with revenues of that period (called *direct costing* or *variable costing*).
2. Matching some or all of the fixed manufacturing costs to units of product and matching all other fixed costs with revenues of the period. The fixed manufacturing costs that are matched with units of product are then expensed as part of the income statement's cost of goods sold

figure when those units are sold. This is called *absorption costing* or *full absorption costing,* and is required by generally accepted accounting principles and by tax regulations.

These alternatives give the same reported results in the long run, but yield a different profit for individual short periods such as years. They are examined in more detail in Chapter 20.

Choosing Among Alternatives

Cost accounting is the source of information concerning the different revenues and different costs which might result from alternative courses of action. Based on this information, management must make both short-range and long-range decisions that involve such matters as entering new markets, developing new products, discontinuing products or whole product lines, buying versus making a necessary component of a product, and buying versus leasing equipment. In adding new products and discontinuing existing products, reliable cost information is especially crucial to the competitive success of the firm. Misstated costs create the possibility that undesirable business might be initiated or continued, and that desirable business might be rejected.

Cost Accounting and Manufacturing Technology

ROBOTICS

Factory automation has grown at an accelerated pace. Automation results in capital-intensive processes, often with computerized systems that may involve the use of robot-controlled machinery. Automation is expensive, however, and is not a cure-all for the problems of an obsolete production process. Many problems are rooted in systems and attitudes, and by focusing on those areas first, the firm can reap even greater gains from automation. Employee involvement and motivation represent the first step, and simplification of the existing production system is second. Only then should a large investment in automation be considered. Innovative and experimental applications, including changes in systems and attitudes, now permeate manufacturing from product design and engineering, to production scheduling, the manufacturing process, inventory management, quality control, and strategic decision making.

QUALITY CONTROL

JUST-IN-TIME

Changes in manufacturing technology have spawned a long list of new terminology, including computer-aided design (CAD), computer-aided engineering (CAE), computer-aided manufacturing (CAM), just-in-time production (JIT), computer numerical control machinery (CNC), optimized production technology (OPT), flexible manufacturing systems (FMS), and computer-integrated manufacturing (CIM). These innovations will be discussed in appropriate places in this text.

Such innovative technology and management are drastically changing the nature of costs, e.g., lower inventory levels, less use of labor, and increasing levels of fixed costs. In this new environment, cost accounting systems are being challenged to evolve and take on increased relevance, because reliable cost accounting information has become a competitive weapon.

Inflation's Impact

In the various activities of furnishing relevant information to management, the impact of inflation must be considered. Thus, in the development and use of budgets, in using cost control data, in pricing decisions, in evaluating profit, and in choosing among alternatives, the effect of any change in the purchasing power of the dollar becomes important for the intelligent use of information. Also, the use of physical measures of performance (e.g., pounds of product produced per machine hour of usage) avoids the confusion of the impact of inflation on historical cost financial data.

■ CERTIFICATION AND ETHICS

The subject matter of this textbook, which is broadly described as cost accounting, encompasses the concepts outlined above. These concepts are discussed in detail in the chapters that follow. Those engaged in the activities of cost accounting may be referred to as "management accountants" or "internal accountants." They may also be referred to by their professional certification, *Certified Management Accountant (CMA)*, which was established by the National Association of Accountants (NAA) in 1972 as a formal means of recognizing professional competence and educational achievement in this field.

Requirements for the CMA certificate include passing a four-part examination offered by the Institute of Certified Management Accountants and completing two years of professional experience in management accounting within seven years of having passed the examination. The four parts of the examination are:

1. Economics, finance, and management.
2. Financial accounting and reporting.
3. Management reporting, analysis, and behavioral issues.
4. Decision analysis and information systems.

In 1983, the NAA issued a code of ethics for management (internal or cost) accountants, whether CMAs or not. While individuals practicing as independent certified public accountants have been subject to a code of conduct for many decades, these standards are the first ever issued for management accountants. Such standards should contribute to the public's faith in the integrity of the business community.

The *Standards of Ethical Conduct for Management Accountants* present fifteen responsibilities grouped under four main headings:[4]

Competence

Management accountants have a responsibility to:
- Maintain an appropriate level of professional competence by ongoing development of their knowledge and skills.
- Perform their professional duties in accordance with relevant laws, regulations, and technical standards.
- Prepare complete and clear reports and recommendations after appropriate analyses of relevant and reliable information.

Confidentiality

Management accountants have a responsibility to:
- Refrain from disclosing confidential information acquired in the course of their work except when authorized, unless legally obligated to do so.
- Inform subordinates as appropriate regarding the confidentiality of information acquired in the course of their work and monitor their activities to assure the maintenance of that confidentiality.
- Refrain from using or appearing to use confidential information acquired in the course of their work for unethical or illegal advantage either personally or through third parties.

Integrity

Management accountants have a responsibility to:
- Avoid actual or apparent conflicts of interest and advise all appropriate parties of any potential conflict.
- Refrain from engaging in any activity that would prejudice their ability to carry out their duties ethically.
- Refuse any gift, favor, or hospitality that would influence or would appear to influence their actions.
- Refrain from either actively or passively subverting the attainment of the organization's legitimate and ethical objectives.
- Recognize and communicate professional limitations or other constraints that would preclude responsible judgment or successful performance of an activity.
- Communicate unfavorable as well as favorable information and professional judgments or opinions.
- Refrain from engaging in or supporting any activity that would discredit the profession.

Objectivity

Management accountants have a responsibility to:
- Communicate information fairly and objectively.
- Disclose fully all relevant information that could reasonably be expected to influence an intended user's understanding of the reports, comments, and recommendations presented.

The standards also outline procedures for management accountants to follow if they have knowledge of, or think they are being asked to do, something unethical. The procedures call for discussion with each superior level of management including the board of directors, if necessary, until the matter is resolved. If the management accountant's superior appears to be involved, the problem should be presented initially to the next higher managerial level.

---

[4]"Standards of Ethical Conduct" (New York: National Association of Accountants, 1989). Copyright June 1, 1983 by the National Association of Accountants. All rights reserved. Reprinted by permission.

If no internal resolution is achieved, the standards specify that the accountant should resign. Communication of internal problems to authorities or individuals outside the organization is not considered appropriate unless required by law.

■ THE INFLUENCE OF PRIVATE AND GOVERNMENTAL ORGANIZATIONS

In the private sector, major research and pronouncements by professional organizations contribute to the development, improvement, and revision of both financial and cost accounting theory and practice. These organizations include the Financial Accounting Standards Board (FASB), the Governmental Accounting Standards Board (GASB), the American Institute of Certified Public Accountants (AICPA), the National Association of Accountants (NAA), the American Accounting Association (AAA), and the Financial Executives Institute (FEI). In addition, accounting is influenced by public accounting firms, nonprofit organizations, university research, individuals, and private companies.

The rapid growth of international business activities has led several international organizations to become involved in setting standards of accounting and reporting. These organizations include the International Accounting Standards Committee (IASC) and the Organization for Economic Cooperation and Development (OECD).

In the public sector, federal, state, and local governments prescribe regulations that may often be embodied in the accounting system. At the federal level, the Securities and Exchange Commission (SEC), the Internal Revenue Service (IRS), and the pronouncements of the Cost Accounting Standards Board (CASB) have a significant influence on financial and cost reporting.

Securities and Exchange Commission

The federal government, through the actions of the SEC and other regulatory agencies, is showing an increasing interest in the external reports of private companies. In *Regulation S-X*, requirements are set forth for financial statements filed with the SEC.

Congress and the Internal Revenue Code

Federal income tax liability is determined in accordance with the Internal Revenue Code[5] as enacted and amended by Congress. The Treasury Department, acting under authority granted by Congress, issues regulations[6] which

---

[5]*Title 26 of the United States Code.*
[6]*Title 26 of the Code of Federal Regulations.*

interpret the tax statutes enacted by Congress. Although the Internal Revenue Service (IRS) is actually the Treasury Department's enforcement branch, charged with the responsibility of collecting the tax, it issues rulings and procedures as guidance to taxpayers.[7] The influence of the income tax statutes, regulations, rulings, and procedures on financial statements and cost accounting procedures cannot be ignored. Any meaningful analysis for planning and decision making must carefully consider federal as well as state and local tax consequences.

Cost Accounting Standards Board

On August 15, 1970, Congress established the Cost Accounting Standards Board. The purposes of the board, as outlined in an amendment to Section 719 of the Defense Production Act of 1950, were stated as follows:

> *The Board shall from time to time promulgate cost-accounting standards designed to achieve uniformity and consistency in the cost-accounting principles followed by defense contractors and subcontractors under Federal contracts. Such promulgated standards shall be used by all relevant Federal agencies and by defense contractors and subcontractors in estimating, accumulating, and reporting costs in connection with the pricing, administration, and settlement of all negotiated prime contract and subcontract national defense procurements with the United States in excess of $100,000, other than contracts or subcontracts where the price negotiated is based on (1) established catalog or market prices of commercial items sold in substantial quantities to the general public, or (2) prices set by law or regulation. In promulgating such standards . . . the Board shall take into account the probable costs of implementation . . . compared to the probable benefits. . . . Such regulations shall require defense contractors and subcontractors as a condition of contracting to disclose in writing their cost-accounting principles, including methods of distinguishing direct costs from indirect costs and the basis used for allocating indirect costs, and to agree to a contract price adjustment, with interest, for any increased costs paid to the defense contractor by the United States because of the defense contractor's failure to comply with duly promulgated cost-accounting standards or to follow consistently his disclosed cost-accounting practices in pricing contract proposals and in accumulating and reporting contract performance cost data.*

On September 30, 1980, the CASB was dissolved because Congress believed that the board's purpose of establishing basic cost accounting standards had been accomplished. However, the board's standards, rules, and regulations are incorporated into all major federal procurement regulations, and they are currently in effect. The board was reestablished by Congress in 1988 and was given the same authority as before.

Significant Standards Issued. The CASB has issued a series of Cost Accounting Standards (CASs), which govern the determination and allocation of specific costs. These standards are defined as formal statements that (1) enunciate a principle or principles to be followed, (2) establish practices to be applied, or (3) specify criteria to be employed in selecting from alternative principles and practices in estimating, accumulating, and reporting costs of

---

[7]Revenue Rulings and Revenue Procedures are published weekly in the *Internal Revenue Bulletin* and semiannually in the *Cumulative Bulletin*.

contracts subject to the rules of the board. To achieve increased uniformity and consistency in accounting for costs of negotiated contracts, the standards provide criteria for the allocation of the cost of resources used to cost objectives. Cost in this discussion is the monetary value of the resources used. As defined by the board, a cost objective is "a function, organizational subdivision, contract, or other work unit for which cost data are desired and for which provision is made to accumulate and measure the cost of processes, products, jobs, capitalized projects, etc." CASs deal with all aspects of cost allocability, including:

1. The definition and measurement of costs which may be allocated to cost objectives.
2. The determination of the cost accounting period to which such costs are assignable.
3. The determination of the methods by which costs are to be allocated to cost objectives.

The board's pronouncements adhere to the concept of full costing whenever appropriate. Full allocation of all costs of a period, including general administrative expenses and all other indirect costs, is considered to be the basis for determining the cost of negotiated defense contracts.

Although specific CASs are discussed as appropriate in subsequent chapters, it should be noted here that three of the standards—CASs 409, 414, and 417—have the potential for impact far beyond the government contracting area. CAS 409 requires contractors to depreciate their assets for contract costing purposes over lives that are based on documented historical usefulness, irrespective of the lives used for either financial or income tax purposes. CASs 414 and 417 recognize as a contract cost the imputed cost of capital committed to facilities, thereby overturning the government's longstanding practice of disallowing interest and other financing-type costs.

Contractor's Coverage. The CASB standards are to be followed by defense contractors and subcontractors in estimating, accumulating, and reporting costs for negotiated contracts in excess of $100,000. Since all nondefense agencies have also implemented the CASB's standards, rules, and regulations, most negotiated contracts and subcontracts in which the United States is a party are subject to these standards. The standards have also been adopted by some state and local governments.

On January 1, 1975, smaller contractors and business units with insignificant amounts of government business were removed from the CASB's coverage. Coverage now extends only to business units (segments or profit centers) of a contractor that has received a covered prime or subcontract in excess of $500,000. Once a business unit receives such a contract, it must comply with applicable standards for all subsequently awarded prime or subcontracts in excess of $100,000 unless otherwise exempt. The coverage ceases only when all covered contracts in excess of $100,000 are completed by a contractor and becomes operative again for contracts in excess of $100,000 upon acceptance of an award exceeding $500,000. A firm qualifying as a small business under the regulations of the Small Business Administration is exempt from the CASB's requirements.

In 1978, the Board issued a rule exempting contracts and subcontracts awarded to foreign concerns and governments from most CASB standards. The exemptions are intended to remove impediments to efficient and successful contracting with foreign groups.

Statement of Disclosure. As a condition of contracting, contractors can be required to disclose in writing their cost accounting practices. For this purpose, the board provided for a detailed disclosure statement. The instructions pertaining thereto indicate that a contractor must state the practices of each profit center, division, or similar organizational unit. A *profit center* is defined as "the smallest organizationally independent segment of a company which has been charged by management with profit and loss responsibility."

Although a detailed presentation of the disclosure statement is beyond the scope of this text, it should be noted that the statement requires information regarding the three major elements of direct costs (direct materials, direct labor, and other direct costs); the methods used to charge out materials (fifo, lifo, standard costs, or others); the accumulation of variances; the method of charging direct labor (individual/actual rates, average rates, standard cost rates, or others) and a description of the types of variances; the method used to cost interorganizational transfers; and the allocation bases used for charging indirect costs to government contracts or similar cost objectives.

DISCUSSION QUESTIONS

Q1-1. Define the concepts of planning and control and discuss how they relate to each other and contribute to progress toward achieving objectives.

Q1-2. Distinguish between short-range and long-range plans.

Q1-3. Distinguish between long-range plans and strategic plans.

Q1-4. Is responsibility accounting identical with the concept of accountability? Explain.

Q1-5. In what manner does the controller exercise control over the activities of other members of management?

Q1-6. Discuss the functions of the cost department.

Q1-7. Numerous nonaccounting departments require cost data and must also feed basic data to the cost department. Discuss.

Q1-8. Why must the controller be aware of the latest developments in the field of communications?

Q1-9. Why is the budget an essential tool in cost planning?

Q1-10. Will the *Standards of Ethical Conduct for Management Accountants* prevent management fraud? Explain.

Q1-11. How are CASB standards defined and what degree of authority do they have?

CASES

C1-1. Planning and control. In practice, planning and control are inseparable. One example of their inseparability is the fact that the results of control activity serve as inputs for the next planning cycle, i.e., a control effort or investigation may point to a flaw in planning, and the flaw is then corrected in formulating the next period's plans.

Required: Give at least two other examples showing how planning and control are inextricably linked.

C1-2. Planning. Identify each of the following as an example of one of the three kinds of planning in business by writing A, B, or C for each item.

> A = an example of a short-range plan
> B = an example of a long-range plan
> C = an example of a strategic plan

(1) The number of units of product expected to be sold in the next year.
(2) A plan for discontinuing one of the two divisions of the company.
(3) A forecast, made in the year 19A, of total sales revenue expected for the years 19B, 19C, and 19D.
(4) A plan to be the first company to establish a biomedical research lab on an orbiting space station.
(5) Estimates of quarterly net income for the remaining three quarters of the current year.
(6) A 1993 sinking-fund agreement calling for annual cash deposits sufficient to retire outstanding bonds that will mature in the year 2000.

C1-3. Control. Each of the following paragraphs describes a kind of control:

(a) After suffering heavy casualties in a three-day battle, allied units gained control of Hill 334 and captured the enemy communications post at that location.
(b) A student desires to earn a grade average of at least 90% in a cost accounting course. On the first quiz, the student receives a grade of 80%. Upon learning of this grade, the student decides to study more earnestly and to work more homework problems before each of the remaining quizzes.
(c) A homeowner has worked hard to make a lawn free of weeds, and wants to keep it that way during an upcoming two-year vacation. Before leaving, the homeowner contracts with the local franchise of Weed-Chem Company for five lawn treatments per year for two years. The treatments are guaranteed to control weeds.
(d) It is desired to keep water in a tank at a level between one and two inches below the brim. A water pressure line is installed in the tank with a valve to start and stop the flow, an arm attached to the valve, and a hollow plastic float on the end of the arm. Whenever the water level is two inches or more below the brim, the float drops low enough to open the valve. When the water level is one inch from the brim, the float raises the arm which closes the valve.

Required:

(1) Determine which one of the four paragraphs describes a kind of control that comes closest to what control means in managing a business. Explain.
(2) Take each one of the other three paragraphs in turn, and tell why it lacks some essential attribute(s) of management control.

C1-4. Ethics. Joseph Rodriquez is the controller of the Ceramics Division (CD) of Northeastern Company. Joseph reports directly to the CD general manager, Susan Czeisla. One of Joseph's responsibilities is obtaining data from all CD department managers to prepare annual budgets. The current year's budget reflects a CD sales increase of 8% over last year, compared with the usual 4% to 6% annual sales increases experienced in the past. The CD sales manager has assured Joseph that the 8% increase is attainable, and the CD production manager has pointed out that the plant operated at only 75 % of capacity last year, so ample production capacity is available to sustain the planned sales increase.

At the end of the first quarter of the current year, CD sales were 1% below budget. Joseph was then instructed by Susan to revise the budget to reflect a 12% sales increase over last year. Joseph expressed surprise at this request but was assured by Susan that ". . . our sales-people can produce a 12% increase over last year, and the budget should show it that way. . . . the budget must show it that way to help us convince the bank that we'll be able to repay the loan that we'll be applying for in the second quarter." With this assurance, Joseph revised the budget to reflect the 12% increase.

At the end of the second quarter, CD sales were 3% below the revised budget, and Susan instructed Joseph to revise the budget again, this time to reflect a 14% sales increase over last year: "In preparing our application for the bank loan, we found the figures weren't coming out quite right for the size loan we need. We'll be applying at a different bank now, and the 14% sales increase will take care of the problem with the figures. I've been assured by our salespeople that if a 14% increase is what the company needs, then they can give me 14%, so that's what we're going to do. They're team players, Joseph, and I know you'll be a team player, too."

Required: Answer the following questions:

(1) Which of the fifteen responsibilities in the *Standards of Ethical Conduct for Management Accountants* apply to Joseph's situation?
(2) What might Joseph have done differently to avoid or mitigate this problem?
(3) In addition to his ethical responsibilities to CD, what other ethical responsibilities does Joseph have to consider?

C1-5. Ethics. Mary Jones is Controller of the Non-Ferrous Metals Division of Southeast Manufacturing Incorporated (SMI) in Tuscaloosa, Alabama. Last year, she served as her division's representative on an SMI corporate-level task force charged with developing specific objectives and performance specifications for a new computer system that is to be purchased this year. Due to her pivotal role on that task force, she has just been named to a new SMI corporate-level committee charged with reviewing, evaluating, and ranking the ten to twenty proposals that SMI expects to receive from computer vendors now that SMI has put the proposed system out for bids.

A single parent, Mary expects to incur over $400,000 of medical expenses resulting from treatments of her youngest child, who has contracted a potentially fatal disease. Approximately $150,000 of that amount will not be covered by insurance. Due to this personal financial situation, Mary has investigated some career opportunities that would involve higher salary and more generous insurance benefits, but no position has been offered to her. Her most recent interview was for the controller position at Crimson Systems, a supplier of large-scale computer hardware and custom-designed software.

Crimson Systems' vice-president for finance declined to offer Mary the controller position, but instead said, "We're offering you a temporary consulting engagement—Sunday afternoons for the next four months—helping us write our proposal for the SMI job; your fee will be $500 per hour."

Required: Answer the following questions:

(1) Which of the fifteen responsibilities in the *Standards of Ethical Conduct for Management Accountants* apply to Mary's situation?
(2) What might Mary have done in her interview with Crimson Systems to precipitate this problem?
(3) What might Mary have done differently to avoid or mitigate this problem?
(4) In addition to her ethical responsibilities to SMI, what other ethical responsibilities does Mary have to consider?

CHAPTER 2

Cost Concepts and the Cost Accounting Information System

Cost accounting was once considered to apply only to manufacturing operations. In today's economy, however, every type and size of organization should benefit from the use of cost accounting concepts and techniques. For example, cost accounting principles may be applied by financial institutions, transportation companies (airlines, railroads, bus companies), other service and professional firms, hospitals, churches, schools, colleges, universities, and governmental units, as well as the marketing and administrative activities of manufacturing firms. These numerous applications of cost accounting are examined in this text.

◼ THE COST CONCEPT

Cost concepts and terms have developed according to the needs of accountants, economists, and engineers. Accountants have defined cost as "an exchange price, a forgoing, a sacrifice made to secure benefit. In financial accounting, the forgoing or sacrifice at date of acquisition is represented by a current or future diminution in cash or other assets."[1]

Frequently the term "cost" is used synonymously with the term "expense." However, an expense may be defined as a measured outflow of goods or services, which is matched with revenue to determine income, or:

> . . . the decrease in net assets as a result of the use of economic services in the creation of revenues or of the imposition of taxes by governmental units. Expense is measured by the amount of the decrease in assets or the increase in liabilities related to the production and delivery of goods and the rendering of services . . . expense in its broadest sense includes all expired costs which are deductible from revenues.[2]

When the term "cost" is used specifically, it should be modified by such descriptions as direct, prime, conversion, indirect, fixed, variable, controllable, product, period, joint, estimated, standard, sunk, or out-of-pocket.

---

[1]Robert T. Sprouse and Maurice Moonitz, *Accounting Research Study No. 3,* "A Tentative Set of Broad Accounting Principles for Business Enterprises," (New York: American Institute of Certified Public Accountants, 1962), p. 25.

[2]*Ibid.,* p. 49.

23

Each modification implies a certain attribute which is important in measuring cost, and which may be recorded and accumulated for assigning costs to inventories, preparing financial statements, planning and controlling costs, making strategic plans and decisions, choosing among alternatives, motivating personnel, and evaluating performance. The accountant who is involved in planning, analyzing, and decision making must also work with future, replacement, imputed, differential, or opportunity costs, none of which is recorded and reported in external financial statements.

Cost Objects

A *cost object* is defined as any unit, activity, or phenomenon for which an arrangement is made to accumulate and measure cost. The unit, activity, or phenomenon may consist of a product unit, a batch or lot of like units, all units ever produced of a particular product, a job order, contract, project, process, function, goal, organization department, segment, location or other subdivision of a business entity. Such accumulations in cost accounting systems are multidimensional because of the multiple needs in cost finding, planning, and control. For example, it is necessary to assign costs to each product unit, but it is also necessary to plan and control costs for which individual managers are assigned responsibility, i.e., on a departmental, geographical or functional basis. To plan and control the amounts expended toward attaining different strategic objectives, it is necessary to also accumulate costs according to the strategic goal benefitted by the expenditure of each amount of cost; for example, all costs expended toward the goal of improving product quality would be accumulated in one classification. The design of accounting systems and their implementation must address these multiple cost object requirements. (Cost objects are also called *cost objectives*.)

QUALITY CONTROL

The concept of a cost object is one of the most pervasive ideas in cost accounting. A particular choice of cost object is always present, at least implicitly, whenever any measurement, accumulation, allocation, or reporting of costs occurs. In other words, the concept of cost object is at the heart of what cost means. The selection of a cost object provides the answer to the most fundamental question about cost: "The cost of what?"

Traceability of Costs to Cost Objects

Once the cost object is selected, measurement of costs depends heavily on the *traceability* of costs to the cost object. The traceability of costs determines how objective, reliable, and meaningful the resulting cost measure will be, and therefore how confident a decision maker can be in understanding and relying on the cost measure as a basis for prediction and decision making.

The traceability of costs to a cost object varies by degree. A common way of characterizing costs is to label them as either direct or indirect costs of a particular cost object, as if there were only two degrees of traceability. In fact, degrees of traceability exist along a continuum, as pictured below:

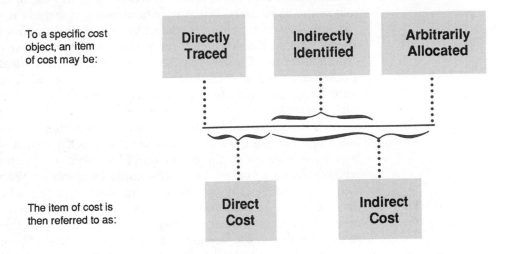

To a specific cost object, an item of cost may be:

Directly Traced   **Indirectly Identified**   **Arbitrarily Allocated**

The item of cost is then referred to as:

Direct Cost   **Indirect Cost**

Continuum of Cost Traceability

To illustrate the different degrees of traceability on the continuum, the cost object is defined here as a product unit. This is the most commonly used definition; for example, when the terms "direct cost" and "indirect cost" are used without specifying a cost object, it is customary to assume that a single unit of product is understood to be the cost object.

At the extreme of directly traceable costs are those items that can be physically or contractually identified as components of the finished unit of product. For example, the unit could be examined, weighed, and measured to find the type and quantity of each raw material and component part incorporated in it, and royalty or patent license agreements can be read to find what fee may be owed to a patent holder for permission to manufacture the unit.

Near that extreme are the costs that can be empirically traced to the unit's production by observing the production process. These include touch labor, consisting of labor expended to convert raw materials into finished product and some material handling labor; paper patterns and other materials that are consumed in the production of each unit but are not physically incorporated in it; and some energy costs. Of course, not all the items that are physically or empirically traceable to a unit will be important enough to justify the clerical effort required to record the traced amounts. Whether tracing is justified depends on how precise a measure of direct costs is needed and how difficult the tracing will be. For that reason, cost accounting systems generally treat as direct costs only some of the cost items that could conceivably be traced directly to the product unit.

Beyond those cost items that are physically, contractually, or empirically traceable, some degree of arbitrariness enters any attempt to identify additional costs with a product unit. For example, the traceable material and labor costs of the small number of defective units that are normally produced along with any large number of good units could logically be included as part of the cost of the good units. But exactly how much to include is subject to debate: The average actual amount of defectives' cost? The amount expected to occur on the next production run? The actual amount that does occur on the next production run? The amount that would occur under ideal conditions? The amount expected under realistic but very efficient conditions? Even when the purpose of the ultimate cost measure is known in advance, the answer to such a question is not always clear.

Moving nearer the middle of the continuum, there are costs traceable to a batch or lot of like units of the product, such as the cost of setting up (adjusting) the machinery on the production line before the batch can be produced, which is called *setup cost*. Setup cost could be identified with a single product unit in the batch only by means of an allocation: the setup costs could be divided by the actual number of units produced in a batch, or by the normal number, or by the ideal number. Again, an essentially arbitrary choice is required if these costs are to be allocated to each unit of product. (Notice that if the batch were defined as the cost object, setup costs would be classified as directly traceable.)

Next on the continuum there are costs traceable to all the units of a particular product that were ever produced. These include the costs of initial product design, engineering, and worker training. To identify these with a single product unit would require allocation over the total number of units of the product to be produced in the entire product life cycle. That number of units would generally be difficult to predict, and even the most experienced manager in the industry would estimate such a quantity with considerable forecasting error.

The pattern followed along the continuum should now be clear: next would be the costs traceable to the process used in making the product, then the costs traceable to the department in which the process is carried out, then the costs traceable to the building or plant location in which the department is located, and so on. (In each of these steps, a sufficiently broad redefinition of the cost object would cause the costs to be reclassified as directly traceable costs.)

At the far extreme of the continuum are those costs that can be identified with a unit of product only by the most arbitrary and indefensible allocations. An example would be to allocate a small fraction of general corporate-level costs, such as income taxes and bond interest, to each unit of product produced by each department, of each plant, of each division of the corporation. The number of arithmetic steps involved in such an allocation, and the very arbitrary choices of methods used and quantities estimated at each step, make the results questionable for practically any purpose related to prediction or decision making.

Among those manufacturers who have come to view cost accounting information as a competitive weapon, and who have begun to thoroughly reexamine and restructure their cost accounting systems, there is a trend toward relying on traceability as the most important basis for classifying and understanding costs.

Cost Traceability in Service Industries

Some service businesses provide excellent examples of the distinction between the role of cost information for external reporting of inventory cost and the role of cost information for determining product costs for all other purposes. (In Chapter 1, these were listed as the #4 and #3 tasks of cost accounting, respectively.) Specifically, consider a service business consisting of a chain of walk-in medical clinics, auto oil change and lubrication shops, or hairdressers, in which all jobs are of such short duration that there are no fully or partially completed jobs on hand at the end of a business day. In such a setting, the inventory costing role in external reporting (task #4) simply does not arise, but product costs (task #3) must still be known by management to permit decisions such as which services to provide and what prices to charge.

The traceability of costs is as important for decision making in all service businesses as it is in manufacturing, regardless of whether there is any need to determine the cost of inventories for external reporting. For routine pricing decisions, bidding on jobs, and dropping or adding a service in the line of services offered, knowing the costs of different services is of paramount importance in any competitive environment, and the traceability of costs is as fundamental in calculating the cost of a service as it is in calculating the cost of a manufactured good.

A simple and common example is found in the hotel business. Room service menus commonly include a statement such as "A $2 delivery charge will be added to each order." Why not adjust the listed prices of all items on the menu by just enough to recover delivery costs, rather than apply a separate delivery charge? Because an arbitrary allocation would be required to calculate the amount of delivery cost that should be added to each item. Should it be the same for a $1 item as for a $30 item? Should it be large enough to justify delivering a single-item order? The obvious answer is that the price necessary to justify the costs of delivering an order should be applied to each order, rather than applying some fraction of it to each item.

Notice the explicit use of multiple cost objects in the room service example. The room service menu lists each item with a separate price, and in determining that price, management treats an individual unit of each item as the cost object. In determining the delivery charge to be added to each order, the order was treated as the cost object. This is a reasonable pattern of pricing because the cost of a delivery is not traceable to an item, only to the delivery of an order. Also, do not be confused by the trivial case in which an order consists of a single item. The delivery cost of a single-item order is traceable to the item only because the item and the order are identical in that instance. In general, it is the order, of any size, that causes the delivery cost to be incurred.

■ THE COST ACCOUNTING INFORMATION SYSTEM

To manage an enterprise, systematic and comparative cost information as well as analytical cost and profit data are needed. This information helps management set the company's profit goals, establish departmental targets which direct middle and operating management toward the achievement of the final goal, evaluate the effectiveness of plans, pinpoint successes or failures in terms of specific responsibilities, and analyze and decide on adjustments and improvements to keep the entire organization moving forward, in balance, toward established objectives. An integrated and coordinated information system should provide only that information which is needed by each responsible manager. To accomplish these objectives, the system must be designed to provide information promptly. Furthermore, the information must be communicated effectively. Cost control needs and profit opportunities may be delayed or missed because of poor communication.

The accumulation of accounting data requires many forms, methods, and systems due to the varying types and sizes of businesses. A successful information system should be tailored to give the blend of sophistication and simplicity that is most efficient and economical for a specific organization. Designing a cost accounting information system requires a thorough understanding of the organizational structure of the company and the type of cost information required by all levels of management. This interface between the system, management, and employees has significant behavioral implications. The system may enhance or thwart the achievement of desired results, depending on the extent to which sound behavioral judgment is applied in developing, administering, and improving the system and in educating employees to fulfill the system's requirements.

The cost accounting information system must be closely associated with the division of authority, so that individual managers can be held accountable for the costs incurred in their departments. The system should be designed to promote the concept of management by exception; i.e., it should provide information that enables management to take prompt remedial action. The system should also reflect the manufacturing and administrative procedures of the particular company for which it is designed. Although the accounting records will not provide all the necessary information for effective management, the accountant who designs the system must know how employees are paid, how inventories are controlled, how equipment is costed, machine capacities, and other operating information.

The information system should provide the proper focus for management's attention. Certain significant aspects of performance may be difficult to measure, while more easily measured but less significant factors may cause the firm to pursue or overemphasize activities that are not in its long-run best interest. Managers should be informed as to the appropriate, intended uses as well as the limitations of information. At the same time, the information system's utility should be extended if possible.

Requirements for record keeping and reporting may be imposed on an organization by external forces, such as the Internal Revenue Code, the Federal Insurance Contributions Act, the Securities and Exchange Commission, Cost Accounting Standards, other governmental regulatory agencies and taxing authorities, as well as creditors and labor unions. These legal and contractual requirements must be met by a system that is designed in a cost-conscious manner. Any sophistication in a system, beyond the basic requirements, must be justified solely on the basis of its value to management.

The Chart of Accounts

Every profit and nonprofit organization, irrespective of its size and complexity, must maintain some type of general ledger accounting system. For such a system to function effectively, data must be collected, identified, and coded for recording in journals and posting to ledger accounts. The prerequisite for efficiently accomplishing these tasks is a well-designed *chart of accounts* for classifying costs and expenses.

In constructing a chart of accounts, the following basic considerations should be observed:

1. Accounts should be arranged and designated to give maximum information with a minimum of supplementary analysis.
2. Account titles should reflect the purpose rather than the nature of expenditures.
3. Manufacturing, marketing, and administrative cost accounts should receive particular attention because these accounts are used to highlight variations in operating efficiency. They should be identifiable with the manager responsible for the costs involved.

A typical chart of accounts is divided into (1) balance sheet accounts for assets, liabilities, and capital, and (2) income statement accounts for sales, cost of goods sold, factory overhead, marketing expenses, administrative expenses, and other expenses and income. Account numbers are commonly employed to avoid the confusion created by different spellings and abbreviations of the same account title. The use of numbers to represent accounts is the simplest form of symbolizing, which is essential to the processing of information, especially when electronic data processing equipment is being used. A condensed chart of accounts is illustrated as follows, using simple three-digit account numbers:

BALANCE SHEET ACCOUNTS (100-299)

Current Assets (100-129)	Current Liabilities (200-219)
Property, Plant, and Equipment (130-159)	Long-Term Liabilities (220-229)
Intangible Assets (170-179)	Capital (250-299)

INCOME STATEMENT ACCOUNTS (300-899)

Sales (300-349)	Administrative Expenses (600-699)
Cost of Goods Sold (350-399)	Other Expenses (700-749)
Factory Overhead (400-499)	Other Income (800-849)
Marketing Expenses (500-599)	Income Taxes (890-899)

Electronic Data Processing

Successful management of a business is essentially a continuous process of decision making. The decision making becomes even more complex when multiple plants are located throughout the nation and in foreign countries; when product lines carry an array of sizes, colors, and options; when various reports are necessary for taxing authorities, regulatory agencies, employees, and stockholders; and when policies and objectives must be communicated from executive management to several operating levels. The information system aids the decision-making process by collecting, classifying, analyzing, and reporting business data. These activities are called *data processing,* and the procedures, forms, and equipment used in the process are called the *data processing system.* Any accounting system, even a cash register in a supermarket, is a data processing system that should be designed to provide pertinent and timely information to management.

The speed and flexibility of computers have led many businesses to convert the processing of data to electronic systems, which replace paper documents and ledgers with magnetic tape or magnetic disks as media for recording and storing account data. These systems can handle routine information easily, verify its accuracy, automatically write checks and remittance statements, classify and post data files, prepare general and subsidiary records and analytical reports, and compute ratios and other statistics for analytical purposes.

An electronic data processing system may be used to recognize and report any circumstances which deviate from a norm or standard. The concept of management by exception is thereby applied efficiently. The system also greatly expands the ability of management to use mathematical models or simulations to plan operations. For example, with a computer, it is possible to simulate a complete operating budget and manipulate product mix, price, cost factors, and the marketing program. By studying alternative combinations of the variables, the uncertainty in making decisions is reduced.

When an electronic data processing system is used, accounting procedures must be carefully programmed for the system. The programming process includes analyzing the procedure, preparing extensive flowcharts that reduce the procedure to a logical design for the system, and writing the detailed code of instructions for the system to follow. As a result of the extensive analysis required in programming, an inherent advantage of an electronic data processing system is that possibly vague accounting procedures become more concise, efficient, and well understood.

The use of electronic data processing systems enables controllers and their staffs to become the nerve centers of large corporations. With such systems, controllers can assemble data concerning human resources, money, materials, and machines, which may form the basis for proposing alternatives in planning crucial operations. The data are based on (1) the company's historical costs and revenues, (2) management's evaluation of the present and future, and (3) economic forecasts originating outside the company.

Sensitivity to Changing Methods

ROBOTICS

JUST-IN-TIME

It is vital that cost accounting systems and procedures be in harmony with the manufacturing methods in current usage. For example, highly automated, robotics-oriented manufacturing processes may employ little if any direct labor (labor directly traceable to the production of each product unit). This condition minimizes the focus of planning and controlling direct labor cost and requires non-labor-related bases for allocating factory overhead costs to production. Also, some manufacturing methods are based on the *just-in-time (JIT) philosophy*, which seeks to reduce dramatically the investments in raw materials as well as in work in process inventories. Systems design, redesign, and implementation must be responsive to changing methods and must account for them in a manner that is representative of current operations.

Management accountants have always been called on to identify, measure, accumulate, report, and interpret a variety of types of useful information. The cost accounting information system has never been restricted to information that is exclusively financial (i.e., measured in dollars). For example, cost accounting reports routinely include physical measures of output produced each period and the percentage of total output that is defective, neither of which necessarily requires measurement in dollars before it is meaningful for use in planning, control, performance evaluation, and decision making. Now robotics, JIT, intensified competition, and other changes in the manufacturing environment have created a need to modify and further broaden the range of information with which management accountants deal, whether such information is integrated into the accounting journals and ledgers or not. This has led to increased attention to non-financial performance measures as a topic with implications for the design of cost accounting systems.

Non-Financial Performance Measures

Many management accountants and other managers have found that the usefulness of non-financial performance measures is not limited to performance evaluation. The reasons for the increased attention being given to these measures include:

1. Dissatisfaction with exclusive reliance on financial measures. Comprehensive financial performance measures, such as total cost or accounting income reported for a product line or a division, are not always regarded as serving any particular decision-making purpose. This limited usefulness is a result of their being produced by an accounting system that serves many purposes simultaneously, including external financial and income tax reporting, routine planning and control of operations, planning and control of unusual or nonrecurring events and decisions, strategic planning, and the evaluation of managers, departments, products and product lines.

2. Growing recognition among non-accountants that the financial measures generated by a company's basic accounting system, including cost accounting measures, are affected by phenomena that are not always relevant to the particular purpose at hand. Examples of these phenomena are the essentially arbitrary choices of calculation methods, such as the cost flow assumptions (first-in, first-out versus weighted average) and the many different ways in which fixed costs may be allocated.

3. Dissatisfaction with the slow pace at which a company's accounting and central data processing departments can add, delete, or modify traditional financial measures when the need arises. Accounting data, including cost accounting measures, are typically processed by large, highly systematized, somewhat unresponsive data processing systems. In such systems, any proposal for a system change is carefully examined for its auditability, compliance with applicable income tax and other regulations, and vulnerability to misstatement, unauthorized access, and misuse. Often the result is a considerable delay in responding to users' requests for modifications of performance measures.

4. Dissatisfaction with financial measures of plant utilization. These measures are easily misinterpreted as encouraging inappropriate overuse of available capacity merely to improve the reported utilization measure. Examples of these utilization measures are fixed overhead volume and idle capacity variances, which are examined in Chapters 13, 14, 15, 18, and 19.

5. Dissatisfaction with financial measures of processing efficiency. In practice, some cost systems fail to take advantage of the flexibility of various control measures, producing reports that are criticized as being too late, too aggregated, too difficult to interpret, or simply misleading.

Non-financial performance measures provide a response to these perceived problems by using simple physical data rather than allocated accounting data, by being unconnected to the general financial accounting system, by being selected to measure only one specific aspect of performance rather than to be "all things for all purposes," or by a combination of these factors. Some non-financial performance measures are simple counts or percentages of desirable or undesirable events, and are intended to measure the efficiency or effectiveness of a production process. Examples are the number of defective units produced, number of good units produced, good units as a percentage of total units, hours of machine downtime, unscheduled downtime as a percentage of total downtime, number of days operating on schedule, days operating on schedule as a percentage of total days operating, weight of scrap material produced, and scrap weight as a percentage of shipped weight.

JUST-IN-TIME   Other non-financial performance measures have arisen in JIT environments. These provide indirect signals of overall processing efficiency by measuring the extent to which the factory has achieved the JIT ideal of minimum inventories or its corollaries, maximum material velocity and optimal material throughput. Examples are the average number of units in process, the maximum number of units in process during a period, total lead time between receipt of a customer order and shipment, and processing time as a percentage of the total time a unit is in the factory.[3]

A third type are those measures of the firm's success in simplifying a process. Simplification is an important step in improving the management of costs and is a precondition for successful automation of a process. Examples of non-financial measures that are relevant to planning and controlling a simplification effort are the average number of times a unit is handled in the factory, the average number of times a unit is retrieved from and returned to a storage location, the average number of times a unit is moved between any two locations, and the total distance a unit is moved within the factory before shipment. (The three types of measures presented thus far are not mutually exclusive; for example, gradual implementation of JIT is a popular way of achieving simplification, so many of the JIT-related measures can also be measures of simplification, and vice versa.)

All three of the types of non-financial measures mentioned thus far can serve as tools for planning and controlling production processes and for evaluating the performance of a department, a team of workers and managers, a product, or a plant. A very different use of those and other non-financial performance measures is in planning and controlling the firm's progress toward strategic objectives, or the attainment of what are referred to as "critical success factors." For example, in pursuing an objective of excellent customer service and satisfaction, non-financial performance measures would include the percentage of on-time deliveries and the number of units or orders returned by customers. In pursuing the objective of world-class employee involvement and motivation, non-financial measures would include the average number of written suggestions made by each employee per year (typically between one and six, but now approaching 100 in some firms).

The increased interest in non-financial performance measures originated outside of the operations of cost accounting systems, and in part it is a response to perceived problems with traditional accounting measures. It would be counter-productive, though, to view this development as a threat to the management accountant's role. Rather, the essential skills of the management accountant should be constructively applied to the identification, measurement, verification, classification, summarization, reporting, and interpretation of any useful performance measure, whether it is preceded by a dollar sign or not.

---

[3]Processing time as a percentage of total time is called *manufacturing cycle efficiency*, calculated by multiplying 100% by the following ratio:

$$\frac{\text{Processing Time}}{\text{Processing Time + Waiting Time + Moving Time + Inspection Time}}$$

Only processing time adds any value to the product, so it is desirable for processing time to be as large a fraction of total time as possible, which means the measure of cycle efficiency should be as high as possible. Unfortunately, cycle efficiencies are generally less than 10%, and levels as low as 1% are not unheard of.

A useful parallel can be drawn with the financial accountant's role. The conservatism built into financial accounting and auditing were historically defended as a necessary counter-weight to offset top management's natural optimism about a firm's success, which could mislead external users of the financial statements. A similar tempering may be useful in internal management reporting. For example, if a firm's production engineers or salespeople begin ignoring financial measures (because they are viewed as being too late, too aggregated, or too unresponsive to changing needs), they may develop their own non-financial measures of each department's performance, such as those measures mentioned above. If the engineers or salespeople seem to regard these measures as the truer, more timely, or more relevant indicators of successes and failures, then top management may begin to request such information, in which case the management accountant would be required, after the fact, to verify the information and explain its financial impact. It would be more efficient for the management accountant to become involved early in the process to help establish efficient and verifiable data gathering and reporting systems.

Rather than a threat to management accountants' position as the firm's internal information consultants, non-financial performance measures can be a signal that management accounting is more important than ever. The essential challenge to management accountants and to accounting systems is clear and simple: their roles must be defined broadly enough to involve measures that are not preceded by dollar signs, and that are not tied to the financial accounting system.

■ CLASSIFICATIONS OF COSTS

Cost classifications are needed for the development of cost data that will aid management in achieving its objectives. The most commonly used classifications are based on the relationship of costs to:

SERVICE ENTITIES

1. The product (a single lot, batch, or unit of a good or service).
2. The volume of production.
3. The manufacturing departments, processes, cost centers, or other subdivisions.
4. The accounting period.
5. A proposed decision, action, or evaluation.

Costs in Relation to the Product

The process of classifying costs and expenses may begin by relating costs to the different phases in the operation of a business. In a manufacturing concern, total operating cost consists of (1) manufacturing cost and (2) commercial expenses. The following chart illustrates this division of total operating cost and identifies some of the elements included in each division.

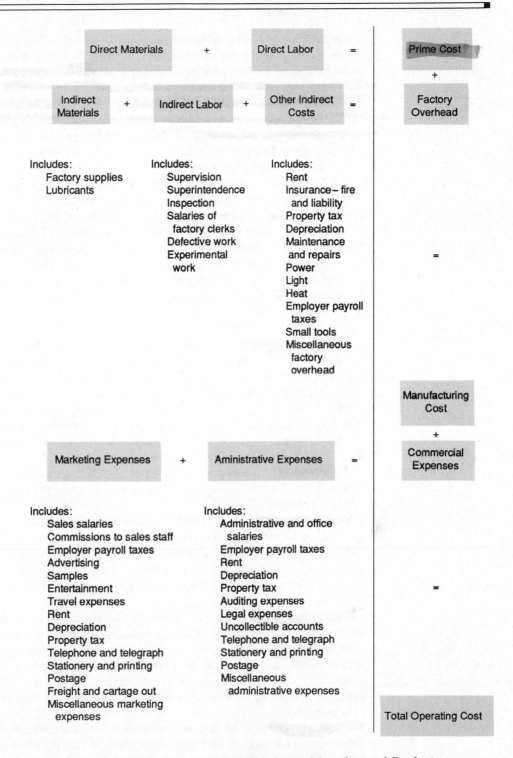

Classification of Costs in Relation to a Manufactured Product

Manufacturing Costs. *Manufacturing cost*—often called production cost or factory cost—is usually defined as the sum of three cost elements: direct materials, direct labor, and factory overhead. Direct materials and direct labor may be combined into another classification called *prime cost.* Direct labor and factory overhead may be combined into a classification called *conversion cost,* which represents the cost of converting direct materials into finished products. In highly automated factories, two problems often arise in attempting to identify direct labor as a separate cost element: (1) the same workers perform many kinds of tasks, and they may shift between direct labor tasks and indirect labor tasks so quickly and so frequently that direct labor cost is difficult or impossible to distinguish from indirect labor cost; (2) direct labor may be a trivial fraction of total production costs, making it difficult to justify the effort of identifying direct labor as a separate cost element. In settings where one or both of these circumstances exist, a single conversion cost classification is appropriate, leaving direct material as the only cost element traced directly to the product. The point is that for any cost item, the feasibility of tracing the cost and the precision needed in the final cost measure are both important in determining whether the cost accounting system should treat the item as a direct cost.

Direct materials are all materials that form an integral part of the finished product and that can be included directly in calculating the cost of the product. Examples of direct materials are the lumber to make furniture and the crude oil to make gasoline. The ease with which the materials items may be traced to the final product is a major consideration in classifying items as direct materials. For example, tacks to build furniture undoubtedly form part of the finished product, but to cost the furniture expeditiously, such items may be classified as indirect materials.

Direct labor is labor expended to convert direct materials into the finished product. It consists of employees' wages which can feasibly be assigned to a specific product.

Factory overhead—also called manufacturing overhead, manufacturing expenses, or factory burden—may be defined as the cost of indirect materials, indirect labor, and all other manufacturing costs that cannot be charged directly to specific products. Simply stated, factory overhead includes all manufacturing costs except those accounted for as direct costs, i.e., direct materials and direct labor.

Indirect materials are those materials needed for the completion of a product, but the consumption of which is so minimal, or the tracing so complex, that treating them as direct materials is futile or uneconomical. Examples include nails, screws, glue, and staples. Factory supplies, a form of indirect materials, consist of such items as lubricating oils, grease, cleaning rags, and brushes needed to maintain the working area and machinery in a usable and safe condition.

Indirect labor may be defined as expended labor which does not directly affect the construction or the composition of the finished product. Indirect labor includes the wages of supervisors, shop clerks, general helpers, maintenance workers, and, usually, material handlers. In a service business, indirect labor cost includes the wages of receptionists, file clerks, supply clerks, and secretaries.

While only direct materials and direct labor are generally traced to a single unit of product, there are other levels of traceability that are useful in understanding the nature of production costs. These were illustrated earlier in the discussion of the cost concept and cost objects: setup costs are directly traceable to a batch, but are indirect to a single unit in the batch; product design costs are directly traceable to the sum of all units ever produced of that particular product, but are indirect to a single unit or batch; and so on. This suggests one of the fundamental tenets of cost accounting: different costs are meaningful and useful for different purposes. For example, the costs of producing one more batch of a product include the costs traceable to a batch and the costs traceable to each of the units in the batch.

Most cost accounting systems include in factory overhead all costs that are not traceable to the product. In such systems, the manufacturing costs directly traceable to a batch, a customer order, an entire production facility, a new product or product variation, or a strategic goal are combined in a single overhead classification, because none of these costs is viewed as being directly traceable to the product.

For any careful analysis of what causes costs or of ways to better manage costs, disaggregation of overhead into different categories is an important but often difficult step. Without careful disaggregation, for example, the difference in the cost of running a large number of small batches of many different products, rather than a few large batches of a few products, is not discernable. A manufacturer may be so inefficient in managing some part of overhead costs that a competitive disadvantage can result, but the large and growing amount of the mismanaged cost item may not be reported to any responsible manager. Instead, the mismanaged cost item may simply be one of many components of a large and growing total of overhead costs, representing some of the indirect labor reported, some of the indirect materials, some energy costs, etc. *Computer-integrated manufacturing* (CIM), employing database management technology on a large, company-wide scale, may provide a remedy for these shortcomings of the information systems of today.

Commercial Expenses. *Commercial expenses* fall into two large classifications: (1) marketing (selling and distribution) expenses and (2) administrative (general and administrative) expenses. *Marketing expenses* begin at the point where the factory costs end, i.e., when manufacturing has been completed and the product is in salable condition. These expenses include the expenses of selling and delivery. *Administrative expenses* include expenses incurred in directing and controlling the organization. Some of these expenses, such as the salary of a vice-president in charge of manufacturing, may be allocated as a manufacturing cost, and the salary of a vice-president in charge of marketing may be allocated as a marketing expense.

Costs in Relation to the Volume of Production

Some costs vary in proportion to changes in the volume of production or output, while others remain relatively fixed in amount. The tendency of costs to vary with output must be considered by management if it desires to plan a company's strategy intelligently and control costs successfully.

Variable Costs. In general, *variable costs* have the following characteristics: (1) variability of total amount in proportion to volume, (2) relatively constant cost per unit as volume changes within a relevant range, (3) assignable, with reasonable ease and accuracy, to operating departments, and (4) controllable by a specific operating level supervisor. The costs which have these characteristics generally include direct materials and direct labor. Some factory overhead and nonmanufacturing costs are also variable. The following list identifies overhead costs which are usually classified as variable:

VARIABLE FACTORY OVERHEAD

Supplies	Royalties
Fuel	Communication costs
Small tools	Overtime premium
Spoilage, salvage, reclamation expenses	Materials handling
Receiving costs	

Fixed Costs. The characteristics of *fixed costs* are: (1) fixed total amount within a relevant output range, (2) decrease in per unit cost as volume increases within a relevant range, (3) assignable to departments on the basis of arbitrary managerial decisions or cost allocation methods, and (4) control responsibility resting with executive management rather than operating supervisors. The following overhead costs are usually classified as fixed:

FIXED FACTORY OVERHEAD

Salaries of production executives	Insurance—property and liability
Depreciation	Wages of security guards and janitors
Property tax	Maintenance and repairs of buildings and grounds
Patent amortization	Rent

Fixed costs may be thought of as the costs of being in business, while variable costs are the costs of doing business. In some cases, management actions may determine whether a cost is classified as fixed or variable. For example, if a truck is rented at a rate per mile, the cost is variable. If the truck is purchased and subsequently depreciated by the straight-line method, the cost is fixed.

Semivariable Costs. Some costs contain fixed and variable elements. These *semivariable costs* include an amount that is fixed within a relevant range of output and an amount that varies proportionately with output changes. For example, electricity cost may be semivariable. Electricity used for lighting tends to be a fixed cost, since lights will be needed when the plant is operating, regardless of the level of output. Conversely, electricity used as power to operate equipment will vary depending upon the usage of the equipment. Other examples of semivariable overhead costs are given at the top of the next page.

For analytical purposes, all manufacturing and nonmanufacturing costs usually are classified as either fixed or variable. Therefore, semivariable costs must be divided into their fixed and variable components. Methods of accomplishing this division are discussed in Chapter 12.

SEMIVARIABLE FACTORY OVERHEAD

Supervision	Maintenance and repairs of machinery and plant equipment
Inspection	Compensation insurance
Payroll department services	Health and accident insurance
Personnel department services	Payroll taxes
Factory office services	Industrial relations expenses
Materials and inventory services	Heat, light, and power
Cost department services	Water and sewage

Costs in Relation to Manufacturing Departments, Processes, or Other Segments

For administrative purposes, a business may be divided into segments having any of a variety of names. The division of a factory into departments, processes, work cells, cost centers, or cost pools also serves as the basis for classifying and accumulating product costs and assigning responsibility for cost control. As a product passes through a department or cost center, it is charged with directly traceable costs (typically direct materials and direct labor) and a share of indirect costs (factory overhead).

To achieve the greatest degree of control, department managers should participate in the development of budgets for their respective departments or cost centers. Such budgets should clearly identify those costs about which the manager can make decisions and for which the manager accepts responsibility. At the end of a reporting period, the efficiency of a department and the manager's success in controlling costs may be measured by comparing actual costs with the budgeted costs.

Producing and Service Departments. The departments of a factory generally fall into two categories: (1) producing departments and (2) service departments. In a *producing department*, manual and machine operations, such as forming and assembling, are performed directly upon the product or its parts. The costs incurred by such departments are charged to the product. If two or more different types of machines perform operations on a product within the same department, the accuracy of product costs may be increased by dividing the department into two or more cost centers.

In a *service department*, service is rendered for the benefit of other departments. In some instances, these services benefit other service departments as well as the producing departments. Although a service department does not directly engage in production, its costs are part of the total factory overhead and must be included in the cost of the product. Service departments which are common to many industrial concerns include maintenance, payroll, cost accounting, data processing, and food services.

Direct and Indirect Departmental Charges. Cost Accounting Standard No. 418, "Allocation of Direct and Indirect Costs," issued in 1980 by the Cost Accounting Standards Board, requires that costs be consistently classified as direct or indirect. In connection with materials and labor, the term "direct" refers to costs which are chargeable directly to a unit of product. Factory overhead is considered "indirect" with regard to units of product. In such a classification system, the product unit is the cost object. The terms "direct" and "indirect" may also be used in connection with charging overhead costs to manufacturing departments and in charging expenses to the departments of nonmanufacturing organizations. If a cost is readily identifiable with (i.e., traceable to) the department in which it originates, it is referred to as a *direct* departmental cost. The salary of the departmental supervisor is an example of a direct cost. If a cost is shared by several departments that benefit from its incurrence, it is referred to as an *indirect* or *nontraceable* cost. Building rent and building depreciation are examples of indirect costs which are allocated to departments. In this cost classification system, the department is the cost object. When costs of a multi-division conglomerate company are allocated among its various divisions, the division is serving as the cost object. When reporting the amounts expended to improve product quality, customer service, and employee involvement, strategic goals are the cost objects.

Service department costs are also indirect costs for other departments. When all service department costs have been allocated, each producing department's overhead will consist of its own direct and indirect departmental cost and the apportioned charges from service departments.

Common Costs and Joint Costs. Both common costs and joint costs are types of indirect costs. *Common costs* are costs of facilities or services employed by two or more operations. Common costs are particularly prevalent in organizations with many departments or segments. The degree of segmentation increases the tendency of costs to be common costs. For example, in general, the salary of the marketing vice-president would not be a common cost shared with the corporation's human resources department. However, if the marketing department provides its service to several segments of the entire firm it would be a common cost shared by those segments.

Joint costs occur when the production of one product may be possible only if one or more other products are manufactured at the same time. The meat-packing, oil and gas, and liquor industries are excellent examples of production that involves joint costs. In such industries, joint costs can be allocated to joint products only by arbitrary procedures. Therefore, data resulting from joint cost allocation must be very carefully treated in some decisions, as explained in Chapter 7.

Costs in Relation to an Accounting Period

Costs may be classified as capital expenditures or as revenue expenditures. A *capital expenditure* is intended to benefit future periods and is reported as an asset. A *revenue expenditure* benefits the current period and is reported as an expense. Ultimately, an asset will flow into the expense stream as it is consumed or when it loses its usefulness.

The distinction between capital and revenue expenditures is essential to the proper matching of costs and revenue and to the accurate measurement of periodic income. However, a precise distinction between the two classifications is not always feasible. In many cases, the initial classification depends upon management's attitude toward such expenditures and the nature of the company's operations. The amount of the expenditure and the number of detailed records required are also factors that influence the distinction between these two classifications. For example, trash barrels purchased for $10 each may be recorded as expenses as an expedient, although they will be used for many years.

Costs in Relation to a Proposed Decision, Action, or Evaluation

When deciding among a number of possible actions or alternatives, it is important to identify the costs (and the revenues, cost reductions, and cost-savings) that are relevant to the choice. Consideration of irrelevant items can be a significant waste of time and can divert attention from relevant items. More importantly, an irrelevant factor may be misused as if it were relevant. *Differential cost* is one name for a cost that is relevant to a choice among alternatives. Differential cost is sometimes called *marginal cost* or *incremental cost*. If an amount of differential cost will be incurred only if one particular alternative is chosen, then that cost may also be called an *out-of-pocket cost* of that alternative. An amount of revenue or other benefit that will be missed or lost if a particular alternative is chosen is called an *opportunity cost* of that alternative. A cost that has already been incurred and, therefore, is irrelevant to a decision is referred to as a *sunk cost*. In a decision to discontinue a product or division, some of the product's or division's costs may be unaffected by the decision; these are called *unavoidable* costs. The *avoidable* costs, in contrast, are relevant to the decision. These decision-making concepts are discussed in Chapter 21.

In evaluating the performance of a manager, an important step is to classify costs that are *controllable* by that manager. Costs that are *uncontrollable* by the manager are generally irrelevant to evaluations of the manager's performance, and the manager should not be held responsible for them. These aspects of responsibility accounting are discussed in Chapter 15.

DISCUSSION QUESTIONS

Q2-1. (a) Explain the meanings of the terms "cost" and "expense" as used for financial reporting in conformity with generally accepted accounting principles. The explanation should indicate distinguishing characteristics of the terms, their similarities and interrelationships.

(b) Classify each of the following items as a cost, expense, or other category, with an explanation of how the classification of each item may change: (1) cost of goods sold; (2) uncollectible accounts expense; (3) depreciation expense for plant machinery; (4) organization costs; (5) spoiled goods.

Q2-2. What are cost objects and why are they important?

Q2-3. (a) Why is the particular choice of a cost object important in classifying costs as direct or indirect?

(b) Give an example of how the choice of a different cost object changes the direct or indirect classification of a single item of cost.

Q2-4. (a) When all manufacturing costs are divided into three elements—direct material, direct labor, and overhead—what choice of a cost object is being used?

(b) For what purpose would a disaggregation of overhead be useful?

(c) What are some choices of cost object that may require disaggregating the total overhead cost?

Q2-5. Define a cost system.

Q2-6. Enumerate the requirements of a good information system.

Q2-7. What is the purpose of a chart of accounts?

Q2-8. What are the advantages of an electronic data processing system?

Q2-9. Increased interest in non-financial performance measures is partly a response to perceived weaknesses of traditional financial measures. What are these perceived weaknesses?

Q2-10. In addition to being measured in a unit other than dollars, what are the attributes of non-financial performance measures that distinguish them from financial measures?

Q2-11. Give four examples of non-financial performance measures and tell what four different aspects of performance they might be used to monitor.

Q2-12. What challenge to cost accountants and cost systems is posed by the increased interest in non-financial performance measures?

Q2-13. Enumerate the most commonly used classifications of costs.

Q2-14. Describe indirect materials and give an appropriate example.

Q2-15. Describe indirect labor and give an appropriate example.

Q2-16. (a) What is a service department? Name several.

(b) How do producing departments classify their apportioned share of service department expenses?

Q2-17. Expenditures may be divided into two general categories: capital expenditures and revenue expenditures.

(a) Distinguish between these two categories of expenditures and their treatment in the accounts.

(b) Discuss the impact on both present and future balance sheets and income statements of improperly distinguishing between capital and revenue expenditures.

(c) What criteria do firms generally use in establishing a policy for classifying expenditures under these two general categories?

EXERCISES

E2-1. Manufacturing costs. The estimated unit costs for Richard & Craig Inc., when operating at a production and sales level of 12,000 units, are as follows:

Cost Item	Estimated Unit Cost
Direct materials	$32
Direct labor	20
Variable factory overhead	15
Fixed factory overhead	6
Variable marketing	3
Fixed marketing	4

Required:

    (1) Identify the estimated conversion cost per unit.

    (2) Identify the estimated prime cost per unit.

    (3) Determine the estimated total variable cost per unit.

    (4) Compute the total cost that would be incurred during a month with a production level of 12,000 units and a sales level of 8,000 units. (ICMA adapted)

E2-2. Fixed and variable costs. In 19A, the Mercaldo Company had sales of $19,950,000, with $11,571,000 variable and $7,623,000 fixed costs. 19B sales are expected to decrease 15% and the cost relationship is expected to remain constant (the fixed costs will not change).

Required: Determine Mercaldo Company's expected operating income or loss for 19B.

E2-3. Non-financial performance measures. Match each of the non-financial performance measures in the first column with the most closely related goal, objective, or other aspect of performance in the second column.

Measures	Aspects of Performance
a. Absenteeism	U. Customer service
b. Number of warranty repairs	V. Process simplification
	W. Product simplification
c. Rejects, as a percentage of units inspected	X. Product innovation
	Y. Product quality
d. Patents applied for	Z. Employee motivation
e. On-time deliveries, as a percentage of all deliveries	
f. Number of times each unit handled during production	
g. Number of unique parts kept in inventory	
h. Number of customer complaints	

E2-4. Manufacturing costs. Rodriquez Company manufactures mainframe computers. In producing a computer, the prime cost is $300,000 and the conversion cost is $400,000, but the total manufacturing cost is only $600,000.

Required: Determine the cost of direct labor per computer.

E2-5. Manufacturing costs. Suboleski Company manufactures diamond-tipped cutting blades. The total manufacturing cost of one blade is $1,000, of which $400 is the conversion cost. The direct labor cost of a blade is one-eighth as large as the direct material cost.

Required: Determine the amount of factory overhead cost per blade.

E2-6. Manufacturing costs. Fuente Company manufactures airbrake systems for long-haul trucks. In producing one system, the prime cost is $800, the conversion cost is $400, and the total manufacturing cost is $1,000.

Required: Determine the cost of direct labor per system.

E2-7. Manufacturing costs. Kallos & Kalogeras Inc. manufactures wave soldering machines. The total manufacturing cost of one machine is $3,000, of which $2,000 is the conversion cost. The direct labor cost of a machine is one-fourth as large as the direct material cost.

Required: Determine the amount of factory overhead cost per machine.

E2-8. Cost objects, traceability, and pricing. Some retail stores that accept bank credit cards will give the customer a discount if a purchase is paid for in cash. The logic behind this practice is that the banks that process credit card transactions charge the merchant a service fee, usually between 1% and 5% of the amount of the credit card transactions each month. If a customer pays the merchant in cash rather than using a credit card, the merchant avoids incurring that extra cost.

Required: Answer the following questions:

  (1) In establishing a price structure where both cash and bank credit card purchases are common, what are the relevant cost objects?

  (2) What does this imply about prices in a store where credit cards are accepted but no discount is given for cash purchases?

  (3) What are the competitive implications for a store like the one described in requirement (2)?

  (4) Instead of offering a discount on cash transactions, why not reduce all the prices in the store and then levy a small additional charge on customers that use credit cards, to cover the banks' processing fees?

E2-9. Cost objects, traceability, and pricing. When Aurora's Small Engine Shop (ASES) repairs a lawn tractor or small garden tractor for a customer, the tractor is picked up and delivered for no extra charge. When Aurora founded ASES, about one-half of its customers transported their own tractors using their trucks, small trailers, vans, or other personal vehicles, rather than waiting for ASES to schedule a pickup.

Over the years, the local market for lawn tractor repair services has become increasingly competitive, and ASES has encountered difficulty in matching the prices offered by competitors and in maintaining market share. A further problem is that the cost of pickups and deliveries has become a financial problem in ASES's cost structure, because nearly all of ASES's remaining customers now request the free pickup and delivery. Most of ASES's original customers who own trucks and similar vehicles now take their tractor repair business to ASES's competitors. ASES competitors all charge extra for pickup and delivery of a tractor.

Required: Answer the following questions:
  (1) What cost objects are relevant to ASES's pricing structure?

  (2) As a lawn tractor owner who also owns a small truck, why might you find that ASES's prices for repair services are not competitive?

E2-10. Manufacturing costs. The estimated unit costs for Bahalia Bookcase Company, when operating at a production and sales level of 2,000 units, are as follows:

Cost Item	Estimated Unit Cost
Lumber......................	$12
Direct labor	2
Variable factory overhead	5
Fixed factory overhead	4
Variable marketing..............	1
Fixed marketing................	3

Required:
  (1) Calculate the estimated conversion cost per unit.

  (2) Calculate the estimated prime cost per unit.

  (3) Calculate the estimated variable manufacturing cost per unit.

  (4) Calculate the estimated total variable cost per unit.

  (5) Calculate the total cost that would be incurred during a month with a production level of 2,000 units and a sales level of 1,900 units.

  (6) Give some examples of items that would be accounted for as indirect materials by Bahalia.

  (7) In the list of cost items and estimated amounts given above, which one would include an estimate of the costs referred to in the answer to requirement (6)?   (ICMA adapted)

E2-11. Manufacturing costs. James Manufacturing produces self-propelled rock-drilling machines for use in mining, road building, and excavation. The direct materials cost of one machine is $12,000, and the total manufacturing cost is $20,000. The overhead cost of one machine is one-third as large as its prime cost.

Required: Determine the direct labor cost of one machine.

CASES

C2-1. Cost objects, traceability, and pricing. The food service manager of Too-Simple Hotel is planning a new price structure for room service. It has been determined that the hotel's cost of a glass of orange juice is $0.20. To provide the normal 75% profit margin on sales, a price of $0.80 would be required; profit would then be $0.80 – $0.20 = $0.60, which is 75% of the $0.80 sales price.

For room service, a higher price will be charged to cover the cost of delivery to a guest's room. The cost of a delivery is $0.60 (not counting the cost of whatever menu items are delivered). To earn a normal profit, additional revenues averaging $2.40 must be earned on a delivery. The profit would then be $2.40 – $0.60 = $1.80, which is 75% of the $2.40 delivery revenue.

The food service manager estimates that an average delivery will involve two items, so $1.20, or one-half of the necessary $2.40 delivery revenue, will be added to the menu price of every room service item. That brings the room service price of a glass of orange juice to $0.80 + $1.20 = $2.

Required: Answer the following questions:

(1) What percentage of profit margin on sales will be earned on a room service order consisting of four glasses of orange juice?

(2) What percentage of profit margin on sales will be earned on a room service order consisting of one glass of orange juice?

(3) What is the food service manager treating as the cost object in setting room service prices?

(4) What refinement of the definition of cost object(s) would result in the planned 75% profit margin on sales?

(5) Using the refinement of requirement (4), what would be the percentages of profit margins in requirements (1) and (2)?

(6) What would be the competitive implications of the food service manager's planned price structure, compared with the implications of the refined price structure?

C2-2. Cost objects and traceability. RWC Company produces over 100 different variations of its basic product, and has expended $400,000 in perfecting its newest variation, Zeggo, to the point of starting production. This amount includes the costs of routine design improvement efforts, testing, assembly line modifications, and training.

Zeggo's production will share an assembly line with several of RWC's other product variations, and only one variation can be produced on the line at one time. Each variation requires a different adjustment ("setup") of the machinery on the line. To begin a batch of Zeggo, the machines on the line must first be set up at a cost of $1,000.

Each unit of Zeggo that is produced results in $5 of cost that the RWC cost accounting system traces directly to the product unit, plus another $1 of cost that could be traced, but only with great difficulty, so the RWC system classifies the $1 as indirect cost.

RWC's cost accounting system allocates a share of factory overhead to each unit produced; this factory overhead amount includes an allocation of all the manufacturing costs that are not directly traced to the product. Each unit of Zeggo is to be allocated $10 of factory overhead.

Required:

(1) Name every cost object for which some amount of cost is identified in the information given, and determine the amount of cost for each cost object.

(2) In addition to the cost objects named in your answer to requirement (1), name other items which are mentioned in the case that could serve as cost objects for some purpose. For each one, describe a purpose for which it would serve as the cost object.

(3) Calculate the total cost expected to result from producing the first batch of Zeggo, which will be a batch of 300 units.

(4) RWC plans to produce one more unit of Zeggo. No setup will be required, because the assembly line has just finished a Zeggo production run. Determine the amount of cost that would be expected to result from producing the one additional unit.

(5) Determine the total cost that the RWC cost accounting system will report for the batch

of 300 units referred to in requirement (3).
(Your answer should be larger than the answer to requirement (3).)

(6) Determine the cost that the RWC cost accounting system will report for the one additional unit referred to in requirement (4). (Your answer should be larger than the answer to requirement (4).)

(7) Determine why the results of requirements (5) and (6) are larger than those of requirements (3) and (4). Specifically: (a) What are the types of activities whose costs are included in the amounts reported by the cost accounting system but which do not result from producing a batch or a unit of Zeggo? Give examples of these activities. (b) What other kinds of costs account for the difference, other than the costs of activities? Give examples.

▼

PART

2

Cost Accumulation

▼

CHAPTER 3

Cost Systems and
Cost Accumulation

Many varieties of cost systems are used in practice, and several will be introduced in this chapter. One of the fundamental roles of any cost system is cost accumulation, which consists of identifying, measuring, and recording cost information in relevant categories or classifications. Several cost accumulation methods are in use, and this chapter will introduce and compare three basic methods. Some cost accumulation consists of a blending of the features of the basic methods, and examples of such blended methods will also be discussed. It is necessary to understand only the three basic methods to be able to identify and understand the important aspects of a blended method. Before the three basic cost accumulation methods and the several varieties of cost systems are presented, the logical pattern by which costs flow through an accounting system will be examined.

■ THE FLOW OF COSTS IN A MANUFACTURING ENTERPRISE

Cost accounting neither adds new steps to the familiar accounting cycle nor discards the principles studied in financial accounting. Cost accounting is concerned with precise recording and measurement of cost elements as they originate and flow through the productive processes. This flow is illustrated in the diagram at the top of the next page.

The diagram shows that all manufacturing costs, regardless of their fixed or variable behavior, flow through the work in process and finished goods inventory accounts. This reflects the full absorption cost assumption that was mentioned in Chapter 2.

The manufacturing process, the physical arrangement of the factory, and the decision-making needs of managers are the basis for determining how costs will be accumulated. Generally, the accounts which describe manufacturing operations are: Materials, Payroll, Factory Overhead Control, Work in Process, Finished Goods, and Cost of Goods Sold. These accounts are used to recognize and measure the flow of costs in each fiscal period—from the acquisition of materials, through factory operations, to the cost of products sold. Cost accounts are expansions of general accounts and are related to general accounts, as shown in the diagram at the bottom of the next page.

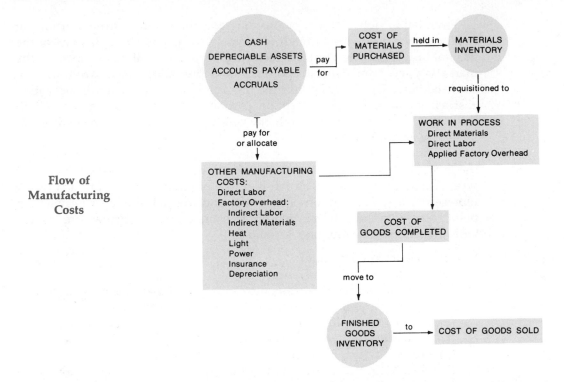

Flow of Manufacturing Costs

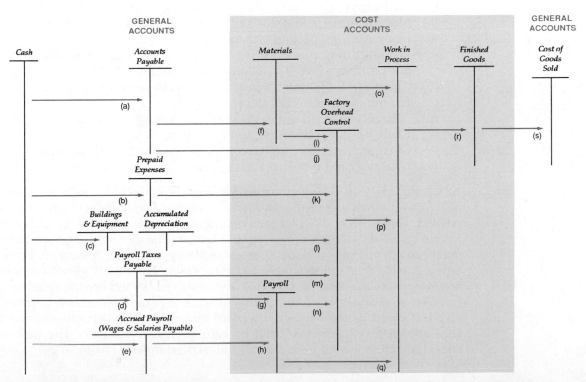

Relationship Between General Accounts and Cost Accounts (Under Full Absorption Costing)

From left to right in the previous diagram, the manufacturing portions of costs are shown flowing through the cost accounts and through some of the general accounts. The nonmanufacturing portions of all costs, such as the marketing and administrative portions of depreciation and payroll, are not depicted here. This diagram, like the preceding one, reflects a full absorption cost assumption. In full absorption costing, all manufacturing costs, both fixed and variable, flow through the work in process and finished goods inventory accounts.

Not only do the arrows in the diagram depict the flow of costs through the accounting system, but each individual arrow also represents a specific type of accounting entry. The left-hand or origination point of each arrow represents the credit portion of an entry, and the right-hand or termination point represents the debit portion of the same entry. The arrows are labeled with the letters (a) through (r) as follows:

(a) Payments on account.
(b) Expenses paid in advance.
(c) Purchases and improvements of long-lived manufacturing assets.
(d) Payments of payroll taxes to the taxing authorities.
(e) Payments of wages and salaries, net of employee taxes withheld.
(f) Purchases of raw materials and factory supplies on credit.
(g) Recording that portion of payroll which is withheld.
(h) Recording that portion of payroll which is due to employees.
(i) Issuing factory supplies (indirect materials) to production.
(j) Incurring various indirect manufacturing costs on credit.
(k) Manufacturing portion of any prepayments that have expired.
(l) Manufacturing portion of depreciation.
(m) Manufacturing portion of employer's payroll taxes (unemployment taxes and employer's matching portion of FICA tax).
(n) Charging all types of indirect labor cost to production.
(o) Issuing direct materials to production.
(p) Charging manufacturing overhead costs to production.
(q) Charging direct labor cost to production.
(r) Charging completed units' cost to the finished goods account.
(s) Charging sold units' cost to the cost of goods sold account.

Cost accounting makes extensive use of a control account-subsidiary record format when detailed information about general ledger accounts is needed. Hundreds of different materials items, for example, may be included in one materials account in the general ledger. The general ledger's factory overhead account may include indirect labor, supplies, rent, insurance, taxes, repairs, and other indirect manufacturing costs. Each such general ledger account, called a *controlling account* or *control account*, would be supported by a number of subsidiary accounts or records. A separate materials subsidiary account would be used for each type of material, and a separate overhead subsidiary account would be used for each overhead cost item. The various subsidiary accounts are described and illustrated in later chapters.

Similarly, control accounts supported by subsidiary records are used in the general accounts. For example, because the diagram shows a single account for payroll taxes payable, it would be supported by individual records for each type of payroll tax the company is required to withhold from employees' paychecks, including FICA, state income tax, and federal income tax. The diagram also shows a single accounts payable account; it would be supported by individual accounts payable, one for each creditor, or by individual vouchers payable, one for each bill to be paid.

The flow of costs to ledger accounts is based on source or transaction documents, which are verified and vouchered before they are journalized and posted. These documents are the fundamental evidence of an economic event, and they may exist in paper or electronic form. Some of the typical source documents which support transactions involving the elements of manufacturing cost are identified in the following table:

Cost	Source Document
Materials	Purchase invoices, materials requisitions, materials returned slips, etc.
Labor	Time tickets or time sheets, clock cards, job tickets, etc.
Factory overhead	Vouchers prepared to set up depreciation or prepaid expenses, vendors' invoices, utility bills, time sheets, etc.

The flow of accounting information from source document to ledger accounts may be facilitated by using the journal voucher control system. Whether manual or computerized, this system involves the use of journal vouchers on which information from the source documents is summarized and identified according to the chart of accounts. The journal voucher is the basis for the preparation of journal entries which record the transactions for a given period and the posting of these transactions to the ledger accounts. The journal voucher should indicate the voucher number, the date, the accounts with their numbers or codes, the amounts to be debited or credited, and the voucher approval. Columns may be added to accommodate the subsidiary ledger details, or these details may be posted directly from the source documents.

To illustrate the flow of costs in a manufacturing enterprise, assume that New Hope Manufacturing Company begins a new fiscal year with the financial position as shown in the balance sheet at the top of page 52.

During the month of January, New Hope completed transactions which are summarized, recorded, and posted to the ledger accounts as shown on pages 52-55. The revenue and expense accounts are not closed at the end of January, because in practice, such formal closing is usually done only at year end.

New Hope Manufacturing Company
Balance Sheet
January 1, 19—

Assets

Current assets:
Cash	$ 183,000	
Marketable securities	76,000	
Accounts receivable	313,100	
Inventories:		
Finished goods	$ 68,700	
Work in process	234,300	
Materials	135,300	438,300
Prepaid expenses		15,800
Total current assets		$1,026,200

Property, plant, and equipment:
Land	$ 41,500	
Buildings	$ 580,600	
Machinery and equipment	1,643,000	
	$2,223,600	
Less accumulated depreciation	1,010,700	1,212,900
Total property, plant, and equipment		1,254,400
Total assets		$2,280,600

Liabilities

Current liabilities:
Accounts payable	$ 553,000	
Estimated income tax payable	35,700	
Due on long-term debt	20,000	
Total current liabilities		$ 608,700
Long-term debt		204,400
Total liabilities		$ 813,100

Stockholders' Equity

Common stock	$ 528,000	
Retained earnings	939,500	
Total stockholders' equity		1,467,500
Total liabilities and stockholders' equity		$2,280,600

Perpetual Inventory →

NEW HOPE MANUFACTURING COMPANY

Transactions	Journal Entries

(a) Materials purchased and received
    on account $100,000

Materials...*Inventory*.... 100,000
  Accounts Payable........ 100,000

This is a summary entry. The materials account is an inventory control account; subsidiary records will indicate the details of the materials received.

(b) Materials requisitioned during the month:
    For production................... $ 80,000
    For indirect factory use............ 12,000

Work in Process....*Direct*.... 80,000
Factory Overhead Control—*indirect* 12,000
  Materials................ 92,000

The indirect factory materials are kept in the inventory control account as well as in subsidiary records to control their purchase and usage.

(c) Total gross payroll. $160,000
     Payroll was paid to employee for the
     month, after deducting 7.5% FICA tax
     and 11.5% federal income tax withheld* . .   129,600

     *Here and in later chapters, the various tax rates are
     used for illustration only. Current rates and wage
     bases to which the taxes apply may be found in pub-
     lished government regulations. Regulations require
     prompt remittance of payroll taxes to taxing authori-
     ties. For brevity, these routine payments are not illus-
     trated here.

(d) The distribution of the payroll was:
     Direct labor 65%
     Indirect factory labor   15
     Marketing salaries.   13
     Administrative salaries   7

(e) An additional 10% is recorded for the
     employer's payroll taxes:
     FICA tax 7.5%
     Federal unemployment insurance tax   .8
     State unemployment insurance tax . .   1.7

     Payroll taxes are distributed in the same proportion as
     the distribution of payroll. Payroll taxes related to
     factory activities (direct and indirect labor) are charged
     to the factory overhead control account.

(f) Factory overhead consisting of:
     Depreciation $8,500
     Prepaid insurance.   1,200

(g) General factory overhead costs
     (not itemized) $26,340
     70% of these expenses were paid in cash; the bal-
     ance was credited to Accounts Payable.

(h) Amount received from customers in
     payment of their accounts $205,000

(i) The following liabilities were paid:
     Accounts payable $227,000
     Estimated income tax   35,700

(j) Factory overhead accumulated in the factory over-
     head control account was transferred to the work in
     process account.

(k) Work completed and transferred to
     finished goods $320,000

Payroll.   160,000
  Employees Income Tax
    Payable   18,400
  FICA Tax Payable   12,000
  Accrued Payroll. . . . . _Cash_   129,600

Accrued Payroll   129,600
  Cash   129,600

The accrued payroll account is used to establish a record
until the payroll department has prepared the paychecks to
be distributed to the employees.

Work in Process. _D.L_.   104,000
Factory Overhead Control _Indirect Lab_   24,000   x10%
Marketing Expenses Control . . .   20,800
Administrative Expenses Control   11,200
  Payroll.   160,000

Factory Overhead Control   12,800
Marketing Expenses Control . . .   2,080
Administrative Expenses Control   1,120
  FICA Tax Payable   12,000
  Federal Unemployment Tax
    Payable   1,280
  State Unemployment Tax
    Payable   2,720

The company is required to pay the same amount of FICA
tax as the employees. In addition, the company must pay
federal and state unemployment taxes, from which the employee is exempt. The state unemployment tax rate is
lower if the employer stabilizes employment; otherwise, it
may be as high as 5.4%.

Factory Overhead Control   9,700
  Accumulated Depreciation . .   8,500
  Prepaid Expenses   1,200

Factory Overhead Control   26,340
  Cash   18,438
  Accounts Payable   7,902

Cash   205,000
  Accounts Receivable   205,000

Accounts Payable.   227,000
Estimated Income Tax Payable. .   35,700
  Cash   262,700

Work in Process.   84,840
  Factory Overhead Control . .   84,840

Finished Goods   320,000
  Work in Process   320,000

(l) Sales............................. $384,000

     40% was paid in cash; the balance was charged to Accounts Receivable. The cost of goods sold was 75% of sales.

(m) Provision for income tax.............. $ 26,000

Cash......................	153,600
Accounts Receivable.........	230,400
Sales..................	384,000
Cost of Goods Sold..........	288,000
Finished Goods..........	288,000
Provision for Income Tax *expense*...	26,000
Estimated Income Tax *liability*	
Payable..............	26,000

Cash

1/1	183,000	(c)	129,600
(h)	205,000	(g)	18,438
(l)	153,600	(i)	262,700
	541,600		410,738
	130,862		

Marketable Securities

1/1	76,000	

Accounts Receivable

1/1	313,100	(h)	205,000
(l)	230,400		
	543,500		
	338,500		

Finished Goods

1/1	68,700	(l)	288,000
(k)	320,000		
	388,700		
	100,700		

Work in Process

1/1	234,300	(k)	320,000
(b)	80,000		
(d)	104,000		
(j)	84,840		
	503,140		
	183,140		

Accrued Payroll

(c)	129,600	(c)	129,600

Materials

1/1	135,300	(b)	92,000
(a)	100,000		
	235,300		
143,300			

Prepaid Expenses

1/1	15,800	(f)	1,200
14,600			

Land

1/1	41,500	

Buildings

1/1	580,600	

Machinery and Equipment

1/1	1,643,000	

Accumulated Depreciation

		1/1	1,010,700
		(f)	8,500
			1,019,200

Accounts Payable

(i)	227,000	1/1	553,000
		(a)	100,000
		(g)	7,902
			660,902
		433,902	

Estimated Income Tax Payable

(i)	35,700	1/1		35,700
		(m)		26,000
				61,700
			26,000	

Federal Unemployment Tax Payable

	(e)	1,280

State Unemployment Tax Payable

	(e)	2,720

Due on Long-Term Debt

	1/1	20,000

Long-Term Debt

	1/1	204,400

Common Stock

	1/1	528,000

Retained Earnings

	1/1	939,500

Sales

	(l)	384,000

Cost of Goods Sold

(l)	288,000

Employees Income Tax Payable

	(c)	18,400

FICA Tax Payable

	(c)	12,000
	(e)	12,000
		24,000

Factory Overhead Control

(b)	12,000	(j)	84,840
(d)	24,000		
(e)	12,800		
(f)	9,700		
(g)	26,340		
	84,840		

Actual costs coming thru

Payroll

(c)	160,000	(d)	160,000

Marketing Expenses Control

(d)	20,800	
(e)	2,080	
	22,880	

Administrative Expenses Control

(d)	11,200	
(e)	1,120	
	12,320	

Provision for Income Tax

(m)	26,000	

■ REPORTING THE RESULTS OF OPERATIONS

The results of operations of a manufacturing enterprise are reported in the conventional financial statements. These statements summarize the flow of costs and revenues, and show the financial position at the end of a period of operations.

Income Statement

The following statement shows the revenues and expenses of New Hope Manufacturing Company for the month of January, based on the transactions listed on the preceding pages:

New Hope Manufacturing Company
Income Statement
For Month Ended January 31, 19—

Sales.....................................		$384,000
Less cost of goods sold (Schedule 1)........		288,000
Gross profit.............................		$ 96,000
Less commercial expenses:		
Marketing expense....................	$22,880	
Administrative expense.................	12,320	35,200
Income from operations...................		$ 60,800
Less provision for income tax		26,000
Net income............................		$ 34,800

In the income statement, the cost of goods sold is shown in one figure. Although this practice is followed in published reports, additional information is necessary for internal uses. Therefore, a supporting schedule of the cost of goods sold is usually produced, illustrated as follows for New Hope:

New Hope Manufacturing Company
Schedule 1
Cost of Goods Sold Statement
For Month Ended January 31, 19—

① Direct materials:			
Materials inventory, January 1, 19--..........................		$135,300	
Purchases..		100,000	
Materials available for use.................................		$235,300	
Less: Indirect materials used.................	$ 12,000		
Materials inventory, January 31.....	143,300	155,300	
Direct materials consumed..			$ 80,000
② Direct labor..			104,000
③ Factory overhead:			
Indirect materials.......................................		$ 12,000	
Indirect labor...		24,000	
Payroll taxes..		12,800	
Depreciation...		8,500	
Insurance..		1,200	
General factory overhead........................		26,340	84,840
Total manufacturing cost...			$268,840
④ Add work in process inventory, January 1...................			234,300
			$503,140
Less work in process inventory, January 31...............			183,140
Cost of goods manufactured..			$320,000
⑤ Add finished goods inventory, January 1......................			68,700
Cost of goods available for sale.................................			$388,700
Less finished goods inventory, January 31..................			100,700
Cost of goods sold...			$288,000

① The direct materials section is comprised of the beginning materials inventory, purchases, and the ending inventory of materials, with an adjustment for the indirect materials that were added to factory overhead. This section identifies the cost of materials that became part of the finished product.

② The direct labor section indicates the cost of labor which can be identified directly with the products manufactured.

③ Factory overhead includes all costs that are indirectly involved in manufacturing the product. (Note: The next chapter and the factory overhead chapters will introduce and demonstrate the use of a predetermined factory overhead rate.)

④ The total manufacturing costs incurred during the period are adjusted for the work in process inventories at the beginning and end of the period.

⑤ The cost of goods manufactured during the period is adjusted for the finished goods inventory at the beginning and end of the period.

Balance Sheet

The balance sheet complements the income statement. Neither statement alone offers a sufficiently clear picture of the status and progress of a company. The balance sheet on the following page shows the financial position of New Hope Manufacturing Company at the end of January.

Statement of Cash Flows

The statement of cash flows is prepared using data from the income statement, the balance sheet and other company records. Whenever the income statement and balance sheet are reported externally, generally accepted accounting principles require that they be accompanied by the statement of cash flows. For a period as short as one month, as in the New Hope Manufacturing Company example, external reporting is very rare, so a statement of cash flows is not illustrated here. Introductory and intermediate financial accounting textbooks can be consulted for an illustration of how a statement of cash flows is prepared.

■ COST SYSTEMS

The previous section presented an overall view of the flow of costs, generally known as the manufacturing cost accounting cycle for cost determination. The remainder of this chapter discusses refinements in accounting for the flow of costs by distinguishing among different cost systems and among different methods of cost accumulation. Backflush costing, a method of cost accumulation used when cycle times are very fast, is then described and illustrated.

Costs which are allocated to units of production may be actual costs or standard costs. In an *actual* or *historical* cost system, cost information is collected as cost is incurred, but the presentation of results is delayed until all

New Hope Manufacturing Company
Balance Sheet
January 31, 19--

Assets

Current assets:			
Cash....................		$ 130,862	
Marketable securities..........		76,000	
Accounts receivable............		338,500	
Inventories:			
Finished goods.............	$ 100,700		
Work in process.............	183,140		
Materials................	143,300	427,140	
Prepaid expenses		14,600	
Total current assets			$ 987,102
Property, plant, and equipment:			
Land........................		$ 41,500	
Buildings....................	$ 580,600		
Machinery and equipment.......	1,643,000		
	$2,223,600		
Less accumulated depreciation...	1,019,200	1,204,400	
Total property, plant, and equipment			1,245,900
Total assets			$2,233,002

Liabilities

Current liabilities:			
Accounts payable..............		$ 433,902	
Estimated income tax payable ...		26,000	
Other current liabilities..........		46,400	
Due on long-term debt..........		20,000	
Total current liabilities........			$ 526,302
Long-term debt			204,400
Total liabilities................			$ 730,702

Stockholders' Equity

Common stock....................		$ 528,000	
Retained earnings:			
Balance, January 1	$ 939,500		
January net income...........	34,800	974,300	
Total stockholders' equity			1,502,300
Total liabilities and stockholders' equity.............			$2,233,002

SERVICE ENTITIES

manufacturing operations of the accounting period have been performed or, in a service business, until the period's services have been rendered. In a *standard* cost system, products, operations, and processes are costed based on predetermined quantities of resources to be used and predetermined prices of those resources. Actual costs are also recorded, and variances or differences between actual costs and standard costs are collected in separate accounts. The presentation in this and subsequent chapters is in the context of cost systems that measure costs primarily at actual amounts, with the details of standard cost systems deferred to Chapters 18 and 19.

As stated in Chapter 2, the costs allocated to units of production may include all manufacturing costs (called full absorption costing) or only the variable manufacturing costs (called direct or variable costing). The presentation in this and subsequent chapters is in the context of full absorption costing, with direct costing deferred to Chapter 20.

Four possible cost systems can be constructed by recognizing that costs may be measured at either actual or standard amounts, in either direct costing or full absorption costing. Actually, a classification of costing systems includes many more possibilities, all based on the cost accounting terminology introduced in Chapter 2. On the question of which cost elements are allocated to production, three possibilities are prime costing, direct (variable) costing, and full absorption costing. On the question of how the cost elements are measured, two possibilities have been mentioned already: all costs may be measured at historical (actual) amounts, or all at predetermined (standard) amounts. A third possibility is to use a hybrid of historical and predetermined measures: direct materials and direct labor at historical amounts, and overhead at a predetermined rate. This hybrid system is encountered often in practice and is discussed in Chapters 13, 14, and 15. It also is referred to often in Chapters 4, 5, 6, and 7.

The following matrix summarizes these possibilities:

MANUFACTURING COST ELEMENTS ALLOCATED TO PRODUCTION

COSTS MEASURED AT:	Direct Material, Direct Labor	Direct Material, Direct Labor, Variable Overhead	Direct Material, Direct Labor, Variable Overhead, Fixed Overhead
Historical Amounts	(1) Actual Prime Costing	(4) Actual Direct Costing	(7) Actual Full Absorption Costing
Historical Amounts for Direct Material & Direct Labor, Predetermined Amount for Overhead	(2) Actual Prime Costing	(5) A Hybrid Direct Costing	(8) A Hybrid Full Absorption Costing
Predetermined Amounts	(3) Standard Prime Costing	(6) Standard Direct Costing	(9) Standard Full Absorption Costing

A Classification of Cost Systems

Although the authoritative literature in financial accounting is not entirely clear on this point, most financial accountants agree that generally accepted accounting principles require actual full absorption costing, which is represented by cell (7) in the matrix. Some manufacturing firms actually use some other system, and are able to meet external reporting requirements by making summary adjustments at the end of each reporting period. For tax reporting, the Tax Reform Act of 1986 requires certain purchasing and storage costs to be allocated to inventory, which represents a step beyond the full absorption of manufacturing costs. This new tax requirement is known as *super absorption* or *super-full absorption*.

A recent survey[1] indicates that in defense-related industries, where cost-plus contracting is the dominant form of business, actual cost is the measure most commonly used in cost accounting systems, and full absorption costing is more common than direct costing. Outside the defense-related industries, many more respondents to the survey reported using standard costing than actual costing, and about three times as many reported using full absorption costing as direct costing.

■ COST ACCUMULATION

Any of the cost systems mentioned above may be used with job order costing, with process costing, or with other cost accumulation methods. Job order costing and process costing will be introduced first. They are the two most widely used cost accumulation methods, they have several aspects in common, and they are discussed in detail in later chapters. Although the ultimate cost object in both of these methods is the product, the two methods differ fundamentally in their emphasis on cost tracing. In job order costing, the focus of cost tracing is an individual job, batch, lot, or contract. In process costing, the focus of cost tracing is a process, cost center, or department within the factory.

Job Order Costing

In *job order costing*, which is discussed in detail in Chapter 4, costs are accumulated by job or specific customer order. This method is used when the products manufactured within a department or cost center are heterogeneous, and it presupposes the possibility of physically identifying the jobs produced and of charging each job with its own cost. Job order costing is applicable to made-to-order work in factories, workshops, and repair shops; to work by builders, construction engineers, and printers; and to service businesses that have only a small number of engagements underway at one time, such as medical, legal, architectural, accounting, and consulting firms.

SERVICE ENTITIES

A variation of the job order cost method is that of costing orders by lots. A lot is the quantity of product which can conveniently and economically be

---

[1]Robert A. Howell, James D. Brown, Stephen R. Soucy, and Allen H. Seed, *Management Accounting in the New Manufacturing Environment*, (Montvale, NJ: National Association of Accountants, 1987), pp. 36 and 96.

produced and costed. In the shoe manufacturing industry, for example, a contract typically is divided into lots which consist of 100 to 250 pairs of one size and style of shoe. The costs then are accumulated for each lot.

When a job produces a specific quantity for inventory, job order costing permits the computation of a unit cost for product costing purposes. When jobs are performed on the basis of customer specifications, job order costing permits the computation of a profit or loss on each order. Since costs are revealed as an order goes through production, these costs may be compared with estimates which were made when an order was taken. Job order costing thereby provides opportunities for controlling costs and for evaluating the profitability of a contract, product, or product line.

ROBOTICS

Many modern manufacturing processes are becoming highly automated. Increasingly, labor-intensive production processes such as assembly lines are being automated through the use of robotics. Manufacturing changes can be made more efficiently in such systems than in labor-intensive systems because the learning period required by humans is eliminated. In a robotics production process, the first unit of product is produced as efficiently as the last unit. As a consequence, robotics systems can enhance the likelihood of manufacturing many different products and using job order costing to accumulate some or all manufacturing costs, provided the costs are traceable to individual jobs in a reasonably accurate, practical manner. However, if traceability of costs to individual jobs is not feasible or practical, then process costing may be required.

Process Costing

Process costing, which is discussed in detail in Chapters 5 and 6, accumulates costs by production process or by department. This method is used when all units manufactured within a department or cost center are essentially homogeneous, or when there is no need to distinguish among units. Essentially, process costing accumulates all the costs of operating a process for a period of time, and then divides the costs by the number of product units that passed through that process during the period. The result is a unit cost. Because of the nature of the output and of the cost accumulation, the product of one process may become the material of the next process, in which case a unit cost must be computed for each process. The process cost method is applicable to industries such as flour mills, breweries, chemical plants, and textile factories where large quantities of one (or few) products are produced. It is also applicable to assembly and testing operations involving large numbers of similar items such as power tools, electrical parts, or small appliances.

JUST-IN-TIME

Most firms using process costing maintain continuous high-volume production, and unless the just-in-time philosophy is applied, a considerable amount of partially processed inventory typically is on hand in each department at the end of each accounting period. A partially processed unit obviously should not be assigned a full amount of cost; therefore, some adjustment of the basic unit cost is needed. The calculations necessary to explicitly account for partially completed inventory represent one of the fundamental characteristics of the process cost method. These calculations are discussed in Chapter 5.

In an actual (historical) cost system that uses process costing, the presence of partially completed inventory at the end of an accounting period results in a second accounting problem: the treatment of the cost of that inventory in the next accounting period. The solution is to select a cost flow assumption like those used in accounting for nonmanufacturing inventories. In practice, the most common cost flow assumption for process costing is the weighted average cost, which averages or blends the costs of the incomplete beginning inventory with all the costs incurred in the current period. Professional licensing examinations for accountants also require familiarity with the first-in, first-out cost flow assumption. Both of these cost flow assumptions are discussed in detail in Chapter 6.

Aspects Common to Both Job Order and Process Costing

SERVICE ENTITIES

Although the textbook discussion of job order and process costing emphasizes manufacturing activity, the job order and process costing methods also can be used by service organizations. For example, an automobile repair shop uses job order costing to accumulate the costs associated with work performed on each automobile. Process costing may be used by an airline to accumulate costs per passenger mile, or by a hospital to accumulate costs per patient day.

When the job order or process cost methods are used, costs must be accumulated for control purposes according to the physical unit in which the product cost is to be stated. For example, coal is measured by the ton, chemicals by the gallon, and lumber by board feet. Products such as machines, automobiles, and shoes are measured either by the individual unit or by a multiple of units, such as a dozen or a gross. The unit selected must conform to the type of product and the manufacturing processes, and it should not be too large or too small. If the unit is too large, the averaging of costs may cause significant cost trends to pass unnoticed. If the unit is too small, unnecessarily detailed and expensive clerical work may be required.

In both job order and process costing, considerable attention is devoted to detailed calculations of the cost of work in process. In job order costing, the general ledger's work in process account is supported by subsidiary records of jobs' costs, with a separate record showing detailed costs of each job currently in production. In process costing, the general ledger's work in process account may be supported by subsidiary records of departments' costs, with one record for each department; or a separate general ledger account may be maintained for each department's costs instead of a single work in process controlling account. The detailed tracking of work in process distinguishes these two cost accumulation methods from the third method, called backflush accounting or backflush costing, in which little or no separate accounting is done for the work in process inventory.

Many companies use both the job order and the process cost methods. For example, a company manufacturing a railway car to the customer's specifications uses job order costing to accumulate the cost per railway car. However, the multiple small metal stampings required are manufactured in a department which uses fast and repetitive stamping machines. The cost of these stampings is accumulated by the process cost method. Although the company is using both the job order and process cost accumulation methods in this example, there is no real blending of the two methods because they are employed in separate operations. Other systems exist in which a real blending of job order and process costing methods does occur.

Blended Methods

In some manufacturing, different units have significantly different direct materials costs, but all units undergo identical conversion in large quantities. In these cases, direct materials costs are accumulated using job order costing, and conversion costs are accumulated using process costing.

An example is the production of sets of faucet handles and other metal hardware for bathrooms. Most sets of hardware are plated with an inexpensive metal such as nickel, but some are gold-plated. Other than this significant difference in materials costs, all manufacturing steps and costs are identical for all sets. A second example is a simple assembly operation in which inexpensive brass-plated lamps and expensive solid brass lamps are assembled in large numbers. Identical labor steps are performed on all units and identical wiring and switches (direct materials) are installed. A high-quality cloth shade is attached to the solid brass bases, and a low-cost cloth or plastic shade is attached to the brass-plated bases. The cost differences for bases and shades are significant, while all other costs are identical for all units. In both these examples, a workable solution is to trace the direct material cost to the specific batch, lot, or job by using job order cost accumulation for direct materials, and to use process cost accumulation for labor and overhead costs.

FLEXIBLE MANUFACTURING SYSTEM

A more general example of the need for a blended costing method is provided by some *flexible manufacturing systems* (FMS). Increasing numbers of factories are moving from manufacturing processes involving manual and/or fixed automated systems toward FMS. FMS consist of an integrated collection of automated production processes, automated materials movement, and computerized system controls to efficiently manufacture a highly flexible variety of products. The extent of product variety is constrained by the need for the products to share certain broad characteristics that allow grouping within a particular family of products while maintaining considerable flexibility. For example, at the General Electric plant in Erie, Pennsylvania, diesel engines of substantially different sizes can be manufactured on the same automated production line, without significant retooling and setups.

Flexible manufacturing systems impact upon and alter many of the factors that management should consider in evaluating a system. The effect of each system—manual, fixed automation, and flexible manufacturing—on these factors is summarized as follows:[2]

THREE MANUFACTURING SYSTEMS COMPARED

Factor	Manual Systems	Fixed Automation Systems	Flexible Manufacturing Systems
Numbers of kinds of products	Many	Only one	Several
Viable production volumes.......	Low	High range	Middle
Product quality	Varies	Tightly constrained	Consistent
Setup times	High (learning curve)	Very high	Short
Learning curve effect	Substantial	Depends on degree of automation	None
Lead times (per unit) to supply customer demands...........	Usually high	Moderate	Moderate/low
Direct labor cost (per unit)	High	Low	Very low
Direct labor cost (in total).......	High	High	Very low
Inventories: Materials*	High	High	High
Work in process*	High	High	Low
Machine utilization	Low	High	High
Space required...............	Extensive	Extensive	Moderate
Capital cost.................	Low	High	High
Sensitivity to effects of breakdowns of single machine or group of machines..........	Low	High	Low
Responsiveness to changes in demand...................	High	Low	High

*Incorporation of a just-in-time inventory system will cause inventories to be low.

JUST-IN-TIME

A comparison of these factors makes the flexible manufacturing system attractive. However, there is a need to consider the substantial capital cost and the scarcity of expert knowledge in the field. Nevertheless, the rate of growth of such modernized factory processes is expected to accelerate.

In an FMS, a group of related machines is coordinated by computer. Each manufacturing step in the production of any one of a variety of products is capable of being performed by one or more of the machines in the group. The computer's software includes detailed instructions for each machine's work in the production of each product. If all units of all products are to pass through the FMS at the same speed, then all units are responsible for the same amount of conversion cost, because the time spent in the FMS is the measure of conversion effort. If speeds differ, conversion costs are charged to units on the basis of processing time.

For example, suppose the function of the last machine in the FMS is to test all electronic components in every unit of product. The simplest product made by the FMS may have only three electronic components to be tested, while the most elaborate product made by the same FMS may have twenty. If the testing machine takes three seconds to perform all the tests needed by a

---

[2]David M. Dilts and Grant W. Russell, "Accounting for the Factory of the Future," *Management Accounting*, Vol. LXVI, No. 9, pp. 34-40. Copyright March, 1985 by the National Association of Accountants. All rights reserved. Reprinted by permission.

unit, regardless of the number of components to be tested, then each unit of any product consumes the same amount of testing resources. The same is true of a multi-point soldering robot that takes five seconds to solder any number of connections on a unit. In such a setting, all units of all products can be treated identically with respect to conversion costs, making process costing appropriate for accumulating conversion costs. But because the amount and cost of materials and parts vary significantly from one product to another, job order costing is appropriate for accumulating material costs.

■ BACKFLUSH COSTING

JUST-IN-TIME

In recent years, some manufacturing facilities and parts of facilities have so successfully implemented the just-in-time philosophy that their average elapsed time between receipt of raw materials and production of finished work has been reduced from a matter of weeks or months to a matter of hours. Not surprisingly, these developments question the usefulness of the conventional job order or process costing methods, with the detailed tracking of the costs of work in process that both of these methods entail.

First, a total cycle time of a few hours means an extremely small amount of work is in process at any time. As a result, accurate assignment of costs to the very small work in process inventory is generally a trivial issue, both for financial reporting and for controlling work in process. For financial reporting, an end-of-period estimate of the cost of a very small inventory is sufficient; and for controlling a fast-moving work in process inventory, physical measures and visual observation are used. Second, even if a manager had some reason for wanting to carefully track the costs of work in process in these circumstances, there may be no way to achieve it with the data processing technology employed by most companies.

Backflush costing is a workable way to accumulate manufacturing costs in a factory or part of a factory in which processing speeds are extremely fast. It is workable because it bypasses the routine cost accounting entries that are required in subsidiary records for job order and process cost accumulation, thus saving considerable data processing time. Where there is insufficient time and insufficient incentive to track the detailed costs of work in process, backflushing provides a method of cost accumulation by working backwards through the available accounting information after production is completed, i.e., at the end of each accounting period.

The Essence of Backflush Costing

The purpose of backflush costing is to reduce the number of cost accounting entries that must be measured and recorded routinely. Compared to job order and process costing, backflush costing is notable for its lack of detailed tracking of the cost of work in process, in other words, for its simplicity.

Concisely stated, the work in process account is not adjusted throughout the accounting period to reflect all the costs of units in process—its balance is corrected by means of a single end-of-period journal entry—and there are no detailed subsidiary records maintained for work in process. Refer now to the diagrams on page 49 depicting the flow of manufacturing costs and the relationship between general accounts and cost accounts. Backflush costing eliminates some of the accounting steps shown or combines them with other steps, and some of the general ledger accounts may be combined.

The accounting for materials, as well as for work in process, may be altered by backflush costing. This is because in a successful just-in-time application where backflush costing is used, there may be no separate accounting for a materials inventory—materials received may be immediately put into production, with materials and work in process costs combined in a single account. Different versions of backflush costing are therefore possible, depending on whether a separate work in process account exists and, if it does exist, whether some or all of the cost elements are charged to it before the end of the accounting period. Similarly, the finished goods inventory account may be charged with some cost elements only by a single end-of-period entry. (There may be no finished goods inventory account at all, but that is not unique to backflush costing—any factory that can produce only for customers' orders and that can ship completed work immediately will have no finished goods inventory.)

In job order and process cost accumulation, the cost of completed work is determined by assigning all cost elements—direct material, direct labor, and overhead—to the work in process inventory at various stages during production. In contrast, backflush costing determines some or all elements of the cost of completed work only after the work is completed. The cost of completed work is subtracted from the balance of the work in process account, or an equivalent combined account, in a step called *postdeduction* or *postmanufacturing deduction*.[3] In this terminology, *post* simply means after, and *deduction* refers to the subtraction of the amount of cost. (In actual practice, there may be other items to be postdeducted, such as the estimated cost of scrapped materials, the cost of materials returned to vendors, shortages in material counts, and, in a standard cost system, the cost variances.[4])

The backflush calculation uses end-of-period estimates of the material and conversion cost components of all unfinished work, including any unprocessed raw material. These cost estimates are made at the time of a physical inventory count, which is likely to be done monthly or weekly. Estimates of the material cost components are derived from recent supplier invoices. Estimates of conversion cost amounts can be derived by: (a) estimating the conversion cost of a finished unit, and then (b) assigning a part of that per-unit

---

[3]Bruce R. Neumann and Pauline R. Jaouen, "Kanban, ZIPS and Cost Accounting: A Case Study" *Journal of Accountancy*, Vol. 162, No. 2 pp. 132-141.

[4]C. J. McNair, William Mosconi, and Thomas Norris, *Meeting the Technology Challenge: Cost Accounting in a JIT Environment*, (Montvale, New Jersey: National Association of Accountants, 1988), pp. 102-104.

conversion cost to the partly finished units on hand. The conversion cost of a finished unit can be estimated by dividing total conversion cost incurred in the period by the number of units started, or by the number of units completed, or by the total of units completed and unfinished units on hand, or any similar total for the period. (In a mature JIT application where backflush costing is likely to be used, all these will give approximately the same result, because so few units are on hand at any time. Whether units on hand are included in the total count of units will affect the total by perhaps one percent or less.)

Before illustrating backflush costing, an example drawn from basic financial accounting will be used to demonstrate the logic of backflush costing and the differences between it and other methods.

A Basic Financial Accounting Example

In an introductory financial accounting course, two different inventory methods are demonstrated for use by nonmanufacturing companies: periodic and perpetual. In the perpetual method, the merchandise inventory account is debited to record each purchase of goods and is credited to record the cost of each sale of goods. The objective is to record each increase or decrease in the merchandise inventory account, so that it provides a perpetual record of the cost of merchandise on hand. A significant amount of detailed accounting for merchandise inventory is done in this method, and it is analogous to the detailed tracking of work in process that the job order and process cost methods entail for a manufacturing company.

In contrast, the periodic inventory method leaves the beginning balance of the merchandise inventory account unchanged through the accounting period and makes a single end-of-period adjustment to arrive at an ending balance corresponding to the physical inventory count. Cost of goods sold, which is the total outflow of merchandise for the accounting period, is calculated and recorded only at the end of the period—this is done by adding the beginning merchandise inventory cost to the total of purchases and subtracting the ending inventory cost. A journal entry adjusts the merchandise inventory account to the correct ending balance and records cost of goods sold for the period. The obvious analogy is that no detailed accounting for merchandise inventory is done in the periodic method, just as no detailed tracking of work in process inventory is done by a manufacturer using backflush costing—both rely on end-of-period calculations and adjustments of inventory account balances.

Illustration of Backflush Costing

McIntire Company produces electronic equipment using purchased materials and components. Cycle time is a matter of hours, and the total time from receipt of raw material to completion of a unit is less than two days. McIntire maintains a small inventory of finished goods, but due to the mature JIT system that governs production, the raw material and work in process inventories are minimal. The cost of raw material on hand, which includes all parts and other items treated as direct material, is combined with work in process cost into a single inventory account entitled Raw and In Process (RIP), for which no detailed subsidiary records are maintained. A separate supplies account is maintained for indirect materials.

Like other manufacturers with greatly reduced levels of inventories, McIntire Company uses frequent physical inventory counts as a routine control procedure. All inventories are physically counted at the end of each month, and estimates are then made of the amount of conversion cost that should be assigned to the finished goods inventory and to the small number of partially completed units in RIP. Because inventory levels change very little from month to month, these conversion cost estimates generally vary little from those of the preceding month.

Raw material cost is backflushed from RIP to the finished goods account and from Finished Goods to Cost of Goods Sold based on the monthly physical counts. (If standard costs were used, backflushing could be done daily or for each individual unit—the number of units would simply be multiplied by the standard per-unit material cost to arrive at the amount to be backflushed.) Direct labor and overhead costs are expensed to the cost of goods sold account. The estimated conversion cost components of the RIP and finished goods inventory account balances are adjusted at the end of each month, with the offsetting entry representing a correction of Cost of Goods Sold.[5]

Before illustrating general journal entries of McIntire Company for comparison with those of New Hope Manufacturing Company on pages 52-54, two important observations can be made. First, the most important difference between backflush costing and other cost accumulation methods is one which will not become apparent by comparing general journal entries but which is an enormous difference in actual practice: no subsidiary detailed records will be maintained for units in production. For example, Chapter 4 discusses the detailed subsidiary records used in accounting for work in process in the job order costing method, but backflush costing entails no such detailed tracking of costs during production. This savings in clerical detail alone can justify the use of backflush costing.

Second, the number of general journal entries to be demonstrated for McIntire Company will not be appreciably different from those shown on pages 52-54 for New Hope Manufacturing. This is because only one general ledger account is being eliminated. The first change to be noticed in the general journal entries is that any material cost amount that would be entered into the materials or work in process inventory accounts under job order or process cost accumulation (as illustrated by New Hope Manufacturing Company) will instead be entered into the RIP account in McIntire Company's backflush costing. A second change is that conversion costs will be expensed

---

[5]Neumannn and Jaouen, Op. cit.

as incurred, bypassing the inventory accounts entirely, with any necessary adjustments made at the end of the month.

Selected transactions and other information for the McIntire Company for January 19A are described and journalized as follows. For brevity, transactions that do not deal with manufacturing costs, such as sales and cash collections, are not listed; they would be handled in the usual manner as illustrated for New Hope Manufacturing Company on pages 52-54. To facilitate comparison with the journal entries for New Hope Manufacturing Company, the portions of journal entries that differ due to backflush costing are shown in italics:

January 1 balances in inventory accounts:

Raw and In Process	$ 21,000
Finished Goods.	170,000
Supplies.	20,000

(The RIP balance consisted of a $20,100 cost of materials, most of which were not yet in process, plus a $900 conversion cost estimate assigned to partially processed work. The Finished Goods balance consisted of $84,000 material cost and an $86,000 estimate of conversion cost.)

January 31 inventories based on physical count:

Raw and In Process	$ 23,000
Finished Goods.	174,000
Supplies.	5,000

(The RIP amount consisted of a $21,600 cost of materials, most of which were not yet in process, plus a $1,400 conversion cost estimate assigned to partially processed work. The Finished Goods amount consisted of $85,800 material cost and an $88,200 estimate of conversion cost.)

MCINTIRE COMPANY

Transactions		Journal Entries		
(a) Direct material received from suppliers . .	$406,000	*Raw and In Process. . . . .*	*406,000*	
		Accounts Payable		*406,000*
		A summary entry for all receipts of raw materials during the period. As direct materials are used, no entry is needed, because they remain a part of RIP.		
(b) Indirect materials used	$15,000	Factory Overhead Control	15,000	
		Supplies		15,000
		Indirect materials are recorded as used.		
(c) Gross payroll of $160,000 was recorded; the payroll was paid, net of 7.5% FICA and 12.5% federal income tax withheld.		Payroll.	160,000	
		Employees Income Tax Payable		20,000
		FICA Tax Payable		12,000
		Accrued Payroll.		128,000
		Accrued Payroll	128,000	
		Cash		128,000

(d) The payroll distribution was:

Direct labor	$25,000
Indirect factory labor	45,000
Marketing salaries	50,000
Administrative salaries	40,000

Cost of Goods Sold	25,000	
Factory Overhead Control	45,000	
Marketing Expenses Control	50,000	
Administrative Expenses Control	40,000	
Payroll		160,000

Direct labor is expensed to the cost of goods sold account. (In job order or process cost accumulation, direct labor would be charged to the work in process account.)

(Due to the small amount of direct labor cost compared to total manufacturing costs, McIntire Company might use a single conversion cost account for direct labor and overhead. To facilitate comparison with New Hope Company, direct labor will be accounted for separately in this illustration.)

(e) Employer payroll taxes of 7.5% FICA, 0.8% federal unemployment, and 1.7% state unemployment tax were recorded.

Factory Overhead Control	7,000	
Marketing Expenses Control	5,000	
Administrative Expenses Control	4,000	
FICA Tax Payable		12,000
Federal Unemployment Tax Payable		1,280
State Unemployment Tax Payable		2,720

(f) Factory overhead costs:

Depreciation	$290,000
Insurance	2,000

Factory Overhead Control	292,000	
Accumulated Depreciation		290,000
Prepaid Insurance		2,000

(g) Miscellaneous factory overhead costs:

Paid in cash	$17,000
On account	4,000

Factory Overhead Control	21,000	
Cash		17,000
Accounts Payable		4,000

(h) The factory overhead accumulated in the factory overhead control account was expensed to Cost of Goods Sold.

Cost of Goods Sold	380,000	
Factory Overhead Control		380,000

Overhead is expensed to the cost of goods sold account. (In job order or process cost accumulation, the overhead would be charged to the work in process account.)

(i) The material cost component of completed work is backflushed from RIP.

Finished Goods	404,500	
Raw and In Process		404,500

To backflush material cost from RIP to Finished Goods. This is a postdeduction. The calculation is:

Material in January 1 RIP balance	$ 20,100
Material received during January	406,000
	$426,100
Material in January 31 RIP, per physical count	21,600
Amount to be backflushed	$404,500

(j) The material cost component of work sold is backflushed from Finished Goods.

Cost of Goods Sold	402,700	
Finished Goods		402,700

To backflush material cost from Finished Goods to Cost of Goods Sold. The calculation is:

Material in Jan. 1 finished goods	$ 84,000
Material cost transferred from RIP	404,500
	$488,500
Material in Jan. 31 finished goods, per physical count. . . .	85,800
Amount to be backflushed. . . .	$402,700

(k) Ending balances are established in inventory accounts by adjusting their conversion cost components.

Raw and In Process.	500	
Finished Goods.	2,200	
Cost of Goods Sold.		2,700

Conversion costs in the inventory accounts are adjusted to the estimates made in the Jan. 31 physical count. For RIP, the adjustment is from the $900 of Jan. 1 to $1,400 on Jan. 31; for Finished Goods, the adjustment is from the $86,000 of Jan. 1 to $88,200 on Jan. 31. The offsetting entry is made to the cost of goods sold account, where all conversion costs were charged during January. (If a conversion cost component had decreased during the month, an inventory account would be credited.)

Because this application of backflush costing expenses all conversion costs directly to the cost of goods sold account, the effects of the general journal entries can be more readily understood by examining the three McIntire Company accounts shown here:

Raw and In Process			
1/1	21,000	(i)	404,500
(a)	406,000		
(k)	500		
	427,500		
23,000			

Finished Goods			
1/1	170,000	(j)	402,700
(i)	404,500		
(k)	2,200		
	576,700		
174,000			

Cost of Goods Sold			
1/1	–0–	(k)	2,700
(d)	25,000		
(h)	380,000		
(j)	402,700		
	807,700		
805,000			

To illustrate a second version of backflush costing, suppose Lightning Fast Company produces only for customer order, has an average elapsed time of less than two days between receipt of raw material and shipment of finished work, and keeps no finished goods on hand, but all other data are the same as those given above for McIntire Company. General journal entries are shown below.

LIGHTNING FAST COMPANY

(a)-(h) These entries will be identical to entries (a) through (h) in the previous illustration of McIntire Company.

(i) *Cost of Goods Sold*   404,500
     Raw and In Process   404,500
     To backflush material cost from RIP to Cost of Goods Sold. This is the postdeduction step.

(j) Not applicable, because there is no finished goods inventory.

(k) *Raw and In Process*   500
     Cost of Goods Sold   500
     Conversion cost in the RIP account is adjusted from the $900 of Jan. 1 to the $1,400 estimate made in the Jan. 31 physical count. The offsetting entry is made to the cost of goods sold account, where all conversion costs were charged during January.

The effects of the general journal entries on two Lightning Fast Company general ledger accounts are shown here:

Raw and In Process					*Cost of Goods Sold*			
1/1	21,000	(i)	404,500		1/1	–0–	(k)	500
(a)	406,000				(d)	25,000		
(k)	500				(h)	380,000		
	427,500				(i)	404,500		
23,000						404,500		
						809,500		
					809,000			

Backflush costing is used by a small but growing number of manufacturers. Except where the backflush costing method is specifically mentioned, the discussion throughout the remainder of this text is in the context of the job order and process costing methods, illustrated by New Hope Manufacturing Company on pages 52-55. A comparison of backflush costing and other cost accumulation methods is given in the exhibit on page 73.

DISCUSSION QUESTIONS

Q3-1. Enumerate the five parts of the cost of goods sold section of the income statement.

Q3-2. Discuss the complementary relationship between the balance sheet and the income statement.

Aspects of Typical System	METHODS			
	Job Order	Blended	Process	Backflush
Cost object to which costs are physically traced	A specific job batch, lot or contract	Material, to a specific job; conversion, to a process or department	A process or department of a production facility	A production facility
Amount of output produced before processing may change	One job, batch, lot or contract	Material may change for each job	Thousands or hundreds of thousands of units of output	Unlimited
Cost elements that differ from one output to another	All cost elements may differ	Material may differ dramatically; conversion, by small degrees	All cost elements may differ by small degree	Only material cost differs
Amount of detailed accounting done for work in process	High	High	Moderate (summarized for each department or process)	None
Source of information used to control processing	Financial and physical data recorded	Financial and physical data recorded	Financial and physical data recorded	Visual observation

Comparison of Cost Accumulation Methods

Q3-3. A corporation's annual financial statements and reports were criticized because it was claimed that the income statement does not by any means give a clear picture of annual earning power, and the balance sheet does not disclose the true value of the plant assets. Considering the criticism made, offer an explanation of the nature and purpose of the income statement and of the balance sheet, together with comments on their limitations.

Q3-4. If a company uses actual full absorption process costing, what attribute of the cost accounting system is described by each of the three terms—actual, full absorption, and process?

Q3-5. What is the distinction among prime, direct, and absorption costing systems?

Q3-6. What is the distinction between actual costing and standard costing?

Q3-7. What are the distinctions among the process, job order, and backflush cost accumulation methods?

Q3-8. In defense-related industries, where cost-plus contracting is the dominant form of business, what difference is found in cost accounting systems?

Q3-9. What is meant by super-full absorption?

Q3-10. What are some industries in which job order costing would be common?

Q3-11. What are some industries in which process costing would be common?

Q3-12. What are some important aspects common to both job order and process costing?

Q3-13. What is meant by a blended costing method?

Q3-14. What characterizes flexible manufacturing systems?

Q3-15. What are the advantages of a flexible manufacturing system over other manufacturing systems?

Q3-16. How does the initial cost of creating a flexible manufacturing system compare with that of other manufacturing systems?

Q3-17. What distinguishes the kind of manufacturing setting suited for backflush costing from those suited for job order or process costing?

Q3-18. In what ways does backflush costing alter the accounting for work in process inventory?

Q3-19. Why might the materials and work in process inventory accounts be combined into a single account in backflush costing?

Q3-20. What is meant by postdeduction?

Q3-21. What basic inventory accounting method used by merchandising companies is analogous to backflush costing used by manufacturing companies?

Q3-22. If all conversion costs are expensed to the cost of goods sold account in a backflush costing system, how is the correct amount of conversion cost included in the inventory accounts when a balance sheet is prepared?

EXERCISES

E3-1. Cost of goods manufactured; cost of goods sold. During the past month, the Moss Company incurred these costs: direct labor, $120,000; factory overhead, $108,000; and direct materials purchases, $160,000. Inventories were costed as follows:

	Beginning	Ending
Finished Goods........	$27,000	$30,000
Work in Process	61,500	67,500
Materials	37,500	43,500

Required: Calculate (1) the cost of goods manufactured and (2) the cost of goods sold.

E3-2. Manufacturing costs; cost of goods manufactured; inventories. Shown below are cost data on the activities of Calabash Manufacturing for December:

(a) Account balances:

	Nov. 30	Dec. 31
Finished Goods	$45,602	$?
Work in Process	60,420	52,800
Stores (direct material)	10,250	12,700
Supplies (indirect material)	5,600	5,180

(b) Transactions in December:

Supplies purchased	$ 16,500
Cost of goods sold	290,000
Raw materials purchased.........................	105,000
Indirect labor.....................................	22,000
Factory heat, light, and power	11,220
Factory rent......................................	18,500
Factory insurance...............................	2,000
Sales commissions...............................	48,000
Administrative expenses.........................	25,000
Production supervisor's salary....................	5,000

(c) 4,250 direct labor hours were worked in December. Laborers work a 40-hour week and are paid $22 per hour for the regular shift and time-and-a-half for each hour of overtime. Of the 4,250 hours, 250 hours were worked in overtime in December. Calabash treats the overtime premium as a part of overhead.

Required:
(1) Calculate the factory overhead incurred in December.
(2) Determine the cost of goods manufactured in December.
(3) Determine the ending balance in finished goods at December 31.   (SMAC adapted)

E3-3. Journal entries for the cost accounting cycle. Selected transactions of the Daniel Company for January are as follows:
(a) Material purchased on account, $40,000.
(b) Materials requisitioned: $33,000 for production and $2,000 for indirect factory use.
(c) Total gross payroll was $40,000, with withholdings of 12% income tax, 7.5% FICA tax, and $280 union dues.
(d) The wages due to the employees were paid.
(e) Of the total payroll, $32,000 was direct labor and $8,000 was indirect factory labor.
(f) An additional 10% is entered for employer's payroll taxes, representing 7.5% FICA tax, 0.8% federal unemployment tax, and 1.7% state unemployment tax.
(g) Various factory overhead costs totaling $18,000 were incurred on account.
(h) Other factory overhead consisted of $2,100 depreciation, $780 expired insurance, and $1,250 accrued property taxes.
(i) Factory overhead was transferred to the work in process account.
(j) Cost of completed production transferred to storage, $92,000.
(k) Sales on account were $80,000, 50% of which was collected. The cost of goods sold was 75% of the sales price.

Required: Prepare journal entries for these transactions.

E3-4. Journal entries for the cost accounting cycle. On January 1, the ledger of the Pacific Bearings Company contained, among other accounts, the following: Finished Goods, $15,000; Work in Process, $30,000; Materials, $25,000. During January the following transactions were completed:

(a) Materials were purchased at a cost of $13,500.

(b) Bar steel in the amount of $17,500 was issued from the storeroom.

(c) Storeroom requisitions for indirect materials and supplies amounted to $1,800.

(d) The total payroll for January amounted to $27,000, including marketing salaries of $5,000 and administrative salaries of $3,000. Labor time tickets show that $17,000 of the labor cost was direct labor. Federal income tax was withheld at the rate of 15% of wages earned, and FICA tax of 7.5% was deducted. A payroll clearing account is used.

(e) The employer's payroll taxes consist of 7.5% FICA, 4.9% state unemployment tax, and 0.8% federal unemployment tax.

(f) Various indirect manufacturing costs were incurred for $8,500 on account.

(g) Total factory overhead is transferred to the work in process account.

(h) Cost of production completed in January totaled $60,100, and finished goods in the shipping room on January 31 totaled $15,100.

(i) Customers to whom shipments were made during the month were billed for $75,000.

Required: Prepare journal entries for these transactions.

E3-5. Cost of goods manufactured statement. Norton Industries, a manufacturer of cable for the heavy construction industry, closes its books and prepares financial statements at the end of each month. The preclosing trial balance as of May 31, 19A, is presented below (in thousands of dollars):

	Debit	Credit
Cash and Marketable Securities.............	$ 54	
Accounts and Notes Receivable.............	210	
Finished Goods (4/30/19A).................	247	
Work in Process (4/30/19A)................	150	
Direct Materials (4/30/19A)................	28	
Property, Plant, and Equipment (net)........	1,140	
Accounts, Notes, and Taxes Payable........		$ 70
Bonds Payable...........................		600
Paid-in Capital...........................		100
Retained Earnings........................		930
Sales....................................		1,488
Sales Discounts..........................	20	
Interest Revenue.........................		2
Purchases of Direct Materials..............	510	
Direct Labor.............................	260	
Indirect Factory Labor....................	90	
Office Salaries...........................	122	
Sales Salaries...........................	42	
Utilities..................................	135	
Rent.....................................	9	
Property Tax.............................	60	
Insurance................................	20	
Depreciation.............................	54	
Interest Expense.........................	6	
Freight In................................	15	
Freight Out...............................	18	
	$3,190	$3,190

Additional information is as follows:

(a) 80% of the utilities are related to manufacturing cable; the remaining 20% are related to the sales and administrative functions in the office building.

(b) All of the rent was for the office building.

(c) The property taxes were assessed on the manufacturing plant.

(d) 60% of the insurance is related to manufacturing cable; the remaining 40% is related to the sales and administrative functions.

(e) Depreciation expense follows:

Manufacturing plant	$20,000
Manufacturing equipment	30,000
Office equipment	4,000
	$54,000

(f) May 31, 19A inventory balances:

Finished Goods	$175,000
Work in Process	220,000
Direct Materials	23,000

Required: Prepare a cost of goods manufactured statement for Norton Industries for May, 19A.(ICMA adapted)

SS **E3-6. Cost of goods sold statement.** The following data are provided with respect to operations of the Star Company for the year ended December 31, 19A:

Raw materials on hand, December 31	$ 24,000
Work in process, December 31	30,000
Finished goods, December 31	40,000
Factory supplies on hand, December 31	14,000
Sales	1,100,000
Factory maintenance	38,400
Administrative salaries	108,000
Discounts on raw materials purchases	4,200
Delivery expenses	16,000
Interest income	1,000
Factory supplies used	22,400
Common stock ($10 par value)	2,000,000
Retained earnings	525,000
Trade accounts payable	273,500
Accumulated depreciation—factory building and equipment	47,500
Building and equipment	500,000
Trade accounts receivable	450,000
Cash	170,000
Finished goods, January 1, 19A	37,500
Direct labor	180,000
Bad debt expense	2,500
Factory power and heat	19,400
Advertising	8,400
Insurance expired—factory building and equipment	4,800
Work in process, January 1, 19A	84,000
Depreciation—factory building and equipment	17,500
Factory superintendence	100,000
Interest expense	1,500
Raw materials purchased	400,000
Indirect factory labor	20,000
Sales returns	2,200
Sales discounts	1,300

Required: Prepare the cost of goods sold statement.

CGA-Canada (adapted) Reprint with permission.

E3-7. Backflush costing. The Stillville Manufacturing Company uses a raw and in process (RIP) inventory account and expenses all conversion costs to the cost of goods sold account. At the end of each month, all inventories are counted, their conversion cost components are estimated, and inventory account balances are adjusted accordingly. Raw material cost is backflushed from RIP to Finished Goods. The following information is for the month of March:

Beginning balance of RIP account, including $1,000 of conversion cost	$ 10,000
Raw materials received on credit.	200,000
Ending RIP inventory per physical count, including $1,300 conversion cost estimate	10,500

Required: Prepare journal entries involving the RIP account.

E3-8. Backflush costing. The Pensawater Manufacturing Company uses a raw and in process (RIP) inventory account and expenses all conversion costs to the cost of goods sold account. At the end of each month, all inventories are counted, their conversion cost components are estimated, and inventory account balances are adjusted accordingly. Raw material cost is backflushed from RIP to Finished Goods. The following information is for the month of April:

Beginning balance of RIP account, including $1,400 of conversion cost	$ 31,000
Raw materials received on credit.	367,000
Ending RIP inventory per physical count, including $1,800 conversion cost estimate	33,000

Required: Prepare journal entries involving the RIP account.

E3-9. Backflush costing with no finished goods account. The Highspeed Manufacturing Company produces only for customer order, and most work is shipped within thirty-six hours of the receipt of an order. Highspeed uses a raw and in process (RIP) inventory account and expenses all conversion costs to the cost of goods sold account. Work is shipped immediately upon completion, so there is no finished goods account. At the end of each month, inventory is counted, its conversion cost component is estimated, and the RIP account balance is adjusted accordingly. Raw material cost is backflushed from RIP to Cost of Goods Sold. The following information is for the month of May:

Beginning balance of RIP account, including $1,300 of conversion cost	$ 12,300
Raw materials received on credit.	246,000
Ending RIP inventory per physical count, including $2,100 conversion cost estimate	12,100

Required: Prepare journal entries involving the RIP account.

PROBLEMS

P3-1. Cost of goods manufactured; prime and conversion costs. Madeira Company's purchases of materials during March totaled $110,000, and the cost of goods sold for March was $345,000. Factory overhead was 50% of direct labor cost. Other information pertaining to Madeira Company's inventories and production for March is as follows:

Inventories:	Beginning	Ending
Finished Goods.	$102,000	$105,000
Work in Process	40,000	36,000
Materials	20,000	26,000

Required:
(1) Prepare a schedule of cost of goods manufactured for March.
(2) Compute the prime cost charged to work in process during March.
(3) Compute the conversion cost charged to work in process during March.   (AICPA adapted)

P3-2. Income statement relationships. The following information is available for three companies at the end of their fiscal years:

Company A:	Finished goods, January 1	$ 600,000
	Cost of goods manufactured	3,800,000
	Sales	4,000,000
	Gross profit on sales.	20%
	Finished goods inventory, December 31	?
Company B:	Freight in	$ 20,000
	Purchases returns and allowances	80,000
	Marketing expense	200,000
	Finished goods, December 31	190,000
	Cost of goods sold	1,300,000
	Cost of goods available for sale	?
Company C:	Gross profit	$ 96,000
	Cost of goods manufactured	340,000
	Finished goods, January 1	45,000
	Finished goods, December 31	52,000
	Work in process, January 1	28,000
	Work in process, December 31	38,000
	Sales	?

Required: Determine the amounts indicated by the question marks for each company.   (AICPA adapted)

P3-3. Cost accounting cycle entries in T accounts. Dekker-Lopez Company charges the total actual factory overhead to Work in Process. Following are selected account balances for September:

	September 1	September 30
Finished Goods	$34,000	$ 30,000
Work in Process	7,000	?
Materials and Supplies.	20,000	15,000
Accrued Payroll (ignore payroll taxes)	13,000	9,000
Accounts Receivable	54,000	22,000
Accounts Payable	18,000	6,000
Sales		500,000

Additional information:
  (a) All sales are on account.
  (b) The accounts payable account is used for the purchase of materials and supplies only.
  (c) Dekker's markup is 30% of sales.
  (d) Work in process at the end of September had $2,000 of materials, $6,000 of direct labor, and $3,000 of factory overhead charged to it.
  (e) Actual factory overhead costs for September were:

Supplies.	$20,000
Indirect labor	55,000
Depreciation.	10,000
Insurance.	2,000
Miscellaneous	13,000

  (f) Materials and supplies purchased on account, $65,000.

Required: Using T accounts, determine:
  (1) Materials issued to production.
  (2) Direct labor.
  (3) Total factory overhead.
  (4) Cost of goods manufactured.
  (5) Cost of goods sold.
  (6) Payment of accounts payable.
  (7) Collection of accounts receivable.
  (8) Payment of payroll.   CGA-Canada (adapted) Reprint with permission.

P3-4. Journal entries for the cost accounting cycle. Jaedicke-Shenkir Company incurred $50,000 direct labor cost in 19A and had the following selected account balances at the beginning and end of 19A:

	January 1	December 31
Finished Goods	$28,000	$ 45,000
Work in Process.	12,000	14,000
Materials.	17,000	24,000
Cost of Goods Sold		140,000
Factory Overhead Control		25,000

Required: Reconstruct the journal entries that recorded the above information in 19A.

CGA-Canada (adapted) Reprint with permission.

P3-5. The cost accounting cycle. The Hopkins & White Company's January 1 account balances are:

Dr.		Cr.	
Cash.	$20,000	Accounts Payable	$15,500
Accounts Receivable	25,000	Accrued Payroll.	2,250
Finished Goods	9,500	Accumulated Depreciation	10,000
Work in Process.	4,500	Common Stock.	60,000
Materials.	10,000	Retained Earnings	21,250
Machinery.	40,000		

During January, the following transactions were completed:
- (a) Materials purchased on account, $92,000.
- (b) Miscellaneous factory overhead incurred on account, $18,500.
- (c) Labor, accumulated and distributed using a payroll account, was consumed as follows: for direct production, $60,500; indirect labor, $12,500; sales salaries, $8,000; administrative salaries, $5,000. 9.5% of the wages is withheld for income tax. The state and federal unemployment tax rates are 2.7% and .8%, respectively; the employer and employee FICA tax rate is 7.5% each. The total accrued payroll was paid.
- (d) Materials were consumed as follows: direct materials, $82,500; indirect materials, $8,300.
- (e) Factory overhead charged to production was $47,330.
- (f) Work finished and placed in stock cost $188,000.
- (g) All but $12,000 of the finished goods were sold, terms 2/10, n/60. The markup was 30% above production cost. The sale and the receivable are recorded in the gross amount.
- (h) Of the total accounts receivable, 80% was collected, less 2% discount. (Round to the nearest dollar.)
- (i) A liability was recorded for various marketing and administrative expenses totaling $30,000. Of this amount, 60% was marketing and 40% was administrative.
- (j) The check register showed payments of $104,000 for liabilities other than payrolls.

Required:
- (1) Prepare T accounts with January 1 balances.
- (2) Prepare journal entries and post January transactions into the ledger accounts. Open new accounts as needed.
- (3) Prepare a trial balance as of January 31.

P3-6. Backflush costing. The La Jolla Manufacturing Company has a mature JIT production system with average cycle time of less than one day. Total time from receipt of raw material to completion of finished product is less than three days. La Jolla uses a finished goods account and a combined raw and in process (RIP) inventory account; there is a separate account, entitled Supplies, for indirect factory materials. La Jolla expenses all conversion costs to the cost of goods sold account. At the end of each month, all inventories are counted, their conversion cost components are estimated, and inventory account balances are adjusted accordingly. Raw material cost is backflushed from RIP to Finished Goods and from Finished Goods to Cost of

Goods Sold. The following information is a summary of selected transactions and other information for the month of May:

Beginning balances in inventory accounts:

Raw and In Process	$ 31,300
Finished Goods.	280,000
Supplies.	27,000

(The May 1 RIP balance consisted of a $30,000 cost of materials, most of which were not yet in process, plus a $1,300 conversion cost estimate assigned to partially processed work. The Finished Goods balance consisted of $150,000 material cost and a $130,000 estimate of conversion cost.)

May 31 inventories based on physical count:

Raw and In Process	$ 37,100
Finished Goods.	294,000
Supplies.	17,000

(The May 31 RIP amount consisted of a $35,000 cost of materials, most of which were not yet in process, plus a $2,100 conversion cost estimate assigned to partially processed work. The Finished Goods amount consisted of $160,000 material cost and a $134,000 estimate of conversion cost.)

(a) Direct material received on credit $620,000
(b) Indirect materials used. . . . . $ 10,000
(c) Gross payroll of $300,000 was recorded; the payroll was paid, net of 7.5% FICA and 12.5% federal income tax withheld.
(d) The payroll distribution was:

Direct labor	$50,000
Indirect factory labor.	90,000
Marketing salaries	90,000
Administrative salaries	70,000

(e) Employer payroll taxes of 7.5% FICA, 0.8% federal unemployment, and 1.7% state unemployment tax were recorded.
(f) Factory overhead costs:

Depreciation	$500,000
Insurance	9,000

(g) Miscellaneous factory overhead costs:

Paid in cash	$26,000
On account.	7,000

(h) The factory overhead accumulated in the factory overhead control account was expensed to Cost of Goods Sold.
(i) The material cost component of completed work is backflushed from RIP.
(j) The material cost component of work sold is backflushed from Finished Goods. Sales are on credit for a total of $2,250,000.
(k) Ending balances are established in inventory accounts by adjusting their conversion cost components.

Required:
   (1) Prepare journal entries based on the above information.
   (2) Prepare completed T accounts for RIP, Finished Goods, and Cost of Goods Sold.

CHAPTER 4

Job Order Costing

The previous chapter discussed and illustrated backflush costing and briefly introduced the job order and process methods of cost accumulation. This chapter describes and illustrates job order costing in detail.

In job order costing, the cost of each order produced for a given customer or the cost of each lot to be placed in stock is recorded on a *job order cost sheet*, sometimes called simply a *cost sheet*. A cost sheet may be in paper or electronic form. Cost sheets are subsidiary records controlled by the general ledger's work in process account. Although several jobs or orders may go through a factory at the same time, each cost sheet is designed to collect the direct and indirect costs charged to a specific job. Each cost sheet is assigned a job number, which is entered on each materials requisition and each labor time ticket used in connection with a job. These paper or electronic records for materials and labor are totaled daily or weekly by job number, for summary journal entries, and the details are entered on the cost sheets. The indirect manufacturing costs charged to a job are usually an estimate rather than the actual costs incurred. As discussed later in the chapter, the amount of indirect costs computed and charged to jobs is referred to as *applied factory overhead*.

Cost sheets differ in form, content, and arrangement from one business to another. An example of a completed job order cost sheet is shown on page 83. The upper section of each cost sheet provides space for the job number, the name of the customer, a description of the items to be produced, the quantity, the date started, and the date completed. The lower section summarizes the production costs, the marketing and administrative expenses, and the profit for the job when it is completed to customer specifications. The job cost sheet also may provide space for estimated costs and a comparison of actual costs to the estimated amounts. In the cost sheet for a departmentalized operation, the materials, labor, and factory overhead applied are shown separately for each department or cost center.

In the remainder of the chapter, job order cost accumulation is described and illustrated for Rayburn Company. The journal entries and descriptions that follow will illustrate some of the cost amounts appearing on the completed job order cost sheet on page 83. That job order cost sheet would be completed only after all relevant cost amounts are entered on it, including those cost amounts that will be illustrated here. The flow of costs for Rayburn Company is summarized in the diagram on page 84.

Rayburn Company

1101 Maple Street. Cincinnati, OH 45227

FOR: Lawrenceville Construction Co.

PRODUCT: #14 Maple Drain Boards

SPECIFICATION: 12'x 20"x 1" Clear Finishes

QUANTITY: 10

Job Order No. **5574**

DATE ORDERED: 1/10

DATE STARTED: 1/14

DATE WANTED: 1/22

DATE COMPLETED: 1/18

DIRECT MATERIALS

DATE	REQ. NO.	AMOUNT	TOTAL
1/14	516	$1,420.00	
1/17	531	780.00	
1/18	544	310.00	
			$2,510.00

DIRECT LABOR

DATE	HOURS	COST	
1/14	40	$ 320.00	
1/15	32	256.00	
1/16	36	288.00	
1/17	40	320.00	
1/18	48	384.00	
	196		$1,568.00

FACTORY OVERHEAD APPLIED

DATE	RATE OF APPLICATION	COST	
1/14	16.2	$ 684.00	
1/16	10.0	400.00	
1/17	3.2	128.00	
	29.4		$1,176.00

Direct Materials.....	$2,510.00	Selling Price...................	$7,860.00
Direct Labor........	1,568.00	Factory Cost $5,254.00	
Factory Overhead		Marketing Expense 776.00	
Applied	1,176.00	Admin. Expense .. 420.00	
		Cost to Make	
Total Factory Cost..	$5,254.00	and Sell	6,450.00
		Profit	$1,410.00

Cost Sheet for a Nondepartmentalized Plant

■ ACCOUNTING FOR MATERIALS

In manufacturing enterprises, materials and supplies are usually recorded in one control account entitled Materials, although supplies may be recorded in a separate account called Supplies or Indirect Materials. Cost accounting for materials involves (1) the purchase of materials and (2) the issuance of

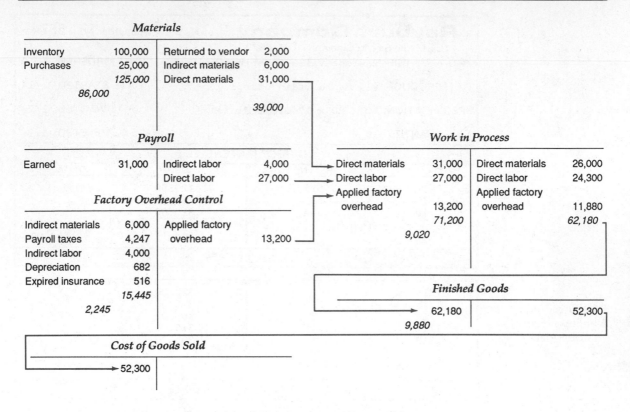

Flow of Costs in Rayburn Company

materials for factory use. Both are discussed in greater detail in Chapters 8 and 9.

Recording the Purchase and Receipt of Materials

Cost accounting techniques for the purchase of materials are similar to those studied in general accounting for a perpetual inventory method. As materials are received, the account debited is Materials or Materials Inventory (rather than Purchases, as in a periodic inventory method):

Materials 25,000
    Accounts Payable 25,000

The quantity received, unit cost, and amount of each purchase also are entered on materials ledger cards. One materials ledger card is maintained for each materials item. Materials ledger cards function as a subsidiary ledger and provide a perpetual inventory record of each item. Materials ledger cards and related transaction documents used to account for materials may exist in paper or electronic form.

Recording the Issuance of Materials

When a job is started, the necessary materials are issued to the factory on the basis of materials requisitions, which are prepared by production scheduling clerks or other employees. The requisition bears the job order number and specifies the type and quantity of materials required. A copy of the requisition is sent to the storekeeper, who assembles the materials called for on the requisition. The quantity, unit cost, and the total cost of each item is entered on the requisition and posted to the materials ledger cards.

The flow of direct materials from storeroom to factory is recorded as a transfer of materials from the materials account to the work in process account. Materials requisitions are summarized and recorded as follows:

Work in Process	31,000	
Materials..		31,000

A copy of each requisition is sent to the cost department. In this department, the requisitions are totaled, sorted by job numbers, and entered in the materials section of the cost sheets for the jobs indicated. In this way, the quantity and cost of materials used in each job are accumulated.

When materials originally requisitioned for a job are not used, a returned materials report is prepared and the materials are returned to the storeroom. The return requires a journal entry in which Materials is debited and Work in Process is credited. Entries on the materials ledger card and the job order cost sheet are also required.

Materials requisitions are used to secure indirect materials or supplies from the storeroom. Supplies that are to be used in locations other than the factory are charged to marketing or administrative expense accounts. Supplies to be used by the factory are charged to the factory overhead control account when the supplies are issued, as shown in the following entry:

	Subsidiary Record	Dr.	Cr.
Factory Overhead Control		6,000	
Indirect Materials.......	6,000		
Materials			6,000

For control, the requisitions for factory supplies must be recorded in a subsidiary ledger for overhead, which may be in the form of a work sheet called a *factory overhead analysis sheet.*

The accounting entries required when materials are purchased and used are illustrated in the two-stage diagram on page 86. In Stage 1, an invoice for materials purchased in the amount of $500 is recorded. In Stage 2, materials requisition number 544 calls for $310 of materials for use on job order number 5574 as illustrated on the completed sheet appearing on page 83. Another requisition for $50 of this same material for use as indirect materials is also recorded. Notice that because the $50 of materials cost is treated as indirect, it is not charged to job order number 5574. It is charged to factory overhead, as is any indirect manufacturing cost.

STAGE 1 MATERIALS PURCHASED	STAGE 2 MATERIALS USED

Journal Entry:
Materials...................... 500
   Accounts Payable.............   500
	Journal Entries:
	Work in Process................. 310
	   Materials 310
	
	Factory Overhead Control
	   (Indirect Materials)........... 50
	   Materials 50

STAGE 1 — General Ledger:

Materials

500	

STAGE 2 — General Ledger:

Materials

500	310
	50

Work in Process

310	

Factory Overhead Control

50	

STAGE 1 — Subsidiary Record:

Materials Ledger Card[1]		
Received	Issued	Balance
$500		$500

STAGE 2 — Subsidiary Records:

Materials Ledger Card		
Received	Issued	Balance
$500		$500
	$310	190
	50	140

Job Order Cost Sheet		
Direct Materials Section		
Date	Req. No.	Cost
1/18	544	$310

Factory Overhead Analysis Sheet			
Date			Indirect Materials
1/26			$50

[1]A separate card is maintained for each type of material.

Entries Required for Materials Purchased and Used

Other materials requisitions for job order number 5574 would be handled similarly to materials requisition number 544; their amounts are all recorded on the job order cost sheet.

■ ACCOUNTING FOR LABOR

The accounting for labor, discussed in detail in Chapters 10 and 11, may be divided into two distinct phases:

1. Collection of payroll data, computation of earnings, calculation of payroll taxes, and payment of wages.
2. Distribution and allocation of labor costs to jobs, departments, and other cost classifications.

In most factories, time clocks register workers' hours on individual clock cards which the workers punch as they enter and leave the plant. These clock cards are used by the timekeeper for maintaining a record of the days or hours worked by each employee and are also the basis for computing the gross earnings of employees who are paid hourly wages.

To compute the direct and indirect labor cost, the time spent on each job during a day must be recorded on labor time tickets for each worker. The time tickets for the various jobs are sorted, priced, and summarized, and the time ticket hours are reconciled periodically with the clock card hours. Time tickets and clock cards may exist in paper or electronic form. (In an automated factory with very little direct labor and a single conversion cost classification, all factory labor is treated in the way described here for indirect labor. No direct labor is then charged to any job, and cost sheets contain sections only for direct materials and conversion cost.)

At regular intervals, usually daily or weekly, the direct labor time and cost for each job are entered on the job order cost sheets. For each payroll period—weekly, biweekly, or monthly—the summary of employees' earnings and the liabilities for payments are journalized and posted to the general ledger.

Entries to record and distribute the payroll costs for Rayburn Company are shown in the two-stage diagram on page 88. Rayburn Company recorded $13,800 of labor costs on the 15th of the month and $17,200 of labor costs on the 31st. Of the $31,000 total labor cost incurred during the month, $27,000 was direct labor and $4,000 was indirect labor. Deductions from gross earnings include 15% for employees income tax and 7.5 % for FICA tax. The gross earnings might also be subject to deductions for pension payments, personal insurance policies, savings bonds, union dues, and charitable contributions. The company incurs additional payroll costs for FICA tax (7.5%), federal unemployment tax (.8%), and state unemployment tax (5.4%). These tax rates, which apply to earnings up to certain maximum amounts, are used here for illustration only. Current rates and bases may be found in published government regulations. The company might incur additional labor-related fringe benefit costs, such as a share of pension payments and insurance premiums.

The payroll account is a clearing account in which labor costs are accumulated pending their distribution to the proper cost accounts. This distribution usually is recorded monthly in the general ledger. The payroll account and employer payroll taxes account may include amounts applicable to marketing and administrative personnel; if so, those amounts would be charged to marketing and administrative expense accounts.

STAGE 1 PAYROLL COMPUTED AND PAID	STAGE 2 PAYROLL COSTS DISTRIBUTED

Journal Entries:
 	
15th
Payroll.................... 13,800
 Employees Income Tax
  Payable   2,070
 FICA Tax Payable   1,035
 Accrued Payroll...........   10,695
 	
Accrued Payroll............. 10,695
 Cash   10,695
 	
31st
Payroll.................... 17,200
 Employees Income Tax
  Payable   2,580
 FICA Tax Payable   1,290
 Accrued Payroll...........   13,330
 	
Accrued Payroll............. 13,330
 Cash   13,330
 	
Factory Overhead Control
 (Payroll Taxes)...........   4,247
 FICA Tax Payable   2,325
 State Unemployment Tax
  Payable   1,674
 Federal Unemployment
  Tax Payable............   248
 	
General Ledger:
 	
Factory Overhead Control
―――――――――――――――――――
   4,247 |
 	
Subsidiary Records:
 Employees' earnings records
 Employees' tax records
  and other deduction records
	Journal Entry:
	
	31st
	Work in Process 27,000
	Factory Overhead Control
	 (Indirect Labor) 4,000
	 Payroll 31,000
	
	General Ledger:
	
	Work in Process
	―――――――――――――――――
	   27,000 |
	
	Factory Overhead Control
	―――――――――――――――――
	   4,247
	   4,000 |
	
	Subsidiary Records:

For Stage 2, the subsidiary records:

Job Order Cost Sheet		
Direct Labor Section[1]		
Date	Hours	Amount
1/18	48	$384

Factory Overhead Analysis Sheet			
Date	Payroll Taxes	Indirect Labor	Indirect Materials
1/31	$4,247	$4,000	

[1]There is a separate cost sheet for every job. Entries in the direct labor section of all jobs worked on during the period are made daily and total $27,000, as shown by the work in process account.

Entries Required for Labor Cost

■ ACCOUNTING FOR FACTORY OVERHEAD

If a planing mill contracts to make fifty cabinet assemblies for an apartment complex, the materials used and the labor expended can be charged to the cabinets on the basis of requisitions and time tickets. The amount of factory overhead which should be charged to the cabinets is more difficult to determine. Some of the overhead costs, such as rent or depreciation of the factory building, insurance, property taxes, and the plant manager's salary, are fixed regardless of the amount of production. Other expenses, such as power and lubricating oil, vary with the quantity of goods manufactured. To overcome these difficulties, overhead is usually charged to jobs by using a rate based on a production-volume-related factor such as direct labor hours, direct labor cost, machine usage, processing time, material usage, some other volume-related factor which exhibits a relationship to factory overhead, or some combination of two or more of such factors. As automation increases and the use of direct labor decreases, the rate used will more likely be based on factors other than direct labor hours or direct labor cost, such as machine hours, processing time, material cost, or material weight. In some factories, production-volume-related factors may not serve well as the only bases for determining overhead rates. Alternatives to production-volume-related factors are provided by measures of the internal activities or transactions that cause much overhead cost to be incurred in these factories. Examples of these internal activities or transactions are the number of setups, total setup time, number of movements of materials or product, and the number of design changes made during production. A costing system using non-volume-related factors is called an *activity costing system*.

ACTIVITY COSTING

Many of the overhead costs may not be known until the end of a fiscal period, long after a job has been completed. Therefore, actual overhead cannot be charged to jobs on a timely basis. To permit timely application of overhead cost to jobs in such cases, it is common to use a *predetermined overhead rate*, which is based on an estimate of factory overhead and an estimate of production activity.

For example, assume that an accountant for Rayburn Company determines that the strongest relationship exists between machine hours and factory overhead.[1] The accountant estimates that machine hours will total 7,500 and factory overhead will total $300,000 for the year. These estimates produce a predetermined overhead rate of $40 ($300,000 divided by 7,500 hours). The amount of factory overhead charged to any job, called *applied factory overhead*, is then determined by multiplying the predetermined overhead rate by the number of machine hours used on that job. If the Rayburn Company's machine logs show that a total of 29.4 machine hours were used on job order number 5574, then applied factory overhead of $1,176 (29.4 machine hours multiplied by the $40 predetermined rate) is entered on the job order cost sheet as shown on page 83.

---

[1]For discussion of why machine hours might be selected as the base, see Robin Cooper, "When Should You Use Machine-Hour Costing?" *The Journal of Cost Management for the Manufacturing Industry,* Vol. 2, No.1, pp. 33-39.

The applied factory overhead entered on the job order cost sheets for all jobs worked on during some period of operations (typically a month) is debited to the work in process control account at the end of the period. For Rayburn Company, the total applied overhead for the period is $13,200 for 330 total machine hours used. The offsetting credit may be made directly to Factory Overhead Control, or a separate account entitled Applied Factory Overhead may be used as shown in the following entry:

Work in Process	13,200	
Applied Factory Overhead (330 machine hours × $40)		13,200

At the end of the accounting period, the separate applied factory overhead account is closed to the factory overhead control account. For illustrative purposes, assume the preceding entry of $13,200 is the only entry to the applied factory overhead account during the period. The closing entry is:

Applied Factory Overhead	13,200	
Factory Overhead Control		13,200

If an applied factory overhead account is used, it keeps applied overhead and actual overhead costs in separate accounts. Companies that do not use the separate applied factory overhead account will credit Factory Overhead Control when Work in Process is debited. This procedure eliminates the need to close Applied Factory Overhead to Factory Overhead Control, and it has the same overall effect on Factory Overhead Control as the procedure illustrated in the preceding journal entries.

Some manufacturing operations are of the job order costing type in the sense that direct materials are issued to specific jobs, but direct labor is not accounted for separately from overhead. In these situations, a predetermined rate is used for total conversion costs, much like the predetermined overhead rate illustrated here.

Some actual overhead costs, such as indirect materials, indirect labor, and payroll taxes, are charged to Factory Overhead Control as they are incurred. Other overhead costs, such as depreciation and expired insurance, are charged to Factory Overhead Control when adjusting entries are recorded. For example, factory depreciation and expired insurance are recorded at the end of the accounting period by the following entries:

	Subsidiary Record	Dr.	Cr.
Factory Overhead Control		682	
Depreciation	682		
Accumulated Depreciation—Machinery			682
Factory Overhead Control		516	
Insurance	516		
Prepaid Insurance			516

These entries are posted to the factory overhead control account shown in the diagram on page 91. This account shows on the debit side the $6,000 of indirect materials (a summary amount that would include the $50 of indirect materials recorded earlier in this illustration), the $4,247 of payroll taxes on

STAGE 1 ACTUAL FACTORY OVERHEAD INCURRED	STAGE 2 ESTIMATED FACTORY OVERHEAD APPLIED

STAGE 1 — ACTUAL FACTORY OVERHEAD INCURRED

General Ledger:

Factory Overhead Control

6,000	13,200
4,247	
4,000	
682	
516	
2,245 15,445	

Materials

	Indirect materials	6,000

Payroll

	Indirect labor	4,000

Payroll Taxes Payable

	Taxes on factory payroll	4,247

Accumulated Depreciation—Machinery

	682

Prepaid Insurance

	516

Subsidiary Record:

Factory Overhead Analysis Sheet

Date	Depr.	Payroll Taxes	Insurance	Indirect Labor	Indirect Materials
1/31	682	$4,247	$516	$4,000	$6,000

STAGE 2 — ESTIMATED FACTORY OVERHEAD APPLIED

General Ledger:

Work in Process

13,200	

Applied Factory Overhead

13,200	13,200

Subsidiary Record:

Job Order Cost Sheet

Factory Overhead Section[1]

Date	Machine Hours	Amount
1/18	29.4	$1,176

[1]There is a separate cost sheet for every job.

Flow of Factory Overhead Through Accounting Records

factory labor, the $4,000 of indirect labor, the $682 of depreciation, and the $516 of expired insurance. The $13,200 on the credit side is the applied factory overhead.

The $2,245 debit balance in the factory overhead control account indicates that actual overhead costs incurred exceeded the amount applied to the job orders. Stated differently, overhead was underapplied by $2,245. Underapplied overhead is often interpreted as an unfavorable variance. The cost control significance of an underapplied or overapplied balance, and the disposition of it, are discussed in Chapter 13. Typically, a relatively small balance is charged to the cost of goods sold. An in-depth discussion of accounting for factory overhead, including departmentalization and responsibility accounting, is included in Chapters 13, 14, and 15.

■ ACCOUNTING FOR JOBS COMPLETED AND PRODUCTS SOLD

During a month's operations, the amounts charged to the work in process account represent the total of the direct costs charged to jobs (typically direct materials placed in process and direct labor used) and the factory overhead applied. As jobs are completed, cost sheets are moved from the in-process category to a finished work file. When a job for replenishing stock for sale is completed, the quantity and cost are recorded on finished goods ledger cards, which are subsidiary records for the finished goods account. The following entry is recorded in the general journal, assuming a total cost of $62,180:

```
Finished Goods.......................................  62,180
    Work in Process....................................          62,180
```

When finished goods are delivered or shipped to customers, sales invoices are prepared, and the sales and the cost of goods sold are recorded. General journal entries are as follows, assuming total sales of $70,000 and total cost of goods sold of $52,300:

```
Accounts Receivable...................................  70,000
    Sales .............................................          70,000

Cost of Goods Sold....................................  52,300
    Finished Goods ....................................          52,300
```

If an entire job is produced for a specific customer, the sale is recorded at the same time that the completed job's cost is debited directly to Cost of Goods Sold. This is illustrated for Rayburn Company's job number 5574 as follows:

```
Accounts Receivable...................................  7,860
    Sales .............................................          7,860

Cost of Goods Sold....................................  5,254
    Work in Process....................................          5,254
```

When the purpose of a job is to replenish the stock of a component used in subsequent manufacturing processes, the completed job is charged to Materials rather than to Cost of Goods Sold and no sale is recognized.

■ SCRAP, SPOILED GOODS, AND DEFECTIVE WORK

Generally, manufacturing operations cannot escape the occurrence of certain losses or output reduction due to scrap, spoilage, or defective work.

Management and all other personnel of an organization should cooperate to reduce such losses to a minimum. Indeed, an important aspect of recent Japanese manufacturing success results from a philosophy that losses such as those attributable to defects can be eliminated. Advocates of this zero-defect approach claim that measures to reduce these losses are cost effective because total long-term manufacturing costs decrease as the percentage of defects decreases.[2] Many just-in-time applications have shown enormous reductions in these losses, while the more traditional settings continue to experience considerable amounts. As long as losses do occur, they must be accounted for and, with the aid of effective reporting, better controlled.

JUST-IN-TIME

Scrap and Waste

In many manufacturing processes, waste and scrap result from (1) the processing of materials, (2) defective and broken parts, (3) obsolete stock, (4) revisions or abandonment of experimental projects, and (5) worn-out or obsolete machinery. This scrap should be collected and placed in storage for sale to scrap dealers. At the time of sale, the following entry may be made, assuming the scrap is sold for $100:

```
Cash (or Accounts Receivable)..................................    100
    Scrap Sales (or Other Income) ..............................           100
```

The full amount realized from the sale of scrap and waste can be included in income of the period in either of two ways:

1. The amount accumulated in Scrap Sales may be closed directly to Income Summary and shown on the income statement under Scrap Sales or Other Income.
2. The amount accumulated may be credited to Cost of Goods Sold, thereby reducing the total costs charged against sales revenue for the period, which results in the same increase in income as when the amount is reported as Scrap Sales or Other Revenue.

Alternatively, the amount received for the sale of scrap may be credited to Factory Overhead Control. If the amount can be estimated, it should be included in the predetermined factory overhead rate, which will reduce the total factory overhead charged to goods manufactured during the period. Even if the amount is not subject to prediction (because it is not expected to occur), it may nevertheless be credited to Factory Overhead Control with the expectation that it will reduce the amount of underapplied factory overhead or increase the amount of overapplied factory overhead for the period. In either case, the entry would be:

```
Cash (or Accounts Receivable)..................................    100
    Factory Overhead Control ...................................           100
```

---

[2]Robert S. Kaplan, "Measuring Manufacturing Performance: A New Challenge for Managerial Accounting Research," *The Accounting Review,* Vol. LVIII, No. 4, p. 690.

When scrap is collected from a job or department, the amount realized from the sale of scrap is often treated as a reduction in the materials cost charged to the individual job (or the product or department, if process costing is used). In this case, the entry to record the sale would be:

```
Cash (or Accounts Receivable)..................................  100
    Work in Process..............................................       100
```

When the quantity and value of scrap material is relatively high, it should be stored in a designated place under the supervision of a storekeeper. One of the following procedures may then be used:

1. The materials ledger clerk may open a materials ledger card, filling in the quantity only. The dollar value would not be needed. When the scrap is sold, the entries and treatment of the income item might be handled as discussed previously.
2. The quantity as well as the dollar value of the scrap delivered to the storekeeper may be recorded. The value would be based on scrap prices quoted on the market at the time of entry. The entry would be:

```
Scrap Materials ...............................................  100
    Scrap Sales (or Other Income or Factory
        Overhead Control or Work in Process) .......................       100
```

When the scrap is sold, the entry would be:

```
Cash (or Accounts Receivable)..................................  100
    Scrap Materials ...........................................       100
```

Any difference between the price at the time the inventory is recorded and the price realized at the time of sale would be a plus or minus adjustment in the scrap sales account, the work in process account, or the factory overhead control account, consistent with the account credited in the first entry.

To reduce accounting for scrap to a minimum, often no entry is made until the scrap is actually sold. At that time, Cash or Accounts Receivable is debited, while Scrap Sales or Other Income is credited. This method is expedient and is justified when a more accurate accounting becomes expensive and burdensome, the scrap value is relatively small, or the price is uncertain.

Proceeds from the sale of scrap are in reality a reduction in production cost. As long as the amounts are relatively small, the accounting treatment is not a major consideration. What is important is an effective scrap control system based on periodic reporting to responsible supervisory personnel. Timely scrap reports for each producing department call attention to unexpected items and unusual amounts and should induce prompt corrective action.

Spoiled Goods

Cost accounting should provide product costs and cost control information. In the case of spoilage, the first requirement is to know the nature and cause of the spoiled units. The second requirement, the accounting problem, is to record the cost of spoiled units and to accumulate spoilage costs and report them to responsible personnel for corrective action.

Attaining the degree of materials and machine precision and the perfection of labor performance necessary to eliminate spoiled units entirely may, in some cases, involve incurring costs in excess of the costs of a normal or tolerable level of spoilage. The related cost vs. benefit must be considered in setting such tolerances. (The zero-defects approach views the benefits of eliminating spoilage as being extremely or immeasurably great, thus justifying a zero tolerance.) The following discussion and illustrations of accounting for spoiled goods pertain to job order costing. The appropriate procedures for process costing are covered in Chapter 5.

Two accounting treatments of the cost of spoilage are appropriate, depending upon the circumstances. These circumstances are described in the four columns of the exhibit below; that exhibit should be referred to throughout this discussion. First, if spoilage is normal but does not occur at a fairly uniform rate with each job (Column 1 of the exhibit), then the cost of the spoiled units in excess of their net realizable value should be charged to Factory Overhead Control. Because the cost of normal spoilage is generally subject to estimation, an amount estimated from previous experience should be included in the predetermined factory overhead rate, thereby spreading the expected cost of such spoilage over all of the jobs produced during the period.

	SPOILAGE		
1	**2**	**3**	**4**
Nature of Spoilage: Normal but does not occur uniformly	Abnormal and due to an event not expected to recur	Normal and occurs at a fairly uniform rate	Directly attributable to a customer-imposed requirement
Accounting Treatment of the Actual Spoilage Identified: Cost of spoilage (less net realizable value) is charged to factory overhead control.			Cost of spoilage (less net realizable value) is charged directly to that job.
Measurement of Spoilage: An estimate of cost, based on experience, can be included in the predetermined overhead rate.	Cost is measured currently.	An estimate of cost, based on experience, can be included in the predetermined overhead rate.	Cost is measured currently but for control purposes only.

Second, the spoilage may be abnormal and attributable to an event that is not expected to recur, such as a setup error, an accident attributable to carelessness or inexperience, or an employee's failure to follow instructions (Column 2). The cost of the spoiled units in excess of their net realizable value should again be charged to Factory Overhead Control. Because such costs were not expected and thus were not included in the predetermined factory overhead rate, an unfavorable variance would be created in factory overhead for the period; i.e., the amount of underapplied factory overhead would be increased or the amount of overapplied factory overhead would be decreased.

Third, if spoilage is normal and occurs at a fairly uniform rate with each job, then the cost of the spoiled units in excess of their net realizable value can be charged to the job and excluded from the overhead rate (right-hand side of Column 3). Alternatively, as described in the left-hand side of Column 3, the periodic amount could be estimated from previous experience and included in the predetermined factory overhead rate, as is done when spoilage is not uniform from job to job. If spoilage is included in the predetermined rate, each job is charged with a share of the cost whenever factory overhead is applied to the job using the predetermined rate. To avoid double charging the job in such a case, the unrecoverable cost of such spoilage must be determined and charged to Factory Overhead Control. Whether the cost of uniformly occurring normal spoilage is charged to the job on which it occurs or is included in the predetermined factory overhead rate, the amount charged to each good unit produced during the period will be approximately the same. However, charging such costs to the job is more economical because the cost of spoiled units need not be separately determined, removed from the job in which spoilage occurs, and then tracked over time, as would be required if spoilage were included in the predetermined factory overhead rate.

Fourth, the spoilage may be directly attributable to requirements imposed by the customer, such as changes made after the job was begun or unusually close production tolerances (Column 4). The cost of the spoiled units in excess of their net realizable value should be charged to the job and excluded from the overhead rate. If the customer is responsible for the spoilage, the job should be charged for the spoilage cost so that the costs can be passed on to the customer during the billing process.

Spoiled Materials Charged to Factory Overhead Control. Nevada Products Company has a monthly capacity to manufacture 125,000 three-inch coil springs for use in mechanical brakes. Production is scheduled in response to orders received. Spoilage is caused by a variety of unpredictable factors and averages $.05 per spring. During November, 100,000 springs were produced with a materials cost of $.40 per unit, a labor cost of $.50 per unit, and factory overhead charged to production at a rate of 150% of the direct labor cost. This rate is based on an estimate that includes $.05 per spring for spoilage. The entry to record work put into production during the month is:

Work in Process	165,000	
Materials		40,000
Payroll		50,000
Applied Factory Overhead		75,000

On the last working day of the month, the entire day's production of 4,000 units is spoiled due to improper heat treatment; however, these units can be sold for $.50 each in the secondhand market. To record this normal loss on spoiled goods and the possible resale value, the entry that charges all production during the period with a proportionate share of the spoilage is:

	Subsidiary Record	Dr.	Cr.
Spoiled Goods		2,000	
Factory Overhead Control		4,600	
Loss on Spoiled Goods	4,600		
Work in Process			6,600

The spoilage loss is the sum of the materials, labor, and factory overhead in the spoiled units, reduced by the recovery or sales value of the units: $1,600 materials + $2,000 labor + $3,000 factory overhead – $2,000 cost recovery = $4,600 spoilage loss. The spoilage loss is transferred from Work in Process to Factory Overhead Control. Any difference between the sales price of the spoiled units when the inventory was recorded and the price realized at the time of sale would be a plus or minus adjustment to Factory Overhead Control (Loss on Spoiled Goods).

Each of the 96,000 good units produced during the month has a charged-in cost of $.05 for spoilage (96,000 × $.05 = $4,800); the actual spoilage during the period is $4,600. The good units produced on the order where the spoilage occurred carry a cost of $.40 for materials, $.50 for labor, and $.75 for overhead because the normal spoilage is charged to all production—not to the lot or order which happens to be in process at the time of actual spoilage. In other words, the $165,000 monthly production cost less the $6,600 credit resulting from spoiled units leaves $158,400 of cost for the 96,000 good units. $158,400 divided by the 96,000 good units gives a cost of $1.65 per good unit. The entry transferring the good units to Finished Goods is:

Finished Goods	158,400	
Work in Process		158,400

During the month, the amounts charged to Factory Overhead Control represent the depreciation, insurance, taxes, indirect materials, and indirect labor actually experienced, along with the $4,600 spoilage cost. All production during the month is charged with overhead of $.75 per unit. Overhead analysis reveals a $200 favorable variance ($4,600 actual minus $4,800 applied) attributable to the spoilage units.

Spoiled Materials Charged to a Particular Job. Nevada Products Company has a contract to manufacture 10,000 heavy-duty coil springs for Tri-State Supply Company. This order requires a steel wire that is harder and slightly heavier than stock normally used, but the production process, labor time, and overhead factors are identical to those of the standard product. Materials cost for each of these springs is $.60. This special order requires exacting specifications, and normal spoilage is to be charged to the order. The $.05 per unit spoilage factor is now eliminated from the overhead rate, and 140% of direct labor cost ($.70 per unit) is the rate used on this job. The order is put into production the first day of December, and sampling during the first hour of production indicates that eleven units of production are required to secure ten good springs. The entry to record costs placed into production for 11,000 units is:

Work in Process	19,800	
Materials		6,600
Payroll		5,500
Applied Factory Overhead		7,700

One thousand units, a normal number, did not meet specifications, but can be sold as seconds for $.45 per unit. The entry to record the spoilage is:

Spoiled Goods	450	
Work in Process		450

The entry made upon completing and shipping the job would be:

Cost of Goods Sold	19,350	
Work in Process		19,350

The net result of this treatment is to charge the spoilage loss of $1,350 ($1,800 – $450 cost recovery) to the 10,000 good units that are delivered at the original contract price. The unit cost of completed springs is $1.935 ($19,350 ÷ 10,000 units).

Any difference between the price when the spoiled goods inventory was recorded and the price realized at the time of sale should be an adjustment to Work in Process, Finished Goods, or Cost of Goods Sold, depending on the completion status of the particular job order. As an expedient, the difference might be closed to Factory Overhead Control.

In the situation just described in which spoilage is charged to the particular job, the overhead rate is adjusted downward from 150% to 140%. This adjustment, which eliminates the normal spoilage cost factor, is the theoretically correct procedure. For expediency, however, a firm may elect not to make an adjustment in the overhead rate if such a charge to a specific job is an unusual occurrence.

Defective Work

In the manufacturing process, imperfections may arise because of faults in materials, labor, or machines. The cost of such occurrences, both before and after delivery to customers, must be compared to the related cost of their prevention. The zero-defects approach should be adopted whenever the long-run cost of defects is believed to exceed the long-run cost of prevention.

If a defective unit can be reprocessed in one or more stages and made into a standard salable product, it is often profitable to rework the defective unit. Although spoiled work usually cannot be made into a first-class finished unit without uneconomical expenditures, defective work can be corrected to meet specified standards by adding materials, labor, and factory overhead.

Similar to the accounting for spoilage, two methods of accounting for the added cost to upgrade defective work are appropriate in job order costing, depending upon the circumstances:

1. If defective work is experienced in regular manufacturing but does not occur at a fairly uniform rate from job to job, or if the defective work is the result of an unusual event that is not expected to recur (for example, an employee error), then the additional cost to correct the defective units should be charged to Factory Overhead Control. If the defects are normal, an amount based on past experience can be included in the predetermined factory overhead rate. When the cost is included in the predetermined factory overhead rate, all jobs produced during the period are charged with a portion of the rework cost as overhead is applied to production. If the cost is not included in the predetermined factory overhead rate, the cost of rework will create an unfavorable factory overhead variance.

   To illustrate, assume that a company has an order for 500 units of a product that has direct production costs of $5 for materials and $3 for labor. Factory overhead is charged to production at 200% of labor cost, including a 5% allowance for reworking defective units. Fifty units are found to be defective and are to be reworked at a total cost of $30 for materials, $60 for labor, and overhead at 200% of direct labor cost. The entries are:

	Subsidiary Record	Dr.	Cr.
Work in Process		7,000	
Materials			2,500
Payroll			1,500
Applied Factory Overhead			3,000
Factory Overhead Control		210	
Defective Work.	210		
Materials			30
Payroll			60
Applied Factory Overhead			120
Finished Goods.		7,000	
Work in Process			7,000

   The unit cost of the completed units is $14 ($7,000 ÷ 500 units).

2. If defective work is expected to occur at a fairly uniform rate from job to job, or if it is directly attributable to requirements imposed by the customer, the additional cost to correct the defective units should be charged to the job. For example, suppose that the company in the preceding example received a special order for 500 units, with the agreement stating that any defective work is chargeable to the contract. During production, 50 units are improperly assembled. The total cost to correct these defective units is $30 for materials, $60 for labor, and 195% of the direct labor cost for factory overhead. Observe that the factory overhead rate has been reduced by the 5% allowance for reworking defective units, because the rework cost is to be charged directly to the job instead of to factory overhead. The entries in this case are:

Work in Process..	6,925	
Materials......................................		2,500
Payroll..		1,500
Applied Factory Overhead......................		2,925
Work in Process..	207	
Materials......................................		30
Payroll..		60
Applied Factory Overhead......................		117
Finished Goods..	7,132	
Work in Process..............................		7,132

The unit cost is $14.264 ($7,132 ÷ 500 units) instead of $14. In this second case in which the particular job is charged for defective work, the overhead rate is adjusted downward from 200% to 195%. As with spoilage this adjustment, which eliminates the allowance for reworking defective units from the overhead rate, is the theoretically correct procedure. However, for expediency such an adjustment in the overhead rate could be avoided if such charge to a specific job is an unusual occurrence.

If defective work is expected to occur at a fairly uniform rate, the cost of correcting the defective units could be included in factory overhead instead of being charged directly to the job, as was discussed in accounting for spoiled goods. But in such a case, charging the defective work cost to the job is more economical for the same reasons discussed for spoiled goods (see page 96).

The preceding discussion has dealt with the accounting for rework of defective units in job order costing. The appropriate procedure in process costing is simply to charge the rework cost to the process or department involved. If the amount of the rework cost is within normal limits, it becomes part of the cost of all units produced. Any portion not within normal limits is treated as a loss in the department, and may be written off immediately as a loss or charged to Factory Overhead Control.

■ JOB ORDER COSTING WITH MULTIPLE OVERHEAD RATES

ACTIVITY COSTING

The preceding discussion of spoilage and defectives contains examples of predetermined overhead rates based on direct labor cost, while in the Rayburn Company illustration earlier in this chapter, the predetermined overhead rate was based on machine hours. In a single company, there may be a significant amount of labor-related overhead, machine-related overhead, materials-related overhead, or a combination of these volume-related phenomena. Further, other components of overhead cost may not be closely related to the usage of labor, machinery, materials, or any other measure of production volume; they may be related to activities or transactions such as the number of setups or the number of product design changes, neither of which is a measure of production volume.

The presence of overhead amounts related to two or more bases or activities in a single business is common, and it does not present any particular product costing problem if a simple product line is being produced—a few similar products or various flavors and colors of the same basic product. Reasonable product cost information can be obtained in these circumstances by selecting a single activity base upon which to allocate factory overhead to production. (Typically the base is direct labor cost or direct labor hours, for which accurate measurements are available already. If direct labor is an insignificant part of total cost, or if it is not measured separately, machine hours or some other easily measured activity may be used.) Such a simple product line, however, would be more closely associated with the use of process costing than job order costing.

Many job order settings involve a diverse product line—a number of different basic products, each of which can be produced not only in several sizes but also in several grades, configurations, or types. For example, a machine tool manufacturer may produce a variety of machine tools. One particular size of one metal-cutting tool may be manufactured with manual, automatic, or computerized controls, digital or analog displays, and any of a variety of lubrication, noise-reduction, and safety devices. Some of these variations in the product's manufacture may result in greater amounts of material-related overhead, others in greater amounts of labor-related overhead, so that reliable product cost data cannot be obtained by using any single predetermined overhead rate.

One useful approach is the division of overhead costs into two or more categories, called overhead cost pools, and calculation of a predetermined overhead rate for each pool.[3] Machine hours might serve as the basis of the predetermined rate for a machine-related overhead cost pool, labor hours as the basis of the predetermined rate for a labor-related overhead cost pool, and the number of parts or cost of material used as the basis of the predetermined rate for a material-related overhead cost pool. In determining the cost of a job, the result would be a multiple-part overhead cost calculation within a single responsibility center. This approach could be interpreted as resulting in two or more overhead cost centers. The job order cost sheet for a nondepartmentalized plant might still include the three usual cost sections—direct material costs, direct labor costs, and applied factory overhead—but with the overhead applied section showing two or more calculations, each based on a different predetermined rate.

Do not confuse this approach to multiple overhead rates with the existence of multiple departments within a factory, which is discussed in Chapter 14. If multiple departments exist, each department is a separate responsibility center, and a job order cost sheet will show direct material, direct labor, and applied overhead for each department. A labor-driven department is likely to apply its overhead cost based on labor hours or labor cost, and a machine-driven department may apply its overhead cost based on machine hours, but within each department there still may be only one overhead cost pool and one allocation base. In contrast, the use of multiple cost pools in one depart-

---

[3]For an example, see John W. Jonez and Michael A. Wright, "Material Burdening: Management Accounting Can Support Competitive Strategy," *Management Accounting*, Vol. 69, No. 2, pp. 27-31.

ment or in a nondepartmentalized factory means that within one responsibility center, two or more forms of overhead application are carried out simultaneously, and their sum is the total overhead charged to jobs.

Refer to the Rayburn Company's completed job order cost sheet shown on page 83. Separate departments do not exist within Rayburn Company. Suppose Rayburn Company expects to incur $100,000 of labor-related overhead and $200,000 of machine-related overhead and to use 20,000 direct labor hours and 10,000 machine hours during the period. Further assume that some of Rayburn Company's jobs require much machine time and little labor, while others require the opposite mix. A single predetermined overhead rate based on labor would assign too much cost to labor-intensive jobs and too little to machine-intensive jobs, and a single predetermined overhead rate based on machine hours would do just the opposite. A solution is to calculate two predetermined overhead rates: $5 per direct labor hour ($100,000 of expected labor-related overhead divided by 20,000 expected direct labor hours) and $20 per machine hour ($200,000 of expected machine-related overhead divided by 10,000 expected machine hours). The cost sheet for job order number 5574, appearing on page 83, would have a two-part calculation in its overhead applied section:

$$
\begin{array}{lrr}
196 \text{ direct labor hours} \times \$ 5 = & \$ & 980 \\
29.4 \text{ machine hours} \quad \times \$20 = & & 588 \\
\hline
\text{Factory overhead applied} \quad = & \$1{,}568 \\
\end{array}
$$

■ ACTIVITY COSTING

A costing system which uses one or more non-volume-related factors in allocating multiple overhead cost pools is called an *activity costing system*, (ACS), *activity-based costing* (ABC), or simply *activity costing*.[4] In activity costing, the bases used to allocate overhead costs are called *cost drivers*. Hundreds of manufacturing companies have found that activity-based costing not only provides more reliable product cost data, but also aids in understanding and reducing overhead costs, in designing products and processes, and in selecting strategies. A tenet of activity costing is that a conventional costing system, in which only volume-related bases are used to allocate overhead costs, may not assign costs to different products appropriately.

Compared to conventional costing, activity costing represents a more thorough application of the concept of cost traceability. Conventional costing traces only direct material and direct labor to the output produced. Activity costing recognizes that many overhead costs are in fact traceable, if not to output, then to some other level called an activity.

---

[4]Robin Cooper, "The Rise of Activity-Based Costing," *Journal of Cost Management*, Vol. 2, No. 2, pp. 45-54.

Conventional costing systems allocate all overhead costs according to some measure of product volume, usually a measure of direct labor or machine usage. Activity costing, in contrast, treats overhead costs as being caused by internal events called *transactions* or *activities*. Products cause or consume activities, and it is the activities that consume resources and thus cause overhead costs to be incurred. Examples of activities in a factory are setups, design changes, material receipts, material requisitions, material movements, vendor orders, inspections, and work orders. Determining the costs of these activities is often a first step toward substantial cost savings, because if activities that add no value to the product are found to have high costs, it becomes clear that such activities should be reduced or eliminated. If activities are reduced, both the firm's cost structure and the activity costing system can become simpler.

Many manufacturers with complex cost structures and diverse product lines have found that conventional costing systems report distorted product costs. A complex cost structure is present if a high proportion of overhead costs are not related to product volume. A diverse product line is one in which different products consume different mixes of volume-related and non-volume-related costs. For example, suppose a specialty product is made in batches of one unit each and its design is changed with practically every batch, while a more common product is made in batches of a thousand units with very rare design changes. The specialty product consumes a large amount of setup and design activities compared to its low volume—regardless of whether volume is measured by direct labor usage, machine usage, or other measures—while the common product consumes an opposite mix; such differences are the essential feature of a diverse product line. If setup costs and design costs make up a significant part of total overhead cost, then the cost structure is complex, and overhead costs cannot be assigned appropriately by a conventional costing system.

Refer to the Rayburn Company example used previously in which 10,000 machine hours and $200,000 of machine-related overhead are expected for the period. Suppose Rayburn's accountants have determined that a significant amount of machine-related overhead cost is caused by machine setups. Two possible setup cost drivers have been examined, total setup time and number of setups, and the latter is found to explain total setup cost better and to be more easily measured.[5] Out of the expected $200,000 of machine-related overhead cost, setup-related costs are expected to represent $80,000 for the period, and 200 setups are expected to be performed. The remaining $120,000 of machine-related overhead will be charged on a machine-hour basis. Rayburn will calculate three predetermined overhead rates as shown on the following page.

---

[5]For additional discussion of how the base may be selected, see the section entitled "Transactions Base" in Chapter 13.

Overhead Related to	(a) Expected Amount	(b) Expected Level of Allocation Base	(a) ÷ (b) Overhead Rate
Direct labor usage	$100,000	20,000 labor hours	$ 5
Machine usage	120,000	10,000 machine hours	12
Machine setups	80,000	200 setups	400
Total	$300,000		

If job number 5574 required two setups, the overhead section of its job order cost sheet would be calculated as follows:

$$
\begin{array}{lr}
\text{196 direct labor hours} \times \$5 = \$ & 980.00 \\
\text{29.4 machine hours} \times \$12 = & 352.80 \\
\text{2 setups} \times \$400 \qquad\qquad = & 800.00 \\
\hline
\text{Factory overhead applied} \quad = \$2{,}132.80 &
\end{array}
$$

This is an example of activity costing because the bases used for charging overhead cost include a non-volume-related factor, setups. In practice, an activity costing system may use many non-volume-related factors to allocate overhead costs.

■ JOB ORDER COSTING IN SERVICE BUSINESSES

In service businesses with not all jobs alike, several varieties of job order costing are commonly used. Such service businesses include repair shops and professional services such as legal, architectural, engineering, accounting, and consulting. In these businesses, direct labor and labor-related costs are usually larger than any other kind of cost, often by a wide margin, so the predetermined overhead rate typically is based on direct labor cost. It is also common to combine the labor cost rate with the predetermined overhead cost rate. The amount charged to a job for each hour of labor time then represents both labor and overhead.

The only remaining items to be charged to each job are the directly traceable costs other than labor. In a repair shop, this category usually includes only the cost of parts, which corresponds to the direct material cost in a factory. But in a professional service business, there are many directly traceable costs other than labor. Examples are travel, meals, entertainment, long distance telephone charges, photocopying, and subcontracted services. In accumulating these costs and charging them to jobs, one crucial link in the control system of a professional service business is the fact that many of these costs are incurred initially by the firm's personnel, who then are entitled to be reimbursed by the firm.

For example, when requesting reimbursement for travel, meals, entertainment, and any other cost paid by an employee, the employee is required to supply several pieces of information as part of the reimbursement request: date of the expenditure, client's name or job number of the engagement, nature of the cost, and, for larger amounts, an original receipt. This information is necessary to establish the legitimacy of the reimbursement, but it also enables the costs to be traced directly to jobs. For photocopying costs, the data needed to trace costs directly to jobs is gathered by requiring all photocopies to be entered on a log kept near the photocopy machine; for tracing long distance telephone charges, each employee is required to keep a log of all phone calls.

Weekly or monthly summaries of all costs are prepared and entered on job cost sheets, which may be called by any of several names depending on the type of business. A partially completed job cost sheet for a law firm is illustrated on page 106. Notice that there is no separate category for overhead, because the predetermined overhead cost rate is included in the hourly charges for labor.

DISCUSSION QUESTIONS

Q4-1. The statement has often been made that an actual product cost does not exist in the sense of absolute authenticity and verifiability. Why?

Q4-2. What is the primary objective in job order costing?

Q4-3. What is the rationale supporting the use of process costing instead of job order costing for product costing purposes?

Q4-4. Describe the uses of a job order cost sheet.

Q4-5. What is the function of the work in process account in job order costing?

Q4-6. How is control over prime costs achieved in job order costing?

Q4-7. Distinguish between actual and applied factory overhead.

Q4-8. Several methods of accounting for scrap materials are discussed in this chapter. Which method could be regarded as most accurate?

Q4-9. In the control of materials cost, why is the knowledge that there is excessive waste likely to be of greater value than the income derived from the sale of scrap?

Q4-10. In some situations, labor and materials costs incurred on defective work are treated as factory overhead. In other cases the cost of perfecting defective work is charged directly to the job. Explain the appropriate use of each accounting treatment.

Q4-11. Within a single department of a factory, or within a nondepartmentalized factory, the use of a single overhead rate may not give accurate product cost information if a complex product line is being produced. What is one approach to solving this product costing problem?

Q4-12. Some service businesses use job order costing. What characteristics of a service business make it likely that job order costing will be used?

Vise, Freud, & Graff, Attorneys at Law

Summary of Engagement Account

Client Name:	Charles Harmed		Date Contracted:	5/9/19A
Engagement Type:	Civil		Date Terminated:	
Engagement Number:	1057		Supervising Partner:	Vise

PARTNERS' TIME:

Period Ending	Hours	Rate	Amount	
5/31/19A	30	$150*	$4,500.00	
6/30/19A				
Subtotals:				$

Job Cost Sheet for a Service Business

ASSOCIATES' TIME:

Period Ending	Hours	Rate	Amount	
5/31/19A	200	$60*	$12,000.00	
6/30/19A				
Subtotals:				$
Total time:				$

OTHER:

Period Ending	5/31/19A	6/30/19A		
Travel	$ 391.00			
Meals	206.00			
Photocopies	52.60			
Telephone	143.49			
Detective	300.00			
Witnesses	900.00			
Total other:	$1,993.09			$
Total for engagement:				$

*Represents the sum of direct labor cost and the predetermined overhead rate based on direct labor.

EXERCISES

E4-1. Manufacturing costs. The work in process account of Highroad Company showed:

Work in Process

Materials	$15,500	Finished goods	$37,500
Direct labor	14,750		
Factory overhead	11,800		

Materials charged to the one job still in process amounted to $3,200. Factory overhead is applied as a predetermined percentage of direct labor cost.

Required: Compute the following:
(1) The amount of direct labor cost in finished goods.
(2) The amount of factory overhead in finished goods.

E4-2. Manufacturing costs. Data relating to Weldco Company's manufacturing activities for December follow:

	Inventories	
	December 1	December 31
Finished goods...............	$12,000	
Direct materials		$5,000
Direct labor...............		$3,000
Machine time		60 hours
Work in process..............	3,000 units	2,000 units
Direct materials, $2.40 per unit		
Direct labor, $0.80 per unit		
Machine time	48 hours	32 hours
Materials....................	$9,000	$4,500

Total December manufacturing cost was $180,000, of which $30,000 was direct labor cost. A total of 600 machine hours were used in the month. Weldco uses a predetermined overhead rate of $100 per machine hour to assign factory overhead to work in process and finished goods inventories. Materials purchased in December were $84,000 and freight-in on these purchases totaled $1,500.

Required: Compute the following:
(1) Materials used in December.
(2) Work in process at December 31.
(3) December cost of goods manufactured.
(4) Finished goods at December 31.
(5) December cost of goods sold.

CGA-Canada (adapted) Reprint with permission.

E4-3. Manufacturing costs. Selected data concerning last year's operations of Televancia Company are as follows (in thousands of dollars):

	Inventories	
	Beginning	Ending
Finished Goods.........	$90	$110
Work in Process	80	30
Materials	75	85

Other data:

Materials used	$326
Total manufacturing costs charged to jobs during the year (includes materials, direct labor, and factory overhead applied at a rate of 60% of direct labor cost).	686
Cost of goods available for sale	826
Marketing and administrative expenses	25

Required: Compute the following:
  (1) Cost of materials purchased.
  (2) Direct labor cost charged to production.
  (3) Cost of goods manufactured.
  (4) Cost of goods sold.   (ICMA adapted)

E4-4. Manufacturing costs. Krieger Company is to submit a bid on the production of 11,250 ceramic plates. It is estimated that the cost of materials will be $13,000, and the cost of direct labor will be $15,000. Factory overhead is applied at $2.70 per direct labor hour in the Molding Department and at 35% of the direct labor cost in the Decorating Department. It is estimated that 1,000 direct labor hours at a cost of $9,000 will be required in Molding. The company wishes a markup of 45% of its total production cost.

Required: Determine the following:
  (1) Estimated cost to produce.
  (2) Estimated prime cost.
  (3) Estimated conversion cost.
  (4) Bid price.

E4-5. Job order cost sheet. Wadsworth Machine Works collects its cost data by job order cost accumulation. For Job 909, the following data are available:

Direct Materials		Direct Labor	
9/14 Issued	$600	Week of Sept. 20	90 hrs. @ $6.20/hr.
9/20 Issued	331	Week of Sept. 26	70 hrs. @ $7.30/hr.
9/22 issued	200		

Factory overhead is applied at the rate of $80 per machine hour. Ten machine hours were used on Job 909 on Sept. 20.

Required:
  (1) Enter the appropriate information on a job order cost sheet.
  (2) Determine the sales price of the job, assuming that it was contracted with a markup of 40% of cost.

E4-6. Journal entries for job order costing. The following job order cost detail pertains to the three jobs that were in process at the Nautical Boat Company during January.

	Job 66	Job 67	Job 68
Cost charged in prior period.	$40,000	$15,000	$ —
Costs added in January:			
Direct materials	35,000	45,000	25,000
Direct labor.	45,000	40,000	35,000
Factory overhead ($50 per machine hour)	?	?	?
January machine hours used	720	640	560

Required: Prepare the appropriate journal entry (including subsidiary ledger detail for job orders) to record each of these January transactions:

(1) Direct materials were issued from the materials storeroom to work in process.
(2) The payroll was distributed to work in process.
(3) Factory overhead was applied to production for the period.
(4) Job orders 66 and 67 were completed and transferred to the finished goods storeroom.

E4-7. Journal entries for job order costing. Chandler Company's July transactions included the following:
  (a) Purchased materials on account, $25,000.
  (b) Requisitions for $8,000 of direct materials and $2,000 of indirect materials were filled from the storeroom.
  (c) Factory payroll totaling $9,400 consisted of $7,600 direct labor and $1,800 indirect labor. Payroll deductions were $658 for FICA and $1,200 for employees income tax.
  (d) Depreciation of $1,200 on factory equipment was recorded.
  (e) A job order was completed with $1,830 of direct labor and $1,450 of materials being previously charged to the order. Factory overhead is to be applied at 66 2/3% of direct labor cost.
  (f) Miscellaneous factory overhead of $1,250 was accrued.
  (g) The job order referred to in transaction (e) was shipped to Dixon Associates, who were billed for $5,400.

Required: Prepare journal entries to record the transactions.

E4-8. Flow of costs through T accounts. The Neilson Company had the following inventories at the beginning and end of January:

	January 1	January 31
Materials	$10,000	$ 38,000
Work in Process	?	110,000
Finished Goods.	50,000	150,000

During January, the cost of materials purchased was $138,000 and factory overhead of $90,000 was applied at a rate of 50% of direct labor cost. January cost of goods sold was $200,000.

Required: Prepare completed T accounts showing the flow of the cost of goods manufactured and sold.
CGA-Canada (adapted) Reprint with permission.

E4-9. Accounting for spoiled work. Ariba Company had a production run of 4,000 pairs of jeans during the last week of June, with the following unit costs:

Direct materials.	$ 5.00
Direct labor	4.00
Factory overhead (includes a $.50 allowance for spoiled work)	3.50
	$12.50

Final inspection revealed that 300 pairs, a normal number, did not meet quality standards, but can be sold as seconds at a price of $7 a pair.

Required: Prepare journal entries for all of the described transactions if:
  (1) The loss is charged to Factory Overhead Control.
  (2) The loss is due to exacting specifications and is charged to the production run.

E4-10. Journal entries to correct defective work. The Los Angeles Fabricators manufacture jacks and other lifting equipment. One order from the Seattle Supply House for 1,000 jacks showed the following costs per unit: direct materials, $3.50; direct labor, $1.25; and factory overhead applied at 140% of direct labor cost if defective work is charged to the job, 150% if it is not.

Final inspection revealed that 50 of the units were improperly riveted. These units were disassembled, properly riveted, and reassembled. The per-unit cost of correcting the defective jacks consists of $0.15 for rivets, $0.25 for direct labor, and factory overhead at the predetermined rate.

Required: Prepare journal entries to record the rework of the defective units and the transfer to Finished Goods if:

(1) The Seattle Supply House order is to be charged with the cost of defective units.

(2) The cost of reworking the defective units is not charged to the Seattle Supply House order.

E4-11. Journal entries to correct defective work. The Watertown Company manufactures jacks and other lifting equipment. One order from the Midwestern Supply Company for 1,500 jacks showed the following costs per unit: direct materials, $7.50; direct labor, $2.63; and factory overhead applied at 150% of direct labor cost, which includes a 5% allowance for reworking defective units.

Final inspection revealed that 100 of the units were improperly riveted. These units were disassembled, properly riveted, and reassembled. The per-unit cost of correcting the defective jacks consists of $0.30 for rivets, $0.45 for direct labor, and factory overhead at the predetermined rate.

Required: Give general journal entries to record all production costs, rework, and the transfer to Finished Goods if:

(1) The rework cost is charged to Factory Overhead.

(2) The rework cost is charged to the job.

E4-12. Multiple overhead rates. Smith Metal Fabricators (SMF) has a diverse product line and a complex cost structure, with some jobs requiring much labor and little machine use and others requiring the opposite mix. Because no single base for a predetermined overhead rate will provide SMF management with reliable product cost information, overhead is classified into two cost pools and two predetermined overhead rates are used. For 19A, it is estimated that total overhead costs will consist of $200,000 of overhead related to the usage of direct labor hours and $300,000 of overhead related to machine usage. Total machine usage is expected to be 4,000 hours for the year, and total direct labor hours are expected to be 16,000.

Job 345 required $2,000 of direct material, 30 hours of labor at $10 per hour, and 10 hours of machine time.

Required:

(1) Calculate SMF's predetermined overhead rates for 19A.

(2) Prepare a completed job cost sheet for Job 345.

E4-13. Activity Costing. Eddie's Machine Tool Incorporated (EMT) produces a varied product line without the use of direct labor. An extensive setup procedure is required. Because no single base for a predetermined overhead rate will provide Eddie with reliable product cost information, overhead is classified into two cost pools and two predetermined overhead rates are used. For 19A, it is estimated that total overhead costs will consist of $525,000 of overhead related to setups and $900,000 of overhead related to machine usage. Total machine usage is expected to be 3,600 hours for the year, and the total number of setups is expected to be 300.

Job 103 required parts and materials costing $56,000, 70 hours of machine time, and four setups.

Required:

(1) Calculate EMT's predetermined overhead rates for 19A.

(2) Prepare a completed job cost sheet for Job 103.

PROBLEMS

P4-1. Manufacturing costs. Last month, Jorge Company put $60,000 of materials into production. The Grinding Department used 8,000 labor hours at $5.60 per hour, and the Machining Department used 4,600 hours at a cost of $6 per hour. Factory overhead is applied at a rate of $6 per labor hour in the Grinding Department and $8 per labor hour in the Machining Department. Inventory accounts had the following beginning and ending balances:

	Beginning	Ending
Finished Goods.........	$22,000	$17,000
Work in Process	15,000	17,600
Materials	20,000	18,000

Required: Without preparing a formal income statement, compute the following:
(1) Total cost of work put into process.
(2) Cost of completed jobs.
(3) Cost of jobs sold.
(4) Conversion cost.
(5) Cost of materials purchased.

P4-2. Manufacturing costs. Cleghorn Assembly Works uses job order cost accumulation and applies overhead based on direct labor hours. Any underapplied or overapplied overhead is adjusted directly to Cost of Goods Sold at the end of each month. On April 1, job cost sheets indicated the following:

	Job 201	Job 202	Job 203	Job 204
Direct materials..........	$3,590	$2,000	$1,480	$2,000
Direct labor	2,700	1,500	1,000	1,200
Applied overhead	2,160	1,200	800	960
Total cost...............	$8,450	$4,700	$3,280	$4,160
Job status	Finished	In Process	In Process	In Process

On April 30, Finished Goods contained only Jobs 204 and 207, which had the following total costs:

	Job 204	Job 207
Direct materials..........	$2,970	$2,450
Direct labor	2,200	1,900
Applied overhead	1,760	1,520
Total cost...............	$6,930	$5,870

Besides working on Jobs 204 and 207 in April, Cleghorn continued work on Jobs 202 and 203 and started work on Jobs 205 and 206. A summary of direct materials used and direct labor hours worked on Jobs 202, 203, 205, and 206 during April showed the following:

	Job 202	Job 203	Job 205	Job 206
Direct materials	$1,250	$555	$2,500	$1,980
Direct labor hours	100	75	105	50

Other information:
(a) On April 30, the only jobs still in process were 203 and 206.
(b) All workers are paid $20 per hour. Wage rates have been stable throughout the year.
(c) Cleghorn maintains only one raw materials account (Materials Control) from which it issues both direct and indirect materials. The balance in this account was $2,750 on April 1.
(d) All sales are billed on account at 150% of total cost.
(e) Other items in April:

Depreciation, factory equipment	$ 1,375
Raw materials purchased	11,500
Indirect labor	2,500
Factory rent and utilities	2,700
Indirect materials used	2,790

Required:
1. (1) Determine the April 30 balances for Materials Control and for Work in Process.
2. (2) Prepare all journal entries required for Job 202 in April.
3. (3) Calculate the cost of goods manufactured in April. (A complete statement of cost of goods manufactured is not required.)
4. (4) Calculate the over- or underapplied overhead for April.
5. (5) Calculate gross profit for April.   (SMAC adapted)

P4-3. Manufacturing cost computations with T accounts. The following information pertains to the Cloverdale Company:

	Account Balances	
	Beginning	Ending
Finished Goods	$80,000	$?
Work in Process.	20,000	?
Materials.	15,000	23,000
Accounts Payable.	7,000	5,000
Accrued Payroll	11,000	14,000
Accounts Receivable	45,000	65,000

(a) All sales were on account, with a markup of 28% of cost.
(b) The accounts payable account was used for materials purchases only.
(c) Factory overhead was applied at 150% of direct labor cost.
(d) Miscellaneous factory overhead cost totaled $60,000.
(e) Direct materials issued to production cost $80,000.
(f) Payment of accounts payable totaled $102,000.
(g) There was only one job in process at the end of the period, with charges to date of materials costing $10,000 and direct labor of $8,000.
(h) Collection of accounts receivable totaled $480,000.
(i) Cost of goods manufactured was $320,000.
(j) Payroll payment totaled $172,000.

Required: Using T accounts, compute:
1. (1) Materials purchased.
2. (2) Cost of goods sold.
3. (3) Finished goods ending inventory.
4. (4) Work in process ending inventory.
5. (5) Direct labor cost.
6. (6) Applied factory overhead.
7. (7) Over- or underapplied factory overhead.
8. (8) Assuming the over- or underapplied overhead is relatively small, what disposition should be made of it?
                                                      CGA-Canada (adapted) Reprint with permission.

SS **P4-4. Income statement; cost of goods sold statement; factory overhead analysis.** On October 1, the accountant of Columbus Company prepared a trial balance from which the following accounts were extracted:

Finished Goods (2,800 units)	$ 9,800	
Work in Process (1,200 units).	4,070	
Materials and Supplies	40,700	
Buildings	48,000	
Accumulated Depreciation—Buildings		$ 6,000
Machinery and Equipment	96,000	
Accumulated Depreciation—Machinery and Equipment		37,500
Office Equipment	3,200	
Accumulated Depreciation—Office Equipment		1,000
Accrued Payroll		650

The following transactions and other data have been made available for October:

Purchased materials and supplies	$ 24,800
Paid factory overhead	20,100
Paid marketing expenses.	25,050
Paid administrative expenses	19,700
Requisitions for: Direct materials.	29,800
Indirect materials	3,950

Depreciation:
  Building, 5% (75% to manufacturing, 15% to
    marketing, and 10% to administrative expenses)
  Machinery and equipment, 10%
  Office equipment, 15% (40% to marketing and
    60% to administrative expenses)

Sales (20,700 units)	144,900
Sales returns and allowances	1,300
Cash payments for: Accounts payable	75,000
Payroll	21,800
Distribution of payroll earned: Direct labor	18,600
Indirect labor	4,400
Cash collected from customers	116,900
Applied factory overhead based on machine hours used	27,450
Transferred to finished goods, 20,400 units	
Cost of goods sold is calculated on the fifo basis.	
Work in process inventory on October 31	4,440

Required:
(1) Prepare in detail the cost of goods sold section of the income statement for October, assuming that over- or underapplied factory overhead is deferred until the end of the calendar year.
(2) Prepare the income statement for October.
(3) Calculate the amount of over- or underapplied factory overhead for October.

P4-5. Balance sheet; income statement. On December 31, 19A, Morrisville Canning Company, with outstanding common stock of $30,000, had the following assets and liabilities:

Cash	$ 5,000	Materials	$ 4,000
Accounts receivable	10,000	Prepaid expenses	500
Finished goods	6,000	Property, plant, and equipment (net)	30,000
Work in process	2,000	Current liabilities.	17,500

During 19B, the retained earnings account increased 50% as a result of the year's business. No dividends were paid during the year. Balances of accounts receivable, prepaid expenses, current liabilities, and common stock were the same on December 31, 19B, as they had been on December 31, 19A. Inventories were reduced by exactly 50%, except for the finished goods inventory, which was reduced by 33 1/3%. Plant assets (net) were reduced by depreciation of $4,000, charged 3/4 to factory overhead and 1/4 to administrative expense. Sales of $60,000 were made on account, costing $38,000. Direct labor cost was $9,000. Factory overhead was applied at a rate of 100% of direct labor cost, leaving $2,000 underapplied that was closed into the cost of goods sold account. Total marketing and administrative expenses amounted to 10% and 15%, respectively, of the gross sales.

Required:
(1) Prepare a balance sheet as of December 31, 19B.
(2) Prepare an income statement for the year 19B, with details of the cost of goods manufactured and sold.   (AICPA adapted)

P4-6. Job order costing. Tropez Inc. had the following inventories on March 1:

Finished Goods.	$15,000
Work in Process	19,070
Materials	14,000

The work in process account controls three jobs:

	Job 621	Job 622	Job 623
Materials	$2,800	$3,400	$1,800
Labor	2,100	2,700	1,350
Applied factory overhead	1,680	2,160	1,080
Total	$6,580	$8,260	$4,230

The following information pertains to March operations:
- (a) Materials purchased and received, $22,000; terms, n/30.
- (b) Materials requisitioned for production, $21,000. Of this amount, $2,400 was for indirect materials; the difference was distributed: $5,300 to Job 621; $7,400 to Job 622; and $5,900 to Job 623.
- (c) Materials returned to the storeroom from the factory, $600, of which $200 was for indirect materials, the balance from Job 622.
- (d) Materials returned to vendors, $800.
- (e) Payroll, after deducting 7.5% for FICA tax and 11.5% for employees income tax, was $30,780. The payroll amount due the employees was paid during March.
- (f) Of the payroll, direct labor represented 55%; indirect labor, 20%; sales salaries, 15%; and administrative salaries, 10%. The direct labor cost was distributed: $6,420 to Job 621; $8,160 to Job 622; and $6,320 to Job 623.
- (g) An additional 13.7% was entered for employer payroll taxes, representing the employer's 7.5% FICA tax, 5.4% state unemployment insurance tax, and .8% federal unemployment insurance tax. Employer payroll taxes related to direct labor are charged to the factory overhead control account.
- (h) Factory overhead, other than any previously mentioned, amounted to $5,500. Included in this figure were $2,000 for depreciation of factory building and equipment and $250 for expired insurance on the factory. The remaining overhead, $3,250, was unpaid at the end of March.
- (i) Factory overhead applied to production: 80% of the direct labor cost to be charged to the three jobs based on the labor cost for March.
- (j) Jobs 621 and 622 were completed and transferred to the finished goods warehouse.
- (k) Both Jobs 621 and 622 were shipped and billed at a gross profit of 40% of the cost of goods sold.
- (l) Cash collections from accounts receivable during March were $69,450.

Required:
- (1) Prepare job order cost sheets to post beginning inventory data.
- (2) Journalize the March transactions with current postings to general ledger inventory accounts and to job order cost sheets.
- (3) Prepare a schedule of inventories on March 31.

P4-7. Ledger accounts covering cost accounting cycle and job order cost accumulation. The books of Rio Grande Products Company show the following account balances as of March 1:

Finished Goods	$ 78,830
Work in Process	292,621
Materials	65,000
Over- or Underapplied Factory Overhead	12,300 (Cr.)

The work in process account is supported by the following job order cost sheets:

Job	Item	Direct Materials	Direct Labor	Factory Overhead	Total
204	80,000 Balloons	$ 15,230	$ 21,430	$ 13,800	$ 50,460
205	5,000 Life Rafts	40,450	55,240	22,370	118,060
206	10,000 Life Belts	60,875	43,860	19,366	124,101
		$116,555	$120,530	$ 55,536	$292,621

During March, the following transactions occurred:
- (a) Purchase of materials, $42,300.
- (b) Purchase of special materials, $5,800, for new Job 207, which calls for 4,000 life jackets.
- (c) Payroll data for March:

Job	Amount	Hours
204	$26,844	3,355.5
205	22,750	3,250.0
206	28,920	3,615.0
207	20,370	2,910.0

Indirect labor cost, $9,480; factory superintendence, $3,000. Payroll deductions: FICA tax, 7.5%; employees income tax, 11.5%.
- (d) Employer's payroll taxes: FICA, 7.5%; state unemployment, 5.4%; federal unemployment, .8%. These taxes are charged to Factory Overhead Control.
- (e) Materials issued:

Job 204	$ 9,480
Job 205	11,320
Job 206	10,490
Job 207	16,640 (excluding $5,800 of special materials, which are also issued at this time)

- (f) Other factory overhead incurred or accrued (credit Various Credits):

Insurance on factory	$830	Coal expense	$1,810
Tax on real estate	845	Power	3,390
Depreciation—machinery	780	Repairs and maintenance	2,240
Depreciation—factory building	840	Indirect supplies	1,910
Light.	560		

- (g) Factory overhead is applied at the rate of $2.30 per direct labor hour. An applied factory overhead account is used.
- (h) Job 204 was shipped and billed at a contract price of $117,500.

Required:
- (1) Construct ledger accounts, inserting beginning balances and entering transactions for March. (Factory overhead is to be posted to the control account only.)
- (2) In itemized form, compute the total cost of each job at the end of March.
- (3) Determine the amount remaining in the over- or underapplied factory overhead account.

P4-8. Job order cost cycle; general and subsidiary ledgers; cost of goods sold statement. On January 1, the general ledger of Mid-State Company contained the following accounts and balances:

Cash.	$47,000	Machinery	$ 45,300
Accounts Receivable	50,000	Accumulated Depreciation—Machinery	10,000
Finished Goods	32,500	Accounts Payable	59,375
Work in Process.	7,500	Common Stock	100,000
Materials.	22,000	Retained Earnings.	34,925

Details of the three inventories are:

Finished goods inventory: Item X—1,000 units @ $12.50.	$12,500
Item Y—2,000 units @ $10.00.	20,000
Total	$32,500

Work in process inventory:	Job 101	Job 102
Direct materials: 500 units of A @ $5	$2,500	
200 units of B @ $3		$ 600
Direct labor: 500 hours @ $4.	2,000	
200 hours @ $5.		1,000
Factory overhead applied at the rate		
of $2 per direct labor hour	1,000	400
Total	$5,500	$2,000

Materials inventory: Material A—2,000 units @ $5		$10,000
Material B—4,000 units @ $3		12,000
Total		$22,000

During January, the following transactions were completed:
(a) Purchases on account: Material A, 10,000 units @ $5.20; Material B, 12,000 units @ $3.75; indirect materials, $17,520.
(b) Payroll totaling $110,000 was accrued, and the amount payable to employees was paid. Payroll deductions consisted of $14,950 for employees income tax and 7.5% for FICA tax.
(c) Payroll was distributed as follows: Job 101, 2,500 direct labor hours @ $8; Job 102, 4,000 direct labor hours @ $10; Job 103, 3,000 direct labor hours @ $6; indirect labor, $12,000; marketing and administrative salaries, $20,000. Employer's payroll taxes were: FICA, 7.5%; state unemployment, 4.9%; federal unemployment, .8%.
(d) Materials were issued on a fifo basis as follows: Material A, 10,000 units (charged to Job 101); Material B, 12,000 units (charged to Job 102); Material A, 1,000 units, and Material B, 2,500 units (charged to Job 103). (Note: Transactions are to be taken in consecutive order.) Indirect materials amounting to $7,520 were issued.
(e) Factory overhead was applied to Jobs 101, 102, and 103, based on a rate of $4.50 per direct labor hour.
(f) Jobs 101 and 102 were completed and sold on account for $120,000 and $135,000, respectively. (Use a finished goods subsidiary account, titled "Completed Jobs.")
(g) After allowing a 5% cash discount, a net amount of $247,000 was collected on accounts receivable.
(h) Marketing and administrative expenses (other than salaries) paid during the month amounted to $15,000. Miscellaneous factory overhead of $10,800 was paid. Depreciation on machinery was $2,000.
(i) Payments on account, other than payrolls paid, amounted to $85,000.
(j) The over- or underapplied factory overhead is to be closed to the cost of goods sold account.

Required:
(1) Open general and subsidiary ledger accounts and record January 1 balances.
(2) Journalize the January transactions, including subsidiary ledger detail.
(3) Post January transactions to the general ledger and the subsidiary ledgers for materials, work in process, finished goods, and factory overhead incurred.
(4) Prepare a trial balance of the general ledger as of January 31, reconciling control accounts with subsidiary ledgers.
(5) Prepare a cost of goods sold statement for January.

P4-9. Journal entries for spoiled work. Fannin Company had a production run of 8,000 pairs of slacks during the last week of June, at the following costs per pair:

Materials	$5
Labor.	4
Factory overhead (includes $.70 allowance for spoiled work).	3

Final inspection revealed 600 pairs not meeting quality standards, salable as seconds at $4 a pair.

Required: Prepare the journal entries to record all related costs if:
  (1) The loss is to be charged to the production run.
  (2) The loss is to be charged to Factory Overhead Control.

P4-10. Journal entries to correct defective work. Lindale Fabricators manufactures jacks and other lifting equipment. One order from Athens Supply House for 1,000 jacks showed the following costs per unit: materials, $4; labor, $1.75; factory overhead applied at 160% of direct labor cost (150% in cases in which any defective unit costs are to be charged to a specific order).

Final inspection revealed that 75 of the units were improperly riveted. Correction of each defective unit requires $.20 for materials, $.30 for labor, and factory overhead at the appropriate rate.

Required: Prepare entries to record all costs related to the order when:
  (1) The order is charged with the cost of defective work.
  (2) The cost of correcting defective work is not charged to a specific order.

P4-11. Multiple overhead rates. Better Engine Works (BEW) has a diverse product line and a complex cost structure, with some jobs requiring much labor and little machine use, and others requiring the opposite mix. Because no single base for a predetermined overhead rate will provide BEW management with reliable product cost information, overhead is classified into two cost pools and two predetermined overhead rates are used. For 19A, it is estimated that total overhead costs will consist of $400,000 of overhead related to the usage of direct labor hours and $600,000 of overhead related to machine usage. Total machine usage is expected to be 20,000 hours for the year, and total direct labor hours are expected to be 16,000 hours.

Job 564 required $1,000 of direct materials, 30 hours of labor at $10 per hour, and 10 hours of machine time. Job 632 required $1,000 of direct material, 30 hours of labor at $10 per hour, and 60 hours of machine time.

Required:
  (1) Calculate BEW's predetermined overhead rates for 19A.
  (2) Determine the total cost of Job 564.
  (3) Determine the total cost of Job 632.
  (4) If BEW had used a single predetermined overhead rate based on direct labor hours to apply all overhead costs, then:
      (a) What would the predetermined rate be?
      (b) What would be reported as the total cost of Job 564?
      (c) What would be reported as the total cost of Job 632?
  (5) Compare the two total cost amounts for Job 564 calculated in parts (2) and (4)(b). Compare the two total cost amounts for Job 632 calculated in parts (3) and (4)(c). What would be the competitive implications of using the single predetermined overhead rate and quoting prices at cost plus a small markup?

CHAPTER 5

Process Costing: Cost of Production Report

Cost accumulation procedures used by manufacturing concerns generally are classified as either (1) job order costing or (2) process costing. In this chapter, the basic aspects of process costing are discussed. These aspects include the cost of production reports for producing departments, the calculation of departmental unit costs, the computation of cost transferred to other departments or to the finished goods storeroom, the costing of work in process, the effect of lost units on unit costs, and the effect of adding materials in departments other than the first. Chapter 6 discusses beginning work in process inventories and Chapter 7 deals with the problem of assigning costs to by-products and joint products.

■ PROCESS COST ACCUMULATION

The objective of either job order or process costing is to match costs of a period with units produced in the same period. The type of manufacturing operations performed determines the cost procedures that must be used. For example, a company manufacturing custom machinery will use job order cost procedures, whereas a chemical company will use process cost procedures. In the case of the machinery manufacturer, a job order cost sheet accumulates materials, labor, and factory overhead costs for each order. In contrast, the chemical company cannot identify materials, labor, and factory overhead with each order, for each order is part of a batch or a continuous process. The individual order identity is lost, and the cost of a completed unit must be computed by dividing the total cost incurred during a period by total units completed.

Process costing is used when products are manufactured under conditions of continuous processing or under mass production methods. These conditions exist in industries that produce such commodities as plastics, petroleum, textiles, steel, flour, and sugar. Process costing is used by firms that manufacture bolts and small electrical parts, and by assembly-type industries (automobiles, airplanes, and household appliances), especially if traceability of costs to individual jobs is not feasible or practical. Some utilities (gas, water, and electricity) cost their products by using process costing methods.

The characteristics of process costing are:

1. Costs are charged to departmental work in process accounts.
2. A cost of production report is used to collect, summarize, and compute total and unit costs. Unit costs are determined by dividing the total cost charged to a department by the total production of the department for a specific period.
3. Production in process at the end of a period is restated in terms of equivalent units.
4. Costs of completed units of a department are transferred to the next processing department in order to arrive eventually at the total cost of the finished products during a period, and costs are assigned to units still in process.

Costing by Departments

In manufacturing firms, production may take place in several departments. Each department performs a specific operation or process leading to the completion of the product. In a process costing situation, for example, the first department performs the starting phase of work on the product and transfers the units to a second department. The second department completes its work and transfers the units to a third department which completes them and sends them to the finished goods storeroom. The costs of materials, labor, and factory overhead are charged to work in process accounts which are maintained for each department. When the units are transferred from one producing department to another, the accumulated costs are transferred to the subsequent department.

In process costing, departmental total and unit costs are summarized in a cost of production report, which is described and illustrated in this chapter. The cost of a completed unit is used in determining the cost of units transferred out and still in process. This breakdown of departmental costs not only accommodates the purposes of inventory costing and income determination but also provides summary cost control data.

Product Flow

A product can move through a factory in a variety of ways. Three product flow formats associated with process costing—sequential, parallel, and selective—are illustrated here to indicate that the same basic costing procedures can be applied to all types of product flow situations.

Sequential Product Flow. In a sequential flow, each product is processed in the same series of steps. In a company with three departments, such a flow may be illustrated as shown at the top of page 120.

The processing of materials begins in the Blending Department, and labor and factory overhead costs are added. When the work is finished in this department, it moves to the Testing Department. Any succeeding processes

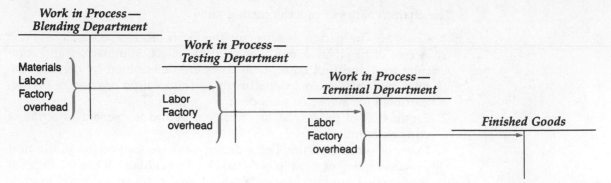

may add more materials or simply work on the partially completed input from the preceding process, adding only labor and factory overhead, as in this example. After the product has been processed by the Terminal Department, it is complete and becomes a part of Finished Goods.

Parallel Product Flow. In a parallel product flow, certain portions of the work are done simultaneously and then brought together in a final process or processes for completion and transfer to Finished Goods. The following accounts illustrate a parallel flow for a production process in which materials are added in subsequent departments:

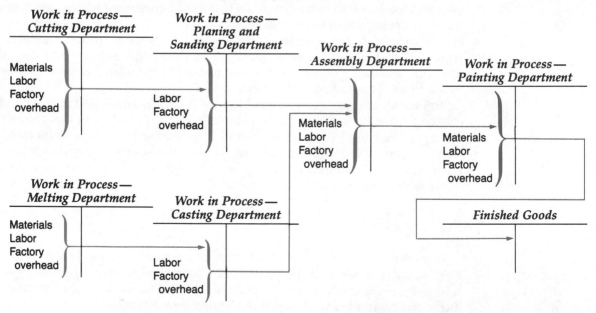

Selective Product Flow. In a selective flow, the product moves to different departments within the plant, depending upon the desired final product. The following accounts illustrate a selective flow in a meat processing plant. After the initial butchering process is completed, some of the product goes directly to the Packaging Department and then to Finished Goods; some goes to the Smoking Department and then to the Packaging Department and Finished Goods; some goes to the Grinding Department, then to the Packaging Department and finally to Finished Goods.

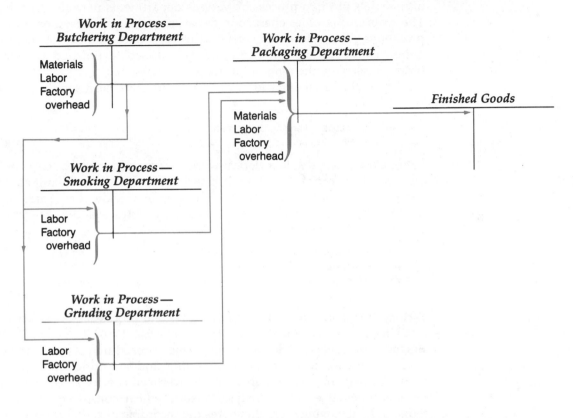

Accumulation of Materials, Labor, and Factory Overhead Costs

The details involved in process cost procedures are usually fewer than those in job order costing, where accumulation of costs for many orders may become unwieldy. The job order procedures for accumulating materials, labor, and factory overhead costs generally apply, however, to process costing. Costs are charged to departments or processes by appropriate journal entries.

Materials Costs. In job order costing, materials requisitions are the basis for charging direct materials to specific jobs. If requisitions are used in process costing, the details are reduced considerably because materials are charged to departments rather than to jobs and the number of departments using materials is usually less than the number of jobs which a firm handles at a given time. Frequently materials are issued only to the process-originating department; subsequent departments add labor and factory overhead.

Materials requisition forms may be useful for materials control purposes. If the requisitions are not priced individually, the cost of materials used may be determined at the end of the production period through inventory difference procedures; i.e., adding purchases to beginning inventory and deducting ending inventory. Consumption reports which state the cost or quantity of materials put into process by various departments may also may be used. The costs or quantities charged to departments may be based on formulas or prorations. These formulas specify the type and quantity of materials required in the various products and are applied to finished production in order to calculate the amount of materials consumed.

A typical journal entry to record the direct materials used during a period is as follows:

Work in Process—Blending Department	24,500	
Materials		24,500

Labor Costs. The detailed clerical work of accumulating labor costs by jobs is eliminated in process costing because labor costs are identified by and charged to departments. Daily time tickets or weekly clock cards are used instead of job time tickets. A summary entry distributes the direct manufacturing payroll to departments, as follows:

Work in Process—Blending Department	29,140	
Work in Process—Testing Department	37,310	
Work in Process—Terminal Department	32,400	
Payroll		98,850

Factory Overhead Costs. In both job order and process costing, factory overhead should be accumulated in a factory overhead subsidiary ledger for producing and service departments. This procedure is consistent with requirements for responsibility accounting and reporting. As expenses are incurred, they are recorded in a factory overhead control account and posted to departmental expense analysis sheets, which constitute the subsidiary ledger. The following entry illustrates the recording of actual factory overhead in the general ledger:

Factory Overhead Control	81,500	
Accounts Payable		24,500
Accumulated Depreciation—Machinery		42,500
Prepaid Insurance.		8,000
Materials (for indirect materials and supplies)		4,500
Payroll (for indirect labor)		2,000

At the end of each period, either actual overhead or overhead using actual or predetermined rates is charged to the producing departments. When rates are used to apply overhead in process costing, the rates are multiplied by the respective actual activity base (e.g., machine hours) for each producing department. The following entry illustrates this procedure for Clonex Corporation, using predetermined rates:

Work in Process—Blending Department	28,200	
Work in Process—Testing Department	32,800	
Work in Process—Terminal Department	19,800	
Applied Factory Overhead		80,800

The $700 difference between the actual factory overhead of $81,500 and the applied amount of $80,800 represents underapplied factory overhead. The significance and disposition of such a balance, either overapplied or underapplied, is discussed in detail in Chapter 13.

Combining Labor and Factory Overhead Costs. Increasing levels of automation cause direct labor to be a decreasing proportion of total manufacturing cost. Furthermore, tasks performed by workers often blur the distinction between direct and indirect labor. Concomitantly, factory overhead costs increase with automation, e.g., equipment depreciation and maintenance. As a result, a company may combine the labor and factory overhead cost elements and refer to them as conversion cost (which represents the cost of converting direct materials into finished products) or perhaps simply as factory overhead. The direct labor may be charged directly to work in process when the payroll is distributed, or may be charged to factory overhead and included as a part of the overhead rate.

■ THE COST OF PRODUCTION REPORT

In process costing, all costs chargeable to a department are summarized in a departmental *cost of production report*. This report is a device for presenting the amount of costs accumulated and disposed of during a month. It is also the source of information for preparing summary journal entries which record activity in the cost accounts.

A cost of production report for a department shows (1) total and unit costs transferred from a preceding department; (2) materials, labor, and factory overhead added by the department; (3) unit costs added by the department; (4) total and unit costs accumulated at the end of operations in the department; (5) the cost of the beginning and ending work in process inventories, which are in various stages of completion; and (6) cost transferred to a succeeding department or to the finished goods storeroom. The cost section of the report usually is divided into two parts: one showing total costs for which the department is accountable, the other showing the disposition of these costs. The cost of production report or a supporting schedule should indicate the cost elements for each department because these detailed data are needed for cost control and for determining the cost of the ending work in process inventories.

The cost of production report also includes a quantity schedule which shows the total number of units for which a department is accountable and the disposition of these units. Information in this schedule, adjusted for equivalent production, is used to determine the unit costs added by a department, the costing of the ending work in process inventory, and the cost to be transferred out of the department.

To illustrate the details involved in the preparation of cost of production reports, the cost procedures of Clonex Corporation are discussed on the following pages. This company manufactures one product in three producing departments: Blending, Testing, and Terminal. The Clonex reports are condensed to show the total materials, labor, and factory overhead charged to departments. Unit costs are computed for each cost element rather than for each item of expense.

Blending Department

The cost of production report of the Blending Department, the originating department of Clonex Corporation, is shown below. The quantity schedule of this report shows that the Blending Department put 50,000 units in process. Of these 50,000 units for which the department was responsible, 45,000 units were transferred to the next department (Testing), 4,000 units are still in process, and 1,000 units were lost in processing.

Clonex Corporation
Blending Department
Cost of Production Report
For January, 19—

Quantity Schedule

Units started in process.		50,000
Units transferred to next department	45,000	
Units still in process (all materials; $1/2$ labor and factory overhead)	4,000	
Units lost in process (all normal).	1,000	50,000

	Total Cost	Unit Cost
Cost Charged to the Department		
Cost added by department:		
Materials.	$24,500	$ .50
Labor	29,140	.62
Factory overhead	28,200	.60
Total cost to be accounted for.	**$81,840**	**$1.72**

Cost Accounted for as Follows		
Transferred to next department (45,000 × $1.72)		$77,400
Work in process—ending inventory:		
Materials (4,000 × $.50)	$ 2,000	
Labor (4,000 × $1/2$ × $.62)	1,240	
Factory overhead (4,000 × $1/2$ × $.60).	1,200	4,440
Total cost accounted for.		**$81,840**

Additional Computations:

Equivalent production: Materials = 45,000 + 4,000 = 49,000 units

$$\text{Labor and factory overhead} = 45,000 + \frac{4,000}{2} = 47,000 \text{ units}$$

Unit costs: Materials $= \dfrac{\$24,500}{49,000} = \$.50$ per unit

Labor $= \dfrac{\$29,140}{47,000} = \$.62$ per unit

Factory overhead $= \dfrac{\$28,200}{47,000} = \$.60$ per unit

The units reported by the Blending Department are assumed to be measured in gallons. Generally, each department should report units in terms of the finished product. If materials issued to a department are stated in pounds, for example, and the finished product is reported in gallons, units in the quantity schedule should be stated in gallons by using a product conversion table.

Equivalent Production. To assign costs equitably to the ending work in process inventory and to transferred units, the stage of completion of the in-process inventory must be analyzed by a supervisor or by the use of formulas. Units still in process must be restated in terms of completed units and added to units actually completed in order to arrive at the equivalent production figure for the period. Units in process at the beginning of the period also must be restated and considered in computing equivalent production. The discussion of this latter procedure is deferred to Chapter 6.

The *equivalent production figure* represents the number of units for which materials, labor, and overhead issued or used during a period were sufficient to complete those units. To compute unit costs by elements, the equivalent production figure is divided into the materials, labor, and overhead costs.

If the cost elements are at different stages of completion with respect to units in process, separate equivalent production figures must be computed for each element. In many manufacturing processes, all materials are issued at the start of production. Unless stated otherwise, the illustrations in this discussion assume such a procedure. The 4,000 units still in process in the Clonex factory have all the materials needed for their completion, but only 50 percent of the labor and factory overhead needed to complete the units has been used. In terms of equivalent production, labor and factory overhead in process are sufficient to complete 2,000 units.

Unit Costs. Department cost of production reports indicate the cost of units as they leave each department. These individual departmental unit costs are accumulated into a completed unit cost for the period. The report for the Blending Department shows a materials cost of $24,500, labor cost of $29,140, and factory overhead of $28,200. The materials cost of $24,500 is sufficient to complete 49,000 units (the 45,000 units transferred out of the department as well as the work in process for which enough materials are in process to complete 4,000 units). The unit materials cost is $.50 ($24,500 ÷ 49,000). To determine the number of units actually and potentially completed with the labor and overhead costs, the 2,000 equivalent units in process are added to the 45,000 units completed and transferred. When this production figure of 47,000 units is divided into the labor cost of $29,140 for the month, a unit cost of $.62 ($29,140 ÷ 47,000) for labor is computed. The unit cost for factory overhead is $.60 ($28,200 ÷ 47,000).

The *departmental unit cost*, or the cost added by the department, is $1.72, which is the sum of the materials, labor, and overhead unit costs. This departmental unit cost figure cannot be determined by dividing total departmental costs of $81,840 by a single equivalent production figure. No such figure exists, since units in process are at different stages of completion as to materials, labor, and factory overhead.

Proper unit costs are required in order to identify the cost of units transferred out, the cost of an abnormal loss of units (as will be discussed later in this chapter), and the cost of units in work in process inventory. In some manufacturing operations, the costs assigned to work in process inventory as well as finished goods inventory may be relatively small. In any situation, however, unit costs provide vital information for cost control and for decision making.

Disposition of Departmental Costs. In the departmental cost report, the section titled "Cost Charged to the Department" shows a total departmental cost of $81,840. The section titled "Cost Accounted for as Follows" shows the disposition of this cost. The 45,000 units transferred to the next department have a cost of $77,400 (45,000 units multiplied by the departmental completed unit cost of $1.72). The balance of the cost to be accounted for, $4,440 ($81,840 – $77,400), is the cost of the ending work in process inventory.

The work in process inventory must be broken down into its component parts. The $2,000 cost of materials in process is obtained by multiplying 4,000 total units in process by the materials unit cost of $.50. The costs of labor and factory overhead in process are similarly calculated by multiplying equivalent units by unit cost. Since the amount of labor and overhead in process is sufficient to complete only 50 percent of the units in process, the cost of labor in process is $1,240 (2,000 × $.62) and the cost of factory overhead in process is $1,200 (2,000 × $.60).

Lost Units. Continuous operating and processing lead to the possibility of waste, seepage, shrinkage, defects, and other factors which cause loss or spoilage of production units, referred to as lost units for purposes of this discussion. Lost units, units reported as complete, and units still in process must be reconciled with the quantities put in process. One method of making such reconciliations is to establish the *expected process yield*; i.e., the finished production that should have resulted from processing the various materials. This yield is computed as follows:

$$\text{Percent Yield} = \frac{\text{Weight of finished product}}{\text{Weight of materials charged in}} \times 100$$

QUALITY CONTROL

Various yields are established as normal. Yields below normal are measures of inefficiencies and sometimes are used to compute lost units. The yield figure is useful in controlling materials consumption and ties in closely with a firm's quality control procedures as the cost vs. benefit of improvement is considered.

When units are lost during processing in the first department, the total cost must be spread over a reduced number of units. Therefore, the effect of losing units is an increase in the unit cost of the remaining good units. The assumption here is that the loss is normal, i.e., within acceptable tolerance limits, and that it is applicable to all units, whether they are transferred out or in ending inventory. Losses are applicable to all units provided that the losses occur evenly throughout the process, or provided that the ending inventory units have passed the point at which losses are identified. Other factors in accounting for lost units are discussed later in this chapter (pages 131-135). If 1,000 units had not been lost in the Blending Department, the equivalent production figure would have been 50,000 units for materials and 48,000 units for labor and factory overhead. The unit cost for materials would have been $.49 instead of $.50; labor, $.607 instead of $.62; and factory overhead, $.588 instead of $.60.

Testing Department

The Blending Department transferred 45,000 units to the Testing Department, where labor and factory overhead were added before the units were transferred to the Terminal Department. Costs incurred by the Testing Department resulted in additional departmental as well as cumulative unit costs.

The cost of production report of the Testing Department, shown on page 128, differs from that of the Blending Department in several respects. Several additional calculations are made, for which space has been provided on the report. The additional information includes (1) costs received from the preceding department, (2) an adjustment of the preceding department's unit cost because of lost units, and (3) costs received from the preceding department to be included in the cost of the ending work in process inventory.

The quantity schedule for the Testing Department shows that the 45,000 units received from the Blending Department were accounted for as follows: 40,000 units were sent to the Terminal Department, 3,000 units are still in process, and 2,000 units were lost. An analysis of the work in process indicates that units in process are only one-third complete as to labor and factory overhead. Therefore, equivalent production of the Testing Department is 41,000 units (40,000 + (1/3 × 3,000)), the labor unit cost is $.91 ($37,310 ÷ 41,000), and the factory overhead unit cost is $.80 ($32,800 ÷ 41,000). No materials were added by the department, so the departmental unit cost is the sum of the labor unit cost of $.91 and the factory overhead unit cost of $.80, or $1.71.

The cost of production report for the Testing Department indicates that this department is responsible for the cost of units received from the Blending Department. This cost is included in the section titled "Cost Charged to the Department." The cost transferred in was $77,400, which was previously shown in the cost report of the Blending Department as cost transferred out of that department. This cost was charged to the Testing Department by the following entry:

Work in Process—Testing Department   77,400
    Work in Process—Blending Department   77,400

Since the work in process account of the Testing Department is charged with $70,110 of departmental labor and factory overhead, a total cost of $147,510 must be accounted for by the department.

Clonex Corporation
Testing Department
Cost of Production Report
For January, 19—

Quantity Schedule

Units received from preceding department		45,000
Units transferred to next department	40,000	
Units still in process (1/3 labor and factory overhead)	3,000	
Units lost in process	2,000	45,000

Cost Charged to the Department	Total Cost	Unit Cost
Cost from preceding department:		
Transferred in during the month (45,000 units)...........	$ 77,400	$1.72
Adjusted cost from preceding department ($77,400 ÷ (45,000 units − 2,000 lost units))		$1.80
Cost added by department:		
Labor	$ 37,310	$ .91
Factory overhead....................................	32,800	.80
Total cost added.....................................	$ 70,110	$1.71
Total cost to be accounted for....................	**$147,510**	**$3.51**

Cost Accounted for as Follows		
Transferred to next department (40,000 × $3.51)		$140,400
Work in process—ending inventory:		
Adjusted cost from preceding department (3,000 × $1.80)..	$ 5,400	
Labor (3,000 × 1/3 × $.91)	910	
Factory overhead (3,000 × 1/3 × $.80).................	800	7,110
Total cost accounted for........................		**$147,510**

Additional Computations:

Equivalent production: Labor and factory overhead = $40,000 + \dfrac{3,000}{3} = 41,000$ units

Unit costs: Labor = $\dfrac{\$37,310}{41,000}$ = $.91 per unit

Factory overhead = $\dfrac{\$32,800}{41,000}$ = $.80 per unit

Units Lost in Departments Subsequent to the First. The Blending Department's unit cost was $1.72 when 45,000 units were transferred to the Testing Department. However, because 2,000 of these 45,000 units were lost during processing in the Testing Department, the $1.72 unit cost figure must be adjusted. The total cost of the units transferred remains at $77,400, but 43,000 units must now absorb this total cost, causing an increase of $.08 in the cost per unit, from $1.72 to an adjusted cost of $1.80 ($77,400 ÷ (45,000 units − 2,000 lost units)).

The $1.80 "Adjusted cost from preceding department" and the $1.71 departmental unit cost are totaled to obtain the $3.51 cumulative unit cost for work done up to the end of operations in the Testing Department. The departmental unit cost of $1.71 does not have to be adjusted for units lost, since the cost of any Testing work on lost units has been automatically absorbed in the departmental unit costs by using the equivalent production figure of 41,000 instead of 43,000 units.

As was the case for the Blending Department, the assumption in both the Testing and Terminal departments is that the loss is normal and that it is applicable to all units. Other assumptions in accounting for lost units are discussed beginning on page 131.

Disposition of Testing Department Costs. The cost of production report on page 128 shows a total cost of $147,510 to be accounted for by the Testing Department. The department completed and transferred 40,000 units to the Terminal Department at a cost of $140,400 (40,000 × $3.51). The remaining cost is assigned to the work in process inventory and is broken down by the various costs in process. When the cost of the ending work in process inventory of any department subsequent to the first is computed, costs received from preceding departments must be included.

The 3,000 units still in process but completed by the Blending Department at a unit cost of $1.72 were later adjusted by $.08 (to $1.80) because of the loss of some of the units transferred. Therefore, the Blending Department's cost of the 3,000 units still in process is $5,400 (3,000 × $1.80). The separate cost elements in this $5,400 figure are not identified, since such information is not pertinent to the Testing Department's operations. However, the amount is listed separately in the cost of production report because it is part of the Testing Department's ending work in process inventory.

Materials (if any), labor, and factory overhead added by a department are costed separately to arrive at the total work in process. Since the Testing Department added no materials to the units received, the ending inventory shows no materials in process. However, labor and factory overhead costs were incurred. The work in process analysis indicates that labor and factory overhead used on the units in process were sufficient to complete 1,000 units. The cost of labor in process is $910 (1,000 × $.91) and factory overhead in process is $800 (1,000 × $.80). The total cost of the 3,000 units in process is $7,110 ($5,400 + $910 + $800). This cost and the $140,400 transferred to the Terminal Department account for the $147,510 total cost charged to the Testing Department.

Terminal Department

The cost of production report of the Terminal Department of Clonex Corporation is illustrated on page 130. Total and unit cost figures were derived by using procedures discussed for the cost of production report of the Testing Department (page 128). Costs charged to the Terminal Department come from the payroll distribution and the department's expense analysis sheet. These costs include costs transferred from the Testing Department when the following journal entry was recorded:

Work in Process—Terminal Department	140,400	
Work in Process—Testing Department.		140,400

Clonex Corporation
Terminal Department
Cost of Production Report
For January, 19—

Quantity Schedule

Units received from preceding department		40,000
Units transferred to finished goods storeroom	35,000	
Units still in process (1/4 labor and factory overhead)	4,000	
Units lost in process	1,000	40,000

Cost Charged to the Department	Total Cost	Unit Cost
Cost from preceding department:		
Transferred in during the month (40,000 units)...........	$140,400	$3.51
Adjusted cost from preceding department ($140,400 ÷ (40,000 units – 1,000 lost units))		$3.60
Cost added by department:		
Labor	$ 32,400	$ .90
Factory overhead	19,800	.55
Total cost added..................................	$ 52,200	$1.45
Total cost to be accounted for...................	**$192,600**	**$5.05**

Cost Accounted for as Follows

Transferred to finished goods storeroom (35,000 × $5.05).....		$176,750
Work in process—ending inventory:		
Adjusted cost from preceding department (4,000 × $3.60)..	$ 14,400	
Labor (4,000 × 1/4 × $.90)	900	
Factory overhead (4,000 × 1/4 × $.55).................	550	15,850
Total cost accounted for.........................		**$192,600**

Additional Computations:

Equivalent production: Labor and factory overhead $= 35,000 + \dfrac{4,000}{4} = 36,000$ units

Unit costs: Labor $= \dfrac{\$32,400}{36,000} = \$.90$ per unit

Factory overhead $= \dfrac{\$19,800}{36,000} = \$.55$ per unit

Since the Terminal Department is the final processing department, the work completed is transferred to the finished goods storeroom. This transfer is recorded as follows:

Finished Goods	176,750	
Work in Process—Terminal Department		176,750

Combined Cost of Production Report

The three cost of production reports for Clonex Corporation have been discussed and computed separately. These reports would most likely be consolidated in a single report summarizing manufacturing operations of the firm for a specified period. Such a report, illustrated on page 131, emphasizes the interrelationship of the various departmental reports.

Clonex Corporation
Cost of Production Report
All Producing Departments
For January, 19—

Quantity Schedule	Blending		Testing		Terminal	
Units started in process	50,000					
Units received from preceding department			45,000		40,000	
Units transferred to next department	45,000		40,000			
Units transferred to finished goods storeroom					35,000	
Units still in process	4,000		3,000		4,000	
Units lost in process	1,000	50,000	2,000	45,000	1,000	40,000

Cost Charged to the Department	Total Cost	Unit Cost	Total Cost	Unit Cost	Total Cost	Unit Cost
Cost from preceding department: Transferred in during the month			$ 77,400	$1.72	$140,400	$3.51
Adjusted cost from preceding department (lost units).				$1.80		$3.60
Cost added by department:						
Materials	$24,500	$ .50	$ 37,310	$ .91	$ 32,400	$ .90
Labor	29,140	.62	32,800	.80	19,800	.55
Factory overhead.	28,200	.60				
Total cost added	$81,840	$1.72	$ 70,110	$1.71	$ 52,200	$1.45
Total cost to be accounted for . .	**$81,840**	**$1.72**	**$147,510**	**$3.51**	**$192,600**	**$5.05**

Cost Accounted for as Follows						
Transferred to next department.	$77,400		$140,400			
Transferred to finished goods storeroom					$176,750	
Work in process—ending inventory:						
Adjusted cost from preceding department.			$ 5,400		$ 14,400	
Materials	$ 2,000					
Labor	1,240		910		900	
Factory overhead.	1,200	4,440	800	7,110	550	15,850
Total cost accounted for		**$81,840**		**$147,510**		**$192,600**

■ OTHER FACTORS IN ACCOUNTING FOR LOST UNITS

In the Testing Department as well as in the Blending and Terminal Departments of Clonex Corporation, it was assumed that the loss of units applied to all good units and was within normal tolerance limits. Thus the loss of units resulted in an increase in the unit cost of the remaining good units, i.e., the units completed and the units still in process. Other lost unit situations require the application of the procedures that are discussed in the following paragraphs.

Timing of Lost Units

Situations may arise in which the cost of lost units does not pertain to the ending work in process inventory, because the identification of lost units occurs at a point beyond the stage of completion of the units still in process. Thus, any measured loss pertains only to units completed. No part of the loss is charged to units still in process.

To illustrate, assume that the 2,000 units lost by the Testing Department of Clonex Corporation were the result of spoilage which was discovered by the Quality Control Department at its final inspection. The cost of these units would be charged only to the 40,000 finished units, as illustrated in the cost of production report for the Testing Department on page 133.

Since the lost units were discovered after completion in the Testing Department, unit costs are based on equivalent production for good units plus lost units. Therefore, no adjustment of the preceding department unit cost is required, and none of the cost of the spoiled units is included in the cost assigned to the ending work in process inventory. Only the cost transferred to the next department includes the full cost of the spoiled units.

The differences between the two cost of production reports for the Testing Department (pages 128 and 133) as to amounts for costs of units transferred and work in process inventory are as follows. A comparison of the differences indicates that the increases and decreases are offsetting.

Cost of units transferred:		Work in process inventory:	
On page 128	$140,400	On page 128	$7,110
On page 133	140,720	On page 133	6,790
Increase	$ 320	Decrease	$ 320

In this illustration, the 2,000 lost units identified at the end of the process were assumed to be complete as to all costs. However, lost units may not be entirely complete when the loss actually occurs, even though the loss is not identified until the end of the process. In other instances the loss may be discovered when production checks are made prior to the end of the process, but, again, the loss cannot be associated with units still in process if they have not yet reached that stage of processing. In both of these cases, the lost units should be adjusted for their equivalent stage of completion. For instance, 2,000 units lost at the 90 percent stage of conversion in the Testing Department would appear as 1,800 equivalent units with regard to labor and factory overhead costs and would be added to the good units in determining equivalent production for use in computing unit costs.

Normal vs. Abnormal Loss of Units

Units are lost through evaporation, shrinkage, substandard yields, spoiled work, poor workmanship, or inefficient equipment. In many instances, the nature of operations makes certain losses normal or unavoidable.

Clonex Corporation
Testing Department
Cost of Production Report
For January, 19--

Quantity Schedule

Units received from preceding department		45,000
Units transferred to next department	40,000	
Units still in process (¹/₃ labor and factory overhead)	3,000	
Units lost in process (at end of process)	2,000	45,000

Cost Charged to the Department	Total Cost	Unit Cost
Cost from preceding department:		
Transferred in during the month (45,000 units).	$ 77,400	$1.72
Cost added by department:		
Labor	$ 37,310	$ .87
Factory overhead	32,800	.76
Total cost added.	$ 70,110	$1.63
Total cost to be accounted for.	**$147,510**	**$3.35**

Cost Accounted for as Follows

Transferred to next department (40,000 units × ($3.35 +		
$.1675) or (40,000 × $3.35) + (2,000 lost units × $3.35)). . .		$140,720*
Work in process—ending inventory:		
From preceding department (3,000 × $1.72).	$ 5,160	
Labor (3,000 × ¹/₃ × $.87).	870	
Factory overhead (3,000 × ¹/₃ × $.76).	760	6,790
Total cost accounted for.		**$147,510**

Additional Computations:

Equivalent production: Labor and factory overhead $= 40,000 + \dfrac{3,000}{3} + 2,000$ lost units

$$= 43,000 \text{ units}$$

Unit costs: Labor $= \dfrac{\$37,310}{43,000} = \$.87$ per unit

Factory overhead $= \dfrac{\$32,800}{43,000} = \$.76$ per unit

Lost unit cost = $3.35 × 2,000 units = $6,700; $6,700 ÷ 40,000 units = $.1675 per unit to be added to $3.35 to make the transfer cost $3.5175.

*40,000 units × $3.5175 = $140,700. To avoid a decimal discrepancy, the cost transferred is computed: $147,510 − $6,790 = $140,720.

When such losses are determined to be within normal tolerance limits for human and machine errors, the cost of the lost units does not appear as a separate item of cost but is spread over the remaining good units.

A different situation is created by abnormal or avoidable losses that are not expected to arise under normal, efficient operating conditions. In fact, some processes have a goal of zero defects. In such cases, any loss is considered to be abnormal. Again, the procedure involves computing unit costs based on equivalent production for good units plus lost units. Therefore, no adjustment of the preceding department unit cost is required. The lost units are multiplied by the resulting unit costs to determine the cost applicable to the abnormal loss. This cost is charged to Factory Overhead or to a current-period expense account which is reported as a separate item in the income statement. Charging abnormal spoilage cost to a current-period expense account would be mandatory if a predetermined factory overhead rate is not used. Otherwise, the actual factory overhead rate would include this cost, thereby assigning it to the cost of units produced.

The $6,700 loss in the Testing Department will be used for illustration. If the cost of the abnormal loss is charged to Factory Overhead, as shown in the following entry, it will be reported as an additional unfavorable factory overhead variance, since abnormal spoilage is not included in the overhead rate.

	Subsidiary Record	Dr.	Cr.
Factory Overhead Control		6,700	
Abnormal Lost Units	6,700		
Work in Process—Testing Department			6,700

The cost of production report would show the abnormal spoilage or loss as follows:

Transferred to next department (40,000 units × $3.35)	$134,020*
Transferred to factory overhead—cost of abnormal loss (2,000 lost units × $3.35)	6,700

*40,000 units × $3.35 = $134,000. To avoid decimal discrepancy, the cost transferred is computed: $147,510 − $6,790 ending inventory − $6,700 = $134,020.

When the lost units are only partially complete, their stage of completion should be considered, and the costing of the abnormal loss should be weighted accordingly.

If one part of a loss is normal and another part abnormal, each portion should be treated in accordance with the above illustrations and discussion. The critical factor in distinguishing between the normal and abnormal portions of a loss is the degree of controllability. Normal or unavoidable loss is produced under efficient operating conditions and is uncontrollable. Abnormal or avoidable loss is considered unnecessary, because the conditions resulting in the loss are controllable. For this reason, within the limits set by the refinement of the production process, the difference is a short-run condition. In the long run, management would attempt to adjust and control all factors of production and eliminate all abnormal conditions.

For some kinds of products the spoiled units have a salvage value. Although any value assigned to spoiled units may be credited to a sales account, it preferably should be credited (1) to the work in process account if the spoilage is normal, or (2) to either Factory Overhead or the appropriate current period expense account if the spoilage is abnormal. If the market for these spoiled units is reasonably stable and reliable, and if the value is relatively high, the entry should occur at the time the physical units can be measured; otherwise, the entry should await the time of sale. These situations are discussed in more detail in Chapter 7.

Defective Work

Any cost necessary to correct defective work is reported as additional cost of materials, labor, and factory overhead provided the rate of defectives is within normal limits. Equivalent units of production are unaffected. For cost control purposes, however, management may wish to have an additional supplemental report of the portion of the cost elements expended for rework of the defective units. The cost of defective work outside normal limits should be reported separately and should be expensed in the current accounting period.

■ ADDITION OF MATERIALS

The addition of materials in departments subsequent to the first has two possible effects on units and costs in process:

1. The additional materials increase the unit cost, since these materials become a part of the product manufactured, but do not increase the number of final units. For example, in a finishing plant of a textile company, the material added is often a bleach; in a wire company, a plating mixture; in an automobile assembly plant, additional parts. These materials are needed to give the product certain specified qualities, characteristics, or completeness. Or,
2. The added materials increase the number of units and cause a change in unit cost. For example, in processing a chemical, water is often added to a mixture. As a result, the number of units increases and costs are spread over a greater number of units.

Increase in Unit Cost

In the simplest case, added materials, such as parts of an automobile, do not increase the number of units but increase the total cost and unit costs. A materials unit cost must be computed for the department, and a materials cost must be included in the work in process inventory.

The cost of production report of the Terminal Department of Clonex Corporation (page 136) is used to illustrate the different effects of the addition of materials on total and unit costs of a department. Assume that additional materials costing $17,020 are placed in process and charged to the Terminal Department. Assume further that these materials are sufficient to complete 2,000 of the 4,000 units in ending inventory; that is, units in process at the

Clonex Corporation
Terminal Department
Cost of Production Report
For January, 19—

Quantity Schedule

Units received from preceding department		40,000
Units transferred to finished goods storeroom	35,000	
Units still in process ($1/2$ materials; $1/4$ labor and factory overhead)	4,000	
Units lost in process	1,000	40,000

Cost Charged to the Department	Total Cost	Unit Cost
Cost from preceding department:		
Transferred in during the month (40,000 units)	$140,400	$3.51
Adjusted cost from preceding department ($140,400 ÷ (40,000 units − 1,000 lost units))		$3.60
Cost added by department:		
Materials	$ 17,020	$ .46
Labor	32,400	.90
Factory overhead	19,800	.55
Total cost added	$ 69,220	$1.91
Total cost to be accounted for	**$209,620**	$5.51

Cost Accounted for as Follows

Transferred to finished goods storeroom (35,000 × $5.51)		$192,850
Work in process—ending inventory:		
Adjusted cost from preceding department (4,000 × $3.60) . .	$ 14,400	
Materials (4,000 × $1/2$ × $.46)	920	
Labor (4,000 × $1/4$ × $.90)	900	
Factory overhead (4,000 × $1/4$ × $.55)	550	16,770
Total cost accounted for		**$209,620**

Additional Computations:

Equivalent production: Materials $= 35,000 + \dfrac{4,000}{2} = 37,000$ units

Labor and factory overhead $= 35,000 + \dfrac{4,000}{4} = 36,000$ units

Unit costs: Materials $= \dfrac{\$17,020}{37,000} = \$.46$ per unit

Labor $= \dfrac{\$32,400}{36,000} = \$.90$ per unit

Factory overhead $= \dfrac{\$19,800}{36,000} = \$.55$ per unit

end of the period are 50 percent complete as to materials cost. The effect of the additional materials cost is shown in the above cost report.

The main differences in the two cost reports (pages 130 and above) are the $17,020 materials cost charged to the department and the $.46 materials unit cost ($17,020 ÷ 37,000). The additional materials cost is reflected also in the total cost to be accounted for, in the cost of units transferred to finished goods, and in the ending work in process inventory.

Increase in Units and Change in Unit Cost

When additional materials result in additional units, different computations are necessary. The greater number of units causes a decrease in unit cost, which necessitates an adjustment of the preceding department's unit cost, since the increased number of units will absorb the same total cost transferred from the preceding department.

To illustrate this situation, assume Terminal Department costs for labor and factory overhead of $32,400 and $19,800, respectively, an additional materials cost of $17,020, and an increase of 8,000 units as the result of added materials. The effect of these assumptions on the Terminal Department's cost of production report is shown on page 138.

The additional 8,000 units are entered in the department's quantity schedule as "Additional units put into process." The quantity schedule reports that 44,000 units were completed and transferred to the finished goods storeroom and that 4,000 units are still in process, 50 percent complete as to materials and 25 percent complete as to labor and factory overhead. Therefore, equivalent production is 46,000 units for materials and 45,000 units for labor and factory overhead. Dividing departmental materials, labor, and factory overhead costs for the period by these production figures results in a unit cost of $.37 ($17,020 ÷ 46,000) for materials, $.72 ($32,400 ÷ 45,000) for labor, and $.44 ($19,800 ÷ 45,000) for factory overhead.

These computations do not differ from those already discussed. Peculiar to this situation of additional materials is the adjustment of the preceding department's unit cost. Total cost charged to the Terminal Department as cost transferred in from the preceding department must now be allocated over a greater number of units, thereby reducing the unit cost of work done in the preceding department.

In the illustration on page 136, the $140,400 cost transferred to the Terminal Department was absorbed by 40,000 units, resulting in a unit cost of $3.51. Because of the increase in units, the $140,400 cost must now be spread over 48,000 units, resulting in a unit cost of $2.925 for the preceding department. This adjusted cost is inserted in the production report on page 138 as "Adjusted cost from preceding department" and is added to departmental unit costs to arrive at the unit cost accumulated to the end of operations in the Terminal Department.

When additional materials increase the number of units being processed, it is still possible to have lost units. However, if both an increase and a loss occur, a separate calculation for the lost units is not necessarily required, and net units added can be used. In the illustration above, 8,000 additional units resulted from added materials. It is quite possible, though, that the materials added should have yielded 10,000 additional units. If 2,000 units were lost in processing, the effect is similar to that of units lost in the first department; that is, the cost is absorbed within the department as an increase in unit costs. However, if desired, it also is possible to report separately the effect of the loss, which can be determined as follows: (1) compute the unit cost of

Clonex Corporation
Terminal Department
Cost of Production Report
For January, 19—

Quantity Schedule

Units received from preceding department	40,000	
Additional units put into process..........................	8,000	48,000
Units transferred to finished goods storeroom	44,000	
Units still in process (¹/₂ materials; ¹/₄ labor and factory overhead)...	4,000	48,000

		Total Cost	Unit Cost
Cost Charged to the Department			
Cost from preceding department:			
Transferred in during the month (40,000 units)............		$140,400	$3.510
Adjusted cost from preceding department ($140,400 ÷ (40,000 units + 8,000 additional units))			$2.925
Cost added by department:			
Materials...		$ 17,020	$ .370
Labor		32,400	.720
Factory overhead		19,800	.440
Total cost added.................................		$ 69,220	$1.530
Total cost to be accounted for....................		**$209,620**	**$4.455**

Cost Accounted for as Follows			
Transferred to finished goods storeroom (44,000 × $4.455)....			$196,020
Work in process—ending inventory:			
Adjusted cost from preceding department (4,000 × $2.925).		$ 11,700	
Materials (4,000 × ¹/₂ × $.370)		740	
Labor (4,000 × ¹/₄ × $.720)		720	
Factory overhead (4,000 × ¹/₄ × $.440)................		440	13,600
Total cost accounted for........................			**$209,620**

Additional Computations:

Equivalent production: Materials $= 44,000 + \dfrac{4,000}{2} = 46,000$ units

Labor and factory overhead $= 44,000 + \dfrac{4,000}{4} = 45,000$ units

Unit costs: Materials $= \dfrac{\$17,020}{46,000} = \$.370$ per unit

Labor $= \dfrac{\$32,400}{45,000} = \$.720$ per unit

Factory overhead $= \dfrac{\$19,800}{45,000} = \$.440$ per unit

work done in preceding departments and in the Terminal Department as if no loss had occurred; (2) compute the loss by multiplying the unit cost obtained in the preceding computation by the 2,000 lost units. The lost units are then accounted for, following the procedures discussed in this chapter.

DISCUSSION QUESTIONS

Q5-1. Within the general objective, common to both job order and process costing, of matching costs with units produced in a period, what is the basic goal of process costing?

Q5-2. Job order and process costing procedures are used by different types of industries. Discuss the procedure appropriate for each type.

Q5-3. For the following products, indicate whether job order or process cost procedures would be required:

(a) Gasoline
(b) Sewing machines
(c) Chocolate syrup
(d) Textbooks
(e) Dacron yarn
(f) Cigarettes
(g) Space capsules
(h) Men's and women's suits

Q5-4. What are the distinguishing characteristics of process cost procedures?

Q5-5. Discuss three product flow formats.

Q5-6. Compare the cost accumulation and summarizing procedures of job order costing and process costing.

Q5-7. Can predetermined overhead rates be used in process costing?

Q5-8. What is the purpose of a cost of production report?

Q5-9. What are the various sections of a cost of production report?

Q5-10. Separate cost of production reports are prepared for each producing department. Why is this method used in preference to one report for the entire firm?

Q5-11. Are month-to-month fluctuations in average unit costs computed in a cost of production report meaningful data in attempting to control costs?

Q5-12. What is equivalent production? Explain in terms of its effect on computed unit costs.

Q5-13. What is the justification for spreading the cost of lost units over the remaining good units? Should the cost of these units ever be charged to overhead? Will the answer be different if units are lost (a) in the originating department, (b) at the beginning of a department's operations, (c) during operations, or (d) at the end of operations?

Q5-14. What are the possible effects on units and costs in process when materials are added in subsequent departments?

EXERCISES

E5-1. Equivalent production. During April, 20,000 units were transferred in from Department A at a cost of $39,000. Materials cost of $6,500 and conversion cost of $13,500 were added in Department B. On April 30, Department B had 5,000 units of work in process 60% complete as to conversion cost. Materials are added in the beginning of the process in Department B. The department combines manufacturing labor and factory overhead, and the total amount is termed conversion cost.

Required:
(1) Compute equivalent production for materials and conversion cost.
(2) Calculate the cost per equivalent unit for conversion cost. (AICPA adapted)

E5-2. Costing of units transferred; lost units. Fulton Inc. instituted a new process in October, during which it started 10,000 units in Department A. Of the units started, 1,000 units, a normal number, were lost during the process; 7,000 were transferred to Department B; and 2,000 remained in work in process inventory at the end of the month, 100% complete as to materials and 50% complete as to conversion cost. Materials and conversion costs of $27,000 and $40,000, respectively, were charged to the department in October. The department treats all manufacturing labor as a part of factory overhead and the combined amount is the conversion cost.

Required:
  (1) Compute the total cost transferred to Department B.
  (2) Prepare the journal entry transferring cost out of Department A and into Department B.

(AICPA adapted)

E5-3. Cost of production report; no lost units. A company's Department 2 costs for June were:

Cost from Department 1	$16,320
Cost added in Department 2:	
Materials.	43,415
Labor	56,100
Factory overhead	58,575

The quantity schedule shows 12,000 units were received during the month from Department 1; 7,000 units were transferred to finished goods; and 5,000 units in process at the end of June were 50% complete as to materials cost and 25% complete as to conversion cost.

Required: Prepare the following:
  (1) A cost of production report.
  (2) The journal entry transferring cost out of Department 2.

E5-4. Cost of production report; normal spoilage. Meadowbrook Company uses process costing. All materials are added at the beginning of the process. The product is inspected when it is 80% converted, and spoilage is identified only at that point. Normal spoilage is expected to be 5% of good output.

During March, 10,500 units were put into process. Current costs were $52,500 for materials, $39,770 for labor, and $63,050 for factory overhead. The 3,000 units still in process at the end of March were estimated to be 90% complete. A total of 7,000 units were transferred to finished goods.

Required: Prepare the following:
  (1) A cost of production report for March.
  (2) The journal entry transferring cost out of the work in process account.

E5-5. Cost of production report; normal loss. For December, the Production Control Department of Lauren Chemical Inc. reported the following production data for Department 2:

Transferred in from Department 1	55 000 liters
Transferred out to Department 3	39 500 liters
In process at end of December (with 1/3 labor and factory overhead).	10 500 liters

All materials were put into process in Department 1. The Cost Department collected these figures for Department 2:

Unit cost for units transferred in from Department 1	$1.80
Labor cost in Department 2.	$27,520
Applied factory overhead.	$30,960

Required: Prepare the following:
  (1) A cost of production report for Department 2 for December.
  (2) The journal entry transferring cost out of Department 2.

E5-6. Cost of production report; spoilage at end of process, all normal. Lexington Company produces toy plastic boats which require processing in two departments. During May, 160,000 units were completed in Department 1 at a total cost of $320,000 and were transferred to the next department. Of these units, Department 2 completed and transferred out 123,000 units. All materials are put into process in Department 1. The May 31 work in process inventory of Department 2 was 34,500 units, 1/2 completed as to labor and factory overhead. Spoilage in Department 2, a normal amount, occurs at the end of processing. Department 2's labor cost for May was $45,680, and applied factory overhead was $22,840.

Required: Prepare the following:
    (1) A cost of production report for Department 2.
    (2) The journal entry transferring cost out of Department 2.

E5-7. Cost of production report; abnormal loss. During February, the Assembly Department received 60,000 units from the Cutting Department at a unit cost of $3.64. Costs added in the Assembly Department were: materials, $41,650; labor, $101,700; and factory overhead, $56,500. There was no beginning inventory. Of the 60,000 units received, 50,000 were completed and transferred out to the Packaging Department; 9,000 units were in process at the end of the month (all materials, 2/3 converted); 1,000 lost units were 1/2 complete as to materials and conversion costs. The department has a zero-defects goal; therefore, the entire loss is considered abnormal and is to be charged to factory overhead.

Required: Prepare the following:
    (1) A cost of production report.
    (2) The journal entry transferring cost out of the Assembly Department.

E5-8. Cost of production report; addition of materials. Marks Inc. produces a cologne, Mi Esencia, which requires processing in three departments. In the third department, materials are added, doubling the number of units. The following data pertain to the operations of Department 3 for March:

Units received from Department 2		20,000
Units transferred to finished goods storeroom		32,000
The balance of the units are still in process—100% complete as to materials, 50% complete as to labor and overhead.		
Cost transferred from Department 2		$30,000
Cost added by the department:		
Materials	$ 8,800	
Labor	9,000	
Factory overhead	10,800	$28,600

There was no beginning work in process inventory.

Required: Prepare the following:
    (1) A cost of production report for Department 3 for March.
    (2) The journal entry transferring cost out of Department 3.

PROBLEMS

P5-1. Equivalent production. Garner Manufacturing Company uses a process cost system to account for the cost of its only product, known as Nino. Production begins in the Fabrication Department, where units of raw material are molded into various connecting parts. After fabrication is complete, the units are transferred to the Assembly Department. There is no material added in the Assembly Department. After assembly is complete, the units are transferred to the Packaging Department, where the units are packaged for shipment. At the completion of this process, the units are complete and are transferred to the Shipping Department.

At year end, December 31, the following inventory of Nino is on hand:
  (a) No unused raw material or packaging material.
  (b) Fabrication Department: 6,000 units, 25% complete as to raw material and 40% complete as to direct labor.
  (c) Assembly Department: 10,000 units, 75% complete as to direct labor.
  (d) Packaging Department: 3,000 units, 60% complete as to packaging material and 75% complete as to direct labor.
  (e) Shipping Department: 8,000 units.

Required: As of December 31, compute:
  (1) The number of equivalent units of raw material in all inventories.
  (2) The number of equivalent units of Fabrication Department direct labor in all inventories.
  (3) The number of equivalent units of Packaging Department material and direct labor in the Packaging Department inventory.   (AICPA adapted)

P5-2. Quantity and equivalent production schedules; lost units. Holman Laboratories Inc. produces an antibiotic product in its three producing departments. The following quantitative and cost data have been made available:

	Department		
	Blending	Testing	Terminal
Production data:			
Started into production.	8 000 kg	5 400 kg	3 200 kg
Transferred to next department	5 400	3 200	
Transferred to finished goods storeroom			2 100
In process (100% materials, 1/3 labor and overhead)	2 400	1 800	
In process (100% materials, 2/3 labor and overhead)			900
Cost charged to departments:			
Materials	$20,670	$ 7,980	$14,400
Labor	11,160	5,016	11,520
Factory overhead	8,370	2,280	5,040
Total	$40,200	$15,276	$30,960

Lost units are normal and apply to all production.

Required:
  (1) Prepare a quantity schedule for each of the three departments.
  (2) Prepare an equivalent production schedule for each of the three departments.
  (3) Compute the unit cost of factory overhead in the Blending Department.
  (4) Compute the adjusted cost from preceding department in the Testing Department if the unit cost transferred in from the Blending Department is $5.80.

P5-3. Cost of production report; normal and abnormal spoilage. Smith Company uses process costing. In Department B, conversion costs are incurred uniformly throughout the process. Materials are added following inspection, which occurs at the 90% stage of completion. Normal spoilage is discovered during the inspection and is expected to be 5% of good output.
  The following information relates to Department B for January:

	Units	Dollars
Received from Department A	12,000	$84,000
Transferred to finished goods	9,000	
Ending inventory (95% conversion cost; all materials)	2,000	
Cost incurred:		
Materials		18,000
Labor and factory overhead		45,200

Department B combines manufacturing labor and factory overhead into a total amount.

Required: Prepare the following:
  (1) A cost of production report for Department B. Compute unit costs to the nearest cent.
  (2) The journal entry transferring cost out of Department B.

P5-4. Cost of production report; normal and abnormal spoilage. Wisdom Company uses process costing in accounting for its production department, which uses two materials. Material A is added at the beginning of the process. Inspection is at the 90% stage. Material B is then added to the good units. Normal spoilage units amount to 5% of good output. Company records contain the following information for January:

Started during the period....................................	10,000 units
Material A...	$13,370
Material B...	$ 9,000
Direct labor cost..	$37,580
Factory overhead.......................................	$46,975
Transferred to finished goods	7,000 units
Ending inventory (95% complete, and includes all Material B)	2,000 units

Required: Prepare the following:
  (1) A cost of production report.
  (2) The journal entry transferring cost out of the work in process account.

P5-5. Cost of production report; spoilage at end of process, both normal and abnormal. Process costing is used in Department 1 of The Arlington Company. Materials are added at the beginning of the process. An inspection occurs at the end of the process. Normal spoilage is expected to be 5% of the good units that pass inspection, while abnormal spoilage is charged to a current period expense account.
  Department 1 records for April show:

Units started in process....................................	10,000
Units transferred to Department 2...........................	8,000
Units still in process (100% materials; 25% conversion cost)	1,200
Materials cost...	$50,000
Conversion cost	$45,500

This department combines manufacturing labor and factory overhead, described here as conversion cost.

Required: Prepare the following:
  (1) A cost of production report for Department 1 for April.
  (2) The journal entry transferring cost out of Department 1.

P5-6. Cost of production report; normal and abnormal spoilage. Menninger Inc. uses process costing in its two producing departments. In Department 2, inspection takes place at the 96% stage of completion, after which materials are added to good units. A spoilage rate of 3% of good output is considered normal. Abnormal spoilage is charged to Factory Overhead.
  Department 2 records for April show:

Received from Department 1	30,000 units
Cost	$135,000
Materials	$ 25,000
Conversion cost.................................	$139,340
Transferred to finished goods	25,000 units
Ending work in process inventory (50% complete)	4,200 units

Department 2 combines manufacturing labor and factory overhead and the combined amount is included in conversion cost.

Required:
  (1) Prepare a cost of production report for Department 2.
  (2) Prepare the journal entry transferring cost out of Department 2.

P5-7. Cost of production report; normal and abnormal spoilage. Trenton Company uses process costing in its two producing departments. The following information pertains to Department 2 for November.

Normal spoilage is 5% of good output; inspection and identification of spoilage take place at the 90% stage of completion; materials are added after inspection. Abnormal spoilage is charged to Factory Overhead.

Department 2 received 14,000 units from Department 1 at a cost of $140,000. Department 2 costs were $24,000 for materials and $89,250 for conversion costs. Department 2 treats all manufacturing labor as a part of factory overhead and the total amount is described as conversion cost.

A total of 8,000 units were completed and transferred to finished goods. At the end of the month, 5,000 units were still in process, estimated to be 60% complete as to conversion costs.

Required: Prepare the following:
  (1) A cost of production report for Department 2.
  (2) The journal entry transferring cost out of Department 2.

P5-8. Cost of production report; addition of materials. Ferry Inc. manufactures a product in two departments. Materials are added in each department, increasing the number of units manufactured. A summary of the cost information for the company's first month of operations (January) is as follows:

	Dept. 1	Dept. 2
Materials...............	$ 90,000	$ 67,500
Labor..................	39,000	41,400
Factory overhead	7,800	20,700
Total...............	$136,800	$129,600

The production supervisor reports that 300,000 units were put into production in Department 1. Of this quantity, 75,000, a normal number, were lost in production, and 180,000 were completed and transferred to Department 2. The units in process at the end of the month were complete as to materials, but only one-third complete as to labor and factory overhead.

In Department 2, 45,000 units of materials were purchased outside and added to the units received from Department 1; 195,000 units were completed and transferred to finished goods inventory. The units in process at the end of the month were complete as to materials, but only 40% complete as to labor and factory overhead.

Required: Prepare the following:
  (1) A cost of production report for January for both departments.
      (Carry unit cost computations to three decimal places.)
  (2) The journal entries transferring cost out of Departments 1 and 2.

CHAPTER 6

Process Costing: Average and Fifo Costing

The previous process costing chapter discussed the fundamentals of the cost of production report, lost unit calculations, and the effect of adding materials in departments other than the first. The discussion of process costing is now continued to include the effect of beginning work in process inventories.

■ BEGINNING WORK IN PROCESS INVENTORIES

The cost of production reports illustrated in Chapter 5 list ending work in process inventories. These inventories become beginning inventories of the next period. Two of the possible methods of accounting for these beginning inventory costs are:

1. *Average costing.* Beginning inventory costs are added to the costs of the new period.
2. *First-in, first-out (fifo) costing.* Beginning inventory costs are kept separate from the new costs necessary to complete the work in process inventory.

Average Costing

The average costing method of accounting for beginning work in process inventory costs involves merging these costs with the costs of the new period. To accomplish this relatively simple task, representative average unit costs must be determined.

The February cost reports of the three departments reviewed in Chapter 5 are used to illustrate the treatment of beginning work in process inventory and to show the relationship of costs from one period to the next. Ending inventories in January departmental cost reports become beginning work in process inventories for February and are summarized as follows:

	Blending	Testing	Terminal
Units..........................	4,000	3,000	4,000
Cost from preceding department	—	$5,400	$14,400
Materials in process	$2,000	—	—
Labor in process	1,240	910	900
Factory overhead in process.........	1,200	800	550

145

Blending Department. The February 1 work in process inventory of the Blending Department shows a $2,000 materials cost, a $1,240 labor cost, a $1,200 factory overhead cost, and 4,000 units in process. During February, additional charges to the department are: materials, $19,840; labor, $24,180; and factory overhead, $22,580. The additional materials put into process are for the production of 40,000 units. Therefore, units to be accounted for total 44,000 (4,000 + 40,000). Of the total units put into process, 39,000 are completed, with 38,000 units transferred to the Testing Department and 1,000 units awaiting transfer. At month end, 3,000 units are in process, 100 percent complete as to materials but only 66 2/3 percent complete as to labor and overhead. During the month, 2,000 units were lost. In the Blending Department as well as in the subsequent departments in this illustration, it is assumed that the loss applies to all good units and that the loss is within normal tolerance limits. Therefore, the effect of losing units is an increase in the unit cost of the remaining good units. The above facts are illustrated in the cost of production report on page 147.

The unit cost of work done in the Blending Department is $1.72, consisting of $.52 for materials, $.62 for labor, and $.58 for factory overhead. The $.52 unit cost for materials is computed by adding the materials cost in the beginning work in process inventory to the materials cost for the month ($2,000 + $19,840) and dividing the $21,840 total by the equivalent production figure of 42,000 units. These units include the 38,000 units completed and transferred, the 1,000 units completed but still on hand, and the 3,000 units in process, which are complete as to materials. The cost of materials already in process is added to the materials cost for the month before being divided by the equivalent production figure. This method results in an average unit cost for work done in the current and preceding periods.

The same procedure is followed in computing unit costs for labor and factory overhead. The $.62 unit cost for labor is the result of dividing equivalent production of 41,000 units (39,000 + (2/3 × 3,000)) into the sum of the beginning inventory labor cost of $1,240 and the departmental labor cost of $24,180 for the month. The factory overhead unit cost is $.58 (($1,200 + $22,580) ÷ 41,000).

Of the total cost charged to the department, $65,360 is transferred to the Testing Department when the following entry is recorded:

```
Work in Process—Testing Department......................   65,360
    Work in Process—Blending Department..................             65,360
```

The cost remaining in the Testing Department, $5,680, is assigned to the ending work in process inventory. The work in process inventory consists of $1,720 (1,000 units × $1.72) for units completed and on hand and of the following costs assigned to units still in process: $1,560 (3,000 units × $.52) for materials; $1,240 (2,000 units × $.62) for labor; and $1,160 (2,000 units × $.58) for factory overhead. The 1,000 units completed but on hand are listed as work in process in the Blending Department because this department is still responsible for these units.

Clonex Corporation
Blending Department
Cost of Production Report—Average Costing
For February, 19—

Quantity Schedule

Units in process at beginning (all materials; $\frac{1}{2}$ labor and factory overhead)	4,000	
Units started in process	40,000	44,000
Units transferred to next department	38,000	
Units completed and on hand	1,000	
Units still in process (all materials; $\frac{2}{3}$ labor and factory overhead)	3,000	
Units lost in process	2,000	44,000

Cost Charged to the Department	Total Cost	Unit Cost
Cost added by department:		
Work in process—beginning inventory:		
Materials	$ 2,000	
Labor	1,240	
Factory overhead	1,200	
Cost added during period:		
Materials	19,840	$ .52
Labor	24,180	.62
Factory overhead	22,580	.58
Total cost to be accounted for	**$71,040**	**$1.72**

Cost Accounted for as Follows

Transferred to next department (38,000 × $1.72)		$65,360
Work in process—ending inventory:		
Completed and on hand (1,000 × $1.72)	$ 1,720	
Materials (3,000 × $.52)	1,560	
Labor (3,000 × $\frac{2}{3}$ × $.62)	1,240	
Factory overhead (3,000 × $\frac{2}{3}$ × $.58)	1,160	5,680
Total cost accounted for		**$71,040**

Additional Computations:

Equivalent production: Materials = 38,000 + 1,000 + 3,000 = 42,000 units
Labor and factory overhead = 38,000 + 1,000 + ($\frac{2}{3}$ × 3,000)
= 41,000 units

Unit costs: Materials = $2,000 + $19,840 = $21,840; $\dfrac{\$21,840}{42,000}$ = $.52 per unit

Labor = $1,240 + $24,180 = $25,420; $\dfrac{\$25,420}{41,000}$ = $.62 per unit

Factory overhead = $1,200 + $22,580 = $23,780; $\dfrac{\$23,780}{41,000}$ = $.58 per unit

Testing Department. Accounting for the beginning work in process inventory cost in a department other than the first requires additional analysis. When the prior period's ending work in process inventory was computed, part of the cost of this inventory came from costs added by the preceding department. Because costs assigned to the beginning work in process inventory are added to costs incurred during the period and the total is divided by equivalent production, the beginning work in process inventory of departments other than the first must be split into the following two parts:

1. Cost transferred from preceding departments.
2. Cost added by the department itself.

The portion of the beginning work in process inventory cost from preceding departments is entered in the section of the cost report entitled "Cost from preceding department." It is added to the cost of transfers received from the preceding department during the current period. An average unit cost for work done in preceding departments is then computed. The other portion of the beginning inventory cost, which was added by the Testing Department, is entered as a departmental cost to be added to other departmental costs incurred during the current period. Average unit costs are then computed for each element of cost.

The cost of production report of the Testing Department presented on page 149 illustrates these procedures. The analysis of the beginning work in process inventory of this department (page 145) lists 3,000 units in process with a cost of $5,400 from the preceding department, a labor cost of $910, and $800 for factory overhead. The following costs pertain to February: cost from the preceding department, $65,360; labor, $34,050; factory overhead, $30,018. Units completed and transferred to the Terminal Department totaled 36,000; 4,000 units are in process, 50 percent complete as to labor and factory overhead; 1,000 units were lost in process.

The $5,400 portion of the beginning work in process inventory, which is cost from the preceding department, is entered in the current month's cost report as work in process—beginning inventory. It is added to the $65,360 of cost transferred from the Blending Department to the Testing Department during the month. The average unit cost for work done in the preceding department is $1.726, computed by dividing total cost received from the Blending Department, $70,760 ($5,400 + $65,360), by 41,000 units. These units consist of 3,000 units in the beginning work in process inventory and 38,000 units received during the month. The unit cost is a weighted average, since it considers all units and costs received from the preceding department. It is not the average of the two unit costs, $1.80 and $1.72. A simple average would not be accurate, since there are more units with a unit cost of $1.72 (38,000 units) than with a unit cost of $1.80 (3,000 units).

The $1.726 average unit cost for work done in the Blending Department pertains to the 41,000 units transferred to the Testing Department. However, because 1,000 of these 41,000 units were lost during processing in the Testing Department, the $1.726 unit cost figure must be adjusted. The "Adjusted cost from preceding department" is computed on the assumption that units lost cannot be identified as coming from either units in process at the beginning or from units received during the period, but proportionately from both sources. Recall that this illustration assumes not only that the loss applies to

Clonex Corporation
Testing Department
Cost of Production Report—Average Costing
For February, 19—

Quantity Schedule

Units in process at beginning (¹/₃ labor and
factory overhead)   3,000
Units received from preceding department   38,000   41,000

Units transferred to next department   36,000
Units still in process (¹/₂ labor and factory overhead)   4,000
Units lost in process   1,000   41,000

Cost Charged to the Department		Total Cost	Unit Cost
Cost from preceding department:			
Work in process—beginning inventory (3,000 units)		$ 5,400	$1.800
Transferred in during this period (38,000 units)		65,360	$1.720
Total (41,000 units)		$ 70,760	$1.726
Adjusted cost from preceding department			
($70,760 ÷ (41,000 units − 1,000 lost units))			$1.769
Cost added by department:			
Work in process—beginning inventory:			
Labor		$ 910	
Factory overhead		800	
Cost added during period:			
Labor		34,050	$ .920
Factory overhead		30,018	.811
Total cost added		$ 65,778	$1.731
Total cost to be accounted for		**$136,538**	**$3.500**

Cost Accounted for as Follows

Transferred to next department (36,000 × $3.500) $126,000
Work in process—ending inventory:
Adjusted cost from preceding department (4,000 × $1.769). $ 7,076
Labor (4,000 × ¹/₂ × $.920)   1,840
Factory overhead (4,000 × ¹/₂ × $.811)   1,622   10,538
Total cost accounted for **$136,538**

Additional Computations:

Unit cost from preceding department = $\frac{\$70,760}{41,000}$ = $1.726 per unit

Equivalent production: Labor and factory overhead = $36,000 + \frac{4,000}{2} = 38,000$ units

Unit costs: Labor = $910 + $34,050 = $34,960; $\frac{\$34,960}{38,000}$ = $.920 per unit

Factory overhead = $800 + $30,018 = $30,818; $\frac{\$30,818}{38,000}$ = $.811 per unit all good units but also that it is normal. The total cost of the units transferred remains at $70,760, but 40,000 units must now absorb this total cost, causing an increase of $.043 in the cost per unit, from $1.726 to an adjusted cost of $1.769 ($70,760 ÷ (41,000 units − 1,000 lost units)).

Departmental unit costs for labor and factory overhead are computed as explained in discussing the cost report of the Blending Department. The $910 of labor in process at the beginning is added to labor put in process during the month, $34,050. The total of these two labor costs, $34,960, is divided by an equivalent production figure of 38,000 units (36,000 + (4,000 × 1/2)) to arrive at a unit cost of $.920. The factory overhead unit cost of $.811 is the result of dividing total factory overhead, $30,818 ($800 + $30,018), by equivalent production of 38,000 units. The departmental unit cost is the sum of these two unit costs, $.920 + $.811, or $1.731. The departmental unit cost of $1.731 does not have to be adjusted for units lost, since the cost of any testing work on lost units has been absorbed automatically in the departmental unit cost by excluding lost units from the equivalent production figure. The $1.769 "Adjusted cost from preceding department" and the $1.731 departmental unit cost are totaled to give a cumulative unit cost figure of $3.50.

The total cost to be accounted for is $136,538. Of this total, $126,000 is the cost of the 36,000 units completed and transferred. The balance is cost assigned to the ending work in process inventory. The following entry transfers the cost of the 36,000 units to the next department:

Work in Process—Terminal Department....................	126,000	
Work in Process—Testing Department		126,000

Terminal Department. To complete this discussion of operations for February, the cost of production report of the Terminal Department is shown on page 151. The following entry transfers the cost of the 36,000 finished units to finished goods:

Finished Goods	182,160	
Work in Process—Terminal Department		182,160

Combined Cost of Production Report—Average Costing. Although the cost reports of each department are presented separately, operations for the month would also be combined in a single cost report as illustrated on page 152.

Other Factors in Accounting for Lost Units—Average Costing. Timing of lost units so that the cost of lost units does not pertain to the ending work in process inventory was discussed in Chapter 5 (page 132). The illustration on page 153, using the Testing Department for February and assuming that the loss of units is normal and is identified at the end of the process, demonstrates how such a situation is treated using average costing.

If the 1,000 lost units were abnormal, then $3,412 (1,000 lost units × $3.412) would be charged to Factory Overhead or to a current-period expense account. If the lost units are only partially complete, their stage of completion should be considered. And if one part of the loss is normal and another part abnormal, each portion should be treated in accordance with the above discussion.

Clonex Corporation
Terminal Department
Cost of Production Report—Average Costing
For February, 19—

Quantity Schedule

Units in process at beginning ($1/4$ labor and factory overhead)..	4,000	
Units received from preceding department	36,000	40,000
Units transferred to finished goods storeroom	36,000	
Units still in process ($1/3$ labor and factory overhead)	3,000	
Units lost in process	1,000	40,000

Cost Charged to the Department		Total Cost	Unit Cost
Cost from preceding department:			
Work in process—beginning inventory (4,000 units)		$ 14,400	$3.60
Transferred in during this period (36,000 units)		126,000	$3.50
Total (40,000 units)		$140,400	$3.51
Adjusted cost from preceding department ($140,400 ÷ (40,000 units − 1,000 lost units))			$3.60
Cost added by department:			
Work in process—beginning inventory:			
Labor....................................		$ 900	
Factory overhead		550	
Cost added during period:			
Labor....................................		33,140	$ .92
Factory overhead		19,430	.54
Total cost added		$ 54,020	$1.46
Total cost to be accounted for		**$194,420**	**$5.06**

Cost Accounted for as Follows

Transferred to finished goods storeroom (36,000 × $5.06)		$182,160
Work in process—ending inventory:		
Adjusted cost from preceding department (3,000 × $3.60)..	$ 10,800	
Labor (3,000 × $1/3$ × $.92)	920	
Factory overhead (3,000 × $1/3$ × $.54)	540	12,260
Total cost accounted for........................		**$194,420**

Additional Computations:

Unit cost from preceding department $= \dfrac{\$140,400}{40,000} = \$3.51$ per unit

Equivalent production: Labor and factory overhead $= 36,000 + \dfrac{3,000}{3} = 37,000$ units

Unit costs: Labor $= \$900 + \$33,140 = \$34,040; \dfrac{\$34,040}{37,000} = \$.92$ per unit

Factory overhead $= \$550 + \$19,430 = \$19,980; \dfrac{\$19,980}{37,000} = \$.54$ per unit

Clonex Corporation
All Producing Departments
Cost of Production Report—Average Costing
For February, 19—

Quantity Schedule	Blending		Testing		Terminal	
Units in process at beginning..........	4,000		3,000		4,000	
Units started in process	40,000	44,000				
Units received from preceding department...............			38,000	41,000	36,000	40,000
Units transferred to next department	38,000		36,000			
Units transferred to finished goods storeroom					36,000	
Units completed and on hand	1,000					
Units still in process	3,000		4,000		3,000	
Units lost in process	2,000	44,000	1,000	41,000	1,000	40,000

Cost Charged to the Department	Total Cost	Unit Cost	Total Cost	Unit Cost	Total Cost	Unit Cost
Cost from preceding department:						
Work in process—beginning inventory .			$ 5,400	$1.800	$ 14,400	$3.60
Transferred in during this period.....			65,360	$1.720	126,000	$3.50
Total			$ 70,760	$1.726	$140,400	$3.51
Adjusted cost from preceding department...................				$1.769		$3.60
Cost added by department:						
Work in process—beginning inventory:						
Materials.....................	$ 2,000					
Labor	1,240		$ 910		$ 900	
Factory overhead	1,200		800		550	
Cost added during period:						
Materials.....................	19,840	$ .52				
Labor	24,180	.62	34,050	$ .920	33,140	$ .92
Factory overhead	22,580	.58	30,018	.811	19,430	.54
Total cost added..............	$71,040	$1.72	$ 65,778	$1.731	$ 54,020	$1.46
Total cost to be accounted for .	**$71,040**	**$1.72**	**$136,538**	**$3.500**	**$194,420**	**$5.06**

Cost Accounted for as Follows						
Transferred to next department........		$65,360		$126,000		
Transferred to finished goods storeroom .						$182,160
Work in process—ending inventory:						
Completed and on hand	$ 1,720					
Adjusted cost from preceding department..			$ 7,076		$ 10,800	
Materials	1,560					
Labor	1,240		1,840		920	
Factory overhead................	1,160	5,680	1,622	10,538	540	12,260
Total cost accounted for		**$71,040**		**$136,538**		**$194,420**

Clonex Corporation
Testing Department
Cost of Production Report—Average Costing
For February, 19—

Quantity Schedule

Units in process at beginning (1/3 labor and factory overhead) . .	3,000	
Units received from preceding department	38,000	41,000
Units transferred to next department	36,000	
Units still in process (1/2 labor and factory overhead)	4,000	
Units lost in process (at end of process)	1,000	41,000

Cost Charged to the Department		Total Cost	Unit Cost
Cost from preceding department:			
Work in process—beginning inventory	(3,000 units)	$ 5,400	$1.800
Transferred in during this period	(38,000 units)	65,360	$1.720
Total	(41,000 units)	$ 70,760	$1.726
Cost added by department:			
Work in process—beginning inventory:			
Labor.		$ 910	
Factory overhead		800	
Cost added during period:			
Labor.		34,050	$ .896
Factory overhead		30,018	.790
Total cost added		$ 65,778	$1.686
Total cost to be accounted for		**$136,538**	**$3.412**

Cost Accounted for as Follows

Transferred to next department (36,000 × (3.412 + $.095))		
or ((36,000 × $3.412) + (1,000 lost units × $3.412))		$126,262*
Work in process—ending inventory:		
From preceding department (4,000 × $1.726)	$ 6,904	
Labor (4,000 × 1/2 × $.896)	1,792	
Factory overhead (4,000 × 1/2 × $.790)	1,580	10,276
Total cost accounted for		**$136,538**

Additional Computations:

Equivalent production: Labor and factory overhead $= 36,000 + \dfrac{4,000}{2} + 1,000$ lost units

$$= 39,000 \text{ units}$$

Unit costs: Labor $= \$910 + \$34,050 = \$34,960; \dfrac{\$34,960}{39,000} = \$.896$ per unit

Factory overhead $= \$800 + \$30,018 = \$30,818; \dfrac{\$30,818}{39,000} = \$.790$ per unit

Lost unit cost $= \$3.412 \times 1,000$ units $= \$3,412; \dfrac{\$ 3,412}{36,000} = \$.095$ per unit to be
added to $3.412 to make the transfer cost $3.507.

*36,000 units × $3.507 = 126,252. To avoid a decimal discrepancy, the cost transferred is computed:
$136,538 – $10,276 = $126,262.

First-In, First-Out (Fifo) Costing

The first-in, first-out (fifo) method may be used to account for beginning work in process inventory costs in process costing. Under this method, the beginning work in process inventory costs are separated from costs incurred in the current period and are not averaged with the additional new costs. This procedure gives one unit cost for units completed from the beginning work in process inventory and another for units started and finished in the same period. The cost of completing units in process at the beginning of the period is computed first, followed by the computation of the cost of units started and finished within the period.

To illustrate the fifo method, the February cost of production reports for Clonex Corporation are presented on the following pages, using the same data and assumptions as were used in the average costing illustration. This includes the assumption that lost units are within normal tolerance limits and that they pertain to the ending inventory as well as to units transferred out. A comparison of these reports with those illustrated for the average costing method indicates that the two methods do not result in significantly different unit costs, since manufacturing operations in industries using process costing are more or less uniform from period to period.

Blending Department. The February cost of production report of the Blending Department, using the fifo method, is shown on page 156. When the report is compared to the average costing report on page 147, the following differences are apparent:

1. Under fifo costing, the beginning work in process inventory cost of $4,440 is kept separate and is not broken down into its component parts.
2. Under fifo costing, the degree of completion of the beginning work in process inventory must be stated in order to compute completed unit costs.

Under fifo costing, the cost of completing the 4,000 units in process at the beginning of February must be computed first. No additional materials were needed; but since these units were only 50 percent complete as to labor and factory overhead, more labor and overhead costs must be added.

To determine costs expended in completing the units in the beginning inventory and to arrive at the cost of units started and finished within the current period, unit costs are computed for materials, labor, and factory overhead added during the period. Materials added during February, costing $19,840, were sufficient to complete an equivalent production of 38,000 units. Of these 38,000 units, 34,000 were started and completed during the period, 3,000 units are in process at month end, with all the necessary materials, and 1,000 units were complete but still on hand. Therefore, the unit cost for materials is $.522 ($19,840 ÷ 38,000).

The labor cost for February is $24,180, and the overhead cost is $22,580. The labor and overhead unit costs are computed after determining the number of units that could have been completed from these total costs. The labor cost and the overhead cost were sufficient to complete (1) 50 percent or 2,000 of the 4,000 units in the beginning inventory; (2) 34,000 units started and completed this period; (3) 1,000 units still on hand; and (4) 2/3 or 2,000 of the 3,000 units still in process. Therefore, the equivalent production for labor and overhead is 39,000 units. The unit cost for labor is $.620 ($24,180 ÷ 39,000), and the unit cost for factory overhead is $.579 ($22,580 ÷ 39,000).

In average costing, the cost of the units transferred to the next department was computed by multiplying the number of units transferred by the final unit cost. Under fifo costing, units in process at the beginning must be completed first and usually will have a completed unit cost that is different from the unit cost for work started and finished during the period. Two separate computations determine the total cost transferred to the next department.

No additional materials were needed to complete the beginning work in process inventory. The cost of labor and factory overhead used during the period in completing the beginning inventory units is added to the $4,440 already included as a cost of these units. Labor and overhead were added at unit costs of $.620 for labor and $.579 for factory overhead to complete the equivalent of 2,000 of the 4,000 units in process. The labor cost added was $1,240 (2,000 × $.620), and factory overhead was $1,158 (2,000 × $.579). The total cost of the 4,000 units completed and transferred was $6,838 ($4,440 + $1,240 + $1,158). The other 34,000 units were transferred at a unit cost of $1.721, or at a total of $58,517. The remaining $5,685 cost to be accounted for is in work in process at the end of the period and is computed as shown on the cost of production report on page 156.

The following entry transfers the total cost of the 38,000 units sent to the next department:

Work in Process—Testing Department......................	65,355	
Work in Process—Blending Department..................		65,355

Testing Department. The cost report of the Testing Department is illustrated on page 158. Although the cost transferred out of the Blending Department was the result of two separate computations, the total cost transferred into the Testing Department is shown as only one amount in its cost report. The unit cost of $1.72 is obtained by dividing the 38,000 total units received into the total cost received of $65,355 ($6,838 + $58,517). This procedure seems to cancel out some of the intended effects of the fifo method and has been criticized by some writers.

The balance of the Testing Department report is consistent with the fifo method of costing. The beginning work in process inventory, valued at $7,110, is shown in total and is not broken down into its component parts. Labor and factory overhead costs needed to complete the units in the beginning inventory are added to this figure to determine the completed cost of these units which are transferred to the next department. The $.920 unit cost for labor and the $.811 unit cost for factory overhead are computed by dividing the equivalent production figure of 37,000 units for labor and factory overhead into the labor cost of $34,050 and factory overhead of $30,018, respectively. The equivalent production figure of 37,000 units consists of (1) 2,000 units of beginning inventory completed; (2) 33,000 units started and

Clonex Corporation
Blending Department
Cost of Production Report—Fifo Costing
For February, 19—

Quantity Schedule

Units in process at beginning (all materials; $1/2$ labor and factory overhead)	4,000	
Units started in process	40,000	44,000
Units transferred to next department	38,000	
Units completed and on hand	1,000	
Units still in process (all materials; $2/3$ labor and factory overhead)	3,000	
Units lost in process	2,000	44,000

Cost Charged to the Department	Total Cost	Unit Cost
Work in process—beginning inventory	$ 4,440	
Cost added by department:		
Materials	$19,840	$ .522
Labor	24,180	.620
Factory overhead	22,580	.579
Total cost added	$66,600	$1.721
Total cost to be accounted for	**$71,040**	

Cost Accounted for as Follows

Transferred to next department—		
From beginning inventory:		
Inventory cost	$4,440	
Labor added (4,000 × $1/2$ × $.620)	1,240	
Factory overhead added (4,000 × $1/2$ × $.579)	1,158	$ 6,838
From current production:		
Units started and finished (34,000 × $1.721)	58,517*	$65,355
Work in process—ending inventory:		
Completed and on hand (1,000 × $1.721)	$ 1,721	
Materials (3,000 × $.522)	1,566	
Labor (3,000 × $2/3$ × $.620)	1,240	
Factory overhead (3,000 × $2/3$ × $.579)	1,158	5,685
Total cost accounted for		**$71,040**

Additional Computations:

Equivalent production:	Materials	Labor and Factory Overhead
Transferred out	38,000	38,000
Less beginning inventory (all units)	4,000	4,000
Started and finished this period	34,000	34,000
Add beginning inventory (work this period)	–0–	2,000
Add ending inventory:		
Completed and on hand	1,000	1,000
Still in process (work this period)	3,000	2,000
	38,000 units	39,000 units

*34,000 units × $1.721 per unit = $58,514. To avoid a decimal discrepancy, the cost transferred from current production is computed as follows: $71,040 – ($6,838 + $5,685) = $58,517.

$$\text{Unit costs: Materials} = \frac{\$19,840}{38,000} = \$.522 \text{ per unit}$$

$$\text{Labor} = \frac{\$24,180}{39,000} = \$.620 \text{ per unit}$$

$$\text{Factory overhead} = \frac{\$22,580}{39,000} = \$.579 \text{ per unit}$$

finished this period; and (3) 2,000 of the 4,000 units in the ending work in process inventory. The labor cost added to the beginning work in process inventory was $1,840 (2,000 × $.920), and factory overhead added was $1,622 (2,000 × $.811). These two amounts are added to the beginning inventory cost of $7,110 to give a total cost of $10,572. This is the completed cost of the 3,000 units in the beginning inventory transferred to the Terminal Department.

Because 1,000 units were lost during February, computation of the cost accumulated to the end of operations in the Testing Department requires an adjustment for lost units. This adjustment is determined by dividing the previous department's total cost of $65,355 by the good units (37,000) of the period, resulting in an adjusted unit cost of $1.766. In fifo costing, the lost units must be identified as all units from the beginning inventory, all new units started during the period, or a portion in each of these two categories. The identification is needed to determine which unit cost(s) should be adjusted. Such a determination in fifo costing is also required in cases involving the addition of materials in departments subsequent to the first, when an increase in units and a resulting change in unit cost occur. In this illustration, the loss is assumed to apply to good units started this period, whether transferred out or in ending inventory, and the loss is assumed to be normal. Other factors in accounting for lost units under fifo costing are discussed on page 159.

For the various lost units conditions or when the addition of materials increases the number of units, the unit costs include not only the cost from the preceding department but the unit costs for materials, labor, and factory overhead that originate in the respective producing departments. For each element of cost, the source of the loss must be determined when fifo costing is used. This illustration, for all three departments, is consistent with the assumption used in the Testing Department for adjusting the preceding department unit cost. That is, for all unit costs, the lost units are assumed to come entirely from those units started in process during the current period, adjusted for the effect of beginning and ending work in process inventories on the computed equivalent production for the current period.

The Testing Department completed and transferred 36,000 units, of which 3,000 units came from those in process at the beginning of the period. The cost of the 3,000 units is $10,572. The remaining 33,000 units came from units started and finished during the month. These units are transferred at a cumulative unit cost of $3.497 and a total cost of $115,435. The following entry transfers the cost of the 36,000 units to the next department:

Work in Process—Terminal Department....................	126,007	
Work in Process—Testing Department		126,007

Clonex Corporation
Testing Department
Cost of Production Report—Fifo Costing
For February, 19—

Quantity Schedule

Units in process at beginning (1/3 labor and factory overhead) . .	3,000	
Units received from preceding department	38,000	41,000
Units transferred to next department	36,000	
Units still in process (1/2 labor and factory overhead)	4,000	
Units lost in process	1,000	41,000

Cost Charged to the Department	Total Cost	Unit Cost
Work in process—beginning inventory	$ 7,110	
Cost from preceding department:		
Transferred in during the month (38,000 units)	$ 65,355	$1.720
Adjusted cost from preceding department ($65,355 ÷ (38,000 units – 1,000 lost units))		$1.766
Cost added by department:		
Labor	$ 34,050	$ .920
Factory overhead	30,018	.811
Total cost added	$ 64,068	$1.731
Total cost to be accounted for	**$136,533**	$3.497

Cost Accounted for as Follows

Transferred to next department—			
From beginning inventory:			
Inventory cost $7,110			
Labor added (3,000 × 2/3 × $.920) 1,840			
Factory overhead added (3,000 × 2/3 × $.811). . 1,622		$ 10,572	
From current production:			
Units started and finished (33,000 × $3.497)		115,435*	$126,007
Work in process—ending inventory:			
Adjusted cost from preceding department (4,000 × $1.766) . .		$ 7,064	
Labor (4,000 × 1/2 × $.920)		1,840	
Factory overhead (4,000 × 1/2 × $.811)		1,622	10,526
Total cost accounted for			**$136,533**

Additional Computations:

Equivalent production:	Labor and Factory Overhead
Transferred out	36,000
Less beginning inventory (all units)	3,000
Started and finished this period	33,000
Add beginning inventory (work this period)	2,000
Add ending inventory (work this period)	2,000
	37,000 units

*33,000 units × $3.497 per unit = $115,401. To avoid a decimal discrepancy, the cost transferred from current production is computed as follows: $136,533 – ($10,572 + $10,526) = $115,435.

$$\text{Unit costs: Labor} = \frac{\$34,050}{37,000} = \$.920 \text{ per unit}$$

$$\text{Factory overhead} = \frac{\$30,018}{37,000} = \$.811 \text{ per unit}$$

The remaining $10,526 cost to be accounted for is the ending work in process inventory, which is computed in the conventional manner.

Terminal Department. To complete the illustration of fifo costing, the cost of production report of the Terminal Department is presented on page 160. Based on this report, the entry to transfer the cost of the 36,000 finished units is:

Finished Goods	182,166	
Work in Process—Terminal Department		182,166

Combined Cost of Production Report—Fifo Costing. The illustration on page 161 is a combined cost of production report for February, using fifo costing. This report should be compared with the report (page 152) in which average costing is used.

Other Factors in Accounting for Lost Units—Fifo Costing. If the loss is normal but does not pertain to the ending inventory or if the loss is abnormal, it is again necessary in fifo costing to identify the extent to which the loss is from units started during the period or from beginning inventory. This determination is required in order to calculate equivalent production and unit costs properly. To illustrate the timing of lost units for a case in which their cost does not pertain to the ending work in process, the Testing Department for February is used, assuming fifo costing. Here the loss is identified at the end of the process and is assumed to come entirely from units started during February.

If the 1,000 lost units were abnormal, then $3,406 (1,000 lost units × $3.406) would be charged to Factory Overhead or to a current-period expense account. If the lost units are only partially complete, their stage of completion should be considered in assigning cost to them. And if one part of the loss is normal and another part abnormal, each portion should be treated in accordance with the above discussion.

Average Costing vs. Fifo Costing

Both average costing and fifo costing have certain advantages. It would be arbitrary to state that one method is either simpler or more accurate than the other. The selection of either method depends entirely upon management's opinion regarding the most appropriate and practical cost determination procedures. Each firm should select the method which offers reliable figures for managerial guidance.

The basic difference between the two methods concerns the treatment of beginning work in process inventory. The average method adds beginning

Clonex Corporation
Terminal Department
Cost of Production Report—Fifo Costing
For February, 19—

Quantity Schedule

Units in process at beginning ($1/4$ labor and factory overhead) . .	4,000	
Units received from preceding department	36,000	40,000
Units transferred to finished goods storeroom	36,000	
Units still in process ($1/3$ labor and factory overhead)	3,000	
Units lost in process	1,000	40,000

Cost Charged to the Department	Total Cost	Unit Cost
Work in process—beginning inventory	$ 15,850	
Cost from preceding department:		
Transferred in during the month (36,000 units)	$126,007	$3.500
Adjusted cost from preceding department ($126,007 ÷ (36,000 units – 1,000 lost units))		$3.600
Cost added by department:		
Labor	$ 33,140	$ .921
Factory overhead	19,430	.540
Total cost added	$ 52,570	$1.461
Total cost to be accounted for	**$194,427**	$5.061

Cost Accounted for as Follows

Transferred to finished goods storeroom—		
From beginning inventory:		
Inventory cost $15,850		
Labor added (4,000 × $3/4$ × $.921) 2,763		
Factory overhead added (4,000 × $3/4$ × $.540) . . 1,620	$ 20,233	
From current production:		
Units started and finished (32,000 × $5.061)	161,933*	$182,166
Work in process—ending inventory:		
Adjusted cost from preceding department (3,000 × $3.60) . .	$ 10,800	
Labor (3,000 × $1/3$ × $.921)	921	
Factory overhead (3,000 × $1/3$ × $.540)	540	12,261
Total cost accounted for		**$194,427**

Additional Computations:

Equivalent production:	Labor and Factory Overhead
Transferred out	36,000
Less beginning inventory (all units)	4,000
Started and finished this period	32,000
Add beginning inventory (work this period)	3,000
Add ending inventory (work this period)	1,000
	36,000 units

*32,000 × $5.061 per unit = $161,952. To avoid a decimal discrepancy, the cost transferred from current production is computed as follows: $194,427 – ($20,233 + $12,261) = $161,933.

$$\text{Unit costs: Labor} = \frac{\$33,140}{36,000} = \$.921 \text{ per unit}$$

$$\text{Factory overhead} = \frac{\$19,430}{36,000} = \$.540 \text{ per unit}$$

Clonex Corporation
All Producing Departments
Cost of Production Report—Fifo Costing
For February, 19—

	Blending		Testing		Terminal	
Quantity Schedule						
Units in process at beginning..........	4,000		3,000		4,000	
Units started in process	40,000	44,000				
Units received from preceding department...............			38,000	41,000	36,000	40,000
Units transferred to next department	38,000		36,000			
Units transferred to finished goods storeroom					36,000	
Units completed and on hand	1,000					
Units still in process	3,000		4,000		3,000	
Units lost in process	2,000	44,000	1,000	41,000	1,000	40,000
	Total Cost	**Unit Cost**	**Total Cost**	**Unit Cost**	**Total Cost**	**Unit Cost**
Cost Charged to the Department						
Work in process—beginning inventory...	$ 4,440		$ 7,110		$ 15,850	
Cost from preceding department: Transferred in during the month			$ 65,355	$1.720	$126,007	$3.500
Adjusted cost from preceding department...................				$1.766		$3.600
Cost added by department:						
Materials	$19,840	$ .522				
Labor	24,180	.620	$ 34,050	$ .920	$ 33,140	$ .921
Factory overhead.................	22,580	.579	30,018	.811	19,430	.540
Total cost added	$66,600	$1.721	$ 64,068	$1.731	$ 52,570	$1.461
Total cost to be accounted for ...	**$71,040**	**$1.721**	**$136,533**	**$3.497**	**$194,427**	**$5.061**
Cost Accounted for as Follows						
Transferred to next department— From beginning inventory:						
Inventory Cost	$ 4,440		$ 7,110		$ 15,850	
Labor added.................	1,240		1,840		2,763	
Factory overhead added	1,158	$ 6,838	1,622	$ 10,572	1,620	$ 20,233
From current production: Units started and finished		58,517		115,435		161,933
		$65,355		$126,007		$182,166
Work in process—ending inventory:						
Completed and on hand	$ 1,721					
Adjusted cost from preceding department			$ 7,064		$ 10,800	
Materials	1,566					
Labor	1,240		1,840		921	
Factory overhead.................	1,158	5,685	1,622	10,526	540	12,261
Total cost accounted for		**$71,040**		**$136,533**		**$194,427**

Clonex Corporation
Testing Department
Cost of Production Report—Fifo Costing
For February, 19—

Quantity Schedule

Units in process at beginning (1/3 labor and factory overhead) . .	3,000	
Units received from preceding department	38,000	41,000
Units transferred to next department	36,000	
Units still in process (1/2 labor and factory overhead)	4,000	
Units lost in process (at end of process)	1,000	41,000

Cost Charged to the Department	Total Cost	Unit Cost
Work in process—beginning inventory	$ 7,110	
Cost from preceding department:		
Transferred in during the month (38,000 units)	$ 65,355	$1.720
Cost added by department:		
Labor	$ 34,050	$ .896
Factory overhead	30,018	.790
Total cost added	$ 64,068	$1.686
Total cost to be accounted for	**$136,533**	**$3.406**

Cost Accounted for as Follows

Transferred to next department—			
From beginning inventory:			
Inventory cost $7,110			
Labor added (3,000 × 2/3 × $.896) 1,792			
Factory overhead added (3,000 × 2/3 × $.790). . 1,580		$ 10,482	
From current production:			
Units started and finished (33,000 × ($3.406 + $.103)			
or (33,000 × $3.406) + (1,000 lost units × $3.406)) . .		115,799*	$126,281
Work in process—ending inventory:			
From preceding department (4,000 × $1.720)		$ 6,880	
Labor (4,000 × 1/2 × $.896)		1,792	
Factory overhead (4,000 × 1/2 × $.790)		1,580	10,252
Total cost accounted for			**$136,533**

Additional Computations:

Equivalent production:	Labor and Factory Overhead
Transferred out	36,000
Less beginning inventory (all units)	3,000
Started and finished this period	33,000
Add beginning inventory (work this period)	2,000
Add ending inventory (work this period)	2,000
Add units lost in process	1,000
	38,000 units

*33,000 units × $3.509 per unit = $115,797. To avoid a decimal discrepancy, the cost transferred from current production is computed as follows: $136,533 – ($10,482 + $10,252) = $115,799.

$$\text{Unit costs: Labor} = \frac{\$34,050}{38,000} = \$.896 \text{ per unit}$$

$$\text{Factory overhead} = \frac{\$30,018}{38,000} = \$.790 \text{ per unit}$$

Lost unit cost = \$3.406 × 1,000 units = \$3,406; \$3,406 ÷ 33,000 units = \$.103 per unit to be added to \$3.406 to make the transfer cost \$3.509.

work in process inventory cost to the cost from the preceding department and to materials, labor, and factory overhead costs incurred during the period. Unit costs are determined by dividing these costs by equivalent production figures. Units and costs are transferred to the next department as one cumulative figure.

The fifo method retains the beginning work in process inventory cost as a separate figure. Costs necessary to complete the beginning inventory units are added to this total cost. The sum of these two cost totals is transferred to the next department. Units started and finished during the period have their own unit cost, which is usually different from the completed unit cost of units in process at the beginning of the period. The fifo method thus separately identifies for management the current period unit cost originating in a department. Unfortunately, these costs are averaged out in the next department, resulting in a loss of much of the value associated with the use of the fifo method.

If the fifo method is used, units lost or added during a period must be identified as to whether they came from units in process at the beginning or from units started or received during the period. Also, in computing equivalent production figures in fifo costing, the degree of completion of both the beginning and ending work in process inventories must be considered.

The principal disadvantage of fifo costing is that if several unit cost figures are used at the same time, extensive detail is required within the cost of production report, which can lead to complex procedures and even inaccuracy. Whether the extra detail yields more representative unit costs than the average costing method is debatable. Where production is continuous and more or less uniform, and, therefore, appreciable fluctuations in unit costs are not expected to develop, and where work in process inventories are relatively small in quantity, the average costing method leads to more satisfactory cost computations.

The fifo method has little to recommend it. However, as long as the CPA and other professional examinations continue to require a knowledge of this method, it is advisable to study the related procedures.

■ DIFFICULTIES ENCOUNTERED IN PROCESS COST ACCOUNTING

The following difficulties in using process costing may be encountered in actual practice:

1. The determination of production quantities and their stages of completion presents problems. Every computation is influenced by these figures. Since the data generally come to the cost department from operating personnel often working under circumstances that make a precise count difficult, a certain amount of doubtful counts and unreliable estimates are bound to exist. Yet, the data submitted form the basis for the determination of inventory costs.

2. Materials cost computations frequently require careful analysis. In the illustrations, materials cost is generally part of the first department's cost. In certain industries, materials costs are not even entered on production reports. When materials prices are influenced by fluctuating market quotations, the materials cost may be recorded in a separate report designed to facilitate management decisions in relation to the materials market.

3. Industries using process costing are generally of the multiple product type. Joint processing cost must be allocated to the products resulting from the processes. Weighted unit averages or other bases are used to prorate the joint cost to the several products. If units manufactured are used as a basis for cost allocation, considerable difficulties may arise in determining reasonable unit costs.

Management must decide whether economy and low operational cost are compatible with increased information, based on additional cost computations and procedures. Some companies use both job order and process costing procedures for various purposes in different departments. The basis for using either method should be reliable production and performance data for product costing which, when combined with output, budget, or standard cost data, will provide the foundation for effective cost control and analysis.

DISCUSSION QUESTIONS

Q6-1. Distinguish between the fifo and average methods of process costing.

Q6-2. Why are units completed and on hand in a processing department included in the department's work in process?

Q6-3. The Wiring Department is the second stage of Riley Company's production cycle. On May 1, the beginning work in process contained 25,000 units which were 60% complete as to conversion costs. During May, 100,000 units were transferred in from the first stage of Riley's production cycle. On May 31, the ending work in process contained 20,000 units which were 80% complete as to conversion costs. Materials costs are added at the end of the process. Using the average method, compute the equivalent units of production.   (AICPA adapted)

Q6-4. Maurice Company adds materials at the beginning of the process in the Forming Department, which is the first of two stages of its production cycle. Information concerning the materials used in the Forming Department in April is as follows:

	Materials	
	Units	Cost
Work in progress, April 1...............	12,000	$ 6,000
Units started during April	100,000	51,120
Units completed and transferred to next department during April	88,000	

Using the average method, what was the materials cost of the work in process at April 30?   (AICPA adapted)

Q6-5. How are equivalent production figures computed when fifo costing is used?

Q6-6. Sussex Corporation's production cycle starts in the Mixing Department. The following information is available for April:

	Units
Work in process, April 1 (50% complete)	40,000
Started in April	240,000
Work in process, April 30 (60% complete)	25,000

Materials are added in the beginning of the process in the Mixing Department. Using the average method, what are the equivalent units of production? (AICPA adapted)

Q6-7. Using the data from discussion question 6, what are the equivalent units of production assuming the fifo method?

Q6-8. What are some of the disadvantages of the fifo costing method?

Q6-9. Noble Manufacturing Company uses the average method of process costing when computing manufacturing cost per equivalent unit. The work in process inventory at the beginning of the period was complete as to materials, and one-third complete as to conversion costs. The work in process inventory at the end of the period was complete as to materials, and one-quarter complete as to conversion costs.
(a) Describe how the cost of the beginning work in process inventory is handled using the average method of process costing when computing manufacturing cost per equivalent unit. Do not describe determination of equivalent units.
(b) Identify the conditions under which the average method of process costing would be inappropriate.
(c) Specify the advantages of the average method of process costing in contrast to the first-in, first-out method.
(d) How would Noble compute the amount of the conversion cost portion of its ending work in process inventory using the average method? (AICPA adapted)

Q6-10. Enumerate several of the basic difficulties frequently encountered in process costing.

Q6-11. Express an opinion as to the usefulness of data, derived from process costing, for the control of costs.

EXERCISES

E6-1. Computation of equivalent production. TSA Company operates two producing departments, whose quantity reports appear as follows:

	Department 1	Department 2
Beginning inventory:		
Department 1—all materials; 25% conversion cost	200	
Department 2—60% conversion cost		80
Started in process	2,260	2,160
	2,460	2,240

Transferred out.	2,160	2,000
Ending inventory:		
Department 1—all materials; 60% conversion cost	300	
Department 2—80% conversion cost		240
	2,460	2,240

Required: Compute equivalent production figures for each department, using: (1) average costing and (2) fifo costing.

E6-2. Computation of equivalent production. The following data have been compiled:
- (a) Started in process, 12,000 units; in process at end of period, 4,000, complete as to materials, 3/4 complete as to labor and factory overhead; transferred 8,000 units to finished goods.
- (b) Beginning inventory, 6,000 units, 1/2 complete as to materials, 1/3 complete as to labor and factory overhead; transferred out, 15,000 units; units lost at end of production, 2,000; in process at end of period, 8,400, 1/4 complete as to materials, 1/8 complete as to labor and factory overhead.
- (c) Beginning inventory, 6,600 units, complete as to materials, 1/3 complete as to labor and factory overhead; started in process, 16,000 units; in process at end of period, 1,600, complete as to materials, 1/4 complete as to labor and factory overhead; and 1,500, complete as to materials, 1/3 complete as to labor and factory overhead; units lost at the 1/8 stage of the process, 2,000, a normal quantity.

Required: Determine equivalent production figures, using (1) the average costing method and (2) the fifo costing method.

E6-3. Average costing. Information concerning Department B of LeRoy Company is as follows:

Units in beginning inventory	5,000
Units transferred in	35,000
	40,000
Units completed.	37,000
Units in ending inventory.	3,000

	Costs			
	Transferred In	Materials	Conversion	Total Cost
Beginning inventory.	$ 2,900	—	$ 3,400	$ 6,300
Units transferred in	17,500	$25,500	15,000	58,000
	$20,400	$25,500	$18,400	$64,300

Conversion costs were 20% complete as to the beginning inventory and 40% complete as to the ending inventory. Department B treats all manufacturing labor as a part of factory overhead and the combined amount is included in conversion cost. All materials are added at the end of the process. LeRoy uses average costing.

Required:
- (1) Compute the cost per equivalent unit for conversion costs, rounded to the nearest cent.
- (2) Determine the portion of the total cost of ending inventory attributable to transferred-in cost.

(AICPA adapted)

E6-4. Inventory costing; average vs. fifo costing. The Cutting Department is the first stage of Starnes Company's production cycle. Conversion cost for this department was 80% complete as to the beginning work in process and 50% complete as to the ending work in process. Information as to conversion cost in the Cutting Department for January is as follows:

	Units	Conversion Cost
Work in process at January 1	25,000	$ 22,000
Units started and costs incurred during January	135,000	143,000
Units completed and transferred to next department during January	100,000	

Required: Compute the conversion cost of the Cutting Department's January 31 work in process inventory, using (1) the average method and (2) the fifo method. (Carry unit cost computations to three decimal places.)

(AICPA adapted)

E6-5. Cost of production report; average costing. Tyler Corporation is a manufacturer that uses average costing to account for costs of production. Tyler manufactures a product that is produced in three separate departments: Molding, Assembling, and Finishing. The following information was obtained by the Assembling Department for June:

Work in process, June 1—2,000 units, composed of:

	Amount	Degree of Completion
Transferred in from the Molding Department	$32,000	100%
Cost added by the Assembling Department:		
Direct materials	20,000	100
Direct labor.	7,200	60
Factory overhead	5,500	50

The following activity occurred during June:
  (a) 10,000 units were transferred in from the Molding Department at a cost of $160,000.
  (b) $150,000 of costs were added by the Assembling Department: direct materials, $96,000; direct labor, $36,000; and factory overhead, $18,000.
  (c) 8,000 units were completed and transferred to the Finishing Department.

At June 30, 4,000 units were still in work in process, with the following degrees of completion: direct materials, 90%; direct labor, 70%; and factory overhead, 35%.

Required:
  (1) Prepare the June cost of production report for the Assembling Department.
  (2) Record the journal entry transferring cost out of the Assembling Department.   (AICPA adapted)

E6-6. Cost of production report; average costing; normal spoilage. The Thornton Company uses average costing in accounting for a single product which is produced in one department. All material is added at the beginning of the process. The product is inspected when it is 80% complete. Normal spoilage is expected to be 5% of good output.

At the beginning of October, 2,500 units were in process, approximately 40% complete. Costs already charged to these units were $12,000 for materials and $6,700 for conversion.

During October, 8,000 more units were put into process. Current month costs were $40,500 for materials and $64,000 for conversion. The company combines manufacturing labor and factory overhead; the total is the conversion cost. Units still in process at the end of October (3,000) were estimated to be 90% complete, with 7,000 units having been transferred to finished goods inventory.

Required:
  (1) Prepare the October cost of production report. Compute unit costs to the nearest cent.
  (2) Prepare the journal entry transferring cost out of the work in process account.

CGA-Canada (adapted) Reprint with permission

E6-7. Process costing; average costing; normal and abnormal spoilage. A manufacturer uses average process cost accumulation for its only product. For each unit of finished product, two pounds of Material A are introduced at the start of the process, and one pound of Material B is added when the process is 60% complete. Labor and factory overhead costs are incurred uniformly throughout the process.

Inspection occurs at the 50% stage of completion and any spoiled units are scrapped with no recovery. Normal spoilage at that stage is expected to be 3% of the units processed up to that point. Normal spoilage costs are added to the cost of the good units completed, and abnormal spoilage costs are treated as an expense of the period.

The following information applies to November operations:

	Units	Percent Complete	Cost
Work in process, November 1.	2,000	80%	—
Work in process, November 30.	1,000	20	—
Total units spoiled, including abnormal spoilage	800	50	—
Good units completed	21,200	—	—
Unit costs incurred:			
Material A per pound	—	—	$4
Material B per pound	—	—	2
Conversion costs per equivalent unit	—	—	5

Required:
(1) Compute the pounds of Material A and of Material B that were put into production in November.
(2) How much should be charged to November expense for abnormal spoilage cost?
(3) Compute the total cost of the units transferred out during November.   (CIA adapted)

E6-8. Manufacturing costs; fifo costing. Yukon Motors is engaged in the production of a standard type of electric motor. Manufacturing costs for April totaled $66,000. At the beginning of April, inventories appeared as follows:

Motors in production, estimated 80% complete (2,500 units)	$32,000
Motors on hand and in finished goods (1,200 units)	19,200

During the month, 5,500 completed units were placed in finished stock. At the end of April, inventories were:

Motors in production, estimated 50% complete.	1,000 units
Motors on hand, completed and in finished goods	1,400 units

The company uses fifo costing for work in process and finished goods inventories. In costing finished goods, the unit cost for units completed from beginning work in process inventory is kept separate from the unit cost of motors started and completed during the month.

Required:
(1) Compute the cost assigned to the ending work in process inventory.
(2) Compute the cost assigned to the ending finished goods inventory.
(3) Compute the cost of goods sold.   CGA-Canada (adapted) Reprint with permission

E6-9. Cost of production report; fifo costing; normal loss. Dentex Plastics Corporation produces non-breakable containers for cosmetics, using three departments: Mixing, Molding, and Finishing. On July 1, the work in process inventory in the Molding Department was 1,000 units, 50% complete as to materials and conversion costs, while the July 31 work in process inventory consisted of 2,800 units, 75% complete as to materials and conversion costs. During July, the Finishing Department received 20,000 units from the Molding Department. In the Molding Department, 800 units (a normal quantity) that came from the Mixing Department in July were lost during processing. Fifo costing is used.

Relevant cost data are as follows:

Work in process, July 1	$ 6,000
July costs:	
Cost from Mixing Department	97,632
Materials	16,200
Labor	26,568
Factory overhead	21,600

Required:

(1) Using the fifo costing method, prepare the cost of production report for the Molding Department for July. Round unit costs to the nearest cent.

(2) Prepare the journal entry transferring cost out of the Molding Department.

PROBLEMS

P6-1. Computation of equivalent production. The Brown Company manufactures hair spray in a three-department process. The Molding Department produces the plastic bottles and caps in which the product is placed. The Mixing Department combines the raw materials for the hair spray and puts the mixture into bottles. In the Packaging Department, the product is boxed and sealed in cellophane.

A description of the departmental activities as well as the units associated with the work in process at the beginning of March follows:

Molding Department:

In the Molding Department, the plastic is added at the beginning of the process, overhead is uniformly incurred, and the only direct labor occurs at the end of the process. A worker trims the bottle and cap and places them on a conveyer for transport to the Mixing Department. The work in process at March 1 was 1,000 units estimated to be 1/2 complete.

Mixing Department:

All the materials for the hair spray are combined in a large vat, thoroughly mixed, and pumped into the plastic bottles conveyed from the Molding Department. The overhead costs for the Mixing Department are uniformly incurred during the mixing process. Materials and direct labor are added at the beginning of the process. At the beginning of March, no work in process existed in the Mixing Department.

Packaging Department:

The capped bottles are conveyed to the Packaging Department where they are automatically boxed. At the end of the process, the boxes are sealed in cellophane and a worker packs them in cases of 24 bottles each. The individual box is added at the beginning of the process and the cellophane, direct labor, and casing are added at the end of the process. Overhead is incurred uniformly. On March 1, the 960 units in process were considered to be 40% complete.

Plastic for 100,000 bottles and caps was added into production in the Molding Department. The work in process inventories at the end of March included: 2,000 units 80% complete in the Molding Department; 1,000 units 50% complete in the Mixing Department; and 640 units 25% complete in the Packaging Department.

The Molding and Mixing Departments use average process costing, while the Packaging Department uses first-in, first-out process costing.

Required: Compute equivalent units of production for March for the three departments. Assume that no spoilage occurs in any of the processes. CGA-Canada (adapted) Reprint with permission

P6-2. Cost of production report; fifo vs. average costing; normal loss. Deterra Inc. uses three departments to produce a detergent. The Finishing Department is the third and last step before the product is transferred to storage.

All materials needed to give the detergent its final composition are added at the beginning of the process in the Finishing Department. Any lost units occur only at this point and are considered to be normal.

The company uses fifo costing. The following data for the Finishing Department for October have been made available:

Production data:

In process, October 1 (labor and factory overhead, 3/4 complete)	10,000 gals.
Transferred in from preceding department	40,000
Finished and transferred to storage	35,000
In process, October 31 (labor and factory overhead, 1/2 complete)	10,000

Additional data:

Work in process inventory, October 1:	
Cost from preceding department	$ 38,000
Cost from this department:	
Materials	21,500
Labor	39,000
Factory overhead	42,000
Total work in process inventory, October 1	$140,500
Transferred in during October	$140,000
Cost added in this department:	
Materials	$ 70,000
Labor	162,500
Factory overhead	130,000
Total cost added	$362,500
Total cost to be accounted for	$643,000

Required:
   (1) Prepare a cost of production report for the Finishing Department for October using fifo costing.
   (2) Prepare a cost of production report for the Finishing Department for October using average costing. (Carry unit cost computations to three decimal places, and round up the digit "5" in the fourth decimal place.)
   (3) Prepare the journal entries transferring cost out of the Finishing Department, assuming (a) fifo costing, and (b) average costing.   (AICPA adapted)

P6-3. Inventory costing; average method. In attempting to verify the costing of the December 31, 19A inventory of work in process and finished goods recorded on Windsor Corporation's books, the auditor finds:

Finished goods, 200,000 units	$1,009,800
Work in process, 300,000 units, 50% complete as to labor and factory overhead	660,960

The company uses average costing. Materials are added to production at the beginning of the manufacturing process, and factory overhead is applied at the rate of 60% of direct labor cost. Windsor's inventory cost records disclosed zero finished goods on January 1, 19A, and the following additional information for 19A:

		Costs	
	Units	Materials	Labor
Work in process, January 1 (80% complete as to labor and factory overhead)	200,000	$ 200,000	$ 315,000
Units started in production	1,000,000		
Materials cost		$1,300,000	
Labor cost			$1,995,000
Units completed	900,000		

Required:
   (1) Compute the equivalent units of production.
   (2) Compute the unit production costs of materials, labor, and factory overhead.

(3) Cost the ending finished goods and work in process inventories and compare to book balances.

(4) Prepare the necessary journal entry to correctly state the finished goods and work in process ending inventories.   (AICPA adapted)

P6-4. Cost of production report; average costing; normal loss. Gulf Shores Company produces sleeping pills in two departments: Mixing, and Compounding and Packaging. The company uses average costing. For February, in the Mixing Department, the ending inventory is complete as to materials and 1/2 complete as to labor and factory overhead, and lost units occur at the end of the department's processing. In the Compounding and Packaging Department, the ending inventory is 2/3 complete as to labor and factory overhead.

	Mixing Department	Compounding and Packaging Department
Production data:		
Beginning inventory	1,000 units	500 units
Started in process	15,000	—
Received from prior department	—	12,500
Transferred out	12,500	11,500
Ending inventory	3,000	1,500
Lost units (all normal)	500	—
Cost summary:		
Beginning inventory:		
Cost from prior department	—	$ 650
Materials	$ 980	—
Labor	230	175
Factory overhead	400	100
Cost for February:		
Materials	15,020	—
Labor	5,570	6,700
Factory overhead	8,300	4,275

Required:

(1) Prepare a cost of production report for both departments for February.

(2) Prepare the journal entries transferring cost out of each of the departments.

P6-5. Cost of production report; average costing; normal and abnormal spoilage. Blanchard Inc. uses average process costing in accounting for its product, which moves through two manufacturing departments. In Department 2, materials are not added until the product is 95% complete. Inspection takes place when the product is 80% complete and it is expected that 3% of the units inspected will be defective.

Information for Department 2 for September is as follows:

	Units	Dollars
Beginning inventory, 40% complete	1,000	
Department 1 cost		$ 5,700
Department 2 cost		980
Received from Department 1	10,000	60,300
Department 2 cost:		
Materials		5,760
Conversion cost (direct labor and factory overhead)		25,000
Transferred to finished goods	9,600	
Ending inventory, 90% complete	1,050	

Required:

(1) Prepare a cost of production report for Department 2 for September. Round unit costs and allocated amounts to the nearest cent.

(2) Record the journal entry transferring cost out of Department 2. Abnormal spoilage is charged to factory overhead.   CGA-Canada (adapted) Reprint with permission

P6-6. Cost of production report; average method; spoilage near end of process, both normal and abnormal. Breiner Company uses the average process costing method for its two production departments. In

Department 2, inspection takes place at the 96% stage of completion. Material is added to good units following inspection. A spoilage rate of 3% of good output is considered normal. Cost attributable to abnormal spoilage is charged to the factory overhead account.

Department 2 records for October show the following:

	Units	Costs
Beginning inventory (70% complete)	2,000	
Department 1 cost		$ 17,600
Conversion cost		13,200
Received from Department 1	13,000	117,400
Materials used		12,500
Conversion cost		126,140
Transferred to finished goods	12,500	
Ending inventory (50% complete)	2,100	

Required:
(1) Prepare a cost of production report for Department 2.
(2) Prepare the journal entry transferring cost out of Department 2.

CGA-Canada (adapted) Reprint with permission

SS **P6-7. Cost of production report; average costing; addition of materials.** Pain-Away Company manufactures liquid aspirin in three departments and accounts for production using average process costing. In Department 2, five gallons of liquid, weighing 8 pounds per gallon, are added to each pound of powder transferred from Department 1. Each Department 2 unit weighs one pound. The following information is available for August:

	Units	Dollars
Beginning inventory (all materials; 1/2 labor and factory overhead)	30,000	
Cost from preceding department		$ 57,000
Materials		29,100
Labor		5,300
Factory overhead		41,000
Ending inventory (all materials; 1/2 labor and factory overhead)	20,000	
Cost added during August:		
Cost from preceding department	10,000 lbs.	823,000
	of powder	
Materials	400,000	410,900
Labor		209,700
Factory overhead		1,679,000

Required:
(1) Prepare a cost of production report for Department 2 for August.
(2) Prepare the journal entry transferring cost out of Department 2.

P6-8. Cost of production report—fifo method; materials added. The Brittlesboro Corporation produces one principal product in two processes. Materials are started in Process One, and other materials added in Process Two increase the number of units by 50%. The company uses the fifo method for costing work in process inventories. The following data for April are available:

	Process One	Process Two
Beginning work in process inventory	$ 2,600	$ 6,200
	(4,000 units;	(12,000 units;
	all materials;	all materials;
	50% labor and	75% labor and
	factory overhead)	factory overhead)
Started in process	75,000 units	
Transferred to next process or to finished goods	70,000 units	110,000 units

Ending work in process inventory...................	9,000 units (all materials; 60% labor and factory overhead)	7,000 units (all materials; 50% labor and factory overhead)
Materials put in process	$56,250	$52,500
Labor put in process	36,700	41,800
Factory overhead put in process....................	44,040	31,350

Required:

(1) Prepare the April cost of production report for each process, using the fifo method. Compute unit costs to four decimal places.

(2) Record the journal entries transferring cost out of Processes One and Two.

P6-9. Cost of production report; average and fifo costing; normal loss. Relaxo Company manufactures tranquilizers. Production is divided into three processes: Mixing, Compounding, and Packaging. Average costing is used in the first two departments, and fifo costing is used in the Packaging Department.

The following data are available for September:

Quantity schedule:	Mixing	Compounding	Packaging
Units in process at beginning................	4,000	2,000	2,000
Units started in process	60,000	—	—
Units received from preceding department	—	50,000	46,000
	64,000	52,000	48,000
Units transferred to next department	50,000	46,000	
Units transferred to finished goods			41,600
Units lost during process*..................	2,000		4,000**
Units still in process	12,000	6,000	2,400
	64,000	52,000	48,000

*Losses are within normal tolerance limits and pertain to ending inventories as well as to units transferred out.
**Loss is assumed to be entirely from units transferred in this period.

	Mixing	Compounding	Packaging
Stage of completion of units in process at beginning of period:			
Materials.........................	1/1	—	1/2
Labor and factory overhead...........	5/6	2/3	1/2
Stage of completion of units in process at end of period:			
Materials.........................	1/1	—	1/6
Labor and factory overhead...........	1/2	2/3	1/6
Cost data:			
Work in process—beginning inventory:			
Cost from preceding department.....	—	$ 2,260	$3,000
Materials........................	$ 1,960	—	60
Labor...........................	770	350	130
Factory overhead	1,060	200	100
Cost added during period:			
Materials........................	29,040	—	1,230
Labor...........................	10,430	13,400	2,870
Factory overhead	15,740	8,550	2,460

Required:

(1) Compute the equivalent units of production for each department.

(2) Prepare a combined cost of production report for September. (Carry unit cost computations to five decimal places.)

(3) Prepare the journal entries transferring cost out of each producing department.

CHAPTER 7

Costing By-Products and Joint Products

Many industrial concerns are confronted with the difficult and often rather complicated problem of assigning costs to their by-products and/or joint products. Chemical companies, petroleum refineries, flour mills, coal mines, lumber mills, dairies, canners, meat packers, and many others produce in their manufacturing or conversion processes a multitude of products to which some costs must be assigned. Assignment of costs to these various products is required for inventory costing, for income determination, and for financial statement purposes. By-product and joint product costing also furnishes management with data that may be useful in planning maximum profit potentials and evaluating actual profit performance. However, management should recognize the limited usefulness of arbitrary cost allocations in the analysis of individual products. The last section of this chapter elaborates on this limitation.

■ BY-PRODUCTS AND JOINT PRODUCTS DEFINED

The term *by-product* is generally used to denote one or more products of relatively small total value that are produced simultaneously with a product of greater total value. The product with the greater value, commonly called the "main product," is usually produced in greater quantities than the by-products. Ordinarily, the manufacturer has only limited control over the quantity of the by-product that comes into existence. However, the introduction of more advanced engineering methods, such as those used in the petroleum industry, has permitted greater control over the quantity of residual products. For example, one company, which formerly paid a trucker to haul away and dump certain waste materials, discovered that the waste was valuable as fertilizer. This by-product is now an additional source of income for the entire industry.

Joint products are produced simultaneously by a common process or series of processes, with each product possessing a more than nominal value in the form in which it is produced. The definition emphasizes the point that the manufacturing process creates products in a definite quantitative relationship. An increase in one product's output will bring about an increase in the quantity of the other products, or vice versa, but not necessarily in the same proportion. To the point of split-off or to the point where these several products emerge as individual units, the cost of the products forms a homogeneous whole.

Nature of By-Products and Joint Products

The accounting treatment of by-products necessitates a reasonably complete knowledge of the technological factors underlying their manufacture, since the origins of by-products may vary. By-products arising from the cleansing of the main product, such as gas and tar from coke manufacture, generally have a residual value. In some cases, the by-product is leftover scrap or waste, such as sawdust in lumber mills. In other cases, the by-product may not be the result of any manufacturing process but may arise from preparing raw materials before they are used in the manufacture of the main product. The separation of cotton seed from cotton, cores and seeds from apples, and shells from cocoa beans are examples of this type of by-product.

By-products can be classified into two groups according to their marketable condition at the split-off point: (1) those sold in their original form without need of further processing and (2) those which require further processing in order to be salable.

The classic example of joint products is found in the meat-packing industry, where various cuts of meat and numerous by-products are processed from one original carcass with one lump-sum cost. Another example of joint product manufacturing is the production of gasoline, where the derivation of gasoline inevitably results in the production of such items as naphtha, kerosene, and distillate fuel oils. Other examples of joint product manufacturing are the simultaneous production of various grades of glue and the processing of soybeans into oil and meal. Joint product costing is also found in industries that must grade raw material before it is processed. Tobacco manufacturers (except in cases where graded tobacco is purchased) and virtually all fruit and vegetable canners face the problem of grading. In fact, such manufacturers have a dual problem of joint cost allocation: (1) materials cost is applicable to all grades; (2) subsequent manufacturing costs are incurred simultaneously for all the different grades.

Joint Costs

A *joint cost* may be defined as that cost which arises from the common processing or manufacturing of products produced from the same process. Whenever two or more different joint or by-products are created from a single cost factor, a joint cost results. A joint cost is incurred prior to the point at which separately identifiable products emerge from the same process.

The chief characteristic of a joint cost is the fact that the cost of several different products is incurred in an indivisible sum for all products, rather than in individual amounts for each product. The total production cost of multiple products involves both joint cost and separate, individual product costs. These separable product costs are identifiable with the individual product and, generally, need no allocation. However, a joint production cost requires allocation or assignment to the individual products.

Difficulties in Costing By-Products and Joint Products

By-products and joint products are difficult to cost because a true joint cost is indivisible. For example, an ore might contain both lead and zinc. In the raw state, these minerals are joint products, and until they are separated by reduction of the ore, the cost of finding, mining, and processing is a joint cost; neither lead nor zinc can be produced without the other prior to the split-off stage. The cost accumulated to the split-off stage must be borne by the difference between the sales price and the cost to complete and sell each mineral after the split-off point.

Because of the indivisibility of a joint cost, cost allocation and apportionment procedures used for establishing the unit cost of a product are far from perfect and are, indeed, quite arbitrary. The costing of joint products and by-products highlights the problem of assigning costs to products whose origin, use of equipment, share of raw materials, share of labor costs, and share of other facilities cannot truly be determined. Whatever methods of allocation are employed, the total profit or loss figure is not affected—provided there are no beginning or ending inventories—by allocating costs to the joint products or by-products, since these costs are recombined in the final income statement. However, a joint cost is ordinarily allocated to the products on some acceptable basis to determine product costs needed for inventory carrying costs. For this reason, there is an effect on periodic income, because different amounts may be allocated to inventories of the numerous joint products or by-products under various allocation methods.

The allocation of costs to joint products may be required for such special purposes as justifying sales prices before governmental regulatory bodies. However, the validity of splitting a joint cost to determine fair, regulated prices for products has been questioned by both accountants and economists.

■ METHODS OF COSTING BY-PRODUCTS

The accepted methods for costing by-products fall into two categories:

1. A joint production cost is not allocated to the by-product. Any revenue resulting from sales of the by-product is credited either to income or to cost of the main product. In some cases, costs subsequent to split-off may be offset against the by-product revenue. For inventory costing, an independent value may be assigned to the by-product. The methods most commonly used in industry are:

Method 1. Revenue from sales of the by-product is listed on the income statement as:

a. Other income.

b. Additional sales revenue.

c. A deduction from the cost of goods sold of the main product.

d. A deduction from the total production (manufacturing) cost of the main product.

Method 2. Revenue from sales of the by-product less the costs of placing the by-product on the market (marketing and administrative expenses) and less any additional processing cost of the by-product is shown on the income statement in a manner similar to that indicated in Method 1.

2. Some portion of the joint production cost is allocated to the by-product. Inventory costs are based on this allocated cost plus any subsequent processing cost. In this category, the following methods are used:

Method 3. The replacement cost method.

Method 4. The market value (reversal cost) method.

Method 1: Recognition of Gross Revenue

Method 1 is a typical noncost procedure in which the final inventory cost of the main product is overstated to the extent that some of the cost belongs to the by-product. However, this shortcoming is somewhat removed in Method 1 (d), although a sales value rather than a cost is deducted from the production cost of the main product.

By-Product Revenue as Other Income. To illustrate this procedure, the following income statement is presented:

Sales (main product, 10,000 units @ $2)		$20,000
Cost of goods sold:		
Beginning inventory (1,000 units @ $1.50)	$ 1,500	
Total production cost (11,000 units @ $1.50)	16,500	
Cost of goods available for sale	$18,000	
Ending inventory (2,000 units @ $1.50)	3,000	15,000
Gross profit		$ 5,000
Marketing and administrative expenses		2,000
Operating income		$ 3,000
Other income: Revenue from sales of by-product		1,500
Income before income tax		$ 4,500

By-Product Revenue as Additional Sales Revenue. In this case, the income statement above would show the $1,500 revenue from sales of the by-product as an addition to sales of the main product. As a result, total sales revenue would be $21,500, and gross profit and operating income would increase accordingly. All other figures would remain the same.

By-Product Revenue as a Deduction from the Cost of Goods Sold. In this case, the $1,500 revenue from the by-product would be deducted from the

$15,000 cost of goods sold figure, thereby reducing the cost and increasing the gross profit and operating income. The income before income tax remains at $4,500.

By-Product Revenue Deducted from Production Cost. In this case, the $1,500 revenue from by-product sales is deducted from the $16,500 total production cost, giving a net production cost of $15,000. This revised cost results in a new average unit cost of $1.3625 for the main product. The final inventory consequently will be $2,725 instead of $3,000. Similarly, the beginning inventory of $1.35 per unit results from crediting revenue from by-product sales in the prior period to the main product's production costs incurred in that period. None of the three preceding treatments of by-product revenue affected the unit cost of the main product. This is an important distinction for product costing, although presumably the dollar amount of the difference will be relatively small. The income statement would appear as follows:

Sales (main product, 10,000 units @ $2)			$20,000
Cost of goods sold:			
Beginning inventory (1,000 units @ $1.35)		$ 1,350	
Total production cost (11,000 units @ $1.50)	$16,500		
Revenue from sales of by-product	1,500		
Net production cost		15,000	
Cost of goods available for sale (12,000 units @ $1.3625 average cost)		$16,350	
Ending inventory (2,000 units @ $1.3625)		2,725	13,625
Gross profit			$ 6,375
Marketing and administrative expenses			2,000
Operating income			$ 4,375

The preceding methods require no complicated journal entries. The revenue received from by-product sales is debited to Cash (or Accounts Receivable). In the first three cases, Income from Sales of By-Product is credited; in the fourth case, the production cost of the main product is credited.

Conceptual justification exists for subtracting by-product revenue from the cost of the main product in recognition that the main product is the principal reason for the production process. That is, the by-product is incidental to the main product. Also, such a procedure is expedient and cost-effective. However, there is a resulting reduction in the usefulness of the reporting system's information. The by-product may be neglected when by-product revenue or cost are absorbed in costing the main product. An approach is needed that provides and highlights relevant information, that encourages managerial attention to by-products, that promotes good decision making and control, and that identifies and rewards good performance.[1] These objectives are better met by separately recognizing and reporting the revenue and associated costs of each by-product. Such an approach would employ Method 2 with separate reporting on the income statement as other income.

---

[1]John P. Fertakis, "Responsibility Accounting for By-Products and Industrial Wastes," *Journal of Accountancy,* Vol. 161, No. 5, pp. 142, 144, and 145.

Method 2: Recognition of Net Revenue

Method 2 recognizes the need for assigning traceable cost to the by-product. It does not attempt, however, to allocate any joint production cost to the by-product. Any costs involved in further processing or marketing the by-product are recorded in separate accounts. All figures are shown on the income statement, following one of the procedures described in Method 1.

Journal entries in Method 2 would involve charges to by-product revenue for the additional work required and perhaps for factory overhead. The marketing and administrative expenses might be allocated to the by-product on some equitable predetermined basis. Some firms carry an account called By-Product, to which all additional expenses are debited and all income is credited. The balance of this account would be presented in the income statement, following one of the procedures outlined in Method 1. However, accumulated manufacturing costs applicable to by-product inventory should be reported on the balance sheet.

Method 3: Replacement Cost Method

The replacement cost method ordinarily is applied by firms whose by-products are used within the plant, thereby avoiding the necessity of purchasing certain materials and supplies from outside suppliers. The production cost of the main product is credited for such materials, and the offsetting debit is to the department that uses the by-product. The cost assigned to the by-product is the purchase or replacement cost existing in the market. In the steel industry, for example, many by-products are sold in the open market. Other products, such as blast furnace gas and coke oven gas, are mixed and used for heating in open-hearth furnaces. The waste heat from open hearths is used again in the generation of steam needed by the various producing departments. The resourceful use of these by-products and their accounting treatment are indicated by the following procedure used by a steel company:

1. Coke oven by-products are credited to the cost of coke at the average sales price per unit for the month.
2. Coke oven and blast furnace gas are credited respectively to the cost of coke and the cost of pig iron at a computed value based on the cost of fuel oil yielding equivalent heat units.
3. Tar and pitch used as fuel are credited respectively to the cost of coke at a computed value based on the cost of fuel oil yielding equivalent heat units.
4. Scrap steel remelted is credited to the cost of finished steel at market cost of equivalent grades purchased.
5. Waste heat from furnaces used to generate steam is credited to the steel ingot cost at a computed value based on the cost of coal yielding equivalent heat units.[2]

---

[2]Howard C. Greer, "Accounting for By-Products and Joint Products," *NA(C)A Bulletin*, Vol. XVII, No. 24, Section 1, p. 1413.

The costing of by-products that are used within a plant actually is a form of intracompany transfer pricing, which is discussed in Chapter 25. In this chapter, alternatives to the use of a replacement cost or market price are discussed. For example, a price based on the cost to produce the by-product, a negotiated price, or an arbitrary price might be used. Whatever the price used, the credit is made to the production cost of the main product from which the by-product comes and the offsetting debit is made to the department that uses the by-product.

Method 4: Market Value Method

The market value (reversal cost) method is basically similar to the last technique illustrated in Method 1. However, it reduces the manufacturing cost of the main product, not by the actual revenue received, but by an estimate of the by-product's value at the time of recovery. This estimate must be made prior to split-off from the main product. Dollar recognition depends on the stability of the market as to price and salability of the by-product; however, control over quantities is important as well. The by-product account is charged with this estimated amount and the production (manufacturing) cost of the main product is credited. Any additional costs of materials, labor, or factory overhead incurred after the by-product is separated from the main product are charged to the by-product. Marketing and administrative expenses might be allocated to the by-product on some equitable basis. The proceeds from sales of the by-product are credited to the by-product account. The balance in this account can be presented on the income statement in one of the ways outlined for Method 1, except that the manufacturing cost applicable to by-product inventory should be reported in the balance sheet.

The market value (reversal cost) method of ascertaining main product and by-product costs may be illustrated as follows:

Item	Main Product	By-Product
Materials.	$ 50,000	
Labor	70,000	
Factory overhead	40,000	
Total production cost (40,000 units)	$160,000	
Market value (5,000 units @ $1.80)		$9,000
Estimated gross profit consisting of:		
Assumed operating profit (20% of sales price)	$1,800	
Marketing and administrative expenses		
(5% of sales price)	450	2,250
		$6,750
Estimated production costs after split-off:		
Materials	$1,000	
Labor	1,200	
Factory overhead	300	2,500
Estimated value of by-product at split-off		
to be credited to main product	4,250	$4,250
Net cost of main product	$155,750	
Add back *actual* production cost after split-off		2,300
Total		$6,550
Total number of units	40,000	5,000
Unit cost	$ 3.894	$1.31

This illustration indicates that an estimated value of the by-product at the split-off point results when estimated gross profit and production cost after split-off are subtracted from the by-product's ultimate market value. Alternatively, if the by-product has a market value at the split-off point, the by-product account is charged with this market value, less its estimated gross profit, and the main product's production cost would be credited. It is also possible to use the total market values of the main product and the by-product at the split-off point as a basis for assigning a share of the prior-to-split-off cost to the by-product, applying the offsetting credit to the production cost of the main product. In any event, subsequent-to-split-off cost related to the by-product would be charged to the by-product.

Method 4 is based on the theory that the cost of a by-product is related to its sales value. It is a step toward the recognition of a by-product cost prior to its split-off from the main product. It is also the nearest approach to methods employed in joint product costing.

Underlying Accounting Theory

Because the total value of a by-product in relationship to a jointly produced main product is relatively small, the effect on periodic income of using one method versus another may be judged as immaterial. Furthermore, joint costs cannot be traced to a by-product. Nevertheless, preference for a particular by-product method is rightfully related to generally accepted concepts in accounting theory. If costs can be traced to a by-product, as would be the case with separate processing cost, they should be charged to the by-product.

The asset recognition concept argues for the recording of by-product inventory in the period of production at an amount approximating its cost to produce, provided there is a market for the by-product. And the matching concept requires expensing inventory in the period in which its sale is recorded. These concepts, balanced against the materiality concept, should be considered in selecting the by-product costing method. Whichever method is chosen, it should be applied consistently from period to period.

■ METHODS OF ALLOCATING JOINT PRODUCTION COST TO JOINT PRODUCTS

Joint production cost, incurred up to the split-off point, can be allocated to joint products by using one of the following methods:

1. The market or sales value method, based on the relative market values of the individual products.
2. The average unit cost method.
3. The weighted average method, based on a predetermined standard or an index of production.
4. The quantitative or physical unit method, based on some physical measurement unit such as weight, linear measure, or volume.

Market or Sales Value Method

Proponents of the market or sales value method often argue that the market value of any product is to some extent a manifestation of the cost incurred in its production. The contention is that if one product sells for more than another, it is because more cost was expended to produce it. In other words, were it not for such a cost, a sales value would not exist. Yet, by definition, the effort required to produce each of the joint products cannot be determined. If it could be determined, the allocation could be made on the basis of the relative amount of effort expended on each of the joint products. Furthermore, according to economic theory, prices in a competitive market economy are determined on the basis of the relative scarcity of goods demanded by consumers, not on the basis of the relative cost of producing those goods.

Another argument for using the market value method of allocating joint costs is that it is neutral, i.e., it does not affect the relative profitability of the joint products. Thus, decisions which must be based on an analysis of the relative profitability of the various joint products are not distorted by arbitrary cost allocations.

The choice between this and other methods tends to be arbitrary when the proportions of the joint products composing the output mix are fixed and cannot be changed. However, the choice is not arbitrary if the proportions can be varied and there is a relationship between the total joint cost and the total value of the output. Thus, especially strong rational support for the market or sales value method occurs if, for given inputs to the joint manufacturing process, two conditions hold: (1) the physical mix of output can be altered by incurring more (or less) total joint cost relative to other production costs and (2) this alteration produces more (less) total market value.[3]

Joint Products Salable at Split-Off. The market value method prorates the joint cost on the basis of the relative market values of the items produced. The method is based on a weighted market value, using the total market or sales value of each product (quantity produced multiplied by the unit sales price). To illustrate, assume that joint products A, B, C, and D are produced at a total joint production cost of $120,000. Quantities produced are: A, 20,000 units; B, 15,000 units; C, 10,000 units; and D, 15,000 units. Product A sells for $.25; B, for $3; C, for $3.50; and D, for $5. These prices are market or sales values for the products at the split-off point; i.e., it is assumed that they can be sold at that point. Management may have decided, however, that it is more profitable to process certain products further before they are sold. Nevertheless, this condition does not destroy the usefulness of the sales value at the split-off point for the allocation of the joint production cost. The proration of this joint cost is made in the following manner:

---

[3]William L. Cats-Baril, James F. Gatti, and D. Jacque Grinnell, "Joint Product Costing for the Semiconductor Industry," *Management Accounting,* Vol. LXVII, No. 8, p. 29.

Product	Units Produced	Market Value per Unit	Total Market Value	Ratio of Product Value to Total Market Value	Apportionment of Joint Production Cost
A	20,000	$ .25	$ 5,000	3.125%	$ 3,750
B	15,000	3.00	45,000	28.125	33,750
C	10,000	3.50	35,000	21.875	26,250
D	15,000	5.00	75,000	46.875	56,250
Total....................			$160,000	100.000%	$120,000

The same results can be obtained if the total joint production cost ($120,000) is divided by the total market value of the four products ($160,000). The resulting 75 percent is the percentage of joint cost in each individual market value. By multiplying each market value by this percentage, the joint cost will be apportioned as shown in the preceding table.

Under the market value method, each joint product yields the same unit gross profit percentage, assuming that the units are sold without further processing. This can be illustrated as follows, assuming no beginning inventories:

	Total	A	B	C	D
Sales—units	52,000	18,000	12,000	8,000	14,000
Ending inventories	8,000	2,000	3,000	2,000	1,000
Sales—dollars.............	$138,500	$ 4,500	$36,000	$28,000	$70,000
Production cost............	$120,000	$ 3,750	$33,750	$26,250	$56,250
Less ending inventory.......	16,125	375*	6,750	5,250	3,750
Cost of goods sold	$103,875	$ 3,375	$27,000	$21,000	$52,500
Gross profit	$ 34,625	$ 1,125	$ 9,000	$ 7,000	$17,500
Gross profit percentage	25%	25%	25%	25%	25%

*$3,750 production cost ÷ 20,000 units produced = $.1875; $.1875 × 2,000 units in ending inventory = $375.

Joint Products Not Salable at Split-Off. Products not salable in their stage of completion at the split-off point and therefore without any market value require additional processing to place them in marketable condition. In such cases, the basis for allocation of the joint production cost is a hypothetical market value at the split-off point. To illustrate the procedure, the following assumptions are added to the preceding example:

Product	Ultimate Market Value per Unit	Processing Cost After Split-Off
A	$ .50	$ 2,000
B	5.00	10,000
C	4.50	10,000
D	8.00	28,000

To arrive at the basis for the apportionment, it is necessary to use a working-back procedure, whereby the after-split-off processing cost is subtracted from the ultimate sales value to find a hypothetical market value. After-split-off marketing and administrative expenses traceable to specific products and an allowance for profit should also be considered if their amounts are proportionately different among the joint products, because the joint cost apportionment would be affected. The following table indicates the steps to be taken:

Product	Ulti-mate Market Value per Unit	Units Pro-duced	Ultimate Market Value	Processing Cost After Split-Off	Hypo-thetical Market Value*	Apportion-ment of Joint Production Cost**	Total Production Cost	Total Production Cost Percent-age***
A	$ .50	20,000	$ 10,000	$ 2,000	$ 8,000	$ 4,800	$ 6,800	68.0
B	5.00	15,000	75,000	10,000	65,000	39,000	49,000	65.3
C	4.50	10,000	45,000	10,000	35,000	21,000	31,000	68.8
D	8.00	15,000	120,000	28,000	92,000	55,200	83,200	69.3
Total			$250,000	$50,000	$200,000	$120,000	$170,000	68.0

*At the split-off point
**Percentage to allocate joint production cost (using the joint cost total determined on page 183):

$$\frac{\text{Total joint production cost}}{\text{Total hypothetical market value}} = \frac{\$120,000}{\$200,000} = .60 = 60\%;$$

60% × hypothetical market value = apportionment of joint production cost

***The production cost percentage is calculated by dividing total production cost by the ultimate market value; e.g.,

$$\frac{\$49,000}{\$75,000} = .653 = 65.3\% \text{ for Product B, and } \frac{\$170,000}{\$250,000} = .68 = 68\% \text{ for all products combined.}$$

If in a given situation, certain of the joint products are salable at the split-off point while others are not, the market values at the split-off point would be used for the former group. For the latter group, hypothetical market values would be required.

The following gross profit statement uses the same number of units sold as was used in the preceding illustration, but the sales prices have been increased as a result of additional processing.

	Total	A	B	C	D
Sales—units	52,000	18,000	12,000	8,000	14,000
Ending inventories	8,000	2,000	3,000	2,000	1,000
Sales—dollars	$217,000	$ 9,000	$60,000	$36,000	$112,000
Cost of goods sold:					
Joint production cost	$120,000	$ 4,800	$39,000	$21,000	$ 55,200
Further processing cost	50,000	2,000	10,000	10,000	28,000
Total	$170,000	$ 6,800	$49,000	$31,000	$ 83,200
Less ending inventory	22,227	680*	9,800	6,200	5,547
Cost of goods sold	$147,773	$ 6,120	$39,200	$24,800	$ 77,653
Gross profit	$ 69,227	$ 2,880	$20,800	$11,200	$ 34,347
Gross profit percentage	32%	32%	35%	31%	31%

*$6,800 production cost ÷ 20,000 units produced = $.34; $.34 × 2,000 units in ending inventory = $680.

Since the statement has often been made that every joint product should be equally profitable, the sales value technique may be modified by using the overall gross profit percentage to determine the gross profit for each product. In the following table, the gross profit (32 percent) is deducted from the sales value to find the total cost, which is reduced by each product's further processing cost to find the joint cost allocation for each product.

	Total	A	B	C	D
Ultimate sales value	$250,000	$10,000	$75,000	$45,000	$120,000
Less 32% gross profit........	80,000	3,200	24,000	14,400	38,400
Total cost	$170,000	$ 6,800	$51,000	$30,600	$ 81,600
Further processing cost	50,000	2,000	10,000	10,000	28,000
Joint cost.................	$120,000	$ 4,800	$41,000	$20,600	$ 53,600

If sales value, gross profit percentage, or further processing costs are estimated, the balance labeled "Joint cost" would serve as the basis for allocating the actual joint cost to the four products.

Average Unit Cost Method

The average unit cost method attempts to apportion the total joint production cost to the various products on the basis of an average unit cost obtained by dividing the total number of units produced into the total joint production cost. Companies using this method argue that all products turned out by the same process should receive a proportionate share of the total joint production cost based on the number of units produced. As long as all units produced are measured in terms of the same unit and do not differ greatly, this method can be used without too much misgiving. When the units produced are not measured in like terms or the units differ markedly, the method should not be applied.

Using figures in the market value example, the average unit cost method can be illustrated as follows:

$$\frac{\text{Total joint production cost}}{\text{Total number of units produced}} = \frac{\$120,000}{60,000} = \$2 \text{ per unit}$$

Product	Units Produced	Apportionment of Joint Production Cost
A	20,000	$ 40,000
B	15,000	30,000
C	10,000	20,000
D	15,000	30,000
	60,000	$120,000

Weighted Average Method

In many industries, the average unit cost method does not give a satisfactory answer to the joint cost apportionment problem because individual units of the various joint products differ markedly. For this reason, weight factors often are assigned to each unit, based upon size of the unit, difficulty of manufacture, time consumed in making the unit, difference in type of labor employed, amount of materials used, etc. Finished production of every kind is multiplied by weight factors to apportion the total joint cost to individual units.

Using figures from the previous example, weight factors assigned to the four products might be as follows:

Product A— 3 points
Product B—12 points
Product C—13.5 points
Product D—15 points

The joint production cost allocation would result in the following values:

Product	Units Produced	× Points =	Weighted Units	Cost Per × Unit* =	Apportionment of Joint Production Cost
A	20,000	3	60,000	$.20	$ 12,000
B	15,000	12	180,000	.20	36,000
C	10,000	13.5	135,000	.20	27,000
D	15,000	15	225,000	.20	45,000
			600,000		$120,000

$$* \quad \frac{\text{Total joint production cost}}{\text{Total number of weighted units}} = \frac{\$120,000}{600,000} = \$.20 \text{ per unit}$$

Quantitative Unit Method

The quantitative unit method attempts to distribute the total joint cost on the basis of some unit of measurement, such as pounds, gallons, tons, or board feet. However, if the joint products are not measurable by the basic measurement unit, the joint units must be converted to a denominator common to all units produced. For instance, in the manufacture of coke, products such as coke, coal tar, benzol, sulfate of ammonia, and gas are measured in different units. The yield of these recovered units is measured on the basis of quantity of product extracted per ton of coal.

The following table illustrates the use of weight as a quantitative unit method of joint cost allocation:

Product	Yield in Pounds of Recovered Product per Ton of Coal	Distribution of Waste to Recovered Products	Revised Weight of Recovered Products	Materials Cost of Each Product Per Ton of Coal
Coke	1,320.0 lbs.	69.474 lbs.*	1,389.474 lbs.	$27.790**
Coal tar	120.0	6.316	126.316	2.526
Benzol	21.9	1.153	23.053	.461
Sulfate of ammonia	26.0	1.368	27.368	.547
Gas	412.1	21.689	433.789	8.676
Waste (water)	100.0			
Total	2,000.0 lbs.	100.000 lbs.	2,000.000 lbs.	$40.000

*(1,320 ÷ (2,000 − 100)) = 69.474
**(1,389.474 ÷ 2,000) × $40 = $27.790

The average unit cost, weighted average, and quantitative unit methods could result in product cost for one (or more) of the joint products that exceeds that product's market value. In that case, the product would appear unprofitable while at the same time the other joint products appear profitable. Since the choice of costing method affects product cost and is an arbitrary choice, it is argued that a method should be chosen that does not result in an artificial loss, i.e., a loss for one joint product and a profit for another. A family of joint products is either all profitable or all unprofitable at the point of separation. Avoidance of the problem of artificially creating different rates of profitability for the joint products is the widely touted virtue of the market or sales value method. That is, if an arbitrary allocation must be made, it should at least be neutral.

■ FEDERAL INCOME TAX LAWS AND THE COSTING OF JOINT PRODUCTS AND BY-PRODUCTS

Federal income tax laws concerning the costing of joint products and by-products are not numerous. Legislators recognize the impossibility of establishing a specific code of law for every conceivable situation involving this type of cost problem. Consequently, the written pronouncement of the law does not precisely establish the boundaries of acceptable procedures. A digest of legal viewpoint is given in the Federal Income Tax Regulations, which state the following:

> *Inventories of miners and manufacturers. A taxpayer engaged in mining or manufacturing who by a single process or uniform series of processes derives a product of two or more kinds, sizes, or grades, the unit cost of which is substantially alike, and who in conformity to a recognized trade practice allocates an amount of cost to each kind, size, or grade of product which in the aggregate will absorb the total cost of production, may, with the consent of the Commissioner [of the Internal Revenue Service], use such allocated cost as a basis for pricing inventories, provided such allocation bears a reasonable relation to the respective selling values of the different kinds, sizes, or grades of product.[4]*

The quotation does not fully and unequivocally authorize the utilization of the market value theory of costing joint products and by-products. The words "in conformity to a recognized trade practice" and "with the consent of the Commissioner" clearly imply that the multiplicity of conceivable situations is far too great to be covered by definite rules that allow or prohibit a particular costing procedure.

Clearly, tax laws have not solved the problem of costing joint products and by-products for the accountant and the manufacturer. Tax officials find themselves in exactly the same predicament as any coke producer, petroleum refiner, or chemical manufacturer, even though their immediate objective may be limited to collecting a proper tax. The necessity of defining and interpreting accepted practices in a given industry proves, at least partially, that if the

---

[4]*Regulations*, Section 1.471-7.

present income tax law on joint product and by-product costing—with its implication that the market value method is desirable—is unfair or manifestly inaccurate and illogical, it can and will be changed if industry and the accounting profession can offer better reasons for the use of other procedures.

■ JOINT COST ANALYSIS FOR MANAGERIAL DECISIONS AND PROFITABILITY ANALYSIS

Joint cost allocation methods indicate forcefully that the amount of the cost to be apportioned to the numerous products emerging at the point of split-off is difficult to establish for any purpose. Furthermore, the acceptance of an allocation method for the assignment of the joint production cost does not solve the problem. The thought has been advanced that no attempt should be made to determine the cost of individual products up to the split-off point; rather, it seems important to calculate the profit margin in terms of total combined units. Of course, costs incurred after the split-off point will provide management with information needed for decisions relating to the desirability of further processing to maximize profits.

Using the example from pages 183-185, assume that Product B, which has an ultimate market value of $75,000, alternatively could be sold for $60,000 at the split-off point, without further processing. The same example specifies that processing cost after split-off and traceable to Product B is $10,000. The difference in revenue of $15,000 ($75,000 − $60,000) minus the $10,000 after split-off cost results in a $5,000 positive contribution. This makes further processing appear to be a desirable option in this case. Furthermore, in the short run, any portion of the $10,000 cost that is fixed rather than variable would add to the contribution from further processing. But, in the long run, the margin of contribution (revenue minus variable cost) must be sufficient to recover fixed cost and provide a reasonable profit. Also, consideration should be given to non-quantifiable factors, such as the impact on employment, if further processing of a product is not carried out. Observe that, in any case, the allocated joint cost is not relevant to the decision.

Production of joint products is greatly influenced by both the technological characteristics of the processes and by the markets available for the products. This establishment of a product mix which is in harmony with customer demands appears profitable but often is physically impossible. It is interesting to note that cost accounting in the meat-packing industry serves primarily as a guide to buying, since aggregate sales realization values of the various products that will be obtained from cutting operations are considered in determining the price that a packer is willing to pay for livestock. Sales realization values are also considered when deciding to sell hams or other cuts in a particular stage or to process them further.

A joint cost is often incurred for products that are either interchangeable or not associated with each other at all. Increasing the output of one will in most joint cost cases unavoidably increase to some extent the output of the other. Evaluation of output in joint cost situations falls into the category of the cost-volume-profit relationship and differential cost analysis (Chapters 20 and 21). The many alternative combinations of output can lead to time-consuming computations. Often such evaluations are carried out on a computer using sophisticated simulation techniques. Developments in operations research procedures have provided techniques helpful in solving such problems (Chapter 21 linear programming discussion).

For profit planning, and perhaps as the only reliable measure of profitability, management should consider a product's contribution margin after separable or individual costs are deducted from sales. This contribution margin allows management to predict the amount that a segment or product line will add to or subtract from company profits. This margin is not the product's net profit figure. It only indicates relative profitability in comparison with other products. "Net profit determined by allocating to segments an 'equitable' share of all costs, both separable and joint, associated with the group of segments is not a reliable guide to profit planning decisions because these data cannot be used for predicting the outcome of decisions in terms of the change in aggregate net profit."[5] For these reasons, attempts to allocate joint marketing cost to products and customers by time studies of salespersons' activities, as well as attempts to allocate the joint production cost, often yield results which are unreliable for appraising segment profitability.

DISCUSSION QUESTIONS

Q7-1. Distinguish between joint products and by-products.

Q7-2. How may the revenue from the sale of by-products be shown on the income statement?

Q7-3. Does the showing of revenue from by-products on the income statement influence the unit cost of the main product?

Q7-4. By what method can production cost be relieved of the value of a by-product that can be further utilized in production processes? Explain.

Q7-5. By-products which require no additional processing after the point of separation are often accounted for by assigning to them a cost of zero at the point of separation and crediting the cost of production of the main product as sales are made.
(a) Justify the above method of treating by-products.
(b) Discuss the possible shortcomings of the treatment. (AICPA adapted)

Q7-6. Are by-products ever charged with any cost? Explain.

Q7-7. Describe methods for allocating the total joint production cost to joint products.

Q7-8. Discuss the advantages and disadvantages of the market value and average unit cost methods of joint cost allocation.

Q7-9. When is it necessary to allocate joint costs to joint products?

---

[5]Walter B. MacFarland, *Concepts for Management Accounting* (New York: National Association of Accountants, 1966), p. 49.

Q7-10. Does the Internal Revenue Service prescribe any definite joint product or by-product cost allocation methods for tax purposes? Explain.

Q7-11. Oregon Logging Company obtains its cost information by dividing total cost by the number of board feet of lumber produced. The president states that money is lost on every foot of low grade lumber sold but is made up on the high grades. Appraise the statement.

Q7-12. In making a decision about the further processing of joint products, what costs are relevant?

EXERCISES

E7-1. By-product costing and entries. Okalala Soap Company produces a product known as Okay. In the manufacturing of Okay, a by-product results which can be sold as is for $.36 per pound or processed further and sold for $1.30 per pound. The additional processing for each pound of by-product requires $.125 for materials, $.075 for labor, and $.10 for factory overhead.

For May, production costs of the main product and by-product up to the point of separation were: materials, $250,000; labor, $200,000; and factory overhead, $170,000. These costs were charged to the main product. During the month, 315,000 pounds of Okay and 80,000 pounds of by-product were produced.

Required: Prepare journal entries for the by-product when it is:
(1) Stored without assigning it any cost and later sold on account at $.36 per pound, with no additional costs incurred.
(2) Stored and costed at $.36 per pound, reducing the main product cost by the amount allocated to the by-product.
(3) Further processed and stored, with no cost prior to separation allocated to it.
(4) Further processed and stored, with the market value method being used to allocate the cost prior to separation, the cost of the main product being reduced by the cost allocated to the by-product, and the main product selling at $3 per pound.

E7-2. By-product costing and entries. Nicolaus Confectioners Inc. makes a candy bar called Sunshine which sells for $.50 per pound. The manufacturing process also yields a by-product known as Rainbow. Without further processing, Rainbow sells for $.10 per pound; with further processing, Rainbow sells for $.30 per pound. During April, total joint manufacturing costs up to the point of separation consisted of the following charges to work in process:

Raw materials..........	$75,000
Direct labor............	60,000
Factory overhead	15,000

Production for the month aggregated 394,000 pounds of Sunshine and 30,000 pounds of Rainbow. To complete Rainbow during April and to obtain a sales price of $.30 per pound, further processing of Rainbow would entail the following additional costs:

Raw materials..........	$2,000
Direct labor.............	1,500
Factory overhead	500

Required: Prepare the April journal entries for Rainbow if Rainbow is:
(1) Transferred as a by-product at sales value to the warehouse without further processing, with a corresponding reduction of Sunshine's manufacturing cost.

(2) Further processed as a by-product and transferred to the warehouse, with prior-to-separation cost being assigned to Rainbow at the market value at the split-off point, and a corresponding reduction of Sunshine's manufacturing cost, thus assuming no gross profit attributable to Rainbow at the split-off point.

(3) Further processed as a by-product and transferred to finished goods, with cost prior to separation being allocated between Sunshine and Rainbow based on relative sales value at the split-off point. The joint cost assigned to Rainbow correspondingly reduces Sunshine's manufacturing cost. (AICPA adapted)

E7-3. By-product costing—market value (reversal cost) method. Thunman Company manufactures one main product and two by-products, A and B. For April, the following data are available:

	Main Product	By-Product A	By-Product B	Total
Sales	$75,000	$6,000	$3,500	$84,500
Manufacturing cost after separation	$11,500	$1,100	$ 900	$13,500
Marketing and administrative expenses	6,000	750	550	7,300
Manufacturing cost before separation.........				37,500

Profit allowed for A and B is 15% and 12%, respectively.

Required:
(1) Calculate manufacturing cost before separation for by-products A and B, using the market value (reversal cost) method.
(2) Prepare an income statement, detailing sales and costs for each product.

E7-4. By-product costing—net revenue and market value methods. In the manufacture of its main product, the Welsh Company produces a by-product. Joint production cost incurred to the point of separation totaled $200,000. After separation, cost of $150,000 was incurred to complete the main product, and $5,000 was incurred to complete the by-product. The main product had a final market value of $400,000, and the by-product had a final market value of $20,000. There is no ending inventory.

Required:
(1) Assume that the net revenue method is used to account for the by-product as other income and that the by-product's marketing and administrative expenses are zero. How much other income should be reported on the income statement?
(2) Assume that management wants to allocate $2,000 of marketing and administrative expenses to the by-product and still have a profit of 10% of the sales price. Using the market value (reversal cost) method, how much of the joint cost should be allocated to the by-product?

E7-5. Joint product cost allocation—market value method. Gulf Breeze Corporation manufactures products W, X, Y, and Z from a joint process. Additional information follows:

Product	Units Produced	Market Value at Split-Off	If Processed Further Additional Cost	Market Value
W	6,000	$ 80,000	$ 7,500	$ 90,000
X..........	5,000	60,000	6,000	70,000
Y..........	4,000	40,000	4,000	50,000
Z..........	3,000	20,000	2,500	30,000
Total	18,000	$200,000	$20,000	$240,000

Required: Assuming that the market value method is used, allocate a share of the total joint production cost of $160,000 to each product. (AICPA adapted)

E7-6. Cost allocation—joint and by-products. Grafton Company produces joint products A and B from a process which also yields by-product W. Product A and by-product W are sold after separation, but B must be further processed in a subsequent department before it can be sold. The cost assigned to the by-product is its market value less $.40 per pound for delivery expense. Information related to July production is:

Product	Production (in pounds)	Sales Price per Pound
A	2,000	$4.50
B	4,000	9.00
W	500	1.50

July joint cost was $18,000 and the further processing cost for B was $10,000.

Required:
(1) Compute B's market value to be used in allocating the joint cost.
(2) Compute the amount of joint cost to be allocated to the joint products.   (AICPA adapted)

E7-7. Joint product cost allocation—market value method; by-product cost allocation—market value (reversal cost) method. Alba Company manufactures joint products X and Y as well as by-product Z. Cumulative joint cost data for the period show $204,000, representing 20,000 completed units processed through the Refining Department at an average cost of $10.20. Costs are assigned to X and Y by the market value method, which considers further processing costs in subsequent operations. To determine the cost allocation to Z, the market value (reversal cost) method is used. Additional data:

	Z	X	Y
Quantity processed	2,000 units	8,000 units	10,000 units
Sales price per unit	$6	$20	$25
Further processing cost per unit	2	5	7
Marketing and administrative expenses per unit	1	—	—
Operating profit per unit	1	—	—

Required: Compute the joint cost allocated to Z, then the amount to X and Y.

E7-8. Joint product cost allocation—market value method. The Pacific Company produces three different products, P, C, and F. Costs up to the split-off point were: raw materials, $160,000; conversion, $176,000. Beyond the split-off point, further processing costs, production, and sales were as follows:

	P	C	F
Further processing costs	$51,200	$97,600	$20,800
Production in units	4,800	8,000	1,600
Sales in units	4,500	7,000	1,400
Unit sales price	$40	$50	$86

Required:
(1) Compute the cost of goods sold for each product and in total using the market value method for allocating joint cost. Calculate unit costs to the nearest cent.
(2) Suppose that Pacific finds a customer who is willing to buy all its production of F at the split-off point at a unit price of $75. Should Pacific accept this offer?   CGA-Canada (adapted) Reprint with permission

SS E7-9. Joint product cost allocation—market value method. Langley Company manufactures three products—A, B, and C—as a result of a joint process. During October, joint processing costs totaled $288,000. Details regarding each of the three products show:

	Product		
	A	B	C
Units produced	1,000	3,000	5,000
Units sold	800	2,500	4,300
Further processing costs	$25,000	$60,000	$105,000
Sales price per unit	100	80	50

Required:
(1) Compute the cost assigned to the ending inventory of each product and in total, using the market value method for joint product cost allocation. There were no units in finished goods on October 1.
(2) Customers have been found who would be willing to buy all of the output of each product at the split-off point for the following prices: A, $60; B, $65; and C, $25. Show which of the products should be sold at the split-off point.
(3) Would your answer to part (2) change if Product B's further processing cost of $60,000 included $18,000 of allocated fixed costs? Why or why not?
(4) Now suppose the $60,000 cost of B's further processing includes $18,000 of allocated fixed costs, and the facilities that would be used to further process B have an alternative use. If B is not processed further, the alternative use of these facilities will generate revenues of $6,000 and variable costs of $1,000. Should B be processed further?   CGA-Canada (adapted) Reprint with permission

SS **E7-10. Joint product cost allocation.** Jackson Inc. produces four joint products having a manufacturing cost of $70,000 at the split-off point. Data pertinent to these products follow:

Product	Units Produced	Ultimate Market Value per Unit	Processing Cost After Split-Off	Weight Factors
K	5,000	$5.50	$1,500	3.0 points
L	20,000	1.60	3,000	2.0 points
M	15,000	1.50	2,500	4.0 points
N	10,000	3.00	5,000	2.5 points

Required: Allocate joint products cost using:
(1) The average unit cost method.
(2) The weighted average method.
(3) The market or sales value method.

E7-11. Joint product cost allocation—weighted average method. A department's production schedule shows 10,000 units of X and 8,000 units of Y. Both articles are made from the same raw materials, but units of X and Y require estimated quantities of materials in the ratio of 3:2, respectively. Both articles pass through the same conversion process, but X and Y require estimated production times per unit in the ratio of 5:4, respectively.

Required: Compute the unit materials and conversion costs for each product if the total costs are: materials, $92,000; conversion cost, $123,000.

PROBLEMS

P7-1. Joint product cost allocation—average unit cost and market value methods. Carson Products Company produces three products from a joint source. A single raw material is introduced into Process I from which products A, B, and C emerge. Product A is considered to be a by-product and is sold immediately after split-off. Products B and C are processed further in Process II and Process III, respectively, before they are sold as Butine and Cantol.
    Production costs for February were as follows:

Process I (24 000 kg of raw materials)	$ 590,000
Process II.	580,000
Process III	720,000
Total production cost	$1,890,000

The number of units (kg) of product produced and sold in February was as follows:

	Process I	Process II	Process III	Units Sold
Product A	4 000 kg	—	—	4 000 kg
Product B	10 000 kg	10 000 kg	—	9 000 kg (Butine)
Product C	10 000 kg	—	10 000 kg	9 500 kg (Cantol)

The average price per unit sold in February for each of the products was as follows:

Product A	$ 15 per kg
Butine	130
Cantol	120

There were no inventories of intermediate products B and C at the beginning or end of February and there was no waste or spoilage in any of the processes. The by-product is not accounted for separately; instead, revenue from sales of the by-product is treated as a deduction from joint cost.

Required:

(1) Calculate the cost of the finished goods inventories if the average unit cost method of joint cost allocation is used.

(2) Calculate the value of cost of goods sold if the market value method of joint cost allocation is used. Round allocated joint cost to nearest one thousand dollars.

(3) The company controller argued that the market value method of allocation is the most accurate way to allocate joint cost. The president replied that the average unit cost method is simpler and easier to understand, especially if he has to make a decision about whether to drop a product or continue to process it. The controller claims that using the market value method to analyze a drop or continue decision would be better. Respond to both the president's and controller's comments, and briefly explain the reasons for allocating joint cost. (SMAC adapted)

P7-2. Joint product cost allocation—market value method. Colgor Company manufactures three products—D, F, and L. The first part of the manufacturing process is joint and the current period joint costs total $100,000. Other current information is as follows:

Product	Processing Cost After Split-Off	Number of Units Produced	Number of Units Sold	Unit Sales Price
D	$ 60,000	5,000	4,000	$20
F	40,000	2,000	1,500	30
L	140,000	7,000	6,300	40

Required:

(1) Compute the dollars that should be assigned to finished goods inventory for financial statement presentation, allocating joint cost by the market value method.

(2) Colgor now discovers that it would be possible to sell products D and F at the split-off point for $10 and $8, respectively. Should the company sell these products at the split-off point or process them further? CGA-Canada (adapted) Reprint with permission

P7-3. Cost allocation—joint products and by-product. Brooks Corporation produces three products, Alpha, Beta, and Gamma. Alpha and Gamma are joint products, while Beta is a by-product of Alpha. No joint cost is to be allocated to the by-product. The production processes for a given year are as follows:

(a) In Department 1, 110,000 pounds of material Rho are processed at a total cost of $120,000. After processing, 60% of the units are transferred to Department 2 and 40% of the units (now Gamma) are transferred to Department 3.

(b) In Department 2, the material is further processed at a total additional cost of $38,000. Seventy percent of the units (now Alpha) are transferred to Department 4 and 30% emerge as Beta, the by-product, to be sold at $1.20 per pound. The marketing expense related to Beta is $8,100.

(c) In Department 4, Alpha is processed at a total additional cost of $23,660. After processing, Alpha is ready for sale at $5 per pound.

(d) In Department 3, Gamma is processed at a total additional cost of $165,000. In this department, a normal loss of units of Gamma occurs, which equals 10% of the good output of Gamma. The remaining good output is sold for $12 per pound.

Required:

(1) Prepare a schedule showing the allocation of the $120,000 joint cost between Alpha and Gamma, using the market value at split-off point and treating the net realizable value of Beta as an addition to the sales value of Alpha.

(2) Prepare a statement of gross profit for Alpha, independent of the answer to requirement (1), assuming that:

  (a) $102,000 of total joint cost was appropriately allocated to Alpha.

  (b) 48,000 pounds of Alpha and 20,000 pounds of Beta were available for sale.

  (c) During the year, sales of Alpha were 80% of the pounds available for sale. There was no beginning inventory.

  (d) The net realizable value of Beta available for sale is to be deducted from the cost of producing Alpha. The ending inventory of Alpha is to be based on the net cost of production.

  (e) All other costs, sales prices, and marketing expenses are those presented in the facts of the original problem.   (AICPA adapted)

P7-4. Cost allocation—joint products and by-product. State Chemical Company manufactures several products in its three departments:

(a) In Department 1, the raw materials amanic acid and bonyl hydroxide are used to produce Amanyl, Bonanyl, and Am-Salt. Amanyl is sold to others, who use it as a raw material in the manufacture of stimulants. Bonanyl is not salable without further processing. Although Am-Salt is a commercial product for which there is a ready market, the company does not sell this product, preferring to submit it to further processing.

(b) In Department 2, Bonanyl is processed into the marketable product, Bonanyl-X. The relationship between Bonanyl used and Bonanyl-X produced has remained constant for several months.

(c) In Department 3, Am-Salt and the raw material colb are used to produce Colbanyl, a liquid propellant. As an inevitable part of this process, Demanyl is also produced. Demanyl was discarded as scrap until discovery of its usefulness as a catalyst in the manufacture of glue. For two years, State Chemical has been able to sell all of its Demanyl production.

In its financial statements, the company states inventory at the lower of cost (on the first-in, first-out basis) or market. Unit costs of the items most recently produced must therefore be computed. The cost allocated to Demanyl is computed so that after allowing $.04 per pound for packaging and selling costs, no profit or loss will be recognized on sales of this product.

The following data on October production and inventories are available:

Raw materials	Pounds Used	Total Cost
Amanic acid.	6,300	$ 5,670
Bonyl hydroxide.	9,100	6,370
Colb.	5,600	2,240

Conversion costs (labor and factory overhead)	Total Cost
Department 1.	$33,600
Department 2.	3,306
Department 3.	22,400

	Pounds Produced	Inventories in Pounds September 30	October 31	Sales Price per Pound
Amanyl	3,600	—	—	$ 6.65
Bonanyl	2,800	210	110	—
Am-Salt	7,600	400	600	6.30
Bonanyl-X	2,755	—	—	4.20
Colbanyl	1,400	—	—	43.00
Demanyl	9,800	—	—	.54

Required: Prepare schedules for the following items for October, with supporting computations prepared in good form and answers rounded to the nearest cent:
  (1) Cost per pound of Amanyl, Bonanyl, and Am-Salt produced, using the market or sales value method.
  (2) Cost per pound of Amanyl, Bonanyl, and Am-Salt produced, using the average unit cost method.
  (3) Cost per pound of Colbanyl produced, assuming that the cost per pound of Am-Salt produced was $3.45 in September and $3.55 in October.   (AICPA adapted)

P7-5. Cost of production report—average and fifo process costing methods; joint products and by-product. The following were gathered from the records of Rodomontade Company for February:

	Process 1	Process 2	Process 3
Unit data:			
Beginning work in process inventory (1/3 complete in Processes 2 and 3) . . .	—	3,000	3,000
Started or received	32,000	10,000	20,000
	32,000	13,000	23,000
Transferred to Process 2	10,000	—	—
Transferred to Process 3	20,000	—	—
Transferred to finished goods storeroom	—	9,000	20,000
Transferred out as by-product	2,000	—	—
Normal loss	—	—	1,000
Ending work in process inventory (1/4 complete in Process 2 and 1/2 complete in Process 3)	—	4,000	2,000
	32,000	13,000	23,000
Partial summary of costs:			
Beginning work in process inventory			
Transferred from Process 1	—	$ 6,000	$11,500
Labor and factory overhead	—	2,000	3,000
Cost added by department:			
Materials	$58,000	—	—
Labor and factory overhead	30,000	18,000	60,000
	$88,000		
Less market value of by-product	4,000		
	$84,000		

Materials are issued in Process 1. At the end of processing in Process 1, the by-product appears and the balance of production is transferred out; some to Process 2 for additional processing of one main product and the rest to Process 3 for additional processing of the other main product.

The joint cost of Process 1, less the market value of the by-product, is apportioned to the main products using the market value method at the split-off point. Sales prices for the finished products of Processes 2 and 3 are $10 and $15, respectively. The by-product sells for $2.

Required:
  (1) Prepare a departmental cost of production report for February, assuming that the company uses the average costing method. (Carry unit cost computations to four decimal places and round off multiplications to the nearest dollar.)

(2) From requirement (1) computations, prepare the journal entries transferring cost from each of the three processes.
(3) Repeat requirement (1), assuming that the company uses the fifo costing method and that the normal loss in Process 3 is from units transferred in during February.
(4) From requirement (3) computations, prepare the journal entries transferring cost from each of the three processes.

CASES

C7-1. Joint cost allocation—market value method. Minimax Corporation is a chemical manufacturer that produces two main products, Pepco-1 and Repke-3, and a by-product, SE-5, from a joint process. If Minimax had the proper facilities, it could process SE-5 further into a main product. The ratio of output quantities to input quantity of direct material used in the joint process remains consistent with the processing conditions and activity level.

Minimax currently uses the quantitative method of allocating joint costs to the main products. The fifo inventory method is used to cost the main products. The by-product is inventoried at its net revenue, and this figure is

used to reduce the joint production costs before the joint costs are allocated to the main products.

Jim Simpson, Minimax's controller, wants to implement the market value method of joint cost allocation. He believes that inventoriable cost should be based on each product's ability to contribute to the recovery of joint production cost. The market value of the by-product would be treated in the same manner as with the quantitative method.

Data regarding Minimax's operations for November are presented below. The joint cost of production amounted to $2,640,000 for November.

	Main Products		By-Product
	Pepco-1	Repke-3	SE-5
Finished goods inventory in gallons on November 1	20,000	40,000	10,000
November sales in gallons.	800,000	700,000	200,000
November production in gallons	900,000	720,000	240,000
Sales value per gallon at split-off point	$2.00	$1.50	$.55*
Additional processing cost after split-off	$1,800,000	$720,000	—
Final sales value per gallon.	$5.00	$4.00	—

*Marketing costs of $.05 per gallon will be incurred in order to sell the by-product.

Required:
(1) Describe the market value method and explain how it accomplishes Jim Simpson's objective.
(2) Assuming Minimax Corporation adopts the market value method for internal reporting purposes:
  (a) Calculate how the joint production cost for November would be allocated.
  (b) Determine the cost assigned to finished goods inventories for Pepco-1, Repke-3, and SE-5 as of November 30.
(3) Minimax Corporation plans to expand its production facilities to enable the further processing of SE-5 into a main product. Discuss how the allocation of the joint

production cost under the market value method would change when SE-5 becomes a main product. (ICMA adapted)

C7-2. Costing joint products. Hayes Products Company produces three products, X, Y, and Z, from a single joint process. The company uses the average unit cost method for allocating the joint production cost. Some spoilage normally occurs in the joint process, but the company also has been experiencing some unexpected spoilage in the separable process to Product Y. In costing the three products for sale, all spoilage costs, together with joint and separable process costs, are included in product cost.

Over the past year, the company has been losing money on Product Z. Sentiments are mixed as to whether to drop Z or make modifications. The controller is convinced that the entire costing system needs to be revised and she has hired a consultant to present a proposal for a cost study.

Required: As the consultant, prepare a brief proposal for Hayes Products Company, outlining the aspects of its product costing which need to be reviewed. Explain why the areas cited need to be studied.   (SMAC adapted)

C7-3. Joint cost analysis for managerial decisions. Talor Chemical Company is a highly diversified chemical processing company. The company manufactures swimming pool chemicals, chemicals for metal processing companies, specialized chemical compounds for other companies, and a full line of pesticides and insecticides.

Currently, the Noorwood plant is producing two derivatives, RNA-1 and RNA-2, from the chemical compound VDB developed by Talor's research labs. Each week 1,200,000 pounds of VDB is processed at a cost of $246,000 into 800,000 pounds of RNA-1 and 400,000 pounds

of RNA-2. The proportion of these two outputs from this joint process is fixed and cannot be altered. RNA-1 has no market value until it is converted into a product with the trade name Fastkil. The cost to process RNA-1 into Fastkil is $240,000. Fastkil wholesales at $50 per 100 pounds.

RNA-2 is sold as is for $80 per hundred pounds. However, Talor has discovered that RNA-2 can be converted into two new products through further processing. The further processing would require the addition of 400,000 pounds of compound LST to the 400,000 pounds of RNA-2. This additional joint process would yield 400,000 pounds each of DMZ-3 and Pestrol—the two new products. The additional raw materials and related processing costs would be $120,000. DMZ-3 and Pestrol would each be sold for $57.50 per 100 pounds. Talor management has decided not to process RNA-2 further, based on the analysis presented below. Talor uses the average unit cost method to allocate costs arising from joint processing.

The following analysis of the two options has been prepared:

	Sell as RNA-2	Process Further		
		DMZ-3	Pestrol	Total
Production in pounds.	400,000	400,000	400,000	
Revenue	$320,000	$230,000	$230,000	$460,000
Costs:				
VDB cost*	$ 82,000	$ 61,500	$ 61,500	$123,000
Additional raw materials (LST) and processing of RNA-2 . .		60,000	60,000	120,000
Total cost.	$ 82,000	$121,500	$121,500	$243,000
Weekly gross profit.	$238,000	$108,500	$108,500	$217,000

*If RNA-2 is sold as is, the allocation basis is 1,200,000 pounds; if RNA-2 is processed further, the allocation basis is 1,600,000 pounds for VDB cost.

A new staff accountant who was to review the analysis commented that it should be revised, stating: "Product costing of products such as these should be done on a sales value basis, not an average unit cost basis."

Required:
(1) Discuss whether the use of the sales value method would provide data more relevant for the decision to market DMZ-3 and Pestrol.

(2) Critique Talor's analysis and make any revisions that are necessary. The critique and analysis should indicate:

(a) Whether Talor Chemical Company made the correct decision.
(b) The gross savings (loss) per week of Talor's decision not to process RNA-2 further, if different from the company-prepared analysis.   (ICMA adapted)

PART

3

Planning and Control
of the Elements of Cost

CHAPTER 8

Materials: Controlling and Costing

Effective materials management is essential in order to (1) provide the best service to customers, (2) produce at maximum efficiency, and (3) manage inventories at predetermined levels to control investments in inventories. Successful materials management requires the development of a highly integrated and coordinated system involving sales forecasting, purchasing, receiving, storage, production, shipping, and actual sales. Both the theory of costing materials and other inventories and the practical mechanics of cost calculations and record keeping must be considered.

Costing materials presents some important, often complex, and sometimes highly controversial questions concerning the costing of materials used in production and the cost of inventory remaining to be consumed in a future period. In financial accounting, the subject usually is presented as a problem of inventory valuation; in cost accounting, the primary problem is the determination of the cost of various materials consumed in production and a proper charge to the cost of goods sold. The discussion of materials management in this chapter deals with:

1. Procedures for materials procurement and use.
2. Materials costing methods.
3. Inventory valuation at cost or market, whichever is lower.
4. Inventory pricing and interim financial reporting.

■ ACCOUNTING FOR MATERIALS PROCUREMENT AND USE

Although production processes and materials requirements vary according to the size and type of industry, the cycle of procurement and use of materials usually involves the following steps:

1. *Engineering, planning,* and *routing* determine the design of the product, the materials specifications, and the requirements at each stage of operations. Engineering and planning not only determine the maximum and minimum quantities to run and the bill of materials for given

products and quantities, but they also cooperate in developing standards where applicable.

2. The *production budget* provides the master plan from which details concerning materials requirements are eventually developed.

3. The *purchase requisition* informs the purchasing agent concerning the quantity and type of materials needed.

4. The *purchase order* contracts for appropriate quantities to be delivered on specified dates to assure uninterrupted operations.

QUALITY
CONTROL

5. The *receiving report* certifies quantities received and may report results of inspection and testing for quality.

6. The *materials requisition* notifies the storeroom or warehouse to deliver specified types and quantities of materials to a given department at a specified time and is the authorization for the storeroom to issue materials to departments.

7. The *materials ledger cards* record the receipt and the issuance of each class of materials and provide a perpetual inventory record.

Procedures for materials procurement and use involve forms and records necessary for general ledger financial accounting as well as those necessary for costing a job, process, or department, and for maintaining perpetual inventories and other statistical summaries. These documents may be hard copy, as components of either a manual or computerized accounting system. Increasingly, however, in computerized systems they are in the form of electronic documents, with the capability of screen display and hard-copy printouts where and when needed.

Some of these forms and records are identified in the flowchart on page 202, which shows procedures for purchasing, receiving, recording, and paying for materials, i.e., the procurement phase.

Purchases of Productive Materials

The actual purchase of all materials usually is made by the purchasing department headed by a general purchasing agent. In some small and medium-size companies, however, department heads or supervisors have authority to purchase materials as the need arises. In any case, systematic procedures should be in writing in order to fix responsibility and to provide full information regarding the ultimate use of materials ordered and received.

The purchasing department should (1) receive purchase requisitions for materials, supplies, and equipment; (2) keep informed concerning sources of supply, prices, and shipping and delivery schedules; (3) prepare and place purchase orders; and (4) arrange for adequate and systematic reports between the purchasing, the receiving, and the accounting departments. An additional function of the purchasing department in some enterprises is to verify and approve for payment all invoices received in response to purchase orders placed by the department. This procedure has the advantage of centralizing the verification and approval of invoices in the department that originates the purchases and that has complete information concerning items and

Flowchart for Purchasing, Receiving, Recording, and Paying for Materials

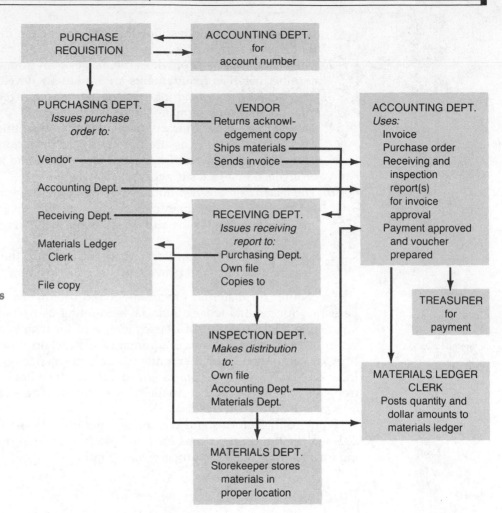

quantities ordered, prices, terms, shipping instructions, and other conditions and details of the purchases. However, invoice verification and approval by the purchasing department may violate sound procedures and principles of internal control, particularly if the same individual prepares an order and later approves the invoice. Consequently, invoice audit and approval in many instances have been made a function of the accounting department, which receives a copy of the purchase order. The purchase order carries all necessary information regarding price, discount agreement, and delivery stipulations, as well as the number of the account to which the order is to be charged. Furthermore, the centralization of invoice approval in the accounting department helps avoid delaying payments beyond the discount period.

JUST-IN-TIME   In a just-in-time system, raw materials and parts may be covered by a blanket purchase order stating the total quantities expected to be needed over a period of three or six months. The exact quantity and date of each shipment then is established by a telephone call or by a direct computer link-up between buyer and seller.

Purchases of Supplies, Services, and Repairs

The procedure followed in purchasing productive materials should apply to all departments and divisions of a business. Purchase requisitions, purchase orders, and receiving reports are appropriate for accounting department supplies and equipment, the company cafeteria, the first aid unit, and the treasurer's office, as well as all other departments. If, for example, the accounting department needs new forms printed, a requisition should be sent to the purchasing department in the usual manner, and a purchase order should be prepared and sent to the printer.

In the case of magazine subscriptions, trade and professional association memberships for company officials, and similar services, the official or department head may send in a requisition in the usual manner. A requisition, a purchase order, and an invoice for all goods and services purchased are a necessity in properly controlling purchases.

Repair contracts on an annual basis for typewriters, electronic data processing equipment, and some types of factory equipment may be requisitioned and ordered in the usual manner. In other cases, a department head or other employee may telephone for service in order to have a machine repaired and back in operation quickly. In such cases, the purchasing agent issues a so-called blanket purchase order that allows approval of all repair and service costs of a specific type without having to know the actual amount that will be charged. When the repair bill is received, the invoice clerk checks the amount of the bill with the head of the department where the repairs took place and then approves the invoice for payment.

Purchasing Forms

The principal forms required in purchasing are the purchase requisition and the purchase order.

Purchase Requisition. The purchase requisition originates with (1) a stores or warehouse clerk, who observes that the quantity on hand is at a set ordering minimum, (2) a materials ledger clerk, who may be responsible for notifying the purchasing agent when to buy, (3) a works manager, who foresees the need for special materials or unusual quantities, (4) a research, engineering, or other department employee or supervisor, who needs materials or supplies of a special nature, or (5) a computer that has been programmed to produce replenishment advice for the purchasing department. One copy remains with the originator, and the original is sent to the purchasing department for execution of the request. The document may sometimes be in electronic rather than hard-copy form. For standard materials, the requisition may indicate only the stock number of an item, and the purchasing agent uses judgment and established policy concerning where to buy and the quantity to order. For other purchase requests, it may be necessary to give meticulous descriptions, blueprints, catalog numbers, weights, standards, brand names, exact quantities to order, and suggested prices.

Purchase Order. The purchase order, signed by the purchasing agent or other official, is authorization to a vendor to supply specified quantities of described goods at agreed terms and at a designated time and place. As a convenience, the vendor's order forms may be used. In typical practice, however, the order forms are prepared by the purchasing company, and the form is adapted to the particular needs of the purchaser. As a matter of record and for accounting control, a purchase order should be issued for every purchase of materials, supplies, or equipment. When a purchase commitment is made by mail, telephone, or a sales representative, the purchase order serves as confirmation to the vendor and places the required documents in the hands of those concerned in the purchasing company.

The purchase order gives the vendor a complete description of the goods and services desired, the terms, the prices, and the shipping instructions. When necessary, the description may refer to attached blueprints and specification pages. The original and an acknowledgment copy are sent to the vendor. Other copies are distributed as shown in the flowchart on page 202. The vendor is asked to sign and return the acknowledgment copy to the purchaser, indicating that the order was received and will be delivered according to the specifications enumerated in the purchase order.

Electronic Data Interchange. Paperwork savings within a company occur by using electronic data transfer for purchasing as well as for many other purposes. Paperwork savings are further enhanced by use of *electronic data interchange* (EDI) to provide information for monitoring and controlling the acquisition and movement of materials. EDI is the exchange of documents and transactions by a computer in one company with the computer of another company. In the traditional paper exchange environment, even when a company has a computerized inventory management system, purchase orders, invoices, and disbursement checks are prepared and exchanged in hard-copy form. But with EDI, transactions are machine readable and the computers can transfer data between companies without extensive paperwork. Purchase orders, the location and status of materials orders, invoices, and cash transfers to payee banks are examples of the types of data which are transferable with EDI.[1]

Vendor Certification

JUST-IN-TIME

Modern inventory management, especially in a just-in-time (JIT) environment, emphasizes reducing the number of vendors or suppliers and improving the quality of procurements. The objective is to deliver materials directly to the plant floor with little or no inspection. A policy of a single vendor is desired for each material, with perhaps a second vendor to be used to ensure sufficient supply in periods when demand is unusually high. Selecting vendors and the monitoring of those selected requires a vendor performance

---

[1]Arjan T. Sadhurani and M. H. Sarhan, "Electronic Systems Enhance JIT Operations," *Management Accounting,* Vol. LXIX, No. 6, pp. 25-26.

appraisal procedure, rating each supplier on timely deliveries, quality of materials, and price competitiveness. The buying firm should develop long-term vendor relationships, rather than consistently seeking short-run price breaks. The importance of certifying the best vendors calls for an objectively quantifiable procedure rather than a subjective approach.[2]

Obstacles to JIT purchasing exist, such as: layout of the production process, frequency of schedule changes, and distance from suppliers. While problems admittedly exist, many can be overcome, with a resulting reduction in manufacturing cost and improvement in product quality.

Receiving

The functions of the receiving department are to (1) unload and unpack incoming materials; (2) check quantities received against the shipper's packing list; (3) identify goods received with descriptions on the purchase order; (4) prepare a receiving report; (5) notify the purchasing department of discovered discrepancies; (6) arrange for inspection when necessary; (7) notify the traffic department and the purchasing department of any damage in transit; and (8) route accepted materials to the appropriate factory location.

The receiving report shows the purchase order number, the account number to be charged, the name of the vendor, details relating to transportation, and the quantity and type of goods received. The form also provides a space for the inspection department to note either the complete approval of the shipment or the quantity rejected and the reason for the rejection.

If inspection does not take place immediately after receipt of the materials, the receiving report is distributed as follows: (1) the receiving department keeps one copy and sends another copy to the purchasing department as notice of the arrival of the materials; (2) all other copies go to the inspection department, and are distributed when inspection is completed. After inspection, one copy of the receiving report, with the inspection result noted thereon, is sent to the accounting department, where it is matched with the purchase order and the vendor's invoice and then paid. Other copies go to various departments such as materials and production planning. One copy accompanies the materials, so that the storekeeper knows the quantity and the kind of materials received. Alternatively, the receiving report data may be entered using a computer terminal and electronically transferred to appropriate recipients.

Invoice Approval and Data Processing

By the time materials reach the receiving department, the company usually will have received the invoice from the vendor. This invoice and a copy of

---

[2]For an illustration of a formalized, objective vendor certification procedure, see Michael A. Robinson and John E. Timmerman, "How Vendor Analysis Supports JIT Manufacturing," *Management Accounting*, Vol. LXIX, No. 6, pp. 20-24.

the purchase order are filed in the accounting department. When the receiving report with its inspection report arrives, the receiving report and the invoice are compared to see that materials received meet purchase order specifications as to items, quantities, prices, price extensions, discount and credit terms, shipping instructions, and other possible conditions. If the invoice is found to be correct or has been adjusted because of rejects as noted by the inspection department, the invoice clerk approves it, attaches it to the purchase order and the receiving report, and sends these documents to another clerk for the preparation of the voucher.

Invoice approval is an important step in the materials control procedure, since it verifies that the goods have been received as ordered and that payment can be made. The verification procedure is handled by responsible invoice clerks, thus assuring systematic examination and handling of the documentation necessary for adequate control of materials purchases.

The preparation of a voucher is based on an approved invoice. The voucher data are entered first in the purchases journal and are posted to the subsidiary records. They then are entered in the cash payments journal according to the due date for payment. The original voucher and two copies are sent to the treasurer for issuance of the check. The treasurer mails the check with the original voucher to the vendor, files one copy of the voucher, and returns another copy to the accounting department for the vendor's file. Purchase transactions entered in the purchases journal affect the control accounts and the subsidiary records as shown in the chart on the next page.

In an electronic data processing (EDP) system, upon receipt of the invoice (the source document) or electronic data interchange, the accounts payable clerk determines the account distribution which then is directly entered into the computer data bank via a terminal device. The data are edited, audited, and merged with the purchase order and the receiving order data, both of which have been stored in the computer data bank. The common matching criterion on all documents is the purchase order number. Quantities, dollar values, due dates, terms, and unit prices are matched. When in agreement, the cost data are entered in the accounts payable computer file with a date for later payment, or a printout of a check is transmitted for payment. Listings in journal form can be produced as needed.

The above procedure deals with the accounts payable phase of a purchase transaction. Of equal importance is the need for posting the data in quantities and dollar values to the materials inventory. In an EDP system, the information enters from either the invoice or the invoice approval form, which includes all computer-necessary data. The internal computer program updates the materials inventory file. The withdrawal of materials is computerized also so that manual postings to the materials inventory file, as well as other manual operations, are eliminated.

Correcting Invoices

When the purchase order, receiving report, and invoice are compared, various adjustments may be needed as a result of the following circumstances:

| TRANSACTION | GENERAL LEDGER CONTROL | | SUBSIDIARY RECORDS |
	Debit	Credit	
Materials purchased for stock	Materials	Accounts Payable	Entry in the Received section of the materials ledger record
Materials purchased for a particular job or department	Work in Process	Accounts Payable	Entry in the Direct Materials section of the production report or job order cost sheet
Materials and supplies purchased for factory overhead purposes	Materials	Accounts Payable	Entry in the Received section of the materials ledger record
Supplies purchased for marketing and administrative offices	Materials Marketing Expenses Control Administrative Expenses Control	Accounts Payable	Entry in the Received section of the materials ledger record or in the proper columns of the marketing or administrative expense analysis sheets
Purchases of services or repairs	Factory Overhead Marketing Expenses Control Administrative Expenses Control	Accounts Payable	Entry in the proper account columns of the expense analysis sheets
Purchases of equipment	Equipment	Accounts Payable	Entry on the equipment ledger record

1. Some of the materials ordered are not received and are not included on the invoice. In this case, no adjustment is necessary, and the invoice may be approved for immediate payment. On the purchase order, the invoice clerk will make a notation of the quantity received in place of the quantity ordered. If the vendor is out of stock or otherwise unable to deliver specified merchandise, an immediate ordering from other sources may be necessary.

2. Items ordered are not received but are included on the invoice. In this situation, the shortage is noted on the invoice and is deducted from the total before payment is approved. A letter to the vendor explaining the shortage is the usual procedure.

3. The seller ships a quantity larger than called for on the purchase order. The purchaser may (a) keep the entire shipment and add the excess to the invoice, if the seller has not already invoiced the excess; (b) return the excess to the seller; or (c) hold the excess pending in-

structions from the seller. Some companies issue a supplementary purchase order that authorizes the invoice clerk to pay the overshipment.

4. Materials of a wrong size or quality, defective parts, and damaged items are received. If the items are returned, a correction should be made on the invoice before payment is approved. It may be advantageous to keep damaged or defective shipments if the seller makes adequate price concessions, or the items may be held subject to the seller's instructions.

5. It may be expedient for a purchaser to pay transportation charges, even though the purchase agreement quotes delivered prices. The amount paid by the purchaser is deducted on the invoice, and the paid freight bill is attached to the invoice as evidence of payment.

Cost of Acquiring Materials

A guiding principle in accounting for the cost of materials is that all costs incurred in entering a unit of materials into factory production be included. Acquisition costs, such as the vendor's invoice price and transportation charges, are the most visible costs of the purchased goods. Less obvious costs of materials entering factory operations are the costs of purchasing, receiving, unpacking, inspecting, insuring, storing, and accounting.

Controversial concepts and certain practical limitations often necessitate a compromise in implementing the principles of costing materials, even with respect to easily identified acquisition costs. Calculating a number of cost additions and adjustments to each invoice involves clerical expenses which may be greater than the benefits that might be derived from the increased accuracy. Therefore, materials are commonly carried at the invoice price paid the vendor, although all acquisition costs and price adjustments affect the materials cost. As a result, acquisition costs are generally charged to factory overhead when it is not practical to follow a more accurate costing procedure.

Purchases Discounts. Choosing the best way to handle discounts on purchases is a challenge in accounting for materials costs. Trade discounts and quantity discounts normally are not on the accounting records but are treated as price reductions. Cash discounts should be handled as price adjustments. At times, however, cash discounts are accounted for as other income, although income is not produced by the act of buying. A lower purchase cost may well widen the margin between sales price and cost, but it takes the sale to produce income. When the vendor quotes terms such as 2/10, n/30 on a $100 invoice, is the sales price $100 or $98? The purchaser has two dates to make payment: on the tenth day (which allows time to receive, unpack, inspect, verify, voucher, and pay for the goods) or twenty days later. For the additional twenty days, an additional charge or penalty of 2 percent is assessed. If regarded as interest, the extra charge is 36 percent per year ((360 days ÷ 20 days) × 2%). On these terms the seller is pricing essentially on a cash basis, since the purchaser has no reasonable choice except to buy on the cash basis in order to avoid a 36 percent short-term financing rate.

Although the nature of a purchases discount is readily understood, for practical reasons the gross materials unit cost of the invoice may be recorded in the materials account and the cash discount recorded as a credit account item. Otherwise it would be necessary to compute the discount on each item.

Freight In. Freight or other transportation charges on incoming shipments are obviously costs of materials, but differences occur in the allocation of these charges. A vendor's invoice for $600 may show 25 items, weighing 1,700 pounds, shipped in five crates, with the attached freight bill showing a payment of $48. The delivered cost is $648. But how much of the freight belongs to each of the invoice items, and what unit price should go on the materials ledger card? When the purchased units are not numerous and are large in size and unit cost, computation of actual amounts of freight may be feasible; otherwise, some logical, systematic, and expedient procedure is necessary.

If freight charges are debited to Materials, the total amount should be added proportionately to each materials card affected. This might be done by assuming that each dollar of materials cost carries an equal portion of the freight. For example, freight of $48 on materials costing $600 would add $.08 ($48 ÷ $600) to each dollar on the invoice. Alternatively, the relative weight of each item on the invoice might be determined and used as a basis for calculating the applicable freight. If an invoice item is estimated to weigh 300 pounds, then $8.47 ((300 ÷ 1,700) × $48) would be added for freight. This procedure is likely to result in unit costs having four or more decimal places on the materials ledger cards.

To simplify procedures, all freight costs on incoming materials and supplies may be charged to Freight In. As materials are issued for production, an applied rate for freight charges might be added to the unit price on the ledger cards. The same amount is included in the debit to Work in Process or Factory Overhead (Indirect Materials), and Freight In is credited. Any balance in Freight In at the end of a period is closed to Cost of Goods Sold or prorated to Cost of Goods Sold and inventories.

Another method of accounting for incoming freight costs on materials is to estimate the total for an accounting period and include this amount in computing the factory overhead rate. Freight In would then become one of the accounts controlled by Factory Overhead. For materials or supplies used in marketing and administrative departments, freight, transportation, or delivery costs should be charged to the appropriate nonmanufacturing account.

Applied Acquisition Costs. If it is decided that the materials cost should include other acquisition costs as well, an applied rate might be added to each invoice and to each item, instead of charging these costs directly to factory overhead. A single rate for these costs could be used, but a more accurate method would be to use separate rates for each class of costs, as follows:

$$\frac{\text{Estimated purchasing department cost for budget period}}{\text{Estimated number of purchases or estimated amount of purchases}} = \frac{\text{Rate per purchase or}}{\text{rate per dollar purchased}}$$

$$\frac{\text{Estimated receiving department cost for budget period}}{\text{Estimated number of items to be received during period}} = \text{Rate per item}$$

$$\frac{\text{Estimated materials department cost for budget period}}{\text{Estimated number of items, feet of space, dollar value, etc.}} = \begin{array}{l}\text{Rate per item, cubic} \\ \text{foot, dollar value, etc.}\end{array}$$

$$\frac{\text{Estimated applicable accounting department cost for budget period}}{\text{Estimated number of transactions}} = \begin{array}{l}\text{Rate per} \\ \text{transaction}\end{array}$$

ACTIVITY COSTING

The logic of this approach is the same as that of activity costing, as introduced in Chapter 4. This procedure results in the following accounting treatment:

Materials	xxx	
Applied Purchasing Department Expenses		xxx
Applied Receiving Department Expenses		xxx
Applied Materials Department Expenses		xxx
Applied Accounting Department Expenses		xxx

Actual expenses incurred by each of the departments for which applied rates are used will be debited to the applied accounts. Differences between the expenses incurred by the departments during the period and the expenses applied to the materials cost would represent over- or underapplied expenses and would be closed to Cost of Goods Sold or prorated to Cost of Goods Sold and inventories.

Inventory Costing for Income Tax Purposes. The Tax Reform Act of 1986 requires new inventory costing procedures.[3] The "uniform capitalization rules" require inclusion in inventory of certain costs that previously either were or could be charged to expense for tax reporting purposes. Costs such as depreciation for tax purposes in excess of the amount for financial reporting, rework labor, scrap and spoilage, materials procurement, warehousing and handling expenses, factory administrative expenses, and office salaries related to production services now must be inventoried for tax purposes. Generally, these costs are properly capitalizable for financial reporting purposes as well, with the exception of excess depreciation and conditions wherein rework labor, scrap, and spoilage are more properly expensed.

Storage and Use of Materials

Materials, together with a copy of the receiving report, are forwarded to the storeroom from the receiving or inspection department. The storekeeper and assistants are responsible for safeguarding the materials, which means that materials and supplies are placed in proper bins or other storage spaces, that they are kept safely until required in production, and that all materials taken from the storeroom are properly requisitioned. It is good policy to restrict admittance to the storeroom to employees of that department only

---

[3]*Internal Revenue Code of 1986,* Section 263A.

and to have these employees work behind locked doors, issuing materials through cage windows.

Since the cost of storing and handling materials may be substantial unless a just-in-time system is implemented, careful design and arrangement of storerooms can result in significant cost savings. Materials can be stored according to (1) the materials account number; (2) the frequency of use of the item; (3) the factory area where the item is used; or (4) the nature, size, and shape of the item. In practice, no single base is likely to be suitable, but the size and shape of materials usually dictate the basic storeroom arrangement. Variations can then be introduced, such as placing the most frequently used items nearest the point of issue and locating materials used primarily in one factory area nearest that area.

Bin cards or *stock cards* are effective ready references that may be attached to storage bins, shelves, racks, or other containers. Bin cards usually show quantities of each type of material received, issued, and on hand. They are not a part of the accounting records as such, but they show the quantities on hand in the storeroom at all times and should agree with the quantities on the materials ledger records in the accounting department.

Issuing and Costing Materials

Control of the quantity and cost of materials, supplies, and services requires a systematic and efficient system of purchasing, recording, and storing. Equally necessary is a systematic and efficient procedure for issuing materials and supplies.

Materials Requisition. The materials requisition is an authorization to the storekeeper to deliver materials or supplies to the place designated or to give the materials to the person presenting a properly executed requisition. It is drawn by someone who has the authority to requisition materials for use in the department. The authorized employee may be a production control clerk, a department head, a supervisor, a group leader, an expediter, or a materials release analyst. It is distinguished from a purchase requisition, discussed earlier, which is used to initiate an order to a vendor.

The materials requisition is the basic document used to withdraw materials from the storeroom. Its preparation results in entries in the Issued section of the materials ledger record and in postings to the job order cost sheets, production reports, or the various expense analysis sheets for individual departments. All withdrawals result in debits to Work in Process or to control accounts for factory overhead, marketing expenses, or administrative expenses and in credits to Materials. A materials requisition in hard-copy form is illustrated at the top of the next page.

Materials Requisitioned Journal. With the postings to the materials ledger records, the job order cost sheets, the production reports, and the expense analysis sheets completed, it is still necessary to post the materials withdrawals to the proper ledger control accounts. This task is greatly facilitated

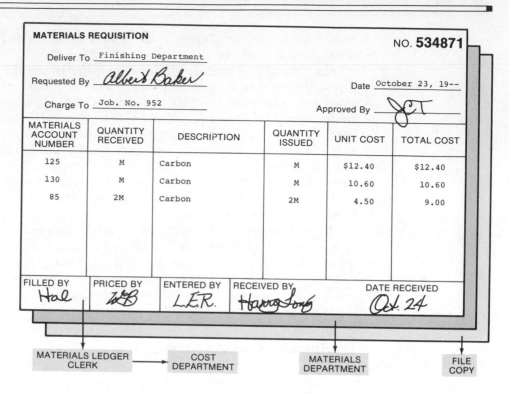

by the use of a *materials requisitioned journal*. This journal, illustrated as follows, is a form of materials summary. At the end of the month, the totals of the various columns are posted directly to the ledger accounts, except for the Sundries column from which items are posted individually.

MATERIALS REQUISITIONED JOURNAL

Date		Credit Materials	Description	Req. No.	Job or Acct. No.	Work in Process	Factory Overhead Control	Marketing Expenses Control	Administrative Expenses Control	Sundries Acct. No.	Sundries Post. Ref.	Sundries Amount
19--												
Oct.	1	600 00	Direct materials	4101	5317	600 00						
	1	225 00	Indirect materials	4102	411		225 00					
	3	1,800 75	Direct materials	4103	5318	1,800 75						
	3	195 50	For installation.......	4104						135	√	195 50
	4	75 00	Supplies.............	4105	630				75 00			
	4	112 80	Supplies.............	4106	530			112 80				
		41,160 90				36,400 00	2,280 00	1,525 40	760 00			195 50

Electronic Data Processing for Materials Requisitions. Through electronic data processing, materials requisition transactions would be entered from the materials requisition form to the computer data bank. Rather than a written requisition document, an electronic requisition may be entered using a computer terminal device. The computer program would produce a materials summary, similar to the materials requisitioned journal, and post to the appropriate subsidiary ledger and ledger control accounts.

Bill of Materials. The *bill of materials,* a kind of master requisition, is a printed or duplicated form that lists all materials and parts necessary for a typical job or production run. Time is saved and efficiency is promoted through the use of a bill of materials. When a job or production run is started, all the materials listed on the bill of materials are sent to the factory or are issued on a prearranged time schedule. The bill of materials is a rather cumbersome medium for posting purposes. Electronic data processing can greatly improve the procedure by utilizing a computer program which will provide printouts of the bill of materials and process the information internally, thus updating the accounting records.

Just-in-Time Inventory Procedures. Manufacturing processes are increasingly being based on the receipt of raw materials from suppliers "just-in-time" for their use on the plant floor. When a firm's raw materials can be handled in this immediate use mode, the traditional storeroom receipt, storage, and issuance procedures are abbreviated. Storage, except for brief periods directly on the plant floor, is eliminated. Receipt and issuing documentation can be combined, and backflush costing procedures described in Chapter 3 can be employed. As a result, there is a savings in record keeping and, more importantly, a savings in inventory investment, storage, and handling costs.

*BACKFLUSH
COSTING*

Materials Ledger Record—Perpetual Inventory

A perpetual inventory accounting system enters each increase and each reduction of inventory in order to maintain up-to-date material ledger records. These records, either on hard copy or in computer memory, constitute a subsidiary ledger controlled by the materials or inventory accounts in the general ledger. In addition to showing quantities and prices of each type of material received, issued, and on hand, the records commonly detail the account number, description or type of material, locations, unit measurement, and maximum and minimum quantities to carry. New materials ledger subsidiary accounts are prepared and old ones are deleted as changes occur in the types of materials carried in stock. The ledger record arrangement is in effect the familiar debit, credit, and balance columns under the descriptions of Received, Issued, and Inventory and a printed version is illustrated in presenting the materials costing methods. Additional columns can be added to record receipt and requisition identification numbers.

The approved invoice with supporting documents, such as the purchase order and receiving report, goes to the materials ledger clerk. These documents enable the clerk to make the necessary entries in the Received section of the materials ledger record. Each receipt increases the balance on hand, and the new balance is extended upon entry of the receipt.

Ideally, unsatisfactory goods or defective units should be detected by the inspection department before being stored and before being paid for. The receiving report should show materials actually accepted, and the ledger entries should be made after adjustments. However, goods which have been accepted in the storeroom may be found unsatisfactory later, after part of a shipment has been used in the factory. The balance may then be returned to the vendor. Since these units were entered in the Received and Balance sections of the materials ledger record when they were placed in the storeroom, an adjustment must be made. The recommended procedure is to enter the quantity and the cost of the returned shipment in brackets in the Received section and to reduce the balance accordingly.

When the storekeeper issues materials, a copy of the requisition is sent to the materials ledger clerk, who then makes an entry in the Issued section of the materials ledger record, showing the date; requisition number; job, lot, or department number; quantity; and cost of the issued materials. The new balance is computed and entered in the Balance column. As already explained, these manual operations are performed in an EDP system via a computer program designed for materials transactions.

Physical Inventory. The alternative to a perpetual inventory system is the periodic inventory system, whereby purchases are added to the beginning inventory, the ending (remaining) inventory is counted and costed, and the difference is considered the cost of materials issued. Regardless of whether a periodic or a perpetual inventory system is used, periodic physical counts are necessary to discover and eliminate discrepancies between the actual count and the balances on materials ledger records. These discrepancies may be due to errors in transferring invoice data to the records, mistakes in costing requisitions, unrecorded invoices or requisitions, or spoilage, breakage, and theft. In some enterprises, plant operations are suspended periodically during a seasonal low period or at the end of the fiscal year to allow a physical inventory to be taken. In others, an inventory crew or members of the internal audit department make a count of one or more stock classes every day throughout the year, presumably on a well-planned schedule, so that every materials item will be inventoried at least once during the year.

Adjusting Materials Ledger Records and Accounts to Conform to Inventory Count. When the inventory count differs from the balance on the materials ledger record, the ledger record is adjusted to conform to the actual count. If the ledger record balance shows more materials units than the inventory count, an entry is made in the Issued section, and the Inventory section is reduced to equal the verified count. In case the materials ledger balance is less than the physical count, the quantity difference may be entered in brackets in the Issued section or may be entered in the Received section, with the Inventory section being increased to agree with the actual count.

In addition to the corrections on the materials ledger records, the materials account must be adjusted for the increase or decrease. For example, if the inventory count is less than that shown on the materials ledger record, the following entry should be recorded:

	Subsidiary Record	Dr.	Cr.
Factory Overhead Control.		xxxx	
Inventory Adjustment to Physical Count	xxxx		
Materials			xxxx

■ MATERIALS COSTING METHODS

Whenever significant amounts of inventories are held, one important objective in cost accounting is the production of accurate and meaningful figures for the cost of goods sold. These figures can be used for purposes of control and analysis and are eventually matched against revenue in order to determine operating income.

After the unit cost and total cost of incoming materials are entered in the Received section of a materials ledger record, the next step is to cost these materials as they move either from storeroom to factory accounts as direct or indirect materials or from storeroom to marketing and administrative accounts as supplies. The more common methods of costing materials issued and inventories are:

1. First-in, first-out (fifo).
2. Average cost.
3. Last-in, first-out (lifo).
4. Other methods—such as market price at date of issue, last purchase price, or standard cost.

These methods relate to assumptions as to the flow of costs. The physical flow of units may coincide with the method of cost flow, though such a condition is not a necessary requirement. Although this discussion deals with materials inventory, the same costing methods are also applicable to finished goods inventories.

As in the previous discussion, the following illustrations assume use of a perpetual inventory system. Such a procedure is especially useful in enhancing materials control and is needed to identify accurately the various general and subsidiary ledger accounts to which materials issued should be charged. Cost flow assumptions other than fifo, however, may result in unit costs that differ, depending on whether the perpetual or periodic inventory system is used.

First-In, First-Out (Fifo) Method of Costing

The first-in, first-out (fifo) method of costing is used to introduce the subject of materials costing. This illustration is based on the following transactions:

Feb. 1   Beginning balance: 800 units @ $6 per unit.
     4   Received 200 units @ $7 per unit.
    10   Received 200 units @ $8 per unit.
    11   Issued 800 units.
    12   Received 400 units @ $8 per unit.
    20   Issued 500 units.
    25   Returned 100 excess units from the factory to the storeroom—to be
          recorded at the latest issued price (or at the actual issued price if
          physically identifiable).
    28   Received 600 units @ $9 per unit.

Calculations for these transactions are as follows:

FIFO COSTING METHOD ILLUSTRATED

Date	Received Quantity	Received Unit Cost	Received Total Cost	Issued Quantity	Issued Unit Cost	Issued Total Cost	Inventory Quantity	Inventory Unit Cost	Inventory Total Cost	Balance
Feb. 1							800	$6.00	$4,800	$4,800
4	200	$7.00	$1,400				800	6.00	4,800	
							200	7.00	1,400	6,200
10	200	8.00	1,600				800	6.00	4,800	
							200	7.00	1,400	
							200	8.00	1,600	7,800
11				800	$6.00	$4,800	200	7.00	1,400	
							200	8.00	1,600	3,000
12	400	8.00	3,200				200	7.00	1,400	
							600	8.00	4,800	6,200
20				200	7.00	1,400				
				300	8.00	2,400	300	8.00	2,400	2,400
25	100*	8.00	800				400	8.00	3,200	3,200
28	600	9.00	5,400				400	8.00	3,200	
							600	9.00	5,400	8,600
	*Returns to storeroom.									

The fifo method of costing issued materials follows the principle that materials used should carry their actual experienced cost. The method assumes that materials are issued from the oldest supply in stock and that the cost of those units when placed in stock is the cost of those same units when issued. However, fifo costing may be used even though physical withdrawal is in a different order. Advantages claimed for the fifo costing method are:

1. Materials used are drawn from the cost records in a logical and systematic manner.
2. Movement of materials in a continuous, orderly, single-file manner represents a condition necessary to and consistent with efficient materials control, particularly for materials subject to deterioration, decay, and style changes.

The fifo method is recommended whenever (1) the size and cost of materials units are large, (2) materials are easily identified as belonging to a particular purchased lot, and (3) not more than two or three different receipts of the materials are on a materials card at one time. Fifo costing is definitely awkward if frequent purchases are made at different prices and if units from several purchases are on hand at the same time. Additional costing difficulties arise when returns to vendors or to the storeroom occur.

Average Costing Method

Issuing materials at an average cost assumes that each batch taken from the storeroom is composed of uniform quantities from each shipment in stock at the date of issue. Often it is not feasible to mark or label each materials item with an invoice price in order to identify the used unit with its acquisition cost. It may be reasoned that units are issued more or less at random as far as the specific units and the specific costs are concerned and that an average cost of all units in stock at the time of issue is a satisfactory measure of materials cost. However, average costing may be used even though the physical withdrawal is in an identifiable order. If materials tend to be made up of numerous small items low in unit cost and especially if prices are subject to frequent change, average costing is advantageous because:

1. It is a realistic costing method useful to management in analyzing operating results and appraising future production.
2. It minimizes the effect of unusually high or low materials prices, thereby making possible more stable cost estimates for future work.
3. It is a practical and less expensive perpetual inventory system.

The average costing method divides the total cost of all materials of a particular class by the number of units on hand to find the average price. The cost of new invoices is added to the total in the Balance column; the units are added to the existing quantity; and the new total cost is divided by the new quantity to arrive at the new average cost. Materials are issued at the established average cost until a new purchase is recorded. Although a new average cost may be computed when materials are returned to vendors and when excess issues are returned to the storeroom, for practical purposes it seems sufficient to reduce or increase the total quantity and cost, allowing the unit price to remain unchanged. When a new purchase is made and a new average is computed, the discrepancy created by the returns will be absorbed.

Using the data of the fifo illustration (page 216), the transactions can be summarized as shown at the top of the next page.

AVERAGE COSTING METHOD ILLUSTRATED

	Received			Issued			Inventory			
Date	Quantity	Unit Cost	Total Cost	Quantity	Unit Cost	Total Cost	Quantity	Unit Cost	Total Cost	Balance
Feb. 1							800	$6.00		$4,800
4	200	$7.00	$1,400				1,000	6.20		6,200
10	200	8.00	1,600				1,200	6.50		7,800
11				800	$6.50	$5,200	400	6.50		2,600
12	400	8.00	3,200				800	7.25		5,800
20				500	7.25	3,625	300	7.25		2,175
25	100*	7.25	725				400	7.25		2,900
28	600	9.00	5,400				1,000	8.30		8,300
	*Returns to storeroom.									

To insure quick costing and early reporting of completed jobs or products, some companies at the close of each month establish an average cost for each kind of material on hand and use this cost for all issues during the following month. When perpetual inventory costing procedures are not used, a variation of this method is to wait until the end of a costing period to compute the cost of materials consumed. The cost used is obtained by adding both quantities and dollars of purchases to beginning inventory figures, thus deriving an average cost.

Last-In, First-Out (Lifo) Method of Costing

The last-in, first-out (lifo) method of costing materials issued is based on the premise that outgoing materials units should carry the cost of the most recent purchase, although the physical flow may actually be different. The method assumes that the most recent cost (the approximate cost to replace the consumed units) is most significant in matching cost with revenue in the income determination process.

Under lifo procedures, the objective is to charge the cost of current purchases to work in process or other operating expenses and to leave the oldest costs in the inventory. Several alternatives can be used to apply the lifo method. Each procedure results in different costs for materials issued and the ending inventory, and consequently in a different profit. It is mandatory, therefore, to follow the chosen procedure consistently.

The fifo data on page 216 are used to illustrate lifo costing, as shown at the top of the next page.

LIFO COSTING METHOD ILLUSTRATED

Date	Received Quantity	Received Unit Cost	Received Total Cost	Issued Quantity	Issued Unit Cost	Issued Total Cost	Inventory Quantity	Inventory Unit Cost	Inventory Total Cost	Balance
Feb. 1							800	$6.00	$4,800	$4,800
4	200	$7.00	$1,400				800	6.00	4,800	
							200	7.00	1,400	6,200
10	200	8.00	1,600				800	6.00	4,800	
							200	7.00	1,400	
							200	8.00	1,600	7,800
11				200	$8.00	$1,600				
				200	7.00	1,400				
				400	6.00	2,400	400	6.00	2,400	2,400
12	400	8.00	3,200				400	6.00	2,400	
							400	8.00	3,200	5,600
20				400	8.00	3,200				
				100	6.00	600	300	6.00	1,800	1,800
25	100*	6.00	600				400	6.00	2,400	2,400
28	600	9.00	5,400				400	6.00	2,400	
							600	9.00	5,400	7,800
	*Returns to storeroom.									

In this illustration, a new inventory balance is computed after each issue of materials, with the ending inventory consisting of 1,000 units costed at $7,800. If, however, a periodic rather than a perpetual inventory procedure is used, the issues would be determined at the end of the period by ignoring day-to-day outflows and subtracting total ending inventory from the total of the beginning balance plus the receipts. The ending inventory would consist of:

800 units @ $6, on hand in the beginning inventory	$4,800
200 units @ $7, from the oldest purchase, Feb. 4	1,400
1,000 units, lifo inventory at the end of February.........	$6,200

Both procedures often are referred to as the *item-layer identification method* of applying lifo and are acceptable variations of the lifo method, even though the cost of materials used and the ending inventory figures differ.

Regardless of the cost flow assumption, the latter procedure is particularly appropriate in process costing where individual materials requisitions are seldom used and where the materials move into process in bulk lots, as in flour mills, spinning mills, oil refineries, and sugar refineries. The procedure also functions smoothly for a company that charges materials to work in process from month-end consumption sheets which provide the cost department with quantities used.

Lifo Advantages and Disadvantages. The advantages of the lifo costing method are:

1. Materials consumed are priced in a systematic and realistic manner. It is argued that current acquisition costs are incurred for the purpose of meeting current production and sales requirements; therefore, the most recent costs should be charged against current production and sales.
2. Unrealized inventory gains and losses are minimized, and reported periodic operating profits are stabilized in industries subject to sharp materials price fluctuations.
3. Inflationary prices of recent purchases are charged to operations in periods of rising prices, thus reducing profits, resulting in a tax saving, and therewith providing a cash advantage through deferral of income tax payments. The tax deferral creates additional working capital as long as the economy continues to experience inflation.

The disadvantages of the lifo costing method are:

1. In a period of declining volume and/or disinflation, the lifo method will result in increasing profits, thus increasing taxes and therewith causing a cash disadvantage. This same phenomenon may occur in high-technology companies because the effect of rapid technological improvements means that the first costs may be higher than the last costs; hence, the fifo method may actually result in a lower taxable income (and cash savings) than lifo.[4]
2. The election of lifo for income tax purposes is binding for all subsequent years unless a change is authorized or required by the Internal Revenue Service (IRS).[5]
3. Lifo is a "cost only" method, with no write-down to the lower of cost or market allowed for income tax purposes. Furthermore, the IRS requires that when lifo is adopted, an adjustment must be made to restore any previous write-downs from actual cost. Should the market fall below lifo cost in subsequent years, the business would be at a tax disadvantage. When prices drop, the only option may be to charge off the older (higher) costs by liquidating the inventory. However, liquidation for income tax purposes must take place at year end. According to

---

[4]Eugene H. Flegm, *Accounting: How to Meet the Challenges of Relevance and Regulation* (New York: John Wiley & Sons, Inc., 1984), p. 191.

[5]*Internal Revenue Code of 1986*, Section 472(e).

IRS regulations, liquidation during the fiscal year is not acceptable if the inventory returns to its original level at the end of the year.[6]

4. Lifo must be used in financial statements if it is elected for income tax purposes. However, for financial reporting purposes, the lower of lifo cost or market can be used without violating IRS lifo conformity rules.[7]

5. Record keeping requirements under lifo, as well as fifo, are substantially greater than those under alternative costing and pricing methods.

6. Under lifo, the balance sheet reflects the earliest inventory costs incurred. Consequently, in periods of rising prices, the company's inventory, current and total assets, and stockholders' equity are understated.

7. End-of-period variations in the level of inventory purchases can permit income manipulation, using lifo procedures, that would not occur with the use of fifo.

Since the use of lifo reduces profits during periods of rising prices, managers whose rewards are based on immediate profits may not be inclined to use lifo. Therefore, if lifo is in the best interests of the firm, it may be necessary to modify the management reward system.

Dollar-Value Lifo. The item-layer identification method and the previous illustrations of the characteristics of lifo costing are generally not practicable for a company that has a wide variety of inventory items. The item-layer identification method is also particularly unsuitable for a company whose range or mix of inventory frequently changes. Use of this method under such conditions virtually ensures frequent liquidation of lifo layers and a corresponding loss of the benefits from using lifo. As a result, companies in using lifo may employ some version of the *dollar-value lifo* method for financial reporting and for income tax purposes.[8] This method reduces the cost of administering lifo and reduces the likelihood of liquidating lifo layers. Also, the income tax savings during periods of rising prices is greater if dollar-value lifo is used, rather than the item-layer identification method. Thus, units issued to jobs or products are costed according to the company's established cost flow assumptions, whatever they may be, for internal costing purposes, and inventories are adjusted to dollar-value lifo figures for financial reporting and for income tax purposes.

The distinguishing feature of the dollar-value method is that similar inventory items are grouped into a pool and layers are determined, based upon the pool's total dollar changes. Under this method, year-end inventory costed at current prices is first adjusted to its base period cost, using the current period price index. The inventory change is then determined by comparing the ending inventory measured in base period dollars with the beginning inventory measured in base period dollars. Increases are adjusted back to current cost, using the current year price index, and are then added to the prior year's reported inventory. Decreases are adjusted by using the price

---

[6]*Regulations*, Section 1.472-2(b), (c), and (d).

[7]*Regulations*, Section 1.472-2(e) (1) and (7).

[8]*Regulations*, Section 1.472-8.

index in effect when the depleted inventory layer was added to inventory and are then subtracted from the prior year's reported inventory.[9]

Other Materials Costing Methods

Although fifo, average cost, and lifo are commonly used methods of costing materials units into work in process, various other methods exist.

Market Price at Date of Issue or Last Purchase Price. Materials precisely standardized and traded on commodity exchanges, such as cotton, wheat, copper, or crude oil, are sometimes costed into production at the quoted price at date of issue. In effect, this procedure substitutes replacement cost for experienced or consumed cost and has the virtue of charging materials into production at a current and significant cost. This method of materials costing and that of using the last purchase price are often used for small, low-priced items.

Standard Cost. This method charges issued materials at a predetermined or estimated cost reflecting a normal or an expected future cost. Receipts and issues of materials are recorded in quantities only on the materials ledger records, thereby simplifying the record keeping and reducing clerical or data processing costs.

For materials purchases, the difference between actual and standard cost is recorded in a purchase price variance account. The variance account enables management to observe the extent to which actual materials costs differ from planned objectives or predetermined estimates. Materials are charged into production at the standard price, thereby eliminating the erratic costing inherent in the actual cost methods. Standard quantities for normal production runs at standard prices enable management to detect trouble areas and take corrective action immediately. Materials pricing under standard costs is discussed in Chapters 18 and 19.

Analysis and Comparison of Costing Methods

The several methods of costing materials represent industry's intense effort to measure costs. Undoubtedly, there is no one best method applicable to all situations. Methods may vary even within the same company, since the same method need not be used for the entire inventory of a business. Whatever method of costing is chosen, it should be followed consistently from period to period.

The various costing methods represent different views of the cost concept. The best method to use is the one that most clearly reflects periodic income when consumed cost is subtracted from current revenue. Perhaps no costing method will reflect consumed materials cost with complete accuracy at all times in all situations. The most appropriate method will, as nearly as pos-

---

[9]For a detailed discussion of dollar-value lifo, retail-dollar-value lifo, and other simplifying procedures, see Jay M. Smith, Jr. and K. Fred Skousen, *Intermediate Accounting*, 10th ed., (Cincinnati: South-Western Publishing Co., 1990), Chapter 10.

sible, (1) relate current cost to current sales; (2) reflect the procurement, manufacturing, and sales policies of a particular company; and (3) carry forward to the new fiscal period a previously incurred residual cost which will be consumed in subsequent periods.

Adequate comparison of the various methods of costing is difficult and involved. However, certain generalizations can be made relative to the use of fifo, average cost, and lifo. In periods of rising prices, fifo costing will result in materials being charged out at lowest costs; lifo will result in materials being charged out at highest costs; and average costing will result in a figure between the two. In a period of falling prices, the reverse situation will develop, with fifo showing the highest cost of materials consumed, lifo showing the lowest cost of materials used, and average cost showing a result between the other two methods.

For internal costing purposes, the average method dominates because of the advantages already described for it and because of the awkwardness of both the fifo and lifo methods. For external purposes, i.e., for financial reporting and for income tax purposes, the lifo method is more likely to be used, largely because of the income tax advantage associated with patterns of rising prices. Lifo for external costing purposes will usually be dollar-value lifo. To restate inventory from the cost assigned for internal costing purposes to the amounts computed for external purposes, an end-of-the-period inventory adjustment is required, with the offset debited or credited to Cost of Goods Sold. The adjustment is then reversed at the beginning of the next accounting period.

JUST-IN-TIME

Increasingly, companies emphasize the minimization of inventory investment and employ just-in-time inventory procedures to achieve a reduction in inventories and to more efficiently manage production planning and control. Such efforts to reduce inventory de-emphasize the impact on financial statements that result from selecting one costing method versus another. In the extreme case of a fully implemented just-in-time system, the total cost of inventories, and certainly the impacts of different costing methods, are immaterial to the firm's overall financial condition.

CASB Costing of Materials

In accounting for government contracts to which CASB regulations apply, materials may be charged directly to a contract if the contract is specifically identified at the time of purchase or manufacture. Materials drawn from company-owned inventory can be priced using fifo, lifo, average, or the standard costing method. However, the method(s) selected must be used consistently for similar categories of materials. Furthermore, the contractor must prepare in writing the procedure for accumulating and allocating the cost of materials.[10]

---

[10]*Standards, Rules and Regulations, Part 411,* "Accounting for Acquisition Costs of Materials" (Washington, D. C.: Cost Accounting Standards Board, 1975), p. 226.

Transfer of Materials Cost to Finished Production

The ultimate, intended destination of direct materials is finished products delivered to customers. The cost of materials used on each job or in each department is transferred from the materials requisition to the job order cost sheet or to the cost of production report. When the job or process is completed, the effect of materials used, as well as labor distributed and factory overhead applied, is expressed in the following entry:

```
Finished Goods. . . . . . . . . . . . . . . . . . . . . . . . . . . . . . . . . . . . . . . . . . . . . .    xxxx
      Work in Process . . . . . . . . . . . . . . . . . . . . . . . . . . . . . . . . . . . . . . . .         xxxx
```

If a considerable portion of production is to be used for stock, a finished goods ledger is advantageous in maintaining adequate and proper control over the inventory. The finished goods ledger, controlled by the finished goods account in the general ledger, is similar in form and use to materials ledger records.

In production devoted to filling specific customer orders, cost sheets should provide sufficient information for a charge directly to the cost of goods sold account. Furthermore, the material cost to be assigned to ending work in process and finished goods inventories may be a result of backflush costing procedures, such as those discussed in Chapter 3, in a just-in-time production environment.

Some production may consist of components manufactured for use in subsequent manufacturing operations. If the units move directly into these operations, the transfer is simply from one departmental work in process account to the next. However, if the components must be held in inventory, their cost should be debited to Materials and credited to Work in Process.

■ INVENTORY VALUATION AT COST OR MARKET, WHICHEVER IS LOWER

American accounting principles follow the practice of pricing year-end inventories (materials as well as work in process and finished goods) at *cost or market, whichever is lower.* This departure from any experienced cost basis is generally defended on the grounds of conservatism. A more logical justification for cost or market inventory valuation is that a full stock is necessary to expedite production and sales. If physical deterioration, obsolescence, and price declines occur, or if stock when finally utilized cannot be expected to realize its stated cost plus a normal profit margin, the reduction in inventory value is an additional cost of the goods produced and sold during the period when the decline in value occurred.

Cost or Market Rules

Generally accepted accounting principles state that cost may properly be determined by any of the common methods already discussed in this chapter, but that cost must be abandoned in valuing inventory when the usefulness of goods is no longer as great as cost. This principle of *cost or residual useful cost, whichever is lower,* is described as follows:

> *Where there is evidence that the utility of goods, in their disposal in the ordinary course of business, will be less than cost whether due to physical deterioration, obsolescence, changes in price levels, or other causes, the difference should be recognized as a loss of the current period. This is generally accomplished by stating such goods at a lower level commonly designated as* market.
>
> *As used in the phrase* lower of cost or market, *the term "market" means current replacement cost (by purchase or by reproduction, as the case may be) except that:*
>
> 1. *Market should not exceed the net realizable value (i.e., estimated selling price in the ordinary course of business less reasonably predictable costs of completion and disposal); and*
> 2. *Market should not be less than net realizable value reduced by an allowance for an approximately normal profit margin.*[11]

In analyzing the cost or market approach to inventory valuation, it is clear that the rules do not indicate that a replacement cost should be used for inventory value merely because it is lower than the acquisition cost figure. The real test is the usefulness of the inventory (whether it will sell at its cost). The rules in regard to inventory valuation may be interpreted as follows:

1. In principle, inventories are to be priced at cost.
2. Where cost cannot be recovered upon sale in the ordinary course of business, a lower figure is to be used.
3. This lower figure is normally market replacement cost, except that the amount should not exceed the expected sales price less a deduction for costs yet to be incurred in making the sale. On the other hand, this lower market figure should not be less than the expected amount to be realized in the sale of the goods, reduced by a normal profit margin.

To illustrate, assume that a certain commodity sells for $1; the marketing expense is $.20; the normal profit is $.25. The lower of cost or market as limited by the foregoing concepts is developed in each case as shown on the top of the next page.[12]

The lower of cost or market procedure may be applied to each inventory item, to major inventory groupings, or to the inventory as a whole. Application of this procedure to the individual inventory items will result in the lowest inventory value. However, application to inventory groups or to the inventory as a whole may provide a sufficiently conservative valuation with less effort. The application method selected by a company must be followed consistently from period to period. The mix within a group or within the total inventory should not change erratically from period to period, so that inventory value is not distorted by the mix changes.

---

[11]*Accounting Research and Terminology Bulletins—Final Edition* (New York: American Institute of Certified Public Accountants, 1961), pp. 30-31.

[12]Adapted from Jay M. Smith, Jr. and K. Fred Skousen, *Intermediate Accounting,* 10th ed. (Cincinnati: South-Western Publishing Co., 1990), Chapter 10.

Case	Cost	Replace-ment Cost	Market — Floor (Estimated Sales Price Less Costs of Completion and Disposal and Normal Profit)	Market — Ceiling (Estimated Sales Price Less Costs of Completion and Disposal)	Market (Limited by Floor and Ceiling Values)	Lower of Cost or Market
A	$.65	$ .70	$.55	$.80	$.70	$.65
B	.65	.60	.55	.80	.60	.60
C	.65	.50	.55	.80	.55	.55
D	.50	.45	.55	.80	.55	.50
E	.75	.85	.55	.80	.80	.75
F	.90	1.00	.55	.80	.80	.80

A: Market is not limited by floor or ceiling; cost is less than market.
B: Market is not limited by floor or ceiling; market is less than cost.
C: Market is limited to floor; market is less than cost.
D: Market is limited to floor; cost is less than market.
E: Market is limited to ceiling; cost is less than market.
F: Market is limited to ceiling; market is less than cost.

Adjustments for Cost or Market, Whichever Is Lower

The problem of year-end inventory valuation is primarily a matter of sepa-rating: (1) the materials cost consumed in products manufactured and sold to customers from (2) the cost assignable to goods in inventory ready to move into production and to be available for sales the next fiscal period. This is important because the materials ledger records would have to be adjusted for any change in unit prices if there is a departure from cost. However, the detailed task of changing hundreds of individual inventory subsidiary ledger accounts may be cumbersome and time-consuming, if not impossible. The difficulty arises from the lower of cost or market procedure, which may be applied to inventory groups or to the inventory as a whole and the fact that the new unit price generally is not available to the materials ledger clerk until some time after the year-end inventory is priced. Instead of adjusting the subsidiary ledger records, companies may create an inventory valuation ac-count, as illustrated by the following journal entry:

	Subsidiary Record	Dr.	Cr.
Cost of Goods Sold (or Factory Overhead Control)........		5,000	
Inventory Adjustment—Lower of Cost or Market	5,000		
Materials—Allowance for Inventory Decline to Market...			5,000

If the debit is to Factory Overhead Control, the effect is to increase the amount of the underapplied factory overhead or decrease the amount of overapplied factory overhead.

Use of the valuation account retains the cost of the inventory and at the same time reduces the materials inventory for statement purposes to the desired cost or market, whichever is lower valuation, without disturbing the mate-rials subsidiary ledger records. The preceding entry should result in the fol-lowing balance sheet presentation:

Materials, at cost $100,000
Less allowance for inventory decline to market   5,000
Materials, at cost or market, whichever is lower. $95,000

The net charge to Cost of Goods Sold may be shown in the cost of goods sold statement or deducted from the ending inventory at cost, thus increasing the cost of materials used. In the subsequent fiscal period, Materials—Allowance for Inventory Decline to Market is closed out to Cost of Goods Sold (or Factory Overhead Control) to the extent necessary to bring the materials consumed that are still carried at a higher cost to the desirable lower cost level.

Whenever the lower of cost or market procedure is applied to each inventory item and the adjustment of individual materials ledger records to a lower market figure is not burdensome, and when the data are available early in the next year, the adjustment should be made by dating the entry as the last day of the fiscal period just ended and entering in the Inventory section the units on hand at the unit price determined for inventory purposes. In such a case, the credit portion of the adjusting entry would be to the materials account.

■ INVENTORY PRICING AND INTERIM FINANCIAL REPORTING

In general, companies should use the same inventory pricing methods and should make provisions for interim-period write-downs to market on the same basis as that used when preparing annual financial statements. However, the following exceptions are appropriate at interim reporting dates:

1. Some companies use estimated gross profit rates to determine the cost of goods sold during interim periods or use other methods different from those used at annual inventory dates. These companies should disclose the method used at the interim date and any significant adjustments that result from reconciliations with the annual physical inventory.

2. Companies that use the lifo method may encounter a liquidation of base period inventories at an interim date that is expected to be replaced by the end of the annual period. In such cases the inventory at the interim reporting date should not give effect to the lifo liquidation, and cost of sales for the interim reporting period should include the expected cost of replacement of the liquidated lifo base.

3. Inventory losses from market declines should not be deferred beyond the interim period in which the decline occurs. Recoveries of such losses on the same inventory in later interim periods of the same fiscal year through market price recoveries should be recognized as gains in the later interim period. Such gains should not exceed previously recognized losses. Some market declines at interim dates, however, can reasonably be expected to be restored in the fiscal year. Such *temporary*

market declines need not be recognized at the interim date, since no loss is expected to be incurred in the fiscal year.[13]

The second exception indicates that if the liquidation of base period inventories is considered temporary and is expected to be replaced prior to year end, the company should charge Cost of Goods Sold at current prices. The difference between the carrying value of the inventory and its current replacement cost is a current liability for replacement of temporarily depleted lifo base inventory. When the liquidated inventory is replaced, inventory is debited for the original lifo value, and the liability is removed from the books.

■ SUMMARY OF MATERIALS MANAGEMENT

Materials managers are constantly confronted with the following problems and requirements:

1. Inventories account for a sizable portion of the working capital requirements of many businesses. This fact makes materials and/or inventory management a major concern requiring constant attention.
2. The need for materials management has become even more acute due to market conditions and inflation.
3. Effective materials management and materials control is found in an organization in which individuals have been vested with responsibility for, and authority over, the various details of procuring, maintaining, and disposing of inventory. Such persons must have the ability to obtain, coordinate, and evaluate the necessary facts and to take action when and where needed.

DISCUSSION QUESTIONS

Q8-1. List the documents most frequently used in the procurement and use of materials.

Q8-2. How is an invoice approved for payment?

Q8-3. If a firm purchases raw materials from its supplier on a 2/10, n/60 cash discount basis, what is the equivalent annual interest rate (using a 360-day year) of foregoing the cash discount?

Q8-4. Diane Company, a retailer and wholesaler of national brand name household lighting fixtures, purchases its inventories from various suppliers.
(a) What criteria should be used to determine which of Diane's costs are inventoriable?
(b) Are Diane's administrative costs inventoriable? Explain.
(AICPA adapted)

---

[13]*Opinion of the Accounting Principles Board, No. 28,* "Interim Financial Reporting" (New York: American Institute of Certified Public Accountants, 1973), par 14.

Q8-5. What is the purpose of just-in-time inventory procedures?

Q8-6. Describe the fundamental cost flow assumptions of the average cost, fifo, and lifo inventory costing methods.

Q8-7. Discuss the reasons for using lifo in an inflationary economy.

Q8-8. During a period of oil price decline, oil companies were accused of making excess profits when the prices at the pump did not fall as quickly as the prices at the well head. In order to report a lower profit to offset the criticism, would lifo or fifo be used. Explain.   CGA-Canada (adapted)
Reprint with permission

Q8-9. Proponents of lifo and fifo procedures ascribe certain merits to each. Identify the inventory procedure, lifo or fifo, to which the following features are attributed:
(a) Matches actual physical flow of goods.
(b) Matches old costs with new prices.
(c) Costs inventory at approximate replacement cost.
(d) Matches new costs with new prices.
(e) Emphasizes the balance sheet.
(f) Emphasizes the income statement.
(g) Opens door for profit manipulation.
(h) Understates the current ratio in a period of inflation.

(i) Overstates inventory turnover in a period of inflation.
(j) Gives higher profits in a period of inflation.
(k) Matches current cost with current revenue.
(l) Reflects more accurately the profit available to owners.
(m) Gives lower profits in a period of deflation.
(n) Results in a procession of costs in the same order as incurred.
CGA-Canada (adapted)
Reprint with permission

Q8-10. Does the method of inventory costing have its principal effect on the balance sheet or on the income statement?

Q8-11. From the viewpoint of accounting theory, why are inventories valued at cost or market, whichever is lower?

Q8-12. Explain how market is determined in the application of the lower cost or market rules.

Q8-13. In applying inventory valuation at cost or market, whichever is lower, the replacement cost of the inventories is below the net realizable value less a normal profit margin, which, in turn, is below the original cost. What amount should be used to value the inventories? Why?
(AICPA adapted)

EXERCISES

E8-1. **Cost of acquiring materials—freight in.** An invoice for Part A, Part B, and Part C is received from the Icerman Company. Invoice totals are: Part A, $8,600; Part B, $5,060; and Part C, $3,840. The freight charges on this shipment weighing 1 400 kilograms is $280. Weights for the respective materials are 630, 490, and 280 kilograms.

Required:
(1) Allocate freight to materials based on cost.
(2) Allocate freight to materials based on shipping weight.

SS E8-2. **Materials costing methods.** Landry Company made the following materials purchases and issues during January:

Inventory: January 1—500 units @ $1.20   Issues: January 15—560
Receipts: January 6—200   @ 1.25   27—400
                  10—400   @ 1.30
                  25—500   @ 1.40

Required: Compute the cost of materials consumed and the cost assigned to the inventory at the end of the month, using a perpetual inventory system and:

(1) Average costing, rounding unit costs to the nearest cent.
(2) Fifo costing.
(3) Lifo costing.

E8-3. Materials costing methods. John Company, which uses a perpetual inventory system, has the following July data for one of its inventory items.

Inventory: July 1—200 units @ $40
Receipts: July 9— 50 units @ 50
               15—100 units @ 60
               20—100 units @ 65
Issues: July 14— 80 units
               26—150 units

Required: Compute the cost of materials consumed and the cost assigned to the inventory at the end of July using:

(1) Average costing, rounding unit costs to the nearest cent.
(2) Fifo costing.
(3) Lifo costing.   CGA-Canada (adapted) Reprint with permission

E8-4. Average costing method—perpetual and periodic inventory costing. The following information was available from Wentz Company's January inventory records:

	Units	Unit Cost	Total Cost
Balance at January 1	2,000	$ 9.775	$19,550
Received			
January 6	1,500	10.300	15,450
January 26	3,400	10.750	36,550
Issued			
January 7	1,800		
January 31	3,200		
Balance at January 31	1,900		

Required: Compute the cost of materials used and the cost assigned to the January 31 inventory, using (1) perpetual inventory records and the average costing method, and (2) the periodic inventory costing system at average cost. For (2), round the unit cost to the nearest cent and add the rounding difference to the cost of materials used.   (AICPA adapted)

E8-5. Lifo costing method—perpetual and periodic inventory costing. Transaction during December for the inventory of model XL water pump gaskets were as follows:

December 1 (balance on hand) ....   90 @ $5.00
Purchases:
    December 4 ....   310 @ 5.10
    December 14 ....   425 @ 5.00
    December 20 ....   475 @ 4.80
Sales:
    December 7 ....   300 @ 7.00

| December 16..................... | 200 @ 7.00 |
| December 22..................... | 400 @ 7.00 |

Required: Compute the December cost of goods sold assuming:
  (1) Lifo perpetual.
  (2) Lifo periodic.   CGA-Canada (adapted) Reprint with permission

E8-6. Inventory costing related to gross profit. Financial data for Cassidy Company for May include the following for one of its stock items:

	Units	Total Dollars
Beginning Inventory	200	$10,000
Purchases:		
May 5................	400	22,000
May 19...............	500	26,500
Sales:		
May 23...............	700	40,000 (sales dollars)

Required:
  (1) Assuming that a perpetual inventory system is used, compute gross profit for each of the following cost flow assumptions: average, fifo, and lifo. Detail cost of goods sold, including beginning and ending inventory.
  (2) If a periodic inventory system were in use, would the answers in (1) be different in this particular situation?   CGA-Canada (adapted) Reprint with permission

E8-7. Inventory costing method related to income computation. Ajax Company uses lifo in costing inventory. During its first three years of operations, the year-end inventory, computed by different methods for comparative purposes, was as follows:

	Ending Inventory		
	19A	19B	19C
Lifo................	$360,000	$400,000	$320,000
Fifo................	300,000	320,000	280,000
Average cost	340,000	420,000	300,000

Operating income computed using the lifo method was: 19A, $80,000; 19B, $140,000; 19C, $60,000.

Required: Determine operating income, using the (a) fifo method and (b) average cost method.
                                        CGA-Canada (adapted) Reprint with permission

E8-8. Fifo, lifo, and cash flow. Due to rising prices for materials, the problem of using the most appropriate inventory costing method has become acute. With the wide variety of methods available to account for inventories, it is important to select one that will be the most beneficial for a company. To illustrate, assume that two companies are almost identical, except that one uses fifo and the other lifo costing. Both companies have a beginning inventory of 200 units @ $2 per unit. The ending inventory is 240 units. The price paid for all purchases during the fiscal period was $2.40 per unit, and sales totaled 180 items at a sales price of $3.60. The income tax rate is 50% for both companies.

Required:
  (1) Compute the amount of total materials available for sale.
  (2) Prepare income statements showing aftertax earnings for both companies.
  (3) Compute the cost assigned to the ending inventory, based on the fifo and lifo costing methods.
  (4) Determine the cash position at the end of the fiscal year, assuming that all transactions, materials purchases, sales, and income tax were paid in cash.
  (5) Write a brief evaluation of the results.

E8-9. Inventory valuation at cost or market, whichever is lower. The following information has been gathered for four inventory items:

Item	Original Cost	Replacement Cost	Sales Price	Estimated Cost to Complete and Sell	Normal Profit Margin
Delta	$ .67	$ .62	$ .72	$.04	$.08
Sigma	2.20	2.12	2.22	.12	.08
Beta	.19	.20	.24	.03	.01
Nu	.93	.87	.97	.05	.04

Required: Determine the unit value that would be assigned to each item for inventory valuation purposes, using the lower of cost or market rules.

E8-10. Materials costing methods and cost or market, whichever is lower. The following lots of a particular material were available for use during the year:

Beginning inventory	20 units @ $80
First purchase.	20 @ 82
Second purchase	30 @ 85
Third purchase	30 @ 87
Ending inventory.	25

The company uses a periodic inventory system.

Required:
(1) Compute the cost assigned to ending inventory, assuming fifo as the costing method.
(2) Compute the cost assigned to ending inventory, assuming fifo as the costing method, if the current replacement cost is $86 per unit and if this replacement cost is between the ceiling and the floor of the rules for cost or market, whichever is lower.
(3) Compute the cost assigned to ending inventory, assuming the average costing method.
(4) Compute the cost assigned to ending inventory, assuming lifo as the costing method.

CGA-Canada (adapted) Reprint with permission

E8-11. Inventory valuation at cost or market, whichever is lower. EAH Corporation uses the lower of cost or market rules to value inventory. Data regarding items in work in process inventory are as follows:

	Inventory Item		
	Markers	Pens	Highlighters
Cost	$12,000	$ 9,440	$15,000
Sales price	18,000	18,000	18,000
Estimated cost to complete	2,400	2,400	3,400
Replacement cost.	10,400	8,400	15,900
Normal profit margin as a percentage of sales price	25%	25%	10%

Required:
(1) Identify the value for cost to be used in the lower of cost or market comparison for markers.
(2) Compute the market value to be used in the lower of cost or market comparison for pens.
(3) Determine the inventory valuation for highlighters, using the lower of cost or market method.

(ICMA adapted)

E8-12. Journal entries to correct materials accounts. The following transactions were completed by Patterson Company:
(a) The inventory of materials on the average costing basis was $4,200 and represented a book quantity of 8,000 units. An actual count showed 7,780 units.
(b) Materials of $150 issued to Job 182 should have been charged to the Repair Department.
(c) Excess materials returned from the factory amounted to $382 for Job 257.

(d) Materials returned to vendor amounted to $165. Freight out on this shipment, to be borne by Patterson Company, was $14, paid in cash.

(e) Finished goods returned by customers: cost, $1,500; sales price, $2,100.

(f) Materials requisitions totaled $4,814.50, of which $214.50 represented supplies used.

(g) Materials purchased and placed in stockroom, $6,150, of which $500 represented supplies. Freight in paid, applicable to direct materials, was $70.

(h) Supplies returned to the storeroom, $150.

Required: Prepare the journal entries or adjustments, if any, for each of the above transactions. Carry all computations to three decimal places. Indicate the appropriate subsidiary ledger account for debits or credits to Factory Overhead Control.

PROBLEMS

P8-1. Applied acquisition costs. Franklin Industries, Inc. records incoming materials at invoice price less cash discounts plus applied receiving and handling cost. For product Cango, the following data are available:

	Budgeted for the Month	Actual Cost for the Month
Freight in and cartage in	$ 2,500	$ 2,580
Purchasing Department cost	4,800	4,500
Receiving Department cost	3,900	4,200
Storage and handling	4,200	3,800
Testing, spoilage, and rejects	2,600	3,120
Total	$18,000	$18,200

The purchasing budget shows estimated net purchases of $144,000 for the month. Actual invoices net of discounts total $148,500 for the month.

Required:
(1) Determine the applied acquisition costing rate for the month.
(2) Determine the amount of applied cost added to materials purchased during the month.
(3) Indicate the possible disposition to be made of the variance.

P8-2. Materials costing methods. Adams Corporation had the following purchases and issues during March:

March	1	Beginning balance: 750 units @ $20 per unit
	3	Purchased 400 units @ $19.50 per unit
	5	Issued 600 units
	12	Purchased 350 units @ $21.50 per unit
	15	Issued 500 units
	18	Purchased 500 units @ $22 per unit
	22	Issued 400 units
	26	Purchased 550 units @ $21 per unit
	28	Issued 650 units
	31	Purchased 200 units @ $20 per unit

Required: Compute the cost of units issued and the cost assigned to the March 31 inventory by each of these perpetual inventory costing methods:
(1) First-in, first-out.
(2) Last-in, first-out.
(3) Average, rounding unit cost to 1/10 cent.

P8-3. Inventory costing methods. A corporation that uses a perpetual inventory system had the following transactions during June:

June	1	Beginning balance: 200 units @ $3.00 per unit.
	2	Purchased 500 units @ $3.20 per unit.
	7	Issued 400 units.
	11	Purchased 300 units @ $3.30 per unit.
	14	Issued 400 units.
	17	Purchased 400 units @ $3.20 per unit.
	21	Issued 200 units.
	24	Purchased 300 units @ $3.40 per unit.
	26	Purchased 400 units @ $3.50 per unit.
	29	Issued 600 units.

Sales were 1,600 units @ $7 per unit. Marketing and administrative expenses totaled $2,100.

Required:
(1) Prepare comparative statements based on the transactions for June, using the lifo and fifo methods and a 40% income tax rate.
(2) For each costing method, determine the cash position at the end of June, assuming that all transactions, purchases, sales, and nonmanufacturing expenses were paid in cash.

P8-4. Inventory costing methods. The records of the Redgrave Trading Company show the following data about Item A:

Balance, January 1. . . . .   200 units @ $10 per unit

		Purchases	
	Units	Purchase Price per Unit	Sales Units
January 12	100	$11	
February 1			200
April 16	200	12	
May 1			100
July 15	100	14	
November 10			100
December 5	200	17	
	600		400

The sales price for Item A was $15 per unit throughout the year.

Required:
(1) Compute the cost of the ending inventory under the fifo method when a periodic inventory system is used.
(2) Compute the cost of the ending inventory under the lifo method (a) when a periodic inventory system is used and (b) when a perpetual inventory system is used.
(3) Assume the sale of February 1 was on credit, that perpetual inventory records were maintained, and the cost per unit sold was $10. Prepare the required journal entries to record this transaction.

                                                   CGA-Canada (adapted) Reprint with permission

P8-5. Inventory costing and valuation. Grant Company uses perpetual inventory costing for inventory Item 407, which it purchases for resale. The company began its operations on January 1 and is in the process of preparing its first financial statements.

Upon examining the inventory ledger and other accounting records, the following information was gathered pertaining to the first four months of operations:

	Purchases			Sales	
	Units	Cost per Unit			Units
January 2.........	2,000	$5	January 15		500
February 2	1,200	6	January 31		700
March 2	1,500	8	February 15		600
April 2............	1,900	7	February 28		900
			March 15		600
			March 31		800
			April 15.............		700
			April 30.............		700

On April 30, the following additional information was obtained:
(a) Current replacement cost, $6.50 per unit.
(b) Net realizable value, $8 per unit.
(c) Net realizable value reduced by a normal profit margin, $5 per unit.

Management has not decided which of the following three inventory costing methods should be selected to evaluate the cost of goods sold:
(a) Average method.
(b) First-in, first-out method.
(c) Last-in, first-out method.

Required:
(1) Prepare the perpetual inventory ledger for Item 407, using each of the above methods. (Carry all computations to three decimal places.)
(2) Prepare a comparative statement showing the effect of each method on gross profit. The sales price is $10 per unit.
(3) Prepare the necessary adjusting journal entry under each of the three inventory costing methods, assuming that the company decides to show its April 30 inventory at the lower of cost or market.

CGA-Canada (adapted) Reprint with permission

P8-6. Cost or market, whichever is lower. WorthCo manufactures radios and quartz clocks for the automobile industry, and clock radios that are sold to several national retailers. WorthCo assumes a first-in, first-out cost flow and uses normal absorption costing in its perpetual inventory system. Actual costs are used for all manufacturing costs except overhead. All overhead is applied to production by means of predetermined overhead rates. The balances of the inventory accounts at the end of WorthCo's fiscal year on November 30, 19A, are as shown below. The inventories are stated at cost before any year-end adjustments.

Finished goods.........	$400,000
Work in process	75,000
Raw materials..........	200,000
Factory supplies	45,000

The following information pertains to WorthCo's inventory and operations. All amounts are to be considered material in relation to WorthCo's financial statements taken as a whole.
(a) The finished goods inventory is comprised of the items listed at the top of page 236 that have been analyzed for inventory valuation purposes.
(b) One half of the LED clock radios (both AM/FM and stereo) in the finished goods inventory are held by retailers on consignment. The $7,500 cost of shipping these radios to the consignees was charged to delivery expense.
(c) One fourth of the raw materials balance represents microchips acquired at a contracted price 25% greater than the current market price. The market value of the rest of the raw materials is $151,500.
(d) For all elements of the work in process inventory, cost is significantly below market value.

	Cost	Market
Radios:		
Model I.............	$ 62,500	$ 51,600
Model II	42,500	57,000
Total radios	$105,000	$108,600
Clocks:		
LED	$ 57,800	$ 58,300
Analog	23,000	19,900
Total clocks	$ 80,800	$ 78,200
Clock radios:		
LED AM/FM	$ 58,000	$ 62,000
LED stereo	92,000	97,000
Analog AM/FM	38,100	39,800
Analog stereo.....	26,100	24,900
Total clock radios ..	$214,200	$223,700
Total finished goods..	$400,000	$410,500

(e) Included in the factory supplies are obsolete items having no disposal value and with a historical cost of $8,000. The market value of the remaining factory supplies is $34,000.

(f) WorthCo applies the lower of cost or market rule to the total of the components of each major category in its finished goods inventory. For each of the other three inventory accounts, WorthCo applies the lower of cost or market rule to the total of each inventory account.

Required: Prepare the inventory section of WorthCo's balance sheet of November 30, 19A, including any inventory related note(s) that would be required.   (ICMA adapted)

P8-7. Fifo and cost or market, whichever is lower. Kenny Company, a food wholesaler, supplies independent grocery stores in the immediate region. The company has a fifo inventory system for all of its food products. Kenny records all purchases, net of purchases discounts, and takes all purchases discounts. The following transactions and other related information regarding two items (instant coffee and sugar) are given for October, the last month of Kenny's fiscal year.

	Instant Coffee	Sugar
Standard unit of packaging:	Case containing 24 one-pound jars	Baler containing 12 five-pound bags
Inventory, October 1:	1,200 cases @ $53.22 per case	600 balers @ $6.50 per baler
Purchases (before purchases discounts):	October 10—1,600 cases @ $56.40 per case plus freight of $480. October 20—1,600 cases @ $57 per case plus freight of $480.	October 5—640 balers @ $5.76 per baler, plus freight of $320. October 16—640 balers @ $5.40 per baler, plus freight of $320. October 24—640 balers @ $5.04 per baler, plus freight of $320.
Purchase terms:	2/10, net/30, FOB shipping point	Net 30 days, FOB shipping point
October sales:	3,400 cases @ $76 per case	2,200 balers @ $7.80 per baler
Sales terms:	1/10, net/30, FOB shipping point	1/10, net/30 FOB shipping point
Returns and allowances:	A customer returned 50 cases which had been shipped by error. The customer's account was credited for $3,800.	As the October 16 purchase was unloaded, 20 balers were discovered to be damaged. A representative of the trucking firm confirmed the damage and the balers were discarded. Credit of $108 for the merchandise and $10 for the freight was received by Kenny.

	Instant Coffee	Sugar
October 31:		
Most recent quoted price (before deducting purchases discounts, excluding freight)	$56.65 per case	$5.30 per baler
Net realizable value	$60.80 per case	$5.20 per baler
Net realizable value less a normal markup	$53.20 per case	$4.55 per baler

Required:

(1) Compute the number of units in inventory and the related unit cost for instant coffee and sugar as of October 31.

(2) Compute the total dollar amount of the October 31 instant coffee and sugar inventory, applying the lower of cost or market rules on an individual product basis.

(3) State whether or not the company could apply the lower of cost or market rule to groups of products or to the inventory as a whole, rather than on an individual product basis.   (ICMA adapted)

CHAPTER 9

Materials: Quantitative Models for Planning and Control

The planning and control of inventory from product design to final delivery are of considerable strategic significance to management. Inventories serve as a cushion between the production and consumption of goods and exist in various forms: materials awaiting processing; partially completed products or components; and finished goods at the factory, in transit, at warehouse distribution points, and in retail outlets. At each of these stages, a sound economic justification for the inventory should exist, since each additional unit carried in inventory generates some additional costs.

Any inventory planning and control method should have but one goal that might be expressed in two ways: (1) to minimize total cost or (2) to maximize profit within specified time and resource allocations. For example, the size of inventory at production sites should reflect the profitability inherent in large production runs, in the economic ordering, handling, and shipping of lots, and in the need for flexibility to meet uncertain future demand.

■ PLANNING MATERIALS REQUIREMENTS

Materials planning begins with the design of a product. Whether it is a regular product or a special contract, a series of planning stages is necessary to get materials into production. In the preliminary stages, the engineering department studies the proposal, design, blueprints, and other available specifications and prepares a product requirement statement. The tooling department studies the work details necessary to manufacture the product in a particular plant. The manufacturing control department examines production in terms of existing and contemplated production schedules. The materials planning and cost estimating departments study the cumulative information and submit a cost estimate for the production proposal. The long-range or economic planning section suggests a product price based on considerations of present product lines, economic conditions and expectations, company policies, and expansion plans. Executive management must finally decide whether to proceed with, reject, or modify the proposal.

To plan manufacturing requirements, every stock item or class of items must be analyzed periodically to:

1. Forecast demand for the next month, quarter, or year.
2. Determine acquisition lead time.
3. Plan usage during the lead time.
4. Establish quantity on hand.
5. Place units on order.
6. Determine reserve or safety stock requirements.

These six steps are illustrated below in determining the quantity to order in September for a November delivery. In this illustration, the *lead time*, the time between the order and delivery, is two months. The desired inventory cushion, or *safety stock* is approximately a two weeks' supply.

Planned or forecast usage from review date:		Units
September production		2,500
October production		2,000
November production		2,500
Desired inventory, November 30		1,000
Total to be provided		8,000
Quantity on hand, September 1	1,600	
On order for September delivery	2,000	
On order for October delivery	2,000	5,600
Quantity to order for November delivery		2,400

Future requirements for each purchased or produced item play a central role in materials control. If usage requirements are not accurately planned, even the most elaborate control system will result in the wrong level of inventory during and at the end of a future period.

Materials planning deals with two fundamental factors—the quantity and the time to purchase. Determination of how much and when to buy involves two conflicting kinds of cost—the cost of carrying inventory and the cost of inadequate carrying. The nature of these conflicting costs is indicated in the following comparison:

Cost of Carrying Inventory	Estimate	Cost of Inadequate Carrying
Interest on investment in working capital	10.00%	Extra purchasing, handling, and transportation costs
Property tax and insurance	1.25	Higher prices due to small order quantities
Warehousing or storage	1.80	Frequent stockouts resulting in disruptions of production schedules, overtime, and extra setup time
Handling	4.25	Additional clerical costs due to keeping customer back-order records
Deterioration and shrinkage of stocks	2.60	Inflation-oriented increases in prices when inventory purchases are deferred
Obsolescence of stocks	5.20	Lost sales and loss of customer goodwill
Total	25.10%	

Inventory Carrying and Ordering Costs for Economic Order Quantity Calculations

The *economic order quantity (EOQ)* is the amount of inventory to be ordered at one time for purposes of minimizing annual inventory cost. If a company buys in large quantities, the cost of carrying the inventory is high because of the sizable investment. If purchases are made in small quantities, frequent orders with correspondingly high ordering costs will result. Therefore, the quantity to order at a given time must be determined by balancing two factors: (1) the cost of possessing (carrying) materials and (2) the cost of acquiring (ordering) materials.

JUST-IN-TIME

In balancing these factors, full consideration must be given to the modern emphasis on minimizing inventory investment and the related benefits of achieving more efficient and effective manufacturing processes. The section in this chapter titled "Just-in-Time Materials Control" is especially relevant to contemporary applications and should be recognized as integral to the design and implementation of materials planning and control models and overall manufacturing systems.

The cost factors of carrying an inventory, listed previously, are expressed as percentages of the average inventory investment and can be estimated and measured. These cost factors should include only those costs that vary with the level of inventory. For example, in the case of warehousing or storage, only those costs that will vary with changes in the number of units ordered should be included. The cost of labor and equipment used in the storeroom normally is a fixed cost and should not be considered a part of the carrying charge. Similarly, the insurance cost is included only when the company has a monthly reporting type of policy with premiums charged on the fluctuating inventory value. A standard insurance policy for one year or more should be considered a fixed cost that is irrelevant to the decision.

QUALITY CONTROL

It is difficult to determine the costs of not carrying enough inventory; yet they must be considered in deciding upon order quantities and order points. Such costs include ordering costs, although the fixed cost of placing an order is not relevant. Only the variable or out-of-pocket cost of procuring an order should be included. Ordering costs include preparing the requisition and the purchase order, handling the incoming shipment and preparing a receiving report, communicating in case of quantity/quality errors or delays in receipts of materials, and accounting for the shipment and the payment. Other costs of not carrying enough inventory relate to such questions as savings in freight and quantity discounts as well as to the question of when to order, including an appropriate allowance for safety stock.

Depending upon many factors, it may cost from $10 to $50 or more to process an order and from 10 to 35 percent of the average inventory investment to hold materials. Techniques for analyzing cost behavior, described and illustrated in Chapter 12, should facilitate the determination of realistic carrying and ordering cost estimates, provided due consideration is given to current costs, including the impact of inflation. Mathematical and statistical techniques permit improved planning and control in an endeavor to maximize profits and minimize costs.

JUST-IN-TIME

Only variable costs are relevant in EOQ and order point computations. However, it is desirable to reduce not only variable costs but fixed inventory costs as well. Fixed costs, such as inventory storage space cost, can be reduced through procedures such as just-in-time materials control.

Tabular Determination of the Economic Order Quantity

A tabular arrangement of data relative to a materials item allows the determination of an approximate economic order quantity, and thereby the number of orders that need to be placed annually. To illustrate, assume the following data:

Estimated requirements for next year	2,400 units
Cost of the item per unit	$ .75
Ordering cost (per order)	$20.00
Inventory carrying cost (% of average inventory investment)	20%

Based on these data, various possible order sizes can be evaluated:

QUANTITATIVE DATA

Order size in units	300	400	800	1,200	2,400
Number of orders	8	6	3	2	1
Average inventory (order size ÷ 2)*	150	200	400	600	1,200

*A uniform rate of usage is assumed.

COST DATA

Average inventory investment	$112.50	$150	$300	$450	$900
Total carrying cost (20% of average inventory)	$ 22.50	$ 30	$ 60	$ 90	$180
Total ordering cost	160.00	120	60	40	20
Cost to order and carry	$182.50	$150	$120	$130	$200

Of the order sizes calculated, 800 is the most economical; thus, an order should be placed every four months. However, the most economical order size may not have been calculated; there may be some unit quantity between 400 and 800 or between 800 and 1,200 with a cost to order and carry that is lower than $120.

Graphic Determination of the Economic Order Quantity

The graph on page 242 shows the lowest point of the total-cost-to-order-and-carry curve, about $120, and the most economic order quantity of about 800 units. The ideal order size is the point where the sum of the ordering and carrying costs is at a minimum, i.e., where the total cost curve is at its lowest. This point generally occurs where the annual carrying charges equal the ordering charges, i.e., where these two cost lines intersect.

The Economic Order Quantity Formula

To determine the economic order quantity by a tabular or graphic method is lengthy and may not provide the most accurate answer. Companies using order-point calculations based upon economic order quantities usually prefer to use a formula. With information as to quantity required, unit price, inventory carrying cost percentage, and cost per order, differential calculus makes

Graphic
Determination of
the Economic
Order Quantity

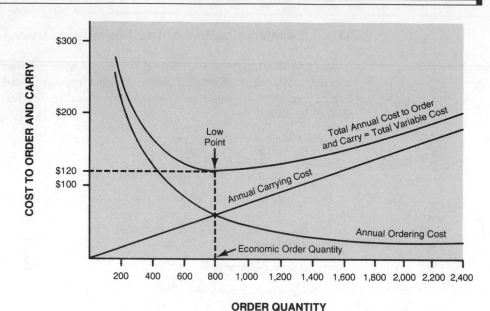

it possible to compute economic order quantity by formula. One formula variation follows:

$$\text{Economic order quantity} = \sqrt{\frac{2 \times \text{Annual required units} \times \text{Cost per order}}{\text{Cost per unit of material} \times \text{Carrying cost percentage}}}$$

$$OR \quad EOQ = \sqrt{\frac{2 \times RU \times CO}{CU \times CC}}$$

Given the terms EOQ, RU, CO, CU, and CC as specified, the formula is based on the following relationships:

$$\frac{RU}{EOQ} = \text{Number of orders placed annually}$$

$$\frac{RU \times CO}{EOQ} = \text{Annual ordering cost}$$

$$\frac{EOQ}{2} = \text{Average number of units in inventory at any point in time}$$

$$\frac{CU \times CC \times EOQ}{2} = \text{Annual carrying cost}$$

$$\frac{RU \times CO}{EOQ} + \frac{CU \times CC \times EOQ}{2} = \begin{array}{l}\text{Total annual cost of ordering and} \\ \text{carrying inventory, designated as AC}\end{array}$$

This latter equation is then solved, utilizing differential calculus to determine the minimum total annual cost of inventory:

$$AC = \frac{RU \times CO}{EOQ} + \frac{CU \times CC \times EOQ}{2}$$

$$AC = RU \times CO \times EOQ^{-1} + \frac{CU \times CC \times EOQ}{2}$$

$$\frac{dAC}{dEOQ} = -RU \times CO \times EOQ^{-2} + \frac{CU \times CC}{2}$$

$$\frac{dAC}{dEOQ} = \frac{-RU \times CO}{EOQ^2} + \frac{CU \times CC}{2}$$

$$Let\ \frac{dAC}{dEOQ} = 0;\quad \frac{-RU \times CO}{EOQ^2} + \frac{CU \times CC}{2} = 0$$

$$\frac{CU \times CC}{2} = \frac{RU \times CO}{EOQ^2}$$

$$EOQ^2 \times CU \times CC = 2 \times RU \times CO$$

$$EOQ^2 = \frac{2 \times RU \times CO}{CU \times CC}$$

$$EOQ = \sqrt{\frac{2 \times RU \times CO}{CU \times CC}}$$

The formula for the economic order quantity, or least-cost order quantity in units, is the square root of a fraction whose numerator is twice the product of the annual unit demand and the cost per order and whose denominator is the product of the unit price and the annual carrying rate. The result is an order quantity that makes the total annual ordering cost exactly equal to the total annual carrying cost. The formula assumes a uniform rate of materials usage. Using the formula, the EOQ for the data on page 241 is:

$$EOQ = \sqrt{\frac{2 \times 2,400 \times \$20}{\$.75 \times 20\%}} = \sqrt{\frac{\$96,000}{\$.15}} = \sqrt{640,000} = 800\ units$$

It is also possible to express EOQ in dollars rather than in units. The following formula is employed:

$$EOQ = \sqrt{\frac{2 \times RU \times CU \times CO}{CC}}$$

Using the data from the previous illustration, the EOQ in dollars is computed as follows:

$$EOQ = \sqrt{\frac{2 \times 2,400 \times \$.75 \times \$20}{20\%}} = \sqrt{\frac{\$72,000}{.20}} = \sqrt{\$360,000} = \$600\ total\ cost$$

The EOQ can be converted to units by dividing the EOQ total cost by the cost per unit ($600 ÷ $.75 = 800 units).

The following example is given to indicate the results when new cost data enter the formula, since any shift in cost data will affect the answer. Again, only those cost components that vary directly with order or production quantities should be used, i.e., the variable costs.

RU = 2,400 units of materials used per year (200 units per month)

CO = $10 ordering cost per order

CU = $1.50 cost per unit of materials

CC = 20% carrying cost as a percent of average inventory investment

$$EOQ = \sqrt{\frac{2 \times 2,400 \times \$10}{\$1.50 \times 20\%}} = \sqrt{\frac{\$48,000}{\$.30}} = \sqrt{160,000} = 400 \text{ units}$$

The economic order quantity for the stock item is 400 units, or six orders per year. Other order quantities resulting in more or less than six orders per year are not so economical, as proven by the following table, which is based on $3,600 (2,400 units × $1.50 cost per unit) annual usage of materials:

Orders per Year	Units per Order	Value per Order	Ordering Cost	Carrying Cost	Total Cost
1	2,400	$3,600	$10	$360	$370
2	1,200	1,800	20	180	200
3	800	1,200	30	120	150
4	600	900	40	90	130
5	480	720	50	72	122
6	400	600	60	60	120
7	343	515	70	52	122
8	300	450	80	45	125

In the EOQ formula as illustrated, the carrying cost per unit (the denominator in the formula) is the product of the acquisition cost per unit of material and the carrying cost expressed as a percentage of the average inventory investment (CU × CC). An alternative is to estimate the carrying cost per unit directly by itemizing each component of carrying cost as a cost per unit of holding items in inventory, rather than as a percentage of average inventory investment. Thus, the denominator in the EOQ formula becomes the carrying cost per unit expressed directly, instead of as CU × CC.

Quantity Price Discounts. By purchasing in quantities larger than the minimum, quantity price discounts and/or freight savings may be realized, resulting in a lower cost per unit and altering the economic order quantity. Buying in larger quantities also alters the frequency of orders, and thus changes the total ordering cost. At the same time, it involves a larger investment in inventories.

To illustrate, assume that annual usage of an inventory item is 3,600 units, costing $1 each, with no quantity discount available. The carrying cost is 20 percent of the average inventory investment, and the cost to place an order is $10. The EOQ is:

$$\sqrt{\frac{2 \times 3,600 \times \$10}{\$1 \times 20\%}} = \sqrt{\frac{\$72,000}{\$.20}} = \sqrt{360,000} = 600 \text{ units}$$

Now assume the availability of the following quantity discounts:

Order Size	Quantity Discount
3,600 units	8%
1,800	6
1,200	5
900	5
720	4½
600	4
450	4

The following table considers the effect of quantity price discounts, using a cost-comparison approach. Observe that the order quantity that minimizes total cost (900 units per order) differs from the EOQ computed when no quantity discount is available (600 units per order).

	Number of orders per year						
	1	2	3	4	5	6	8
List price per unit	$1	$1	$1	$1	$1	$1	$1
Quantity discount	8%	6%	5%	5%	4½%	4%	4%
Discount price per unit	$.92	$.94	$.95	$.95	$.955	$.96	$.96
Size of order in units.	3,600	1,800	1,200	900	720	600	450
Average inventory in units*	1,800	900	600	450	360	300	225
Cost of average inventory	$1,656.00	$ 846.00	$ 570.00	$ 427.50	$ 343.80	$ 288.00	$ 216.00
Annual cost of materials . . .(a)	$3,312.00	$3,384.00	$3,420.00	$3,420.00	$3,438.00	$3,456.00	$3,456.00
Carrying cost (20% of average) . . . .(b)	331.20	169.20	114.00	85.50	68.76	57.60	43.20
Cost to order . . . .(c)	10.00	20.00	30.00	40.00	50.00	60.00	80.00
Total cost per year (a) + (b) + (c)	$3,653.20	$3,573.20	$3,564.00	$3,545.50	$3,556.76	$3,573.60	$3,579.20

*(Size of order in units + 0) ÷ 2

With quantity discounts, the cost of materials is not constant but is affected by the quantity discount. Therefore, the objective becomes the identification of an order quantity that minimizes not only the sum of the ordering and carrying costs ((b) + (c) in the table), but the sum of these costs plus the cost of the materials, i.e., (a) + (b) + (c). Since variable carrying cost in this example is assumed to fluctuate directly with and is expressed as a percentage of the average inventory investment, carrying cost is affected by the quantity discount (since the cost per unit contained in the average inventory investment is reduced by the discount).

The EOQ Formula and Production Runs. The EOQ formula is equally appropriate in computing the optimum size of a production run, in which case CO represents an estimate of the setup cost and CU is the variable manufacturing cost per unit. To illustrate, assume that stock item A88 is manufactured rather than purchased; the setup cost (CO), such as the cost of labor to rearrange and adjust machines, is $62; variable manufacturing cost (CU) is $2 per unit; annual required units total 6,000; and the carrying cost is 20 percent. The optimum size of a production run is computed as follows:

$$\sqrt{\frac{2 \times 6{,}000 \text{ units} \times \$62 \text{ setup cost}}{\$2 \text{ variable manufacturing cost per unit} \times 20\%}} = \sqrt{\frac{\$744{,}000}{\$.40}} = \sqrt{1{,}860{,}000} = 1{,}364 \text{ units}$$

This formulation assumes that the entire production run is transferred to stock at one time; however, this is not always the case in actual practice. Often, while some units are being produced, other units are transferred to stock. At the same time, withdrawals are being made from stock, so that the maximum inventory level does not equal the lot size. As a consequence, average inventory and total carrying cost are less than that computed for the basic EOQ model. Since total annual ordering costs and total annual carrying costs must be equal in order to minimize inventory cost, the production quantity must be increased in order to reduce total annual ordering cost to the same level as total annual carrying cost. To adjust for the effect of this phenomenon, the following correction factor is multiplied times the EOQ formula:

$$\sqrt{\frac{P}{P-D}}$$

where P denotes the production rate and D is the demand (or usage) rate.[1]

Thus, in the example above, if P is 120 units per day and D is 24 units per day, then:

$$\sqrt{\frac{120}{120-24}} = \sqrt{\frac{120}{96}} = \sqrt{1.25} = 1.118$$

This factor is multiplied by the 1,364 units previously computed to obtain the adjusted production run quantity of 1,525 units. In a situation in which P is quite large in comparison to D, the correction factor approaches 1, in which case it would not alter materially the size of the production run and can be ignored.

This model assumes that the setup cost is constant for various production run quantities. In fact, the setup cost to put in place a larger production run may be greater than for a smaller quantity. This possibility should be considered if it is relevant and if it would shift the optimum quantity to a lower figure.

ROBOTICS

The reduction of setup costs permits reduced production runs and an associated lower investment in inventories. Reductions can come from improving equipment design, equipment and assembly line configurations, and worker training and attitude, and from computerized automation. For example, a computer-controlled robot machine tool does not care whether it makes one part 12 times or 12 different items, each just once. This factor alters the need to extend production runs of standard products, so that it only is necessary to produce enough variety of products to keep the factory going day after day and week after week. The savings from reduced investments in inventories thus is enhanced.

---

[1]Charles D. Mecimore and James K. Weeks, *Techniques in Inventory Management and Control* (Montvale, N.J.: National Association of Accountants, 1987), pp. 24-28.

Determining the Time to Order

The EOQ formula answers the quantity problem of inventory planning. However, the question of when to order is equally important. This question is controlled by three factors: (1) time needed for delivery, (2) rate of inventory usage, and (3) safety stock. Unlike the economic order quantity, the order point has no generally applicable and acceptable formula. Determining the order point would be relatively simple if *lead time*—the interval between placing an order and having materials on the factory floor ready for production—and the usage pattern for a given item were definitely predictable. For most stock items, there is a variation in either or both of these factors which almost always causes one of three results: (1) if lead time or usage is below expectation during an order period, the new materials will arrive before the existing stock is consumed, thereby adding to the cost of carrying inventory; (2) if lead time or usage is greater than expected, a *stockout* will occur with the resultant incurrence of costs associated with not carrying enough inventory; (3) if average or normal lead time and usage are used to determine an order point, a stockout could be expected on every other order.

Forecasting materials usage requires the expenditure of time and money. In materials management, forecasts are an expense as well as an aid to balancing the cost to acquire and the cost to carry inventory. Since perfect forecasts are rarely possible, an inventory cushion or safety stock is often the least costly device for protecting against a stockout. The basic problem is to determine the safety stock quantity. If the safety stock is greater than needed, the carrying cost will be too high; if too small, frequent stockouts will occur and inconveniences, disruptions, and additional costs will result. The optimum safety stock is that quantity which results in minimal total annual cost of stockouts and safety stock carrying cost. This carrying cost is determined in the same manner as in calculating the economic order quantity. The annual cost of stockouts depends upon the frequency of occurrence and the actual cost of each stockout.

To illustrate, assume that a company uses an item for which it places 10 orders per year, the cost of a stockout is $30[2], and the carrying cost is $.50 per unit. The following probabilities of a stockout have been estimated for various levels of safety stock:

Probability	Safety Stock Level
40%	0 units
20	50
10	100
5	200

---

[2]If the action taken in the event of a stockout is to stop the job for which there is a materials shortage and start up a new job, the stockout cost would equal the setup cost required for the change order. On the other hand, if production cannot be shifted to another product, it may be necessary to shut down the facility until the materials resupply arrives, in which case the stockout cost would vary depending upon the length of time the facility is shut down. The shut down period would likely be longer on average (and stockout cost higher) for smaller quantities of safety stock than for larger quantities.

The total carrying cost and stockout cost at each level of safety stock is determined as follows:

Safety Stock Level	Expected Annual Stockouts (Probability x Number of Orders)	Total Stockout Cost	Total Carrying Cost	Total Stockout and Carrying Cost
0 units	4.0	$120	-0-	$120
50	2.0	60	$ 25	85
100	1.0	30	50	80
200	.5	15	100	115

In this illustration, the optimum level of safety stock is 100 units, since the total stockout and safety stock carrying cost is minimized at this level. Such an analysis of important stock items leads to smooth operations and effective materials management.

Order Point Formula

Order points are based on usage during the time necessary to requisition, order, and receive materials, plus an allowance for protection against stockout. The *order point* is reached when inventory on hand and quantities due in are equal to the lead time usage quantity plus the safety stock quantity. In equation form, the order point may be expressed as:

$$I + QD = LTQ + SSQ, \text{ where:}$$

I = Inventory balance on hand
QD = Quantities due in from orders previously placed, materials transfers, and returns to stock
LTQ = Lead time quantity equals normal lead time in months, weeks, or days multiplied by normal month's, week's, or day's use
SSQ = Safety stock quantity

The following situations are illustrated, both of which are solved mathematically and graphically:

1. Usage and lead time are known with certainty; therefore, no safety stock is provided.
2. A safety stock is injected into the calculation.

Order Point Illustrated—No Safety Stock. Assume the weekly use of 175 units of a stock item, that a lead time of four weeks establishes an order point at 700 units (175 units × 4 weeks), and that the order quantity is 2,090 units. Each order provides a 12 weeks' supply (2,090 ÷ 175). Figure 1 shows the control pattern of this item if usage and lead time are definitely known. It is apparent that (1) if lead time is more than four weeks, a stockout will result; and (2) if usage exceeds 700 units in any four-week period following an order point, a stockout is inevitable. Since perfect prediction of usage and lead time is usually unrealistic, a safety stock allowance is needed.

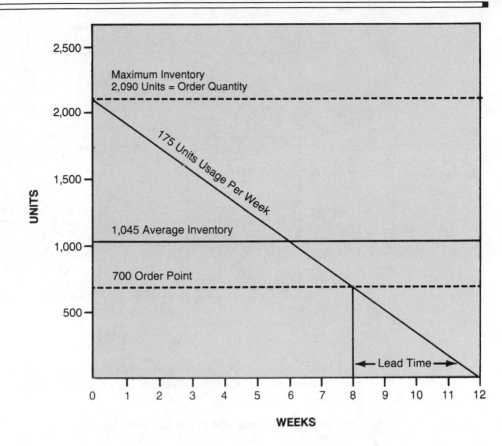

Figure 1—Rate of Usage and Lead Time Known with Certainty

Order Point Illustrated—Safety Stock. Assuming the same usage of 175 units per week, shown in Figure 1, with a lead time of normally four weeks but possibly as long as nine weeks, the order point would be 1,575 units: 700 units usage during normal lead time (175 units × 4 weeks) plus 875 units of safety stock (175 units × 5 weeks). Assuming a beginning inventory of 2,800 units and no orders outstanding, the usage, order schedule, and inventory levels would be:

2,800 units in beginning inventory
1,225 usage to order point (1,225 ÷ 175 weekly usage = 7 weeks)

1,575 order point
  700 usage during normal lead time (700 ÷ 175 weekly usage = 4 weeks)

  875 maximum inventory or safety stock at date of delivery, assuming normal lead time and usage
2,090 order quantity units received

2,965 maximum inventory, assuming normal lead time and usage

Figure 2 on page 250 depicts materials planning under the above assumptions and shows that a stockout would not occur unless lead time exceeds nine weeks, assuming normal usage.

In most businesses, a constant normal usage is not likely to occur because usage depends upon production schedules, and production depends upon sales. For instance, if the usage rate is as high as 210 units per week, with

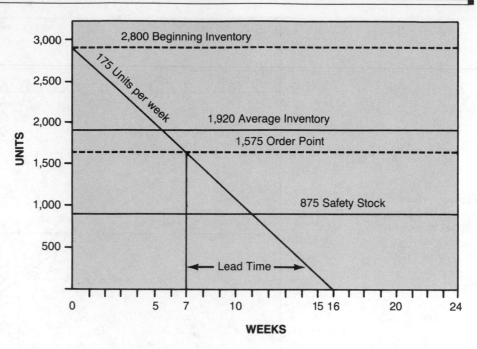

Figure 2—Rate of Usage Known with Certainty and Lead Time Known but Variable

lead time normally four weeks or possibly as long as nine weeks, the safety stock would be 1,190 units and the order point 1,890 units, calculated as follows:

Normal usage for normal lead time of four weeks (175 units × 4 weeks)		700 units
Safety stock:		
Normal usage for five weeks' delay (175 units × 5 weeks)	875	
Usage variation ((210 – 175) × 9 weeks)	315	1,190
Order point		1,890 units

Assuming a beginning inventory of 2,800 units, with no orders outstanding, the usage, order schedule, and inventory levels would be:

2,800 units in beginning inventory
  910 usage to order point (910 ÷ 210 maximum weekly usage = 4.3 weeks)

1,890 order point
  700 normal usage for normal lead time (700 ÷ 175 normal weekly usage = 4 weeks)

1,190 maximum inventory or safety stock at date of delivery, assuming normal lead time and usage
2,090 order quantity units received

3,280 maximum inventory, assuming normal lead time and usage

Figure 3 shows materials planning under the assumptions that the rate of usage and lead time are known but variable.

Safety Stock Calculations by Statistical Methods

The preceding situations tend to provide a safety stock for the extreme boundaries of usage and lead time variability. In other situations, the amount

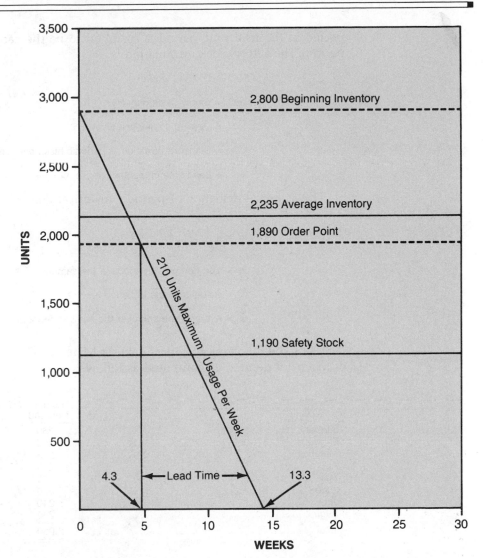

Figure 3—Rate of Usage and Lead Time Known but Variable

of safety stock is often calculated by traditional rules of thumb, such as a two-weeks' supply. These approaches have given way to statistical techniques which provide ways of determining the probability of incurring a stockout at different levels of safety stock, based on historical data. Such methods furnish management with a sound basis for determining the level of safety stock to carry. As the situation increases in complexity, computers may be used for handling calculations.

In the following paragraphs, two statistical techniques are discussed: (1) variability in demand and (2) deviations from forecast demand. The technique selected for use depends on which one most represents the conditions of a specific situation.

Variability in Demand. In this case, periodic demand is assumed to follow a random normal distribution, and the distribution of periodic demand expected in the lead time period is assumed to be the same as in the sample period. The safety stock formulation is:

$$SSQ = D \sigma \sqrt{L}, \text{ where:}$$

$$SSQ = \text{Safety stock quantity}$$

$$D = \text{Desired confidence level}$$

$$\sigma = \text{Standard deviation of periodic historical demand}$$

$$L = \text{Lead time in months, weeks, or days}$$

The standard deviation of periodic historical demand is defined as:

$$\sigma = \sqrt{\frac{\Sigma(x_i - \bar{x})^2}{n-1}}, \text{ where}$$

$$n = \text{The number of periods in the sample}$$

$$x_i = \text{Actual demand in period } i$$

$$\bar{x} = \text{Average demand over the sample period, i.e., } \frac{\Sigma x_i}{n}$$

Using the following historical data for Material J-2, the standard deviation of historical demand is computed as follows:

	x_i Actual Demand	$(x_i - \bar{x})$ Deviations from Mean	$(x_i - \bar{x})^2$ Deviations Squared
January	250	− 6.25	39.0625
February	225	−31.25	976.5625
March	275	18.75	351.5625
April	240	−16.25	264.0625
May	280	23.75	564.0625
June	260	3.75	14.0625
July	240	−16.25	264.0625
August	280	23.75	564.0625
Total	2,050	−0−	3,037.5000

$$\bar{x} = \frac{\Sigma x_i}{n} = \frac{2,050}{8} = 256.25$$

$$\sigma = \sqrt{\frac{\Sigma(x_i - \bar{x})^2}{n-1}} = \sqrt{\frac{3,037.5}{8-1}} = 20.83$$

Although demand usually is assumed to follow a normal distribution, for small samples, as in this illustration, the Student's t distribution is a more appropriate assumption. A table of selected t values follows, based on the assumption that only one tail of the distribution is of interest, i.e., that managers are concerned about the occurrence rather than the nonoccurrence of a stockout:

Degrees of Freedom (df)[3]	Desired Confidence Level			
	95%	97.5%	99%	99.5%
1	6.314	12.706	31.821	63.657
2	2.920	4.303	6.965	9.925
3	2.353	3.182	4.541	5.841
4	2.132	2.776	3.747	4.604
5	2.015	2.571	3.365	4.032
6	1.943	2.447	3.143	3.707
7	1.895	2.365	2.998	3.499
8	1.860	2.306	2.896	3.355
9	1.833	2.262	2.821	3.250
10	1.812	2.228	2.764	3.169
11	1.796	2.201	2.718	3.106
12	1.782	2.179	2.681	3.055
13	1.771	2.160	2.650	3.012
14	1.761	2.145	2.624	2.977
15	1.753	2.131	2.602	2.947
20	1.725	2.086	2.528	2.845
25	1.708	2.060	2.485	2.787
30	1.697	2.042	2.457	2.750
40	1.684	2.021	2.423	2.704
60	1.671	2.000	2.390	2.660
120	1.658	1.980	2.358	2.617
∞	1.645	1.960	2.326	2.576

Given a sample size of 8, the $8 - 1 = 7$ degrees of freedom row in the table indicates that for a 97.5 percent confidence level, 2.365 should be multiplied by the standard deviation. The 97.5 percent figure includes all of the area under the curve plotted for the assumed probability distribution, except for the 2.5 percent right tail of the curve, which represents the probability of a stockout. Thus, the safety stock required to avoid a stockout approximately 97.5 percent of the time in the example above, with a lead time of one month, would be computed as follows:

$$SSQ = D \sigma \sqrt{L} = (2.365)(20.83)(\sqrt{1}) = 49.26 \text{ or about 50 units}$$

The order point would be:

$$LTQ + SSQ = (256.25)(1 \text{ month}) + (49.26) = 305.51 \text{ or about 306 units}$$

As shown in the table, the Student's t distribution approaches the standard normal distribution as the sample size increases. Therefore, for large samples, the appropriate z value for the standard normal distribution may be used. The t values presented in the table above for df $= \infty$ are equal to the z values for the standard normal distribution at the probability levels indicated at the head of each column. For sample sizes of 30 or more, two standard deviations would approximate the appropriate factor at the 97.5 percent confidence level.

---

[3]Degrees of freedom (df) refers to the number of values that are free to vary after certain restrictions have been placed on the data. It is expressed as df $= n - p$, where n is the number of observations and p is the number of unknown parameters. Here, the unknown parameter is the mean of the demand distribution for this statistical procedure. For the next method to be discussed, the unknown parameter is the mean of the forecast error distribution.

Deviations from Forecast Demand. In this application, the safety stock formulation is based on the variability in forecast errors, i.e., the differences between forecast demand and actual demand. The technique assumes that variations between forecast demand and actual demand during the future lead time periods can be modeled by the variations experienced during the sample period. The eight months of actual consumption of Material J-2, previously illustrated, together with the forecast monthly usage, provide the following data for this statistical approach:

	x'_i Forecast Demand	x_i Actual Demand	$(x'_i - x_i)$ Deviations from Forecast	$(x'_i - x_i)^2$ Deviations Squared
January	260	250	10	100
February	218	225	− 7	49
March	260	275	−15	225
April	230	240	−10	100
May	275	280	− 5	25
June	270	260	10	100
July	245	240	5	25
August	270	280	−10	100
Total	2,028	2,050	−22	724

The standard deviation of the periodic forecast demand is defined as:

$$\sigma = \sqrt{\frac{\Sigma(x'_i - x_i)^2 - \dfrac{(\Sigma(x'_i - x_i))^2}{n}}{n - 1}} \text{ , where}$$

n = The number of periods in the sample

x'_i = Forecast demand in period i

x_i = Actual demand in period i

The standard deviation for this illustration is computed as follows:

$$\sigma = \sqrt{\frac{724 - \dfrac{(-22)^2}{8}}{8 - 1}} = \sqrt{\frac{663.5}{7}} = 9.74$$

Since the forecasting model underestimated demand for the sample period, the level of safety stock must be increased by the average forecasting bias, multiplied by the number of periods expected during the lead time. Here, the safety stock required to avoid a stockout approximately 97.5 percent of the time (a confidence level of 97.5 percent) with a lead time of one month, would be:

$$SSQ = (D\sigma\sqrt{L}) - \left(\frac{\Sigma(x'_i - x_i)}{n}(L)\right)$$

$$= ((2.365)(9.74)(\sqrt{1})) - \left(\left(\frac{-22}{8}\right)(1)\right) = 23.035 + 2.75$$

$$= 25.785 \text{ or about 26 units}$$

The order point for September, assuming a forecast demand of 260 and a lead time of one month, would be:

$$LTQ + SSQ = (260)(1 \text{ month}) + (25.785) = 285.785 \text{ or about 286 units}$$

Note that lead time periods must be measured in the same units, such as months, weeks, or days, as those used in computing the standard deviation.

An additional safety stock allowance may be needed if lead time varies, again giving consideration to the degree of protection desired by management. When the inventory stock reaches the order point level, it should trigger an order for the most economical order quantity.

Forecasting Usage

The number of units needed during the lead time and the lead time itself are the two variables which influence the when-to-order decision. Usually it is possible to estimate fairly accurately the time required to receive materials. It is seldom possible to forecast exactly the materials needed even for a short future period; and when thousands of items are involved, the task becomes prodigious even with the aid of a computer. Some forecasting techniques are mentioned briefly in order to indicate the scope and complexity of the task:

1. Factor listing or barometric methods.
2. Statistical methods.
3. Forecasting surveys.

Factor listing involves enumerating the favorable and unfavorable conditions likely to influence sales of the various divisions or products of a company and relies upon the forecaster's judgment to evaluate the degree of the influence factor. *Barometric methods* result in systematized factor listing.

Statistical methods describe historical patterns in time series. The methods may be simple or complex, but the purpose is to reveal patterns that have occurred in the past and project them into the future. The usual procedure results in plotting time series data (such as total sales, sales of specific lines or products, inventory units or dollars, labor hours, or machine hours) on a graph, thus revealing a trend or a seasonal or cyclical pattern. A moving average may be used to smooth a series and remove irregular fluctuations, but the intent is to describe mathematically the growth or decline over a period of time. Regression analysis usually employs the least-squares method (see Chapter 12) to determine economic relationships between a dependent variable and one or more independent variables, such as sales territory, family incomes, advertising expenditures, and price of the product.

Forecasting surveys are used to avoid complete dependence on historical data. They commonly are made in order to determine consumer buying intentions, opinions, or feelings about the business outlook, and capital investment plans.

General Observations

The primary key to good inventory planning is sufficient knowledge of the fundamental techniques to develop enough self-confidence to permit their practical adaptation to the specific needs of the company. Basically, economic order quantity and computed order points assume:

1. Relatively uniform average demand.
2. Uniform rate of inventory usage.
3. Normal distribution of demand forecast errors.
4. Constant purchase price per unit, regardless of order size.
5. Available funds when the order point is reached.
6. Statistical independence of demand for all inventory items.

Aside from the technical and mathematical steps, it is important to remember that the following fundamentals largely determine the success of inventory planning procedures:

1. The order point is a significant factor affecting inventory planning, since it establishes the inventory level. It determines the investment in inventories and the ability to provide satisfactory customer service. The order point depends primarily on the accuracy of the sales or usage forecast.
2. Of equal importance is the establishment of unit costs, carrying and ordering costs, and the investment factor. These elements, along with estimated requirements, are involved in determining the economic order quantity.
3. The inventory model should be sensitive and adaptive to seasonal usage variations and other nonstatic data influencing order point quantity computations.

Computer Simulation for Materials Requirements Planning

Materials requirements planning (MRP) is a computer simulation for managing materials requirements, using each product's bill of materials as well as inventory status and the process of manufacture. A master schedule of items to be produced and due dates are entered into the computer, which then accesses the bill of materials, materials delivery lead times, and on-hand and on-order inventory balances.

The computer then determines component parts requirements and projects the time-phased production demands on various work centers. These demands, when compared with work-center capacities representing machines and personnel, determine the feasibility of meeting the master schedule of products to be produced. If work-center overloads cannot be resolved, the master schedule must be revised.

Only when the master schedule is determined to be feasible is it released, along with purchase order and work-center operation schedules. By using such simulations, the feasibility of schedules can be tested prior to their release.[4]

---

[4]Dale G. Sauers, "Analyzing Inventory Systems," *Management Accounting*, Vol. LXVII, No. 11, p. 31.

■ MATERIALS CONTROL

Materials control is accomplished through functional organization, assignment of responsibility, and documentary evidence obtained at various stages of operations. These stages begin with the approval of sales and production budgets and with the completion of products which are ready for sale and shipment to warehouse stocks or to customers.

Two levels of inventory control exist: unit control and dollar control. Purchasing and production managers are interested primarily in unit control; they think, order, and requisition in terms of units instead of dollars. Executive management is interested primarily in the financial control of inventories. These executives think in terms of an adequate return on capital employed; i.e., dollars invested in inventory must be utilized efficiently and effectively. Inventory control is operating successfully when inventory increases or decreases follow a predetermined and predictable pattern, related in amount and time to sales requirements and production schedules.

QUALITY
CONTROL

The control of materials must meet two opposing needs: (1) maintenance of an inventory of sufficient size and diversity for efficient operations and (2) maintenance of a financially favorable inventory. A basic objective of materials control is the ability to place an order at the appropriate time with the best source to acquire the proper quantity at the right price and quality. Effective inventory control should:

1. Provide a supply of required materials and parts for efficient and uninterrupted operations.
2. Provide ample stocks in periods of short supply (seasonal, cyclical, or strike) and anticipate price changes.
3. Store materials with a minimum of handling time and cost and protect them from loss by fire, theft, elements, and damage through handling.
4. Keep inactive, surplus, and obsolete items to a minimum by systematic reporting of product changes which affect materials and parts.
5. Assure adequate inventory for prompt delivery to customers.
6. Maintain the amount of capital invested in inventories at a level consistent with operating requirements and management's plans.

Control Principles

Inventory control systems and techniques should be based on the following principles:

1. Inventory is created by purchasing (a) materials and parts plus (b) additional labor and overhead to process the materials into finished goods.
2. Inventory is reduced through sales and spoilage.
3. Accurate sales and production schedule forecasts are essential for efficient purchasing, handling, and materials investment.

4. Management policies, which attempt to balance size and diversity of inventory for efficient operations and cost of maintaining that inventory, are the greatest factors in determining inventory investment.
5. Ordering materials is a response to forecasts; scheduling production controls inventory.
6. Inventory records alone do not achieve inventory control.
7. Control is comparative and relative, not absolute. It is exercised by people with varying experiences and judgment. Rules and procedures guide these individuals in making evaluations and decisions. For example, by establishing closer controls, experts in the field of materials control commonly expect to reduce inventory by 15 percent or more without significantly affecting customer service or production scheduling.

Organizing for Materials Control

Materials control is commonly centralized in one department called the materials management or materials control department. Size of the company, number of purchased items in a finished product, time required to manufacture a product, and physical size, weight, and unit value of items are factors that influence the organization and personnel required for effective materials control. A materials management organization may include some or all of the following sections:

Planning and Scheduling	Finished Goods
Purchasing	Warehousing
Receiving	Packing
Inspection	Traffic
Stores	Shipping
Materials Handling	Statistical Analysis

Materials Control Methods

Materials control methods differ primarily in the care and cost expended. Critical items and high-value items require greater attention than do low-value items. For example, for low-cost items, large safety stocks and large orders of three to six months' supply are appropriate, since carrying costs are usually low and the risk of obsolescence is often negligible. Control methods include the order cycling and the min-max method.

The *order cycling* or *cycle review method* examines periodically (e.g., each 30, 60, or 90 days) the status of quantities on hand of each item or class. Different companies use different time periods between reviews and may use different cycles for different types of materials. High-value items and items that would tie up normal operations if out of stock usually require a short review cycle. On low-cost and noncritical items, a longer review cycle is common, since these materials would be ordered in large quantities and a stockout would not be as costly. At each review period in the order cycling system, orders are placed to bring quantities up to some determined and desired level. This quantity often is expressed as a number of days' or weeks' supply and can be adjusted to projected sales for seasonal items.

The *min-max method* is based on the premise that the quantities of most stock items are subject to definable limits. A maximum quantity for each item is established. A minimum level provides the margin of safety necessary to prevent stockouts during a reorder cycle. The minimum level sets the order point, and the quantity to order usually will bring inventory to the maximum level.

Min-max procedures may be based on physical observation or may be keyed to the accounting system. Physical observation that an order point has been reached is illustrated by the *two-bin procedure*, which separates each stock item into two bins, piles, or bundles. The first bin contains enough stock to satisfy usage that occurs between receipt of an order and the placing of the next order; the second bin contains the normal amount used from order date to delivery date plus the safety stock. When the first bin is empty and the second bin is tapped, a requisition for a new supply is prepared. The second bin or reserve quantity is determined originally by estimating usage requirements and adding a safety stock adequate to cover the time required for replenishing the materials. For example, if monthly usage of an item is ten dozen, a one-month safety stock is desired, and 30 days are required to place an order and receive delivery, the second bin should contain 20 dozen units. A purchase order must be prepared when the reserve stock is tapped; otherwise, a stockout is likely to occur. The two-bin or "last bag" system requires little paper work, since reordering takes place when the "last bag" is opened.

The min-max method may be implemented through the accounting system by triggering an order when a materials ledger record shows that the balance on hand has dropped to the order point. The system is especially advantageous in companies using electronic data processing equipment. The materials control department reviews materials items, forecasts usage and lead time, establishes safety stock requirements, and determines economic order quantities. Thereafter, subject to quarterly or semiannual review, receipts and issues are electronically recorded on the materials record. When the quantity on hand drops to the established order point, the information is automatically routed to order clerks who activate orders for the quantity specified. Companies with computers may go even further in their use of the automatic order system. The computer reviews and updates order points, recalculates economic order quantities, and even writes purchase orders.

Just-in-Time Materials Control. The savings that can result from a minimum inventory investment and associated carrying costs has led to increasing interest in *just-in-time (JIT) inventory systems*. Such a procedure calls for heightened coordination with suppliers so that materials arrive immediately prior to their use. Vendors are needed who can make frequent deliveries of small standard lots having zero defects. Emphasis is on reduction of the number of suppliers and on improved quality so that purchases can be delivered directly to the assembly line requiring little or no inspection.

In JIT, authorization for a part to be made at a work station is generated by a requirement for the part at the next work station in the production line. As parts are used in final assembly, the need for production of their replacements is authorized. The process is repeated at all preceding work stations, thus "pulling" parts through the production system as they are needed and in turn pulling raw materials and purchased parts from suppliers.

JIT pertains to raw materials inventory as well as to work in process inventory between interacting work centers. The objective is that both raw materials and work in process inventories are held to absolute minimums.[5] JIT places new emphasis on the desirability of minimum inventory levels and on improving integrated manufacturing processes rather than focusing on individual materials or operations. It is intended to complement the appropriate use of other materials planning and control tools, such as EOQ and safety stock calculations. It is a special case of small EOQs. For JIT to operate properly, machine setup time must be kept short. Furthermore, production flow through the various work stations must be uniform, a usual characteristic of repetitive manufacturing.

A successful just-in-time system requires a change in manufacturing processes to accommodate this new inventory philosophy. What is involved is process management, not merely inventory management. The fundamental objective of JIT is to produce and deliver what is needed, when it is needed, at all stages of the production process—just in time to be fabricated, subassembled, assembled, and shipped to the customer. Although in practice there are no such perfect plants, JIT is an ideal and therefore a worthy goal. The benefits are low inventory, high manufacturing cycle rates, high output per employee, minimum floor space requirements, minimum indirect labor, and perfect in-process control. An associated requirement of a successful JIT operation is the pursuit of perfect quality in order to reduce, to an absolute minimum, delays caused by defective product units.[6]

QUALITY CONTROL

The intent is to reduce total throughput time or cycle time, because the only time that value can be added to a product is when it is being processed. Move time, wait time, and inspection time do not add value. Only process time adds value; the rest solely add cost. Thus reducing total cycle time means reducing cost and increasing competitiveness. One measure of manufacturing cycle efficiency is shown in the following formula:

$$\text{Manufacturing Cycle Efficiency} = \frac{\text{Processing Time}}{\text{Processing Time} + \text{Waiting Time} + \text{Moving Time} + \text{Inspection Time}}$$

And, of course, even processing time should be at a minimum consistent with quality production.

VALUE-ADDED

The object is to eliminate waste in an enlightened manner, recognizing that all costs are not equal. The use of value-added criteria provides a basis

---

[5]*Ibid.*, pp. 31-32.

[6]Larry Utzig, "Reconciling the Two Views of Quality," *Journal of Cost Management*, Vol. 1, No. 1, p. 68.

for analyzing organizational activities, resulting in targeted cost reductions and eliminations.[7]

Parts are provided to the next production stage only as needed. To avoid excessive inventory queues, production along the entire assembly line is stopped if parts are missing at any stage or if defects are found. Defective parts or subassemblies are caught early before they can be built into a large number of units. Thus for reasonable flow rates, the number of defects must be small. Workers are more involved in quality because a defect at any station can shut down the entire production line.

While the focus of JIT is on reducing inventories to zero levels, the underlying philosophy is to get rid of all wastes in the system. This philosophy views inventories as evil and wasteful. Inventories not only are resources not being used but are slack or fat that cover up other wasteful areas in a company.[8]

The objective of reducing inventory to a zero level would be possible only under the following conditions:

1. Low or insignificant setup (or order) times and costs.
2. Lot sizes equal to one.
3. Minimum and almost instantaneous lead times.
4. Balanced and level work loads.
5. No interruptions due to stockouts, poor quality, unscheduled equipment downtimes, engineering changes, or other unplanned changes.

Inventories are carried in virtually all systems because these idealized conditions do not exist. The JIT approach connotes a level of perfection that is unattainable. However, it stimulates a quest for constant improvement in the environmental conditions that necessitate inventories. Thus, JIT is a journey toward continuous improvement, not a destination. This reduction of inventories is achieved with the following process:

1. Inventories are reduced until a problem (bump) is discovered and identified.
2. Once the problem is defined, the inventory level is increased to absorb the shock of this bump and to keep the system operating smoothly.
3. The problem is analyzed and practical ways are identified to reduce or remove the problem.
4. Once the problem is reduced or removed, the inventory level is reduced until another problem is discovered and identified.
5. Steps 2 through 4 of the process are repeated until the minimum possible level of inventories is achieved.

In this iterative way, getting rid of inventory uncovers problems and stimulates the search for practical ways of solving those problems so that continuous improvement in eliminating the system's wastes can be made.[9]

---

[7]C.J. McNair, William Mosconi, and Thomas Norris, *Meeting the Technology Challenge: Cost Accounting in a JIT Environment* (Montvale, N.J.: National Association of Accountants, 1988), pp. 181-182.

[8]Charles D. Mecimore and James K. Weeks, *Techniques in Inventory Management and Control* (Montvale, N.J.: National Association of Accountants, 1987), pp. 6, 124.

[9]*Ibid.*, p. 125.

Selective Control—The ABC Plan. Segregation of materials for *selective control*, called the *ABC plan*, is an analytical approach based upon statistical averages. The ABC plan measures the cost significance of each materials item. "A," or high-value, items would be under the tightest control and the responsibility of the most experienced personnel. Middle-value, "B," items would require moderate control procedures. "C" items would be under simple physical controls, such as the two-bin system with safety stocks. The plan provides an impressive saving in materials cost.

The ABC plan concentrates on important items and is also known as *control by importance and exception (CIE)*. Because it is impractical to give equal attention to all items in inventory, stock items are classified and ranked in descending order on the basis of the annual dollar value of each item, thus providing a proportional value analysis. In most situations, an arbitrary number of items can be selected on a percentage basis to approximate, for example:

> 10% of the items to equal 70% of the dollar cost of materials used
> 30% of the items to equal 25% of the dollar cost of materials used
> 60% of the items to equal 5% of the dollar cost of materials used

The following table suggests the handling of high-, middle-, and low-value items to achieve effective control:

	High-Value Items (A)	Middle-Value Items (B)	Low-Value Items (C)
Quality of personnel	Best available	Average	Low
Records needed	Complete	Simple	Not essential
Order point and quantity used	As guides, frequent review	Infrequent review	Strictly used
Number of orders per year	Generally high	Moderate	Low
Replacement time	As short as possible	Normal	Can be long
Amount of safety stock	Low	Moderate	High
Inventory turnover	High	Moderate	Low

The procedure for segregating materials for selective control consists of six steps:

1. Determining future use in units over the review forecast period—month, quarter, or year.
2. Determining the price per unit for each item.
3. Multiplying the projected price per unit by the projected unit requirement to determine the total cost of that item during the period.
4. Arranging the items in terms of total cost, listing first the item with the highest total cost.
5. Computing for each item its percentage of the total for (a) units—number of units of each item divided by total units of all items, and (b) total cost—total cost of each item divided by total cost of all materials.
6. Plotting the percentages on a graph.

The following table and graph demonstrate ABC inventory classification:

Item	Units	% of Total		Unit Cost	Total Cost	% of Total	
1	800	8	} 12%	$20.00	$16,000	32.0	} 56%—A
2	400	4		30.00	12,000	24.0	
3	1,600	16		4.50	7,200	14.4	
4	1,400	14	} 42%	5.00	7,000	14.0	} 38%—B
5	1,200	12		4.00	4,800	9.6	
6	2,000	20		1.00	2,000	4.0	
7	1,600	16	} 46%	.50	800	1.6	} 6%—C
8	1,000	10		.20	200	.4	
Total	10,000	100			$50,000	100.0	

Distribution of Inventory Usage Values (Cumulative Percentages)

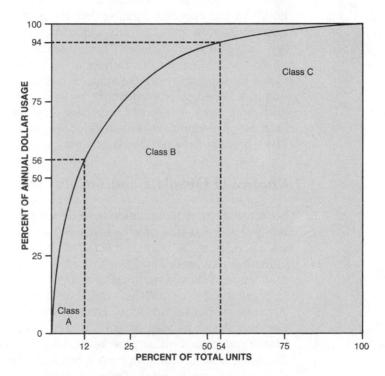

Controlling Materials in Process

As was stressed in the earlier discussion of just-in-time materials control, the materials control responsibility is not ended when materials are requisitioned for production. Until goods are finished, packed, sold, and shipped, inventory control problems and cost savings potentials exist. This is particularly true of in-process inventories, which are intimately related to production processes and schedules.

JUST-IN-TIME

Perhaps the greatest impact of a just-in-time inventory system on organization management is that it focuses on nonvalue processes, i.e., on any activities performed within the company that do not add value to a product.

VALUE-ADDED

Conversely, value-added time is process or running time. This is the time during which a product is actually being manufactured and, of course, even this value-added time should be used as efficiently as possible. The goal is reduction of nonvalue-added time and the associated cost reductions in inventories, product defects, and schedule interruptions, while also increasing manufacturing flexibility. Modern manufacturing systems focus on these reductions through better scheduling, less setup time, improved work stations or cells, and more efficient materials handling.

Controlling Finished Goods

An accurate sales forecast is important to effectively managing finished goods inventories and meeting delivery dates. This forecast must be communicated to production control departments in order to develop production schedules for meeting sales commitments.

To meet customer preferences and competition, many product lines feature a growing array of colors, sizes, and optional equipment. This results in added finished goods inventory as well as more materials inventory items and more work in process inventory. The need for tighter control becomes increasingly important, to satisfy customer requirements while keeping the investment in finished goods at a reasonable level.

Control of Obsolete and Surplus Inventory

Almost every organization is faced with the problem of surplus and obsolete inventory at one time or other. Whatever the many possible reasons for such conditions, some action is required in order to reduce or eliminate these items from inventory and free the related capital. To accomplish a reduction, management should first make certain that the buildup will not continue due to present ordering policies, and should then take steps to dispose of stock. Accurate perpetual inventory records showing acquisition and issue quantities and dates, as well as periodic review of the records, are necessary to identify obsolete and surplus items. Obsolete inventory usually results from changing a design or dropping a product. Prompt sale of the inventory for the first reasonable offer is often the best policy.

Reporting on Inventory Control

Management requires timely information concerning inventory control efforts. This information should be reported in a concise, easily understood form. Quantitative as well as graphic comparisons of actual and budgeted inventory, such as those illustrated on the next page, provide an indication of the efficiency of use of the total inventory and the major categories of raw materials, work in process, and finished goods.[10]

---

[10]Anker V. Andersen, *Graphing Financial Information—How Accountants Can Use Graphs to Communicate* (New York: National Association of Accountants, 1983), p. 39. Copyright 1983 by the National Association of Accountants. All rights reserved. Reprinted by permission.

INVENTORY TRENDS

Total Inventory $

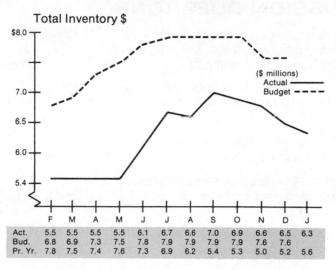

	F	M	A	M	J	J	A	S	O	N	D	J
Act.	5.5	5.5	5.5	5.5	6.1	6.7	6.6	7.0	6.9	6.6	6.5	6.3
Bud.	6.8	6.9	7.3	7.5	7.8	7.9	7.9	7.9	7.9	7.6	7.6	
Pr. Yr.	7.8	7.5	7.4	7.6	7.3	6.9	6.2	5.4	5.3	5.0	5.2	5.6

Raw Materials $

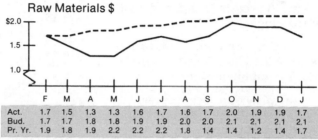

	F	M	A	M	J	J	A	S	O	N	D	J
Act.	1.7	1.5	1.3	1.3	1.6	1.7	1.6	1.7	2.0	1.9	1.9	1.7
Bud.	1.7	1.7	1.8	1.8	1.9	1.9	2.0	2.0	2.1	2.1	2.1	2.1
Pr. Yr.	1.9	1.8	1.9	2.2	2.2	2.2	1.8	1.4	1.4	1.2	1.4	1.7

Work in Process $

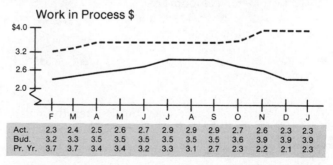

	F	M	A	M	J	J	A	S	O	N	D	J
Act.	2.3	2.4	2.5	2.6	2.7	2.9	2.9	2.9	2.7	2.6	2.3	2.3
Bud.	3.2	3.3	3.5	3.5	3.5	3.5	3.5	3.5	3.6	3.9	3.9	3.9
Pr. Yr.	3.7	3.7	3.4	3.4	3.2	3.3	3.1	2.7	2.3	2.2	2.1	2.3

Finished Goods $

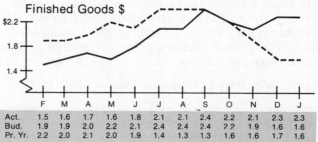

	F	M	A	M	J	J	A	S	O	N	D	J
Act.	1.5	1.6	1.7	1.6	1.8	2.1	2.1	2.4	2.2	2.1	2.3	2.3
Bud.	1.9	1.9	2.0	2.2	2.1	2.4	2.4	2.4	2.2	1.9	1.6	1.6
Pr. Yr.	2.2	2.0	2.1	2.0	1.9	1.4	1.3	1.3	1.6	1.6	1.7	1.6

DISCUSSION QUESTIONS

Q9-1. In designing an inventory control system, what are three key questions which must be answered?

Q9-2. How can a firm benefit from economic order quantity and order point techniques?

Q9-3. What is the purpose of the economic order quantity model?

Q9-4. What types of costs should be considered in deriving the economic order quantity?

Q9-5. What are the consequences of maintaining inadequate inventory levels? What are the difficulties of measuring precisely the costs associated with understocking?

Q9-6. In computing optimum production run size, what alterations to the EOQ formula's components are required?

Q9-7. Why is a correction factor applied to the EOQ formula in computing optimum production run size and how is this correction factor computed?

Q9-8. Explain each of the following terms: (a) order point, (b) lead time, and (c) safety stock.

Q9-9. How is the economic order quantity model affected by an increase in the uncertainty of usage of the inventory item?

Q9-10. Define materials requirements planning (MRP).

Q9-11. Is general management concerned primarily with unit control or financial control of inventory?

Q9-12. The control of materials must meet two opposing needs. What are they?

Q9-13. Discuss the purpose of a just-in-time inventory system.

Q9-14. In what situation are selective control and automatic control of materials effective?

Q9-15. What is the key to controlling finished goods inventory in a manufacturing company?

EXERCISES

E9-1. Quantity to order. On September 1, it is desired to determine the number of units of Material X to order for November delivery. The production schedule calls for 4,200 units of this material for September operations; 4,400 units in October; and 4,750 units in November. On September 1, the inventory record shows 4,500 units on hand, 3,600 units on order for September delivery, and 4,500 units on order for October delivery. The desired inventory to begin December production is 80% of the September 1 inventory.

Required: Compute the quantity for November delivery.

E9-2. Usage forecast and inventory balances. On January 1, a materials analyst is asked to determine the number of units of Material Z to order for March delivery. The production schedule calls for 4,800 units of this material for January operations, 5,000 units for February, and 5,600 units for March. On January 1, the

Material Z inventory is 6,000 units, 3,800 units are on order for January delivery, and 4,600 units are on order for February delivery. The desired inventory level to begin second-quarter production is 80% of the January 1 inventory.

Required:

(1) Compute the quantity to order for March delivery.

(2) If the planned usage occurs and outstanding orders are received on expected delivery dates, compute the number of units on hand (a) on March 1 and (b) on March 31.

E9-3. Computations and applications of the EOQ formula. (Round all answers to the nearest whole number.)

(a) Franklin Inc. has an annual usage of 100 units of Item M, with purchase price of $55 per unit. The following data are applicable to Item M:

Ordering cost. . . . . $5 per order
Carrying cost percentage 15%

Required: Compute the economic order quantity.

(b) Tyler Equipment Company estimates a need for 2,250 Ajets next year at a cost of $3 per unit. The estimated carrying cost is 20%, and the cost to place an order is $12.

Required: Compute the economic order quantity.

(c) Barter Corporation has been buying Product A in lots of 1,200 units which represents a four months' supply. The cost per unit is $100; the order cost is $200 per order; and the annual inventory carrying cost for one unit is $25.

Required: Compute the economic order quantity.   (AICPA adapted)

(d) Shubert Company estimates that it will need 25,000 cartons next year at a cost of $8 per carton. The estimated carrying cost is 25% of average inventory investment, and the cost to place an order is $20.

Required: Compute (1) the economic order quantity and (2) the frequency in days that orders should be placed, based on a 365-day year.

(e) The Alexander Company estimates that it will need 18,000 units of Material X next year at a cost of $15 per unit. The estimated carrying cost is 20% of average inventory and the cost to place an order is calculated to be $15.

Required: Compute (1) the EOQ, (2) the frequency with which orders should be placed, in days, based on a 365-day year, and (3) the EOQ if Material X cost is $6 per unit and other estimates remain unchanged.

(f) The Fairhaven Company estimates that it will need 18,000 Material Y units next year at a cost of $7.50 per unit. The estimated carrying cost is 20% of average inventory investment, and the cost to place an order is calculated to be $15.

Required: Compute (1) the most economical number of units to order, (2) the frequency, in days, for placing orders, based on a 365-day year, and (3) the most economical order quantity if Material Y costs $2.50 per unit and other estimates remain as originally stated.

(g) Zarba Sporting Goods Inc. buys baseballs at $20 per dozen from its wholesaler. Zarba will sell 48,000 dozen balls evenly throughout the year. The firm incurs interest expense of 10% on its average inventory investment. In addition, rent, insurance, and property tax for each dozen baseballs in the average inventory is $.40. The cost involved in handling each purchase order is $10.

Required: Compute (1) the economic order quantity and (2) the total annual inventory expense to sell 48,000 dozen baseballs, if orders of 800 dozen each are placed evenly throughout the year.

(h) A customer has been ordering 5,000 specially designed metal columns at the rate of 1,000 per order during the past year. The variable production cost is $8 per unit: $6 for materials and labor, and $2 for factory overhead. It costs $1,000 to set up for one run of 1,000 columns, and the inventory carrying cost is 20%. Since this customer may buy at least 5,000 columns per year, the company would like to avoid making five different production runs.

Required: Compute the most economical production run. Assume that an adjustment for noninstantaneous receipts is not required.

(i) Pace Company manufactures 10,000 blades annually for its electric lawn mower division. Blades are used evenly throughout the year. The setup cost each time a production run is made is $80, and the cost to carry a blade in inventory is $.40. Management's objective is to produce the blades at the lowest possible cost. The production rate is 200 units per day and the demand rate is 40 units per day.

Required: Compute the most economical number of annual production runs, if each run is scheduled for the same number of blades.

(j) Fulton Company estimates that it will need 12,000 units of Material W next year at a cost of $9 per unit. The estimated carrying cost is 20%, and the cost to place an order is calculated to be $16.

Required: Compute (1) the economic order quantity, (2) the frequency of order placement, and (3) the economic order quantity if forecast usage is changed to 8,000 and the carrying cost percentage is 22%.

(k) An item costs $10, has a yearly usage volume of 500 units, an ordering cost of $6, and a carrying cost of 25%.

Required:

(1) Compute the economic order quantity and the total ordering and carrying cost per year.

(2) Determine the effect on the total ordering and carrying cost if the order quantity is 10% above the EOQ. Comment on the magnitude of the effect.

(l) Bahner Inc. manufactures a line of walnut office products. Management estimates the annual demand for the double walnut letter tray at 6,000 units. The tray sells for $80. The costs relating to the letter tray are (a) the variable manufacturing cost per tray, $50; (b) the cost to initiate a production run, $300; and (c) the annual cost of carrying the tray in inventory, 20%. In prior years, the production of the tray has been scheduled in two equal production runs. Assume that an adjustment for noninstantaneous receipts is not required.

Required: Find the expected annual cost savings the company could experience if it employed the economic order quantity model to determine the number of production runs which should be initiated during the year.

E9-4. Economic order quantity and quantity discount. A particular material is purchased for $3 per unit. Monthly usage is 1,500 units, the ordering costs are $50 per order, and the annual carrying cost is 40%.

Required:

(1) Compute the economic order quantity.

(2) Determine the proper order size if the material can be purchased at a 5% discount in lots of 2,000 units.

E9-5. Ordering and carrying costs, economic order quantity, and quantity discount. Patton Company buys 500 boxes of Item X-100 every 2 months. Order costs are $380 per order; carrying costs are $1 per unit and vary directly with inventory investment. Currently the company purchases the item for $5 each.

Required:

(1) Determine total ordering and carrying costs under current policy.

(2) Determine the economic order quantity and the related ordering and carrying costs.

(3) What is the order-size decision Patton should make, if the supplier offers a 5% discount for order sizes of 3,000 units?   CGA-Canada (adapted) Reprint with permission

E9-6. Safety stock and order point. Eagle Company's usage of Material A is 7,200 units during 240 working days per year. Normal lead time and maximum lead time are 20 working days and 30 working days, respectively.

Required: Assuming Material A will be required evenly throughout the year, what is the safety stock and order point?   (AICPA adapted)

E9-7. Order point computations. Jones Company has obtained the following costs and other data pertaining to one of its materials:

Order quantity	1,500 units
Normal use per day	500 units
Maximum use per day	600 units
Minimum use per day	100 units
Lead time	5 days

Required: Compute the following:
  (1) Safety stock (maximum).
  (2) Order point.
  (3) Normal maximum inventory.
  (4) Absolute maximum inventory.   CGA-Canada (adapted) Reprint with permission

E9-8. Order point computations. The Yew Company is setting up an inventory control system. For one type of material, the following data have been assembled:

Order quantity	3,000 units
Minimum use per day	80 units
Normal use per day	120 units
Maximum use per day	200 units
Lead time	12 days

Required: Compute the following:
  (1) Safety stock (maximum)
  (2) Order point.
  (3) Normal maximum inventory.
  (4) Absolute maximum inventory.   CGA-Canada (adapted) Reprint with permission

E9-9. Safety stock. Jackson & Sons Inc. would like to determine the safety stock to maintain for a product, so that the lowest combination of stockout cost and carrying cost would result. Each stockout will cost $75; the carrying cost for each safety stock unit will be $1; the product will be ordered five times a year. The following probabilities of running out of stock during an order period are associated with various safety stock levels:

Safety Stock Level	Probability of Stockout
10 units	40%
20	20
40	10
80	5

Required: Determine the combined stockout and safety stock carrying cost associated with each level and the recommended level of safety stock.   (AICPA adapted)

E9-10. Safety stock calculation by a statistical method—deviations from forecast demand. Because of erratic customer demand, Atlanta Company has been experiencing stockouts on one of its important inventory items, even though deliveries arrive on a dependable schedule one month from the date of an order. Records provide the usage forecast and the actual consumption on this item for the past nine months. The sum of the deviations squared is 2,888 and the sum of forecast minus units consumed is zero. A 97.5% protection against stockout is desired.

Required:
  (1) Compute the safety stock, using Student's t table on page 253.
  (2) Determine the order point if average usage is 292 units per month.
  (3) Calculate the safety stock for 97.5% protection if four months are required from order to delivery.

E9-11. ABC plan of control. Frontline Industries Inc. is considering a system of selective control of materials, using the following data:

Materials Stock No.	Quarterly Usage in Units	Unit Cost	Total Cost
24	2,000	$20.00	$ 40,000
25	20,400	.25	5,100
26	5,600	10.50	58,800
27	1,000	30.00	30,000
28	18,600	1.00	18,600
29	7,560	2.50	18,900
30	8,880	3.25	28,860
31	4,920	2.00	9,840
32	6,840	2.00	13,680
33	30,000	.50	15,000
34	9,980	1.50	14,970
35	8,220	2.50	20,550
Total	124,000		$274,300

Required:
   (1) Prepare an arrangement of the data for presentation to management, assuming that the ABC plan of selective control is indicated. (Round all percentages to two decimal places.)
   (2) Construct a graph to depict the situation.

PROBLEMS

 P9-1. Economic order quantity—tabular, graphic, and formula determination. Evans Company uses 5,000 units of EL-304 each year. The relevant ordering cost is $250 per order and the carrying cost is $4 per unit per year.

Required:
   (1) For order quantities of 5,000, 2,500, 1,250, 800, 500, 250, and 100 units of EL-304, calculate the annual ordering cost, the annual carrying cost, and the sum of the two types of costs.
   (2) Graphically illustrate the annual ordering cost function, the annual carrying cost function, and the annual total cost function for EL-304.
   (3) In the graph, indicate the EOQ and its approximate value.
   (4) Mathematically determine the EOQ.   CGA-Canada (adapted) Reprint with permission

P9-2. Optimum production run size. A manufacturer expects to produce 100,000 Widgets during the year ending June 30, to supply a demand which is uniform throughout the year. The setup cost for each production run of Widgets is $144 and the variable cost of producing each Widget is $5. The cost of carrying one Widget in inventory is $.20 per year. After a batch of Widgets is produced and placed in inventory, it is sold at a uniform rate, and inventory is exhausted when the next batch of Widgets is completed.

   Management would like to have an equation to describe the above situation and determine the optimum quantity of Widgets in each production run in order to minimize total production and inventory carrying costs.

   Let: AC = Total annual cost of producing and carrying Widgets in inventory.
         X = Number of Widgets to be produced in each production run.

Required: Using the above notation, show (1) the derivation, dAC/dX, of the equation which determines the optimum quantity of Widgets produced during each production run in the fiscal year and (2) the quantity of

Widgets (to the nearest whole number) that should be produced in each production run in the fiscal year in order to minimize total cost. The adjustment for noninstantaneous receipts is not required because production capacity is assumed to be large when compared to annual requirements.   (AICPA adapted)

 P9-3. EOQ formula and safety stock. Esther Company sells a number of products to many restaurants in the area. One product is a special meat cutter with a disposable blade. Blades are sold in a package of 12 at $20 per package. It has been determined that the demand for the replacement blades is at a constant rate of 2,000 packages per month. The packages cost the company $10 each from the manufacturer and require a three-day lead time from date of order to date of delivery. The ordering cost is $1.20 per order, and the carrying cost is 10% per annum. The company uses the economic order quantity formula.

Required:
(1) Compute the economic order quantity.
(2) Compute the number of orders needed per year.
(3) Compute the cost of ordering and of carrying blades for the year.
(4) Determine the date on which the next order should be placed, assuming that there is no reserve (safety stock) and that the present inventory level is 200 packages. (360 days = 1 year.)
(5) Discuss the difficulties that most firms would have in attempting to apply the EOQ formula to their inventory problems.   (ICMA adapted)

P9-4. Order point and inventory levels. Rosedale Company has developed the following figures to assist in controlling one of its inventory items:

Minimum daily use	150 units
Normal daily use.	200 units
Maximum daily use.	230 units
Working days per year	250
Lead time in working days	10
Safety stock.	300 units
Cost of placing an order	$80
Order quantity	4,000 units

Required: Compute the following:
(1) Order point.
(2) Normal maximum inventory.
(3) Absolute maximum inventory.
(4) Assuming demand were uniform and the EOQ formula were applicable, determine the cost of storing one unit for one year.   CGA-Canada (adapted) Reprint with permission

 P9-5. Safety stock. For Product D, ordered 5 times per year, stockout cost per occurrence is $80 and safety stock carrying cost is $3 per unit. Available options are:

Units of Safety Stock	Probability of Running Out of Safety Stock
10	50%
20	40
30	30
40	20
50	10
55	5

Required: Compute the safety stock resulting in the lowest cost.   (AICPA adapted)

 P9-6. Safety stock calculation by a statistical method—variability in demand. Historical data indicating actual demand for Material A88 are as follows:

January.........	640 units	July.............	540 units
February	630	August	550
March	625	September	600
April............	615	October...........	620
May............	595	November.........	615
June	600	December.........	630

Lead time is one month. Management has determined that 97.5% protection against a stockout is adequate.

Required:
    (1) Prepare a schedule showing the safety stock required, using the variability in demand statistical method and Student's *t* table on page 253. (Round all amounts to two decimal places.)
    (2) Compute the safety stock required if the normal lead time is two months.

  P9-7. Safety stock calculation by a statistical method—deviations from forecast demand. The forecast and actual usage data for Material A88 for a 12-month period are as follows:

	Forecast Demand	Actual Demand		Forecast Demand	Actual Demand
January.........	600 units	640 units	July.............	600 units	540 units
February	610	630	August	575	550
March	620	625	September	575	600
April............	620	615	October...........	590	620
May............	610	595	November.........	600	615
June	600	600	December.........	610	630

Lead time can be depended upon to be one month. Management has determined that a 97.5% protection against a stockout is adequate.

Required:
    (1) Prepare a schedule showing the safety stock required, using the deviations from forecast demand statistical method and Student's *t* table on page 253. (Round all amounts to two decimal places.)
    (2) Compute the safety stock required if the normal lead time is two months.

 P9-8. Economic order quantity; order point; safety stock using probabilities. Sanborn Company is a regional distributor of automobile window glass, including windshields for subcompact cars. The expected daily demand for these windshields is 36, and the unit purchase price is $50.

    Other costs associated with ordering and maintaining an inventory of the subcompact car windshields are as follows:
    (a) Cost incurred in the Purchase Order Department for placing and processing orders during the last three years is:

Year	Orders Placed and Processed	Cost
19A	20	$12,300
19B	55	12,475
19C	100	12,700

       Management expects this cost to increase 16% over the amounts and rates experienced the last three years.
    (b) The windshield manufacturer charges Sanborn a $75 shipping fee per order.
    (c) A clerk in the Receiving Department receives, inspects, and secures the windshields as they arrive from the manufacturer. This activity requires 8 hours per order received and the clerk is assigned to other duties when not performing this work. The clerk is paid at the rate of $9 per hour, and related variable overhead costs in this department are applied at the rate of $2.50 per hour.
    (d) Storage space for the windshields is rented as needed in a public warehouse at an estimated cost of $2,500 per year plus $5.35 per windshield.

(e) Breakage cost is estimated to be 6% of each windshield's purchase price.

(f) Property tax and fire insurance on the inventory are $1.15 per windshield.

(g) The interest rate on the inventory investment is 21% of the purchase price.

Six working days are required from the time the order is placed with the manufacturer until it is received. Sanborn uses a 300-day work year when making economic order quantity computations.

Required:
(1) Calculate the following:
   (a) Cost to place an order.
   (b) Carrying cost per unit.
   (c) Economic order quantity.
   (d) The minimum annual relevant cost at the EOQ point.
   (e) The order point in units, with no allowance for safety stock.
(2) Without prejudice to the requirement (1) answer, assume that the EOQ is 400 units, the carrying cost is $28 per unit, and the stockout cost is $12 per unit. Sanborn wants to determine the best safety stock in order to minimize its relevant costs. Using the following schedule of stockout probabilities during the reorder period, determine the proper amount of safety stock.

Safety Stock Level in Units	Stockout in Units	Probability
0	60	12%
	120	5
	180	2
60	60	5
	120	2
120	60	2
180	0	0

(ICMA adapted)

P9-9. Cost impact of just-in-time inventory system. Margro Corporation is an automotive supplier that uses automatic machines to manufacture precision parts from steel bars. Margro's inventory of raw steel averages $600,000 with a turnover rate of four times per year.

John Oates, President of Margro, is concerned about the costs of carrying inventory. He is considering the adoption of the just-in-time inventory system in order to eliminate the need to carry any raw steel inventory. Oates has asked Helen Gorman, Margro's Controller, to evaluate the feasibility of just-in-time for the corporation. Gorman identified the following effects of adopting just-in-time.

(a) Without scheduling any overtime, lost sales due to stockouts would increase by 35,000 units per year. However, by incurring overtime premiums of $40,000 per year, the increase in lost sales could be reduced to 20,000 units. This would be the maximum amount of overtime that would be feasible for Margro.

(b) Two warehouses presently used for steel bar storage would no longer be needed. Margro rents one warehouse from another company at an annual cost of $60,000. The other warehouse is owned by Margro and contains 12,000 square feet. Three-fourths of the space in the owned warehouse could be rented for $1.50 per square foot per year.

(c) Insurance and property tax costs totaling $14,000 per year would be eliminated.

Margro's projected operating results for the current calendar year are presented on the next page.

Long-term capital investments by Margro are expected to produce a rate of return of 12% after income tax. Margro is subject to an effective income tax rate of 40%.

Required:
(1) Calculate the estimated before-tax dollar savings (loss) for Margro Corporation that would result in the current year from the adoption of the just-in-time inventory system.
(2) Identify and explain the conditions that should exist in order for a company to successfully install just-in-time.

(ICMA adapted)

Margro Corporation
Pro Forma Income Statement
For the Year Ending December 31
(In Thousands of Dollars)

Sales (900,000 units)		$10,800
Cost of goods sold:		
Variable	$4,050	
Fixed	1,450	5,500
Gross profit		$ 5,300
Marketing and administrative expenses:		
Variable	$ 900	
Fixed	1,500	2,400
Income before interest and income tax		$ 2,900
Interest.............................		900
Income before income tax		$ 2,000
Income tax...........................		800
Net income		$ 1,200

CASES

C9-1. EOQ and safety stock related to production runs. Clyde Peterson, general manager for Adam Desk Company, is exasperated because the company exhausted its finished goods inventory of Style 103—Modern Desk twice during the previous month. This led to customer complaints and disrupted the normal flow of operations.

"We ought to be able to plan better," declared Peterson. "Our annual sales demand is 18,000 units for this model or an average of 75 desks per day based upon our 240-day work year. Unfortunately, the sales pattern is not this uniform. Our daily demand for that model varies considerably. If we do not have the units on hand when a customer places an order, 35% of the time we lose the sale, 40% of the time we pay an extra charge of $24 per unit to expedite shipping when the unit becomes available, and 25% of the time the customer will accept a back order at no out-of-pocket cost to us. A lost sale reduces the contribution to profit by $60. Thus the weighted average (sometimes called expected value) cost of a stockout on a given day would be:

75 desks per day × $60 × 35%	=	$1,575
75 desks per day × $24 × 40%	=	720
Back order (no out-of-pocket cost) × 25% ..	=	–0–
Stockout cost........................		$2,295

"When we run out of units, we cannot convert immediately because we would disrupt the production of our other products and cause cost increases. The setup process for this model (occurring on any stockout day) results in the destruction of 12 finished desks, leaving no salvageable materials. Once we get the line up, we can produce 200 units per day. I would prefer to have several planned runs of a uniform quantity rather than short unplanned runs often required to meet unfilled customer orders."

The manager of the Cost Accounting Department has suggested that they use an EOQ model to determine optimum production runs and then establish a safety stock to guard against stockouts. The cost data for the Modern Desk that sells for $110 are available from the accounting records and are as follows:

Direct materials.....................	$30.00
Direct labor (2 DLH @ $7.00)..........	14.00
Factory overhead:	
Variable (2 DLH @ $3.00)..........	6.00
Fixed (2 DLH @ $5.00)	10.00
Total manufacturing cost	$60.00

Cost Accounting estimates that the company's carrying costs are 19.2% of the incremental out-of-pocket manufacturing costs. This percentage can be broken down into a 10.8% variable rate and an 8.4% fixed rate.

Required:

(1) Adam Desk Company believes that it can solve part of its production scheduling problems by adapting the EOQ model to determine the optimum production run.
 (a) Explain what costs the company would be attempting to minimize when it adapts the EOQ model to production runs.
 (b) Using the EOQ model, calculate the optimum quantity that Adam Desk Company should manufacture in each production run of Style 103—Modern Desk. Assume that production capacity is large when compared to the annual demand for this product, thus eliminating the need for an adjustment for noninstantaneous receipts.
 (c) Calculate the number of production runs of Modern Desks that Adam Desk Company would schedule during the year based upon the optimum quantity calculated in requirement (1) (b).

(2) Adam Desk Company should establish a safety stock level to guard against stockouts.
 (a) Explain what factors affect the desired size of the safety stock for any inventory item.
 (b) Calculate the minimum safety stock level that Adam Desk Company could afford to maintain for the Style 103—Modern Desk and not be worse off than if it were unable to fill orders equal to an average day's demand.

(ICMA) adapted

C9-2. Setup cost. Pointer Furniture Company manufactures and sells office desks. For efficiency and quality control reasons, the desks are manufactured in batches. For example, 10 high-quality desks might be manufactured during the first two weeks in October and 50 units of a lower-quality desk during the last two weeks. Because each model has its own unique manufacturing requirement, the change from one model to another requires the factory's equipment to be adjusted. Pointer management wishes to determine the most ec-

onomical production run for each of the items in its product lines by adapting the economic order quantity inventory model.

One of the cost parameters that must be determined before the model can be employed is the setup cost incurred when there is a change to a different furniture model. As an example, the Accounting Department has been asked to determine the setup cost for Model JE 40 in its junior executive line.

The Equipment Maintenance Department is responsible for all of the changeover adjustments on production lines, in addition to the preventive and regular maintenance of all the production equipment. The equipment maintenance employees are paid $9 per hour and employee benefits average 20% of wage costs. The other departmental costs, which include such items as supervision, depreciation, and insurance, total $50,000 per year. Two people from the Equipment Maintenance Department are required to make the production change for Model JE 40. Each person spends an estimated 5 hours in setting up the equipment as follows:

Machinery changes..............	3 hours
Testing........................	1 hour
Machinery readjustments	1 hour
Total	5 hours

The production line on which Model JE 40 is manufactured is operated by five workers. During the changeover, these workers assist the maintenance workers when needed and operate the line during the test run. However, they are idle for approximately 40% of the time required for the changeover and cannot be assigned to other jobs. The production workers are paid a basic wage of $7.50 per hour. Two factory overhead bases are used to apply the indirect costs because some of the costs vary in proportion to direct labor hours, while others vary with machine hours. The factory overhead rates applicable for the current year are as follows:

	Based on Direct Labor Hours	Based on Machine Hours
Variable	$2.75	$ 5.00
Fixed	2.25	15.00
	$5.00	$20.00

These department overhead rates are based on an expected activity of 10,000 direct labor hours and 1,500 machine hours for the current year. This department is not scheduled to operate at full capacity because production capability currently exceeds sales potential.

The estimated cost of the direct materials used in the test run totals $200. Salvage materials from the test run should total $50.

Required:

(1) Estimate Pointer's setup cost for desk Model JE 40, for use in the economic production run model.
(2) Identify cost items to include in estimating Pointer's inventory carrying cost.

(ICMA adapted)

C9-3. Cost of carrying inventory. Lacy Products is a regional firm that operates with a typical manufacturing plant involving raw materials, work in process, and finished goods inventories. Raw materials are purchased and stored until their introduction into the manufacturing process. Upon completion, the finished products are stored in the company's warehouse, awaiting final sale.

A recent study indicated that Lacy's annual cost of carrying inventory is more than 25% of the average inventory investment. Management believes that inventory carrying costs might be an excellent area to implement cost reductions and proposes (1) not requesting raw materials from suppliers until near the time needed in the manufacturing process and (2) transferring the finished goods to customers immediately following completion.

Required: Identify and discuss the circumstances necessary to make such a proposal feasible with respect to (1) raw materials inventory and (2) finished goods inventory.

(ICMA adapted)

CHAPTER 10

Labor: Controlling and Accounting for Costs

Labor cost represents the human contribution to production, and in many accounting systems it is an important cost factor requiring constant measurement, control, and analysis. Labor cost consists of basic pay and fringe benefits. The basic pay for work performed is called the *base rate* or *job rate*. A base rate should be established for each operation in a plant or office and grouped by class of operation. An equitable wage rate or salary structure requires an analysis, description, and evaluation of each job within the plant or office. The value of all jobs must relate to wages and salaries paid for similar work in the community and in the industry or business as a whole. Maintaining competitive wage rates and salaries facilitates the acquisition and retention of quality personnel.

Fringe benefits also form a substantial element of labor cost. Fringe costs, such as the employer's share of FICA tax, unemployment taxes, holiday pay, vacation pay, overtime premium pay, insurance benefits, and pension costs, must be added to the base rate in order to arrive at the full labor cost. While these fringe costs generally are included in overhead, they should not be overlooked in management's planning and control responsibilities, in decision-making analyses, or in labor-management wage negotiations. Workers' demands for a 50¢ per hour increase in pay may result in far greater expenditures by the company when related fringe costs are considered.

Wages and fringe benefits are only one element in employer-employee relations, however. Adequate records, easily understood and readily available, also are an important factor in harmonious relations between management, employees, labor unions, government agencies, and the general public.

■ PRODUCTIVITY AND LABOR COSTS

All wage payments are directly or indirectly based on and limited by the productivity and skill of the worker. Therefore, proper planning, motivation, control, and accounting for this human cost factor is one of the most important problems in the management of an enterprise. A cooperative and enthusiastic labor force, loyal to the company and its policies, can contribute greatly toward efficient, low-cost operations.

Labor productivity may be defined as the measurement of production performance using the expenditure of human effort as a yardstick. It is the amount of goods and services a worker produces. In a broader sense, productivity could be described as the efficiency with which resources are converted into commodities and/or services. Greater productivity can be achieved by more efficient production processes, improved or modern equipment, or any other factor that improves the utilization of resources. Changes in the utilization of a labor force often require changes in methods of compensating labor, followed by changes in accounting for labor costs.

Planning Productivity

Improving productivity requires careful planning that transforms productivity improvement from an indirect residual of other planning efforts into a freestanding, tracked effort in its own right. The plan should assign direct responsibilities for productivity improvement action as well as specifying interrelationships with other existing plans (e.g., the operating budget, capital investment, research and technology, and human resource development).

Questions typically answered by the plan include:

1. How does the organization define productivity and quality of work life?
2. What priority should be attached to productivity improvement? Who is responsible?
3. How will executive management's commitment be communicated?
4. How much uniformity of application is desired?
5. How much employee involvement in planning and implementation is appropriate?
6. How will progress be measured?[1]

Measuring Productivity

Once plans have been formulated, productivity should be measured, analyzed, understood, and reported. The objective of productivity measurement is to provide management with a concise and accurate index for the comparison of actual results with a standard of performance. Productivity measurement should recognize the individual contribution of factors such as employees (including management), plant and equipment used in production, products and services utilized in production, capital invested, and government services utilized (as indicated by taxes). One such measure has been developed by American Standards for Productivity Measurement, of Houston, Texas. This measure considers use of capital, raw materials, energy, and labor, related to a plant's output. However, the most generally utilized measurement

---

[1]Carl G. Thor, "Planning Your Productivity Efforts," *Management Accounting,* Vol. LXIV, No. 12, pp. 28-29.

has been physical output per labor hour, which takes into account only one element of input—labor. Thus productivity measurement ratios are, at their best, crude statistical devices that often ignore such essential factors as capital and land. This point is supported by a 1984 study which concluded: "Despite a decade of intense concern for productivity improvement in U.S. industry and some notable advances in techniques, measurement is still in its infancy."[2]

Setting a standard of labor performance is not easy, since it is often accompanied by serious disputes between management and unions. The pace at which the observed person is working is noted and referred to as a *rating* or *performance rating*. The rating factor is applied to the selected task to obtain a *normal time*, i.e., the time it should take a person working at a normal pace to do the job. Allowances are added for personal time, rest periods, and possible delays. The final result is the *standard time* for the job, expressed in minutes per piece or in units to be produced per hour.

The *productivity-efficiency ratio* measures the output of an individual relative to the performance standard. This ratio can also be used to measure the relative operating achievement of a machine, an operation, a department, or an entire organization. To illustrate, if 4,000 hours is standard for a department and if 4,400 hours are used, then there is an unfavorable ratio of 90.9 percent (4,000 ÷ 4,400).

Economic Impact of Productivity

When productivity increases, business profits and the real earnings of workers should also increase. Furthermore, increased productivity enables society to get more and better output from the basic resources of the economy. In recent years, productivity has generally been increasing, resulting in more available goods and services. However, the normal productivity gain has fallen below the average gain of earlier years. This slowdown has given rise to increased costs. When increases in output do not keep pace with rising costs, unit costs—and, therefore, selling prices—increase.

If prices are to be kept from rising, then wage increases should not exceed an amount that reflects the unit cost reduction resulting from increased productivity. In recent years, employment costs—wages, salaries, and fringe benefits—have risen more than output or production per labor hour, leading to inflationary higher prices to meet higher unit costs.

In 1980, the Congressional Joint Economic Committee issued a report, *Productivity and Inflation*, in which the role of productivity in reducing the nation's rate of inflation was assessed. The report stated that each increase of 1 percent in productivity growth would reduce inflation by at least 2.1 percent two years after the change and 2.8 percent four years later. The report further states that productivity growth should be considered in designing any

---

[2]Jerome Kraus, *How U.S. Firms Measure Productivity* (New York: National Association of Accountants, 1984), p. 55.

wage and price standards, and that wage settlements which would otherwise be inflationary might not be, if accompanied by large productivity gains.[3]

Increasing Productivity by Better Management of Human Resources

Better management of human resources offers the prospect of increasing productivity as well as boosting product quality by enabling workers to participate more directly in the management of their work and the overall goals of their company. A long-term rather than short-term perspective is required, involving extensive training and a long-term view of results. Four fundamental assumptions characterize better human resource management:

1. People who do the work are best qualified to improve it.
2. Decision making should be pushed down to the lowest level possible.
3. Worker participation increases both job satisfaction and commitment to company objectives.
4. There is a vast pool of ideas in the work force waiting to be tapped.

Quality Costs

Productivity impacts significantly on product quality and a category of costs that might be labeled "quality of conformance costs." *Quality of conformance* refers to the degree to which a product meets its specifications, i.e., its fitness for use. These costs can be classified into four types:

1. *Prevention costs* are the costs associated with designing, implementing, and maintaining the quality system. They include engineering quality control systems, quality planning by various departments, quality training programs, and working with suppliers to improve the quality of incoming materials.
2. *Appraisal costs* are the costs incurred for activities designed to ensure that materials and products meet quality standards. These activities include the inspection of raw materials, work in process, and the finished product, as well as laboratory tests, quality audits, and field tests.
3. *Internal failure costs* are the costs associated with materials and products that fail to meet quality standards and result in manufacturing losses before a product reaches the customer. Included here are the cost of scrap, repair, and rework of defective products identified before shipment to customers, as well as the cost of downtime or work stoppages caused by defects.

---

[3]For an extended discussion of productivity, see Harold E. Arnett and Neill R. Schmeichel, *Increasing Productivity in the United States—A Political, Social, and Economic Policy Approach* (Montvale, New Jersey: National Association of Accountants, 1984).

4. *External failure costs* are those incurred because inferior quality products are shipped to customers. They include the costs of handling complaints, warranty replacement, repairs of returned products, and the difficult-to-measure, but nevertheless real, cost of damaged company reputation among existing and prospective customers. Damaged company reputation due to external failure can have both immediate and long-term negative effects.[4]

These categories of quality costs are interrelated. As more is invested in appraisal and prevention costs, failure costs decrease, with the objective of lowering total quality costs. Moreover, effective preventive actions reduce failure costs as well as appraisal costs, although the payoff may require some time. Although the total elimination of failure costs may be neither feasible nor cost effective, management should be made aware of the trade-offs associated with these various quality costs and take appropriate action. Therefore, the accounting information system should track these costs by the accounting records to the extent that they are measurable, or by good estimates to the extent that they are not measurable.[5]

Quality of conformance costs occur in many different departments within the organization. Their order of magnitude may be substantial. Not only labor cost, but materials and factory overhead costs, marketing and administrative costs, and the opportunity cost of lost future sales all impact on the total.

SERVICE ENTITIES These costs pertain not just to manufacturing industries, but to service industries as well. Banking institutions are a prime example in the service category.

One recent estimate is that quality costs, while amounting to 10 to 20 percent of sales dollars for many U.S. companies, with proper control should be reduced to about 2.5 percent, which approximates the experience in the Japanese automobile industry. Xerox Corporation offers an example of quality improvement in a U.S. company. Over a recent five-year period, prevention, appraisal, and internal failure costs were cut by more than one half, without a negative impact on external failure costs. Xerox achieved this by improving

JUST-IN-TIME quality through total quality control techniques, coupled with just-in-time control procedures.[6] There is, indeed, tremendous room for improvement, and the accounting system should contribute toward this end. Some of these costs can be measured rather precisely, while others will probably have to be estimated. The more precise measurement is useful as long as the cost of obtaining the added precision is not excessive.

As is the case for cost control in general, the earlier in the production process that poor quality can be identified, the greater the potential quality

---

[4]Harold P. Roth and Wayne J. Morse, "Let's Help Measure and Report Quality Costs," *Management Accounting,* Vol. LXV, No. 2, pp. 50-53. For further discussion, see Wayne J. Morse, Harold P. Roth, and K.M. Poston, *Measuring, Planning, and Controlling Quality Costs* (Montvale, New Jersey: National Association of Accountants, 1987).

[5]James B. Simpson and David L. Muthler, "Quality Costs: Facilitating the Quality Initiative," *Journal of Cost Management,* Vol. 1, No. 1, pp. 25-34.

[6]C.J. McNair, William Masconi, and Thomas Norris, *Meeting the Technology Challenge: Cost Accounting in a JIT Environment* (Montvale, N.J.: National Association of Accountants, 1988) pp. 186-187.

cost savings. For example, if a faulty resistor costing two cents and used in manufacturing a computer is found before it is used, the cost is only the two cents. However, if it is not caught until it is soldered into a computer component, a substantially greater cost results. Even more severe is the cost of not catching the faulty part before shipment to a customer and having to recall and repair a computer that has been delivered.

In summary, productivity and its related costs demand careful planning and measurement if the associated economic impact is to be controlled effectively. Better management of human resources and careful balancing of quality of conformance costs are essential requirements leading to increased productivity.

■ INCENTIVE WAGE PLANS

QUALITY CONTROL

In the modern industrial enterprise with mass production and many employees, a worker's wage is based on negotiated labor contracts, productivity studies, job evaluations, profit sharing, incentive wage plans, and guaranteed annual wages. Because all wages are paid for work performed, an element of incentive is present in all wage plans. In contrast with pay by the hour, week, or month, an incentive wage plan should reward workers in direct proportion to their increased high quality output. A fair day's work standard should be established so that workers can meet and even exceed it with a reasonable effort, thereby receiving full benefit from the incentive wage plan.

The installation and operation of incentive wage plans require not only the combined efforts of the personnel department, labor unions, factory engineers, and accountants, but also the cooperation and willingness of each worker. To be successful, an incentive wage plan must: (1) be applicable to situations in which workers can increase output, (2) provide for proportionately more pay for output above standard, and (3) set fair standards so that extra effort will result in bonus pay. Along with these essentials, the plan needs to be reasonably simple and understandable to workers as well as to managers.

Purpose of an Incentive Wage Plan

The primary purpose of an incentive wage plan is to induce workers to produce more, to earn a higher wage, and at the same time to reduce unit costs. The plan seeks to insure greater output, to increase control over labor cost by insuring more uniform unit costs, and to change the basis for reward from hours served to work accomplished. Naturally, producing more in the same period of time should result in higher pay for workers. Because of the greater number of units produced, it should also result in a lower cost per unit for factory overhead and labor cost combined.

To illustrate, assume that a factory operation takes place in a building that is rented for $2,400 per month ($80 per day or $10 per hour) and that depreciation, insurance, and property tax amount to $64 per day or $8 per hour.

Assume further that 10 workers on an 8-hour day are paid $6 per hour and that each worker produces 40 units of product per day (an individual production rate of 5 units per hour). The workers and the management agree that a rate of $6.60 per hour will be paid if a worker produces 48 units per day, thereby increasing the hourly output from 5 to 6 units.

The following table shows the cost per hour and cost per unit for the two systems, and indicates how a wage incentive can reduce unit costs and at the same time provide workers with higher income.

Cost Factor	Original System, $6 Per Hour (10 workers)			New System, $6.60 Per Hour (10 workers)		
	Amount per Hour	Units per Hour	Unit Cost	Amount per Hour	Units per Hour	Unit Cost
Labor	$60	50	$1.20	$66	60	$1.1000
Rent.....................	10	50	.20	10	60	.1667
Depreciation, insurance, and property tax	8	50	.16	8	60	.1333
Total	$78	50	$1.56	$84	60	$1.4000

Effect of an Incentive Wage Plan on Unit Costs

Although the hourly labor cost of the work crew increases from $60 to $66, the cost of a complete unit of product is reduced from $1.56 to $1.40. The unit cost decrease is caused by two factors: (1) unit output per worker is increased 20 percent, with a 10 percent increase in wages, and (2) the same amount of factory overhead is spread over 60 instead of 50 units of production an hour. For greater precision, such an analysis should include labor-related costs, such as employer's payroll taxes, as well as any other relevant factory overhead that would influence the unit cost. In this example, both labor and factory overhead unit costs were reduced. But even if the incentive wage causes the labor cost per unit to increase, the reduction of factory overhead cost per unit may be sufficient to result in a net reduction in unit cost, thus supporting the desirability of the incentive wage plan.

The lowering of conversion or manufacturing cost resulting from an incentive wage plan, illustrated here on a cost per unit basis, also should be analyzed in terms of differential cost, also called marginal or incremental cost (Chapter 21). The differential revenue associated with the additional output and the differential cost of an incentive wage plan should influence management's decision to install a plan.

Types of Incentive Wage Plans

In actual practice, time wages and output wages are not clear-cut and distinct. Incentive plans typically involve wage rates based upon various combinations of output and time. Many wage incentive systems retain the names of the industrial engineers and efficiency experts who originated the plans—the Taylor differential piece-rate plan, the Halsey premium plan, the Bedaux point system, the Gantt task and bonus plan, and the Emerson efficiency bonus plan. Most of these plans are no longer used, but many adaptations are still in use. To demonstrate the operation of incentive wage plans, the straight piecework plan and the 100 percent bonus plan for individual workers, and the group bonus plan are discussed as representative examples.

Straight Piecework Plan. The *straight piecework plan*, one of the simplest incentive wage plans, pays wages above the base rate for production above the standard. The production standard is computed in minutes per piece and then is translated into money per piece. If time studies determine that 2.5 minutes is to be the standard time required for producing one unit, the standard rate is 24 pieces per hour. If a worker's base pay rate is $7.44 per hour, the piece rate is $.31. Workers are generally guaranteed a base pay rate, even if they fail to earn that amount in terms of output. If a worker's production exceeds 24 pieces per hour, the $.31 per unit still applies. In the table below, the labor cost per unit of output declines until the standard is reached and then remains constant at any level of output above standard.

While piece rates reflect an obvious cause-effect relationship between output and pay, the incentive is effective only when workers can control their individual rates of output. Piece rates would not be effective when output is machine-paced. Also, modification of production standards and labor rates becomes necessary when increases in output are the result of the installation of new and better machines. If rate of output depends on a group effort, then a group rather than an individual incentive plan is appropriate, as discussed on page 285.

Units per Hour	Guaranteed Hourly Rate	Piece Rate	Earned per Hour	Labor Cost per Unit	Overhead per Hour	Overhead per Unit	Conversion Cost per Unit
20	$7.44	$0	$7.44	$.372	$4.80	$.240	$.612
22	7.44	0	7.44	.338	4.80	.218	.556
24	7.44	.31	7.44	.310	4.80	.200	.510
26	7.44	.31	8.06	.310	4.80	.185	.495
28	7.44	.31	8.68	.310	4.80	.171	.481
30	7.44	.31	9.30	.310	4.80	.160	.470
32	7.44	.31	9.92	.310	4.80	.150	.460

Straight Piecework Plan

100 Percent Bonus Plan. The *100 percent bonus plan* is a variation of the straight piecework plan. It differs in that standards are stated not in terms of money, but in time per unit of output. Instead of a price per piece, a standard time is allowed to complete a job or unit, and the worker is paid for the standard time at the hourly rate if the job or unit is completed in standard time or less. Thus if a worker produces 100 units in an 8-hour shift and the standard time is 80 units per shift (or 10 units per hour), the worker would be paid the hourly rate for 10 hours. In other variations of the 100 percent bonus plan, savings are shared with the supervisor and/or the company.

Each payroll period, an efficiency ratio must be figured for every worker before earnings can be computed. Production standards in units of output per hour are set by industrial engineers. Hours of work and units produced are reported to the payroll department, where the reported hours worked are multiplied by the hourly production standard to determine the standard units. The worker's production is then divided by the standard quantity, resulting in the efficiency ratio. The efficiency ratio multiplied by the worker's base rate results in the hourly earnings for the period. The following table illustrates how earnings are computed, assuming that standard production is 15 units per hour.

Worker	Hours Worked	Output Units	Standard Units	Efficiency Ratio	Base Rate	Base × Efficiency Ratio	Total Earned	Labor Cost per Unit	Overhead per Hour	Overhead per Unit	Conversion Cost per Unit
Abrams	40	540	600	.90	$7.50	—*	$300.00	$.5556	$5.40	$.4000	$.9556
Gordon	40	660	600	1.10	7.50	$ 8.250	330.00	.5000	5.40	.3273	.8273
Hanson	40	800	600	1.33	7.50	9.975	399.00	.4988	5.40	.2700	.7688
Jonson	38	650	570	1.14	7.60	8.664	329.23	.5065	5.40	.3157	.8222
Stowell	40	750	600	1.25	8.00	10.000	400.00	.5333	5.40	.2880	.8213
Wiebold	40	810	600	1.35	7.72	10.422	416.88	.5147	5.40	.2667	.7814

*When the efficiency ratio is less than 1.00, no bonus is earned.

100 Percent Bonus Plan

The 100 percent bonus plan has gained in popularity because of the frequency of wage increases. The standards, stated in terms of time and output quantity, need no adjustment when wage rates change. Since the system emphasizes time rather than money, the plan lends itself to the development of controls and efficiency standards.

Group Bonus Plan. Industry uses a great variety of incentive wage plans, some of which depend upon a superior productive performance of a whole department or an entire factory. Factory operations often require employees to work in groups or crews using large machines. Although the work of each employee is essential to the machine operation, it is frequently impossible to separate the work of one member of a crew. A worker on an assembly line cannot increase output without the cooperation of the entire group. Group bonus plans have proven successful in such situations.

Group bonus plans, like those designed for individual incentive, are intended to encourage production at rates above a minimum standard. Each worker in the group receives an hourly rate for production up to the standard output. Units produced in excess of the standard are regarded as time saved by the group, and each worker is in effect paid a bonus for time saved as well as being paid for time worked. Usually, the bonus earned by the group is divided among the group members in accordance with their respective base rates.

Group plans reduce the amount of clerical work necessary to compute labor cost and payrolls and the amount of supervision necessary to operate the incentive system. Group plans may also contribute to better cooperation among workers, and good workers are likely to bring pressure upon poor workers who might jeopardize the group bonus. Group plans quite often lead to the reduction of accidents, spoilage, waste, and absenteeism. For example, a bonus may be paid to a crew or department which has not had an accident for a specified period of time, or which has a reject rate in units of output below a specified ratio.

The following table illustrates the operation of a 100 percent group bonus plan. A crew of 10 workers uses costly equipment, and each is paid $10 an hour for a regular 8-hour shift. Standard production is 50 units per hour, or 400 units per shift; overhead is $320 per 8-hour shift, or $40 per hour.

Units Produced	Standard Hours for Units Produced	Actual Hours	Regular Group Wage	Bonus (Hrs. Saved @ $10)	Total Group Earnings	Labor Cost per Unit	Over-head Cost per Unit	Conversion Cost per Unit
350	70	80	$800	$ 0	$ 800	$2.286	$.914	$3.200
400	80	80	800	0	800	2.000	.800	2.800
425	85	80	800	50	850	2.000	.753	2.753
450	90	80	800	100	900	2.000	.711	2.711
475	95	80	800	150	950	2.000	.674	2.674
500	100	80	800	200	1,000	2.000	.640	2.640

100 Percent Group Bonus Plan

In this illustration, the bonus is computed for each day. In other group or individual incentive plans, it may be computed based on aggregate results for a week, a month, or for some longer period.

Organizational (Gainsharing) Incentive Plans

Management should evaluate the pros and cons of both individual and group incentive plans in order to determine what best meets their organization's needs. The suitability of an individual incentive plan over a group plan will depend upon management's philosophy, objectives, and the way in which the work is organized. However, management may encounter situations whereby it would be desirable to improve the productivity of the organization as a whole. In such cases, an organizational or gainsharing plan may be the best answer.

Organizational incentive plans, otherwise known as *gainsharing plans*, have developed as an answer to the productivity problems which have plagued U.S. industries. These plans have been used with great success by the Japanese. In fact, Japan was probably the first country to use gainsharing as a standard practice. The central characteristic of gainsharing plans is that all individuals have the capacity to make valuable contributions to an organization. Inherent to these plans is an employee-centered management style which places great emphasis on the involvement and participation of all employees.

Gainsharing plans require a management style that is both participative and highly committed to making the incentive plan a success. These plans require a high level of employee participation. Employee suggestions are the heart of a gainsharing plan. Finally, the gains that result from employee suggestions are shared between owners and employees throughout the organization.

Just like individual and group incentive plans, gainsharing plans have requirements for success that must occur in order for management and employees to realize the benefits that can be achieved. The keys to a successful implementation include measurable normal labor costs, a relatively stable ratio of sales value of production to labor costs, and, to all participants, fairness of the incentives and the policies that are established. These factors are important because the incentive equation usually is based on some ratio of labor costs to the value that is added to sales as a result of improved productivity.

One popular form of gainsharing is the Scanlon plan. In this plan, the company sets a predetermined formula comprised of the factors described above. If improvement above a certain amount occurs, an employee incentive payment results. The payment is a stated fraction of the attributable savings. All employees, including management and labor, usually participate in the bonus.

It is interesting to note the connection between management styles and gainsharing plans. The majority of the plans require a management philosophy that is both communicative and cooperative. The gainsharing plans place emphasis on team work and employee involvement. Whether the incentive plan is of the individual, group, or organizational type, it can be important by improving productivity, enhancing relations between management and employees, and improving the overall economic climate of the company.

■ TIME STANDARDS VIA LEARNING CURVE THEORY

Incentive wage plans assume that monetary bonuses will motivate workers to achieve higher productivity rates. However, the previous discussion stressed that motivation is not always based on financial rewards, and studies show that incentive wage plans based on fixed time standards—no matter how scientifically engineered—do not always appear to motivate workers.[7] Even so, incentive wage plans using fixed time standards continue to be used. The deficiencies existing in wage incentive standards can be remedied by means of the learning curve theory.

The *learning curve theory* stipulates that every time the cumulative quantity of units produced is doubled, the cumulative average time per unit is reduced by a given percentage. If this reduction is 20 percent, it means that producing two units requires 80 percent of the cumulative average time per unit required for the first unit; four units require 80 percent of the cumulative average time of the first two; and so on. Based on this theory, the following table of values for an 80 percent learning curve can be computed (assume that 10 direct labor hours are required to produce the first unit):[8]

---

[7]A fixed time standard is best explained by referring to the 100 percent bonus plan (page 284), in which the standard is fixed at 80 units per day (or 10 units per hour).

[8]James A. Broadston, "Learning Curve Wage Incentives," *Management Accounting*, Vol. XLIX, No. 12, pp. 15-23.

Units	×	Cumulative Average Required Labor Hours per Unit	=	Estimated Total Hours Needed To Perform the Task
1		10.0 hours		10.0 hours
2		8.0 (10.0 × 80%)		16.0
4		6.4 (8.0 × 80%)		25.6
8		5.1 (6.4 × 80%)		40.8
16		4.1 (5.1 × 80%)		65.6
32		3.3 (4.1 × 80%)		105.6
64		2.6 (3.3 × 80%)		166.4

The results indicate that the 80 percent rate is constant at each doubling of the accumulated number of times the task is performed. The figures in the third column are the cumulative average hours times the number of units. To estimate the total time needed to perform the task the first 32 times, the calculation is 32 × 3.3, or 105.6 hours.[9]

The 80 percent learning curve is used here for illustrative purposes. The 80 percent rate is frequent among industries, and typically the percentage is no lower than 60 nor higher than 85. The actual percentage will depend on the particular situation. Generally, for more complicated tasks in terms of labor skill, there is more room for learning to occur and, therefore, a greater

---

[9]The underlying learning curve formula is

$$y = ax^b$$

where

y = cumulative average required labor hours per unit
a = the first unit's time
x = number of units, and
b = the learning curve exponent, measured as follows:

$$b = \frac{\log (\% \text{ learning})}{\log (2)}$$

For an 80 percent learning curve,

$$b = \frac{\log .80}{\log 2} = \frac{-.09691}{.301029} = -.3219$$

As an illustration, if x is 4 units and the first unit requires 10 labor hours, then

$$y = (10)(4)^{-.3219}$$
$$\log y = \log 10 + (-.3219) \log 4$$
$$\log y = 1 + (-.3219) .602059$$
$$\log y = .8061972$$
$$y = 6.4$$

This is the cumulative average time learning model and it is assumed in the illustrations, discussion, and end-of-chapter materials of this textbook. Instead, the incremental unit time learning model can be used, in which case y is redefined as the time taken to produce the last unit rather than as the cumulative average time per unit. This model requires the computation of each incremental unit's time in order to sum the resulting amounts to obtain cumulative total time. The total time for a given number of units is then divided by the corresponding number of units to obtain the cumulative average time per unit.

An advantage of the incremental unit model is that it provides an estimate of time for the last unit made, which may be the best basis for predicting future time requirements once a steady state is reached. The incremental unit time model predicts a higher cumulative total time required to produce two or more units than is the case when the cumulative average time model is used. The preferred model is the one most accurately approximating actual behavior. For further discussion of model preference, see Shu S. Liao, "The Learning Curve: Wright's Model vs. Crawford's Model," *Issues in Accounting Education*, Vol. 3, No.2, pp. 302-315.

likelihood of a lower labor input percentage as production increases. For a lower learning curve percentage, i.e., for more rapid learning rates, more of the increase in efficiency occurs earlier as cumulative units are produced.

At the extremes, the actual percentage could range from 100 percent (if no learning occurs) to 50 percent. At the latter extreme, if the average accumulated time for the first unit is 100 minutes, then the time for the second unit must equal zero (i.e., 100 minutes × 50% = 50 minutes = accumulated average time per task unit at the 2 task units level, or a total of 100 minutes for the 2 units). Thus the 50 percent rate is an upper limit of learning—one that can never be reached. If the production period is long or the labor operations routine, a point in production is reached when any improvement through repetition would become imperceptible, and the learning curve would level out to a steady-state condition.

ROBOTICS

It must be observed that in some highly automated modern manufacturing processes, especially in those that are computer-controlled and perhaps include robotics, there is no learning curve. The machine is as efficient producing one item as it is producing one thousand items. Learning curves still may be present, though, in areas where human effort is used.

After the learning curve percentage has been empirically determined for a specific operation, time requirements for successive increments in output can be estimated as long as conditions remain the same. Conditions which may cause deviations from times predicted by an established learning curve include changes in product design, changes in proportions of manufactured and purchased components, and changes in equipment.[10] Of course, conditions may also change because of improvements in engineering design and in manufacturing techniques.

When production is not continuous and there are comparatively long lapses of time or changes in personnel, relearning will be required. Furthermore, there may be a certain element of influence on learning curve behavior that is associated with individual worker variants over time, such as temporary productivity variations caused by health or emotional problems, or the Friday afternoon downturn of production as the weekend approaches. Worker group productivity attitudes may also have their impact.

By means of the learning curve, the time standard used for determining a worker's earnings has now changed to a variable time instead of the fixed time standard. The variable time standard meets the need of an incentive wage system more equitably.

> *The improvement phenomenon, as well as its mathematical model, the learning curve, provides an insight into human capabilities that bears directly upon the ability of workers to do work and the time required for them to learn new skills. An actual learning curve may show small irregularities; yet it will eventually follow an underlying natural characteristic of group or individual human activity.[11]*

---

[10]Walter B. McFarland, *Manpower Cost and Performance Measurement* (New York: National Association of Accountants, 1977), p. 43.

[11]Broadston, *op. cit.*, p. 15.

As soon as workers have passed the learning stage and begin to produce the expected number of units (i.e., reach the standard proficiency), they will begin to draw bonus pay for doing the operation in less than standard time. They may even slow down a little and yet perform the operation in standard time or better, drawing the bonus pay but working less hard for it.

Government procurement agencies have used the learning curve as a tool for cost evaluation in negotiating prices for contracts. When a bid on a contract is entered, the unit labor cost is usually estimated. The learning curve permits the determination of lot costs for various stages of production. As production progresses, the cumulative average unit labor cost should decrease.

By comparing the budgeted cost with the experienced labor cost in the initial stages of production, the trend of the labor cost can be determined. If, for example, an average labor cost of $20 per unit is to be achieved, the following output and cost table with 80, 85, and 90 percent learning curves can be predetermined.[12]

Cumulative Quantity	Learning Curve		
	80%	85%	90%
25	$61.02	$45.06	$33.86
50	48.82	38.30	30.47
100	39.06	32.56	27.43
200	31.25	27.68	24.69
400	25.00	23.53	22.22
800	20.00	20.00	20.00

The learning curve allows projection of the cumulative average unit cost at any stage of production. It predicts labor hours with accuracy and reliability, establishes work load, and allows production control to take advantage of reducing time per unit by increasing lot sizes, thereby maintaining a level work force. It also provides a basis for standard cost variance calculations (Chapter 18), allows judgment of a manager's performance relative to the department's target, and provides a basis for cost control through analysis of undesirable shifts of the curve.

■ ORGANIZATION FOR LABOR COST ACCOUNTING AND CONTROL

Labor costing procedures involve:

1. The employment history of each worker—date hired, wage rate, initial assignment, promotions, tardiness, sickness, and vacations.
2. Adequate information for compliance with union contracts, social security laws, wage and hour legislation, income tax withholdings, and other federal, state, and local government requirements.
3. The establishment of labor time and cost standards for comparative purposes.

---

[12]William H. Boren, "Some Applications of the Learning Curve to Government Contracts," *NAA Bulletin*, Vol. XLVI, No. 2, pp. 21-22.

4. Productivity in relation to type of wage payment, creating the best system of compensation for each kind of work.
5. Each employee's time worked, wage rate, and total earnings for each payroll period.
6. The computation of deductions from gross wages for each employee.
7. The output or accomplishment of each employee.
8. The amount of direct labor cost and hours to be charged to each job, lot, process, or department, and the amount of indirect labor cost. The direct labor cost or hours information may be used as a basis for factory overhead application.
9. Total labor cost in each department for each payroll period.
10. The compilation of cumulative earnings and deductions detail for each employee.

The accounting principles, procedures, and objectives in labor costing are relatively simple, although considerable difficulty in their application may be experienced with large numbers of workers or when workers shift from one type of work to another under various factory conditions. Basically, two sets of underlying detailed records are kept, one for financial accounting and the other for cost accounting. The procedures for labor accounting are outlined as follows. The journal entries associated with these procedures, as well as those pertaining to labor-related costs, are discussed and illustrated in Chapter 11.

FINANCIAL ACCOUNTING

A record is kept of the total time worked and the total amount earned by each worker.

The daily or weekly amount earned by each worker is entered on the payroll record.

Each payroll period, the total amount of wages paid to workers results in the following entry:

	Dr.	Cr.
Payroll...........................	xxx	
Employees Income Tax Payable.....		xxx
FICA Tax Payable................		xxx
Accounts Payable or Cash.........		xxx

COST ACCOUNTING

A record is kept of the time worked on each job, process, or department by each worker and the cost thereof.

The direct labor hours and cost are entered on the respective job cost sheets or production reports; the indirect labor cost is entered on the departmental expense analysis sheets.

The weekly or month-end entry for labor distribution is:

	Subsidiary Record	Dr.	Cr.
Work in Process..........		xxx	
Factory Overhead Control...		xxx	
Indirect Labor.......	xxx		
Payroll..............			xxx

Labor cost control begins with an adequate production planning schedule supported by labor-hour requirements and accompanying labor costs, determined well in advance of production runs. In most manufacturing plants, it is usually possible to establish a reasonably accurate ratio of direct labor hours and number of employees to dollar sales by product lines, and by relating this ratio to the sales forecast, to predict future labor requirements. The relationship between sales volume and personnel needs is perhaps more direct and predictable in wholesale, retail, financial, and service enterprises. The entire labor cost control process begins with the design of the product and continues until the product is sold. The departments that should cooperate in this process include the personnel, production planning, timekeeping, payroll, and cost departments.

Personnel Department

The chief function of a personnel department is to provide an efficient labor force. In a general way, this department is responsible for seeing that an entire organization follows good personnel policies. However, very little of the real personnel work is done by employees of the personnel department. Personnel relations are personal relations—between department heads and their subordinates, between supervisors and workers, and among all employees.

Personnel functions, dealing with the human resources of the organization, involve recruiting and employment procedures, training programs, job descriptions, job evaluations, and time and motion studies. Hiring of employees may be for replacement or for expansion. Replacement hiring starts with a labor requisition sent to the personnel department by a department head or supervisor. Expansion hiring requires authorization by executive management, in which case the authority to hire results from approval of the labor requirements of a production schedule rather than from separate requisitions to fill individual jobs. The personnel department, in conjunction with the department heads concerned, plans the expansion requirements and agrees upon promotions and transfers to be made, the number and kinds of workers to be hired, and the dates at which new employees will report for work.

Employment practices must comply not only with regulations set forth at the federal level (i.e., the Equal Employment Opportunity Commission and the Department of Labor), but also with regulations of human rights commissions in the states.

Production Planning Department

A production planning department is responsible for the scheduling of work, the release of job orders to the producing departments, and the dispatching of work in the factory. The release of orders is generally accompanied by materials requisitions and labor time tickets that indicate the operations to be performed on the product. A specific and understandable listing of detailed labor and machine operations is important if work is to be performed within the time allowed and with the materials provided. Delays caused by lack of materials, machine breakdowns, or need for additional instructions give rise to complaints by the workers and lead to additional labor costs. Production schedules prepared several weeks in advance, utilizing labor time standards for each producing department, lead to cost control through the use of departmental labor budgets similar to the one shown below.

```
                              LABOR BUDGET
     Department  Cooler Assembly              For    October, 19--

                                         Prepared   September 10, 19--
```

Model No.	Units Scheduled	Budgeted Assembly Hours per Unit			Total Budgeted Direct Labor Hours
		Motor	Fan	Freon	
625	2,000	1.5	.25	.5	4,500
748	1,000	1.5	.30	.6	2,400
500	3,000	1.5	.20	.4	6,300
600	1,500	1.3	.40	.5	3,300
	7,500				16,500

Variable and Fixed Costs	Total Cost	Cost per Unit	No. of Employees*
Variable costs:			
Direct labor -- 16,500 hrs. @ $6	$ 99,000	$13.200	94
Indirect labor -- 1,000 hrs. @ $4.80 ..	4,800	.640	6
Total variable labor budget	$103,800	$13.840	
Fixed costs:			
Supervision -- 700 hrs. @ $7	$ 4,900	$ .653	4
Clerical & Packing -- 350 hrs. @ $4.60	1,610	.215	2
Total fixed labor budget	$ 6,510	$ .868	
Total for October	$110,310	$14.708	106

*No. of hrs. ÷ 176 (22 days x 8 hrs.)

Timekeeping Department

Securing an accurate record of the time purchased from each employee is the first step in labor costing. To do so, it is necessary to provide a:

1. Clock card (or time card) as unquestionable evidence of the employee's presence in the plant from the time of entry to departure.
2. Time ticket (or job ticket) to secure information as to the type of work performed.

Both documents are supervised, controlled, and collected by the time-keeping department. Since the earnings of the employee depend mainly upon these two forms and the timekeeper processes them in the first step toward final payment, the timekeeping department forms a most valuable link in harmonious labor-management relationships. In fact, to many workers, the timekeeper is management. Frequently the timekeeper's performance is the basis for a worker's first opinion of the company.

Time Clock. The *time clock* (or *time recorder*) is a mechanical instrument for recording employee time in and out of the office and the factory. Under a typical procedure, each employee is assigned a clock number that identifies the department and the employee. The clock number is used for identification on the payroll and in charging labor time to departments and production orders.

A *clock card* provides space for the name and number of the employee and usually covers an entire payroll period. When completed, the clock card shows the time a worker started and stopped work each day or shift of the payroll period, with overtime and other premium hours clearly indicated.

Time clocks may be electronically on line as a part of the computerized system, making a hard-copy clock card unnecessary. Under such a procedure, each employee is provided a bar-coded identification card. The employee passes the card through a slot in the time clock, which automatically enters employee arrival and departure times directly into the computer data base.

Time Ticket or Report. In accounting for materials, the receiving report and the invoice are evidence that the goods have been received and payment is in order. In accounting for labor, the clock card is evidence that time has been purchased and is comparable to the receiving report. The *time ticket* shows the specific use that has been made of the time purchased and is comparable to the materials requisition. When an individual time ticket is used, a new ticket must be made out for each job worked on during the day. Since this procedure may lead to many tickets per employee, some plants use a *daily time report* on which the worker lists jobs worked on during the day. Increasingly, remote computer terminals are used to report time distributions by direct entry to the computer, thus eliminating the hard-copy time ticket or daily time report.

The best procedure for filling in time tickets depends upon many factors peculiar to shop operations. In some factories, the workers prepare their own time tickets which are approved by the supervisor, or the supervisor prepares them. In other factories, timekeepers, dispatch clerks, and supervisors have desks near the work stations. When changing jobs, employees report to the timekeeper, get a new assignment from the dispatch clerk, secure instructions at the supervisor's desk, and get the required tools at the tool crib. A smooth shift from one job to another is thereby achieved, with time distributions entered by the timekeeper upon approval by the supervisor.

The total time reported on each time ticket is compared with the total hours of each employee's clock card. If there is any difference, an adjustment is made. If the clock card correctly shows more hours than the time tickets, the difference is reported as idle time. If the time tickets show more hours than the clock card, the error is corrected in consultation with the supervisor and the worker.

The degree of accuracy in reporting time varies from plant to plant, but in most situations a report to the exact minute is neither necessary nor practical. Many companies find it advantageous to use a decimal system, which is fast and which measures the hour in ten periods of six minutes each rather than the regular clock interval of five-minute periods and twelve periods per hour. On a decimal system, a job started at 9:23 a.m. and finished at 11:38 a.m. would be reported as 9.4 and 11.6, with an elapsed time of 2.2 hours. The time distribution task is simplified if all of a worker's time is related to only one job or if a worker's time is charged to a single process or department.

Payroll Department

Payroll data are processed in two steps: (1) computing and preparing the payroll and (2) distributing the payroll to jobs, processes, and departments. These steps may be performed by a payroll department, depending on the size and complexity of a company. Some companies require only a small payroll department staffed by one or two payroll clerks; others require an elaborate payroll department with many employees and computerized procedures. In any case, the payroll department is responsible for the important task of recording the job classification, department, and wage rate for each employee. It records hours worked and wages earned, makes payroll deductions, determines the net amount due each employee, maintains a permanent earnings record for each employee, prepares the paychecks or provides the cashier's or treasurer's office with the necessary records to make the payments, and may prepare the payroll distribution.

Payroll Computation and Preparation. The company's payroll is prepared from the clock cards. The final computed payroll may be recorded in a payroll journal or payroll record. The record must show total wages, deductions, and the net payroll. A record of individual employee earnings and deductions also must be maintained.

In most instances, employees are paid by check. Payroll checks may be drawn against the regular checking account or a special payroll deposit. The special payroll bank account is especially advantageous with large numbers of workers. When a payroll fund is deposited in the bank, the payroll department certifies the amount required for a particular payment date, a voucher is drawn for the specified amount, and a check is drawn against the regular deposit account and is deposited in the payroll fund. By utilizing this procedure, only one check, drawn on the general bank account, appears in the cash payments journal each payroll period. For each employee, the paymaster prepares a check drawn against the special payroll account. When computerized methods are used for payroll accounting, the payroll journal, the checks, the check register, and the employees' earnings records are commonly prepared in one simultaneous operation. An additional service provided by payroll may allow employees to authorize the direct electronic deposit of their net pay to their individual checking accounts.

Payroll Distribution. The individual time ticket or daily time report shows the use made of the time purchased from each factory employee. The tickets for each employee must agree with the employee's total earnings for the week. Time tickets are sorted by jobs, departments, and types of indirect labor to permit the distribution of the total payroll to Work in Process and to the departmental expense analysis sheets controlled by Factory Overhead Control. Distribution of the payroll is speeded up when automated methods are used. If the payroll department does not prepare the distribution summary, the time tickets are sent to the cost department, which must perform this task. Labor costs distributed to jobs, processes, or departments must agree with the total amount recorded in the payroll account. The distribution summary may also show the labor hours when they are the basis for the application of factory overhead. In highly automated manufacturing, direct labor may be small relative to other production costs and/or not easily traced to jobs or production lines. In such cases, direct labor might be charged to Factory Overhead Control and included as part of the factory overhead rate rather than being charged directly to Work in Process.

JUST-IN-TIME

BACKFLUSH COSTING

If the labor cost to be assigned to ending work in process and finished goods inventories is encountered in a just-in-time production environment, these costs may be charged directly to Cost of Goods Sold as incurred. An end-of-the-period adjustment would be made adjusting the inventory accounts for the portion of labor and other manufacturing costs appropriate to the units in inventory with the offset to the cost of goods sold account following the backflush costing procedures covered in Chapter 3.

Cost Department

On the basis of the labor distribution summary or the time tickets, the cost department records the direct labor cost on the appropriate job cost sheets or production reports, and the indirect cost on the departmental expense analysis sheets. In some factories, cost accounting activities are decentralized, and cost work becomes largely a matter of organization and direction in carrying out a system for recording payroll information and labor costs. In such a situation, cost clerks may be stationed in producing departments to assist in accumulating and classifying labor costs, using the time tickets to compute production costs and services by job orders, units of output, departmental operations, and product types. In other factories, the cost department may be highly centralized and may not direct and control any timekeeping or payroll preparation.

Summary

The organization chart on page 297 summarizes the departmental interrelationships required for effective labor cost control and accounting.

The preceding labor costing procedures have emphasized manufacturing labor. Labor costing of nonmanufacturing labor, such as marketing and administrative employees, also requires the same detailed cost accumulation and distribution procedures.

■ LABOR PERFORMANCE REPORTS

Production schedules, performance standards, and labor budgets represent plans and expectations, but effective control of labor efficiency and costs

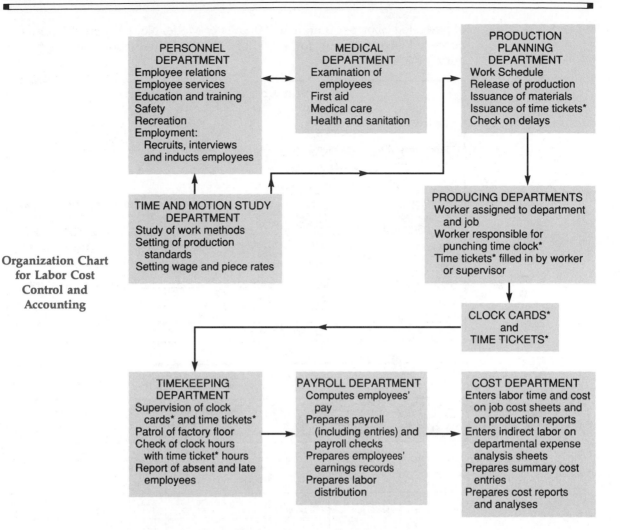

Organization Chart for Labor Cost Control and Accounting

* Or other data entry devices

depends upon meaningful and timely performance reports sent to department heads and supervisors who are directly responsible for departmental production. Labor performance reports are designed to compare budgets and standards with actual results attained, thereby pointing to variances from planned performance. The departmental direct labor cost report, the plant-wide labor cost report issued weekly or monthly, the daily performance report for labor, and daily idle time reports are the media used to provide supervisors and plant managers with information needed for effective cost control.

In the following report, the expected direct labor cost for the week is computed from the October labor budget for the Cooler Assembly Department shown on page 293. For example, in motor assembling, the Cooler Assembly Department produced 600 units of Model No. 625 requiring 1.5 hours of budgeted labor per unit, 800 units of Model No. 500 with 1.5 hours of budgeted labor per unit, and 500 units of Model No. 600 with 1.3 hours of budgeted labor per unit, for a total of 2,750 budgeted labor hours at $6 per hour, or $16,500.

DEPARTMENTAL DIRECT LABOR COST REPORT

Department Cooler Assembly   Supervisor H. Stevenson

Production No. 625--600 units   Week Ending October 12, 19--

No. 500--800 units

No. 600--500 units

Operation	Actual Cost	Budgeted Cost	Variance*	Reasons
Motor........	$16,925.00	$16,500.00	$425 over 2.6%	Reboring hangers
Fan..........	3,000.00	3,060.00	60 under 2.0%	Good group
Freon........	5,675.00	5,220.00	455 over 8.7%	Overtime and reweld
Total...	$25,600.00	$24,780.00	$820 over	

*Expressed as a percentage of budgeted cost, e.g., $425 ÷ $16,500 = 2.6%

LABOR COST REPORT

Plant Midville

Week Ending October 12, 19--

Department	Labor Class	Actual Labor Cost			Estimated Labor Cost		
		This Week	Last Week	Year to Date	This Week	Last Week	Year to Date
Cutting	Direct....	$28,500	$28,200	$1,174,380	$28,200	$28,000	$1,172,500
	Indirect..	2,200	2,250	81,640	2,240	2,200	81,800
	Total..	$30,700	$30,450	$1,256,020	$30,440	$30,200	$1,254,300
Forming	Direct....	$13,600	$13,400	$ 430,525	$13,750	$13,450	$ 431,000
	Indirect..	1,600	1,600	65,600	1,600	1,620	65,700
	Total..	$15,200	$15,000	$ 496,125	$15,350	$15,070	$ 496,700
Cooler Assembly	Direct....	$25,600	$26,100	$1,152,250	$24,780	$24,000	$1,150,000
	Indirect..	2,825	2,800	117,880	2,750	2,750	117,000
	Total..	$28,425	$28,900	$1,270,130	$27,530	$26,750	$1,267,000

Timely reporting is required for effective cost control. While weekly reports, as illustrated above, are informative and serve a useful purpose, daily reports may be required as well. The following daily performance report[13] and daily idle time report show: (1) employee performance, (2) departmental performance, and (3) idle time. Physical factors such as hours are coupled with percentages to improve the effectiveness of these reports.

---

[13]William L. Ferrara, "An Integrated Approach to Control of Production Costs," *NAA Bulletin*, Vol. LXI, No. 9, p. 65. Copyright March, 1960, by the National Association of Accountants. All rights reserved. Reprinted by permission.

DAILY PERFORMANCE REPORT FOR LABOR							
Daily Performance Report by Employees				Daily Performance Report by Departments			
Employee No.	Actual Producing Hours	Standard Hours of Output	Percent Performance	Department	Actual Producing Hours	Standard Hours of Output	Percent Performance
105	8	10	125.0	1	110	90	81.8
110	6	7	116.7	2	280	300	107.1
112	5	4	80.0	3	150	145	96.7

DAILY IDLE TIME REPORT													
Depart-ment	Total Direct Labor Hours	Productive Direct Labor Hours		Idle Time Due To									
				Maintenance		No Materials		Other		Total			
		Amount	%	Amount	%	Amount	%	Amount	%	Amount	%		
1	3,200	2,900	90.6	200	6.2	50	1.6	50	1.6	300	9.4		
2	1,300	1,200	92.3	25	1.9	25	1.9	50	3.9	100	7.7		
3	600	550	91.7	20	3.3	30	5.0			50	8.3		
4	200	180	90.0	10	5.0			10	5.0	20	10.0		
Total	5,300	4,830	91.1	255	4.8	105	2.0	110	2.1	470	8.9		

■ THE COMPUTER'S CONTRIBUTION TO LABOR COST ACCOUNTING AND CONTROL

Payroll procedures were among the first to be programmed for computers because most businesses had well-defined payroll accounting procedures. Computerized labor accounting begins the day an employee is hired and the data for the employee's name, number, job classification, shift, department, direct/indirect pay rate, deductions, etc., are entered in the employee's master file. From that moment on, each employee's activities are entered for payroll data, labor distribution, and a permanent employment data bank. Computerized payroll procedures are depicted in the flowchart on page 300.

Computerized procedures can be used to produce the types of reports that have been illustrated, including use of a computer program to calculate and report each worker's daily earnings and efficiency. Because such a report is too voluminous and impractical for a plant manager or supervisor to use, one procedure is to program for significant unfavorable shifts in performance from one day to the next. This type of report provides for management by exception, whereby the supervisor can work to correct problems of a very few

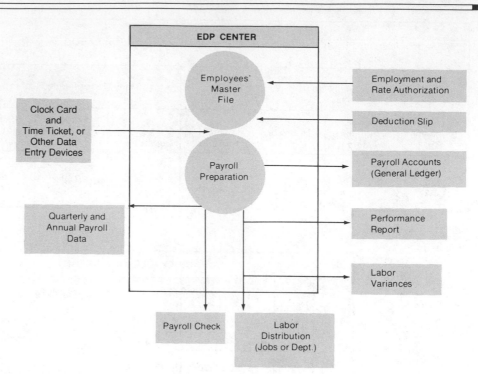

**Flowchart of
Computerized
Payroll Procedures**

workers and prevent chronic difficulties. With a work force of five hundred
employees, a daily report from the computer, identifying significant adverse
changes, might appear as follows. This report is focused on adverse changes
in performance from the workers' historical pattern. For example, Perez is a
highly efficient performer, but the 81% efficiency rate seems too low for this
worker, and management has an opportunity to take early corrective action if
needed.

Employee Performance Report (Significant Adverse Change)				May 19, 19--						
Employee	% Efficiency Last Month			% Efficiency Yesterday	Previous Five Days % Efficiency					Number of Times Reported This Month
	Low	High	Average							
Bowan, T.	72%	84%	78%	64%	76	79	83	81	78	1
Duram, A.	75	91	83	69	71	73	85	90	90	2
Gordon, E.	70	78	74	31	76	71	75	78	74	1
Hoesl, A.	62	88	75	56	80	84	76	65	87	3
Perez, G.	86	98	92	81	85	93	97	94	92	1

With daily efficiency performances in computer storage, management can
be provided with monthly or quarterly reports on chronically inefficient
workers. The following illustration indicates the information needed to increase effectiveness in labor utilization and labor cost control. Even with no

knowledge of the situation, a reading of the illustration suggests that Asbury, Clarke, and probably Varney are not likely to be satisfactory workers in this department if 75% of the standard rate is considered minimal. Dettmer and Mayes seem to be improving, while Shaw appears capable of attaining the desired productivity level.

Employee Performance Report (Chronically Low Performance)				November 30, 19--		
Employee	% Efficiency Last 12 Months			% Efficiency This Month	Previous Five Months % Efficiency Oct. Sep. Aug. Jul. Jun.	Number of Times Reported This Year
	Low	High	Average			
Asbury, M.	33%	43%	38%	40%	42 49 43 51 46	6
Clarke, G.	42	58	50	52	56 45 51 45 51	7
Dettmer, C.	58	74	66	71	70 68 66 58 63	3
Mayes, W.	60	66	63	66	64 60 56 54 50	2
Shaw, T.	70	84	77	68	70 75 68 75 80	5
Varney, M.	45	73	59	64	60 65 68 66 64	4

Effective control is best achieved by careful use of comparisons between actual performance and predetermined standards of performance. Daily or weekly comparisons may be in aggregate (i.e., by department or division), or they may be made for each employee. Departmental labor cost reports can be combined to form a plant summary of operating performance, which is most useful to the plant superintendent and other production officials.

DISCUSSION QUESTIONS

Q10-1. Is it generally true that all wage payments are ultimately limited by and are usually based, directly or indirectly, on the productivity of the worker? Explain.

Q10-2. Define productivity.

Q10-3. Why is productivity important to the firm, to workers, and to society?

Q10-4. What are the four major types of quality of conformance costs and why are these costs important?

Q10-5. How can labor efficiency be determined or measured?

Q10-6. What is the purpose of an incentive wage plan?

Q10-7. In most incentive wage plans, does production above standard reduce the labor cost per unit of output? Discuss.

Q10-8. Wage incentive plans are successful in plants operating near full capacity.

(a) Discuss the desirability of using these plans during periods of curtailed production.

(b) Is it advisable to install an incentive wage plan in a plant operating at 60% of capacity? Discuss.

Q10-9. Describe the straight piecework plan, the 100 percent bonus plan, and the group bonus plan.

Q10-10. What is an organizational (gain-sharing) incentive plan?

Q10-11. State the basic concept underlying the relationship involved in the cumulative average time learning curve model.

Q10-12. Name some situations for the application of the learning curve theory.

Q10-13. Accounting for labor has a two-fold aspect: financial accounting and cost accounting. Differentiate between the two.

Q10-14. In what way are the creation and maintenance of an efficient labor force a cooperative effort?

Q10-15. What is the purpose of determining the labor hours (a) worked by each employee; (b) worked on each job, or in each department?

Q10-16. What purpose is served by the (a) clock card; (b) time ticket?

Q10-17. If employees' clock cards show more time than their time tickets, how is the difference reconciled?

EXERCISES

E10-1. 100 percent bonus plan. J. Pace, employed by the Beach City Canning Company, submitted the following labor data for the first week in June:

	Units	Hours
Monday	270	8
Tuesday	250	8
Wednesday	300	8
Thursday	240	8
Friday.	260	8

Required: Prepare a schedule showing Pace's weekly earnings, the effective hourly rate, and the labor cost per unit, assuming a 100 percent bonus plan with a base wage of $9 per hour and a standard production rate of 30 units per hour. (Round the bonus percentage to two decimal places.)

E10-2. Incentive wage plans. Standard production for an employee in the Assembly Department is 20 units per hour in an 8-hour day. The hourly wage rate is $8.

Required: Compute the employee's earnings under each of the following conditions (carrying all computations to three decimal places):

(1) If an incentive plan is used, with the worker receiving 80% of the time saved each day, and records indicate:

	Units	Hours
Monday	160	8
Tuesday	170	8
Wednesday	175	8

(2) If the 100 percent bonus plan is used and 860 units are produced in a 40-hour week.

(3) If an incentive plan is used, providing an hourly rate increase of 5% for all hours worked each day that quota production is achieved, and records indicate:

	Units	Hours
Monday	160	8
Tuesday	168	8
Wednesday	175	8

E10-3. 100 percent group bonus plan. The Forming Department of the Plastic-Powell Company employs six workers on an 8-hour shift at $12.50 per hour. Factory overhead is $120 per hour. Production for the second week of June shows: Monday, 460 units; Tuesday, 475 units; Wednesday, 492 units; Thursday, 500 units; and Friday, 510 units. The company has recently installed a group 100% bonus system with a standard production for the group of 60 units per hour. The bonus is computed for each day. The controller asks that an analysis of the week's production costs be made.

Required: Prepare a schedule showing earnings in the department, the unit labor cost, the unit overhead cost, and the total cost per unit. (Round unit costs to three decimal places.)

E10-4. Group bonus plan. Ten employees are working as a group in a particular manufacturing department. When the weekly production of the group exceeds the standard number of pieces per hour, each worker in the group is paid a bonus for the excess production in addition to wages at hourly rates. The amount of bonus is computed by first determining the percentage by which the group's production exceeds the standard; one half of this percentage is then applied to a wage rate of $9 to determine an hourly bonus rate. The standard rate of production before a bonus can be earned is 200 pieces per hour for total hours worked.

	Production Record for the Week	
	Hours Worked	Production
Monday	80	17,824
Tuesday	74	16,206
Wednesday	80	18,048
Thursday	76	17,480
Friday.	72	16,733

Required: On the basis of the production record, compute:
(1) The group's bonus for each day and for the week.
(2) The week's earnings of each employee.

E10-5. Organizational (gainsharing) incentive plan. Scarlet Company employs an organizational incentive plan for its entire manufacturing facility. For the year 19B, 755 employees were eligible, and each participated equally.

The plan provides for a gainsharing pool totalling 50% of the value of wages saved. The saving is computed by determining the prior year's productivity ratio, i.e., standard hours for work done divided by total actual direct and indirect labor hours. This ratio (rounded to six decimal places) is then divided into the standard hours for the work done during the current year. The resulting figure is compared to current year actual direct and indirect labor hours.

	19B	19A
Standard hours for work done.	558,510	643,823
Total actual direct and indirect labor hours.	1,284,983	1,525,324

The 19B average hourly pay plus labor fringe benefits was $14.70.

Required: Compute the gainsharing incentive, in total and per employee.

E10-6. Incentive wage plan evaluation. McDaniel Company, a relatively small supplier of computer-oriented parts, is currently engaged in producing a new component for the computer sensory unit. The company has been producing 150 units per week and factory overhead (all fixed) was estimated to be $1,200 per week. The following is a schedule of the pay rates of three workers assigned to the new component:

Employee	Hourly Rate
Clancy, D	$6.00
Luken, T	8.00
Schott, J	7.00

Customers have been calling in for additional units, but management does not want to work more than 40 hours per week. To motivate its workers to produce more, the company decided to institute an incentive wage plan. Under the plan, each worker would be paid a base rate per hour, as shown in the following schedule, and a premium of $1 per unit for all units when the total number exceeds 150.

Employee	Base Rate
Clancy, D	$3.50
Luken, T	5.50
Schott, J	4.50

The first week the plan was put into operation, production increased to 165 units. The shop superintendent studied the results and considered the plan too costly. Production had increased 10%, but the labor cost had increased by approximately 23.2%. The superintendent requested permission to redesign the plan in order to make the labor cost increase proportionate to the productivity increase.

Required:
   (1) Calculate the dollar amount of the 23.2% labor cost increase.
   (2) Give an opinion, supported by figures, as to whether the shop superintendent was correct in assuming that the incentive wage plan was too costly, and discuss other factors to be considered.

E10-7. Learning curve and production cost. A company's new process will be carried out in one department. The production process has an expected learning curve of 80%. The cost subject to the learning effect for the first batch produced by the process was $30,000.

Required: Compute the cumulative average cost per batch subject to the learning effect after the 16th batch has been produced, using the learning curve function.

E10-8. Learning curve and construction time. A construction company has just completed a bridge over the Escambia River. This is the first bridge the company has built and it required 100 weeks to complete. Now, having a bridge construction crew with some experience, the company would like to continue building bridges. Because of the investment in heavy machinery needed continuously by this crew, the company believes it would have to bring the average construction time to less than one year (52 weeks) per bridge in order to earn a sufficient return on investment. The average construction time will follow an 80% learning curve.

Required: Compute the number of additional bridges the crew must build to bring the average construction time (over all bridges constructed) below one year per bridge.   (ICMA adapted)

E10-9. Learning curve. Romer Company uses labor standards in manufacturing its products. Based upon past experience, the company considers the effect of an 80% learning curve when developing standards for direct labor costs.

   The company is planning the production of an automatic electrical timing device requiring the assembly of purchased components. Production is planned in lots of five units each. A steady-state production phase with no further increases in labor productivity is expected after the eighth lot. The first production lot of 5 units required 90 hours of direct labor time at a standard rate of $9 per hour.

Required:
   (1) Compute the standard amount the company should establish for the total direct labor cost required for the production of the first 8 lots.
   (2) Discuss the factors that should be considered in establishing the direct labor standards for each unit of output produced beyond the first 8 lots.   (ICMA adapted)

E10-10. Labor performance report. Heathrow Inc. prepares monthly production budgets for its three departments. Budgeted and actual amounts for April for one of its products are as follows:

Department	Budgeted Hours	Labor Cost	Actual Units Produced
Mixing............	1,100	$ 9,798	740
Processing	3,320	28,275	615
Packaging........	580	3,816	800

The following standards have been adopted for this product:

Department	Standard Hours per Unit	Standard Labor Cost per Hour
Mixing............	1.5	$9.15
Processing	5.0	9.75
Packaging........	0.5	9.00

Required: **Prepare a labor cost report for April, comparing actual and standard labor cost.**

PROBLEMS

P10-1. Incentive wage plans. For the first week in March, the record of M. Roderick shows:

	Hours Worked	Units Produced
Monday	8	180
Tuesday..........	8	200
Wednesday	8	220
Thursday	8	224
Friday............	8	192

Roderick's guaranteed hourly wage rate is $6 and standard production is 24 units per hour. Factory overhead per labor hour is $3.

Required:
(1) Assume Roderick receives 90% of the labor value of time saved during a day. Prepare a schedule to show Roderick's pay, using the following headings:

Day	Premium Wage
Units Produced	Total Pay
Daily Wage	Labor Cost per Unit (four decimal places)
Units Above Standard	Overhead per Unit (four decimal places)
Hours Saved	Conversion Cost per Unit (four decimal places)

(2) Assume the 100 percent bonus plan is used (for each week's total production). Prepare a schedule to show Roderick's pay, using the following headings:

Hours Worked	Base × Efficiency Ratio
Units Produced	Week's Earnings
Standard Production	Labor Cost per Unit (four decimal places)
Efficiency Ratio (nearest %)	Conversion Cost per Unit (four decimal places)
Base Wage	

(3) Assume the daily quota is 192 units and the hourly rate increases 5% for each day the quota is achieved or exceeded. Prepare a schedule to show Roderick's pay, using the following headings:

Day   Amount Earned
Units Produced   Labor Cost per Unit (four decimal places)
Hourly Wage   Conversion Cost per Unit (four decimal places)

P10-2. Incentive wage plans. The company's union steward complained to the Payroll Department that several union members' wages had been miscalculated in the previous week. The following schedule indicates the incentive wage plan, hours worked, and gross wages calculated for each worker involved.

Worker	Incentive Wage Plan	Total Hours	Down-time Hours	Units Pro-duced	Stan-dard Units	Base Rate	Gross Wages per Books
Dodd	Straight piecework	40	5	400	—	$6.00	$284.00
Hare	Straight piecework	46	—	455*	—	6.00	277.20
Lowe	Straight piecework	44	4	420**	—	6.00	302.20
Ober	Percentage bonus plan	40	—	250	200	6.00	280.00
Rupp	Percentage bonus plan	40	—	180	200	5.00	171.00
Suggs	Emerson efficiency system	40	—	240	300	5.60	233.20
Ward	Emerson efficiency system	40	2	590	600 ***	5.60	280.00

   *Includes 45 pieces produced during the 6 overtime hours.
  **Includes 50 pieces produced during the 4 overtime hours. The overtime, brought about by the downtime, was necessary to meet a production deadline.
***Standard units for 40 hours production.

    The minimum wage for a worker is the base rate, which is also paid for any downtime when the worker's machine is under repair or there is no work. Workers are paid 150% of base rates for hours worked beyond the standard work week of 40 hours. The company's union contract contains the following description of each incentive wage plan:
    (a) Straight piecework. The worker is paid at the rate of $.66 per piece produced.
    (b) Percentage bonus plan. Standard quantities of production per hour are established by the Engineering Department. The worker's average hourly production, determined from the total hours worked and the worker's production, is divided by the standard quantity of production to determine an efficiency ratio. The efficiency ratio is then applied to the base rate to determine the worker's hourly earnings for the period.
    (c) Emerson efficiency system. A minimum wage is paid for total hours worked. A bonus, calculated from the following table of rates, is paid when the worker's production exceeds $66\frac{2}{3}\%$ of standard output or efficiency. The bonus rate is applied only to wages earned during productive hours.

Efficiency	Bonus
Up to $66\frac{2}{3}\%$	0
$66\frac{2}{3}$ — 79%	10%
80 — 99%	20%
100 — 125%	45%

Required: Calculate the proper amount of gross wages for each worker in question. Present your results in a schedule comparing each individual's gross wages per books with the gross wages calculated.

(AICPA adapted)

P10-3. Group bonus plans. Employees of Dyson Enterprises work in groups of five, plus a group leader. Standard production for a group is 400 units for a 40-hour week. The workers are paid $6 an hour until production reaches 400 units; then a bonus of $1.20 per unit is paid for production over 400 units, with $1 being divided equally among the five workers and the remainder passing to the group leader (who is also paid a weekly salary of $300). Factory overhead is $7 per direct labor hour and includes the group leader's earnings.

The production record of a group for one week shows:

	Hours Worked	Units Produced
Monday	40	72
Tuesday	40	81
Wednesday	40	95
Thursday	40	102
Friday.	40	102

Required:

(1) Compute the week's earnings of the group (excluding the leader), the labor cost per unit, the overhead cost per unit, and the conversion cost per unit, based upon the above data and bonus plan, and assuming the bonus is computed based on aggregate results for the week. (Round off unit costs to four decimal places.)

(2) Prepare a schedule showing daily earnings of the group (excluding the leader), unit labor cost, unit overhead cost, and the conversion cost per unit, assuming that the company uses the group bonus plan, as described on page 285, and assuming the bonus is computed for the (a) day and (b) week.

P10-4. Quarterly bonus allotment. Ritchie Inc., manufacturers of standard pipe fittings for water and sewage lines, pay a bonus to their employees based upon the production recorded each calendar quarter. Normal production is set at 240,000 units per quarter. A bonus of $.50 per unit is paid for any units in excess of the normal output for each quarter. Distribution of the bonus is made on the following point basis:

Employees Participating	Points Allowed For Each Employee
1 works manager	250
2 production engineers . . .	200
5 shop supervisors.	200
1 storekeeper	100
5 factory office clerks.	10
150 factory workers	20

The employees' earnings are not penalized for any month in which the actual output falls below the monthly average of the normal quarterly production. In such a case, the deficiency is deducted from any excess in subsequent months before any bonus is earned by and paid to the employees.

At the end of March, cumulative actual production amounted to 270,000 units for the quarter.

Required:

(1) Calculate the amount of bonus payable to each group of employees. (Carry all calculations to three decimal places.)

(2) Prepare journal entries at the end of each month to record the bonus liability on the basis of the following production figures: January, 75,000 units; February, 94,000 units; March, 101,000 units. Assume that all of the bonus is charged to Factory Overhead Control.

P10-5. Planning labor costs. Barnes Inc., a relatively new company in the environmental control industry, is experiencing tremendous growth in product demand. To meet customers' increasing demands, management is considering the addition of a nighttime production shift beginning October 1.

Production takes place in three departments: Assembly, Molding, and Finishing. Standard time in the Molding Department is 10 minutes per unit produced, while the Finishing Department averages 12½ items per hour. Employees in these two departments are paid $8 per hour. Two people are needed in the Assembly Department, each with a monthly salary of $1,500, to serve the extra shift. Five cleanup employees are needed, and one supervisor for each 19 workers (including cleanup employees) is required in the Molding and Finishing Departments. Supervisors are paid $1,900 per month, and each member of the cleanup crew is paid $5.50 per hour.

Under normal conditions, the company schedules 20 workdays per month, with a standard monthly production of 120,000 units.

Required: Prepare a monthly labor budget for the extra shift, showing the time required in each department, the labor cost for each department and service, the unit labor cost, and the number of employees required. (Round off unit costs to four decimal places.)

CASES

C10-1. Setting productivity standards. Anvil Inc. intends to expand its Punch Press Department with the purchase of three new presses from Presco Inc. Mechanical studies indicate that for Anvil's intended use, the output rate for one press should be 1,000 pieces per hour. The company has similar presses now in operation that average 600 pieces per hour. This average is derived from these individual outputs:

Worker	Hourly Output (In Pieces)
Allen, W	750
Miller, G	750
Salermo, J	600
Velasquez, E	500
Underwood, P	550
Keppinger, J	450
Total.	3,600
Average hourly output	600

Anvil's management also plans to institute a standard cost accounting system in the very near future. The company's engineers are supporting a standard based upon 1,000 pieces per hour; the Accounting Department, a standard based upon 750 pieces per hour; and the Punch Press Department supervisor, a standard based upon 600 pieces per hour.

Required:

(1) Specify arguments which each proponent could use.
(2) Decide which alternative best reconciles the needs of cost control and employee motivation. Explain.   (ICMA adapted)

C10-2. Learning curve. Kelly Company plans to manufacture a product called Electrocal, which requires a substantial amount of direct labor on each unit. Based on the company's experience with other products that required similar amounts of direct labor, management believes that there is a learning factor in the production process used to manufacture this product.

Each unit of Electrocal requires 50 square feet of raw materials at a cost of $30 per square foot for a total materials cost of $1,500. The standard direct labor rate is $25 per hour. Variable factory overhead is assigned to products at a rate of $40 per direct labor hour. The company adds a markup of 30% on variable manufacturing cost in determining an initial bid price for all products.

Data on the production of the first two lots (16 units) of Electrocal are as follows:

(a) The first lot of eight units required a total of 3,200 direct labor hours.
(b) The second lot of eight units required a total of 2,240 direct labor hours.

Based on prior production experience, Kelly anticipates that there will be no significant improvement in production time after the first 32 units. Therefore, a standard for direct labor hours will be established, based on the average hours per unit for units 17-32.

Required:

(1) What is the basic premise of the learning curve?

(2) Based on the data presented for the first 16 units, what learning rate appears to be applicable to the direct labor required to produce Electrocal?

(3) Calculate the standard for direct labor hours which Kelly Company should establish for each unit of Electrocal.

(4) After the first 32 units were manufactured, Kelly was asked to submit a bid on an additional 96 units. What price should Kelly bid on this order of 96 units?

(5) Knowledge of the learning curve phenomenon can be a valuable management tool. Explain how management can apply the learning curve in the planning and controlling of business operations.

(ICMA adapted)

C10-3. Payroll procedures. A team of internal auditors was assigned to review the Galena Plant's Payroll Department, including the procedures used for payroll processing. Their findings are as follows:

(a) The payroll clerk receives the clock cards from the various department supervisors at the end of each pay period, checks the employee's hourly rate against information provided by the Personnel Department, and records the regular and overtime hours for each employee.

(b) The payroll clerk sends the clock cards to the plant's Data Processing Department for compilation and processing.

(c) The Data Processing Department returns the clock cards with the printed checks and payroll journal to the payroll clerk upon completion of the processing.

(d) The payroll clerk verifies the hourly rate and hours worked for each employee by comparing the detail in the payroll journal to the clock cards.

(e) If errors are found, the payroll clerk voids the computer-generated check, prepares another check for the correct amount, and adjusts the payroll journal accordingly.

(f) The payroll clerk obtains the plant signature plate from the Accounting Department and signs the payroll checks.

(g) An employee of the Personnel Department picks up the checks and holds them until they are delivered to department supervisors for distribution to employees.

Required: Discuss the shortcomings in Payroll Department procedures and suggest corrective action. (ICMA adapted)

C10-4. Production planning and control reports. Kaiman Inc., a supplier of bulk metals and alloys, recently negotiated a contract to supply 3,000 sections of aluminum air-conditioning ductwork for an office building under construction. The order required fabricating, cutting, and assembly. Based on experience, the supervisor prepared the following daily budget:

Department	Sections Scheduled	Hours Budgeted
Fabricating	100	50
Cutting	100	30
Assembly	100	25

Realizing the need for up-to-the-minute production information, the supervisor obtained the following results for the first two days:

	Department	Sections Produced	Hours Required
First day:	Fabricating .	112	48
	Cutting	81	30
	Assembly ..	77	22
Second day:	Fabricating .	120	49
	Cutting	96	30
	Assembly ..	96	23

Required:

(1) Discuss the action to be taken by the supervisor, based on the first day's report.

(2) Discuss the action needed according to the results on the second day's report.

CHAPTER 11

Labor: Accounting for Labor-Related Costs

During the past forty years, American workers have enjoyed a spectacular growth in nonwage benefits because (1) new benefits have been introduced (e.g., insurance for vision, dentistry, and legal needs), (2) benefit costs have increased, (3) the duration of benefits has increased, and (4) more employees are covered by benefits. In recent years, these benefits have tended to stabilize and have declined in some companies. Nevertheless, employee benefits are substantial. Increasingly, employers are offering *cafeteria plans* whereby a specified dollar amount is provided to each employee, which can be apportioned to defray part or all of the cost of various available benefits, such as various types of insurance coverage.

In addition to the basic earnings computed on hours worked or units produced, nonwage benefits are cost elements that enter into labor cost. The following possible labor-related costs that would not be included in the basic wages are expressed as a percentage of straight-time earnings.

FICA tax for employees' old-age, survivors, and disability insurance and the hospital insurance program.	7.5%
Federal unemployment insurance tax (FUTA)	.8
State unemployment insurance tax (representing a typical rate, with most companies paying less than the 5.4% maximum)	4.0
State worker's compensation insurance (rates vary with the hazards—a fraction of 1% to 3% and over)	1.0
Vacation pay and paid holidays (two weeks of vacation and 7 to 10 holidays as a percentage of 52 weeks of 40 hours)	8.0
Contributions to pension fund (probable average)	7.0
Recreation, tuition benefits, life insurance, parental leave, health services, medical care	5.5
Contributions to supplemental unemployment pay funds	2.0
Time off for voting, jury duty, grievance meetings	1.3
Services related to parking lots, income tax, legal advice, meal money, uniforms	1.5
Total	38.6%

Some of the percentages, such as those for FICA, FUTA, and state unemployment insurance tax, apply to a base that may be less than total annual wages, which tends to lower the average annual percentage.

In addition to the elements listed, labor cost usually includes overtime earnings; premium pay for work on holidays, Saturdays, and Sundays when

overtime is not involved; shift bonuses or differentials; bonuses for atten-
dance, length of service, no accidents, and year end; apprenticeship or
trainee costs; and dismissal or severance pay. This chapter discusses the accounting for many of these fringe benefits.

■ OVERTIME EARNINGS

The Fair Labor Standards Act of 1938, commonly referred to as the Federal
Wage and Hour Law, established a minimum wage per hour with time and a
half for hours worked in excess of 40 in one week. Subsequently the act has
been amended, broadening the coverage and raising the minimum wage.
Some types of organizations and workers are exempt from the provisions of
the act and its amendments, or have lower minimums.

A number of payroll practices are mandatory to comply with the Federal
Wage and Hour Law. For each employee, records must show:

1. Hours worked each working day and the total hours worked during
   each workweek.
2. Basis on which wages are paid.
3. Total daily or weekly earnings at straight time.
4. Total extra pay for overtime worked each week.
5. Total wages paid during each pay period, the date of payment, and the
   work period covered by the payment.

Overtime earnings consist of two elements: (1) the regular pay due for the
employee's work and (2) the overtime premium pay, which is an additional
amount for work done beyond the 40-hour workweek or a regular 8-hour
workday (as specified in some labor union contracts). For most workers, an
employer must pay a minimum of one and one-half times the regular rate for
overtime. For example, if an employee is paid $8 per hour for a regular work-
week of 40 hours, but works 45 hours, the gross earnings are:

Regular workweek	40 hours @ $8 =	$320
Overtime	5 hours @ 8 =	40
Overtime premium	5 hours @ 4 =	20
Gross earnings		$380

Charging overtime premium pay to a specific job or product or to factory
overhead primarily depends upon the reason for the overtime work. The
contract price of a particular job, taken as a rush order with the foreknowl-
edge that overtime will be necessary, may include the overtime premium; if
so, the premium should be charged to the specific job. But when regular
orders cannot be completed in the regular working hours, the overtime premium pay should be included in the predetermined factory overhead rate as
factory overhead, because it cannot properly be allocated to work that hap-
pens to be in process during overtime hours.

■ BONUS PAYMENTS

Bonus payments may be a fixed amount per employee or job classification, a percentage of profits, a fraction of one month's wages, or some other calculated amount. The amount of bonus for each employee may be a fixed and long-established tradition of a company, or the amount may vary from year to year. Bonus payments are a production cost, a marketing expense, or an administrative expense. If a direct-labor employee's average weekly earnings are $250 and the company intends to pay two weeks' pay as a bonus at the end of the year, then earnings actually amount to $260 per week, but the additional $10 per week is paid in a lump sum of $500 ($10 × 50 weeks, assuming two weeks of vacation time) at the end of the year. To spread the bonus cost over production throughout the year via the predetermined factory overhead rate, the weekly entry would be:

	Subsidiary Record	Dr.	Cr.
Work in Process		250	
Factory Overhead Control. . .		10	
Bonus Pay	10		
Payroll			250
Liability for Bonus			10

When the bonus is paid, the liability account is debited and Cash and the withholding accounts are credited.

In theory, this and other direct-labor-related costs are additional labor costs that should be charged to Work in Process. In practice, such a procedure usually is impractical, and these costs are generally included in the predetermined factory overhead rate as illustrated in the journal entry above.

■ VACATION PAY

Vacation pay presents cost problems similar to those of bonus payments. When an employee is entitled to a paid vacation of 2 weeks, the vacation pay is accrued over the 50 weeks of productive labor. For example, assume that a direct labor employee has a base wage of $300 per week and is entitled to a paid vacation of 2 weeks. The cost of labor is $300, plus $12 per week. In 50 weeks at $12 per week, the deferred payment of $600 will equal the expected vacation pay. The entry to record the weekly labor cost, including the provision for vacation pay, would be:

	Subsidiary Record	Dr.	Cr.
Work in Process		300	
Factory Overhead Control.		12	
Vacation Pay	12		
Payroll			300
Liability for Vacation Pay. . .			12

When a vacation is taken, the liability account is debited and Cash and the withholding accounts are credited. Similarly, accrual should be made for employer liability pertaining to sick leave, holidays, military training, or other personal activities for which employees receive compensation. If it becomes necessary to use temporary replacements to perform the duties of personnel who are absent, this additional expense should be charged to the department for which the replacement is made.

FASB Statement No. 43, "Accounting for Compensated Absences," requires an employer to accrue a liability for employees' rights to receive compensation for future absences when all of the following conditions are met: (1) the rights are attributable to employees' services already rendered, (2) the rights vest or accumulate, (3) payment is probable, and (4) the amount can be reasonably estimated. While the statement requires accrual of vacation benefits, it generally does not require a liability to be accrued for future sick pay benefits (unless the rights vest), holidays, and similar compensated absences until employees are actually absent.[1] In accounting for government contracts, CASB regulations require the accrual of employer obligations for labor-related costs for personal absences.[2] Conversely, vacation pay accruals are not allowed for income tax purposes.[3] The only exception is for vested plans, which may accrue amounts paid within two and one-half months after year end.

■ GUARANTEED ANNUAL WAGE PLANS

While a guaranteed annual wage plan for all industrial workers is far from realization, a step in that direction has been taken in labor contracts that provide for the company to pay employees who are laid off. The company pay is a supplement to the state unemployment insurance. For example, assume that an unemployed worker is guaranteed 60 percent of normal take-home pay, beginning the second week of layoff and continuing for as long as 26 weeks. To recognize the liability for payments to be made during unemployment periods, a specified amount, such as $.15 an hour for each worker, is accrued by the company.

In principle, if it is assumed that layoffs will eventually occur, it is clear that the employee while working is earning $.15 an hour that is not included in the paycheck at the end of the payroll period. This amount is held in reserve by the company in order to make payments during unemployment periods. For a direct-labor employee whose base pay rate is $8 an hour, the cost effect of unemployment pay for a 40-hour week is illustrated by the following entry:

[1]*Statement of Financial Accounting Standards, No. 43.,* "Accounting for Compensated Absences" (Stamford: Financial Accounting Standards Board, 1980).

[2]*Standards, Rules and Regulations, Part 408* "Accounting for Costs of Compensated Personal Absence" (Washington, D.C.: Cost Accounting Standards Board, 1974).

[3]The Tax Revenue Act of 1987 repealed Section 463 of the Internal Revenue Code.

	Subsidiary Record	Dr.	Cr.
Work in Process		320	
Factory Overhead Control		6	
Unemployment Pay	6		
Payroll.			320
Liability for Unemployment Pay ...			6

■ APPRENTICESHIP AND TRAINING PROGRAMS

In many plants, new workers receive some preliminary training before they become economically productive. The portion of the wages paid in excess of the average or standard paid for the productive output, plus the cost of instruction, is an indirect labor cost to be charged to the total annual output through inclusion in the factory overhead rate. When unusual training programs are needed as a result of the opening of a new plant or the activating of a second or third shift, a case can be made for deferring the training cost as development or starting load cost and amortizing it over a period of time.

■ HUMAN RESOURCE ACCOUNTING

In annual reports, management often speaks in glowing terms of its employees as the company's most valuable asset. Yet management makes little effort to assess the value of this asset, and the company's accounting system does little to provide any assistance. For example, many firms invest heavily in personnel training programs without evaluating the expected payoff or the return on such investments. A firm is apt to send its managers to a variety of executive development programs whose value is essentially taken on faith and which are discontinued when the firm cannot afford them.

Human resource accounting is the process of developing financial assessments of people or groups of people within organizations and society and of monitoring these assessments over time. It deals with the value of investments in human beings and with the related economic results. Managers are being asked to give more serious consideration to human resource investment decisions and to the human resource impact of all their decisions. Thus, the personnel function within an organization may serve more efficiently its role of acquisition, development, and utilization of human resource potential.

A human resource accounting system, separate from and supplemental to the formal accounting system, attempts to identify incurred human resource costs that are to be separated from the firm's other costs. The techniques and procedures used should distinguish between the asset and expense components of human resource costs. The resulting human resource assets would then be classified into functional categories, such as recruiting, hiring, training, development, and familiarization. Such information would purportedly enable management to make decisions based on a realistic cost/benefit analysis and cost amortization and would provide investors with an improved basis to assess the value of an enterprise.

The quantification of human resources appears to be the first stumbling block in the creation of human resource accounting. All companies have methods of measuring sales, profits, investments in plant and equipment, and investments in inventories. Similarly, incurred human resource costs such as training programs can be measured, although determining the time period for amortization may be difficult. But beyond the possibility of capitalizing certain incurred human resource costs, how does a company set a quantitative value for such attributes as loyalty, skills, morale, decision-making ability, and intelligence? Since it seems difficult to quantify these human factors, it seems equally difficult to assign asset status to human resources except when measured incurred costs can be identified. The justification for measuring an asset value is based on the economic concept that an asset is capable of providing future benefits to the firm. It is argued that since the employee group is important to the future success of the company, it has value that should be considered as an asset on the human resource balance sheet. Asset determination for human resources is particularly meaningful for professional sports franchises where a superstar is essentially the asset that creates gate receipts. As with any other asset, the professional athlete can be sold or traded, which increases the litigation involving player contracts.

In spite of the difficulties, a number of proposals have attempted to utilize human resource accounting. Some proposals focus on incurred costs only, while others encompass estimated values. These proposals are:

1. *Capitalizing salaries*—whereby a firm assumes that what the employees are doing will be of some future benefit to the firm and that appropriate rates of capitalization can be determined.
2. *Capitalizing the cost of acquiring an employee*—a plan that would require collecting the costs of acquiring, hiring, and training. (A precedent for this method exists in professional sports.)
3. *Capitalizing startup costs*—involves not only capitalizing startup costs but goes one step further by considering the synergistic components of cost and time required for members of a firm to establish effective cooperative working relationships.
4. *Behavioral variables approach*—involves periodic measurements of the key causal and intervening variables for the corporation as a whole. Statistical variation in leadership styles and technical proficiency levels (causal variables) and the resulting changes in subordinate attitudes, motivations, and behavior (intervening variables) can establish relationships between such variables. These changes would produce changes in the end-result variables such as productivity, innovation, and human resource developments. Trends in earnings could then be predicted. These forecasts are discounted to find the present value of the human resources.

5. *Opportunity costs*—suggest that investment center managers are encouraged to bid for any scarce employee they desire. The winning manager includes the bid in the investment base. The division's benefit is the increased profit produced by the new employee.

6. *Economic value approach*—compares differences in present and future earnings of similar firms in the same industry. Ostensibly, the differences are due to human organization. Future earnings are forecast and discounted to find their present value. A portion thereof is allocated to human resources based on their contribution.

7. *Present value method*—involves determining wage payments over perhaps a five-year period, and then discounting these payments at the rate of return of owned assets in the economy for the most recent year. This calculation yields the present value of the future five-years' wage payments based on this year's return.

8. *Stochastic rewards valuation model*—involves a stochastic process defined as a natural system that changes in time in accordance with the law of probability. To measure an individual's value to an organization requires:
   (a) An estimate of the time interval during which an individual is expected to render services to the organization, and
   (b) A measure of the services expected to be derived from the individual during this interval.
   The resource's expected value is then multiplied by a discount factor to arrive at the present value of expected future services.[4]

Human resource data may be part of a large-scale human resource accounting system or merely part of a specific project application. Although the human resource accounting movement might gain an aura of respectability from inclusion as supplemental data in external reports, these data seem more useful for managerial decisions, i.e., an internal reporting focus.

At present, the value of human resource accounting systems for specific purposes must be determined by designing models and methods which can be empirically tested. Further research is required to demonstrate both the feasibility and the effects of human resource accounting on management's attitude, behavior, and decisions.[5]

■ PENSION PLANS

A *pension plan* is an arrangement whereby a company provides retirement benefit payments for all employees in recognition of their work contribution to the company. A pension plan is probably the most important as well as the most complicated factor associated with labor and labor costs. It influences

---

[4]Roger Jauch and Michael Skigen, "Human Resources Accounting: A Critical Evaluation," *Management Accounting*, Vol. LV, No. 11, pp. 33-36.

[5]For an example of empirical research, see Lawrence A. Tomassini, "Assessing the Impact of Human Resource Accounting: An Experimental Study of Managerial Decision Preferences," *The Accounting Review*, Vol. LII, No. 4, pp. 904-913. In this study, human resources accounting cost data caused different preferences to be expressed between the experimental and control group subjects.

personnel relations, company financing, income determination, income tax considerations, and general economic conditions. It must also comply with governmental regulations.

Pension Cost Estimate

The ultimate cost of a company pension plan depends upon several related factors:

1. The number of employees reaching retirement age each year.
2. The average benefit to be paid to each retired employee.
3. The average period over which benefits will be paid.
4. Income from pension fund investments.
5. Income tax allowances.
6. Expense of administration.
7. Treatment of benefits to employees who leave the company before reaching the pension age.

Pension Cost Allocation

In the case of bonuses and paid vacations, part of the total earnings of an employee is withheld or accrued for a period of months and then paid in a lump sum. In the case of pension payments, the wage is earned and the labor cost is incurred many years before the payment is made. As a matter of principle, if an employee is paid a base wage for a 40-hour week and if the employer's pension cost will amount to $1.50 an hour, the pension cost incurred is $60 per week and is chargeable to factory overhead, marketing expense, or administrative expense. If payment is probable and the amount can be reasonably measured in advance, an employer should accrue postretirement benefits such as health care coverage during the years of employment, rather than expensing them when incurred after retirement.[6]

Employee Retirement Income Security Act of 1974

The Employee Retirement Income Security Act of 1974 (more commonly known as ERISA or the Pension Reform Act of 1974) was enacted in order to make certain that promised pensions are actually paid at retirement. This act sets minimum government standards for vesting, participation, funding, management, and a variety of other matters. The act also covers a wide range of employee welfare plans for health, accident, and death benefits. In addition, it covers pension or retirement plans and establishes both labor standards (administered by the Secretary of Labor) and tax standards (administered

---

[6]For a detailed discussion of accounting for pension plans and postretirement benefits, see Jay M. Smith, Jr. and K. Fred Skousen, *Intermediate Accounting*, 10th ed., Chapter 22, Comprehensive Vol., (Cincinnati: South-Western Publishing Co., 1990)

by the Secretary of the Treasury). The labor and tax standards taken together form a common body of legislation pertaining to practically all employee benefit plans not specifically exempted from the act.

Virtually every private pension, profit-sharing, thrift, or savings plan had to be amended in order to comply with the act. All plans must contend with increased record keeping, compliance, and reporting. Many plans have experienced increased costs and/or funding obligations.

The Pension Reform Act of 1974, including its amendments, is a comprehensive piece of legislation. The presentation here enumerates only a few matters relevant to labor-related costs. Among the more important requirements affecting employers and employees are:

1. New employees cannot be denied participation for more than one year unless an employee is under twenty-five years of age or benefits are fully vested at the end of a three-year waiting period. The law prohibits a plan from excluding an employee because of advanced age if employment began at least five years prior to normal retirement age.
2. An employer's minimum annual contribution generally must include the normal cost for the year plus amortization of initial past service liabilities, liabilities resulting from plan amendments, and experience gains and losses. Amortization payments must be calculated on a level payment basis.
3. In case the assets of a terminated or insolvent plan are not sufficient to pay the insured benefits, the Pension Benefit Guaranty Corporation (PBGC) guarantees certain specified vested benefits for each participant or beneficiary. To finance this insurance program, the PBGC collects a premium from all covered plans.
4. Descriptions of the plan and annual financial, actuarial, and other information must be provided to participants and beneficiaries, the Secretaries of Labor and the Treasury, and the PBGC.

Vesting. A participant of a pension plan is assured of receiving future benefits under a plan when rights to the benefits become vested. *Vesting* means that benefits will not be forfeited even in the event of dismissal or discontinuance of company operations. Employees who resign will still be entitled upon reaching retirement age to receive the benefits in which their rights were vested. The act sets minimum vesting standards that must be met by all plans subject to the participation standards.

Funding. The act establishes minimum funding standards for certain defined benefit plans. The effect of these standards is to impose time limitations for accumulating sufficient assets to pay retirement benefits to participants. Generally, employers must currently contribute the normal cost of the plan for the plan year plus a level funding of past service costs and certain other costs, including interest. The law does not permit the use of the so-called pay-as-you-go method, whereby employers would make periodic pension payments directly to retired employees.

Present Value (PV). Basic to all funding methods is the concept of present value (PV), sometimes referred to as capitalized value. The *present value* principle permits the value at any given point of time to be expressed as the equivalent value at a different point in time under a set of future conditions. The principle is particularly useful in dealing with financial transactions involving a time series, such as periodic contributions and retirement annuities. It permits the computation of an entire series of financial transactions over a period of time to be expressed as a single value at any point in time.

The Role of the Actuary. Computations relating to pension plan costs, contributions, and benefits are made by an *actuary*, an expert in pension, life insurance, and related matters involving life contingencies. An actuary employs mathematical, statistical, financial, and other techniques to compute costs or benefits, to equate costs with benefits, and to evaluate and project actuarial experience under a plan. Membership in the American Academy of Actuaries, or one of the other recognized actuarial organizations, identifies a person as a member of the actuarial profession.

Administrative Problems. The Pension Reform Act of 1974 mandated sweeping changes in the structure and administration of all types of qualified employee benefit plans. In addition, the act created a staggering number of complicated requirements in such areas as disclosure, reporting, investments, and insurance. For example, an employer must report to four government agencies: the Department of Labor, the Pension Benefit Guaranty Corporation, the Internal Revenue Service, and the Secretary of Labor. A summary description report must also be prepared and sent to all participants and beneficiaries.

CASB Pension Cost Standards

In 1975, the Cost Accounting Standards Board promulgated CAS No. 412, "Cost Accounting Standards for Composition and Measurement of Pension Cost," establishing the components of pension cost, the bases for measuring such cost, and the criteria for assigning pension cost to cost accounting periods. This standard is to be used in accounting for government contracts to which CASB regulations apply. This standard is compatible with the requirements of the Pension Reform Act of 1974, although certain of its provisions are more restrictive than the Pension Reform Act. Furthermore, the CASB standard, while attempting to stay within the constraints of generally accepted accounting principles (GAAP), specifies certain features of GAAP which are considered not appropriate for government contract costing purposes. In 1977, CAS No. 413, "Adjustment and Allocation of Pension Cost," declared that actuarial gains and losses should be calculated and gave criteria for assigning pension expense to accounting periods and to segments, as well as for valuing pension fund assets.

■ ADDITIONAL LEGISLATION AFFECTING LABOR-RELATED COSTS

Costing labor and keeping payroll records were relatively simple prior to the first social security act. This legislation made it necessary for many employers to initiate or redesign payroll procedures in order to account accurately for payroll deductions. Later, other state and federal legislation imposed additional requirements affecting the accounting for wages and salaries. For example, the Federal Insurance Contributions Act, federal and state unemployment tax laws, workmen's compensation laws, and federal, state, and city income tax laws require periodic reports.[7] As a result of the multiplicity of forms and regulations, competent personnel are needed in a company's payroll department.

Federal Insurance Contributions Act (FICA)

This legislation is administered and operated entirely by the federal government. Originally enacted in August of 1935, the act provided that employers in a covered industry must withhold 1 percent of the wages paid to each employee up to $3,000 of earnings in any one year, which amounted to a maximum of $30 of FICA tax. The employer was required to contribute an equal amount. Specifically excluded in the 1935 act were agricultural and domestic workers; federal, state, and municipal employees; employees of nonprofit organizations; and a variety of others, including the self-employed.

The Federal Insurance Contributions Act has been amended many times since 1935. The amendments have brought more employees under the act and have increased the benefits, the tax rate, and the wage base, including certain fringe benefits, upon which the tax is levied.[8] Under the 1965 FICA amendments, the Hospital Insurance Program (Medicare) was enacted.[9]

Employers are required to pay a tax equal to the amount paid by the employees. The employer is further required to collect the FICA tax from employees by deducting the current percent from the wages paid each payday up to the current annual limit or base to which the tax applies. Federal income tax withheld and employee and employer FICA taxes must be periodically deposited with either an authorized commercial bank depository or a Federal Reserve Bank, and a quarterly report must be filed.

---

[7]These pages summarize the major provisions. U.S. Treasury Department Internal Revenue Service Circular E, entitled "Employer's Tax Guide," is an excellent source for a more comprehensive coverage of these regulations at the federal government level. A free copy of the current edition can be obtained by writing to the nearest District Director, Internal Revenue Service. State and local laws must be determined as they apply to specific employers.

[8]The Tax Reform Act of 1984 amended the *Internal Revenue Code*, Section 3121(a), to require the inclusion of fringe benefits (not specifically excluded by statute) in wages subject to FICA tax.

[9]A rate of 7.5 percent on an annual wage base of $50,000 per employee for FICA tax, used in the illustrations and in the end-of-chapter material, is not current. The actual rate and wage base change from time to time.

Federal Unemployment Tax Act (FUTA)

Unemployment compensation insurance is another phase of social security legislation affecting labor costs and payroll records. Unlike FICA, which is strictly a federal program, FUTA provides for cooperation between state and federal governments in the establishment and administration of unemployment insurance. When the initial legislation was enacted by the federal government in August, 1935, provisions of FUTA forced various states to pass adequate unemployment laws.

Under the provisions of the Federal Unemployment Tax Act, an employer in covered employment pays an unemployment insurance tax of 6.2 percent. The annual earnings base is $7,000 of each employee's wages paid, with .8 percent payable to the federal government and 5.4 percent to the state. States generally provide an experience rating plan under which an employer who has provided stable employment may pay less than 5.4 percent to the state agency, with zero as a possible payment. State legislation may provide for a higher rate or a larger annual earnings base in computing the state portion of the tax. While the federal act requires no employee contribution, some states also levy an unemployment insurance tax on the employee.[10]

The payroll and personnel departments should work together to earn an experience rating that minimizes the firm's state unemployment tax. An awareness of the effect of claims on the rate may provide stronger incentives for a more stable work force, a desirable condition for the employees as well.

Payment of the FUTA Tax. The federal portion of the unemployment tax is payable quarterly. However, if the employer's tax liability (plus any accumulated tax liability for previous quarters) is $100 or less for the fiscal year, only one payment is required by January 31 of the following year. The related tax return is due annually on January 31.

State Unemployment Reports and Payments. The various state unemployment compensation laws require reports from employers to determine their liability to make contributions, the amount of taxes to be paid, and the amount of benefit to which each employee is entitled if unemployment occurs. While the reports and report forms vary from state to state, the more important requirements are:

1. *Status Report.* The status report determines whether an employer is required to make contributions to the state unemployment insurance fund.
2. *Contribution and Wage Report.* All employers covered by the state unemployment compensation laws are required to file a quarterly contribution and wage report. This report provides a summary of wages paid

---

[10]The earnings base and rates are subject to change. To find the current levels, consult published government regulations. Also, the percentage payable to the federal government may be greater than .8 percent in certain states because those states failed to repay prior year advances that came from the federal government to the state unemployment compensation funds.

during the quarter, a computation of the tax, names of employees, and wages paid to each during the quarter.

3. *Separation Report.* When it becomes necessary to lay off workers, printed materials prepared by the state employment commission are provided, informing employees how to secure new employment and how to make an application for unemployment benefits. An employee who quits without good cause or before working a certain number of weeks, is discharged for ample reason, or has been unemployed for a short period may be ineligible for unemployment payments. In these cases, an employer files a separation notice with the state employment commission. Since any unemployment benefits paid to a former employee may increase the employer's state rate, the separation notice is filed in order to prevent the experience rating adjustment that the state employment commission might otherwise make. Charge statements from the state should be checked by the employer to verify their accuracy.

Worker's Compensation Insurance

Worker's compensation insurance laws provide insurance benefits for workers or their survivors for losses caused by accidents and occupational diseases suffered in the course of employment. In most states, these laws have been in effect for many years. While the benefits, premium costs, and various other details vary from state to state, the total insurance cost is borne by the employer. The employer may have the option of insuring with an approved insurance company or through a state insurance fund. In some cases, if the size and the financial resources are sufficient, the enterprise may carry its own risk.

Withholding of Federal Income Tax, State Income Tax, and City Wage Tax

The employer is required to withhold federal income tax—and state income and city wage taxes if applicable—from employees' compensation, including certain fringe benefits, and to furnish information to the Internal Revenue Service and to state and city taxing authorities showing the amount of compensation paid each employee and the amount of income taxes withheld.[11] The collection of income taxes from employees and the remittance of these taxes affect payroll accounting. Before new employees begin work, they are required to fill out a withholding allowance certificate (W-4 form).

Income taxes are withheld from each wage payment in accordance with the amount of the employee's earnings and the exemptions claimed on the

---

[11]The Tax Reform Act of 1984 amended the *Internal Revenue Code*, Section 61(a)(1), to require the inclusion of employee fringe benefits in the definition of gross income, i.e., income subject to taxation. Consequently, employers must include employee fringe benefits that are not specifically excluded by statute in income subject to withholding.

W-4 form. Employers are required to furnish a written statement or receipt to each employee from whom taxes have been withheld, showing the total wages earned and the amount of taxes withheld (income taxes and FICA) during a calendar year. This withholding statement (W-2 form) must be delivered to the employee on or before January 31 of the following year. If employment is terminated before December 31, the W-2 form, if requested by the employee, must be furnished within 30 days (1) from the date requested or (2) from the last payment of wages, whichever is later. If it is not requested by the employee, the normal January 31 deadline applies.

As mentioned previously, each employer must periodically deposit federal income tax withheld and FICA taxes. Also, a reconciliation of the quarterly reports with duplicate copies of the W-2 forms furnished employees must be filed annually. Therefore, payroll records must show the names of persons employed during the year, the periods of employment, the amounts and dates of payment, and the taxes withheld each payroll date.

The state may also levy an income tax that must be withheld from employees' wages. The tax withheld must be remitted to the taxing authorities along with the required reports. Information must also be supplied to the employee.

A city or municipality may levy a wage earnings tax on an employee working within its boundaries even though the employee is not a resident. Here, too, not only must reports and payments be made to the local taxing authority, but information must also be supplied to the employee.

Recordkeeping

Federal, state, and city taxing authorities require that employers keep payroll tax records, by employee, of:

1. The name, address, social security number, and occupation.
2. The amounts and dates of remuneration payments and the period of service covered by each payment.
3. The amounts and dates of annuity and pension payments.
4. The amounts of payments that constitute taxable wages.
5. The amounts and dates of tax withheld.
6. The amounts of payments and dates covered while absent due to sickness or injury.
7. Copies of employees' withholding allowance certificates.
8. A record of fringe benefits provided.
9. The amounts and dates of tax deposits made by the employer.
10. The amount of contributions paid into each state unemployment compensation fund, showing separately (a) payments made and not deducted from the remuneration of employees and (b) payments made and deducted from the remuneration of employees.
11. Copies of employer tax returns filed, as well as records of all information required to be shown on the prescribed tax returns.

Although the taxing authorities do not order, suggest, or recommend forms or details for securing the required information, the employer must keep records that will enable a government agency to ascertain whether the taxes for which the employer is liable are correctly computed and paid. These records must be kept for at least four years after the date the tax becomes due or the date the tax is paid, whichever is later. Employees are not required to keep records, but each employee should keep accurate and permanent records showing the name and address of each employer, date for beginning and termination of employment, wages earned, and tax withheld during employment.

■ LABOR-RELATED DEDUCTIONS

In addition to compulsory payroll deductions, a variety of other deductions may be withheld from take-home pay, with the consent of the employee.

Insurance

Many companies provide various benefits for their employees, such as health, accident, hospital, and life insurance. It is common for the company and the employees to share the cost, with the employees' share being deducted from wages each payroll period or at regular intervals. If the company pays insurance premiums in advance, including the employees' share, an asset account such as Prepaid Health and Accident Insurance will be debited when the payments are made. The employer's share will subsequently be credited to the asset account and debited to expenses, and the asset account will be credited for the employees' share of the premiums when the payroll deductions are made. In this payroll deduction, as in all similar cases, a subsidiary record showing the contributions of each employee is necessary, and one or more general ledger accounts are maintained.

A company's cost of group life insurance premiums for that portion of an employee's coverage exceeding $50,000 must be included as a part of the employee's gross income for income tax purposes; however, it is not subject to income tax withholding by the employer.[12] This cost also is deemed to be wages for FICA tax purposes, but not for unemployment tax. In addition, the Internal Revenue Code requires that employers must demonstrate that benefits to employees who are highly compensated are nondiscriminatory with respect to other employees. Specific nondiscrimination rules must be met. This requirement applies not only to insurance plans but to other employer-provided fringe benefits as well. Businesses that do not meet these rules must report the extra benefits paid as taxable income to their employees, and these employees must pay tax on it.[13]

---

[12]*Internal Revenue Code of 1986*, Section 79 (a) (1).
[13]*Internal Revenue Code of 1986*, Section 105 (h).

Union Dues

Many enterprises employing union labor agree to a union shop and to a deduction of initiation fees and regular membership dues from the wages of each employee. To account for these deductions, a general ledger account entitled Union Dues Payable shows the liability for amounts withheld from the employees. At regular intervals, the company prepares a report and remits the dues collected to the union treasurer.

U.S. Savings Bonds

To cooperate with the federal government, an employer and an employee frequently agree to some systematic plan of withholding from wages a fixed amount for the purpose of purchasing U.S. Savings Bonds. A general ledger account entitled U.S. Savings Bonds Payable is set up to show the liability for wages withheld for this purpose. When the accumulated amount withheld from a given employee is sufficient to purchase a bond, an entry is made debiting U.S. Savings Bonds Payable and crediting Cash. Similar procedures may be used for other employee savings and investment plans.

Payroll Advances

For a variety of reasons, payroll advances may be made to employees. The advances may be in the form of cash, materials, or finished goods. To provide control, an advance authorization form should be executed by a responsible official and should be sent to the payroll department. The asset account debited for all advances represents a receivable to the company and may be entitled Salary and Wage Advances.

When the advances take the form of merchandise, Materials or Finished Goods is credited. If the merchandise is charged to the employee at a figure above cost, Sales may be credited. When the price is above cost but substantially less than the regular sales price, an account entitled Sales to Employees might be maintained. At the regular payroll date, the employee's earnings are entered in the payroll journal as usual, and the advance is deducted from wages to be paid. The amount of the advance being deducted is credited to Salary and Wage Advances.

■ RECORDING LABOR COSTS

The basic principle of labor costing is simple and straightforward. A record of the labor time "purchased" is made through use of the clock card; a record of the performance received is made through the use of time tickets or the daily time report. These documents may exist in electronic or hard copy form. The accounting entries required are:

1. To record wage payments due employees and the liability for all amounts withheld from wages.
2. To charge the total labor cost to appropriate jobs, processes, and departments.

Weekly, semimonthly, monthly, or as often as a payroll is met, the total amount earned by workers is debited to Payroll, with credits to Accrued Payroll and to the withholding accounts. The cost of labor purchased is summarized and recorded as debits to Work in Process, Factory Overhead Control, Marketing Expenses Control, and Administrative Expenses Control and as a credit to Payroll. Employer payroll taxes and other labor-related costs are recorded, and at appropriate times, payments are made to discharge payroll-related liabilities.

The accounting for labor costs and payroll liabilities is illustrated in general journal form on pages 327 and 328, based upon these assumptions:

1. The payroll period is for January, 19B.
2. The payroll is paid on January 9, 19B, and on January 23, 19B, covering wages earned through the preceding Saturday. Note that the wages of the last week of December, 19A, would be paid on January 9 and that the payment of January 23 would cover work done through January 19. Refer to the following calendar.

JANUARY, 19B

Sun	Mon	Tue	Wed	Thu	Fri	Sat
		1	2	3	4	5
6	7	8	9	10	11	12
13	14	15	16	17	18	19
20	21	22	23	24	25	26
27	28	29	30	31		

3. Payroll figures for wages earned during January are:

Direct factory labor	$38,500
Indirect factory labor	18,000
Sales salaries	20,000
Office and administrative salaries	12,000
Total payroll	$88,500

4. Wages paid during January, 19B: $50,000 on January 9, and $40,000 on January 23. Of the federal income tax withheld, $6,000 is on the payroll of January 9 and $5,500 on that of January 23.
5. Wages earned and unpaid on December 31, 19A, total $26,000. On January 31, the amount is $24,500.
6. The cost of the employer's payroll taxes is recorded when the month-end labor cost distribution entry is made, with separate liability accounts for federal and state agencies. In compliance with the regulations, employees' FICA taxes are recorded when they are withheld and determination of the payment of the total FICA tax (employer and employee portions) is based on the date the wages are paid.

7. Employees' income tax, employees' FICA tax, the employer's matching FICA tax payment, employees' union dues, and U.S. Savings Bonds payments are paid on the same dates that wages are paid to the employees. No other January payroll-related liabilities are paid in that month.

Added assumptions:

FICA tax: 7.5%.
Worker's compensation: 1% of payroll
Unemployment insurance: .8% federal, 5.4% state.
Estimated pension cost: $4,000 per month (direct labor, $1,540; indirect labor, $900; sales salaries, $1,000; office and administrative salaries, $560).
Payroll advances: $2,200 (deducted on January 9 payroll).
Union dues collected: $1,000 each payroll period.
Savings bonds deductions: $1,200 on January 9; $900 on January 23.
Health and accident insurance: 2% of payroll, shared equally (employees' share as wages paid; employer's share as wages earned).
Cost for supplemental unemployment benefits: 2% of factory labor earned.

	Subsidiary Record	Dr.	Cr.
Jan. 2 Accrued Payroll.....................		26,000.00	
Payroll			26,000.00
Reversing entry for wages payable as of December 31............			
9 Payroll		50,000.00	
Accrued Payroll			35,350.00
Employees Income Tax Payable......			6,000.00
FICA Tax Payable			3,750.00
Salary and Wage Advances			2,200.00
Union Dues Payable			1,000.00
U.S. Savings Bonds Payable			1,200.00
Prepaid Health and Accident Insurance			500.00
9 Accrued Payroll.....................		35,350.00	
Employees Income Tax Payable.........		6,000.00	
FICA Tax Payable		7,500.00	
Union Dues Payable..................		1,000.00	
U.S. Savings Bonds Payable		1,200.00	
Cash.............................			51,050.00
23 Payroll		40,000.00	
Accrued Payroll			29,200.00
Employees Income Tax Payable......			5,500.00
FICA Tax Payable			3,000.00
Union Dues Payable			1,000.00
U.S. Savings Bonds Payable			900.00
Prepaid Health and Accident Insurance			400.00
23 Accrued Payroll.....................		29,200.00	
Employees Income Tax Payable.........		5,500.00	
FICA Tax Payable		6,000.00	
Union Dues Payable		1,000.00	
U.S. Savings Bonds Payable		900.00	
Cash.............................			42,600.00
31 Payroll		24,500.00	
Accrued Payroll			24,500.00

	Subs. Rec.	Dr.	Cr.
31 Work in Process		38,500.00	
Factory Overhead Control		8,354.50	
FICA Tax	2,887.50		
Unemployment Insurance Taxes . . .	2,387.00		
Workers' Compensation	385.00		
Pension Expense	1,540.00		
Health and Accident Insurance	385.00		
Estimated Unemployment Expense	770.00		
Payroll			38,500.00
FICA Tax Payable			2,887.50
Federal Unemployment Tax Payable. . .			308.00
State Unemployment Tax Payable			2,079.00
Prepaid Workers' Compensation			385.00
Liability for Pensions			1540.00
Prepaid Health and Accident Insurance			385.00
Liability for Unemployment Pay			770.00
31 Factory Overhead Control		22,086.00	
Indirect Labor	18,000.00		
FICA Tax	1,350.00		
Unemployment Insurance Taxes . . .	1,116.00		
Worker's Compensation	180.00		
Pension Expense	900.00		
Health and Accident Insurance	180.00		
Estimated Unemployment Expense	360.00		
Payroll			18,000.00
FICA Tax Payable			1,350.00
Federal Unemployment Tax Payable. . .			144.00
State Unemployment Tax Payable			972.00
Prepaid Worker's Compensation.			180.00
Liability for Pensions			900.00
Prepaid Health and Accident Insurance			180.00
Liability for Unemployment Pay			360.00
31 Marketing Expenses Control		24,140.00	
Sales Salaries	20,000.00		
FICA Tax	1,500.00		
Unemployment Insurance Taxes . . .	1,240.00		
Worker's Compensation	200.00		
Pension Expense	1,000.00		
Health and Accident Insurance	200.00		
Payroll			20,000.00
FICA Tax Payable			1,500.00
Federal Unemployment Tax Payable. . .			160.00
State Unemployment Tax Payable			1,080.00
Prepaid Worker's Compensation.			200.00
Liability for Pensions			1,000.00
Prepaid Health and Accident Insurance			200.00
31 Administrative Expenses Control		14,440.00	
Office and Administrative Salaries .	12,000.00		
FICA Tax	900.00		
Unemployment Insurance Taxes . . .	744.00		
Worker's Compensation	120.00		
Pension Expense	560.00		
Health and Accident Insurance	120.00		
Payroll			12,000.00
FICA Tax Payable			900.00
Federal Unemployment Tax Payable. . .			96.00
State Unemployment Tax Payable			648.00
Prepaid Worker's Compensation.			120.00
Liability for Pensions			560.00
Prepaid Health and Accident Insurance			120.00

This illustration records the employer's payroll taxes as a liability when the wages are earned, which follows the accrual concept of accounting. As a practical matter, many employers do not accrue payroll taxes at the end of each fiscal period because the legal liability does not occur until the next period when the wages are paid. This latter practice may be considered acceptable if it is consistently applied or if the amounts are not material. It is, however, required for tax purposes, and payments to the Internal Revenue Service must conform, as is done in this illustration.

DISCUSSION QUESTIONS

Q11-1. The hourly wage of an employee is $9, but the labor cost of the employee is considerably more than $9 an hour. Explain.

Q11-2. Discuss the accounting treatment of fringe benefits to factory employees.

Q11-3. Give two costing methods of accounting for the premium costs of overtime direct labor. State circumstances under which each method would be appropriate. (AICPA adapted)

Q11-4. For many years, a company has paid all employees one week's wages as a year-end bonus. It is also company policy to give 2-week paid vacations. What accounting procedures should be followed with respect to the bonus and vacation pay?

Q11-5. The productive efficiency of a company depends upon superior group leaders. The company management suggests that group leaders and selected workers organize a class in personnel administration and group leadership. The class is set up at a nearby university with one of the regular professors in charge. The employees attend the class at night on their own time, but the company pays the tuition charges. How should the company account for this cost?

Q11-6. (a) Define human resource accounting.
(b) What are the objectives of the concept?
(c) State the theoretical proposals that have been made in favor of human resource accounting.
(d) What are some of the more serious drawbacks of this concept?

Q11-7. The total cost of contributions that must be paid ultimately to provide pensions for the present participants in a plan cannot be determined precisely in advance; however, reasonably accurate estimates can be made by the use of actuarial techniques. List the factors entering into the determination of the ultimate cost of a funded pension plan. (AICPA adapted)

Q11-8. The term "pension plan" has been referred to as a formal arrangement for employee retirement benefits, whether established unilaterally or through negotiation, by which specific or implied commitments have been made and used as the basis for estimating costs. Explain the preferable procedure for computing and accruing the costs under a pension plan. (AICPA adapted)

Q11-9. What is meant by the experience-rating provisions of the unemployment compensation laws of various states?

EXERCISES

E11-1. Overtime earnings. An employee in the Assembly Department is paid $7.60 an hour for a regular week of 40 hours. During the week ended April 30, the employee worked 52 hours and earned time and a half for overtime hours.

Required:

   (1) Prepare the journal entry to record the labor cost if the overtime premium is charged to production worked on during the overtime hours.
   (2) Prepare the journal entry to record the labor cost if the overtime premium is not charged to production worked on during the overtime hours.

E11-2. Bonus and vacation pay liability. A production worker earns $1,150 per month and the company pays the worker a year-end bonus equal to one month's wages. The worker is also entitled to a half-month paid vacation per year. Company policy dictates that bonus and vacation benefits be treated as indirect costs and accrued during the 11 1/2 months the employee is at work.

Required: Prepare the journal entry to record and distribute (simultaneously) the labor cost of the production worker for a month. Assume that there are no deductions from gross wages.

E11-3. Bonus and vacation pay liability. Four factory workers and a supervisor comprise a team in the Machining Department. The supervisor earns $10 per hour and the combined hourly direct wages of the four workers is $32. Each employee is entitled to a two-week paid vacation and a bonus equal to four weeks' wages each year. Vacation pay and bonuses are treated as an indirect cost and are accrued over the 50-week work year. A provision in the union contract does not allow these employees to work in excess of 40 hours per week.

Required: Prepare the journal entry to record the bonus and vacation pay liability applicable to one week's production.

E11-4. Pension cost. The Midwest Corporation employs a pension plan for its 100 direct laborers. Normal operations are 50 weeks per year at 40 hours each week. After working 25 years, the workers are to receive a pension of $10,800 annually. It is estimated that 70% of the employees will qualify for eventual retirement and will receive the pension for an average of 10 years. For October, the number of direct labor hours was 16,800. Pension cost is recorded monthly on the basis of labor hours.

Required: Compute the pension cost for October. (For simplicity, assume no discounting for future pension fund earnings.)

E11-5. Fringe benefits. A production worker earns $1,656 a month, and the company pays one month's salary as a bonus at the end of the year. The worker is also entitled to a half-month paid vacation, and the company pays $1,840 a year into a pension fund for the worker. Bonus, vacation pay, and pension costs are charged to production during the 11 1/2 months the employee is at work. The federal and state unemployment insurance tax rates are .8% and 3.6%, respectively. The employer's share of FICA tax is 7.5%. All labor-related fringe benefits for production workers are treated as factory overhead.

Required: Prepare the journal entries to record the March payroll distribution and the cost of fringe benefits.

E11-6. Fringe benefits. A maintenance worker earns $1,334 a month and the company pays one month's salary as a bonus at the end of the year. The worker is entitled to a half-month paid vacation annually, and the company pays $1,104 a year into a pension fund for the worker's retirement. The federal and state unemployment insurance rates are .8% and 1.5%, respectively, and the FICA payroll tax is 7.5%. Labor-related costs are recorded during the 11 1/2 months the employee is at work.

Required: Prepare a combined journal entry to record one month's payroll distribution and to record the cost of fringe benefits.

E11-7. Employer's labor-related expenses. Clarks Company has employees engaged in manufacturing, marketing, and administrative functions. The February payroll was:

Direct labor	$25,000
Indirect labor	10,000
Marketing.	8,000
Administrative	7,000
	$50,000

The company incurs the following labor-related expenses as a percentage of the payroll:

Pension plan.	7.8%
FICA tax	7.5
Federal unemployment insurance	.8
State unemployment insurance	4.6
Worker's compensation	4.0
Medical insurance	1.0

Required: Present the journal entry to record the employer's labor-related expenses.

CGA-Canada (adapted)   Reprint with permission

E11-8. Payroll entries. For the second week in February, Wisconsin Products Company's records show direct labor, $18,000; indirect factory labor, $3,000; sales salaries, $4,200; and administrative office salaries, $1,500. The FICA tax rate is 7.5%; state and federal unemployment compensation insurance taxes are 3.2% and .7%, respectively; state and federal income taxes withheld are $500 and $2,500, respectively; and the city wage tax is 1% on employee gross earnings and is paid by the employee. The company treats employer payroll taxes on factory personnel as an indirect cost.

Required:

(1) Prepare the entry to record the payroll liability.
(2) Prepare the entry to distribute the payroll cost.
(3) Prepare the entry to record the employer's payroll taxes.

E11-9. Payroll entries. For the first payroll in November, the records of Gulfport Company show direct labor, $20,000; indirect labor, $4,000; sales salaries, $5,000; and office salaries, $3,600. FICA tax is applicable to 75% of the payroll in each department, while unemployment insurance tax applies to only 25%. Federal income tax to be withheld totals $3,000, and employees pay a city income tax of 1% on gross earnings.

Required: Prepare the journal entries to record the payroll liability, distribute the payroll, and record the employer's payroll taxes, treated as an indirect cost. The state unemployment tax rate is 3%, the FUTA tax rate is .8%, and the FICA tax rate is 7.5%.

PROBLEMS

P11-1. Overtime earnings. The pay stub of Wilshire Manufacturing employee #1071, who works on the production line, showed the following for a two-week pay period:

Gross earnings	$1,140.00
Income tax withheld.	152.92
FICA tax.	85.50
Company pension plan	83.54
Union dues.	11.00
Net earnings	$ 807.04

The employee works a regular 40-hour week and is paid $12 per hour regular time and time and a half for overtime.

For this employee, the company paid an additional $273.20 in benefits for the two-week pay period with regard to the employer's contribution to the company's pension plan and FICA tax.

Required:

(1) What was the amount charged to work in process for employee #1071 for the two-week period, assuming that any overtime work is not traceable to a particular job order or product?

(2) How much would the department factory overhead control account have been charged for the two-week period for employee #1071?

(3) Assume that in the second week of the pay period, the machine on which this employee worked was being repaired for three hours and the worker was unable to perform regular duties of production during that time. To which account should the cost of idle time be charged?   (SMAC adapted)

P11-2. Entries for payroll and payroll taxes. For the December 1-15 payroll, which totaled $28,000, employees' FICA deductions amounted to only $1,230, since some of the employees had already earned the maximum applicable during the year. For the same period, income tax withheld totaled $2,872.

The company should apportion employer FICA taxes as follows: 60% to factory overhead, 30% to marketing expense, and 10% to general office expense. The state unemployment insurance tax rate is 4%, the FUTA tax rate is .8%, and only $5,000 of the payroll (all factory employees) is subject to this tax, since all other employees had earned more than $7,000 by December 1. The company closed for the year on December 15 and had no more payroll expenses.

Required: Prepare (1) the entry to record the payroll for the period December 1-15, (2) the entry to pay the payroll of December 1-15, (3) the entry to record the employer's payroll taxes for the period December 1-15, and (4) the entry to remit employees income tax and total FICA tax to the Internal Revenue Service.

P11-3. Payroll, tax deductions, and payroll distribution. The following information, taken from the daily time tickets of a producing department, summarizes time and piecework for the week ended April 30:

Employee	Clock No.	Job No.	Hours Worked	Production Pieces	Hourly Rate	Piece Rate
Belcastro, V	90	641	40	960	—	$.30
Cherpack, C	91	—	46	—	$7.00	—
Meadows, A	92	638	40	—	5.80	—
Smeltzer, S	93	—	40	—	7.20	—

The company operates on a 40-hour week and pays time and a half for overtime. Additional information:

(a) A FICA tax deduction of 7.5% should be made for each employee.

(b) An advance of $20 was made to Belcastro on April 26.

(c) A 2% deduction is to be made from each employee's wage for the company's employee health and hospital benefit plan.

(d) Cherpack works in the storeroom issuing materials; Smeltzer is the supervisor; the others work directly on special orders as noted.

(e) Use 10% in computing income tax withheld. The state unemployment tax rate is 4%, and the federal unemployment tax rate is .8%.

Required:

(1) Compute each employee's gross pay, deductions, and net pay.

(2) Prepare journal entries to (a) set up the accrued payroll and other liabilities, (b) pay the payroll, (c) distribute the payroll and record the employer's payroll taxes, and (d) pay the employees income tax and the FICA tax payable. Include subsidiary record detail.

P11-4. Payroll taxes, vacation pay, and payroll. The normal workweek at Oaks Publishing Inc. is Monday through Friday, with payday being the following Tuesday. On April 1, after the reversing entry was posted, the payroll account showed a $2,230 credit balance, representing labor purchased during the last two days of March. (See the following calendar.)

APRIL

Sun	Mon	Tue	Wed	Thu	Fri	Sat
			1	2	3	4
5	6	7	8	9	10	11
12	13	14	15	16	17	18
19	20	21	22	23	24	25
26	27	28	29	30		

Deductions of 7.5% for FICA tax and 9.5% for income tax are withheld from each payroll check.

The labor summary for April shows $16,400 of direct labor and $5,600 of indirect labor. Vacation pay is charged to current production at a rate of 8% of total payroll.

Payrolls were:

April 7	$5,890
14	4,920
21	5,900
28	4,880

Required:

(1) Prepare entries to record each payroll.
(2) Prepare the entry on April 30 to distribute the payroll and to record the employer's payroll taxes for wages earned during April, treating the employer's payroll taxes and vacation pay as factory overhead. The state unemployment tax rate is 4%, and the federal unemployment tax rate is .8%. Include subsidiary record detail.
(3) Prepare T accounts for Payroll and Accrued Payroll and the entry to record accrued wages at the end of April.

P11-5. Payroll entries. Cleanaire Inc. manufactures air pollution control devices. There are four producing departments, supported by two factory service departments, Toolroom and Storeroom. For manufacturing employees, overtime premium wages are treated as factory overhead, as are payroll taxes borne by the employer. The Finished Goods Stockroom and Shipping departments are located in the manufacturing plant facilities but are a part of marketing expenses. The separate sales and administrative offices' payroll expenses are charged to marketing expenses and administrative expenses, respectively.

For the week ended February 14, the following payroll summary was prepared:

Department	Labor Hours	Payroll (Earned Hours)	Overtime Premium	Federal Income Tax Withheld (10%)	FICA Tax (7.5%)	Net Pay
Casting	240	$ 1,620	$108	$ 172.80	$129.60	$1,425.60
Forging	410	2,542	160	270.20	202.65	2,229.15
Machining	560	3,976	120	409.60	307.20	3,379.20
Assembly	160	960	—	96.00	72.00	792.00
Toolroom	84	428	16	44.40	33.30	366.30
Storeroom	82	410	8	41.80	31.35	344.85
Finished Goods Stockroom	40	180	—	18.00	13.50	148.50
Shipping	40	192	—	19.20	14.40	158.40
Total plant payroll	1,616	$10,308	$412	$1,072.00	$804.00	$8,844.00
Sales Office	—	$ 2,200	—	$ 220.00	$165.00	$1,815.00
Administrative Office	—	1,550	$150	170.00	127.50	1,402.50

Required: Prepare journal entries, including subsidiary record detail, to record:

(1) Preparation of the payroll.
(2) Payment of the payroll.
(3) Distribution of the payroll.
(4) Recording of the employer's payroll taxes. (The state unemployment tax rate is 3.2%, and the federal unemployment tax rate is .8%.)
(5) Payment of employees income tax and total FICA tax payable.

P11-6. Payroll cycle. The payroll department of Banderillo Company Inc. prepares its monthly and biweekly payroll using the following payroll data:

(a) The payroll period deals with August and September; the last payment was made on August 25. Refer to the calendars shown below.

(b) The company pays its factory, marketing, and office and administrative personnel on a biweekly basis. The workweek is Monday through Friday; paychecks are distributed on the Friday following the close of the two weeks. Executives, superintendents, and department heads are paid on a monthly basis on the first Friday following the last day of the month. The 4th of September is Labor Day; all employees will be paid, but the direct labor cost is charged to factory overhead.

AUGUST

Sun	Mon	Tue	Wed	Thu	Fri	Sat
		1	2	3	4	5
6	7	8	9	10	11	12
13	14	15	16	17	18	19
20	21	22	23	24	25	26
27	28	29	30	31		

SEPTEMBER

Sun	Mon	Tue	Wed	Thu	Fri	Sat
					1	2
3	4	5	6	7	8	9
10	11	12	13	14	15	16
17	18	19	20	21	22	23
24	25	26	27	28	29	30

(c) The payroll is based on these data:

Monthly salaries:

    2 executives: $3,000 each per month
    3 superintendents: $2,500 each per month
    2 department heads: $2,000 each per month

Hourly workers:

    Direct factory labor: 200 employees; 40 hours per week; average pay, $6 per hour
    Indirect factory labor: 30 employees; 40 hours per week; average pay, $4 per hour

Weekly rates:

    Marketing personnel: 12 employees; average pay, $350 per week
    Office and administrative personnel: 9 employees; average pay, $305 per week

(d) Additional information:

Federal income tax withheld: 15% on monthly salaries; 10% on all others
FICA tax: 7.5% up to a base of $50,000 per employee
Federal unemployment tax: .8% up to a base of $7,000 per employee
State unemployment tax: 5.4% up to a base of $7,000 per employee

All indirect factory labor wages are still subject to the federal and state unemployment taxes, but the cumulative earnings for the year exceed the $7,000 base for all other employees. The FICA tax is recorded as a liability when it is withheld at the payroll date, in compliance with regulations. The employer's payroll taxes are recorded when the cost distribution entry is made; separate liability accounts are kept for federal and state agencies; month-end payroll accrual entries are made only at the end of the calendar year.

Workers' compensation insurance: 1% of total payroll

Pension cost: 5% for monthly salaries, with equal contributions by these employees deducted from their paychecks; 3% for all other employees, with no contributions by them

Union dues: $.50 deducted each payday from each hourly worker

Health insurance: 1% of earnings, shared equally between employees and employer

Required: Prepare journal entries, including subsidiary record detail, to record:

(1) The monthly salaries to be paid in September, with all applicable deductions and employer-borne labor-related costs. Include the payment of employee income tax and total FICA tax. Distribution is to be made as follows: 2 executives to administration; 3 superintendents to factory; 1 department head to marketing; 1 department head to administration (office).

(2) Factory, marketing, and office employees' earnings to be paid in September on a biweekly basis, with all applicable deductions and employer-borne labor-related costs. Include the payment of employee income tax and total FICA tax. Distribution is to be made on the basis of the four categories.

(3) The earnings of one direct factory laborer for the first of the two-week payroll periods, in order to illustrate the procedure required for an individual employee.

CASES

C11-1. Cost principles and cost determination. As a subcontractor under a prime contract with a governmental agency, a company operating a machine shop undertook to produce certain parts on a cost-plus-fixed-fee basis. The hours of operation were about evenly divided between the above contract and the regular business of the company.

Each day, the work required for the regular company business was completed first. The remainder of the day, with whatever overtime was necessary, was devoted to production under the contract. During the contract period, overtime hours represented a substantial portion of the total hours worked. Under an agreement with the employees, time and a half was paid for all hours over eight worked each day.

Job sheets recorded the actual costs of materials and direct labor, including any overtime premium paid. Factory overhead was applied on the basis of the labor cost so recorded, and the job sheets were adjusted each month to eliminate any balance in the overhead variance account.

Required: State objections to the cost accounting principles applied, reasons for any incorrectness of the client's statements, and the procedure for making a revised cost determination.   (AICPA adapted)

C11-2. Accrual of compensated absences. Kristina Company began operations on January 1. Doug Clark, human resources manager, developed the following policies related to compensated absences.

(a) All employees are eligible to receive vacations and sick leave with pay.

(b) The number of vacation days granted depends on the employee's length of service as follows.

Length of Service	Days of Vacation
0-1 year	1 day per month (after 2 months service)
1-4 years	10 days per year
5-14 years	15 days per year
15 years and over	20 days per year

(c) Vacation days earned as of an anniversary date should be taken during the following 12 months. Vacation days earned but not taken are vested and may be carried forward; however, this practice is not encouraged.

(d) Employees earn sick leave at a rate of one day per month of service accumulating to a maximum of 40 days. Sick leave days taken are subtracted from those earned.

(e) Upon termination of employment, the employee will be paid for vacation days earned but not taken. No payment is made for sick leave earned but not taken.

(f) All employees are eligible for holiday pay. Holidays earned but not taken may be taken on another day during the calendar year. Holidays may not be carried forward to the next year.

Diana Seitz, Kristina's controller, has received the information shown below for the Drafting Department.

Record of Compensated Absences
Drafting Department—January 1-December 31

| Employee | Hourly Wage | Vacation Days | | Sick Days | | Holidays Not Taken |
		Earned	Taken	Earned	Taken	
R. Gage........	$15.50	10	8	12	4	0
K. Allen........	14.25	8	8	9	6	0
A. Talbot.......	14.25	10	5	12	2	1
S. Williams.....	13.50	6	6	7	1	2
T. Jenson.......	13.50	7	5	8	0	0
B. Howard......	13.50	10	7	12	5	0

Seitz will be receiving similar information for all of Kristina's employees, and has informed Doug Clarke that she will make the necessary accruals for compensated absences at the end of the year according to *Statement of Financial Accounting Standards (FASB) No. 43,* "Accounting for Compensated Absences." Clarke remarked that he believed it was not necessary to accrue sick days. Seitz replied that sick days can be handled either way, according to FASB No. 43 and that she had chosen to accrue them.

The employees of Kristina work an eight-hour day and a 40-hour week, and the company uses the calendar year as its fiscal year.

Required:

(1) Based on the information presented above, prepare the journal entry to accrue the vacation pay for the Drafting Department at December 31. Debit Factory Overhead Control.

(2) Explain the financial accounting treatment for vacation days earned but not taken when vacation days:
   (a) Do not vest but accumulate.
   (b) Neither vest nor accumulate.

(3) Kristina Company can elect to accrue or not accrue sick leave pay.
   (a) Explain why the accrual of sick leave pay is an election and not a requirement.
   (b) Prepare the journal entry to accrue sick leave pay for the Drafting Department at December 31. Debit Factory Overhead Control.

(4) Explain how Kristina Company should account for holiday benefits.

(ICMA adapted)

C11-3. Human resource accounting. The Consumer Products Division of Liberty Manufacturing Company experienced reduced sales in the first quarter of 19B and has forecasted that the decline in sales will continue through the remainder of the year.

Liberty's executive management believes in a decentralized organization, and division managers have considerable managerial latitude, receiving bonuses of a specified percentage of division profits, in addition to their annual salaries. At the end of the first quarter of 19B, J. Spassen, the Consumer Products Division manager, felt that drastic action was needed to reduce costs and improve the division's performance. Consequently, 20 highly-trained, skilled employees were dismissed as one cost-reduction step. Five of these employees are expected to be available for reemployment when business is projected to return to normal in 19C.

Executive management, upon reviewing the steps taken by Spassen, was concerned about the consequences of dismissing the 20 skilled employees. The company officials had recently attended a seminar on human resource accounting and wondered if Spassen would

have taken that particular action if a cost-based human resource accounting system had been in operation.

Required:

(1) Explain what is accounted for in a cost-based human resource accounting system.
(2) Explain how information generated by such a system might apply to the decision to dismiss the 20 skilled employees.

(ICMA adapted)

CHAPTER 12

Cost Behavior Analysis

Some costs vary in total directly with changes in production activity, while others remain relatively unaffected. Because of the dynamic nature of business, companies often are faced with the need to make changes in the level and mix of their business activities. In order for management to plan a company's activities intelligently and control its costs effectively, the relationship of cost incurrence to changes in activity must be thoroughly understood. This chapter discusses the effect of changes in business activity on costs and classifies costs with respect to activity as fixed, variable, or semivariable. Techniques used to segregate the fixed and variable components of semivariable costs are illustrated. Although the discussion centers on production costs and activities, the concepts and techniques are equally applicable to marketing and administrative activities.

■ CLASSIFYING COST

Success in planning and controlling cost depends upon a thorough understanding of the relationship between the incurrence of cost and business activity. Careful study and analysis of the effect of business activities on costs generally will result in the classification of each type of expenditure as a fixed, variable, or semivariable cost.

Fixed Cost

A *fixed cost* is defined as one that does not change in total as business activity increases or decreases. Although some kinds of costs may have the appearance of being fixed, all costs are variable in the long run. If all business activity decreases to zero and there is no prospect for an increase, a firm will liquidate, thereby avoiding all costs. If activity is expected to increase beyond the capacity of current facilities, fixed costs must be increased to handle the expected increase in volume. For example, factory overhead includes items such as supervision, depreciation, rent, property insurance, and property taxes which are generally considered to be fixed costs. If management expects demand for the company's products to increase beyond the capacity of the present production facilities, it must acquire additional plant and equipment, personnel, and possibly supervisors in order to produce the level of output necessary to meet demand. Such additions would result in an incremental increase in the level of expenditure for each of these items of factory overhead.

For this reason, a particular kind of expenditure should be classified as a fixed cost only within a limited range of activity. This limited range of activity is referred to as the *relevant range*. Total fixed cost will change outside the relevant range of activity. The changes in fixed cost at different levels of activity and the relevant range are depicted in the following graph.

Fixed Cost

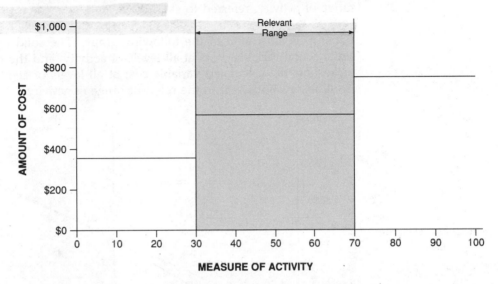

Some expenditures acquire the fixed characteristic through the dictates of management policy. For example, the level of advertising expenditure and the amount of charitable contribution (or the cost of other community service projects) are determined by management and are not directly related to sales or production activity. Such expenses are sometimes referred to as *programmed fixed expenses*. Expenditures that require a series of payments over a long-term period of time are often called *committed fixed expenses*. Examples include interest on long-term debt and rentals on long-term lease agreements.

Variable Cost

A *variable cost* is defined as one that increases in total proportionately with an increase in activity and decreases proportionately with a decrease in activity. Variable costs include the cost of direct materials, direct labor, some supplies, some indirect labor, perishable tools, rework, and normal spoilage. Variable costs can usually be directly identified with the activity that gives rise to the incurrence of cost.

In practice, the relationship between a business activity and the related variable cost usually is treated as if it were linear; that is, total variable cost is assumed to increase by a constant amount for each unit increase in activity.

However, the actual relationship is rarely perfectly linear over the entire range of possible activity. Productive efficiency usually declines when the work load is lighter than normal and, at the opposite extreme, when labor and machinery are pushed to the limit of capacity. When the volume of activity increases to a certain level, management may add newer, more efficient production machinery or replace existing machinery with more productive machinery. As a result of these factors, the cost per unit of activity usually is different at widely varied levels of activity. Nevertheless, within a limited range of activity, referred to as the relevant range, the relationship between an activity and the related cost may closely approximate linearity. This relationship is illustrated in the following graph. The solid line (Line B) represents actual variable costs at all levels of activity, and the dash line (Line A) represents the calculated variable cost at all levels of activity as determined from observations within the relevant range of activity.

Calculated Variable Cost

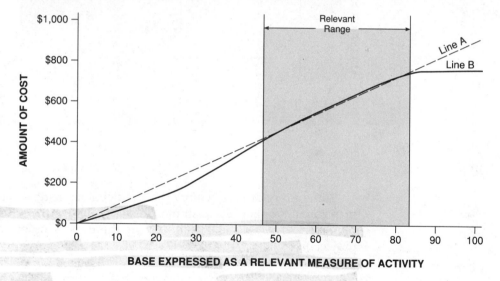

In cases such as the one illustrated in the graph, a constant variable cost rate is a sufficient approximation of the relationship between the variable cost and the related activity within the relevant range. However, to plan and control variable costs effectively, the underlying conditions that give rise to the incurrence of cost should be reviewed frequently to determine whether or not the variable cost per unit of activity has changed. When conditions change or the level of activity is outside the relevant range, a new variable cost rate should be computed.

Semivariable Cost

A *semivariable cost* is defined as one that displays both fixed and variable characteristics. Examples include the cost of electricity, water, gas, fuel oil, coal, some supplies, maintenance, some indirect labor, employee group-term life insurance, pension cost, payroll taxes, and travel and entertainment.

Three reasons for the semivariable characteristic of some types of expenditures are:

1. A minimum of organization may be needed, or a minimum quantity of supplies or services may need to be consumed, in order to maintain readiness to operate. Beyond this minimum level of cost, which is essentially fixed, additional cost varies with volume.
2. Accounting classifications, based upon the object of expenditure or function, commonly group fixed and variable items together. For example, the cost of steam used for heating, which is dependent upon the weather, and the cost of steam used for manufacturing, which is dependent upon the volume of production, may be charged to the same account.
3. Production factors are divisible into infinitely small units. When such costs are charted against their volume, their movements appear as a series of steps rather than as a continuous straight line. This situation is quite noticeable in moving from a one-shift to a two-shift or from a two-shift to a three-shift operation. Such moves result in definite steps in the cost line because a complete set of workers must be added at one point.[1]

A semivariable cost is illustrated in the following graph. The solid line in the graph represents actual costs at all levels of activity. In this illustration, the actual cost line (Line C) is nonlinear. This situation could occur because of the use of different production techniques or equipment and/or because of different degrees of capacity utilization at different levels of activity. The dash lines are linear and represent the calculated fixed and variable components of the semivariable cost (Line A and Line B, respectively) at all levels of activity, as determined from observations within the relevant range. Where Line B

Semivariable Costs

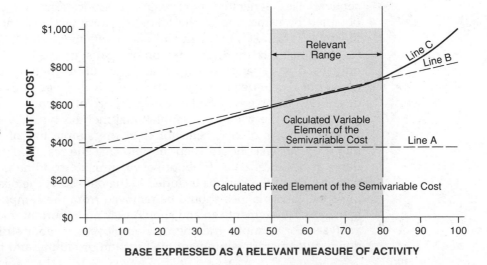

and Line C coincide, the linear assumption closely approximates the actual relationship. This area of coincidence is the relevant range. The use of the calculated fixed cost and the variable cost rate to estimate cost at any level of activity outside of the relevant range would result in unreliable estimates.

■ SEPARATING FIXED AND VARIABLE COSTS

In order to plan, analyze, control, measure, or evaluate costs at different levels of activity, fixed and variable costs must be separated. Those costs that are entirely fixed or entirely variable within the range of activity anticipated must be identified, and the fixed and variable components of semivariable costs must be separated. As discussed in later chapters, the separation of fixed and variable costs is necessary for the following purposes:

1. Predetermined factory overhead rate computation and variance analysis.
2. Flexible budget preparation and variance analysis.
3. Direct costing and contribution margin analysis.
4. Break-even and cost-volume-profit analysis.
5. Differential and comparative cost analysis.
6. Short-run profit maximization and cost minimization analysis.
7. Capital budgeting analysis. won't study here
8. Marketing profitability analysis by territories, products, and customers.

In practice, managerial judgment often is used to classify costs as fixed or variable.[2] In such cases, classification is based on the personal experience of management. Although such an approach is expedient, it often results in unreliable estimates of cost. The behavior of a particular type of cost is not always readily apparent from a casual observation. Furthermore, managers often attempt to simplify the process by classifying all costs as either entirely fixed or entirely variable, thereby ignoring the fact that some costs are semivariable. Generally, more reliable classifications and cost estimates are obtained by using one of the following computational methods which are illustrated below: (1) the high and low points method, (2) the statistical scattergraph method, or (3) the method of least squares. These methods are not only used to separate the fixed and variable components of semivariable costs, but also to determine whether a particular type of cost is entirely fixed or entirely variable within the relevant range of activity.

Although the use of a computational method typically results in a more reliable analysis of cost behavior than the simple use of managerial judgment, the analyst should keep in mind that the results obtained are dependent on historical data. If abnormal or unusual conditions occurred during one or more of the periods included in the data base, the observations reflecting such abnormalities should be removed from the sample. In this respect, managerial judgement can and should play an important role in cost behavior analysis. For example, training new employees, a labor strike or work slowdown, a temporary equipment malfunction or failure, and the purchase of a

---

[2]Maryanne M. Mowen, *Accounting for Costs as Fixed and Variable*, (Montvale, N.J.: National Association of Accountants, 1986), pp. 19-20.

batch of substandard materials or parts are events that could distort the relationship between an activity and a related cost. In order to enhance prediction accuracy, the historical data base should be inspected by experienced management and the abnormal observations should be removed from the sample.

Fixed and variable cost estimates that are based on historical data should be adjusted to reflect changes that are expected to occur during the forecast period. Technological improvements in production techniques or facilities can materially affect the behavior of costs. For example, if management acquires (or plans to acquire) new machinery that is expected to operate more efficiently than machinery used during the sample period, cost behavior estimates based on historical data should be adjusted to reflect the expected improvement in operating or production efficiency. Product design changes, as well as changes in production technology, may affect cost behavior. For example, changes in the kinds of materials or component parts used in a product may make it necessary to operate machinery at a different speed than that required during the sample period. This, in turn, may affect the machinery's rate of energy or fuel consumption and possibly the amount of preventive maintenance required per machine hour. To the extent that such changes are anticipated, cost behavior estimates should be adjusted.

If the historical data base includes observations from several different years, the analyst should consider the potential distorting effects of inflation. If the rate of inflation was substantial during one or more of the periods in the sample, fixed and variable cost estimates are likely to be unreliable. One way to compensate for this problem would be to first restate the cost for each period in the sample to current dollars (i.e., multiply the cost in each period in the sample by the quotient obtained by dividing the price index expected for the forecast period by the price index in effect during the period in which the sample observation was recorded), and then perform the analysis on the inflation-adjusted costs.

To illustrate the three computational methods of determining the fixed and variable elements of a particular type of cost, assume that the following data are taken from Barker Company's records for the preceding year:

Month	Direct Labor Hours	Electricity Expense
January........	34,000	$ 640
February	30,000	620
March	34,000	620
April..........	39,000	590
May...........	42,000	500
June	32,000	530
July	26,000	500
August.........	26,000	500
September	31,000	530
October........	35,000	550
November	43,000	580
December	48,000	680
Total........	420,000	$6,840
Monthly average .	35,000	$ 570

High and Low Points Method

In the high and low points method, the fixed and variable elements of a cost are computed from two data points. The data points (periods) selected from the historical data being analyzed are the high and low periods as to activity level. These periods are usually, but not necessarily, also the highest and lowest figures for the cost being analyzed. If the periods having the highest or lowest activity levels are not the same as those having the highest or lowest level of cost being analyzed, the activity level should govern in making the selection. From a theoretical point of view, activity is presumed to drive cost. The high and low periods are selected because they represent conditions for the two activity levels which are the farthest apart. However, care must be taken not to select data points distorted by abnormal conditions.

Using the data for Barker Company, the fixed and variable elements are determined as follows:

	Activity Level	Expense
High	48,000 hours	$680
Low	26,000 hours	500
Difference	22,000 hours	$180

Variable rate: $180 ÷ 22,000 hours = $.00818 per direct labor hour

	High	Low
Total expense..............	$680	$500
Variable expense* (rounded)	393	213
Fixed expense..............	$287	$287

*Direct labor hours × $.00818

The high and low activity levels differ by 22,000 direct labor hours, with a cost variation of $180. The assumption is that the difference in the costs at the two levels of activity occurred because of differences in the activity being measured and is therefore pure variable cost. The variable rate is determined by dividing the difference in expense ($180) by the difference in activity (22,000 direct labor hours). In this example, the variable rate is determined to be $.00818 per direct labor hour. The total variable expense at either the high or low level of activity can be determined by multiplying the variable rate times the activity level. This results in a total variable cost at the high level of $393 ($.00818 × 48,000 hours) and at the low level, $213 ($.00818 × 26,000 hours). The difference between the total expense and the total variable expense is the fixed expense, which in this example is determined to be $287. The fixed expense is the same, whether computed from the high or low data.[3]

---

[3]The high and low points method is equivalent to solving two simultaneous equations, based on the assumption that both points fall on the locus of the true variable cost line. Using the above figures, equations could be set up and solved as follows:

$$
\begin{array}{rcl}
F + 48{,}000V &=& \$\ 680 \\
- F - 26{,}000V &=& -500 \\
\hline
22{,}000V &=& \$\ 180
\end{array}
$$

$$V = \$180 \div 22{,}000 = \$.00818 \text{ per direct labor hour}$$

With variable and fixed elements established, the expense totals for various levels of activity can be calculated.

The high and low points method is simple, but it has the disadvantage of using only two data points to determine cost behavior, and it is based on the assumption that the other data points lie on a straight line between the high and low points. Because it uses only two data points, it may result in estimates of fixed and variable costs that are biased. As a result, estimates of total cost based on fixed and variable costs computed with the high and low points method often are more inaccurate than estimates derived by other methods that consider a larger number of data points.

Statistical Scattergraph Method

The statistical scattergraph method can be used to analyze cost behavior. In this method, the cost being analyzed (the dependent variable) is plotted on a vertical line (the *y-axis*) and the associated activity (the independent variable, e.g., direct labor dollars, direct labor hours, machine hours, units of output, or percentage of capacity) is plotted along a horizontal line (the *x-axis*).

The data from the electricity expense illustration on page 343 are plotted on the following graph. Each point on the graph represents the electricity expense for a particular month. For instance, the point labeled "Nov." represents the electricity expense for November, when 43,000 direct labor hours

Statistical Scattergraph Representing the Fixed and Variable Elements for Electricity Expense

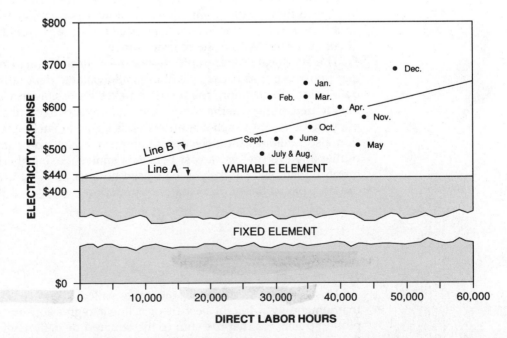

were worked. The x-axis shows the direct labor hours, and the y-axis shows the electricity expense. Line B is plotted by visual inspection. This line represents the trend shown by the majority of data points. Generally, there should be as many data points above as below the line. Another line (Line A) is drawn parallel to the base line from the point of intersection on the y-axis, which is read from the scattergraph as approximately $440. This line represents the fixed element of the electricity expense for all activity levels within the relevant range.

The triangle formed by Lines A and B shows the increase in electricity expense as direct labor hours increase. This increase is computed as follows:

$$
\begin{array}{ccc}
\text{Average monthly} - & \text{Fixed} & = \text{Average monthly variable} \\
\text{expense} & \text{element} & \text{element of expense} \\
\$570 & - \$440 = & \$130
\end{array}
$$

$$
\frac{\text{Average monthly variable element of expense}}{\text{Average monthly direct labor hours}} = \frac{\text{Variable cost per}}{\text{direct labor hour}}
$$

$$
\frac{\$130}{35{,}000 \text{ hours}} = \$.0037 \text{ per direct labor hour}
$$

Thus the electricity expense consists of $440 fixed expense per month and of a variable factor of $.0037 per direct labor hour.

In the statistical scattergraph on page 345, Line B is drawn as a straight line, even though the points do not follow a perfect linear pattern. In most analyses, a straight line is adequate, because it is a reasonable approximation of cost behavior within the relevant range.

The statistical scattergraph method is an improvement over the high and low points method because it utilizes all available data rather than only two data points. In addition, the method makes it possible to visually inspect the data to determine whether or not the cost appears to be related to the activity and whether or not such a relationship is approximately linear. Visual inspection also facilitates the detection of abnormal data (sometimes referred to as outliers). Nevertheless, a cost behavior analysis using the statistical scattergraph method is still likely to be biased because the cost line drawn through the data plot is based on visual interpretation.

Method of Least Squares

The *method of least squares* (sometimes called *regression analysis*) determines mathematically a line of best fit or a linear regression line through a set of plotted points, so that the sum of the squared deviations of each actual plotted point from the point directly above or below it on the regression line is at a minimum.[4] To illustrate this method, the data from page 343 are used in completing the table on page 348.

To prepare this table, the following steps are required:

1. First, determine the average direct labor hours, $\bar{x}$, and the average electricity expense, $\bar{y}$. The total direct labor hours are 420,000. When this amount is divided by the sample size, 12, the average of 35,000

---

[4]The formula for a straight line is $y = a + bx$; consequently, the regression equation is:

$$y_i = a + bx_i + e_i$$

where y_i = dependent variable (expense) at period i
x_i = independent variable (activity) at period i
a = intercept (estimate of fixed expense)
b = slope (estimate of variable expense per unit of activity)
e_i = prediction error, i.e., the difference between y_i (an actual observation) and $a + bx_i$ (an estimate of y_i)

Since the regression line exactly splits the plotted sample y_is, so that the sum of the values of the e_is above the line will exactly equal the sum of the values of the e_is below the line, the e_is will equal zero if they are totaled. To have a value to work with, the e_is are squared before being summed. This sum of the squared error terms, SSE, is expressed as follows:

$$\text{SSE} = \Sigma\,(y_i - a - bx_i)^2 = \Sigma y_i^2 - 2b\Sigma x_i y_i + 2ab\Sigma x_i + b^2\Sigma x_i^2 + na^2 - 2a\Sigma y_i$$

where y, a, b, and x are as previously defined and n is the sample size. For ease of presentation, the subscripts for x and y have been omitted in the remainder of the footnote. To find the minimum value of SSE, first partial derivatives are taken with respect to the two unknowns, i.e., a and b, and set equal to zero as follows:

$$\frac{\partial \text{SSE}}{\partial a} = 2b\Sigma x + 2na - 2\Sigma y = 0$$

$$\frac{\partial \text{SSE}}{\partial b} = 2\Sigma xy + 2a\Sigma x + 2b\Sigma x^2 = 0$$

Rearranging terms and dividing through by 2 yields the so-called normal equations:

$$\Sigma y = na + b\Sigma x$$
$$\Sigma xy = a\Sigma x + b\Sigma x^2$$

The normal equations each contain two unknowns. However, since the two equations are not linear transformations of one another, they can be solved. One way would be to multiply both sides of the first equation by $\Sigma x/n$ and then to subtract the first equation from the second in order to eliminate one of the unknowns (a in this case):

$$\Sigma xy = a\Sigma x + b\,\Sigma x^2$$
$$-\ \frac{\Sigma x \Sigma y}{n} = -a\Sigma x\ -\ \frac{b\Sigma x\Sigma x}{n}$$

$$\Sigma xy\ -\ \frac{\Sigma x \Sigma y}{n} = b\Sigma x^2\ -\ \frac{b\Sigma x\Sigma x}{n} \quad \text{or} \quad n\Sigma xy - \Sigma x\Sigma y = nb\Sigma x^2 - b\Sigma x\Sigma x$$

Solving for b yields:

$$b = \frac{n\Sigma xy - \Sigma x\Sigma y}{n\Sigma x^2 - \Sigma x\Sigma x} = \frac{\Sigma xy - \dfrac{\Sigma x\Sigma y}{n}}{\Sigma x^2 - \dfrac{\Sigma x\Sigma x}{n}} = \frac{\Sigma(x - \bar{x})(y - \bar{y})}{\Sigma(x - \bar{x})^2}$$

where $\bar{x} = \Sigma x/n$ and $\bar{y} = \Sigma y/n$

Since $y = a + bx$, then the remaining unknown, a, is computed as follows:

$$a = \bar{y} - b\bar{x}$$

Month	(1) x_i Direct Labor Hours	(2) $(x_i - \bar{x})$ Difference from Average of 35,000 Hours	(3) y_i Electricity Expense	(4) $(y_i - \bar{y})$ Difference from Average of $570 Electricity Expense	(5) $(x_i - \bar{x})^2$ (2) Squared	(6) $(x_i - \bar{x})(y_i - \bar{y})$ (2) × (4)	(7) $(y_i - \bar{y})^2$ (4) Squared
January	34,000	−1,000	$ 640	$ 70	1,000,000	$ − 70,000	$ 4,900
February	30,000	−5,000	620	50	25,000,000	−250,000	2,500
March	34,000	−1,000	620	50	1,000,000	− 50,000	2,500
April.	39,000	4,000	590	20	16,000,000	80,000	400
May	42,000	7,000	500	−70	49,000,000	−490,000	4,900
June	32,000	−3,000	530	−40	9,000,000	120,000	1,600
July	26,000	−9,000	500	−70	81,000,000	630,000	4,900
August.	26,000	−9,000	500	−70	81,000,000	630,000	4,900
September. . .	31,000	−4,000	530	−40	16,000,000	160,000	1,600
October	35,000	0	550	−20	0	0	400
November . . .	43,000	8,000	580	10	64,000,000	80,000	100
December . . .	48,000	13,000	680	110	169,000,000	1,430,000	12,100
Total	420,000	0*	$6,840	0*	512,000,000	$2,270,000	$40,800

*The sum of these columns is always zero, except for rounding differences.

hours per month results. The total electricity expense is $6,840, or an average of $570 per month ($6,840 ÷ 12).

2. Compute the differences between actual monthly figures for direct labor hours, x_i, and electricity expense, y_i, and their respective monthly averages, $\bar{x}$ and $\bar{y}$ computed in Step 1. These differences are entered in Columns 2 and 4.

3. Next, two multiplications must be made. First, square each of the differences entered in Column 2, $(x_i - \bar{x})$, and enter in Column 5, $(x_i - \bar{x})^2$. Second, multiply each of the differences in Column 2, $(x_i - \bar{x})$, by the corresponding differences in Column 4, $(y_i - \bar{y})$, and enter the products in Column 6, $(x_i - \bar{x})(y_i - \bar{y})$. (The differences entered in Column 4, $(y_i - \bar{y})$, are also squared and entered in Column 7, $(y_i - \bar{y})^2$. This column will be used on page 350 in computing the coefficient of determination.)

The variable rate for electricity expense, b, is computed as follows:

$$b = \frac{\Sigma(x_i - \bar{x})(y_i - \bar{y})}{\Sigma(x_i - \bar{x})^2} = \frac{\text{Column 6 total}}{\text{Column 5 total}} = \frac{\$2,270,000}{512,000,000} = \$.0044 \text{ per direct labor hour}$$

The fixed expense, a, can be computed, using the formula for a straight line as follows:

$$\bar{y} = a + b\bar{x}$$
$$\$570 = a + (\$.0044)(35,000)$$
$$\$570 = a + \$154$$
$$a = \$416 \text{ fixed element of electricity expense per month}$$

The answer above differs somewhat from the figure determined by the scattergraph method because fitting a line visually through the data points is not as accurate as fitting a line mathematically. The mathematical preciseness of the method of least squares injects a high degree of objectivity into the analysis. However, it is still useful to plot the data in order to verify visually the existence of a linear relationship between the dependent variable and the independent variable. Plotting the data makes it easier to spot abnormal data which can distort the least squares estimate of the fixed and variable components of the semivariable cost being analyzed. If abnormal data are found, they should be removed from the sample data set before using the least squares formulas. In this illustration, the sample size was small in order to simplify the computations. In practice, the sample size should be sufficiently large to represent normal operating conditions.

Correlation Analysis. The use of the statistical scattergraph method makes it possible to visually determine whether or not there is a reasonable degree of correlation between the cost and the activity being analyzed. In a statistical sense, *correlation* is a measure of the covariation between two variables—the independent variable (x, or direct labor hours in the illustration) and the dependent variable (y, or electricity expense in the illustration). In addition to computing the fixed cost and the variable rate for semivariable expenses or the variable rate for entirely variable expenses, the correlation between the independent variable and the dependent variable should be assessed. If all plotted points fall on the regression line, perfect correlation exists.

Mathematical measurements may be used to quantify correlation. In statistical theory, the *coefficient of correlation*, denoted r, is a measure of the extent to which two variables are related linearly. When $r = 0$, there is no correlation; and when $r = \pm 1$, the correlation is perfect. If the sign of r is positive, the relationship between the dependent variable, y, and the independent variable, x, is positive, which means that the value of y increases as the value of x increases, and the regression line slopes upward to the right. If the sign of r is negative, the relationship between the dependent variable, y, and the independent variable, x, is negative or inverse, which means that the value of y decreases as the value of x increases, and the regression line slopes downward to the right.

The *coefficient of determination*, r^2, is found by squaring the coefficient of correlation. The coefficient of determination is considered easier to interpret than the coefficient of correlation, r, because it represents the percentage of variance in the dependent variable explained by the independent variable. The larger the coefficient of determination, the closer it comes to the coefficient of correlation until both coefficients equal 1. The word "explained" means that the variations in the dependent variable are related to, but not necessarily caused by, the variations in the independent variable. Although the coefficient of correlation and the coefficient of determination are mathematical measures of covariation, they do not establish a cause-and-effect relationship between the dependent variable and the independent variable. Such a relationship must be theoretically developed or physically observed.

The formula for calculating the coefficient of correlation is:

$$r = \frac{\Sigma(x_i - \bar{x})(y_i - \bar{y})}{\sqrt{\Sigma(x_i - \bar{x})^2 \Sigma(y_i - \bar{y})^2}}$$

where $x_i - \bar{x}$ is the difference between each observation of the independent variable (direct labor hours in the Barker Company illustration) and its average; and $y_i - \bar{y}$ is the difference between each observation of the dependent variable (electricity expense) and its average. The coefficient of correlation, r, and the coefficient of determination, r^2, for the data on page 348 are calculated as follows:

$$r = \frac{\Sigma(x_i - \bar{x})(y_i - \bar{y})}{\sqrt{\Sigma(x_i - \bar{x})^2 \Sigma(y_i - \bar{y})^2}} = \frac{\text{Column 6 total}}{\sqrt{(\text{Column 5 total})(\text{Column 7 total})}}$$

$$= \frac{2{,}270{,}000}{\sqrt{(512{,}000{,}000)(40{,}800)}} = \frac{2{,}270{,}000}{\sqrt{20{,}889{,}600{,}000{,}000}}$$

$$= \frac{2{,}270{,}000}{4{,}570{,}514.2} = +.49666$$

$$r^2 = .24667$$

The coefficient of determination of less than .25 means that less than 25 percent of the change in electricity expense is related to the change in direct labor hours. Apparently, the cost in this case is related not only to direct labor hours but to other factors as well, such as the time of day for production or the season of the year. Furthermore, some other activity, such as machine hours, may be more closely correlated to electricity expense, thereby providing a better basis for predicting electricity expense.

To illustrate a case in which a high degree of correlation exists, the cost of electricity from the previous example is slightly altered, with direct labor hours remaining on the same level. The following solution indicates an almost perfect correlation between the two variables, which means that this relationship could be accepted as the basis for calculating electricity expense for planning and control.

Month	(1) x_i Direct Labor Hours	(2) $(x_i - \bar{x})$ Difference from Average of 35,000 Hours	(3) y_i Electricity Expense	(4) $(y_i - \bar{y})$ Difference from Average of $655 Electricity Expense	(5) $(x_i - \bar{x})^2$ (2) Squared	(6) $(x_i - \bar{x})(y_i - \bar{y})$ (2) × (4)	(7) $(y_i - \bar{y})^2$ (4) Squared
January	34,000	−1,000	$ 660	$ 5	1,000,000	$ −5,000	$ 25
February	30,000	−5,000	590	− 65	25,000,000	325,000	4,225
March	34,000	−1,000	660	5	1,000,000	−5,000	25
April.	39,000	4,000	680	25	16,000,000	100,000	625
May	42,000	7,000	740	85	49,000,000	595,000	7,225
June	32,000	−3,000	610	− 45	9,000,000	135,000	2,025
July	26,000	−9,000	580	− 75	81,000,000	675,000	5,625
August.	26,000	−9,000	550	−105	81,000,000	945,000	11,025
September. . .	31,000	−4,000	630	− 25	16,000,000	100,000	625
October	35,000	0	640	− 15	0	0	225
November . . .	43,000	8,000	750	95	64,000,000	760,000	9,025
December . . .	48,000	13,000	770	115	169,000,000	1,495,000	13,225
Total	420,000	0	$7,860	0	512,000,000	$5,120,000	$53,900

$$r = \frac{\Sigma(x_i - \bar{x})(y_i - \bar{y})}{\sqrt{\Sigma(x_i - \bar{x})^2 \Sigma(y_i - \bar{y})^2}} = \frac{\text{Column 6 total}}{\sqrt{(\text{Column 5 total})(\text{Column 7 total})}} = \frac{5{,}120{,}000}{\sqrt{(512{,}000{,}000)(53{,}900)}}$$

$$= \frac{5{,}120{,}000}{\sqrt{27{,}596{,}800{,}000{,}000}} = \frac{5{,}120{,}000}{5{,}253{,}265.7} = +.97463$$

$$r^2 = .94991$$

Standard Error of the Estimate. The regression equation, which in the Barker Company illustration is $y_i' = \$416 + \$.0044x_i$, can be used to predict expense at a given level of activity. However, since the regression equation is determined from a limited sample and since variables which are not included in the regression equation may have some influence on the expense being predicted, the calculated expense will usually be different from the actual expense at the same level of activity. The visual scatter around the regression line portrayed in the graph on page 345 illustrates that the actual electricity expense will likely vary from what might be estimated using the calculated fixed expense and the variable expense rate. Because some variation can be expected, management should determine an acceptable range of tolerance for use in exercising control over expenses. Expenses within the limits of variation can be accepted. Expenses beyond the limits should be investigated, and any necessary corrective action should be taken.

The *standard error of the estimate* is defined as the standard deviation about the regression line. A small value for the standard error of the estimate indicates a good fit. For an r^2 equal to one, the standard error would equal zero. Management can use this concept to develop a confidence interval which, in turn, can be used to decide whether a given level of cost variance is likely to require management action. To illustrate, the following table can be prepared from the data on page 343.

Month	(1) x_i Direct Labor Hours	(2) y_i Actual Electricity Expense	(3) $(y_i' = a + bx_i)$ Predicted Electricity Expense*	(4) $(y_i - y_i')$ Prediction Error (2) – (3)	(5) $(y_i - y_i')^2$ Prediction Error Squared (4) Squared
January........	34,000	$ 640	$ 566	$ 74	$ 5,476
February.......	30,000	620	548	72	5,184
March	34,000	620	566	54	2,916
April..........	39,000	590	588	2	4
May...........	42,000	500	601	–101	10,201
June	32,000	530	557	– 27	729
July	26,000	500	530	– 30	900
August........	26,000	500	530	– 30	900
September	31,000	530	552	– 22	484
October........	35,000	550	570	– 20	400
November......	43,000	580	605	– 25	625
December......	48,000	680	627	53	2,809
Total........	420,000	$6,840	$6,840	0**	$30,628

*Calculated regression line, y_i', values, (direct labor hours × $.0044) + $416, are rounded to the nearest dollar.
**The sum of this column is always zero, except for rounding differences.

The standard error of the estimate is then calculated as follows:

$$s' = \sqrt{\frac{\Sigma(y_i - y_i')^2}{n-2}} = \sqrt{\frac{\text{Column 5 total}}{12-2}} = \sqrt{\frac{\$30,628}{10}} = \sqrt{\$3,062.80} = \$55.34$$

The prediction errors are usually assumed to follow a standard normal distribution. However, for small samples, the Student's t distribution is a more appropriate assumption. A table of selected t values (based on the assumption that two tails of the distribution are of concern, i.e., that managers are concerned about both favorable and unfavorable variances) is given at the top of page 353.

The acceptable range of actual expense around the predicted expense would be computed for a sample of size n by multiplying the standard error of the estimate by the t value for $n - 2$ degrees of freedom[5] at the desired confidence level, t_p, and by a correction factor for small samples as follows:

$$y_i' \pm t_p s' \sqrt{1 + \frac{1}{n} + \frac{(x_i - \bar{x})^2}{\Sigma(x_i - \bar{x})^2}}$$

where all variables above are as previously defined.

To illustrate the computation and use of the confidence interval, assume that the actual level of activity for a period is 40,000 direct labor hours. The electricity expense computed for the budget from the regression equation determined in the previous example is $592 ($416 + $.0044 (40,000)). Assume further that management wants to be 95 percent confident that the actual electricity expense is within acceptable tolerance limits. Based on the table factor of 2.228 for t at the 95 percent confidence level, with $df = 12 - 2$, and on the standard error of the estimate computed above ($s' = 55.34), the confidence interval would be:

$$y_i' \pm t_{95\%} s' \sqrt{1 + \frac{1}{n} + \frac{(x_i - \bar{x})^2}{\Sigma(x_i - \bar{x})^2}}$$

$$\$592.00 \pm (2.228)(\$55.34) \sqrt{1 + \frac{1}{12} + \frac{(40,000 - 35,000)^2}{512,000,000}}$$

$$\$592.00 \pm (2.228)(\$55.34)(1.064)$$

$$\$592.00 \pm \$131.19$$

Management can expect the actual electricity expense to be between $460.81 ($592.00 - $131.19) and $723.19 ($592.00 + $131.19) about 95 percent of the time. Electricity expense outside of these limits will occur because of random chance only 5 percent of the time. If the actual electricity expense is less than $460.81 or greater than $723.19, management should investigate the cause and take any necessary corrective action.

For large samples, the Student's t distribution approaches the standard normal distribution and the correction factor for small samples (the square root term) approaches one. For large samples, therefore, the computation of the acceptable range of actual expense around the predicted expense may be simplified by omitting the correction factor and using the appropriate z value

---

[5]Degrees of freedom (df) refers to the number of values which are free to vary after certain restrictions have been placed on the data. In general, if a regression equation involves p unknown parameters, then $df = n - p$. In linear bivariate regression there are two unknown parameters, a and b; thus, $df = n - 2$.

Degrees of Freedom	Desired Confidence Level			
	90%	95%	99%	99.8%
1	6.314	12.706	63.657	318.310
2	2.920	4.303	9.925	22.326
3	2.353	3.182	5.841	10.213
4	2.132	2.776	4.604	7.173
5	2.015	2.571	4.032	5.893
6	1.943	2.447	3.707	5.208
7	1.895	2.365	3.499	4.785
8	1.860	2.306	3.355	4.501
9	1.833	2.262	3.250	4.297
10	1.812	2.228	3.169	4.144
11	1.796	2.201	3.106	4.025
12	1.782	2.179	3.055	3.930
13	1.771	2.160	3.012	3.852
14	1.761	2.145	2.977	3.787
15	1.753	2.131	2.947	3.733
20	1.725	2.086	2.845	3.552
25	1.708	2.060	2.787	3.450
30	1.697	2.042	2.750	3.385
40	1.684	2.021	2.704	3.307
60	1.671	2.000	2.660	3.232
120	1.658	1.980	2.617	3.160
∞	1.645	1.960	2.576	3.090

for the standard normal distribution.[6] If the sample size used in computing the regression equation and the standard error of the estimate in the illustration were large, the 95 percent confidence interval for electricity expense at 40,000 direct labor hours would be:

$$\$592.00 \pm (1.960)(\$55.34)$$
$$\$592.00 \pm \$108.47$$

After the fixed and variable components of cost have been computed using the method of least squares, it is useful to plot the regression line against the sample data, so that the pattern of deviations of the actual observations from the corresponding estimates on the regression line can be inspected. Normally, the distribution of observations around the regression line should be uniform for all values of the independent variable (referred to as *homoscedastic*) and randomly distributed around the regression line as depicted in Figure 1 on page 354. However, if the variance differs at different points on the regression line (referred to as *heteroscedastic*) as depicted in Figure 2 or the observations around the regression line appear to be correlated with one another (referred to as *serial correlation* or *autocorrelation*) as depicted in Figure 3, the standard error of the estimate and the confidence intervals based on the standard error are unreliable measures.[7]

---

[6]The *t* values presented in the table on this page for *df* = ∞ are equal to the *z* values for the standard normal distribution at the probability levels indicated at the head of each column.

[7]For a comprehensive discussion, see Chapter 19, "Multiple Regression and Correlation," Michael J. Brennan and Thomas M. Carroll, *Preface to Quantitative Economics & Econometrics* (Cincinnati: South-Western Publishing Co., 1987).

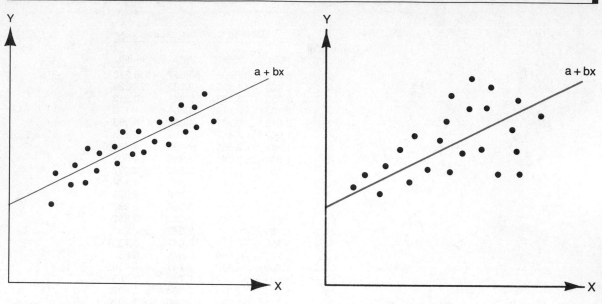

Figure 1-Homoscedasticity-Random Error Term   Figure 2-Heteroscedasticity

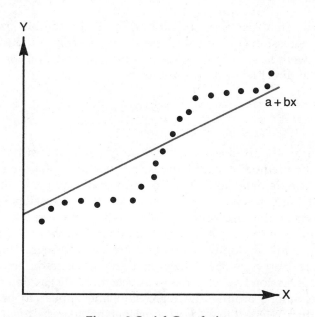

Figure 3-Serial Correlation

Method of Least Squares for Multiple Independent Variables

Typically, cost behavior is shown as dependent upon a single measure of volume or on some other independent variable. In the discussion above, for example, the behavior of the dependent variable, electricity expense, was described by the independent variable, direct labor hours. However, a cost may vary because of more than one factor.

Multiple regression analysis is a further application and expansion of the method of least squares, permitting consideration of more than one independent variable. In multiple regression analysis, the simple least squares equation for a straight line, $y_i = a + bx_i + e_i$, is expanded to include more than one independent variable. For example, in the equation $y_i = a + bx_i + cz_i + e_i$, c is the degree of variability for an additional independent variable z. Although the cost relationship can no longer be shown on a two-dimensional graph and the arithmetical computations become more complex, the widespread availability of computer programs makes the use of multiple regression analysis feasible.

The least-squares concept is fundamentally the same when there are two or more independent variables as when there is only one. The assumption of normality still applies. In the case of multiple regression, however, it is the joint probability distribution of the variables that is assumed to be normally distributed (sometimes referred to as multivariate normal). One additional assumption is that the independent variables are not correlated with one another. When the independent variables are correlated with one another, they are said to be collinear, a condition referred to as *multicollinearity*. When the degree of multicollinearity is high, the relationship between one or more of the independent variables and the dependent variable may be obscured.[8] The presence of multicollinearity would not affect the estimate of cost unless one or more important independent variables—activity measures—were omitted from the regression model because of an apparent lack of relationship to the dependent variable—cost. Omitting important variables from the multiple regression model is referred to as *specification error* and is more of a problem in analyzing the sources of cost incurrence than in estimating cost.

If the cost behavior of a group of expenses in one or more ledger accounts is being described, an alternate to multiple variables (and hence to the considerations necessitated by multiple variables when applying the least squares method) may be possible. That is, expenses may be grouped and classified in sufficient detail so that expenses in a particular group are all largely related to only one independent variable. This would allow the use of the method of least squares as earlier illustrated, i.e., simple regression analysis. If this approach is not feasible, i.e., if more than one independent variable is still required to describe the cost behavior, then multiple regression analysis should be employed.[9]

---

[8]*Ibid.*

[9]*Ibid.*

DISCUSSION QUESTIONS

Q12-1. Explain the difference between fixed, variable, and semivariable costs.

Q12-2. What is meant by the term "relevant range"?

Q12-3. Why should semivariable costs be segregated into their fixed and variable components?

Q12-4. Discuss the advantage and the disadvantage of using managerial judgment to separate fixed and variable costs.

Q12-5. What computational methods are available for separating the fixed and variable components of semivariable costs?

Q12-6. What are the advantages and disadvantages of each of the three different methods of separating fixed and variable components of semivariable costs?

Q12-7. Explain the meaning of the $200 and the $4 in the regression equation, $y_i = \$200 + \$4x_i$, where y_i denotes the total monthly cost of indirect supplies and x_i is machine hours per month.   (ICMA adapted)

Q12-8. Define and explain the difference between the coefficient of correlation and the coefficient of determination.

Q12-9. What is the standard error of the estimate?

Q12-10. With respect to the method of least squares, what is meant by the term "heteroscedasticity," and what problem is likely to occur if it is present?

Q12-11. Define and explain the significance of the term "serial correlation."

Q12-12. What is meant by the term "multicollinearity" as it is applied in multiple regression analysis?

EXERCISES

E12-1 **High and low points method.** Edd Company wishes to segregate the fixed and variable portions of maintenance expense, believed to be a semivariable expense, as measured against machine hours. The following information has been provided for the first six months of the current year:

Month	Machine Hours	Maintenance Expense
January.........	2,500	$1,250
February........	2,200	1,150
March...........	2,100	1,100
April............	2,600	1,300
May.............	2,300	1,180
June	2,400	1,200

Required: Using the high and low points method, compute the variable expense rate and the fixed expense for maintenance expense.

E12-2 **Statistical scattergraph.** Keefer Company production management is interested in determining the fixed and variable components of supplies expense, a semivariable expense, as measured against direct labor hours. Data for the first ten months of the current year follow:

Month	Direct Labor Hours	Supplies Expense
January.	450	$600
February	475	700
March	500	750
April	550	650
May.	725	900
June	750	800
July	675	825
August	525	725
September	600	775
October.	625	850

Required: Graph the data provided and determine the fixed and variable components of supplies expense.

E12-3. Method of least squares. Tiptop Company management is interested in predicting travel and entertainment expense based on the number of expected sales calls on customers. Over the past 50 weeks, the company's Sales Department reported that its sales force made 6,250 calls on customers, an average of 125 calls per week. Travel and entertainment expenses over the same period totaled $500,000, an average of $10,000 per week. The travel and entertainment expense deviations from its average multiplied by the sales call deviations from its average and summed $(\Sigma(x_i - \bar{x})(y_i - \bar{y}))$ is 87,000, and the sales call deviations from its average squared and summed $(\Sigma(x_i - \bar{x})^2)$ is 1,450.

Required: Using the method of least squares, estimate the total cost of travel and entertainment for a week in which the company's sales personnel make 200 sales calls.

DA E12-4. Method of least squares. The management of Clearso Inc. would like to separate the fixed and variable components of shipping expense as measured against sales revenue. Data collected over the most recent twelve months follow:

Month	Shipping Expense	Sales Revenue
January.	$560	$26,500
February	600	30,000
March	600	29,000
April	580	28,000
May.	570	27,000
June	550	25,500
July.	590	30,000
August	610	33,000
September	650	35,000
October.	620	32,000
November.	630	30,500
December.	640	33,500

Required: Using the method of least squares, compute the fixed cost and the variable cost rate for shipping expense. Round the estimate of variable cost to the nearest cent and the estimate of fixed cost to the nearest dollar.

E12-5. Correlation analysis. The controller of Berry Electronics Company would like to know how closely the incurrence of factory overhead in the company's Semiconductor Manufacturing Department correlates with machine hours. Total factory overhead over the past 12 months is $108,000, and 5,760 machine hours were logged in for the same period. The machine hour differences from its average and summed $(\Sigma(x_i - \bar{x})^2)$ are 850, and the factory overhead cost differences from its average and summed $(\Sigma(y_i - \bar{y})^2)$ is $3,400. The machine hour differences from average multiplied by the factory overhead cost differences from average and summed $(\Sigma(x_i - \bar{x})(y_i - \bar{y}))$ is 1,564.

Required: Compute the coefficient of correlation, r, and the coefficient of determination, r^2, for factory overhead and machine hours in the semiconductor manufacturing department.

E12-6. Correlation analysis. The following data were collected for the most recent twelve-month period by the cost accountant in one of Axelrod Company's manufacturing plants.

Month	Electricity Expense	Machine Hours
January...........	$1,500	2,600
February..........	1,510	2,500
March............	1,450	2,450
April	1,600	2,750
May..............	1,460	2,400
June	1,520	2,650
July..............	1,570	2,700
August	1,420	2,400
September	1,530	2,600
October...........	1,440	2,440
November.........	1,400	2,350
December.........	1,480	2,460

Required: Compute the coefficient of correlation, r, and the coefficient of determination, r^2, for electricity expense and machine hours.

E12-7 Cost behavior and correlation analysis. Circle Company total maintenance expense for the past ten months is $50,000. Some of the maintenance activity appears related to the operation of machinery, and the accountant desires to determine whether machine hours should be used as a basis upon which to estimate maintenance expense at various levels of capacity. Machine hours for the same period totaled 40,000 hours. The machine hour differences from average multiplied by the maintenance expense differences from its average and summed $(\Sigma(x_i - \bar{x})(y_i - \bar{y}))$ is 2,400. The machine hour differences from average squared and summed $(\Sigma(x_i - \bar{x})^2)$ is 6,250, and the maintenance expense differences from average squared and summed $(\Sigma(y_i - \bar{y})^2)$ is 1,000.

Required:

(1) Compute the coefficient of correlation, r, and the coefficient of determination, r^2, for maintenance expense and machine hours.
(2) Compute the variable maintenance expense per machine hour, using the method of least squares.
(3) Compute the fixed maintenance expense, using the method of least squares.

E12-8. Choosing appropriate activity measure and separating fixed and variable costs. Total electricity expense for the past 20 months is $42,000. An activity measure upon which to base estimates of electricity expense is needed. The two activity measures being considered are direct labor hours and machine hours. Direct labor hours for the period totaled 180,000, and machine hours totaled 120,000. The direct labor hour differences from average multiplied by the electricity expense differences from its average and summed $(\Sigma(x_i - \bar{x})(y_i - \bar{y}))$ is 5,700. The direct labor hour differences from average squared and summed $(\Sigma(x_i - \bar{x})^2)$ is 28,500. The electricity expense differences from average squared and summed $(\Sigma(y_i - \bar{y})^2)$ is 1,264. The machine hour differences from average multiplied by the electricity expense differences from its average and summed $(\Sigma(x_i - \bar{x})(y_i - \bar{y}))$ is 7,000. The machine hour differences from average squared and summed $(\Sigma(x_i - \bar{x})^2)$ is 50,000.

Required:

(1) Compute the coefficient of correlation, r, and the coefficient of determination, r^2, for direct labor hours and electricity expense.
(2) Compute the coefficient of correlation, r, and the coefficient of determination, r^2, for machine hours and electricity expense.
(3) Which activity measure should be used for the estimation of fixed and variable electricity expense? Explain.

(4) Compute the variable electricity expense rate and the fixed expense, using the method of least squares.

E12-9. Standard error of the estimate. The controller of Fratiani Company used the method of least squares to compute the fixed and variable components of utility expense from the following data:

Month	Utility Expense	Labor Hours
January...........	$3,600	2,650
February..........	4,000	3,000
March............	4,000	2,900
April	3,800	2,800
May.............	3,700	2,700
June	3,500	2,550
July.............	3,900	3,000
August	4,100	3,300
September	4,500	3,500
October...........	4,200	3,200
November.........	4,300	3,050
December.........	4,400	3,350

Required: Assuming that the least squares estimate of fixed cost is $1,000 and the variable rate is $1.00, compute the standard error of the estimate to three decimal places for the data presented above.

E12-10. Standard error of the estimate and confidence interval estimation. The production supervisor of Pylex Inc. would like to know the range of maintenance expense that should be expected about 90 percent of the time at the 1,500 machine hour level of activity. The least squares estimate of maintenance expense at that level of activity is $500. The least squares parameter estimates, i.e., the estimates of fixed cost and the variable cost rate, were derived from a sample of data for a recent 15-month period. The machine hour average for the sample period is 1,300, and the machine hour deviations from its average squared and summed $(\Sigma(x_i - \bar{x})^2)$ is 150,000. The prediction error squared $(\Sigma(y_i - y_i')^2)$ over the same sample period is $49,972.

Required: Compute the standard error of the estimate and the 90 percent confidence interval estimate for maintenance expense at the 1,500 machine hour level of activity.

PROBLEMS

 P12-1. Correlation analysis. The Cost Department of Quick Supply Company attempts to establish a budget to assist in the control of marketing expenses. An examination of individual expenses shows:

Item	Fixed Portion	Variable Portion
Sales staff:		
Salaries	$1,200	none
Retainers	2,000	none
Commissions	none	4% on sales values
Advertising...........	5,000	none
Travel expense.........	?	?

Statistical analysis is needed to split the travel expense satisfactorily into its fixed and variable portions. Before beginning such an analysis, it is thought that the variable portion of the travel expense might vary in accordance either with the number of calls made on customers each month or the value of orders received each month. Records reveal the following details over the past twelve months:

Month	Calls Made	Orders Received	Travel Expense
January.	410	$53,000	$3,000
February.	420	65,000	3,200
March	380	48,000	2,800
April	460	73,000	3,400
May.	430	62,000	3,100
June	450	67,000	3,200
July.	390	60,000	2,900
August	470	76,000	3,300
September	480	82,000	3,500
October.	490	62,000	3,400
November.	440	64,000	3,200
December.	460	80,000	3,400

Required:

(1) Compute the coefficient of correlation, r, and coefficient of determination, r^2, between (a) the travel expense and the number of calls made and (b) the travel expense and orders received. (Round to four decimal places.)
(2) Compare the answers obtained in (1a) and (1b).

P12-2. Choosing appropriate activity measure; cost behavior analysis. The controller of Moore Corporation has asked for help in the selection of the appropriate activity measure to be used in estimating variable supplies expense for the company's budget. The following information about past expenses and two potential activity measures has been supplied:

Month	Supplies Expense	Labor Hours	Machine Hours
January.	$ 1,540	4,000	2,100
February.	1,430	4,100	1,990
March	1,600	4,250	2,140
April	1,550	3,950	2,080
May.	1,480	3,800	1,960
June	1,450	3,950	1,940
July.	1,500	4,200	2,020
August	1,540	4,300	2,070
September	1,610	4,150	2,140
October.	1,570	4,550	2,050
November.	1,530	4,250	2,030
December.	1,620	4,900	2,260
Total	$18,420	50,400	24,780

Required:

(1) Compute the coefficient of correlation, r, and the coefficient of determination, r^2, between supplies expense and each of the two activity measures.
(2) Identify which of the two activity measures above should be used as a basis upon which to estimate the allowable supplies expense.
(3) Using the activity measure selected in requirement (2) above, determine the fixed expense and the variable expense rate by the method of least squares.

P12-3. Cost behavior analysis; correlation analysis; standard error of the estimate. The following data have been collected by the controller of Lynpax Corporation over the past twelve months:

Month	Maintenance Expense	Machine Hours
January...........	$ 2,200	2,500
February..........	2,130	2,350
March.............	2,000	2,000
April	2,170	2,400
May..............	2,050	2,100
June	2,220	2,600
July..............	2,150	2,450
August	2,250	2,550
September	2,290	2,700
October...........	2,150	2,450
November.........	2,210	2,400
December.........	2,100	2,300
Total	$25,920	28,800

Required:

(1) Using the high and low points method, determine the average amount of fixed maintenance expense per month and the variable maintenance rate per machine hour.
(2) Determine the fixed expense and the variable expense rate, using the method of least squares.
(3) Compute the coefficient of correlation, r, and the coefficient of determination, r^2, between the machine hours and the maintenance expense.
(4) Compute the standard error of the estimate.
(5) Determine the 95% confidence interval for maintenance expense at the 2,500 machine hour level of activity.

P12-4. Cost behavior analysis; correlation analysis; standard error of the estimate. The management of the Rest-Time Hotel is interested in an analysis of the fixed and variable costs in the electricity used relative to hotel occupancy. The following data have been gathered from records for the year:

Month	Guest Days	Electricity Cost
January...........	1,000	$ 400
February..........	1,500	500
March.............	2,500	500
April	3,000	700
May..............	2,500	600
June	4,500	800
July..............	6,500	1,000
August	6,000	900
September	5,500	900
October...........	3,000	700
November.........	2,500	600
December.........	3,500	800
Total	42,000	$8,400

Required:

(1) Determine the fixed and variable elements of the electricity cost, using (a) the method of least squares, (b) the high and low points method, and (c) a scattergraph with trend line fitted by inspection. (Round the variable rate to four decimal places.)
(2) What other elements, besides occupancy, might affect the amount of electricity used in any one month?

(3) Compute the coefficient of correlation, r, and the coefficient of determination, r^2, for guest days and electricity expense.

(4) Compute the standard error of the estimate.

(5) Compute the 90% confidence interval for electricity expense at the 2,000 guest days capacity.

 P12-5. Cost behavior analysis; correlation analysis; standard error of the estimate. Randal Company manufactures a wide range of electrical products at several different plant locations. Due to fluctuations, its Franklin plant has been experiencing difficulties in estimating the level of monthly overhead.

Management needs more accurate estimates to plan its operational and financial needs. A trade association publication indicates that for companies like Randal, overhead tends to vary with direct labor hours. Based on this information, one member of the accounting staff proposes that the overhead cost behavior pattern be determined in order to calculate the overhead cost in relation to budgeted direct labor hours. Another member of the accounting staff suggests that a good starting place for determining the cost behavior pattern of the overhead cost would be an analysis of historical data to provide a basis for estimating future overhead costs.

Direct labor hours and the respective factory overhead costs for the past three years are as follows:

	19A		19B		19C	
Month	Direct Labor Hours	Factory Overhead Costs	Direct Labor Hours	Factory Overhead Costs	Direct Labor Hours	Factory Overhead Costs
January............	2,000	$8,500	2,100	$8,700	2,000	$8,600
February..........	2,400	9,900	2,300	9,300	2,300	9,300
March............	2,200	8,950	2,200	9,300	2,300	9,400
April.............	2,300	9,000	2,200	8,700	2,200	8,700
May..............	2,000	8,150	2,000	8,000	2,000	8,100
June	1,900	7,550	1,800	7,650	1,800	7,600
July..............	1,400	7,050	1,200	6,750	1,300	7,000
August	1,000	6,450	1,300	7,100	1,200	6,900
September	1,200	6,900	1,500	7,350	1,300	7,100
October...........	1,700	7,500	1,700	7,250	1,800	7,500
November.........	1,600	7,150	1,500	7,100	1,500	7,000
December.........	1,900	7,800	1,800	7,500	1,900	7,600

Required:

(1) Compute the amount of fixed factory overhead and the variable cost rate, using the method of least squares. (Round fixed factory overhead to the nearest dollar and the variable cost rate to the nearest cent.)

(2) Compute the coefficient of correlation, r, and the coefficient of determination, r^2, for factory overhead costs and direct labor hours. (Round to four decimal places.)

(3) Compute the standard error of the estimate. (Round to the nearest dollar.)

(4) Compute the 95% confidence interval for factory overhead costs at the 2,200 direct labor hour level of activity. (Assume that the sample size is sufficiently large that the standard normal probability distribution can be assumed and that the correction factor for small samples can be omitted. Round to the nearest dollar.)

P12-6. Choosing appropriate activity measure; cost behavior analysis; standard error of the estimate. Based on observation and knowledge of the production process, the controller of Whirlwind Company believes that the bulk of variable maintenance expense is driven by either labor hours or machine hours. Data gathered for the past 24 months follows:

Months	Maintenance Expense	Direct Labor Hours	Machine Hours
January, 19A	$1,195	950	809
February, 19A..........	1,116	1,024	744
March, 19A............	1,390	1,109	987
April, 19A	1,449	1,148	987
May, 19A..............	1,618	1,313	1,186

Months	Maintenance Expense	Direct Labor Hours	Machine Hours
June, 19A	$1,525	1,261	1,154
July, 19A	1,687	1,552	1,291
August, 19A	1,650	1,372	1,238
September, 19A	1,595	1,366	1,186
October, 19A	1,675	1,455	1,246
November, 19A	1,405	1,221	997
December, 19A	1,251	1,150	841
January, 19B	950	999	502
February, 19B	1,175	1,022	733
March, 19B	1,425	1,220	1,090
April, 19B	1,506	1,283	1,135
May, 19B	1,608	1,339	1,174
June, 19B	1,653	1,250	1,246
July, 19B	1,675	1,440	1,264
August, 19B	1,724	1,290	1,323
September, 19B	1,626	1,335	1,230
October, 19B	1,575	1,164	1,165
November, 19B	1,653	1,373	1,237
December, 19B	1,418	1,124	1,035

Required:

(1) Compute the correlation coefficient, r, and the coefficient of determination, r^2, for maintenance expense with each of the two activity measures suggested by the controller.

(2) Using the method of least squares and the activity measure most highly correlated with maintenance expense, compute the variable maintenance expense rate and the estimated fixed maintenance expense.

(3) Compute the standard error of the estimate using the variable rate and estimated fixed cost computed in requirement (2) above.

(4) Compute the 95 percent confidence interval estimate at the 1,100 hour level of activity. Student's t value at the 95 percent level of confidence for a two-tail test is 2.074 for 22 degrees of freedom, 2.069 for 23 degrees of freedom, and 2.064 for 24 degrees of freedom.

CASES

C12-1. Cost behavior analysis using method of least squares. Elisko Inc. is a major book distributor that ships books throughout the United States. Elisko's Shipping Department consists of a manager plus ten other permanent positions—four supervisors and six loaders. The four supervisors and six loaders provide the minimum staff and frequently must be supplemented by additional workers, especially during the weeks when the volume of shipments is heavy. Thus the number of people shipping the orders frequently averages over 30 per week, i.e., 10 permanent persons plus 20 temporary workers. The temporary workers are hired through a local agency.

Elisko must use temporary workers to maintain a minimum daily shipment rate of 95% of orders presented for shipping. The loss of efficiency from using temporary workers is minimal, and the $10.00 per hour cost of temporary workers is less than the $15.00 per hour for the loaders and $22.50 per hour for the supervisors on Elisko's permanent staff. The agency requires Elisko to utilize each temporary worker for at least four hours each day.

Jim Locter, shipping manager, schedules temporary help based on forecasted orders for the coming week. Supervisors serve as loaders until temporary help is needed. A supervisor stops loading when the ratio of loaders to supervisors reaches 7:1. Locter knows that he will need temporary help when the forecasted average daily orders exceed 300. Locter has frequently requested from two to four extra temporary workers per day to guard against unexpected rush orders. If there was not enough work, he would dismiss the extra people at noon after four hours of work. The agency has not been pleased with Locter's practice of overhiring and has notified Elisko that it is changing its policy. From now on, if a person is dismissed before an eight-hour assignment is completed, Elisko will still be charged for an eight-hour day plus mileage back to the agency for reassignment. This policy would go into effect the following week.

Paula Brand, general manager, called Jim Locter to her office when she received the notice from the agency. She told Locter, "Your staffing has to be better. This penalty could cost us up to $500 per week in labor cost for which we receive no benefit. Why can't you schedule better?"

Locter replied, "I agree that the staffing should be better, but I can't do it accurately when there are rush orders. By being able to lay off people at noon, I have been able to adjust for the uncertain order schedule without cost to the company. Of course, the agency's new policy changes this."

Locter and Brand contacted Elisko's controller, Mitch Berg, regarding Locter's problem on how to estimate the number of people needed each week. Berg realized that Locter needed a quick solution until he could study the work flow. Berg suggested a regression analysis using the number of orders shipped as the independent variable and the number of workers (permanent plus temporary) as the dependent variable. Berg indicated that data for the past year are available and that the analysis could be done quickly on the Accounting Department's micro-computer.

Berg completed the two regression analyses below. The first regression was based on the data for the entire year. The second regression excluded the weeks when only the 10 permanent staff persons were used; these weeks were unusual and appeared to be out of the relevant range.

Regression Equation
$$W = a + bS$$

where: W = total workers (permanent plus temporary)
S = orders shipped

	Regression 1 (Daily data for 52 weeks)	Regression 2 (Daily data for 38 weeks)
a..............	5.062	0.489
b..............	0.023	0.028
Standard error (s) of the estimate.......	2.012	0.432
Coefficient of determination (r^2)...	0.962	0.998

Locter was not familiar with regression analysis and, therefore, was unsure how to implement this technique. He wondered which regression data he should employ, i.e., which one was better. When he recognized that the regression was based on actual orders shipped by week, Berg told him he could use the forecasted shipments for the week to determine the number of workers needed.

Required:

(1) Using Regression 1 based on data from a full year, calculate the number of temporary workers that should be hired for a forecast of 1,200 shipments.
(2) Which one of the two regressions appears to be better? Explain.
(3) Explain the circumstances under which this regression should be used in planning for temporary workers.
(4) Explain how the regression might be improved.   (ICMA adapted)

C12-2. Regression and correlation analysis—utility and implementation. Ned McCarty, controller of Arkansas Distribution Company, is responsible for development and administration of the company's internal information system as well as the coordination of the company's budget preparation.

At a meeting with Donna Tuma, the vice-president, McCarty proposed that the company employ regression analysis (the least squares method) and correlation analysis as a standard part of its internal information system relating to sales and expenses. He felt that such analyses, including projections, would be significant decision-making aids.

Tuma admitted that she had forgotten the exact mechanics of regression and correlation analysis. However, she did comment that:

(a) Regression and correlation calculations for weekly or monthly amounts would involve enormous numbers of calculations because the company's budget and control system uses weekly amounts for sales and some expenses and monthly amounts for other expenses.

(b) A great deal of caution must be exercised when relying on predictions calculated by regression analysis techniques.

McCarty agreed that a large number of calculations would be required, but felt that this problem might be overcome by computerizing the analysis. The computerized analysis would have to suit the company's budget and control system and cover all significant sales and expense accounts, of which there are about 100.

The company's microcomputer is not large and operates only with a flexible diskette data storage device. No standard computer programs are available for this kind of analysis. Therefore, a program must be specially written, its accompanying data gathered, and the processing problems solved.

To pursue his idea, McCarty decided to obtain sample data regarding sales and related selling expenses for the past five years. Using regression analysis, he predicted sales of $30,500,000 for the coming year and calculated a coefficient of correlation of .4 between sales and the selling expenses.

Required:

(1) Explain both the advantages and the limitations of using regression and correlation analysis according to McCarty.
(2) Identify those matters that should be considered before the regression analysis is made, based on the sample data collected.
(3) Provide an outline of the programming and operating problems that might be encountered if the analysis is computerized using the available computer.

(CICA adapted)

C12-3. Cost behavior analysis; correlation analysis; standard error of the estimate. A company's cost department has compiled weekly records of production volume (in units), electric power used, and direct labor hours employed. The range of output for which the following statistics were computed is from 500 to 2,000 units per week:

Electric power:

$$y = 1,000 + .4x, \text{ where } y \text{ is electric power}$$
and x is units of production
Standard error of the estimate: 100
Coefficient of correlation: .45

Direct labor:

$$y = 100 + 1.2x, \text{ where } y \text{ is direct labor}$$
hours and x is units of production
Standard error of the estimate: 300
Coefficient of correlation: .70

Required:

(1) Compute the best estimate of the additional number of required direct labor hours, if production for the next period should be 500 units greater than production in this period.
(2) Comment on the reliability of the above equations for estimating electric power and direct labor requirements, together with the necessary assumptions if the estimating equations are to be used to predict future requirements. An interpretation of the coefficient of correlation and the standard error of the estimate should be included.

CGA-Canada (adapted)
Reprint with permission

C12-4. Cost behavior analysis; alternative models. Motorco Corporation plans to acquire several retail automotive parts stores as part of its expansion program. Motorco carries out extensive review of possible acquisitions prior to making any decision to approach a specific company. Projections of future financial performance are one of the aspects of such a review. One form of projection relies heavily on using past performance (normally ten prior years) to estimate future performance.

Currently, Motorco is conducting a preacquisition review of Alpha Auto Parts, a regional chain of retail automotive parts stores. Among the financial data to be projected for Alpha are the future rental costs for its stores.

The following schedule presents the rent and revenues (in millions of dollars) for the past ten years:

Year	Revenues	Annual Rent Expense
19A......	$22	$1.00
19B	24	1.15
19C	36	1.40
19D	27	1.10
19E......	43	1.55
19F......	33	1.25
19G	45	1.65
19H	48	1.60
19I	61	1.80
19J......	60	1.95

The following three alternative methods of estimating future rental expense are being considered:

Alternative A: A linear regression using time as the independent variable was performed. The resultant formula is as follows:

Rental expense $= .93 + .0936y$

$r = .895$

Standard error
of the estimate $= .150$

where y is equal to (actual year – 19A), e.g., 19J = 10.

Alternative B: The annual rental expense was related to annual revenues through linear regression. The formula for predicting rental expense in this case is as follows:

Rental expense $= .5597 + .02219y$

$r = .978$

Standard error
of the estimate $= .070$

where y is equal to (Revenues $÷$ 1,000,000), e.g., y for 19J is 60.

Alternative C: The third alternative is to calculate rental expense as a percentage of revenues using the arithmetical average for the ten-year period of 19A-19J inclusive. The formula for predicting rental expense in this case is as follows:

Rental expense $=$
$(\Sigma E ÷ \Sigma R)y =$
$(14.45 ÷ 399)y = .0362y$

where ΣE is equal to the sum of the rental expenses for the ten-year period, ΣR is equal to the sum of the revenues for the ten-year period, and y is equal to revenue in the prediction year; e.g., y for 19J is 60.

Required:

(1) Discuss the advantages and disadvantages of each of the three alternative methods for estimating the rental expense for Alpha Auto Parts.
(2) Identify one method from Alternatives A, B, or C that Motorco should use to estimate rental expense and explain why that alternative was selected.
(3) Explain whether a statistical technique is an appropriate method in this situation for estimating rental expense.

(ICMA adapted)

C12-5. Multiple regression analysis. Multiple regression is a procedure used to measure the relationship of one variable with two or more other variables. Regression provides a rational statement rather than a causal statement with regard to the relationship. The basic formula for a multiple regression equation is:

$$y_i' = a + bx_i + cz_i + e_i$$

For a regression equation to provide meaningful information, it should comply with the basic criteria of goodness of fit and specification analysis. Specification analysis is determined by examining the data and the relationships of the variables for (1) linearity within a relevant range, (2) constant variance of error terms (homoscedasticity), (3) independence of observations (serial correlation), (4) normality, and (5) multicollinearity.

Required:

(1) Explain what is meant by "regression provides a rational statement rather than a causal statement."
(2) Explain the meaning of each of the symbols which appear in the basic formula of the multiple regression equation above.
(3) Identify the statistical factors which are used to test a regression equation for goodness of fit and, for each item identified, indicate whether a high or low value describes a "good" fit.
(4) Explain what each of the following terms means with respect to regression analysis:

(a) Linearity within a relevant range
(b) Constant variance (homoscedasticity)

(c) Serial correlation
(d) Normality
(e) Multicollinearity   (ICMA adapted)

C12-6. Multiple regression and correlation analysis. John Wood, a financial analyst for a major automobile corporation, has been monitoring the funds used in advertising campaigns and the funds used for automobile factory rebates. Financial data have been accumulated for the last 24 months along with customer sales, i.e., automobiles sold. Wood contends that there may be a relationship between the level of automobile sales and funds expended on advertising and/or factory rebates. If such a relationship can be determined, the company may be able to estimate sales demand based upon various levels of funding commitments for one or both types of expenditures.

Regression equations and supporting statistical values were developed for the various relationships between variables and are as follows:

	Equation	Coefficient of Determination r^2	Standard Error of the Estimate s
Equation 1	$D = 2.455 + 0.188A$	.414	1.325
Equation 2	$D = 2.491 + 0.44R$	.314	1.434
Equation 3	$R = 6.052 + .005A$	.0002	2.202
Equation 4	$D = -.184 + .186A + .437R$	.703	.922

where the notations used in the equations are as follows:

A = advertising funds in $100,000
R = funds for factory rebates in $1,000,000
D = customer sales demand (automobiles sold) in 10,000 units

The appropriate t values for use in determining confidence intervals are as follows:

50% confidence	0.69
95% confidence	2.07

Required:

(1) Assuming the corporation is projecting advertising expenditures amounting to $1,500,000 and factory rebate expenditures amounting to $12,000,000 for the next time period, calculate expected customer demand in units using:

(a) Equation 1.   (b) Equation 2.

(2) Assume that Equation 4 is employed to estimate a total customer demand of 104,160 automobiles for a time period. Using a 50% confidence level, determine the range of automobile sales that could occur during the time period.

(3) Select the regression equation which would be most advantageous to predict customer sales demand and explain why it is the best.

(4) Explain the significance of Equation 3 and how it may be used in evaluating Equation 4.
(ICMA adapted)

CHAPTER 13

Factory Overhead: Planned, Actual, and Applied; Variance Analysis

The use of a predetermined factory overhead rate for the purpose of charging a fair share of factory overhead to products was introduced briefly in earlier chapters. This chapter (1) discusses the methods, procedures, and bases available for applying factory overhead; (2) describes methods and procedures for classifying and accumulating actual factory overhead; (3) shows computations for over- or underapplied factory overhead; and (4) analyzes the total net variance, showing the spending and idle capacity variances. Chapter 14 discusses (1) the departmentalization of factory overhead, (2) the creation and use of separate departmental overhead rates, and (3) departmentalization in nonmanufacturing businesses and nonprofit organizations. Chapter 15 discusses (1) the relationship of product costing to responsibility accounting, (2) monthly overhead variance analysis for use in responsibility accounting and reporting for producing and service departments, and (3) responsibility reporting fundamentals and systems.

■ THE NATURE OF FACTORY OVERHEAD

Factory overhead is generally defined as indirect materials, indirect labor, and all other factory costs that can neither be conveniently identified with nor charged directly to specific jobs, products, or final cost objectives. Other terms used for factory overhead are *factory burden, manufacturing expense, manufacturing overhead, factory expense,* and *indirect manufacturing cost.*

Factory overhead possesses two characteristics that require consideration if products are to be charged with a fair share of this cost. These characteristics deal with the particular relationship of factory overhead to (1) the product itself and (2) the volume of production. Unlike direct materials and direct labor, factory overhead is an invisible part of the finished product. There is no materials requisition or labor time ticket to indicate the amount of overhead, such as factory supplies or indirect labor, that enters into a job or product. Yet factory overhead is as much a part of a product's manufacturing cost as direct materials and direct labor. Since automation has increased in modern manufacturing processes, factory overhead as a percentage of total product cost has increased, while the portion of direct labor has declined.

The second characteristic deals with the change in cost that many items of overhead undergo with a change in production volume; i.e., overhead may be fixed, variable, or semivariable. As discussed in Chapter 12, fixed overhead remains relatively constant regardless of changes in production volume, within the relevant range, while the fixed overhead per unit of output varies inversely with production volume. Variable overhead varies proportionately with production output, again, within the relevant range. Semivariable overhead varies but not in proportion to units produced. As production volume changes, the combined effect of these different overhead patterns can cause unit manufacturing cost to fluctuate considerably, unless some method is provided to stabilize overhead charged to the units produced. The following chart illustrates the relationship of overhead and volume:

Fixed-Variable Cost Relationship to Volume

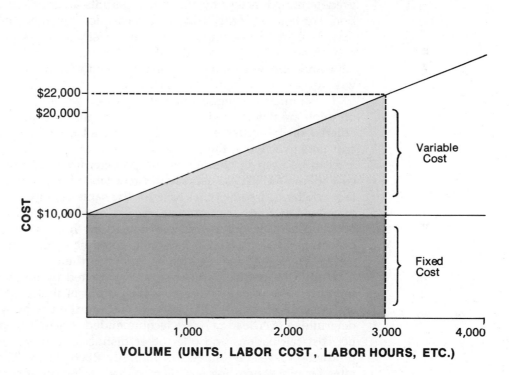

■ THE USE OF A PREDETERMINED FACTORY OVERHEAD RATE

The various overhead costs must be charged to all work done during any period. The problem is how to make such a charge. It is possible to allocate actual overhead to all work completed during the month, using a base such as actual direct labor dollars, direct labor hours, or machine hours. As long as the volume of work completed each month is the same, and costs are within control limits, this method would result in a consistent charge to production each period. As variations occur, work completed during different months would receive a greater or smaller charge—an inequitable situation. For example, costing problems would result if actual costs incurred for repairs and maintenance are charged directly to a job or product when repairs are made. Ordinarily, repairs are necessary because of wear and tear over a much longer period than one month and are made to permit continuous operations in any month. Moreover, since overhead cost needs to be assigned promptly to production and inefficiencies need to be identified, it is argued that factory overhead should be charged to work done on an estimated basis. However, the use of estimates will be less meaningful if underlying data are the result of opinions and judgments. Estimates must be based on careful studies.

Because of the impossibility of tracing all items of factory overhead to specific jobs or specific products, an arbitrary overhead allocation is made. A predetermined factory overhead rate permits an equitable and logical allocation. For both job order and process cost accumulation, it provides the only feasible method of computing product overhead costs promptly enough to serve management needs, identify inefficiencies, and smooth out uncontrollable and somewhat illogical month-to-month fluctuations that would otherwise appear in the reported unit costs.

In job order costing, actual costs of direct materials and direct labor used on a job are determined from materials requisitions and time cards and are entered on job order cost sheets. Overhead costs are predetermined from cost data to arrive at the total amount of overhead estimated for the activity level to be used in computing the predetermined overhead rate. This total cost then is related to estimated direct labor hours, machine hours, direct labor dollars, or some other base for the same activity level, ultimately to be expressed as a rate. For example, factory overhead applicable to a job would be calculated by multiplying actual machine hours used on the job by the predetermined rate, and the amount would be entered on the job order cost sheet. The cost of a job is thereby known at the time the job is completed.

In process costing, unit costs are computed by dividing total weekly or monthly costs of each process by the output of that process. While process costing could produce product costs without the use of overhead rates, predetermined overhead rates are recommended, since they speed up unit product cost calculations and offer other distinct advantages when overhead or production levels are subject to monthly fluctuations. The use of overhead rates for process costing is similar to that for job order costing.

■ FACTORS TO BE CONSIDERED IN THE SELECTION OF OVERHEAD RATES

The types of overhead rates used differ not only from company to company but also from one department, cost center, or cost pool to another within the same company. The type, significance, and use of factory overhead items must be considered when deciding upon applicable rates. At least five main factors influence the selection of overhead rates. The first three of these factors, which are identified as follows, are discussed in this chapter. The last two factors are discussed in Chapters 14 and 15.

I. Base To Be Used
   a. Physical output
   b. Direct materials cost
   c. Direct labor cost
   d. Direct labor hours
   e. Machine hours
   f. Transactions

II. Activity Level Selection
   a. Theoretical capacity
   b. Practical capacity
   c. Expected actual capacity
   d. Normal capacity
      1. Purposes of establishing normal capacity
      2. Factors involved in determining normal capacity

   e. Effect of capacity on overhead rates
   f. Idle capacity vs. excess capacity

III. Including or Excluding of Fixed Overhead
   a. Absorption costing
   b. Direct costing

IV. Use of a Single Rate or Several Rates
   a. Plant-wide or blanket rate
   b. Departmental rates
   c. Subdepartmental and activity rates

V. Use of Separate Rates for Service Activities

Base To Be Used

Selection of the most appropriate base for applying overhead is of utmost importance if a cost system is to provide reasonably proper costs and if management is to receive meaningful and valuable data. Therefore, the primary objective in selecting a base is to ensure the application of factory overhead in a reasonable proportion to the beneficial or causal relationship to jobs, products, or work performed. Since factory overhead rates also are used for estimating total costs, the overhead base quantity needed can be translated easily and efficiently into a factory overhead cost to arrive at total estimated production cost.

Ordinarily, the base selected should be closely related (correlated) to functions represented by the overhead cost being applied. If, for example, factory overhead is predominantly labor-oriented, such as supervision and indirect labor, the proper base is probably direct labor cost or direct labor hours. If overhead items are predominantly investment-oriented, related to the ownership and operation of machinery, then a machine hour base is probably most appropriate. If overhead is mainly materials-oriented, such as costs associated with the purchasing and handling of materials, then the materials cost might be considered as the base. Correlation analysis tools discussed in Chapter 12 are especially useful in selecting the base to be used.

A secondary objective in selecting a base is to minimize clerical cost and effort relative to the benefits attained. When two or more bases provide approximately the same applied overhead cost for specific units of production, the simplest base should be used. Although the cost of administering the various methods differs from one company to another, the direct labor cost base and the direct materials cost base seem to cause the least clerical effort and cost because these data are accumulated in any case. The labor hour and machine hour bases generally require additional clerical work and expense, because special accumulation is required.

Physical Output. The physical output or units of production base, the simplest and most direct method of applying factory overhead, is computed as follows:

$$\frac{\text{Estimated factory overhead}}{\text{Estimated units of production}} = \text{Factory overhead per unit}$$

If the estimated expense is $300,000 and the company intends to produce 250,000 units during the next period, each completed unit would be charged with $1.20 ($300,000 ÷ 250,000 units) as its share of factory overhead. An order with 1,000 completed units would be charged with $1,200 (1,000 units × $1.20) of factory overhead.

The physical output base is satisfactory when a company manufactures only one product; otherwise, the method is either unsatisfactory or subject to extremely arbitrary allocations. However, if the several products manufactured are alike or closely related, their difference being merely one of weight or volume, application of factory overhead can be made on a weight, volume, or point base. The weight base applies overhead according to the weight of each unit of product and is illustrated as follows:

	Product		
	A	B	C
Estimated number of units manufactured ...	20,000	15,000	20,000
Unit weight of product.................	5 lbs.	2 lbs.	1 lb.
Estimated total weight produced	100,000 lbs.	30,000 lbs.	20,000 lbs.
Estimated factory overhead per pound ($300,000 ÷ 150,000).................	$2	$2	$2
Estimated factory overhead for each product	$200,000	$60,000	$40,000
Estimated factory overhead per unit	$10	$4	$2

If the weight or volume base does not seem to yield a reasonable apportionment of overhead, the method can be improved by assigning a certain number of points to each unit to compensate for differences. For example, a company manufacturing Products L, S, M, and F computes an overhead rate per product as follows:

Product	Estimated Quantity	Points Assigned	Estimated Total Points	Estimated Factory Overhead per Point	Estimated Factory Overhead for Each Product	Estimated Factory Overhead Cost per Unit
L	2,000	5	10,000	$3	$ 30,000	$15
S	5,000	10	50,000	3	150,000	30
M	3,000	8	24,000	3	72,000	24
F	4,000	4	16,000	3	48,000	12
			100,000		$300,000	

If products are different in any respect not considered in the allocation base, such as time to produce, difficulty of machinery setup, or method of production, a uniform charge based on physical output may result in inappropriate costing. Other methods must be adopted in such instances.

Direct Materials Cost Base. In some companies, a study of past costs will reveal a correlation between direct materials cost and factory overhead. The study might show that factory overhead has remained approximately the same percentage of direct materials cost. Therefore, a rate based on materials cost might be applicable. In such instances, the charge is computed by dividing total estimated factory overhead by total direct materials cost expected to be used in the manufacturing processes:

$$\frac{\text{Estimated factory overhead}}{\text{Estimated materials cost}} \times 100 = \begin{array}{l}\text{Percentage of overhead}\\ \text{per direct materials cost}\end{array}$$

If the estimated overhead is $300,000 and the estimated materials cost is $250,000, each job or product completed would be charged with an additional 120 percent (($300,000 ÷ $250,000) × 100) of its materials cost as its share of factory overhead. For example, if the materials cost of an order is $5,000, the order would receive an additional charge of $6,000 ($5,000 × 120%) for factory overhead.

The materials-related cost base has only limited use, because in most cases no logical relationship exists between the direct materials cost of a product and factory overhead used in its production. One product might be made from high-priced materials, another from less expensive materials; yet both products might require the same manufacturing process or even the same materials-oriented overhead costs, and thus use approximately the same amount of factory overhead. If the materials cost base is used to charge overhead, the product using expensive materials will, in this case, be charged with more than its share. To overcome this costing problem, two overhead rates might be calculated: one (based on materials cost, weight, volume, number of different parts used, or some other measure of use) for items that are materials-oriented, such as purchasing, receiving, inspecting, handling, and storage costs; the other based on some other more relevant activity for the remaining overhead costs.

Direct Labor Cost Base. The direct labor cost base method of applying overhead to jobs or products entails dividing estimated factory overhead by estimated direct labor cost to compute a percentage:

$$\frac{\text{Estimated factory overhead}}{\text{Estimated direct labor cost}} \times 100 = \text{Percentage of direct labor cost}$$

If estimated factory overhead is $300,000 and total direct labor cost for the next period is estimated at $500,000, the overhead rate would be 60 percent (($300,000 ÷ $500,000) × 100). A job or product with a direct labor cost of $12,000 would be charged with $7,200 ($12,000 × 60%) for factory overhead.

Factory overhead items that are used over a period of time must be taken into consideration. The direct labor cost base does so, since the labor cost is computed by multiplying the number of work hours by an hourly wage rate. The more hours worked, the higher the labor cost, the greater the use of time-related items, and the greater the charge for factory overhead.

The direct labor cost base is relatively easy to use, since information needed to apply overhead is readily available. Its use is particularly favored when (1) a direct relationship between direct labor cost and factory overhead exists and (2) the rates of pay per hour for similar work are comparable. The weekly payroll provides the direct labor cost without any additional record keeping. As long as economy in securing underlying information remains a main prerequisite, the direct labor cost base can be accepted as the best and quickest of the available methods of applying factory overhead in labor-intensive manufacturing.

On the other hand, this method can be objected to for two reasons:

1. Factory overhead must be looked upon as an addition to the value of a job or product. The added value often comes about through depreciation charges of high-cost machinery, which might not bear any relationship to direct labor payroll.
2. Total direct labor cost represents the sum of wages paid to high- and low-wage production workers. By applying overhead on the basis of direct labor cost, a job or product is charged with more overhead when a high-wage operator performs work. Such a method can lead to incorrect distribution of factory overhead, particularly when numerous operators, with different hourly rates in the same department, perform similar operations on different jobs or products.

causes distortion

Direct Labor Hour Base. The direct labor hour base is designed to overcome the second disadvantage of using the direct labor cost base. The overhead rate based on direct labor hours is computed as follows:

$$\frac{\text{Estimated factory overhead}}{\text{Estimated direct labor hours}} = \text{Rate per direct labor hour}$$

If estimated factory overhead is $300,000 and total direct labor hours are estimated to be 60,000, an overhead rate based on direct labor hours would be $5.00 per hour of direct labor ($300,000 ÷ 60,000 hours). A job or product that required 800 direct labor hours would be charged with $4,000 (800 hours × $5.00) for factory overhead.

The use of this method requires accumulation of direct labor hours by job or product. Timekeeping forms and records must be organized to provide the additional data. The use of the direct labor hour base requires, (1) a direct relationship between direct labor hours and factory overhead, and (2) different rates of pay per hour for similar work, caused, for example, by seniority rather than by increased output. As long as labor operations are the chief factor in production processes, the direct labor hour method is acceptable as a base for applying overhead. However, if shop or factory departments use machines extensively, the direct labor hour method might lead to unreasonable costing.

Management goals in manufacturing in recent years have focused on decreasing the amount of direct labor as a component of total cost. The shift has been away from direct labor toward increasing levels of automation. As a result, the use of direct labor cost or direct labor hours for purposes of factory overhead application has become less appropriate, often giving way to the use of machine hours as the preferred base.

In highly automated manufacturing, direct labor may not only be an inappropriate base for factory overhead application, but it also may be a relatively small portion of total manufacturing costs. In this latter case, direct labor may be included with factory overhead in a single conversion cost classification and applied as a part of a conversion cost rate.

Machine Hour Base. When machines are used extensively, machine hours may be the most appropriate base. This method is based on time required to perform identical operations by a machine or group of machines. Machine hours expected to be used are estimated, and a machine hour rate is determined as follows:

$$\frac{\text{Estimated factory overhead}}{\text{Estimated machine hours}} = \text{Rate per machine hour}$$

If factory overhead is estimated to be $300,000 and 20,000 machine hours are estimated, the rate is $15 per machine hour ($300,000 ÷ 20,000 machine hours). Work that required 120 machine hours would be charged with $1,800 (120 hours × $15) for factory overhead.

If a machine or group of machines differ with respect to the overhead costs related to them, then a weighting procedure such as that discussed for the physical output base is required. An alternative is to use a separate rate for each machine or machine group, which requires segmentation of cost estimation, accumulation, and application, following the procedures discussed in the next chapter. A third alternative, increasingly popular in automated settings, is use of process time as the base. *Process time* is the total time that the manufacturing process requires to produce a unit of product.

The machine hour method requires additional clerical work. A reporting system must be designed to assure correct accumulation of all required data for proper overhead accounting. Generally, shop personnel, supervisors, or timekeepers collect machine hour data needed to charge overhead to jobs, products, or work performed. In computerized plants, this data collection effort may be entirely electronic. The machine hour method is considered the most reasonable method of applying overhead if the overhead cost is comprised predominantly of facility-related costs, such as depreciation, maintenance, and utilities. Indeed, with modern manufacturing technology, direct labor becomes an increasingly smaller portion of manufacturing costs, and facility costs become a proportionately greater portion. As a result, more and more situations require the use of a base other than direct labor, such as machine hours or weighted machine hours.

ACTIVITY COSTING

Transactions Base. A group of expenses may be associated with a particular activity in a manner not adequately represented by any of the bases previously discussed. For example, setup costs might more appropriately be assigned to products by a rate per setup, with a weighing scheme that considers each setup's complexity. Each setup is thus viewed as a transaction, with costs assigned to a product or batch of products based on the number of transactions required. This transactions approach may apply to other activities such as scheduling, inspections, materials movements, changes in products and processes, etc. The greater the diversity and complexity in the product line, the greater the number of transactions. Such

JUST-IN-TIME

transactions often are responsible for a large percentage of overhead costs, and the key to managing overhead is controlling the transactions that drive it. This means thinking consciously and carefully about which transactions are necessary and which are not, and about how to apply the necessary ones most effectively. For example, adherence to a just-in-time philosophy of process design permits elimination or reduction of many transactions.[1]

The transactions base approach gives particular consideration to the fact that certain significant overhead costs may not be driven by volume of output. Rather, in modern multiproduct factories, overhead cost may be caused more by the complexity of the product line and by the handling required for special, low volume items than by the total volume of production. To the extent that overhead cost is driven by transactions which are not proportional to output volume, the use of a volume of output base tends to overcost the high volume products and undercost the low volume products. Use of the transactions base corrects this misallocation.[2,3]

The criteria of reasonable correlation and practical reasonableness, as to both clerical efficiency and costing accuracy, should be foremost in seeking the preferred overhead costing base for a given situation, whatever that base may be. The idea of different bases for different cost groups suggests multiple rates rather than a single plant-wide factory overhead rate, and is discussed in detail in Chapters 14 and 15.

Activity Level Selection

In calculating an overhead rate, a great deal depends on the activity level selected. The numerator used in calculating the rate is an estimate of overhead at whatever level of activity the denominator assumes. The greater the assumed activity, the lower the fixed portion of the overhead rate, because fixed overhead will be spread over a greater number of machine hours, direct labor dollars, direct labor hours, etc. The variable portion of the rate will tend to remain constant at various activity levels within the relevant range of activity.

The following terms are used to describe different activity levels: theoretical capacity, practical capacity, expected actual capacity, and normal capacity. These descriptions are discussed in the following paragraphs. Current federal income tax regulations permit the use of expected actual capacity or normal capacity in assigning factory overhead costs to inventories.[4] The Internal Revenue Service does not permit the use of practical capacity nor theoretical capacity, arguing that it is an ". . . exception to the general rules of 'full absorption' accounting that apply to the determination of inventoriable costs."[5]

---

[1]Jeffrey G. Miller and Thomas E. Vollman, "The Hidden Factory," *Harvard Business Review,* Vol. 5, p. 146.

[2]John K. Shank and Vijay Govindarajan, "The Perils of Cost Allocation Based on Production Volumes," *Accounting Horizons,* Vol. 2, No. 4, p. 77.

[3]See Debbie Berlant, Reese Browning, and George Foster, "How Hewlett-Packard Gets Numbers It Can Trust," *Harvard Business Review,* Vol. 68, No. 1, pp. 178-183, for a description of Hewlett-Packard's experience with the transactions base approach.

[4]*Regulations,* Section 1.471-11.

[5]*Regulations,* Section 1.263A-1T(b)(2)(vii).

Theoretical Capacity. The *theoretical capacity* of a department is its capacity to produce at full speed without interruptions. It is achieved if the plant or department produces at 100 percent of its rated capacity.

Practical Capacity. It is highly improbable that any company can operate at theoretical capacity. Allowances must be made for unavoidable interruptions, such as time lost for repairs, inefficiencies, breakdowns, setups, failures, unsatisfactory materials, delays in delivery of materials or supplies, labor shortages and absences, Sundays, holidays, vacations, inventory taking, and pattern and model changes. The number of work shifts must also be considered. These allowances reduce theoretical capacity to the *practical capacity* level. This reduction is caused by internal influences and does not consider the chief external influence—lack of customers' orders. Reduction from theoretical to practical capacity typically ranges from 15 percent to 25 percent, which results in a practical capacity level of 75 percent to 85 percent of theoretical capacity.

Expected Actual Capacity. The short-range or short-term planning and control approach, the *expected actual capacity* concept, advocates a rate in which overhead and production are based on the expected actual output for the next production period. This method usually results in the use of a different predetermined rate for each period, depending on increases or decreases in estimated factory overhead and production figures. The use of expected actual capacity is feasible with firms whose products are of a seasonal nature and whose market and style changes allow price adjustments according to competitive conditions and customer demands. However, the use of a predetermined rate based on expected actual production is more often due to the difficulty of judging current performance on a long-range or normal capacity level.

Normal Capacity. The long-range or long-term planning and control approach, the *normal capacity* concept, advocates an overhead rate in which expenses and production are based on average utilization of the physical plant over a time period long enough to level out the highs and lows. The normal capacity rate is based on the concept that the overhead rate should not be changed because existing plant facilities are used to a greater or lesser degree in different periods; therefore, a more useful unit cost results. A job or product should not cost more to produce in any one accounting period just because production was lower and fixed charges were spread over fewer units. The rate will be changed, however, when prices of certain expense items change or when fixed costs increase or decrease.

As a result of the use of normal production figures for estimating factory overhead and the selected bases, applied overhead will usually differ from actual overhead incurred. The possibility of such a difference or variance must be recognized, but should not serve to discourage the use of an overhead rate or encourage the change of this rate. In fact, when this variance, generally called over- or underapplied factory overhead, is further analyzed, it reveals useful management information (pages 384-387).

Purposes of Establishing Normal Capacity. Although there may be some differences between a normal long-run volume and the sales volume expected in the next period, normal capacity is useful in establishing sales prices and controlling costs. It is fundamental to the entire budget system, and it can be used for the following purposes:

1. Preparing departmental flexible budgets and computing predetermined factory overhead rates.
2. Compiling the standard cost of each product.
3. Scheduling production.
4. Assigning cost to inventories.
5. Determining the break-even point.
6. Measuring the effects of changing volumes of production.

Although other capacity assumptions are sometimes used due to existing circumstances, normal capacity fulfills both long- and short-term purposes. The long-term utilization of the normal capacity level relates the marketing and pricing policy of the business to the production phase over a long period of time, leveling out fluctuations that are of short duration and of comparatively minor significance. The short-term utilization relates to management's analysis of changes or fluctuations that occur during an operating year. This short-term utilization measures temporary idleness and aids in an analysis of its causes.

Factors Involved in Determining Normal Capacity. In determining the normal capacity of a plant, both its physical capacity and average sales expectancy must be considered. Neither plant capacity nor sales potential alone is sufficient. As previously mentioned, sales expectancy should be determined for a period long enough to level out cyclical variations. Unused machinery and machinery bought for future use must be excluded from the considerations which lead to the determination of the normal capacity level.

Calculation of the normal capacity of a plant requires many different judgment factors. Normal capacity should be determined first for the business as a whole and then broken down by plants and departments. Determination of a departmental capacity figure might indicate that for a certain department the planned program is an overload, while in another it will result in excess capacity. The capacities of several departments will seldom be in such perfect balance as to produce an unhampered flow of production. For the department with the overload, often termed the "bottleneck" department, actions such as the following might have to be taken:

1. Working overtime.
2. Introducing an additional shift.
3. Temporarily transferring operations to another department where spare capacity is available.
4. Subcontracting the excess load.
5. Purchasing additional equipment.

If these actions are not taken or are unsuccessful, the excess facilities of other departments should be either shut down or eliminated, or the sales department might be asked to obtain additional orders to utilize the spare capacity in these departments. If there is a bottleneck department, then using the full capacity of all departments merely to increase reported utilization measures will result in excess work in process inventories at points preceding the bottleneck, with no increase in final output.[6]

Effect of Capacity on Overhead Rates. The effect of the various capacity levels on predetermined factory overhead rates is illustrated in the following table. In this illustration, if the 75 percent capacity level (normal capacity) is the selected level, the overhead rate is $2.40 per machine hour. At higher capacity levels, the rate is lower because the fixed overhead is spread over more machine hours.

EFFECT OF VARIOUS CAPACITY LEVELS ON PREDETERMINED FACTORY OVERHEAD RATES					
Item	Expected Actual Capacity	Normal Capacity	Expected Actual Capacity	Practical Capacity	Theoretical Capacity
Percentage of theoretical capacity	70%	75%	80%	85%	100%
Machine hours.	7,000 hrs.	7,500 hrs.	8,000 hrs.	8,500 hrs.	10,000 hrs.
Budgeted factory overhead:					
Fixed	$12,000	$12,000	$12,000	$12,000	$12,000
Variable	5,600	6,000	6,400	6,800	8,000
Total	$17,600	$18,000	$18,400	$18,800	$20,000
Fixed factory overhead rate per machine hour .	$1.71	$1.60	$1.50	$1.41	$1.20
Variable factory overhead rate per machine hour	.80	.80	.80	.80	.80
Total factory overhead rate per machine hour .	$2.51	$2.40	$2.30	$2.21	$2.00

Idle Capacity vs. Excess Capacity. A distinction must be made between idle capacity and excess capacity. *Idle capacity* results from the idleness of production workers and facilities due to a temporary lack of sales. When sales demand increases, the idle production workers and facilities are restored to full use. When idle capacity is budgeted for the period, its cost is usually included in the factory overhead application rate and thus becomes a part of the product cost. When idle capacity is not budgeted, a factory overhead idle capacity variance results which is related to idle facilities. Costs associated with idle production workers are included in the spending variance. An overhead idle capacity variance should be (1) treated as a period cost or (2) allocated to inventories and cost of goods sold. If it is not material, it is typically

---

[6]Eliyahu M. Goldratt and Jeff Cox, *The Goal: Excellence in Manufacturing* (Croton-on-Hudson, New York: North River Press, Inc., 1984).

charged to expense of the period. (See pages 384-387 for further discussion of these variances.)

Excess capacity, conversely, results either from greater productive capacity than the company could ever hope to use, or from an imbalance in equipment or machinery. This imbalance involves the excess capacity of one machine in contrast with the output of other machines with which it must be synchronized. Any expense arising from excess capacity should be excluded from the factory overhead rate and from the product cost. The expense should be treated as a deduction in the income statement. In many instances, it may be wise to dispose of excess plant and equipment.

Including or Excluding of Fixed Overhead Items

Ordinarily, cost accounting applies all factory costs to the output of a period. Under this approach, called *absorption costing, conventional costing,* or *full costing,* both fixed and variable costs are included in overhead rates. Another method of costing, termed *direct costing,* is sometimes used, but only for internal management purposes. Under this method of costing, only variable overhead is included in overhead rates. The fixed portion of overhead cost does not become a product cost but is treated as a period cost, meaning that it is charged off in total each period as are marketing and administrative expenses. It is not included in either work in process or finished goods inventories. Direct costing is discussed in detail in Chapter 20.

Absorption costing and direct costing are the results of two entirely different cost concepts with respect to product cost, period cost, gross profit, and operating income. Although the two methods result in different inventory costs and different period profits, each of the various bases discussed for applying overhead may be used with absorption costing or direct costing. Problems of idle capacity variances and their disposition do not arise under direct costing, however.

■ THE CALCULATION OF A FACTORY OVERHEAD RATE

The first step in calculating the overhead rate is to determine the activity level to be used for the base selected and then estimate or budget each individual cost item at the estimated activity level in order to arrive at the total estimated factory overhead. To illustrate, assume that DeWitt Products estimates a normal capacity level of 20,000 machine hours. The total factory overhead is estimated to be $300,000. This overhead is classified into fixed or variable categories, as shown in the statement on page 381.

The classification of costs according to changes in volume attempts to establish a variability pattern for each item. This classification must, in turn, consider certain specific assumptions regarding plant facilities, prices (including inflation estimates), managerial policy, and the state of technology. Once the classification has been decided upon, the item may remain in this category for a limited period of time. Should underlying conditions change, the original classification must be reviewed and the cost items reclassified as necessary.

Variable costs change with production volume and are considered a function of volume; that is, the amount of variable cost per unit is constant. Fixed costs, on the other hand, are just the opposite. The total amount is fixed, but the cost per unit is different for each production level. Increased production causes a decrease in fixed cost per unit. Knowledge of the effect of fixed and variable costs on the product unit cost is highly important in any study of factory overhead. A knowledge of the behavior of all costs is fundamental to the planning and analytical processes for decision-making purposes as well as for cost control.

DeWitt Products
Estimated Factory Overhead for 19—

Expense	Fixed	Variable	Total
Supervisors	$ 70,000		$ 70,000
Indirect labor	9,000	$ 66,000	75,000
Overtime premium		9,000	9,000
Factory supplies	4,000	19,000	23,000
Repairs and maintenance	3,000	9,000	12,000
Electric power	2,000	18,000	20,000
Fuel	1,000	5,000	6,000
Water	500	500	1,000
Labor fringe benefits	10,500	48,500	59,000
Depreciation—building	5,000		5,000
Depreciation—equipment	13,000		13,000
Property tax	4,000		4,000
Insurance (fire)	3,000		3,000
Total estimated factory overhead	$125,000	$175,000	$300,000

An examination of fixed and variable costs indicates the difficulty of segregating all items as either fixed or variable. Some cost items are partly fixed and partly variable; some are fixed to a certain production level and then increase as production increases. Also, costs may change in step-like fashion at various production levels. Such items are classified as semivariable. Because costs are to be classified as either fixed or variable, the fixed portion of any semivariable expense and the degree of change in the variable portion must be determined.

Chapter 12 (pages 344-349) presented the methods available to aid in finding the constant portion and the degree of variability in the variable portion for determining cost behavior patterns. These procedures determine the relationship between increases in production and increases in total and individual costs. For example, when production is expected to increase 10 percent, it is possible to determine the corresponding increase in total cost as well as the increase in individual cost items such as supplies, power, or indirect labor.

After the activity level for the selected base and the factory overhead have been estimated, the overhead rates can be computed. Assuming that the machine hour base is used and machine hours for the coming year are estimated to be 20,000 (normal capacity level) for DeWitt Products, the factory overhead rate at this selected activity level would be:

$$\text{Factory overhead rate} = \frac{\text{Estimated factory overhead}}{\text{Estimated machine hours}} = \frac{\$300,000}{20,000} = \frac{\$15.00 \text{ per}}{\text{machine hour}}$$

This rate should be used to charge overhead to jobs, products, or work performed. Amounts applied are first entered in subsidiary ledgers such as job order cost sheets and cost of production reports. Machine hours used will determine the amount of overhead chargeable to each job or product.

The factory overhead rate can be further broken down into its fixed and variable components as follows:

$$\frac{\$125,000 \text{ estimated fixed factory overhead}}{20,000 \text{ estimated machine hours}} = \begin{array}{l} \$\ 6.25 \text{ fixed portion of the} \\ \text{factory overhead rate} \end{array}$$

$$\frac{\$175,000 \text{ estimated variable factory overhead}}{20,000 \text{ estimated machine hours}} = \begin{array}{l} 8.75 \text{ variable portion of the} \\ \text{factory overhead rate} \end{array}$$

$$\text{Total factory overhead rate} = \underline{\$15.00} \text{ per machine hour}$$

■ ACTUAL FACTORY OVERHEAD

Deciding upon the base and activity level to be utilized, estimating the factory overhead, and calculating the overhead rate take place prior to the incurrence or recording of the actual costs. Factory overhead is applied as soon as the necessary data, such as machine hours, have been made available. Each day, however, actual overhead transactions are journalized and posted to general and subsidiary ledgers, independent of the application of factory overhead based on the predetermined overhead rate.

A basic objective for accumulating factory overhead is the gathering of information for control. Control, in turn, requires (1) reporting costs to the individual department heads responsible for them and (2) making comparisons with amounts budgeted for the level of operations achieved. The mechanics for collecting overhead items are based on the chart of accounts, which indicates the accounts to which various factory overhead items are to be charged.

The principal source documents used for recording overhead in the journals are (1) purchase vouchers, (2) materials requisitions, (3) labor time tickets, and (4) general journal vouchers. These documents provide a record of the overhead information which must be analyzed and accumulated in proper accounts. To obtain accurate and useful information, each transaction must be properly classified at its inception. Those responsible for this identification must be thoroughly familiar with the names and code numbers of cost accounts as well as with the purpose and function of each account.

Factory overhead includes numerous items which can be classified in many different ways. Every firm, because of its own manufacturing peculiarities, will devise its own particular accounts and methods of classifying them. However, regardless of these possible variations, expenses are summarized in a factory overhead control account kept in the general ledger. Details of this general ledger account are kept in a subsidiary overhead ledger. This subsidiary ledger also can take many forms, and it may be difficult to recognize it as such, particularly when electronic data processing equipment is used. A subsidiary ledger will group various overhead cost items together under significant selective titles as to kinds of costs and may detail the costs chargeable to individual producing and service departments (discussed in Chapter 14), thereby permitting stricter control over factory overhead.

The accumulation of factory overhead in accounting records presents several distinct problems. Due to the many varied potential requests and uses of factory overhead data for managerial decision-making purposes, it is almost impossible to set up an all-purpose system for accumulating factory overhead.

■ APPLIED FACTORY OVERHEAD—OVER- OR UNDERAPPLIED AND VARIANCE ANALYSIS

At the end of the month or year, applied factory overhead and actual factory overhead are analyzed. The comparison between actual and applied figures leads to computation of the spending variance and the idle capacity variance. The following paragraphs present the mechanics of applying factory overhead, determining the over- or underapplied overhead, and analyzing the overhead variances.

The Mechanics of Applying Factory Overhead

The job order cost sheets or the departmental cost of production reports receive postings as soon as direct materials or direct labor data become available. Factory overhead is applied to the work done after the direct materials and the direct labor costs have been recorded. If machine hours or direct labor hours are the basis for overhead charges, these data must also be available to the cost department.

To continue the illustration for DeWitt Products, assume that actual machine hours totaled 18,900 and actual factory overhead totaled $292,000. The overhead applied during the period is $283,500 (18,900 machine hours × $15.00 per hour). The journal entry for summarizing factory overhead applied is:

Work in Process	283,500	
Applied Factory Overhead........................		283,500

Charges made to subsidiary records (the job order cost sheets or departmental cost of production reports) list in detail applied factory overhead charged to jobs or process costing departments. The debit to the work in process control account brings total applied overhead into the general ledger. The applied factory overhead account would subsequently be closed to the factory overhead control account by the following entry:

Applied Factory Overhead.........................	283,500	
Factory Overhead Control		283,500

It is common practice to use an applied factory overhead account because it keeps applied costs and actual costs in separate accounts. However, some companies post the credit directly to Factory Overhead Control.

After the actual and applied overhead have been recorded, the factory overhead control account for DeWitt Products appears as follows:

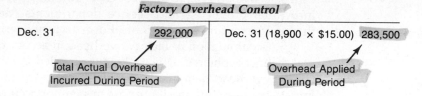

Factory Overhead Control

| Dec. 31 | 292,000 | Dec. 31 (18,900 × $15.00) | 283,500 |

Total Actual Overhead Incurred During Period   Overhead Applied During Period

Factory overhead costs are normally assigned to ending work in process and finished goods inventories, but in a just-in-time production environment, the overhead costs may be charged directly to Cost of Goods Sold as incurred. An end-of-the-period adjustment would be made adjusting the inventory accounts for the portion of factory overhead and other manufacturing costs appropriate to the units in inventory with the offset to the cost of goods sold account, using backflush costing procedures discussed in Chapter 3.

Over- or Underapplied Factory Overhead

Debits to the factory overhead control account are for actual overhead costs incurred during the period, while credits are for applied amounts of cost. There may also be credit adjustments (e.g., the return of supplies to the storeroom) which reduce the total actual factory overhead. Since the debits and credits are seldom equal, there is usually a debit or credit balance in the account. A debit balance indicates that overhead has been underapplied; a credit balance means that overhead has been overapplied. These over- or underapplied balances must be analyzed carefully, because they are the source of much information needed by management for controlling and judging the efficiency of operations and the use of available capacity during a particular period.

For DeWitt Products, applied factory overhead for the period is $8,500 less than the actual factory overhead incurred. Therefore, factory overhead for the period was $8,500 underapplied. This difference must be analyzed to determine the reason or reasons for the underapplied overhead.

Variance Analysis

Two separate variances are computed in analyzing over- or underapplied overhead:

1. Spending variance—a variance due to budget or expense factors.
2. Idle capacity variance—a variance due to volume or activity factors.

The analysis can be made in the following manner, using the factory overhead data given on pages 380-383:

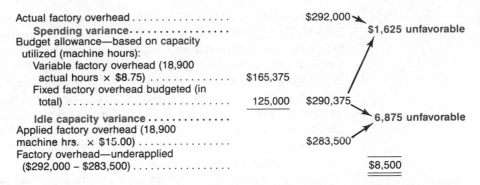

Actual factory overhead		$292,000
Spending variance.		$1,625 unfavorable
Budget allowance—based on capacity utilized (machine hours):		
Variable factory overhead (18,900 actual hours × $8.75)	$165,375	
Fixed factory overhead budgeted (in total)	125,000	$290,375
Idle capacity variance		6,875 unfavorable
Applied factory overhead (18,900 machine hrs. × $15.00)		$283,500
Factory overhead—underapplied ($292,000 − $283,500)		$8,500

Spending Variance. The $1,625 spending variance is the difference between the actual factory overhead incurred and the budget allowance estimated for the capacity utilized, i.e., for the actual activity of 18,900 machine hours. The spending variance can also be computed as follows:

Actual factory overhead incurred during the period	$292,000
Less budgeted fixed overhead	125,000
Actual variable overhead incurred during the period	$167,000
Variable overhead applied during the period (18,900 machine hours × $8.75)	165,375
Spending variance—unfavorable.	$ 1,625

If actual overhead had been less than budgeted, the spending variance would have been favorable. Any difference between actual and budgeted fixed overhead would be included as part of the spending variance or separately identified as an additional variance.

A breakdown of the $1,625 spending variance, as well as a comparison of each actual overhead cost item with its budgeted figure, is useful. Details of the actual costs are recorded in the factory overhead subsidiary ledger. The comparison of actual with budgeted overhead for capacity utilized (18,900 machine hours) is illustrated for DeWitt Products on page 386.

The budgeted figures utilize the concept of the flexible budget discussed in Chapter 17. Basically, the budget figures represent the budget for the level of activity attained. For example, from the estimates for indirect labor on page 381, fixed overhead is $9,000; the variable part of the overhead cost is $3.30 per machine hour ($66,000 estimated variable indirect labor ÷ 20,000 estimated machine hours). The budgeted indirect labor for the activity level attained is $9,000 fixed overhead plus $62,370 (18,900 machine hours × $3.30) variable overhead.

Some of the actual costs exceed while others are less than the budgeted figures. Each difference must be analyzed, the reason for the difference must be determined, and discussion must be initiated with the individual responsible for its incurrence. Corrective action should be taken where needed; likewise, effective and efficient performance should be recognized and rewarded. Observe that even underexpenditures may be undesirable. For example, the $1,305 underspent repairs and maintenance amount may suggest insufficient attention to preventive maintenance.

In deciding which costs to investigate, tolerance limits should be established. The question becomes, "How large a variance should be tolerated before it is considered excessive?" If a variance falls within the tolerance range, it can be considered acceptable. If the variance is outside the range, an investigation should occur if the cost of the investigation is reasonable. Thus, the notion of management by exception can be employed. The tolerance limits may be set by rules of thumb or preferably by applying procedures such as the standard error of the estimate discussed in Chapter 12.

Some of the spending variance may be attributable to inflation. Although budget estimates are intended to incorporate inflationary effects, the level of inflation is difficult to predict and difficult to isolate as part of a variance.

DeWitt Products Comparison of Actual and Factory Overhead Budget Allowance for 19— (Capacity Utilized: 18,900 Machine Hours = 94.5% of Normal)			
	Budget Allowance	Actual	Spending Variance
Variable overhead:			
Indirect labor	$ 62,370	$ 63,550	$1,180
Overtime premium	8,505	8,700	195
Factory supplies	17,955	18,720	765
Repairs and maintenance	8,505	7,200	(1,305)
Electric power	17,010	17,650	640
Fuel	4,725	4,300	(425)
Water	472	500	28
Labor fringe benefits	45,833	46,380	547
Total	$165,375	$167,000	$1,625
Fixed overhead:			
Supervisors	$ 70,000	$ 70,000	———
Indirect labor	9,000	9,000	———
Factory supplies	4,000	4,000	———
Repairs and maintenance	3,000	3,000	———
Electric power	2,000	2,000	———
Fuel	1,000	1,000	———
Water	500	500	———
Labor fringe benefits	10,500	10,500	———
Depreciation—building	5,000	5,000	———
Depreciation—equipment	13,000	13,000	———
Property tax	4,000	4,000	———
Insurance (fire)	3,000	3,000	———
Total	$125,000	$125,000	———
Total	$290,375	$292,000	$1,625 unfav.

Idle Capacity Variance. For DeWitt Products, the rate used for applying factory overhead was $15.00 per machine hour, which was based on 20,000 normal capacity hours. However, machine hours utilized during the period totaled only 18,900 hours; capacity not used was 1,100 machine hours. The capacity attained was 94.5 percent (18,900 ÷ 20,000) of normal.

The $15.00 overhead rate was considered the proper costing price for each machine hour used. The fact that operations were at a level below normal should not increase the factory overhead cost of each unit. The cost of idle capacity should be recorded separately and considered a part of total manufacturing cost. The $6,875 idle capacity variance arises because 1,100 available machine hours were not used. It is computed as follows:

Budget allowance (based on capacity utilized)	$290,375
Applied factory overhead	283,500
Idle capacity variance—unfavorable	$ 6,875

The idle capacity variance can also be computed by multiplying the 1,100 idle hours by the $6.25 fixed cost rate or by multiplying the total budgeted fixed cost of $125,000 by 5.5 percent (100% − 94.5%).

Responsibility for the idle capacity variance rests with executive management, since this variance indicates the under- or overutilization of plant and equipment. The cause of a capacity variance, whether favorable or unfavorable, should always be determined and possible reasons for the variance discovered. One cause may be a lack of proper balance between production facilities and sales.

Disposition of Over- or Underapplied Factory Overhead. Because of its importance, the analysis of the over- or underapplied factory overhead is presented in detail. Disposition of this figure is generally quite simple. Although total over- or underapplied overhead is analyzed, showing spending and idle capacity variances, it need not be journalized and posted in two parts. At the end of the fiscal period, overhead variances may be (1) treated as a period cost or (2) allocated between inventories and the cost of goods sold.

For financial reporting purposes, the procedure often used for disposing of over- or underapplied overhead, provided the amount involved is insignificant, is to close it directly to Income Summary or to Cost of Goods Sold, thereby treating the over- or underapplied overhead as a period cost. The entry to record the underapplied factory overhead on the books of DeWitt Products would be:

Income Summary	8,500	
Factory Overhead Control		8,500

or

Cost of Goods Sold	8,500	
Factory Overhead Control		8,500

In the second case, the $8,500 is subsequently closed to the income summary account as a part of the total cost of goods sold account balance.

The over- or underapplied figure is closed to the cost of goods sold account if the variances are considered a manufacturing function responsibility; if not, the balance is closed to Income Summary. If it is closed to the income summary account, it will appear in the income statement as shown on page 388.

DeWitt Products
Income Statement
For Year Ended December 31, 19—

Sales.		$1,600,000
Less: Cost of goods sold at normal.	$1,193,500	
Underapplied factory overhead.	8,500	1,202,000
Gross profit.		$ 398,000
Less: Marketing expense.	$ 150,000	
Administrative expense	100,000	250,000
Operating income.		$ 148,000

If the over- or underapplied overhead is closed to the cost of goods sold account, it will appear in the cost of goods sold statement. This statement and the income statement would appear as follows:

DeWitt Products
Cost of Goods Sold Statement
For Year Ended December 31, 19—

Direct materials used.	$ 400,000
Direct labor used	500,000
Applied factory overhead.	283,500
Total manufacturing cost	$1,183,500
Less increase in work in process inventory	20,000
Cost of goods manufactured at normal	$1,163,500
Plus decrease in finished goods inventory.	30,000
Cost of goods sold at normal	$1,193,500
Plus underapplied factory overhead	8,500
Cost of goods sold at actual	$1,202,000

DeWitt Products
Income Statement
For Year Ended December 31, 19—

Sales		$1,600,000
Less cost of goods sold at actual.		1,202,000
Gross profit		$ 398,000
Less: Marketing expense	$150,000	
Administrative expense	100,000	250,000
Operating income		$ 148,000

Over- or underapplied overhead may be allocated between inventories and the cost of goods sold. This procedure has the effect of restating applied overhead at amounts approximating actual overhead, and it is appropriate for financial reporting purposes if the variances are significant, because to do otherwise would materially misstate financial results. For example, expensing of a significant underapplied overhead balance would overstate expense, understate income, and understate inventory on the balance sheet.

Internal Revenue Service regulations require that inventories include an allocated portion of significant annual overhead variances. When the amount involved is not significant in relation to total actual factory overhead, an allocation is not required unless such allocation is made for financial reporting purposes. Also, the taxpayer must treat both over- and underapplied overhead consistently.

Regardless of the disposition made of the over- or underapplied figure, the computation, analysis, and reporting of both the spending and idle capacity variances are significant. In the disposition of over- or underapplied factory overhead for financial reporting purposes, companies generally should follow the same procedures at interim dates as are followed at year end. Variances that occur at an interim date and that are expected to be absorbed prior to year end should be deferred rather than disposed of immediately. Further discussion of the disposition of variances is reserved for the standard cost chapters (18 and 19).

■ CHANGING OVERHEAD RATES

Overhead rates are usually reviewed annually. This procedure helps level out costing through the year and ties overhead control in with budget control. If rates are changed during a fiscal or budget period, meaningful comparisons will be difficult. Changes in production methods, prices, efficiencies, and sales expectancy make review and, possibly, revision of overhead rates necessary at least annually. Revisions should be based on a complete review of all factors involved. The extent to which a company revises its overhead rates depends on the frequency of changes, on factors which affect overhead rates, and on management's need and desire for current costs and realistic overhead variance information.

An overhead rate may be incorrect because of misjudgments regarding estimated overhead or anticipated activity. A large over- or underapplied overhead figure does not necessarily mean that the overhead rate was wrong. As mentioned, use of a normal overhead rate is purposely designed to show spending variances as well as the extent to which normal capacity is or is not used. Likewise, when an overhead rate based on expected actual conditions is used, seasonal variations may result in a large amount of over- or underabsorbed overhead, which will tend to even itself out during a full year. The best way to detect an incorrect overhead rate is to analyze the factors used in its predetermination. Since a rate is an estimate, small errors should be expected, and the rate need not be changed for such errors.

■ SUMMARY OF FACTORY OVERHEAD

This chapter's discussion of estimating, accounting for, and analyzing factory overhead is summarized diagrammatically on page 390.

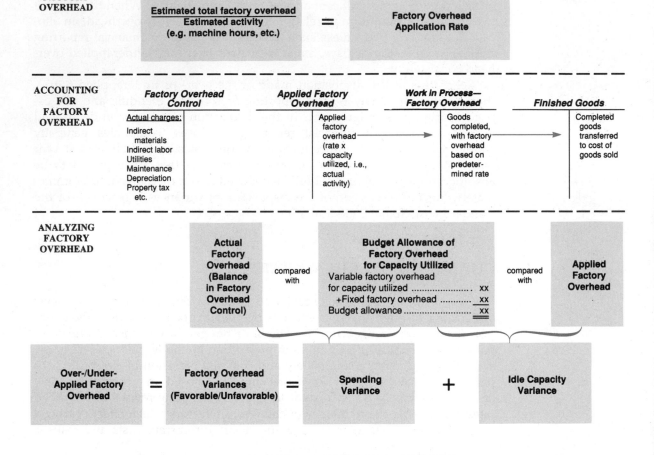

DISCUSSION QUESTIONS

Q13-1. List some of the main costs that are considered to be factory overhead.

Q13-2. Why will factory overhead vary from month to month?

Q13-3. When and why must predetermined factory overhead rates be used? Indicate the impracticalities and inaccuracies of charging actual overhead to jobs and products. (AICPA adapted)

Q13-4. Name six bases used for applying overhead. What factors must be considered in selecting a particular base?

Q13-5. Why is the selection of a proper predetermined rate so essential to reasonable costing? Explain.

Q13-6. Discuss the objectives and criteria that should be used in deciding whether to use direct labor hours or machine hours as the overhead rate base. (AICPA adapted)

Q13-7. Differentiate between (a) theoretical capacity, (b) practical capacity, (c) expected actual capacity, and (d) normal capacity.

Q13-8. How does the selection of normal or maximum capacity affect operating profit in setting the factory overhead rate?

Q13-9. (a) What situations give rise to idle capacity costs? (b) How and why should such costs be accounted for? (c) What is excess capacity cost?

Q13-10. What are the steps involved in accounting for actual factory overhead?

Q13-11. The factory overhead control account has a credit balance at the end of the period. Was overhead over- or underapplied?

Q13-12. Over- or underapplied overhead can be analyzed into two parts called variances. Name these variances, state the reason(s) for their titles, and show their computations.

Q13-13. What are the purposes of a factory overhead variance analysis report, such as the one shown on page 386?

Q13-14. A company applies factory overhead to production on the basis of direct labor dollars. At the end of the year, factory overhead has been overapplied to the extent of $60,000. What factors could cause this situation?

Q13-15. Describe two methods for disposing of over- or underapplied factory overhead and explain how the decision to use one of these methods rather than the other would affect net income.

Q13-16. If large underabsorbed (underapplied) factory overhead variances occur month after month, the factory overhead rate should be revised to make unit costs more accurate. Comment.

EXERCISES

E13-1. Factory overhead application. On September 30, the work in process account of Perdido Company showed:

Work In Process

Materials	25,800	Finished goods	50,600
Direct labor	20,160		
Factory overhead	15,840		

Materials charged to the work still in process amounted to $4,560. Factory overhead is applied as a percentage of direct labor cost.

Required: Compute the individual amounts of factory overhead and direct labor charged to work still in process. (Round all amounts to four decimal places.)

E13-2. Calculation of estimated labor hours. Stetson Company employs 150 people, who work 8 hours, 5 days a week. Normal capacity for the firm is based on the assumption that the equivalent of 48 weeks of work can be expected from an employee.

Required: Calculate the following:

(1) The number of direct labor hours to be used in setting up the firm's factory overhead rate based on normal capacity.
(2) The number of direct labor hours if management and workers agree on a 10-hour, 4-day workweek.

E13-3. Various factory overhead rates. The Greenville Corporation estimates factory overhead of $225,000 for the next fiscal year. It is estimated that 45,000 units will be produced, with materials cost of $500,000. Conversion will require an estimated 56,250 labor hours at a cost of $8 per hour, with an estimated 75,000 machine hours.

Required: Compute the predetermined factory overhead rate to be used in applying factory overhead to production on each of the following bases:

  (1) Units of production
  (2) Materials cost
  (3) Direct labor hours
  (4) Direct labor cost
  (5) Machine hours

E13-4. Normal and expected actual capacity. Normal capacity for Abilene Products Company is 50,000 direct labor hours. The actual capacity attained for the fiscal year ended June 30, 19A, was 43,000 hours. It is estimated that 40,000 hours will be worked in 19B. Fixed factory overhead is $200,000, and variable factory overhead is $6.69 per direct labor hour.

Required:

  (1) Using normal capacity, compute (a) the factory overhead rate, (b) the fixed part of the factory overhead rate, and (c) the 19A idle capacity variance.
  (2) Using expected actual capacity for 19B, compute (a) the factory overhead rate, (b) the fixed part of the factory overhead rate, and (c) the 19B idle capacity variance if actual hours worked were 42,000.

E13-5. Factory overhead—applied, over- or underapplied. Carlo Company budgeted factory overhead at $255,000 for the period for Department A, based on a budgeted volume of 50,000 machine hours. At the end of the period, the actual factory overhead was $270,000 and actual machine hours were 52,500.

Required: Calculate the applied and over- or underapplied factory overhead for the period.

E13-6. Entries for factory overhead. Perry Co. assembles and sells electric mixers. All parts are purchased, and the cost of the parts per mixer totals $40. Labor is paid on the basis of $32 per mixer assembled. Since the company handles only this one product, the unit cost base for applying factory overhead is used. Estimated factory overhead for the coming period, based on a production of 30,000 mixers, is as follows:

Indirect materials	$220,000
Indirect labor	240,000
Light and power	30,000
Depreciation	25,000
Miscellaneous.	55,000

During the period, 29,000 mixers were assembled and actual factory overhead was $561,600. These units were completed but not yet transferred to the finished goods storeroom.

Required:

  (1) Prepare the journal entries to record the above information.
  (2) Determine the amount of over- or underapplied factory overhead.

E13-7 **Variance analysis.** Normal annual capacity for Farthington Company is 48,000 units, with production being constant throughout the year. The October budget shows fixed factory overhead of $1,440 and an estimated variable factory overhead rate of $2.10 per unit. During October, actual output was 4,100 units, with a total factory overhead of $9,000.

Required: Compute the spending and idle capacity variances.

E13-8 **Applied factory overhead and variance analysis.** Normal annual capacity for Maddax Company is 36,000 machine hours, with fixed factory overhead budgeted as $16,920 and an estimated variable factory overhead rate of $2.10 per hour. During October, actual production required 2,700 machine hours, with a total overhead of $7,959.

Required: Compute (1) the applied factory overhead and (2) the spending and idle capacity variances.

E13-9. **Variance analysis.** Quitman Company made the following data available from its accounting records and reports:

(a) $\dfrac{\$600,000 \text{ estimated factory overhead}}{200,000 \text{ estimated machine hours}}$ = $3 predetermined factory overhead rate

(b) Further analysis indicates that one third of the rate is variable-cost oriented.
(c) During the year, the company utilized 210,000 machine hours and actual factory overhead expenditures were $631,000.

Required: Compute the spending and idle capacity variances.

E13-10. **Variance analysis.** The Utah Company has $200,000 of fixed expenses at normal capacity based on 100,000 direct labor hours per month. Labor time tickets for January showed that 130,000 hours were worked, 20,000 of which were recorded as indirect labor. It is known also that factory overhead was overapplied by $9,000 as a result of January operations.

Required: Compute the factory overhead spending and idle capacity variances.

E13-11. **Factory overhead application and analysis.** Normal operating capacity of Mars Inc. is 100,000 machine hours per month, the level used to compute the predetermined factory overhead application rate. At this level of activity, fixed factory overhead is estimated to be $150,000 and variable factory overhead is estimated to be $250,000. During March, actual production required 105,000 machine hours and actual factory overhead totaled $415,000.

Required:

(1) Determine the fixed portion of the factory overhead application rate.
(2) Determine the variable portion of the factory overhead application rate.
(3) Is factory overhead for March over- or underapplied and by how much?
(4) How much is the spending variance and is it favorable or unfavorable?
(5) How much is the idle capacity variance and is it favorable or unfavorable?

E13-12. **Variance analysis.** Kornbrant Company was totally destroyed by fire during June. However, certain fragments of its cost records with the following data were recovered: idle capacity variance, $1,266 favorable; spending variance, $879 unfavorable; and applied factory overhead, $16,234.

Required: Determine (1) the budget allowance, based on capacity utilized, and (2) the actual factory overhead.

PROBLEMS

P13-1. Determining variable and fixed factory overhead cost behavior. Hank Company had the following production, sales, and costs in March and October, 19A, which are considered to be typical months:

	March	October
Production in units	10,000	15,000
Sales in units	12,000	16,000
Costs:		
Depreciation on factory building and equipment	$16,000	$ 16,000
Heat, light, and power (factory)	6,000	8,000
Supplies used (factory)	7,000	10,500
Direct materials used	50,000	75,000
Taxes on factory building	2,000	2,000
Bad debt expense	1,000	1,500
Indirect labor (factory)	60,000	70,000
Advertising expense	6,000	8,000
Maintenance (factory)	12,000	18,000
Direct labor	70,000	105,000

Required:

(1) Compute the variable overhead per unit for each factory overhead cost.
(2) Compute the fixed overhead for each factory overhead cost.

CGA-Canada (adapted) Reprint with permission

P13-2. Factory overhead accumulation and application. Lamb Company uses job order cost accumulation procedures. Manufacturing-related costs for November were:

Work in process, November 1 (Job 50)	$ 54,000
Materials and supplies requisitioned for:	
Job 50	$ 45,000
Job 51	37,500
Job 52	25,500
Supplies	2,000
Factory direct labor hours:	
Job 50	3,500
Job 51	3,000
Job 52	2,000
Labor costs:	
Direct labor wages	$102,000
Indirect labor wages	15,000
Supervisory salaries	6,000
Building occupancy costs	3,500
Factory equipment costs	6,000
Other factory costs	5,000

Jobs 50 and 51 were completed during November. The predetermined factory overhead rate is $4.50 per direct labor hour.

Required:

(1) Compute the total cost of Job 50.
(2) Determine the factory overhead costs applied to Job 52 during November.
(3) Compute the total factory overhead costs applied during November.
(4) Determine the actual November factory overhead incurred.
(5) How should Lamb dispose of any over- or underapplied factory overhead, assuming that the amount is not significant in relation to total factory overhead?

(ICMA adapted)

P13-3. Variance analysis. Following are seven sets of partial factory overhead data, with favorable variances shown in parentheses:

	Actual Factory Overhead	Applied Factory Overhead	Budget Allowance (Based on Capacity Utilized)	Spending Variance	Idle Capacity Variance
(a)	$30,000	$29,000	$32,000	$?	$?
(b)	?	15,000	?	1,000	7,000
(c)	24,000	24,000	?	(6,000)	?
(d)	?	?	18,000	1,000	2,000
(e)	18,000	20,000	?	3,000	?
(f)	27,000	?	?	(6,000)	(2,000)
(g)	16,000	16,000	?	–0–	?

Required: Compute the missing figures.

P13-4. Factory overhead costing; job order cost accumulation. The following manufacturing cost data are available for Department 203:

Work in process—beginning of period:

Job No.	Materials	Labor	Factory Overhead	Total
1376	$17,500	$22,000	$33,000	$72,500

Costs for 19––:

Incurred by Jobs	Materials	Labor	Other	Total
1376	$ 1,000	$ 7,000	—	$ 8,000
1377	26,000	53,000	—	79,000
1378	12,000	9,000	—	21,000
1379	4,000	1,000	—	5,000

Not Incurred by Jobs				
Indirect materials and supplies	15,000	—	—	15,000
Indirect labor......................	—	53,000	—	53,000
Employee benefits	—	—	$23,000	23,000
Depreciation	—	—	12,000	12,000
Supervision......................	—	20,000	—	20,000
Total......................	$58,000	$143,000	$35,000	$236,000

Factory overhead rate for 19––:
Budgeted overhead:

Variable—Indirect materials and supplies...	$ 16,000
Indirect labor..	56,000
Employee benefits..	24,000
Fixed—Depreciation..	12,000
Supervision	20,000
Total..	$128,000
Budgeted direct labor cost..	$ 80,000
Overhead rate per direct labor dollar ($128,000 ÷ $80,000)...........................	160%

Required:

(1) Compute the actual factory overhead.
(2) Determine the over- or underapplied factory overhead.

(3) Calculate the spending variance.

(4) Calculate the amount included in cost of goods sold for Job 1376, which was the only job completed and sold in 19--.

(5) Determine the cost assigned to the work in process account at the end of 19--, unadjusted for any over- or underapplied factory overhead.

(6) Assume that factory overhead was $7,000 underapplied. Compute the underapplied factory overhead charged to Work in Process if it was distributed between this account and Cost of Goods Sold.

(ICMA adapted)

P13-5. Variance analysis. Murdock Goods Company set normal capacity at 60,000 machine hours. The expected operating level for the period just ended was 45,000 hours. At this expected actual capacity, variable expenses were estimated to be $29,250 and fixed expenses, $18,000. Actual results show that 47,000 machine hours were used and that actual factory overhead totaled $50,400 during the period.

Required:

(1) Compute the predetermined factory overhead rate based on normal capacity.

(2) Compute the predetermined factory overhead rate based on expected actual capacity.

(3) Compute the amount of factory overhead charged to production if the company used the normal capacity rate.

(4) Compute the amount of factory overhead charged to production if the company used the expected actual capacity rate.

(5) Would there be a favorable idle capacity variance if the normal capacity rate were used? Illustrate by variance computation.

(6) Would there be a favorable idle capacity variance if the expected actual capacity rate were used? Illustrate by variance computation.

(7) Determine the difference in the amount of the spending variance, depending on whether normal or expected actual capacity was used. Illustrate by variance computation.

P13-6. Inventory costing; overhead analysis; statement of cost of goods sold. The Cost Department of Columbus Company received the following monthly data, pertaining solely to manufacturing activities, from the general ledger clerk:

Work in process inventory, January 1	$ 32,500
Materials inventory, January 1	21,000
Direct labor	256,000
Materials purchased	108,000
Materials returned to suppliers	5,050
Supervision	17,500
Indirect labor	29,050
Heat, light, and power	23,800
Depreciation—factory buildings	7,500
Property tax—factory facilities	4,000
Insurance on factory buildings	3,000
Transportation in (factory overhead)	6,500
Repairs and maintenance—factory equipment	8,250
Depreciation—factory equipment	7,500
Miscellaneous factory overhead	9,900
Finished goods inventory, January 1	18,000
Applied factory overhead	115,200

Additional data:

(a) Physical inventory taken January 31 shows $9,000 of materials on hand.

(b) The January 31 work in process and finished goods inventories show the following direct materials and direct labor contents:

	Direct Materials	Direct Labor
Work in process	$ 9,000	$16,000 (2,000 hrs.)
Finished goods	10,000	40,000 (5,000 hrs.)

(c) Factory overhead is applied to these two ending inventories on the basis of a factory overhead rate of $3.60 per direct labor hour.

Required:

(1) Determine the cost assigned to the ending work in process and finished goods inventories, including factory overhead.
(2) Prepare a schedule of the total actual factory overhead for the month.
(3) Prepare an analysis of the over- or underapplied factory overhead, assuming that the predetermined factory overhead rate was based on the following data:

Variable factory overhead	$70,875
Fixed factory overhead	$42,525
Direct labor hours	31,500

(4) Prepare a detailed cost of goods sold statement, assuming that over- or underapplied overhead is closed to the cost of goods sold account.

CASES

C13-1. Cost behavior analysis; utility of cost behavior information. Tastee-Treat Food Company assigns factory overhead by a predetermined rate on the basis of direct labor hours. Factory overhead costs for two recent years, adjusted for changes using current prices and wage rates, are as follows:

	Year 1	Year 2
Direct labor hours worked.	2,760,000	2,160,000
Factory overhead costs:		
Indirect labor	$11,040,000	$ 8,640,000
Employee benefits.......	4,140,000	3,240,000
Supplies..............	2,760,000	2,160,000
Power................	2,208,000	1,728,000
Heat and light	552,000	552,000
Supervision	2,865,000	2,625,000
Depreciation...........	7,930,000	7,930,000
Property taxes and		
insurance............	3,005,000	3,005,000
Total factory		
overhead cost	$34,500,000	$29,880,000

Required:

(1) The company expects to operate at a 2,300,000 direct labor hour level of activity next year. Using the data from the two recent years, calculate the estimated total factory overhead for next year.

(2) Explain how the company can use the computed cost behavior information for:

(a) Evaluation of product pricing decisions.
(b) Cost control evaluation.
(c) Development of budgets.

(ICMA adapted)

C13-2. Factory overhead rate bases. Herbert Manufacturing Company, a manufacturer of custom designed restaurant and kitchen furniture, uses job order costing. Actual factory overhead costs incurred during the month are applied to the products on the basis of actual direct labor hours required to produce the products and consist primarily of supervision, employee benefits, maintenance costs, property tax, and depreciation.

Herbert recently won a contract to manufacture the furniture for a new fast food chain which is expanding rapidly in the area. In general, this furniture is durable but of a lower quality than the company normally manufactures. To produce this new line, Herbert must produce more molded plastic parts for the furniture than for its current line. Through innovative industrial engineering, an efficient manufacturing process for this new furniture has been developed, requiring only a minimum capital investment. Management is optimistic about the profit improvement the new product line will bring.

At the end of October, the start-up month for the new line, and again in November, the controller prepared a separate income statement for the new product line. On a consolidated basis, the gross profit percentage was normal; however, the profitability for the new line was less than expected. Management is concerned that knowledgeable stockholders will criticize the decision to add this lower-quality product line at a time when profitability appeared to be increasing with their standard product line. Gross profit results for the first nine months, for October, and for November are as follows:

Herbert Manufacturing Company
Statement of Gross Profit
(Thousands of Dollars)

	First Nine Months			October			November		
	Fast Food Furniture	Custom Furniture	Consolidated	Fast Food Furniture	Custom Furniture	Consolidated	Fast Food Furniture	Custom Furniture	Consolidated
Sales	—	$8,100	$8,100	$400	$900	$1,300	$800	$800	$1,600
Direct materials	—	$2,025	$2,025	$200	$225	$ 425	$400	$200	$ 600
Direct labor:									
Forming	—	758	758	17	82	99	31	72	103
Finishing	—	1,314	1,314	40	142	182	70	125	195
Assembly	—	558	558	33	60	93	58	53	111
Factory overhead	—	1,779	1,779	60	180	240	98	147	245
Cost of goods sold	—	$6,434	$6,434	$350	$689	$1,039	$657	$597	$1,254
Gross profit		$1,666	$1,666	$ 50	$211	$ 261	$143	$203	$ 346
Gross profit percentage	—	20.6%	20.6%	12.5%	23.4%	20.1%	17.9%	25.4%	21.6%

The controller contends that the factory overhead allocation based solely on direct labor hours is inappropriate and that only supervision and employee benefits should use this base, with the balance of factory overhead allocated based on machine hours. In the controller's judgment, the increase in custom design furniture profitability is partially a result of overhead misallocation.

The actual direct labor hours and machine hours for the past two months are shown on the next page. The actual factory overhead costs for the past two months were:

	October	November
Supervision	$ 13,000	$ 13,000
Employee benefits	95,000	109,500
Maintenance	50,000	48,000
Depreciation	42,000	42,000
Property tax	8,000	8,000
All other	32,000	24,500
Total	$240,000	$245,000

Required:

(1) Reallocate actual factory overhead for October and November, following the controller's preference. (Round allocated costs to the nearest $100.)

(2) Present support or criticism of the controller's contention, based on requirement (1) results, and include revised statements of gross profit for October and for November.

(3) The controller has also recommended that consideration be given to using predetermined factory overhead rates calculated on an annual basis rather than allocating actual cost over actual volume each month. The controller stated that this is particularly applicable now that the company has two distinct product lines. Discuss the advantages of predetermined factory overhead rates.   (ICMA adapted)

	Fast Food Furniture	Custom Furniture		Fast Food Furniture	Custom Furniture
Machine hours: October:			Machine hours: November:		
Forming	660	10,700	Forming	1,280	9,640
Finishing	660	7,780	Finishing	1,280	7,400
Assembly	—	—	Assembly	—	—
	1,320	18,480		2,560	17,040
Direct labor hours: October:			Direct labor hours: November:		
Forming	1,900	9,300	Forming	3,400	8,250
Finishing	3,350	12,000	Finishing	5,800	10,400
Assembly	4,750	8,700	Assembly	8,300	7,600
	10,000	30,000		17,500	26,250

CHAPTER 14

Factory Overhead: Departmentalization

The preceding chapter discussed the establishment and use of one factory-wide predetermined overhead rate, the accumulation of actual factory overhead, and the analysis of over- or underapplied factory overhead. These phases are now expanded through the use of predetermined departmental factory overhead rates, which improves the charging of overhead to jobs and products and leads to cost control via responsibility accounting.

The computation of predetermined overhead rates requires a series of departmental allocation processes with respect to estimated overhead costs. These allocations are necessary for computing overhead rates prior to the beginning of the fiscal period. Actual overhead accumulated during the month or year should remain with the individual department until the end of the accounting period.

■ THE CONCEPT OF DEPARTMENTALIZATION

Methods for the control of materials and labor costs are discussed in other chapters. However, because each product manufactured requires a certain minimum amount of materials and labor, there is a limit to the amount of cost reduction for materials and labor which can be realized through the use of such methods. The control potential and control methods are different for factory overhead.

Departmentalization of factory overhead means dividing the plant into segments, called departments, cost centers, or cost pools, to which overhead costs are charged. For accounting purposes, dividing a plant into separate departments provides improved costing of jobs and products and responsible control of overhead costs, which is necessary if unit and total costs are to stay within predetermined or budgeted ranges.

Improved costing of jobs and products is possible because departmentalization allows different departmental overhead rates for applying factory overhead. A job or product going through a department is charged with factory overhead for work done in that department, using the department's predetermined overhead rate. Depending on the type and number of departments through which they pass, jobs or products are charged with varying amounts of factory overhead, rather than with a single plant-wide overhead amount.

Responsible control of overhead costs is possible because departmentalization makes the incurrence of costs the responsibility of a supervisor or manager. Costs which originate directly and completely within a department are identified with the individual responsible for the supervision of the department.

The entire process of departmentalizing factory overhead is an extension of methods previously discussed. Estimating or budgeting costs and selecting a proper base for applying them is still necessary; but, in addition, departmentalizing overhead requires separate estimates or budgets for each department. Actual costs of a period must still be recorded in a factory overhead control account and a factory overhead subsidiary ledger, but they must be recorded for each department, according to the nature of the expense. This procedure permits comparison of actual departmental costs with departmentally applied factory overhead. Over- or underapplied factory overhead is computed departmentally and analyzed separately to determine departmental spending and idle capacity variances.

■ PRODUCING AND SERVICE DEPARTMENTS

Departments are classified as either producing or service departments. A *producing department* engages in the actual manufacture of the product by changing the shape, form, or nature of the material worked upon or by assembling the parts into a finished article. A *service department* renders a service that contributes in an indirect manner to the manufacture of the product but which does not itself change the shape, form, or nature of the material that is converted into the finished product. The following table lists examples of producing and service departments:

Producing		Service	
Cutting	Mill Room	Utilities	Shipping
Planing	Plating	Materials Handling	Medical
Assembly	Knitting	Inspection	Production Control
Upholstery	Mixing	Storage	Personnel
Finishing	Refining	Plant Security	Maintenance
Machining		Purchasing	Cafeteria
		Receiving	General Factory Cost Pool

Selection of Producing Departments

A manufacturing company is usually organized along departmental lines for production purposes. Manufacturing processes dictate the type of organization needed to handle the different operations efficiently, to obtain the best production flow, and to establish responsibility for physical control of production.

The cost information system is designed to fit the departmentalization required for production purposes. The system accumulates manufacturing costs according to such departmentalization, whether operations are of the job type or the continuous process type. Factors to be considered in deciding the kinds of departments required for establishing accurate departmental overhead rates with which to control costs are:

1. Similarity of operations, processes, and machinery in each department.
2. Location of operations, processes, and machinery.
3. Responsibilities for production and costs.
4. Relationship of operations to flow of product.
5. Number of departments or cost centers.

The establishment of producing departments for the purposes of product costing and cost control is a problem for the management of every company. Although no hard and fast rules can be given, the most common approach divides the factory along lines of functional activities, with each activity or group of activities constituting a department. Division of the factory into separate, interrelated, and independently governed units is important for the proper control of factory overhead and the reasonable costing of jobs and products.

The number of producing departments used depends on the emphasis the cost system puts on cost control and the development of overhead rates. If the emphasis is on cost control, separate departments might be established for the plant manager and for each superintendent or supervisor. When the development of departmental overhead rates emphasizes costing, fewer or more cost centers or departments might be used. Sometimes the number of departments needed for cost control is larger than that needed for overhead rates. In such cases, the cost control system can be adapted to proper overhead rates by combining departments, thus reducing the number of rates used without sacrificing control of costs.

In certain instances, departments are further subdivided for cost control and overhead rate purposes (particularly when the product line is diverse, the cost structure is complex, or different types of machines are used). This results in a refinement in applying and controlling overhead with respect to the jobs or products passing through a department. For example, different rates can be applied to reflect the cost of more expensive or less expensive machinery employed for one job, or for the processing of one product in a diverse product line.

Selection of Service Departments

The selection and designation of service departments has considerable bearing on effective costing and control. Services available for the benefit of producing departments and other service departments can be organized in several ways by (1) establishing a separate service department for each function, (2) combining several functions into one department, or (3) placing service costs in a department called "general factory cost pool." The specific service is not identified if service costs applicable to producing and service functions are accumulated in a general factory cost pool.

Determination of the kinds and numbers of service departments should consider the number of employees needed for each service function, the cost of providing the service, the importance of the service, and the assignment of supervisory responsibility. Establishing a separate department for every service function is rarely done, even in large companies. When relatively few employees are involved and activities are closely related, service functions are often combined for the sake of economy and expediency. Decisions with respect to combining service functions are governed by the individual circumstances existing in each company. Since factory overhead rates for job and product costing are generally calculated for producing departments only, service department expenses are transferred ultimately to producing departments for rate setting and variance analysis.

CAS 418, "Allocation of Direct and Indirect Costs," states that a department should be homogeneous and specifies that this criterion is met ". . . if each significant activity whose costs are included therein has the same or a similar beneficial or causal relationship . . . as the other activities whose costs are included in the (department)."

■ DIRECT DEPARTMENTAL COSTS IN PRODUCING AND SERVICE DEPARTMENTS

The majority of direct departmental overhead costs can be categorized as follows:

1. Supervision, indirect labor, and overtime.
2. Labor fringe benefits.
3. Indirect materials and factory supplies.
4. Repairs and maintenance.
5. Equipment depreciation.

These expense categories are generally readily identified with the originating department, whether producing or service. In the discussion that follows, detailed attention is given to each of the categories.

Supervision, Indirect Labor, and Overtime

These factory labor categories, in contrast to direct labor, do not alter the shape or content of a product; they are auxiliary to its manufacture. It is important to realize that the labor control and accounting procedures discussed in Chapters 10 and 11 are relevant to supervision, indirect labor, and overtime, as well as to their related labor fringe benefits. Any factory labor not classified as direct labor is automatically classified as factory overhead. Since overhead is allocated to all products, a lax or incorrect classification would cause direct labor that applies to only one product to be allocated as indirect labor in the form of overhead to other products, thereby understating the one product cost and overstating the others. Thus decisions on whether or not to classify costs as direct labor can have an important effect on overhead rates, especially since direct labor cost is sometimes used as the base for determining the rates.

The premium portion of overtime paid should generally be charged as overhead to the departments in which the overtime occurred. This method should be followed for all labor except for special cases, which are discussed in Chapters 10 and 11. However, the straight-time portion of overtime paid to direct labor employees should be charged to direct labor.

Labor Fringe Benefits

Labor fringe benefits include such costs as vacation and holiday pay, FICA tax, state and federal unemployment taxes, worker's compensation insurance, pension costs, hospitalization benefits, and group insurance. In theory, these fringe benefits are additional labor costs and should be added to the direct labor cost when they pertain to direct labor employees. In practice, such a procedure is usually impractical; therefore, these costs that pertain to direct laborers as well as to other factory workers are generally included in factory overhead and become part of the factory overhead rate.

Indirect Materials and Factory Supplies

The materials control and costing procedures and quantitative models discussed in Chapters 8 and 9 are equally appropriate in dealing with indirect materials and factory supplies. However, incorrectly distinguishing between direct and indirect materials (the latter being part of overhead) has the same adverse effects on product costing as failure to make proper distinction between direct and indirect labor. However, distinguishing between direct and indirect materials is usually not as difficult. In a manufacturing operation, direct materials are those which are significant in amount, are changed in form through processing, and become an integral part of the end product. Indirect materials, often referred to as factory supplies, are auxiliary to the processing operations and do not become an essential part of the end product. Although insignificant amounts of direct materials may be distinguishable, they may be charged to overhead as an expediency.

Repairs and Maintenance

With respect to repairs and maintenance costs, it is essential to establish control over the total cost incurred by the repairs and maintenance department and to devise effective means for charging maintenance costs to departments receiving the service. Repairs and maintenance costs are generally traceable to benefiting departments and are thus classified here as direct departmental expenses, even though they first may originate in a maintenance department.

As a rule, the work of repair and maintenance crews is supervised by a maintenance superintendent. If possible and practical, all actual maintenance costs should be charged to a maintenance department, so that the total cost is controlled by the maintenance superintendent and kept within a maintenance budget. However, since maintenance is a service function, its costs must ultimately be distributed to departments that receive the service.

Most maintenance work performed for departments is generally of a recurring nature, and charges are incurred evenly throughout the year. However, certain types of maintenance work, such as breakdowns and overhauls, occur at irregular intervals and often involve large expenditures. In such cases, companies using departmental budgets may spread major repair costs over the year by making monthly charges to operations, based on a predetermined rate. These rates are commonly derived from previous years' experiences. Monthly provisions are charged to Maintenance Expense and credited to an allowance account. Actual repair costs are charged to the allowance account. In this manner, large maintenance costs are charged to operations in direct proportion to the operating rate and presumably approximate the actual deterioration of the equipment.

Equipment Depreciation

Depreciation is usually a cost not controllable by departmental supervisors. However, their use of equipment influences maintenance and depreciation costs. This is true with respect to all types of depreciable assets—machinery and equipment, buildings, vehicles, and furniture and fixtures. For effective costing and controlling, depreciation is usually identified with the departments using the assets, and the cost is charged directly to departments. The recommended method is to compute depreciation by departments, based on the cost of equipment as recorded on detailed plant asset records. When no records are available or equipment is used by more than one department, depreciation is frequently accumulated in the general factory cost pool.

For assets acquired in earlier years, depreciation of historical costs results in failure to consider price-level changes and/or current values, especially in inflationary periods. The result is a mingling of these older costs with newer costs (those acquired with more current dollars). Inflation accounting, while not incorporated in the historical-cost accounting records, should be considered by management in using accounting data for planning and decision making. Discussion of inflation adjustments is left to financial accounting textbooks.

■ INDIRECT DEPARTMENTAL COSTS IN PRODUCING AND SERVICE DEPARTMENTS

Costs such as power, light, rent, and depreciation of factory buildings, when shared by all departments, are not charged directly to a department. These costs do not originate with any specific department. They are incurred for all to use and must, therefore, be prorated to any or all departments using them.

Selecting appropriate bases for the distribution of most indirect departmental costs is difficult and arbitrary. At best, allocations will be intuitively reasonable. To charge every department with its share of an expense, a base using some factor common to all departments must be found. For example, square footage may be used for prorating such expenses as rent. In plants with departments occupying parts of the factory with ceilings of unequal height, cubic measurement rather than square footage might be used. Areas occupied by stairways, elevators, escalators, corridors, and aisles must also be considered. Some of the indirect departmental expenses that require prorating, together with the bases most commonly used, are:

Indirect Departmental Costs	Distribution Bases
Factory rent	Square footage
Property tax	Square footage
Depreciation—buildings	Square footage
Insurance (fire)	Square footage
Building repairs	Square footage
Heat	Square footage
Superintendence	Number of employees
Telephone and telegraph	Number of employees or number of telephones
Worker's compensation insurance	Department payroll
Light	Kilowatt-hours
Freight in	Materials used
Power	Horsepower-hours

At times a service that could be obtained separately by each of several departments can be obtained centrally at a lower aggregate cost. In such cases, the cost if each department obtained the service separately, i.e., the "stand-alone" cost, may be the most equitable base for allocation of the centralized cost.[1] For example, assume that individual departments can obtain necessary rental space separately as follows:

Department	Cost of Rental Space Obtained Separately
A	$ 500,000
B	500,000
C	250,000
D	50,000
	$1,300,000

Assume further that the rental space can be provided under a consolidated rental agreement for a total cost of $1,030,000. Proration of the aggregate cost on a "stand-alone" base would yield the following result:

Department	Aggregate Cost		Allocation Base		Allocated Aggregate Cost
A	$1,030,000	×	$500,000/$1,300,000	=	$ 396,154
B	1,030,000	×	500,000/1,300,000	=	396,154
C	1,030,000	×	250,000/1,300,000	=	198,077
D	1,030,000	×	50,000/1,300,000	=	39,615
					$1,030,000

The Cost Accounting Standards Board Disclosure Statement requires that covered federal government contractors identify and describe allocation bases

---

[1]Richard B. Troxel, "Corporate Cost Allocation Can Be Peaceful . . . Is Sharing the Key?" *Management Focus,* Vol. 38, No. 1, pp. 3-5.

for all factory overhead, service center, and general and administrative cost pools used by the contractor. CAS 418 sets forth guidance for accumulating as well as for allocating indirect costs. The allocation is to be based on one of the following, listed in order of preference: (1) a resource consumption measure, (2) an output measure, or (3) a surrogate that is representative of resources consumed.[2] While specified for costing government contracts, this hierarchy affords guidance for more general cost accounting system uses.

■ ESTABLISHING DEPARTMENTAL OVERHEAD RATES

For convenience, factory overhead is usually applied on the basis of machine hours or direct labor hours or cost when only one factory overhead rate is used for the entire plant. However, the use of departmental rates requires a distinct consideration of each producing department's overhead, which often results in the use of different bases for applying overhead for different departments. For example, it is possible to use a direct labor hour rate for one department and a machine hour rate for another. A further refinement might lead to different bases and rates for cost pools within the same producing department.

*ACTIVITY
COSTING*

This may call for the establishment of subdepartments. For example, a department may be physically divided into one segment that is heavily automated, using machine hours as the overhead allocation base, and another segment that is labor intensive, using labor hours as the allocation base. Instead, the multiple pools within a department might be based on kinds of costs and the activity base that drives them but without the department being physically segmented. For example, there may be a pool of machine-related overhead costs (repair and maintenance, setup, lubricants, and energy) and a pool of labor-related overhead costs (fringe benefits, small tools, supplies) all within the same work center. The result is two overhead rate bases within the same department (one for each cost pool) without requiring the physical segregation of subdepartments.

The logic of such multiple pools can be seen by considering a situation in which small rush orders are produced on semi-automatic machines that require very little setup but only make one part per minute and require the machinist to be present to operate, while larger routine orders are done on more automated machines that require the same machinist to spend half a day setting up and then run essentially untended at a rate of ten parts per minute. If setup costs are considered part of overhead, a part made in a rush order may have little machine-related overhead (utilizing a small inexpensive machine with little setup time required) and a considerable portion of labor-related overhead. Conversely, a part made in a routine order may have just the opposite mix. Neither a single overhead pool based on labor nor a single pool based on machine type and machine time would accurately cost both

---

[2]*Standards, Rules and Regulations, Part 418,* "Allocation of Direct and Indirect Costs" (Washington, D.C.: Cost Accounting Standards Board, 1980).

kinds of jobs. But if the same machinist's skills are required for both, it is logical to have a single department where these people work, so that a machinist who has just set up a long automatic run can be assigned to produce a rush order rather than being idle until the next long run has to be set up. A labor overhead rate and a machine overhead rate in the same department address these kinds of manufacturing settings.

SERVICE ENTITIES

The same kind of need may occur in a service industry. An automobile dealership, for example, may have a parts-related overhead pool whose cost is assigned based on the price of each kind of part and a service-related overhead pool whose cost is assigned based on an hourly service labor rate.

Since all factory overhead, whether from producing departments or from service departments, is ultimately allocated to producing departments, the establishment of departmental factory overhead rates proceeds in the following manner:

1. Estimate total direct factory overhead of producing departments and total direct costs of service departments at selected activity levels and determine, if possible, the fixed and variable nature of each cost category.
2. Prepare a factory survey for the purpose of distributing indirect factory overhead and service department costs.
3. Estimate total indirect factory overhead (such as electric power, fuel, water, building depreciation, property tax, and fire insurance) at selected activity levels and allocate these costs based on selected methods.
4. Distribute service department costs to benefiting departments.
5. Calculate departmental factory overhead rates.

These steps are illustrated with the total estimated factory overhead for DeWitt Products (page 381), which has now been departmentalized. The figures have been modified for ease in calculating departmental rates, but the fixed-variable cost classification has been retained. The illustration uses four producing departments: Cutting, Planing, Assembly, and Upholstery; and four service departments: Materials Handling, Inspection, Utilities, and General Factory.

Materials handling involves the operation of equipment such as cranes, trucks, forklifts, and loaders. Since many departments are served by this function, the preferred method of organization establishes a separate service department for materials handling activities. All handling costs are charged to this department, with a supervisor responsible for their control. Costs charged to such a service department are the same as those charged to any department and include wages and labor benefit costs of the department's employees; supplies, such as batteries and gasoline; and repairs and maintenance of the equipment. In addition to centralizing responsibility for materials handling operations, departmentalization has the advantage of collecting all materials handling costs in one place.

For cost control, inspection costs are treated in the same manner as other service department costs. However, in certain instances, a special work order may require additional inspection or testing. This type of inspection cost is chargeable to the order and must be so identified. To accumulate these specific charges, separate cost centers may be established for the purpose of charging time and materials for special inspections.

Power and fuel are consumed for two major purposes: for operating manufacturing facilities such as machines, electric welders, and cranes, and for what might be termed "working condition" purposes, such as lighting, cooling, and heating. Although a single billing is common for electric power or natural gas, a direct departmental allocation is often possible. Such allocation may require the installation of separate meters to measure power or fuel consumed by specific types of equipment. In other instances, separate power sources (fuel, natural gas, coal, or electricity) may be used for different facilities or equipment.

For purposes of departmental and product costing, two methods of accounting for costs of utilities are recommended:

1. Charge all power and fuel costs to a separate utilities department; then allocate to the benefiting departments.
2. Charge specific departments with power or fuel cost if separate meters are provided, and charge the remaining power and fuel costs to a separate utilities department or to a general factory account; this remainder is then allocated to the benefiting departments.

Allocation of utilities costs to specific departments is based on special studies that determine such information as each department's horsepower of machines and the number of machines.

Certain costs other than those discussed above come under the category "general factory," because they represent a variety of miscellaneous factory services. Therefore, a separate general factory cost pool is established to accumulate and control such expenses. Such an organizational unit is usually the direct responsibility of the plant superintendent. Salaries of management personnel directly concerned with production are charged to this cost pool if they cannot be charged to specific departments except by arbitrary allocations. Janitor labor and supplies may be charged to general factory unless charged to maintenance or to "building occupancy." Unless separate service departments for plant security and yard operation are established, these costs are also charged to general factory.

Estimating Direct Departmental Costs

Estimating or budgeting the direct costs of producing and service departments (Exhibit 1, page 411) is a joint undertaking of department heads, supervisors, and members of the budget or cost department of the company. Labor fringe benefits costs are calculated by the office personnel, since the individual supervisor has little influence or knowledge with respect to the underlying rates and figures. Costs of indirect labor and indirect materials are of greater interest to the supervisor. Repairs and maintenance costs often are disputed items unless a definite maintenance program has been established; and, while not illustrated here, they first may be charged to the maintenance department and then assigned to the benefiting departments. Departmental depreciation charges are based on management's decision regarding depreciation methods and rates. In the illustration, depreciation of equipment is charged directly to the departments on the basis of asset values and rates set by the controller. The plant manager, working with budget personnel, estimates and supervises the general factory costs.

Factory Survey

Before indirect departmental and service department costs can be prorated to benefiting and ultimately to the producing departments, certain underlying data must be obtained. A survey of factory facilities and records usually produces the information needed, such as rated horsepower of equipment in each department, estimated kilowatt-hour consumption, number of employees in each department, estimated payroll costs, square footage, estimated materials consumption, and asset values. Functions performed by each service department must be studied carefully to determine the most reasonable basis for distributing their costs. The factory survey for DeWitt Products appears as follows:

DEWITT PRODUCTS
SCHEDULE A—FACTORY SURVEY PREPARED AT THE BEGINNING OF THE YEAR

Producing Department	Number of Employees*	%	Kilo-watt Hours	%	Horse-power Hours	%	Floor Area (Sq. Ft.)	%	Cost of Materials Requisitioned	%
Cutting.............	8.0	20	12,800	20	200,000	40	5,250	25	$180,000	45
Planing	6.8	17	6,400	10	120,000	24	4,200	20	40,000	10
Assembly...........	12.0	30	19,200	30	80,000	16	6,300	30	40,000	10
Upholstery..........	13.2	33	25,600	40	100,000	20	5,250	25	140,000	35
Total...............	40.0	100	64,000	100	500,000	100	21,000	100	$400,000	100

*Average based on portion of year employed.

Estimating and Allocating Indirect Costs

Indirect departmental costs, such as heat, electric power, fuel, water, and building depreciation, must be estimated and then allocated to either producing and service departments or perhaps only to producing departments. The method depends upon management's decision. In Exhibit 1, indirect departmental costs are prorated in two ways: (1) electric power, fuel, and water are charged to Utilities, from which a distribution is made to producing departments only; (2) depreciation of building, property tax, and fire insurance are prorated only to producing departments on the basis of floor area as shown in the Factory Survey (Schedule A); e.g., 25 percent of $5,000, or $1,250, is charged to the Cutting Department for building depreciation. However, as an alternative, these costs could be allocated to service departments as well as to producing departments. This procedure would more completely measure the

DeWitt Products
Estimated Departmental Factory Overhead
For the Year 19—

Cost Account	F or V	Total	Producing Departments				Service Departments			
			Cutting	Planing	Assembly	Upholstery	Materials Handling	Inspection	Utilities	General Factory
Direct departmental costs:										
Supervisors	F	$ 70,000	$ 9,000	$ 8,000	$ 8,000	$ 8,000	$10,000	$ 6,000	$ 9,000	$12,000
Indirect labor	F	9,000	1,000	2,000	1,000	1,500	1,000	500	1,000	1,000
Labor fringe benefits	V	66,000	9,000	3,000	5,000	5,500	11,000	8,500	10,000	14,000
	F	10,000	1,500	1,000	1,000	1,000	2,000	1,000	1,500	1,000
Indirect materials	V	47,000	10,500	11,800	9,400	8,200	1,800	1,400	1,900	2,000
	F	4,000	500	500	800	1,200	300	200	200	300
Repairs and maintenance	V	19,000	2,500	2,500	3,200	4,800	1,700	800	1,800	1,700
	F	3,000	600	500	700	600			300	300
	V	9,000	1,400	1,500	1,300	1,800	500	200	1,700	600
Depreciation—equipment	F	13,000	1,500	3,500	1,000	3,000				4,000
Total direct departmental cost		$250,000	$37,500	$34,300	$31,400	$35,600	$28,300	$18,600	$27,400	$36,900
Indirect departmental costs:										
Electric power	F	$ 2,000							$ 2,000	
Fuel	V	20,000							20,000	
	F	1,000							1,000	
Water	V	10,000							10,000	
	F	1,000							1,000	
	V	4,000							4,000	
Depreciation—buildings	F	5,000	$ 1,250	$ 1,000	$ 1,500	$ 1,250				
Property tax	F	4,000	1,000	800	1,200	1,000				
Insurance (fire)	F	3,000	750	600	900	750				
Total indirect departmental cost		$ 50,000	$ 3,000	$ 2,400	$ 3,600	$ 3,000			$38,000	
Total departmental factory overhead		$300,000	$40,500	$36,700	$35,000	$38,600	$28,300	$18,600	$65,400	$36,900
Total fixed factory overhead		$125,000	$17,100	$17,900	$16,100	$18,300	$13,300	$ 7,700	$16,000	$18,600
Total variable factory overhead		$175,000	$23,400	$18,800	$18,900	$20,300	$15,000	$10,900	$49,400	$18,300

Exhibit 1

total cost for individual service departments as well as provide information needed for cost planning and control.

Distributing Service Department Costs

The number and types of service departments in a company depend on its operations and the degree of cost control desired. As shown in Exhibit 1, each service department of DeWitt Products is charged with its direct costs. These costs and any indirect departmental costs charged to the service departments should be distributed equitably to either producing departments and service departments or just to producing departments, again depending on management's decision. The distribution might be based on number of employees, kilowatt-hour consumption, horsepower-hour consumption, floor space, asset value, or cost of materials to be requisitioned. The costs of service departments are ultimately transferred to producing departments to establish predetermined factory overhead rates and to analyze variances. The commonly used procedures for allocating service department overhead to benefiting departments are the direct method, the step method, and the algebraic method.

Direct Method. In some companies, service department costs are transferred only to producing departments. This procedure minimizes clerical work. It can be justified for product costing if there is no material difference in the final costs of a producing department when the costs of a service department are not prorated to other service departments. However, this procedure fails to measure the total cost for individual service departments when such information is needed for cost planning and control.

The direct procedure for the distribution of estimated service department costs for DeWitt Products is illustrated in Exhibit 2, page 413. Since the illustration shows no transfer of service department costs to other service departments, the order of distribution does not matter. The distribution begins with Materials Handling. The overhead of this department is distributed on the basis of the estimated cost of materials requisitioned per Schedule A. For example, 45 percent of $28,300, or $12,735, is transferred to the Cutting Department. The Inspection cost is transferred to the Assembly and Upholstery producing departments on a 50-50 basis, because these two departments are the only ones receiving this type of service and they receive it in equal amounts.

The Utilities cost is transferred in a three-fold manner: 20 percent of the cost based on kilowatt-hours; 50 percent, on horsepower-hours; and 30 percent, on floor area. The amount of $13,080 represents 20 percent of $65,400, the total cost of the Utilities Department. According to Schedule A, 20 percent of $13,080, or $2,616, is distributed to the Cutting Department. The same method is followed for the other costs and departments. General Factory is distributed on the basis of number of employees. For example, 20 percent of $36,900, or $7,380, is distributed to the Cutting Department.

DeWitt Products
Distribution of Estimated Service Department Costs
and
Calculation of Departmental Factory Overhead Rates
For the Year 19—

Cost Account	Total	Producing Departments Cutting	Planing	Assembly	Upholstery	Service Departments Materials Handling	Inspection	Utilities	General Factory
Total departmental factory overhead before distribution of service departments	$300,000	$40,500	$36,700	$ 35,000	$38,600	$28,300	$18,600	$65,400	$36,900
Distribution of service department costs:									
Materials handling (Base: estimated cost of materials requisitioned)		$12,735	$ 2,830	$ 2,830	$ 9,905	(28,300)			
Inspection (Base: equally to assembly and upholstery departments)				9,300	9,300		(18,600)		
Utilities: (Bases: 20% on kwh, 50% on hph, 30% on floor area)		2,616 / 13,080 / 4,905	1,308 / 7,848 / 3,924	3,924 / 5,232 / 5,886	5,232 / 6,540 / 4,905			(13,080) / (32,700) / (19,620)	
General factory (Base: no. of employees)		7,380	6,273	11,070	12,177				(36,900)
Total service department cost distributed		$40,716	$22,183	$ 38,242	$48,059				
Total departmental factory overhead after distribution of service departments	$300,000	$81,216	$58,883	$ 73,242	$86,659				
Bases: Direct labor hours / Machine hours / Direct labor cost		20,304	9,200	$122,000	24,070				
Rates		$4.00 per direct labor hour	$6.40 per machine hour	60% of direct labor cost	$3.60 per direct labor hour				

Exhibit 2

Handwritten annotations: 45%, 10%, 10%, 35% (materials handling row); 50%, 50% (inspection); 20%, 17%, 30%, 33% (general factory); "only 2 Depts" near Inspection; "development of OH Rate"; "to be used"; "Same"

The distribution of the service department costs in this illustration is based on percentages in the Factory Survey, page 410. Alternatively, such costs could be allocated by calculating a rate per square foot, per kilowatt-hour, or per employee. For example, the amount of General Factory cost allocated to the Cutting Department may be determined as follows:

$$\frac{\$36,900 \text{ General Factory Cost}}{40 \text{ employees}} = \$922.50 \text{ per employee}$$

$$\$922.50 \times 8 \text{ employees in the Cutting Department} = \$7,380$$

An additional and more compact illustration of the direct method, and other methods to be discussed, is based on the following data for Nickleby Company:

Department	Factory Overhead Before Distribution of Service Departments	Services Provided	
		Dept. Y	Dept. Z
Producing—A	$ 60,000	40%	20%
Producing—B	80,000	40	50
Service—Y	36,300	———	30
Service—Z	20,000	20	———
Total factory overhead	$196,300	100%	100%

Recall that the service provided to other service departments is ignored by the direct procedure because this method allocates service department overhead only to producing departments. Thus the order of distribution does not matter. For Nickleby Company, the distribution is as follows:

Distribution of Service Department Overhead Using the Direct Method

	Total	Producing Departments		Service Departments	
		A	B	Y	Z
Factory overhead before distribution of service departments	$196,300	$60,000	$ 80,000	$36,300	$20,000
Distribution of:					
Department Y		18,150	18,150	(36,300)*	
Department Z		5,714	14,286		(20,000)**
Total factory overhead......	$196,300	$83,864	$112,436		

*40/80 to A, 40/80 to B
**20/70 to A, 50/70 to B

Step Method. An alternate procedure is to transfer the costs of service departments by steps, that is, in a prescribed order by departments, primarily on the basis of producing and other service departments' use of the respective services. To use this procedure, a decision must be made with respect to the service department which should be closed first, second, etc., because no further distributions are made to a service department once its costs have been distributed. Thus a more complete recognition of interrelated benefits among service departments occurs than is the case using the direct method in which no such interrelationships are recognized. However, this procedure is still only a partial consideration of the service departments' mutual benefits, since after distribution of a service department's costs, no further distributions are made to it.

Usually, costs are transferred in the order of the amount of service rendered and received, with the costs of the department serving the greatest number of other departments and receiving service from the smallest number of other departments transferred first, and so on. When service rendered and received by departments cannot be determined reasonably, however, the costs of the service department which has the largest total cost may be distributed first, then distributions may be made by descending cost amount for other departments. With this latter approach, it is assumed that the department with the largest amount of cost provided the greatest amount of service.

The Nickleby Company data can be used to demonstrate the step method, with Department Y distributed first, as follows:

Distribution of Service Department Overhead Using the Step Method

	Total	Producing Departments		Service Departments	
		A	B	Y	Z
Factory overhead before distribution of service departments	$196,300	$60,000	$ 80,000	$36,300	$20,000
Distribution of:					
Department Y		14,520	14,520	(36,300)*	7,260
Department Z		7,789	19,471		(27,260)**
Total factory overhead.	$196,300	$82,309	$113,991		

*40/100 to A, 40/100 to B, 20/100 to Z
**20/70 to A, 50/70 to B

Algebraic Method. When each service department serves the other, incompleteness in proration arises using the step method because one department would be closed out before the other and, therefore, before receiving any cost proration from the other. While the resulting difference in the final costs of a producing department may or may not be material, the direct method and, to a lesser extent, the step method fail to measure the total cost for individual service departments. This total cost information may be quite useful for cost planning and control.

The algebraic method, sometimes referred to as the simultaneous method, offers a means of accomplishing a complete consideration of interrelationships among the various service departments. The Nickleby Company data from page 414 are used to illustrate the procedure. Here the costs of the service departments are allocated simultaneously, using the following algebraic technique.[3] First, each service department's total cost is expressed in the form of an equation as shown on the following page.

[3]Matrix algebra can also be used, and it is especially efficient when there is a large number of service departments and the allocation is done by computer. See Thomas H. Williams and Charles H. Griffin, "Matrix Theory and Cost Allocation," *The Accounting Review,* Vol. XXXIX, No. 3, pp. 671-678, and John L. Livingstone, "Matrix Algebra and Cost Allocation," *The Accounting Review,* Vol. XLIII, No. 3, pp. 503-508.

Let: $Y = \$36{,}300 + .30Z$

$Z = \$20{,}000 + .20Y$

Substituting: $Y = \$36{,}300 + .30\ (\$20{,}000 + .20Y)$

Solving: $Y = \$36{,}300 + \$6{,}000 + .06Y$

$.94Y = \$42{,}300$

$Y = \$45{,}000$

Substituting: $Z = \$20{,}000 + .20\ (\$45{,}000) = \$20{,}000 + \$9{,}000 = \$29{,}000$

The distribution is then accomplished as follows:

Distribution of Service Department Overhead Using the Algebraic Method

	Total	Producing Departments A	Producing Departments B	Service Departments Y	Service Departments Z
Factory overhead before distribution of service departments	$196,300	$60,000	$ 80,000	$36,300	$20,000
Distribution of:					
Department Y		18,000	18,000	(45,000)*	9,000
Department Z		5,800	14,500	8,700	(29,000)**
Total factory overhead.	$196,300	$83,800	$112,500		

*40/100 to A, 40/100 to B, 20/100 to Z
**20/100 to A, 50/100 to B, 30/100 to Y

Calculating Departmental Overhead Rates

After service department costs have been distributed, producing department overhead rates can be calculated in terms of direct labor hours, direct labor cost, machine hours, or some other appropriate base. In Exhibit 2, three different bases are used: direct labor hours, machine hours, and direct labor cost.

This discussion has described procedures by which all factory overhead costs, for both producing and service departments, are assigned to work in process by ultimate accumulation of factory overhead in producing departments and then by use of overhead rates for producing departments only. However, it is possible to assign certain service department costs directly from the service department to work in process. For example, materials handling costs might be accumulated in a materials handling department and a materials-cost-oriented rate used for assigning these costs directly to work in process, with any difference between actual and applied costs analyzed into spending and idle capacity variances. Such an approach may employ a transactions base, discussed on page 375 of the previous chapter.

ACTIVITY COSTING

■ USE OF DEPARTMENTAL FACTORY OVERHEAD RATES

During the fiscal year, as information becomes available at the end of each week or month, factory overhead is applied to a job or product by inserting the applied overhead figure into the overhead section of a job sheet or production report. Amounts applied must be summarized periodically for entry into the general journal. The summary entry applicable to DeWitt Products is illustrated as follows:

Work in Process	285,000
Applied Factory Overhead—Cutting Department (21,005 actual direct labor hours × $4).	84,020
Applied Factory Overhead—Planing Department (8,500 actual machine hours × $6.40)	54,400
Applied Factory Overhead—Assembly Department ($111,700 actual direct labor cost × 60%)	67,020
Applied Factory Overhead—Upholstery Department (22,100 actual direct labor hours × $3.60)	79,560

A separate work in process account may be used for each producing department, instead of the single work in process account illustrated here. In such a case, the debit would be to each of these departmental work in process accounts in the same amount as for the corresponding applied departmental factory overhead figure.

■ ACTUAL FACTORY OVERHEAD—DEPARTMENTALIZED

Actual factory overhead is summarized in the factory overhead control account in the general ledger. Details are entered into the factory overhead subsidiary ledger. Departmentalization of actual factory overhead also involves the detailed adaptation of previously outlined procedures for handling actual factory overhead.

Departmentalization of factory overhead requires that each cost be charged to a department as well as to a specific cost account. Such charges are collected on departmental cost analysis sheets, which serve as the subsidiary ledger. A portion of the form used for both producing and service departments is reproduced as follows:

DEPARTMENTAL COST ANALYSIS SHEET									
Department No. 1—Cutting					For		March, 19--		
Explanation	Date	411	412	413	421	433	451	453	Summary

In this form, each column represents a certain class of factory overhead that will be charged to the department. For example, the column coded 411 represents supervisors, and 412 represents indirect labor. Entries to departmental cost analysis sheets, whether computerized or manual, are facilitated by combining department numbers and cost codes. A code such as 1412 indicates that Department No. 1 (Cutting) is charged with indirect labor

(Code 412). Similar combinations are used for other departments. The chart of accounts establishes the codes.

The subsidiary ledger must also include a sheet for each indirect factory cost not originally charged to a department, so that the total of the subsidiary overhead ledger will equal the total in the factory overhead control account.

■ STEPS AT END OF FISCAL PERIOD

At the end of the fiscal period, actual costs of producing and service departments, as well as those of a general indirect nature, are again assembled in the same manner as for estimated factory overhead at the beginning of the year. When all overhead has been assembled in the producing departments, it is then possible to compare actual with applied overhead and to determine the over- or underapplied factory overhead. The procedures are summarized as follows:

1. Prepare a summary of the actual direct departmental factory overhead of producing departments, direct costs of service departments, and indirect factory overhead. (See Exhibit 3 on page 419.)
2. Prepare a second factory survey based on the actual data experienced during the year. (See Schedule B below.)
3. Allocate actual indirect factory overhead based on the results of the factory survey at the end of the year. (See Exhibit 3 and Schedule B.)
4. Distribute actual service department costs to benefiting departments on the basis of the end-of-the-year factory survey. (See Exhibit 4 on page 420 and Schedule B.)
5. Compare actual total and departmental factory overhead with the total and departmental factory overhead applied to jobs and products during the year. Determine the total and departmental over- or underapplied factory overhead. (See Exhibit 4.)

DEWITT PRODUCTS
SCHEDULE B—FACTORY SURVEY—DECEMBER 31, 19—

Producing Department	Number of Employees*	%	Kilo-watt Hours	%	Horse-power Hours	%	Floor Area (Sq. Ft.)	%	Cost of Materials Requisi-tioned	%
Cutting	9.1	24	16,978	26	210,000	42	5,250	25	$193,500	45
Planing	6.5	17	5,224	8	110,000	22	4,200	20	43,000	10
Assembly	10.6	28	16,325	25	90,000	18	6,300	30	47,300	11
Upholstery	11.8	31	26,773	41	90,000	18	5,250	25	146,200	34
Total	38.0	100	65,300	100	500,000	100	21,000	100	$430,000	100

*Average based on portion of year employed.

DeWitt Products
Actual Departmental Factory Overhead
For the Year 19—

Cost Account	F or V	Total	Producing Departments				Service Departments			
			Cutting	Planing	Assembly	Upholstery	Materials Handling	Inspection	Utilities	General Factory
Direct departmental costs:										
Supervisors	F	$ 70,000	$ 9,000	$ 8,000	$ 8,000	$ 8,000	$10,000	$ 6,000	$ 9,000	$12,000
Indirect labor	F	9,000	1,000	2,000	1,000	1,500	1,000	500	1,000	1,000
	V	63,000	9,800	2,800	4,200	6,000	10,000	7,300	9,000	13,900
Labor fringe benefits	F	10,000	1,500	1,000	1,000	1,000	2,000	1,000	1,500	1,000
	V	45,000	10,000	11,400	9,700	8,000	1,700	1,300	1,600	1,300
Indirect materials	F	4,000	500	500	800	1,200	300	200	200	300
	V	23,000	4,300	3,600	2,900	5,400	1,800	1,200	2,100	1,700
Repairs and maintenance	F	3,000	600	500	700	600			300	300
	V	12,000	1,700	1,800	2,000	2,100	600	300	300	1,000
Depreciation—equipment	F	13,000	1,500	3,500	1,000	3,000			2,500	4,000
Total direct departmental cost		$252,000	$39,900	$35,100	$31,300	$36,800	$27,400	$17,800	$27,200	$36,500
Indirect departmental costs:										
Electric power	F	$ 2,000							$ 2,000	
	V	14,000							14,000	
Fuel	F	1,000							1,000	
Water	F	7,000							7,000	
	V	1,000							1,000	
	V	3,000							3,000	
Depreciation—buildings	F	5,000	$ 1,250	$ 1,000	$ 1,500	$ 1,250				
Property tax	F	4,000	1,000	800	1,200	1,000				
Insurance (fire)	F	3,000	750	600	900	750				
Total indirect departmental cost		$ 40,000	$ 3,000	$ 2,400	$ 3,600	$ 3,000			$28,000	
Total actual departmental factory overhead before distribution of service departments		$292,000	$42,900	$37,500	$34,900	$39,800	$27,400	$17,800	$55,200	$36,500

Exhibit 3

DeWitt Products
Distribution of Actual Service Department Costs
and
Computation of Departmental Over- or Underapplied Factory Overhead
For the Year 19—

Cost Account	Total	Producing Departments				Service Departments			
		Cutting	Planing	Assembly	Upholstery	Materials Handling	Inspection	Utilities	General Factory
Total actual departmental factory overhead before distribution of service departments	$292,000	$42,900	$37,500	$34,900	$39,800	$27,400	$17,800	$55,200	$36,500
Distribution of service department costs:									
Materials handling . . . . (Base: actual cost of materials requisitioned)		$12,330	$ 2,740	$ 3,014	$ 9,316	(27,400)			
Inspection . . . . (Base: equally to assembly and upholstery departments)				8,900	8,900		(17,800)		
Utilities: (Bases: 20% on kwh . . . . 50% on hph . . . . 30% on floor area)		2,870 11,592 4,140	883 6,072 3,312	2,760 4,968 4,968	4,527 4,968 4,140			(11,040) (27,600) (16,560)	
General factory . . . . (Base: no. of employees)		8,760	6,205	10,220	11,315				(36,500)
Total service department cost distributed		$39,692	$19,212	$34,830	$43,166				
Total actual departmental factory overhead after distribution of service departments	$292,000	$82,592	$56,712	$69,730	$82,966				
Total applied factory overhead. . .	285,000	84,020	54,400	67,020	79,560				
(Over-) or underapplied factory overhead	$ 7,000	$ (1,428)	$ 2,312	$ 2,710	$ 3,406				

Exhibit 4

Over- or Underapplied Factory Overhead

With the year-end overhead distribution completed, total actual departmental factory overhead can now be transferred to the individual departmental factory overhead control accounts. Using the figures provided by the overhead distribution sheet (Exhibit 4), the following entry can be made:

Factory Overhead—Cutting Department 82,592	
Factory Overhead—Planing Department 56,712	
Factory Overhead—Assembly Department 69,730	
Factory Overhead—Upholstery Department. 82,966	
Factory Overhead Control	292,000

A comparison of actual and applied overhead of each producing department as well as of the total overhead of the company results in the following (over-) underapplied factory overhead:

Total	Cutting	Planing	Assembly	Upholstery
$7,000	$(1,428)	$2,312	$2,710	$3,406

Spending and Idle Capacity Variance Analysis

In the previous chapter, page 385, the $8,500 underapplied factory overhead was analyzed and a $1,625 unfavorable spending variance and a $6,875 unfavorable idle capacity variance were determined. Neither the $15.00 overhead rate used there, based on 20,000 machine hours, nor the variance results are applicable for the departmentalized illustration. New rates with different bases and variance results have been created. However, it is possible to analyze each departmental over- or underapplied figure and determine a departmental spending and idle capacity variance. What is particularly needed is the amount of overhead budgeted for the level of operation attained (capacity utilized), which, in turn, requires a knowledge of the fixed and variable overhead in each producing department. To develop the budget allowance, the estimates shown in the summaries of the departmental factory overhead (Exhibit 1) and the distribution of service department costs (Exhibit 2) are examined. Exhibit 1 indicates the fixed and variable departmental costs at the bottom line of the estimates. The service department costs distributed to the producing departments, as shown in Exhibit 2, are considered variable costs for the producing departments. The fixed-variable classification does not apply after the distribution.

The following spending and idle capacity variance analysis is prepared for executive management on the basis of the actual annual data after the books have been closed. However, the middle- and operating-management levels require current cost control information at least once a month. With ever greater emphasis placed upon the control of costs by responsible supervisory personnel, control information must be communicated to all levels of management in a manner that permits the charging and discharging of responsibility of cost incurrence. This subject is discussed in Chapter 15.

CALCULATION OF ESTIMATED FIXED AND VARIABLE OVERHEAD RATES

	Producing Departments			
	Cutting	Planing	Assembly	Upholstery
Fixed departmental overhead*...........	$17,100	$17,900	$16,100	$18,300
Variable departmental overhead*........	$23,400	$18,800	$18,900	$20,300
Variable service department costs**......	40,716	22,183	38,242	48,059
Total variable overhead.................	$64,116	$40,983	$57,142	$68,359
Bases:**				
Direct labor hours.................	20,304			24,070
Machine hours....................		9,200		
Direct labor cost			$122,000	
Fixed overhead rate	$ .84	$ 1.95	13%	$ .76
Variable overhead rate	3.16	4.45	47	2.84
Total overhead rate:				
Per direct labor hour...............	$ 4.00			
Per machine hour		$ 6.40		
Of direct labor cost			60%	
Per direct labor hour...............				$ 3.60

*From Exhibit 1, p. 411
**From Exhibit 2, p. 413

CALCULATION OF BUDGET ALLOWANCES*

	Producing Departments			
	Cutting	Planing	Assembly	Upholstery
Variable overhead:				
21,005 direct labor hours × $3.16.....	$66,376			
8,500 machine hours × $4.45........		$37,825		
$111,700 direct labor cost × 47%			$52,499	
22,100 direct labor hours × $2.84.....				$62,764
Fixed overhead......................	17,100	17,900	16,100	18,300
Total budget allowance................	$83,476	$55,725	$68,599	$81,064

*Based on capacity utilized, i.e., actual activity.

SPENDING AND IDLE CAPACITY VARIANCE ANALYSIS

Producing Department	(1) Actual Overhead*	(2) Budget Allowance**	(3) Applied Overhead***	Total Variance (1) – (3)	Spending Variance (1) – (2)	Idle Capacity Variance (2) – (3)
Cutting	$ 82,592	$ 83,476	$ 84,020	$(1,428)	$ (884)	$ (554)
Planing	56,712	55,725	54,400	2,312	987	1,325
Assembly	69,730	68,599	67,020	2,710	1,131	1,579
Upholstery	82,966	81,064	79,560	3,406	1,902	1,504
Total	$292,000	$288,864	$285,000	$ 7,000	$3,136	$3,864

*From Exhibit 4, p. 420.
**From calculations above.
***From journal entry, p. 417.

■ OVERHEAD DEPARTMENTALIZATION IN NONMANUFACTURING BUSINESSES AND NOT-FOR-PROFIT ORGANIZATIONS

SERVICE
ENTITIES

The responsible control of departmental costs is equally essential in non-manufacturing activities. The following large complex entities should be divided into administrative and supervisory departments, sections, or service units for cost planning and control:

Nonmanufacturing segments of manufacturing concerns (e.g., marketing departments—see
    Chapter 24)
Retail or department stores
Financial institutions (banks, savings and loan associations, and brokerage houses)
Insurance companies
Educational institutions (school systems, colleges, and universities)
Service organizations (hotels, motels, hospitals, nursing homes, law firms, accounting firms,
    medical or dental practices, and realtors)
Federal, state, and local governments (and their agencies)

Retail or department stores have practiced departmentalization for many years by grouping their organizations under the following typical headings: administration, occupancy, sales promotion and advertising, purchasing, selling, and delivery. These groups incur costs similar to those in manufacturing businesses. The group "Occupancy" is almost identical with General Factory, and includes such expenses as building repairs, rent and property taxes, insurance on buildings and fixtures, light, heat, power, and depreciation on buildings and fixtures. Again, similar to factory procedures, group costs are prorated to revenue-producing sales departments via a charging or billing rate.

Financial institutions should departmentalize their organizations in order to control expenses and establish a profitability rating of individual activities. The size of the institution and the types of services offered determine the number of departments. The accumulation of departmental costs again follows factory procedure: (1) direct costs, such as salaries, supplies, and depreciation of equipment, are charged directly; (2) general costs such as light, heat, air conditioning, are prorated to the departments on appropriate bases. As income and costs are ascertained, it is possible to create a work cost unit that permits the charging of accounts for services rendered and the analysis of an account's profitability.

The work of insurance companies is facilitated by dividing the office into departments. Some departments have several hundred employees, and the work is highly organized. Insurance companies were one of the first businesses to install computers to reduce the clerical costs connected with the insurance business and to calculate new insurance rates and coverage on a more expanded basis for greater profitability. This quite detailed departmentalization might include actuarial, premium collection, group insurance, policyholders' service, registrar, medical, and legal information. While some costs are unique to the individual group, most are identical with costs incurred in any office.

Educational institutions and service organizations find it increasingly necessary to budget their costs on a departmental basis in order to control costs and be able to charge an adequate cost recovering fee for their services. The services of social security via Medicare make a knowledge of costs mandatory in hospitals and nursing homes. Departmentalization will assist management in creating a costing or charging rate for short- or long-term care, for special services, for nurses' instruction, and for professional services (surgical, medical, X-rays, laboratory examinations, and filling of prescriptions).

The federal government employs a great number of people in a vast number of departments and agencies. A similar situation exists in state and local governments. This discussion uses the municipality as an example, since its varied services are better known to the public. Some common services or departments are street cleaning, street repairing and paving, public works projects, police and fire departments, city hospitals, sewage disposal plants, and trash and garbage collection. These services should be budgeted and their costs controlled on a responsibility accounting basis. Since the costs incurred are generally not revenue- but service-benefit-oriented, an attempt should be made to measure the operating efficiency of an activity based on some unit of measurement such as per capita (police), per mile (street paving and cleaning), and per ton (trash and garbage collection). Increasing costs require additional revenue, which means additional taxes. Taxpayers, however, expect efficient service in return for their tax money.

The state and federal governments must be made equally aware of the need for responsible cost control methods, so that services may be rendered at the lowest cost with greatest efficiency. With their many departments and agencies and huge sums budgeted for all of these units, governments must ensure that these activities are being administered by cost-conscious and service-minded people. The departmentalization process helps to assure the achievement of such a goal in any governmental unit.

DISCUSSION QUESTIONS

Q14-1. State reasons for the preference of departmental overhead rates over a single plant-wide rate.

Q14-2. The statement has been made that the entire process of departmentalizing factory overhead is an extension of methods used when a single overhead rate is used. Explain.

Q14-3. A company uses departmental factory overhead rates based on direct labor hours. Would the sum of departmental over- or underapplied over-head be any different if a plant-wide or blanket rate were used? Would the costs of goods sold and inventory be different?

Q14-4. What is a producing department? A service department? Give illustrations of each.

Q14-5. What are some of the factors that must be considered in deciding the kinds and number of departments required to control costs and to establish accurate departmental overhead rates?

Q14-6. Why might overhead rates be established for subdepartments (cost pools within departments)?

Q14-7. For effective control of overhead, a supervisor, superintendent, manager, or department head can be held accountable for more than one cost center; but responsibility for a single cost center should not be divided between two or more individuals. Discuss.

Q14-8. State reasons for using a general factory cost pool for certain types of overhead instead of allocating it directly to producing and service departments.

Q14-9. Most companies keep plant asset records to identify equipment and its original cost by location or department. However, charges for depreciation, property tax, and fire insurance are often accumulated in general factory accounts and charged to departments on the basis of equipment values. Is this the best method for controlling such costs? If not, suggest possible improvements.

Q14-10. What are the important factors involved in selecting the rate to be used for applying the factory overhead of a producing department?

Q14-11. What are the several steps followed in establishing departmental factory overhead rates?

Q14-12. What questions must be resolved in allocating service department costs to benefiting departments, and how can cost information aid in service department cost control?

Q14-13. What methods can be used for allocating service department costs to producing departments? Which is recommended?

Q14-14. Procedures followed in computing departmental factory overhead rates determine the accounting for actual factory overhead. Explain.

Q14-15. Describe how departmental over- or underapplied overhead is determined, and explain the computations of departmental spending and idle capacity variances.

Q14-16. Overhead control in a nonmanufacturing business can be achieved through departmentalization. Explain.

Q14-17. Federal, state, and local governments should practice cost control via responsibility accounting. Discuss.

EXERCISES

E14-1. **Entries with overhead subsidiary ledger.** The general ledger of Amtech Company contains a factory overhead control account supported by a subsidiary ledger showing details by departments. The plant has one service department and three producing departments. The following table shows details with respect to these departments:

	Machining Dept.	Painting Dept.	Assembly Dept.	General Factory Cost Pool
Building space (sq. ft.)	10,000	4,000	4,000	2,000
Cost of machinery	$300,000	$100,000	$60,000	$20,000
Horsepower rating	1,000	–0–	100	150
Worker's compensation insurance rate (per $100)	$1.50	$1.50	$1.00	$1.00

During January, certain assets expired and some liabilities accrued as follows:

(a) Depreciation on buildings, $3,000.
(b) Depreciation on machinery, $9,600.

(c) Property tax for the year ending December 31 is estimated to be $12,000 (60% on buildings and 40% on machinery).

(d) Worker's compensation insurance for January is based on the following earnings of factory employees: Machining Department, $30,000; Painting Department, $12,000; Assembly Department, $16,000; and General Factory Cost Pool, $6,000.

(e) The power meter reading at January 31 shows 12,500 kilowatt-hours consumed. The rate is $.06 per kilowatt-hour.

(f) The heat and light bill for January is $900.

(g) Supplies requisitions show $1,800 used in the Machining Department, $2,300 in the Assembly Department, and $410 in the General Factory Cost Pool.

Required: Prepare journal entries, with details entered in the departmental factory overhead subsidiary ledger columns.

E14-2. Rate calculation—plant-wide vs. departmental direct method. West Virginia Company uses the direct method in allocating service department costs to producing departments. Costs of Department S1 are allocated on the basis of number of employees, while costs of Department S2 are allocated on the basis of machine hours. The allocation bases used in calculating predetermined overhead rates are machine hours in Department P1 and direct labor hours in Department P2.

	Producing Departments		Service Departments	
	P1	P2	S1	S2
Budgeted factory overhead	$410,000	$304,000	$100,000	$50,000
Number of employees	90	210	20	28
Machine hours.................	64,000	16,000		
Direct labor hours	35,000	100,000		

The following data pertain to Job 437:

	Department P1	Department P2
Materials cost	$90	$40
Direct labor hours	1	2
Machine hours...........	3	1

Required:

(1) Calculate predetermined factory overhead rates for the producing departments and compute the resulting overhead cost of Job 437.

(2) Calculate a plant-wide predetermined factory overhead rate based on direct labor hours and compute the resulting overhead cost of Job 437.   CGA-Canada (adapted) Reprint with permission

E14-3. Rate calculation—plant-wide vs. departmental step method. Abby Company allocates some service department costs to other service departments. However, after a department's costs have been allocated, no costs are assigned back to it. Buildings and Grounds is allocated first, using square feet as a base. The number of employees is used as a base for allocating Factory Administration.

	Machining	Assembly	Buildings and Grounds	Factory Administration
Budgeted factory overhead	$360,000	$420,000	$40,000	$25,000
Square feet....................	9,000	10,000	1,500	1,000
Number of employees	440	460	50	30
Direct labor hours	452,000	567,250		
Machine hours.................	195,600	23,000		

Required:

(1) Compute a plant-wide factory overhead rate, using direct labor hours as a base. Round answer to the nearest cent.
(2) Compute the factory overhead rate for Machining, using machine hours as a base, and for Assembly, using direct labor hours as a base. Round answers to the nearest cent.

CGA-Canada (adapted) Reprint with permission

E14-4. Departmental distribution of estimated overhead—direct method; rate calculation. Naughton Company's factory contains two producing departments, Cutting and Assembly, and two service departments, Maintenance and Administration. Maintenance Department cost is allocated based on square feet, and Administration Department cost is allocated based on number of employees. Service department costs are allocated to producing departments only. Producing department overhead rates are computed based on machine hours.

The estimated annual data are as follows:

	Cutting	Assembly	Maintenance	Administration
Number of employees	150	100	40	30
Square feet.	21,000	9,000	4,000	3,000
Machine hours	30,000	20,000		
Overhead budget	$520,000	$400,000	$200,000	$150,000

Required: Prepare a factory overhead distribution and compute overhead rates.

CGA-Canada (adapted) Reprint with permission

E14-5. Departmental distribution of estimated overhead—step method; rate calculation. The Bayswater Equipment Company has two producing departments, Mixing and Finishing, and two service departments, Cafeteria and Product Design. The company assigns service department costs to other service departments; however, after a department's costs have been allocated, no costs are assigned back to it. Cafeteria is allocated first, based on the number of employees, and Product Design is allocated based on the number of product orders. In calculating predetermined factory overhead rates, machine hours are used as the basis in both producing departments.

The following estimated data are provided:

	Cafeteria	Product Design	Mixing	Finishing
Budget overhead	$10,000	$50,000	$100,000	$200,000
Number of employees	10	5	65	130
Number of product orders			100	200
Machine hours			30,000	80,000

Required: Develop predetermined factory overhead rates for the Mixing and Finishing departments.

CGA-Canada (adapted) Reprint with permission

E14-6. Departmental distribution of estimated overhead—step method; rate calculation. The Morris Company uses the step method in allocating the costs of its two service departments, S1 and S2, to its two producing departments, P1 and P2. S1 is allocated first on the basis of number of employees. S2 is allocated on the basis of machine hours. Departmental overhead rates are based on machine hours in P1 and direct labor hours in P2. The following budget data are available:

	S1	S2	P1	P2
Budgeted overhead	$10,000	$34,750	$200,000	$300,000
Number of employees	15	10	180	210
Machine hours			4,000	3,000
Direct labor hours			5,000	10,000

Required:

   (1) Develop predetermined overhead rates for the producing departments.

   (2) If Morris Company decided to change to a plant-wide rate based on direct labor hours, what would that rate be?

   (3) Why would separate departmental rates be preferable to a single plant-wide rate?

CGA-Canada (adapted) Reprint with permission

 E14-7. Departmental distribution of estimated overhead—step method; rate calculation; job order costing. Wassail Company has two producing departments, Machining and Assembly, and two service departments, Maintenance and Personnel. The step method is used in allocating service department costs to producing departments, with Maintenance allocated first, based on square feet. In calculating predetermined factory overhead rates, machine hours are used as a base in Machining and direct labor hours are used as a base in Assembly.

Budgeted monthly cost and other operating data are as follows:

	Maintenance	Personnel	Machining	Assembly
Factory overhead	$30,000	$15,000	$150,000	$75,000
Square feet.	2,000	4,000	19,000	17,000
Number of employees	5	3	40	80
Machine hours			22,700	
Direct labor hours			8,000	16,625

Cost and related data pertaining to Job No. 3752 are:

Machining:	Machine hours	10
	Materials.	$60
	Direct labor. . . . . 4 hours @	$6
Assembly:	Materials.	$7
	Direct labor. . . . . 11 hours @	$9

Required:

   (1) Develop predetermined factory overhead rates for Machining and Assembly.

   (2) Compute the total cost of Job No. 3752.   CGA-Canada (adapted) Reprint with permission

 E14-8. Departmental distribution of estimated overhead—algebraic method. The estimated departmental factory overhead for Producing Departments S and T and the estimated costs of Service Departments E, F, and G (before any service department allocations) are:

Producing Department		Service Department	
S	$60,000	E	$20,000
T	90,000	F	20,000
		G	10,000

The interdependence of the departments is as follows:

	Services Provided By		
Department	E	F	G
Producing—S.	——	30%	40%
Producing—T.	50%	40	30
Service—E.	——	20	——
Service—F.	20	——	——
Service—G.	30	10	——
Marketing	——	——	20
General Office	——	——	10
	100%	100%	100%

Required:

(1) Compute the final amount of estimated overhead of each service department after reciprocal transfer costs have been calculated algebraically.
(2) Compute the total factory overhead of each producing department and the amount of Department G cost assigned to the Marketing Department and to General Office.

E14-9. Departmental distribution of actual overhead—step method. The Colorado Mining Corporation has producing departments A and B, and service departments C, D, E, and F. Costs are distributed from F first, D second, C third, and E fourth. It is the company's policy that once a service department's costs have been allocated, no costs from other service departments are to be allocated to it. F distributes one half of its costs to A and the remainder to D and E on the basis of the number of employees. D distributes its costs on the basis of investment in equipment, C's are assigned to B, and E's are distributed on the basis of floor space. The following information pertains to the month just ended:

Department	Cost	Square Feet	Employees	Investment in Equipment
A	$15,000	2,000	40	$170,000
B	12,000	3,000	20	80,000
C	12,000	4,000	20	130,000
D	8,000	2,000	30	70,000
E	2,000	1,500	20	50,000
F	2,000	2,500	10	30,000
Total......	$51,000	15,000	140	$530,000

Required: Make the distribution of service department overhead.

E14-10. Departmental distribution of actual overhead—step method; variance analysis. Boyd Company has two producing departments, A and B, and four service departments, C, D, E, and F. Costs are distributed from Department F first, D second, C third, and E fourth. The company assigns some service department costs to other service departments; however, after a department's costs have been allocated, no costs are assigned back to it.

Department F distributes one-half of its costs to A and the remainder, on the basis of the number of employees, to Departments D and E. Department D distributes its costs on the basis of the investment in equipment. C's costs are assigned to B, and E's expenses are distributed on the basis of floor space.

The following information is available for March:

Department	Actual Costs	Square Feet	Employees	Investment in Equipment (In Thousands)
A	$100,000	1,500	20	$12,500
B	80,000	2,500	10	6,000
C	120,000	3,000	10	10,000
D	56,000	1,500	15	5,000
E	15,000	1,000	10	4,000
F	30,000	1,200	5	2,000
Total......	$401,000	10,700	70	$39,500

Required:

(1) Distribute service department costs, based on the data given.
(2) Department A's predetermined overhead rate is based on machine hours. The total rate is $4, 25% of which is fixed. Fixed factory overhead budgeted is $40,000. The actual machine hours for March were 38,500. Compute the spending and idle capacity variances for Department A.

E14-11. Departmental distribution of actual overhead—algebraic method; variance analysis. Happy Company has decided to distribute the costs of service departments by the algebraic method. The producing departments are P1 and P2, the service departments are S1 and S2, and the monthly data are:

	Actual Factory Overhead Costs Before Distribution	Services Provided By	
		S1	S2
P1	$94,000	40%	50%
P2	85,000	50	30
S1	20,000	——	20
S2	17,600	10	——

Required:

(1) Compute the total factory overhead of producing department P1 after distribution of service department costs.

(2) P1's predetermined overhead rate is based on direct labor hours. The total rate is $3, 40% of which is fixed. Fixed factory overhead budgeted is $46,000. The actual direct labor hours for the month were 34,000. Compute the spending and idle capacity variances for department P1.

PROBLEMS

P14-1. Revision of departmental overhead rates. Upton Inc. manufactures a line of home furniture. The company's single manufacturing plant consists of the Cutting, Assembly, and Finishing Departments. Upton uses departmental rates for applying factory overhead to production and maintains separate factory overhead control and applied factory overhead accounts for each of the three production departments.

The following predetermined departmental factory overhead rates were calculated for Upton's fiscal year ending May 31, 19B.

Department	Rate
Cutting.	$2.40 per machine hour
Assembly.	5.00 per direct labor hour
Finishing	1.60 per direct labor dollar

Information regarding actual operations for Upton's plant for the six months ended November 30, 19A is presented below.

	Department		
	Cutting	Assembly	Finishing
Factory overhead costs	$22,600	$56,800	$98,500
Machine hours	10,800	2,100	4,400
Direct labor hours	6,800	12,400	16,500
Direct labor dollars.	$40,800	$62,000	$66,000

Based upon this experience and updated projections for the last six months of the fiscal year, Upton revised its operating budget. Projected data regarding factory overhead and operating activity for each department for the six months ending May 31, 19B, are as follows:

	Department		
	Cutting	Assembly	Finishing
Factory overhead costs	$23,400	$57,500	$96,500
Machine hours	9,200	2,000	4,200
Direct labor hours	6,000	13,000	16,000
Direct labor dollars.	$36,000	$65,000	$64,000

Diane Potter, Upton's controller, plans to develop revised departmental factory overhead rates that will be more representative of efficient operations for the current fiscal year ending May 31, 19B. She has decided to combine the actual results for the first six months of the fiscal year with the projections for the next six months to develop the revised departmental application rates. She then plans to adjust the applied factory overhead accounts for each department through November 19A to recognize the revised application rates. The analysis presented below was prepared by Potter from general ledger account balances as of November 30, 19A.

Account	Direct Material	Direct Labor	Factory Overhead	Account Balance
Work in Process Inventory	$ 53,000	$ 95,000	$ 12,000	$ 160,000
Finished Goods.	96,000	176,000	48,000	320,000
Cost of Goods Sold	336,000	604,000	180,000	1,120,000
	$485,000	$875,000	$240,000	$1,600,000

Required:

(1) Determine the balance of the applied factory overhead accounts as of November 30, 19A, before any revision for the:

 (a) Cutting Department.
 (b) Assembly Department.
 (c) Finishing Department.

(2) Calculate the revised departmental factory overhead rates that Upton Inc. should use for the remainder of the fiscal year ending May 31, 19B.

(3) Prepare an analysis that shows how the applied factory overhead account for each production department of Upton Inc. should be adjusted as of November 30, 19A, and prepare the adjusting entry to correct all general ledger accounts that are affected.   (ICMA adapted)

P14-2. Departmental distribution of estimated overhead—step method; rate calculation. The president of Mellow Products Company has been critical of the product costing methods whereby factory overhead is charged to products by a plant-wide overhead rate. The chief accountant suggested a departmentalization of the factory for the purpose of calculating departmental factory overhead rates. The following estimated direct departmental overhead data were accumulated on an annual basis:

Overhead Items	Producing Departments			Service Departments		
	Dept. 10	Dept. 12	Dept. 14	Store-room	Repairs and Maintenance	General Factory Cost Pool
Supervision	$20,500	$16,000	$14,000	$ 7,200	$ 8,000	$24,000
Indirect labor	5,400	6,000	8,000	6,133	7,200	18,000
Indirect supplies.	4,850	5,600	5,430	1,400	3,651	1,070
Labor fringe benefits	6,872	9,349	10,145	640	760	2,100
Equipment depreciation.	6,000	8,000	10,000	560	1,740	1,100
Property tax, depreciation of buildings, etc. . . .						20,000
Total	$43,622	$44,949	$47,575	$15,933	$21,351	$66,270

The annual light and power bill is estimated at $9,300 and is allocated on the basis of electricity usage. The order and bases of distribution of service department costs (using the step method) are as follows:

 (a) General Factory Cost Pool—area occupied
 (b) Storeroom—estimated requisitions
 (c) Repairs and Maintenance—estimated repairs and maintenance hours

The following departmental information is provided:

	Dept 10	Dept. 12	Dept. 14	Store-room	Repairs and Maintenance	General Factory Cost Pool
Percentage of usage of electricity	20%	25%	30%	3%	12%	10%
Area occupied (sq. ft.)	21,000	25,200	29,400	3,360	5,040	——
Estimated number of requisitions	124,200	81,000	40,500	——	24,300	——
Estimated number of repairs and maintenance hours.	4,800	4,200	6,000	——	——	——
Estimated machine hours.	8,000	9,000	8,000	——	——	——

Required: Prepare a factory overhead distribution sheet, with calculation of overhead rates for the producing departments based on machine hours.

P14-3. Departmental distribution of estimated overhead—direct vs. algebraic method; rate calculation. Bayside Corporation is developing departmental overhead rates based upon direct labor hours for its two production departments—Molding and Assembly. The Molding Department employs 20 people, and the Assembly Department employs 80 people. Each person in these two departments works 2,000 hours per year. The production-related overhead costs for the Molding Department are budgeted at $200,000, and the Assembly Department costs are budgeted at $320,000. Two service departments, Repair and Power, support the two production departments and have budgeted costs of $48,000 and $250,000, respectively. The production departments' overhead rates cannot be determined until the service departments' costs are properly allocated. The following schedule reflects the use of the Repair Department's and Power Department's output by the various departments.

	Services Provided	
Department	Repair Hours	KWH
Molding	1,000	840,000
Assembly	8,000	120,000
Repair.	——	240,000
Power	1,000	——
	10,000	1,200,000

Required:

(1) Calculate the overhead rates per direct labor hour for the two producing departments, allocating service department costs to producing departments only. (Round rates to the nearest cent.)
(2) Calculate the overhead rates per direct labor hour for the two producing departments, using the algebraic method to distribute service department costs. (Round rates to the nearest cent.)
(3) Explain the difference between the methods and indicate arguments to support the algebraic method.

(ICMA adapted)

P14-4. Departmental distribution of actual overhead—direct, step, and algebraic methods. De Luna Company operates with two producing departments, P1 and P2, and two service departments, S1 and S2. Actual factory overhead before distribution of service department costs, together with the usage of services from the service departments, follows:

Department	Actual Factory Overhead Before Distribution of Service Department Costs	Services Provided By	
		S1	S2
P1	$20,000	40%	20%
P2	23,800	50	40
S1	7,200	——	40
S2	9,000	10	——
	$60,000	100%	100%

Required:

(1) Determine the total factory overhead (including service department costs) for each producing department, allocating service department costs to producing departments only.

(2) Determine the total factory overhead (including service department costs) for each producing department, allocating service department costs stepwise, beginning with Department S2. After a department's expenses have been allocated, no expenses are assigned back to it.

(3) Determine the total factory overhead (including service department costs) for each producing department, using the algebraic method.

 P14-5. Departmental distribution of actual overhead—algebraic method; variance analysis. The controller of Sansing Corporation instructs the cost supervisor to use an algebraic procedure for allocating service department costs to producing departments. The corporation's three producing departments are served by three service departments, each of which consumes part of the services of the other two. After primary but before reciprocal distribution, the account balances of the service departments and the interdependence of the departments were tabulated as follows:

Department	Departmental Overhead Before Distribution of Service Departments	Services Provided		
		Powerhouse	Personnel	General Factory
Mixing.................	$200,000	25%	35%	25%
Refining	90,000	25	30	20
Finishing..............	105,000	20	20	20
Powerhouse	16,000	——	10	20
Personnel	29,500	10	——	15
General Factory	42,000	20	5	——
	$482,500	100%	100%	100%

Required:

(1) Compute the final amount of overhead of each service department after reciprocal transfer costs have been calculated algebraically.

(2) Compute the total factory overhead of each producing department.

(3) The Mixing Department's predetermined overhead rate is based on machine hours. The total rate is $6, 40% of which is fixed. Fixed factory overhead budgeted is $96,000. The actual machine hours for the period were 37,000. Compute the spending and idle capacity variances for the Mixing Department.

P14-6. Cost center rates and variance analysis. The Cost Department of Montpelier Company applies factory overhead to jobs and products on the basis of predetermined cost center overhead rates. In each of the two producing departments, two cost centers have been set up. For the coming year, the following estimates and other data have been made available:

	Estimated Annual Factory Overhead			Estimated Annual Hours
Department 10	Fixed	Variable	Total	
Cost Center 10-1	$14,040	$23,400	$37,440	15,600
Cost Center 10-2	26,910	43,290	70,200	23,400
Department 20				
Cost Center 20-1	$ 8,320	$21,580	$29,900	26,000
Cost Center 20-2	6,240	19,760	26,000	20,800

Required:

(1) Compute the annual normal cost center overhead rates, based on the estimated machine hours in Department 10 and the estimated direct labor hours in Department 20.

(2) Apply factory overhead to the four cost centers on the basis of these actual machine or labor hours used or worked during February:

Cost Centers	10-1	10-2	20-1	20-2
Machine hours	1,220	2,000		
Labor hours			2,250	1,650

(3) Compute the spending and the idle capacity variances for the two producing departments. Actual factory overhead in Department 10 amounted to $9,430 and in Department 20 to $4,005.

(4) Analyze the total idle capacity variance of Department 10, determining the idle capacity variances of the two cost centers. Use 1/12 of the total annual estimated hours as normal monthly hours.

P14-7. Transfer entries and variance analysis. The distribution of a company's actual factory overhead for the past year is given as follows. Budgeted factory overhead for the four producing departments (including apportioned service department costs) is also given for two levels of activity.

	A	B	C	D	X	Y	Z	Total
			Actual Factory Overhead					
Actual costs. . .	$11,000	$16,000	$4,000	$8,000	$3,000	$5,000	$6,000	$53,000
Z's costs	1,500	750	1,250	500	1,000	1,000	(6,000)	
Y's costs	1,800	1,200	1,800	600	600	(6,000)		
X's costs	2,000	1,000	1,200	400	(4,600)			
Total	$16,300	$18,950	$8,250	$9,500				$53,000

	Budgeted Factory Overhead	
	20,000 Hours (Normal)	16,000 Hours
Department A	$17,800	$15,000
Department B	20,200	17,800
Department C	10,600	9,400
Department D	10,600	9,400
Total	$59,200	$51,600

The company uses a predetermined rate for each producing department, based on labor hours at the normal capacity level. Actual hours worked last year were 17,000 for Department A and 18,000 for Department B.

Required:

(1) Prepare entries to record:

    (a) The transfer of the actual factory overhead to producing departments, assuming that the actual factory overhead was accumulated in a single factory overhead control account.

    (b) The applied factory overhead for Department A and for Department B.

(2) Compute the spending and idle capacity variances for Department A and for Department B.

CASES

C14-1. Departmental factory overhead rates. The Cheetah Company produces custom-made stuffed toy animals and competes in a highly competitive marketplace. The company establishes its selling prices as being equal to the cost of production plus a 30% mark-up. The production process consists of two departments:

(1) The Skins Department where the outside liners (skins) are hand-made for each toy animal from specially ordered materials.

(2) The Stuffing Department where the skins are filled by machine with a standard stuffing material to complete the toys.

These two production departments (the Skins and Stuffing Departments) both receive services from the company's two service departments (the Purchasing Department and the Cleaning and Maintenance Department). A description of each service department's operations and of how the costs of these two departments are allocated is shown below:

Purchasing:

(a) Purchases all materials and supplies required for all departments.
(b) Its fixed cost is allocated to the two production departments based on the number of square feet each department occupies.
(c) Its variable cost is allocated based on total volume of materials ordered by each department.

Cleaning and Maintenance:

(a) Cleans the entire building and maintains all of the equipment in the company.
(b) Both variable and fixed costs of the department are allocated to the two production departments on the basis of the number of square feet each department occupies.

Required:

(1) Should the company use a plant-wide overhead rate or departmental overhead rates? Explain.
(2) Comment on the company's cost allocation methods, and, where necessary, suggest improvements. Fully justify any suggested improvements. (SMAC adapted)

C14-2. Types of factory overhead rates. Valley View Inc. engages the services of a CPA firm for the installation of a job order cost system. Preliminary investigation of manufacturing operations discloses these facts:

(a) The company makes a line of light fixtures and lamps. The materials cost of any particular item ranges from 15% to 60% of total factory cost, depending on the kind of metal and fabric used.
(b) The business is subject to wide cyclical fluctuations, since the sales volume follows new housing construction.
(c) About 60% of the manufacturing is normally finished during the first quarter of the year.

(d) For the whole plant, the direct labor wage rates range from $6.50 to $12 an hour. However, within each of the eight individual departments, the spread between the high and low wage rate is less than 5%.
(e) Each product requires the use of all eight of the manufacturing departments, but not proportionately.
(f) Within the individual manufacturing departments, factory overhead ranges from 30% to 80% of conversion cost.

Required: Prepare a letter to the president of Valley View Inc., explaining whether its cost system should use the following procedures, and including the reasons supporting each of these recommendations:

(1) A predetermined overhead rate or an actual overhead rate—departmental or plant-wide.
(2) A method of factory overhead distribution based on direct labor hours, direct labor cost, or prime cost. (AICPA adapted)

C14-3. Assigning costs to activity centers in a data processing department. Fitzgerald Associates recently reorganized its computer and data processing activities. In the past, small computer units were located in accounting departments at the firm's plants and subsidiaries. These units have been replaced with a single Electronic Data Processing Department at corporate headquarters. The new department has been in operation for two years, regularly producing reliable and timely data for the past twelve months.

Because the department has focused its activities on converting applications to the new system and producing reports for the plant and subsidiary managements, little attention has been devoted to data processing costs. Now that the department's activities are operating relatively smoothly, company management has requested that the department manager recommend a cost accumulation system to facilitate cost control and the development of suitable service charging rates.

For the past two years, the data processing costs have been recorded in one account. The costs have then been allocated to user departments on the basis of computer time used. Following are the costs and charging rate for the current year:

(a) Salaries and benefits	$ 622,600
(b) Supplies	40,000
(c) Equipment maintenance contract . . .	15,000
(d) Insurance	25,000
(e) Heat and air conditioning	36,000
(f) Electricity	50,000
(g) Equipment and furniture depreciation	285,400
(h) Building improvement depreciation .	10,000
(i) Building occupancy and security . . .	39,300
(j) Corporate administrative charge	52,700
Total cost	$1,176,000

Computer hours for user processing*	2,750
Hourly rate ($1,176,000 ÷ 2,750) . . .	$428

*Use of available computer hours:	
Testing and debugging programs	250
Setup of jobs	500
Processing jobs	2,750
Downtime for maintenance	750
Idle time	742
Total	4,992

The department manager recommends that the data processing costs be accumulated by five activity centers within the department: Systems Analysis, Programming, Data Preparation, Computer Operations (processing), and Administration. The Administration activity cost should be allocated to the other four activity centers before a separate rate for charging users is developed for each of the first four activities.

The manager noted that the subsidiary accounts within the department contained the following charges:

(a) Salaries and benefits—the salary and benefit costs of all employees in the department.

(b) Supplies—diskette cost, paper cost for printers, and a small amount for miscellaneous other costs.

(c) Equipment maintenance contracts—charges for maintenance contracts covering all equipment.

(d) Insurance—cost of insurance covering the equipment and the furniture.

(e) Heat and air conditioning—a charge from the corporate Heating and Air Conditioning Department estimated to be the differ-

ential costs which meet the special needs of the Electronic Data Processing Department.

(f) Electricity—the charge for electricity, based upon a separate meter within the department.

(g) Equipment and furniture depreciation—the depreciation charges for all owned equipment and furniture within the department.

(h) Building improvement depreciation—the depreciation charges for the building changes which were required to provide proper environmental control and electrical service for the computer equipment.

(i) Building occupancy and security—the department's share of the depreciation, maintenance, heat, and security costs of the building; these costs are allocated to the department on the basis of square feet occupied.

(j) Corporate administrative charge—the department's share of the corporate administrative cost which is allocated to the department on the basis of number of employees in the department.

Required:

(1) State whether each of the ten cost items (lettered a through j) should be allocated to the five activity centers. For each cost item which should be distributed, specify the basis upon which the distribution should be made. Justify your answer in each case, including an indication as to whether the cost would be included in a rate designed to include only variable costs as opposed to a full cost rate.

(2) Calculate the total number of hours that should be employed to determine the charging rate for Computer Operations, using the analysis of computer utilization shown as a footnote to the department cost schedule, and assuming that the Computer Operations activity cost will be charged to the user departments on the basis of computer hours. Explain.

(ICMA adapted)

C14-4. Overhead analysis and causes for variances. Beachmont Company uses predetermined departmental overhead rates. The rate for the Fabricating Department is $4 per direct labor hour. Direct labor employees are paid $10.50 per hour. A total of 15,000 direct labor hours were worked in the department during the year. Total overhead charged to the department for supervisors' salaries, indirect labor, labor fringe benefit costs, indirect materials, and service department costs was $65,000.

Required:

(1) Determine the over- or underapplied factory overhead.
(2) Determine the effect on the amount of over- or underapplied factory overhead in each of the following situations. Discuss each item separately as though the other factors had not occurred.

(a) Direct laborers worked one hundred overtime hours for which time-and-a-half was paid. Overtime premium, the amount in excess of the regular rate, is charged as overhead to the department in which the overtime is worked.
(b) A $.35 per hour wage increase was granted November 1. Direct labor hours worked in November and December totaled 2,500.
(c) The company cafeteria incurred a $1,500 loss, which was distributed to producing departments on the basis of number of employees. Nine of the 120 employees work in the Fabricating Department. No loss was anticipated when predetermined overhead rates were computed.

CHAPTER 15

Factory Overhead: Responsibility Accounting and Reporting

Factory overhead creates two distinct problems:

1. Allocation to products for inventory costing and profit determination.
2. Control of factory overhead with the aid of responsibility accounting.

The well-designed information system should yield product costs for inventory costing and profit determination. It should also provide a control mechanism encompassing *responsibility accounting* and make meaningful cost data available for setting policies and making decisions. The predetermined or budgeted revenue and cost items form the foundation for comparison with actual results, leading to variance analysis and management by exception.

The establishment of such a system allows and maintains the most efficient and profitable balance between manufacturing and marketing. On the one hand, management needs to decide the kinds and costs of its products; on the other hand, it must decide the prices of its products. The greatest profit results from the proper balance of these considerations. For these reasons, product costs must be fairly accurate, include all relevant costs, and recognize cost differentials between products.

■ RESPONSIBILITY ACCOUNTING AND CONTROL OF FACTORY OVERHEAD

Webster's dictionary defines being *responsible* as "liable to be called upon to answer." Kohler's *A Dictionary for Accountants* defines *responsibility* as "the obligation prudently to exercise assigned or imputed authority attaching to the assigned or imputed role of an individual or group participating in organizational activities or decisions." The N.A.(C.)A. Research Series, No. 22, says: "A responsibility may be defined as an organizational unit having a single head accountable for activities of the unit."

Responsibility Accounting—Basic Concepts

The following concepts are prerequisites to the initiation and maintenance of a responsibility accounting system:

1. Responsibility accounting is based on a classification of managerial responsibilities (departments) at every level in the organization for the purpose of establishing a budget for each. The individual in charge of each responsibility classification should be responsible and accountable for the costs of his or her activity. This concept introduces the need for the classification of costs into controllable and not controllable by a department head. Generally, costs charged directly to a department, with the exception of fixed costs, are controllable by the department's manager.

2. The starting point for a responsibility accounting information system rests with the organization chart in which the spheres of jurisdiction have been determined. Authority leads to the responsibility for certain costs which, with the knowledge and cooperation of the supervisor, department head, or manager, are presented in the budget.

3. Each individual's budget should clearly identify the costs controllable by that person. The chart of accounts should be adapted to permit recording of controllable or accountable expenses within the jurisdictional framework.

Factors Influencing Responsible Cost Control

The fundamental tenet of responsibility accounting limits the individual's control effort to controllable costs. Yet, studies have shown that in departmental situations, several factors may influence the extent of controllability and the effectiveness of the departmental control efforts. These factors are summarized in the following performance model.[1]

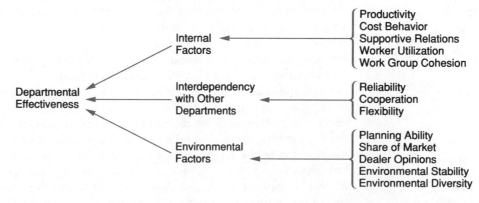

Performance Model

---

[1]David C. Hayes, "The Contingency Theory of Managerial Accounting," *The Accounting Review*, Vol. LII, No. 1, pp. 22-39.

Human Behavior in Responsibility Accounting

A program to develop management accounting controls must be considered a prime responsibility of executive management, with the accounting department providing technical assistance. To assure the follow-through of the program and its ultimate success, management must provide a complete clarification of the objectives and responsibilities of all levels of the organization. This prerequisite requires an understanding by middle and operating management of executive management's goals. The acceptance of responsibility for certain costs does not always follow the issuance of directives and orders. Supervisory personnel, particularly at the foreman level, need guidance and training to achieve the control and/or profit results expected from them. Control responsibility does not happen naturally, but requires a certain fundamental attitude or frame of mind for the task.

One of the most beneficial influences is executive management's own exemplary adherence to the cost-and-profit responsibility it created. Of equal importance is the motivation for corrective action by the responsible individual. The issuance of reports based on the organization's responsibility concept is not sufficient. The successful achievement of effective management control depends upon the lines of communication between the accounting department, the responsible supervisors, and their superiors. Responsibility accounting requires teamwork in the truest sense of the word.

Responsibility for Overhead Costs

As the preceding factory overhead chapters indicate, many overhead items are directly chargeable to a given department and become the direct responsibility of the departmental supervisor. Other overhead items must be allocated or distributed in order to calculate a departmental factory overhead rate that will charge all costs to a job, a product, or the work performed. This allocation procedure, however, is not necessary or useful for cost control, i.e., for responsibility accounting. For responsibility accounting purposes, any allocated charges should be limited to those expenses for which control and responsibility have been assumed by the originating department. However, the assignment of responsibility depends a great deal upon the methods of cost accumulation and allocation used by a firm.

In some firms, the cost system provides for a normal volume distribution of service hours, use hours, and/or maintenance hours to producing or other service departments. The distribution can be looked upon as a purchase by the recipient department and a sale by the providing service department. The distribution to the recipient department is based on what is termed a predetermined *billing rate*, a *sold-hour rate*, a *charging rate*, or a *transfer rate*. The method is based on the idea that these departments purchase the services in the same manner as direct materials and direct labor.

The determination of the billing rate follows the procedures discussed in the previous factory overhead chapters.

1. Estimate or budget the costs of any service department according to their nature (supervision, supplies, electricity, etc.).
2. Classify costs as fixed or variable. This classification often leads to the realization that many costs of service departments are fixed over fairly wide ranges of service volume.
3. Determine a rate by dividing total estimated departmental cost by the number of use hours the service is expected to be needed.

The establishment of the use hours is as important for billing rates as it is for factory overhead rates. The hours can be based either on past experience in a representative period or on future activity or volume as expressed in the budget. A refinement of the rate is the apportionment of fixed costs to cost centers on the basis of service capacity, i.e., readiness or ability to provide services, as defined for each benefiting department. The variable cost is then assigned on the basis of actual usage.[2]

The comparison of actual and budgeted costs is made (1) in the service department to which the expenses are originally charged, by comparing actual costs with charged-out or sold-out amounts; and (2) in the benefiting (recipient) departments in which the charges for service departments' services are linked with the budget allowances. This step is the control phase of the service department's charging-out procedure. The supervisor of the service department is responsible for the actual cost versus the cost for services charged out to benefiting departments. The benefiting department supervisor is responsible for the number of service department hours purchased and the resulting cost charged to his or her department. Variances for service and producing departments are calculable.

Billing Rates for Electronic Data Processing Services. Electronic data processing (EDP) services offer an excellent illustration of the need for careful attention to the use of appropriate billing rates. EDP services usually start as a support group, with costs classified as general overhead. These costs may be allocated to broad functional classifications, such as manufacturing (factory overhead), marketing, and administrative expenses. As data processing matures and becomes an integral part of the organization's operations, more precise cost accounting mechanisms are considered. The EDP center might apportion costs to users on the basis of a percentage of general utilization; e.g., assigning 10 percent of the costs to one department, 15 percent to another, and so forth. This approach has limitations, because it fails to contribute to efficient use of the EDP facility and does not aid the recipient in making selective judgments about the application requested. Users need to understand the cost and value of the services which they require.

The electronic data processing department should develop a price (charge) for the services which users can include in their departmental budgets. The price of a given system is a predetermined rate including fixed and

---

[2]An example of more sophisticated allocation procedures is found in Daniel L. Jensen's "A Class of Mutually Satisfactory Allocations," *The Accounting Review,* Vol. LII, No. 4, pp. 842-856.

variable costs, or a fixed amount plus a variable amount per transaction, the volume of which would affect the total processing time. The difference between actual price and actual cost provides one measure of the data processing department's efficiency.[3]

The general, one-rate allocation to functional classifications may be superseded by the partitioning of the computer into cost centers, with major costs classified as direct costs to a cost center where possible. To illustrate, a budget for a data processing department which has been partitioned into eight cost centers is shown on page 443.[4]

The "percent utilization expected" is important to a data processing department. Experience indicates that available hours are often utilized at only a 70 to 80 percent rate. The difference between utilized and available hours represents nonproductive activity which, for a systems analyst or a programmer, consists of vacation, holiday, illness, training, staff meetings, administrative tasks, professional societies, initial examination of requests, and other miscellaneous tasks. In this illustration, the budgeted hourly rates are the predetermined billing rates for each cost center, based on expected productive hours and including both variable and fixed costs.

Time recording procedures established in all cost centers would allow the data processing administration to:

1. Keep a close watch over the productive utilization percentage and take action if and when it gets out of line.
2. Calculate the cost of each project or system, based on actual time incurred multiplied by the budgeted hourly rates.
3. Compare the actual productive hours to budgeted productive hours, and be aware of variances on a weekly or monthly basis.
4. Note the variance between total actual monthly data processing cost and the summation of project and system costs.
5. For subsequent years, estimate more accurately the expected productive hours by cost centers.

The use of a "budgeted hourly rate" provides the following benefits:

1. Aids in controlling or reducing data processing costs.
2. Permits accurate and realistic costing of all work performed by project, system, user department, and/or line of business served.
3. Provides realistic rates to be used in estimating the cost of requested or proposed projects.
4. Permits a comparison of actual costs of processing a system to those costs which were estimated prior to implementation.
5. Aids in evaluating the operating efficiency of a data processing installation.

---

[3]Adapted from "The Fair Measure," *Data Processor*, Vol. 18, No. 2, pp. 10-13.

[4]Adapted from "Costing in the Data Processing Department" by John E. Finney, *Management Accounting*, Vol. LVI, No. 4, pp. 29-35. Copyright October, 1974, by the National Association of Accountants. All rights reserved. Reprinted by permission.

how to control costs at recipient level (producing)

service level (Service Dept)

DATA PROCESSING BUDGET BY COST CENTER

Item	Annual Budget	Systems	Program-ming	Computer Back-ground	Computer Fore-ground 1	Computer Fore-ground 2	Off-Line Devices	Data Entry	Data Control
Data processing administration	$ 48,000	$ 7,400	$ 5,200	$ 4,700	$ 8,900	$ 5,600	$ 500	$ 13,000	$ 2,700
Group managers and secretaries	82,000	20,000	15,000	5,000	10,000	10,000	2,000	10,000	10,000
Other salaries and fringe benefits	528,300	114,000	84,000	10,000	23,000	15,000	4,000	230,000	48,300
Training costs	11,000	3,500	3,500	300	900	500	200	1,600	500
Supplies	34,600	2,300	1,700	1,000	8,000	12,600	2,000	6,000	1,000
Travel	7,700	4,000	2,000	500	700	500			
Consulting fees	9,000	6,000	3,000						
Rent, insurance, and utilities	78,000	13,500	13,500	8,000	11,000	9,000	2,000	17,000	4,000
Equipment rental and depreciation	356,000			80,000	150,000	77,000	1,000	47,000	1,000
Equipment maintenance	30,700			8,000	12,000	10,000	500		200
Depreciation on furniture and fixtures	6,100	1,700	1,700	200	400	400	300	400	1,000
Employment agency fees	7,000	4,000	3,000						
Dues and subscriptions	1,600	1,000	600						
Total budgeted cost	$1,200,000	$177,400	$133,200	$117,700	$224,900	$140,600	$12,500	$325,000	$68,700
Available or purchased hours		14,560	14,560	7,488	7,488	7,488	1,040	60,320	12,480
Percent utilization expected		70	80	35	60	20	85	86	80
Expected productive hours		10,192	11,648	2,621	4,493	1,498	884	51,875	9,984
Budgeted hourly rate		$ 17.41	$ 11.44	$ 44.91	$ 50.06	$ 93.86	$ 14.14	$ 6.27	$ 6.88

6. Provides one measure of profitability for each data processing cost center and for the entire department in those cases where services are charged to a user or customer.

Maintenance Costs. Maintenance cost, like other factory cost, is charged ultimately to producing departments in order to be included in the calculation of overhead rates. The basic problem is assigning responsibility for this cost. Maintenance supervisors often believe that their department really incurs no cost at all, since any cost incurrence is for the benefit and at the request of other departments. Factory supervisors, on the other hand, may argue that they have no influence on either personnel or machinery costs of the maintenance department. The control is in reality twofold: the factory supervisors control the amount of maintenance work, while maintenance engineers or supervisors control the number of people and quantity of materials required to serve the various departments. Since maintenance work is done at the request of production supervisors, the problem arises as to whether control should be exercised at the source level or the recipient level.

At the source level, maintenance labor is organized and supervised. Control at this point requires predetermination of labor-hour requirements in each of the producing and service departments for each maintenance function. At the recipient level, the cost system establishes budget allowances for this indirect cost. Budget allowances based on planned levels of production permit the determination of the labor-hour budgets and advance scheduling of the work force of each shop service or maintenance unit. Preplanning is the heart of the control, providing an opportunity for corrective action before the hours are worked. Maintenance department supervisors are apprised of the maintenance allowance or budgeted service for individual recipient cost centers, but the distribution or scheduling of the work is left largely to their discretion.[5]

One major problem, however, is how much maintenance or repair work is needed in a department. Up to a point, the costs of preventive maintenance services generally will be more than offset by reductions in cost due to fewer equipment failures. Beyond this point, costs of providing additional preventive maintenance services will outweigh the benefits gained and total cost will increase. A basic problem of maintenance, therefore, is the determination of the balance—in terms of both effectiveness and cost—between prevention of equipment failure and correction of equipment failure.[6]

The solution may be determined by the executive management group. When a factory is laid out and the machinery installed, a maintenance program should be planned. The size of the maintenance department, the type or class of workers (carpenters, plumbers, electricians, pipefitters, masons, millwrights, machinists, etc.), and the kind of equipment and tools are

---

[5]For additional discussion and illustration of responsibility accounting for maintenance, see James H. Bullock, *Maintenance Planning and Control* (New York: National Association of Accountants, 1979), pp. 29-33.

[6]*Ibid.*, p. 14.

greatly influenced by early decisions. On the other hand, experience indicates that such maintenance objectives are lacking in many companies due to management's own lack of interest as well as alleged difficulties in planning, measuring, and controlling the maintenance function. Although many organizations engage the services of outside firms for part or all of their maintenance, the need for careful planning and control of maintenance cost is not negated.

When management and the supervisors of the producing, service, and maintenance engineering departments agree on a preventive maintenance program, their objective is to keep equipment in such condition that breakdowns and the need for emergency repairs are within control. Preventive maintenance facilitates the scheduling of maintenance work and helps to obtain better utilization of the maintenance work force and the productive equipment.

A preventive maintenance program can work automatically so that inspection, minor repairs, adjustments, and lubrication are completed as a matter of course. The method further provides for a check on the effectiveness of the maintenance work by the supervisor of the serviced or buying unit. The maintenance supervisor, in turn, is responsible for the inspection and the upkeep of the facilities.

Responsibility for Other Costs

The discussion has intentionally focused on factory overhead items, since their assignment and control occupies the attention of many executives, department heads, and supervisors. However, other cost elements as well as functions in administration and marketing also require supervision and control by responsible managers.

The best approach to assigning responsibility for any cost element is to identify those individuals who are in the most favored position to keep the costs under control. The assignment of responsibility for overhead costs to supervisors and department heads provides a certain degree of control. Nevertheless, certain costs (e.g., maintenance costs) are often troublesome. Many individuals may be assigned responsibility for direct materials and direct labor costs incurred. This responsibility often becomes obscure and nearly impossible to identify, making it advisable to assign responsibility on the basis of relative control rather than absolute control.

For direct materials, the variances or deviations from a predetermined norm or standard will result in (1) materials price variances, (2) materials quantity, or mix and yield variances, and/or (3) excessive defective work, rejects, or scrap costs. For direct labor, the variances or deviations from a predetermined norm or standard will result in (1) pay rate variations, (2) efficiency variations, (3) and/or overtime costs.

There are other variances for which a manager may be held responsible. Deviations from budgeted gross or net profit figures require explanation, as illustrated in later chapters. The changes in sales prices, sales volume, and sales mix are the responsibility of the marketing department. Yet the gross profit and net profit figures contain elements of cost as well, so that a further investigation is warranted.

Cost Control Characteristics

An effective cost control system has two major characteristics:

1. A sound technical design with goals set at a challenging but attainable performance level and with a reporting system that distinguishes controllable costs within each managerial responsibility from costs controllable elsewhere in the organization.
2. A managerial style sensitive to the behavior of people in a particular organizational setting. This requires a proper blend of:
   (a) Involvement by managers in setting goals for their own activities.
   (b) Leadership provided by executive management.
   (c) Open communication channels through which individual managers feel their views receive serious consideration.
   (d) Review procedures which disclose and discourage suboptimization and individual gains at the expense of the whole organization.

Cost control techniques are effective only with sufficient managerial appreciation of the behavioral aspects of control systems.[7]

Suboptimization everything geared to 1 certain function to the disregard of all else ex. acctg functions

Variance Analysis for Responsibility Accounting

Today—with the emphasis on responsible control of financial results via the return-on-capital-employed concept—assets, liabilities, net worth, revenue, and costs form a vast area in which the entire management spectrum, from the top executive to the supervisor, holds some share of responsibility. Like blocks within a pyramid (page 453), the responsibility travels from the lowest to the highest level of supervision. All supervisors are responsible for costs incurred by their subordinates.

To exercise this control, the cost and/or budget department should issue frequent reports that compare actual results with predetermined amounts or budget allowances. An analysis prepared at the end of the annual fiscal period, as shown in Chapter 14, is not very helpful for immediate control actions. Reports on a monthly or a more frequent basis are advisable to allow short-range comparisons of those costs for which operating management is responsible.

In general, variable costs are controllable at the departmental level, while fixed costs are not. In some circumstances, however, certain variable costs may be controlled at a higher level in the organization; e.g., employee fringe benefits may be determined by negotiations between executive management

[7]Walter B. McFarland, *Manpower Cost and Performance Measurement* (New York: National Association of Accountants, 1977), p. 101.

and the labor union or by government regulations. Such costs should be analyzed and separately identified to relieve a department manager of this responsibility. Conversely, a department manager may have some control over certain fixed costs—those that involve a long-term commitment (sometimes called *committed fixed costs*), such as equipment depreciation or lease payments, and those that can be readily changed in the short run (sometimes called *programmed fixed costs*), such as the number of supervisors in the department. These costs should be individually identified as to whether they are controllable by the manager of the department. Whether fixed or variable, some costs may be indirect or common with respect to two or more departments and thus may require arbitrary allocation. Accordingly, their controllability by a single department manager is restricted.

Attention must be called to the fact that in the long run, all costs are controllable at some level within the organization. Variable costs are generally controllable over short time periods. Some fixed costs, such as supervisory labor or equipment rental, can also be altered on short notice. Other fixed costs, such as depreciation of plant assets or a long-term lease agreement, involve a fixed commitment over a long period of time. Finally, some costs possess a dual short- and long-run controllability characteristic. For example, a five-year contract as to the price of a raw material, representing a long-term commitment, is not immediately controllable and the contract may be negotiable only at a higher management level. However, waste and spoilage of the same material is immediately controllable by the department. Generally, department managers should be well enough informed to explain cost variances, even though the control or certain aspects of the control do not fall within their scope of authority and responsibility. In other words, responsibility should not be equated with fault or blame. *But unfortunately it is,*

To illustrate monthly variance analysis on a departmental basis, the DeWitt Products data used in Chapter 14 are modified to accommodate a monthly comparison, and for conciseness of the illustration only one service department, Utilities, is used. The four departmental factory overhead rates computed in Chapter 14 are maintained as follows:

Cutting Department	$4.00 per direct labor hour
Planing Department	$6.40 per machine hour
Assembly Department	60% of direct labor cost
Upholstery Department	$3.60 per direct labor hour

At the end of January, the following actual data for DeWitt Products are assembled:

Department	Actual Hours (Labor or Machine) or Labor Cost	Actual Consumption for the Month kwh	Actual Consumption for the Month hph	Actual Departmental Overhead Before Billing Out Utilities
Cutting	1,523 direct labor hours	1,180	19,000	$3,575
Planing	810 machine hours	700	10,800	3,125
Assembly	$11,400 direct labor cost	1,700	7,000	2,900
Upholstery	2,050 direct labor hours	1,980	8,000	3,570
Utilities				5,860
		5,560	44,800	

Based on the actual production and cost data, the cost department would apply the following amounts of factory overhead to products passing through the four departments:

Cutting Department, 1,523 direct labor hours × $4.00	$6,092
Planing Department, 810 machine hours × $6.40	5,184
Assembly Department, $11,400 direct labor cost × 60%	6,840
Upholstery Department, 2,050 direct labor hours × $3.60	7,380

To determine and analyze the amount of over- or underapplied factory overhead, service department costs must be added to the actual direct and indirect departmental overhead to put actual and applied figures on a comparable basis. These procedures were presented in Chapter 14.

Spending Variance. In responsibility accounting, the emphasis rests upon the comparison of actual departmental costs with budgeted or estimated costs before service department costs are allocated, because it is at these departmental points of origin that costs are best controlled. Furthermore, many accountants believe that only the variable portion of these point-of-origin costs should be compared and not the total overhead, since these variable costs tend to be the most readily controllable at the department level. Naturally, the procedures for different organizations vary.

In this example, both procedures are illustrated for the four producing departments and one service department. The first computation shows total actual departmental overhead, both fixed and variable, compared with budgeted or predetermined departmental overhead. The second computation shows only variable actual departmental overhead compared with its budgeted or predetermined amount. In both situations, the analysis is made for producing and service departments prior to any service department cost allocation.

PROCEDURE 1

	Departments				
	Cutting	Planing	Assembly	Upholstery	Utilities
Actual departmental overhead	$3,575	$3,125	$2,900	$3,570	$5,860
Budget allowances:					
Variable overhead:					
1,523 hours × $1.1525*	$1,755				
810 hours × $2.0435*		$1,655			
$11,400 × 15.5%*			$1,767		
2,050 hours × $.8434*				$1,729	
5,560 kwh × $.1544*					$ 858
44,800 hph × $.0494*					2,213
1,750 sq. ft.** × $.7057*					1,235
Fixed overhead (1/12 annual fixed cost; e.g.,					
$17,100*** ÷ 12 = $1,425)	1,425	1,492	1,342	1,525	1,333
Budget allowances	$3,180	$3,147	$3,109	$3,254	$5,639
Spending variances	$ 395	$ (22)	$ (209)	$ 316	$ 221
	unfav.	fav.	fav.	unfav.	unfav.

*Variable cost rate, as calculated on the next page.
**1,750 sq. ft. is 1/12 of 21,000 sq. ft. (to convert to a one-month period), as shown on page 410.
***Estimated fixed cost for the Cutting Department, page 411.

PROCEDURE 2

Just Variable

subtract fixed o/h

	Departments				
	Cutting	Planing	Assembly	Upholstery	Utilities
Actual variable departmental overhead (e.g., $3,575 – $1,425 fixed cost)..	$2,150	$1,633	$1,558	$2,045	$4,527
Budgeted variable overhead	1,755	1,655	1,767	1,729	4,306
Spending variances	$ 395	$ (22)	$ (209)	$ 316	$ 221
	unfav.	fav.	fav.	unfav.	unfav.

The variable cost rates for the producing departments are calculated by dividing the variable departmental overhead, before service department distribution, by the predetermined or estimated direct labor hours, direct labor cost, or machine hours, using data from pages 411 and 413.

	Estimated Variable Departmental Overhead	÷	Estimated			=	Variable Departmental Cost Rates
			Direct Labor Hours	Direct Labor Cost	Machine Hours		
Cutting	$23,400		20,304				$1.1525
Planing	$18,800				9,200		$2.0435
Assembly	$18,900			$122,000			15.5%
Upholstery	$20,300		24,070				$ .8434

In the producing departments, actual hours or actual costs for the month are multiplied by the variable cost rate to arrive at the budgeted or estimated variable cost.

The variable rates for Utilities (using data from pages 410, 411, and 413) are calculated as follows:

Total departmental expense	$65,400
Less fixed expense	16,000
Total variable expense..........	$49,400

$49,400 × 20% = $ 9,880 ÷ 64,000 kwh = $.1544 variable rate per kwh
$49,400 × 50% = $24,700 ÷ 500,000 hph = $.0494 variable rate per hph
$49,400 × 30% = $14,820 ÷ 21,000 sq. ft. = $.7057 variable rate per sq. ft.

The estimated allowance for Utilities is based on the actual monthly consumption figures multiplied by the corresponding variable rates.

Idle Capacity Variance. Responsibility accounting stresses the control of variable costs and the calculation of the departmental spending variance. It is possible, however, to continue the analysis and calculate an idle capacity variance based entirely on departmental costs without any allocation of service department costs or charges. To illustrate, the data from page 411 are used in determining the idle capacity variance for the Cutting Department, as shown in the table on page 450.

(1)	(2)	(3)	(4)	(5)	(6)
Actual Overhead	Budget Allowance	Applied Overhead	Total Variance (1) − (3)	Spending Variance (1) − (2)	Idle Capacity Variance (2) − (3)
$3,575	$3,180	$3,038*	$537 unfav.	$395 unfav.	$142** unfav.

*1,523 actual hours × $1.9947 = $3,038
**1,692 (20,304 hours ÷ 12 months) predetermined hours − 1,523 actual hours = 169 idle hours; 169 idle hours × $.8422 = $142

The Cutting Department's total estimated overhead cost is $40,500, with $17,100 fixed and $23,400 variable. The variable overhead rate is $1.1525 and the fixed rate is $.8422 ($17,100 ÷ 20,304 estimated hours), providing a total of $1.9947. In the Cutting Department, a factory overhead rate of $4 per direct labor hour is used for product costing purposes. The difference of $2.0053 ($4.00 − $1.9947) is accounted for by service department costs assigned to this department.

A similar analysis can be made as follows for the service department, Utilities:

(1)	(2)	(3)	(4)	(5)	(6)
Actual Overhead	Budget Allowance	Utilities Cost Charged Out	Total Variance (1) − (3)	Spending Variance (1) − (2)	Idle Capacity Variance (2) − (3)
$5,860	$5,639	$5,701*	$159 unfav.	$221 unfav.	$(62) fav.

*The amount of cost charged out is based on the total predetermined utilities cost of $65,400 (from page 411), which was to be distributed 20% or $13,080 based on kwh, 50% or $32,700 on hph, and 30% or $19,620 on floor area, resulting in these charging rates: $.2044 ($13,080 ÷ 64,000 kwh); $.0654 ($32,700 ÷ 500,000 hph); and $.9343 ($19,620 ÷ 21,000 sq. ft.). The $5,701 is the result of:

$$
\begin{array}{rr}
5,560 \text{ actual kwh} \times \$.2044 = & \$1,136 \\
44,800 \text{ actual hph} \times \$.0654 = & 2,930 \\
1,750 \text{ sq. ft. converted to a one-month period (1/12 of 21,000 sq. ft.)} \times \$.9343 = & 1,635 \\
\hline
& \$5,701 \\
\end{array}
$$

Responsibility for Service Department Variances. While the responsibility for the cost incurred is, generally speaking, easily identifiable in the producing departments, a service department's cost variances need a great deal of additional investigation. With a service department such as Utilities, the analysis is not so easy because:

1. Utilities can be charged accurately to consuming departments only when departmental or cost center meters are used.
2. Even with meters, the quantity used might differ from the quantity produced, due to line losses. The pinpointing of the responsibility for these losses is often impossible.
3. Since any utility can often be either purchased from outside or manufactured inside, it could be possible that the interchangeable use of one source with another will give rise to variances for which the cause is also difficult to detect.

Similar difficulties regarding the pinpointing of responsibility for the cost incurrence and the resulting variance are experienced with any service department. The maintenance department has already been cited as an example. In many instances, service department costs are largely fixed, at least over a relevant range of activity or volume. For this reason, responsibility is difficult to establish. The idle capacity variance is particularly troublesome when calculated on a monthly basis. The spending variance is somewhat more meaningful, since actual and budgeted costs can be compared with their increases and decreases.

As a rule, the manager of the service department is responsible for the variance between the actual cost and the cost based on the number of hours or service units charged out or sold. The manager of the producing or services received department, together with the service department supervisor, is responsible for the number of hours or service units consumed in the department. This statement indicates that a kind of dual responsibility exists between the charges to the services received departments and the credits to the services rendered departments. The consuming department's cost must be compared with the allowed or budgeted service cost to determine the cost increase or decrease in that department, while the service department must examine its cost on the basis of the quantity consumed or sold.

RESPONSIBILITY REPORTING — *Know Summarizators up chain*

Responsibility accounting is a program encompassing all operating management for which the accounting, cost, or budget divisions provide technical assistance in the form of daily, weekly, or monthly control reports. Responsibility reporting includes the reporting phase of responsibility accounting. In fact, the terms, "responsibility accounting" and "responsibility reporting" are generally considered synonymous.

Reporting to the various levels of management can be divided into responsibility-performance reporting and information reporting. A clear distinction between the two is important; each serves different goals or objectives. *Responsibility-performance reports* are accountability reports with two purposes:

1. To inform managers and superiors of their performance in responsible areas.
2. To motivate managers and superiors to generate the direct action necessary to improve performance.

Information reports are issued for the purpose of providing managers with information relevant to their areas of interest, although not necessarily associated directly with their specific responsibility for performance. Information reports serve a broader and different set of goals than performance reports. In the short view, responsibility-performance reports are more important than information reports because of the immediate and pressing needs to keep the business on course. However, from the long view, information reports bearing on the progress and growth of the business are also important.

Fundamentals of Reports

Reports should be based on the following fundamental qualities and characteristics:

to be useful!

1. Reports should fit the organization chart; that is, they should be addressed primarily to the individuals responsible for controlling the items covered by the reports. Managers must be educated to use the results of the reporting system.

2. Reports should be consistent in form and content each time they are issued. Changes should be made only for good reasons and with clear explanations to users.

3. Reports should be prompt and timely. Prompt issuance of a report requires that cost records be organized so that information is available when it is needed.

4. Reports should be issued with regularity. Promptness and regularity are closely tied in with the mechanical aids used to assemble and issue reports.

5. Reports should be easy to understand. Often they contain accounting terminology that managers with little or no accounting training find difficult to understand, and vital information may be incorrectly communicated. Therefore, accounting terms should be explained or modified to fit the user. Management should have some knowledge of the kind of items chargeable to an account as well as the methods used to compute overhead rates, allocate costs, and analyze variances.

6. Reports should convey sufficient but not excessive detail. The amount and nature of the detail depend largely on the management level receiving the report. Reports to management should neither be flooded with immaterial facts nor so condensed that management lacks vital information essential to carrying out its responsibilities.

7. Reports should give comparative figures (a comparison of actual with budgeted figures, or of predetermined standards with actual results) and should isolate variances.

8. Reports should be analytical. Analysis of underlying records, such as time tickets, scrap tickets, work orders, and materials requisitions, provides reasons for poor performance which might have been due to power failure, machine breakdown, an inefficient operator, poor quality of materials, or other similar factors.

9. Reports for operating management should be stated in physical units as well as in dollars, since dollar information may be irrelevant to a supervisor not trained in the language of the accountant. Also, dollars may be more difficult to compare over time because of the impact of inflation.

10. Reports may tend to highlight supposed departmental efficiencies and inefficiencies. Care should be exercised to see that such reports do not encourage departmental activities aimed at "making a good showing" regardless of the effect on the entire organization. Also,

any tendency to place blame should be avoided. The emphasis should be on obtaining information to explain variances, not on placing blame.

To be of value, information must be used; to be used, it must be effectively communicated. Both the form and the method of the reporting techniques are critical, whether written or oral.

The written report should include tabular presentation as well as the use of charts and graphs.[8] Narrative comments are useful for conveying qualitative information and for analyzing and interpreting quantitative data. Oral presentations are especially effective in offering opportunities to convey information, raise questions, and voice opinions.

Responsibility-Reporting Systems Illustrated

The first step in a responsibility-reporting system is the establishment of lines of responsibility and responsibility areas. Each block in a company's organization chart represents a segment (cost center, division, department, etc.) that is reported upon and that receives reports on the functions responsible to it. Any report prepared according to this concept easily fits into one of the blocks illustrated in the following organization chart for a manufacturing concern:

Organization Chart for a Manufacturing Concern

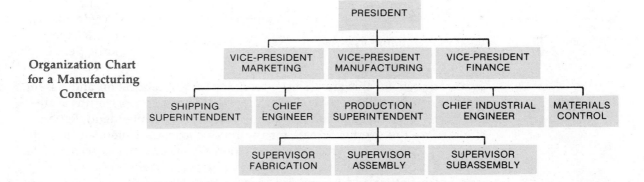

The following reports illustrate the factory overhead reporting structure for each level of responsibility and the relationship of each report to the next higher echelon of responsibility.[9] Starting with Report D (bottom of the pyramid), the Subassembly Department supervisor is provided with the factory

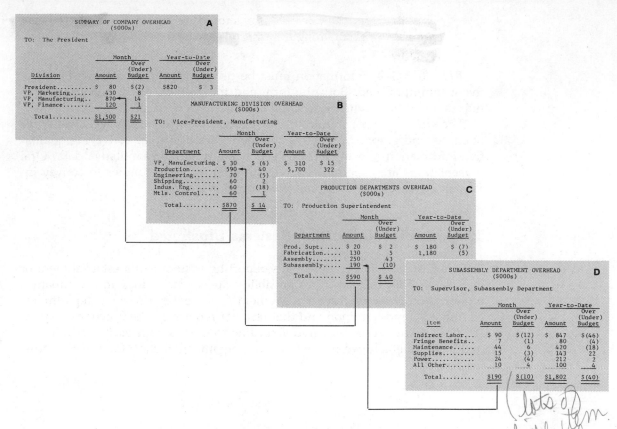

Flow of Responsibility Reporting in a Manufacturing Concern

overhead costs for this area. The supervisors for the Fabrication and Assembly Departments also receive similar reports. The supervisors of these three departments are responsible to the production superintendent. Report C summarizes the overhead costs for the production superintendent and the three departments for which the production superintendent is accountable. Report B provides the vice-president of manufacturing with performance figures for this office and for the five responsibility areas within this division. Finally, the president receives a summary, Report A, indicating overhead costs not only for the president's own area but also for the three divisions (Marketing, Manufacturing, Finance) reporting to that office.

The illustration on page 455 depicts responsibility reporting in a bank, utilizing a reporting system that accurately identifies and reports expenses along the bank's organizational lines.[10] This permits effective expense control through the proper assignment of responsibility and control at each manage-

---

[10]Edward T. Kennedy, "Computer-Based Bank Financial Information Systems," *The Arthur Andersen Chronicle* (Chicago: Arthur Andersen & Co.), Vol. 29, No. 2, p. 28.

ment level, with expenses at each management level identified by area of responsibility as well as by natural classification.

Flow of Responsibility Reporting in a Bank

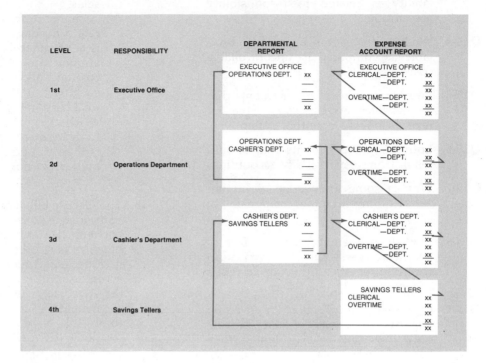

Reviewing the Reporting Structure

To provide all levels of management with all the facts when needed, the reporting system should be geared to the requirements of all managerial personnel. Each report should be so arranged that exceptions are highlighted and brought to the attention of the responsible manager without too much searching and extensive reading. The number of reports issued and sent to a manager also needs constant examination. Too many times a reporting system is cluttered with old, detailed, and voluminous reports, without consideration of the cost of their preparation or their justification. No reporting system is ever perfect. It requires continuous checking and examination in the light of changing times and the fluctuations of business itself.

DISCUSSION QUESTIONS

Q15-1. Explain responsibility accounting and the classification of revenues and costs under this concept.

Q15-2. Responsibility accounting does not involve a drastic change in accounting theory or principles. Discuss.

Q15-3. Explain what is meant by controllable costs and how the idea of controllability is related to responsibility accounting.

Q15-4. What is the significance of controllable as compared to uncontrollable costs?

Q15-5. Enumerate general requirements that are absolutely necessary for a successful responsibility accounting system.

Q15-6. Enumerate the benefits that should result from responsibility accounting.

Q15-7. Why is some knowledge of human behavior important to responsibility accounting?

Q15-8. The departmentalization of factory overhead is essential for maximum control of overhead. Explain in terms of responsibility reporting.

Q15-9. Overhead control reports received by department heads should include only those items over which they have control. Explain.

Q15-10. Why are service department costs included in the overhead rates? Why should actual service department costs be accumulated in service department accounts instead of being charged directly to production department accounts?

Q15-11. Although service department costs are included in departmental overhead rates, actual costs of these departments need not be distributed to departments serviced each period. Explain.

Q15-12. The following charges are found on the monthly report of a division which manufactures and sells products primarily to outside companies. State which, if any, of these charges are consistent with the responsibility accounting concept. Support each answer with a brief explanation.

(a) A charge for general corporation administration at 10% of division sales.
(b) A charge for the use of the corporate computer facility. The charge is determined by taking the actual annual Computer Department cost and allocating an amount to each user on the ratio of its use to total corporation use.
(c) A charge for goods purchased from another division. (The charge is based upon the competitive market price for the goods.)

(ICMA adapted)

Q15-13. The electric bill of the Emmons Company increased from $5,000 to $7,500 between January and February. As a bill is received, its cost is allocated to various departments on the basis of actual usage.
(a) What factors may have caused the increase?
(b) Is this an effective way of handling this cost? If not, suggest a better procedure.

Q15-14. A charging rate is frequently used to charge Maintenance Department cost to departments using its services. The charge is determined by multiplying the number of labor hours of service by a charging rate which is computed by the following formula:

$$\frac{\text{Total actual Maintenance Department cost}}{\text{Total labor hours worked}}$$

The superintendent of the Stamping Department was upset by a $15,000 maintenance charge for work that involved approximately the same number of labor hours as work done in a previous month when the charge was $12,000.
(a) What factors may have caused the increased charge?
(b) What improvements can be made in the distribution of this company's Maintenance Department cost?

Q15-15. Discuss the information which a well-designed cost report should give to the management from the point of view of production and of control. Is there any other information with which the cost figures should be amplified? In what terms should such information be given?

Q15-16. On what fundamentals should the method of presenting cost data to management be based?

Q15-17. Why is usefulness of the figures so important in accounting?

Q15-18. A frequent complaint made by management is that cost reports arrive too late to be of any value to the executives. What are the main contributing causes of this condition, and how can it be remedied?

EXERCISES

E15-1. Billing rates; variance analysis in service departments. Baars Company uses predetermined departmental overhead rates to apply factory overhead. In computing these rates, every attempt is made to transfer service department costs to producing departments on the most equitable bases. Budgeted cost and other data for Baar's two service departments, Maintenance and General Factory, are as follows:

	Maintenance	General Factory
Monthly fixed cost.............	$7,500	$30,000
Variable cost	$8.50 per maintenance labor hour	$20 per employee (producing departments only)
Normal level of activity	15,000 maintenance hours per month	1,000 producing department employees
Actual November results:		
Total cost	$130,000	$49,500
Actual level of activity	14,000 maintenance hours	980 producing department employees

Required:

(1) Compute the charging or billing rates to be used to transfer estimated maintenance and general factory costs to other departments, together with a description of the method used.

(2) Compute the spending and idle capacity variances for the service departments.

E15-2. Sold-hour rates; variance analysis in service departments. A company's two service departments provide the following data:

Service Center	Monthly Budget	Service-Hours Available	Actual Monthly Expense
Carpenter Shop	$20,000	2,000	$19,800
Electricians...........	30,000	2,500	28,900

The two service departments serve three producing departments that show the following budgeted and actual cost and service-hours data:

Department No.	Estimated Services Required		Actual Services Used	
	Carpenter Shop	Electricians	Carpenter Shop	Electricians
1	600 hrs.	900 hrs.	400 hrs.	1,000 hrs.
2	750 hrs.	1,000 hrs.	800 hrs.	850 hrs.
3	650 hrs.	600 hrs.	450 hrs.	550 hrs.

Required:

(1) Compute the sold-hour rates for the two service departments.
(2) Compute the amounts charged to the producing departments for services rendered.
(3) Compute the spending variances for the two service departments, assuming that 70% of the budgeted expense is fixed in the Carpenter Shop and 80% for Electricians.

E15-3. Billing rates; variance analysis in service departments. The plant manager of the Lehigh Company suggested in a management meeting that the charging of the cost of service departments to producing and other service departments should be examined in the light of management's attempt to secure better control over service departments' costs. The supervisors of the budget and cost departments investigated the matter and assembled the following monthly data for the Maintenance Department and the Payroll Department:

	Maintenance Department		Payroll Department	
	Fixed Cost	Variable Cost per Maintenance Hour	Fixed Cost	Variable Cost per Employee
Supervision, foreman	$ 4,000	–0–	$1,500	–0–
Maintenance, workers.	12,000	$0.25		
Payroll clerks.			2,560	$0.35
Supplies, etc.	1,200	1.00	2,100	0.20
Miscellaneous	1,000	0.10	1,000	0.20
Totals	$18,200	$1.35	$7,160	$0.75

Maintenance hours at normal capacity	1,000 hours	
Number of company employees at normal level	250 employees	
Actual data at end of month:		
Maintenance Department	$20,300 for 945 hours	
Payroll Department	$ 7,380 for 268 employees	

Required:

(1) Compute a billing or charging rate for each department.
(2) Compute the spending and idle capacity variance for each department.
(3) Explain what should be done concerning disposition of the variances in the service departments.

E15-4. Readiness-to-serve and billing rates. During November, the actual cost of operating a power plant was $12,800, of which $6,000 was considered a fixed cost. The schedule of horsepower-hours for the producing and service departments is as follows:

	Producing Departments		Service Departments	
	A	B	X	Y
Needed at capacity production	10,000	20,000	12,000	8,000
Used during November	8,000	13,000	7,000	6,000

Required:

(1) Compute the dollar amounts of the power plant cost to be allocated to each producing and service department. The fixed cost is assigned on the basis of the power plant's readiness to serve.

(2) State reasons for allocating one service department's cost to other service departments as well as to producing departments.

E15-5 **Readiness-to-serve and billing rates; variance analysis.** The Fairhope Company operates its own power-generating plant. Power cost is distributed to the producing departments by charging the fixed cost according to the standby capacity provided and the variable cost on the basis of a predetermined rate multiplied by actual consumption. The rated standby capacity of the three departments, A, B, and C, is 50,000, 37,500, and 12,500 kwh, respectively, per month.

The following information relative to the producing departments and the power plant for January through May is available:

| | Consumption in Kilowatt-Hours | | | Power Plant | |
	Dept. A	Dept. B	Dept. C	Fixed	Variable
January.........	45,000	40,000	10,000	$30,000	$19,600
February	55,000	35,000	11,000	30,000	20,000
March	47,500	38,000	11,000	30,000	19,800
April...........	53,800	37,000	12,500	30,000	21,800
May	44,000	33,000	13,000	30,000	19,000

The predetermined variable power cost rate is $.20 per kwh.

Required:

(1) Separately identify the fixed and variable power cost charged to each department for each of the five months.

(2) Compute the over- or underdistributed variable cost (i.e., the spending variance) of the power plant for each of the five months.

SS E15-6. **Overhead analysis; report to supervisor.** The cost and operating data on April factory overhead for Department 10 are as follows: *W report*

	Budgeted Factory Overhead	Actual Factory Overhead
Variable departmental overhead:		
Supplies	$ 2,000	$ 1,800
Repairs and maintenance	800	600
Indirect labor.....................	4,000	3,800
Power and light....................	1,200	1,150
Heat..............................	400	350
Subtotal......................	$ 8,400	$ 7,700
Fixed departmental overhead:		
Depreciation—buildings	$ 800	$ 840
Depreciation—machinery.............	2,400	2,400
Property tax and insurance	400	420
Subtotal......................	$ 3,600	$ 3,660
Total	$12,000	$11,360
Operating data:		
Normal capacity hours...............	8,000	
Factory overhead rate per hour	$1.50	
Actual hours		6,400

Required:

(1) Prepare a variance analysis of the factory overhead for Department 10.

(2) Prepare a departmental report for the supervisor of Department 10, with explanations regarding the format used.

PROBLEMS

P15-1. Variance analysis in producing and service departments. Sanders Products Inc. decided to push for a greater amount of cost consciousness and cost responsibility among its departmental supervisors. The allocation of service department costs to the producing departments, using predetermined rates, has been in use for some time. Now the management asks the Cost Department, with the cooperation of the departmental supervisors, not only to prepare departmental budgets but also to give the supervisors monthly reports for cost control information.

The company operates with three producing departments, A, B, and C, and two service departments, Repairs and Maintenance, and Utilities. For the year 19-, the Cost Department prepared the following departmental factory overhead budgets and determined the factory overhead rates based on machine hours:

| | Producing Departments | | | Service Departments | |
	A	B	C	Repairs and Maintenance	Utilities
Total budgeted cost	$52,000	$52,450	$41,900	$56,000	$49,000
Allocation of service departments:					
Utilities (based on kilowatt-hours)	14,000	15,750	12,250	7,000	(49,000)
Repairs and maintenance (based on machine hours)	18,000	27,900	17,100	(63,000)	
Total	$84,000	$96,100	$71,250		
Bases:					
Kilowatt-hours.	40,000	45,000	35,000	20,000	
Machine hours	20,000	31,000	19,000		
Service department allocation rates				$.90 per machine hour	$.35 per kilowatt-hour
Departmental overhead rates	$4.20 per machine hour	$3.10 per machine hour	$3.75 per machine hour		

Actual cost and operating data before allocation of service department costs at the end of the budget period are:

| | Producing Departments | | | Service Departments | |
	A	B	C	Repairs and Maintenance	Utilities
Total actual cost	$56,020	$52,850	$42,580	$56,320	$50,040
Operating data:					
Machine hours	20,480	29,850	20,100		
Kilowatt-hours	39,300	46,200	35,800	18,950	

Required:

(1) Compute the amount of factory overhead applied for each of the three producing departments.
(2) Compute the amount of over- or underapplied factory overhead for each of the three producing departments, charging them with service department costs on the basis of actual kilowatt-hours or machine hours multiplied by the billing rate.
(3) Compute the total variance for each of the two service departments.

P15-2. Billing rate; variance analysis in producing and service departments. The Croesus Corporation has three producing departments: Assembling, Painting, Finishing and Packing; and one service department: General Factory. Overhead is applied to the product via departmental overhead rates that include a share of the service department's costs. The following monthly predetermined and actual costs and production data are available:

| | Departments | | | |
| | Production | | | Service |
	Assembly	Painting	Finishing and Packing	General Factory
Variable cost per direct labor hour	$ .50	$ .25	$ .30	$ 1.00
Fixed cost.	$2,800	$4,000	$2,280	$ 6,000
Normal monthly activity (direct labor hours)	2,000	1,600	2,400	
Actual monthly results:				
Cost	$4,400	$4,100	$3,300	$12,600
Hours worked	2,050	1,500	2,200	

The service department's costs are distributed to the producing departments via a predetermined billing rate on the basis of direct labor hours.

Required:

(1) Determine the charging or billing rate of the General Factory service department.
(2) Compute the factory overhead rate for each of the three producing departments with the service department's cost being prorated on the basis of the billing rate calculated in (1).
(3) Calculate the spending and idle capacity variances for each of the three producing departments.
(4) Calculate the spending and idle capacity variances for the General Factory service department.

P15-3. Billing rates; variance analysis in producing and service departments. Perdido Tool Co. has two producing departments, Planers and Radial Drills, and two service departments, Maintenance and Utilities. The following data were collected:

| | Producing Departments | | Service Departments | |
	Planers	Radial Drills	Maintenance	Utilities
Estimated data for 19––:				
Fixed overhead	$18,000	$15,000	$ 6,000	$ 4,800
Variable overhead	15,000	9,000	4,500	3,600
Total	$33,000	$24,000	$10,500	$ 8,400
Machine hours	12,000	7,500		
Maintenance hours	2,500	1,000	3,500	
Kilowatt-hours	45,000	25,000		70,000
Actual data for January 19––:				
Fixed overhead	$ 1,500	$ 1,250	$ 500	$ 400
Variable overhead	1,620	1,050	670	310
Total	$ 3,120	$ 2,300	$ 1,170	$ 710
Machine hours	1,020	680		
Maintenance hours	320	80	400	
Kilowatt-hours	4,000	2,000		6,000

Required:

(1) Compute the billing (or charging) rate for each of the two service departments.
(2) Calculate the total predetermined factory overhead for each of the two producing departments and their departmental factory overhead rates based on machine hours. Service department costs are to be distributed on the basis of the billing rates calculated in (1). (Carry all computations to three decimal places.)
(3) Prepare an analysis of the over- or underapplied factory overhead of each of the two producing departments for January, including the spending and idle capacity variances. Service department costs are to be charged on the basis of actual hours (maintenance or kilowatt) multiplied by the billing rate. This method treats these costs as being wholly variable.

(4) Prepare a calculation and analysis of the over- or underapplied factory overhead in each of the two service departments, including the spending and idle capacity variances. (Round all amounts to four decimal places.)

(5) Prepare a reconciliation of the total variances.

P15-4. Budget allowance; variance analysis in producing and service departments. The controller of Cole Corporation prepared the following forecast income statement for the year:

		Amount	Unit
Sales (60,000 units)		$600,000	$10.00
Cost of goods sold (Schedule 1)		384,000	6.40
Gross profit		$216,000	$ 3.60
Commercial expenses:			
Marketing expense	$80,000		
Administrative expense	70,000	150,000	2.50
Income before income tax		$ 66,000	$ 1.10
Schedule 1—Estimated cost of goods sold:			
Direct materials		$102,000	$ 1.70
Direct labor		162,000	2.70
Factory overhead		120,000	2.00
Total		$384,000	$ 6.40

The product's manufacturing processes require two producing departments that make use of the services of Department 76, Maintenance, and Department 95, Janitorial. To charge the products moving through the two departments, the cost accountant has prepared an overhead distribution sheet and calculated predetermined factory overhead rates as follows:

	Producing Departments		Service Departments	
	Dept. 10	Dept. 12	Dept. 76 Maintenance	Dept. 95 Janitorial
Production units	60,000	60,000		
Direct labor hours	15,000	12,000		
Direct labor cost	$90,000	$72,000		
Factory overhead:				
Variable overhead	$27,000	$22,800	$ 5,100	$2,700
Fixed overhead	17,520	34,230	8,400	7,200
			$13,500	$9,900
Share of Department 76	7,500	6,000	(13,500)	
Share of Department 95	1,980	2,970		(4,950)
Total factory overhead	$54,000	$66,000		
To marketing and administrative expenses				(4,950)
Factory overhead rate (based on direct labor hours)	$3.60	$5.50		

Actual hours and costs at the end of the month:

	Dept. 10	Dept. 12	Dept. 76	Dept. 95
Hours worked	1,340	1,030		
Actual factory overhead:				
Variable overhead	$2,700	$2,240	$650	$440
Fixed overhead	1,500	3,000	700	600

The Department 76 cost was allocated to the two producing departments on the basis of the direct labor hours. The Department 95 cost was prorated 50% to the factory and 50% to the general offices. The two producing departments shared the 50% factory allocation on a 40:60 basis, respectively.

For January, the Planning Department scheduled 5,000 units. At the end of the month, sales and production showed the following results:

Sales	4,900 units
Production—completed in both departments	5,200 units

Required:

(1) Compute the budget allowance for each of the two producing departments for January, based on (a) scheduled production hours and (b) actual production hours.
(2) Compute the spending and idle capacity variances for each of the two producing departments, based on actual production hours.
(3) Compute the spending variance for each of the two service departments. (Round all amounts to three decimal places.)

P15-5. Overhead rates; variance analysis in producing and service departments. Roderick Products Co. prepared the following budgeted and actual data:

		Budgeted Data, 19——		Actual Data March, 19——	
Department	Machine Hours	Factory Overhead		Machine Hours	Factory Overhead Cost
		Fixed	Variable		
Machining	22,000	$12,840	$14,400	2,130	$3,586*
Assembly.	28,000	14,100	18,300	2,310	3,341*
Tools and Supplies	-0-	3,600	5,600	-0-	920
Materials Handling	-0-	5,700	6,000	-0-	1,090

* Includes service departments

The fixed cost of the service departments is apportioned to the producing departments on a 60:40 basis and the variable cost at a predetermined rate on the basis of machine hours. Budgeted machine hours are based on normal capacity utilization. Factory overhead is applied on the basis of machine hours.

Required:

(1) Compute the departmental factory overhead rates for the producing departments. (Round all amounts to three decimal places.)
(2) Compute the spending and idle capacity variances of producing and service departments for March. (Round calculations to three decimal places.)

P15-6. Setting sewage treatment usage charge rates. The city of Mineola, Texas, estimates its sewage treatment costs for next year as follows:

Fixed

Debt service cost associated with excess capacity	$350,000
Costs attributable to infiltration and inflow (basically rain water and subsurface ground water):	
Debt service	150,000
Operating and maintenance.	140,000
Administration and office overhead	250,000
Remaining debt service	110,000

Variable

Sewage volume and strength processing costs	$1,000,000

Its user census profile is estimated to be:

User Class	Number of Users	Volume/Strength Units
Wet industry.....................	3	80,000
Commercial and dry industry........	150	50,000
Residential.....................	8,675	120,000
Total	8,828	250,000

Required:

(1) Compute the user charging rate, based on volume/strength units.

(2) Compute the fixed and variable user charging rates, assuming that:

    (a) Excess capacity cost and infiltration and inflow debt service cost are excluded from rates and recovered through property tax, and

    (b) All other fixed costs are charged to industry/commercial users and residential users at a per user ratio of 25:1, which is based on the user's relative size of lateral pipe.

(3) Calculate allocations to user classes, based on (1) and (2), and identify the more equitable method, giving reasons.

CASES

C15-1. Cost responsibility and the attitude of managers. Declining profits compelled the management of the Wilmington Corporation to approach employees to work for production economy and increased productivity. Production managers were promised a monetary incentive based on cost reductions.

The production managers responded with (1) an increased rate of production; (2) a higher rejection rate for quantities of raw materials and parts received from the storeroom; (3) a postponement of repairs and maintenance work; and (4) a reliance on quick emergency repairs to avoid breakdowns.

The repair and maintenance policy is causing serious conflicts. The maintenance supervisor argues that the postponement of certain repairs and the use of emergency repair techniques could result in increased costs later, could reduce the life of machines, and could make them less safe.

Even more serious is the growing bitterness caused by pressures placed on the mainte-nance managers by individual production managers to obtain service. Also, in several instances, some production departments whose production has been halted due to machine breakdown have had to wait while another production department, with an aggressive manager, has received repair service on machines not needed in the current production run. Furthermore, the demand for immediate service sometimes results in substandard repair work.

The production departments are charged with the actual cost of the repairs. A record of the repair work conducted in individual production departments is prepared by the maintenance managers. This record, when completed in the Accounting Department, shows the repair hours, the hourly rate of the maintenance worker, the maintenance overhead charge, and the cost of any parts. The record serves as the basis for the charges to production departments. Production managers have complained about the charging system, claiming that charges depend upon which maintenance worker does the work (hourly rate and efficiency), when the work is done (the production department is charged for the overtime premium), and how careful the worker is in recording the time on the job.

Required:

(1) Identify and briefly explain the motivational factors which may cause friction between the production and maintenance managers.
(2) Develop a plan which revises the system employed to charge production departments for repair costs, so that the production departments' complaints are eliminated or reduced.   (ICMA adapted)

C15-2. Maintenance cost control. Mobile Company is a medium-size manufacturer in a capital-intensive industry. The corporation's profitability is low at the moment and, as a result, investment funds are limited and hiring is restricted. These consequences of the corporation's problems have placed a strain on the plant's repair and maintenance program. The result has been a reduction in work efficiency and cost control effectiveness in the repair and maintenance area.

The controller proposes the installation of a maintenance work order system to overcome these problems. This system would require a work order to be prepared for each repair request and for each regular maintenance activity. The maintenance superintendent would record the estimated time to complete a job and would send one copy of the work order to the department in which the work was to be done. The work order would also serve as a job cost sheet. The actual cost of the parts and supplies used on the job as well as the actual labor costs incurred in completing the job would be recorded directly on the work order. A copy of the completed work order with the actual costs would be the basis of the charge to the department in which the repair or maintenance activity occurred.

The maintenance superintendent opposes the program on the grounds that the added paperwork will be costly and nonproductive.

He states that the departmental clerk who now schedules repair and maintenance activities is doing a good job without all the extra forms the new system would require. The real problem, in the superintendent's opinion, is that the Maintenance Department is understaffed.

Required:

(1) Discuss how the maintenance work order system would aid cost control.
(2) Explain how the maintenance work order system might aid the maintenance superintendent in obtaining authorization to employ more mechanics. (ICMA adapted)

C15-3. Readiness-to-serve and billing rates. The Independent Underwriters Insurance Co. (IUI) established a Systems Department two years ago to implement and operate its own data processing systems. IUI believed that its own department would be more cost effective than the service bureau it had been using.

IUI's three departments—Claims, Records, and Finance—have different requirements with respect to hardware and other capacity-related resources and operating resources. The system was designed to recognize these differing needs. In addition, the system was designed to meet IUI's long-term capacity needs. The excess capacity designed into the system would be sold to outside users until needed by IUI. The estimated resource requirements used to design and implement the system are shown in the following schedule:

	Hardware and Other Capacity-Related Resources	Operating Resources
Records	30%	60%
Claims	50	20
Finance	15	15
Expansion (outside use)	5	5
Total	100%	100%

IUI currently sells the equivalent of its expansion capacity to a few outside clients.

The three user departments have complained about the cost distribution method since the Systems Department was established. The Records Department's monthly costs have been as much as three times the costs experienced with the service bureau. The Finance Department is concerned about the costs distributed to the outside user category because these allocated costs form the basis for the fees billed to the outside clients.

At the time the system became operational, management decided to redistribute total expenses of the Systems Department to the user departments, based on actual computer time used. The actual costs for the first quarter of the current fiscal year were distributed to the user departments as follows:

Department	Percentage Utilization	Amount
Records	60%	$330,000
Claims	20	110,000
Finance	15	82,500
Outside	5	27,500
Total	100%	$550,000

James Dale, IUI's controller, decided to review the distribution method by which the Systems Department's costs have been allocated for the past two years. The additional information he gathered for his review is reported in the three tables on page 467.

Dale has concluded that the method of cost distribution should be changed to show more directly the actual benefits received by the departments. He believes that the hardware and capacity-related costs should be allocated to the user departments in proportion to the planned, long-term needs. Any difference between actual and budgeted hardware costs would not be allocated to the departments but remain with the Systems Department.

The remaining costs for software development and operations would be charged to the user departments, based on actual hours used multiplied by a predetermined hourly rate based on annual budget data. The hourly rates that would be used for the current fiscal year are as follows:

Function	Hourly Rate
Software development	$ 30
Operations:	
Computer related	$200
Input/output related	$ 10

Dale plans to use first quarter activity and cost data to illustrate his recommendations. The recommendations will be presented to the Systems Department and the user departments for their comments and reactions. He then expects to present his recommendations to management for approval.

Required:

(1) Calculate the amount of data processing costs that would be included in the Claims Department's first quarter budget according to the method James Dale has recommended.

(2) Prepare a schedule to show how the actual first quarter costs of the Systems Department would be charged to the users if Dale's recommended method was adopted.

(3) Explain whether Dale's recommended system for charging costs to the user departments will:

(a) Improve cost control in the Systems Department.

(b) Improve planning and cost control in the user departments.

(c) Be a more equitable basis for charging costs to user departments.

(ICMA adapted)

C15-4. Reviewing the reporting structure. McCumber Company employs a computer-based data processing system for maintaining all company records. The present system was developed in stages over the last five years and has been fully operational for the last 24 months.

When the system was being designed, all department heads were asked to specify the types of information and reports they would need for planning and controlling operations. The Systems Department attempted to meet the specifications of each department head. Company management specified that certain other reports be prepared for department heads. During the five years of systems development and operations, there have been changes in the department head positions due to attrition and promotions. New department

Table 1
Systems Department Costs and Activity Levels

| | Annual Budget | | First Quarter | | | |
| | | | Budget | | Actual | |
	Hours	Dollars	Hours	Dollars	Hours	Dollars
Hardware and other capacity-related costs	——	$ 600,000	——	$150,000	——	$155,000
Software development	18,750	562,500	4,725	141,750	4,250	130,000
Operations:						
Computer related.	3,750	750,000	945	189,000	920	187,000
Input/Output related	30,000	300,000	7,560	75,600	7,900	78,000
		$2,212,500		$556,350		$550,000

Table 2
Historical Utilization by Users

| | Hardware and Other Capacity Needs | Software Development | | Operations | | | |
| | | | | Computer | | Input/Output | |
		Range	Average	Range	Average	Range	Average
Records.	30%	0-30%	12%	55-65%	60%	10-30%	20%
Claims.	50	15-60	35	10-25	20	60-80	70
Finance	15	25-75	45	10-25	15	3-10	6
Outside	5	0-25	8	3-8	5	3-10	4
	100%		100%		100%		100%

Table 3
Utilization of Systems Department's Services
in Hours—First Quarter

| | | Operations | |
	Software Development	Computer Related	Input/ Output
Records.	425	552	1,580
Claims.	1,700	184	5,530
Finance	1,700	138	395
Outside	425	46	395
Total	4,250	920	7,900

heads have often requested additional reports according to their specifications; the Systems Department has complied with all of these requests. Consequently, the data processing system has generated a large quantity of reports each reporting period. Occasionally, a report has been discontinued upon request by a department head, but only if it was not a standard report required by executive management.

Company management became concerned about the quality of information being produced by the system, and the Internal Audit Department was asked to evaluate the effectiveness of these reports. The audit staff noted the following reactions to this information overload:

(a) Many department heads would not act on certain reports during periods of peak activity. The department head would let these reports accumulate with the hope of catching up during a subsequent lull.

(b) Some department heads had so many reports that they did not act at all upon the information or made incorrect decisions because of misuse of the information.

(c) Frequently, action required by the nature of the report data was not taken until the department head was reminded by someone who needed the decision. These department heads did not appear to have developed a priority system for acting on the information produced by the data processing system.

(d) Department heads often would develop the information they needed from alternative, independent sources, rather than utilize the reports generated by the data processing system. This was often easier than trying to search among the reports for the needed data.

Required:

(1) Explain whether each of the observed reactions is a functional or dysfunctional behavioral response.

(2) Recommend procedures that the company could employ to eliminate any dysfunctional behavior and to prevent its recurrence.

(ICMA adapted)

Budgeting and Standard Costing

CHAPTER 16

Budgeting: Profits, Sales, Costs, and Expenses

Management sets goals and objectives for the company and then formulates plans for achieving these goals and objectives. The expected financial impacts of management's plans are developed and evaluated via the budgeting process. Once the accepted plans are set into motion, effective control of operations then depends upon cost accounting, which provides management with detailed statements of the actual cost of materials, labor, factory overhead, marketing expenses, and administrative expenses. Comparisons and analyses of these actual costs and expenses with those budgeted enable management to identify deviations from its plans, which in turn provides a basis for controlling operations. Significant deviations signal the need for analysis and corrective action. The reasons for significant deviations from the budget should be determined and appropriate corrective action taken.

This chapter begins with a discussion of the profit planning concept, including long-range and short-range budgets. The principles of budgeting are discussed next, after which a detailed illustration of the periodic budget is presented. The chapter concludes with a discussion of computerized budgeting and prospective financial information for external users. Specific budgets, such as capital expenditures, research and development, and cash budgets, along with other budgeting topics (budgeting for nonmanufacturing business and not-for-profit organizations, zero-base budgeting, PERT and PERT/cost, probabilistic budgets, and flexible budgeting) are discussed in Chapter 17.

■ PROFIT PLANNING

The terms "profit planning" and "budgeting" can be viewed as synonymous. *Profit planning* is a well thought-out operational plan with its financial implications expressed in the form of long- and short-range income statements, balance sheets, and cash and working capital projections. A budget is simply a plan expressed in financial and other quantitative terms. Profit planning is directed to the ultimate objectives of the organization and serves as a guide to maintaining a definite course of activity.

Budgets should be distinguished from forecasts. A profit plan or budget represents the expected profit level or target which management strives to achieve, whereas a forecast is a level of revenue or cost that the organization predicts will occur. The notion of a weather forecast illustrates the distinction: one forecasts the weather; one does not budget the weather.

Sound and intelligent planning of profits is a difficult task, because external forces (such as changes in technology, the actions of competitors, the economy, demographics, consumer tastes and preferences, social attitudes, and political factors) exert strong influences on business. Such forces are not generally controllable by the firm, and the magnitude and direction of changes are often difficult to predict.

Setting Profit Objectives

Fundamentally, three different procedures can be followed in setting profit objectives:

1. The *a priori* method, in which the profit objectives take precedence over the planning process. At the outset, management specifies a given rate of return, which it seeks to realize in the long run by means of planning toward that end.
2. The *a posteriori* method, in which the determination of profit objectives is subordinated to the planning, and the objectives emerge as the product of the planning itself.
3. The *pragmatic* method, in which management uses a profit standard that has been tested empirically and sanctioned by experience. By using a target rate of profit derived from experience, expectations, or comparisons, management establishes a relative profit standard which is considered satisfactory for the company.[1]

In setting profit objectives, management needs to consider the following factors:

1. Profit or loss resulting from a given volume of sales.
2. Sales volume required to recover all consumed costs, to produce a profit adequate to pay dividends on preferred and common stock, and to retain sufficient earnings in the business for future needs.
3. Break-even point.
4. Sales volume that the present operating capacity can produce.
5. Operating capacity necessary to attain the profit objectives.
6. Return on capital employed.

Public expectations with regard to social responsibilities compel companies to consider the social consequences of profit objectives. Increasingly, important actions must be evaluated in a context that includes social as well as economic impacts. Potential social impacts specifically pertain to ". . . environmental pollution, the consumption of nonrenewable resources, and

---

[1]*Research Report No. 42,* "Long-Range Profit Planning" (New York: National Association of Accountants, 1964), pp. 60-65.

other ecological factors; the rights of individuals and groups; the maintenance of public service; public safety; health and education; and many other social concerns."[2]

Long-Range Profit Planning

Business has become increasingly aware of a need to develop long-range profit plans. *Long-range planning* has been defined as "the continuous process of making present decisions systematically and, with the best possible knowledge of their futurity, organizing systematically the efforts needed to carry out these decisions, and measuring the results of these decisions against the expectations through organized, systematic feedback."[3] Long-range plans are not stated in precise terms, nor are they expected to be completely coordinated future plans. They deal rather with specific areas such as sales, capital expenditures, extensive research and development activities, and financial requirements.

In long-range profit planning, management attempts to find the most probable course of events. Of greatest importance, however, is the ability to be flexible and adaptable to changing conditions. Long-range planning does not eliminate risk, for risk taking is the essence of economic activity. An end result of successful long-range profit planning is a capacity to take a greater risk, which is a fundamental way to improve entrepreneurial performance.

Market trends and economic factors, inflation, growth of population, personal consumption expenditures, and indexes of industrial production form the background for long-range planning. Quantitative and dollar sales estimates for a three- to five-year forecast may be developed from this information. A prospective income statement can then be prepared, showing anticipated sales, fixed and variable costs (factory, marketing, and administrative), contribution margin, and operating income by years. A balance sheet by years should indicate anticipated cash balances, inventory levels, accounts receivable balances, and liabilities. This financial long-range plan might also be supported by a cash flow statement.

The rate of return on capital (total assets) employed is an important statistic in long-range profit planning and in setting profit objectives. To measure the effectiveness with which management is likely to use the assets, rates of return are computed for each individual year covered in the long-range plan. These figures show whether planned increases in total net income will keep pace with increases in assets at the corporate as well as divisional or operating levels. Though return on capital employed is the basic measure of profit performance (discussed in detail in Chapter 25), companies typically use several other measures, such as the ratio of net income to sales, the ratio of sales to shareholders' capital, and earnings per common share.[4]

---

[2]Robert K. Elliott, "Social Accounting and Corporate Decision-Making," *Management Controls*, Vol. XXI, No. 1, p. 2.

[3]Peter F. Drucker, "Long-Range Planning," *Management Science*, Vol. 5, No. 3, p. 240.

[4]*Research Report No. 42, loc. cit.*

Short-Range Plans or Budgets

Management's long-range plans can only be achieved through successful long-run profit performance, which requires growth and a reasonably high and stable level of profit. Long-range plans with their future expectancy of profits and growth, however, must be incorporated into a shorter-range budget for both planning and control of the contemplated course of action. Although one year is the usual planning period, the short-range budget may cover periods of three, six, or twelve months, depending upon the nature of the business. For efficient planning, the annual budget should be expanded into an eighteen-month budget, allowing for a three-month period at the end of the old year, twelve months for the regular budget period, and an additional three months into the third year. These overlapping months are needed in order to allow transition from year to year and to make adjustments based on prior months' experience. The budget period should:

1. Be divided into months.
2. Be long enough to complete production of the various products.
3. Cover at least one entire seasonal cycle for a business of a seasonal nature.
4. Be long enough to allow for the financing of production well in advance of actual needs.
5. Coincide with the financial accounting period to compare actual results with budget estimates.

Some organizations use a continuous budget, by which a month or quarter in the future is added as the month or quarter just ended is dropped, and the budget for the entire period is revised and updated as needed. This procedure forces management to think continuously about its short-range plans.

Advantages of Profit Planning

Profit planning, or budgeting, has the following benefits and advantages:

1. Profit planning provides a disciplined approach to problem identification and problem solving. Management is obliged to systematically study and evaluate every aspect of the business in developing the periodic budget. This affords the opportunity to periodically reappraise every facet of operations and re-examine the company's basic policies and procedures.
2. Profit planning provides a sense of direction and purpose to all levels of management. It helps to develop an atmosphere of profit-mindedness throughout the organization and to encourage an attitude of cost-consciousness and maximum resource utilization.
3. Profit planning enhances coordination of business activity. It provides a way to coordinate the efforts of all segments of the business in achieving the goals and objectives of the firm. The budgeting process

makes it possible to spot and eliminate bottlenecks before they occur and to channel capital and effort into the most profitable activities.

4. Profit planning provides a vehicle to enlist the ideas and cooperation of all levels of management. The skill and knowledge of all members of the management team should be utilized in developing the most effective plan possible. Participation by personnel at all levels not only brings the best ideas to light, but it also provides a way to communicate objectives and gain support for the final plan. Managers who participate in the budget process learn what is expected of them and develop a sense of commitment to work to achieve the budget goals they help establish.

5. The budget provides a yardstick or standard that can be used to evaluate actual performance and gauge the managerial judgment and ability of individual executives. This in turn encourages managers to perform efficiently, thereby increasing output and reducing cost.

Limitations of Profit Planning

While the advantages of profit planning are unquestionably impressive and far-reaching, the following limitations and pitfalls should be mentioned:

1. Forecasting is not an exact science; a certain amount of judgment is present in any estimate. Since a budget must be based on forecasts of future events, a revision or modification of the budget should be made when variations from the estimates warrant a change of plans. Flexibility should be built into the budget wherever possible, and management should keep the effect of forecast error in mind when using the budget as an evaluation tool. If actual performance deviates substantially from the budget, the reason may simply be the result of a forecasting error.

2. The budget could focus a manager's attention on goals (e.g., high production, high credit sales, etc.) which are not necessarily in harmony with the organization's overall objectives. Thus care must be used in setting goals in order to properly channel the managers' efforts. To accomplish this task, managers must be motivated to strive for attainment of their personal objectives in congruence with the organization's objectives. A budgetary system is inadequate whenever it motivates an individual to take an action that is not in the best interest of the organization. Regardless of how sophisticated budgetary systems become, their effectiveness ultimately depends upon how they influence human behavior and attitudes.[5]

3. A profit planning program must have the commitment of top management and the cooperation and participation of all members of the

[5]Paul J. Carruth and Thurrell O. McClendon, "How Supervisors React to 'Meeting the Budget' Pressure," *Management Accounting,* Vol. LXVI, No. 5, p. 54.

management team in order to be successful. The basis for success is executive management's sustained adherence to and enthusiasm for the profit plan. Too often a profit plan has failed because executive management has paid only lip service to its execution. If top management does not continually support the budget process, lower level management will quickly begin to view the budget process as a meaningless exercise and, as a result, the quality of the budget will deteriorate. Also, involvement of all levels of management is needed to avoid the feeling at lower levels that the budget is being imposed on them without their participation.

4. Excessive use of the budget as an evaluation tool can result in disfunctional behavior. Managers who are to be evaluated may attempt to build slack into the budget so that they will look good when final results are compared to the budget. This in turn can result in mediocre levels of performance and could result in coordination inefficiencies between segments of the business.

5. Profit planning does not eliminate or take over the role of administration. Executives should not feel restricted by the budget. Rather, the profit plan is designed to provide detailed information that allows the executives to operate with strength and vision toward achievement of the organization's objectives.

6. Installation takes time. Management often becomes impatient and loses interest because it expects too much too soon. The budget must first be sold to the responsible people; and they, in turn, must then be guided, trained, and educated in the fundamental steps, methods, and purposes of a budgetary system.

■ PRINCIPLES OF BUDGETING

A company's organization chart and its chart of accounts form the basic framework on which to build a coordinated and efficient system of managerial planning and budgetary control. The organization chart defines the functional responsibilities of executives and thereby justifies their budgets. Although final responsibility for the budget rests with executive management, all managers are responsible for the preparation and execution of their departmental budgets. If a budgetary control system is to be successful, these managers must fully cooperate and must understand their role in making the budget system successful. The budget must be the joint effort of many people—a working document that forms the basis for action.

The Budget Committee

The budgeting process usually is directed by a budget committee, which is composed of the sales manager, the production manager, the chief engineer, the treasurer, and the controller. The principal functions of the budget committee are to:

1. Decide on general policies.
2. Request, receive, and review individual budget estimates.
3. Suggest revisions in individual budget estimates.
4. Approve budgets and later revisions.
5. Receive and analyze budget reports.
6. Recommend actions designed to improve efficiency where necessary.

In performing these functions, the budget committee becomes a management committee. It is a powerful force in coordinating the various activities of the business and in controlling operations.

Budget Development and Implementation

The procedure used in developing a budget may be as important as its content and should include these fundamental principles:

1. Provide adequate guidance so that all management levels are working on the same assumptions, targeted objectives, and agenda. All managers should understand the limitations and constraints of their participation and the bounds of their decision making. Participants should be told, prior to the time the budget is established, how their activities will fit into the entire organization and what constraints will be placed upon them and their activities by upper-level administrative decisions.

2. Encourage participation in the budgeting process at each level within the organization. Structure the activity of developing the budget to involve the people who will be responsible for implementing the budget and who will be rewarded according to its accomplishments. The participation of those who are responsible for implementation will improve the quality of the budget by utilizing the widest possible base of expertise. In addition, managers who are responsible for implementation will gain understanding and commitment by participating in the development of the budget.

3. Structure the climate of budget preparation to eliminate anxiety and defensiveness. Individuals should have the freedom and authority to influence and accept their own performance levels, and should assume the responsibility for accomplishment. Budget preparation should be oriented to the problems and opportunities of the participants in order to reduce their anxiety and, thereby, alleviate their desire to incorporate slack into the budget.

4. Structure the preparation of the budget so that there is a reasonably high probability of successful attainment of objectives. When challenging but attainable objectives are achieved, feelings of success, confidence, and satisfaction are produced and aspiration levels are raised. If objectives are not accomplished, the reasons for this failure should

be clear. A careful distinction should be made between controllable factors for which individuals should be responsible and for uncontrollable factors for which they are not.

5. Evaluate numerous sets of assumptions in developing the budget. This iterative process is facilitated by the use of computers (discussed later in this chapter) and probabilities (discussed in Chapter 17).

If the proper procedure for developing a budget has been followed, implementation difficulties are minimized. Proper budget implementation requires adherence to the following principles:

1. Establish rewards and reward contingencies that will lead to achieving the organizational objectives. Too often, the budgeting process does not provide sufficient rewards to induce employees to accomplish organizational objectives.

2. The organization should focus on rewarding achievement rather than punishing failure. Feelings of success or failure largely determine attitudes toward the budget and the level of performance to which employees will aspire.

3. Provide rapid feedback on the performance of each work team or individual. This principle necessitates the use of reports and reporting procedures that are understandable to workers and supervisors at the department level, so that they can analyze their results and initiate corrective action.[6]

Budgeting and Human Behavior

Anyone who is charged with the task of creating a budget and establishing budget figures, particularly of department overhead, is aware of the irrational and often obstinate behavior of certain supervisors with respect to the contemplated budget program.[7] In some firms, budgeting is perhaps the most unpopular management and/or accounting device for planning and control.

In recent years, considerable attention has been given to the behavioral implications of providing managers with the data required for planning, coordinating, and controlling activities. Cost accounting and budgeting play an important role in influencing individual and group behavior at all of the various stages of the management process including: (1) setting goals, (2) informing individuals what they must do to contribute to the accomplishment of these goals, (3) motivating desirable performance, (4) evaluating performance, and (5) suggesting when corrective action should be taken. In short, accountants cannot ignore the behavioral sciences (psychology, social-

---

[6]J. Owen Cherrington and David J. Cherrington, "Budget Games for Fun and Frustration," *Management Accounting*, Vol. LVII, No. 7, p. 32.

[7]Chris Argyris, *The Impact of Budgets on People* (New York: Financial Executives Research Foundation; formerly Controllership Foundation, Inc., 1952).

psychology, and sociology) because the "information for decision making" function of accounting is essentially a behavioral function.[8]

For budget building, James L. Pierce advises:

> *In the field of cost control, use the budget as a tool to be placed in the foreman's hands—not as a club to be held over their heads. To implement this rule, it may be a good idea to design an educational program. Meetings attended by line and staff supervisors may prove an effective vehicle. Cost reduction must be placed on the basis of mutual effort toward a common aim. The creation of this atmosphere is an essential, definite step in budget practice.[9]*

An individual manager's attitude toward the budget will depend greatly upon the existing good relationship within the management group. If properly guided by the company plan, with an opportunity for increased compensation, greater satisfaction, and eventually promotion, the middle and lower management group can achieve remarkable results. On the other hand, a discordant management group, unwilling to accept the budget's underlying figures, can perform so poorly that top management will be compelled "to defer trying the planning and control idea until it has put its house in order."[10] Peirce further states that:

> *We are beginning to learn that no tool can be used effectively unless the hand that guides it is rightly motivated. Like all other techniques of business, the budget should be a door open to more satisfying and profitable work—not an instrument of torture.*
>
> *Then it will be known that what you can do without a budget you can do better with one. It will be seen that the entire planning and control procedure is a device for freeing men to do their best work—not a machine of restriction and condemnation.*
>
> *Planning is but another word for the vision that sees a creative achievement before it is manifest. Control is but a name for direction. The genius of management cannot fail to turn the budget idea finally into positive channels, so that people individually as well as business leadership generally will reap the harvest that it promises.[11]*

The remarks quoted from Pierce's article indicate that no budget can be successful as long as people are unwilling to accept it. The problem of motivating a company's personnel, however, is difficult to solve. As pointed out in Chapter 10, pay incentives for factory workers do not necessarily lead to greater productivity. Motivational requirements that have been suggested include the following:

1. A compensation system that builds and maintains a clearly understood relationship between results and rewards.
2. A system for performance appraisal that employees understand with regard to their individual effectiveness and key results, their tasks and

---

[8]For references explaining behavioral implications of accounting in some detail, see William J. Bruns, Jr., and Don T. DeCoster, *Accounting and Its Behavioral Implications* (New York: McGraw-Hill Book Company, 1969) and Edwin H. Caplan, *Management Accounting and Behavioral Science* (Reading, Mass.: Addison-Wesley Publishing Co., Inc., 1971).

[9]Reprinted by permission of *Harvard Business Review*. An excerpt from "The Budget Comes of Age" by James L. Pierce, Vol. 32, No. 3 (May/June 1954), p. 65. Copyright 1954 by the President and Fellows of Harvard College; all rights reserved.

[10]*Ibid.*, pp. 58-66.

[11]*Ibid.*, p. 66.

their responsibilities, their degree and span of influence in decision making, as well as the time allowed to judge their results.

3. A system of communication that allows employees to query their superiors with trust and honest communication.

4. A system of promotion that generates and sustains employee faith in its validity and judgment.

5. A system of employee support through coaching, counseling, and career planning.

6. A system that not only considers company objectives, but also employees' skills and capacities.

7. A system that will not settle for mediocrity, but which reaches for realistic and attainable standards, stressing improvement and providing an environment in which the concept of excellence can grow.[12]

■ THE COMPLETE PERIODIC BUDGET

A complete set of budgets generally consists of:

1. A sales budget.
2. Estimates of inventory and production requirements.
3. Budgets of materials, labor, and factory overhead, combined into a cost of goods manufactured and sold schedule.
4. Budgets for marketing and administrative expenses.
5. Estimates of other income and expense items and income tax.
6. A budgeted income statement.
7. A budget of capital expenditures and of research and development expenditures.
8. A cash receipts and disbursements budget.
9. A budgeted balance sheet showing the estimated financial position of the company at the end of the budget period.

Items 1 through 5 form the basis for preparing the budgeted income statement. They, along with items 6 and 9, are discussed and illustrated in the remainder of this chapter, while items 7 and 8 are covered in the first portion of Chapter 17.

The following data are used to illustrate the budget components that comprise the income statement. As each budget component is discussed, the relevant data are used to illustrate the preparation of the related budget schedule. Subsequent schedules are cross-referenced to show the linkage between the various budget parts, building to the budgeted income statement. Assume that Franklin Company manufactures three products, A, B, and C, which are marketed in two territories, the Midwest and the Southwest. The production departments are designated Cutting, Assembling, and Finishing.

[12]Paul E. Sussman, "Motivating Financial Personnel," *The Journal of Accountancy*, Vol. 141, No. 2, p. 80.

The management and the department heads have made the following estimates for the coming year ending December 31:

1. Sales:

Product	Midwest	Southwest	Sales Price
A	4,000 units	3,000 units	$200 per unit
B	6,000	5,000	150
C	9,000	6,000	100

2. Inventories:
   Materials:

Material	Beginning Inventory Units	Ending Inventory Units	Unit Cost
X	30,000	40,000	$ 1.00
Y	10,000	12,000	14.00
Z	2,000	2,500	2.50

Work in process: None at the beginning or end of the period.
Finished goods (fifo):

Product	Beginning Inventory Units	Unit Cost	Ending Inventory Units
A	200	$125.70	250
B	400	82.50	200
C	500	64.00	400

3. Materials quantity requirements and unit cost:

	Material		
	X	Y	Z
Product A	12	5	2
Product B	8	3	1
Product C	6	2	1
Materials unit cost	$1.00	$14.00	$2.50

4. Labor time requirements and rate per hour:

	Cutting	Assembling	Finishing
Product A.	.500 hour	2.500 hours	.800 hour
Product B.	.375	2.000	.500
Product C	.375	1.750	.500
Rate per hour	$8.00	$10.00	$9.00

5. Unit overhead rates:

Product	Cutting	Assembling	Finishing	Total
A	$3.00	$7.50	$4.80	$15.30
B	2.25	6.00	3.00	11.25
C	2.25	5.25	3.00	10.50

6. Marketing expenses: $450,000.
   Administrative expenses: $270,000.
   Other income: $70,000.
   Other expenses: $105,000.
   Income tax rate: 40%.

To achieve a concise yet comprehensive illustration, only annual data are shown. As previously noted, however, monthly budget details are not only desirable but often necessary. Also, customer group classifications for sales are omitted, and factory overhead, marketing and administrative expenses, and other income and expense items are not shown in detail.

Sales Budget

One of the most important elements in a budgetary control system is a realistic sales estimate that is based on analyses of past sales and the present market. Yet the sales variable is often the budget component that is the most difficult to predict with reasonable precision. The demand for an entity's products or services normally depends on forces and factors largely beyond the scope of management's control. In most instances, this uncertainty makes expected sales the focal point of the planning process.[13]

The task of preparing the sales budget is usually approached from two different angles: (1) judging and evaluating external influences and (2) considering internal influences. These two influences are brought together in a workable sales budget. External influences include the general trend of industrial activity, actions of competitors, governmental policies, cyclical phases of the nation's economy, price-level expectations, purchasing power of the population, population shift, and changes in buying habits and modes of living. Internal influences are sales trends, factory capacities, new products, plant expansion, seasonal products, sales estimates, and establishment of quotas for salespeople and sales territories. The profit desired by the company is a highly significant consideration.

The annual sales budget on page 482 for Franklin Company, detailed by product and by territory, is prepared from the data on page 480.

Estimating Sales. The preparation of sales estimates usually is the responsibility of the marketing manager, assisted by individual salespeople and market research personnel. Because of the many dissimilarities in the marketing of products, actual methods used to estimate sales vary widely. One method used by many companies is the preparation of sales estimates by individual salespeople. All salespeople supply their district managers with estimates of probable sales in their territories. These estimates are consolidated and adjusted by the district marketing manager and then forwarded to the general marketing manager, who makes further adjustments. These adjustments in-

---

[13]Eugene A. Imhoff, Jr., *Sales Forecasting Systems* (Montvale, N.J.: National Association of Accountants, 1986), pp. 5-6.

Franklin Company
Sales Budget
For the Year Ending December 31, 19—

	Territories		
	Midwest	Southwest	Total
Product A			
Units	4,000	3,000	7,000
Unit price	$200	$200	$200
Total	$ 800,000	$ 600,000	$1,400,000
Product B			
Units	6,000	5,000	11,000
Unit price	$150	$150	$150
Total	$ 900,000	$ 750,000	$1,650,000
Product C			
Units	9,000	6,000	15,000
Unit price	$100	$100	$100
Total	$ 900,000	$ 600,000	$1,500,000
Total sales	$2,600,000	$1,950,000	$4,550,000

Schedule 1

clude allowances for expected economic conditions and competitive conditions of which salespeople are unaware, as well as allowances for expected canceled orders and sales returns that salespeople would likely disregard because their estimates are based on the orders they expect to procure. During the budget preparation process, it is not unusual for sales estimates to be revised a number of times. The ultimate sales estimates tend to be improved when forecasts from several sources, such as a group of managers, are averaged.

In estimating sales as well as expenditures, the tendency to over- or underestimate plans must be recognized. Individuals tend to be overly pessimistic or optimistic in setting goals and in making plans. Therefore, the budgeting system should be designed to monitor this tendency in order to keep goals and plans within reasonable bounds.

In most large organizations, the estimating procedure usually starts with known factors; namely, (1) the company's sales of past years broken down by product groups and profit margins, (2) industry or trade sales volume and perhaps profits, and (3) unusual factors influencing sales in the past. The company's past sales figures often require a restudy or reclassification due to changes in products, profit margins, competition, sales areas, distribution methods, or changes within the industry. Industry or trade sales and profits are secured from trade associations, trade publications, and various business magazines. For some industries, the U.S. Department of Commerce publishes information that is useful as background data. Unusual factors influencing past sales are inventory conditions, public economic sentiment, competition, and customer relations.

Charting a company's volume in units of various products for a three- to five-year period and comparing it with the industry's volume will disclose the company's sales trend and will pinpoint factors that affected past sales. However, a recent study indicated that, for most companies, the use of historical sales data is generally limited to the most recent two years. Thus the amount of time-series data used is reduced. The study also finds that managers tend to use current and prospective information in preference to historical trends, even though there is research evidence that time-series models are often good predictors of future sales.[14]

Although the feeling frequently exists that the sales budget is a crystal-ball area, a sound basis for estimating future sales often can be established by using time-series models and by applying probability analysis techniques to the consideration of general business conditions, the industry's prospects, the company's potential share of the total industry market, and the plans of competitive companies.

Seasonal Variations. When the annual sales estimate has been approved, it must be placed on an operating period basis, which is usually a month. The monthly sales budget should show seasonal sales patterns for each product manufactured. These patterns are evident from the company's experience and from records of a product's trend during past years. Any fluctuations in a trend should be considered, as well as the causes of fluctuations, such as customs or habits based on local or national traits, climate, holidays, or even the influences of other companies in the firm's own industry.

The seasonal or operating sales budget is of great help in judging the records of individual salespeople. Averaging sales over a budget period is not sufficient to assure success of a sales program. Too many times, low sales in one month have been excused with the optimistic statement that sales in the following month will make up the difference. When this does not happen, the sales budget and the entire budget plan suffer.

Sales Budget on a Territory and Customer Basis. A sales budget should not only be placed on a monthly basis for each product, but should also be classified by territories or districts and by types of customers. The customer classification should show sales to jobbers, wholesalers, retailers, institutions, governmental agencies, schools and colleges, foreign businesses, etc. Such a breakdown indicates the contribution of each territory and customer class to total sales and profits. An analysis of this type often reveals that certain territories or classes of customers are not given sufficient attention by sales managers and sales representatives. A detailed sales budget can be a strong means for analyzing possible new trade outlets. It assists in identifying reasons for a drop in sales, in investigating such a decrease, and in taking remedial steps.

Estimating Production and Inventory Requirements. Prior to the final acceptance of a sales budget, the factory's capacity to produce the estimated quantities must be determined. The production level should maintain inventories that are sufficient to fulfill periodic sales requirements.

---

[14]*Ibid.*, pp. 20, 36.

If factory capacity is available, production should be planned at a level that will keep workers and equipment operating all year. Serious fluctuations in employment are expensive and do not promote good labor relations. If the sales budget indicates that factory employment in certain months would fall below a desirable level, it would be necessary to attempt to increase sales volume or increase inventories. At the same time, the investment in inventories should be held to a level consistent with sound financial policy. If estimated sales are higher than available capacity, the purchase or rental of new machinery and factory space must be considered as a means of increasing plant capacity.

Sales Estimate Follow-Up. Follow-up review should occur at intervals influenced by the frequency of change in the company, its industry, and general economic conditions. The review should determine (1) the accuracy of past estimates, (2) the location of the major estimation errors, (3) the best method by which to update estimates, and (4) the steps needed for improvement of the making and monitoring of future estimates.

Past errors indicate the reliance that can be placed on sales estimates and provide insight into the company and the personal bias built into the estimate. When estimates are monitored, comparison with actual results should extend beyond financial results to include consideration of the underlying factors and key assumptions. Such comparisons might require the monitoring of unit sales volumes, prices, production rates, backlogs of sales orders, changes in capacity, and economic indicators.

Production Budget

The production budget deals with the scheduling of operations, the determination of volume, and the establishment of maximum and minimum quantities of finished goods inventories. It provides the basis for preparing the budgets of materials, labor, and factory overhead.

A production budget is stated in physical units. As shown in the following illustration, this budget is the budgeted sales quantity adjusted for any inventory changes.

Franklin Company
Production Budget
For the Year Ending December 31, 19--

	Products		
	A	B	C
Units required to meet sales budget (Schedule 1)............	7,000	11,000	15,000
Add desired ending inventory.............................	250	200	400
Total units required.....................................	7,250	11,200	15,400
Less beginning inventory.................................	200	400	500
Planned production for the year..........................	7,050	10,800	14,900

Schedule 2

JUST-IN-TIME

If there is work in process inventory, the equivalent number of such units in the ending inventory would be added to, and units in the beginning inventory would be subtracted from, the above calculations in order to determine the units to be produced. In a just-in-time system, work in process inventory may be so small that changes in the level of work in process inventory are ignored in preparing the production budget.

The production budget, like other budgets, may be detailed by months or quarters as well as annually. For comparison with actual production, the detailed budget should be broken down by work stations. The nature of this division will be determined by plant layout, type of production, and other factors.

For a company that does not manufacture standard products but produces only on orders, a detailed production budget may not be possible. In special-order work, the primary problem is to be prepared for production when orders are received. Work must be routed and scheduled through the factory, so that delays are prevented and production facilities are fully utilized.

No division of a manufacturing business has made so much progress in scientific management as the production department. Constant effort is directed toward devising new ways and shortcuts that will lead to more efficient production and cost savings which will be reflected in earnings.

Manufacturing Budgets

With the forecast sales translated into physical units in the production budget, the estimated manufacturing costs essential to the sales and production program can be computed. Detailed budgets are prepared for direct materials and direct labor in order to identify these costs with products and responsible managers. Factory overhead is budgeted in detail by responsibility centers or departments. This budget information becomes part of the master budget to be used as a standard or target against which the performance of the individual department is judged and evaluated.

Direct Materials Budget. The budgeting of direct materials specifies the quantity and cost of materials required to produce the predetermined units of finished goods. It (1) leads to the determination of quantities of materials that must be on hand, (2) permits the purchasing department to set up a purchasing schedule that assures delivery of materials when needed, and (3) establishes a means by which the treasurer can include in the cash budget the necessary funds for periodic purchases as well as for all other cash payments. Although the materials budget usually deals only with direct materials, these budgeting procedures are also applicable to supplies and indirect materials that are included in the factory overhead budget and the commercial expenses budget.

The schedules for Franklin Company on pages 486 and 487 consist of (1) the direct materials budget expressed in units required for production (Schedule 3), (2) the purchases budget, specifying inventory levels and units as well as the cost of purchases (Schedule 4), and (3) the calculation of the cost of materials required for production (Schedule 5).

The production planning department determines the quantity and type of materials required for the various products manufactured by a company. Most companies have standard parts lists and bills of materials which detail all materials requirements. These requirements are given to the purchasing department, which sets up a buying schedule. This schedule is based on the

JUST-IN-TIME

objective of providing sufficient materials, without overstocking, and entails an increasing trend by manufacturers to minimize inventory by utilizing a

Franklin Company
Direct Materials Budget in Units
For the Year Ending December 31, 19—

	Materials		
	X	Y	Z
Product A			
Units of A to be manufactured (Schedule 2)............	7,050	7,050	7,050
Materials quantity required per unit of A...............	12	5	2
Units of materials required.........................	84,600	35,250	14,100
Product B			
Units of B to be manufactured (Schedule 2)............	10,800	10,800	10,800
Materials quantity required per unit of B...............	8	3	1
Units of materials required.........................	86,400	32,400	10,800
Product C			
Units of C to be manufactured (Schedule 2)............	14,900	14,900	14,900
Materials quantity required per unit of C...............	6	2	1
Units of materials required.........................	89,400	29,800	14,900
Total units of materials required	260,400	97,450	39,800

Schedule 3

Franklin Company
Purchases Budget
For the Year Ending December 31, 19—

	Materials			
	X	Y	Z	Total
Units required for production (Schedule 3)	260,400	97,450	39,800	
Add desired ending inventory........	40,000	12,000	2,500	
Quantity required..................	300,400	109,450	42,300	
Less beginning inventory	30,000	10,000	2,000	
Units to be purchased..............	270,400	99,450	40,300	
Unit cost	$1.00	$14.00	$2.50	
Total cost of purchases.............	$270,400	$1,392,300	$100,750	$1,763,450

Schedule 4

Franklin Company
Cost of Materials Required for Production
For the Year Ending December 31, 19—

| | Materials | | | |
	X	Y	Z	Total
Product A				
Units of materials required for production (Schedule 3)	84,600	35,250	14,100	
Unit cost......................	$1.00	$14.00	$2.50	
Total	$ 84,600	$ 493,500	$35,250	$ 613,350
Product B				
Units of materials required for production (Schedule 3)	86,400	32,400	10,800	
Unit cost......................	$1.00	$14.00	$2.50	
Total	$ 86,400	$ 453,600	$27,000	567,000
Product C				
Units of materials required for production (Schedule 3)	89,400	29,800	14,900	
Unit cost......................	$1.00	$14.00	$2.50	
Total	$ 89,400	$ 417,200	$37,250	543,850
Total cost of materials required for production	$260,400	$1,364,300	$99,500	$1,724,200

Schedule 5

just-in-time inventory stocking policy. In preparing a buying schedule, the purchasing department must consider changes in possible delivery promises by the supplier and changes in the rate of materials consumption because of unforeseen circumstances. In a just-in-time materials inventory system, materials inventory may be so small that inventory changes can be ignored in preparing the direct materials budget. In such a situation, there may be no separate accounting for a materials inventory; instead, Materials and Work in Process may be combined into a single asset account.

Direct Labor Budget. The annual budget is the principal tool for the overall planning for human resources. When the budget is completed and approved, it should include a human resources plan that is coordinated with planned sales and production activities as well as the profit goal.

The direct labor budget, based on specifications drawn up by product engineers, guides the personnel department in determining the number and type of workers needed. If the labor force has been with the firm for several years and if the production schedule does not call for additional workers, the task of the personnel department is rather easy. If an increase in the labor force is required, the personnel department must make plans in advance to assure the availability of workers. Frequently, the personnel department must provide a training program which provides workers to the production department at the proper time. When workers are to be laid off, the personnel department must prepare a list of those affected, giving due recognition to skill and seniority rights. In many companies, this schedule is prepared in collaboration with union representatives in order to protect employees from any injustice or hardship.

For each type of labor, the hours or the number of workers must be translated into dollar values. Established labor rates as agreed upon in union contracts generally are used. If conditions indicate that labor rates might change, the new rates should be used, so that the financial budget reflects the most recent figures available. The following direct labor budget for Franklin Company is prepared from the data on page 480:

Franklin Company
Direct Labor Budget
For the Year Ending December 31, 19—

	Cutting	Assembling	Finishing	Total
Product A				
Hours required per unit	.500	2.500	.800	
Units to be manufactured (Schedule 2).	7,050	7,050	7,050	
Hours of labor required	3,525	17,625	5,640	
Labor cost per hour	$8	$10	$9	
Total.	$ 28,200	$176,250	$ 50,760	$255,210
Product B				
Hours required per unit	.375	2.000	.500	
Units to be manufactured (Schedule 2).	10,800	10,800	10,800	
Hours of labor required	4,050	21,600	5,400	
Labor cost per hour	$8	$10	$9	
Total.	$ 32,400	$216,000	$ 48,600	297,000
Product C				
Hours required per unit	.375	1.750	.500	
Units to be manufactured (Schedule 2).	14,900	14,900	14,900	
Hours of labor required	5,587.5	26,075	7,450	
Labor cost per hour	$8	$10	$9	
Total.	$ 44,700	$260,750	$ 67,050	372,500
Total direct labor cost	$105,300	$653,000	$166,410	$924,710

Schedule 6

Indirect labor is included in the factory overhead budget and consists of such employees as helpers in producing departments, maintenance workers, crane operators, materials clerks, and receiving clerks. In addition, if direct labor is not traceable to the products manufactured, as is often the case in fully automated manufacturing plants, no separate direct labor budget would be prepared. Instead, the cost of employees who operate production machinery and equipment would be included in the factory overhead budget, along with indirect labor. In such a system, direct labor is charged to products via the factory overhead rate. Labor requirements for marketing and administrative activities must be budgeted as part of the commercial expenses budget.

Factory Overhead Budget. The detailed factory overhead budget is prepared on the basis of the chart of accounts, which properly classifies expense accounts and details the various cost centers for planning and control and assignment of factory overhead to product cost. As discussed and illustrated in Chapter 14, expenses are grouped according to:

1. Natural expense classification, such as indirect materials and supplies, indirect labor, freight, light, and power.
2. Departmental or functional classification according to the producing or service department or cost center in which the expense originated.
3. Behavior, i.e., variable and fixed, using the cost behavior analysis tools described in Chapter 12.

The natural expense (primary account) classification alone is not useful for budget purposes, since expenses usually are incurred by various departments. By classifying expenses according to individual departments, the value and importance of budgetary control for expenses becomes significant.

Preparation of any expense budget should be guided by the principle that every expense is chargeable to a department, and that an executive, department head, or supervisor should be held accountable and responsible for expenses incurred. Those expenses for which the department supervisor is directly responsible should be identified in the supervisor's budget. Allocated expenses for which the supervisor has little or no responsibility also should be identified.

If department supervisors accept the budget, they are more likely to cooperate in its execution. Therefore, supervisors should be asked to prepare their own estimates of departmental expenses, based on the department's projected activity for the budget period. These estimates and any revisions should be reviewed and coordinated with other budgets before they are incorporated into the overall budget.

Once the factory overhead budgets for the production departments have been prepared, including service department cost allocations, factory overhead rates can be determined (as illustrated in Chapter 14). These rates then are used to estimate factory overhead for the units of the products to be manufactured as determined from the production budget. For Franklin Company, these costs are shown in Schedule 7.

Beginning and Ending Inventories. Not only must inventory quantities be determined for materials, work in process, and finished goods, but the inventories must be costed in order to make available the necessary information leading to preparation of a budgeted cost of goods manufactured and sold statement and ultimately to an income statement and a balance sheet. For Franklin Company, beginning and ending inventory quantities and costs are summarized on Schedule 8. Observe that the ending inventory unit costs for finished goods are the summation of estimates for direct materials, direct labor, and factory overhead.

Budgeted Cost of Goods Manufactured and Sold Statement. This statement requires no new estimates. Figures taken from various manufacturing sched-

Franklin Company
Factory Overhead Budget
For the Year Ending December 31, 19—

	Cutting	Assembling	Finishing	Total
Product A				
Units to be manufactured (Schedule 2)..	7,050	7,050	7,050	
Estimated departmental factory overhead per unit.............	$3.00	$7.50	$4.80	
Total.......................	$21,150	$ 52,875	$ 33,840	$107,865
Product B				
Units to be manufactured (Schedule 2)..	10,800	10,800	10,800	
Estimated departmental factory overhead per unit...............	$2.25	$6.00	$3.00	
Total.......................	$24,300	$ 64,800	$ 32,400	121,500
Product C				
Units to be manufactured (Schedule 2)..	14,900	14,900	14,900	
Estimated departmental factory overhead per unit..............	$2.25	$5.25	$3.00	
Total.......................	$33,525	$ 78,225	$ 44,700	156,450
Total factory overhead	$78,975	$195,900	$110,940	$385,815

Schedule 7

ules are arranged in the form of a cost of goods manufactured and sold
statement, illustrated on Schedule 9. Source schedules are referenced to indicate
the linkage with the budget components previously discussed and illustrated.

Budgeting Commercial Expenses

The company's chart of accounts is the basis for budgetary control of
commercial expenses, which include both marketing (selling or distribution)
and administrative expenses. These expenses may be classified by primary
accounts and by functions.

Budgeting and analyzing commercial expenses by primary accounts is the
simplest method of classification. This method stresses the nature or the type
of expenditure, such as salaries, commissions, repairs, light and heat, rent,
telephone and telegraph, postage, advertising, travel expenses, sales promotion, entertainment, delivery expense, freight out, insurance, donations, depreciation, taxes, and interest. As expenses are incurred, they are recorded in
primary expense accounts, posted to ledger accounts, and then taken directly
to the income statement. No further allocation is made. At the end of an
accounting period, actual expenses are compared with either budgeted expenses or expenses of the previous month or year.

To control commercial expenses effectively, it is necessary to group them
by functional activities or operating units. Classification by function emphasizes departmental activities, such as selling, advertising, warehousing, billing, credit and collection, transportation, accounting, purchasing, engineering,

Franklin Company
Beginning and Ending Inventories
For the Year Ending December 31, 19—

	Beginning Inventory			Ending Inventory		
	Units	Cost	Total	Units	Cost	Total
Materials:						
X..........	30,000	$ 1.00	$ 30,000	40,000	$ 1.00	$ 40,000
Y..........	10,000	14.00	140,000	12,000	14.00	168,000
Z..........	2,000	2.50	5,000	2,500	2.50	6,250
Total.....			$175,000			$214,250
Work in process: None						
Finished goods:						
Product A ...	200	$125.70	$ 25,140	250	$138.50*	$ 34,625
Product B ...	400	82.50	33,000	200	91.25	18,250
Product C ...	500	64.00	32,000	400	72.00	28,800
Total.....			$ 90,140			$ 81,675
Total inventories.			$265,140			$295,925

* Ending inventory unit costs for finished goods determined as follows:

	Product A	Product B	Product C
Materials:			
X: 12 × $ 1.00..........................	$ 12.00		
8 × 1.00..........................		$ 8.00	
6 × 1.00..........................			$ 6.00
Y: 5 × $14.00..........................	70.00		
3 × 14.00..........................		42.00	
2 × 14.00..........................			28.00
Z: 2 × $ 2.50..........................	5.00		
1 × 2.50..........................		2.50	
1 × 2.50..........................			2.50
Direct labor:			
Cutting: .500 × $ 8...................	4.00		
.375 × 8...................		3.00	
.375 × 8...................			3.00
Assembling: 2.500 × $10...................	25.00		
2.000 × 10...................		20.00	
1.750 × 10...................			17.50
Finishing: .800 × $ 9...................	7.20		
.500 × 9...................		4.50	
.500 × 9...................			4.50
Factory overhead:			
Cutting.......................	3.00	2.25	2.25
Assembling	7.50	6.00	5.25
Finishing	4.80	3.00	3.00
Total unit costs	$138.50	$91.25	$72.00

Schedule 8

and financing. Such a classification is consistent with the concept of responsibility accounting and may be compared to collecting factory overhead by departments or cost centers. A departmental classification adds to rather than replaces the process of classifying expenses by primary accounts, because primary account classifications are maintained within each department.

Franklin Company
Budgeted Cost of Goods Manufactured and Sold Statement
For the Year Ending December 31, 19—

Materials:		
Beginning inventory (Schedule 8)	$ 175,000	
Add purchases (Schedule 4)	1,763,450	
Total materials available for use.	$1,938,450	
Less ending inventory (Schedule 8).	214,250	
Cost of materials used (Schedule 5)		$1,724,200
Direct labor (Schedule 6).		924,710
Factory overhead (Schedule 7)		385,815
Total manufacturing cost		$3,034,725
Add beginning finished goods inventory (Schedule 8)		90,140
Cost of goods available for sale		$3,124,865
Less ending finished goods inventory (Schedule 8).		81,675
Cost of goods sold.		$3,043,190

Schedule 9

When a departmental classification system is used, it is important that each expense be charged to a department, and that the classification conforms to the company's organization chart at the corporate level as well as each marketing territory level. However, it is impossible to suggest exact classifications, since organizational structures vary so much in business organizations. Departments known by the same name may perform widely differing functions.

Commercial expenses grouped by department may be subclassified as direct and indirect expenses. Direct expenses, such as salaries and supplies, are charged directly to a department. Indirect expenses are general or service department expenses that are prorated to benefiting departments. Expenses such as rent, insurance, and utilities, when shared by several departments, constitute this type of expense. Also, expenses should be estimated and identified as to their variable and fixed components, again utilizing the cost behavior analysis tools described in Chapter 12. Such identification will help highlight control responsibility.

To identify an outlay of cash or the incurrence of a liability with a function requires considerably more work than is required by the primary account method. However, the chart of accounts will normally provide the initial breakdown of expenses. Usually the allocation of expenses to departments and the identification of the primary account classification within each department can be made when the voucher is prepared. This procedure requires coding the expenditure when it is requisitioned for purchase. Any increase in expenses caused by the use of this functional method is more than offset by the advantages of improved cost control. Furthermore, to the extent that the identifications are practical and meaningful, commercial expenses may be assigned to individual products or product groups and to individual marketing territories.

Commercial expenses are not detailed in the Franklin Company illustration, but rather are shown only in summary form in the budgeted income statement. Budget detail for primary accounts as well as for functional activities, products, and territories is shown in Chapter 24, using marketing expenses as the basis for illustration.

Marketing Expenses Budget. A company's marketing activities can be divided into two broad categories:

1. Obtaining the order—involves the functions of selling and advertising.
2. Filling the order—involves the functions of warehousing, packing and shipping, credit and collection, and general accounting (for marketing).

The supervisors of functions connected with marketing activities should prepare budget estimates of these costs. Some estimates are based on individual judgment, while others are based on the costs experienced in previous years, modified by expected sales volume. Expenses such as depreciation and insurance depend upon the policy established by management.

Administrative Expenses Budget. Administrative expenses include some costs which are peculiar to the administrative function, such as directors' fees, franchise taxes, capital stock taxes, and professional services of accountants, lawyers, and engineers. Other expenses, such as purchasing, engineering, personnel, and research, are shared by the production and marketing as well as the administrative functions.

As a result of the problem of classifying certain expenses, the budgeting and control of administrative expenses often is quite difficult. The difficulty is increased because the persons responsible for the control of certain of these expenses may not be identifiable. However, an attempt should be made to place every item of expense under the jurisdiction and control of an executive, such as the chief executive, treasurer, controller, general accounting supervisor, or office manager. This person should be responsible for estimating the administrative expenses of a specific section or division, and should have authority to control the incurrence of the division's expenses. For example, the office manager should supervise filing clerks, mail clerks, librarians, stenographers, secretaries, and receptionists. This arrangement permits better control and more intense utilization of personnel in clerical jobs, where overlapping and over expansion are common.

■ BUDGETED INCOME STATEMENT — *Pro Forma Statement*

A budgeted income statement contains summaries of the sales, manufacturing, and expense budgets. It projects net income, the goal toward which all efforts are directed, and it offers management the opportunity to judge the accuracy of the budget work and to investigate causes for variances. The budgeted income statement for Franklin Company is presented in Schedule 10.

The sales budget gives expected sales revenue, from which the budgeted cost of goods sold is deducted to give the estimated gross profit. Budgeted marketing and administrative expenses are subtracted from estimated gross profit to arrive at income from operations, which then is adjusted for other

Franklin Company
Budgeted Income Statement
For the Year Ending December 31, 19—

			Amount	% of Sales
Sales (Schedule 1)			$4,550,000	100.0%
Cost of goods sold (Schedule 9)			3,043,190	66.9%
Gross profit			$1,506,810	33.1%
Commercial expenses:				
Marketing expenses	$450,000	9.9%		
Administrative expenses	270,000	5.9%	720,000	15.8%
Income from operations			$ 786,810	17.3%
Other (income) expense			35,000	.8%
Income before income tax			$ 751,810	16.5%
Less provision for income tax			300,724	6.6%
Net income			$ 451,086	9.9%

Schedule 10

income and expense to determine income before income tax. Finally, the provision for income tax is deducted to determine net income. The inclusion of percentages of sales may aid in determining whether various income statement components are in line with expectations.

The budgeted income statement and related supporting budgets may be shown by months or quarters. They may also be segmented by individual products or product groups and by individual marketing territories.

■ BUDGETED BALANCE SHEET

A balance sheet for the beginning of the budget period is the starting point in preparing a budgeted balance sheet for the end of the budget period. The budgeted balance sheet for Franklin Company (Schedule 11) incorporates any changes in assets, liabilities, and stockholders' equity in the budgets submitted by the various departments, functions, or segments.

The finished goods and materials inventory balances agree with those shown in the company's budgeted cost of goods manufactured and sold statement on page 492. While these inventory account changes are directly related to income statement transactions, other accounts may be affected in part by non-income statement transactions. For example, in the case of cash, proceeds from a bank loan or the payment of a cash dividend to stockholders are of the latter type of transaction.

Numerous advantages result from the preparation of a budgeted balance sheet. One advantage is that it discloses unfavorable ratios which management may wish to change for various reasons. Unfavorable ratios can lower credit ratings or cause a drop in the value of the corporation's securities. A second advantage is that it serves as a check on the accuracy of all other budgets. Still another advantage is that a return-on-investment ratio can be computed by relating net income to capital employed. An inadequate return on investment would suggest a need for budget changes.

Franklin Company
Budgeted Balance Sheet
At December 31, 19—

Assets

Cash		$ 245,750
Accounts receivable	$ 370,265	
Less allowance for doubtful accounts	7,400	362,865
Inventories:		
Finished goods	$ 81,675	
Materials	214,250	295,925
Plant and equipment	$1,604,740	
Less accumulated depreciation	418,610	1,186,130
Other assets		143,834
Total assets		$2,234,504

Liabilities and Stockholders' Equity

Current liabilities		$ 327,942
Long-term debt		450,000
Common stock		800,000
Retained earnings		656,562
Total liabilities and stockholders' equity		$2,234,504

Schedule 11

■ COMPUTERIZED BUDGETING[15]

The time required to assemble the periodic budget and to achieve a consensus of the managers involved is so great that the budgeting process often is inhibited. Time constraints may be handled more effectively, however, by converting the elements of the conventional budgeting process into a functional planning tool through the use of computer modeling techniques. Tedious arithmetic can be eliminated by converting budgeting procedures into a computerized set of straightforward algebraic formulas. The resulting computerized model entails the following primary components:

1. A line-by-line outline which describes the format of the desired output of budget schedules and statements.
2. A structure of algebraic logic or procedures which demonstrates the computational processes in simple formulas.
3. Elements of data which, when passed through the computational process, will generate the desired output.

The development of a computerized budgeting process can result in substantial benefits. These benefits include:

QUALITY CONTROL

1. Shortening the planning cycle time. By reducing computational effort, it frequently is possible to delay the start of budget preparation until

---

[15]This discussion adapted from Richard C. Murphy, "A Computerized Model Approach to Budgeting," *Management Accounting*, Vol. LVI, No. 12, pp. 34-36, 38.

more accurate inputs are available. Thus the quality of sales and cost estimates may be improved.

2. Reconsidering planning assumptions. Time savings make it feasible to reconsider planning assumptions early in the budgeting process. Cost and profit implications of various assumptions can be estimated before any commitment is made.

3. Continuous budgeting. Plans can be updated continuously throughout the budget period and, in some cases, planning horizons can be extended beyond the current budget period.

4. Operating analysis capability. If procedures and data are maintained in current form, the computerized model is available to produce instant answers to "what if" questions. More alternatives can be evaluated when such a model is used.

5. Discipline. Development of a model requires precise understanding and definition of the organization and its accounting system. Therefore, the discipline of developing the relationships inherent in a computerized budgeting model is of itself a valuable learning experience.

■ PROSPECTIVE FINANCIAL INFORMATION FOR EXTERNAL USERS

Recent years have seen increasing recognition of the importance of prospective financial information for external users, because investors and potential investors seek to enhance the process of predicting the future. What has happened in the past, as reported in the financial statements, may be viewed as an indicator of the future. Often, however, past results may not be indicative of future expectations and may need to be tempered accordingly.

The question of whether prospective information should be included in external financial statements is controversial. Opponents point out that the uncertainty of such information and the potential dangers of undue reliance upon it could result in added legal liability, a drop in credibility, or both. These concerns and potentially advantageous disclosures to competitors have been cited as causes of widespread opposition by management. On the positive side, however, it has been argued that the inclusion of prospective information in external financial statements "should be provided when it will enhance the reliability of user's predictions."[16]

In 1985, the AICPA issued a statement which establishes detailed procedures and reporting standards for engagements to examine, compile, or apply agreed-upon procedures to prospective financial information. Included are financial forecasts and financial projections. Financial forecasts are defined as an entity's expected financial position, results of operations, and changes in cash flow, reflecting conditions expected to exist and the course of

---

[16]Report of the Study Group on the Objectives of Financial Statements, *Objectives of Financial Statements* (New York: American Institute of Certified Public Accountants, 1973), p. 46.

action expected to be taken. A financial forecast may be expressed in specific monetary amounts as a single point estimate of forecasted results or as a range.

Financial projections present an entity's financial statements based on one or more hypothetical assumptions. One or more hypothetical courses of action may be presented for evaluation, as in a response to a question such as "What would happen if. . . ?" The presentation reflects conditions expected to exist and the course of action expected to be taken, given the assumptions. A projection, like a forecast, may contain a range.

The AICPA statement includes minimum presentation guidelines. Generally, the prospective financial information should be in the format of the historical financial statements and should include a description of what management intends to present, a statement that the assumptions are based on information existing at the time the prospective information was prepared, a caveat that the prospective results may not be achieved, and a summary of significant assumptions.[17]

Securities and Exchange Commission regulations presently encourage but do not require inclusion of prospective financial data in external financial reports. Furthermore, a safe harbor rule gives SEC-regulated companies and their auditors protection from legal liability should public prospective information fail to materialize. For the rule to apply, forecasts and projections must be made on a reasonable basis, in good faith, with assumptions disclosed. The Commission requires that materially incorrect predictions be corrected in subsequent financial reports. SEC guidelines are in harmony with AICPA requirements.

DISCUSSION QUESTIONS

Q16-1. Profit planning includes a complete financial and operational plan for all phases and facets of the business. Discuss.

Q16-2. Distinguish between a budget and a forecast.

Q16-3. Discuss the three different procedures that a company's management might follow to set profit objectives.

Q16-4. Differentiate between long-range profit planning and short-range budgeting.

Q16-5. What is a budget and how is it related to the control function?

Q16-6. The development of a budgetary control program requires specific systems and procedures needed in carrying out management's functions of planning, organizing, and control. Enumerate these steps.

Q16-7. Explain whether the periodic budget represents a formal or informal communication channel within a company.   (ICMA adapted)

---

[17]*Statement on Standards for Accountants' Services on Prospective Financial Information*, "Financial Forecasts and Projections" (New York: American Institute of Certified Public Accountants, 1985).

Q16-8. "Budgets are meaningless in my business because I simply cannot estimate my sales for next year. Only if you can tell me which of my bids will be accepted can I prepare a meaningful budget," protested the president of a small custom manufacturer of die-cast parts for the automobile industry. Discuss, with respect to the above statement, the role of budgets and explain to the president how budgeting could help in bidding.

CGA-Canada (adapted)
Reprint with permission

Q16-9. The human factors in budget preparation are more important than its technical intricacies. Explain.

Q16-10. While the budget is usually thought to be an important and necessary tool for management, it has been subject to some criticism from managers and researchers studying organizations and human behavior.
(a) Describe and discuss the benefits of budgeting from the behavioral point of view.
(b) Describe and discuss the criticisms leveled at the budgeting processes from the behavioral point of view.
(c) What solutions are recommended to overcome the criticisms described in (b) above?   (ICMA adapted)

Q16-11. Commercial expenses are generally identified as marketing and administrative expenses. How should these expenses be grouped for budgetary purposes?

Q16-12. The budgeted income statement may be viewed as the apex of budgeting. Explain this statement.

Q16-13. The budgeted balance sheet may indicate an unsatisfactory financial condition. Discuss.

Q16-14. What governing criterion has been suggested for determining whether to include prospective information in external financial statements?

EXERCISES

E16-1. Sales budget. Clifton Brothers is a wholesaler for three chemical compounds, Rex-Z, Sip-X, and Tok-Y, for which the following information relates to the year 19A:

Product	Sales (In Pounds)	Average Sales Price per Pound	Gross Profit per Pound
Rex-Z........	10,000	$30	$10
Sip-X	9,000	23	8
Tok-Y	7,500	18	5

Demand for Rex-Z has greatly increased and is expected to double in 19B. Sip-X will probably experience a 40% increase in demand, while demand for Tok-Y is expected to remain constant. In line with the overall economy, sales prices will increase by 5%, except for Rex-Z, whose sales price will increase by 15%. Unit costs of goods sold are expected to increase by the following amounts: Rex-Z, 25%; Sip-X, 20%; Tok-Y, 10%.

Required: Prepare a schedule presenting budgeted sales revenue and gross profit, by product, for 19B.

E16-2. **Production budget.** Schwankenfelder Company's sales forecast for the next quarter, ending June 30, indicates the following:

Product	Expected Sales
Ceno	21,000 units
Nepo	37,500
Teno.........	54,300

Inventories at the beginning and desired quantities at the end of the quarter are as follows:

Product	March 31	June 30
Ceno	5,800 units	6,200 units
Nepo	11,000	10,500
Teno.........	14,500	12,200

Required: Prepare a production budget for the second quarter.

E16-3. **Production budget.** Magic Enterprises produces three perfumes. The sales department prepared the following tentative sales budget for the first quarter of the coming year:

Perfume	Units
Moon Glow	250,000
Enchanting	175,000
Day Dream	300,000

The following inventory levels have been established:

	Work in Process				Finished Goods	
	Beginning		Ending		Beginning	Ending
Perfume	Units	% Processed	Units	% Processed	Units	Units
Moon Glow	4,000	50%	7,000	60%	16,000	15,000
Enchanting	6,000	30	5,000	40	12,000	10,000
Day Dream	8,000	80	8,000	75	25,000	20,000

Required: Prepare a production budget, by product.

E16-4. **Production budget and raw materials purchases requirements.** Manford Industries produces television antennas and has estimated sales for the next six-month period as follows:

Model Number	Units
1001	200
1002	150
1003	425
2001	175
2002	325
2003	215

Raw materials requirements for each model are:

	Raw Materials in Pounds	
Model Number	X	Y
1001	5	2
1002	7	2
1003	10	3
2001	4	1.5
2002	6	2
2003	8	2.5

Estimated inventories are:

	Beginning Inventory	Ending Inventory
Raw Materials:		
X	5,000 lbs.	7,000 lbs.
Y . . . . :	2,000	1,500
Finished Goods:		
1001	50 units	40 units
1002	25	25
1003	75	60
2001	15	20
2002	35	35
2003	20	20

Required:

(1) Prepare a production budget, by product.
(2) Compute the raw materials purchases requirements, by raw material.

E16-5. **Sales budget, production budget, and materials budget.** The Maverick Company manufactures and sells three products: X, Y, and Z. In September, 19A, Maverick's budget department gathered the following forecast data related to its operations in the coming year.

Projected Sales for Fourth Quarter

Product	Quantity	Unit Price
X	4,500	$12
Y	2,000	25
Z	3,000	20

Inventories in Units

Item	Beginning	Desired Ending
Product X	600	900
Product Y	500	400
Product Z	400	500
Material A	2,000	2,500
Material B	1,500	2,000
Material C	2,500	2,000

Materials Production Requirements for Each Unit of Product

Product	Units of Material A	Units of Material B	Units of Material C
X	3	1	2
Y	2	2	4
Z	1	3	2

There is no beginning or ending inventory in work in process. Budgeted unit costs for Materials A, B, and C are $.50, $2.00, and $1.50, respectively.

Required:

(1) Prepare a sales budget which includes quantities and revenues for each of the three products.
(2) Prepare a production budget for all three products.
(3) Prepare a materials usage budget.
(4) Prepare a materials purchases budget.

E16-6. Production budget, purchase requirements, and manufacturing costs. Provence Company prepared the following figures as a basis for its annual budget:

Product	Expected Sales	Estimated per Unit Sales Price	Required Materials per Unit	
			A	B
Tribolite	80,000 units	$1.50	1 kg	2 kg
Polycal.........	40,000	2.00	2	—
Powder X	100,000	.80	—	1

Estimated inventories at the beginning and desired quantities at the end of the year are:

Material	Beginning	Ending	Purchase Price per Kilogram
A	10 000 kg	12 000 kg	$.20
B	12 000	15 000	.10

Product	Beginning	Ending	Direct Labor Hours per 1,000 Units
Tribolite	5,000 units	6,000 units	50.0
Polycal.........	4,000	2,000	125.0
Powder X	10,000	8,000	12.5

The direct labor cost is budgeted at $8 per hour and variable factory overhead at $6 per hour of direct labor. Fixed factory overhead, estimated to be $40,000, is a common cost and is not allocated to specific products in developing the manufacturing budget for internal management use.

Required:

(1) Prepare a production budget.
(2) Prepare a purchases budget for each material.
(3) Prepare a budget of manufacturing costs, by product and in total.

E16-7. Budgeted cost of goods sold statement. Sandersen Inc, with $20,000,000 of par stock outstanding, plans to budget earnings of 6%, before income tax, on this stock. The Marketing Department budgets sales at $12,000,000. The budget director approves the sales budget and expenses as follows:

Marketing	15% of sales
Administrative	5%
Financial	1%

Labor is expected to be 50% of the total manufacturing cost; materials issued for the budgeted production will cost $2,500,000; therefore, any savings in manufacturing cost will have to be in factory overhead. Inventories are to be as follows:

	Beginning of Year	End of Year
Finished goods.........	$800,000	$1,000,000
Work in process	100,000	300,000
Materials..............	500,000	400,000

Required: Prepare the budgeted cost of goods manufactured and sold statement, showing the budgeted purchases of materials and the adjustments for inventories of materials, work in process, and finished goods.

E16-8. Budgeted income statement. Patz Company has just received a franchise to distribute air conditioners. The company began business on January 1 with the following assets:

Cash...	$ 60,000
Inventory	90,000
Warehouse, office, and delivery facilities and equipment	800,000

All facilities and equipment have a useful life of 20 years and no residual value. First quarter sales are expected to be $500,000 and should be doubled in the second quarter. Third quarter sales are expected to be $1,200,000. Two percent of sales are considered to be uncollectible. The gross profit margin should be 40%. Variable marketing expenses (except uncollectible accounts) are budgeted at 10% of sales and fixed marketing expenses at $50,000 per quarter, exclusive of depreciation. Administrative expenses are all considered to be fixed expenses and should total $40,000 per quarter, exclusive of depreciation.

Required: Prepare a budgeted income statement for the second quarter.

CGA-Canada (adapted) Reprint with permission

E16-9. Budgeted income statement. Calcor Company has been a wholesale distributor of automobile parts for domestic automakers for 20 years. Calcor has suffered through the recent slump in the domestic auto industry, and its performance has not rebounded to the levels of the industry as a whole. Calcor's income statement for the year ended November 30, 19A, is as follows:

Calcor Company
Income Statement
For the Year Ended November 30, 19A
(In Thousands)

Net sales	$8,400
Expenses:	
Cost of goods sold	$6,300
Marketing expenses	780
Administrative expenses	900
Interest expense	140
Total expense	$8,120
Income before income tax	$ 280
Income tax	112
Net income	$ 168

Calcor's management team is considering the following actions for fiscal 19B, which they expect will improve profitability and result in a 5% increase in unit sales:

(a) Increase sales prices 10%.
(b) Increase advertising by $420,000 and hold all other marketing and administrative expenses at fiscal 19A levels.
(c) Improve customer service by increasing average current assets (inventory and accounts receivable) by a total of $300,000, and hold all other assets at fiscal 19A levels.
(d) Finance the additional assets at an annual interest rate of 10% and hold all other interest expense at fiscal 19A levels.
(e) Improve the quality of products carried; this will increase the unit cost of goods sold by 4%.

Calcor's 19B effective income tax rate is expected to be 40%—the same as in fiscal 19A.

Required: Prepare a budgeted income statement for Calcor Company for the year ending November 30, 19B, assuming that Calcor's planned actions would be carried out and that the 5% increase in unit sales would be realized.

(ICMA adapted)

PROBLEMS

P16-1. Sales and manufacturing budgets. Scarborough Corporation manufactures and sells two products, Thingone and Thingtwo. In July, 19A, Scarborough's Budget Department gathered the following data in order to project sales and budget requirements for 19B:

19B projected sales:

Product	Units	Price
Thingone	60,000	$ 70
Thingtwo	40,000	100

19B inventories (in units):

Product	Expected January 1, 19B	Desired December 31, 19B
Thingone	20,000	25,000
Thingtwo	8,000	9,000

To produce one unit of Thingone and Thingtwo, the following raw materials are used:

	Amount Used per Unit	
Raw Material	Thingone	Thingtwo
A	4 lbs.	5 lbs.
B	2 lbs.	3 lbs.
C	–	1 unit

Projected data for 19B with respect to raw materials are as follows:

Raw Material	Anticipated Purchase Price	Expected Inventories January 1, 19B	Desired Inventories December 31, 19B
A	$8	32,000 lbs.	36,000 lbs.
B	5	29,000 lbs.	32,000 lbs.
C	3	6,000 units	7,000 units

Projected direct labor requirements and rates for 19B are as follows:

Product	Hours per Unit	Rate per Hour
Thingone	2	$8
Thingtwo	3	9

Factory overhead is applied at the rate of $2 per direct labor hour.

Required: Based on the above projections and budget requirements for 19B for Thingone and Thingtwo, prepare the following 19B budgets:

(1) Sales budget.
(2) Production budget.
(3) Raw materials purchases budget.
(4) Direct labor budget.
(5) Budgeted finished goods inventory at December 31, 19B.   (AICPA adapted)

P16-2. Production and direct labor budget. Roletter Company makes and sells artistic frames for pictures of weddings, graduations, christenings, and other special events. Lynn Anderson, controller, is responsible for preparing Roletter's budget and has accumulated the following information for 19B:

	January	February	March	April	May
Estimated unit sales	10,000	12,000	8,000	9,000	9,000
Sales price per unit.	$50.00	$47.50	$47.50	$47.50	$47.50
Direct labor hours per unit	2.0	2.0	1.5	1.5	1.5
Wage per direct labor hour.	$ 8.00	$ 8.00	$ 8.00	$ 9.00	$ 9.00

Labor-related costs include pension contributions of $.25 per hour, workers' compensation insurance of $.10 per hour, employee medical insurance of $.40 per hour, and social security and unemployment taxes of 10% of wages. The cost of employee benefits paid by Roletter on its employees is treated as a direct labor cost.

Roletter has a labor contract that calls for a wage increase to $9 per hour on April 1, 19B. New labor saving machinery has been installed and will be fully operational by March 1, 19B.

Roletter expects to have 16,000 frames on hand at December 31, 19A, and has a policy of carrying an end-of-month inventory of 100% of the following month's sales plus 50% of the second following month's sales.

Required:

(1) Prepare a production budget and a direct labor budget for Roletter Company by month and for the first quarter of 19B. Both budgets may be combined in one schedule. The direct labor budget should include direct labor hours and show the detail for each direct labor cost category.

(2) For each item used in Roletter's production budget and its direct labor budget, identify the other component(s) of the periodic budget that would also use these data.   (ICMA adapted)

P16-3. Production and manufacturing budgets. The following data are provided for Hanska Corporation:

Sales:

Sales through June 30, 19A, the first six months of the current year, are 24,000 units. Expected sales for the full year are 60,000 units. Actual sales in units for May and June and estimated unit sales for the next four months are as follows:

May.	4,000 units
June	4,000
July.	5,000
August	6,000
September	7,000
October.	7,000

Direct materials:

At each month end, Hanska desires to have sufficient materials on hand to produce the next month's estimated sales. Data regarding materials are as follows:

Direct Material	Units of Material Required	Cost per Unit	Inventory Units, June 30, 19A
101	6	$2.40	35,000
211	4	3.60	30,000
242	2	1.20	14,000

Direct labor:

Process	Hours per Unit	Hourly Labor Rate
Forming	.80	$8.00
Assembly.	2.00	5.50
Finishing	.25	6.00

Factory overhead:

The company produced 27,000 units during the six-month period through June 30,19A, and expects to produce 60,000 units during the year. The actual variable factory overhead costs incurred during this six-month period are as follows. The controller believes that these costs will be incurred at the same rate during the remainder of 19A.

Supplies.	$ 59,400
Electricity.	27,000
Indirect labor	54,000
Other	21,600
Total variable factory overhead	$162,000

The fixed factory overhead costs incurred during the first six months of 19A amounted to $93,000. Fixed overhead costs are budgeted for the full year as follows:

Supervision......................	$ 60,000
Property tax	7,200
Depreciation	86,400
Other...........................	32,400
Total fixed factory overhead	$186,000

Finished goods inventory:

The desired monthly ending finished goods inventory in units is 80% of the next month's estimated sales. There are 5,600 finished units in the June 30, 19A inventory.

Required:

(1) Prepare the production budget for the third quarter ending September 30, 19A.
(2) Prepare the direct materials purchases budget for the third quarter.
(3) Prepare the direct labor budget for the third quarter.
(4) Prepare the factory overhead budget for the six months ending December 31, 19A, presenting two figures, i.e., for total variable and fixed overhead.   (ICMA adapted)

P16-4. Sales budget; purchases and materials requirements. The management of Bannister Food Products decided to install a budgetary control system under the supervision of a budget director and a committee. Among its products, the company manufactures a patented breakfast food that is sold in packages of two sizes—1 lb. and 2 lb. The cereal is made from two types of grain, called R(rye) and S(soy) for this purpose. There are two operations: (a) processing and blending and (b) packaging. The grains are purchased by the bushel measure, a bushel of R containing 70 lbs. and a bushel of S containing 80 lbs. Three bushels of grain mixed in the proportion of 2R:1S produce 198 lbs. of finished product. The entire loss occurs in the first department.

To prepare estimated sales figures for the first six months of the coming year, the budget committee first asked the salespeople to prepare sales estimates in units. The following data were submitted:

	Territories				
	I	II	III	Other	6-Month Total
1-lb. package	10,000	15,000	12,000	613,000	650,000
2-lb. package	12,000	18,000	12,000	783,000	825,000
Total	22,000	33,000	24,000	1,396,000	1,475,000

The figures submitted are analyzed by the budget committee in the light of general business conditions. The company uses the Federal Reserve Board Index together with its own trade index to prepare a trend percentage that exists in the business. The trend percentage indicates that a .90 general index figure should be applied to the estimates in order to arrive at the final sales figures. The finished goods inventory is to be kept at zero if possible. The work in process inventory is to be kept near the present level, which is about 160,000 lbs. of blended material.

Factory facilities permit processing sales requirements as stated in the sales budget. The production manager decided to accept the monthly sales figures for the production budget.

Purchases of grains in bushels have been arranged as follows:

	Type R Quantity	Type R Price	Type S Quantity	Type S Price
January.	5,000 bu.	$1.30	2,000 bu.	$1.20
February	2,000	1.40	1,000	1.20
March	-0-	-0-	3,000	1.25
April.	8,000	1.50	3,000	1.00
May.	3,000	1.50	-0-	-0-
June	4,000	1.60	4,000	1.00
Beginning inventory, Jan. 1	10,000	1.20	3,000	1.00

Materials are charged into production on the fifo basis.

Required:

(1) Prepare a revised sales budget in units for the six-month period, based on the index.
(2) Prepare a sales budget in dollars, assuming that the 1-lb. package sells for $.25 and the 2-lb. package for $.50.
(3) Prepare a schedule of materials purchases.
(4) Prepare a computation of materials requirements for production. (Round to the nearest whole amount.)
(5) Prepare a schedule of the materials account (fifo basis), in units and dollars, indicating beginning inventory, purchases, usage, and ending inventory for the six-month period taken as a whole.

P16-5. Budgeted income statement. The president of a hardware manufacturing company has asked the controller to prepare an income forecast for the next year, by quarters, with sales reported for each of the two major segments—commercial and government.

The Marketing Department provided the following sales estimates:

	1st Quarter	2d Quarter	3d Quarter	4th Quarter
Commercial sales	$250,000	$266,000	$275,000	$300,000
Government sales	100,000	120,000	110,000	115,000

The controller's office assembled these figures:

(a) Cost of goods sold: 46% of total sales.
(b) Advertising expenditures: $6,000 each quarter.
(c) Selling expenses: 10% of total sales.
(d) Administrative expenses: 16.8% of gross profit.
(e) General office expenses: 12% of gross profit.
(f) Other income: $8,000 per quarter.
(g) Corporate income tax rate: 40%.

Required:

(1) Prepare a budgeted income statement, by quarters and in total. All figures should be shown in thousands of dollars and rounded to the nearest thousand, adding four quarters across to obtain total figures.
(2) Prepare an analysis of the effect of a 5% increase in commercial sales revenue, using the same income statement format as for (1).

P16-6. Preliminary profit plan. Yorio Food Manufacturing Company is a medium-size publicly held corporation, producing a variety of consumer food and specialty products. Current-year data were prepared as follows for the salad dressing product line, using five months of actual expenses and a seven-month projection:

Projected Income Statement
For the Year Ending December 31, 19A
(5 months actual; 7 months projected)
(In Thousands)

Volume in gallons	5,000
Gross sales	$30,000
Freight, allowances, and discounts	3,000
Net sales	$27,000
Less manufacturing costs:	
Variable	$13,500
Fixed	2,100
Depreciation	700
Total manufacturing cost	$16,300
Gross profit	$10,700
Less expenses:	
Marketing	$ 4,000
Brokerage	1,650
General and administrative	2,100
Research and development	500
Total expense	$ 8,250
Income before income tax	$ 2,450

The current-year projection was accepted as being accurate, but it was agreed that the projected income was not at a satisfactory level. The president wants, at a minimum, a 15% increase in gross sales dollars and not less than 10% before-tax profit on gross sales for 19B. The president also intends to reduce general and administrative expenses $200,000 to help achieve the profit goal.

Both the vice-president—marketing and the vice-president—production felt that the president's objectives would be difficult to achieve; however, they offered the following suggestions to reach the objectives:

(a) Sales volume. Yorio's current share of the salad dressing market is 15% and the total salad dressing market is expected to increase by 5% for 19B. Yorio's current market share can be maintained by a marketing expenditure of $4,200,000. The two vice-presidents estimated that the market share could be increased by additional expenditures for advertising and sales promotion. For an additional expenditure of $525,000, the market share can be raised by one percentage point until the market share reaches 17%. To achieve further market penetration, an additional $875,000 must be spent for each percentage point until the market share reaches 20%. Any advertising and promotion expenditures beyond this level are not likely to increase the market share to more than 20%.

(b) Sales price. The sales price, which will remain at $6 per gallon, is very closely related to the cost of the ingredients, which is not expected to change in 19B from that experienced in 19A.

(c) Variable manufacturing cost. Variable manufacturing cost is projected at 50% of the net sales dollar (gross sales less freight, allowances, and discounts).

(d) Fixed manufacturing cost. An increase of $100,000 is projected for 19B.

(e) Depreciation. A projected increase in equipment will increase depreciation by $25,000 over the 19A projection.

(f) Freight, allowances, and discounts. The current rate of 10% of gross sales dollars is expected to continue in 19B.

(g) Brokerage expense. A rate of 5% of gross sales dollars is projected for 19B.

(h) General and administrative expense. A $200,000 decrease in general and administrative expense from the 19A forecast is projected, an amount consistent with the president's commitment.

(i) Research and development expense. A 5% increase from the absolute dollars in the 19A forecast will be necessary to meet divisional research targets.

Required: Prepare a profit plan (budgeted income statements) for 15% through 20% market shares, in 1% increments, indicating the market share percentage most in harmony with the president's objectives.

(ICMA adapted)

SS **P16-7. Budgeted income statement and related schedules.** A1 Sound Systems manufactures speakers for component stereo systems. Three models are produced: Model 150, Model 100, and Model 50. The speakers are marketed in two regions, the South and Southwest. The production departments are designated Cutting, Assembling, and Finishing. Lumber, speakers, and a finishing compound are the materials used in producing the speakers. The following estimates have been made for the coming year:

(a) Sales forecast:

Model	South	Southwest	Sales Price
150	3,000 units	4,000 units	$175 per unit
100	5,000	7,000	120
50	7,000	8,000	90

(b) Inventories:
   Materials:

	Beginning Inventory Units	Ending Inventory Units	Unit Cost
Lumber (board feet)	40,000	30,000	$ .75
Speakers.	10,000	8,000	15.00
Finish (pints).	1,500	2,000	2.00

   Work in process: None at the beginning or end of the period.
   Finished goods (fifo):

Model	Beginning Inventory Units	Beginning Inventory Unit Cost	Ending Inventory Units	Ending Inventory Unit Cost
150	200	$98.00	200	$105.50
100	300	62.00	400	66.75
50	400	47.00	300	50.25

(c) Materials requirements:

Model	Lumber (Board Feet)	Speakers	Finish (Pints)
150	12	5	2
100	8	3	1
50	6	2	1

(d) Estimated materials cost:
   Lumber, $.75 per board foot
   Speakers, $15 per speaker
   Finish, $2 per pint

(e) Estimated labor cost:

	Cutting	Assembling	Finishing
Rate per hour	$6.00	$5.00	$4.00

   Estimated labor time requirements:

Model	Cutting	Assembling	Finishing
150	.375 hour	2.0 hours	.375 hour
100	.375	1.5	.250
50	.375	1.5	.250

(f) Factory overhead budgets show the following unit overhead rates:

Model	Cutting	Assembling	Finishing
150	$1.00	$2.00	$.75
100	1.00	1.50	.50
50	1.00	1.50	.50

(g) Marketing expenses: $500,000.
Administrative expenses: $300,000.
Income tax rate: 50%.

Required: Prepare annual budget schedules utilizing the budget estimates provided. The schedules should be designed to provide essential data in an easily understood form. Titles and schedule numbers to be used are as follows. Cross-references should be made using schedule numbers.

Schedule	Title
(1)	Sales budget—by models and by sales regions
(2)	Production budget—by models and by units
(3)	Direct materials budget in units—by materials and by models
(4)	Purchases budget—by materials and by cost
(5)	Cost of materials required for production—by materials and by models
(6)	Direct labor budget—by models and by departments
(7)	Factory overhead budget (applied overhead)—by models and by departments
(8)	Beginning and ending inventories—by materials and by models
(9)	Budgeted cost of goods manufactured and sold statement
(10)	Budgeted income statement—with each item shown as a percentage of sales (round percentages to the nearest tenth of a percent)

P16-8. Prospective financial statements. CL Corporation appears to be experiencing a good year, with sales in the first quarter of 19B one third ahead of last year and the Sales Department predicting continuation of this rate throughout the year. The controller has been asked to prepare a new forecast for the year and to analyze the differences from 19A results. The forecast is to be based on actual results obtained in the first quarter plus the expected costs of programs to be carried out in the remainder of the year. Various department heads (production, sales, etc.) have provided the necessary information which is summarized and the results are presented in the prospective trial balance on page 510.

Adjustments for the change in inventory and for income tax have not been made. The scheduled production for 19B is 450 million units, while the sales volume will reach 400 million units. Sales and production volume in 19A was 300 million units. A full-cost, first-in, first-out inventory system is used. The company is subject to a 40% income tax rate. The actual financial statements for 19A are presented on pages 510 and 511.

Required:

(1) Prepare prospective financial statements (statement of income and retained earnings, and balance sheet) for 19B.

(2) Using the 19A information provided for comparison:

(a) Evaluate the 19B prospective profit performance.
(b) Specify areas of 19B operating performance to be investigated.
(c) Recommend programs for improved management performance. (ICMA adapted)

CL Corporation
Prospective Trial Balance
For December 31, 19B
(In Thousands)

Cash	1,200	
Accounts Receivable	80,000	
Inventory (1/1/19B, 40,000 units)	48,000	
Plant and Equipment	130,000	
Accumulated Depreciation		41,000
Accounts Payable		45,000
Accrued Payables		23,250
Notes Payable (due within one year)		50,000
Common Stock		70,000
Retained Earnings		108,200
Sales		600,000
Other Income		9,000
Cost of Goods Sold		—
Manufacturing costs:		
Materials	213,000	
Direct Labor	218,000	
Variable Factory Overhead	130,000	
Depreciation	5,000	
Other Fixed Factory Overhead	7,750	
Marketing:		
Salaries	16,000	
Commissions	20,000	
Promotion and Advertising	45,000	
General and administrative:		
Salaries	16,000	
Travel	2,500	
Office Costs	9,000	
Income Tax	—	
Dividends	5,000	
	946,450	946,450

CL Corporation
Balance Sheet
December 31, 19A
(In Thousands)

Assets

Current assets:		
Cash	$ 23,000	
Accounts receivable	50,000	
Inventory	48,000	$121,000
Plant and equipment	$130,000	
Less accumulated depreciation	36,000	94,000
Total assets		$215,000

Liabilities and Shareholders' Equity

Current liabilities:		
Accounts payable	$ 13,000	
Accrued payables	12,800	
Notes payable	11,000	$ 36,800
Shareholders' equity:		
Common stock	$ 70,000	
Retained earnings	108,200	178,200
Total liabilities and shareholders' equity		$215,000

CL Corporation
Statement of Income and Retained Earnings
For Year Ended December 31, 19A
(In Thousands)

Revenue:			
Sales		$450,000	
Other income		15,000	$465,000
Expenses:			
Cost of goods manufactured and sold:			
Materials	$132,000		
Direct labor	135,000		
Variable factory overhead	81,000		
Fixed factory overhead	12,000		
	$360,000		
Beginning inventory	48,000		
	$408,000		
Ending inventory	48,000	$360,000	
Marketing:			
Salaries	$ 13,500		
Commissions	15,000		
Promotion and advertising	31,500	60,000	
General and administrative:			
Salaries	$ 14,000		
Travel	2,000		
Office costs	8,000	24,000	
Income tax		8,400	452,400
Net income			$ 12,600
Beginning retained earnings			100,600
			$113,200
Less dividends			5,000
Ending retained earnings			$108,200

P16-9. Time budget, billing rates, and budgeted income statement. In June, 19A, after ten years with a large CPA firm, Anna B. Johnson, CPA, opened an office as a sole practitioner. In 19C, Walter L. Smith, CPA, joined Johnson as a senior accountant. The partnership of Johnson and Smith was organized July 1, 19H, and a fiscal year ending June 30 was adopted and approved by the Internal Revenue Service.

Continued growth of the firm has required additional personnel. The current complement, including approved salaries for the fiscal year ending June 30, 19N, is as follows:

Partners:	
Anna B. Johnson, CPA	$60,000
Walter L. Smith, CPA	40,000
Professional staff:	
Manager:	
Harold S. Vickers, CPA	31,200
Senior accountant:	
Duane Lowe, CPA	24,960
Staff accountants:	
James M. Kennedy	20,800
Viola O. Quinn	20,800
Secretaries:	
Livia A. Garcia	14,560
Johnnie L. Hammond	12,480
Mary Lyons	12,480

During a severe illness which kept Johnson away from the office for over four months in late 19L, the firm suffered, mainly because other personnel lacked knowledge about the practice. After Johnson's return, a plan was developed for delegation of administrative authority and responsibility and for standardization of procedures. The goals of the plan included income objectives, standardized billing procedures (with flexibility for adjustments by the partners), and assignment schedules to eliminate overtime and to allow for nonchargeable time such as vacations and illness. The firm plans a 52-week year with five-day, forty-hour weeks.

The partners would like to achieve an annual income target of at least $80,000 (after deducting partners' salaries). The budget for fiscal year 19N is 700 hours of chargeable time at $90 per hour for Johnson and 1,100 hours at $70 for Smith. Johnson and Smith are to devote all other available time, except as specified below, to administration. The billing rates for all other employees including secretaries are to be set at a level to recover their salaries plus the following overhead items: fringe benefits of $35,000, other operating expenses of $62,370, and a contribution to the targeted income of at least $50,000.

The partners agree that salary levels are fair bases for allocating overhead in setting billing rates, with the exception of salary costs of the secretaries' nonchargeable time, which are to be added to overhead to arrive at total overhead to be allocated. Thus the billing rates for each secretary will be based upon the salary costs of chargeable time plus a share of the total overhead. No portion of total overhead is to be allocated to partners' salaries.

The following information is available for nonchargeable time:

(a) Because of the recent illness, Johnson expects to be away an additional week. Smith expects no loss of time from illness. All other employees are to be allowed one illness day per month.

(b) Allowable vacations are as follows:

Johnson	1 month (173 hours)
Smith.	1 month (173 hours)
Vickers	3 weeks
Garcia	3 weeks
All other employees	2 weeks

(c) If any of the holidays observed (7 annually) falls on a weekend, the office is closed the preceding Friday or the following Monday.

(d) Kennedy and Quinn should each be allotted three days to sit for the November 19N CPA examination.

(e) Hours are budgeted for other miscellaneous activities of personnel as follows:

Name	Firm Projects	Professional Development	Professional Meetings	Community Activities	Miscellaneous Office Time	Total
Johnson	48	80	184	80	0	392
Smith	148	80	120	40	0	388
Vickers	88	56	40	40	84	308
Lowe	64	40	40	24	72	240
Kennedy	89	40	16	16	0	161
Quinn	39	50	16	16	0	121
Garcia	248	24	24	12	1,000	1,308
Hammond . . .	8	16	8	0	716	748
Lyons	8	24	8	0	808	848

(f) Unassigned time should be budgeted for Lowe, Kennedy, and Quinn as 8, 38, and 78 hours, respectively.

Required:

(1) Prepare a time allocation budget for each partner and each employee that begins with maximum hours available (without incurring overtime) and ends with chargeable hours.

(2) Prepare a schedule computing the billing rates for each employee (excluding the partners) for the year ending June 30, 19N. The schedule should show the proper allocation of appropriate expenses and

target income contribution to salaries applicable to chargeable time in accordance with the objective established by the partners.

(3) Prepare a condensed statement of budgeted income for the year ending June 30, 19N.(AICPA adapted)

CASES

C16-1. Need for profit planning. George Mai invented a special valve for application in the paper manufacturing industry. At the time of its development, he could not find any company willing to manufacture the valve. As a result, he formed Maiton Company to manufacture and sell the valve.

Maiton Company grew quite slowly. George Mai found it difficult to persuade paper companies to try this new valve designed and manufactured by an unknown company. However, the company has prospered and now has a number of smaller paper companies as regular customers. In fact, there is increasing interest by a number of large paper companies because of the very good results experienced by the smaller paper companies.

The size of the potential new customers and their probable needs over the next several years will dramatically increase the sales of the valve. George Mai was an engineer for a large company prior to his invention. His business experience is limited to the activities of Maiton Company.

Required:

(1) Explain why it is important for George Mai to introduce business planning and budgeting activities into his company at this time.
(2) Identify major problems that likely would be disclosed as Maiton Company attempts to prepare a five-year plan. Explain why the problems identified were selected.

(ICMA adapted)

C16-2. Long-range planning; periodic sales budget. Marval Products manufactures and wholesales several lines of luggage. Each luggage line consists of various pieces and sizes. One line is a complete set of luggage designed to be used by both men and women, but some lines are designed specifically for men or women. Some lines also have matching at-

tache cases. Luggage lines are discontinued and introduced as tastes change or as product improvements are developed.

Marval Products also manufactures luggage for large retail companies according to each company's specifications. This luggage is marketed under the retail companies' own private labels rather than the Marval label.

Marval has been manufacturing several lines of luggage under its own label and private lines for retail companies for the last ten years.

Required:

(1) Identify the factors Marval Products needs to consider in its periodic review of long-range planning.
(2) Identify the factors Marval Products needs to consider when developing its sales component of the annual budget.

(ICMA adapted)

C16-3. Budget preparation. RV Industries manufactures and sells recreation vehicles. The company has eight divisions strategically located near major markets. Each division has a sales force and two to four manufacturing plants. These divisions operate as autonomous profit centers responsible for purchasing, operations, and sales.

Dale Collins, the corporate controller, described the divisional performance measurement system as follows: "We allow the divisions to control the entire operation from the purchase of raw materials to the sale of the product. We, at corporate headquarters, only get involved in strategic decisions, such as developing new product lines. Each division is responsible for meeting its market needs by providing the right products at a low cost on a timely basis. Frankly, the divisions need to focus on cost control, delivery, and services to customers in order to become more profitable.

"While we give the divisions considerable autonomy, we watch their monthly income statements very closely. Each month's actual performance is compared with the budget in considerable detail. If the actual sales or contribution margin is more than 4 or 5% below the budget, we jump on the division people immediately. I might add that we don't have much trouble getting their attention. All of the management people at the plant and division level can add appreciably to their annual salaries with bonuses if their actual profit is considerably greater than budget."

The budgeting process begins in August when division sales managers, after consulting with their sales personnel, estimate sales for the next calendar year. These estimates are sent to plant managers who use the sales forecasts to prepare production estimates. At the plants, production statistics, including raw material quantities, labor hours, production schedules, and output quantities, are developed by operating personnel. Using the statistics prepared by the operating personnel, the plant accounting staff determines costs and prepares the plant's budgeted variable cost of goods sold and other plant expenses for each month of the coming calendar year.

In October, each division's accounting staff combines plant budgets with sales estimates and adds additional division expenses. "After the divisional management is satisfied with the budget," said Collins, "I visit each division to go over their budget and make sure it is in line with corporate strategy and projections. I really emphasize the sales forecasts because of the volatility in the demand for our product. For many years, we lost sales to our competitors because we didn't project high enough production and sales, and we couldn't meet the market demand. More recently, we were caught with large excess inventory when the bottom dropped out of the market for recreational vehicles.

"I generally visit all eight divisions during the first two weeks in November. After that, the division budgets are combined and reconciled by my staff and they are ready for approval by the board of directors in early December. The board seldom questions the budget.

"One complaint we've had from plant and division management is that they are penalized for circumstances beyond their control.

For example, they failed to predict the recent sales decline. As a result, they didn't make their budget and, of course, they received no bonuses. However, I point out that they are well rewarded when they exceed their budget. Furthermore, they provide most of the information for the budget, so it's their own fault if the budget is too optimistic."

Required: Discuss the following:

(1) Biases which corporate management should expect in the communication of budget estimates prepared by its division and plant personnel.
(2) Sources of information which corporate management can use to monitor the budget estimates prepared by its divisions and plants.
(3) Services which corporate management could offer the divisions to aid them in their budget development, without appearing to interfere with division budget decisions.
(4) Factors which corporate management should consider in deciding whether or not it should become more involved in the budget process.   (ICMA adapted)

C16-4. Evaluation of budget procedures. Schaffer Company, a large multidivisional firm with several plants in each division, uses a comprehensive budgeting system for planning operations and measuring performance. The annual budgeting process begins in August, five months prior to the beginning of the fiscal year. At this time, the division managers submit proposed budgets for sales, production and inventory levels, and expenses. Capital expenditure requests also are formalized at this time. The expense budgets include direct labor and all factory overhead items, separated into fixed and variable components. Direct materials are budgeted separately in developing the production and inventory schedules.

The expense budgets for each division are developed from each plant's results, as measured by the percent variation from an adjusted budget in the first six months of the current year, and a target expense reduction percentage established by the corporation.

To determine plant percentages, the plant budget for the just completed half-year period is revised to recognize changes in operating procedures and costs outside the control of plant management (e.g., labor wage rate changes and product style changes). The difference between this revised budget and the actual expenses is the controllable variance, expressed as a percentage of the actual expenses. If unfavorable, this percentage is added to the corporate target expense reduction percentage. A favorable plant variance percentage is subtracted from the corporate target. If a plant had a 2% unfavorable controllable variance and the corporate target reduction was 4%, the plant's budget for next year should reflect costs approximately 6% below this year's actual costs.

Next year's final budgets for the corporation, its divisions, and plants are adopted after corporate analysis of the proposed budgets and a careful review with each division manager of the changes made by corporate management.

Division profit budgets include allocated corporate costs, and plant profit budgets include allocated division and corporate costs.

Required: Evaluate the budget procedures of Schaffer Company with respect to its effectiveness for planning and controlling operations.

(ICMA adapted)

C16-5. Setting Segment Profit Objectives. The Noton Company has operated a comprehensive budgeting system for many years. This system is a major component of the company's program to control operations and costs at its widely scattered plants. Periodically the plants' general managers gather to discuss the overall company control system with the top management.

At this year's meeting the budgetary system was severely criticized by one of the most senior plant managers. He said that the system discriminated unfairly against the older, well-run and established plants in favor of the newer plants. The impact was lower year-end bonuses and poor performance ratings. In addition, there were psychological consequences in the form of lower employee morale. In his judgment, revisions in the system were needed to make it more effective. The basic factors of Noton's budget include:

(a) Announcement of an annual improvement percentage target established by top management.

(b) Plant submission of budgets implementing the annual improvement target.
(c) Management review and revision of the proposed budget.
(d) Establishment and distribution of the final budget.

To support his arguments, he compared the budget revisions and performance results. The older plants were expected to achieve the improvement target but often were unable to meet it. On the other hand, the newer plants were often excused from meeting a portion of this target in their budgets. However, their performance was usually better than the final budget.

He further argued that the company did not recognize the operating differences which made attainment of the annual improvement factor difficult, if not impossible. His plant has been producing essentially the same product for its 20 years of existence. The machinery and equipment, which underwent many modifications in the first five years, have had no major changes in recent years. Because they are old, repair and maintenance costs have increased each year, and the machines are less reliable. The plant management team has been together for the last ten years and works well together. The labor force is mature, with many of the employees having the highest seniority in the company. In his judgment, the significant improvements have been "wrung out" of the plant over the years and merely keeping even is difficult.

For comparison he noted that one plant opened within the past four years would have an easier time meeting the company's expectations. The plant is new, containing modern equipment that is in some cases still experimental. Major modifications in equipment and operating systems have been made each year as the plant management has obtained a better understanding of the operations. The plant's management, although experienced, has been together only since its opening. The plant is located in a previously nonindustrial area and therefore has a relatively inexperienced work force.

Required:

(1) Evaluate the manufacturing manager's views.
(2) Equitable application of a budget system

requires the ability of corporate management to remove "budgetary slack" in plant budgets. Discuss how each plant could conceal "slack" in its budget.

(ICMA adapted)

C16-6. Budgetary control. Two divisional managers of the same company were overheard in conversation:

Manager X: "You know, comparison of my division's performance against the budget shows my group falling further and further behind each month. I'm really depressed. Conditions in our markets have changed so much since the budget was established that there is no way I can achieve those figures. In fact, our divisional performance is worse and worse by comparison with the budget for the balance of the year."

Manager A: "Yes, I know what you mean and sympathize with you. I had that problem last year. But this year I'm in the opposite situation. Our actual performance vis-a-vis the budget just gets better and better. It's nothing we're doing—conditions in our markets have changed for the good since the budget was established. We are, in a sense, just along for the ride, but it sure makes me look good at the head office."

Required: Discuss the role of the budgeting process in achieving objectives and what (if anything) is wrong with the process in this company.   CGA-Canada (adapted)
Reprint with permission

C16-7. The budget and human behavior. Drake Inc. is a multiproduct firm with several manufacturing plants. Management generally has been pleased with the operation of all but the Swan Plant, whose poor operating performance has been traced to poor control over plant costs. Four plant managers have resigned or been terminated during the last three years.

David Green was appointed the new manager of the Swan Plant on February 1, 19B. Green is a young and aggressive individual who had progressed rapidly in Drake's management development program and had performed well in lower level management positions.

Green had been recommended for the position by Susan Bradley, Green's immediate supervisor. Bradley was impressed by Green's technical ability and enthusiasm. Bradley explained to Green that the assignment as Swan Plant manager was approved despite the objections of some of the other members of the executive management team. Bradley told Green that she had complete confidence in him and his ability and was sure that Green wanted to prove that she had made a good decision. Therefore, Bradley expected Green to have the Swan Plant on budget by June 30.

As a result of Swan Plant's past difficulties, Susan Bradley has had responsibility for formulating the last four annual budgets for the plant. The 19B budget was prepared during the last six months of 19A before Green had been appointed plant manager. The budget report covering the three-month period ended March 31, 19B, showed that Swan's costs were slightly over budget. At a meeting with Bradley, Green described the changes he had instituted during the last month. Green was confident that the costs would be held in check with these changes and the situation would get no worse for the rest of the year.

Bradley repeated that she not only wanted the cost controlled but she expected Swan Plant to be on budget by June 30. Green pointed out that the Swan Plant had been in poor condition for three years. He further stated that, while he appreciated the confidence Bradley had in him, he had only been in charge two months.

Susan Bradley then replied, "I am expected to meet my figures. The only way that can occur is if my subordinates exercise control over their costs and achieve their budgets. Therefore, to assure that I achieve my goals, get the Swan Plant on budget by June 30 and keep it on budget for the rest of the year."

Required:

(1) Critically evaluate the budget practices described in the case.
(2) What are the likely immediate and long-term effects on David Green and Drake Inc. if the present method of budget administration is continued?

(ICMA adapted)

CHAPTER 17

Budgeting: Capital Expenditures, Research and Development Expenditures, and Cash; PERT/Cost; The Flexible Budget

Budgeting is usually an iterative process. Budgets are prepared, reviewed, and revised until executive management is satisfied that the result represents the best plans that can be devised under existing circumstances. Furthermore, management may develop contingency plans for dealing with various eventualities. As the planning period unfolds, budget revisions may be required, and such revisions will be facilitated if management has anticipated alterations called for by changing circumstances and conditions.

This chapter discusses specific budgets, such as capital expenditures and research and development budgets, which play a significant part in the long- and short-range plans of any management. Closely related thereto is the cash budget, which reveals excesses or shortages of funds. Budgeting for non-manufacturing businesses and not-for-profit organizations, zero-base budgeting, PERT and PERT/cost, probabilistic budgets, and the flexible budget conclude the presentation.

■ CAPITAL EXPENDITURES BUDGET — *equipment w/ useful life of over 1 year*

Capital expenditures are long-term commitments of resources to realize future benefits. Budgeting capital expenditures is one of the most important managerial decision-making functions. Facility improvements and plant expansion programs must be geared to a limited supply of funds from internal operations and external sources. The magnitude of funds involved in each expenditure and the length of time required to recover the investment call for penetrating analysis and capable judgment. Decisions regarding current manufacturing operations can always be changed, but because substantial amounts are invested in a capital project which can be recovered only over a fairly extended length of time, managerial errors could be quite costly.

517

Evaluating Capital Expenditures

To minimize the number of capital expenditure errors, many firms have established definite procedures for evaluating the merits of a project before funds are released. True control of capital expenditures is exercised in advance by requiring that each request be based on evaluation analyses, described and illustrated in Chapters 22 and 23. Managerial control requires facts regarding engineering estimates, expected sales volumes, production costs, and marketing costs. Management usually has a firm conviction as to what is consistent with the long-range objectives of the business. It is fundamentally interested in making certain that the project will contribute to the earnings position of the company.

Short- and Long-Range Capital Expenditures

Capital expenditure programs involve both short- and long-range projects. Short-range projects must be examined in the light of their economic worth as compared with other projects seeking final approval. The process of budgeting provides the only opportunity to examine these projects side by side and to evaluate their contribution to future periods. For short-range capital expenditures, the current budget should include a detailed capital expenditures budget as well as a determination of the impact on budgeted depreciation expense, cash, fixed asset, and liability accounts.

Long-range projects which will not be implemented in the current budget period need only be stated in general terms, since the exchange and addition of capital assets are only significant in the current budget period. Primarily, long-range capital expenditure plans are a management responsibility and are translated into budget commitments only as the opportune time for their implementation approaches. Timing is very important to the achievement of the most profitable results in planning and budgeting capital expenditures.

■ RESEARCH AND DEVELOPMENT BUDGET

Research and development (R & D) activities have been defined as follows:

1. *Research* is planned search or critical investigation aimed at discovery of new knowledge with the hope that such knowledge will be useful in developing a new product or service (hereinafter "product") or a new process or technique (hereinafter "process") or in bringing about a significant improvement to an existing product or process.
2. *Development* is the translation of research findings or other knowledge into a plan or design for a new product or process or for a significant improvement to an existing product or process whether intended for sale or use. It includes the conceptual formulation, design, and testing of product alternatives, construction of prototypes, and operation of pilot plants. It does not include routine or periodic alterations to exist-

ing products, production lines, manufacturing processes, and other ongoing operations even though those alterations may represent improvements, and it does not include market research or market testing activities.[1]

The managements of many firms are acutely aware of the increased necessity for and rapid growth of research and development activities and of the need to consider their costs from both the long- and short-range points of view. From the long-range viewpoint, management must assure itself that a program is in line with future market trends and demands and that the future cost of a program is not at odds with forecast economic and financial conditions. From the short-range viewpoint, management must be assured that experimental efforts are being expended on programs which promise a satisfactory rate of return on the dollars invested.

R & D projects compete with other projects for available financial resources. The value of the research and development program must be shown as clearly as possible, so that management can compare it with similar programs and other investment opportunities. Therefore, the motivation and intent of experimental activities must be carefully identified.

R & D efforts may require significant resources and may involve considerable risk. The cost of the resources may be estimated by using a "rule of sevens." That is, if an incremental technology to be sold through existing channels costs $1 million for R & D, it will likely cost $7 million for design and $7 million more to produce the first commercial unit. To these costs must be added working capital requirements and consideration of lead time. Studies have shown that generally if the time to complete the research is one year, the time to produce the first unit is another three years, with still another two years before significant profit occurs.[2]

As to risk, on average the probabilities are .6, .6, and .7, respectively, of successfully completing the phases of (1) determining that the product is technologically sound, (2) deciding that the product can be commercially successful, and (3) actually achieving commercial success. Thus, one in four projects can be expected to succeed (.6 × .6 × .7 = .25). Therefore, while many businesses require R & D efforts, they should be planned with a realistic understanding of the associated resource commitment and risk.[3]

The research and development budget involves identifying program components and estimating their costs. Other planning devices are used at times, but the budget is considered best for (1) balancing the research and development program, (2) coordinating the program with the company's other projects, and (3) checking certain phases of nonfinancial planning. The budget forces management to think in advance about planned expenditures, both in total amounts and in sphere of effort. It helps achieve coordination, because

---

[1]*Statement of Financial Accounting Standards, No. 2,* "Accounting for Research and Development Costs" (Stamford: Financial Accounting Standards Board, 1974), par. 8.

[2]Francis W. Wolek, "The Business of Technology, Part 1: A Board Guide to Progress and Profits," *Directors & Boards,* Vol. 9, No. 4, p. 33.

[3]*Ibid.*

it presents an overall picture of proposed R & D activities which can be reviewed and criticized by other operating managers. Exchange of opinions and information at planning meetings is management's best control over the program.

Another important purpose of research and development budgeting is to coordinate these plans with the immediate and long-term financial plans of the company. The budget also forces the R & D director and staff to think in advance about major aspects of the program: personnel requirements, individual or group work loads, equipment requirements, special materials, and necessary facilities. These phases of the research and development program are often overlooked or duplicated.

Forms of a Research and Development Budget

Management expects the R & D staff to present ideas along with a complete and detailed budget which can be evaluated as part of the entire planning program. The controller's staff may assist in the preparation of budgets with clearly defined goals and properly evaluated cost data.

Submission of data takes many forms. Information regarding segmentation and allocation of time and effort to various phases of the program is of particular interest to executive management as well as to divisional managers. The following example of a research and development budget has been proposed.[4]

RESEARCH AND DEVELOPMENT BUDGET
PROGRAM PLANNED FOR 19—
(Percentages of Total Effort by Area of Inquiry and by Phase)

Phase	Cost Reduction			Improved Products			New Products			Total
	A*	B	C	A	B	C	A	B	C	
Basic research	4%	3%	3%	2%	4%	4%	1%	1%	3%	25%
Applied research	5	12	3	4	1		2		3	30
Development	7	6	2	5			10		15	45
Total by product lines	16%	21%	8%	11%	5%	4%	13%	1%	21%	100%
Total by area of inquiry		45%			20%			35%		

*A, B, and C refer to product lines.

The overall R & D program should be supported by a specific budget request which indicates the jobs or steps within each project, the necessary labor hours, the service department time required, and required direct departmental funds. Each active project should be reviewed monthly, comparing projected plans with results attained.

---

[4]J. B. Quinn, "Study of the Usefulness of Research and Development Budgets," *NAA Bulletin*, Vol. XL, No. 1, pp. 79-90: Copyright July, 1958, by the National Association of Accountants. All rights reserved. Reprinted by permission.

The Franklin Company illustration from the preceding chapter did not include budgeted research and development expenditures. Such a budget could be detailed in dollars, using a format similar to the budget shown on page 520. The dollar amount would be included in the budgeted income statement, consistent with the accounting procedures described in the following paragraph.

Accounting for Research and Development Costs

Research and development costs generally should be expensed in the period incurred because of the uncertainty of the extent or length of future benefit to the company. An exception to the expensing requirement applies to costs of R & D expenditures that are (1) conducted for others, (2) unique to extractive industries, or (3) incurred by a government-regulated enterprise, such as a public utility, which often defers research and development costs because of the rate-regulated aspects of its business. Equipment and purchased intangibles having alternative future uses should be recorded as assets and expensed through depreciation or amortization. R & D costs, when expensed, should be reported as one item in the operating expense section of the income statement.[5]

For government contract costing, the Cost Accounting Standards Board promulgated a standard dealing with accounting for independent research and development costs and bid and proposal costs. It provides criteria for (1) accumulation of such costs, (2) their allocation among contractor divisions, and (3) allocation of these costs to contracts.[6]

■ CASH BUDGET

— responsibility of Treasurer not Controller

does 2 things
1. receipts
2. disbursements

A *cash budget* involves detailed estimates of anticipated cash receipts and disbursements for the budget period or some other specific period. It has generally been recognized as an extremely useful and essential management tool. Planning and controlling cash is basic to good management.

Effective cash management entails having the right amounts of cash in the right places at the right times. It involves the management of flows of cash by looking at an organization's liquid funds as an income-producing asset rather than simply as currency for paying bills. Even if a company does not prepare extensive budgets for sales and production, it should set up a budget or estimate of cash receipts and disbursements as an aid to cash management.

---

[5]*Statement of Financial Accounting Standards, No. 2, op. cit.,* pars. 2, 3, and 11-14.

[6]For specifics, see *Standards, Rules and Regulations, Part 420,* "Accounting for Independent Research and Development Costs and Bid and Proposal Costs" (Washington, D.C.: Cost Accounting Standards Board, 1980).

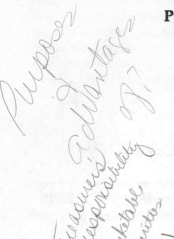

Purpose and Nature of a Cash Budget

A cash budget:

1. Indicates cash requirements needed for current operating activities.
2. Aids in focusing on cash usage priorities currently required and unavoidable versus postponable or permanently avoidable.
3. Indicates the effect on the cash position of seasonal requirements, large inventories, unusual receipts, and slowness in collecting receivables.
4. Indicates the availability of cash for taking advantage of discounts.
5. Indicates the cash requirements for a plant or equipment expansion program.
6. Assists in planning the financial requirements of bond retirements, income tax installments, and payments to pension and retirement funds.
7. Shows the availability of excess funds for short-term or long-term investments.
8. Shows the need for additional funds from sources such as bank loans or sales of securities and the time factors involved. In this connection, it might also exert a cautionary influence on plans for plant expansion, leading to a modification of capital expenditure decisions.
9. Serves as a basis for evaluating the actual cash management performance of responsible individuals, using measurement criteria such as the target average daily balance as compared with the actual average daily balance in each cash account.

The cash budget for different time spans has different uses and origins. A long-range cash projection, which may cover periods ranging from three to five years, is useful in planning business growth, investments in projects, and introduction of new products. It focuses primarily on significant changes in the firm's cash position. A medium-range cash budget is related to the overall periodic, usually yearly, budgeting procedures for the business, detailed by quarters and months. Improved cash utilization within this time frame is obtained through control of accounts payable policies, control of inventory turnover, and a review of credit, billing, and collection procedures. The short-range cash budget details the daily availability of cash for current operations, usually 30 to 60 days, and indicates any need for short-term financing. This kind of projection generally is based on records of current transactions of the business.[7]

Preparation of a Periodic Cash Budget

Preparation of a periodic cash budget involves estimating cash receipts and disbursements by time periods. All anticipated cash receipts, such as cash sales, cash collections of accounts receivable, dividend income, interest income, proceeds from sales of assets, royalty income, borrowings from

---

[7]Robert A. Leitch, John B. Barrack, and Sue H. McKinley, "Controlling Your Cash Resources," *Management Accounting*, Vol. LXII, No. 4, p. 59.

banks, bond issues, and stock sales, are carefully estimated. Likewise, cash requirements for materials purchases, supplies, payroll, interest payments, repayment of loans, dividend payments to shareholders, taxes, and purchases of plant or equipment must be determined.

The primary sources of cash receipts are cash sales and collections of accounts receivable. Estimates of collections of accounts receivable are based on the sales budget and on the company's collection experience. A study is made of a representative period to determine how customers pay their accounts, how many take the discount offered, and how many pay within 10 days, 30 days, and so forth. These experiences are set up in a schedule of anticipated collections from credit sales. Collections during a month will be the result of (1) this month's sales and (2) accounts receivable of prior months' sales. Seasonal variations also should be considered if they affect the collections pattern. To illustrate, assume that during each month, collections of credit sales show the following pattern:

From current month's sales	10.8%
From prior months' accounts receivable:	
Last month's sales	77.4
2 months old	6.3
3 months old	2.1
4 months old	1.2
Cash discounts taken	1.2
Doubtful accounts	1.0
	100.0%

On the basis of these percentages, collections for January, as an illustrative month, are computed as follows:

Month	Assumed Estimate of Credit Sales	%	Collections
January	$400,000	10.8	$ 43,200
December	385,000	77.4	297,990
November.	420,000	6.3	26,460
October	360,000	2.1	7,560
September	340,000	1.2	4,080
Total collections for January			$379,290

Estimated cash disbursements are computed from the:

1. Purchases budget, which shows planned purchases of materials and supplies.
2. Direct labor budget, which indicates direct labor wages to be paid.
3. Various types of expense budgets, both factory overhead and commercial, which indicate expenses expected to be incurred. Noncash expenses such as depreciation are excluded.
4. Plant and equipment budget, which details cash needed for the purchase of new equipment or replacements.
5. Treasurer's budget, which indicates requirements for items such as dividends, interest and payments on loans and bonds, donations, and income tax.

For each item, the estimated timing of the cash disbursements is required. If indebtedness does not occur uniformly, variations in the pattern should be considered in estimating the timing of cash disbursements.

A cash budget includes no accrual items. For example, assume that direct labor payroll accrued at the beginning and the end of January is $14,800 and $13,300, respectively, and the budget shows that $90,000 will be earned by direct labor employees. The treasurer computes the monthly cash requirement for the direct labor payroll as follows:

Accrued payroll at beginning of January	$ 14,800
Add payroll earned as per budget.	90,000
	$104,800
Deduct accrued payroll at end of January	13,300
Amount of cash to be paid out during January	$ 91,500

A similar approach can be used to estimate the timing of other cash disbursements as well. Alternatively, a cash payment may be estimated in the following manner. Assume that direct materials purchases and other items such as factory overhead and commercial expenses occur fairly uniformly throughout each month and that approximately ten days (1/3 month) normally elapse between the recording of an indebtedness and its payment. Assume further that cash discounts are always taken and that they average 2 percent. Using data that would be obtained from the direct materials budget, the January cash disbursement for direct materials purchased is:

December purchases (($200,000 – 2% cash discount) × 1/3 paid in January) . .	$ 65,333
January purchases (($130,000 – 2% cash discount) × 2/3 paid in January)	84,933
January cash disbursement for direct materials purchased	$150,266

After all the cash receipts and cash disbursements have been estimated for each month of the budget year, the year-end cash balance for inclusion in the budgeted balance sheet can be determined. This amount is the beginning of the budget year's cash balance, plus the estimated total annual cash receipts from all sources, less the estimated total annual disbursements necessary to satisfy all cash demands. An illustrated cash budget for the month of January follows:

January 1, cash balance		$181,506
Budgeted cash receipts:		
Collections of accounts receivable.	$379,290	
Dividend and interest income.	9,000	
Issue of long-term debt	50,000	438,290
Cash available during January		$619,796
Budgeted cash disbursements:		
Payroll	$ 91,500	
Payment of accounts payable for materials purchases.	150,266	
Pension plan payments	9,000	
Insurance, utilities, and miscellaneous expenses	11,000	
Repayment of bank loans	50,000	
Interest payment on bank loans.	6,000	
Purchases of new machinery.	60,000	377,766
January 31, cash balance		$242,030

Development of Daily Cash Budget Detail

Daily cash receipts and disbursements schedules are necessary for prudent and efficient cash management. Such schedules bring the focus of the cash budget to the most relevant time frame.

Development of daily cash budget detail begins with identification of the timing of major cash flows for items such as taxes, dividends, lease payments, debt service, and wages. Most major cash flows are either easily forecast or, if not forecastable, are offset by a single financial transaction, such as the use of short-term borrowing for an outflow or short-term investing for an inflow.

Numerous small receipts and payments may also occur. These minor flows are amenable to some combination of two basic approaches—distribution and scheduling. *Distribution* refers to using statistical estimation to spread a forecast of the total monthly minor flow components over the days of the month in order to reflect the known intramonth cash flow.[8] *Scheduling* refers to the construction of a forecast from information-system-based data, such as disbursement data from invoices, purchase authorizations, production schedules, and work plans.

Electronic Cash Management

The basic premise of cash management is that dollars in transit are not earning assets. They cannot be utilized until they are available as deposits. Similarly, cash lying idle in checking accounts contributes little to corporate profitability.

Organizations with multiple, geographically dispersed units, or firms with a widespread customer base making individual payments to dispersed collecting units, can especially benefit from electronic cash management systems. The system involves cash concentration by means of nationwide electronic transfers which accelerate the collection of deposits from local banks into a central account on a same-day basis. By drawing checks on its centrally located account, the firm has the additional advantage of *float* for the time it takes the check to be cleared back to the central bank account.

For whatever number of bank accounts a firm may have, electronic balance reporting affords a valuable aid to efficient and effective cash management. This bank service provides accurate, up-to-date, and on-line daily information on amounts and locations of available cash. Depending on the level of service, the information furnished may be highly detailed, via a computer terminal, or abbreviated by means of a telephone-to-computer inquiry that results in each bank's computer "telling" the firm's balances. This information is especially useful in the short-term investment management of the day-to-day difference between the firm's book balance of cash and the bank's balance, that is, in the management of float.

---

[8]For an illustration of this procedure, see Bernell K. Stone and Robert A. Wood, "Daily Cash Forecasting: A Simple Method for Implementing the Distribution Approach," *Financial Management*, Vol. 6, No. 3, pp. 40-50.

Another and broader electronic cash management application is found in *electronic funds transfer systems* (EFTS). These systems are designed to reduce the number of paper documents and to increase the use of electronic data in carrying out banking cash transfer functions, thus reducing bank transaction costs and expediting cash transfers. These developing cash payment systems include unstaffed customer banking facilities, automated clearinghouses for interbank cash transfers, point-of-sale facilities, pay-by-phone service, and corporate funds transfers.[9] For the manager, the potential for virtually instantaneous receipts and payments of cash requires consideration in the management of cash resources.

PLANNING AND BUDGETING FOR NONMANUFACTURING BUSINESSES AND NOT-FOR-PROFIT ORGANIZATIONS

Many industrial concerns still pay only lip service to the suggested steps, methods, and procedures of budgeting. To an even greater extent, nonmanufacturing businesses—and especially not-for-profit organizations—lack effective planning and control mechanisms. However, examples of effective budgeting do exist.

Nonmanufacturing Businesses

Under the guidance of the National Retail Merchants Association, department stores have followed merchandise budget procedures that have a long and quite successful history. A budget for a retail store is a necessity, since the profit per dollar of sales generally is low, usually from 1 to 3 percent. Planning, budgeting, and control administration is strongly oriented toward profit control on the total store as well as on a departmental basis. The merchandise budget shows predetermined sales and profits, generally on a six-month basis following the two merchandising seasons: spring-summer and fall-winter. The merchandise budget includes sales, purchases, expenses, capital expenditures, cash, and annual statements.

Although it is logical for a department store or a wholesaler to plan and budget its activities, banks, savings and loan associations, and insurance companies also should create a long-range profit plan coordinating long-term goals and objectives of the institution. In these businesses, forecasting would deal with deposit size and mix, number of insured and mix of policies, capital requirements, types of earning assets, physical facilities, personnel requirements, operational changes, and new, additional, or changed depositor or client services. The long-range goal should be translated into short-range budgets, starting at the lowest level of responsibility, building and combining

---

[9]Howard C. Johnson and Edward C. Arnold, "The Emerging Revolution in Electronic Payments," *Price Waterhouse Review*, Vol. 22, No. 3, pp. 26-31.

the various organizational units into a whole. Similarly, such needs exist for professional service organizations, e.g., law firms, accounting firms, medical and dental practices, and realtors.

Not-for-Profit Organizations

While business organizations are concerned with profits, the not-for-profit sector is concerned with programs. Yet neither can succeed without sound budgeting. Management in a not-for-profit organization, as in any entity, is a process that entails planning, resource allocation, execution, and evaluation. Budgeting is the common denominator that links these management activities.

Periodic budgets in any enterprise, not-for-profit or business, are usually conceived at the bottom of the organizational hierarchy and then passed upward for refinement and approval. Department managers in not-for-profit organizations develop their program needs in the context of policies, priorities, and assumptions expressed in long-range plans and in accordance with periodic budget guidelines established by senior management. A comprehensive budget format is required—presented by program to indicate the purpose of expenditures and with adequate detail to establish control. Each program should emphasize the relationship between the input of resources and the output of services to be performed, including the measures necessary to evaluate achievement of program objectives.[10]

Measuring the benefits or outputs of programs poses difficulties. A private enterprise measures its benefits in terms of increased revenue or decreased cost. In the nonprofit sector, however, social problems complicate the measurement of benefits. Consequently, such endeavors often have resulted in relatively meaningless monetary outcome data. Problems encountered in monetary output measurements suggest that monetary inputs (costs) might be more meaningfully related to nonmonetary outcomes for specific programs.[11]

Annual budgets for governments at all levels in the United States are now well in excess of one trillion dollars—an enormous sum of money. Yet, in spite of the many decades in which governmental budgeting has been practiced, the general public is increasingly critical of services received for money spent. While the federal government might be under more obvious attack, state, county, and municipal governments are equally criticized not only for the lack of a satisfactory control system, but also for the ill-conceived procedure for planning the costs and revenues needed to govern. Therefore, a budget based on a managerial approach would go a long way toward responsibly meeting these criticisms.

An example of such an effort in government is found in the concept of a planning, programming, budgeting system, commonly referred to as PPBS.

---

[10]R. Schuyler Lesher, Jr., and Craig Becker, "Total Recall," *Management Focus*, Vol. 30, No. 5, pp. 13, 15.

[11]For additional discussion and illustration, see James E. Sorensen and Hugh D. Grove, "Cost-Outcome and Cost-Effectiveness Analysis: Emerging Nonprofit Performance Evaluation Techniques," *The Accounting Review*, Vol. LII, No. 3, pp. 658-675.

PPBS might be defined as an analytical tool to assist management (1) in the analysis of alternatives as the basis for rational decision making and (2) in allocating resources to accomplish stated goals and objectives over a designated time period. It had its origin in the Defense Department's attempt to quantify huge expenditures in terms of benefits derived from activities and programs of the public sector. This analysis technique is closely related to cost-benefit analysis, focusing upon the outputs or final results, rather than the inputs or the initial dollars expended. The outputs are directly relatable to the planned objectives through the use of performance budgets.

The idea that governmental programs should be undertaken in the light of final benefits has caused agencies in the field of health, education, and welfare services as well as other nonprofit organizations to apply PPBS to their activities and programs. However, PPBS has been criticized because its required specification of objectives cannot be transformed readily into operational outcome quantities or statistics. PPBS, if effective, needs a great deal of refinement and innovation, an understanding of its aims and methods, and active participation of executive and middle management.

In the same way that governmental units have become budget and cost conscious, not-for-profit organizations, such as hospitals, churches, school districts, colleges, universities, fraternal orders, libraries, and labor unions, are adopting strong measures of budgetary control. In the past, efforts to control costs were generally exercised through pressure to reduce budget increases rather than through method improvements or program changes. Long-range planning was seldom practiced.

Basically, the objectives of not-for-profit organizations are directed toward the economic, social, educational, or spiritual benefit of individuals or groups who have no vested interest in such organizations in the form of ownership or investment. The presidents, boards of directors, trustees, or administrative officers, like their counterparts in profit-seeking enterprises, are charged with the stewardship of economic resources, except that their job is primarily to use or spend these resources instead of trying to derive monetary gain. It is expressly for this not-for-profit objective that these organizations should install adequate and effective methods and procedures in planning, budgeting, and cost control.[12]

■ ZERO-BASE BUDGETING

Customarily, those in charge of an established budgetary program are required to justify only the increase sought above last year's appropriation. What they are already spending is usually accepted as necessary, with little or no examination. *Zero-base budgeting*, however, is a budget-planning procedure for the reevaluation of an organization's program and expenditures. It

[12]Budgeting for not-for-profit organizations other than governmental, health care, and higher education is discussed in considerable detail in *Financial Planning and Evaluation for the Nonprofit Organization*, by Anthony J. Gambino and Thomas J. Reardon (New York: National Association of Accountants, 1981).

Requires 3 budgets

1. Bare bones - survival only

2. Median → to do good job

3. Enhanced - what you would do w/ extra money

requires each manager to justify the entire budget request in detail and places the burden of proof on the manager to justify why authorization to spend any money at all should be granted. It starts with the assumption that zero will be spent on each activity—thus, the term "zero-base." What a manager is spending already is not accepted as a starting point.

Managers are asked to prepare for each activity or operation under their control a *decision package* that includes an analysis of cost, purpose, alternative courses of action, measures of performance, consequences of not performing the activity, and benefits. The zero-base budgeting approach asserts that in building the budget from zero, two types of alternatives should be considered by managers: (1) different ways of performing the same activity and (2) different levels of effort in performing the activity.

A decision package identifies an activity in a definitive manner for evaluation and comparison with other activities. Devising these decision packages, ranking them, and making funding decisions according to the rank order comprise the heart of the zero-base budgeting process.

Success in implementing zero-base budgeting requires:

1. Linkage of zero-base budgeting to the short- and long-range planning process.
2. Sustained support and commitment from executive management.
3. Innovation among the managers who make up the budget decision packages.
4. Sale of the procedure to the people who must perform the work necessary to keep the concept vigorous.

■ PERT AND PERT/COST SYSTEMS FOR PLANNING AND CONTROL

Skip

The accountant's involvement in management planning and control has led to the use of network analysis systems for planning, measuring progress to schedule, evaluating changes to schedule, forecasting future progress, and predicting and controlling costs. These systems are variously referred to as PERT (Program Evaluation and Review Technique) or CPM (Critical Path Method). The origin of PERT is military; it was introduced in connection with the Navy Polaris program. CPM's origin is industrial.

Many companies use these methods in planning, scheduling, and costing such diverse projects as constructing buildings, installing equipment, and research and development. There is also an opportunity for using PERT in business administration tasks, such as scheduling the closing of books, revising standard cost data, scheduling the time elements for the preparation of departmental budgets, cash flows, and preparing the annual profit plan, as well as for audit planning and control. In conjunction with PERT and critical path techniques, computer systems provide executive management with far better means for directing large-scale, complex projects. Management can measure cost, time, and technical performance on an integrated basis. Actual results can be compared with the network plan and revisions made as needed.

The PERT System

PERT is a probabilistic diagram of the interrelationships of a complex series of activities. Whether a military, industrial, or business administration task, time is the fundamental element of any of these activities. The major burden of PERT is the determination of the longest time duration for the completion of the entire project. This calculation is based on the length of time required for the longest sequence of activities.

All of the individual tasks to complete a given job or program must be visualized in a *network* of events and activities. An *event* represents a specified accomplishment at a particular instant in time, such as B or E in the following network. An *activity* represents the time and resources necessary to move from one event to another, e.g., B→E in the chart. Some of the activities may be in series; e.g., market research cannot be performed before the research design is planned. Other activities may be parallel; e.g., the engines for a ship can be built at the same time the hull is being constructed.

**PERT Network with
Time Estimates
in Weeks**

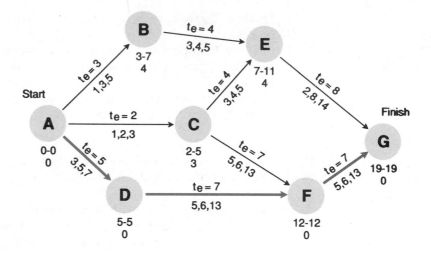

Time estimates for PERT are made for each activity on a three-way basis, i.e., optimistic (t_o), most likely (t_m), and pessimistic (t_p). In the network illustrated, the three time estimates, expressed in units of one week, are indicated under each activity line. From these estimates, an expected time (t_e) is calculated for each activity. The expected time represents the average time an activity would require if it were repeated a large number of times. The calculation is generally based on the assumption that the distribution of activity times closely approximates a Beta probability distribution. Such distributions may be symmetrical or skewed. The following formula is used to compute the mean of the Beta probability distribution, which is the expected time:

$$t_e = \frac{(t_o + 4t_m + t_p)}{6}$$

For example, the activity D-F has a value of $t_e = 7$, determined as follows:

$$\text{If: } t_o = 5$$
$$t_m = 6$$
$$t_p = 13$$
$$\text{Then: } t_e = \frac{(5 + 4(6) + 13)}{6} = \frac{42}{6} = 7$$

Below each event in the network are noted the earliest expected and latest allowable times, and below these two numbers, the slack time is shown. The *earliest expected time* is the earliest time that an activity can be expected to start, because of its relationship to pending activities. The *latest allowable time* is the latest time that an activity may begin and not delay completion of the project.

The Critical Path. The longest path through the network is known as the *critical path* and is denoted on the flowchart by the arrows connecting A-D-F-G. Shortening of total time can be accomplished only by shortening the critical path. However, if the critical path A-D-F-G is shortened from nineteen weeks to fifteen weeks, A-C-F-G (assuming F-G remains unchanged) would then become the critical path because it would be the longest.

Slack Time. Activities along the critical path (A-D-F-G) have a slack of zero. All noncritical activities have positive slack. The less the amount of slack time, the more critical an activity or path, and vice versa.

Slack is computed by subtracting the earliest expected time from the latest allowable time. It is determinable only in relation to an entire path through the network. When multiple activities lead to an event, the event's earliest expected starting time is always the largest sum of expected times of the preceding activities. When multiple activities lead from an event, the latest allowable time at that event is always the smallest figure found by subtracting from total project time the sum of expected times of subsequent network activities. For example, path A-C-E-G at event C has an earliest expected time of two weeks and a latest allowable time of five weeks (19 – (7 + 7)), for a slack time of three weeks. At event E, the earliest expected time is seven weeks (3 (A-B) + 4 (B-E)) and the latest allowable time is eleven weeks (19 – 8), for a slack time of four weeks. However, if any slack time is used up, that is, if a noncritical activity utilizes more than the expected time, the slack times for subsequent activities must be recomputed. Recomputation also may be necessary when less than the expected times are required.

Slack allows management some flexibility. If available slack time is not exceeded, noncritical activities can be delayed without delaying the project's completion date. Slack time information provides useful data for initial planning and continuous project monitoring when the project's status is compared with the plan.

The PERT/Cost System

PERT/cost is an integrated management information system designed to furnish management with timely information for planning and controlling schedules and costs of projects. The PERT/cost system is really an expansion of PERT. It assigns cost to time and activities, thereby providing total financial planning and control by functional responsibility.

The predetermination of cost is in harmony with the accountant's budgeting task and follows the organizational and procedural steps used in responsibility accounting. The PERT/cost estimates are activity- or project-oriented, and the addition of the cost component permits analyses involving time/cost tradeoffs. Each activity is defined at a level of detail necessary for individual job assignments and supervisory control. Control is on scheduled tasks, with time and cost as the common control factors. Cost accumulation methods must be devised to be compatible with PERT/cost control concepts.

In the following network, the activities noted by the dark circles, A, B, C, and D, represent completed events. The dollar figures in the white blocks represent estimated costs, e.g., $30,000 for activity F-G. Figures in the lightly shaded blocks to the right of the estimates are actual costs. Estimated times (t_e) and actual times (t_a) are shown below the activity lines.

PERT/Cost Network with Time (in Weeks) and Cost (in Thousands of Dollars)

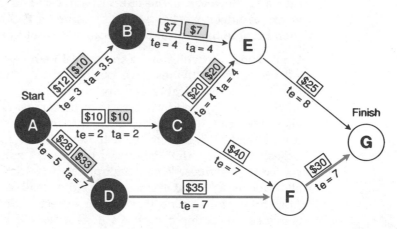

Activities A-B, A-C, and A-D have been completed. A-B required one-half week more time than planned; however, it is not on the critical path and will not affect total project duration. If excess time were such that another path became long enough to be the critical path, then total time would be involved.

The actual activity cost of $10,000 for A-B compared to a budget of $12,000 indicates an underrun of $2,000. Activity A-C budget and actual figures coincide for time and cost. A-D had an overrun of $5,000 and a two-week slippage. The slippage requires immediate attention because A-D is on the critical path. Immediate investigation and corrective action seem needed for B-E and C-E. According to the present status report, both activities have consumed the budgeted time and cost and one or both are not yet completed.

While comparison of actual versus planned time and cost figures is essential, comparison alone is not enough to evaluate a project. Evaluation of performance is needed to complete the process. For example, a project is not necessarily in financial trouble when actual expenditures exceed budgeted.

Progress may be correspondingly ahead of schedule. Nor is a project necessarily meeting performance standards when it is within the budget. To evaluate the true status, management needs to study performance, cost, and timing.

Computer Applications

Computer support provides distinct advantages to PERT and PERT/cost applications. PERT and PERT/cost procedures are mathematically oriented and therefore are ideally suited to the high-speed response of computers for deriving the critical path, slack times, and costs, and for storing and reporting results to management. Revisions to all schedule elements, whether during the initial estimating phase or during the active project phase, can be updated and the revised results promptly reported.

■ PROBABILISTIC BUDGETS

The budget may be developed based on one set of assumptions as to the most likely performance in the forthcoming period. However, there is increasing evidence that several sets of assumptions are evaluated by management before the budget is finalized. One possibility is the PERT-like three-level estimates—optimistic, most likely, and pessimistic. This involves estimating each budget component assuming each of the three conditions. Probability trees can be used in which several variables can be considered in the analysis, e.g., number of units sold, sales price, and variable manufacturing and marketing costs.

To each discrete set of assumptions, a probability can be assigned, based on past experience and management's best judgment about the future, thus revealing to management not only a range of possible outcomes but also a probability associated with each. Further statistical techniques can then be applied, including an expected (weighted, composite) value, the range, and the standard deviation for the various budget elements, such as sales, manufacturing cost, and marketing cost. For example, the expected value for sales may be $960,000, with a range from a low of $780,000 to a high of $1,200,000 and a standard deviation of $114,600.

The computational capability of the computer facilitates the consideration of complex sets of assumptions and permits the use of simulation programs, making it possible to develop more objectively determined probabilities.[13]

---

[13]An exhaustive treatment of these techniques is beyond the scope of this discussion. For expanded discussion and illustrations, see:

William L. Ferrara and Jack C. Hayya, "Toward Probabilistic Profit Budgets," *Management Accounting*, Vol. LII, No. 3, pp. 23-28.

Belverd E. Needles, Jr., "Budgeting Techniques: Subjective to Probabilistic," *Management Accounting*, Vol. LIII, No. 6, pp. 39-45.

Edmund J. Hall and Richard J. Kolkmann, "A Vote for the Probabilistic Pro Forma Income Statement," *Management Accounting*, Vol. LVII, No. 7, pp. 45-48.

Davis L. S. Chang and Shu S. Liao, "Measuring and Disclosing Forecast Reliability," *The Journal of Accountancy*, Vol. 143, No. 5, pp. 76-87, (Monte Carlo simulation).

■ THE FLEXIBLE BUDGET FOR PLANNING AND CONTROL

Budgets are based on certain definite assumed conditions and results. The budgets discussed and illustrated in Chapter 16 and up to this point in the present chapter are known as fixed or expected budgets, while the budgets discussed in this section are known as flexible budgets. The term "fixed" is misleading, however, since a fixed budget is subject to revision. *Fixed* merely denotes that the budget is not adjusted to actual volume attained. It represents a prefixed point of sales and cost estimates with which actual results are compared. A *flexible budget*, however, is adjusted to actual volume.

Both fixed and flexible budgets provide management with information necessary to attain the major objectives of budgetary control, which include:

1. An organized procedure for planning.
2. A means for coordinating the activities of the various divisions of a business.
3. A basis for cost control.

Cost control is predicated on the idea that actual costs will be compared with budgeted costs, relating what did happen with what should have happened. When a company's activities can be estimated within close limits, the fixed budget is satisfactory. However, completely predictable situations exist in only a few cases. If actual volume differs from that planned, a comparison of actual results with a fixed budget may be misleading. For example, suppose that 1,000 units of product were planned at a budgeted cost of $10,000, but that 1,100 units actually are produced at a cost of $10,500. A simple comparison of budgeted costs with actual costs indicates an unfavorable variance of $500. However, further examination reveals that actual production exceeds that planned by 100 units. Since budgeted and actual costs contain both fixed and variable costs, it is not clear whether the variance is favorable or unfavorable. To make such a determination, actual costs must be compared with a budget based on the actual volume. A flexible budget provides an acceptable measure of what costs should be under any given set of conditions, i.e., a budget adjusted to actual volume.

Preparing a Flexible Budget

To prepare a flexible budget, a formula must be developed for each account within each department or cost center using one of the techniques described in Chapter 12. Each formula indicates the fixed cost and/or the variable cost rate for the account. The variable portion of the formula is a rate of cost in relation to some measure of activity such as direct labor hours, machine hours, or units of production. The fixed amount and the variable rate remain constant within prescribed ranges of activity.

The application of these formulas to the level of activity actually experienced produces allowable budget expenditures for the volume of activity actually attained. These budget figures are compared with actual costs in order to compute the spending and idle capacity variances discussed in Chapters 13 through 15 and, thus, to measure the performance of each department or cost center.

Originally, the flexible budget was applied principally to the control of departmental factory overhead. Now, however, the idea is applied to the entire budget, so that marketing and administrative budgets as well as manufacturing budgets are prepared on a flexible budget basis. The flexible budget also is a useful planning tool because it provides cost behavior information that can be used to evaluate the effects of different volumes of activity on profits and on the cash position and to establish the approved periodic budget.

The following illustration is devoted to the preparation of a flexible budget for a producing department in a factory. It is not intended to convey the idea, however, that the factory overhead budget outranks the budgets for other functions of the business, because these other functions can also utilize the flexible budget concept. Any increase or decrease in business activity must be reflected throughout the enterprise. In some activities or departments, changes will be greater or smaller than in others. Certain departments have the ability to produce more without much additional cost. In others, costs increase or decrease in more or less direct proportion to production increases or decreases. The flexible budget attempts to deal with this problem.

When the fixed dollar amount and the variable rate of a cost have been determined, following the cost behavior analysis covered in Chapter 12, budget allowances for any level within a relevant range of activity can be computed without difficulty. For example, a budget allowances schedule, based on normal capacity for the Machining Department of a manufacturing company, is as follows:

BUDGET ALLOWANCE FOR MACHINING DEPARTMENT

Activity Base: 1,000 machine hours per month at normal capacity, which is 80% of rated capacity.

Cost	Fixed Cost	Variable Rate per Machine Hour
Indirect labor	$ 5,000	$ .50
Supervision	3,000	
Factory supplies	1,500	.90
Power	900	1.10
Rework operations	500	.50
Payroll taxes	1,000	.15
Repair and maintenance	1,000	.75
Total controllable cost	$12,900	$3.90
Property insurance	$ 800	
Property taxes	600	
Vacation pay	2,200	
Employee pension costs	1,400	
Employee health plan	600	
Machinery depreciation	3,400	
Water and heat	800	
Building occupancy cost allocation	1,300	
General factory cost allocation	2,000	$ .10
Total noncontrollable cost	$13,100	$ .10
Total cost	$26,000	$4.00

(Continued)

Summary:
Fixed cost..	$26,000	
Variable cost (1,000 machine hours × $4 variable rate)	4,000	
Total cost at normal capacity.........................	$30,000	
Factory overhead rate for Machining Department at normal capacity ($30,000 ÷ 1,000 machine hours)...............	$ 30.00	per machine hour

The schedule of budget allowances is the basis for the following flexible budget. One approach to preparing a flexible budget would be to compute the variable cost for each item of factory overhead at several different levels of activity (i.e., multiply each level of activity being considered by the variable rate for each item of overhead) and prepare a flexible budget as follows:

ONE MONTH FLEXIBLE BUDGET FOR MACHINING DEPARTMENT

Operating level:				
Based on machine hours ..	875	1,000	1,125	1,250
Percentage of capacity	70%	80%*	90%	100%
Variable cost:				
Indirect labor	$ 437.50	$ 500.00	$ 562.50	$ 625.00
Factory supplies..........	787.50	900.00	1,012.50	1,125.00
Power..................	962.50	1,100.00	1,237.50	1,375.00
Rework operations........	437.50	500.00	562.50	625.00
Payroll taxes	131.25	150.00	168.75	187.50
Repair and maintenance...	656.25	750.00	843.75	937.50
General factory	87.50	100.00	112.50	125.00
Total variable cost	$ 3,500.00	$ 4,000.00	$ 4,500.00	$ 5,000.00
Fixed cost:				
Indirect labor	$ 5,000.00	$ 5,000.00	$ 5,000.00	$ 5,000.00
Supervision	3,000.00	3,000.00	3,000.00	6,000.00
Factory supplies..........	1,500.00	1,500.00	1,500.00	1,500.00
Power..................	900.00	900.00	900.00	900.00
Rework operations........	500.00	500.00	500.00	975.00
Payroll taxes	1,000.00	1,000.00	1,000.00	1,000.00
Repair and maintenance...	1,000.00	1,000.00	1,000.00	1,000.00
Property insurance	800.00	800.00	800.00	800.00
Property taxes	600.00	600.00	600.00	600.00
Vacation pay	2,200.00	2,200.00	2,200.00	2,500.00
Employee pension costs ...	1,400.00	1,400.00	1,400.00	1,600.00
Employee health plan	600.00	600.00	600.00	700.00
Machinery depreciation....	3,400.00	3,400.00	3,400.00	3,400.00
Water and heat	800.00	800.00	800.00	800.00
Building occupancy.......	1,300.00	1,300.00	1,300.00	1,300.00
General factory	2,000.00	2,000.00	2,000.00	2,000.00
Total fixed cost	$26,000.00	$26,000.00	$26,000.00	$30,075.00**
Total cost	$29,500.00	$30,000.00	$30,500.00	$35,075.00
Factory overhead rate per machine hour	$33.714	$30.000	$27.111	$28.060

*Normal capacity
**See footnote #14 on page 537.

Service department charges to user departments that are not based on a predetermined rate or that are charged on the basis of a noncontrollable activity may not be controllable. In such a case controllable costs should be separated from those that are not controllable by the department supervisor. (See discussion of responsibility accounting and reporting concepts in Chapter 15.) Although fixed and variable costs could be reported separately for both controllable and noncontrollable costs, it may be more convenient to simply add the fixed and variable costs together for each item of cost within each category. In such a case, the flexible budget could be presented in the following format:

Flexible Budgets are used basically for control ←

ONE MONTH FLEXIBLE BUDGET FOR MACHINING DEPARTMENT

Operating level:				
Based on machine hours	875	1,000	1,125	1,250
Percentage of capacity	70%	80%*	90%	100%
Cost category:				
Indirect labor	$ 5,437.50	$ 5,500.00	$ 5,562.50	$ 5,625.00
Supervision	3,000.00	3,000.00	3,000.00	6,000.00
Factory supplies............	2,287.50	2,400.00	2,512.50	2,625.00
Power....................	1,862.50	2,000.00	2,137.50	2,275.00
Rework operations..........	937.50	1,000.00	1,062.50	1,600.00
Payroll taxes	1,131.25	1,150.00	1,168.75	1,187.50
Repair and maintenance.....	1,656.25	1,750.00	1,843.75	1,937.50
Controllable cost	$16,312.50	$16,800.00	$17,287.50	$21,250.00
Property insurance	$ 800.00	$ 800.00	$ 800.00	$ 800.00
Property taxes	600.00	600.00	600.00	600.00
Vacation pay	2,200.00	2,200.00	2,200.00	2,500.00
Employee pension costs	1,400.00	1,400.00	1,400.00	1,600.00
Employee health plan	600.00	600.00	600.00	700.00
Machinery depreciation......	3,400.00	3,400.00	3,400.00	3,400.00
Water and heat	800.00	800.00	800.00	800.00
Building occupancy.........	1,300.00	1,300.00	1,300.00	1,300.00
General factory	2,087.50	2,100.00	2,112.50	2,125.00
Noncontrollable cost	$13,187.50	$13,200.00	$13,212.50	$13,825.00
Total cost	$29,500.00	$30,000.00	$30,500.00	$35,075.00
Factory overhead rate per machine hour	$33.714	$30.000	$27.111	$28.060

*Normal capacity

In this budget, the factory overhead rate declines steadily as production moves to the 90 percent operating level. As production approaches theoretical capacity, the overhead rate increases, because items such as rework operations, supervision and employee benefit costs related to increased supervision[14] increase faster than at lower operating levels. While such cost increases are revealed through the flexible budget, the situation indicates a

---

[14]Supervision and employee benefits related to increased supervision are generally regarded as fixed costs. However, recall from the discussion in Chapter 12 that a cost may be regarded as fixed only within a relevant range of activity. When production activity increases beyond the relevant range, additional demands on capacity may necessitate an increase in one or more fixed costs.

possible departure from the use of the equation for a straight line, $y = a + bx$, for all levels of activity. In cost behavior terms, this simply means that the 100% capacity level lies outside the relevant range. However, it should be emphasized that one definite level must be agreed upon and used for setting the predetermined factory overhead rate, for applying overhead cost to production, and for computing the spending and idle capacity variances, including a determination of the spending variance related to each cost category (discussed and illustrated in Chapter 13). Significant variances could indicate the need to take corrective action in order to control costs, or it could indicate a need to change the factory overhead rate in the next period for the sake of more meaningful cost control and product costing. In any case, the effective use of cost data for planning, control, and decision-making purposes requires reasonably accurate knowledge of cost behavior.

To illustrate the determination of variances in a flexible budgeting system, assume that the Machining Department actually incurred 1,075 machine hours during the month and the following actual costs:

Indirect labor..............	$ 5,750.00
Supervision...............	3,000.00
Factory supplies	2,625.50
Power	2,107.75
Rework operations	1,088.25
Payroll taxes	1,182.50
Repair and maintenance	1,525.75
Property insurance	830.00
Property taxes.............	625.00
Vacation pay	2,200.00
Employee pension costs.....	1,400.00
Employee health plan.......	600.00
Machinery depreciation	3,400.00
Water and heat	825.75
Building occupancy	1,300.00
General factory............	2,315.25
Total actual cost	$30,775.75

If the flexible budget shows variable and fixed costs separately, as in the illustration on page 536, the variance report would appear as on page 539.

On the other hand, if the items of overhead are separated according to their controllability in the flexible budget, the variance report would appear as given on page 540.

In the flexible budget for the Machining Department, the factory overhead rate based on machine hours means that variable costs are more related to this activity base than any other. Typically some overhead items within a department will be closely related to one activity while other overhead items are closely related to some other activity. For example, the amount of factory supplies, power, rework, and repair and maintenance may be driven by machine hours, whereas the amount of indirect labor and payroll taxes may be driven by direct labor hours. Alternatively, the nature of activities within a single department may differ, e.g., one operation within the department may be machine intensive while another operation is labor intensive, in which

COST DRIVER

like activity base

MACHINING DEPARTMENT
Variance Report
For the Month Ending March 31, 19—

Flexible Budget

	Budget Allowance Normal Capacity	Budget Allowance Actual Capacity	Actual Cost	Spending Variance (Favorable) Unfavorable
Based on machine hours.......	1,000	1,075		
Percentage of capacity.........	80%	86%		
Variable cost:				
Indirect labor..............	$ 500.00	$ 537.50	$ 750.00	$212.50
Factory supplies	900.00	967.50	1,125.50	158.00
Power..................	1,100.00	1,182.50	1,207.75	25.25
Rework operations	500.00	537.50	588.25	50.75
Payroll taxes	150.00	161.25	182.50	21.25
Repair and maintenance.....	750.00	806.25	525.75	(280.50)
General factory	100.00	107.50	315.25	207.75
Total variable cost	$ 4,000.00	$ 4,300.00	$ 4,695.00	
Fixed cost:				
Indirect labor..............	$ 5,000.00	$ 5,000.00	$ 5,000.00	0.00*
Supervision	3,000.00	3,000.00	3,000.00	0.00
Factory supplies	1,500.00	1,500.00	1,500.00	0.00*
Power..................	900.00	900.00	900.00	0.00*
Rework operations	500.00	500.00	500.00	0.00*
Payroll taxes	1,000.00	1,000.00	1,000.00	0.00*
Repair and maintenance.....	1,000.00	1,000.00	1,000.00	0.00*
Property insurance	800.00	800.00	830.00	30.00
Property taxes.............	600.00	600.00	625.00	25.00
Vacation pay	2,200.00	2,200.00	2,200.00	0.00
Employee pension costs.....	1,400.00	1,400.00	1,400.00	0.00
Employee health plan........	600.00	600.00	600.00	0.00
Machinery depreciation......	3,400.00	3,400.00	3,400.00	0.00
Water and heat	800.00	800.00	825.75	25.75
Building occupancy.........	1,300.00	1,300.00	1,300.00	0.00
General factory	2,000.00	2,000.00	2,000.00	0.00*
Total fixed cost..........	$26,000.00	$26,000.00	$26,080.75	
Total cost	$30,000.00	$30,300.00	$30,775.75	$475.75
				Unfav.

Applied factory overhead ($30 rate × 1,075 actual hours)............................	32,250.00	
Idle capacity variance	$(1,950.00)	Fav.
Actual factory overhead cost................	$30,775.75	
Applied factory overhead....................	32,250.00	
Overapplied factory overhead	$(1,474.25)	
Spending variance........................	$ 475.75	Unfav.
Idle capacity variance	(1,950.00)	Fav.
Overapplied factory overhead	$(1,474.25)	

*These cost items contain both fixed and variable components. Any separation of the spending variance into fixed and variable components would be arbitrary. As a consequence, the spending variance for each item of cost is typically reported as variable.

case the department may be divided into sub-departments or cost centers. In addition, more meaningful cost control and product costing would result by using more than one factory overhead rate within the department. However,

MACHINING DEPARTMENT Variance Report For the Month Ending March 31, 19—				
	Budget Allowance Normal Capacity	Budget Allowance Actual Capacity	Actual Cost	Spending Variance (Favorable) Unfavorable
Based on machine hours	1,000	1,075		
Percentage of capacity	80%	86%		
Cost category:				
Indirect labor	$ 5,500.00	$ 5,537.50	$ 5,750.00	$212.50
Supervision	3,000.00	3,000.00	3,000.00	0.00
Factory supplies ...., ...	2,400.00	2,467.50	2,625.50	158.00
Power.....................	2,000.00	2,082.50	2,107.75	25.25
Rework operations	1,000.00	1,037.50	1,088.25	50.75
Payroll taxes	1,150.00	1,161.25	1,182.50	21.25
Repair and maintenance.....	1,750.00	1,806.25	1,525.75	(280.50)
Controllable cost	$16,800.00	$17,092.50	$17,279.75	$187.25
Property insurance	$ 800.00	$ 800.00	$ 830.00	$ 30.00
Property taxes.............	600.00	600.00	625.00	25.00
Vacation pay	2,200.00	2,200.00	2,200.00	0.00
Employee pension costs.....	1,400.00	1,400.00	1,400.00	0.00
Employee health plan	600.00	600.00	600.00	0.00
Machinery depreciation......	3,400.00	3,400.00	3,400.00	0.00
Water and heat	800.00	800.00	825.75	25.75
Building occupancy.........	1,300.00	1,300.00	1,300.00	0.00
General factory	2,100.00	2,107.50	2,315.25	207.75
Noncontrollable cost	$13,200.00	$13,207.50	$13,496.00	$288.50
Total cost	$30,000.00	$30,300.00	$30,775.75	$475.75
				Unfav.
Applied factory overhead ($30 rate × 1,075 actual hours)...........................		32,250.00		
Idle capacity variance		$(1,950.00)	Fav.	

the use of multiple rates within a department is costly, and the benefits to be derived from such added precision may not outweigh the costs of gathering and providing such information. As a consequence, a single factory overhead rate is commonly used within a department, and that single rate is based on the one activity that is related to most of the variable cost incurred within the department. On the other hand, because the nature of the work performed in each department differs, the activity base used to allocate factory overhead in each department may differ. It is, therefore, essential to study the correlation of volume in physical terms, such as units produced, labor hours worked, or machine hours used, with the dollar cost for each item or group of items (see Chapter 12).

Flexible Budgeting Through Computers and Step Charts

The determination of the fixed and variable elements in each departmental cost is a time-consuming task, particularly when computations, calculations, and analyses are performed either manually or by a desk calculator. The application of computerized techniques can eliminate this tedious chore and at the same time provide the necessary tools for budgetary control and responsibility reporting throughout the year.

Predetermined rates usually are used. However, when increases or decreases in certain costs are anticipated due to a change in the product or a change in processing, the projected overhead amounts are adjusted accordingly. Some costs are budgeted on a step-chart basis which is in harmony with the relevant range idea mentioned previously.

The following step chart indicates the allowance for nonproduction personnel at various levels of production activity. Each bisected square is an indication as to the number of nonproduction personnel (upper left-hand corner) and salary levels allowable (lower right-hand corner) at each step. The levels are based on the number of production workers.

Step Chart for a Producing Department

Department _____

How a fixed cost (supervision) would incr. w/diff levels of production

MONTHLY DEPARTMENTAL ALLOWANCE FOR NONPRODUCTION PERSONNEL

NUMBER OF PRODUCTION PERSONNEL — From	To	DEPARTMENT HEAD	SUPERVISOR	ASSISTANT SUPERVISOR	MFG. QUALITY ANALYST					
0	10	1 / 1674								
11	20	1 / 1674	1 / 1000		1 / 1050					
21	30	1 / 1674	2 / 2000		1 / 1050					
31	40	1 / 1674	4 / 4000		2 / 2100					
41	50	1 / 1674	5 / 5000	1 / 1200	2 / 2100					
51	60	1 / 1674	5 / 5000	1 / 1200	3 / 3150					
61	70	1 / 1674	6 / 6000	1 / 1200	3 / 3150					
71	80	1 / 1674	6 / 6000	1 / 1200	4 / 4200					
81	90	1 / 1674	7 / 7000	1 / 1200	4 / 4200					
91	100									

In a step chart for a service department, the levels might be based on the total number of production hours in all producing departments. Such detailed data enhance the development of monthly departmental budgets by sub-classifications.

Flexible Budget for a Service Department

Flexible budgets for service departments permit (1) comparison of actual costs with allowed expenses at the prevailing level of operations and (2) establishment of a fairer use rate or sold-hour rate by charging operating departments with fixed costs regardless of activity and with a variable cost based on departmental activity. In the following flexible budget for the Maintenance Department of a company, the expenses of the department are estimated at a fixed amount of $4,200. At 80 percent capacity, the total expense is $27,000. Assuming that the company has two producing departments and two service departments to which a fixed cost of $1,200, $2,000, $600, and $400, respectively, is charged as the readiness-to-serve expense of the Maintenance Department, the remaining balance of $22,800 is divided by the total number of maintenance hours, 2,400, to arrive at a variable rate of $9.50 per hour.

FLEXIBLE BUDGET FOR MAINTENANCE DEPARTMENT

Operating level:				
Based on maintenance hours	2,100	2,400	2,700	3,000
Percentage of capacity	70%	80%	90%	100%
Monthly allowances for expenses:				
Artisans	$12,600	$14,400	$16,200	$18,000
Supervision	2,000	2,000	2,000	2,000
Factory supplies	5,950	6,800	7,650	8,500
Tools	1,400	1,600	1,800	2,000
Depreciation	1,400	1,400	1,400	1,400
Building occupancy	800	800	800	800
Total expense	$24,150	$27,000	$29,850	$32,700
Fixed expense	$ 4,200	$ 4,200	$ 4,200	$ 4,200
Variable expense	19,950	22,800	25,650	28,500
Variable charging rate per maintenance hour	$9.50	$9.50	$9.50	$9.50

Flexible Marketing and Administrative Budgets

In contrast to the factory overhead budget, which bases its cost levels in most cases on direct labor hours, machine hours, or direct labor dollars, the budget for commercial expenses often is based on net sales, as shown in the following illustration. This practice has been criticized, and other methods are suggested in Chapter 24.

FLEXIBLE MARKETING AND ADMINISTRATIVE BUDGET

Net sales		$600,000	$700,000	$800,000	$900,000	$1,000,000
	Based on Sales					
Monthly allowances for marketing expenses:						
Sales salaries	5%	$30,000	$35,000	$40,000	$45,000	$50,000
Advertising	1%	6,000	7,000	8,000	9,000	10,000
Sales expenses	2%	12,000	14,000	16,000	18,000	20,000
Misc. expenses	5%	3,000	3,500	4,000	4,500	5,000
Depreciation	Fixed	10,000	10,000	10,000	10,000	10,000
Total marketing		$61,000	$69,500	$78,000	$86,500	$95,000
	Based on Sales					
Monthly allowances for administrative expenses:						
Executives' salaries	Fixed	$20,000	$20,000	$20,000	$30,000	$50,000
General expenses	3%	18,000	21,000	24,000	27,000	30,000
Depreciation	Fixed	5,000	5,000	5,000	5,000	5,000
Insurance	Fixed	3,000	3,000	3,000	3,000	3,000
Taxes	Fixed	4,000	4,000	4,000	4,000	4,000
Total administrative		$50,000	$53,000	$56,000	$69,000	$92,000

DISCUSSION QUESTIONS

Q17-1. What is meant by a capital expenditure? How does it differ from a revenue expenditure?

Q17-2. Name some purposes of and some reasons for a research and development program.

Q17-3. Companies should establish budgetary procedures to provide control and accounting systems for research and development expenditures. What are such procedures specifically designed to achieve?

Q17-4. Managers consider a cash budget an extremely useful management tool. Why?

Q17-5. Discuss the need for planning and budgeting in (a) nonmanufacturing businesses and (b) not-for-profit organizations.

Q17-6. What is the objective of the control concept generally referred to as PPBS?

Q17-7. (a) Describe zero-base budgeting.
(b) Explain how zero-base budgeting differs from traditional budgeting.

Q17-8. What strengths and weaknesses might be associated with zero-base budgeting?
(CICA adapted)

Q17-9. Discuss the conditions determining when PERT is appropriate.

Q17-10. Explain the computation of slack in the PERT network.

Q17-11. State the relationship between PERT and PERT/cost systems.

Q17-12. What does computer support offer to PERT and PERT/cost users?

Q17-13. Discuss how PERT/cost would be used in planning the audit of a state government's highway construction and maintenance operation.

(CIA adapted)

Q17-14. Contrast the probabilistic budget and the traditional budget in terms of information provided to management.

Q17-15. Name some relative advantages in the use of a flexible budget over a fixed budget.

Q17-16. What is the underlying principle of a flexible budget?

Q17-17. A company has been operating a budget system for a number of years. Production volume fluctuates widely, reaching its peak in the fall, but is quite low during the rest of the year. Manufacturing for stock during the dull period as a means of smoothing out the volume fluctuations is im-practical because of frequent and sudden changes in specifications prescribed by the customers. Actual annual volume has been substantially below normal. The budget produces large unfavorable capacity variances since overhead rates are computed from normal volume and are inadequate to absorb the overhead which should be charged into production during the low-volume periods. This fixed type of budget based on an unrealistic normal production volume fails to serve its planning and control purpose. As a consultant, diagnose the situation and offer advice.

Q17-18. Can service departments' costs be planned using flexible budget procedures? What makes the situation difficult? Suggest how the expenses can be allocated meaningfully to producing departments.

EXERCISES

E17-1. Budgeted cash collections and accounts receivable. A company's actual sales on account were:

Month	Sales on Account
February	$160,000
March	100,000
April	180,000

Experience has shown that such sales are usually collected as follows:

Month of sale	20%
Month after sale	50
Second month after sale	25
Never collected and written off in third month after sale	5
	100%

Required:

(1) Compute the budgeted cash collections in May, if May sales on account are budgeted at $150,000.
(2) Compute the balance of accounts receivable at April 30.
(3) Compute the balance of accounts receivable at May 31.
(4) What steps could the company take to reduce the balance in accounts receivable as of May 31st? Evaluate both the risks and advantages.

(CIA adapted)

E17-2. Cash budget. The management of Easterly Corporation requested a cash budget for the coming quarter, October through December. The budget is to be prepared from the following data:

Item	August	September	October	November	December
Sales (on account)	$60,000	$70,000	$50,000	$70,000	$60,000
Payroll.	20,000	22,000	21,000	22,000	23,000
Purchases (on account)	15,000	20,000	15,000	25,000	20,000
Depreciation expense.	5,000	5,000	5,000	5,000	5,000
Miscellaneous cash operating expenses. .	5,000	6,000	6,000	7,000	6,000
Cash dividend to owners					30,000

Collections of accounts receivable amount to 40% in the month of sale, 50% in the first month after sale, 5% in the second month after sale, and 5% written off as uncollectible. Purchases are paid off at the rate of 30% in the month of purchase and 70% in the first month following purchase. Cash on hand at October 1 is $10,000.

Required: Prepare a cash budget for October, November and December.

E17-3. Budgeted cash disbursements. Olney Company is preparing its cash budget. The sales budget specifies the following budgeted monthly sales, in units:

April	9,000
May	10,000
June	12,000
July.	11,000

The company's inventory policy is to budget for finished goods inventory equal to 20% of the following month's sales, and to budget for materials inventory equal to 40% of the following month's production requirements. Each unit of finished goods requires three pieces of material at a predicted price of $20 each. However, Olney intends to take advantage of a 2/10, n/30 discount.

Required: Compute the budgeted cash disbursements during May for payment of accounts payable for material purchases. Assume material purchases are made evenly throughout the month.

CGA-Canada (adapted) Reprint with permission

E17-4. Cash budget for inventory purchases. Partee Company manufactures a product called Par. Each unit of Par requires 3 pieces of a material called Tee, whose standard price per piece is $5. Budgeted inventory levels are as follows:

	Par	Tee
June 1	5,000	20,000
July 1	3,000	14,000
August 1	3,000	11,000

Budgeted sales of Par are 50,000 for June and 30,000 for July. The company intends to take advantage of a 2/10, n/30 discount. Assume one third of the purchases of any month due for discount are paid in the following month.

Required: Compute the cash required in July for purchases of Tee.

CGA-Canada (adapted) Reprint with permission

E17-5. Cash budget. Crockett Company is preparing a cash budget for July. The following estimates were made:

(a) Expected cash balance, July 1, $5,000.
(b) Income tax rate is 40%, based on accounting income for the month, payable in the following month.
(c) Crockett's customers pay for 50% of their purchases during the month of purchase and the balance during the following month. Bad debts are expected to be 2%.

(d) Merchandise is purchased on account for resale, with 25% of purchases paid for during the month of purchase and the balance paid during the following month.

(e) Marketing and administrative expenses are all paid in the current month.

(f) Dividends of $15,000 are expected to be declared and paid during July.

(g) Crockett's desire is to have a minimum month-end cash balance of $5,000.

(h) Other budgets include the following estimates:

	June	July
Sales (all on account)	$30,000	$40,000
Purchases	10,000	15,000
Depreciation expense	5,000	6,000
Cost of goods sold	12,000	16,000
Other marketing and administrative expenses	9,000	10,000

Required:

(1) Prepare a cash budget for July.

(2) What financial action needs to be taken as a result of this cash budget?

CGA-Canada (adapted) Reprint with permission

E17-6. PERT network. Crespi Construction Company will soon begin work on a building for Echelon Savings Bank. Work on the building was started by another construction firm that has gone out of business. Crespi has agreed to complete the project. Crespi's schedule of activities and related expected completion times for the Echelon Savings Bank project are presented in the following table:

Activity Code	Activity Description	Estimated Time (in weeks)
1-2	Obtain on-site work permit	1
2-5	Repair damage done by vandals	4
2-3	Inspect construction materials left on site	1
3-5	Order and receive additional construction materials	2
3-4	Apply for waiver to add new materials	1
4-5	Obtain waiver to add new materials	1
5-6	Perform electrical work	4
6-7	Complete interior partitions	2

Required:

(1) Prepare the PERT network.

(2) Identify the critical path and determine the expected time in weeks for the project.

(3) Explain the effect on the critical path and expected time for the project if Crespi were not required to apply for and obtain the waiver to add new materials. (ICMA adapted)

E17-7. PERT network. A company is faced with the following PERT network situation (time in days):

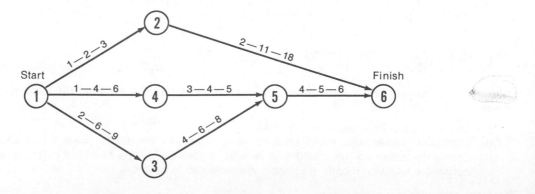

Required:

(1) Calculate t_e (expected time) for each activity, to two decimal places. For each activity, the estimates are t_o, t_m, and t_p, in that order.

(2) Calculate the total time for each path, and identify the critical path as well as total time for other paths.
CGA-Canada (adapted) Reprint with permission

E17-8. PERT network. The following PERT network has been prepared for a project, with expected time calculated in days, as shown.

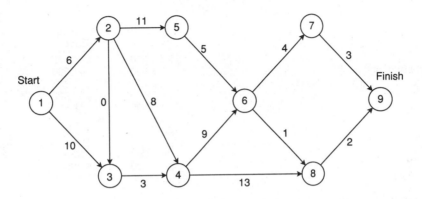

Required:

(1) Identify the critical path.

(2) Determine the slack time at each event.
CGA-Canada (adapted) Reprint with permission

E17-9. PERT network. The following time estimates in days have been obtained for each activity required for a certain construction project.

Activity	t_o	t_m	t_p	t_e	
0-1				4	t_o = most optimistic time
1-2				3	t_m = most likely time
1-3				4	t_p = most pessimistic time
					t_e = estimated completion time
2-6				6	
3-4	1	2	9	?	
3-5				6	
4-6				3	
4-7				6	
5-7				6	
6-7				5	

Required:

(1) Compute the expected completion time for activity 3-4.

(2) Construct a PERT network of the activities and events necessary to complete the construction project.

(3) Determine the estimated time required to complete each path through the PERT network, and identify the critical path.

(4) What is the slack time for event 2?

E17-10. Flexible budget for performance evaluation. The University of Boyne offers an extensive continuing education program in many cities throughout the state. For the convenience of its faculty and administrative staff and to save costs, the university employs a supervisor to operate a motor pool. The motor pool operated with 20 vehicles until February, when an additional automobile was acquired. The motor pool furnishes gasoline, oil, and other supplies for its automobiles. A mechanic does routine maintenance and minor repairs. Major repairs are done at a nearby commercial garage.

Each year, the supervisor prepares an operating budget, which informs the university administration of the funds needed for operating the pool. Depreciation (straight-line) on the automobiles is recorded in the budget in order to determine the cost per mile.

The following schedule presents the annual budget approved by the university, with March's actual costs compared to one twelfth of the annual budget:

University Motor Pool
Budget Report for March

	Annual Budget	One-Month Budget	March Actual	(Over) Under
Gasoline	$ 52,500	$ 4,375	$ 5,323	$(948)
Oil, minor repairs, parts, and supplies	3,600	300	380	(80)
Outside repairs	2,700	225	50	175
Insurance	6,000	500	525	(25)
Salaries and benefits	30,000	2,500	2,500	—
Depreciation	26,400	2,200	2,310	(110)
	$121,200	$10,100	$11,088	$(988)
Total miles	600,000	50,000	63,000	
Cost per mile	$ .2020	$ .2020	$ .1760	
Number of automobiles	20	20	21	

The annual budget was constructed upon these assumptions:

    (a) 20 automobiles in the pool.
    (b) 30,000 miles per year per automobile.
    (c) 16 miles per gallon per automobile.
    (d) $1.40 per gallon of gasoline.
    (e) $.006 per mile for oil, minor repairs, parts, and supplies.
    (f) $135 per automobile for outside repairs.

The supervisor is unhappy with the monthly report comparing budget and actual costs for March, claiming it presents an unfair picture of performance. A previous employer used flexible budgeting to compare actual costs to budgeted amounts.

Required:

    (1) Prepare a report showing budgeted amounts, actual costs, and monthly variations for March, using flexible budget techniques. (Round computations to four decimal places.)
    (2) Explain the basis of the budget figure for outside repairs.   (ICMA adapted)

E17-11. Flexible budget. Basston Company produces electrical appliances. Its Assembly Department operates under a flexible budget, with monthly allowances established at 20% intervals. The following information shows fixed and total expenses at the 80% and 100% levels:

	Fixed	Total Cost 80%	Total Cost 100%
Direct materials		$16,000	$20,000
Direct labor		9,000	11,250
Supervision	$ 500	500	500
Indirect materials	250	1,450	1,750
Property tax	300	300	300
Maintenance	600	1,400	1,600
Power	200	280	300
Insurance	175	175	175
Depreciation	1,600	1,600	1,600

Required: Prepare a flexible budget at the 92% level.

E17-12. Flexible budget. One month budget allowances for the Fabricating Department of Willow Corporation follow:

Activity Base: 1,800 machine hours per month at normal capacity which is 90% of rated capacity.

Category of Cost	Fixed Cost	Variable Rate per Machine Hour
Indirect labor	$ 3,000.00	$1.50
Supervision . . . . :	2,400.00	
Factory supplies	900.00	2.30
Power.	1,200.00	1.00
Rework operations	600.00	0.50
Payroll taxes	2,000.00	0.40
Repair and maintenance	400.00	1.40
Controllable cost	$10,500.00	$7.10
Property insurance	$ 550.00	
Property taxes.	700.00	
Vacation pay	2,150.00	
Employee pension costs.	1,500.00	
Employee health plan.	800.00	
Machinery depreciation.	3,000.00	
Water and heat	600.00	
Building occupancy.	1,200.00	
General factory	1,500.00	$0.40
Noncontrollable cost	$12,000.00	$0.40
Total cost	$22,500.00	$7.50

Summary:

Fixed expense.	$22,500.00
Variable expense (1,800 machine hours × $7.50 variable rate).	13,500.00
Total cost at normal capacity	$36,000.00
Factory overhead rate for Fabricating Department at normal capacity ($36,000 ÷ 1,800 hours).	$20.00 per machine hour

Required: Prepare a flexible budget for the Fabricating Department at the 80%, 90%, 100%, and 110% rated capacity levels. Assume that fixed costs are not expected to change between the 80% and 110% levels of capacity.

PROBLEMS

P17-1. Cash and purchases budget for a manufacturer. Huntsville Company seeks assistance in developing cash and other budget information for May, June, and July. On April 30, the company had cash of $5,500, accounts receivable of $437,000, inventories of $309,400, and accounts payable of $133,055. The budget is to be based on the following assumptions:

Sales:

(a) Each month's sales are billed on the last day of the month.

(b) Customers are allowed a 3% discount if payment is made within 10 days after the billing date. Receivables are recorded at the gross sales price.

(c) Sixty percent of the billings are collected within the discount period; 25% by the end of the month; 9% by the end of the second month; and 6% prove uncollectible.

Purchases:

(a) Fifty-four percent of all purchases of materials and a like percentage of marketing, general, and administrative expenses are paid in the month purchased, with the remainder paid in the following month.

(b) Each month's units of ending materials inventory are equal to 130% of next month's production requirement.

(c) The cost of each unit of inventory is $20.

(d) Wages and salaries earned each month by employees total $38,000.

(e) Marketing, general, and administrative expenses (of which $2,000 is depreciation) are equal to 15% of the current month's sales.

Actual and projected sales are as follows:

March	$354,000	June	$342,000
April	363,000	July	360,000
May	357,000	August	366,000

Actual and projected materials needed for production:

March	11,800 units	June	11,400 units
April	12,100	July	12,000
May	11,900	August	12,200

Accrued payroll at the end of each month is as follows:

March	$3,100	June	$3,400
April	2,900	July	3,000
May	3,300	August	2,800

Required: Compute the following:

(1) Budgeted cash disbursements during June.

(2) Budgeted cash collections during May.

(3) Budgeted units of inventory to be purchased during July.   (AICPA adapted)

P17-2. Cash and purchases budgets. Russon Corporation is a retailer whose sales are all made on credit. Sales are billed twice monthly, on the 10th of the month for the last half of the prior month's sales and on the 20th of the month for the first half of the current month's sales. The terms of all sales are 2/10, n/30, from the billing date. Based upon past experience, the collection experience of accounts receivable is as follows:

Within the discount period .	80%
On the 30th day	18
Uncollectible	2

Sales for May and forecast sales for the next four months are:

May (actual)	$500,000
June	600,000
July..............	700,000
August	700,000
September	400,000

Russon's average markup on its products is 20% of the sales price. Russon purchases merchandise for resale to meet the current month's sales demand and to maintain a desired monthly ending inventory of 25% of the next month's sales. All purchases are on credit, with terms of net 30. Russon pays for one half of a month's purchases in the month of purchase and the other half in the month following the purchase. All sales and purchases occur uniformly throughout the month.

Required: Compute the following:

(1) Russon's budgeted cash collections in July.
(2) Russon's budgeted cash collections in September from August sales.
(3) Desired August 31 inventory.
(4) Budgeted June purchases.   (ICMA adapted)

P17-3. Cash budget. Mayne Manufacturing Co. has incurred substantial losses for several years and has become insolvent. On March 31, 19A, Mayne petitioned the court for protection from creditors and submitted the following balance sheet:

Mayne Manufacturing Co.
Balance Sheet
March 31, 19A

Assets	Net Book Value	Liquidation Value
Accounts receivable......................	$100,000	$ 50,000
Inventories	90,000	40,000
Plant and equipment	150,000	160,000
Total	$340,000	$250,000
Liabilities and Stockholders' Equity		
Accounts payable—general creditors	$600,000	
Common stock outstanding................	60,000	
Deficit.................................	(320,000)	
Total	$340,000	

Mayne's management informed the court that the company has developed a new product, and that a prospective customer is willing to sign a contract for the purchase of 10,000 units of this product during the year ending March 31,19B,12,000 units during the year ending March 31, 19C, and 15,000 units during the year ending March 31, 19D, at a price of $90 per unit. This product can be manufactured using Mayne's present facilities. Monthly production with immediate delivery is expected to be uniform within each year. Receivables are expected to be collected during the calendar month following sales. Unit production costs of the new product are expected to be as follows:

Direct materials	$20
Direct labor	30
Variable overhead	10

Fixed costs (excluding depreciation) will amount to $130,000 per year. Purchases of direct materials will be paid during the calendar month following purchase. Fixed costs, direct labor, and variable overhead will be paid as incurred. Inventory of direct materials will be equal to 60 days' usage. After the first month of operations, 30 days' usage of direct materials will be ordered each month.

The general creditors have agreed to reduce their total claims to 60% of their March 31, 19A balances, under the following conditions:

(a) Existing accounts receivable and inventories are to be liquidated immediately, with the proceeds turned over to the general creditors.
(b) The balance of reduced accounts payable is to be paid as cash is generated from future operations, but in no event later than March 31, 19C. No interest will be paid on these obligations.

Under this proposed plan, the general creditors would receive $110,000 more than the current liquidation value of Mayne's assets.

Required: Ignoring any need to borrow and repay short-term funds for working capital purposes, prepare a cash budget for the years ending March 31, 19B and 19C, showing the cash expected to be available to pay the claims of the general creditors, payments to general creditors, and the cash remaining after payment of claims.

(ICMA adapted)

P17-4. Cash budget. J. Jones decided to start a business which would require the purchase of assets at a total cost of $200,000. He started his business with a cash investment of $50,000 and on January 1, 19A, took out a long-term loan from the bank in the amount of $150,000. The terms of the note stipulated that interest of 2% (monthly) would be paid at the end of each month and a payment of $30,000, to be applied towards the principal, would be payable at the end of each quarterly period. The proceeds of the loan were used to purchase equipment. The company would produce a product with the following budgeted revenues and expenses, based on an expected monthly production volume of 5,000 units:

Selling price per unit		$150.00
Manufacturing costs per unit:		
Direct materials		$ 20.00
Direct labor		30.00
Variable factory overhead:		
Utilities	$ 5.00	
Supplies	6.00	
Indirect labor	4.00	15.00
Fixed factory overhead:		
Factory rent	$10.00	
Depreciation on machinery	15.00	25.00
Total manufacturing cost per unit		$ 90.00
Selling and administrative costs:		
Sales commissions per unit of product sold		$ 8.00
Bad debt expense per unit of product sold		3.00
Office equipment rentals per month		12,000.00
Equipment depreciation per month		5,000.00

Other information includes the following:

(a) Expected sales total $360,000 for January, $450,000 for February, $480,000 for March, and $600,000 for April.

(b) All sales are on credit, with terms 2/10, net 30 days. Collection of accounts receivable are expected to be in the following pattern:

    30% will be collected in the month of the sale (of which 80% will take the discount).
    30% will be collected in the month after the sale.
    38% will be collected two months after the sale.
    2% will be uncollected.

(c) A direct materials inventory of $2,000 will have to be maintained at all times.

(d) In order to meet fluctuations in customer demand, a finished goods inventory equal to 100 units plus 10% of the expected demand for the following month (in units) will have to be maintained.

(e) All direct material purchases are expected to be incurred uniformly throughout the month with payments being made in the month of purchase.

(f) Wages payable at the end of each month are expected to average $7,500.

(g) A minimum cash balance of $10,000 is to be maintained at all times.

Required: Prepare a cash budget for the first quarterly period ending on March 31. Include any supporting schedules and/or budgets which are appropriate and indicate what financing (if any) may be required.

(SMAC adapted)

P17-5. Cash budget for not-for-profit organization. Triple-F Health Club (Family, Fitness, and Fun) is a not-for-profit family-oriented health club. The club's board of directors is developing plans to acquire more equipment and expand the club facilities. The board plans to purchase about $25,000 of new equipment each year and wants to begin a fund to purchase the adjoining property in four or five years. The adjoining property has a market value of about $300,000.

The club manager, Jane Crowe, is concerned that the board has unrealistic goals in light of its recent financial performance. She has sought the help of a club member with an accounting background to assist her in preparing for the board a report supporting her concerns.

The club member reviewed the club's records, including the following cash basis income statement. The review and discussions with Jane Crowe disclosed the additional information which follows the statement.

Triple-F Health Club
Statement of Income (Cash Basis)
For Years Ended October 31
(In Thousands)

	19B	19A
Cash revenues:		
Annual membership fees...........................	$355.0	$300.0
Lesson and class fees............................	234.0	180.0
Miscellaneous.....................................	2.0	1.5
Total cash received............................	$591.0	$481.5
Cash expenses:		
Manager's salary and benefits......................	$ 36.0	$ 36.0
Regular employees' wages and benefits..............	190.0	190.0
Lesson and class employee wages and benefits........	195.0	150.0
Towels and supplies...............................	16.0	15.5
Utilities (heat and light)	22.0	15.0
Mortgage interest.................................	35.1	37.8
Miscellaneous.....................................	2.0	1.5
Total cash expenses...........................	$496.1	$445.8
Cash income	$ 94.9	$ 35.7

Additional Information:

(a) Other financial information as of October 31, 19B:

    (1) Cash in checking account, $7,000.
    (2) Petty cash, $300.
    (3) Outstanding mortgage balance, $360,000.
    (4) Accounts payable arising from invoices for supplies and utilities which are unpaid as of October 31, 19B, $2,500.

(b) No unpaid bills are expected to exist on October 31, 19C.

(c) The club purchased $25,000 worth of exercise equipment during the current year 19B. Cash of $10,000 was paid on delivery, and the balance was due on October 1 but was not paid as of October 31, 19B.

(d) The club began operations six years ago in rental quarters. Two years later it purchased its current property (land and building) for $600,000, paying $120,000 down and agreeing to pay $30,000 plus 9% interest annually on November 1 until the balance was paid off.

(e) Membership rose 3% during 19B. This is approximately the same annual rate the club has experienced since it opened.

(f) Membership fees were increased by 15% in 19B. The board has tentative plans to increase the fees by 10% in 19C.

(g) Lesson and class fees have not been increased for three years. The board policy is to encourage classes and lessons by keeping the fees low. The members have taken advantage of this policy and the number of classes and lessons have grown significantly each year. The club expects the percentage growth experienced in 19B to be repeated in 19C.

(h) Miscellaneous revenues are expected to grow at the same percentage as experienced in 19B.

(i) Operating expenses are expected to increase. Hourly wage rates and the manager's salary will need to be increased 15% because no increases were granted in 19B. Towels and supplies, utilities, and miscellaneous expenses are expected to increase 25%.

Required:

(1) Construct a cash budget for 19C for Triple-F Health Club.
(2) Identify and explain any operating problem(s) that this budget discloses for Triple-F Health Club.
(3) Is Jane Crowe's concern that the board's goals are unrealistic justified? Explain.   (ICMA adapted)

P17-6. Budgeted cash receipts and disbursements. Vincent Hospital provides a wide range of health services in its community. Vincent's board of directors has authorized the following capital expenditures:

Inter-aortic balloon pump	$1,100,000
CT scanner	700,000
X-ray equipment	600,000
Laboratory equipment.	1,400,000
	$3,800,000

The expenditures are planned for October 1, 19A, and the board wishes to know the amount of borrowing, if any, necessary on that date. M. Kelly, the controller, has gathered the following information to be used in preparing an analysis of future cash flows.

(a) Billings, made in the month of service, for the first six months of 19A are listed below:

Month	Amount
January	$4,400,000
February	4,400,000
March	4,500,000
April.	4,500,000
May	5,000,000
June	5,000,000

Ninety percent of Vincent's billings are made to third parties such as federal or state governments and private insurance companies. The remaining 10% of the billings are made directly to patients. Historical patterns of billing collections are presented below:

	Third Party Billings	Direct Patient Billings
Month of service	20%	10%
Month following service	50	40
Second month following service	20	40
Uncollectible.	10	10

Estimated billings for the last six months of 19A are listed below. The same billing and collection patterns that have been experienced during the first six months of 19A are expected to continue during the last six months of the year.

Month	Estimated Amount
July	$4,500,000
August	5,000,000
September	5,500,000
October.	5,700,000
November.	5,800,000
December.	5,500,000

(b) The purchases that have been made during the past three months and the planned purchases for the last six months of 19A are presented in the following schedule:

Month	Amount	Month	Amount
April	$1,100,000	September	1,850,000
May	1,200,000	October	1,950,000
June	1,200,000	November	2,250,000
July	1,250,000	December	1,750,000
August	1,500,000		

All purchases are made on account, and accounts payable are remitted in the month following the purchase.

(c) Salaries for each month during the remainder of 19A are expected to be $1,500,000 per month plus 20% of that month's billings. Salaries are paid in the month of service.

(d) Vincent's monthly depreciation charges are $125,000.

(e) Vincent incurs interest expense of $150,000 per month and makes interest payments of $450,000 on the last day of each calendar quarter.

(f) Endowment fund income is expected to continue to total $175,000 per month.

(g) Vincent has a cash balance of $300,000 on July 1, 19A, and has a policy of maintaining a minimum end-of-month cash balance of 10% of the current month's purchases.

(h) Vincent Hospital employs a calendar year reporting period.

Required:

(1) Prepare a schedule of budgeted cash receipts by month for the third quarter of 19A.

(2) Prepare a schedule of budgeted cash disbursements by month for the third quarter of 19A.

(3) Determine the amount of borrowing, if any, necessary on October 1, 19A, to acquire the capital items totaling $3,800,000 and still maintain the minimum required cash balance.   (ICMA adapted)

P17-7. PERT/cost network. The following network has been prepared for a project:

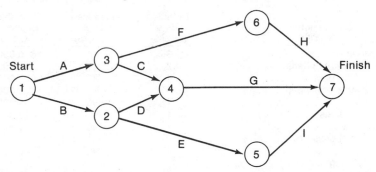

Expected time and cost estimates are:

Activity	Time	Cost
A	5 days	$ 4,000
B	5	4,000
C	10	15,000
D	7	3,500
E	5	10,000
F	7	14,000
G	5	5,000
H	10	20,000
I	10	30,000

Costs for each activity occur uniformly; e.g., activity A requires $800 each day.

Required:

    (1) Identify the critical path.

    (2) Prepare a daily activity and cost schedule.   CGA-Canada (adapted) Reprint with permission

P17-8. PERT network and project planning. The following diagram and accompanying schedule have been prepared for a proposed retail store opening. The schedule describes the activities, the expected time (in weeks), the expected cost of each activity, and the possible reduced time (in weeks) and related incremental cost for those activities which can be accomplished in a shorter time period. It is estimated that the store should produce a contribution of about $2,000 per week to operating income.

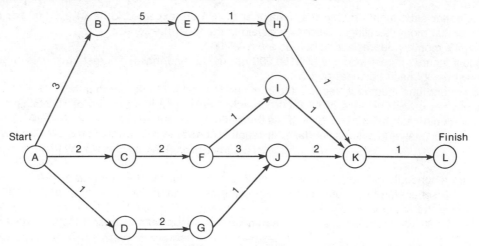

Activity	Description of Activity	Expected Time (weeks)	Reduced Time (weeks)	Possible Expected Cost	Incremental Cost To Achieve Reduced Time
A-B	Design exterior	3	1	$ 5,000	$4,500
A-C	Determine inventory needs...........	2	NC	500	0
A-D	Develop staffing plan	1	NC	500	0
B-E	Do exterior structural work	5	3	27,000	3,500
E-H	Paint exterior	1	NC	4,000	0
H-K	Install exterior signs	1	NC	15,000	0
C-F	Order inventory	2	NC	1,500	0
F-I	Develop special prices for opening	1	NC	2,000	0
I-K	Advertise opening and special prices	1	NC	8,000	0
F-J	Receive inventory	3	2	4,000	2,000
D-G	Acquire staff.......................	2	1	3,000	1,000
G-J	Train staff.........................	1	NC	5,000	0
J-K	Stock shelves	2	1	3,500	1,500
K-L	Final preparations for grand opening....................	1	NC	6,000	0

NC denotes no change in time is possible.

Required:

    (1) Determine the normal critical path, its length in weeks, and the normal cost to be incurred in opening the store.

(2) Compute the minimum time in which the store could be opened and the costs incurred to achieve the earlier opening.

(3) Explain whether the store should be opened following the normal schedule or the reduced program.

(ICMA adapted)

P17-9. Flexible budget and variance analysis. A one-month budget allowance schedule for the Assembly Department of the Rosebud Company follows:

Activity Base: 1,350 direct labor hours per month at normal capacity which is 90% of rated capacity.

Category of Cost	Fixed Cost	Variable Rate per Direct Labor Hour
Indirect labor	$ 2,500.00	$2.25
Supervision	1,800.00	
Factory supplies	500.00	1.20
Power	150.00	0.35
Rework operations	600.00	0.50
Payroll taxes	1,000.00	0.35
Repair and maintenance	350.00	0.15
Controllable cost	$ 6,900.00	$4.80
Property insurance	$ 150.00	
Property taxes	200.00	
Vacation pay	1,800.00	
Employee pension costs	1,200.00	
Employee health plan	500.00	
Machinery depreciation	450.00	
Water and heat	400.00	
Building occupancy	900.00	
General factory	1,000.00	$0.20
Noncontrollable cost	$ 6,600.00	$0.20
Total cost	$13,500.00	$5.00

Summary:

Fixed cost	$13,500.00
Variable cost (1,350 direct labor hours × $5 variable rate)	6,750.00
Total cost at normal capacity	$20,250.00

Factory overhead rate for Assembly Department at normal capacity ($20,250 ÷ 1,350 hours) .... $15.00 per direct labor hour

Actual costs for the month of August follow:

Indirect labor	$ 5,750.00
Supervision	1,800.00
Factory supplies	2,154.00
Power	615.00
Rework operations	1,088.25
Payroll taxes	1,451.50
Repair and maintenance	1,525.75
Property insurance	165.00
Property taxes	210.50
Vacation pay	2,200.00
Employee pension costs	1,200.00
Employee health plan	500.00
Machinery depreciation	450.00
Water and heat	465.00
Building occupancy	900.00
General factory	1,385.00
Total cost for August	$21,860.00

Required:

(1) Prepare a flexible budget for the Assembly Department of the Rosebud Company at the 80%, 90%, 100%, and 110% levels of the rated capacity. Assume that fixed costs are not expected to change between the 80% and 110% levels of capacity.

(2) Prepare a variance report for August assuming that factory overhead was charged to production on the basis of predetermined rate for normal capacity (i.e., 90% of rated capacity). The variance report should show the spending variance for each item of departmental cost and a single figure for the department's idle capacity variance.

P17-10. Flexible budget. The controller of Oakhill Corporation decided to prepare a flexible factory overhead budget ranging from 80% to 100% of capacity for the next year, with 50,000 hours as the 100% level. The data available are based on either past experiences, shop supervisors' figures, or management's decisions. For expenses of a semivariable nature, the fixed amount and the variable rate are determined via the high and low points method. The direct labor rate is $7.50 per hour. Additional data for factory overhead are:

Annual fixed expenses:

Depreciation...	$ 9,000
Insurance...	1,500
Maintenance cost (including payroll taxes and fringe benefits)........	24,000
Property tax..	1,500
Supervisory staff (including payroll taxes and fringe benefits).........	36,000

Variable expenses:

Shop supplies	$	.10	per direct labor hour
Indirect labor (excluding inspection)	$	.45	per direct labor hour
Payroll taxes and fringe benefits................................		18%	of labor cost, direct and indirect

Semivariable expenses (from previous five years):

Year	Direct Labor Hours	Power and Light	Inspection (including Payroll Taxes and Fringe Benefits)	Other Semi-Variable Expenses
19A	44,000	$1,500	$ 9,200	$8,000
19B	40,000	1,400	9,000	7,400
19C	45,000	1,600	9,200	8,200
19D	49,000	1,650	10,000	8,800
19E	50,000	1,700	10,200	8,900

Required: Prepare a flexible factory overhead budget ranging from 80% to 100% of capacity, with 10% intervals.

P17-11. Flexible budget and overapplied fixed factory overhead. Salsbury Corporation uses a flexible budgeting system. The flexible budget at the top of page 559 is provided for 80% and 100% of normal capacity.

Required:

(1) Prepare the allowable flexible budget on the assumption that 2,600 units are actually produced in the current period.

(2) If the factory overhead application rate were based on 100% of actual capacity and actual production costs were equal to the allowable budget for 2,600 units, what would be the amount of over- or under-applied factory overhead?

	80% Capacity	100% Capacity
Units of production	2,000	2,500
Direct labor	$ 4,000	$ 5,000
Direct materials	6,000	7,500
Total prime cost	$10,000	$12,500
Factory overhead:		
Utilities	$ 900	$ 1,000
Supplies	800	1,000
Indirect labor	1,000	1,250
Depreciation of plant and equipment	3,000	3,000
Miscellaneous indirect factory costs	1,000	1,200
Total factory overhead	$ 6,700	$ 7,450
Total budgeted manufacturing cost	$16,700	$19,950

CASES

C17-1. PERT network analysis. Caltron Inc. produces computer-controlled components for a wide variety of military hardware. As a defense contractor, the company is often under severe time and scheduling constraints. The development of a new component, Vector-12, is no exception. The project has the potential for future contracts that could generate substantial revenue if development and testing can be accomplished in the allotted time.

The planning of the Vector-12 project has been assigned to Norm Robertson. This is Robertson's first assignment as a Project Director for Caltron, and he is eager to demonstrate his abilities.

This project, like many of Caltron's projects, cuts across departments. Therefore, scheduling and coordination among departments is crucial. Caltron's management has long been an advocate of the Project Evaluation and Review Technique (PERT). Therefore, Robertson prepared the PERT diagram for the Vector-12 project that is presented below.

The circles with letters inside correspond to the completion of a significant activity while the arrows connecting the circles correspond to an activity. The numbers by the activity arrows represent the expected time in weeks required to complete each activity. The responsibility for the critical path, Start-B-C-F-I-J-Finish,

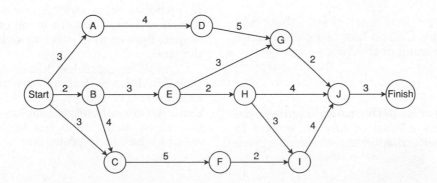

is shared by two departments, Electro-Mechanical Engineering (EME) and Fabrication (FAB). Resource Appropriation and Processing (RAP) is responsible for Start-A-D-G-J.

Robertson developed the PERT diagram with minimial input from the department directors affected. He did review the preliminary diagrams with the Directors of EME and FAB. Robertson was unable to contact the Director of RAP, Shiela Neill, and Robertson neglected to talk with Neill when she returned to the office. The Directors of EME and FAB offered suggestions to Robertson on how to revise the diagrams in terms of ordering activities and time estimates. They also indicated how Neill's activities would coordinate with their activities. However, none of the directors reviewed the final PERT diagram shown above.

As the Vector-12 project entered its fourth week, Robertson requested progress reports from the department directors. Neill told Robertson that activity A-D would take 10 to 12 weeks. When Robertson asked Neill to explain the delay, Neill replied, "I could have told you there would be a problem, but you never asked for my input. The time for activity A-D is understated as is, and I cannot even start until activity B-E is completed by FAB."

Required:

(1) Discuss the advantages and disadvantages of network analysis as a means of organizing and coordinating projects.
(2) Identify the specific reason that would cause Norm Robertson to be concerned about the delay in activity A-D.
(3) Critique the way Norm Robertson developed the PERT diagram for the Vector-12 project.
(4) Discuss the behavioral problems that could arise within Caltron Inc. as a consequence of the planning of the Vector-12 project.
(ICMA adapted)

C17-2. Critique of performance report. Jewell Company uses a fixed or forecast budget to measure its performance against the objectives set by the forecast and to help in controlling costs. At the end of a month, management received the following report, which compares actual performance with budgeted figures:

Items of Cost	Budget	Actual
Units produced	75,000	73,500
Direct materials	$39,000	$37,020
Direct labor	6,000	5,950
Factory supplies	1,500	1,550
Indirect labor	726	710
Repairs and maintenance	2,250	2,300
Insurance and property tax	355	350
Rent	2,000	2,000
Depreciation	2,200	2,200
Total	$54,031	$52,080

Required: What conclusions can be drawn from this report? Indicate weaknesses, if any, of this type of budget.

C17-3. Flexible budget for performance evaluation. Berwin Inc. is a manufacturer of small industrial tools with an annual sales volume of approximately $3.5 million. Sales growth has been steady during the year, and there is no evidence of cyclical demand. Production has increased gradually during the year and has been distributed evenly throughout each month. The company employs a sequential processing system. The four manufacturing departments—Casting, Machining, Finishing, and Packaging—are all located in the same building. Fixed factory overhead is assigned using a plant-wide rate.

Berwin has always been able to compete with other manufacturers of small industrial tools. However, its market has expanded only in response to product innovation. Thus research and development is important and has helped Berwin to expand as well as maintain demand.

Carla Viller, controller, has designed and implemented a new budget system in response to concerns voiced by George Berwin, president. An annual budget that has been divided into 12 equal segments has been prepared to assist in the timely evaluation of monthly per-

Berwin Inc.
Machining Department Performance Report
For the Month Ended May 31, 19A

	Budget	Actual	(Over) Under Budget
Volume in units	3,000	3,185	(185)
Variable manufacturing costs:			
Direct materials . . .	$24,000	$ 24,843	$ (843)
Direct labor	27,750	29,302	(1,552)
Variable factory overhead	33,300	35,035	(1,735)
Total variable manufacturing cost	$85,050	$ 89,180	$(4,130)
Fixed factory overhead:			
Indirect labor	$ 3,300	$ 3,334	$ (34)
Depreciation	1,500	1,500	
Taxes	300	300	
Insurance.	240	240	
Other	930	1,027	(97)
Total fixed overhead cost.	$ 6,270	$ 6,401	$ (131)
Corporate costs:			
Research and development	$ 2,400	$ 3,728	$(1,328)
Marketing and administrative . . .	3,600	4,075	(475)
Total corporate cost.	$ 6,000	$ 7,803	$(1,803)
Total cost	$97,320	$103,384	$(6,064)

formance. Berwin was visibly upset upon receiving the performance report for May for the Machining Department, shown below. Similar performance reports were prepared for the other three departments.

Berwin exclaimed, "How can they be efficient enough to produce nine extra units every working day and still miss the budget by $300 a day?" Gene Jordan, Machining Department supervisor, could not understand "all the red ink," when he knew the department had operated more efficiently in May than it had in several months. Jordan stated, "I was expecting a pat on the back and instead the boss tore me apart. What's more, I don't even know why!"

Required:

(1) Review the May performance report for the Machining Department of Berwin Inc. Based upon the information presented in the report:

(a) Discuss the strengths of the new budget system in general.

(b) Identify the weaknesses of the performance report and explain how the report should be revised to eliminate each weakness.

(2) Prepare a revised performance report for the Machining Department, using the data given for May.   (ICMA adapted)

CHAPTER 18

Standard Costing: Setting Standards and Analyzing Variances

A *standard cost* is the predetermined cost of manufacturing a single unit or a specific quantity of product during a specific period. It is the planned cost of a product under current and/or anticipated operating conditions. A standard cost has two components: a physical standard (i.e., a standard quantity of inputs per unit of output) and a price standard (i.e., a standard cost or rate per unit of input).

A standard is like a norm. Whatever is considered normal can generally be accepted as standard. For example, if a score of 72 is the standard for a golf course, a golfer's score is judged on the basis of this standard. In industry, the standards for making a desk, assembling a microcomputer, refining crude oil, or manufacturing automobiles are based on carefully determined quantitative and qualitative measurements and engineering methods. A standard should be thought of as a norm in terms of specific production inputs, such as units of materials, hours of labor, and percentage of plant capacity used.

To provide a foundation for understanding and effectively utilizing a standard cost system, this chapter begins by discussing the usefulness of standard costs and the setting of standards. This foundation is followed by a section which explains and illustrates the computation of the standard cost variances for materials, labor, and factory overhead. The chapter concludes with a discussion about the responsibility and control of these variances. Incorporating standards into the accounting records is discussed in Chapter 19.

■ USEFULNESS OF STANDARD COSTS

A standard cost system may be used in connection with either the process or job order cost accumulation method. Standard costing is most readily adaptable to manufacturing environments where production technology is relatively stable and the products manufactured are homogeneous within the cost accumulation unit, i.e., the department or the job. It is difficult to establish standards if the manufacturing technology changes rapidly or if each product manufactured is unique. Consequently, standard costing typically is found in firms that use process cost accumulation (e.g., manufacturers of petroleum and chemical products, building supplies, steel, and soft drinks), and in firms that use job order cost accumulation where homogeneous units are batch produced on each job (e.g., manufacturers of radios and televisions, furniture, paper products, and processed foods).

Standard cost systems aid in planning and controlling operations and in gaining insights into the probable impact of managerial decisions on costs and profits. Standard costs are used for:

1. Establishing budgets.
2. Controlling costs by motivating employees and measuring efficiencies.
3. Simplifying costing procedures and expediting cost reports.
4. Assigning costs to materials, work in process, and finished goods inventories.
5. Forming the basis for establishing contract bids and for setting sales prices.

Standards are quite useful in preparing budgets. With the use of standard costs, the preparation of budgets for any volume and mixture of products is more reliably and speedily accomplished. Reliability is enhanced because the standards are based on detailed analyses of the production processes. The time required to prepare the operating budget is reduced because production requirements already are documented for each product.

The effectiveness of controlling costs depends greatly upon a thorough understanding of both the processes that give rise to cost incurrence and the motivation of the personnel who control those processes. Standards provide performance goals for employees and a basis for evaluating actual operating results. Executives and supervisors become cost-conscious as they become aware of results. This cost-consciousness tends to reduce costs and encourage economies in all phases of the business.

The use of standard costs for accounting purposes simplifies costing procedures through the reduction of clerical labor and expense. A complete standard cost system usually is accompanied by standardization of productive operations. Production or manufacturing orders, which call for standard quantities of production and specific labor operations, can be prepared in advance of actual production. Materials requisitions, labor time tickets, and operation cards can be prepared in advance of production, and standard costs can be compiled. As orders for a part are placed into the shop, previously established standards are used to determine the quantities, production processes, and costs that will apply. As the production process becomes more standardized, the clerical effort becomes simpler. Reports can be systematized to present complete information regarding standards, actual costs, and variances.

Although some companies that use standard costs for planning and control do not record inventories at standard cost, the incorporation of standard costs into the regular accounting records leads to increased efficiency and accuracy in clerical work. A complete standard cost file by parts and operations simplifies assigning costs to materials, work in process, and finished goods inventories. Inventory costs are easily determined by multiplying the quantities of each product in inventory by the standard unit cost and adding the total cost for each product. The use of standard costs also tends to stabilize the influence of fluctuating input prices and capacity utilization on inventory costs. Incorporation of standard costs into the accounting records through journal entries is discussed and illustrated in Chapter 19.

The process of determining contract bids and establishing sales prices for products is greatly enhanced by utilization of a standard cost system. The computation of costs to be incurred on a contract is simplified and made more reliable by using standard costs for the products to be produced or, if a unique product is to be produced, by using standard costs for the production operations that will be required. Standards are useful in establishing sales prices for products by providing reliable, up-to-date cost information. When the market price of a product is not readily observable, as would be the case for new products or products that are in some way differentiated from those of competitors, product cost typically provides the starting point in establishing the sales price.

■ SETTING STANDARDS

Calculation of a standard cost is based on physical standards—two types, basic and current, are often discussed in the literature. A basic standard is a yardstick against which both expected and actual performances are compared. It is similar to an index number against which all subsequent results are measured. *Current standards* are of three types:

1. The *expected actual standard* is a standard set for an expected level of operation and efficiency. It is a reasonably close estimate of actual results.
2. The *normal standard* is a standard set for a normal level of operation and efficiency, intended to represent challenging yet attainable results.
3. The *theoretical standard* is a standard set for an ideal or maximum level of operation and efficiency. Such standards constitute goals to be aimed for rather than performances that can be currently achieved.

Materials and labor costs are generally based on normal, current operating conditions, allowing for expected changes in prices and rates and tempered by the desired efficiency level. Factory overhead is based on normal operating conditions and volume at the desired efficiency level.

The success of a standard cost system depends on the reliability, accuracy, and acceptance of the standards. Extreme care should be taken to make sure that all factors are considered in the establishment of standards. In some cases, standards are set on the basis of an average of the actual results of previous periods. However, the most effective standards are set by industrial engineers on the basis of careful studies of product components and production operations, using appropriate sampling techniques and including participation by those individuals whose performance is to be measured by the standards.

Standards must be set, and the system implemented, in an atmosphere that gives full consideration to the behavioral characteristics of managers and workers. In the long run, workers and plant management will tend to react negatively if they feel threatened by imposed standards. If they participate in setting standards, they can more easily understand the basis upon which the standards are determined and more readily identify with the standard costing procedure. Under ideal conditions, employees will accept standards as personal production goals.

Standards which are too loose or too tight generally will have a negative impact on worker motivation. If standards are too loose, workers will tend to set their goals at this low level, thereby reducing productivity to a level below what is attainable. If the standard is too tight, workers will quickly realize the impossibility of attaining the standards, will become frustrated, and will soon begin to ignore the standard. A reasonable standard which can be attained under normal working conditions is likely to contribute to the workers' motivation to achieve the designated level of activity or production.

Mature products are better candidates for cost minimization and measures of productivity than are new products for which innovative behavior may be more appropriate. The new product is likely to begin in a somewhat fluid form, with process standardization evolving with maturity. Otherwise, ". . . managers introducing new products, but who are evaluated on the basis of cost minimization and productivity, may not be as responsive to customer needs, will freeze the design specifications of the products prematurely in an attempt to standardize production, and may not pay sufficient attention to producing consistently high-quality products."[1]

To be utilized effectively in the control and analysis of costs, standards must be established for a definite period of time. Standards usually are computed for a six- or twelve-month period, although a longer period sometimes is used. Standards should be changed only when underlying conditions change or when they no longer reflect the original concept. Changing physical standards more than once a year usually weakens their effectiveness and increases clerical details. Frequent changes in the physical standards create confusion and tend to give employees the impression that supervisors are not in control and do not know what level of efficiency can be achieved. Nevertheless, physical standards should be continuously monitored and frequently reviewed to determine their appropriateness. Excellence is desired, and excellence is a process of continual improvement.

Events, rather than time, are the factors that determine when standards should be revised. These events may be classified as internal or external.

---

[1]Robert S. Kaplan, "Measuring Manufacturing Performance: A New Challenge for Managerial Accounting Research," *The Accounting Review*, Vol. LVIII, No. 4, p. 695.

Internal events such as technological advances, design revisions, method changes, labor rate adjustments, and changes in physical facilities are to some degree controllable by management. In contrast, external events such as price changes (including the impact of inflation), market trends, specific customer requirements, and changes in the competitive situation are generally not controllable by management. Consequently, price standards and product configuration standards may require frequent change as controlling external events occur.[2]

Once standards are set, standard cost cards should be prepared, on which the itemized cost of each materials part, labor operation, and overhead cost is shown. A master standard cost card, illustrated as follows, gives the standard cost for a single unit of product.[3]

Standard Cost Card

DATE OF STANDARD _July 1, 19--_			STANDARD COST CARD FOR PRODUCT _Paxel_				
DIRECT MATERIALS			**DEPARTMENT**				**TOTAL COST**
ITEM CODE	QUANTITY	STANDARD UNIT PRICE	1	2	3	4	
1-234	4	$6.25/pc.	$25.00				
3-671	24	3.75/doz.			$ 7.50		
3-561	8	2.45/gal.			19.60		
4-489	2	7.50/pc.				$15.00	$ 67.10
DIRECT LABOR							
OPERATION NUMBER	STANDARD HOURS	STANDARD RATE PER HOUR					
1-11	1/4	$11.00	$ 2.75				
3-10	3/4	10.00			$ 7.50		
3-14	1/2	10.00			5.00		
4-25	1/3	12.00				$ 4.00	19.25
FACTORY OVERHEAD							
OPERATION NUMBER	ALLOCATION BASIS	STANDARD HOURS RATE					
1-11	Machine hours	1/2 $21.50	$10.75				
3-10	Labor hours	3/4 24.80			$18.60		
3-14	Processing time	1-1/2 18.50			27.75		
4-25	Labor hours	1/3 27.00				$ 9.00	66.10
TOTAL MANUFACTURING COST PER UNIT							$152.45

The master standard cost card is supported by individual cards that indicate how the standard cost was compiled and computed. Each subcost card represents a form of standard cost card.

---

[2]Some firms facing technological change experiment with the use of standards that are essentially very recent actual costs, or a rolling average of past actual costs. Such standards may be redetermined as often as every month. For some examples, see C. J. McNair, William Mosconi, and Thomas Norris, *Meeting the Technology Challenge: Cost Accounting in a JIT Environment* (Montvale, NJ: National Association of Accountants, 1988).

[3]The illustration shows no costs in Department 2 since this particular product does not require any processing in that department.

■ DETERMINING STANDARD PRODUCTION

The preceding discussion deals with the determination of the standards per unit of production. To determine the standard allowed for each cost component, the standard quantity allowed per unit of product must be multiplied by the number of equivalent units of product produced during the period. This determination must consider the stage of completion of work in process inventories. Because the emphasis of standard cost variance analysis is on control, it is essential to compute the production standard and identify the associated variances for the current period production only. To illustrate, assume that there were 864 units of Paxel in process in Department 4 at the beginning of the month, one-half complete as to materials and one-third complete as to conversion cost (i.e., labor and factory overhead). During the month, 4,200 units were completed and transferred to finished goods inventory. There were 900 units in process at the end of the month, complete as to materials and two-thirds complete as to labor and factory overhead. The equivalent units of product for each cost element would be determined as follows:

	Materials	Conversion Cost
Units completed and transferred out	4,200	4,200
Less beginning inventory (all units)	864	864
Units started and completed this period.	3,336	3,336
Add beginning inventory (work this period)	432	576
Add ending inventory (work this period)	900	600
Equivalent units of production this period	4,668	4,512

Generally, standards include an allowance for normal spoilage. In such a case, equivalent unit computations for standard costing are based on good units only. By this procedure, the cost of excess or abnormal spoilage becomes a part of the computed variances. However, if management wishes to segregate the cost of abnormal spoilage for separate identification and evaluation, equivalent production computations must include both good units and abnormal spoilage.

■ DETERMINING STANDARD COST VARIANCES

For each item of direct material, for each labor operation, and for factory overhead attributable to each department (or each cost center, if multiple cost pools are used within a department), actual costs are measured against standard costs, resulting in differences. These differences are analyzed and identified as specific types of standard cost variances. If the actual cost exceeds the standard cost, the variance is referred to as "unfavorable" because the excess has an unfavorable effect on income. Conversely, if the standard cost exceeds the actual cost, the variance is referred to as "favorable" because it has a favorable effect on income.

The analysis does not end with such labeling, however. A standard cost variance is a question, not an answer. To achieve cost control, managers must determine reasons for the occurrence of each significant variance by investigating the circumstances that caused it. Effective management action can be taken only when the causes of cost variances are known. The responsibility and control of variances is more fully discussed later in this chapter.

Materials Standards and Variances

Two standards must be developed for direct materials costs:

1. A materials price standard.
2. A materials quantity standard (sometimes referred to as a materials usage standard).

Price standards permit (1) checking the performance of the purchasing department and detecting the influence of various internal and external factors on materials cost and (2) measuring the effect of materials price increases or decreases on the company's profits. Determining the price or cost to be used as the standard cost often is difficult because materials prices are controlled more by external factors than by a company's management. Prices selected should reflect current market prices, and the standards should be revised at inventory dates or whenever there is a major change in the market price of any of the principal materials or parts. Typically, prices are determined at the beginning of the accounting period and used throughout the period. However, during periods of rapidly changing prices, it may be necessary to change the price standard frequently, especially if inventory is recorded in the accounting records at standard.

If the actual price paid is more or less than the standard price, a price variance occurs. Materials price variances may be recorded at the time the materials are purchased (referred to as a *materials purchase price variance*) or at the time the materials are issued to the factory (referred to as a *materials price usage variance*). To hold the purchasing department fully accountable for price variances at the date they occur, the variances should be recorded at the time of purchase. Otherwise, materials used in the current period may include price variances related to materials purchased in a prior period, or price variances applicable to current period purchases may be inventoried. In either case, the materials price usage variance would be difficult to interpret because of the compounding effects of inventory changes. On the other hand, in a just-in-time inventory system, there would be little if any distinction between the two alternatives because there would be practically no materials inventory. In such a case, the timing and quantity of purchases and usages would differ only trivially.

JUST-IN-TIME

To illustrate the computation of a materials purchase price variance, assume that 10,000 units of Item 4-489 on the standard cost card for Paxel (page 566) are purchased at a unit price of $7.44. The materials purchase price variance is computed as follows:

	Quantity	×	Unit Cost	=	Amount
Actual quantity purchased	10,000		$7.44 actual		$74,400
Actual quantity purchased	10,000		7.50 standard		75,000
Materials purchase price variance	10,000		$ (.06)		$ (600) fav.

The $600 materials purchase price variance is favorable because the actual price is less than the standard price (i.e., the actual cost is $.06 per unit less than the standard permitted). As an alternative, the materials price usage variance could be computed. For example, if 9,500 units of Item 4-489 were issued and used by production, the materials price usage variance would be computed as follows:

	Quantity	×	Unit Cost	=	Amount
Actual quantity used	9,500		$7.44 actual		$70,680
Actual quantity used	9,500		7.50 standard		71,250
Materials price usage variance	9,500		$ (.06)		$ (570) fav.

The $600 favorable materials purchase price variance is $30 greater than the $570 favorable materials price usage variance. The reason for this difference is that 500 units of Item 4-489 which were purchased this period at a favorable variance of $.06 per unit (500 × $.06 = $30) were added to inventory and not used this period.

Quantity or usage standards generally are developed from materials specifications prepared by the departments of engineering (mechanical, electrical, or chemical) or product design. In a small or medium-size company, the superintendent or the departmental supervisors will provide basic specifications regarding type, quantity, and quality of materials needed and operations to be performed. Quantity standards should be set after the most economical size, shape, and quality of the product and the results expected from the use of various kinds and grades of materials have been analyzed. The standard quantity should be increased to include allowances for acceptable levels of waste, spoilage, shrinkage, seepage, evaporation, and leakage. The determination of the percentage of spoilage or waste should be based on figures that prevail after the experimental and development stages of the product have been completed.

The *materials quantity (or usage) variance* is computed by comparing the actual quantity of materials used with the standard quantity allowed, both priced at standard cost. The standard quantity allowed is determined by multiplying the quantity of materials that should be required to produce one unit of product (the standard quantity allowed per unit) by the actual number of units produced during the period. The units produced are the equivalent units of production for the materials cost being analyzed.

To illustrate the computation of the materials quantity (or usage) variance, recall that 4,668 equivalent units of Paxel were produced in Department 4 during the period with respect to material Item 4-489. Since the standard cost card calls for two units of Item 4-489 per unit of Paxel produced, the standard quantity of material Item 4-489 allowed is 9,336 units (4,668 × 2). The materials quantity (or usage) variance for material Item 4-489 is computed as shown at the top of page 570.

	Quantity	×	Unit Cost	=	Amount
Actual quantity used..................	9,500		$7.50 standard		$71,250
Standard quantity allowed	9,336		7.50 standard		70,020
Materials quantity variance	164		7.50 standard		$ 1,230 unfav.

The $1,230 materials quantity (or usage) variance is unfavorable because the actual quantity used exceeded the standard quantity allowed by 164 units at a standard cost of $7.50 each.

Labor Standards and Variances

Two standards also must be developed for direct labor costs:

1. A rate (wage or cost) standard.
2. An efficiency (time or usage) standard.

In many plants, the standard is based on rates established in collective bargaining agreements that define hourly wages, piece rates, and bonus differentials. Without a union contract, rates are based on the earnings rate as determined by agreement between the employee and the personnel department. Since rates generally are based on definite agreements, labor rate variances are infrequent. If they occur, they usually are due to unusual short-term conditions existing in the factory.

To assure fairness in rates paid for each operation performed, job rating has become a recognized procedure in industry. When a rate is revised or a change is authorized temporarily, it must be reported promptly to the payroll department to avoid delays, incorrect pay, and faulty reporting. Any difference between the standard and actual rates results in a *labor rate (wage or cost) variance.*

To illustrate the computation of the labor rate variance for Operation 4-25 on the standard cost card for Paxel (page 566), assume that 1,632 hours are actually worked at an actual rate of $12.50 per hour to produce 4,512 equivalent units of Paxel (page 567). The labor rate variance is computed as follows:

	Hours	×	Rate	=	Amount
Actual hours worked..................	1,632		$12.50 actual		$20,400
Actual hours worked..................	1,632		12.00 standard		19,584
Labor rate variance	1,632		$ .50		$ 816 unfav.

The labor rate variance of $816 is unfavorable because the actual rate exceeded the standard rate by $.50 per hour. The actual labor hours worked excludes nonproductive time, which is charged to factory overhead. Idle labor cost, to the extent that it is not included as a budgeted overhead item, will ultimately become part of the controllable variance in the two-variance method or the spending variance in the three- and four-variance methods, which are discussed later in the chapter.

Determination of labor efficiency standards is a specialized function. Therefore, they are best established by industrial engineers, using time and motion studies. Standards are set in accordance with scientific methods and accepted practices. They are based on actual performance of a worker or group of workers possessing average skill and using average effort while performing manual operations or working on machines operating under normal conditions. Time factors for acceptable levels of fatigue, personal needs, and delays beyond the control of the worker are studied and included in the standard. Such allowances are an integral part of the labor standard, but time required for setting up machines, waiting, or a breakdown is included in the factory overhead standard.

The establishment of time standards requires a detailed study of manufacturing operations. Standards based on operations should be understood by supervisors and used to enhance labor efficiency. However, time standards are of limited use "where operating times are strongly influenced by factors which cannot be standardized and controlled by management or where output from highly mechanized work is a function of machine time and speed rather than of labor hours worked."[4]

When a new product or process is started, the labor efficiency standard for costing and budget development should be based on the learning curve phenomenon (Chapter 10). The learning curve may well be, at least in part, an explanation of the labor efficiency variance associated with employees assigned to existing tasks that are new to them. Labor-related factory overhead costs and perhaps materials usage also might be affected.

The *labor efficiency variance* is computed at the end of any reporting period (day, week, or month) by comparing actual hours worked with standard hours allowed, both at the standard labor rate. The standard hours allowed is determined by multiplying the number of direct labor hours established or predetermined to produce one unit (the standard labor hours per unit) times the actual number of units produced during the period for which the variances are being computed. The units produced are the equivalent units of production for the labor cost being analyzed. The standard hours allowed for the 4,512 equivalent units of Paxel produced during the month is 1,504 (4,512 equivalent units × 1/3 standard hour per unit).

The labor efficiency variance for Operation 4-25 is computed as follows:

	Hours ×	Rate	= Amount
Actual hours worked...................	1,632	$12.00 standard	$19,584
Standard hours allowed	1,504	12.00 standard	18,048
Labor efficiency variance	128	12.00 standard	$ 1,536 unfav.

The unfavorable labor efficiency variance of $1,536 is due to the use of 128 hours in excess of standard hours allowed. In fully automated production systems, it may be impossible to directly trace labor to individual products produced during the period. In such a case, labor is likely to be treated as part of overhead, and no separate labor variances would be computed. The labor variances simply become a part of the factory overhead controllable variance in the two variance method or the factory overhead spending vari-

---

[4]Walter B. McFarland, *Manpower Cost and Performance Measurement* (New York: National Association of Accountants, 1977), p. 60.

ance in the three- and four-variance methods. These alternative methods of computing factory overhead variances are explained in the following section.

Factory Overhead Standards and Variances

Procedures for establishing and using standard factory overhead rates are similar to the methods discussed in Chapters 13 and 14, dealing with the determination of predetermined factory overhead rates by department and their application to jobs and products. First, a factory overhead budget must be prepared for each department or cost center. This process involves estimating each item of factory overhead cost that is expected to be incurred within each department or cost center at some predetermined level of activity, typically normal capacity or expected actual capacity. Next, budgeted service department costs are allocated to producing departments on the basis of services that are expected to be provided. When all budgeted factory overhead costs have been allocated to producing departments, each producing department's standard factory overhead rate is determined by totaling the budgeted direct and indirect factory overhead in the department and dividing the total by the predetermined level of the allocation base used by the department, such as direct labor hours, direct labor dollars, machine hours, direct materials cost, or units of product.

The activity measure used as an allocation base may vary from department to department, depending upon the nature of the production process in each department. There are two important considerations in selecting the appropriate allocation base. First, in order to assign costs to products on a reasonably accurate basis, the activity measure chosen should be the one that reflects the primary source of cost incurrence within the department. For example, if the production process is labor intensive in one department and capital intensive in another, direct labor hours or direct labor cost should be used in the first department and machine hours in the latter. However, if only one product is produced within the department, the equivalent units of product is a reasonable allocation base, regardless of the nature of the production process. If one activity within a department does not appear to be substantially related to most of the costs within that department and different products are produced within the department, multiple rates may be needed to improve costing accuracy. In such a case, a different overhead rate based on a different activity is used for each different cost pool within the department.[5] Although more accurate, the cost of developing and administering such a system is high and must be weighed against the potential need for improved accuracy.

Second, the activity measure chosen must be one that is capable of being reasonably and accurately monitored on a per unit or per job basis within the

ACTIVITY
COSTING

---

[5]See Chapter 13 for additional information about transactions base accounting.

existing data gathering system or with inexpensive modification to that system. If machine hours are selected, a data gathering system that can accurately record the number of machine hours incurred in the production of each unit or job must be in place. Because such data normally are not collected and because the installation and operation of a system that would accurately collect such data are costly, manufacturers traditionally have used readily available measures such as direct labor hours or direct labor cost to allocate factory overhead to production. However, with the increasing use of *ROBOTICS* robotics in manufacturing, direct labor is becoming a less significant, and in some cases an insignificant, cost.[6] Consequently, many modern manufacturing companies are being forced to redesign their cost accounting systems and find new ways of allocating factory overhead.

The data from the following flexible budget for Department 4, which is involved in producing Paxel (page 566), are used to illustrate the computation of the standard overhead rate and the overhead variances:

Department 4 Monthly Flexible Budget				
Capacity	80%	90%	100%	
Standard production	3,840	4,320	4,800	
Direct labor hours (DLH)	1,280	1,440	1,600	
Variable factory overhead:				
Indirect labor	$ 1,280	$ 1,440	$ 1,600	$1.00 per DLH
Supplies	3,200	3,600	4,000	2.50
Payroll taxes	1,600	1,800	2,000	1.25
Repair and maintenance	1,920	2,160	2,400	1.50
Utilities	960	1,080	1,200	.75
Total variable overhead	$ 8,960	$10,080	$11,200	$7.00
Fixed factory overhead:				
Supervision	$ 3,200	$ 3,200	$ 3,200	
Indirect labor	5,400	5,400	5,400	
Payroll taxes	2,400	2,400	2,400	
Vacation expense	6,000	6,000	6,000	
Machinery depreciation	5,000	5,000	5,000	
Building rent	1,200	1,200	1,200	
Property taxes and insurance	600	600	600	
Utilities	900	900	900	
Repair and maintenance	3,200	3,200	3,200	
General factory	4,100	4,100	4,100	
Total fixed overhead	$32,000	$32,000	$32,000	
Total factory overhead	$40,960	$42,080	$43,200	$32,000 per month plus $7.00 per DLH

(handwritten note: represents normal capacity)

Assuming that the 100% column represents normal capacity, the standard factory overhead rate is computed as follows:

$$\frac{\text{Total factory overhead}}{\text{Direct labor hours}} = \frac{\$43,200}{1,600} = \$27 \text{ per standard direct labor hour}$$

---

[6]Allen H. Seed, III, "Cost Accounting in the Age of Robotics," *Management Accounting*, Vol. LXVI, No. 4, pp. 39-43.

At the 100% capacity level, the rate consists of:

$$\frac{\text{Total variable factory overhead}}{\text{Direct labor hours}} = \frac{\$11,200}{1,600} = \$\ 7.00 \text{ variable factory overhead rate}$$

$$\frac{\text{Total fixed factory overhead}}{\text{Direct labor hours}} = \frac{\$32,000}{1,600} = 20.00 \text{ fixed factory overhead rate}$$

Total factory overhead rate at normal capacity. . $27.00 per standard direct labor hour

The standard cost of factory overhead chargeable to each job or process is determined by multiplying the standard number of units of the allocation base allowed, direct labor hours in this illustration, by the predetermined standard factory overhead rate. The standard number of units of the allocation base allowed is determined by multiplying the standard number of units of the allocation base allowed per unit of product by the actual number of equivalent units of product produced during the period. At the end of each period, usually a month, the factory overhead actually incurred is compared with the standard cost of factory overhead chargeable to work in process for the period. The difference between these two amounts is referred to as the *overall (or net) factory overhead variance*. If the standard cost system is fully integrated into the regular accounting records, i.e., inventories are recorded in the accounts at standard, the overall factory overhead variance is equal to over- or underapplied factory overhead (see Chapter 19).

For illustration purposes, assume that Paxel is the only product produced in Department 4 during the month and that the following data are available at the end of the month:

Actual factory overhead.	$43,685
Standard hours allowed for actual production (4,512 units × ⅓ standard labor hour per unit)	1,504
Actual direct labor hours used	1,632

The overall factory overhead variance is computed as follows:

Actual factory overhead.	$43,685
Factory overhead chargeable to work in process at standard (1,504 standard hours allowed × $27 standard overhead rate)	40,608
Overall (or net) factory overhead variance	$ 3,077 unfav.

The overall factory overhead variance must be further analyzed to reveal the sources of the variance in order to provide a guide to management in determining its causes. Causes must be determined before effective remedial action can be taken. The overall variance can be broken down for analysis in many different ways; however, the most frequently used approaches are to compute two, three, or four factory overhead variances. Regardless of the method used, the sum of the variances computed must equal the overall factory overhead variance.

Two-Variance Method. The two-variance method is the most frequently used method in actual practice, perhaps because it is the easiest to compute. The two variances are (1) the controllable variance and (2) the volume variance.

The *controllable variance* is the difference between the actual factory overhead incurred and the budget allowance based on the standard number of units of the allocation base allowed for actual production. The budget allowance may be thought of as the amount of factory overhead that would have been budgeted at standard if the actual quantity produced had been known in advance, i.e., total budgeted variable overhead at standard for actual production plus total budgeted fixed factory overhead.

The controllable variance is the responsibility of department managers to the extent that they can exercise control over the costs to which the variances relate. It is composed of two elements: (1) the difference between actual variable factory overhead and standard variable factory overhead allowed and (2) the difference between actual fixed factory overhead and budgeted fixed factory overhead. Based on the data presented above for Department 4, the controllable variance is computed as follows:

Actual factory overhead..		$43,685
Budget allowance based on standard hours allowed:		
Variable factory overhead (1,504 standard hours × $7.00 variable overhead rate)............................	$10,528	
Budgeted fixed factory overhead......................	32,000	42,528
Controllable variance...		$ 1,157 unfav.

The *volume variance* is the difference between the budget allowance based on the standard number of units of the allocation base allowed for actual production and the standard factory overhead chargeable to work in process. It indicates the cost of capacity available but not utilized efficiently and, therefore, may be the responsibility of the department manager (to the extent caused by variances in production efficiencies) or of executive management (to the extent caused by unexpected changes in sales demand). The volume variance for Department 4 is computed as follows:

Budget allowance based on standard hours allowed (computed above).....	$42,528
Factory overhead chargeable to work in process at standard (1,504 standard hours allowed × $27 standard overhead rate)...............	40,608
Volume variance	$ 1,920 unfav.

When standard cost rather than actual cost is charged to production, the volume variance can be thought of as the amount of over- or underapplied budgeted fixed factory overhead. It is the difference between budgeted fixed factory overhead and the amount of fixed factory overhead chargeable to production, based on the standard number of units of the allocation base allowed for actual production. Consequently, the volume variance for Department 4 could be computed as follows:

Budgeted fixed factory overhead................................	$32,000
Fixed factory overhead chargeable to production, based on the standard hours allowed for units produced (1,504 standard hours allowed × $20.00 fixed overhead rate)............................	30,080
Volume variance	$ 1,920 unfav.

Alternatively, it also can be computed as follows:

Normal (or budgeted) capacity in labor hours	1,600
Standard hours allowed for actual production	1,504
Capacity hours not utilized or not utilized efficiently	96
Fixed factory overhead rate	× $20
Volume variance	$1,920 unfav.

The controllable variance plus the volume variance equals the overall factory overhead variance for Department 4, as follows:

Controllable variance	$1,157 unfav.
Volume variance	1,920 unfav.
Overall factory overhead variance	$3,077 unfav.

Three-Variance Method. One of the problems with the two-variance method is that it conceals the over- or underutilization of the variable input used as the factory overhead allocation base, which is direct labor hours in the Department 4 illustration. The three-variance method attempts to remedy this problem. There are two commonly found alternative approaches for dividing the overall factory overhead variance into three variances. One method, referred to throughout this text as three-variance method A, requires the computation of (1) the spending variance, (2) the idle capacity variance, and (3) the efficiency variance. The other method, referred to throughout this text as three-variance method B, requires the computation of (1) the spending variance, (2) the variable efficiency variance, and (3) the volume variance. Each alternative provides a different view of the overall variance for management analysis.

Method A. The spending variance and the idle capacity variance computed in three-variance method A are the same variances discussed in Chapter 13. In this method, only the efficiency variance is unique to standard costing. The *spending variance* is the difference between the actual factory overhead incurred and the budget allowance based on the actual number of units of the allocation base used in actual production. It is composed of (1) the difference between the actual variable factory overhead incurred and the amount that would have been budgeted at the actual level of activity and (2) the difference between the actual fixed factory overhead and the budgeted fixed factory overhead. For Department 4, the spending variance would be computed as follows:

Actual factory overhead incurred		$43,685
Budget allowance based on actual hours:		
Variable factory overhead (1,632 actual hours × $7.00 variable overhead rate)	$11,424	
Budgeted fixed factory overhead	32,000	43,424
Spending variance		$ 261 unfav.

By basing the budget allowance on actual hours instead of on standard hours allowed, as shown above in the controllable variance, the manager of

Department 4 receives a more favorable allowance, which reduces the variance from $1,157 to $261. This reduction, which is identified later in this chapter as the variable efficiency variance, is caused by the inefficient use of the variable production input used as the allocation base for factory overhead.

The *idle capacity variance* is the difference between the budget allowance based on the actual number of units of the allocation base used in actual production and the amount of factory overhead chargeable to production in the absence of a standard cost system (i.e., the actual number of units of the allocation base used multiplied by the factory overhead rate). It is a measure of the over- or underutilization of production capacity and is computed for Department 4 in the illustration as follows:

Budget allowance based on actual hours (computed above)	$43,424
Actual hours (1,632) × factory overhead rate ($27)	44,064
Idle capacity variance.	$ (640) fav.

Conceptually, the idle capacity variance is the difference between the budgeted fixed factory overhead and the fixed factory overhead that would be charged to production on the basis of the actual capacity employed. Consequently, it can be computed as follows:

Budgeted fixed factory overhead	$32,000
Actual hours (1,632) × fixed overhead rate ($20)	32,640
Idle capacity variance.	$ (640) fav.

Alternatively, it can also be computed as follows:

Normal (or budgeted) capacity in labor hours	1,600
Actual labor hours.	1,632
Capacity hours utilized in excess of normal capacity	(32)
Fixed factory overhead rate	× $20
Idle capacity variance.	$ (640) fav.

The *efficiency variance* is the difference between the actual number of units of the allocation base used and the standard number of units of the allocation base allowed for actual production, multiplied by the standard factory overhead rate. It is largely the responsibility of department management because it reflects the efficient or inefficient use of the variable production input used as the allocation base. When labor hours are used as the basis for applying factory overhead, this variance reflects the efficient or inefficient use of labor, and when machine hours are used as the allocation base, this variance reflects the efficiency of machine usage. This variance is affected by inexperienced labor, fatigue, poor employee morale, changes in operating procedures, new or worn-out machinery, and poor quality of materials.

The efficiency variance for Department 4 is computed as follows:

Actual hours (1,632) × standard overhead rate ($27)	$44,064
Factory overhead chargeable to production at standard (1,504 standard hours × $27 overhead rate)	40,608
Efficiency variance.	$ 3,456 unfav.

Alternatively, it can be computed as follows:

Actual hours worked	1,632
Standard hours allowed for actual units produced	1,504
Excess of actual hours over standard hours allowed	128
Standard factory overhead rate	× $27
Efficiency variance	$3,456 unfav.

The sum of the three variances computed under method A equals the overall factory overhead variance for Department 3, as follows:

Spending variance	$ 261	unfav.
Idle capacity variance	(640)	fav.
Efficiency variance	3,456	unfav.
Overall factory overhead variance	$3,077	unfav.

Method B. The spending variance computed in three-variance method B is the same as the spending variance computed in three-variance method A, and the volume variance is the same volume variance as computed in the two-variance method. The *variable efficiency variance* is the difference between the actual number of units of the allocation base used and the standard number of units of the allocation base allowed for actual production, multiplied by the variable factory overhead rate. It is the portion of the efficiency variance that measures the effect of the efficient or inefficient use of the input used as an allocation base on the cost of the variable factory overhead. The variable efficiency variance may be computed as follows:

Budget allowance based on actual hours worked (computed above)	$43,424	
Budget allowance based on standard hours allowed (computed above)	42,528	
Variable efficiency variance	$ 896	unfav.

Alternatively, it can be computed as follows:

Actual hours worked	1,632	
Standard hours allowed for actual units produced	1,504	
Excess of actual hours over standard hours allowed	128	
Variable factory overhead rate	× $7	
Variable efficiency variance	$ 896	unfav.

The unfavorable spending variance of $261 plus the unfavorable variable efficiency variance of $896 equals the unfavorable controllable variance of $1,157 computed under the two-variance method illustrated for Department 4.

As is the case with method A, the sum of the three variances computed under method B equals the overall factory overhead variance for Department 4, as follows:

Spending variance	$ 261	unfav.
Variable efficiency variance	896	unfav.
Volume variance	1,920	unfav.
Overall factory overhead variance	$3,077	unfav.

The primary difference in method A and method B is that since the volume variance is computed in method B, the effect of the efficient or inefficient use of the input used to allocate factory overhead is impounded in the measure of capacity utilization and not separately stated. Under method A, the idle capacity variance is computed along with the efficiency variance. The efficiency variance segregates the effects of production efficiency from the measure of capacity utilization. The effect of the efficient or inefficient use of the input used to allocate factory overhead on capacity utilization can be observed in the difference between the volume variance and the idle capacity variance, a measure identified in the next section as the fixed efficiency variance. If department management has no control over capacity utilization, the method B approach seems reasonable. On the other hand, if department management has some control over the level of capacity utilized, the method A approach seems more desirable because it charges management with the effect of productive efficiency on capacity utilization.

Four-Variance Method. The four-variance method is similar to the three-variance method A, except that the efficiency variance is divided into its fixed and variable components. The four variances are (1) the spending variance, (2) the variable efficiency variance, (3) the fixed efficiency variance, and (4) the idle capacity variance. The spending variance and the idle capacity variance are computed in the same manner as in the three-variance method A, and the variable efficiency variance is computed in the same manner as in the three-variance method B. All three of these variances were illustrated previously. The fourth variance, the *fixed efficiency variance,* is the difference between the amount of fixed factory overhead that would be charged to production if based on the actual number of units of the allocation base used and the amount that would be charged to production based on the standard number of units of the allocation base allowed for actual production. Based on the information provided for Department 4, the fixed efficiency variance would be computed as follows:

Actual hours (1,632) × fixed overhead rate ($20)	$32,640
Standard hours allowed (1,504) × fixed overhead rate ($20)	30,080
Fixed efficiency variance	$ 2,560 unfav.

Alternatively, it may be computed as follows:

Actual hours worked	1,632
Standard hours allowed for actual units produced	1,504
Excess of actual hours over standard hours allowed	128
Fixed factory overhead rate	× $20
Fixed efficiency variance	$2,560 unfav.

When all four variances for Department 4 in the illustration are added together, the total is equal to the overall factory overhead variance, as follows:

Spending variance	$ 261	unfav.
Variable efficiency variance	896	unfav.
Fixed efficiency variance	2,560	unfav.
Idle capacity variance	(640)	fav.
Overall factory overhead variance	$3,077	unfav.

The presentation of four different methods of computing factory overhead variances may seem overwhelming at first; however, upon closer inspection, it becomes readily apparent that the different methods illustrated here are merely different combinations of essentially the same basic variance computations. These relationships are illustrated below:

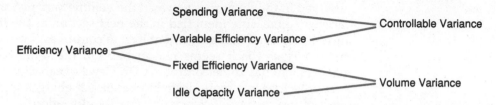

The four-variance method reconciles to the two-variance method by simply combining the spending variance and variable efficiency variance to get the controllable variance, and then combining the fixed efficiency variance and the idle capacity variance to get the volume variance. These relationships for the Department 4 illustration are demonstrated as follows:

Spending variance	$ 261	unfav.
Variable efficiency variance	896	unfav.
Controllable variance	$1,157	unfav.
Fixed efficiency variance........	$2,560	unfav.
Idle capacity variance	(640)	fav.
Volume variance	$1,920	unfav.

The four-variance method reconciles to the three-variance method A by keeping the spending and idle capacity variances separated, and combining the variable efficiency and the fixed efficiency variances to get the efficiency variance. These relationships for the Department 4 illustration are demonstrated as follows:

Spending variance	$ 261	unfav.
Variable efficiency variance	$ 896	unfav.
Fixed efficiency variance........	2,560	unfav.
Efficiency variance	$3,456	unfav.
Idle capacity variance	$ (640)	fav.

The four-variance method reconciles to the three-variance method B by keeping the spending and variable efficiency variances separated, and combining the fixed efficiency variance and the idle capacity variance to get the volume variance. These relationships for the Department 4 illustration are demonstrated as follows:

Spending variance	$ 261	unfav.
Variable efficiency variance	$ 896	unfav.
Fixed efficiency variance........	$2,560	unfav.
Idle capacity variance	(640)	fav.
Volume variance	$1,920	unfav.

The relationships between each of these four alternative methods of computing factory overhead variances are illustrated graphically below:

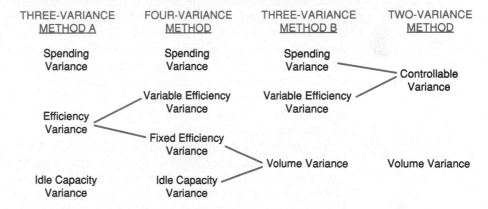

THREE-VARIANCE METHOD A	FOUR-VARIANCE METHOD	THREE-VARIANCE METHOD B	TWO-VARIANCE METHOD
Spending Variance	Spending Variance	Spending Variance	
			Controllable Variance
	Variable Efficiency Variance	Variable Efficiency Variance	
Efficiency Variance			
	Fixed Efficiency Variance		
		Volume Variance	Volume Variance
Idle Capacity Variance	Idle Capacity Variance		

Other Methods. There are numerous other methods of breaking down the overall factory overhead variance for analysis. For example, any portion of the spending or controllable variance attributable to the difference between budgeted and actual fixed factory overhead may be isolated separately and labeled as the fixed spending variance. It also is possible to break down the spending variance into price and quantity variances for each item of factory overhead expense (illustrated on page 590). The variance system chosen by management should be the one that it finds most useful in identifying the causes of the overall factory overhead variance. However, as a practical matter, management must weigh the costs of alternative data gathering and reporting systems with their expected benefits.

■ MIX AND YIELD VARIANCES

Basically, the establishment of a standard product cost requires the determination of price and quantity standards. In many industries, particularly of the process type, materials mix and materials yield play significant parts in the final product cost, in cost reduction, and in profit improvement.

Materials specification standards generally are set up for various grades of materials and types of secondary materials. In most cases, specifications are based on laboratory or engineering tests. Comparative costs of various grades of materials are used to arrive at a satisfactory materials mix, and changes often are made when it seems possible to use less costly grades of materials or substitute materials. In addition, a substantial cost reduction might be achieved through the improvement of the yield of good product units in the factory. At times, trade-offs may occur; e.g., a cost saving resulting from use of a less costly grade of materials may result in a poorer yield, or vice versa. A variance analysis program identifying and evaluating the nature, magnitude, and causes of mix and yield variances is an aid to operating management.

Mix Variance

After the standard specification has been established, a variance representing the difference between the standard cost of formula materials and the standard cost of the materials actually used can be calculated. This variance is generally recognized as a *mix (or blend) variance*, which is the result of mixing basic materials in a ratio different from standard materials specifications. In a woolen mill, for instance, the standard proportions of the grades of wool for each yarn number are reflected in the standard blend cost. Any difference between the actual wool used and the standard blend results in a blend or mix variance.

Industries like textiles, rubber, and chemicals, whose products must possess certain chemical or physical qualities, find it quite feasible and economical to apply different combinations of basic materials and still achieve a perfect product. In cotton fabrics, it is common to mix cotton from many parts of the world with the hope that the new mix and its cost will contribute to improved profits. In many cases, the new mix is accompanied by either a favorable or unfavorable yield of the final product. Such a situation may make it difficult to judge correctly the origin of the variances. A favorable mix variance, for instance, may be offset by an unfavorable yield variance, or vice versa. Thus any apparent advantage created by one may be canceled out by the other.

Yield Variance

Yield can be defined as the amount of prime product manufactured from a given amount of materials. The *yield variance* is the result of obtaining a yield different from the one expected on the basis of input.

In sugar refining, a normal loss of yield develops because, on the average, it takes approximately 102.5 pounds of sucrose in raw sugar form to produce 100 pounds of sucrose in refined sugars. Part of this sucrose emerges as black strap molasses, but a small percentage is completely lost.

In the canning industry, it is customary to estimate the expected yield of grades per ton of fruit purchased or delivered to the plant. The actual yield should be compared to the one expected and should be evaluated in terms of cost. If the actual yield deviates from predetermined percentages, cost and profit will differ.

Illustration of Mix and Yield Variances

To illustrate the calculation of mix and yield variances, assume that the Springmint Company, a manufacturer of chewing gum, uses a standard cost system. Standard product and cost specifications for 1,000 lbs. of chewing gum are as follows:

Material	Quantity	×	Unit Cost	=	Amount
A	800		$.25 per lb.		$200
B	200		.40		80
C	200		.10		20
Input	1,200 lbs.				$300	($300 ÷ 1,200 lbs. = $.25 per lb.*)
Output	1,000 lbs.				$300	($300 ÷ 1,000 lbs. = $.30 per lb.*)

Standard

*Weighted averages.

The production of 1,000 lbs. of chewing gum requires 1,200 lbs. of raw materials. Hence the expected yield is 1,000 lbs. ÷ 1,200 lbs., or 5/6 of input. *yield ratio*
Materials records indicate:

Material	Beginning Inventory	Purchases in January	Materials Available	Ending Inventory	Materials Used
A	10,000 lbs.	162,000 lbs. @ $.24	172,000 lbs.	15,000 lbs.	157,000 lbs.
B	12,000	30,000 @ .42	42,000	4,000	38,000
C	15,000	32,000 @ .11	47,000	11,000	36,000

231,000

Actual finished production for January is 200,000 lbs.

The materials variances for January consist of (1) price variances, (2) a mix variance, (3) a yield variance, and (4) quantity variances. The company computes the materials price variances as follows, using the procedure illustrated on page 569, and recognizes these variances when the materials are purchased.

Material	Quantity	Actual Cost	Standard Cost	Unit Cost Variation	Price Variance	
A	162,000	$.24	$.25	$(.01)	$(1,620)	fav.
B	30,000	.42	.40	.02	600	unfav.
C	32,000	.11	.10	.01	320	unfav.
Net materials purchase price variance					$ (700)	fav.

The materials mix variance results from combining materials in a ratio different from the standard materials specifications. It is computed as follows:

Actual quantities at individual *by* standard materials costs:

154,000	A	157,000 lbs.	@ $.25 =	$39,250
38,500	B	38,000	@ .40 =	15,200
38,500	C	36,000	@ .10 =	3,600	$58,050
		231,000 lbs.		

Actual quantity at weighted average of standard
materials cost input (231,000 lbs. × $.25). 57,750*
Materials mix variance . . . . $ 300   unfav.

*This figure can also be determined by multiplying the standard (expected) output from actual input (192,500 lbs., or 5/6 of 231,000 lbs.) by $.30 weighted average of standard materials cost output.

The influence of individual raw materials on the total materials mix variance can be computed in the following manner:

Combined Materials mix Variance

Individual materials mix Variance

Material	Actual Total Quantity in Actual Mix	Actual Total Quantity in Standard Mix	Quantity Variation	Standard Unit Cost	Materials Mix Variance	
A	157,000 lbs.	154,000 lbs.*	3,000 lbs.	$.25	$750	unfav.
B	38,000	38,500 **	(500)	.40	(200)	fav.
C	36,000	38,500 ***	(2,500)	.10	(250)	fav.
	231,000 lbs.	231,000 lbs.	0		$300	unfav.

*(800 lbs. of A ÷ 1,200 lbs. total on standard cost card) × 231,000 lbs.
**(200 lbs. of B ÷ 1,200 lbs. total on standard cost card) × 231,000 lbs.
***(200 lbs. of C ÷ 1,200 lbs. total on standard cost card) × 231,000 lbs.

The yield variance is computed as follows:

Actual input quantity at weighted average of standard materials cost.......	$57,750
Actual output quantity at weighted average of standard materials cost (200,000 lbs. × $.30)...	60,000*
Materials yield variance.......................................	$ (2,250) fav.

*This figure can also be determined by multiplying the input needed to produce 200,000 lbs. (240,000 lbs.) by $.25.

The yield variance occurred because the actual production of 200,000 lbs. exceeded the expected output of 192,500 lbs. (5/6 of 231,000 lbs.) by 7,500 lbs. The yield difference multiplied by the standard weighted materials cost of $.30 per output pound equals the favorable yield variance of $2,250.

The materials quantity variance can be computed for each item as follows, using the procedure illustrated on page 570:

Material	Quantity	× Standard Unit Cost	= Amount	Materials Quantity Variance
A: Actual quantity used......	157,000 lbs.	$.25	$39,250	
Standard quantity allowed .	160,000 lbs.*	.25	40,000	$ (750) fav.
B: Actual quantity used......	38,000 lbs.	$.40	$15,200	
Standard quantity allowed .	40,000 lbs.**	.40	16,000	(800) fav.
C: Actual quantity used......	36,000 lbs.	$.10	$ 3,600	
Standard quantity allowed .	40,000 lbs.***	.10	4,000	(400) fav.
Total materials quantity variance............				$(1,950) fav.

*An output of 200,000 lbs. should require an input of 240,000 lbs., with a standard yield of 1,000 lbs. output for each 1,200 lbs. input. Then the 240,000 lbs. × (800 lbs. ÷ 1,200 lbs.) Material A portion of the formula = 160,000 lbs.
**The 240,000 lbs. × (200 lbs. ÷ 1,200 lbs.) Material B portion of the formula = 40,000 lbs.
***The 240,000 lbs. × (200 lbs. ÷ 1,200 lbs.) Material C portion of the formula = 40,000 lbs.

The total materials quantity variance can also be determined by comparing actual quantities at standard prices, $58,050 ($39,250 + $15,200 + $3,600), to actual output quantity at the weighted average of standard materials cost, $60,000 (200,000 lbs, × $.30) for a total favorable variance of $1,950. The mix and yield variances separate the materials quantity variance into two parts:

Materials mix variance.........	$ 300 unfav.
Materials yield variance........	(2,250) fav.
Materials quantity variance	$(1,950) fav.

■ RESPONSIBILITY AND CONTROL OF VARIANCES

Management scrutinizes variances in an attempt to determine why they occur, what corrective action can be taken, and how efficient and effective performance should be rewarded. There is no substitute for competent supervision, but variance reporting can be a valuable aid to the supervisor in carrying out control responsibilities. However, management should recognize that explanations for variations in costs have limited usefulness in improving the future control of costs because the explanations seldom suggest the corrective action that should be taken. If cost control is to be effective, the results of corrective action taken must be measured and reported.

The extent of variance investigation should be based on the estimated cost of making the investigation versus the value of the anticipated benefits. If the costs to be saved from investigating a variance and taking corrective action are expected to exceed the cost of making the investigation, management should investigate to determine the cause of the variance. Variances should be identified and reported to management as frequently as economically feasible. The closer the detection and reporting is to the point of occurrence, the more effective is the remedial action and the larger is the amount of cost that can be saved. It may also be desirable to report variances in physical units as well as in dollars of cost.

Causes of Variances

QUALITY CONTROL

A variance is a signal. Large variances, whether favorable or unfavorable, should be investigated and critically analyzed. A variance may be caused by some random event that is not expected to recur, or it may be the result of some systematic problem that can be corrected. It is also possible that the standard is simply out-of-date. For example, the manufacturing process may change, thus changing physical standards, or unexpected price changes may cause monetary standards to be out of date. In some cases, variances in different departments may be related. Determination of such a relationship is particularly important where favorable variances in one area are more than offset by related unfavorable variances in another area. For example, a favorable materials price variance resulting from the purchase of inexpensive materials may be more than offset by unfavorable labor efficiency variances that result from increased labor time required to work with the poorer quality materials.

The purchasing department carries the primary responsibility for materials price variances. To be useful, variance reports should list the variance for each item of materials purchased during the period. Control of prices is obtained by getting several quotations, buying in economical lots, taking advantage of cash discounts, and selecting the most economical means of delivery. However, economic conditions and unexpected price changes by suppliers may be outside the limits of the department's control and may be caused by unexpected inflation, an excess or shortage of the quantity available in the market, or a fortunate buy. Thus a materials price variance may be more a measure of forecasting ability than a failure to buy at predetermined prices.

Internal factors, such as costly rush orders requiring materials shipments on short notice or in smaller than economical quantities, may have a negative impact on the materials price variance but would not be the fault of the purchasing department.

Materials quantity variances may result from many causes, which must be identified if the variances are to be controlled. Materials variance reports should be prepared on a departmental basis and should list the materials quantity variance for each item of materials used during the period. If the materials are of substandard quality, the fault may be with the person who prepared the purchase requisition informing the purchasing department about the quality of materials needed. If the materials purchased varied from the purchase requisition specification, the fault may lie with the purchasing department. Perhaps the faulty materials were not discovered during inspection when received. Other causes relate to the production activity and include inexperienced or inefficient labor, pilferage or theft, badly worn or new machinery, changes in production methods, faulty product planning, or lack of proper production supervision.

Labor rate variances tend to be fairly minor because labor rates usually are set by management for the period or by long-term union contract. Rate variances may occur, however, because of the use of a single average rate for a department, operation, or craft, while several different rates exist for the individual workers. In such cases, absenteeism or the assignment of workers to tasks that normally pay different rates can result in a rate variance. In this case, the planning or scheduling of work assignments would be the cause of the variance.

Labor efficiency variances may occur for a multitude of reasons. These reasons include a lack of materials or faulty materials, inexperienced workers and the related learning curve phenomenon (pages 287-290), badly worn or obsolete machinery, machinery breakdowns, new and unfamiliar machinery, changes in production methods, poor or incorrect production planning and scheduling, faulty blueprints or product design specifications, worker dissatisfaction, or work interruptions. From the point of view of department managers, the most useful labor efficiency report would be one that reports an efficiency variance for each worker. However, because of the high cost of such reports, labor efficiency variances usually are reported on a departmental or production operation basis.

Factory overhead variances relate to the variable and the fixed portions of factory overhead. The variance computation methods discussed previously segregate controllable variances from capacity variances. The idle capacity variance and the volume variance are measures of capacity utilization. Capacity variances are generally attributed to executive management. The decision regarding the utilization of plant capacity and the setting of predetermined factory overhead rates rests with the planning group. Within the range of fixed costs, however, changes occur due to changes in depreciation rates, increases in insurance premiums and taxes, and increases in salaries of top-level managers. Such changes generally become a part of the controllable variance or the spending variance.

Unless the portion of the controllable variance or spending variance attributable to each item of factory overhead expense is computed and reported to responsible management, large variances may go undetected. An itemized variance report can highlight a situation in which a large favorable variance for one item of cost is substantially offset by a large unfavorable variance for another item. An example of such a report for Department 4 is illustrated below, using the two-variance method. For this report, the budget allowance based on standard hours is determined for each item of overhead by multiplying the standard overhead rate per labor hour for each item of factory overhead (from the flexible budget on page 573) by the standard hours allowed for the work produced during the period. The controllable variance for

Department 4
Factory Overhead Variance Report
For Month Ending March 31, 19A

	(1) Budget Allowance Normal Capacity	(2) Budget Allowance Standard Hours	(3) Actual Cost	(4) Controllable Variance Unfav. (Fav.) (3) – (2)
Direct labor hours..............	1,600	1,504		
Capacity	100%	94%		
Variable factory overhead:				
Indirect labor................	$ 1,600	$ 1,504	$ 1,824	$ 320
Supplies	4,000	3,760	4,380	620
Payroll taxes	2,000	1,880	2,040	160
Repair and maintenance	2,400	2,256	2,080	(176)
Utilities.....................	1,200	1,128	1,216	88
Total variable cost	$11,200	$10,528	$11,540	
Fixed factory overhead:				
Supervision..................	$ 3,200	$ 3,200	$ 3,200	0
Indirect labor................	5,400	5,400	5,400	0
Payroll taxes	2,400	2,400	2,400	0
Vacation expense	6,000	6,000	6,000	0
Machinery depreciation........	5,000	5,000	5,000	0
Building rent	1,200	1,200	1,200	0
Property taxes and insurance...	600	600	645	45
Utilities.....................	900	900	900	0
Repair and maintenance	3,200	3,200	3,200	0
General factory	4,100	4,100	4,200	100
Total fixed cost............	$32,000	$32,000	$32,145	
Total factory overhead	$43,200	$42,528	$43,685	$ 1,157 unfav.
Standard factory overhead chargeable to work in process (1,504 standard hours × $27 rate)		40,608		
Volume variance.........................		$ 1,920 unfav.		

Reconciliation of variances:
Actual factory overhead				$43,685
Standard factory overhead chargeable to work in process				40,608
Overall factory overhead variance				$ 3,077 unfav.
Controllable variance				$ 1,157 unfav.
Volume variance				1,920 unfav.
Overall factory overhead variance				$ 3,077 unfav.

each item shown in the report on page 589 is computed by subtracting the actual cost of each item from its budget allowance (i.e., the value in column 3 minus the value in column 2).

The controllable variance can be broken down into the spending variance and the variable efficiency variance. The variable efficiency variance is caused by the efficient or inefficient use of the input used to allocate factory overhead, and the spending variance results from the efficient or inefficient use of the various items of factory overhead. An example of such a report for Department 4 is illustrated below, using three-variance method B. In addition to the budget allowance based on standard hours computed for the two-variance method above, the budget allowance based on actual hours must be computed for each item by multiplying its standard overhead rate per labor hour (from the flexible budget on page 573) by the actual labor hours worked during the period. The variable efficiency variance for each item of cost shown in the report is computed by subtracting its budget allowance based on standard hours from its budget allowance based on actual hours (i.e., the value in column 3 minus the value in column 2), and the spending variance for each item is computed by subtracting the actual cost of each item from its budget allowance based on actual hours (i.e., the value in column 4 minus the value in column 3).

To further enhance the usefulness of the standard cost variance report, the spending variance could be broken down into price and quantity variances for each item of factory overhead cost. The computational procedures are similar to those used in computing price and quantity variances for direct materials and direct labor. To break the spending variance down into price and quantity variances, more data are needed. The standard cost per unit, the actual cost per unit, and the actual quantity of each item of variable factory overhead must be available. To illustrate, assume the following additional data are available for Department 4 at the end of the month of March:

Item of Variable Overhead	(1) Standard Cost per Unit	(2) Actual Cost per Unit	(3) Actual Quantity Used	(4) Actual Quantity Used at Standard Unit Cost (3) × (1)	(5) Actual Quantity Used at Actual Unit Cost (3) × (2)
Indirect labor	$ 8.00	$ 8.00	228 hours	$1,824	$1,824
Supplies	1.80	2.00	2,190 units	3,942	4,380
Payroll taxes	1.25	1.25	1,632 hours	2,040	2,040
Repair and maintenance . . .	15.00	16.00	130 hours	1,950	2,080
Utilities	.90	.95	1,280 kwh	1,152	1,216

The spending quantity variance for each item of factory overhead is determined first by computing the actual quantity of input at the standard unit cost for each item (i.e., for each item of variable factory overhead, multiply its standard cost per unit by the actual quantity of the item used), and then subtracting it from its budget allowance based on actual hours. The spending price variance for each item is determined by subtracting the actual quantity of input used at the standard unit cost for each item from its actual cost.

Department 4
Factory Overhead Variance Report
For Month Ending March 31, 19A

	(1) Budget Allowance Normal Capacity	(2) Budget Allowance Standard Hours	(3) Budget Allowance Actual Hours	(4) Actual Cost	(5) Variable Efficiency Variance Unfav. (Fav.) (3) − (2)	(6) Spending Variance Unfav. (Fav.) (4) − (3)
Direct labor hours	1,600	1,504	1,632			
Capacity	100%	94%	102%			
Variable factory overhead:						
Indirect labor.....................	$ 1,600	$ 1,504	$ 1,632	$ 1,824	$128	$192
Supplies	4,000	3,760	4,080	4,380	320	300
Payroll taxes	2,000	1,880	2,040	2,040	160	0
Repair and maintenance	2,400	2,256	2,448	2,080	192	(368)
Utilities	1,200	1,128	1,224	1,216	96	(8)
Total variable cost	$11,200	$10,528	$11,424	$11,540		
Fixed factory overhead:						
Supervision......................	$ 3,200	$ 3,200	$ 3,200	$ 3,200	0	0
Indirect labor....................	5,400	5,400	5,400	5,400	0	0
Payroll taxes	2,400	2,400	2,400	2,400	0	0
Vacation expense	6,000	6,000	6,000	6,000	0	0
Machinery depreciation	5,000	5,000	5,000	5,000	0	0
Building rent	1,200	1,200	1,200	1,200	0	0
Property taxes and insurance	600	600	600	645	0	45
Utilities	900	900	900	900	0	0
Repair and maintenance	3,200	3,200	3,200	3,200	0	0
General factory...................	4,100	4,100	4,100	4,200	0	100
Total fixed cost	$32,000	$32,000	$32,000	$32,145		
Total factory overhead	$43,200	$42,528	$43,424	$43,685	$896	$261
					unfav.	unfav.

Standard factory overhead chargeable to work in process (1,504 standard hours × $27 rate)		40,608	
Volume variance..............................		$ 1,920	unfav.

Reconciliation of variances:

Actual factory overhead...	$43,685	
Standard factory overhead chargeable to work in process	40,608	
Overall factory overhead variance......................................	$ 3,077	unfav.
Spending variance...	$ 261	unfav.
Variable efficiency variance..	896	unfav.
Volume variance..	1,920	unfav.
Overall factory overhead variance......................................	$ 3,077	unfav.

These variances are illustrated in the factory overhead variance report for Department 4 on page 590.

A variance report is an integral part of the system of cost control. It provides a way for upper level management to monitor the efficiency of department supervisors or other operating level managers, and it provides a way for responsible managers to identify problems which require attention. In its efficiency monitoring capacity, upper level management typically is not concerned about the variances for each item of overhead, except to make sure

Department 4
Factory Overhead Variance Report
For Month Ending March 31, 19A

	(1) Budget Allowance Normal Capacity	(2) Budget Allowance Standard Hours	(3) Budget Allowance Actual Hours	(4) Actual Quantity Used at Standard Unit Cost	(5) Actual Cost	(6) Variable Efficiency Variance Unfav. (Fav.) (3) – (2)	(7) Spending Variance Unfav. (Fav.) (5) – (3)	(8) Spending Quantity Variance Unfav. (Fav.) (4) – (3)	(9) Spending Price Variance Unfav. (Fav.) (5) – (4)
Direct labor hours	1,600	1,504	1,632						
Capacity	100%	94%	102%						
Variable factory overhead:									
Indirect labor	$ 1,600	$ 1,504	$ 1,632	$ 1,824	$ 1,824	$128	$192	$ 192	$ 0
Supplies	4,000	3,760	4,080	3,942	4,380	320	300	(138)	438
Payroll taxes	2,000	1,880	2,040	2,040	2,040	160	0	0	0
Repair and maintenance	2,400	2,256	2,448	1,950	2,080	192	(368)	(498)	130
Utilities	1,200	1,128	1,224	1,152	1,216	96	(8)	(72)	64
Total variable cost	$11,200	$10,528	$11,424	$10,908	$11,540	$896	$261	$(516)	$777
Fixed factory overhead:									
Supervision	$ 3,200	$ 3,200	$ 3,200	$ 3,200	$ 3,200	0	0	0	0
Indirect labor	5,400	5,400	5,400	5,400	5,400	0	0	0	0
Payroll taxes	2,400	2,400	2,400	2,400	2,400	0	0	0	0
Vacation expense	6,000	6,000	6,000	6,000	6,000	0	0	0	0
Machinery depreciation	5,000	5,000	5,000	5,000	5,000	0	0	0	0
Building rent	1,200	1,200	1,200	1,200	1,200	0	0	0	0
Property taxes and insurance	600	600	600	600	645	0	45	0	45
Utilities	900	900	900	900	900	0	0	0	0
Repair and maintenance	3,200	3,200	3,200	3,200	3,200	0	0	0	0
General factory	4,100	4,100	4,100	4,100	4,200	0	100	0	100
Total fixed cost	$32,000	$32,000	$32,000	$32,000	$32,145				
Total factory overhead	$43,200	$42,528	$43,424	$42,908	$43,685	$896 unfav.	$261 unfav.	$(516) fav.	$777 unfav.

Standard factory overhead chargeable to work in process (1,504 standard hours × $27 rate) 40,608

Volume variance .... $ 1,920 unfav.

Reconciliation of variances:
Actual factory overhead $43,685
Standard factory overhead chargeable to work in process 40,608
Overall factory overhead variance .... $ 3,077 unfav.

Spending variance:
Spending quantity variance .... $ (516) fav.
Spending price variance ....   777 unfav.
                      $ 261 unfav.
Variable efficiency variance ....   896 unfav.
Volume variance ....   1,920 unfav.
Overall factory overhead variance ...... $ 3,077 unfav.

that subordinates do not cut desirable expenditures in one area to offset inefficiencies in another. For example, in the absence of a detailed variance report to upper level management, a department supervisor who expects a large unfavorable supplies quantity variance during the period may be tempted to cut maintenance expenditures in order to mitigate or eliminate the overall unfavorable variance.

At the operating level, more detail may be desirable. Because managers are evaluated on the basis of standard cost variances, they typically pay close attention to operating activities. As a consequence, they often are aware of inefficiencies and their causes before receiving a variance report at the end of the period. In such a case, a highly detailed variance report may not be necessary. On the other hand, even in situations where managers closely monitor activity, surprises sometimes occur. Managers generally pay close attention to those activities that have been problems in the past and less attention to those areas that have not. As a consequence, inefficiencies may go undetected in the absence of a detailed variance report. In addition, a detailed variance report can be useful in that it identifies the magnitude of variances. Furthermore, a manager may be too busy to closely monitor operations and may, therefore, be unaware of inefficient activities. Even if a manager is aware of an inefficiency, it may be ignored on the grounds that the amount of cost involved is insignificant compared to the cost of correcting the problem.

In deciding the amount of detail to report to responsible managers, the cost of gathering and recording additional data must be weighed against the expected benefit. If there is a high probability that significant controllable inefficiencies can occur and go undetected by operating level managers, the potential cost savings may exceed the additional cost of providing detailed variance reports. This is more apt to be the case in situations where inefficiencies are not easily observed or in situations where the responsible manager does not have sufficient time to closely monitor operating activities.

Tolerance Limits for Variance Control

All managers have many important time-consuming responsibilities other than variance investigation; therefore, their efforts should be concentrated on large variances first because they have the greatest impact on cost and profit. Some variance in cost measurements can be expected as a result of imperfect measurement techniques. Typically, the activity measure used to estimate a cost does not explain all of the variation in the cost. The question that should be asked is "How large a variance from standard should be tolerated before the variance should be investigated?" In other words, some tolerance limit or range should be established, so that if the cost variance falls within this range, it can be considered acceptable. If the variance is outside the range, an investigation should be made if the cost of doing so is reasonable. In this manner, the practice of management by exception can be employed effectively and efficiently.

Each reported variance should be highlighted in a manner indicating whether the variance is within the control limit. Such information enables the responsible manager or supervisor to accept deviations from the standard as a valuable tool for the control of costs and lessens the dangers of their being more averse to risk than upper-level managers prefer. A manager who is unduly concerned about the penalty for even small variances may perform in a manner that hinders rather than enhances efficient operations.

Past data on established operations, tempered by estimated changes in the future, may furnish reliable bases for estimating expected costs and calculating control limits that serve to indicate good as well as poor operation and that aid in the decision to investigate a variance. The limits may be expressed as minimum dollar amounts or as percentage differences. Their determination may be based on subjective judgments, hunches, guesses, and biases, or on careful analyses and estimates, including the possible use of statistical procedures such as the standard error of the estimate (pages 351-353). In setting and applying tolerance limits, it is important to recognize that the relative magnitude of a variance is more significant than its absolute value. Furthermore, the cost versus benefit of tighter controls must be considered as tolerance reduction alternatives are explored.

To illustrate the use of tolerance limits, assume that maintenance cost is a semivariable cost which appears in factory overhead budget for the period and that the method of least squares is used to estimate maintenance costs. The standard error of the estimate for maintenance cost, based on a statistical analysis of data gathered over the past 30 months, is $750. Company policy is to investigate any variance that exceeds the 95 percent confidence interval estimate, which in this case would be the estimated maintenance expense based on actual machine hours plus or minus $1,500 (i.e., the value of two standard errors).[7] The budget allowance based on actual machine hours for the current period indicates that maintenance costs should be $12,500; however, actual maintenance costs are $14,300. The current period spending variance for maintenance expense is unfavorable in the amount of $1,800. Since the unfavorable spending variance exceeds two standard deviations, investigation of the causes of this excess is required.

If the actual maintenance cost were only $13,800, the unfavorable spending variance would be $1,300. Since this variance would be less than two standard deviations, investigation would not appear to be warranted. However, if the unfavorable variance were to persist in subsequent reporting periods, the causes should be examined because they would be significant in the long run.

---

[7]In this situation the sample size is sufficiently large to treat maintenance cost as normally distributed, thereby making it possible to ignore the correction factor for small samples and Student's *t* distribution discussed on pages 351-353.

DISCUSSION QUESTIONS

Q18-1. (a) Define standard costs.
(b) Name some advantages of a standard cost system.

Q18-2. A team of management consultants and company executives concluded that a standard cost installation was a desirable vehicle for accomplishing the objectives of a progressive management. State some uses of standard costs that can be associated with the above decision.

Q18-3. The use of standard costs in pricing and budgeting is quite valuable, since decisions in the fields of pricing and budgetary planning are made before the costs under consideration are incurred. Discuss.

Q18-4. Explain how standards relate to job order and process cost accumulation procedures.

Q18-5. Discuss the criteria to be used when selecting the operational activities for which standards are to be set.
(ICMA adapted)

Q18-6. Identify two uses of standards for which "normal" or "currently attainable" standards are preferable to "theoretical" or "ideal" standards.
(SMAC adapted)

Q18-7. Discuss the behavioral issues to be considered when selecting the level of performance to be incorporated into a standard cost. (ICMA adapted)

Q18-8. Discuss the role that each of the following departments should play in establishing standard costs:

(a) Accounting department.
(b) The department whose performance is being measured.
(c) The industrial engineering department. (ICMA adapted)

Q18-9. What is indicated by a factory overhead variable efficiency variance?
(SMAC adapted)

Q18-10. What is indicated by a factory overhead spending variance?

Q18-11. What is indicated by a factory overhead volume variance?
(SMAC adapted)

Q18-12. In a standard cost system, the computation of variances is a first step. What steps should follow?

Q18-13. Discuss the meaning of variance control and responsibility by various levels of management.

Q18-14. (a) Describe the features of tolerance limits.
(b) Discuss potential benefits of tolerance limits to an organization.
(c) Identify and discuss potential behavioral problems which can occur in using tolerance limits.
(ICMA adapted)

EXERCISES

 E18-1. Materials variance analysis. The standard cost per unit of material M-12 is $13.50 per pound. During the month, 4,500 pounds of M-12 were purchased at a total cost of $60,300. In addition, 4,000 pounds of M-12 were used during the month; however, the standard quantity allowed for actual production is 3,800 pounds.

Required: Compute the materials purchase price variance, price usage variance, and quantity variance, indicating whether the variances are favorable or unfavorable.

E18-2. Materials price variance analysis. The standard cost per unit of component part K-45 is $4. During the month, 6,000 units of K-45 were purchased at a total cost of $25,200. In addition, 7,100 units of K-45 were used during the month; however, the standard quantity allowed for actual production is 6,900 units.

Required:

(1) Compute the materials purchase price variances and the materials quantity variances and indicate whether the variances are favorable or unfavorable.
(2) Assume that materials are inventoried at actual cost and that the beginning inventory of K-45 contained 2,000 units at a total cost of $8,240. Compute the materials price usage variance assuming that the average cost method is used for materials inventories.

 E18-3. Labor variance analysis. During the month, 1,200 units of Topo were produced. Actual direct labor required 650 direct labor hours at an actual total cost of $6,435. According to the standard cost card for Topo, one-half hour of labor should be required per unit of Topo produced, at a standard cost of $10 per labor hour.

Required: Compute the labor rate and efficiency variances, indicating whether the variances are favorable or unfavorable.

 E18-4. Materials and labor variance analysis. The following data pertain to the first week of operations during the month of June:

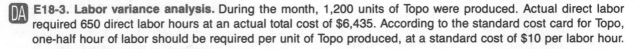

Materials:	Actual purchases	1,500 units at $ 3.80 per unit
	Actual usage.	1,350 units
	Standard usage	1,020 units at $ 4.00 per unit
Direct labor:	Actual hours	310 hours at $12.10 per hour
	Standard hours.	340 hours at $12.00 per hour

Required: Compute the following variances, indicating whether the variances are favorable or unfavorable:

(1) Materials purchase price variance, price usage variance, and quantity variance.
(2) Labor rate and efficiency variances.

 E18-5. Factory overhead variance analysis, two-variance method. The normal capacity of the Assembly Department is 12,000 machine hours per month. At normal capacity, the standard factory overhead rate is $12.50 per machine hour, based on $96,000 of budgeted fixed expenses per month and a variable expense rate of $4.50 per machine hour. During April, the department operated at 12,500 machine hours, with actual factory overhead of $166,000. The number of standard machine hours allowed for the production actually attained is 11,000.

Required: Compute the overall factory overhead variance and analyze it using the two-variance method. Indicate whether the variances are favorable or unfavorable.

 E18-6. Factory overhead variance analysis, three-variance method A. The normal capacity of Department 3 is 6,000 direct labor hours per month. At normal capacity, the standard factory overhead rate is $22 per direct labor hour, based on $96,000 of budgeted fixed expenses per month and a variable expense rate of $6 per direct labor hour. During November, the department operated at 5,600 direct labor hours, with actual factory overhead of $130,000. The number of standard direct labor hours allowed for the production actually attained is 5,700.

Required: Compute the overall factory overhead variance and analyze it using the three-variance method A. Indicate whether the variances are favorable or unfavorable.

 E18-7. Factory overhead variance analysis, three-variance method B. The normal capacity of the Die Cutting Department is 4,500 machine hours per month. At normal capacity, the standard factory overhead rate is $24.80 per machine hour, based on budgeted fixed factory overhead of $85,500 per month and a variable expense rate of $5.80 per machine hour. During July, the department operated at 4,600 machine hours, with actual factory overhead of $121,000. The number of standard machine hours allowed for the production actually attained is 4,200.

Required: Compute the overall factory overhead variance and analyze it using the three-variance method B. Indicate whether the variances are favorable or unfavorable.

DA **E18-8. Factory overhead variance analysis, four-variance method.** Standard direct labor hours budgeted for February production were 2,000, with factory overhead at that level budgeted at $10,000, of which $3,000 is variable. Actual labor hours for the month were 1,900; however, the number of standard labor hours allowed for actual February production is 2,050. Actual factory overhead incurred during the month was $10,500.

Required: Compute the overall factory overhead variance and analyze it using the four-variance method. Indicate whether the variances are favorable or unfavorable.

DA **E18-9. Factory overhead variance analysis.** Montana Machine Company has developed the following standard factory overhead costs for each SX unit assembled in Department 6, based on a monthly capacity of 80,000 direct labor hours:

Variable overhead..............................	2 hours @ $6 per hour = $12
Fixed overhead.................................	2 hours @ $3 per hour = 6
Department 6 factory overhead per unit of SX........	$18

During the month of August, 38,000 units of SX were actually produced. Actual direct labor hours totaled 77,500, and actual factory overhead totaled $700,000.

Required: Determine the overall factory overhead variance and analyze it with each of the following variance analysis methods, indicating whether the variances computed are favorable or unfavorable.

(1) Two-variance method.
(2) Three-variance method A.
(3) Three-variance method B.
(4) Four-variance method.

SS **E18-10. Factory overhead variance analysis report.** The Cost Department of Benjamin Products Company prepared the following flexible budget for Department 2 for June:

Production quantity based on standard........	9,600	10,800	12,000
Direct labor hours at standard	4,800	5,400	6,000
Capacity utilization at standard..............	80%	90%	100%
Variable overhead:			
Indirect labor	$ 1,920	$ 2,160	$ 2,400
Manufacturing supplies	1,680	1,890	2,100
Repairs................................	640	720	800
Heat, power, and light	80	90	100
Total variable overhead	$ 4,320	$ 4,860	$ 5,400
Fixed overhead:			
Superintendence	$ 6,000	$ 6,000	$ 6,000
Indirect labor	5,400	5,400	5,400
Manufacturing supplies	1,020	1,020	1,020
Maintenance	960	960	960
Heat, power, and light	120	120	120
Machinery depreciation	540	540	540
Insurance and taxes	360	360	360
Total fixed overhead..................	$14,400	$14,400	$14,400
Total budgeted factory overhead.............	$18,720	$19,260	$19,800

Factory overhead is charged to production at the rate of $3.30 per direct labor hour. The overhead rate was determined on the basis of 100% capacity utilization, considered to be normal. At the end of the month, cost records showed 10,200 units of product were manufactured, 5,040 direct labor hours were worked, and actual factory overhead was as follows:

Superintendence	$ 6,200
Indirect labor.......................	7,500
Manufacturing supplies	2,825
Repairs	650
Maintenance.......................	960
Heat, power, and light	225
Machinery depreciation	540
Insurance and taxes.................	372
Total actual factory overhead	$19,272

Required: Prepare a departmental factory overhead variance report which shows the controllable variance for each item of factory overhead and a single departmental volume variance. For each item of expense that contains both a fixed and a variable portion, assume that the actual fixed portion is equal to the budgeted fixed portion and that the balance of the actual expense is variable. Indicate whether the variances are favorable or unfavorable.

E18-11. Price, mix, and yield variances. Chocolate manufacturing operations require close control of daily production and cost data. The computer printout for a batch of one ton of cocoa powder indicates the following materials standards:

Ingredients	Standard Quantity (Pounds)	Standard Unit Cost	Standard Batch Cost
Cocoa beans	800	$.60	$ 480
Milk	3,700	.50	1,850
Sugar..............	500	.40	200
Total batch	5,000		$2,530

On December 7, the company's Commodity Accounting and Analysis Section reported the following production and cost data for the December 6 operations:

Ingredients Put in Process	Actual Quantity (Pounds)	×	Actual Unit Price	=	Actual Total Cost
Cocoa beans	325,000		$.62		$201,500
Milk...............	1,425,000		.48		684,000
Sugar..............	250,000		.39		97,500
Total	2,000,000				$983,000

Cocoa powder transferred to finished goods inventory totaled 387 tons. There was no work in process inventory.

Required: Compute the materials price, mix, and yield variances.

E18-12. Materials price, mix, and yield variances. Energy Products Company produces a gasoline additive, Gas Gain. This product increases engine efficiency and improves gasoline mileage by creating a more complete burn in the combustion process.

Careful controls are required during the production process to ensure that the proper mix of input chemicals is achieved and that evaporation is controlled. If the controls are not effective, there can be loss of output and efficiency.

The standard cost of producing a 500-liter batch of Gas Gain is $135. The standard materials mix and related standard cost of each chemical used in a 500-liter batch are as follows:

Chemical	Standard Input Quantity (Liters)	Standard Cost per Liter	Total Cost
Echol.........	200	$.200	$ 40.00
Protex	100	.425	42.50
Benz	250	.150	37.50
CT-40.........	50	.300	15.00
	600		$135.00

The quantities of chemicals purchased and used during the current production period are shown in the schedule below. A total of 136 batches of Gas Gain were manufactured during the current production period. Energy Products determines its cost and chemical usage variations at the end of each production period.

Chemical	Quantity Purchased (Liters)	Total Purchase Price	Quantity Used (Liters)
Echol.........	25 000	$ 5,365	26 800
Protex	13 000	6,240	12 660
Benz	40 000	5,840	37 400
CT-40.........	7 500	2,220	7 140
	85 500	$19,665	84 000

Required:

(1) Calculate the purchase price variances by chemical for Energy Products Company.
(2) Compute the materials mix and yield variances.   (ICMA adapted)

PROBLEMS

P18-1. Variance analysis: materials, labor, and factory overhead. Armando Corporation manufactures a product with the following standard costs:

Direct materials—20 yards @ $1.35 per yard	$27
Direct labor—4 hours @ $9 per hour..	36
Factory overhead—4 direct labor hours @ $7.50 per hour; ratio of variable to fixed factory overhead is 2:1	30
Total standard cost per unit of output.......................................	$93

Standards are based on normal monthly capacity of 2,400 direct labor hours. The following information pertains to July, 19A:

Units produced in July.......................................	500
Direct materials purchased—18,000 yards @ $1.38 per yard	$24,840
Direct materials used—9,500 yards	
Direct labor—2,100 hours @ $9.15 per hour	19,215
Actual factory overhead	16,650

Required:

(1) Compute the variable factory overhead rate per direct labor hour and the total fixed factory overhead based on normal monthly capacity.
(2) Compute two variances each for materials, labor, and factory overhead.   (AICPA adapted)

P18-2. Variance analysis: materials, labor, and factory overhead; process costing. Trutch Company manufactures a product which is accounted for using a standard process costing system with the following standards:

Materials—2 pieces @ $.48 each...........................	$ .96
Labor—1/2 hour @ $7.60 per hour	3.80
Variable factory overhead—1/2 hour @ $1.40 per hour	.70
Fixed factory overhead—1/2 hour @ $.40 per hour	.20
	$5.66

The company's standards include an allowance for normal spoilage. Equivalent production computations for standard costing are made for good units only. By this procedure, excess spoilage becomes a contributing factor to the computed variances. The following data are available for September:

Beginning inventory (all materials, 50% converted)......	10,000 units
Started in process..................................	40,000 units
Transferred to finished goods	42,000 units
Ending inventory (all materials, 90% converted)	5,000 units
Fixed factory overhead budgeted....................	$ 8,000
Materials used (76,000 pieces)......................	$ 38,000
Labor (22,500 hours)...............................	$180,000
Variable factory overhead incurred..................	$ 33,800
Fixed factory overhead incurred....................	$ 8,200

Required: Compute two variances for materials and labor, and compute three variances for factory overhead, using three-variance method A. Indicate whether the variances are favorable or unfavorable.

CGA-Canada (adapted) Reprint with permission

 P18-3. Equivalent units and variance analysis for materials, labor, and factory overhead. Hatzig Company manufactures one product for which it has developed the following standard cost per unit:

Direct materials	3 kg. @ $ 4 =	$12.00
Direct labor	1/2 hr. @ 11 =	5.50
Variable overhead	1/2 hr. @ 6 =	3.00
Fixed overhead	1/2 hr. @ 8 =	4.00
Standard cost per unit of Beta produced		$24.50

Materials are added at the beginning of the process. Inspection takes place at the end of the process and spoilage is considered to be abnormal. Actual activity for November follows:

(a) Budgeted fixed factory overhead for the month was $80,000.

(b) There were 4,000 units in process on November 1 and they were 20% complete as to conversion costs.

(c) 60 000 kg of materials were purchased at a unit cost of $3.95. The materials price variance is determined at the date the materials are purchased.

(d) 16,000 units of product were started during November.

(e) 50 000 kg of materials were issued to production.

(f) The direct labor payroll was $108,000 for 9,000 hours.

(g) 17,000 units of product were transferred to finished goods inventory.

(h) There were 2,150 units in process on November 30 and they were 40% complete as to conversion costs.

(i) Actual factory overhead totaled $134,900.

Required:

(1) Compute equivalent units for materials and conversion costs.

(2) Compute two variances for materials and labor, and reconcile the overall factory overhead variance using three-variance method B. Indicate whether the variances are favorable or unfavorable.

CGA-Canada (adapted) Reprint with permission

P18-4. Variance analysis: materials, labor, and factory overhead. Terry Company manufactures a commercial solvent used for industrial maintenance. This solvent, which is sold by the drum, generally has a stable selling price. Terry produced and sold 60,000 drums in December.

The following information is available regarding Terry's operations for the month:

(a) Standard costs per drum of product manufactured were:

Materials:	
10 gallons of raw material	$20
1 empty drum.	1
Total materials.	$21
Direct labor: 1 hour	$ 7
Fixed factory overhead per direct labor hour	$ 4
(normal capacity is 68,750 direct labor hours)	
Variable factory overhead per direct labor hour	6
Total factory overhead per direct labor hour	$10

(b) Costs incurred during December were:

Raw materials:
  600,000 gallons purchased at a cost of $1,150,000.
  700,000 gallons used.

Empty drums:
  85,000 drums purchased at a cost of $85,000.
  60,000 drums used.

Direct labor:
  65,000 hours worked at a cost of $470,000.

Factory overhead:	
Depreciation of building and machinery (fixed)	$230,000
Supervision and indirect labor (semivariable)	360,000
Other factory overhead (variable).	76,500
Total factory overhead	$666,500

Required: Compute two variances for each material and for labor and four variances for factory overhead. The materials price variance is determined at the time of purchase. Indicate whether the variances are favorable or unfavorable. (AICPA adapted)

 P18-5. Equivalent production and standard costing variance analysis. Moose Company uses a standard process costing system in accounting for costs in its one production department. Material A is added at the beginning of the process, and Material B is added when the units are 90% complete. Conversion costs are incurred uniformly throughout the process. Inspection takes place at the end of the process, and all spoilage is expected to be abnormal. The standard cost of abnormal spoilage is charged to a current period expense account. Normal capacity is 7,800 direct labor hours per month.

The standard cost per unit is as follows:

Material A: 4 gallons @ $1.20	$ 4.80
Material B: 2 square feet @ $.70	1.40
Direct labor: 1 hour @ $11.50	11.50
Variable factory overhead: 1 hour @ $1.80	1.80
Fixed factory overhead: 1 hour @ $5.00	5.00
Total	$24.50

Additional data for January:

    (a) Beginning work in process inventory—3,000 units ($33^1/_3$% converted).
    (b) Started in process during the month—11,000 units.
    (c) Finished during the month—8,000 units.
    (d) Ending work in process inventory—5,000 units (40% converted).
    (e) Actual costs incurred:

Material A used	50,000 gallons @ $1.00
Material B used	18,000 sq. ft. @ $.75
Direct labor............	10,200 hours @ $12.00
Factory overhead	$60,100

Required:

    (1) Compute the January equivalent production for Material A, Material B, and for conversion costs.
    (2) Compute two variances each for Material A, Material B, direct labor, and factory overhead. Indicate whether the variances are favorable or unfavorable.   CGA-Canada (adapted) Reprint with permission

P18-6. Standard process costing; cost of production report at standard; variance analysis. Weissritter Company uses a standard process costing system in accounting for its one product, which is produced in one department. All materials are added at the beginning of the process. Inspection takes place at the end of the process. Any spoiled units revealed by inspection are considered abnormal and complete as to all cost elements, and the related standard cost is charged to a current period expense account.
    Standard cost per unit:

Materials: 3 square meters @ $.60	$1.80
Direct labor: $1/4$ hour @ $10.00	2.50
Variable factory overhead: $1/4$ hour @ $2.00	.50
Fixed factory overhead: $1/4$ hour @ $2.80	.70
Total	$5.50

Normal capacity is 8,750 direct labor hours per month.
Actual data for November follow:

    (a) Beginning work in process inventory—5,000 units (40% converted).
    (b) Started in process during the month—30,000 units.
    (c) Spoiled during November—1,000 units.
    (d) Ending work in process inventory—2,000 units (80% converted).
    (e) Actual costs incurred:

Materials purchased	100 000 square meters @ $.64 (recorded at standard cost)
Materials used................	92 000 square meters
Direct labor	8,000 hours @ $10.60
Variable factory overhead	$17,000
Fixed factory overhead	$25,000

Required:

    (1) Prepare a cost of production report at standard for November.
    (2) Compute two variances each for materials and direct labor and three for factory overhead (method A). Indicate whether the variances are favorable or unfavorable.

CGA-Canada (adapted) Reprint with permission

P18-7. Equivalent production and standard costing variance analysis. Steeler Manufacturing Company manufactures product AB in a process which involves two departments, Department A and Department B. Units are transferred from Department A to Department B and from Department B to the Finished Goods Storeroom.

In Department B, units are inspected at the end of the process, and material is added only to those units that pass inspection. All spoilage is considered to be normal. The company uses a standard cost system; therefore, the cost of normal spoilage becomes a part of the computed standard cost variances. Steeler Manufacturing has set the following standards for Department B production of one unit of product AB:

Materials	1 pound @ $1.90 =	$ 1.90
Direct labor	2 hours @ $8.00 =	16.00
Variable overhead	2 hours @ $ .75 =	1.50
Fixed overhead	2 hours @ $1.50 =	3.00
		$22.40

Normal capacity is 17,000 units of product AB (34,000 direct labor hours). The following information pertains to April:

Beginning inventory (50% complete), 2,000 units	$ 28,800
Received from Department A, 18,000 units	190,100
Transferred to Finished Goods, 15,000 units	
Ending inventory (75% complete), 4,000 units	
Costs added in Department B this period:	
Materials (14,800 lbs. @ $2.00 actual cost)	29,600
Direct labor (38,000 hours @ $7.80)	296,400
Variable factory overhead	28,000
Fixed factory overhead	56,500

Required:

(1) Compute the equivalent production for prior department costs, materials, and conversion costs for the month of April.

(2) Compute two variances each for materials and labor, and compute three variances for factory overhead using method B. Indicate whether variances are favorable or unfavorable.

CGA-Canada (adapted) Reprint with permission

P18-8. Variance analysis: materials, labor, and factory overhead; job order costing. Fancy Fashions Inc. manufactures ladies' blouses of one quality, produced in lots to fill each special order from its customers, comprised of department stores located in various cities. Fancy sews the particular stores' labels in the blouses. The standard costs for a dozen blouses are:

Direct materials	24 yards @ $1.10 =	$26.40
Direct labor	3 hours @ $4.90 =	14.70
Factory overhead	3 hours @ $4.00 =	12.00
Standard cost per dozen		$53.10

During June, Fancy worked on three orders, for which the month's job cost records disclose the following:

Lot No.	Units in Lot (dozens)	Material Used (yards)	Hours Worked
22	1,000	24,100	2,980
23	1,700	40,440	5,130
24	1,200	28,825	2,890

The following information is also available:

(a) Fancy purchased 95,000 yards of material during June at a cost of $106,400. The materials price variance is recorded when goods are purchased. All inventories are carried at standard cost.

(b) Direct labor during June amounted to $55,000. According to payroll records, production employees were paid $5 per hour.

(c) Factory overhead during June amounted to $45,600.

(d) A total of $576,000 was budgeted for factory overhead for 19A, based on estimated production at the plant's normal capacity of 48,000 dozen blouses annually. Factory overhead at this level of production is 40% fixed and 60% variable. Factory overhead is applied on the basis of direct labor hours.

(e) There was no work in process at June 1. During June, Lots 22 and 23 were completed. All material was issued for Lot 24, which was 80% completed as to direct labor.

Required:

(1) Prepare a schedule showing the computation of standard cost of Lots 22, 23, and 24 for June.

(2) Prepare a schedule showing the computation of the materials price variance for June.

(3) Prepare a schedule showing, for each lot produced during June, computations of the following variances, indicating whether they are favorable or unfavorable:

   (a) Materials quantity variance.
   (b) Labor efficiency variance.
   (c) Labor rate variance.

(4) Prepare a schedule showing computations of the total controllable and volume factory overhead variances for June. Indicate whether the variances are favorable or unfavorable.   (AICPA adapted)

P18-9. Factory overhead variance analysis report. The Cost Department of Claffy Manufacturing Company prepared the following flexible budget for Department 2 for February:

Production quantity based on standard	6,400	7,200	8,000
Processing time in hours at standard.	4,800	5,400	6,000
Capacity utilization at standard.	80%	90%	100%
Variable overhead:			
Indirect labor	$ 1,600	$ 1,800	$ 2,000
Manufacturing supplies	1,920	2,160	2,400
Repairs.	800	900	1,000
Heat, power, and light	240	270	300
Total variable overhead	$ 4,560	$ 5,130	$ 5,700
Fixed overhead:			
Superintendence	$ 4,000	$ 4,000	$ 4,000
Indirect labor	6,200	6,200	6,200
Manufacturing supplies	2,000	2,000	2,000
Maintenance	1,100	1,100	1,100
Heat, power, and light	1,400	1,400	1,400
Machinery depreciation	4,500	4,500	4,500
Insurance and taxes	900	900	900
Total fixed overhead.	$20,100	$20,100	$20,100
Total budgeted factory overhead.	$24,660	$25,230	$25,800

Factory overhead is charged to production at the rate of $4.30 per standard hour of processing time. The overhead rate was determined on the basis of 100% capacity utilization, considered to be normal. At the end of the month, cost records showed 7,600 units of product were manufactured during 5,840 processing hours, and actual factory overhead was as follows:

Superintendence	$ 4,000
Indirect labor.	8,120
Manufacturing supplies	4,325
Repairs	1,050
Maintenance.	1,080
Heat, power, and light	1,725
Machinery depreciation	4,500
Insurance and taxes.	970
Total actual factory overhead	$25,770

Required: **Prepare a departmental factory overhead variance report which shows the spending variance and the variable efficiency variance for each item of factory overhead, along with a single departmental volume variance. For each item of expense that contains both a fixed and a variable portion, assume that the actual fixed portion is equal to the budgeted fixed portion and that the balance of the actual expense is variable. Indicate whether the variances are favorable or unfavorable.**

P18-10. Factory overhead variance analysis report. The Cost Department of Coffman Manufacturing Company prepared the following flexible budget for Department X for the month of January:

Machine hours	4,000	4,500	5,000
Capacity utilized	80%	90%	100%
Variable factory overhead:			
Indirect labor	$ 2,800	$ 3,150	$ 3,500
Supplies.	2,000	2,250	2,500
Machinery repairs	800	900	1,000
Electric power	4,000	4,500	5,000
Total variable overhead	$ 9,600	$10,800	$12,000
Fixed factory overhead:			
Supervision	$ 3,000	$ 3,000	$ 3,000
Supplies.	1,700	1,700	1,700
Machinery maintenance	3,000	3,000	3,000
Depreciation of machinery	6,500	6,500	6,500
Insurance.	1,800	1,800	1,800
Property tax.	1,000	1,000	1,000
Gas heating.	600	600	600
Electricity (lighting)	400	400	400
Total fixed overhead.	$18,000	$18,000	$18,000
Total factory overhead.	$27,600	$28,800	$30,000

Factory overhead is allocated to production on the basis of machine hours. The factory overhead rate is computed on the basis of normal capacity, which is 5,000 machine hours. At the end of January, 4,650 machine hours were actually worked; however, based on the standard cost card, 4,800 machine hours were allowed for the actual quantity of production output. The following cost data have also been compiled by the cost department for January:

	Actual Quantity of Input at Standard Unit Costs	Actual Quantity of Input at Actual Unit Costs
Supervision	$ 3,000	$ 3,100
Indirect labor	3,300	3,400
Variable supplies	2,600	2,200
Fixed supplies	1,700	1,650
Machinery repairs	950	960
Machinery maintenance	3,200	3,200
Depreciation of machinery	6,500	6,500
Insurance.	1,800	1,900
Property tax.	1,000	1,100
Gas heating.	700	845
Variable electricity	4,700	4,740
Fixed electricity	400	405
Total factory overhead	$29,850	$30,000

Required: **Prepare a departmental factory overhead variance report which includes (a) a variable efficiency variance, a spending variance, a spending quantity variance, and a spending price variance for each item of factory overhead expense, and (b) a single departmental volume variance. Indicate whether the variances are favorable or unfavorable.**

CASES

C18-1. Motivation via standard costing. Kelly Company manufactures and sells pottery items. All manufacturing takes place in one plant, having four departments, with each department producing only one product. The four products are plaques, cups, vases, and plates. Sam Kelly, the president and founder, credits the company's success to well-designed, quality products and to an effective cost control system which was installed early in the firm's existence to improve cost control and to serve as a basis for planning.

With the participation of plant management, the company establishes standard costs for materials and labor. Each year, the plant manager, the department heads, and the time-study engineers are invited by executive management to recommend changes in the standards for the next year. Executive management reviews these recommendations and the records of actual performance for the current year before setting the new standards. As a general rule, tight standards representing very efficient performance are established so that no inefficiency or slack will be included in cost goals. The plant manager and department heads are charged with control responsibility and the variances from standard costs are used to measure their performance in carrying out this charge.

No standards are set for factory overhead because management believes it is too difficult to predict and relate overhead to output. The actual factory overhead for the departments and the plant is accumulated in one "pool." The actual overhead is then allocated to the departments on the basis of departmental output.

The company's executives are convinced that more effective cost control can be obtained than is currently being realized from the standard cost system. A review of cost performance for recent years disclosed several factors that led them to this conclusion:

(a) Unfavorable variances were the norm rather than the exception, although the size of the variances was quite uniform.
(b) Employee motivation, especially among first-line supervisors, appeared to be low.

Required:

(1) Identify the probable effects on motivation of plant managers and department heads resulting from:

  (a) The participative standard cost system.
  (b) The use of tight standards.

(2) State the effect on the motivation of department heads to control overhead costs when actual factory overhead costs are applied on the basis of actual units.

(ICMA adapted)

C18-2. Standard setting. John Stevens, plant manager of the Fairlee Plant of Lockstead Corporation called together the twenty-five employees of Department B and told them that production standards established several years previously were now too low in view of the recent installation of automated equipment. He gave the workers an opportunity to discuss the mitigating circumstances and to decide among themselves, as a group, what their standards should be. Stevens, on leaving the room, believed they would doubtlessly establish much higher standards than he himself would have dared propose.

After an hour of discussion, the group summoned Stevens and notified him that, contrary to his opinion, their group decision was that the standards were already too high, and since they had been given the authority to establish their own standards, they were making a reduction of 10%. These standards, Stevens knew, were far too low to provide a fair profit on the owner's investment. Yet it was clear that his refusal to accept the group decision would be disastrous.

Required:

(1) Identify the errors made by Stevens.
(2) Suggest a course of action to be taken by Stevens.   CGA-Canada (adapted)
Reprint with permission

C18-3. Implementing a standard cost system. Ogwood Company is a small manufacturer of wooden household items. A. Rivkin, corporate controller, plans to implement a standard cost system for Ogwood. Rivkin has information from several co-workers that will be useful in developing standards for Ogwood's products.

One of Ogwood's products is a wooden cutting board. Each cutting board requires 1.25 board feet of lumber and 12 minutes of direct labor time to prepare and cut the lumber. The cutting boards are inspected after they are cut. Because the cutting boards are made of natural material that has imperfections, one board is normally rejected for each five that are accepted. Four rubber foot pads are attached to each good cutting board. A total of fifteen minutes of direct labor time is required to attach all four foot pads and finish each cutting board. The lumber for the cutting boards costs $3.00 per board foot, and each foot pad costs $.05. Direct labor is paid at the rate of $8.00 per hour.

Required:

(1) Develop the standard cost for the direct cost components of the cutting board. The standard cost should identify (a) the standard quantity, (b) the standard rate, and (c) the standard cost per board for each direct cost component.
(2) Identify the advantages of implementing a standard cost system.
(3) Explain the role of each of the following persons in developing standards:

   (a) Purchasing manager.
   (b) Industrial engineer.
   (c) Cost accountant.   (ICMA adapted)

C18-4. Factory overhead variance analysis. Stringfellow Industries uses a standard cost system and budgets the following sales and costs for 19—:

Unit sales	20,000
Sales	$200,000
Total production cost at standard	130,000
Gross profit	70,000
Beginning inventories	None
Ending inventories	None

The 19— budgeted sales level was the normal capacity level used in calculating the factory overhead predetermined standard cost rate per direct labor hour.

At the end of 19—, Stringfellow Industries reported production and sales of 19,200 units. Total factory overhead incurred was exactly equal to budgeted factory overhead for the year and there was underapplied total factory overhead of $2,000 at December 31. Factory overhead is applied to the work in process inventory on the basis of standard direct labor hours allowed for units produced. Although there was a favorable labor efficiency variance, there was neither a labor rate variance nor materials variances for the year.

Required: Write an explanation of the underapplied factory overhead of $2,000, being as specific as the data permit and indicating the overhead variances affected. Stringfellow uses three-variance method A to analyze the total factory overhead.   (AICPA adapted)

C18-5. Price, mix, and yield variances and their use. LAR Chemical Company manufactures a wide variety of chemical compounds and liquids for industrial uses. The standard mix for producing a single batch of 500 gallons of one liquid is as follows:

Liquid Chemical	Quantity in Gallons	Cost per Gallon	Total Cost
Maxan	100	$2.00	$200
Salex	300	.75	225
Cralyn	225	1.00	225
	625		$650

There is a 20% loss in liquid volume during processing due to evaporation. The finished liquid is put into 10-gallon bottles for sale. Thus the standard materials cost for a 10-gallon bottle is $13.

A total of 4,000 bottles (40,000 gallons) were produced during November. The actual quantities of raw materials and the respective cost of the materials placed in production during November were as follows:

Liquid Chemical	Quantity in Gallons	Total Cost
Maxan	8,480	$17,384
Salex	25,200	17,640
Cralyn	18,540	16,686
	52,220	$51,710

Required:

(1) Compute the materials price, mix, and yield variances, including an analysis of the portion of the mix variance attributable to each material.
(2) Explain how LAR Chemical could use each of these variances to help control the cost to manufacture this liquid compound.
                                     (ICMA adapted)

C18-6. Variance analysis; variance control responsibility. Cappels Corporation manufactures and sells a single product, using a standard cost system. The standard cost per unit of product is:

Materials: 1 pound of plastic @ $2	$ 2.00
Direct labor: 1.6 hours @ $4	6.40
Variable factory overhead cost per unit	3.00
Fixed factory overhead cost per unit	1.45
	$12.85

The factory overhead cost per unit was calculated from the following annual overhead cost budget for a 60,000-unit volume:

Variable factory overhead cost:	
Indirect labor (30,000 hours @ $4)	$120,000
Supplies (oil—60,000 gallons @ $.50) . . .	30,000
Allocated variable service department	
cost	30,000
Total variable factory overhead cost	$180,000
Fixed factory overhead cost:	
Supervision	$ 27,000
Depreciation	45,000
Other fixed costs	15,000
Total fixed factory overhead cost	$ 87,000
Total budgeted annual factory overhead cost	
for 60,000 units	$267,000

The charges to the Manufacturing Department for November, when 5,000 units were produced, were:

Materials (5,300 pounds @ $2)	$10,600
Direct labor (8,200 hours @ $4.10)	33,620
Indirect labor (2,400 hours @ $4.10)	9,840
Supplies (oil—6,000 gallons @ $.55)	3,300
Allocated variable service department cost . . .	3,200
Supervision	2,475
Depreciation	3,750
Other fixed costs	1,250
Total	$68,035

The Purchasing Department normally buys about the same quantity of plastic as is used in production during a month. In November, 5,200 pounds were purchased at a price of $2.10 per pound.

The company has divided its responsibilities so that the Purchasing Department is responsible for the price at which materials and supplies are purchased, while the Manufacturing Department is responsible for the quantities of materials used.

The Manufacturing Department manager performs the timekeeping function and, at various times, an analysis of factory overhead and direct labor variances has shown that the manager has deliberately misclassified labor hours (e.g., direct labor hours might be classified as indirect labor hours and vice versa), so that only one of the two labor variances is unfavorable. It is not economically feasible to hire a separate timekeeper.

Required:

(1) Calculate these variances from standard costs for the data given: (a) materials purchase price variance; (b) materials quantity variance; (c) direct labor rate variance; (d) direct labor efficiency variance; (e) factory overhead controllable variance, analyzed for each expense classification.
(2) Explain whether the division of responsibilities should solve the conflict between price and quantity variances.
(3) Prepare a report which details the factory overhead budget variance. The report, which will be given to the Manufacturing Department manager, should display only that part of the variance that is the manager's responsibility and should highlight information useful to that manager in evaluating departmental performance and in considering corrective action.
(4) Suggest a solution to the company's problem involving the classification of labor hours.   (ICMA adapted)

C18-7. In-depth analysis of labor variances. Technowave Company manufactures a complete line of radios. Since a large number of models have plastic cases, the company has its own molding department for producing them.

The month of April was devoted to the production of the plastic case for one of the portable radios—Model SX76.

The Molding Department has two operations—molding and trimming; there usually is no interaction of labor in these two operations. The standard labor cost for producing 10 plastic cases for Model SX76 is as follows:

Molding: 1/2 hour @ $6	$3
Trimming: 1/4 hour @ $4	1
	$4

During April, 70,000 plastic cases were produced in the Molding Department; however, 10% of these cases had to be discarded because they were found to be defective at final inspection. The Purchasing Department had changed to a new plastic supplier to take advantage of a lower price for comparable plastic. The new plastic turned out to be of a lower quality, resulting in the rejection of the 7,000 cases.

Direct labor hours worked and direct labor costs charged to the Molding Department are as follows:

Molding: 3,800 hours @ $6.25	$23,750
Trimming: 1,600 hours @ $4.15	6,640
Total labor charges...................	$30,390

As a result of poor scheduling by the Production Scheduling Department, the supervisor of the Molding Department had to shift molders to the trimming operation for 200 hours during April. The company paid the molding workers their regular hourly rate, even though they were performing a lower-rated task. There was no significant loss of efficiency caused by the shift. In addition, as a result of unexpected machinery repairs required during the month, 75 hours and 35 hours of idle time occurred in the molding and trimming operations, respectively.

The monthly report which compares actual costs with standard cost of output for April shows the following labor variance for the Molding Department:

Actual labor cost for April	$30,390
Standard labor cost of output (63,000 × ($4 ÷ 10))..................	25,200
Unfavorable labor variance	$ 5,190

This variance is significantly higher than normal.

Required:

(1) Prepare a detailed analysis of the unfavorable labor variance for the Molding Department, showing the variance resulting from (a) labor rates; (b) labor substitution; (c) material substitution; (d) operating efficiency; and (e) idle time.
(2) Evaluate the Molding Department supervisor's argument that the variances due to labor substitution and change in raw materials should not be charged to the department. (ICMA adapted)

C18-8. Revision of standards. NuLathe Company produces a turbo engine component for jet aircraft manufacturers. A standard cost system has been used for years with good results. Unfortunately, NuLathe has recently experienced production problems. The source for its direct material went out of business. The new source produces a similar but higher quality material. The price per pound from the original source has averaged $7.00 while the price from the new source is $7.77. The use of the new material results in a reduction in scrap. This scrap reduction reduces the actual consumption of direct material from 1.25 to 1.00 pound per unit. In addition, the direct labor is reduced from 24 to 22 minutes per unit because there is less scrap labor and machine setup time.

The direct material problem was occurring at the same time that labor negotiations resulted in an increase of over 14% in hourly direct labor costs. The average rate rose from $12.60 per hour to $14.40 per hour. Production of the main product requires a high level of labor skill. Because of a continuing shortage in that skill area, an interim wage agreement had to be signed.

NuLathe started using the new direct material on April 1, the same date that the new labor agreement went into effect. NuLathe has been using standards that were set at the beginning of the calendar year. The direct material and direct labor standards for the turbo engine component are as follows:

Direct material—(1.2 lbs. @ $6.80 per lb.)	$ 8.16
Direct labor—(20 min. @ $12.30 per DLH).....	4.10
Standard prime cost per unit of product.......	$12.26

H. Foster, cost accounting supervisor, had been examining the performance report shown below that had been prepared at the close of business on April 30. When J. Keene, assistant controller, came into Foster's office, Foster said, "Look at this performance report. Direct material price increased 11% and the labor rate increased over 14% during April. I expected greater variances, yet prime costs decreased over five percent from the $13.79 we experienced during the first quarter of this year. The proper message just isn't coming through."

"This has been an unusual period," said Keene. "With all the unforeseen changes, perhaps we should revise our standards based on current conditions and start over."

Foster replied, "I think we can retain the current standards but expand the variance analysis. We could calculate variances for the specific changes that have occurred to direct material and direct labor before we calculate the normal price and quantity variances. What I really think would be useful to management right now is to determine the impact the changes in direct material and direct labor had in reducing our prime costs per unit from $13.79 in the first quarter to $13.05 in April—a reduction of $.74."

NuLathe Company
Standard Prime Cost Variance Analysis
For April, 19—

	Standard	Price Variance		Quantity Variance		Actual
Direct materials	$ 8.16	($.97 × 1.0)	$.97 U	($6.80 × .2)	$1.36 F	$ 7.77
Direct labor	4.10	($2.10 × 22/60)	.77 U	($12.30 × 2/60)	.41 U	5.28
	$12.26					$13.05

NuLathe Company
Comparison of Actual Prime Costs
For April, 19—

	First Quarter Costs	April Costs	Percentage Increase (Decrease)
Direct materials	$ 8.75	$ 7.77	(11.2)%
Direct labor	5.04	5.28	4.8 %
	$13.79	$13.05	(5.4)%

Required:

(1) Discuss the advantages of each of the following alternatives:

  (a) Immediately revise the standards.
  (b) Retain the current standards and expand the analysis of variances.

(2) Prepare an analysis that reflects the impact the new direct material and new labor contract had on reducing NuLathe's prime costs per unit from $13.79 in the first quarter to $13.05 in April. The analysis should show the changes in prime costs per unit that are due to (a) the use of new direct material, and (b) the new labor contract. This analysis should be in sufficient detail to identify the changes due to direct materials price, direct labor rate, the effect of direct material quality on direct material usage, and the effect of direct material quality on direct labor usage.

CHAPTER 19

Standard Costing: Incorporating Standards Into the Accounting Records

Some companies prefer to use standard costs for planning, motivation, and evaluation purposes only. In such cases, standard costs do not enter into the company's journals and ledgers. However, the incorporation of standard costs into the regular accounting system permits the most efficient use of a standard cost system and leads to savings and increased accuracy in clerical work. In either case, variances can be analyzed for cost control, and standard costs can be used in developing budgets, bidding on contracts, and setting prices. The accumulation of standard costs in the company's accounts and the disposition of standard cost variances are presented in this chapter. The illustrative data and the resulting variance computations used are the same as for Chapter 18.

■ RECORDING STANDARD COST VARIANCES IN THE ACCOUNTS

Standard costs should be viewed as costs which pass through the data processing system into financial statements. However, variations exist in the methods of accumulating these costs. Some systems employ the partial plan; others, the single plan. Both plans center around the entries to the work in process account. Under either plan, the work in process account can be broken down by individual cost elements (materials, labor, and factory overhead) and/or by departments. The plans are summarized as follows:

Partial Plan		Single Plan	
Work in Process		*Work in Process*	
Actual cost	Standard cost	Standard cost	Standard cost

The Partial Plan

In the partial plan, the work in process account is debited for the actual cost of materials, labor, and factory overhead and is credited at standard cost when goods are completed and transferred to finished goods inventory. Any balance remaining in the work in process account consists of two elements: (1) the standard cost of work still in process and (2) the variances between actual and standard costs. To isolate these variances, additional analysis is needed.

The Single Plan

Since timely identification and reporting are major control features of standard cost accounting, prompt communication for very short time frames may be required. The single plan debits and credits the work in process account at standard costs only, and variances are recorded in separate variance accounts. These entries are periodic summaries of standard costs, actual costs, and resulting variances. They are discussed in detail in the following pages and are used in the exercises and problems of this chapter.

■ STANDARD COST ACCOUNTING FOR MATERIALS

The recording of materials purchased can be handled by three different methods:

1. *Record the price variance when materials are received and placed in stores.* The general ledger control account, Materials, is debited at standard cost and the materials ledger records are kept in quantities only. A standard price is noted on the record when the standards are set. As purchases are made, no prices are recorded in these records. This procedure results in clerical savings and speedier postings.

2. *Record the materials at actual cost when received, and determine the price variance when the materials are requisitioned for production.* The general ledger control account, Materials, is debited at actual cost and the materials ledger records show quantities and dollar values as in a historical cost system.

3. *Use a combination of methods (1) and (2).* Calculate price variances when the materials are received, but defer charging them to production until the materials actually are placed in process. At that time, only the price variance applicable to the quantity used will appear as a current charge, the balance remaining as a part of the materials inventory. This method results in two types of materials price variances: (1) a materials purchase price variance originating when materials purchases are first recorded, and (2) a materials price usage variance when materials are used. The occurrence of the materials price usage variance is a reduction of the materials purchase price variance.

For control purposes, the price variance should be determined when the materials are received. If it is not computed and reported until the materials are requisitioned for production, then remedial action is difficult because the time of computation is far removed from the time of purchase. In addition, if the materials are charged to inventory at actual price rather than standard, the actual cost used in determining the price variance will depend upon the cost flow assumption used to cost inventory (i.e., average, lifo, or fifo). On the other hand, in a just-in-time inventory system, these differences would be trivial since materials inventory would not be significant. In such a system, the quantity of materials purchased would essentially equal the quantity used.

JUST-IN-TIME

The methods for recording materials purchased are illustrated below, using the following data for Item 4-489 used in Department 4 in the production of Paxel (pages 569-570):

Standard unit price as per standard cost record	$7.50
Purchased	10,000 pieces @ $7.44
Requisitioned.	9,500 pieces
Standard quantity allowed for actual production	9,336 pieces

Method 1

The journal entry when materials are purchased is:

Materials*	75,000	
Accounts Payable**		74,400
Materials Purchase Price Variance***		600

    *$7.50 standard price × 10,000 pieces purchased
    **$7.44 actual price × 10,000 pieces purchased
    ***$.06 favorable price variance per piece × 10,000 pieces purchased

When materials issued to the factory are recorded, the entry is:

Work in Process*	70,020	
Materials Quantity Variance**	1,230	
Materials***		71,250

    *$7.50 standard price × 9,336 pieces (standard quantity allowed)
    **$7.50 standard price × 164 piece unfavorable quantity variance
    ***$7.50 standard price × 9,500 pieces actually used

Method 2

When materials are purchased, no variance is computed and the entry is:

Materials*	74,400	
Accounts Payable		74,400

    *$7.44 actual price × 10,000 pieces purchased

When materials issued to production are recorded, the entry is:

Work in Process*	70,020	
Materials Quantity Variance**	1,230	
Materials***		70,680
Materials Price Usage Variance****		570

    *$7.50 standard price × 9,336 pieces (standard quantity allowed)
    **$7.50 standard price × 164 piece unfavorable quantity variance
    ***$7.44 actual price × 9,500 pieces used
    ****$.06 favorable price variance per piece × 9,500 pieces used

For this computation, the actual cost used is $7.44 per piece. The assumption here is that there is no beginning materials inventory and that there are no other purchases during the period. In practice, the actual cost used would depend upon the type of inventory costing methods employed, such as perpetual or periodic, and the inventory cost flow assumptions, such as fifo, lifo, or average costing.

In this method, the materials price usage variance account appears on the books after the materials are issued, and then only for the quantity issued—not for the entire purchase. The price variance occurred because the actual cost of the materials issued was $.06 less than the standard price; the quantity variance occurred because 164 pieces were used in excess of the standard quantity allowed. Notice that the cost charged to Work in Process and the amount recorded as the quantity variance are the same for Method 1 and Method 2. Only the price variance and the charge to the materials inventory are different.

Method 3

The following entry, identical with the first entry in Method 1, would be made when the materials are purchased:

```
Materials* .............................................  75,000
    Accounts Payable** ...................................          74,400
    Materials Purchase Price Variance*** ...................             600
```

```
  *$7.50 standard price × 10,000 pieces purchased
 **$7.44 actual price × 10,000 pieces purchased
***$.06 favorable price variance per piece × 10,000 pieces purchased
```

When the materials issued are recorded, two entries are made. The following entry, identical with the second entry in Method 1, recognizes the 164 pieces of material used in excess of the standard quantity allowed.

```
Work in Process* ......................................  70,020
Materials Quantity Variance** ...........................   1,230
    Materials*** .........................................          71,250
```

```
  *$7.50 standard price × 9,336 pieces (standard quantity allowed)
 **$7.50 standard price × 164 piece unfavorable quantity variance
***$7.50 standard price × 9,500 pieces actually used
```

The next entry transfers $570 from the purchase price variance account to the price usage variance account.

```
Materials Purchase Price Variance.........................   570
    Materials Price Usage Variance* .......................            570
```

```
*$.06 favorable price variance per piece × 9,500 pieces actually used
```

In Method 3, any balance remaining in the materials purchase price variance account at the end of the accounting period is used to adjust the inventory to actual cost. This balance is shown in the partial balance sheet presented at the top of the next page.

Materials purchased (at standard cost)		$75,000
Materials used during period (at standard cost)		71,250
Materials in ending inventory (at standard cost)		$ 3,750
Materials purchase price variance (favorable)	$(600)	
Materials price usage variance (favorable)	(570)	(30)
Materials in ending inventory (adjusted to actual cost)		$ 3,720

■ STANDARD COST ACCOUNTING FOR LABOR

The payroll is computed on the basis of clock cards, job tickets, and other labor time information furnished to the payroll department. In a standard cost system, these basic records supply the data for the computation of labor variances.

The necessary journal entries are illustrated with the following data for Operation 4-25 in Department 4 (pages 570-571):

Actual hours worked	1,632
Actual rate paid per hour	$12.50
Standard hours allowed for actual production	1,504
Standard rate per hour	$12.00

The following journal entry records the total actual direct labor payroll, assuming that there were no payroll deductions:

Payroll	20,400	
Accrued Payroll*		20,400

*$12.50 actual labor rate × 1,632 actual hours worked

To distribute the payroll and to set up the variance accounts, the journal entry is:

Work in Process*	18,048	
Labor Rate Variance**	816	
Labor Efficiency Variance***	1,536	
Payroll		20,400

*$12.00 standard labor rate × 1,504 standard hours allowed
**$.50 unfavorable labor rate × 1,632 actual hours worked
***$12.00 standard labor rate × 128 excess actual hours over standard

■ STANDARD COST ACCOUNTING FOR FACTORY OVERHEAD

The close relationship between standard costs and budgetary control methods is particularly important for the analysis of factory overhead. Actual factory overhead is measured not only against the applied overhead cost, but also against a budget based on actual and standard activity allowed for actual production.

The following data for Department 4 (pages 573-581) are used to illustrate the journal entries for the two-variance, three-variance, and four-variance methods.

Normal capacity in direct labor hours (DLH)		1,600 DLH
Total factory overhead at normal capacity:		
Variable...	$11,200	
Fixed...	32,000	$43,200
Factory overhead rate per direct labor hour:		
Variable...	$ 7.00	
Fixed...	20.00	$ 27.00
Actual factory overhead..................................		$43,685
Actual direct labor hours...............................		1,632
Standard hours allowed for actual production		1,504

In actual practice, numerous entries would be entered in the general journal during each month of the year to record the incurrence of actual factory overhead. A single entry is used as follows to illustrate the recording of actual factory overhead for the entire period:

Factory Overhead Control................................	43,685	
Various Credits*....................................		43,685

*Accounts credited during the period typically include Payroll (for indirect labor and supervision), Materials (for indirect materials and supplies), Accumulated Depreciation, Prepaid Expenses, Accounts Payable, Accrued Vacation Pay, Pension Liability, Payroll Tax Liabilities, and Cash.

Typically, an entry to record the factory overhead charged to Work in Process would be entered in the general journal at least once a month. Again, a single entry is used to illustrate the application of factory overhead to Work in Process:

Work in Process*.......................................	40,608	
Applied Factory Overhead............................		40,608

*$27.00 factory overhead rate × 1,504 standard hours allowed

At the end of the period, when Applied Factory Overhead is closed, the entry would be as follows:

Applied Factory Overhead................................	40,608	
Factory Overhead Control............................		40,608

The factory overhead control account now has a debit balance of $3,077, which will be closed to the appropriate factory overhead variance accounts. The two-variance, three-variance, and four-variance methods are illustrated and discussed in detail in Chapter 18. The journal entries to record each of the alternative methods are illustrated here.

Two-Variance Method

In the two-variance method, the balance in the factory overhead control account is divided between the controllable variance and the volume variance. The entry to close the factory overhead control account and to record the controllable and volume variances is as follows:

Factory Overhead Volume Variance* 1,920
Factory Overhead Controllable Variance** 1,157
   Factory Overhead Control*** 3,077

   *$20.00 fixed factory overhead rate × 96 hours (i.e., the difference between normal capacity (1,600 hours) and the standard hours allowed (1,504 hours))
  **The amount required to balance the entry (see page 575 for an illustration of the computation of the controllable variance)
 ***The amount of underapplied factory overhead (i.e., the difference between actual factory overhead ($43,685) and applied factory overhead ($40,608))

Three-Variance Method A

In the three-variance method A, the amount of over- or underapplied factory overhead can be analyzed as spending, idle capacity, and efficiency variances. The entry to close the factory overhead control account and to record these three variances is as follows:

Factory Overhead Efficiency Variance* 3,456
Factory Overhead Spending Variance** 261
   Factory Overhead Idle Capacity Variance*** 640
   Factory Overhead Control**** 3,077

   *$27.00 factory overhead rate × 128 hours (i.e., the difference between the actual hours required (1,632 hours) and the standard hours allowed (1,504 hours))
  **The amount required to balance the entry (see page 576 for an illustration of the computation of the spending variance)
 ***$20.00 fixed factory overhead rate × 32 hours (i.e., the difference between normal capacity (1,600 hours) and the actual hours required (1,632 hours))
 ****The amount of underapplied factory overhead (i.e., the difference between actual factory overhead ($43,685) and applied factory overhead ($40,608))

Three-Variance Method B

In the three-variance method B, the amount of over- or underapplied factory overhead can be analyzed as spending, variable efficiency, and volume variances. The entry to close the factory overhead control account and to record these three variances is as follows:

Factory Overhead Volume Variance* 1,920
Factory Overhead Variable Efficiency Variance** 896
Factory Overhead Spending Variance*** 261
   Factory Overhead Control**** 3,077

   *$20.00 fixed factory overhead rate × 96 hours (i.e., the difference between normal capacity (1,600 hours) and the standard hours allowed (1,504 hours))
  **$7.00 variable factory overhead rate × 128 hours (i.e., the difference between the actual hours required (1,632 hours) and the standard hours allowed (1,504 hours))
 ***The amount required to balance the entry (see page 576 for an illustration of the computation of the spending variance)
 ****The amount of underapplied factory overhead (i.e., the difference between actual factory overhead ($43,685) and applied factory overhead ($40,608))

Four-Variance Method

In the four-variance method, the amount of over- or underapplied factory overhead is divided into the spending, idle capacity, variable efficiency, and fixed efficiency variances. The entry to close the factory overhead control account and to record these four variances is as follows:

Factory Overhead Variable Efficiency Variance*	896	
Factory Overhead Fixed Efficiency Variance**	2,560	
Factory Overhead Spending Variance***	261	
Factory Overhead Idle Capacity Variance****		640
Factory Overhead Control*****		3,077

    *$7.00 variable factory overhead rate × 128 hours (i.e., the difference between the actual hours required (1,632 hours) and the standard hours allowed (1,504 hours))
    **$20.00 fixed factory overhead rate × 128 hours (i.e., the difference between the actual hours required (1,632 hours) and the standard hours allowed (1,504 hours))
    ***The amount required to balance the entry (see page 576 for an illustration of the computation of the spending variance)
    ****$20.00 fixed factory overhead rate × 32 hours (i.e., the difference between normal capacity (1,600 hours) and the actual hours required (1,632 hours))
    *****The amount of underapplied factory overhead (i.e., the difference between actual factory overhead ($43,685) and applied factory overhead ($40,608))

■ STANDARD COST ACCOUNTING FOR COMPLETED PRODUCTS

The completion of production requires the transfer of cost from the work in process account of one department to the work in process account of another department, or, in the case of the last department, to the finished goods inventory account. The cost transferred is the standard cost of the completed products.

Recall from the data in the Chapter 18 illustration presented on page 567 that 4,200 units of Paxel were completed during the period and transferred to finished goods inventory. The standard cost card for Paxel (page 566) indicates that the total cost of manufacturing a unit is $152.45. The journal entry to record the transfer of the 4,200 finished units follows:

Finished Goods	640,290	
Work in Process*		640,290

    *$152.45 standard cost per unit × 4,200 completed units

The finished goods ledger card will show quantities only, because the standard cost of the units remains the same during a period unless substantial cost changes occur. The entry to record the sale of 4,000 units of Paxel during the year is:

Cost of Goods Sold	609,800	
Finished Goods*		609,800

    *$152.45 standard cost per unit × 4,000 units sold

■ DISPOSITION OF VARIANCES

Variances may be disposed of in either of the following ways: they may be (1) treated as period expenses (i.e., closed to Cost of Goods Sold or directly to Income Summary) or (2) treated as adjustments to Cost of Goods Sold and ending inventories.

Variances Treated as Period Expenses

Usually, standard cost variances are considered to be a manufacturing function responsibility. If the net amount of the variances is not material, the variances are closed to the cost of goods sold account. To illustrate, assume Radford Manufacturing Company has the following variances at the end of the year:

	Debit	Credit
Materials purchase price variance	$1,200	
Labor efficiency variance.	1,800	
Factory overhead controllable variance		$600
Factory overhead volume variance	1,300	

The entry to close the variance accounts would appear as follows:

Cost of Goods Sold.	3,700	
Factory Overhead Controllable Variance	600	
Materials Purchase Price Variance		1,200
Labor Efficiency Variance		1,800
Factory Overhead Volume Variance		1,300

The total amount in Cost of Goods Sold (the standard cost of units sold adjusted for the standard cost variances) would then be closed to Income Summary along with other revenue and expense accounts. When variances are closed to the cost of goods sold account, they appear in the cost of goods sold statement. Financial statement presentation for Radford Manufacturing Company is illustrated below:

Radford Manufacturing Company
Income Statement
For Year Ending December 31, 19--

Sales.		$78,000
Cost of goods sold (Schedule 1)		43,700
Gross profit.		$34,300
Less commercial expenses:		
Marketing expenses	$16,000	
Administrative expenses.	10,000	26,000
Operating income.		$ 8,300

Schedule 1
Cost of Goods Sold
For Year Ending December 31, 19—

Materials (at standard)		$16,000
Direct labor (at standard)		10,000
Applied factory overhead (at standard)		18,000
Total cost added to work in process		$44,000
Add beginning work in process inventory		14,000
		$58,000
Deduct ending work in process inventory		16,000
Cost of goods manufactured		$42,000
Add beginning finished goods inventory		23,000
Cost of goods available for sale		$65,000
Deduct ending finished goods inventory		25,000
Cost of goods sold (at standard)		$40,000
Adjustments for standard cost variances:		
Materials purchase price variance	$ 1,200	
Labor efficiency variance	1,800	
Factory overhead controllable variance	(600)	
Factory overhead volume variance	1,300	3,700
Cost of goods sold		$43,700

As an alternative, variances may be closed to Income Summary rather than directly to Cost of Goods Sold. At the end of the period, the variance accounts for Radford Manufacturing Company would be closed as follows:

Income Summary	3,700	
Factory Overhead Controllable Variance	600	
Materials Purchase Price Variance		1,200
Labor Efficiency Variance		1,800
Factory Overhead Volume Variance		1,300

This procedure makes it possible to keep work in process, finished goods inventory, and cost of goods sold at standard costs, thereby facilitating comparison of sales revenue and standard cost by product class. Unfavorable (or debit) manufacturing cost variances are deducted from the gross profit calculated at standard cost. Favorable (or credit) variances are added to the gross profit computed at standard cost. The treatment of manufacturing cost variances using this method for Radford Manufacturing Company is depicted in the income statement on page 619.

Accountants who use these procedures believe that only the standard costs should be considered the true costs. Variances are treated not as increases or decreases in manufacturing costs but as deviations from contemplated costs, due to abnormal inactivity, extravagance, inefficiencies or efficiencies, or other changes of business conditions. This viewpoint leads to the closing of all variances to the income summary account, which is an acceptable procedure as long as standards are reasonably representative of what costs ought to be. However, some proponents of this procedure suggest that the unused portion of the materials purchase price variance should be linked with materials still on hand and shown on the balance sheet as part of the cost of the ending materials inventory.

Radford Manufacturing Company
Income Statement
For Year Ending December 31, 19—

Sales		$78,000
Cost of goods sold (at standard)—Schedule 1		40,000
Gross profit (at standard)		$38,000
Adjustments for standard cost variances:		
Materials purchase price variance	$ 1,200	
Labor efficiency variance	1,800	
Factory overhead controllable variance	(600)	
Factory overhead volume variance	1,300	3,700
Gross profit (adjusted)		$34,300
Less commercial expenses:		
Marketing expenses	$16,000	
Administrative expenses	10,000	26,000
Operating income		$ 8,300

Schedule 1
Cost of Goods Sold
For Year Ending December 31, 19—

Materials (at standard)	$16,000
Direct labor (at standard)	10,000
Applied factory overhead (at standard)	18,000
Total cost added to work in process	$44,000
Add beginning work in process inventory	14,000
	$58,000
Deduct ending work in process inventory	16,000
Cost of goods manufactured	$42,000
Add beginning finished goods inventory	23,000
Cost of goods available for sale	$65,000
Deduct ending finished goods inventory	25,000
Cost of goods sold (at standard)	$40,000

If an adjustment is made for the materials purchase price variance, whereby a part of the variance is attached to the materials inventory, the following computation would be made in the Radford Manufacturing Company example:

Balance in materials inventory: $4,000 or 20% of purchases made
Materials purchase price variance: $1,200
Variance transferred to the materials account: $240 (20% of $1,200)

Since the materials purchase price variance is unfavorable, the materials account would be increased and the amount closed to Income Summary would be decreased, thereby increasing the operating income from $8,300 to $8,540. The journal entry to close the variance accounts would be:

Income Summary	3,460	
Materials	240	
Factory Overhead Controllable Variance	600	
Materials Purchase Price Variance		1,200
Labor Efficiency Variance		1,800
Factory Overhead Volume Variance		1,300

Variances Allocated to Cost of Goods Sold and Ending Inventories

With respect to the cost of inventories, Accounting Research Bulletin No. 43 implies that significant variances are to be allocated between cost of goods sold and inventories:

> Standard costs are acceptable if adjusted at reasonable intervals to reflect current conditions so that at the balance-sheet date standard costs reasonably approximate costs computed under one of the recognized bases. In such cases descriptive language should be used which will express this relationship, as, for instance, "approximate costs determined on the first-in, first-out basis," or, if it is desired to mention standard costs, "at standard costs, approximating average costs."[1]

CASB regulations require that significant standard cost variances be included in inventories. Current federal income tax regulations also require the inclusion of a portion of significant variances in inventories. With respect to factory overhead variances, when the amount involved is not significant in relation to total actual factory overhead for the year, an allocation is not required by the IRS unless such allocation is made for financial reporting purposes.[2] Also, the taxpayer must treat both favorable and unfavorable variances consistently. Although the tax law does not specifically mention the treatment of material and labor variances, they should be treated in the same manner as factory overhead variances, i.e., when the amount involved is significant in relation to total cost, it should be allocated between ending inventories and cost of goods sold.

To illustrate the allocation of variances, the percentage of cost elements in the inventories and cost of goods sold of the previous example are:

Account	Materials Amount	%	Labor Amount	%	Factory Overhead Amount	%
Work in Process	$ 6,000	37.5	$ 2,000	20	$ 7,200	40
Finished Goods	2,000	12.5	2,000	20	1,800	10
Cost of Goods Sold	8,000	50.0	6,000	60	9,000	50
Total	$16,000	100.0	$10,000	100	$18,000	100

The allocation of the variances shown on page 617 is summarized in the table at the top of page 621. The materials purchase price variance of $960 ($1,200 – $240 allocated to Materials) is multiplied by the respective percentage of materials in the inventories and cost of goods sold accounts (37.5%, 12.5%, and 50.0%). The labor and factory overhead variances are allocated in a similar manner.

---

[1]*Accounting Research Bulletin*, No. 43, "Inventory Pricing" (New York: American Institute of Certified Public Accountants, 1953), Chapter 4, par. 6.

[2]See *Code of Federal Regulations*, Section 1.471-11(d)(3) and Temporary Section 1.263A-1T(b)(3)(iii)(3)(D).

Account	Total Amount	Work in Process	Finished Goods	Cost of Goods Sold
Materials Purchase Price Variance	$ 960	$ 360	$120	$ 480
Labor Efficiency Variance	1,800	360	360	1,080
Factory Overhead Controllable Variance	(600)	(240)	(60)	(300)
Factory Overhead Volume Variance	1,300	520	130	650
Total	$3,460	$1,000	$550	$1,910

Assuming that variances in the preceding period were charged to period expense because they were not material, the proration of the current period variances to Work in Process, Finished Goods, and Cost of Goods Sold results in the following income statement:

Radford Manufacturing Company
Income Statement
For Year Ending December 31, 19--

Sales		$78,000
Cost of goods sold (standard adjusted to actual)—		
Schedule 1		41,910
Gross profit (actual)		$36,090
Less commercial expenses:		
Marketing expenses	$16,000	
Administrative expenses	10,000	26,000
Operating income		$10,090

Schedule 1
Cost of Goods Sold
For Year Ending December 31, 19--

	Standard	Variance	Actual
Materials	$16,000		
Materials purchase price variance		$ 960	$16,960
Direct labor	10,000		
Labor efficiency variance		1,800	11,800
Applied factory overhead	18,000		
Controllable variance		(600)	
Volume variance		1,300	18,700
Total cost added to work in process	$44,000	$3,460	$47,460
Add beginning work in process inventory	14,000	0	14,000
	$58,000	$3,460	$61,460
Deduct ending work in process inventory	16,000	1,000	17,000
Cost of goods manufactured	$42,000	$2,460	$44,460
Add beginning finished goods inventory	23,000	0	23,000
Cost of goods available for sale	$65,000	$2,460	$67,460
Deduct ending finished goods inventory	25,000	550	25,550
Cost of goods sold	$40,000	$1,910	$41,910

The $1,790 difference between the operating income of $10,090 reported in the income statement above and the operating income of $8,300 shown in the income statement on page 619 occurs as a result of charging a portion of the unfavorable variances of the period to ending inventories rather than period expense. The $1,790 difference is reconciled as follows on page 622.

Cost added to: Materials	$ 240
Work in process	1,000
Finished goods	550
Total	$1,790

Entries transfer the prorated amounts to the respective accounts in the general ledger only. Subsidiary inventory accounts and records are not adjusted. The various adjustment accounts could be shown on the balance sheet as valuation or contra accounts against standard inventory values, or combined with them to form one amount. At the beginning of the next period, the portion of these proration entries that affects inventory accounts is reversed in order to return beginning inventories to standard costs. At the end of that period, new variances are allocated in the same manner as before, based on the elements of cost added to work in process that pertain to ending inventory and cost of goods sold account balances. The amount reversed from the previous period is allocated based on where the units are that gave rise to the variances.

In connection with closing variances, a problem arises in the allocation of variances to product or commodity groups. Preferably, standard cost variances are shown as deductions in total and are not allocated to major commodity groups to determine the profit and loss per commodity. Experience has shown that it is almost impossible to do otherwise. The basic idea of variance analysis is misconstrued when such prorations are attempted. The isolation of variances is for the purpose of controlling costs and determining what the variances are, where they occurred, and what caused them.

The Logic of Disposition of Variances

The treatment of variances depends upon the (1) type of variance (materials, labor, or factory overhead), (2) size of variance, (3) experience with standard costs, (4) cause of variance (e.g., incorrect standards), and (5) timing of variance (e.g., a variance caused by seasonal fluctuations). Therefore, determining the most acceptable treatment requires consideration of more than the argument that only actual costs should be shown in the financial statements. The determination of an actual cost may be impossible, and to argue that charging off variances in the period in which they arise might distort the operating income reveals a misunderstanding of standard costs.

One view of the disposition of variances has been expressed as follows:

1. Where the standards are current and attainable, companies would "state their inventories at standard cost and charge the variances against the income of the period in which the variances arise. They justify this practice on the grounds that variances represent inefficiencies, avoidable waste not recoverable in the selling price, and random fluctuations in actual cost."

2. Where standards are not current, "the general practice is to divide the variances between inventories and cost of goods sold or profit and loss

thereby converting both inventories and cost of sales to approximate actual costs."[3]

Another view asserts that:

1. Any variances which are caused by inactivity, waste, or extravagance (outside acceptable tolerance limits) should be written off, since they represent losses. They should not be deferred by capitalizing them in the inventory accounts. This would include quantity variances on materials and labor as well as idle time (capacity) and efficiency variances on overhead. To assign a portion of such costs to inventory may cloud the product pricing decision. For example, "the inclusion of idle capacity costs in product costs has the effect of raising (inventory) costs when it is most difficult to raise prices (low volume periods) and lowering (inventory) costs when it is easiest to ask for higher prices (high volume periods)."[4]

2. An inventory reserve account should be established and charged with part of the price (spending and rate) variances (and quantity, capacity, and efficiency variances within acceptable tolerance limits) to an extent which would bring the materials, work in process, and finished goods inventories up to, but not in excess of, current market values. The rest of the price (spending and rate) variance amounts (as well as those variances described in (1) above) should be written off, since they represent excess costs. In this way, the inventory accounts themselves will be stated at standard cost while the inventories on the balance sheet will, as a whole, be shown at reasonable costs through the use of the inventory reserve account. In addition, losses caused by excessive costs and inefficiencies will be shown in the operating statement for the period in which they occur.[5]

Disposition of Variances for Interim Financial Reporting

The AICPA takes the following position concerning variance disposition for interim financial reporting in published financial statements:

Companies that use standard cost accounting systems for determining inventory and product costs should generally follow the same procedures in reporting purchase price, wage rate, usage or efficiency variances from standard cost at the end of an interim period as followed at the end of a fiscal year. Purchase price variances or volume or capacity cost variances that are planned and expected to be absorbed by the end of the annual period, should ordinarily be deferred at interim reporting dates. The effect of unplanned or unanticipated purchase price or volume variances, however, should be reported at the end of an interim period following the same procedures used at the end of a fiscal year.[6]

---

[3]*NAA Research Report, Nos. 11-15,* "How Standard Costs Are Being Used Currently" (New York: National Association of Accountants, 1948), pp. 65-66.

[4]Edwin Bartenstein, "Different Costs for Different Purposes," *Management Accounting,* Vol. LX, No. 2, p. 46.

[5]W. Wesley Miller, "Standard Costs and Their Relation to Cost Control," *NA(C)A Bulletin,* Vol. XXVII, No. 15, p. 692.

[6]*Opinions of the Accounting Principles Board, No. 28,* "Interim Financial Reporting" (New York: American Institute of Certified Public Accountants, 1973), par. 14.

■ REVISION OF STANDARD COSTS

As discussed in Chapter 18, standards should be changed only when underlying conditions change or when they no longer reflect the original concept. The idea that standards should be changed more than once a year weakens their effectiveness and increases operational details. Nevertheless, standard costs require continuous review and should be changed when conditions dictate.

When standard costs are changed, any adjustment to inventory should be made with care so that inventories are not written up or down arbitrarily. The National Association of Accountants made the following comments concerning adjustments to ending inventory for such changes:

1. *If the new standard costs reflect conditions which affected the actual cost of the goods in the ending inventory, most firms adjust inventory to the new standard cost and carry the contra side of the adjusting entry to cost of sales by way of the variance accounts. In effect, this procedure assumes that the standard costs used to cost goods in the inventory have been incorrect and that restatement of inventory cost is needed to bring inventories to a correct figure on the books. Since the use of incorrect standards has affected the variance accounts as well as the inventory, the adjustment is carried to the variance accounts.*

2. *If the standard costs represent conditions which are expected to prevail in the coming period but which have not affected costs in the past period, ending inventories are costed at the old standards. It appears to be common practice to adjust the detailed inventory records to new standard costs.*

    In order to maintain the control relationship which the inventory accounts have over subsidiary records, the same adjustment is entered in the inventory control accounts; and the contra entry is carried to an inventory valuation account. Thus, the net effect is to state the inventory in the closing balance sheet at old standard costs. In the next period the inventory valuation account is closed to cost of sales when the goods to which the reserve relates move out of inventories. By use of this technique, the detailed records can be adjusted to new standards before the beginning of the year while at the same time the net charge to cost of sales in the new period is for old standard cost since the latter cost was correct at the time the goods were acquired.[7]

■ BROAD APPLICABILITY OF STANDARD COSTING

The use of standard costing is not limited to manufacturing situations. This powerful working tool for planning and control can be used in other aspects of business organizations. For example, standards can be used for marketing activities, as discussed in Chapter 24, and for maintenance work.[8] The not-for-profit organization sector (hospitals, governmental agencies, etc.) also affords many opportunities to utilize standard costing concepts and techniques. Though standard costs may not be formally recorded in the accounts, many relatively small organizations, such as automotive repair shops and

---

[7]*NAA Research Report, Nos. 11-15, op. cit.,* p. 64.

[8]See James H. Bullock, *Maintenance Planning and Control* (New York: National Association of Accountants, 1979), Chapter 6, "Maintenance Standards and Performance Measurement," pp. 99-111.

construction contractors, can utilize the comparison of actual to standard quantities, times, and costs for bidding, pricing of jobs or projects, and the planning and control of routine operating activities.

DISCUSSION QUESTIONS

Q19-1. Some firms incorporate standard costs into their accounts; others maintain them only for statistical comparisons. Discuss these different uses of standard costs.

Q19-2. Compare the use of actual cost methods to standard costing systems for inventory costing.

Q19-3. Differences between actual costs and standard costs may be recorded in variance accounts. What considerations might determine the number of variance accounts?

Q19-4. Name several advantages of using standard costs for finished goods and cost of goods sold.

Q19-5. The determination of periodic income depends greatly upon the cost assigned to materials, work in process, and finished goods inventories. What considerations determine the costing of inventories at standard or approximate actual costs by companies using standard costs?

Q19-6. Present arguments in support of each of the following three methods of treating standard cost variances for purposes of financial reporting:
(a) As deferred charges or credits on the balance sheet.
(b) As charges or credits on the income statement.
(c) Allocated between inventories and cost of goods sold.
(AICPA adapted)

EXERCISES

E19-1. Journal entries for materials; variance analysis. Blackrock Electronics Company uses a standard costing system. The standard for one of its products, Tekal, is 2 units of component part F-25 at a cost of $.42 per unit. During September, 8,200 units of Tekal were manufactured. During September, 20,000 units of component part F-25 were purchased at a total actual cost of $8,800, and 16,500 units were used in production.

Required: Prepare the journal entries for the purchase and issue of component part F-25 using the three methods for recording materials.

E19-2. Journal entries for labor; variance analysis. The processing of one unit of product Gaplock requires a standard of 3/4 hours of direct labor at $9.50 per hour. During the month, 2,400 units of Gaplock were manufactured. Actual production required 1,920 direct labor hours at a total cost of $17,856.

Required: Prepare the journal entries required to record direct labor charged to production, including variances.

E19-3. Journal entries for factory overhead; two-variance analysis. Factory overhead is charged to production in Department A on the basis of the standard machine hours allowed for actual production. The following data relate to the results of operations for the month of May:

Normal capacity in machine hours	15,000
Standard machine hours allowed for actual production	12,000
Actual machine hours..................................	13,000

The factory overhead rate based on normal capacity machine hours follows:

Variable overhead	$ 37,500 ÷ 15,000 hours =	$2.50
Fixed overhead	67,500 ÷ 15,000 hours =	4.50
Total factory overhead	$105,000 ÷ 15,000 hours =	$7.00

Actual factory overhead incurred during the month of May totaled $90,000.

Required: Prepare the journal entries necessary to record each of the following:

(1) The incurrence of actual factory overhead.
(2) The factory overhead actually charged to production.
(3) The closing of the applied factory overhead account.
(4) The closing of the factory overhead control account into the controllable variance and the volume variance accounts.

E19-4. Journal entries for factory overhead: three-variance method A. Factory overhead is charged to production in the Assembly Department of Indiana Manufacturing Company on the basis of the standard direct labor hours allowed for actual production. The following data relate to the results of operations for December:

Normal capacity in direct labor hours	10,000
Standard labor hours allowed for actual production	11,000
Actual direct labor hours worked	10,500

The factory overhead rate based on normal capacity direct labor hours follows:

Variable overhead	$30,000 ÷ 10,000 hours =	$3.00
Fixed overhead	20,000 ÷ 10,000 hours =	2.00
Total factory overhead	$50,000 ÷ 10,000 hours =	$5.00

Actual factory overhead incurred during December totaled $56,000.

Required: Prepare the journal entries necessary to record each of the following:

(1) The incurrence of actual factory overhead.
(2) The factory overhead actually charged to production.
(3) The closing of the applied factory overhead account.
(4) The closing of the factory overhead control account into three factory overhead variance accounts (method A).

E19-5. Journal entries for factory overhead; three-variance method B. Factory overhead is charged to production in the Machining Department of Texas Tool Company on the basis of the standard machine hours allowed for actual production. The following data relate to the results of operations for November:

Normal capacity in machine hours	5,000
Standard machine hours allowed for actual production	4,800
Actual machine hours................................	5,200

The factory overhead rate based on normal capacity machine hours follows:

Variable overhead	$20,000 ÷ 5,000 hours =	$ 4.00
Fixed overhead	60,000 ÷ 5,000 hours =	12.00
Total factory overhead	$80,000 ÷ 5,000 hours =	$16.00

Actual factory overhead incurred during November totaled $78,000.

Required: Prepare the journal entries necessary to record each of the following:

(1) The incurrence of actual factory overhead.
(2) The factory overhead actually charged to production.
(3) The closing of the applied factory overhead account.
(4) The closing of the factory overhead control account into three factory overhead variances (method B).

E19-6. Journal entries for factory overhead; four-variance method. Factory overhead is charged to production in the Finishing Department of Franklin Furniture Company on the basis of the standard direct labor hours allowed for actual production. The following data relate to the results of operations for February:

Normal capacity in direct labor hours	8,000
Standard labor hours allowed for actual production	7,000
Actual direct labor hours worked	7,600

The factory overhead rate based on normal capacity direct labor hours follows:

Variable overhead	$64,000 ÷ 8,000 hours =	$ 8.00
Fixed overhead	24,000 ÷ 8,000 hours =	3.00
Total factory overhead	$88,000 ÷ 8,000 hours =	$11.00

Actual factory overhead incurred during February totaled $86,000.

Required: Prepare the journal entries necessary to record each of the following:

(1) The incurrence of actual factory overhead.
(2) The factory overhead actually charged to production.
(3) The closing of the applied factory overhead account.
(4) The closing of the factory overhead control account into four factory overhead variance accounts.

E19-7. Factory overhead variance analysis and journal entries. The theoretical capacity of Winslow Manufacturing Company is 5,000 units of product Dupto. At the normal capacity level (80% of theoretical), the following factory overhead amounts have been budgeted:

Fixed	$16,500
Variable	4,500

Standards were set as follows:

Processing time, 1.5 hours per unit of Dupto
Factory overhead, $3.50 per hour of processing

Actual data for November were:

Production, 3,450 units of Dupto
Processing time, 5,320 hours
Factory overhead, $21,230

Required:

(1) Compute the variances resulting when the two-, three-, and four-variance methods are used. For the three-variance method, use both methods A and B.
(2) For each method, prepare the journal entries to record actual factory overhead, applied factory overhead, and variances.

E19-8. Disposition of variances. Nanron Company uses a standard process cost system for all its products. All inventories are carried at standard. Inventories and cost of goods sold are adjusted for financial statement purposes for all variances considered material in amount at the end of the fiscal year. All products are considered to flow through the manufacturing process to finished goods and ultimate sale in a first-in, first-out pattern.

The standard cost of one of Nanron's products is as follows:

Materials......................	$2
Direct labor (.5 DLH @ $8)	4
Factory overhead................	3
Total standard cost............	$9

There is no work in process inventory of this product due to the nature of the product and the manufacturing process.

The following schedule reports the manufacturing and sales activity measured at standard cost for the current fiscal year:

	Units	Dollars
Product manufactured.................	95,000	$855,000
Beginning finished goods inventory	15,000	135,000
Goods available for sale	110,000	$990,000
Ending finished goods inventory...........	19,000	171,000
Cost of goods sold..................	91,000	$819,000

The balance of the Finished Goods Inventory, $140,800, reported on the balance sheet at the beginning of the year, included a $5,800 adjustment for variances from standard cost. The unfavorable standard cost variances for labor for the current fiscal year consisted of a wage rate variance of $32,000 and a labor efficiency variance of $20,000 (2,500 hours @ $8). There were no other variances from standard cost for this year.

Required: Assuming the unfavorable labor variances totaling $52,000 are considered material in amount by management and are to be allocated to finished goods inventory and to cost of goods sold, compute the amount that will be shown on the year-end balance sheet for Finished Goods Inventory and the amount for Cost of Goods Sold on the income statement prepared for the fiscal year.   (ICMA adapted)

E19-9. Disposition of variances. Atlantic Manufacturing Corporation uses standard costing in accounting for manufacturing costs. Variances are allocated to the cost of goods sold and ending inventories. The following information was extracted from the corporation's books for March:

	Debit	Credit
Materials purchase price variance		$ 150
Materials quantity variance..............	$ 500	
Labor rate variance....................	600	
Labor efficiency variance	1,200	
Controllable variance	1,500	
Volume variance		1,800

The following inventories were on hand on March 31:

Finished goods.........	1,200 units
Work in process........	1,500 units
Raw materials..........	none

The work in process inventory was fully complete as to materials and 1/3 complete as to direct labor and factory overhead. During January, 3,300 units were sold.

Required: Allocate the variances. Round distribution percentages to the nearest whole percent and allocations to the nearest cent.

PROBLEMS

P19-1. Journal entries; variance analysis. Glibb Company manufactures a product called Primostuff, which has the following standard costs:

Materials..	6 units @ $ 2 =	$12.00
Labor	1/4 hr. @ 8 =	2.00
Variable factory overhead	3/4 hr. @ 4 =	3.00
Fixed factory overhead (normal capacity is 5,000 hours of processing time)	3/4 hr. @ 12 =	9.00
Total standard cost		$26.00

The following information pertains to actual production activity for the month of August:

(a) 6,000 equivalent units of Primostuff were produced with respect to materials, 5,800 equivalent units with respect to labor, and 5,500 equivalent units with respect to factory overhead.
(b) 33,000 units of materials were purchased at a total cost of $64,350. The materials price variance is recorded when the materials are purchased.
(c) 40,000 units of materials were issued to production and used during the period.
(d) Direct labor cost was $11,644 for 1,420 actual hours. Assume that the liability has already been recorded, but not yet distributed.
(e) Actual processing required during August totaled 4,350 hours.
(f) Actual factory overhead was $72,125.
(g) 5,200 units were completed and transferred to finished goods inventory during the month.
(h) 5,500 units of Primostuff were sold during the month for $40 each.

Required: Prepare the journal entries to record the above information, including two variances for each cost element.

P19-2. Journal entries; variance analysis. Alexandria Manufacturing Inc. produces custom-made, tie-dyed sweat shirts for distribution on college campuses. The following standards have been established.

Materials:	
Cotton cloth: 2 yards @ $1	$2.00
Dyes: 1 pint @ $.50	.50
Labor: 1/2 hour @ $6..................	3.00
Factory overhead: 1/2 hour @ $1	.50
Total standard cost.............	$6.00

The yearly production budget is based upon normal plant operations of 20,000 hours, with fixed factory overhead of $6,000.

Inventories at January 1 were:

Cotton Cloth (2,000 yards @ $1)	$2,000
Dye (1,000 pints @ $.50)	500
Work in Process (1,000 units; 1/4 finished as to conversion; all materials issued)	3,375
Finished Goods (500 @ $6)	3,000

Production for January:

> 3,000 units completed
> 750 units 1/3 converted, all materials added

Transactions for January:

Cotton cloth purchased	5,000 yds. @ $1.10
Dyes purchased.	2,500 pints @ $.49
Cotton cloth issued to factory	5,600 yards
Dyes issued to factory	2,700 pints
Direct labor payroll.	1,550 hours @ $5.90
Actual factory overhead.	$1,620
Sales on account.	3,100 sweat shirts @ $9

Required: Prepare the journal entries to record the January transactions, accounting for work in process at standard cost and recognizing variances in the proper accounts. Use the two-variance method in computing materials and labor, and three-variance method A in computing factory overhead variances; recognize the materials price variance at the time of purchase. Use separate inventory and variance accounts for each material. Close all variances to Cost of Goods Sold.

P19-3. Journal entries; variance analysis. Cimarron Manufacturing Company uses a standard cost system in its accounting records. The standard costs for its one product are as follows:

Materials	9 kilograms	@	$ 2.00 =	$18.00
Direct labor	2 hours	@	10.50 =	21.00
Variable overhead.	2 hours	@	3.00 =	6.00
Fixed overhead.	2 hours	@	10.00 =	20.00
Total standard cost				$65.00

Normal capacity is 2,000 direct labor hours per month. Materials, work in process, and finished goods are recorded in inventory at standard cost. The following information is taken from last month's records:

Production	900 units
Materials purchased.	10 000 kilograms @ $ 1.95
Materials used in production	8 600 kilograms
Direct labor payroll	1,740 hours @ $11.55
Actual overhead	$24,000

Required: Prepare the journal entries to record the above information. Use the two-variance method to compute materials and labor variances and three-variance method B to compute overhead variances.

CGA-Canada (adapted) Reprint with permission

P19-4. Journal entries; variance analysis. The following information pertains to production operations of Groff Company for April:

Inventories:

Work in process: Beginning, 2,000 units, all materials,
$1/2$ converted; ending, 3,000 units,
all materials, $1/3$ converted; no spoilage.

Finished goods: No beginning or ending inventory.

Standard and actual costs:

Materials: Standard quantity, 5 square feet per unit;
50,000 square feet were purchased @ $.52;
the unfavorable materials purchase price
variance was $1,000; 29,500 square feet
of materials were requisitioned from the
storeroom.

Labor: Standard per unit, $1/2$ hour at $9 per hour;
actual labor rate was $9.05 per hour for 2,600
hours.

Factory overhead: Normal capacity, 2,000 labor hours; fixed factory
overhead standard, $2 per unit or $4 per labor
hour; actual factory overhead was $5,500 variable
and $8,200 fixed; efficiency variance, $400
unfavorable; spending variance, $700 unfavorable.

Five thousand units were sold for cash at $15 each.

Required: Prepare the journal entries to record the cost accounting cycle transactions, using standard costing. Variances will not be disposed of until June, the end of the fiscal year.

CGA-Canada (adapted) Reprint with permission

P19-5. Income statement; variance analysis. Ensley Corporation manufactures Product G, which sells for $25 per unit. Material M is added before processing starts, and labor and overhead are added evenly during the manufacturing process. Production capacity is budgeted at 110,000 units of G annually. The standard costs per unit of G are:

Direct materials: 2 pounds of material M @ $1.50		$ 3.00
Direct labor: 1.5 hours at $8 per hour		12.00
Factory overhead:		
Variable	$1.50	
Fixed	1.10	2.60
Total standard cost per unit		$17.60

A process cost system is used. Inventories are costed at standard cost. All variances from standard costs are charged or credited to Cost of Goods Sold in the year incurred.

Inventory data for 19A:

	January 1	December 31
Material M	50,000 pounds	60,000 pounds
Work in process:		
All materials, $2/5$ processed	10,000 units	
All materials, $1/3$ processed		15,000 units
Finished goods inventory	20,000 units	12,000 units

During 19A, 250,000 pounds of M were purchased at an average cost of $1.485 per pound; and 240,000 pounds were transferred to work in process inventory. Direct labor costs amounted to $1,313,760 at an average hourly labor rate of $8.16.

Actual factory overhead for 19A:

Variable	$181,500
Fixed	114,000

A total of 110,000 units of G were completed and transferred to finished goods inventory. Marketing and administrative expenses were $681,000.

Required: Prepare an income statement for 19A, including all manufacturing cost variances and using the two-variance method for factory overhead.   (AICPA adapted)

P19-6. Income statement. The Kalman Company, a subsidiary of the Camper Corporation, submits interim financial statements. Camper combines these statements with similar statements from other subsidiaries to prepare its quarterly statements. The following data are taken from the records and accounts of the Kalman Company.

(a) Sales forecasts for the year are:

Quarter	Stove Units	Percent
First.	450,000	30%
Second	600,000	40
Third	150,000	10
Fourth	300,000	20
	1,500,000	100%

Sales have been achieved as forecasted in the first and second quarters of the current year.

(b) Management is considering increasing the selling price of a stove from $30 to $34. However, management is concerned that this price increase may reduce the already low sales volume forecasts for the third and fourth quarters.

(c) The production schedule calls for 1,500,000 stoves this year. The manufacturing facilities can produce 1,720,000 units per year or 430,000 units per quarter during regular hours. The quarterly production schedule shown below was developed to meet the seasonal sales demand and is being followed as planned.

Quarter	Scheduled Production (in units)	Percent
First.	465,000	31%
Second	450,000	30
Third	225,000	15
Fourth	360,000	24
	1,500,000	100%

(d) The standard manufacturing cost of a stove unit, as established at the beginning of the current year, is shown below. This standard cost does not incorporate any charges for overtime.

Materials	$ 4.00
Labor.	9.00
Variable factory overhead.	2.00
Fixed factory overhead.	3.00
Standard cost per stove	$18.00

(e) A significant and permanent price increase in the cost of raw materials resulted in a material price variance of $270,000 for the materials used in the second quarter. Unplanned variances which are significant and permanent in nature are prorated to the applicable accounts during the quarter in which they occur.

(f) There was a $36,000 unfavorable direct labor efficiency variance in the second quarter, which occurred as a result of unexpected inefficiencies. These inefficiencies are not regarded as significant, and they are not expected to recur.

(g) The second quarter unfavorable factory overhead spending variance of $126,000 was partially due to overtime paid during the second quarter and partially due to unexpected inefficiencies. Since overtime was incurred in order to produce enough product to meet the sales forecasts, the portion of the spending variance attributable to overtime is prorated between quarters on the basis of budgeted sales. Management does not expect to incur overtime in the last half of the year. The overtime premium is 50% of the standard labor rate.

(h) Total fixed factory overhead expected to be incurred and budgeted for the year is $4,500,000. Through the first two quarters, $2,745,000 of fixed factory overhead was applied to production. Of this amount, $1,350,000 was applied in the second quarter. The high production activity resulted in a total favorable fixed factory overhead volume variance of $495,000 for the first two quarters. However, since the fixed overhead rate is based on annual expected production of 1,500,000 units, a volume variance is reported on interim statements only if actual production differs from the planned production schedule.

(i) Selling expenses are 10% of sales and are expected to total $4,500,000 for the year.

(j) Administrative expenses are $6,000,000 annually and are incurred uniformly throughout the year.

(k) Inventory balances as of the end of the second quarter follow:

Materials (at actual cost)...............	$400,000
Work in Process (50% complete—	
at standard cost)	72,000
Finished Goods (at standard cost)	900,000

(l) The stove product line is expected to earn $7,500,000 before taxes this year. The estimated state and federal income tax expenses for the year are $4,050,000.

Required: Prepare the second quarter interim income statement for the Kalman subsidiary of Camper Corporation.

P19-7. Variance analysis; journal entries; income statement. The following information concerns Pacific Manufacturing Company, which manufactures a single product called Westco. The standard cost card for Westco follows:

Materials: A: 1 unit @ $14	$14
B: 6 units @ $2	12
Direct labor: $1/2$ hour @ $10...........................	5
Variable factory overhead: $1/3$ machine hour @ $3	1
Fixed factory overhead: $1/3$ machine hour @ $24	8
	$40

Other information available for the year ending December 31, 19A, includes the following:

(a) Materials price variances are recorded when the materials are purchased. Transactions related to materials follow:

Material	Beginning Inventory	Purchased	Issued
A	1,200 units @ $14	15,000 units @ $13	14,200 units
B	6,300 units @ $ 2	80,000 units @ $ 3	82,300 units

(b) Beginning work in process contained 6,000 units of Westco, complete with respect to material A, $2/3$ complete with respect to material B, $1/2$ complete with respect to direct labor, and $2/3$ complete with respect to machining.

(c) Ending work in process contains 5,000 units of Westco, complete with respect to material A, $1/2$ complete with respect to material B, $1/4$ complete with respect to direct labor, and $1/2$ complete with respect to machining.

(d) 15,000 units of Westco were transferred completed and transferred to finished goods during the period. There were 4,000 units of Westco in finished goods at the beginning of the period and 3,600 units at the end of the period. Westco sells for $60 a unit.

(e) During the period, 6,500 direct labor hours were worked at a total cost of $71,500.

(f) Production machining time totaled 4,400 hours. The standard factory overhead rate is determined on the basis of a normal operating capacity of 5,000 machine hours.

(g) Actual factory overhead for the period totaled $122,000.

(h) Marketing and administrative expenses for the period totaled $120,000, and the effective income tax rate is 40%.

Required:

(1) Prepare the journal entries to record the purchase and issue of materials, the production charge for labor and factory overhead, and the closing of the two factory overhead accounts (i.e., Factory Overhead Control and Applied Factory Overhead), along with the appropriate standard cost variances. Use the three-variance method B for factory overhead.

(2) Prepare the journal entry to close the variance accounts into Income Summary.

(3) Prepare an income statement for the year ending December 31, 19A.

P19-8. Journal entries; variance analysis; income statement. Halifax Company uses the following standard costs in accounting for its only product:

Materials: 3 liters × $4	$12.00
Direct labor: $1/2$ hour × $7	3.50
Variable factory overhead: $1/2$ hour × $6	3.00
Fixed factory overhead: $1/2$ hour × $9	4.50
Total standard cost	$23.00

Fixed factory overhead budgeted was $49,500 per month. Actual activity for November was:

(a) 40 000 liters of material were purchased for $159,200. The related price variance is recorded at the time of purchase.

(b) 10,000 units were produced.

(c) There was no work in process at the beginning or end of November.

(d) 31 000 liters of material were issued to production.

(e) The direct labor payroll to be distributed (credit the payroll account) is $35,616 for 4,800 hours.

(f) Actual factory overhead cost of $81,500 was incurred.

(g) 8,000 units were sold on account at $40 each.

(h) Marketing and administrative expenses of $60,000 were incurred.

Required:

(1) Prepare journal entries to record the November activity. (Ignore overhead variances.)

(2) Prepare a four-variance analysis of under- or overapplied factory overhead.

(3) Prepare an income statement, assuming that all variances are to be closed to Cost of Goods Sold.

CGA-Canada (adapted) Reprint with permission

SS **P19-9. Allocating variances.** Hamm Corporation commenced doing business on December 1. The corporation uses a standard cost system for the manufacturing costs of its only product, Hamex. The standard costs for a unit of Hamex are:

Materials: 10 kilograms @ .70		$ 7
Direct labor: 1 hour @ $8		8
Factory overhead (applied on the basis of $2 per direct labor hour)		2
Total standard cost		$17

The following data were extracted from the corporation's books for December:

	Units	Debit	Credit
Budgeted production	3,000		
Units sold	1,500		
Sales			$45,000
Sales discounts		$ 500	
Materials price usage variance		1,500	
Materials quantity variance		660	
Direct labor rate variance		250	
Factory overhead spending variance			300
Discounts lost		120	

The company records purchases of materials net of discounts. The amounts shown for discounts lost and materials price usage variance are applicable to materials used in manufacturing operations during December. Inventory data at December 31 indicate the following inventories were on hand:

Finished goods	900 units
Work in process	1,200 units
Materials	None

The work in process inventory was 100% complete as to materials and 50% as to direct labor and factory overhead. The corporation's policy is to allocate variances to the cost of goods sold and ending inventories, i.e., work in process and finished goods.

Required: Prepare schedules:

(1) Allocating the variances and discounts lost on purchases to the ending inventories and to cost of goods sold.

(2) Computing the cost of goods manufactured at standard cost and at actual cost for December. Amounts for materials, labor, and factory overhead should be shown separately.

(3) Computing the actual cost of materials, labor, and factory overhead included in the work in process inventory and in the finished goods inventory at December 31.   (AICPA adapted)

CASES

C19-1. Disposition of Variances. Jonesboro Company manufactures office equipment. The company historically has utilized standard costing to aid management decisions. Variances from standard usually have been minor and always have been expensed in the audited financial statements. However, two problems have been encountered this year. First, variances from standard are large because of rapid increases in labor and materials costs and because of a slowdown in production during the last quarter. Second, a considerable portion of manufactured inventory remains unsold. The company wishes to expense the variances from standard.

Required: Discuss the acceptability of the proposal insofar as external reporting is concerned.   (CICA adapted)

C19-2. Standard costs in inventory and variance disposition. Many advocates of standard costing take the position that these costs are a proper basis for inventory costing for external reporting purposes. Accounting Research Bulletin No. 43, however, reflects the widespread view that standard costs are not acceptable unless "adjusted at reasonable intervals to reflect current conditions so that at the balance-sheet date standard costs reasonably approximate costs computed under one of the recognized bases."

Required:

(1) Discuss the conceptual merits of using standard costs as the basis for inventory costing for external reporting purposes.

(2) Prepare general journal entries for three alternative dispositions of a $1,500 unfavorable variance, when all goods manufactured during the period are included in the ending finished goods inventory. Assume that a formal standard cost system is in operation, that $500 of the variance resulted from actual costs exceeding normal (attainable) standard cost, and that $1,000 of the variance resulted from the difference between the theoretical (ideal) standard and a normal standard.

(3) Discuss the conceptual merits of each of the three alternative methods of disposition requested in (2) above.

(AICPA adapted)

PART

5

Analysis of
Costs and Profits

CHAPTER 20

Direct Costing and Cost-Volume-Profit Analysis

The factory overhead chapters (Chapters 13, 14, and 15) presented the use of the factory overhead rate for product costing. All budgeted factory overhead costs were combined into a composite, predetermined rate which was then used as the basis for charging factory overhead to products manufactured during the period. To construct this rate, all factory overhead for the accounting period must be budgeted and the total divided by the expected volume of the activity measure used to allocate factory overhead to production. The objective of this process is to assign a portion of each item of factory overhead incurred during the period to each unit of product produced during the period. Since this process results in the assignment of a share of both fixed and variable factory overhead to production, it is referred to as *absorption, full,* or *conventional costing.*

Since the amount of factory overhead assigned to production is a function of the predetermined rate and the actual volume of production activity, actual factory overhead and the amount charged to production typically differ. This difference may be the result of differences in costs (i.e., actual factory overhead for the period is not the same as budgeted factory overhead adjusted to the actual level of activity) or differences in activity (i.e., the actual volume of production activity is not the same as the budgeted level of activity used in computing the predetermined rate) or both. When actual and budgeted activity differ, fixed factory overhead will be over- or underabsorbed. Whether this fixed cost variance is charged to period expense or ratably allocated between ending inventories and the cost of goods sold, fluctuations in the unit product cost occur as a result of differences in activity between periods.

An additional problem occurs when absorption costing is used because most fixed costs cannot be traced to individual products. As a consequence, the fixed cost allocated to any particular product may have little relationship to actual costs that must be incurred to manufacture the product. A change in the mix of products manufactured and sold during a period may have an unanticipated effect on the total amount of fixed cost absorbed (i.e., charged to production) and on profits.

In a competitive business environment, management needs information that will enable it to determine the effects of changes in volume and mix on profit. Since product cost determined on the absorption costing basis contains an arbitrarily allocated element of fixed cost which is based on budgeted production capacity and product mix, such cost is of limited usefulness for internal decision making. Reliance on such costs can result in poor decisions and unprofitable actions. Direct costing was designed to enhance the usefulness of product costs in internal decision making by eliminating the fixed cost element in product cost. Cost-volume-profit analysis is a short-run planning tool that effectively utilizes direct costing data to analyze the relationships between costs, profits, product mix, and sales volume.

know all definitions

■ DIRECT COSTING

Direct costing, also referred to as *variable costing* or *marginal costing,* charges units of product with only those manufacturing costs that vary directly with volume. Prime costs (direct materials and direct labor) plus variable factory overhead are assigned to inventories (both work in process and finished goods) and to the cost of goods sold. Thus only variable manufacturing costs are charged to the product, while all fixed manufacturing costs are expensed in the period in which they are incurred. Fixed manufacturing costs, such as depreciation, insurance, taxes, supervisory salaries, and the salaries of janitors, guards, maintenance, and office personnel, are excluded from the cost of the product. Because the incurrence of fixed costs appears to be more closely associated with the passage of time than with production activity, such costs are often referred to as period costs and are charged to period expense rather than to inventories. In contrast, variable costs are often referred to as *product costs* and are assigned to inventories because they are more closely associated with production activity than with the passage of time.

Direct costing focuses attention on the product and the costs directly traceable to changes in production activity. This focus is directed in two ways: (1) to internal uses of the fixed-variable cost relationship and the contribution margin concept, and (2) to external uses involving the costing of inventories, income determination, and financial reporting. The internal uses deal with the application of direct costing in profit planning, product pricing, other phases of decision making, and in cost control. These facets of direct costing can be presented as follows:

Facets of Direct Costing

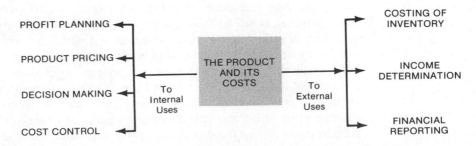

Contribution Margin Defined

The *contribution margin*, sometimes referred to as *marginal income*, is the difference between sales revenue and variable costs. It is computed by subtracting all variable costs, both manufacturing and nonmanufacturing, from sales revenue. In direct costing, the contribution margin may be computed in total (for the entire firm or for each product line, sales territory, operating division, etc.) or on a per unit basis. However, income per unit is not computed. Total income is computed by subtracting total fixed costs from the total contribution margin, as shown in the following illustration. This illustration is based on the assumption that unit variable cost remains constant at $42 for all levels of activity, and that the fixed cost is fixed in total for all levels of activity.

	Per Unit	Total	Percentage of Sales
Sales (10,000 units)	$70	$700,000	100
Less variable cost.......	42	420,000	60
Contribution margin	$28	$280,000	40
Less fixed cost		175,000	25
Operating income		$105,000	15

Internal Uses of Direct Costing

Executive managers, including marketing executives, production managers, and cost analysts, frequently praise the planning, control, and analytical potentialities of direct costing. Fixed costs calculated on a unit cost basis under absorption costing tend to vary for various volumes of production and sales. Such variability in unit costs makes the use of absorption costing for many types of internal analysis difficult at best and misleading at worst. In contrast, variable unit costs and the contribution margin per unit tend to remain constant at all levels of activity (at least within the relevant range). Consequently, managers often find direct costing more understandable and more useful than absorption costing for most types of internal analysis.

ROBOTICS

Many modern manufacturing plants are highly automated. In some cases, robotics technology has been used to replace direct labor, thereby significantly reducing variable manufacturing costs. In fully automated plants, variable costs may comprise no more than one or two percent of the total manufacturing cost. At first glance, one might assume that direct costing would be of little value to decision makers if variable costs comprise such a small component of the total cost of manufacturing. However, quite the opposite may be true. Since fixed costs comprise a larger share of total costs, the inclusion of fixed costs in the cost of the product will result in larger changes in product costs as production volume fluctuates between periods. Consequently, reliance on absorption costing figures can be even more misleading than in cases where fixed costs comprise a smaller share of the total cost of manufacturing.

Direct Costing as a Profit-Planning Tool. A *profit plan*, often called a *budget* or *plan of operations*, covers all phases of future operations to attain a stated profit goal. Although such a plan includes both long- and short-range operations, direct costing is quite useful in planning for short periods, in pricing special orders, or in making current operating decisions.

The variable cost and the contribution margin allow quick and fairly reliable profit approximations for making decisions in the short run. To be reliable in such situations, the change or shift of a small segment within the total volume must not require major changes in capacity, which would change fixed or period costs. Period costs that are specific or relevant to a single product, product line, or segment of the business should be isolated and attached to that unit in order to increase the usefulness of these costs for decision-making purposes.

With its separation of variable and fixed costs and its calculation of the contribution margin, direct costing facilitates analysis of the cost-volume-profit relationship. Direct costing aids in identifying the relevant analytical data for determining the break-even point, the rate of return on investment, the contribution margin by a segment of total sales, and the total profit from all operations based on a given volume. Direct costing also aids management in planning and evaluating the profit resulting from a change of volume, a change in the sales mix, make-or-buy situations, and the acquisition of new equipment. A knowledge of the variable or out-of-pocket costs, fixed costs, and contribution margin provides a basis for evaluating the profitability of products, customers, territories, and other segments of the entire business. These uses are discussed in later chapters.

Direct Costing as a Guide to Product Pricing. In a highly competitive market, prices are determined through the interaction of supply and demand. The best or optimum price is the one which will yield the maximum excess of total revenue over total cost. The volume at which the increase in total cost due to the addition of one more unit of volume is just equal to the increase in total revenue (i.e., the point at which marginal revenue is equal to marginal cost) is the profit-maximizing volume. The price at which this volume can be obtained is the optimum price. A higher price will lower the quantity demanded and decrease total profit. A lower price will increase the quantity demanded but decrease total profit. Although management can control supply, demand is a function of such factors as the tastes and preferences of consumers and their financial capacity, over which management has little control. Direct costing provides the marginal cost of the product necessary to determine the profit-maximizing volume.

In multiproduct pricing, management needs to know whether each product can be priced competitively and still contribute sufficiently to the company's total contribution margin for fixed cost recovery and profit. Direct costing provides the data necessary to compute the contribution margin from each product line for different unit sales prices and different levels of sales. Although such information is useful in short-term pricing decisions, a long-run pricing policy should ensure that all fixed costs are fully recovered.

Direct Costing for Managerial Decision Making. Installation of a direct costing system requires a study of cost trends and a segregation of fixed and variable costs. The classification of costs as either fixed or variable, with semivariable expenses properly subdivided into their fixed and variable components, provides a framework for the accumulation and analysis of costs. This also provides a basis for the study of contemplated changes in production levels or proposed actions concerning new markets, plant expansion or contraction, or special promotional activities. Of course, it is important to recognize that a study of cost behavior that identifies fixed and variable costs can be accomplished without the use of a formal direct costing system.

In NAA Research Report No. 37, findings on the usefulness of direct costing are summarized as follows:

> *Companies participating in this study generally feel that direct costing's major field of usefulness is in forecasting and reporting income for internal management purposes. The distinctive feature of direct costing which makes it useful for this purpose is the manner in which costs are matched with revenues.*
>
> *The marginal income (contribution margin) figure which results from the first step in matching costs and revenues in the direct costing income statement is reported to be a particularly useful figure to management because it can be readily projected to measure increments in net income which accompany increments in sales. The theory underlying this observed usefulness of the marginal income figure in decision making rests upon the fact that within a limited volume range, period costs tend to remain constant in total when volume changes occur. Under such conditions, only the direct costs are relevant in costing increments in volume.*
>
> *The tendency of net income to fluctuate directly with sales volume was reported to be an important practical advantage possessed by the direct costing approach to income determination because it enables management to trace changes in sales to their consequence in net income. Another advantage attributed to the direct costing income statement was that management has a better understanding of the impact that period costs have on profits when such costs are brought together in a single group.*[1]

Direct Costing as a Control Tool. The direct costing procedure is designed to improve the usefulness of the income statement prepared for management. With absorption costing, inverse fluctuations of production costs and sales revenues can result from fixed manufacturing cost allocations between inventories and cost of goods sold. Such allocations do not occur in direct costing. By adopting direct costing, management and marketing management in particular believe that a more meaningful and understandable income statement can be furnished by the accountant. However, reports issued should serve not only the marketing department but all divisions of an enterprise. It seems appropriate, therefore, to prepare reports for all departments or responsibility centers based on standard costs, flexible budgets, and a division of all costs into their fixed and variable components.

The marketing manager should receive a statement placing sales and production costs in direct relationship to one another. Differences between intended sales and actual sales caused by changes in sales price, sales volume, or sales mix, which are the direct responsibility of the marketing manager,

---

[1] *NAA Research Report, No. 37,* "Applications of Direct Costing" (New York: National Association of Accountants, 1961), pp. 84-85.

should be detailed for analysis as discussed in Chapter 24. Control of marketing costs also is vital to the total cost control framework.

Other managers can examine and interpret their reports with respect to the production cost variances originating in their respective areas of responsibility. The production manager is able to study the materials quantity variance, the labor efficiency variance, and the controllable overhead variance. Variable expenses actually incurred can be analyzed by comparing them with the budget allowance for work actually performed. The purchasing agent or manager can be held accountable for the purchase price variance, and the personnel manager for labor rate variances. General management, which originally authorized and approved plant capacity in the form of labor and machines, is primarily responsible for utilization of existing facilities. In direct costing, however, no variances result with respect to fixed expenses, because all fixed costs are charged against revenue of the period instead of to the product.

External Uses of Direct Costing

The proponents of direct costing believe that the separation of fixed and variable expenses, and the accounting for each according to some direct costing plan, simplifies both the understanding of the income statement and the assignment of costs to inventories.

To keep fixed overhead out of the reported product costs, variable and fixed expenses should be recorded in separate accounts. Therefore, the chart of accounts should be expanded so that each natural classification has two accounts, as needed—one for the variable and one for the fixed portion of the expense. Also, instead of one overhead control account, two should be used: Factory Overhead Control—Variable Expenses, and Factory Overhead Control—Fixed Expenses. When a predetermined overhead rate is used to charge variable expenses to Work in Process, an applied overhead account labeled Applied Variable Factory Overhead is credited. The difference between actual and applied variable overhead is a spending variance, or, if a standard cost system is used, the difference is a controllable variance. The controllable variance can be broken down into two components, a spending variance and a variable efficiency variance. Because fixed expenses are not charged to Work in Process, they are excluded from the predetermined overhead rate. The total fixed expense accumulated in the account, Factory Overhead Control—Fixed Expenses, is charged directly to Income Summary.

To illustrate the effects of direct costing on the income statement, assume that the normal capacity of a plant that produces only one kind of product is 20,000 units per quarter, or 80,000 units per year. Variable standard costs per unit are: direct materials, $30; direct labor, $22; and variable factory overhead, $8. Fixed factory overhead is budgeted at $1,200,000 per year ($300,000 per quarter or $15 per unit under the absorption costing method at normal capacity). The units of production basis is used for applying factory overhead. Fixed marketing and administrative expenses are $200,000 per quarter, or $800,000 per year; and variable marketing expense is $5 per unit. The sales price per unit is $100.

Materials variances, labor variances, and the factory overhead controllable variance have a net unfavorable total of $15,000, $9,000, $14,000, and $17,000 for the first, second, third, and fourth quarters, respectively. These variances are not considered to be material and are closed to Cost of Goods Sold each quarter, whether absorption costing or direct costing is used, because they relate to variable costs which are included in the cost of the product under both methods. However, the factory overhead volume variance (i.e., the over- or underapplied fixed factory overhead) is computed and closed to Cost of Goods Sold only for the absorption costing method because fixed costs are not added to the cost of the product under direct costing.

In this illustration there is no work in process inventory. Standard costs are assigned to finished goods, and the standard costs for the previous year are the same as the standard costs for the current year. If work in process inventories were present, they would also be assigned standard costs. If standard costs were not used or if standard costs in the current period were different from standard costs in the prior period, an assumption about the flow of costs would be required to cost inventories. That is, the average, fifo, or lifo cost flow assumption would be used to cost inventories.

There are 4,000 units in finished goods inventory at the beginning of the first quarter. Actual production, planned production, and sales in units are:

	First Quarter	Second Quarter	Third Quarter	Fourth Quarter
Planned production in units.................	20,000	20,000	20,000	20,000
Actual production in units	20,000	18,000	20,000	22,000
Actual sales in units.......................	20,000	20,000	18,000	18,000

From this information, income statements can be prepared. The following income statement (based on absorption costing) includes the fixed factory overhead in the unit cost of the product and also in the costs assigned to inventory:

	First Quarter	Second Quarter	Third Quarter	Fourth Quarter
Sales.......................	$2,000,000	$2,000,000	$1,800,000	$1,800,000
Standard cost of goods sold	$1,500,000	$1,500,000	$1,350,000	$1,350,000
Materials, labor, and controllable variances	15,000	9,000	14,000	17,000
Volume variance*..............	0	30,000	0	(30,000)
Adjusted cost of goods sold	$1,515,000	$1,539,000	$1,364,000	$1,337,000
Gross profit..................	$ 485,000	$ 461,000	$ 436,000	$ 463,000
Marketing and administrative expenses	300,000	300,000	290,000	290,000
Operating income..............	$ 185,000	$ 161,000	$ 146,000	$ 173,000

*The volume variance is determined as follows:	First Quarter	Second Quarter	Third Quarter	Fourth Quarter
Budgeted fixed overhead	$300,000	$300,000	$300,000	$300,000
Actual production in units......................	20,000	18,000	20,000	22,000
Fixed factory overhead rate	× $15	× $15	× $15	× $15
Applied fixed overhead........................	$300,000	$270,000	$300,000	$330,000
Volume variance, unfavorable (favorable)...........	$ 0	$ 30,000	$ 0	$ (30,000)

The following income statement (based on direct costing) excludes the fixed factory overhead in the unit cost of products and also from the costs assigned to inventory:

	First Quarter	Second Quarter	Third Quarter	Fourth Quarter
Sales	$2,000,000	$2,000,000	$1,800,000	$1,800,000
Standard variable cost of goods sold	$1,200,000	$1,200,000	$1,080,000	$1,080,000
Materials, labor, and controllable variances	15,000	9,000	14,000	17,000
Adjusted variable cost of goods sold	$1,215,000	$1,209,000	$1,094,000	$1,097,000
Gross contribution margin	$ 785,000	$ 791,000	$ 706,000	$ 703,000
Variable marketing expenses	100,000	100,000	90,000	90,000
Contribution margin	$ 685,000	$ 691,000	$ 616,000	$ 613,000
Fixed factory overhead	$ 300,000	$ 300,000	$ 300,000	$ 300,000
Fixed marketing and administrative expenses	200,000	200,000	200,000	200,000
Total fixed expenses	$ 500,000	$ 500,000	$ 500,000	$ 500,000
Operating income	$ 185,000	$ 191,000	$ 116,000	$ 113,000

Costs Assigned to Inventory. To determine the costs assigned to ending finished goods inventory, the number of units in ending inventory must first be computed:

	First Quarter	Second Quarter	Third Quarter	Fourth Quarter
Units in beginning inventory	4,000	4,000	2,000	4,000
Units produced during period	20,000	18,000	20,000	22,000
Units available for sale	24,000	22,000	22,000	26,000
Units sold	20,000	20,000	18,000	18,000
Units in ending inventory	4,000	2,000	4,000	8,000

Since standard costs are assigned to inventory and since the standard costs have not changed between periods, the cost assigned to the finished goods ending inventory under the absorption costing method and the direct costing method can be determined as follows:

	First Quarter	Second Quarter	Third Quarter	Fourth Quarter
Units in ending inventory	4,000	2,000	4,000	8,000
Standard full cost per unit.	× $75	× $75	× $75	× $75
Cost of ending inventory under absorption costing	$300,000	$150,000	$300,000	$600,000

	First Quarter	Second Quarter	Third Quarter	Fourth Quarter
Units in ending inventory	4,000	2,000	4,000	8,000
Standard variable cost per unit.	× $60	× $60	× $60	× $60
Cost of ending inventory under direct costing	$240,000	$120,000	$240,000	$480,000

	First Quarter	Second Quarter	Third Quarter	Fourth Quarter
Cost of ending inventory under absorption costing...........................	$300,000	$150,000	$300,000	$600,000
Cost of ending inventory under direct costing...........................	240,000	120,000	240,000	480,000
Difference	$ 60,000	$ 30,000	$ 60,000	$120,000

These differences occur because fixed factory overhead is included in inventory in absorption costing but excluded in direct costing. In absorption costing, fixed factory overhead becomes a part of the predetermined factory overhead rate and, therefore, becomes a part of the product's cost. In direct costing, fixed factory overhead is charged to period expense and does not become a part of the product's cost.

Operating Profits. The inclusion or exclusion of fixed cost from inventories and the cost of goods sold causes the gross profit to vary considerably from the gross contribution margin. The gross contribution margin (sales less variable manufacturing cost) is greater than the gross profit in absorption costing. This difference has also resulted in some criticism of direct costing. Some opponents argue that a greater gross contribution margin might mislead marketing personnel about product profitability, thereby resulting in requests for lower product prices and demands for higher bonuses or benefits. In most cases, however, sales prices and bonuses are based not on gross profit but on operating income.

The income statements on pages 644 and 645 also show differences in operating income. These differences are the result of charging fixed factory overhead to inventory under the absorption costing method but expensing it under direct costing. These differences are summarized and reconciled as follows:

	First Quarter	Second Quarter	Third Quarter	Fourth Quarter
Operating income under absorption costing...........................	$185,000	$ 161,000	$146,000	$173,000
Operating income under direct costing ..	185,000	191,000	116,000	113,000
Difference	$ 0	$ (30,000)	$ 30,000	$ 60,000
Inventory change under absorption costing:				
Ending inventory	$300,000	$ 150,000	$300,000	$600,000
Beginning inventory..............	300,000	300,000	150,000	300,000
Increase (decrease)..............	$ 0	$(150,000)	$150,000	$300,000
Inventory change under direct costing:				
Ending inventory	$240,000	$ 120,000	$240,000	$480,000
Beginning inventory..............	240,000	240,000	120,000	240,000
Increase (decrease)..............	$ 0	$(120,000)	$120,000	$240,000
Difference	$ 0	$ (30,000)	$ 30,000	$ 60,000

Since standard costing is used in this illustration, the differences in operating income determined under absorption costing and direct costing may be computed by multiplying the difference between the quantity produced and the quantity sold for each quarter by the fixed portion of the factory overhead rate used in absorption costing, as follows:

	First Quarter	Second Quarter	Third Quarter	Fourth Quarter
Units produced	20,000	18,000	20,000	22,000
Units sold	20,000	20,000	18,000	18,000
Unit change in inventories, increase (decrease)	0	(2,000)	2,000	4,000
Fixed factory overhead rate under absorption costing	× $15	× $15	× $15	× $15
Difference in operating income	$ 0	$(30,000)	$30,000	$60,000

The amount of fixed cost charged to inventory is affected not only by the quantities produced and sold but also by the inventory costing method employed—a fact that frequently is overlooked. In the illustrations presented above, the operating profit is larger in absorption costing than in direct costing when the quantity produced exceeds the quantity sold (third and fourth quarters). Conversely, the operating profit is smaller in absorption costing than in direct costing when the quantity produced is less than the quantity sold (second quarter). These relationships hold only for the standard costing method when the standard cost does not change between periods (as in the illustration) and for the lifo inventory method. Under the fifo and the average costing methods, the results may differ from those demonstrated, depending upon the magnitude and the direction of the changes in costs.[2]

The inventory change in this illustration is for finished goods only. If there were work in process inventories, they too would be included in the inventory change in order to reconcile the difference in operating income. Also, any volume variances (i.e., over- or underapplied fixed factory overhead) deferred on the balance sheet, rather than being expensed currently, would be a reconciling item in explaining the difference in operating income.

The operating income will be the same in each method when no inventories exist or, as demonstrated in the first quarter of the illustration, when no change in the total cost assigned to inventory occurs from the beginning to the end of the period. Although the illustrations of direct costing and absorption costing are prepared on a quarterly basis, they are equally representative of statements prepared on a monthly or an annual basis.

As previously explained, many managers favor direct costing because there is a direct correspondence between sales figures and cost figures. The variable cost of goods sold varies directly with sales volume, and the influence of production volume on profit is eliminated. The idea of "selling overhead to inventories" might sound plausible and appear pleasing at first; but when the prior period's inventories become this period's beginning inventories, the apparent advantages cancel out. The results of the third and fourth quarters with absorption costing offer good examples of the effects of large production with current period cost being deferred in inventories to be charged against income in a future period. The absorption costing income statement also demonstrates the effect of expensing the volume variance (i.e.,

[2]Yuri Ijiri, Robert K. Jaedicke, and John L. Livingstone, "The Effect of Inventory Costing Methods on Full and Direct Costing," *Journal of Accounting Research*, Vol. 3, No. 1, pp. 63-74.

the over- or underapplied fixed factory overhead resulting from fluctuations in production volume).

Financial Reporting. The use of direct costing for financial reporting is not accepted by the accounting profession as a generally accepted accounting principle. In addition, the Securities and Exchange Commission refuses to accept financial reports prepared on the basis of direct costing, and the Internal Revenue Service will not permit the computation of taxable income on the direct costing basis. The position of these groups generally is based on their opposition to excluding fixed costs from inventories.

The Position of the Accounting Profession. The basis for the accounting profession's position on direct costing is Accounting Research Bulletin No. 43. The "Inventory Pricing" chapter begins by stressing that "a major objective of accounting for inventories is the proper determination of income through the process of matching appropriate costs against revenues."

The bulletin continues by stating that "the primary basis of accounting for inventories is cost, which has been defined generally as the price paid or consideration given to acquire an asset. As applied to inventories, cost means in principle the sum of the applicable expenditures and charges directly or indirectly incurred in bringing an article to its existing condition and location." In discussing the second point, the bulletin states quite emphatically that "it should also be recognized that the exclusion of all overheads from inventory costs does not constitute an accepted accounting procedure." This last statement seems to apply to direct costing. Proponents of direct costing might argue, however, that while the exclusion of all overhead is not acceptable, by inference the exclusion of some is acceptable. This argument might sound true, but it does not seem to have any bearing on the accounting profession's acceptance of direct costing, since in an earlier discussion of cost, the bulletin states that "under some circumstances, items such as idle facility expense, excessive spoilage, double freight, and rehandling costs may be so abnormal as to require treatment as current period charges rather than as a portion of the inventory cost." This appears to be the type of overhead that the bulletin recognizes as excludable from inventories.

The Position of the IRS. The Internal Revenue Service position is directed by Section 1.471-3(c) of the Regulations, which defines inventory cost in the case of merchandise produced to be: "(1) the cost of raw materials and supplies entering into or consumed in connection with the product, (2) expenditures for direct labor, and (3) indirect production costs incident to and necessary for the production of the particular article, including in such indirect production costs an appropriate portion of management expenses. . . ." Furthermore, Section 1.471-11(a) of the Regulations specifically requires the use of the full absorption method of inventory costing. As a result of the Tax Reform Act of 1986, Section 263A of the Internal Revenue Code requires the capitalization of the indirect as well as the direct costs incurred in the manufacture of products held for sale to customers.

The Position of the SEC. The SEC's refusal to accept annual financial reports prepared on the basis of direct costing generally is the result of (1) its policy to favor consistency among reporting companies as far as possible and (2) its attitude that direct costing is not generally accepted accounting procedure. In filing reports with the SEC, a firm that uses direct costing must adjust its inventories and reported income to what they would have been had absorption costing been used.

Adjustment of Direct Costing Figures for External Reporting Purposes. Companies using direct costing internally make adjustments in preparing income tax returns and external financial reports. In actual practice, comparatively simple procedures frequently are used to determine the amount of periodic adjustment necessary to convert inventories recorded on the direct costing basis to the absorption costing basis required for external reporting purposes. According to NAA Research Report No. 37, one company reported that fixed factory overhead for the period is divided by actual production to create a costing rate which is applied to the units in the ending inventory. Another company expresses these fixed expenses as a rate per dollar of variable expenses at normal volume. The dollar amount of variable expenses in the ending inventory is then multiplied by the foregoing rate to arrive at the fixed factory overhead component.[3] In both cases, the excess of the fixed factory overhead incurred during the period over the amount charged to the ending inventory is closed to the cost of goods sold, and the adjustment to the ending inventory is reversed at the beginning of the next accounting period.

■ COST-VOLUME-PROFIT ANALYSIS

Cost-volume-profit analysis is concerned with determining the sales volume and mix of products necessary to achieve a desired level of profit with available resources. It is an analytical tool that provides management with important information about the relationship between costs, profits, product mix, and sales volume. Cost-volume-profit analysis is based on the assumptions that all costs can be segregated into fixed and variable portions, that fixed costs are constant over the range of the analysis, and that variable costs are proportional to volume (i.e., that variable cost per unit is constant over the range of activity being analyzed).

Break-even analysis is used to determine the level of sales and the mix of products which are required to just recover all costs incurred during the period. The *break-even point* is the point at which cost and revenue are equal. There is neither a profit nor a loss at the break-even point. Since the objective of cost-volume-profit analysis is to determine the level of sales and the mix of products which are required to achieve a targeted level of profit, break-even

---

[3]*NAA Research Report, No. 37*, op. cit. pp. 94-95.

analysis may be thought of as a special case of cost-volume-profit analysis, i.e., the determination of the level of sales and the mix of products necessary to achieve a zero level of profit.

Although management typically plans for a profit each period, the break-even point is of concern. If sales fall below the break-even point, losses will be incurred. Management must determine the break-even point in order to compute the *margin of safety*, which indicates how much sales may decrease from the targeted level before the company will incur losses. The margin of safety is a criterion used to evaluate the adequacy of planned sales.

Break-even and cost-volume-profit analysis may be based on historical data, past operations, or projected sales and costs. However, data for break-even and cost-volume-profit analysis cannot be taken directly from the absorption or full costing income statement, because the effect of activity on costs cannot be readily determined. Each item of expense must be analyzed to determine its fixed and variable components. In contrast to the absorption or full costing income statement, the direct or variable costing income statement segregates fixed costs from variable costs and, therefore, is quite useful in break-even and cost-volume-profit analysis. The flexible budget and standard cost cards are also good sources of data because fixed and variable costs are segregated in both data sources. Consequently, the data available in each source can be used directly and without alteration for break-even and cost-volume-profit analysis.

Break-even and cost-volume-profit analysis is based on the following accounting relationship:

$$\text{Profit} = \text{Total Revenues} - (\text{Total Variable Costs} + \text{Total Fixed Costs})$$

which is equivalent to saying that:

$$\text{Total Revenues} = \text{Total Fixed Costs} + \text{Total Variable Costs} + \text{Profit}$$

Since total fixed cost and the variable cost per unit are assumed to remain constant within the range of activity being analyzed, the basic accounting relationship can be expressed in the form of a linear equation as follows:

$$R = F + (V \times R) + \pi$$

where: R = Total sales revenue
F = Total fixed cost
V = Variable cost per dollar of sales revenue
(i.e., total variable cost divided by total sales revenue)
π = Total profit

The objective of break-even and cost-volume-profit analysis is to determine the volume of sales and the mix of products required to achieve a targeted level of profit (zero profit in the case of break-even analysis). If only one product is produced, as assumed initially, the only unknown of concern is the volume of sales. The volume of sales can be measured in terms of sales revenue or in terms of units of product. To determine the required level of sales revenue, the equation above can be solved for R, as follows:

$$R = F + (V \times R) + \pi$$
$$R - (V \times R) = F + \pi$$
$$R(1 - V) = F + \pi$$
$$R = \frac{F + \pi}{1 - V} = \frac{\text{Total fixed cost} + \text{Profit}}{\text{Contribution margin per sales dollar}}$$

If profit were set equal to zero, the break-even point measured in sales revenue, R(BE), would be computed as follows:

Break Even Revenue

$$R(BE) = \frac{F}{1 - V} = \frac{\text{Total fixed cost}}{\text{Contribution margin per sales dollar}}$$

The contribution margin per sales dollar, also referred to as the *contribution margin ratio (C/M)*, is the portion of each sales dollar available to recover fixed costs and provide a profit. Below the break-even point, it is the portion of each sales dollar used to recover fixed cost. Above the break-even point, it is the portion of each sales dollar that provides an increase in profit. To illustrate the computation of the break-even point, assume that the following data are taken from the flexible budget of Northstar Company:

Total sales revenue at normal capacity	$6,000,000
Total fixed costs.	1,600,000
Total variable costs at normal capacity	3,600,000
Sales price per unit.	400
Variable costs per unit	240

The break-even point would be computed as follows:

$$R(BE) = \frac{F}{1 - V}$$

$$= \frac{\$1,600,000}{1 - (\$3,600,000 \div \$6,000,000)} \quad \text{or} \quad \frac{\$1,600,000}{1 - (\$240 \div \$400)}$$

$$= \frac{\$1,600,000}{.40}$$

$$= \$4,000,000$$

Once fixed costs have been recovered, the contribution margin from each additional dollar of sales revenue provides a profit. Consequently, if the sales revenue required to break even has already been computed, the sales revenue required to achieve a targeted level of profit can be determined by simply dividing the targeted profit by the contribution margin per sales dollar and adding the quotient to the sales revenue required to break even. For example, based on the data provided in the Northstar Company illustration, a targeted profit of $400,000 would require sales of $1,000,000 beyond the break-even point ($400,000 profit divided by $.40 contribution margin per dollar of sales). Therefore, total sales of $5,000,000 would be required to yield a profit of $400,000 ($4,000,000 of sales to break even plus $1,000,000 of sales beyond the break-even point). Alternatively, the required level of sales can be determined directly by adding the targeted level of profit to fixed costs and dividing the sum by the contribution margin per sales dollar, as indicated by the formula derived above and demonstrated at the top of page 652.

$$R = \frac{F + \pi}{1 - V}$$

$$= \frac{\$1,600,000 + \$400,000}{1 - (\$3,600,000 \div \$6,000,000)} \text{ or } \frac{\$1,600,000 + \$400,000}{1 - (\$240 \div \$400)}$$

$$= \frac{\$2,000,000}{.40}$$

$$= \$5,000,000$$

Since each unit sells for $400, the total quantity of product to be sold to break even would be 10,000 units ($4,000,000 break-even sales divided by $400 sales price per unit), and the total quantity to be sold to meet a targeted profit of $400,000 would be 12,500 units ($5,000,000 of sales divided by $400 sales price).

A units-of-product approach rather than the sales-revenue approach is sometimes taken in break-even and cost-volume-profit analyses. For some types of analyses, it is more expedient and convenient to work with units of product rather than sales revenue. Both approaches are conceptually the same. In the units-of-product approach, the basic equation is altered to include the quantity of product, the unit sales price, and the unit variable cost. Recall that the equation used in developing the sales-revenue approach to cost-volume-profit analysis on page 650 is:

$$R = F + (V \times R) + \pi$$

Since sales revenue, R, is equal to the unit sales price multiplied by the quantity of product sold, and total variable cost, $(V \times R)$, is equal to the variable cost per unit multiplied by the quantity of product sold, the equation above can be restated as follows:

$$P \times Q = F + (C \times Q) + \pi$$
where: P = Sales price per unit
Q = Quantity of product sold
F = Total fixed cost
C = Variable cost per unit
π = Total profit

The unknown in the modified equation is the quantity of product, Q. Solving for Q yields:

$$P \times Q = F + (C \times Q) + \pi$$
$$(P \times Q) - (C \times Q) = F + \pi$$
$$Q \times (P - C) = F + \pi$$
$$Q = \frac{F + \pi}{P - C}$$

If profit is set equal to zero, then the break-even point in units of product, Q(BE), would be:

$$Q(BE) = \frac{F}{P - C}$$

Based on the data provided in the Northstar Company illustration, the break-even point in units of product would be computed as follows:

$$Q(BE) = \frac{F}{P-C} = \frac{\$1,600,000}{\$400 - \$240} = \frac{\$1,600,000}{\$160} = 10,000 \text{ units}$$

A targeted profit of $400,000 would require sales of:

$$Q = \frac{F + \pi}{P - C}$$

$$= \frac{\$1,600,000 + \$400,000}{\$400 - \$240}$$

$$= \frac{\$2,000,000}{\$160}$$

$$= 12,500 \text{ units}$$

Constructing a Break-Even Chart

Break-even computations can be presented graphically on a break-even chart, where the cost line and the sales line intersect at the break-even point. The data needed to construct this chart are forecast sales and fixed and variable costs.

A conventional break-even chart for Northstar Company is illustrated as follows:

Break-Even Chart—Conventional

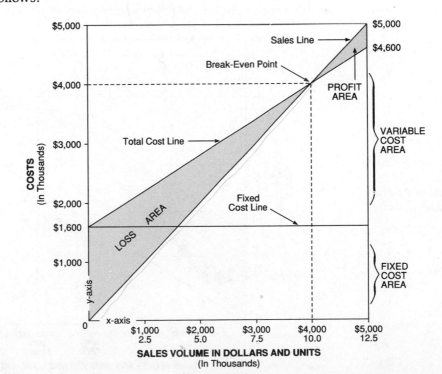

The conventional break-even chart is constructed as follows:

1. A horizontal base line, the x-axis, is drawn and spaced into equal distances to represent the sales volume in dollars or in number of units, or as a percentage of some specified volume.
2. A vertical line, the y-axis, is drawn at the extreme left and right sides of the chart. The y-axis at the left is spaced into equal parts and represents sales and costs in dollars.
3. A fixed cost line is drawn parallel to the x-axis at the $1,600,000 point of the y-axis.
4. A total cost line is drawn from the $1,600,000 fixed cost point on the left y-axis to the $4,600,000 cost point on the right y-axis.
5. The sales line is drawn from the 0 point on the left side of the graph (the intersection of the x-axis and y-axis) to the $5,000,000 point on the right y-axis.
6. The total cost line intersects the sales line at the break-even point, representing $4,000,000 sales or 10,000 units of sales.
7. The shaded area to the left of the break-even point is the loss area, while the shaded area to the right is the profit area.

In the conventional break-even chart, the fixed cost line is parallel to the x-axis and variable cost is plotted above the fixed cost. Such a chart emphasizes fixed cost at a definite amount for various levels of activity. Many analysts, however, prefer an alternative form of chart, in which the variable cost is drawn first and fixed cost is plotted above the variable cost line. An example of this type of chart is as follows, using Northstar Company data:

Break-Even Chart with Fixed Cost Plotted Above Variable Cost

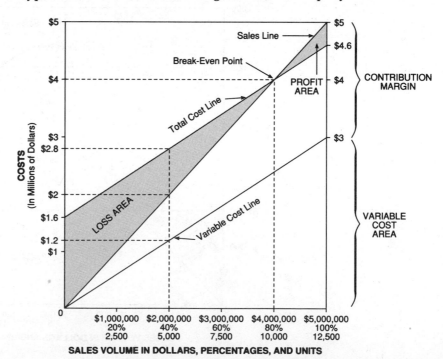

The space between the variable cost line and the sales line represents the contribution margin. Where the total cost line intersects the sales line, the break-even point has been reached. The space between the sales line and the total cost line beyond the break-even point represents the profit for the period at any volume. The space between the total cost line and the sales line to the left of the break-even point indicates the fixed costs not yet recovered by the contribution margin and is the loss for the period at any volume below the break-even point.

This alternative break-even chart indicates the recovery of fixed costs at various percentages of capacity and at various levels of dollar sales or unit sales. If sales, for example, drop to $2,000,000, variable costs would be $1,200,000 (60 percent of $2,000,000) while fixed costs remain at $1,600,000. The loss at this point would be $800,000 ($2,000,000 − ($1,200,000 + $1,600,000)). The chart shows $2,000,000 on the sales line to be $800,000 below the total cost line. In columnar form, the analysis can be illustrated as follows:

(1) Number of Units	(2) Sales	(3) Variable Cost	(4) Contribution Margin (2)–(3)	(5) Fixed Cost	(6) Profit (Loss) (4)–(5)
2,500	$1,000,000	$ 600,000	$ 400,000	$1,600,000	$(1,200,000)
5,000	2,000,000	1,200,000	800,000	1,600,000	(800,000)
7,500	3,000,000	1,800,000	1,200,000	1,600,000	(400,000)
10,000	4,000,000	2,400,000	1,600,000	1,600,000	None
12,500	5,000,000	3,000,000	2,000,000	1,600,000	400,000

A break-even chart can be constructed in even greater detail by breaking down fixed and variable costs into subclassifications. Variable expenses, for example, may be classified as direct materials, direct labor, variable factory overhead, and variable marketing and administrative expenses. Fixed expenses may be divided in a similar manner, showing fixed factory overhead and fixed marketing and administrative expenses separately. Even the profit wedge might be subdivided to indicate application of the profit to income tax, interest and dividend payments, and retained earnings. Such a chart is illustrated at the top of page 656.

Break-Even and Cost-Volume-Profit Analysis for Decision Making

The accounting data involved, the assumptions made, the manner in which the information is obtained, and the way the data are expressed are limitations that must be considered in connection with the results of cost-volume-profit analysis. The break-even chart is fundamentally a static analysis. In most cases, changes can only be shown by drawing a new chart or a series of charts. The concept of relevant range as discussed in Chapter 12 is applicable. That is, the amount of fixed and variable costs, as well as the slope of the sales line, is meaningful only in a defined range of activity and

**Break-Even Chart
with Detailed Fixed
and Variable Costs**

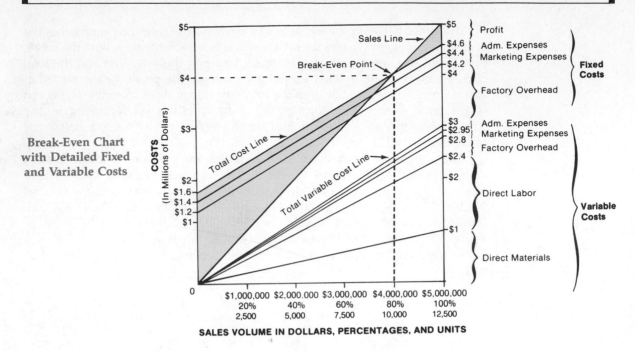

must be redefined for activity outside the relevant range. Furthermore, costs and revenue are assumed to be linear with respect to activity.[4]

Despite its limitations, cost-volume-profit analysis offers wide application for testing proposed actions, for considering alternatives, or for other decision-making purposes. For example, the technique permits determination of the effect on profit of a shift in fixed and/or variable expenses when old machinery is replaced by new equipment. Firms with multiple plants, products, and sales territories may prepare charts which show the effects of the shift in sales quantities, sales prices, and sales efforts. With such information, management is able to direct the firm's operations into the most profitable channels. For a company with numerous divisions, the analysis is particularly valuable in determining the influence on profits of an increase in divisional fixed cost. If, for example, a company's overall contribution margin ratio is 25 percent, a division manager should realize that for every $1 of proposed increase in fixed cost, sales revenue must increase by no less than $4 if the existing profit position is to be maintained ($1 ÷ 25% = $4).

In using cost-volume-profit analysis, management should understand that:

1. A change in per unit variable cost changes the contribution margin ratio and the break-even point.
2. A change in sales price changes the contribution margin ratio and the break-even point.

---

[4]Calculus can be employed in dealing with nonlinear functions. See Travis P. Goggans, "Break-Even Analysis with Curvilinear Functions," *The Accounting Review,* Vol. XL, No. 4, pp. 867-871.

3. A change in fixed cost changes the break-even point but not the contribution margin ratio.
4. A combined change in fixed and variable costs in the same direction causes an extremely sharp change in the break-even point.

Changes in Fixed Cost. If Northstar Company management were able to reduce fixed expense to $1,450,000, the break-even point would be $3,625,000 ($1,450,000 ÷ .40). If sales remained at the $5,000,000 figure, the profit would increase from $400,000 to $550,000, and the break-even point would be 72.5 percent of sales instead of 80 percent. The change in the break-even point resulting from a reduction in fixed cost is shown by the broken lines in the chart below.

The effects of changes in the per unit variable cost or in the unit sales price could also be charted. Thus a dynamic dimension could be added to the analysis.

Break-Even Chart with a Reduction in Fixed Cost

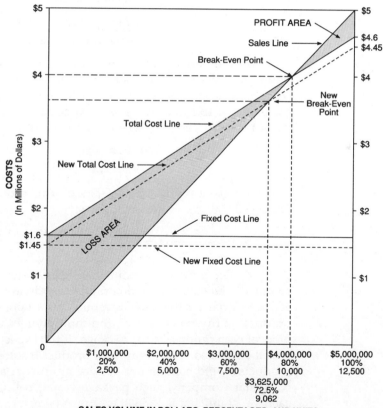

SALES VOLUME IN DOLLARS, PERCENTAGES, AND UNITS

Multiple Products and Shifts in the Sales Mix. When firms produce more than one product, the variable costs per dollar of sales revenue may be different for different products. In such cases, the contribution margin ratio would be different for different sales mixes. As a consequence, the break-even point and the level of sales required to achieve targeted profit levels would be different for different mixes of products. The mathematical computations in the multiple-product case are essentially the same as those in the single-product case, except that the analyst must remember that the results are valid only for the sales mix used in the analysis. If the sales mix is expected to change, the results should be recomputed for the new mix.

To illustrate the computations in a multiple-product case, assume that Northstar Company expects the following product mix to be sold in the coming period:

Product	Unit Sales Price	Variable Cost per Unit	Expected Sales Mix
A	$180	$100	1
B	110	70	2

If the product mix is expected to remain constant at all levels of sales, the variable cost per dollar of sales revenue would be determined as follows:

$$V = \frac{\text{Variable cost}}{\text{Sales revenue}} = \frac{\$100 + (2 \times \$70)}{\$180 + (2 \times \$110)} = \frac{\$240}{\$400} = .60$$

Once the variable cost per dollar of sales is computed, the break-even point and the sales revenue required to achieve a targeted level of profit are computed in the same manner as in the single-product case. To illustrate, assume that fixed costs are still expected to be $1,600,000. The break-even point measured in sales revenue would be:

$$R(BE) = \frac{F}{1-V} = \frac{\$1,600,000}{1-.60} = \frac{\$1,600,000}{.40} = \$4,000,000$$

To achieve a profit of $400,000 with this product mix, sales revenue must be $5,000,000, computed as follows:

$$R = \frac{F + \pi}{1-V} = \frac{\$1,600,000 + \$400,000}{1-.60} = \frac{\$2,000,000}{.40} = \$5,000,000$$

Once the break-even point has been determined, the quantity of each product to be sold can be determined by dividing the sales revenue required to break even by the sales revenue of a hypothetical package of the firm's products at the expected mix and multiplying the quotient by the number of units of each product in the package. If the expectation is that 1 unit of product A will be sold for every 2 units of product B sold, the hypothetical package of products would contain one unit of product A and 2 units of product B. For Northstar Company, each package would sell for $400 ((l unit of A × $180 each) + (2 units of B × $110 each)). As a result, the quantity of each product to be sold to break even with this sales mix can be determined as follows:

$$Q(BE) = \frac{R(BE)}{\$400} = \frac{\$4,000,000}{\$400} = 10,000 \text{ hypothetical packages}$$

10,000 packages × 1 unit of A per package = 10,000 units of A
10,000 packages × 2 units of B per package = 20,000 units of B

The quantity of each product to be sold at this mix to achieve sales revenue of $5,000,000 and a profit of $400,000 would be determined as follows:

$$Q = \frac{R}{\$400} = \frac{\$5,000,000}{\$400} = 12,500 \text{ hypothetical packages}$$

12,500 packages × 1 unit of A per package = 12,500 units of A
12,500 packages × 2 units of B per package = 25,000 units of B

Alternatively, the quantity of hypothetical packages to be sold to break even or achieve a targeted level of profit can be computed directly using the units-of-product approach. In this case, the unit used in the formula presented on page 653 is the hypothetical package of the firm's products. For Northstar Company, the break-even point in hypothetical packages of product containing 1 unit of product A and 2 units of product B would be determined as follows:

Sales revenue per package = (1 unit of A × $180 each) + (2 units of B × $110 each) = $400

Variable cost per package = (1 unit of A × $100 each) + (2 units of B × $70 each) = $240

$$Q(BE) = \frac{F}{P-C} = \frac{\$1,600,000}{\$400 - \$240} = \frac{\$1,600,000}{\$160} = 10,000 \text{ packages}$$

The units of each product required to break even would then be computed by multiplying the number of hypothetical packages by the number of units of each product in the hypothetical package, as follows:

10,000 packages × 1 unit of A per package = 10,000 units of A
10,000 packages × 2 units of B per package = 20,000 units of B

The number of hypothetical packages required to achieve a targeted profit of $400,000 would be:

$$Q = \frac{F + \pi}{P-C} = \frac{\$1,600,000 + \$400,000}{\$400 - \$240} = \frac{\$2,000,000}{\$160} = 12,500 \text{ packages}$$

The number of units of each product would be:

12,500 packages × 1 unit of A per package = 12,500 units of A
12,500 packages × 2 units of B per package = 25,000 units of B

In this multiple-product case, the break-even point and the sales revenue required to achieve a targeted level of profit would be different for a different product mix because the variable cost and the contribution margin per dollar of sales would be different. For example, if the expected sales mix were 1 unit of product A for every 3 units of product B, the variable cost per dollar of sales would change from $.60 to $.607843, determined as follows:

$$V = \frac{\text{Variable cost}}{\text{Sales revenue}} = \frac{\$100 + (3 \times \$70)}{\$180 + (3 \times \$110)} = \frac{\$310}{\$510} = \$.607843$$

The increase in variable cost per dollar of sales revenue would result in a decline in contribution margin per dollar of sales revenue and an increase in the sales revenue required to break even. The sales revenue required to break even would increase from \$4,000,000 to \$4,080,000, determined as follows:

$$R(BE) = \frac{F}{1-V} = \frac{\$1,600,000}{1-.607843} = \frac{\$1,600,000}{.392157} = \$4,080,000$$

As a result of this change in sales mix, the quantity of each product that must be sold to break even also changes. The number of hypothetical packages required to break even would be determined as follows:

$$Q(BE) = \frac{R(BE)}{\$510} = \frac{\$4,080,000}{\$510} = 8,000 \text{ hypothetical packages}$$

or equivalently:

$$Q(BE) = \frac{F}{P-C} = \frac{\$1,600,000}{\$510-\$310} = \frac{\$1,600,000}{\$200} = 8,000 \text{ hypothetical packages}$$

The number of units of each product that must be sold to break even with this mix would be:

8,000 packages × 1 unit of A per package =   8,000 units of A
8,000 packages × 3 units of B per package = 24,000 units of B

A change in the mix of products sold can have a material effect on not only the break-even point but also profitability. Based on a sales mix of 1 unit of product A to 2 units of product B, Northstar Company should have a \$400,000 profit if it can generate sales revenue of \$5,000,000. However, if the actual sales mix is 1 unit of product A to 3 units of product B, sales revenue of approximately \$5,000,000 will result in only \$360,800 of profit, determined as follows:

Sales: Product A (9,804 units @ \$180).....................	\$1,764,720	
Product B (29,412 units @ \$110)....................	3,235,320	\$5,000,040
Less variable cost of goods sold:		
Product A (9,804 units @ \$100).....................	\$ 980,400	
Product B (29,412 units @ \$70)....................	2,058,840	3,039,240
Contribution margin......................................		\$1,960,800
Less fixed costs..		1,600,000
Operating income.......................................		\$ 360,800

Because of uncertainty in the market place, this sort of situation is not uncommon. It illustrates the desirability of considering alternative sales mixes in break-even and cost-volume-profit analysis. One way to overcome this difficulty is to prepare a separate analysis for each product. However, if arbitrarily allocated common or joint costs are included in the analysis, the results are of limited value. Another approach is to evaluate the sensitivity of the results of the targeted, or most probable, sales mix by preparing a separate analysis for each of several possible alternative sales mixes and comparing the results. This approach makes it possible for management to identify an acceptable range of profit.

The Unit Profit Graph. A break-even chart generally is prepared on the basis of total revenue and expense. These dollar sales and expense figures can be translated into a profit-per-unit graph in order to show more vividly the influence of fixed cost on the product unit cost. Assume, for example, the following: normal capacity, 100 percent; total sales, $50,000 (500 units @ $100); variable cost, $30,000; fixed cost, $15,000; profit, $5,000. The break-even point is $37,500 ($15,000 ÷ .40) or 75 percent of normal capacity ($37,500 ÷ $50,000). The variable cost is $60 per unit, and the fixed cost is $30 per unit if 500 units are made and sold. As volume decreases, the fixed cost per unit increases. This relationship is illustrated in the graph below.

The effect of varying volume on the fixed cost per unit also can be expressed as follows:

	Units					
	100	200	300	375	400	500
Variable unit cost	$ 60	$ 60	$ 60	$ 60	$ 60.00	$ 60
Fixed unit cost	150	75	50	40	37.50	30
Total unit cost	$ 210	$135	$110	$100	$ 97.50	$ 90
Unit sales price	100	100	100	100	100.00	100
Profit (loss) per unit	$(110)	$ (35)	$ (10)	Break even	$ 2.50	$ 10

Unit Profit Graph Showing the Influence of Fixed and Variable Costs on Unit Cost

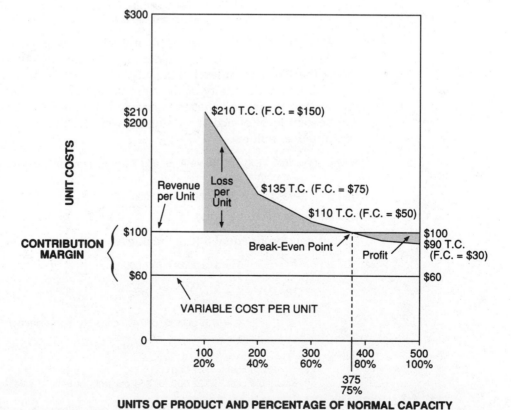

The analysis illustrated in the unit profit graph and in the tabular presentation, together with a break-even analysis, are important tools in determining which unit cost(s) should be used in setting sales prices. A break-even chart will help in understanding the effect on total profits when sales prices and fixed and variable costs are related to sales volume.

Unit Cost Formulas. The unit profit graph and the tabular presentation show a total unit cost that varies from a high of $210 per unit to a low of $90 per unit. To obtain a true comparison, unit costs must be computed at all levels of activity. When unit costs of various products are compared, the analyst must observe the production rates of each product, each of which may be at a different level.

Formulas can aid in determining the effect of changing costs or level of activity. For example, the following formula can be used to determine unit costs under conditions of fluctuating activity levels:

$$\text{Unit cost} = \frac{A + BX}{CX}$$

Where: A = total fixed cost
B = total variable cost at normal capacity
C = units of production at normal capacity
X = level of activity, expressed as a percentage
of normal capacity

Using figures from the example introduced on page 661, the total cost of $45,000 ($15,000 + $30,000) divided by total units (500) gives a unit cost of $90 at the 100 percent level of activity.

To illustrate the utility of the formula, assume that the fixed expense increases to $17,000 and that the variable expense decreases to $27,000 at the 100-percent level of activity. Using these facts, the new break-even point is computed as follows:

New profit = (SX – BX) – A, where A, B, and X are as previously defined and S = total sales
at normal capacity

New profit = ($50,000X – $27,000X) – $17,000

New profit = $23,000X – $17,000

Let new profit equal 0 (the break-even point) and solve for X:

$$0 = \$23,000X – \$17,000$$

$$X = \frac{\$17,000}{\$23,000}$$

$$X = .739 \times 100, \text{ or } 74\% \text{ capacity (approximate)}$$

(or)

Fixed cost = $17,000
Variable cost = $27,000, or $54 per unit, or 54% of sales

$$\frac{\$17,000}{1 – .54} = \frac{\$17,000}{.46} = \$37,000, \text{ or } 74\% \text{ capacity, or } 370 \text{ units}$$

The unit cost at the new break-even point can then be computed as follows:

$$\text{Unit cost} = \frac{A + BX}{CX}$$

$$= \frac{\$17,000 + \$27,000(.74)}{500(.74)}$$

$$= \frac{\$17,000 + \$19,980}{370}$$

$$= \$100 \text{ (approximate)}$$

Assuming the same changes in the fixed and variable expenses, the unit cost at 90 percent of capacity would be determined as follows:

$$\text{Unit cost} = \frac{\$17,000 + \$27,000(.90)}{500(.90)}$$

$$= \frac{\$17,000 + \$24,300}{450}$$

$$= \$92 \text{ (approximate)}$$

The above equations permit the development of unit costs using data included in the budget. They further permit quick and easy computations in connection with problems raised by changing conditions. Budget data expressed in equation form permit quicker analysis of the effects of a variety of changes on unit costs.

Margin of Safety. Information developed from a break-even and cost-volume-profit analysis offers additional useful control data such as the *margin of safety,* which indicates how much sales may decrease from a selected sales figure before the company will break even, i.e., before the company will begin to suffer a loss. From the Northstar Company illustration on page 651, where sales are $5,000,000, the margin of safety is $1,000,000 ($5,000,000 – $4,000,000). The margin of safety expressed as a percentage of sales is called the *margin of safety ratio (M/S)* and is computed as follows:

$$\text{Margin of safety ratio (M/S)} = \frac{\text{Selected sales figure} - \text{Break-even sales}}{\text{Selected sales figure}}$$

$$= \frac{\$5,000,000 - \$4,000,000}{\$5,000,000}$$

$$= 20\%$$

Observe that the margin of safety and the margin of safety ratio would be negative if the break-even sales exceed the selected sales figure.

The margin of safety is directly related to profit. Using the same illustration from page 651, with a contribution margin ratio of 40 percent and a margin of safety ratio of 20 percent, then:

$$\text{Profit ratio} = \text{Contribution margin ratio} \times \text{Margin of safety ratio}$$
$$\text{PR} = \text{C/M} \times \text{M/S}$$
$$= 40\% \times 20\%$$
$$= 8\%$$

This computation indicates that of the margin of safety dollars, i.e., the sales above the break-even point, the contribution margin ratio portion is available for profit. Thus, 8 percent (40 percent of 20 percent) is the profit ratio, i.e., the percentage of the total selected sales figure that is profit.

$$\begin{aligned} \text{Profit} &= \text{Margin of safety dollars} \times \text{Contribution margin ratio} \\ &= \$1{,}000{,}000 \times 40\% \\ &= \$400{,}000 \end{aligned}$$

and

$$\begin{aligned} \text{Profit} &= \text{Selected sales figure} \times \text{Profit ratio} \\ &= \$5{,}000{,}000 \times 8\% \\ &= \$400{,}000 \end{aligned}$$

If the contribution margin ratio and the profit ratio are known, the margin of safety ratio is:

$$\text{M/S} = \frac{\text{PR}}{\text{C/M}} = \frac{8\%}{40\%} = 20\%$$

The Profit-Volume Analysis Graph

Break-even analysis and cost-volume-profit analysis also employ the *profit-volume (P/V) analysis graph*, which relates profit to volume. Using the figures from the illustration on page 651, a P/V analysis graph is illustrated below.

Profit-Volume
Analysis Graph

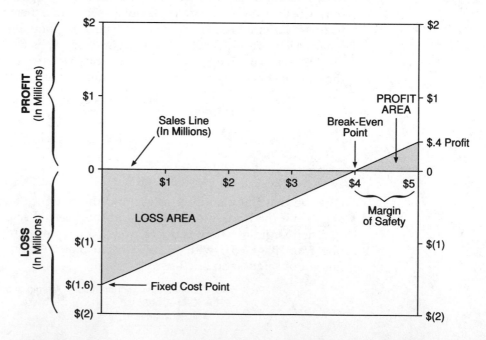

The P/V analysis graph is constructed as follows:

1. The graph is divided into two parts by the sales line.
2. The total fixed cost is marked off below the sales line on the left-hand vertical line. The computed profit or loss figure is located by moving horizontally to the point representing assumed sales dollars, then moving vertically to the point representing the computed profit or loss.
3. Fixed cost and profit points are joined by a diagonal line which crosses the sales line at the break-even point.

When management is considering various courses of action, a tabular report can present the possible results. For example, the effect of possible sales price increases and decreases for a product are shown in the following report:

| | Decrease | | Normal | Increase | |
	20%	10%	Volume	10%	20%
Units	200,000	200,000	200,000	200,000	200,000
Sales	$320,000	$360,000	$400,000	$440,000	$480,000
Variable cost	200,000	200,000	200,000	200,000	200,000
Contribution margin	$120,000	$160,000	$200,000	$240,000	$280,000
Fixed cost	160,000	160,000	160,000	160,000	160,000
Profit	–	0	$ 40,000	$ 80,000	$120,000
Loss....................	$ 40,000	0	–	–	–
Profit per unit	–	–	$.20	$.40	$.60
Loss per unit.............	$.20	–	–	–	–
% change in profit	–200%	–100%	–	+100%	+200%
Return on investment of $200,000	–20%	0%	20%	40%	60%
Break-even point..........	$426,667	$360,000	$320,000	$293,333	$274,286

In this illustration, a 10 percent drop in price reduces the profit to the break-even point, and a 20 percent drop in price causes a $40,000 loss. However, the 10 percent and 20 percent price increases cause profit to increase $40,000 and $80,000, respectively. These effects are indicated more effectively, however, in a P/V analysis graph, as follows:

P/V Analysis Graph Illustrating the Effect of Possible Sales Price Changes on Profit

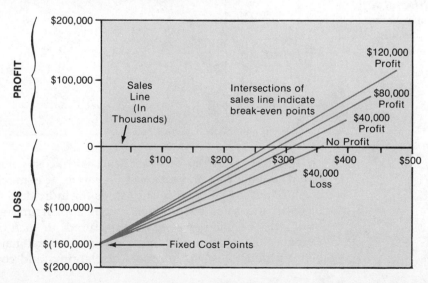

As another example of the use of a P/V analysis graph, assume that a company's management has the following plans regarding sales, costs, volume, and profit:

Plan 1		Plan 2	
Decrease in price	10%	Increase in price	10%
Increase in volume	12%	Decrease in volume........	12%
Variable cost increase	4%	Variable cost decrease	4%
Fixed cost increase........	5%	Fixed cost decrease........	5%

The effect of these plans is summarized as follows:

	Plan 1	Normal Volume	Plan 2
Units.............................	224,000	200,000	176,000
Sales..............................	$403,200	$400,000	$387,200
Variable cost......................	232,960	200,000	168,960
Contribution margin	$170,240	$200,000	$218,240
Fixed cost........................	168,000	160,000	152,000
Profit............................	$ 2,240	$ 40,000	$ 66,240
Profit per unit	$.01	$.20	$.3763
% change in profit	−94.4%		+ 65.6%
Return on investment of $200,000	1.12%	20%	33.1%
Break-even point	$397,895	$320,000	$269,677

The following graph, based on the summary data, is a composite, highly informative P/V analysis graph:

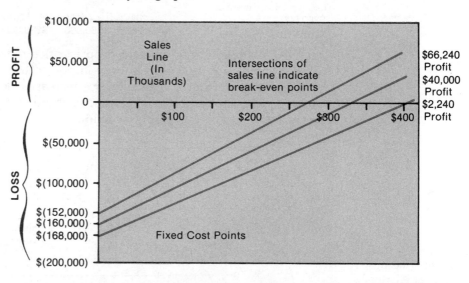

P/V Analysis Graph
Illustrating the
Effect of All
Profit-Volume
Factors

The discussion so far has dealt with cost-volume-profit relationships based on total cost and total sales revenue. It is much more desirable, however, to investigate these relationships for individual products. A breakdown of costs and sales by products might appear impractical, especially when hundreds of small items are manufactured. In such instances, it is advisable to reduce the large number of products to several major lines. To determine a better product cost for purposes of planning and control, many firms have departmentalized their sprawling factory output. With such departmentalization, the contribution that each product or product group makes to the total contribution margin can be gauged more satisfactorily.

Variable costs used in previous illustrations are a composite of the variable costs of the several manufacturing cost centers, the marketing departments, and administrative divisions. However, it is possible to determine the variable cost of each product line because:

1. Direct materials and direct labor costs can be based on standard costs.
2. Variable factory overhead can be based on normal production hours, labor cost, or machine hours established for the cost centers of the plant. The flexible budget for each cost center serves as an excellent basis for the determination of product factory overhead.
3. Variable marketing and administrative expenses can be charged directly to products or allocated on the basis of the sales value of each product or gross profit return or other bases discussed in Chapter 24. Of course, allocations of either nonmanufacturing or manufacturing costs are arbitrary, a limitation that should not be overlooked.

Once the sales value and the variable cost of each product have been determined, it will be apparent that each product has a different contribution margin and a C/M ratio. To illustrate cost-volume-profit analysis by products, the figures of the Normal Volume column of the summary on page 666 are divided between four products, resulting in the following data:

Product	Sales Value of Production	Variable Cost	% of Variable Cost to Sales	Contribution Margin	C/M Ratio
A	$120,000	$100,000	83%	$ 20,000	17%
B	140,000	60,000	43	80,000	57
C	90,000	30,000	33	60,000	67
D	50,000	10,000	20	40,000	80
Total	$400,000	$200,000	50	$200,000	50

Less fixed cost.   160,000

Profit. . . . . $ 40,000

$$\text{Break-even point} = \frac{\$160,000}{.50} = \$320,000$$

The contribution margin and C/M ratio are shown for each product and in total. The C/M ratio varies from 17 percent for Product A to 80 percent for Product D. If the present sales mix can be altered or if sales can be expanded, products with higher C/M ratios afford greater relative contributions to profit per dollar of sales. But the product's C/M ratio, sales dollars, and contribution margin must be related to facility utilization. The product offering the higher C/M ratio is desirable only if the resulting contribution margin (C/M ratio × sales dollars) is greater than could be achieved by some alternative use of the same limited facilities. If unused or idle facilities are available, perhaps both alternatives can be pursued profitably.

The following P/V analysis graph indicates the profit path for each product, A, B, C, and D:

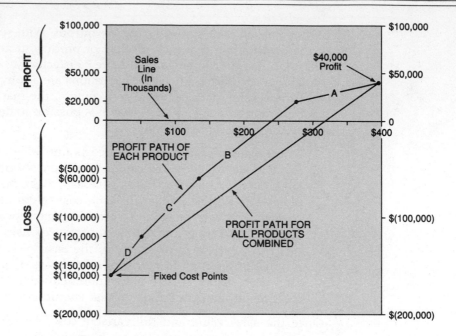

This P/V analysis graph is constructed as follows:

1. The horizontal line 00 represents sales and is marked off from zero to $400,000.
2. The profit path for all products combined is then drawn, starting at the $(160,000) fixed cost point in the loss area and ending at the $40,000 profit point in the profit area. The break-even point is at the point of crossover from the loss to the profit area.
3. The profit path of each product is plotted next. It starts with the product with the highest C/M ratio, Product D. The line begins at the total fixed cost point and is drawn to the $(120,000) point in the loss area directly below the $50,000 sales volume point. The plotting indicates that $40,000 of the $160,000 fixed cost has been recovered.
4. The profit path of Product C starts at the point where D's path ended. The line for Product C ends opposite the loss figure of $(60,000) and below the sales volume figure of $140,000. The $(60,000) figure shows that $60,000 additional fixed cost was recovered. The $140,000 point on the sales line is the accumulated sales total of Products D and C ($50,000 + $90,000).
5. The profit path for Product B begins at the end of C's path and leads across the sales line into the profit area to the $20,000 profit point immediately above the sales volume figure of $280,000.
6. Product A with the lowest C/M ratio is charted last. It adds $20,000 to the profit, and its path ends at the $40,000 profit figure.

The plotting of the profit path of each product provides management with an interesting pictorial report—the steeper the slope, the higher the C/M ratio. If any product did not have a contribution margin, its path or slope would be downward. Also, the dollar amount of each product's contribution margin can be read from the graph by measuring the vertical distance from one plotted point to the next. Similar graphs can be prepared for the analysis of sales by territories, salespersons, and classes of customers. It is then possible to portray the profitability of territories, the effectiveness of salespersons' selling activities, and the type of customers whose purchases mean greatest profit to the company. In this way, sales effort is measured by marginal contributions toward fixed cost and profit—and not by sales volume.

DISCUSSION QUESTIONS

Q20-1. Differentiate between direct costs and direct costing.

Q20-2. Distinguish between product and period costs and relate this distinction to direct costing.

Q20-3. Describe the difference between direct costing and the current generally accepted method of costing inventory for external reporting.

Q20-4. What is the theoretical justification for excluding fixed manufacturing costs from inventories in direct costing?

Q20-5. What would be the rationale for using the direct costing method for internal reporting?   (AICPA adapted)

Q20-6. List the arguments for the use of direct costing.

Q20-7. List the arguments against the use of direct costing.

Q20-8. Assuming that the quantity of ending inventory is larger than the quantity of beginning inventory and that the lifo method is being used, would operating income using direct costing be different from operating income using absorption costing? If so, specify whether operating income would be larger or smaller and explain the rationale for your answer.
                    (AICPA adapted)

Q20-9. What is the break-even point?

Q20-10. What is the contribution margin?

Q20-11. Give the formulas commonly used by firms with a single product to determine the break-even point (a) in dollars of sales revenue and (b) in units of product.

Q20-12. Identify the numbered components of the following break-even chart:

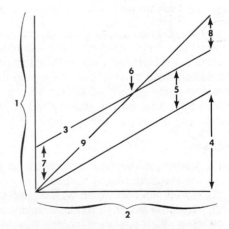

Q20-13. Discuss the significance of the concept of the relevant range to break-even analysis.

Q20-14. Discuss weaknesses inherent in the preparation and uses of break-even analysis.

Q20-15. How does the break-even point move when changes occur in (a) variable cost? (b) fixed cost?

Q20-16. The break-even chart and the unit profit graph intend to show the same information but seem to differ. How?

Q20-17. What is the margin of safety?

Q20-18. What is meant by the term "cost-volume-profit relationship?" Why is

this relationship important in business management?

Q20-19. Why is a cost-volume-profit analysis by products valuable to management?

Q20-20. Describe how the contribution of each product to the recovery of fixed expense and to the total profit of a company can be presented in graphic form.

EXERCISES

E20-1. Operating income using direct costing. Dayton Manufacturing Company began its operations on January 1, 19A, and produces a single product that sells for $12 per unit. During 19A, 100,000 units of the product were produced, 90,000 of which were sold. There was no work in process inventory at the end of the year.

Manufacturing costs and marketing and administrative expenses for 19A were as follows:

	Fixed	Variable
Materials	—	$2.00 per unit produced
Direct labor	—	1.50 per unit produced
Factory overhead.................	$200,000	.50 per unit produced
Marketing and administrative	100,000	.20 per unit sold

Required: Prepare an operating income statement for 19A using direct costing.   (AICPA adapted)

E20-2. Absorption costing vs. direct costing. Murphy Products began operations on January 3 of the current year. Standard costs were established in early January assuming a normal production volume of 160,000 units. However, Murphy Products produced only 140,000 units of product and sold only 100,000 units at a selling price of $180 per unit during the current year. Variable costs totaled $7,000,000, of which 60% were manufacturing and 40% were selling. Fixed costs totaled $11,200,000, of which 50% were manufacturing and 50% were selling. Murphy had no raw materials or work in process inventories at the end of the year. Actual input prices per unit of product and actual input quantities per unit of product were equal to standard.

Required:

(1) Determine Murphy Products' cost of goods sold at standard cost, using full absorption costing (excluding standard cost variances).
(2) How much cost would be assigned to Murphy Products' ending inventory using direct costing?
(3) Compute Murphy Products' factory overhead volume variance for the year.
(4) How much operating income would Murphy Products have using direct costing?   (ICMA adapted)

E20-3. Income statements—absorption costing vs. direct costing. The following data pertain to April operations for Klinger Company:

Beginning inventory....................	3,000
Units sold...........................	9,000
Units produced	8,000
Sales price per unit....................	$30
Direct manufacturing cost per unit	$10

Fixed factory overhead—total	$40,000
Fixed factory overhead—per unit	$5
Commercial expense (all fixed)	$30,000

Required:

(1) Prepare an income statement using absorption costing.

(2) Prepare an income statement using direct costing.

(3) Provide computations explaining the difference in operating income between the two methods.

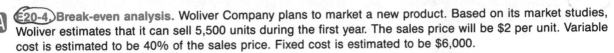 **E20-4. Break-even analysis.** Woliver Company plans to market a new product. Based on its market studies, Woliver estimates that it can sell 5,500 units during the first year. The sales price will be $2 per unit. Variable cost is estimated to be 40% of the sales price. Fixed cost is estimated to be $6,000.

Required: Compute the break-even point in dollars and in units.

E20-5. Break-even and cost-volume-profit analysis. Kenton Company produces only one product. Normal capacity is 20,000 units per year, and the unit sales price is $5. Relevant costs are:

	Unit Variable Cost	Total Fixed Cost
Materials	$1.00	
Direct labor	1.20	
Factory overhead	.50	$15,000
Marketing expenses	.30	5,000
Administrative expenses		6,000

Required: Compute (1) the break-even point in units of product, (2) the break-even point in dollars of sales, (3) the number of units of product that must be produced and sold to achieve a profit of $10,000, and (4) the sales revenue required to achieve a profit of $10,000.

E20-6. Margin of safety. Marvel Corporation plans sales of $2,000,000 for the coming period, which top management expects will result in a profit of $200,000. The break-even point has been determined to be $1,500,000 of sales.

Required: Compute the margin of safety and the margin of safety ratio.

E20-7. Break-even analysis and profit formula. A month's operations of Sureflite Company show fixed cost of $9,300, an M/S ratio of 25%, and a C/M ratio of 62%.

Required: Compute (1) break-even sales, (2) actual sales, and (3) profit for the month.

E20-8. Break-even analysis and profit formula. Operations of Gilley Company for the year disclosed an M/S ratio of 20% and a C/M ratio of 60%. Fixed cost amounted to $30,000.

Required: Compute (1) break-even sales, (2) the amount of profit, and (3) the contribution margin.

E20-9. Cost-volume-profit analysis. Semiconductor Company is planning to produce and sell 100,000 units of Chip A at $4 a unit and 200,000 units of Chip B at $3 a unit. Variable costs are 50% of sales for Chip A and 60% of sales for Chip B.

Required: If total planned operating profit is $140,000, what must the total fixed cost be?   (AICPA adapted)

E20-10. Break-even analysis with multiple products. Outback Furniture Company manufactures two products, tables and chairs. Tables sell for $100 each and chairs for $30 each. Four times as many chairs are sold each year as tables. Variable costs per unit are $53 and $17 for tables and chairs, respectively. Total fixed cost is $668,250.

Required: Compute the break-even point in sales dollars and in units of product.

E20-11. Break-even and cost-volume-profit analysis. Puma Company manufactures two products, L and M. L sells for $20 and M for $15. Variable costs per unit are $12 and $10 for L and M, respectively. Total fixed cost is $372,000. Puma management has targeted profit for the coming period at $93,000. Two units of L are expected to sell for every three units of M sold during the period.

Required: Compute (1) the break-even point in units of product and in sales dollars and (2) the level of sales in units of product and dollars necessary to achieve Puma's profit goal.

 E20-12. Cost-volume-profit analysis. Citation Company expects to incur the following costs to produce and sell 70,000 units of its product:

Variable manufacturing cost	$210,000
Fixed manufacturing cost	80,000
Variable marketing expense	105,000
Fixed marketing and administrative expenses	60,000

Required:

(1) What price would Citation have to charge for the product in order just to break even if all 70,000 units produced are sold?
(2) If Citation decides upon a price of $8 and has a profit objective of 10% of sales, what sales volume would be required?
(3) Citation plans to expand capacity next year to 100,000 units. The increased capacity will increase fixed manufacturing costs to $100,000. If the sales price of each unit of product remains at $8, how many units must Citation sell in order to produce a profit of 15% of sales?

CGA-Canada (adapted) Reprint with permission

E20-13. Break-even chart. Groff Company expects annual sales of 10,000 units of its product at $20 per unit. Variable cost is $10 per unit, and fixed cost is expected to total $70,000.

Required: Prepare a break-even chart for Groff Company.

PROBLEMS

P20-1. Direct costing income statement. Quebec Company wishes to use direct costing in accounting for its only product, with standard unit manufacturing costs as follows:

Materials	$ 5
Direct labor	4
Variable factory overhead	3
	$12

The fixed factory overhead budget is $160,000, and normal capacity is 80,000 units. During 19A, Quebec's first year of operations, 85,000 units were produced, of which 75,000 were sold at $25 each. Actual costs were:

Materials used	$434,000
Direct labor	350,000
Variable factory overhead	250,000
Fixed factory overhead	162,000
Variable marketing and administrative expenses	75,000
Fixed marketing and administrative expenses	100,000

Required:

(1) Prepare a direct costing income statement, assuming variances are written off in the current period.

(2) Determine the difference in operating income if absorption costing were used. (An income statement is not required.) CGA-Canada (adapted) Reprint with permission

P20-2. Absorption costing vs. direct costing. Roberts Corporation developed the following standard unit costs at 100% of its normal production capacity, which is 50,000 units per year:

Direct materials	$ 6
Direct labor	3
Variable factory overhead	1
Fixed factory overhead	5
	$15

The selling price of each unit of product is $25. Variable commercial expenses are $1 per unit sold and fixed commercial expenses total $200,000 for the period. During the year, 49,000 units were produced and 52,000 units were sold. There are no work in process beginning or ending inventories, and finished goods inventory is maintained at standard cost, which has not changed from the preceding year. For the current year, there is a net unfavorable variable cost variance in the amount of $2,000. All standard cost variances are charged to cost of goods sold at the end of the period.

Required:

(1) Prepare an income statement on the absorption costing basis.

(2) Prepare an income statement on the direct costing basis.

(3) Compute and reconcile the difference in operating income for the current year under absorption costing and direct costing.

P20-3. Absorption costing vs. direct costing. Placid Corporation developed the following standard unit costs at 100% of its normal production capacity, which is 50,000 units per year:

Direct materials	$2
Direct labor	3
Variable factory overhead	1
Fixed factory overhead	3
	$9

The selling price of each unit of product is $16. Variable commercial expenses are $1 per unit sold and fixed commercial expenses total $100,000 for the period. During the year, 51,000 units were produced and 48,000 units were sold. There are no work in process beginning or ending inventories, and finished goods inventory is maintained at standard cost, which has not changed from the preceding year. For the current year, there is a net unfavorable variable cost variance in the amount of $1,000. All standard cost variances are charged to cost of goods sold at the end of the period.

Required:

(1) Prepare an income statement on the absorption costing basis.

(2) Prepare an income statement on the direct costing basis.

(3) Compute and reconcile the difference in operating income for the current year under absorption costing and direct costing.

 P20-4. Income statements—absorption costing vs. direct costing. On January 2, Commerce Reel Company began production of a new model. First quarter sales were 20,000 units and second quarter sales were 26,000 units at a unit price of $10. Unit production costs each quarter were: direct materials, $1; direct labor,

$2; and variable factory overhead, $1.50. Fixed factory overhead was $62,400 each quarter and, for absorption costing, is assigned to inventory based on actual units produced.

Marketing and administrative expenses consisted of a $15,000 fixed portion each quarter and a variable portion which was 5% of sales. Units produced in the first quarter and the second quarter totaled 30,000 and 20,000, respectively. The fifo inventory costing method is used.

Required:

(1) Prepare comparative income statements for the first and second quarters under the absorption costing method.
(2) Prepare comparative income statements for the first and second quarters under the direct costing method.
(3) Compute and reconcile the differences in operating income under the two methods for each quarter.

 P20-5. Break-even analysis. Kimbrell Company has decided to introduce a new product. The new product can be manufactured by either a capital-intensive method or a labor-intensive method. The manufacturing method will not affect the quality of the product. The estimated unit manufacturing costs by the two methods follow:

	Capital Intensive	Labor Intensive
Materials	$5.00	$5.60
Direct labor	6.00	7.20
Variable factory overhead	3.00	4.80

Directly traceable incremental fixed factory overhead is expected to be $2,440,000 if the capital-intensive method is chosen and $1,320,000 if the labor-intensive method is chosen. Kimbrell's market research department has recommended an introductory unit sales price of $30. Regardless of the manufacturing method chosen, the incremental fixed marketing expenses are estimated to be $500,000 per year plus a variable marketing expense of $2 for each unit sold.

Required:

(1) Calculate the estimated break-even point for the new product in annual units of sales, if Kimbrell Company uses the:

    (a) Capital-intensive manufacturing method.
    (b) Labor-intensive manufacturing method.

(2) Determine the annual unit sales volume at which Kimbrell Company would be indifferent between the two manufacturing methods.   (ICMA adapted)

 P20-6. Break-even and cost-volume-profit analysis. Castleton Company has analyzed the costs of producing and selling 5,000 units of its only product to be as follows:

Direct materials	$60,000
Direct labor	40,000
Variable factory overhead	20,000
Fixed factory overhead	30,000
Variable marketing and administrative expenses	10,000
Fixed marketing and administrative expenses	15,000

Required:

(1) Compute the number of units to break even at a per unit sales price of $38.50.
(2) Determine the number of units that must be sold to produce an $18,000 profit, at a $40 per unit sales price.
(3) Determine the price Castleton must charge at a 5,000-unit sales level, in order to produce a profit equal to 20% of sales.   CGA-Canada (adapted) Reprint with permission

P20-7. Cost-volume-profit analysis. The Desousa Company produces and sells two distinct products (B2 and B4). Available data for the year ending December 31, 19A, follows:

	B2	B4
Sales volume..................	20,000	40,000
Selling price per unit...........	$180	$160
Direct materials	$ 65	$ 40
Direct labor	40	40
Variable factory overhead	16	16
Fixed factory overhead	25	25
Full cost per unit	$146	$121
Gross profit per unit	$ 34	$ 39

Other information pertaining to operations during the year ending December 31, 19A, follow:

(a) Variable selling costs were 5% of sales.
(b) Fixed selling and administrative costs were $207,330 (with a capacity to handle volumes of up to twice that of 19A).
(c) The present plant facilities provide a capacity of 60,000 units; this can be increased to a capacity of 100,000 units at an additional cost of $80,000.
(d) The company is taxed at a rate of 40%.

Expected changes for the year ending December 31, 19B, include the following:

(a) The selling price of B4 is expected to increase by 10%, but no other changes are expected in costs or selling prices for either product.
(b) The sales mix for 19B is expected to be in the ratio of 2 units of B2 to 3 units of B4.

Required: Calculate the number of units of each product that the company would have to sell in order to earn an after-tax net income of $135,000 for the year ending December 31, 19B. (SMAC adapted)

P20-8. Break-even and cost-volume-profit analysis. Cabot Electronics produces and markets tape recorders and electronic calculators. Its 19A income statement follows:

Cabot Electronics
Income Statement
For Year Ended December 31, 19A

	Tape Recorders		Electronic Calculators		
	Total (In Thousands)	Per Unit	Total (In Thousands)	Per Unit	Total (In Thousands)
Sales	$1,050	$15.00	$3,150	$22.50	$4,200.00
Production costs:					
Materials.............................	$ 280	$ 4.00	$ 630	$ 4.50	$ 910.00
Direct labor..........................	140	2.00	420	3.00	560.00
Variable factory overhead	140	2.00	280	2.00	420.00
Fixed factory overhead	70	1.00	210	1.50	280.00
Total production cost	$ 630	$ 9.00	$1,540	$11.00	$2,170.00
Gross profit	$ 420	$ 6.00	$1,610	$11.50	$2,030.00
Fixed marketing and administrative expenses					1,040.00
Income before income tax.......					$ 990.00
Income tax (55%).........................					544.50
Net income...........................					$ 445.50

The tape recorder business has been fairly stable in recent years, and the company has no plans to change the tape recorder price. However, because of increasing competition and market saturation, management has decided to reduce its calculator price to $20, effective January 1, 19B, and to spend an additional $57,000 in 19B for advertising. As a result, Cabot estimates that 80% of its 19B revenue will be from electronic calculator sales. The sales units mix for tape recorders and calculators was 1:2 in 19A and is expected to be 1:3 in 19B at all volume levels. For 19B, materials costs are expected to drop 10% and 20% for the tape recorders and calculators, respectively; however, all direct labor costs are to increase 10%.

Required:

(1) Compute the number of tape recorders and electronic calculators to break even, using 19A data.
(2) Determine the sales dollars required to earn an aftertax profit of 9% on sales, using 19B estimates.
(3) Compute the number of tape recorders and electronic calculators to break even, using 19B estimates.

(ICMA adapted)

 P20-9. Break-even and cost-volume-profit analysis; direct costing. The following data relate to a year's budgeted activity for Mariemont Corporation, which manufactures one product:

Beginning inventory	30,000 units
Production	120,000 units
Available for sale	150,000 units
Sales	110,000 units
Ending inventory	40,000 units
Sales price	$5.00 per unit
Variable manufacturing cost	1.00 per unit
Variable marketing cost	2.00 per unit
Fixed manufacturing cost (based on 100,000 units)	.25 per unit
Fixed marketing cost (based on 100,000 units)	.65 per unit

A special order is received for 10,000 units, in addition to budgeted sales, to be used in an unrelated market. The total fixed cost remains unchanged within the relevant range of 45,000 units to total capacity of 135,000 units.

Required: Compute the following:

(1) Projected annual break-even sales in units.
(2) Projected operating income for the year from budgeted sales (a) under direct costing; (b) under absorption costing, charging all variances to Cost of Goods Sold.
(3) Price per unit to be charged on the special order, given the original data, so that the operating income will increase by $5,000.
(4) Number of units to be sold to generate a profit equal to 10% of the contribution margin, assuming that the sales price increases by 20%; the variable manufacturing cost increases by 10%; the variable marketing cost remains the same; and the total fixed cost increases to $104,400.   (AICPA adapted)

P20-10. Break-even and cost-volume-profit analysis. Seco Corporation, a wholesale supply company, engages independent sales agents to market the company's lines. These agents currently receive a commission of 20% of sales, but they are demanding an increase to 25% of sales made during the year ending December 31, 19A. Seco had already prepared its 19A budget before learning of the agents' demand for an increase in commissions. The pro forma income statement on the next page is based on this budget.

Seco is considering the possibility of employing its own salespersons. Three individuals would be required, at an estimated annual salary of $30,000 each, plus commissions of 5% of sales. In addition, a sales manager would be employed at a fixed annual salary of $160,000. All other fixed costs, as well as the variable cost percentages, would remain the same as the estimates in the 19A pro forma income statement.

Required:

(1) Compute Seco's estimated break-even point in sales dollars for the year ending December 31, 19A, based on the pro forma income statement prepared by the company.

Seco Corporation
Pro Forma Income Statement
For the Year Ending December 31, 19A

Sales		$10,000,000
Cost of goods sold		6,000,000
Gross profit		$ 4,000,000
Selling and administrative expenses:		
Commissions	$2,000,000	
All other costs (fixed)	100,000	2,100,000
Income before income tax		$ 1,900,000
Income tax (30%)		570,000
Net income		$ 1,330,000

(2) Compute Seco's estimated break-even point in sales dollars for the year ending December 31, 19A, if the company employs its own salespersons.

(3) Compute the estimated volume in sales dollars that would be required for the year ending December 31, 19A, to yield the same net income as projected in the pro forma income statement, if Seco continues to use the independent sales agents and agrees to their demand for a 25% sales commission.

(4) Compute the estimated volume in sales dollars that would generate an identical net income for the year ending December 31, 19A, regardless of whether Seco employs its own salespersons or continues to use the independent sales agents and pays them a 25% commission. (AICPA adapted)

CASES

C20-1. Sales and production volume effects— absorption costing vs. direct costing. Star Company, a wholly-owned subsidiary of Orbit Inc., produces and sells three main product lines. The company employs a standard cost accounting system for record-keeping purposes.

At the beginning of the year, the president of Star Company presented the budget to the parent company and accepted a commitment to contribute $15,800 to Orbit's consolidated profit in 19A. The president has been confident that the year's profit would exceed the budget target, since the monthly sales reports have shown that sales for the ear will exceed the budget by 10%. The president is both disturbed and confused when the controller presents an adjusted forecast as of November 30, indicating that profit will be 11% under budget. The two forecasts are shown at the right.

There have been no sales price changes or product mix shifts since the January 1 forecast. The only cost variance on the income statement is the underapplied factory overhead.

This arose because the company used only 16,000 standard machine hours (budgeted machine hours were 20,000) during the year as a result of a shortage of raw materials. Fortunately, Star Company's finished goods inventory was large enough to fill all sales orders received.

	Forecasts as of	
	Jan. 1	Nov. 30
Sales	$268,000	$294,800
Cost of goods sold at standard.	212,000*	233,200
Gross profit at standard	$ 56,000	$ 61,600
Less underapplied factory overhead	—	6,000
Gross profit at actual	$ 56,000	$ 55,600
Marketing expense	$ 13,400	$ 14,740
Administrative expense	26,800	26,800
Total commercial expense	$ 40,200	$ 41,540
Income from operations	$ 15,800	$ 14,060

*Includes fixed factory overhead of $30,000.

Required:

(1) Analyze and explain the forecast profit decline, in spite of increased sales and good cost control.
(2) Explain and illustrate an alternative internal cost reporting procedure which would avoid the confusing effect of the present procedure.   (ICMA adapted)

C20-2. Sales and production volume effects— absorption costing vs. direct costing. RGB Corporation is a manufacturer of a synthetic element. A. B. Meek, president of the company, has been eager to get the operating results for the fiscal year just completed. Meek was surprised when the income statement revealed that operating income dropped to $645,000 from $900,000, although sales volume had increased by 100,000 units. This drop in operating income occurred even though Meek had implemented the following changes during the past 12 months to improve the profitability of the company.

(1) In response to a 10% increase in production costs, the sales price of the company's product was increased by 12%. This action took place on December 1, 19A.
(2) The managements of the selling and administrative departments were given strict instructions to spend no more in fiscal 19B than they did in fiscal 19A.

RGB's accounting department prepared and distributed to top management the following comparative income statements:

RGB Corporation
Statements of Operating Income
For the Years Ended November 30, 19A and 19B
(In Thousands)

	19A		19B	
Sales revenue .		$9,000		$11,200
Cost of goods sold	$7,200		$8,560	
Volume variance, (favorable) unfavorable ..	(600)	6,600	495	9,055
Gross profit ...		$2,400		$ 2,145
Selling and administrative expenses		1,500		1,500
Operating income		$ 900		$ 645

The accounting staff also prepared related financial information that is presented in the following schedule to assist management in evaluating the company's performance. RGB uses the fifo inventory method for finished goods.

RGB Corporation
Selected Operating and Financial Data
For 19A and 19B

	19A	19B
Sales price per unit........	$10.00	$11.20
Materials cost per unit......	1.50	1.65
Direct labor cost per unit ...	2.50	2.75
Variable factory overhead per unit	1.00	1.10
Fixed factory overhead per unit...................	3.00	3.30
Total fixed factory overhead .	$3,000,000	$3,300,000
Total selling and administrative expenses ...	1,500,000	1,500,000
Quantity of units budgeted (normal capacity)........	1,000,000	1,000,000
Quantity of units actually produced	1,200,000	850,000
Quantity of units sold	900,000	1,000,000
Quantity of units in beginning inventory	0	300,000
Quantity of units in ending inventory	300,000	150,000

Required:

(1) Explain to A. B. Meek why RGB Corporation's net income decreased in the current fiscal year, despite the sales price and sales volume increase.
(2) A member of RGB's accounting department has suggested that the company adopt direct costing for internal reporting purposes.

   (a) Prepare an operating income statement for the fiscal years ending November 30, 19A and 19B, for RGB Corporation using the direct costing method.
   (b) Present a numerical reconciliation of the difference in operating income between the absorption costing method currently in use and the direct costing method proposed.

(3) Identify and discuss some of the advantages and disadvantages of using the direct costing method for internal reporting purposes.   (ICMA adapted)

C20-3. Break-even and cost-volume-profit analysis. Daly Company has determined the number of units of Product Y that Daly would have to sell in order to break even. However, Daly would like to attain a profit of 20% on sales of Product Y.

Required:

(1) Explain how cost-volume-profit analysis can be used to determine the number of units of Product Y that Daly would have to sell to attain a 20% profit on sales.

(2) If variable cost per unit increases as a percentage of the sales price, how would that affect the number of units of Product Y that Daly would have to sell in order to break even? Explain why.

(3) Identify the limitations of break-even and cost-volume-profit analysis in managerial decision making.   (AICPA adapted)

CHAPTER 21

Differential Cost Analysis

In order to achieve the goals and objectives of the company, management must make frequent decisions about the potential cost or profitability of alternative actions. The cost or managerial accountant facilitates this process by providing information to management that is relevant to the decisions that must be made. Different decision problems require the use of different decision models which in turn utilize different kinds of information. In order to provide relevant information, the accountant must understand the nature of the problem being evaluated and the decision model being used.

This chapter focuses on short-term decision making, i.e., on decisions that affect activities that do not extend beyond one year. The first section of the chapter defines differential cost and illustrates its relevance in solving numerous different short-term decision problems. The second section discusses linear programming and its application to short-term decision problems. Decisions that have long-term effects are discussed in Chapter 22, and the problems of making short-term and long-term decisions under uncertainty are discussed in Chapter 23.

■ DIFFERENTIAL COST STUDIES

Differential cost studies are undertaken to determine the profitability of alternative uses of resources. This is accomplished by comparing the revenue to be derived from an alternative (referred to as *marginal revenue* or *incremental revenue*) with its differential cost. *Differential cost* (often referred to as *marginal cost* by economists and as *incremental cost* by industrial engineers) is essentially the total cash outlay that is required to undertake a project or to extend a project beyond its original goal, and it may include an expenditure classified as a fixed cost as well as those classified as variable. The required cash outlay sometimes is referred to as *out-of-pocket cost*. Similarly, differential cost may be thought of as the expenditure that can be avoided if a project is abandoned or discontinued. In this sense, it may be referred to as *avoidable cost*. Differential cost does not include cost that must be incurred regardless of whether the project is undertaken or not. Consequently, *sunk costs* (such as the excess of the book value of an asset over its salvage value) and allocated fixed costs (such as building depreciation and supervisory salaries) are not differential costs. Since sunk costs cannot be recovered and allocated fixed costs must be incurred regardless of whether the project is undertaken or extended, they are not relevant to any decision concerning the desirability of undertaking or extending the project.

Variable costs are relevant in differential cost studies because they are costs that must be incurred if a project is undertaken or extended and can be avoided if the project is not undertaken. In contrast, fixed costs usually are not affected by short-run increases or decreases in activity and, therefore, are not relevant to any decision about the relative cost or profitability of alternatives. If, however, fixed cost must be increased in order to expand capacity to the level required to undertake or extend a project, the additional fixed cost should be considered a differential cost. For purposes of determining the cost to be incurred in undertaking or extending a project, any out-of-pocket expenditure required to provide sufficient capacity is relevant to the decision. For example, if a company currently operating at 95 percent of capacity must rent additional machinery in order to expand production to 110 percent of capacity, the cost of renting the additional machinery is a differential cost (even though it is also a fixed cost) because it is an out-of-pocket expenditure.

Opportunity costs related to alternative uses of resources also are relevant to differential cost studies. An *opportunity cost* may be defined as the measurable value of the best forgone alternative, i.e., the measurable value of an opportunity bypassed by rejecting the best alternative use of resources. For example, money could either be spent in producing and selling a product or it could be invested in an interest-earning asset, such as a bond. If money were spent producing and selling a product, the interest that could have been earned from the alternative investment in the interest-earning asset would be an opportunity cost. Similarly, a machine could either be used in the manufacture of a product or it could be sold for salvage. The salvage value of the machine is an opportunity cost. Although opportunity costs are not routinely reported in financial statements, they should be considered in evaluating alternatives in order to determine the most profitable use of resources.

Imputed costs may also be relevant to differential cost studies. *Imputed costs* are hypothetical costs representing the cost of a resource measured by its use value. Imputed costs ordinarily do not appear in conventional accounting records and do not necessarily entail dollar outlays. An imputed cost is similar to an opportunity cost, except that an imputed cost may be an arbitrary measure. A common example of an imputed cost is the inclusion of "interest" on ownership equity as a part of operating expenses.

Historical costs drawn from the accounting records generally do not give management the differential cost information needed to evaluate alternative courses of action. However, a flexible budget[1] with costs computed for different levels of capacity utilization can be useful in differential cost analyses.

---

[1]See Chapter 17 for a discussion of flexible budgets, including an illustration of the computations required to determine costs at various levels of activity.

The following flexible budget shows costs at different levels of production capacity. It indicates that some costs increase proportionately with an increase in capacity, while other costs remain comparatively unchanged through various levels of activity.

FLEXIBLE BUDGET FOR DIFFERENT RATES OF OUTPUT
(100,000 Units = 100% Normal Capacity)

Capacity	60%	80%	100%	120%
Variable costs:				
Direct manufacturing costs:				
Direct materials	$102,000	$136,000	$170,000	$204,000
Direct labor	93,000	124,000	155,000	186,000
Total	$195,000	$260,000	$325,000	$390,000
Indirect manufacturing costs:				
Heat	$ 720	$ 960	$ 1,200	$ 1,440
Light and power	1,440	1,920	2,400	2,880
Repairs and maintenance	2,460	3,280	4,100	4,920
Supplies	1,260	1,680	2,100	2,520
Indirect labor	9,120	12,160	15,200	18,240
Total	$ 15,000	$ 20,000	$ 25,000	$ 30,000
Commercial expenses:				
Clerical help	$ 11,580	$ 15,440	$ 19,300	$ 23,160
Wages, general	6,960	9,280	11,600	13,920
Supplies	1,260	1,680	2,100	2,520
Total	$ 19,800	$ 26,400	$ 33,000	$ 39,600
Fixed costs:				
Indirect manufacturing costs:				
Foremen	$ 15,250	$ 20,500	$ 20,500	$ 25,750
Superintendent	15,000	15,000	15,000	17,750
Setup crew	5,000	7,500	7,500	8,500
Depreciation and rent	8,000	9,400	9,400	9,400
Property taxes and insurance	2,600	2,600	2,600	2,600
Total	$ 45,850	$ 55,000	$ 55,000	$ 64,000
Commercial expenses:				
Executives' salaries	$ 28,000	$ 35,000	$ 35,000	$ 40,000
Assistants' salaries	11,200	16,400	16,400	19,200
Property taxes	3,400	3,400	3,400	3,400
Advertising	6,000	7,200	7,200	8,600
Total	$ 48,600	$ 62,000	$ 62,000	$ 71,200
Total cost	$324,250	$423,400	$500,000	$594,800
Units of output	60,000	80,000	100,000	120,000
Average unit cost	$5.40	$5.29	$5.00	$4.96
Differential cost total		$99,150	$76,600	$94,800
Differential cost per unit		$4.96	$3.83	$4.74

In the flexible budget illustrated above, the $5.40 average unit cost at 60 percent of normal capacity is computed by dividing the total cost at that capacity by the number of units produced ($324,250 ÷ 60,000 units). The total differential cost is determined by subtracting the total estimated cost for one level of activity from that of another level (e.g., $423,400 – $324,250 = $99,150, which is the differential cost between the 80-percent and 60-percent levels). The differential unit cost is computed by:

1. Subtracting one level of output from the next higher level (80,000 units output at 80 percent of capacity minus 60,000 units output at 60 percent of capacity = 20,000 units).
2. Dividing the total differential cost between these two levels of capacity by the difference in the number of units ($99,150 ÷ 20,000 units = $4.96).

Differential cost studies typically are short-term in orientation. If the alternatives being evaluated extend beyond one year, one or more of the capital expenditure evaluation techniques discussed in Chapter 22 should be used. Some examples of short-term decisions that may require differential cost analysis include:

1. Accepting or refusing certain orders.
2. Reducing the price of a single, special order.
3. Making a price cut in a competitive market.
4. Evaluating make-or-buy alternatives.
5. Expanding, shutting down, or eliminating a facility.
6. Increasing, curtailing, or stopping production of certain products.
7. Determining whether to sell or process further.
8. Choosing among alternative routings in product manufacture.
9. Determining the maximum price that can be paid for raw materials.

Accepting Additional Orders

Differential cost is the cost that should be considered when a decision involves a change in output. The differential cost of added production is the difference between the cost of producing the present smaller output and that of the contemplated, larger output. If available capacity is not fully utilized, a differential cost analysis might indicate the possibility of selling additional output at a figure lower than the existing average unit cost. The additional business will be profitable as long as the revenue from the additional output exceeds the differential cost of manufacturing and selling the additional output.

To illustrate, assume that a plant has a maximum production capacity of 100,000 units, but normal capacity is set at 80,000 units. The predetermined overhead rate is computed so that budgeted fixed overhead is fully absorbed when operating at the 80,000-unit level (i.e., all of the budgeted fixed overhead will be applied to the products produced during the period). If fewer units are produced, fixed overhead will be underapplied. If more units are produced, fixed overhead will be overapplied. If this company makes only one unit, its total cost for the period and its unit cost would be equal because the one unit produced must absorb all production cost incurred during the period. The total cost per unit would be:

Variable cost per unit	$ 5
Total fixed cost.	100,000
Total cost per unit	$100,005

At normal capacity, the fixed cost per unit is reduced to $1.25 ($100,000 ÷ 80,000 units), and the total cost per unit is:

Variable cost per unit	$5.00
Share of fixed cost	1.25
Total cost per unit	$6.25

Notice that the differential cost of the additional 79,999 units is $5 per unit, i.e., the variable cost, because no additional fixed costs are incurred. If additional capacity can be utilized to produce an additional 1,000 units, the differential cost of these units would be only the $5 variable cost per unit, unless the production of the additional 1,000 units requires the incurrence of additional fixed cost. Assuming that the sales price is $9 per unit, a differential cost analysis comparing present operating results with the total results after 1,000 additional units are produced and sold might appear as follows:

	Present Business	With Additional Business
Sales	$720,000	$729,000
Variable cost	400,000	405,000
Contribution margin	$320,000	$324,000
Fixed cost	100,000	100,000
Profit[2]................	$220,000	$224,000

The additional business requires the additional incurrence of variable cost only. Since adequate unused capacity is available to produce the additional 1,000 units, additional fixed cost need not be incurred. If the 1,000 units are sold at any price above the $5 variable cost each, the sale would yield a positive contribution to short-run profit.

The illustration above also can be presented in the following manner to highlight the differential revenue of $9,000 and cost of $5,000:

	Present Business	Additional Business	Total
Sales	$720,000	$9,000	$729,000
Variable cost	400,000	5,000	405,000
Contribution margin	$320,000	$4,000	$324,000
Fixed cost	100,000	0	100,000
Profit	$220,000	$4,000	$224,000

Reducing the Price of a Special Order

Differential cost analysis is an aid to management in deciding at what price the firm can afford to sell additional goods. To illustrate, assume that a company manufactures 450,000 units using 90 percent of its normal capacity. The fixed factory overhead is $1,250,000, which is $2.50 for each unit manufactured when operations are at 100 percent of normal capacity ($1,250,000 ÷ 500,000 units). The variable factory overhead rate is $.50 per unit. The direct

---

[2]The term "profit" in this discussion denotes operating income before income tax.

materials cost is $1.80, and the direct labor cost is $1.40 per unit. Each unit sells for $10. Variable marketing expense (shipping expense and sales commission) is $.50 per unit. Fixed marketing and administrative expenses total $800,000. On the basis of these data, the accountant would prepare the following statement:

Sales (450,000 units @ $10)		$4,500,000
Cost of goods sold:		
Direct materials (450,000 units @ $1.80)	$ 810,000	
Direct labor (450,000 units @ $1.40)	630,000	
Variable factory overhead (450,000 units @ $.50)	225,000	
Fixed factory overhead (450,000 units @ $2.50)	1,125,000	2,790,000
Gross profit		$1,710,000
Underapplied fixed factory overhead ((500,000 units – 450,000 units) @ $2.50)		125,000
Gross profit (adjusted)		$1,585,000
Less commercial expenses:		
Variable marketing expense (450,000 units @ $.50)	$ 225,000	
Fixed marketing and administrative expenses	800,000	1,025,000
Income from operations		$ 560,000

The sales department reports that a customer has offered to pay $6 per unit for an additional 100,000 units. To make the additional units, an annual rental cost of $10,000 for additional equipment would be incurred. Using absorption cost data, the accountant might compute the gain or loss on this order as follows:

Sales (100,000 units @ $6)		$600,000
Differential cost of goods sold:		
Direct materials (100,000 units @ $1.80)	$180,000	
Direct labor (100,000 units @ $1.40)	140,000	
Variable factory overhead (100,000 units @ $.50)	50,000	
Fixed factory overhead (100,000 units @ $2.50)	250,000	620,000
		$ (20,000)
Variable marketing expense (100,000 units @ $.50)		50,000
Loss on this order		$ (70,000)

There are two problems with this calculation: the $10,000 additional cost of equipment rental has been ignored, and fixed overhead which is not affected by the decision has been allocated to the additional business as if it were a differential cost. The use of absorption cost data in this case would cause management to reject the offer. In this computation, all cost elements use the existing unit costs, and fixed overhead is allocated on the basis of the established rate ($2.50 per unit). A second look, however, reveals the following effect of the new order on total fixed factory overhead:

Fixed factory overhead (at present)		$1,250,000
Fixed factory overhead (because of additional business)		10,000
Total fixed factory overhead		$1,260,000
Fixed factory overhead charged into production:		
For 450,000 units (old business)	$1,125,000	
For 100,000 units (additional business)	250,000	1,375,000
Overapplied fixed factory overhead		$ 115,000

Instead of underapplied fixed factory overhead of $125,000, the additional business would result in overapplied factory overhead of $115,000, or an increase of $240,000 in applied factory overhead. The increase of $240,000 may also be computed by subtracting the additional fixed cost that must be incurred ($10,000 equipment rental) from the amount of fixed factory overhead allocated to the additional 100,000 units produced under the absorption costing method (100,000 units × $2.50 each = $250,000). This $240,000 minus the computed $70,000 loss on the order results in a gain of $170,000. This gain is shown more clearly in the following statement, which includes only the differential costs and revenue:

Sales (100,000 units @ $6)		$600,000
Cost of goods sold:		
Direct materials (100,000 units @ $1.80)	$180,000	
Direct labor (100,000 units @ $1.40)	140,000	
Variable factory overhead (100,000 units @ $.50)	50,000	
Additional fixed cost to produce this order	10,000	380,000
		$220,000
Variable marketing expense (100,000 @ $.50)		50,000
Gain on this order		$170,000

The cost of manufacturing and selling each additional unit can be computed as follows:

Differential manufacturing cost per unit:

$$\frac{\text{Differential cost of goods sold}}{\text{Additional units}} = \frac{\$380,000}{100,000} = \$3.80$$

Variable marketing expense per unit 50

Total differential cost per unit $4.30

Because the $4.30 differential cost is less that the $6 sales price, it is clear that the effect on profit will be favorable.

In practice, it is often very difficult to determine whether the offer to buy additional output is really additional business.[3] An annual sales budget does not normally specify the quantities to be sold to each customer because the forecasts involved are generally based on historical trends in product sales and economic factors expected to affect demand during the forecast period. As a consequence, it is often difficult to evaluate whether or not a particular offer is incremental business or a component of the original budget. If the offer is actually an offer to purchase units included in the original sales forecast, the profits expected from the differential cost analysis will not materialize. If the price reduction and quantity of units involved in the order are large, total sales revenue might not even cover total fixed costs, in which case a loss would occur for the period.

[3]Bernard A. Coda and Barry G. King, "Manufacturing Decision-Making Tools," *Journal of Cost Management*, Vol. 3, No. 1, p. 34.

If management decides that an offer to purchase at a reduced price is indeed additional business, the long-run effect of the sale on other customers and the reaction of competitors should also be considered. If regular customers become aware that the product has been sold to anyone at a reduced price, they may demand similar cost concessions, which if not granted could result in the loss of business and if granted could result in a reduced profit margin. The firm must also be careful not to violate the Robinson-Patman Act (discussed in Chapter 24) and other governmental pricing restrictions. If the product sold at a reduced price affects the sales of competitors, they might retaliate by cutting their prices. Such actions could result in a price war and lost profits for all concerned.

Make-or-Buy Decisions

Another short-term decision that involves differential cost analysis is that of deciding whether to make or buy component parts for a finished product. The importance of the make-or-buy decision is evidenced by the fact that most manufacturing firms at some time during the course of their operations will have to make such a decision. The choice of whether to manufacture an item internally or purchase it from outside the firm can be applied to a wide variety of decisions that are often major determinants of profitability and that can be significant to the company's financial health.

The objective of a make-or-buy decision should be to best utilize the firm's productive and financial resources. The problem often arises in connection with the possible use of idle equipment, idle space, and even idle labor. In such situations, a manager is inclined to consider making certain units instead of buying them in order to utilize existing facilities and to maintain work-force stability. Commitments of new resources may also be involved.

To illustrate a make-or-buy analysis, assume that a company plans to introduce a new product which will require a component part that can be purchased from an outside vendor at a cost of $5 per unit, or manufactured in house. The company has sufficient excess capacity to manufacture 10,000 units of the component part, the quantity needed during the first year. The prime cost per unit for the component part is expected to be $1.80 for materials and $1.20 for direct labor. The factory overhead rate is 200 percent of direct labor cost ($1.20 direct labor cost per unit × 200% = $2.40 overhead per unit); however, only 25 percent of factory overhead budgeted for the year is variable. In order to manufacture the component part, specialized equipment must be rented at an annual cost of $7,200.

If the full absorption cost of the component part were compared to the vendor's price, management would decide to purchase the component part from the outside vendor, because the purchase price of $5 per unit is less than the full absorption cost $5.40 per unit ($1.80 materials + $1.20 labor + $2.40 overhead). Such a decision would be inappropriate because the full absorption cost in this situation is not equal to the differential cost. The fixed portion of the overhead charged to each unit is a sunk cost, which is not relevant to the decision ($2.40 overhead per unit × 75 percent fixed = $1.80 sunk cost per unit). In addition, the $7,200 rental of specialized equipment, which is not included in the absorption cost computation, is an out-of-pocket fixed cost that is relevant to this decision. To evaluate the economic effect of the two alternatives, the differential costs of manufacturing the component part should be computed and compared to the cost of purchasing it from an outside vendor. Instead of purchasing the component part in this case, the company should manufacture it, as indicated by the following cost comparison:

Cost to purchase the part (10,000 units @ $5).....................		$50,000
Differential cost to manufacture the part:		
Materials (10,000 units @ $1.80)...........................	$18,000	
Direct labor (10,000 units @ $1.20).........................	12,000	
Variable factory overhead (10,000 units × $1.20 labor		
cost × 200% × 25% variable)	6,000	
Incremental fixed factory overhead	7,200	43,200
Savings from manufacturing the part		$ 6,800

Despite its importance, studies indicate that surprisingly few firms give adequate objective study to their make-or-buy problems.[4] Not only is this type of decision important to the firm, but it is also complicated by a host of factors, both financial (quantitative) and nonfinancial (qualitative) that must be considered. Faced with a make-or-buy decision, management should:

1. Consider the quantity, quality, and dependability of supply of the items as well as the technical know-how required, weighing such requirements for both the short-run and long-run period.
2. Compare the cost of making the items with the cost of buying them.
3. Compare the making of the items with possibly more profitable alternative uses that could be made of the firm's own facilities if the items are purchased.
4. Consider differences in the required capital investment and the timing of cash flows (Chapters 22 and 23).
5. Adopt a course of action related to the firm's overall policies. Customers' and suppliers' reactions often play a part in these decisions. Retaliation or ill will could result. Whether it is profitable to make or buy depends upon the circumstances surrounding the individual situation.

The managerial accountant should present a statement that compares the company's cost of making the items with the vendor's price. A cost study with only the differential costs and with no allocation of existing fixed overhead or of profit indicates possible short-run cost savings. In practice, such studies seem to favor making rather than buying the items in the majority of cases. However, if management were asked to sell the items at the differential cost, it might be unwilling to do so, since, in the long run, the full cost must

---

[4]Anthony J. Gambino, *The Make-or-Buy Decision* (New York: National Association of Accountants and Hamilton, Ontario: The Society of Management Accountants of Canada, 1980), pp. 9-10.

be covered and a reasonable profit achieved. Furthermore, if there is only a slight advantage in favor of making, purchasing may be the most desirable alternative because more reliance can be put on a known cost to buy rather than an estimated cost to make.[5]

A study by the National Association of Accountants makes the following observations about cost considerations:

> To evaluate the alternatives properly, costs to make vs. costs to buy must be based on the same underlying assumptions. Thus, costs for each of the alternatives must be based on the identical product specifications, quantities, and quality standards.
>
> Determination of the "cost to buy" cannot be limited to existing costs shown on supplier invoices. The competitive nature of supplier pricing requires that current optimum third-party prices based upon identical specifications and quantities be used for evaluation of this alternative. There are many examples of lower prices being obtained from suppliers for larger quantities, standardization of specifications, etc., as well as from the use of competitive bids and/or the threat of self-manufacture. All direct and indirect costs of functions and facilities which are properly allocable to the "buy" alternative, under the "full cost" concept must be considered. Cost to buy must also include the "full cost" to bring the product to the same condition and location as if self-manufactured—including freight, handling, purchasing, incoming inspection, inventory carrying costs, etc.
>
> Determination of the "cost to make" cannot be limited to those identified as manufacturing costs or used in the valuation of inventories. All direct and indirect costs of functions and facilities which are properly allocable to self-manufacture under the "full cost" concept must be considered.
>
> It is concluded that in the case of short-run decisions, differential costs become more significant. However, . . . it is recommended that the long-term and full-cost consideration also be developed. The short-term judgments can then be properly evaluated against the alternative choices which will be required at a later date.
>
> The long-term nature of most make-or-buy decisions requires that cost determinations not only consider present costs but also projections of future costs resulting from inflationary factors, technological changes, productivity, mechanization, etc. More specifically, the projection of the future cost to make and the cost to buy must give full consideration to what the costs "should be" under obtainable conditions and reflect all possible improvements—not just what may be achieved under existing operating conditions.[6]

Decisions to Shut Down Facilities

Differential cost analysis also is used when a business is confronted with the possibility of a temporary shutdown of manufacturing and marketing facilities. In the short run, a firm may be better off operating than not operating, as long as the products or services sold recover the variable cost and make a contribution toward the recovery of the fixed cost. A shutdown of facilities does not eliminate all costs. Depreciation, interest, property tax, and insurance continue during complete inactivity.

---

[5]*Ibid.*, p. 21.

[6]*NAA Statement, No. 5*, "Criteria for Make-or-Buy Decisions" (New York: National Association of Accountants, June 21, 1973), pp. 5-8. Copyright June, 1973, by the National Association of Accountants. All rights reserved. Reprinted by permission.

Even if sales do not recover the variable cost and the portion of fixed cost that is avoidable, the firm may still be better off operating than shutting down the facility. Closing a facility and subsequently reopening it is a costly process. The shutdown may necessitate the incurrence of maintenance procedures in order to preserve machinery and buildings during periods of inactivity (e.g., rust inhibitors, dust covers, security equipment, etc.). The shutdown also may require the incurrence of legal expenditures and employee maintenance pay. During the shutdown period, some employees will probably be lost (i.e., they may not wait until the facility is reopened to go back to work), in which case the investment in the training of those employees will be lost. The morale of other employees, as well as community goodwill, may be adversely affected, and the recruiting and training of replacement workers that must be incurred when the facility is later reopened add to costs. Although difficult to quantify, the loss of established market share is also a factor to be considered. When a company leaves a market for a while, its customers tend to forget about the company's product. As a consequence, reentering the market at a later time will probably require reeducating consumers about the company's product. These shutdown costs must be weighed against losses from continued operations.

To illustrate an analysis of a possible temporary shutdown, assume that Nigent Company has three production facilities which produce different kinds of products. The following projected income statement based on absorption costing relates to the coming period:

	Company Total	Plant 1	Plant 2	Plant 3
Sales	$200,000	$90,000	$70,000	$ 40,000
Less cost of goods sold	110,000	40,000	31,000	39,000
Gross profit	$ 90,000	$50,000	$39,000	$ 1,000
Less commercial expenses...............	50,000	20,000	16,000	14,000
Operating income (loss)	$ 40,000	$30,000	$23,000	$(13,000)

Plant 3 appears to be unprofitable; however, an evaluation of the relative profitability of the plants is obscured because some unavoidable common fixed costs have been allocated to each of the plants. Assuming that $32,000 of the commercial expenses is unavoidable common fixed cost allocated to the plants under the absorption cost method, a clearer picture of the expected operating efficiency of the various plants is obtained by preparing a contribution margin analysis (i.e., an income statement based on direct costing) as shown on the following page.

Based on the contribution margin analysis, Plant 3 still appears to be losing money. If Plant 3 is closed during the coming period, variable costs of $20,000 could be avoided ($19,000 of variable manufacturing costs and $1,000 of variable commercial costs); however, revenues of $40,000 also would be lost. This would result in a net reduction of the contribution margin in the amount of $20,000 ($40,000 revenue less $20,000 variable costs). If no more than $20,000 of Plant 3's traceable fixed cost can be avoided by closing, the plant should remain open. If unavoidable fixed cost such as depreciation, interest, insurance, and property taxes exceeds $3,000 at Plant 3, the avoidable fixed cost would be less than the $20,000 lost contribution margin. As a result, the most profitable short-run decision would be to continue operations.

	Company Total	Plant 1	Plant 2	Plant 3
Sales.	$200,000	$90,000	$70,000	$40,000
Less variable costs of goods sold	58,500	23,000	16,500	19,000
Gross contribution margin	$141,500	$67,000	$53,500	$21,000
Less variable commercial expenses	4,500	2,000	1,500	1,000
Contribution margin	$137,000	$65,000	$52,000	$20,000
Less traceable fixed costs:				
Manufacturing.	$ 51,500	$17,000	$14,500	$20,000
Commercial.	13,500	5,000	5,500	3,000
Total traceable fixed costs	$ 65,000	$22,000	$20,000	$23,000
Margin available to cover common expenses and provide a profit	$ 72,000	$43,000	$32,000	$ (3,000)
Common commercial fixed expenses	32,000			
Operating profit	$ 40,000			

Even if more than $20,000 of traceable fixed cost could be avoided by shutting down Plant 3, the shutdown costs (i.e., the costs of closing and reopening the plant, rehiring and retraining replacement employees, and reestablishing a market for the products manufactured by Plant 3) should be weighed against the potential savings before making a decision to discontinue operations. Even if all of the $23,000 of traceable fixed costs could be avoided, Plant 3 should be shut down only if the shutdown costs are less than $3,000. If the shutdown costs exceed $3,000, the plant should continue operations unless the losses are expected to continue for more than one period, in which case the cost savings from a shutdown for several periods would have to be weighed against the shutdown costs.

Decisions to Discontinue Products[7]

While an entire facility may not be closed or eliminated, management may decide to discontinue certain individual products because they are producing no profit or an inadequate profit. Decisions to discontinue products require careful analysis of relevant differential cost and revenue data through a structured and continuous product evaluation program. Several benefits can accrue from an effectively administered evaluation program that has as its objective the timely identification of products that should be eliminated or

---

[7]This discussion is adapted from Stanley H. Kratchman, Richard T. Hise, and Thomas A. Ulrich, "Management's Decision to Discontinue a Product," *The Journal of Accountancy*, Vol. 139, No. 6, pp. 50-54.

that can be made more profitable through appropriate corrective action. These benefits include:

1. Expanded sales.
2. Increased profits.
3. Reduced inventory levels.
4. Executive time freed for more profitable activities.
5. Important and scarce resources, such as facilities, materials, and labor, made available for more promising projects.
6. Greater management concern with why products get into difficulty or fail, thus enabling the institution of policies that will reduce the rate of product failure.

Care must be taken not only to consider the profitability of the product being analyzed but also to evaluate the extent to which sales of other products will be adversely affected when one product is removed. An unprofitable product may be part of a line of products that must be complete in order to attract customers to more profitable products. The unprofitable product may also be a complement to more profitable products, in which case some customers may buy the more profitable products because the unprofitable product is also available from the same company. If the expected sales decrease of related products is severe enough, it probably would be desirable to retain the product being scrutinized.

Management needs data that will permit development of warning signals for products that may be in trouble. Such warning signals include:

1. Increasing number of customer complaints.
2. Increasing number of shipments returned.
3. Declining sales volume.
4. Product sales volume decreasing as a percentage of the firm's total sales.
5. Decreasing market share.
6. Malfunctioning of the product or introduction of a superior competitive product.
7. Past sales volume not up to projected amounts.
8. Expected future sales and market potential not favorable.
9. Return on investment below a minimum acceptable level.
10. Variable cost approaching or exceeding revenue.
11. Various costs consistently increasing as a percentage of sales.
12. Increasing percentage of executive time required.
13. Price which must be constantly lowered to maintain sales.
14. Promotional budgets which must be consistently increased to maintain sales.

Studies have shown that firms often do a poor job of identifying products that are in difficulty and that should be eliminated. Probably the major deficiency is the lack of timely, relevant data. To determine what data are required for a successful product monitoring program and its effective implementation and operation, management must draw on the accountant's experience and expertise.

The conditions that bring about the need to evaluate products or facilities may be permanent or even long-term in nature. If profitable alternative asset usage is not foreseen, asset divestment may be needed.[8]

To illustrate the product abandonment decision, assume that Plant 3 of Nigent Company produces three different products: tape cleaner, disk cleaner, and cleaning solvent. Operations for the coming period are expected to be as follows:

	Plant 3 Total	Tape Cleaner	Disk Cleaner	Cleaning Solvent
Sales	$40,000	$16,000	$14,000	$10,000
Less variable costs of goods sold	19,000	7,000	6,000	6,000
Gross contribution margin	$21,000	$ 9,000	$ 8,000	$ 4,000
Less variable commercial expenses	1,000	400	400	200
Contribution margin	$20,000	$ 8,600	$ 7,600	$ 3,800
Less traceable fixed cost	15,000	4,000	3,200	7,800
Margin available to cover Plant 3 and company common cost	$ 5,000	$ 4,600	$ 4,400	$ (4,000)
Common fixed cost	8,000			
Margin available to cover company common cost	$ (3,000)			

Since the contribution margin from the expected sales of cleaning solvent is $3,800 compared to traceable fixed cost of $7,800, it appears that the contribution margin available to cover company common costs would be improved by $4,000 if cleaning solvent were dropped from the product line. However, a portion of the $7,800 of fixed cost traceable to cleaning solvent may not be avoidable. If the unavoidable amount is less than $4,000, the profitability of operating Plant 3 would be improved by dropping cleaning solvent from the product line. On the other hand, if the unavoidable amount exceeds $4,000, dropping cleaning solvent from the product line would reduce profits even further. Even if the unavoidable cost is less than $4,000, before cleaning solvent is dropped from the product line, management should evaluate the potential effect on the sales of the other two products, tape cleaner and disk cleaner, as discussed above.

Additional Applications of Differential Cost Analysis

In the following pages, differential cost analysis is applied to the alternatives which confront the management of an oil refinery. The hypothetical cases, which illustrate the methods that may be employed in solving such problems, demonstrate additional examples of differential cost analysis and can be generalized for other industry settings.[9]

---

[8]For an expanded development of this topic, see Douglas M. Lambert, *The Product Abandonment Decision* (Montvale, N.J.: National Association of Accountants, and Hamilton, Ontario: The Society of Management Accountants of Canada, 1985).

[9]Adapted from a study prepared by John L. Fox, later published in *NA(C)A Bulletin*, Vol. XXXI, No. 4, pp. 403-413, under the title, "Cost Analysis Budget to Evaluate Operating Alternatives for Oil Refiners."

The oil refining industry is characterized by processes that require management to choose between alternatives at various points during the processes. The basic function of oil refining is the separation, extraction, and chemical conversion of the crude oil's component elements, employing skillful utilization of heat, pressure, and catalytic principles. The basic petroleum products are obtained through a physical change caused by the application of heat through a wide temperature range. Within a temperature differential of 300° (275°F to 575°F), the different liquid products (called fractions, ends, or cuts) pass off as vapors and are then condensed back into liquids. The initial application of heat drives off the lightest fractions—the naphthas and gasoline; the successively heavier fractions, such as kerosene and fuel oil, follow as the temperature rises. This process of vaporizing the crude oil and condensing the gaseous vapors to obtain the various cuts is commonly referred to as primary distillation.

Certain cuts (such as gasoline) are marketable with little treating. Other products may undergo further processing in order to make them more salable. Thus, heavier fractions, such as kerosene and fuel oil, may be subjected to cracking, which will cause them to yield more valuable products such as gasoline. Cracking is a process during which, by the use of high temperatures and pressures and perhaps in the presence of a catalyst, a heavy fraction is subjected to destructive distillation and converted to a lighter hydrocarbon possessing different chemical characteristics, one of which is a lower boiling point. The heaviest of the fractions resulting from primary distillation is known as residuum or heavy bottoms. This residuum, after further processing, treating, and blending, forms lubricating oils and ancillary wax or asphalt products.

The management of a refinery must decide what to do with each distillate or fraction and at what stage of refining each should be sold; whether additional fractions should be bought from other refineries and what price should be paid for the additional units; or whether the company should enlarge the plant in order to handle a greater volume. They must also determine what alternate courses should be taken in order to break into the most profitable market at the moment.

The accountant can help management through the preparation of flexible budgets for the secondary operating departments in which further processing might take place. These departmental flexible budgets are called *cost analysis budgets*. They differ from the flexible budget used for control purposes in several respects: (1) all expenses (controllable as well as non-controllable costs) are included; (2) budgeted expenses of service departments are allocated to operating departments at corresponding capacity levels; and (3) their aim is to discover the departmental differential costs.

The amounts stated for each class of expense at each production level are computed on separate work sheets in which various individual expenses are separated into their fixed and variable elements. This separation is necessary to arrive at the estimated expenses for each level of production.

Analysis budgets for various activities for the following departments, which represent secondary processing or finishing operations, are prepared:

Treating	Solvent Extraction
Filters and Burners	Wax Specialties
Cracking	Canning
Solvent Dewaxing	Barrel House

The analysis budget for cracking fuel oil in the Cracking Department is as shown below:

ANALYSIS BUDGET

Department: Cracking

Period Budgeted: _____ to _____

Supervisor: _____

Normal Capacity (100%) 100,000 gallons of throughput of fuel oil

	Shut-Down	60%	80%	100%	120%
Direct costs	$6,000	$14,000	$16,000	$17,000	$23,000
Allocated costs	1,000	2,000	3,000	4,000	6,000
Total costs	$7,000	$16,000	$19,000	$21,000	$29,000
Throughput:					
Total gallons		60,000	80,000	100,000	120,000
Differential gallons		60,000	20,000	20,000	20,000
Total differential cost		$9,000	$3,000	$2,000	$8,000
Differential cost per unit		$.1500	$.1500	$.1000	$.4000
Average cost per unit		$.2667	$.2375	$.2100	$.2417

Cracking analysis budget:
   Present operations, 80% of normal capacity
   Differential cost (80% to 100%) = $.10 per gallon of input
Cracking yields: 75% gasoline; 15% residual fuel oil; 10% loss

Sell or Process Further. A refiner has on hand 20,000 gallons of fuel oil and must decide whether to sell it as fuel oil or crack it into gasoline and residual fuel oil. The following current prices per gallon are available:

Fuel oil	$1.40
Gasoline	1.68

The refiner can then prepare the following differential income computation, utilizing the Cracking Department analysis budget:

Potential revenue—products from cracking:			
Gasoline (15,000 gallons @ $1.68)		$25,200	
Fuel oil (3,000 gallons @ $1.40)		4,200	
		$29,400	
Less differential cost (20,000 gallons @ $.10)		2,000	$27,400
Net potential revenue—fuel oil (20,000 gallons @ $1.40)			28,000
Loss from cracking of fuel oil			$ 600*

*Not an accounting loss per se, but a loss of profit that would result from an improper choice of alternatives.

Thus, judging from a quantitative standpoint, it would be more profitable to sell the 20,000 gallons of fuel oil as such rather than to process them further.

Choice of Alternate Routings. A refiner is trying to decide whether to treat and sell the kerosene fraction or to crack it for its gasoline content. The current decision involves 10,000 gallons of raw kerosene. Pertinent available information follows (from an analysis budget for cracking kerosene):

```
Current prices per gallon:
    Kerosene .........................................................    $1.20
    Gasoline..........................................................     1.68
    Fuel oil..........................................................     1.40
Cracking yields:
    Gasoline..........................................................      85%
    Residual fuel oil.................................................       5
        Loss .........................................................      10
Differential costs associated with potential gallons throughput of
  kerosene:
    Cracking..........................................................    $.12   per gallon
    Treating .........................................................     .08
```

Using the above amounts, the refiner can prepare the following analysis:

```
Net potential revenue—products from cracking:
    Gasoline (8,500 gallons @ $1.68) ...........................    $14,280
    Fuel oil (500 gallons @ $1.40)..............................        700
                                                                   $14,980
        Less differential cost (10,000 gallons @ $.12)..............     1,200    $13,780
Net potential revenue—kerosene:
    Total revenue (10,000 gallons @ $1.20) .....................    $12,000
        Less differential cost (10,000 gallons @ $.08)              800      11,200
Gain from cracking rather than treating ........................              $ 2,580
```

In this situation, the more profitable alternative is to crack the kerosene fraction.

Price to Pay for an Intermediate Stock. A refiner has been offered 10,000 gallons of cylinder stock. The usual bargaining process will determine the final price. The refiner is interested in knowing how high a price it can pay and still make a profit. The stock purchased would be processed into conventional bright stock and sold at that stage, since the blending unit for making finished motor oils is currently working at full capacity. Available information is as follows:

Cylinder stock is of such a quality and type that it will probably yield:
   90% bright stock
    5% petrolatum
    5% loss
Current prices: bright stock, $1 per gallon; petrolatum—no market

Differential costs associated with processing 10,000 gallons of cylinder stock through several stages (from analysis budgets) are:

```
        Solvent dewaxing......    $.06 per gallon
        Solvent extracting .....     .06
        Filtering .............     .03
            Total .............    $.15 per gallon
```

Using this information, the refiner's position can be analyzed and a bargaining margin can be determined:

Revenue—bright stock (9,000 gallons @ $1)	$9,000
Differential cost (10,000 gallons @ $.15).	1,500
Margin.	$7,500
Margin per gallon of cylinder stock	$ .75

The refiner is now ready to bargain for the purchase of the cylinder stock, knowing that a purchase price of $.75 a gallon represents a critical maximum point—to pay more would produce a loss, to pay less would result in a gain. Management can then decide how much profit is required to justify the purchase. Here the concept of opportunity costs also enters into the final decision. If the available capacity could be more profitably used for another purpose, then perhaps the proposed purchase should not be consummated.

Proposed Construction of Additional Capacity. A refiner discovers that the market for finished neutrals is such that present capacity will not satisfy the demand. The refiner feels certain that an addition to the solvent dewaxing and solvent extracting units would prove profitable. The additional wax distillate stock required would be purchased on the open market at the current rate. However, before going ahead with the construction, the chief accountant is consulted and presents the following information.

Unit differential cost:
    Capacity from 100% (normal) to 120% (increase of 10,000 gallons throughput)
    Solvent Dewaxing Department—$.10 per gallon throughput
    Solvent Extracting Department—$.10 per gallon throughput
Assumed yield from wax distillate:
    90% Viscous neutral
    1.5% Paraffin (8 pounds per gallon)
    8.5% Loss
Current market prices:
    Viscous neutrals—$1.50 per gallon
    Paraffin—$.24 per pound
    Wax distillate stock—$1.20 per gallon*

*Not a published market price, but the price management believes it will have to pay to acquire the stock.

Using this information, the following analysis is prepared:

Differential revenue:		
9,000 gallons viscous neutrals @ $1.50	$13,500	
1,200 pounds paraffin @ $.24	288	
	$13,788	
Less cost of wax distillate stock (10,000 gallons @ $1.20)	12,000	
Margin to apply against differential costs		$1,788
Differential costs:		
Solvent Dewaxing Department (10,000 gallons @ $.10).	$ 1,000	
Solvent Extracting Department (10,000 gallons @ $.10)	1,000	2,000
Potential loss from differential production		$ 212

The accountant's analysis indicates that the proposed increase in the productive capacity would not be justified under the stated conditions. Furthermore, even a potential profit should yield a satisfactory return on the additional capital investment.

■ LINEAR PROGRAMMING

QUALITY CONTROL

A short-term resource allocation problem may become complex when several products are involved and numerous constraints are imposed. One approach to solving the problem would be for the decision maker to model the production process and to make an educated guess about the appropriate level of inputs and outputs. Alternatively, after modeling the production process, the decision maker could input numerous different combinations of decision variables and select the combination that results in the best outcome from among those combinations evaluated. In contrast to the trial and error approach, *linear programming* is a quantitative decision tool that will permit the decision maker to find the optimal solution to a short-term resource allocation problem without guessing.

Maximization of Contribution Margin

The contribution margin is a measure of business success, which often is used as a measure of management performance. To maximize company profits, management must maximize the total contribution margin from the production and sale of products.

To illustrate the application of linear programming to the problem of maximizing the total contribution margin, assume that a machine shop manufactures two models of a product, standard and deluxe. Each unit of the standard model requires two hours of grinding and four hours of polishing. Each unit of the deluxe model requires five hours of grinding and two hours of polishing. The manufacturer has three grinders and two polishers; therefore, in a 40-hour work week there are 120 hours of grinding capacity and 80 hours of polishing capacity available. A unit of the standard model sells for $9, and a unit of the deluxe model sells for $12. The variable costs of producing and selling one unit total $6 and $8 for the standard model and the deluxe model, respectively. Consequently, the contribution margins from the production and sale of a standard unit and a deluxe unit are $3 and $4, respectively. Market demand for both products is strong enough to absorb all units that the company can produce and sell with its present capacity. To maximize the total contribution margin, management must decide on (1) the allocation of the available production capacity between the standard and deluxe models and (2) the resulting number of units of each model to produce.

The relevant information required to solve the problem is summarized as follows:

	Grinding Time	Polishing Time	Sales Price	Variable Cost	Contribution Margin
Standard model.............	2 hours	4 hours	$ 9	$6	$3
Deluxe model..............	5	2	12	8	4
Plant capacity	120	80			

The problem can be expressed mathematically as follows:

1. First, the total contribution margin the manager can obtain from the production and sale of the two models of products (called the *objective function*) is written mathematically. Let x and y represent the quantities of the standard model and the deluxe model, respectively, to be produced and sold. Since a contribution margin of $3 is expected for each unit of the standard model and $4 for each unit of the deluxe model, the total contribution margin available would be 3x + 4y. Therefore, the objective function is:

$$\text{Maximize CM} = 3x + 4y$$

2. Next, the resource limitations in the problem (called *constraints*) are expressed in mathematical form. In the illustration, there are two constraints available, grinding time and polishing time. There are 120 hours of grinding time available. It takes 2 hours of grinding to produce one unit of the standard model (denoted x) and 5 hours of grinding to produce one unit of the deluxe model (denoted y). Therefore, the grinding constraint can be expressed mathematically as follows:

$$2x + 5y \leq 120$$

Since there are 80 hours of polishing time available and it takes 4 hours to produce a unit of the standard model and 2 hours to produce a unit of the deluxe model, the polishing constraint can be expressed mathematically as follows:

$$4x + 2y \leq 80$$

Both constraints in this example are less-than-or-equal-to constraints, i.e., the amount of constraint that may be used must be less than or equal to the amount of constraint available. Maximization problems may also include equal-to constraints (i.e., all of the available constraint must be used) and/or greater-than-or-equal-to constraints (i.e., the amount of resource used must be greater than or equal to the amount specified on the right-hand side of the constraint inequality). These two types of constraints are illustrated in the linear programming minimization problem beginning on page 702.

When a linear programming problem involves only two variables, a two-dimensional graph can be used to determine the optimal solution. In this example, the maximum quantity of each model that can be produced, given the limited grinding and polishing capacity, is determined as follows:

	Maximum Production Quantity	
Production Operation	Standard Model (x)	Deluxe Model (y)
Grinding	120 hrs. ÷ 2 = 60	120 hrs. ÷ 5 = 24
Polishing	80 hrs. ÷ 4 = 20	80 hrs. ÷ 2 = 40

The smallest quantity in each of the two columns is the maximum quantity that can be produced with the limited capacity available. The company can produce no more than 20 units of the standard model, which would result in a contribution margin (CM) of $60 (20 units × $3 CM per unit), or 24 units of the deluxe model, which would result in a contribution margin of $96 (24 units × $4 CM per unit). However, producing a combination of standard and deluxe models would result in a different, perhaps better, solution.

To determine the production combinations possible, the constraints can be plotted on a graph. Once graphed, the production combinations can be evaluated to determine which alternative would result in the maximum contribution margin. Since the relationship between the usage of each available constraint and the quantity of each model produced in this example is linear, the polishing and grinding constraints may be drawn by connecting the points, plotted on each axis, representing the maximum number of units of each model that can be produced with each constraint. These points are:

When x = 0: y ≤ 24 for the grinding constraint
y ≤ 40 for the polishing constraint

When y = 0: x ≤ 60 for the grinding constraint
x ≤ 20 for the polishing constraint

A graph of the constraints for the illustrated problem appears as follows:

Graph Depicting Feasible Area

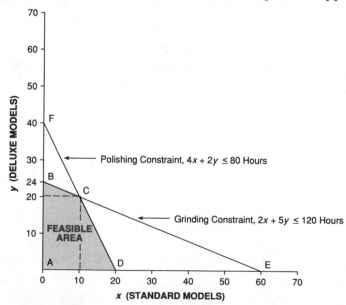

The feasible solution space (referred to as the *feasible area*) is bounded by the lines AB, BC, CD, and DA on the graph above. Any combination of standard and deluxe units that falls on or within the boundaries of the feasible area can be physically produced. Any combination that falls outside the feasible area cannot be produced because there is not enough constraint available.

The best feasible solution is found at one of the corner points, labeled A, B, C, and D in the graph. To determine which corner point is best, each must be evaluated as follows:

$$
\begin{array}{lll}
A\ (x = 0, y = 0) & = (\$3)(0) + (\$4)(0) & = \$\ \ \ 0\ \text{CM} \\
B\ (x = 0, y = 24) & = (\$3)(0) + (\$4)(24) & = \$\ 96\ \text{CM} \\
C\ (x = 10, y = 20) & = (\$3)(10) + (\$4)(20) & = \$110\ \text{CM} \\
D\ (x = 20, y = 0) & = (\$3)(20) + (\$4)(0) & = \$\ 60\ \text{CM}
\end{array}
$$

In this case, the total contribution margin is maximized when 10 standard models and 20 deluxe models are produced and sold, i. e., the combination indicated at corner point C.

The fact that the optimal solution is found at one of the corner points can be demonstrated graphically. Notice in the graph that the largest quantities for each product combination occur at the farthest distances from point A (i.e., the farthest away from 0 units of each product). Consequently, the production and sale of the product mix indicated at one of the points that lies on the line defining the outermost limit of the feasible area (i.e., the line defined by points B, C, and D, which will be called line BCD) would result in the maximum contribution margin possible, given the constraints imposed on the problem. To determine which of those points is optimal, a series of contribution margin lines (CM lines) can be constructed (the green lines on the graph on page 702). The production and sale of each combination of products represented by the points on a single CM line will result in the same total contribution margin. The total contribution margin will increase the farther the CM line is from point A.

The slope of a CM line is determined by multiplying –1 by the quotient of the contribution margin available from the sale of one unit of the product designated by the horizontal axis, divided by the contribution margin available from the sale of one unit of the product designated by the vertical axis. For products x and y in the illustration the slope is –3/4. Since the total contribution margin in this example is $3x + $4y, a CM line can be constructed by drawing a line between a point plotted on the horizontal axis (indicating the quantity of x's required to yield the contribution margin represented by the line, given that y is zero) and a point plotted on the vertical axis (indicating the quantity of y's required to yield the same contribution margin, given that x is zero). The following points are computed for the CM lines on the graph:

CM	Quantity of x's Required when y = 0			Quantity of y's Required when x = 0		
$ 48	$ 48CM ÷ $3	= 16	units	$ 48CM ÷ $4	= 12	units
60	60CM ÷ 3	= 20	units	60CM ÷ 4	= 15	units
84	84CM ÷ 3	= 28	units	84CM ÷ 4	= 21	units
96	96CM ÷ 3	= 32	units	96CM ÷ 4	= 24	units
110	110CM ÷ 3	= 36 2/3	units	110CM ÷ 4	= 27 1/2	units

**Graph Depicting
CM Lines and
Optimal Solution**

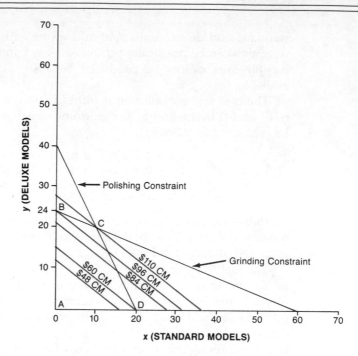

Notice in the graph above that the CM line is farthest from point A when it intersects point C.[10] Full utilization of all available resources will occur only at the point of common intersection of all of the constraint equations in the problem (point C in this example). However, utilization of all available resources does not necessarily result in an optimal solution. For example, if the contribution margin from the sale of a unit of x were $1 instead of $3, the optimal solution would be found at point B instead of point C (i.e., $1(0) + $4(24) = $96 contribution margin at point B would be greater than $1(10) + $4(20) = $90 contribution margin at point C). Therefore, to find the optimal solution, the contribution margin available from the production and sale of the combination of products indicated at each corner point must be computed and compared.

Minimization of Cost

The previous problem dealt with the maximization of the total contribution margin. Linear programming can also be used in problems where the objective is minimization of cost. To illustrate the cost minimization problem, assume that a pharmaceutical firm is planning to produce exactly 40 gallons

---

[10]If the contribution margin changes for either product or for both products, the slope of the CM line would change. If the change in slope is sufficiently large, the optimal solution would shift to a different corner point. If the slope of the CM line were equal to the slope of line BC, all points on line BC would be equally profitable; however, notice that it would never be possible for a point on line BC between points B and C to be more profitable than points B and C.

of a mixture in which the basic ingredients, x and y, cost $8 per gallon and $15 per gallon, respectively. No more than 12 gallons of x can be used, and at least 10 gallons of y must be used. The firm wants to minimize cost.

The objective function can be written as:

$$\text{Minimize cost} = 8x + 15y$$

subject to the following constraints:

$$x + y = 40$$
$$x \leq 12$$
$$y \geq 10$$

The optimal solution in this case is obvious. Since x is cheaper than y, the maximum amount of x permitted by the constraint should be used first (12 gallons), and then the remaining required quantity (28 more gallons to meet the 40-gallon total requirement) should be filled with the more expensive y. However, in more complex problems, a solution may not be so obvious, especially if there are many ingredients, each having different constraints.

The graphic method can be applied to minimization problems in the same manner as for maximization problems. As with maximization problems, the constraints define the solution space for minimization problems when they are graphed. The constraints for the illustration may be graphed as follows:

Graph Depicting Feasible Solutions

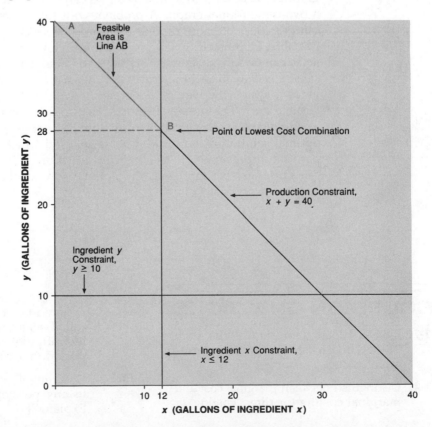

The feasible area in this example is confined to the points on line AB. Any combination of x and y that lies on line AB will result in a total production quantity of exactly 40 gallons, of which more than 10 gallons will be y and no more than 12 gallons will be x. As in the case of the maximization problem, the optimal solution will be on one of the corner points of the feasible area, in this case point A or B. Consequently, the corner points must be evaluated to find the combination of inputs that minimizes the objective function, i.e., cost. The values at each of the two corner points are:

A (x = 0, y = 40)   = $8(0)   + $15(40) = $600 total cost
B (x = 12, y = 28) = $8(12) + $15(28) = $516 total cost

To minimize total cost, the company should use 12 gallons of x and 28 gallons of y, which will result in a total cost of $516.

Simplex Method

Although linear programming problems with more than two constraints can be solved fairly easily using the graphic method, such an approach is not practical in solving problems with more than two variables in the objective function. A problem with three variables would require a three-dimensional graph, which, while not impossible, is certainly more difficult to handle than a two-dimensional graph. A problem with four or more variables would require a four- or more-dimensional graph, which would not be physically tractable. Fortunately, linear programming problems with more than two variables can be solved algebraically with an iterative procedure referred to as the *simplex method*. Based on matrix (or linear) algebra, the simplex method provides a systematic way of algebraically evaluating each corner point in the feasible area. The process begins at the origin (point A in the maximization example) and systematically moves from one corner point to another until the optimal solution is found. Moves are selected which will provide the largest per unit improvement in the objective function. When the objective function can no longer be improved, the optimal solution has been found, and the iterative process stops.

DISCUSSION QUESTIONS

Q21-1. Give a broad definition of the term "differential cost." What other terms are often used and by whom?

Q21-2. Distinguish between marginal cost and marginal costing (or direct costing).

Q21-3. Differential costs have also been called alternative costs. Why is the identification of alternative costs important in decision making?

Q21-4. Differential costs do not correspond to any possible accounting category. Explain.

Q21-5. How does the flexible budget assist in the preparation of differential cost analyses?

Q21-6. Why are historical costs usually irrelevant for decision making?

Q21-7. Why is variable cost so important in differential cost studies?

Q21-8. What are sunk costs?

Q21-9. Explain how a fixed cost can be relevant in deciding between alternative choices.

Q21-10. Define opportunity costs.

Q21-11. What is linear programming?

Q21-12. What kind of unit costs are used in linear programming?

Q21-13. Examine the graph on page 700 and answer the following questions:
(a) The area bounded by the lines AB, BC, CD, and AD is called the feasible area. Why?
(b) The triangles BCF and CDE are not part of the feasible area. Why?
(c) Which point in the feasible area designates the optimal solution? How can it be identified?

Q21-14. What is the simplex method?

EXERCISES

E21-1. Analysis of proposed new business. Saugus Insecticide Company is currently producing and selling 30 000 kilograms of Sta Ded monthly. This volume is 70% of capacity for Sta Ded. A wholesaler outside the Saugus marketing area offers to buy 5 000 kilograms of this product per month on a two-year contract at $1.80 per kilogram, provided the present pinkish color can be changed to green. The product will be marketed under the wholesaler's brand name.

To change the color, a special mixing machine will need to be purchased at a cost of $3,000, but it will have no value at the end of the two-year contract period. Ingredients to change the color in the finished product will cost $.01 per kilogram.

Marketing expense will not be increased if the new business is accepted, but additional administrative expense of $150 per month is estimated. No additional cost for supervision or property tax is contemplated. Additional payroll taxes will be $210.

A monthly income statement for the current operations follows:

Sales..............................		$72,000
Cost to manufacture:		
Direct materials....................	$18,000	
Direct labor	15,000	
Factory overhead:		
Indirect labor	6,000	
Supervisory labor	4,000	
Power ($180 fixed)..............	780	
Supplies.......................	600	
Maintenance and repair	810	
Depreciation	3,000	
Insurance.......................	210	
Property tax.....................	125	
Payroll taxes	1,250	
Cost of goods produced and sold		49,775
Gross profit........................		$22,225
Marketing expense...................	$11,000	
Administrative expense	4,500	15,500
Income before income tax		$ 6,725

Required: Prepare a differential cost analysis to show whether the company should accept the proposed new business.

E21-2. Differential cost analysis. The Budgeting Department of Yarborough Products Corporation prepared the following schedule of factory overhead at various levels of production:

	40% of Capacity	60% of Capacity	80% of Capacity	100% of Capacity
Units of product................	100,000	150,000	200,000	250,000
Variable factory overhead........	$ 50,000	$ 60,000	$ 67,000	$ 80,000
Fixed factory overhead..........	90,000	91,400	91,400	94,000

Yarborough manufactures gaskets for natural gas pipelines. In recent months, legislation unfavorable to gas transmission firms has been pending in Congress, and customer orders have been minimal. For example, in December only 150,000 gaskets, representing 60% of capacity, were manufactured at the following costs:

Materials.............	$ 42,000
Direct labor..........	49,200
Factory overhead:	
Variable...........	60,000
Fixed.............	91,400
	$242,600

Economic indicators point to rising production costs in the near future. Accordingly, management is considering stepping up January production to 80% of capacity (an additional 50,000 units) in order to build up an inventory of relatively low cost product during this slack period.

Required:

(1) Determine the cost of the additional 50,000 units of product.
(2) Compute the total cost of producing 200,000 units in January.
(3) Determine the sales price required for January production in order to achieve a 20% markup on production cost.

E21-3. Acceptance of a special order. Pacific Palmer Company has been producing and selling 10,000 units of its product per month, with the following total costs:

Direct materials	$20,000
Direct labor......................................	35,000
Variable factory overhead	15,000
Fixed factory overhead	24,000
Variable marketing and administrative expenses	10,000
Fixed marketing and administrative expenses	13,000

The normal sales price is $15 and plant capacity is 18,000 units. The company has received an offer from a special customer who would like to buy exactly 5,000 units of Pacific Palmer's product for $9 per unit. Marketing and administrative expenses related to this special order would be $1,500.

Required:

(1) Present computations showing whether or not Pacific Palmer should accept this special order.
(2) Determine the effect on the answer to requirement (1) if the plant capacity were only 13,000 units.

CGA-Canada (adapted) Reprint with permission

E21-4. Make-or-buy decision. Huntington Products manufactures 10,000 units of Part M-1 annually for use in its production. The following costs are reported:

Direct materials	$ 20,000
Direct labor	55,000
Variable factory overhead	45,000
Fixed factory overhead	70,000
	$190,000

Lufkin Company has offered to sell Huntington 10,000 units of Part M-1 annually for $18 per unit. If Huntington accepts the offer, some of the facilities presently used to manufacture Part M-1 could be rented to a third party at an annual rental of $15,000. Additionally, $4 per unit of the fixed factory overhead applied to Part M-1 would be totally eliminated.

Required: Should Huntington accept Lufkin's offer, and why? (AICPA adapted)

E21-5. Make-or-buy decision. Montrose Inc. manufactures Part 345 for use in one of its main products. Normal annual production for Part 345 is 100,000 units. The cost per 100-unit lot of the part follows:

Direct materials	$260
Direct labor	100
Factory overhead:	
Variable	120
Fixed	160
Total cost per 100 units	$640

Kalispell Inc. has offered to sell Montrose all 100,000 units it will need during the coming year for $600 per 100 units. If Montrose accepts the offer from Kalispell, the facilities used to manufacture Part 345 could be used in the production of Part 789. This change would save Montrose $90,000 in fixed cost related to the rental of capacity necessary to produce Part 789. In addition, a $50,000 cost item included in fixed factory overhead which is specifically related to Part 345 (rental of special equipment not usable in the manufacture of other products) would be eliminated.

Required: Determine whether or not Montrose Inc. should make Part 345 or buy it from Kalispell Inc.

(ICMA adapted)

E21-6. Decision to drop a product. The Montreal Company manufactures and sells three products, Mift, Tift, and Lift. For the coming year, sales are expected to be as follows:

Product	Sales Price	Quantity	Total Sales
Mift	$10	5,000	$ 50,000
Tift	6	7,000	42,000
Lift	15	3,000	45,000
			$137,000

At the expected sales quantity and mix, the manufacturing cost per unit follows:

	Mift	Tift	Lift
Materials	$2	$2	$ 4
Direct labor	2	1	3
Factory overhead:			
Variable	1	1	2
Fixed	1	1	3
	$6	$5	$12

Variable marketing expense is $1 per unit for Mift and Tift and $2 per unit for Lift. Budgeted fixed marketing expenses for the coming year are $3,000, and budgeted fixed administrative expenses are $6,000.

The sales manager has recommended dropping Tift from the product line and using the production capacity currently committed to the production of Tift to produce more Mift. The production manager reports that 4,000 additional units of Mift could be produced with the production capacity now used in manufacturing Tift. In order to sell 4,000 additional units of Mift, the sales manager believes that the advertising budget will have to be increased by $5,000.

Required:

(1) Should the sales manager's proposal be accepted? Support your answer by computing the change in profitability that would result from this action.

(2) In addition to the factors mentioned by the production manager and the sales manager, what other factors should be considered?   CGA-Canada (adapted) Reprint with permission

E21-7. Sell or process further. Enid Company produces a variety of cleaning compounds and solutions for both industrial and household use. One of its products, a coarse cleaning powder called Grit 337, has a variable manufacturing cost of $1.60 and sells for $2 per pound.

A small portion of this product's annual production is retained for further processing in the Mixing Department, where it is combined with several other ingredients to form a paste which is marketed as a silver polish selling for $4 per jar. The further processing requires one-fourth pound of Grit 337 per jar; other ingredients, labor, and variable factory overhead associated with further processing cost $2.50 per jar, while unit variable marketing cost is $.30. If a decision were made to cease silver polish production, $5,600 of fixed Mixing Department costs could be avoided.

Required: Calculate the minimum number of jars of silver polish that must be sold to justify further processing Grit 337.   (ICMA adapted)

E21-8. Minimum bid price. Hall Company specializes in packaging bulk drugs in standard dosages for local hospitals. The company has been in business since 19A and has been profitable since its second year of operation. D. Greenway, director of cost accounting, installed a standard cost system after joining the company in 19E.

Wyant Memorial Hospital has asked Hall to bid on the packaging of one million doses of medication at full cost plus a return on full cost of no more than 9% after income taxes. Wyant defines cost as including all variable costs of performing the service, a reasonable amount of nonvariable overhead, and reasonable administrative costs. The hospital will supply all packaging materials and ingredients. Wyant has indicated that any bid over $.015 per dose will be rejected.

Greenway accumulated the following information prior to the preparation of the bid.

Direct labor	$5.00 per hour
Variable factory overhead	$2.00 per direct labor hour
Fixed factory overhead	$5.00 per direct labor hour
Administrative costs.	$1,000 for the order
Production rate	1,000 doses per direct labor hour

Hall Company is subject to an effective income tax rate of 40%.

Required:

(1) Calculate the minimum bid price per dose that Hall Company would bid for the Wyant Memorial Hospital job that would not reduce Hall's net income.

(2) Calculate the bid price per dose using the full cost criterion and the maximum allowable return specified by Wyant Memorial Hospital.

(3) Without prejudice to your answer in requirement (2) above, assume that the price per dose that Hall Company calculated using the cost-plus criterion specified by Wyant Memorial Hospital is greater than the maximum bid of $.015 per dose specified by Wyant. What factors should Hall Company consider before deciding whether or not to submit a bid at the maximum price of $.015 per dose?

(4) What factors should Wyant Memorial Hospital have considered before deciding whether or not to employ cost-plus pricing?   (ICMA adapted)

E21-9. Alternative cash collection procedures. Kleenvu Corporation is a franchisor of automatic car washes in the southeast. Kleenvu has 420 franchisees that operate seven days per week. The average gross revenue for each location is $500 per day. Kleenvu collects 25% of the gross revenue as its franchise fee. The cash collection procedure requires each franchisee to mail one check, on a daily basis, to Kleenvu headquarters in Miami. The check is supposed to be mailed by noon each day. Many of the franchisees are lax, however, and payments are forwarded an average of two days late. Once mailed, the checks take an average of one and one-half days in the mail and another three days to be processed in Kleenvu's receivables department.

Kleenvu's management is considering a change in the company's cash collection procedure. The two proposals it is considering are presented below. Kleenvu has a 15% before-tax opportunity cost and is subject to an income tax rate of 40%.

(1) The first proposal would be to use local messenger services to collect and mail the checks. This would save the two days of late check forwarding. The cost of the messenger service is $20,000 per year.

(2) The second proposal would be to combine the messenger service with a lock-box arrangement for a combined savings of five days. The cost of the second proposal is $20,000 per year for the messenger service plus $15,000 in a compensating balance required by the bank servicing the lock-box.

Required: Compute the annual change in Kleenvu's before-tax income that would result from the adoption of each of the two alternative proposals. (ICMA adapted)

E21-10. Choice of production method. Circutech Company is evaluating the use of AZ-17 Photo Resist for the manufacture of printed circuit boards. The major advantages in the utilization of this process versus the present silk-screen method are:

(a) Anticipated reduced manufacturing cycle and cost due to elimination of the need for silk circuit screens and shorter operator time to produce circuit boards.

(b) Improved ease of registration between front and back patterns.

(c) The ability to achieve finer line widths and closer spacing between circuit paths.

The proposed AZ-17 process is described as follows:

(a) Fabricate through the completion of the drilling and copper plating of inside holes.

(b) Pressure spray AZ-17 Photo Resist on one side, oven bake for 10 minutes, and repeat for other side.

(c) Use the photo negative and expose each side for seven minutes in a Nu-Arc Printer.

(d) Develop in AZ-17 Developer and proceed through normal operations for making printed circuit board.

Total direct labor time for the proposed AZ-17 process is 30 minutes. The original silk-screen method uses a wire mesh stencil film, screening ink, and frames. The direct labor time to prepare the screen for each circuit board is 1 1/2 hours. The direct labor time to screen patterns on the printed wire board is 20 minutes. The hourly direct labor rate is $6.50. The monthly cost for materials and for equipment rental and operation needed for the proposed process is $4,000 greater than for the silk-screen method, excluding the direct labor. The company manufactures 20,000 circuit boards annually.

Required: Compute the annual savings or added cost from changing from the silk-screen method to the new AZ-17 process. (Round all computations to the nearest dollar.)

E21-11. Linear programming problem formulation—contribution margin maximization. Smythe Company manufactures two types of display boards that are sold to office supply stores. One board is hard-finished marking board that can be written on with a water-soluble felt-tip marking pen and then wiped clean with a cloth. The other is a conventional cork-type tack board.

Both boards pass through two manufacturing departments. All of the raw materials (board base, board covering, and aluminum frames) are cut to size in the Cutting Department. Both types of boards are the same size and use the same aluminum frame. The boards are assembled in one of Smythe Company's two assembly operations (the Automated Assembly Department or the Labor Assembly Department). The Automated Assembly Department is a capital intensive assembly operation. This department has been in operation for 18 months and was intended to replace the Labor Assembly Department. However, Smythe Company's business expanded so rapidly that both assembly operations are needed and used. The final results of the two assembly operations are identical. The only difference between the two is the proportion of machine time versus direct labor in each department and, thus, different costs. However, workers have been trained for both operations so that they can be switched between the two operations.

Data regarding the two products and their manufacture follow:

	Marking Board	Tack Board
Sales price per unit	$60.00	$45.00
Variable marketing expenses.	3.00	3.00
Materials:		
Base	6.00	6.00
Covering	14.50	7.75
Frame	8.25	8.25
Direct labor:		
Cutting Department	2.00	2.00
Automated Assembly Department	.60	.60
Labor Assembly Department	3.00	3.00
Variable factory overhead:		
Cutting Department	2.45	2.45
Automated Assembly Department	3.30	3.30
Labor Assembly Department	2.25	2.25

Machine Hour Data

	Cutting Department	Automated Assembly Department	Labor Assembly Department
Machine hours required per board	.15	.05	.02
Monthly machine hours available	25,000	5,000	1,500
Annual machine hours available	300,000	60,000	18,000

Smythe Company produced and sold 600,000 marking boards and 900,000 tack boards last year. Management estimates that the total unit sales volume for the coming year could increase 20% if the units can be produced. Smythe Company has contracts to produce and sell 30,000 units of each board each month. Sales, production, and cost incurrence are uniform throughout the year. Smythe Company has a monthly maximum labor capacity of 30,000 direct labor hours in the Cutting Department and 40,000 direct labor hours for the assembly operations (Automated Assembly and Labor Assembly Departments combined). It takes 12 minutes of labor in the Cutting Department for both kinds of boards. The Automated Assembly Department requires 3 minutes of labor for each board, regardless of type, and the Labor Assembly Department requires 15 minutes of labor per board.

Required: Assuming that Smythe Company wants to maximize its profits, give the appropriate linear programming objective function and constraints for the production of the two boards.   (ICMA adapted)

 E21-12. Linear programming contribution margin maximization problem—graphic method. An office supply company makes two types of paper pads, legal and regular. A box of legal pads requires 20 minutes to produce and a box of regular pads requires 10 minutes to produce. Two people work on the production line which operates 7.5 hours per day, 5 days a week. The company can sell any combination of boxes of legal and regular pads up to a maximum of 300 boxes of pads per week. The legal pads sell for $18 a box and the regular pads sell for $12 a box.

Required: Determine the quantity of legal and regular pads that should be produced daily in order to maximize total contribution margin, using the graphic method.   CGA-Canada (adapted) Reprint with permission

E21-13. Linear programming contribution margin maximization problem—graphic method. Merz Inc. manufactures two kinds of leather belts—Belt A (a high-quality belt) and Belt B (of a lower quality). The respective contribution margins are $4 and $3 per belt. Production of Belt A requires twice as much time as for Belt B; and if all belts were of the Belt B type, Merz Inc. could produce 1,000 per day. The leather supply is sufficient for only 800 belts per day (both Belt A and Belt B combined). Belt A requires a fancy buckle, and only 400 buckles per day are available for this belt.

Required: Determine the quantity of each type belt to be produced to maximize the contribution margin, using the graphic method.

 E21-14. Linear programming cost minimization problem—graphic method. A company produces three products, A, B, and C, which use common materials, X and Y. Material X costs $3 per ton and Y $4 per ton. The amount of materials required per ton of product and the required weight per ton of product are:

	Product A	Product B	Product C
Material X	4 lbs.	7 lbs.	1.5 lbs.
Material Y	8	2	5
Minimum weight required	32	14	15

Required: Determine the number of tons of each material needed to meet the requirements at minimum cost, using the graphic method.

 E21-15. Linear programming cost minimization problem—graphic method. Deane Pulp Paper Company uses softwood and hardwood pulp as basic materials for producing converter-grade paper. Hardwood is 80% pulp fiber and 20% pulp binder, while softwood is 50% pulp fiber and 50% pulp binder. The cost per pound for hardwood and softwood is $.50 and $.40, respectively.

The company's quality control expert specifies that in order for the product to meet quality standards, each batch must contain at least 12,000 pounds of pulp fiber and at least 6,000 pounds of pulp binder. Because of equipment limitations, the size of a batch cannot exceed 24,000 pounds.

The production department recently received a new standard from the Cost Department, allowing $8,200 per batch. The production manager feels that this amount is too low, because such costs have never been less than $8,400.

Required: Determine the hardwood and softwood mix necessary to minimize the cost per batch, using the graphic method.

PROBLEMS

P21-1. Special order analysis. Auer Manufacturing Company received an order from Jaycor Company for a piece of special machinery, but just as the machine was completed, Jaycor Company defaulted on the order and forfeited the 10% deposit paid on the $72,500 sales price. Auer's manufacturing manager identified the costs already incurred in the production of the special machinery for Jaycor as follows:

Direct materials used............................		$16,600
Direct labor incurred		21,400
Factory overhead applied:		
Variable......................................	$10,700	
Fixed..	5,350	16,050
Fixed marketing and administrative expenses		5,405
Total cost		$59,455

KaTee Corporation would be interested in buying the special machinery if it is reworked to KaTee's specifications. Auer offered to sell the reworked special machinery to KaTee for a net price of $68,400. The additional identifiable costs to rework the machinery to the specifications of Katee are as follows:

Direct materials	$ 6,200
Direct labor	4,200
	$10,400

A second alternative available to Auer is to convert the special machinery to the standard model, which lists for $62,500. The additional identifiable costs to make the conversion are:

Direct materials	$2,850
Direct labor	3,300
	$6,150

A third alternative for Auer Manufacturing Company is to sell, as a special order, the machine as is (e.g., without modification) for a net price of $52,000.

The following additional information is available regarding Auer's operations:

(a) The sales commission rate on sales of standard models is 2%, while the sales commission rate on special orders is 3%. All sales commissions are calculated on net sales price (i.e., list price less cash discount, if any).

(b) Normal credit terms for sales of standard models are 2/10, n/30. Customers take the discounts, except in rare instances. Credit terms for special orders are negotiated with the customer.

(c) The application rates for factory overhead and the fixed marketing and administrative costs are as follows:

Factory overhead:
    Variable: 50% of direct labor cost
    Fixed: 25% of direct labor cost
Marketing and administrative:
    Fixed: 10% of the total of direct materials, direct labor, and factory overhead costs

Required:

(1) Compute the dollar contribution that each of the three alternatives will add to Auer's profit.

(2) If KaTee makes Auer a counter offer, determine the lowest price Auer should accept from KaTee.

(ICMA adapted)

P21-2. Special order analysis. Framar Inc. manufactures automation machinery according to customer specifications. The company is relatively new and has grown each year. Framar operated at about 75% of practical capacity during its most recent fiscal year ended September 30, with the operating results on page 713.

Framar management has developed a pricing formula based on current operating costs, which are expected to prevail for the next year. This formula was used in developing the following bid for APA Inc.:

Direct materials cost	$ 29,200
Direct labor cost.	56,000
Factory overhead calculated at 50% of direct labor.	28,000
Corporate overhead calculated at 10% of direct labor.	5,600
Total cost. excluding sales commission	$118,800
Add 25% for profit and tax	29,700
Suggested price (with profit) before sales commission	$148,500
Suggested total price (suggested price divided by .9 to adjust for 10% sales commission)	$165,000

Sales		$25,000
Less sales commissions		2,500
Net sales		$22,500
Expenses:		
Direct materials		$ 6,000
Direct labor.		7,500
Factory overhead—variable:		
Supplies	$ 625	
Indirect labor.	1,500	
Power	125	2,250
Factory overhead—fixed:		
Supervision.	$ 500	
Depreciation	1,000	1,500
Corporation administration.		750
Total expense		$18,000
Income before income tax.		$ 4,500
Income tax (40%)		1,800
Net income.		$ 2,700

Required:

(1) Compute the impact on net income if APA accepts the bid.
(2) Determine the suggested decision if APA is willing to pay only $127,000.
(3) Calculate the lowest price Framar can quote without reducing current net income.
(4) Determine the effect on the most recent fiscal year's profit if all work were done at prices similar to APA's $127,000 counteroffer. (ICMA adapted)

P21-3. Comparative differential costs. Valbec Company manufactures and distributes toy doll houses. Because the toy industry is a seasonal business, a large portion of Valbec's sales occur in the late summer and fall. The projected sales in units for 19A follow:

January	8,000		July.	12,000
February	8,000		August	12,000
March	8,000		September	13,000
April.	8,000		October.	13,000
May	8,000		November.	12,000
June	10,000		December.	8,000

With a sales price of $10 per unit, sales revenue for 19A is projected to be $1,200,000. Valbec scheduled its production in the past so that finished goods inventory at the end of each month, exclusive of a safety stock of 4,000 units, would equal the next month's sales. One-half hour of direct labor is required to produce each unit under normal operating conditions. January, 19B sales are estimated to be 8,000 units.

The present labor force limits monthly production capacity to 8,000 units (4,000 direct labor hours). While overtime is feasible, management wishes to consider two other possible alternatives: (a) hire temporary help from an agency during the peak months, or (b) expand its labor force and adopt a level production schedule. Use of a second shift was not considered.

Factory employees are paid $6 per hour for regular time and the fringe benefits average 20% of regular pay. For work in excess of 4,000 hours per month, employees receive time and one-half; however, fringe benefits only average 10% on these additional wages. Past experience has shown that when overtime is required, labor inefficiencies occur during overtime work which increases the overtime normally expected by 5% (i.e., the number of overtime hours increases by 5%). Temporary workers can be hired through an agency at the same labor rate of $6, but there would be no fringe benefit costs. Management estimates that the temporary workers would require 25% more time than the regular employees to produce a unit of product. If Valbec goes to a level production schedule, the labor force would be expanded; however, no overtime would be required. The same labor rate of $6 and fringe benefit rate of 20% would apply.

Manufacturing facilities have the capacity to produce 18,000 units per month and on-site storage facilities for completed units are adequate. The estimated annual cost of carrying inventory is $1 per unit. Valbec is subject to a 40% income tax rate.

Required:

(1) Compare the costs associated with each of the company's three alternatives: (a) schedule overtime hours, (b) hire temporary workers, and (c) expand the labor force and schedule level production of 10,000 units per month.

(2) What noncost factors should Valbec Company consider before making a final decision?

(ICMA adapted)

P21-4. Comparative cost study to make or buy new product components. Meyers Surgical Products Company produces diverse lines of surgical instruments. It is considering a proposal, suggested by one of its sales managers, to produce dissection instrument sets for use by medical and premedical students. There is little competition in the market for the instrument sets, and the firm's present sales force could be used for effective distribution coverage. Moreover, the sales manager believes that the company could produce the instruments with the present facilities, except for the addition of certain minor auxiliary equipment.

Company management assigned two members of its Sales Department, two members from the Production Department, and an accounting staff representative to analyze the proposal. The team has assembled the following information:

(a) The proposed dissection instrument sets include:

(1) Dissection knives	3
(2) Scissors	2
(3) Tweezers.	2
(4) Scalpels	2
(5) Clamps	4
(6) Glass slides	100
(7) Cover slips	400
(8) Case	1

(b) The market price for such sets ranges from $55 to $65. An estimate of the total annual market demand ranges between 5,000 and 7,000 sets, and Meyers expects to sell 2,000 sets at $60.

(c) Set components can be purchased from suppliers at the following prices per unit:

(1) Dissection knives	$3.20
(2) Scissors	3.00
(3) Tweezers.	2.97
(4) Scalpels	3.30
(5) Clamps	3.28
(6) Glass slides	.03
(7) Cover slips	.01
(8) Cases	6.00

(d) Meyers has the option of manufacturing all of the components, except glass slides, cover slips, and the cases. The remaining components can be grouped into two categories for production and for product costing purposes:

(1) Group I—dissection knives and scalpels

(2) Group II—scissors, tweezers, and clamps

(e) Production costs were analyzed to be as follows:

	Group I	Group II
Materials	1 lb. of steel for 25 units @ $3.27 per lb.	1 lb. of steel for 20 units @ $3.60 per lb.
Labor	2.5 hrs for 25 units @ $9.48 per hr.	2 hrs. for 20 units @ $12.16 per hr.
Variable factory overhead	150% of labor cost	150% of labor cost

(f) Set assembly and packing costs will average $3 per set.

(g) Additional fixed factory overhead directly related to the sets will be $7,040 and $6,000 annually for Groups I and II, respectively.

(h) The new product will have the following amounts of presently existing annual fixed overhead allocated to it:

  (1) Group I manufacturing. $4,000
  (2) Group II manufacturing   6,000
  (3) All other dissection sets' production activity.   7,000

(i) All sales are FOB Meyers' plant.

Required: Advise management on the desirability of the proposal, including supporting computations. Compute unit costs to 1/10 of one cent.

P21-5. Minimum bid price. Chemco Inc. manufactures a combination fertilizer/weed-killer under the name Fertikil, the only product produced at the present time. Fertikil is sold nationwide, through normal marketing channels, to retail nurseries and garden stores.

National Nursery Company plans to sell a similar fertilizer/weed-killer compound through its regional nursery chain under its own private label. National Nursery has asked Chemco to submit a bid for a 25,000-pound order of the private brand compound. While the chemical composition of the National Nursery compound differs from Fertikil, the manufacturing process is similar.

The National Nursery compound would be produced in 1,000-pound lots. Each lot would require 60 direct labor hours and the following chemicals:

Chemicals	Quantity in Pounds
CW-3	400
JX-6	300
MZ-8	200
BE-7	100

The first three chemicals (CW-3, JX-6, and MZ-8) are all used in the production of Fertikil. BE-7 was used in a compound that Chemco has discontinued. This chemical was not sold or discarded because it does not deteriorate, and there have been adequate storage facilities. Chemco could sell BE-7 at the prevailing market price less $.10 per pound for selling and handling expenses.

Chemco also has on hand a chemical called CN-5, which was manufactured for use in another product that is no longer produced. CN-5, which cannot be used in Fertikil, can be substituted for CW-3 on a one-for-one basis without affecting the quality of the National Nursery compound. The quantity of CN-5 in inventory has a salvage value of $500.

Inventory and cost data for the chemicals which can be used to produce the National Nursery compound follow:

Chemical	Pounds in Inventory	Inventory Cost per Pound	Market Price per Pound
CW-3	22,000	$ .80	$ .90
JX-6	5,000	.55	.60
MZ-8	8,000	1.40	1.60
BE-7	4,000	.60	.65
CN-5	5,500	.75	salvage

The current direct labor rate is $7 per hour. The factory overhead rate is established at the beginning of the year and is applied consistently throughout the year, using direct labor hours (DLH) as the base. The predetermined overhead rate for the current year, based on a two-shift capacity of 400,000 total DLH with no overtime, follows:

Variable factory overhead.	$2.25 per DLH
Fixed factory overhead.	3.75 per DLH
Combined factory overhead rate	$6.00 per DLH

Chemco's production manager reports that the present equipment and facilities are adequate to manufacture the National Nursery compound. However, Chemco is within 800 hours of its two-shift capacity this month before it must schedule overtime. If need be, the National Nursery compound could be produced on regular time by shifting a portion of Fertikil production to overtime. Chemco's rate for overtime is one and one-half times the regular pay rate, or $10.50 per hour. There is no allowance for any overtime premium in the factory overhead rate.

Chemco's standard markup policy for new products is 25% on the full manufacturing cost.

Required:

(1) Calculate the lowest price Chemco should bid for the order and not reduce its net income. Assume that Chemco has decided to submit a bid for a 25,000-pound order of National Nursery compound. The order must be delivered by the end of the current month. It is presumed to be a one-time order (i.e., it will probably not be repeated).

(2) Without prejudice to your answer in requirement (1) above, calculate the price Chemco should quote National Nursery for each 25,000-pound lot of the compound, assuming that National Nursery plans to place regular orders for 25,000-pound lots of the new compound during the coming year. Chemco expects the demand for Fertikil to remain strong again in the coming year. Therefore, the recurring orders from National Nursery will put Chemco over its two-shift capacity. However, production can be scheduled so that 60% of each National Nursery order can be completed during regular hours, or Fertikil production could be shifted temporarily to overtime, so that the National Nursery orders could be produced on regular time. Chemco's production manager has estimated that the prices of all chemicals will stabilize at the current market rates for the coming year, and that all other manufacturing costs are expected to be maintained at the same rates or amounts.   (ICMA adapted)

P21-6. Proposed construction of additional capacity. Westmore Company is considering expanding its production facilities with a building costing $260,000 and equipment costing $84,000. Building and equipment depreciable lives are 25 and 20 years, respectively, with straight-line depreciation and no salvage value. Of the additional depreciation cost, 5% is expected to be allocated to inventories.

The plant addition will increase volume by 50%; the product's sales price is expected to remain the same. The new union contract calls for a 5% increase in wage rates. Because of the increased plant capacity, quantity buying will yield an overall 6% decrease in materials cost. One additional supervisor must be hired at a salary of $15,000.

The following data pertain to last year:

Sales, 50,000 units @ $10 per unit
Direct materials, $2 per unit

Direct labor, $4 per unit
Variable factory overhead, $1.30 per unit
Fixed factory overhead, $72,500
Variable marketing expense, $12,000
Fixed marketing expense, $7,000

With the volume increase, advertising, which is 10% of present fixed marketing expense, will be increased 25%.

Required: Prepare an analysis estimating the contribution margin and operating income for the present and the proposed plant capacities.

P21-7. Evaluating production alternatives. Mowen Corporation has manufacturing plants in Boston and Chicago. Both plants produce the same product, Xoff, which sells for $20 per unit. Budgeted revenues and costs (in thousands) for the coming year are as follows:

	Total	Boston	Chicago
Sales	$6,200	$2,200	$4,000
Variable factory costs:			
Direct materials	$1,550	$ 550	$1,000
Direct labor	1,660	660	1,000
Variable factory overhead	1,140	440	700
Fixed factory overhead	1,600	700	900
Fixed regional promotional cost	200	100	100
Allocated home office cost	310	110	200
Total costs	$6,460	$2,560	$3,900
Operating income (loss)	$ (260)	$ (360)	$ 100

Home office costs are fixed and are allocated to manufacturing plants on the basis of relative sales levels. Fixed regional promotional costs are discretionary advertising costs needed to obtain budgeted sales levels. Because of the budgeted operating loss, Mowen is considering the possibility of ceasing operations at its Boston plant. If Mowen were to cease operations at its Boston plant, proceeds from the sale of plant assets would exceed their book value and exactly cover all termination costs. Fixed factory overhead costs of $50,000 would not be eliminated. Mowen is considering the following three alternative plans:

Plan A. Expand Boston's operations from the budgeted 110,000 units of Xoff to a budgeted 170,000 units. It is believed that this can be accomplished by increasing Boston's fixed regional promotional expenditures by $120,000.

Plan B. Close the Boston plant and expand Chicago's operations from the current budgeted 200,000 units of Xoff to 310,000 units in order to fill Boston's budgeted production of 110,000 units. The Boston region would continue to incur promotional costs in order to sell the 110,000 units. All sales and costs would be budgeted through the Chicago plant.

Plan C. Close the Boston plant and enter into a long-term contract with a competitor to serve the Boston region's customers. This competitor would pay Mowen a royalty of $2.50 per unit of Xoff sold. Mowen would continue to incur fixed regional promotional costs in order to maintain sales of 110,000 units in the Boston region.

Required:

(1) Without considering the effects of implementing Plans A, B, and C, compute the number of units of Xoff required by the Boston plant to cover its fixed factory overhead cost and fixed regional promotional cost.

(2) Prepare a schedule by plant and in total, computing Mowen's budgeted contribution margin and operating income resulting from the implementation of each of the three alternative plans.

(AICPA adapted)

P21-8. Evaluating new purchasing procedure. The Lex Glass Company uses silica in the production of three different lines of glassware. The company plans to introduce a new line of glassware without expanding its present facilities. The company would like to purchase the required silica at a lower price in order to increase its profits. The present purchase price of silica is $2 per ton, and the company consumes approximately 120,000 tons per year. Silica is used at a fairly uniform rate throughout the year. The company's policy has been to place an order for materials once a month and to maintain a minimum inventory of 5,000 tons. This represents one half of one month's consumption and results in an average inventory of 10,000 tons (i.e., 1/2 of the 10,000 ton monthly requirement + 5,000 ton minimum).

Other firms in the same industry and the same manufacturing area purchase the silica in small lots for $2.20 a ton. The purchasing manager contacted suppliers and determined that a price of $1.80 per ton can be obtained if the company purchases 400,000 tons of silica a year or more. The purchasing manager, then, contacted other manufacturers in the area and offered to sell silica to them for $2 a ton. Most of the manufacturers accepted the offer; however, they asked the purchasing manager to keep an inventory of at least one half of one month's consumption in storage at all times to be available for their use. The annual consumption of these manufacturers is expected to be 300,000 tons per year, and consumption is expected to be uniform each month. Lex Glass plans to continue its once a month ordering policy.

In order to handle the additional volume of silica required by these other manufacturers, Lex Glass would have to increase its labor force at an annual cost of $20,000 and incur $10,000 of additional administrative expenses annually. The company could borrow the additional funds necessary from the local bank at an interest rate of 5%. The additional materials could be stored in a company-owned warehouse which is now being leased to another company for $10,000 a year.

Required: Determine whether or not the Lex Glass Company should take advantage of the quantity discount.

Source: *Management Accounting Campus Report* (Montvale, N.J.: National Association of Accountants), pp. 4–5. Copyright Spring, 1987, by the National Association of Accountants. All rights reserved. Reprinted by permission.

SS P21-9. Evaluation of alternatives for a charitable foundation. J. Watson recently was appointed executive director of a charitable foundation. The foundation raises money for its activities in a variety of ways, but the most important source of funds is an annual mail campaign. Although large amounts of money are raised each year from this campaign, the year-to-year growth in the amount derived from this solicitation has been lower than expected by the foundation's board. In addition, the board wants the mail campaign to project the image of a well-run and fiscally responsible organization in order to build a base for future contributions. Consequently, the major focus of Watson's first-year efforts will be devoted to the mail campaign.

The campaign takes place in the spring of each year. The foundation staff makes every effort to secure newspaper, radio, and television coverage of the foundation's activities for several weeks before the mailing. In prior years, the foundation has mailed brochures that described its charitable activities to a large number of people and requested contributions from them, The addresses for the mailing are generated from the foundation's own file of past contributors and from mailing lists purchased from brokers.

The foundation staff is considering three alternative brochures for use in the upcoming campaign. All three will be 8 1/2″ × 11″ in size. The simplest and the one most likely to be available on a timely basis for bulk mailing is a sheet of white paper with a printed explanation of the foundation's program and a request for funds. A more expensive brochure on colored stock will contain pictures as well as printed copy. However, this brochure may not be ready in time to take advantage of bulk postal rates, but there is no doubt that it can be ready in time for mailing at first-class postal rates. The third alternative would be an elegant, multicolored brochure printed on glossy paper with photographs as well as printed copy. The printer assures the staff that it will be ready on time to meet the first-class mailing schedule, but asks for a delivery date one week later just in case there are production problems.

The foundation staff has assembled the following cost and gross revenue information for mailing the three alternative brochures to 2,000,000 potential contributors:

Type of Brochure	Design	Brochure Costs Type-setting	Unit Paper Cost	Unit Printing Cost	Gross Revenue Potential (In Thousands) Bulk Mail	First Class	Late First Class
Plain paper	$ 300	$ 100	$.005	$.003	$1,200	–	–
Colored paper	1,000	800	.008	.010	2,000	$2,200	–
Glossy paper	3,000	2,000	.018	.040	–	2,500	$2,200

The postal rates are $.04 per item for bulk mail and $.26 per item for presorted first-class mail. First-class mail is more likely to be delivered on a timely basis than bulk mail. The charge by outside companies who will be hired to handle the mailing is $.01 per unit for the plain and colored paper brochures and $.02 per unit for the glossy paper one.

Required:

(1) Calculate the net revenue potential for each brochure for each viable mailing alternative.
(2) The foundation must choose one of the three brochures for this year's campaign. The criteria established by the board—net revenue potential, image as a well-run organization, and image as a fiscally responsible organization—must be considered when making the choice. Evaluate the three alternative brochures in terms of the three criteria. (ICMA adapted)

P21-10. Elimination of market. Justa Corporation produces and sells three products, A, B, and C. The three products are sold in a local market and in a regional market. At the end of the first quarter of the current year, the following income statement was prepared:

	Total	Local	Regional
Sales	$1,300,000	$1,000,000	$300,000
Cost of goods sold	1,010,000	775,000	235,000
Gross profit	$ 290,000	$ 225,000	$ 65,000
Marketing expense	$ 105,000	$ 60,000	$ 45,000
Administrative expense	52,000	40,000	12,000
	$ 157,000	$ 100,000	$ 57,000
Operating income	$ 133,000	$ 125,000	$ 8,000

Management has expressed special concern with the regional market because of the extremely poor return on sales. This market was entered a year ago because of excess capacity. It was originally believed that the return on sales would improve with time, but after a year, no noticeable improvement can be seen from the results as reported in the quarterly statement.

In attempting to decide whether to eliminate the regional market, the following information has been gathered:

	A	B	C
Sales	$500,000	$400,000	$400,000
Variable manufacturing expense as a percentage of sales	60%	70%	60%
Variable marketing expense as a percentage of sales	3%	2%	2%

Product	Sales by Markets Local	Regional
A	$400,000	$100,000
B	300,000	100,000
C	300,000	100,000

All fixed expense is based upon a prorated yearly amount. All administrative expense and fixed manufacturing expense are common to the three products and the two markets and are fixed for the period, regardless of whether a market is eliminated. Remaining marketing expense is fixed for the period and separable by market. All separable cost would be eliminated with the dropping of a market.

Required:

(1) Prepare the quarterly income statement, showing contribution margins by markets. Include a total column, combining the two markets.
(2) Assuming that there are no alternative uses for Justa Corporation's present capacity, should the regional market be dropped? Why or why not?
(3) Prepare the quarterly income statement, showing contribution margins by products.
(4) It is believed that a new product to replace Product C could be ready for sale next year if Justa Corporation decides to go ahead with continued research. The new product could be produced by simply converting equipment presently used in producing Product C. This conversion would increase fixed costs by $10,000 per quarter. Calculate the minimum contribution margin per quarter for the new product if Justa Corporation is to be no worse off financially than at present. (ICMA adapted)

CASES

C21-1. Special order acceptance. Sportech Company manufactures and sells baseball spikes and ice skates. The baseball spikes are produced from January until the end of April. From May to December the company produces exclusively its three skate models, sold under brand names XL-100, XL-200, and XL-300.

At the beginning of April, 19A, the president analyzed the new budget for May through December, 19A, which had been revised by the controller on the basis of the new sales forecast prepared by the marketing manager:

(a) Budgeted operating income:

	XL-100	XL-200	XL-300	Total
Sales:				
Number of pairs.............	20,000	18,000	10,000	
Prices per pair..............	× $14.00	× $15.00	× $25.00	
	$280,000	$270,000	$250,000	$800,000
Manufacturing costs	200,000	207,000	180,000	587,000
Gross profit	$ 80,000	$ 63,000	$ 70,000	$213,000
Commercial expenses:				
Delivery	$ 5,000	$ 4,500	$ 2,500	$ 12,000
Salaries and commissions	16,800	16,200	15,000	48,000
Salespersons' expenses	5,600	5,400	5,000	16,000
Advertising.................	15,000	15,000	15,000	45,000
Other fixed expenses	21,000	20,250	18,750	60,000
	$ 63,400	$ 61,350	$ 56,250	$181,000
Operating income	$ 16,600	$ 1,650	$ 13,750	$ 32,000
Underabsorbed fixed factory overhead				20,800
Adjusted operating income				$ 11,200

(b) Budgeted manufacturing costs (per unit):

	XL-100	XL-200	XL-300
Direct materials:			
Blades.....................................	$ 2.00	$ 2.00	$ 3.00
˙ Other (leather, cap, etc.)..................	3.00	3.50	5.00
Direct labor*................................	2.00	2.40	4.00
Applied factory overhead (150% of direct labor)...	3.00	3.60	6.00
	$10.00	$11.50	$18.00

*Direct labor was budgeted at $4 per hour.

(c) These budgeted figures were accompanied by the following explanatory notes:

(1) Fixed factory overhead costs ($144,000) are applied on the basis of the practical capacity of the plant (36,000 direct labor hours). Variable factory overhead costs are budgeted to be $.50 per direct labor dollar. Total factory overhead rate is determined as follows:

$$\text{Fixed rate} = \frac{\$144,000}{36,000 \text{ DLH} \times \$4} = \$1.00$$

Variable rate.................. .50

Rate per direct labor dollar $1.50

(2) Budgeted direct labor hours:

XL-100 (20,000 units × .5 hour) = 10,000
XL-200 (18,000 units × .6 hour) = 10,800
XL-300 (10,000 units × 1 hour) = 10,000
                                      30,800

(3) Each of five salespersons receives a monthly salary of $400 and a commission of 4% of all sales to the customers visited regularly, even if they order directly from the company.

(4) Variable salespersons' expenses, other marketing expenses (fixed), and administrative expenses are allocated as a percentage of sales.

(5) Advertisements in newspapers, on radio, and on television always mention the three models. Therefore, the expense is split evenly among the three models.

The president realizes that the plant is not operating at practical capacity for the first time in many years, and that idle capacity will be costly for the company.

A few days after receiving the revised budget, the president received a letter from the purchasing agent of Sunset Inc., which operates a large chain of department stores in the metropolitan area where Sportech's plant is located. This letter stated that Sunset would buy 10,000 pairs of each model of skates before the end of the year on the following conditions:

(a) Sportech would deliver 1/4th of the order on the last day of each of the last four months of the year at Sunset's central warehouse.

(b) Sunset would pay for the goods before the 10th of the month following the delivery.

(c) Cash and quantity discounts would amount to 15% of regular sales prices.

The president immediately called a meeting with the production manager, the sales manager, and the controller. The production manager saw an opportunity to wipe out the unabsorbed fixed factory overhead and mentioned that there would be no problem in hiring enough workers to operate at full capacity. The union contract provides for an overtime premium of 50% after a regular 8-hour day or 40-hour work week. Overtime is limited to three hours a day during the week, but employees can work four hours on Saturday mornings. The production manager estimated that of the additional direct labor hours needed to produce the order for Sunset, 15,800 would be overtime hours (all within the constraints specified in the union contract). Fixed manufacturing costs would increase by $3,000 a month; however, some of this cost could be offset because the blades manufacturer would agree to a price reduction of 10% on all blades, if the annual purchases totaled 60,000 pairs or more. The sales manager agreed to take care of all relations with Sunset but insisted that all regular orders be accepted. No sales commission would be paid on this special order.

After a brief discussion, the controller and the sales manager agreed to prepare an analysis of all the important factors, qualitative as well as quantitative, that might affect the decision.

Required:

(1) Compute the effect of this offer on operating income.
(2) What nonquantitative factors may have a bearing on the decision?   (CICA adapted)

C21-2. Plant closing decision. Big-Auto Corporation manufactures automobiles, vans, and trucks. The Denver Cover Plant, one of Big-Auto's plants, produces coverings made primarily of vinyl and upholstery fabric which are sewn at Denver Cover and used to cover interior seating and other surfaces of Big-Auto products.

T. Vosilo is the plant manager for Denver Cover. The Denver Cover Plant was the first Big-Auto plant in the region. As other area plants were opened, Vosilo, in recognition of his management ability, was given responsibility for managing them. Vosilo functions as a regional manager although the budget for him and his staff is charged to the Denver Cover Plant.

Vosilo has just received a report indicating that Big-Auto could purchase the entire annual output of Denver Cover from outside suppliers for $30,000,000. Vosilo was astonished at the low outside price because the budget for Denver Cover's operating costs for the coming year was set at $52,000,000. Vosilo believes that Big-Auto will have to close down operations at Denver Cover in order to realize the $22,000,000 in annual cost savings.

The budget for Denver Cover's operating costs for the coming year is at the top of the next column. Additional facts regarding the plant's operations follow.

Denver Cover Plant
Budget for Operating Costs
For the Year ending December 31, 19A
(In Thousands)

Materials		$12,000
Direct labor		13,000
Factory overhead:		
Supervision	$3,000	
Indirect labor	4,000	
Depreciation—equipment	5,000	
Depreciation—building.	3,000	
Pension expense	4,000	
Plant manager and staff	2,000	
Corporate allocation.	6,000	27,000
Total budgeted costs		$52,000

(a) Due to Denver Cover's commitment to use high quality fabrics in all of its products, the Purchasing Department was instructed to place blanket purchase orders with major suppliers to ensure the receipt of sufficient materials for the coming year. If these orders are cancelled as a consequence of the plant closing, termination charges would amount to 15% of the cost of direct materials.

(b) Approximately 700 plant employees will lose their jobs if the plant is closed. This includes all of the direct laborers and supervisors as well as the plumbers, electricians, and other skilled workers classified as indirect plant workers. Some would be able to find new jobs while many others would have difficulty. All employees would have difficulty matching Denver Cover's base pay of $9.40 an hour, which is the highest in the area. A clause in Denver Cover's contract with the union may help some employees; the company must provide employment assistance to its former employees for 12 months after a plant closing. The estimated cost to administer this service would be $1,000,000 for the year.

(c) Some employees would probably elect early retirement because Big-Auto has an excellent pension plan. In fact, $3,000,000 of the 19A pension expense would continue whether Denver Cover is open or not.

(d) Vosilo and his staff would not be affected by the closing of Denver Cover. They would still be responsible for administering three other area plants.

(e) Denver Cover considers equipment depreciation to be a variable cost and uses the units-of-production method to depreciate its equipment; Denver Cover is the only Big-Auto plant to use this depreciation method. However, Denver Cover uses the customary straight-line method to depreciate its building.

Required:

(1) Without regard to costs, identify the advantages to Big-Auto Corporation of continuing to obtain covers from its own Denver Cover Plant.

(2) Big-Auto Corporation plans to prepare a numerical analysis that will be used in deciding whether or not to close the Denver Cover Plant.

   (a) Identify the recurring annual budgeted costs that can be avoided by closing the plant.

   (b) Identify the recurring annual budgeted costs that are not relevant to the plant-closing decision, and explain why they are not relevant.

   (c) Identify any nonrecurring costs that arise due to the closing of the plant, and explain how they affect the decision.

   (d) Identify any revenues or costs not specifically mentioned in the case that Big-Auto should consider before making the decision.   (ICMA adapted)

C21-3. New product proposal. Calco Corporation, a producer and distributor of plastic products for industrial use, is considering a proposal to produce a plastic storage unit designed especially for the consumer market. The product is well suited for Calco's manufacturing process, with no costly machinery modifications or Assembly Department changes required. Adequate manufacturing capacity is available because of recent facility expansion and a leveling of sales growth in its industrial product line.

Management is considering two alternatives for marketing the product. The first is to add this responsibility to Calco's current Marketing Department. The other alternative is to acquire a small, new company named Jasco Inc. at a

nominal cost. This company was started by some former employees of a firm which specialized in marketing plastic products for the consumer market when they lost their jobs because of a merger. Jasco has not yet started operations.

The Product Engineering Department has prepared the following unit manufacturing cost estimate for the new storage unit at both the 100,000- and the 120,000-unit levels of production:

Direct materials	$14.00
Direct labor.	3.50
Factory overhead (25% variable)*.	10.00
Total.	$27.50

*Total fixed factory overhead will be $750,000 at the 100,000-unit level and $900,000 at the 120,000-unit level.

Calco's Marketing Department has used its experience in the sale of industrial products to develop a proposal for the distribution of the new consumer product. The Marketing Department would be reorganized so that several positions which were scheduled for elimination now would be assigned to the new product. The Marketing Department's forecast of the annual financial results for its proposals to market the storage units is as follows:

Sales (100,000 units @ $45)	$4,500,000
Costs:	
Cost of units sold (100,000 units	
@ $27.50 each).	$2,750,000
Marketing costs:	
Positions that were to be eliminated .	600,000
Sales commission (5% of sales). . . .	225,000
Advertising program.	400,000
Promotion program	200,000
Share of current Marketing	
Department's management	
costs.	100,000
Total cost	$4,275,000
Income before income tax	$ 225,000

The Jasco founders also prepared a forecast of the annual financial results, based upon their experience in marketing consumer products. The following forecast was based upon the assumption that Jasco would become part of Calco and be responsible for marketing the storage unit:

Sales (120,000 units @ $50)	$6,000,000
Costs:	
Cost of units sold (120,000 units	
@ $27.50)	$3,300,000
Marketing costs:	
Personnel—sales.	660,000
Personnel—sales management.	200,000
Commission (10%)	600,000
Advertising program.	800,000
Promotion program	200,000
Office rental (the annual rental of a	
long-term lease already signed	
by Jasco)	50,000
Total cost	$5,810,000
Income before income tax	$ 190,000

Required:

(1) List factors Calco should consider before entering the consumer products market.
(2) Alter financial forecasts for use in deciding between the alternatives, if Calco decides to enter the consumer market.
(3) Compare the reliability of the two proposals.
(4) Identify the nonquantitative factors Calco should consider when choosing between the alternatives. Indicate whether or not any one of these factors is sufficiently important to warrant selection of one alternative over the other, regardless of the estimated financial effect on profit.

(ICMA adapted)

C21-4. Elimination of a product. Precision Gauge Corporation produces three gauges. These gauges, which measure density, permeability, and thickness, are known as D-gauges, P-gauges, and T-gauges, respectively. For many years, the company has been profitable and has operated at capacity. In the last two years, however, prices on all gauges were reduced and selling expenses increased to meet competition and to keep the plant operating at full capacity. The following third quarter results are representative of recent experiences:

			(In Thousands)	
	D-gauge	P-gauge	T-gauge	Total
Sales	$900	$1,600	$ 900	$3,400
Cost of goods sold	770	1,048	950	2,768
Gross profit	$130	$ 552	$ (50)	$ 632
Selling and admin-				
istrative expenses	185	370	135	690
Income before				
income tax	$ (55)	$ 182	$(185)	$ (58)

Marvin Caplan, president of the company, is very concerned about the results of the pricing, selling, and production policies. After reviewing the third quarter results, he announced that he would ask his management staff to consider a course of action that includes the following three suggestions:

(a) Discontinue the T-gauge line immediately. T-gauges would not be returned to the line of products unless the problems with the gauge could be identified and resolved.
(b) Increase quarterly sales promotion by $100,000 on the P-gauge product line in order to increase sales volume 15%.
(c) Cut production on the D-gauge line by 50%, a quantity sufficient to meet the demand of customers who purchase P-gauges. In addition, the traceable advertising and promotion for this line would be cut to $20,000 each quarter.

Joan Garth, who is the controller, suggested that a more careful study of the financial relationships be made to determine the possible effect on the company's operating results as a consequence of the president's proposed course of action. The president agreed, and Tom Kirk, assistant controller, was assigned the analysis. To prepare the analysis, Tom gathered the following information:

(a) All three gauges are manufactured with common equipment and facilities.
(b) The quarterly general selling and administrative expenses of $170,000 are allocated to the three gauge lines in proportion to their dollar sales volume.
(c) Special selling expenses (primarily advertising, promotion, and shipping) are incurred for each gauge as follows:

	Quarterly Advertising and Promotion	Shipping Expense
D-gauge	$100,000	$ 4 per unit
P-gauge	210,000	10 per unit
T-gauge.	40,000	10 per unit

(d) The unit manufacturing costs for the three products are as follows:

	D-gauge	P-gauge	T-gauge
Direct materials	$17	$ 31	$ 50
Direct labor..........	20	40	60
Variable factory			
overhead...........	30	45	60
Fixed factory overhead..	10	15	20
	$77	$131	$190

(e) The unit sales prices for the three products are $90, $200, and $180 for the D-gauge, P-gauge, and T-gauge, respectively.

(f) The company is manufacturing at capacity and is selling all the gauges it produces.

Required:

(1) Tom Kirk has suggested that the Precision Gauge Corporation product-line income statement presented for the third quarter of 19A is not suitable for analyzing proposals and making decisions such as the ones suggested by Marvin Caplan.

    (a) Explain why the product-line income statement presented is not suitable for analysis and decision making.

    (b) Describe an alternative income statement format that would be more suitable for analysis and decision making, and explain why it is better.

(2) Using the operating data presented for Precision Gauge Corporation and assuming that the president's proposed course of action had been implemented at the beginning of the third quarter of 19A, evaluate the president's proposed course of action by specifically responding to the following points:

    (a) Are each of the three suggestions cost effective? The discussion should be supported by a differential cost analysis that shows the net impact on income before tax for each of the three suggestions.

    (b) Was the president correct in eliminating the T-gauge line? Explain.

    (c) Was the president correct in promoting the P-gauge line rather than the D-gauge line? Explain.

    (d) Does the proposed course of action make effective use of Precision's capacity? Explain.

(3) Are there any nonquantitative factors that Precision Gauge Corporation should consider before it considers dropping the T-gauge line? Explain.   (ICMA adapted)

C21-5. Linear programming problem formulation—contribution margin maximization. Leastan Company manufactures a line of carpeting which includes a commercial carpet and a residential carpet. Two grades of fiber—heavy duty and regular—are used in manufacturing both types of carpeting. The mix of the two grades differs in each type of carpeting, with the commercial grade using a greater amount of heavy duty fiber.

Leastan will introduce a new line of carpeting in two months to replace the current line. The present fiber in stock will not be used in the new line; therefore, management wants to exhaust the present stock during the last month of production.

Data regarding the current line of commercial and residential carpeting are:

	Commercial	Residential
Sales price per roll........	$1,000	$800
Production specifications per roll of carpet:		
Heavy duty fiber.......	80 lbs.	40 lbs.
Regular fiber..........	20 lbs.	40 lbs.
Direct labor hours......	15 hrs.	15 hrs.
Standard cost per roll of carpet:		
Heavy duty fiber ($3/lb.).	$ 240	$120
Regular fiber ($2/lb.)....	40	80
Direct labor ($10/DLH)..	150	150
Variable factory overhead	90	90
Fixed factory overhead..	180	180
Total standard cost per roll...............	$ 700	$620

Leastan has 42,000 pounds of heavy duty fiber and 24,000 pounds of regular fiber in stock. All fiber not used in the manufacture of the present types of carpeting during the last month of production can be sold as scrap at $.25 a pound.

There is a maximum of 10,500 direct labor hours available during the month. The labor force can work on either type of carpeting.

Sufficient demand exists for the present line of carpeting so that all quantities produced can be sold.

Required:

(1) Compute the number of rolls of commercial carpet and residential carpet that Leastan must manufacture during the last month of production in order to exhaust completely the heavy duty and regular fiber still in stock.

(2) Explain whether or not the requirement (1) solution quantities can be manufactured during the last month of commercial and residential carpet production.

(3) Explain why linear programming would be useful in this application.

(4) Formulate the objective function and the constraints, so that this problem can be solved by linear programming.

(ICMA adapted)

C21-6. Linear programming—product mix contribution margin. The illustration beginning on page 698 assumes that the market for standard and deluxe models was stable and that the $3 and $4 per unit was maintainable for at least the near future. Increased demand for the deluxe model suggests the desirability of raising the price well above the level that produced the original $4 contribution margin.

Required:

Determine the following:

(1) The product mix to be attained if deluxe models are priced to yield a $6 unit contribution margin.

(2) The product mix to be attained if deluxe models are priced to yield a $10 contribution margin.

(3) The contribution margin figure per deluxe model to make it possible to abandon production of standard units and operate at less than full capacity, maintaining maximum profits.

CHAPTER 22

Capital Expenditures: Planning, Evaluating, and Controlling

Capital expenditure planning, evaluating, and controlling, sometimes called *capital budgeting*, is the process of planning the continuing investment and reinvestment of an organization's resources and monitoring that investment. Capital expenditures involve long-term commitments of resources to realize future benefits. They reflect basic company objectives and have a significant, long-term effect on the economic well-being of the firm.

In order to survive in the long run, a firm must earn a reasonable return on invested funds. As a consequence, considerable attention has been devoted to techniques for evaluating capital expenditure proposals. Yet evaluation is only one essential requirement for the effective administration of a capital expenditure program. Equally important is the effective planning and control of such expenditures, because (1) the long-term commitment increases financial risk, (2) the magnitude of expenditures is substantial and the economic penalties for unwise decisions usually are severe, and (3) the decisions made in this area provide the structure that supports the operating activities of the firm.

■ PLANNING FOR CAPITAL EXPENDITURES

Planning for capital expenditures consists of relating plans to objectives, structuring the framework, searching for proposals, budgeting the expenditures, and requesting authority for expenditures.

Relating Plans to Objectives

Individual projects must be consistent with the objectives of the firm and must be capable of being blended into a firm's operations. To achieve consistency, all levels of an organization need to be conscious of objectives and the different roles played by each level relative to these objectives. Ideally, executive management sets broad goals and objectives; managers of functional activities formulate specific policies and programs for action which, when approved, are executed by operating-level management. The lower the level at which a decision is authorized, the greater the need for guidelines extending to detailed procedures and standards. Investment projects not conducive to such detail require handling at a higher level.

Structuring the Framework

An organization's established capital expenditure framework forms the basis for implementing the capital expenditure program. The framework is important because the very nature of performing tasks implies a sound frame of reference. Several factors influence the molding and revision of a firm's framework: the company's organizational structure, its philosophy and application of principles of organization, its size, the nature of its operations, and the characteristics of individual projects.

A company manual may be used to detail policies and procedures and to illustrate forms required for administering the capital expenditure program. Such manuals should be stripped down to helpful levels and should (1) encourage people to work on and submit ideas, (2) focus attention on useful analytical tasks, and (3) facilitate rapid project development and expeditious review.

Searching for Proposals

A capital investment program yields the best results only when the best available proposals are considered and all reasonable alternatives of each proposal have been brought into the analysis for screening and evaluation. Ideas should come from all segments of the enterprise. Everyone in the organization should participate in the search activity within the bounds of their technical knowledge and ability, their authority and responsibility, their awareness of operating problems, and existing management guidelines regarding desirable projects. Care must be taken to create and maintain an incentive to search out and bring good projects into the system. This incentive is strong when there is a genuine feeling that all proposals will be reviewed in a fair and objective manner.

Budgeting Capital Expenditures

The capital expenditures budget typically is prepared for a one-year period. It presents management's investment plans at the time the budget is prepared for the coming period.

Some projects never materialize; others are added through amendments to the budget during the budget year. Thus, the budget must be adaptable to changing needs. The capital expenditures budget is not an authorization to commit funds; it merely affords an opportunity to consolidate plans by looking at projects for the total organization, side by side. The capital expenditures budget should be reconciled with the other periodic budgeting activities of the firm, e.g., expense and cash budgets (as discussed in Chapters 16 and

17), and the annual capital budget should be reconciled with long-range capital investment and operating plans and objectives.

The capital expenditures budget passes through several management levels as it moves toward final approval at the executive management level. It follows that a clear explanation of the content of the approved budget should be transmitted to the various management levels to avoid misunderstandings.

Requesting Authority for Expenditures

The periodic budget is usually an approval of ideas and does not grant automatic approval to commit funds. Authority to commit funds for other than necessary preliminary administrative costs should come by means of an Authority for Expenditure (AFE). The AFE procedure is, in effect, a second look at budgeted projects, based on an up-to-date set of documents justifying and describing the expenditure. The AFE and supporting detail should be originated at the level at which the expenditure will occur, with staff assistance if needed.

Approval of the AFE should be delegated to the organizational level having the necessary competence to make the decision, as opposed to requesting executive management's approval for each AFE. The philosophy of companies varies as to the extent of decentralization of approval authority. The amount, type, and significance of the expenditure should be considered in determining the required level of approval. Required approvals also may be governed by whether certain designated evaluation criteria are met.

During the budget year, periodic reports should be prepared by categories, comparing approved AFE expenditures with the budget. The reports should be prepared for use by the organization levels originating the requests for expenditures as well as those granting approval. Higher echelons find summaries helpful, with off-budget items reported in detail.

Ethical Considerations

Ethics for cost and managerial accountants was discussed in Chapter 1. Capital budgeting is an area in which the accountant should be especially vigilant, because the capital budgeting process provides both an opportunity and a temptation for unethical behavior. Some common problems are:

1. Pressure to circumvent the approval process is sometimes applied by superiors or associates. In most companies, only projects that require an expenditure in excess of a predesignated level must go through the evaluation and approval process. One way of circumventing such a system would be to break the capital project up into several small purchases, each of which falls below the reporting level of expenditure. If detected by the accountant, the small projects should be grouped into one. Pressure may be applied for the accountant to ignore the situation or to cooperate in subverting the system on the grounds that avoiding the evaluation and approval process would save

time and the project would be accepted anyway. In other cases, pressure may be applied by simple threats, e.g., an executive may threaten to use his or her friendship with or authority over the accountant's immediate supervisor to negatively impact the accountant's career advancement with the company.

2. Pressure may be applied to write off or devalue assets below their true value in order to justify replacement. The pressure may be applied by well-meaning associates who believe that the project will benefit the company in some qualitative way that will not receive adequate consideration in the evaluation process. Alternatively, the pressure may be applied by an executive who wants the project approved for personal prestige or comfort (e.g., new office furniture or a new automobile).

3. The economic benefits of capital expenditure proposals may be exaggerated in order to increase the likelihood of approval. This is a particularly troublesome problem because predictions about the future are never perfectly accurate and necessarily contain some subjectivity. The problem is compounded by the fact that capital projects often have an expected life greater than the period the individual submitting the proposal expects to remain in the current job position. Promotions and job rotations at lower and middle management levels typically occur at fairly short intervals. Therefore, there may be an incentive for the manager to exaggerate the expected benefits of a capital project in order to secure its acceptance, if a subsequent failure of the project to live up to expectations can be blamed on the manager's successor. Although the accountant has access to a considerable amount of data, it often is difficult to determine whether predictions are realistic. Even if predictions are believed to be unrealistic, providing a convincing argument is difficult except in the most extreme cases.

The appropriate course of action in each of these situations (and any other for that matter) depends to a great extent on the character of the individuals involved and nature of the ethical violation. The accountant is clearly and unavoidably obligated to make sure that the company's legitimate policies and procedures are not circumvented and to make sure that the data used in the evaluation of capital projects are as reliable and realistic as possible. In most cases, the accountant should first discuss the perceived ethical problem with the accounting supervisor (in order to clarify the significance of the problem and identify possible courses of action) and then with the individual or individuals involved. If the problem cannot be resolved through discussion, the accountant is obligated to provide a full disclosure of all the details to the executives responsible for evaluating and approving the capital expenditure. If the individual involved is the immediate supervisor, the accountant should consult the next higher level of management.

■ EVALUATING CAPITAL EXPENDITURES

Evaluating capital expenditures refers to the basic concepts, techniques, and procedures employed in appraising and reappraising projects throughout the course of their development. A number of evaluations of a single proposal may be necessary because of:

1. Circumstances that change during the time span from the origin of the project idea to its completion.
2. Alternative solutions of the problem for which the project is designed.
3. Assumptions that vary as to the amount and time pattern of cash flows.

The economic evaluation of capital expenditure proposals has received considerable attention in the literature, and for good reason. In order to survive in the long run, a firm must be profitable. Since capital investments require the commitment of substantial resources for relatively long periods of time, poor investments can have a material long-term effect on the firm's profitability and, consequently, its ability to survive. Four commonly used techniques are discussed in detail in this chapter. Although useful in selecting projects which will maximize company profits, excessive reliance on quantitative answers is dangerous. Since the life of a capital project extends well into the future, the data used in quantitative analysis are fraught with uncertainty. It is difficult to accurately predict what will happen next year, and even more difficult to predict what will happen several years in the future. Furthermore, since predictions about future costs and revenues unavoidably contain elements of subjectivity, such data can be easily manipulated by overzealous or misguided employees.

Strategic considerations and managerial intuition often drive investment decisions rather than evaluations of the results of analytic techniques applied to quantitative data. In some cases, quantitative data are simply not available, or if available, they are not reliable. In other cases, investment decisions are determined by the company's strategic plan or by past choices, in which case quantitative analysis may be unwarranted.[1]

Some capital expenditures are made for qualitative or legal reasons, rather than for purely economic reasons: a manufacturer may be forced to improve product quality, improve delivery and service, increase manufacturing flexibility, or produce a less profitable product in response to competitive pressure; dining or recreation facilities may be installed for employee use; or air and water pollution regulations may necessitate an expenditure for a waste disposal unit.[2] Other projects are musts to the point that use of an evaluation technique is superfluous, e.g., a railway trestle that has been washed out by a flood must be replaced if the section of line affected is to continue in use.

In evaluating capital expenditures, many imponderable factors may affect the decision, such as the actions or reactions of competitors, changes in market demographics or economic prosperity, and changes in social concerns that may spawn new legal requirements and social responsibilities. Further-

[1]Bernard A. Coda and Barry G. King, "Manufacturing Decision-Making Tools," *Journal of Cost Management*, Vol. 3, No. 1, pp. 29-37.

[2]A sample of actual firms suggests that the use of qualitative justification for capital expenditures is common. See Robert A. Howell, James D. Brown, Stephen R. Soucy, and Allen H. Seed, *Management Accounting in the New Manufacturing Environment*, (Montvale, New Jersey: National Association of Accountants, 1987), p. 88.

more, there is a need to select investments that will keep the firm in balance and be consistent with its goals and objectives. Some potentially profitable projects may be rejected because they do not fit into the company's overall plan of operations. Many firms, particularly small and middle-sized ones, are not diversified and invest only in activities related to their particular line of business. This may simply be a matter of choice, or it may be a matter of necessity. One firm may lack expertise while another may lack sufficient funds and be unwilling or unable to secure the necessary financing. The circumstances of each expenditure alternative must be considered in passing judgment on the criteria used. Even then there may be justifiable differences of opinion with respect to governing criteria. The mechanics of various evaluation techniques are important, but of still greater importance is their relationship to the overall capital expenditure planning and control process and the need for creative and thoughtful management.

Classification of Capital Expenditures

Capital expenditure projects can be classified as: (1) equipment-replacement expenditures, (2) expansion investments, and (3) improvements of existing products and/or additions of new products. A proposal may involve more than one classification. For example, a firm may consider a proposal to replace an old printing press, whose maintenance cost has become excessive (an equipment-replacement expenditure), with a new press that will offer an expanded productive capacity (an expansion investment).

Some projects may not be independent of one another and in such cases should be grouped together for evaluation as a compound project. The following quotation illustrates this point:

> *Contingent or dependent projects can arise, for instance, when acceptance of one proposal is dependent on acceptance of one or more other proposals. One simple example would be the purchase of an extra-long boom for a crane which would be of little value unless the crane itself were also purchased; the latter, however, may be justified on its own. When contingent projects are combined with their independent prerequisites, the combination may be called a compound project. Thus, a compound project may be characterized by the algebraic sum of the payoffs and costs of the component projects plus, perhaps, an interaction term.[3]*

Equipment-Replacement Expenditures. Equipment-replacement expenditures include both like-for-like and obsolescence replacements. Historically, the basis for decision making has been the desire for prospective cost savings, i.e., comparing future costs of old equipment with future costs of new equipment. In addition to comparisons of operating costs, the analysis of future costs requires the determination of the prospective purchase price less any ultimate resale or salvage value. One of the most difficult problems is to estimate the probable economic life of the new equipment. This is the core of

---

[3]H. Martin Weingartner, "Capital Budgeting of Interrelated Projects· Survey and Synthesis," *Management Science*, Vol. XII, No. 7, p. 492.

any capital expenditure decision. For the present equipment, the future decline in disposal value must be estimated. The original cost of the present facility is a sunk cost, which is irrecoverable and totally irrelevant to the decision-making process. Accumulated depreciation also is independent of the company's real future costs. Book values of existing assets are not relevant for the replacement decision, except for possible income tax consequences. For example, an increase or decrease in income tax liability might result from the recognition of a gain or loss, respectively, from the sale, exchange, or abandonment of an asset in the year of disposition. On the other hand, in the case of an exchange of like-kind assets, the income tax effect results from an adjustment to the tax basis of the new asset and the amount of depreciation available for tax purposes, which in turn affects the amount of income tax liability over the depreciable life of the asset. An increase or decrease in income tax liability has a direct effect on cash flow and is, therefore, relevant to the capital expenditure decision.

ROBOTICS

FLEXIBLE MANUFACTURING SYSTEM

In the current business environment, there is considerable emphasis on modernizing manufacturing facilities. Although cost savings may occur, the movement toward robotics and flexible manufacturing systems is motivated primarily by strategic considerations. These include the need to improve product quality in the face of increasing competition and the desire to be able to quickly adjust production output, both in quantity and variety, to satisfy rapidly changing consumer demands. The cost of modernization often is very high, and the strategic benefit generally is difficult to quantify.[4]

Expansion Investments. Expansion investments involve plant enlargement and the expansion of existing markets or an invasion into new markets. In these cases, the expected results of expanding and not expanding are compared, with the basis for a decision shifted from cost savings to the expected addition to profits, including the consideration of cash inflow. The expected increase in profit is estimated by preparing a projected income statement showing additional revenue and expense over the life of the project. The degree of uncertainty in this type of investment may be great, but it usually is quantifiable.

Improvements of Existing Products and/or Additions of New Products. Decisions to improve existing products are generally strategic. A firm may be forced to improve product quality or design in order to counter the actions of competitors. Failure to improve existing products can cause deterioration of the market share. Such improvement may require the development of new processes or the modernization of facilities or both. Since no historical basis for making the capital expenditure decision exists and the return on such investments is based on maintaining profits in the face of competition, the benefits often are difficult to quantify. A high degree of sound judgment and business insight is required.

---

[4]Robert A. Howell and Stephen R. Soucy, "Capital Investment in the New Manufacturing Environment," *Management Accounting*, Vol. LXIX, No. 11, pp. 26-32.

Decisions to add new products may involve the decision to drop existing products or to expand the product line. In either case, a capital expenditure may be necessary to either alter or expand existing facilities. In such cases, the capital expenditure is similar to the expansion decision, i.e., the emphasis is generally on profit improvement rather than maintenance. The increase in profits over the life of the capital project must be estimated and compared with its cost in order to determine the value of adding the new product.

Cost of Capital

The *cost of capital* represents the expected return that investors demand for a given level of risk. Although this discussion is brief, the cost of capital as related to capital expenditures is a complex concept. It may refer to a specific cost of capital from a particular financing effort to provide funds for a specific product. Such use of the concept connotes the marginal cost of capital and implies linkage of the financing and investment decisions. This view has been challenged as a useful concept for allocating capital because businesses rely on more than one source of funds to finance their activities. The funds available for one or all capital projects are usually considered to be a commingling of more than one source. Therefore, different costs of capital exist, depending upon the mix of the sources of funds used to finance the business. Companies typically obtain funds from (1) bond issues, (2) preferred and common stock issues, (3) use of retained earnings, and (4) loans from banks. If a company obtains funds by some combination of these sources in order to achieve or maintain a particular capital structure, then the cost of capital (money) is the weighted average cost of each money source. This weighted average considers the joint cost of all sources of funds. The relative proportions and the cost of each source of funds used in computing the weighted cost of capital should be those expected over the investment horizon.[5] In practice, the relative proportions used are likely to be those desired by management in the long run, and the costs used are those currently applicable, adjusted for anticipated inflation. The computation of the weighted average cost of capital may be illustrated as follows:

Funds—Source	Proportion of Funds To Be Provided	Aftertax Cost	Weighted Cost
Bonds.	.20	.05	.01
Preferred stock.	.20	.10	.02
Common stock and retained earnings. . .	.60	.15	.09
	1.00	Weighted average cost of capital	.12 = 12%

[5]*Statement on Management Accounting, No. 4A,* "Cost of Capital" (Montvale, New Jersey: National Association of Accountants, 1984), pp. 3 and 11.

Below is a description of the cost of capital for each source:

1. The cost of bonds is the aftertax rate of interest, i.e., the pretax rate of interest multiplied by one minus the tax rate. If bonds are sold at a premium or a discount, the rate used should be the market yield rate.
2. The cost of preferred stock is the dividend per share divided by the present market price.
3. The cost of common stock and retained earnings is the expected earnings per share, after income tax and after preferred dividends are paid, divided by the present market price.[6]

Inflationary Considerations in Estimating Cash Flows

Just as a company's cost of capital is affected by inflation, so too are estimates of cash flow. In order for the cash flows to be on an equivalent basis with the acceptance criterion, i.e., the weighted average cost of capital, cash flow estimates must include an allowance for the effect of anticipated inflation. To illustrate this effect, assume that Star Company is considering an investment in a project to produce a new product. A sales volume of 1,000 units of the new product is expected for each of the next five years. The planned sales price is $10 per unit and current period cash costs are expected to be $6 per unit, resulting in a net cash inflow of $4 per unit sold. In addition, assume that management expects the general price level to rise at an annual rate of 10 percent. If management believes that its costs will increase at the same rate as inflation and that the sales price of the new product can be increased at the same rate, the estimated cash flows should be adjusted for the effect of inflation as follows:

Year	(1) Unadjusted Estimate of Cash Inflow	(2) General Price-Level Index	(3) Adjusted Estimate of Cash Inflow	(4) Difference (3) – (1)
1	$ 4,000	1.100	$ 4,400	$ 400
2	4,000	1.210	4,840	840
3	4,000	1.331	5,324	1,324
4	4,000	1.464	5,856	1,856
5	4,000	1.610	6,440	2,440
Total	$20,000		$26,860	$6,860

Unless the cash flows are adjusted for inflation's impact, the cash inflows expected over the life of Star Company's project will be understated by $6,860. Such understatement could result in an erroneous rejection of this project. If the impact of inflation is expected to be different for cash inflows and outflows, separate inflation adjustments must be made. For example,

---

[6]Conflicting opinions exist regarding the treatment of the investors' income tax effect on the cost of equity acquired through the retention of earnings.

such a difference would occur when either the sales price of output or the purchase price of input is to be under a fixed price contract.[7]

Another effect of inflation is that it increases the discount rate. In order to obtain the desired return on monetary investments, the financial markets increase the cost of money (i.e., the loan rate on borrowed funds and the rate of return on equity investments) by an amount necessary to offset the expected decline in the value of money over the investment horizon. Such an increase in discount rates biases the decision-making process in favor of short-term projects because, as rates increase, cash flows in more distant years become less significant. These high rates:

> ... serve as a destabilizing factor . . . The high interest rates encourage and even demand that decision makers use high discount rates in their planning. The high discount rates, in turn, tremendously increase the importance of the present—the time horizon becomes biased toward the near future—and the comparative neglect of the long run makes the short run even more unstable.[8]

Income Tax Considerations in Estimating Cash Flows

The effect of income taxes on cash flows is an important consideration in planning and evaluating capital expenditures. The following paragraphs discuss the tax laws regarding depreciation, the investment tax credit, and construction period interest and taxes. Because the tax law changes frequently, the discussion presented in this textbook should be regarded as illustrative only. It is presented to demonstrate the importance of considering the effect of taxes on capital expenditure analysis. Current income tax statutes and regulations should be consulted when planning actual capital expenditures.

Depreciation. Depreciation is not a cash inflow or outflow. However, depreciation allowed for income tax purposes reduces taxable income and, consequently, tax liability, which directly affects cash flow.

The Economic Recovery Tax Act of 1981, with subsequent amendments, represented a substantial change in income tax accounting for capital expenditures. A new system for recovering the cost of capital expenditures, referred to as the Accelerated Cost Recovery System (ACRS), is now used for tangible, depreciable property placed in service after 1980. Although used for federal income tax purposes, some states do not allow the ACRS rates in computing state income taxes. ACRS reduces the impact of inflation by accelerating the recovery of capital expenditures as follows:

1. It eliminates the useful-life concept and replaces it with a shorter recovery period.

---

[7]For an elaboration of the effect of inflation in capital budgeting, see Jon W. Bartley, "A NPV Model Modified for Inflation," *Management Accounting*, Vol. LXII, No. 6, pp. 49-52; Debra D. Raiborn and Thomas A. Ratcliffe, "Are You Accounting for Inflation in Your Capital Budgeting Process?," *Management Accounting*, Vol. LXI, No. 3, pp. 19-22; and Allen H. Seed, III, *The Impact of Inflation on Internal Planning and Control* (New York: National Association of Accountants, 1981), pp. 73-78 and 104-105.

[8]C. Torben Thomsen, "Dangers in Discounting," *Management Accounting*, Vol. LXV, No. 7, pp. 37-39. Copyright January, 1984, by the National Association of Accountants. All rights reserved. Reprinted by permission.

2. It allows more cost recovery in the earlier years of the recovery period, i.e., accelerated depreciation rates.

Under the Tax Reform Act of 1986, Modified ACRS (MACRS) increases the number of property classes and lengthens the recovery periods of most kinds of depreciable property.[9] The 1986 Act provides for the recovery of capital expenditures over periods of 3, 5, 7, 10, 15, 20, 27.5, or 31.5 years, depending upon the type of property. Most of the common depreciable business assets, other than buildings, are classified as 5-year or 7-year property. For example, automobiles, trucks, small aircraft, and technological equipment are classified as 5-year property, and railroad locomotives and cars, commercial aircraft, and most manufacturing machinery are classified as 7-year property. Buildings that qualify as residential rental property are depreciated over 27.5 years, and nonresidential buildings over 31.5 years.

The maximum depreciation rate allowable for 3-year, 5-year, 7-year and 10-year property is 200 percent of the declining balance with an automatic switch to straight-line in the first year in which the straight-line deduction determined as of the beginning of the change year exceeds the declining-balance deduction for the same year. The maximum depreciation rate allowable is reduced to 150 percent of the declining balance for 15-year and 20-year property and to straight-line for residential rental and nonresidential real property. For most tangible personal property, depreciation is computed as if the property were placed into service at the mid-point of the year (referred to as a half-year convention). Depreciation for real property is based on a mid-month convention (i.e., property placed into service in any month is treated as being placed into service in the middle of the month). For all classes of property, salvage value is treated as zero. An example of the cost recovery rates for 3-year, 5-year, and 7-year property classes follows:

Example of MACRS Recovery Percentages by Property Class
(Half-Year Convention and 200% Declining-Balance Method)

Recovery Year	3-Year	5-Year	7-Year
1	.333	.200	.143
2	.444	.320	.245
3	.148	.192	.175
4	.075	.115	.125
5		.115	.089
6		.058	.089
7			.089
8			.045
	1.000	1.000	1.000

Gains on Disposals of Depreciable Property. For federal income tax purposes, gain recognized on the disposal of depreciable property other than buildings is treated as ordinary income to the extent of tax depreciation de-

---

[9]*Internal Revenue Code,* Section 168. Generally, MACRS rules apply to property placed in service after December 31, 1986.

ducted prior to disposal.[10] Gain, if any, in excess of such depreciation is essentially treated as a capital gain.[11] The Tax Reform Act of 1986 repealed the preferential treatment accorded capital gains by removing the capital gain deduction previously available to individuals and by setting the capital gain rate for corporations equal to the ordinary income rate. However, the law still requires that capital gains be computed and reported separately from ordinary income. This requirement was presumably included in order to permit taxpayers to deduct unused capital loss carryovers. It may also have been included in order to keep in place a mechanism that would make it convenient for Congress to reenact some form of preferential tax treatment for capital gains at a later time.

Investment Tax Credit. The investment tax credit was originally enacted in 1962 for the stated purpose of stimulating the economy and generating additional employment by providing an incentive to business to invest and expand. Congress has repealed, reenacted, increased, and expanded the investment tax credit to meet varying economic conditions. The investment tax credit was repealed by the Tax Reform Act of 1986. Although the investment tax credit has not been a stable feature of the income tax law, it is an important capital expenditure consideration during periods when it is available because it reduces income tax expense at the end of the project's first year.

When last a part of the law, the investment tax credit was available on the acquisition of most tangible property (other than buildings). The law has sometimes required that the property's depreciable basis be reduced by all or part of the credit claimed. When repealed in 1986, the most recent version of the investment tax credit required that the property's basis be reduced by 50 percent of the amount of the credit claimed. The regular credit rate was 10 percent. If new property was acquired in exchange for a trade-in of an old machine, the qualified cost for purposes of computing the investment tax credit was the tax basis of the old property plus the cash paid. On the other hand, if used property was acquired in a trade-in, the qualified cost was limited to the cash paid for the property.

Construction Period Interest and Taxes. *Statement of Financial Accounting Standards, No. 34,* "Capitalization of Interest Cost," prescribes the capitalization of interest costs incurred in acquiring assets that require a period of time to be made ready for their intended use, provided the periodic income effect, compared with that of expensing interest, is material. The amount capitalized

---

[10]*Internal Revenue Code,* Section 1245 and *Internal Revenue Code,* Section 1250 generally provide that a gain recognized on the disposition of buildings is to be treated as ordinary income to the extent that the depreciation allowed or allowable exceeds the depreciation that would have been allowed under the straight-line method. The remaining gain recognized, if any, is included in the Section 1231 pool. Since MACRS requires that buildings acquired after 1986 must be depreciated under the straight-line method, on such buildings there will be no excess of accelerated over straight-line depreciation to be recaptured as ordinary income under Section 1250.

[11]*Internal Revenue Code,* Section 1231 provides that all gains (i.e., those recognized in excess of the amount treated as ordinary income) and all losses recognized from the dispositions of trade or business properties during the tax year must be pooled. If the total is a net gain, it is added to the capital gain pool. If the total is a net loss, it is treated as an ordinary loss.

would be recovered through depreciation over the economic life of the new asset. On the other hand, for federal income tax purposes, both construction period interest and taxes must be capitalized.[12] The tax law limits the capitalization of such costs to the acquisition or construction of property that meets any one of the following tests: (1) the property has a class life of 20 years or more, (2) the estimated production period exceeds 2 years, or (3) the estimated production period exceeds one year and the estimated production costs exceed $1,000,000.[13] In addition, the tax law requires the capitalization of not only interest paid or accrued on funds specifically borrowed to construct the property but also a portion of the interest paid or accrued on other liabilities if construction cost exceeds funds borrowed specifically to finance the project.[14]

In evaluating capital expenditure proposals which involve the acquisition or construction of property over a period of time, the initial cash outflow would be increased by both interest and taxes incurred during the construction period. Cash inflows in subsequent periods would be increased by the reduction in income taxes that would result from the amortization of the interest and taxes which had been capitalized during the construction period.

Representative Evaluation Techniques

Despite the fact that many capital expenditures are entered into for strategic or qualitative reasons (and therefore not subjected to economic evaluation), quantitative economic evaluation techniques are frequently and widely used in practice.[15] The following four evaluation techniques are representative tools in current use: (1) the payback (or payout) period method, (2) the average annual return on investment (or accounting rate of return or financial statement) method, (3) the present value method, and (4) the discounted cash flow (or internal rate of return) method (DCF). None of these methods serves every purpose or every firm. The circumstances and needs of a situation determine the most appropriate techniques to be used. A company may use more than one technique (e.g., payback period and DCF) in evaluating each project; however, the same method or methods should be used uniformly for every project throughout the firm. Confusion could arise if Division A used the discounted cash flow method, while Division B used the average annual return on investment method. Trying to compare different projects which have been evaluated with different techniques would be like trying to compare apples and oranges. To evaluate alternative projects, the same evaluation techniques must be used.

---

[12]*Internal Revenue Code*, Section 263A(a)(2)(B) and Section 263A(f).

[13]*Internal Revenue Code*, Section 263A(f)(1)(B).

[14]*Internal Revenue Code*, Section 263A(f)(2)(A).

[15]See Ralph Pope, "Current Capital Budgeting Practices: A Comparison of Small and Large Firms," *Southwest Journal of Business and Economics*, Vol. IV, No. 2, pp. 16-24.

These evaluation techniques, if thoroughly understood by the analysts who use them, should aid management in exercising judgment and making decisions. Certainly the cost of gathering data and applying the evaluation techniques should be justified in terms of the value to management. Moreover, inaccurate raw data used in the calculations or lack of uniform procedures may yield harmful or misleading conclusions.

For purposes of discussing and illustrating the evaluation methods listed, assume that Dartmond Corporation is operating at the limit of the capacity of one of its producing units, and maintenance costs of an existing machine have become excessive. A new machine with greater capacity can be purchased at a cost of $103,000, less a trade-in allowance for the old machine of $8,000, which represents the fair market value of the old machine. Therefore, the initial cash outflow would be $95,000. The old machine has a book value of $5,000 and a tax basis of zero. The net acquisition cost for financial accounting purposes is $100,000 ($95,000 cash price plus $5,000 book value) and for tax purposes is $95,000 ($95,000 cash price plus zero tax basis).[16] The expected economic life of the new unit is eight years. Straight-line depreciation is to be used for financial accounting purposes, with an estimated salvage value of $10,000.[17] For tax purposes, however, the property qualifies as 5-year property under ACRS and salvage value is ignored.

The estimated differential aftertax cash inflows yielded by the utilized additional capacity of the new machine for Dartmond Corporation are calculated in the table on page 741. The pretax estimates of cash inflows include consideration of inflation's impact. The aftertax cash flows are computed under the assumption that the investment tax credit is not available. The aftertax cash inflow estimates computed in the table are used to illustrate the capital expenditure evaluation techniques discussed in the following paragraphs. The numbers given in Columns 2 and 3 are uneven, so that the resulting amounts in Column 8 will be easy to use and to follow in subsequent calculations.

This example involves both a replacement and an expansion investment, in which the cash outlay is restricted to the cost of the plant asset unit. Some projects require the commitment of working capital for inventories, receiv-

---

[16]Both *APB Opinion No. 29* and *IRC Section 1031* require that no gain be recognized on the exchange of similar or like-kind assets. The book value or tax basis of the new asset is the value or tax basis of the old asset plus boot given (cash paid to the vendor). Note, however, that if the old asset is sold outright rather than traded in, an $8,000 taxable gain would be realized on the sale ($8,000 sales price less zero tax basis) and the net acquisition cost would be the cash price of $103,000. The initial cash outflow would be $95,000 ($103,000 cash price less $8,000 cash proceeds from the sale of the old asset) plus the tax paid on the $8,000 gain recognized. Regardless of whether the old asset is sold or traded in, the book value of the old asset is a sunk cost and irrelevant to the decision. The aftertax gain on the sale of the old asset is irrelevant, since the proceeds received from the sale must be used to purchase the new asset at a greater cash outflow than would be required if the old asset were traded in. However, the tax liability incurred on the sale of the old asset is relevant, because it could be avoided by trading in the old asset instead of selling it outright. Since a trade-in results in a smaller initial cash outflow than a sale, it is assumed for this illustration.

[17]Generally accepted accounting principles require that the cost of a depreciable asset be allocated to expense over the expected useful life of the asset, even though that period is different from the cost recovery period used for tax purposes. See "AcSEC Position on Tax and Depreciation Lives," *The CPA Letter*, AICPA, Vol. 61, No. 21, p. 3. The method of depreciation and the treatment of estimated salvage value for financial accounting purposes must also comply with generally accepted accounting principles, even though such treatment may differ from that required for tax purposes.

DARTMOND CORPORATION—AFTERTAX CASH FLOW

(1) Year	(2) Estimated Cash Savings Relating to Present Capacity (Primarily Maintenance)	(3) Estimated Cash Income Relating to Use of Increased Capacity	(4) Total Cash Inflow (2) + (3)	(5) Tax Depre- ciation*	(6) Taxable Income (Loss) (4) − (5)	(7) Federal and State Income Tax (Reduction) (6) × 40%	(8) Net Aftertax Cash Inflow (4) − (7)
1	$9,100	$26,566	$35,666	$19,000	$16,666	$6,666	$ 29,000
2	7,800	25,267	33,067	30,400	2,667	1,067	32,000
3	6,500	26,340	32,840	18,240	14,600	5,840	27,000
4	5,200	25,850	31,050	10,925	20,125	8,050	23,000
5	3,900	23,817	27,717	10,925	16,792	6,717	21,000
6	2,600	23,727	26,327	5,510	20,817	8,327	18,000
7	1,300	22,033	23,333	0	23,333	9,333	14,000
8	0	20,000	20,000	0	20,000	8,000	12,000
							$176,000

Cash inflow from salvage at end of economic life 6,000**

Total aftertax cash inflows. $182,000

*Tax depreciation is determined by multiplying the depreciable basis of $95,000 by the MACRS depreciation rates provided on page 737 for the 5-year property class.

**The salvage value received at the end of the project would be fully taxable because the tax basis would be zero. Thus, the aftertax cash flow would be $6,000 ($10,000 salvage × (1 − .40 tax rate)). Note, however, that no tax would be estimated for salvage if management planned to exchange the asset for a replacement in kind.

ables, etc., as well as expenditures that may not be capitalized. When such commitments and expenditures exist, they should be included as part of the initial investment and, to the extent that they are recoverable, should be shown as cash inflow in the recovery years.

The Payback Period Method. The payback (or payout) period method is widely used in many firms, if only to serve as an initial screening device or to complement the answers of more sophisticated methods. The technique measures the length of time required by the project to recover the initial outlay.[18] The calculated payback period is compared with the payback period acceptable to management for projects of the kind being evaluated. The computation for the Dartmond Corporation project is:

Year	Net Aftertax Cash Flow	Recovery of Initial Outlay Needed	Balance	Payback Years Required
1	$29,000	$95,000	$66,000	1.0
2	32,000	66,000	34,000	1.0
3	27,000	34,000	7,000	1.0
4	23,000	7,000	0	0.3
Total payback period in years.				3.3

[18]The initial outlay used in calculating the payback period should exclude working capital to the extent that the working capital can be recovered through its own liquidation. Investment salvage value at the payback point would further reduce the payback period. Such adjustments result in what is referred to as the "bailout payback."

Because of the effects of variations in business activity, inflation, and accelerated methods of depreciation used for income tax purposes, it is highly unlikely that estimated cash flows for actual projects would be uniform for each year. However, professional examinations, such as the CPA and CMA examinations, may assume uniform cash flows for simplicity in problems requiring the computation of the payback period. In such cases, the payback period can be computed by dividing the cash outflow in the initial period by the annual cash inflow. For example, if the annual cash inflow from the Dartmond Corporation capital project were $30,000 each year, the payback period would be 3.17 years ($95,000 initial cash investment ÷ $30,000 annual cash inflow).

Advantages of using the payback (or payout) method to evaluate capital expenditures are:

1. It is simple to compute and easy to understand.
2. It may be used to select those investments yielding a quick return of cash, thus placing an emphasis on liquidity.
3. It permits a company to determine the length of time required to recapture its original investment, thus offering a possible indicator of the degree of risk of each investment. Such an indicator is especially useful when the danger of obsolescence is great.
4. It is a widely used method that is certainly an improvement over a hunch, rule of thumb, or intuitive method.

Disadvantages and limitations associated with using the payback (or payout) method of evaluating capital expenditures are:

1. It ignores the time value of money. To illustrate this disadvantage, assume that the "Net Aftertax Cash Inflow" for Dartmond Corporation had been: Year 1, $62,000; Year 2, $16,000; Year 3, $14,000; and Year 4, $10,000—with the same 8-year total. The computation would be:

Year	Net Aftertax Cash Flow	Recovery of Initial Outlay Needed	Recovery of Initial Outlay Balance	Payback Years Required
1	$62,000	$95,000	$33,000	1.0
2	16,000	33,000	17,000	1.0
3	14,000	17,000	3,000	1.0
4	10,000	3,000	0	0.3
Total payback period in years...........				3.3

In both this example and the example on page 741, the payback period is 3.3 years. In this example, however, $33,000 more was received in the first year ($62,000 – $29,000). This situation is more desirable from an investment standpoint because money has a time value; that is, a dollar is worth more the earlier it is received because it can be reinvested.

2. It ignores cash flows which may occur beyond the payback period. In the example on page 741, the payback period is 3.3 years, the economic life is 8 years, and the "Net Aftertax Cash Inflow" is $182,000.

Assume that an alternative project indicates a "Net Aftertax Cash Inflow" of $95,000 in the first two years and an economic life of three years, with "Net Aftertax Cash Inflow" of $10,000 in the third year. Although the latter case has a shorter payback period, the original example of a 3.3 year payback and net cash inflow of $182,000 is more desirable when immediate cash problems are not of critical importance.

3. It fails to consider salvage value which may exist after the payback period.

The Average Annual Return on Investment Method. This method sometimes is referred to as the accounting rate of return method or the financial statement method. When this method is used, an investment proposal is evaluated by comparing the estimated average annual rate of return on the investment with a target rate of return. If more than one project exceeds the target rate of return and funds are insufficient to finance all qualified projects, the acceptable projects are ranked and only the most profitable ones selected. The estimated rate of return for the Dartmond Corporation project may be computed as follows:

Net income without deduction for depreciation (net aftertax cash inflow, excluding salvage value)	$176,000
Less financial accounting depreciation ($100,000 acquisition cost less $10,000 salvage value)*	90,000
	$ 86,000
Less tax expense on taxable gain from sale of asset at end of economic life ($10,000 salvage value × 40%)	4,000
Net income over economic life of project	$ 82,000

*Depreciation is assumed to be the only noncash expense and thus is the only adjustment required in converting from cash flow to accrual basis income.

$$\text{Average annual return on } \textit{original} \text{ investment} = \frac{\text{Net income}}{\text{Economic life}} \div \text{Original investment}$$

$$= \frac{\$82,000}{8 \text{ years}} \div \$100,000$$

$$= 10.25\%$$

Another approach to estimating a project's rate of return is to divide the average annual net income by the average investment rather than the original investment. The computation for the Dartmond Corporation project is:

Original investment.	$100,000
Investment at end of economic life (salvage value)	10,000
	$110,000
Average investment ($110,000 ÷ 2)	$ 55,000*

*The original book value and the book value at the end of each year can be averaged if the straight-line depreciation method is not used for financial accounting purposes.

$$\text{Average annual return on } \textit{average} \text{ investment} = \frac{\text{Net income}}{\text{Economic life}} \div \text{Average investment}$$

$$= \frac{\$82,000}{8 \text{ years}} \div \$55,000$$

$$= 18.64\%$$

Advantages of using the average annual return on investment method to evaluate capital expenditures are:

1. It facilitates expenditure follow-up due to more readily available data from accounting records.
2. It considers income over the entire life of the project.

Disadvantages and limitations associated with the use of the average annual return on investment method of evaluating capital expenditures are:

1. It ignores the time value of money. Two projects might have the same average return, yet vary considerably in the pattern of cash flow. In such a case, the recognition of the time value of money would point to the desirability of the alternative having greater cash flow in the earlier periods.
2. Inflation's effect is expected to be included in cash flow estimates. But a calculation of net income based on historical cost depreciation and the expression of net income as a return on an investment, which is also stated at historical cost, may be quite misleading.
3. The average return on the original investment technique is inapplicable, if any of the investment is made after the beginning of the project.

The Present Value Method. A dollar received a year hence is not the equivalent of a dollar received today, because the use of money has a value. To illustrate, if $500 can be invested at 20 percent, $600 will be received a year later ($500 + 20% of $500). The $600 to be received next year has a present value of $500 if 20 percent can be earned ($600 ÷ 120% = $500). The difference of $100 ($600 – $500) represents the time value of money. In line with this idea, the estimated results of an investment proposal can be stated at its present value, i.e., as a cash equivalent at the present time.[19]

Present value tables have been devised to facilitate the application of present value theory. The "Present Value of $1" table on page 754 presents computations to three decimal places and shows today's value, or the present value, of each dollar to be received or paid in the future for various rates of

---

[19]The basic formula for present value is:

$$PV = S\left(\frac{1}{(1+i)^n}\right) \quad \text{or} \quad \frac{S}{(1+i)^n} \quad \text{or} \quad S(1+i)^{-n}$$

where PV = present value of future sum of money
      S = future sum of money
      i = earnings rate for each compounding period
      n = number of periods

interest and periods of time.[20] By multiplying the appropriate factor obtained from the table times an expected future cash flow, the present value of the cash flow is easily determined.

The "Present Value of $1 Received or Paid Annually for Each of the Next N Years" table on page 755 shows the present value of a series of $1 periodic receipts or payments. It is sometimes referred to as the "Present Value of an Ordinary Annuity of $1 per Period." This table is used when the cash flow is estimated to be the same each period. The relationship between this table and the "Present Value of $1" table on page 754 is as follows:

Period	Present Value of $1 at 12%	Present Value of $1 Received or Paid Annually for Each of the Next N Years at 12%
1	.893	.893
2	.797	1.690 (.893 + .797)
3	.712	2.402 (1.690 + .712)
4	.636	3.037 (2.402 + .636)*
5	.567	3.605 (3.037 + .567)*
6	.507	4.111 (3.605 + .507)*
7	.452	4.564 (4.111 + .452)*
8	.404	4.968 (4.564 + .404)

*Difference of .001 results from rounding off the results of the formula.

If the flow is uniform, the flow for one period can be multiplied by the cumulative factor to obtain approximately the same answer as by multiplying the individual factors by the flow for each period and totaling the products. For example, if a project costing $20,000 is expected to yield a uniform annual aftertax cash inflow of $5,000 for seven years, then the present value of the expected cash inflows, discounted at 12 percent, is $5,000 × 4.564, or $22,820, and the net present value is $2,820 ($22,820 – $20,000).[21]

The present value concept can be applied to the Dartmond Corporation problem by discounting at the company's 12 percent estimated cost of capital. For assets requiring a period of time to be made ready for use, the initial cash payment marks the project's origin, at which point the discount factor is 1.000. Subsequent cash payments related to the project's acquisition or construction are shown as outflows to be discounted back to the initial cash outflow date, along with net cash inflows associated with the investment's operating use.

---

[20]Ordinary tables, such as those included in this chapter, assume that all cash flows occur at the end of each period and that interest is compounded at the end of each period. Either or both of these assumptions can be varied by the use of calculus so that, instead of assuming that the cash flows occur at the end of each period, they can occur continuously, and interest can be compounded continuously. Although the continuous assumptions often are more representative of actual conditions, the tables in this chapter are more frequently used in practice.

[21]As noted earlier, although unusual in actual capital expenditure evaluation cases, uniform cash flow analysis is included here because it is occasionally required on professional examinations such as the CPA and CMA examinations.

The computation for Dartmond Corporation is as follows:

Year	Net Aftertax Cash (Outflow) Inflow	Present Value of $1 @ 12%	Present Value of Net Cash Flow
0	$(95,000)	1.000	$(95,000)
1	29,000	.893	25,897
2	32,000	.797	25,504
3	27,000	.712	19,224
4	23,000	.636	14,628
5	21,000	.567	11,907
6	18,000	.507	9,126
7	14,000	.452	6,328
8	18,000*	.404	7,272
Net present value			$ 24,886

*$12,000 + $6,000 aftertax salvage

The positive net present value of $24,886 indicates that the true rate of return is greater than the cost of capital discount rate. A net present value of zero would indicate a rate of return of exactly 12 percent. If investment funds are not rationed (i.e., the company has sufficient funds available to finance all acceptable projects), all projects with a positive net present value would be accepted. On the other hand, if investment funds are being rationed (the typical case in practice), alternative projects would be ranked according to their net present values.

A project's useful life is one of the uncertainties often associated with capital expenditure evaluations. Equipment obsolescence or shifts in market demands may occur. The conventional payback method determines the time necessary to recover the initial outlay, without regard to present value considerations. However, management may wish to know the minimum life for a project necessary to recover the original investment and earn a desired rate of return on the investment. The *present value payback* calculation focuses on this question and is computed for Dartmond Corporation as follows, using the "present value of net cash flow" figures shown in the previous computation:

Year	Present Value of Net Cash Flow	Recovery of Initial Outlay — Needed	Recovery of Initial Outlay — Balance	Present Value Payback Years Required
1	$25,897	$95,000	$69,103	1.00
2	25,504	69,103	43,599	1.00
3	19,224	43,599	24,375	1.00
4	14,628	24,375	9,747	1.00
5	11,907	9,747	0	.82
Total present value payback in years				4.82

Based on the present value of estimated cash flows, 4.82 years will be required to recover the $95,000 original cash investment and earn a desired 12 percent rate of return on the annual unrecovered balance. Additionally, the present value payback will be shortened by the present value of the project's salvage value.

Advantages of using the present value method of evaluating capital expenditures are:

1. It considers the time value of money.
2. It considers cash flow over the entire life of the project.
3. It allows for different discount rates over the life of the project, i.e., the discount rate used to discount the cash flows for each period can be altered to reflect anticipated changes in the cost of capital.

Disadvantages and limitations associated with the use of the present value method of evaluating capital expenditures are:

1. Some argue that this method is too difficult to compute and to understand. Given the pervasive use of computers in business today, such an argument generally is unwarranted.
2. Management must determine a discount rate to be used. A well-informed management should already be aware of its cost of capital that should represent the benchmark for discount rate purposes. However, some firms may set as their discount rate something in excess of the cost of capital or use different rates that depend on risk and uncertainty and other characteristics of a particular project. This procedure is conceptually unsound. Cash received in early periods has more value than cash received in later periods only because early cash inflows can be reinvested. If the discount rate is inflated above the reinvestment rate, the value of the cash inflows is misstated. This problem can be overcome by using the reinvestment rate to compute the future value of the cash inflows at the end of the life of the project and then discounting the total terminal value to the start of the project, using a risk adjusted rate (i.e., the cost of capital rate plus an additional component to compensate for risk).[22] Assuming that the cost of capital rate is a reasonable reinvestment rate, the terminal value for the Dartmond Corporation illustration would be computed as follows:

Year	Net Aftertax Cash Inflow	Future Value of $1 at 12%	Terminal Value of Cash Inflows
1	$29,000	$(1.00 + .12)^7 = 2.211$	$ 64,119
2	32,000	$(1.00 + .12)^6 = 1.974$	63,168
3	27,000	$(1.00 + .12)^5 = 1.762$	47,574
4	23,000	$(1.00 + .12)^4 = 1.574$	36,202
5	21,000	$(1.00 + .12)^3 = 1.405$	29,505
6	18,000	$(1.00 + .12)^2 = 1.254$	22,572
7	14,000	$(1.00 + .12)\ \ = 1.120$	15,680
8	18,000	1.000	18,000
			$296,820

---

[22]See Lester Barenbaum and Thomas Monahan, "Utilizing Terminal Values in Teaching Time Value Analysis," *Journal of Accounting Education*, Vol. 1, No. 2, pp. 79-88.

If a risk premium of 2 percent were added to the 12 percent reinvestment rate, the net present value of the project would be as follows:

Terminal value of aftertax cash inflows	$296,820
Present value of $1 at 14% for 8 periods	.351
Present value of terminal aftertax cash inflows	$104,184
Initial cash outflow	95,000
Net present value of project	$ 9,184

More explicit methods of incorporating risk and uncertainty into the capital expenditure analysis are discussed in Chapter 23.

3. If projects being compared involve different dollar amounts of investment, the project with more profitable dollars, as computed by the present value method, may not be the better project if it also requires a larger investment. For example, a net present value of $1,000 on an investment of $100,000 is not as economically wise as a net present value of $900 on an investment of $10,000, provided that the $90,000 difference in investments can be used to realize a net present value of at least $101 in other projects. In this case, a net present value index should be used rather than the net present value dollar figure. This index places all competing projects on a comparable basis for the purpose of ranking them. For Dartmond Corporation, the computation is:

$$\frac{\text{Net present}}{\text{value index}} = \frac{\text{Net present value}}{\text{Required investment}} = \frac{\$24,886}{\$95,000} = .262$$

This index simplifies finding the optimum solution for competing projects when the total budget for capital outlays is fixed arbitrarily, because it is possible to rank by percentages rather than absolute dollars.

4. It may be misleading when dealing with alternative projects or limited funds under the condition of unequal lives, in that the alternative with the higher net present value may involve longer economic life to the point that it would be less desirable than an alternative having a shorter life. To illustrate, a firm may be faced with the problem of acquiring equipment for a manufacturing operation. Two alternatives are available: Equipment A, expected to last 18 years, and Equipment B, expected to last 5 years. There are three ways to deal with this problem:

(a) Repeat the investment cycle for Equipment B a sufficient number of times to cover the estimated economic life of Equipment A; in the example, 3 3/5 times. An estimate of the salvage value of the fourth equipment investment cycle for Equipment B at the end of the life for Equipment A is needed in order to reflect a common termination date.

(b) The period considered can be the life of the shorter-life alternative, Equipment B, coupled with an estimate of the recoverable value of Equipment A at the end of 5 years. The analysis would then cover only the 5-year period, with the recoverable value of Equipment A being treated as a cash inflow at the end of the period. A serious difficulty rests in the need to estimate a value of the longer-life asset at the end of 5 years. Such an intermediate recoverable value may not be an adequate measure of the service value of the equipment at that point in its useful life.

(c) The net present value of each project can be annualized before being compared. To accomplish this, divide the net present value of Equipment A by the present value of $1 received annually for 18 years (the life of Equipment A) at the company's cost of capital rate and divide the net present value for Equipment B by the present value of $1 received annually for 5 years (the life of Equipment B) at the same cost of capital rate. The alternative with the highest annualized net present value should be selected because it will provide the largest increase in the value of the firm.[23]

The Discounted Cash Flow (DCF) Method. In the present value method, the discount rate is known or at least predetermined. In the discounted cash flow method, the discount rate is not known but is defined as the rate at which the sum of positive present values equals the sum of negative present values. This discount rate is sometimes referred to as the internal rate of return. Present value theory is used, but the analysis is developed further to determine the discounted rate of return, which is then compared with some standard.

The discounted rate of return for Dartmond Corporation can be determined by trial and error, i.e., by computing net present value at various discount rates to find the rate at which the net present value is zero. This computation is illustrated in the following table:

Year	Net Aftertax Cash (Outflow) Inflow	Present Value of $1 @ 20%	Net Present Value of Cash Flow	Present Value of $1 @ 22%	Net Present Value of Cash Flow
0	$(95,000)	1.000	$(95,000)	1.000	$(95,000)
1	29,000	.833	24,157	.820	23,780
2	32,000	.694	22,208	.672	21,504
3	27,000	.579	15,633	.551	14,877
4	23,000	.482	11,086	.451	10,373
5	21,000	.402	8,442	.370	7,770
6	18,000	.335	6,030	.303	5,454
7	14,000	.279	3,906	.249	3,486
8	18,000	.233	4,194	.204	3,672
			$ 656		$ (4,084)

The discounted rate is greater than 20 percent and less than 22 percent. The trial-and-error search should continue until adjacent rates in the table are found—one rate yielding a positive net present value with the other rate yielding a negative net present value, and both as close to zero as possible.

Expanded present value tables permit the determination of a net present value nearer zero. However, an approximation is obtainable by interpolation, as shown at the top of page 750.

---

[23]Jack F. Truitt, "Capital Rationing: An Annualized Approach," *The Journal of Cost Analysis*, Vol. 8, Summer 1988, pp. 63-75.

$$20\% + \left(2\% \times \frac{\$656}{\$656 + \$4,084}\right) = 20\% + ((2\%)(.138)) = .2028 \text{ or } 20.28\%$$

The discounted cash flow method permits management to maximize corporate profits by selecting proposals with the highest rates of return, as long as the rates are higher than the company's cost of capital plus management's allowance for risk and uncertainty and individual project characteristics.

Note that the rate of return, using either the discounted cash flow method or the present value method, is computed on the basis of the unrecovered cash outflow from period to period, not on the original cash investment. In the illustration, the DCF rate of return of 20.28 percent denotes that, over the eight years, the aftertax cash inflow equals the recovery of the original cash investment plus a return of 20.28 percent on the unrecovered cash investment from period to period. The net present value of $24,886 (page 746) indicates that, over the eight years, this additional amount, or a total of $119,886 ($95,000 + $24,886), could have been spent on the machine; and the original cash investment, plus a return of 12 percent on the unrecovered cash investment from period to period, could still have been recovered.

The following are some advantages of using the discounted cash flow rate of return method of evaluating capital expenditures:

1. It considers the time value of money.
2. It considers cash flow over the entire life of the project.
3. The discounted cash flow rate of return is more easily interpreted than the net present value and the net present value index.
4. Alternative projects which require different initial cash outlays and have unequal lives can be ranked logically in accordance with their respective discounted cash flow rates of return.

Some disadvantages and limitations associated with the use of the discounted cash flow rate of return method of evaluating capital expenditures may be:

1. This method is difficult to compute and to understand, particularly when cash flows change signs more than once, in which case the project has more than one rate of return.
2. Discounting at the project's internal rate of return implies that cash inflows can be reinvested to earn the rate earned by the investment being evaluated. In contrast, the present value method implies that cash inflows are reinvested at the discount rate being used, which is usually the weighted average cost of capital. The latter assumption appears more reasonable, particularly when the internal rate of return for the project is high, because the weighted average cost of capital is the company-wide expected earnings rate. Nevertheless, in most circumstances, the use of the discounted cash flow rate of return method instead of the present value method will not seriously alter the ranking of alternative projects.

The Error Cushion. A project whose estimated desirability is near a cutoff point for the type of project being evaluated affords little cushion for errors. For example, if the management of a chain of automotive muffler shops anticipates that a new location should yield a minimum discounted cash flow of 12 percent, there obviously is a greater cushion for errors when the computed rate of return is 20 percent as opposed to 13 percent. Similarly, when one alternative clearly is superior to others for a particular project, there is a better cushion against errors than when two or more of the best alternatives indicate approximately the same expected results.

Reasonably accurate estimates are desirable in evaluating any project. However, a higher degree of sophistication and care, at a higher cost of obtaining the data, may be necessary to add confidence when the evaluation is close to a cutoff point or when two or more project alternatives yield about the same "best" answer. Conversely, in many cases, the desirability of a project or the selection from alternatives for a particular project will be so obvious that the costs of making sophisticated data estimates and using evaluation techniques are not justified.

Purchase vs. Lease. A lease arrangement may be available as an alternative to investment in a capital asset. This possibility can be evaluated by determining the incremental annual cost of leasing versus purchasing. This cost represents purchasing cost savings which, on an aftertax basis, should be sufficient to yield the desired DCF rate of return on the anticipated purchase price.

In evaluating the leasing and purchasing alternatives, the present value method can be used as an alternative to the DCF method in either of two ways:

1. The net present value of the purchase price and the associated aftertax savings is computed, with the resulting net present value used to evaluate the attractiveness of purchasing versus leasing.
2. The net present values of the purchasing alternative and the leasing alternative cash flows are computed separately, each on an aftertax basis. The alternative having the more favorable net present value identifies the preferable choice.

Generally, the capital expenditure or investment decision is first justified, followed by the lease or financing decision. The rationale is that the acquisition must be a sound investment before considering the financing strategy and the operating flexibility, obsolescence, and service/maintenance factors associated with leases versus purchases. With a justified capital expenditure in hand, a lease-purchase decision can be made.[24]

Usually the lease is the more expensive alternative, since a lease involves avoiding various ownership risks for which a price must be paid. In such

---

[24]William L. Ferrara, *The Lease-Purchase Decision: How Some Companies Make It* (New York: National Association of Accountants; Hamilton, Ontario: The Society of Management Accountants of Canada, 1978), p. 7. For a detailed discussion of the lease-purchase decision model, see William L. Ferrara, James B. Thies, and Mark W. Dirsmith, *The Lease-Purchase Decision* (New York: National Association of Accountants, 1980; Hamilton, Ontario: The Society of Management Accountants of Canada, 1979).

cases, a relevant question then becomes whether or not the extra cost entailed in leasing is worth paying in order to avoid risks of ownership. Management may prefer leasing if it is thereby able to improve balance sheet position by avoiding a purchase liability. Also, the rate of return on capital employed would be enhanced by reducing the investment in capital assets.[25] However, generally accepted accounting principles prescribe rules that require the capitalization and the recording of an associated liability for leases that are determined to be, in effect, purchases.[26]

■ CONTROLLING CAPITAL EXPENDITURES

The phase of controlling capital expenditures consists of (1) control and review of a project while it is in process and (2) follow-up or post-completion audit of project results.

Control While in Process

QUALITY
CONTROL

When a project or a series of projects finally has been approved, methods, techniques, and procedures must be set in motion to permit the control and review of all project elements (costs, time, quality, and quantity) until completion. Control responsibility should be clearly designated, recognizing the necessity of assistance from and coordination with many individuals and groups, including those external to the company. Actual results should be compared with approved plans and evaluation results. Variations or trends toward deviations from plans should be reported promptly to responsible authorities in order to facilitate corrective action as quickly as possible. Day-to-day, on-the-scene observation and up-to-date reports should provide good cost control vehicles. Construction engineers have long used such devices as bar charts for planning and controlling the timing of project activities.

PERT/cost (Chapter 17) utilizes the network scheme to show the interrelationships of the multiple activities required to complete the average to large-scale project. Any project (for example, the installation of a single large machine, a complex of machinery and equipment, or the construction of a new factory or office building) will involve many diverse tasks. Some of them can be done simultaneously; others must await the completion of preceding activities. PERT/cost offers a clear and all-inclusive picture of the operation as

---

[25]Lawrence A. Gordon, Danny Miller, and Henry Mintzberg, *Normative Models in Managerial Decision-Making* (New York: National Association of Accountants; Hamilton, Ontario: The Society of Industrial Accountants of Canada, 1975), p. 67.

[26]*Statement of Financial Accounting Standards, No. 13*, "Accounting for Leases" (Stamford: Financial Accounting Standards Board, 1976).

a whole in contrast to the bars on a chart. The use of this technique is particularly appropriate for those evaluation cases where more than one estimate is needed due to risk and uncertainty and there is a desire to expedite and increase the reliability of difficult estimates.

The cost of administering the control phase should be commensurate with the value derived. Overcontrol is an inefficient use of administrative resources.

Follow-Up of Project Results

Follow-up or post-completion audit means comparing and reporting results as related to the outcome predicted when the investment project was evaluated and approved. Follow-up affords a test of the existing planning and control procedure and therein the possibility of reinforcing successful projects, salvaging or terminating failing projects, and improving upon future investment proposals and decisions.

The same techniques used to evaluate the proposed project should be used for follow-up. For example, if the DCF rate of return projected in support of a project proposal is compared in the follow-up procedure with the actual average annual return on investment, the comparison could be quite misleading. Instead, the projected DCF rate should be compared to a DCF rate based on actual data and a reestimation of future data, thus employing the same evaluation technique in the follow-up as in evaluating the project proposal.

Follow-up should aid in determining the optimal point for project abandonment. For example, if the present value of estimated aftertax cash flows for a project's remaining life is less than the aftertax disposal value, it should be abandoned.

Generally, actual work in the area of follow-up lags behind advances made in other capital expenditure phases. Common hindrances to follow-up procedures are management's unwillingness to incur additional administrative costs, difficulty of quantifying the results of certain types of investments, apparent failure of the accounting or cost system to produce needed information, lack of personnel qualified to perform the follow-up tasks, and resentment by those being audited.

Value received as related to the cost of obtaining the follow-up information should determine the extent of the follow-up. For uniformity, efficiency, and independent review, management should designate a centralized group to prescribe procedures and audit the performance of the follow-up activity. The assembled data should be utilized as a control device and be reported to the controlling levels of management. Out-of-line results should then trigger corrective action in harmony with the management by exception principle.

PRESENT VALUE OF $1

Future Years	1%	2%	4%	6%	8%	10%	12%	14%	15%	16%	18%	20%	22%	24%	25%	26%	28%	30%	35%	40%	45%	50%
1	.990	.980	.962	.943	.926	.909	.893	.877	.870	.862	.847	.833	.820	.806	.800	.794	.781	.769	.741	.714	.690	.667
2	.980	.961	.925	.890	.857	.826	.797	.769	.756	.743	.718	.694	.672	.650	.640	.630	.610	.592	.549	.510	.476	.444
3	.971	.942	.889	.840	.794	.751	.712	.675	.658	.641	.609	.579	.551	.524	.512	.500	.477	.455	.406	.364	.328	.296
4	.961	.924	.855	.792	.735	.683	.636	.592	.572	.552	.516	.482	.451	.423	.410	.397	.373	.350	.301	.260	.226	.198
5	.951	.906	.822	.747	.681	.621	.567	.519	.497	.476	.437	.402	.370	.341	.328	.315	.291	.269	.223	.186	.156	.132
6	.942	.888	.790	.705	.630	.564	.507	.456	.432	.410	.370	.335	.303	.275	.262	.250	.227	.207	.165	.133	.108	.088
7	.933	.871	.760	.665	.583	.513	.452	.400	.376	.354	.314	.279	.249	.222	.210	.198	.178	.159	.122	.095	.074	.059
8	.923	.853	.731	.627	.540	.467	.404	.351	.327	.305	.266	.233	.204	.179	.168	.157	.139	.123	.091	.068	.051	.039
9	.914	.837	.703	.592	.500	.424	.361	.308	.284	.263	.225	.194	.167	.144	.134	.125	.108	.094	.067	.048	.035	.026
10	.905	.820	.676	.558	.463	.386	.322	.270	.247	.227	.191	.162	.137	.116	.107	.099	.085	.073	.050	.035	.024	.017
11	.896	.804	.650	.527	.429	.350	.287	.237	.215	.195	.162	.135	.112	.094	.086	.079	.066	.056	.037	.025	.017	.012
12	.887	.788	.625	.497	.397	.319	.257	.208	.187	.168	.137	.112	.092	.076	.069	.062	.052	.043	.027	.018	.012	.008
13	.879	.773	.601	.469	.368	.290	.229	.182	.163	.145	.116	.093	.075	.061	.055	.050	.040	.033	.020	.013	.008	.005
14	.870	.758	.577	.442	.340	.263	.205	.160	.141	.125	.099	.078	.062	.049	.044	.039	.032	.025	.015	.009	.006	.003
15	.861	.743	.555	.417	.315	.239	.183	.140	.123	.108	.084	.065	.051	.040	.035	.031	.025	.020	.011	.006	.004	.002
16	.853	.728	.534	.394	.292	.218	.163	.123	.107	.093	.071	.054	.042	.032	.028	.025	.019	.015	.008	.005	.003	.002
17	.844	.714	.513	.371	.270	.198	.146	.108	.093	.080	.060	.045	.034	.026	.023	.020	.015	.012	.006	.003	.002	.001
18	.836	.700	.494	.350	.250	.180	.130	.095	.081	.069	.051	.038	.028	.021	.018	.016	.012	.009	.005	.002	.001	.001
19	.828	.686	.475	.331	.232	.164	.116	.083	.070	.060	.043	.031	.023	.017	.014	.012	.009	.007	.003	.002	.001	
20	.820	.673	.456	.312	.215	.149	.104	.073	.061	.051	.037	.026	.019	.014	.012	.010	.007	.005	.002	.001	.001	
21	.811	.660	.439	.294	.199	.135	.093	.064	.053	.044	.031	.022	.015	.011	.009	.008	.006	.004	.002	.001		
22	.803	.647	.422	.278	.184	.123	.083	.056	.046	.038	.026	.018	.013	.009	.007	.006	.004	.003	.001	.001		
23	.795	.634	.406	.262	.170	.112	.074	.049	.040	.033	.022	.015	.010	.007	.006	.005	.003	.002	.001			
24	.788	.622	.390	.247	.158	.102	.066	.043	.035	.028	.019	.013	.008	.006	.005	.004	.003	.002	.001			
25	.780	.610	.375	.233	.146	.092	.059	.038	.030	.024	.016	.010	.007	.005	.004	.003	.002	.001	.001			
26	.772	.598	.361	.220	.135	.084	.053	.033	.026	.021	.014	.009	.006	.004	.003	.002	.002	.001				
27	.764	.586	.347	.207	.125	.076	.047	.029	.023	.018	.011	.007	.005	.003	.002	.002	.001	.001				
28	.757	.574	.333	.196	.116	.069	.042	.026	.020	.016	.010	.006	.004	.002	.002	.001	.001	.001				
29	.749	.563	.321	.185	.107	.063	.037	.022	.017	.014	.008	.005	.003	.002	.002	.001	.001	.001				
30	.742	.552	.308	.174	.099	.057	.033	.020	.015	.012	.007	.004	.003	.002	.001	.001						
40	.672	.453	.208	.097	.046	.022	.011	.005	.004	.003	.001	.001										
50	.608	.372	.141	.054	.021	.009	.003	.001	.001	.001												

PRESENT VALUE OF $1 RECEIVED OR PAID ANNUALLY FOR EACH OF THE NEXT N YEARS

Future Years	1%	2%	4%	6%	8%	10%	12%	14%	15%	16%	18%	20%	22%	24%	25%	26%	28%	30%	35%	40%	45%	50%
1	.990	.980	.962	.943	.926	.909	.893	.877	.870	.862	.847	.833	.820	.806	.800	.794	.781	.769	.741	.714	.690	.667
2	1.970	1.942	1.886	1.833	1.783	1.736	1.690	1.647	1.626	1.605	1.566	1.528	1.492	1.457	1.440	1.424	1.392	1.361	1.289	1.224	1.165	1.111
3	2.941	2.884	2.775	2.673	2.577	2.487	2.402	2.322	2.283	2.246	2.174	2.106	2.042	1.981	1.952	1.923	1.868	1.816	1.696	1.589	1.493	1.407
4	3.902	3.808	3.630	3.465	3.312	3.170	3.037	2.914	2.855	2.798	2.690	2.589	2.494	2.404	2.362	2.320	2.241	2.166	1.997	1.849	1.720	1.605
5	4.853	4.713	4.452	4.212	3.993	3.791	3.605	3.433	3.352	3.274	3.127	2.991	2.864	2.745	2.689	2.635	2.532	2.436	2.220	2.035	1.876	1.737
6	5.795	5.601	5.242	4.917	4.623	4.355	4.111	3.889	3.784	3.685	3.498	3.326	3.167	3.020	2.951	2.885	2.759	2.643	2.385	2.168	1.983	1.824
7	6.728	6.472	6.002	5.582	5.206	4.868	4.564	4.288	4.160	4.039	3.812	3.605	3.416	3.242	3.161	3.083	2.937	2.802	2.508	2.263	2.057	1.883
8	7.652	7.325	6.733	6.210	5.747	5.335	4.968	4.639	4.487	4.344	4.078	3.837	3.619	3.421	3.329	3.241	3.076	2.925	2.598	2.331	2.108	1.922
9	8.566	8.163	7.435	6.802	6.247	5.759	5.328	4.946	4.772	4.607	4.303	4.031	3.786	3.566	3.463	3.366	3.184	3.019	2.665	2.379	2.144	1.948
10	9.471	8.983	8.111	7.360	6.710	6.145	5.650	5.216	5.019	4.833	4.494	4.192	3.923	3.682	3.571	3.465	3.269	3.092	2.715	2.414	2.168	1.965
11	10.368	9.787	8.760	7.887	7.139	6.495	5.988	5.453	5.234	5.029	4.656	4.327	4.035	3.776	3.656	3.544	3.335	3.147	2.752	2.438	2.185	1.977
12	11.255	10.575	9.385	8.384	7.536	6.814	6.194	5.660	5.421	5.197	4.793	4.439	4.127	3.851	3.725	3.606	3.387	3.190	2.779	2.456	2.196	1.985
13	12.134	11.348	9.986	8.853	7.904	7.103	6.424	5.842	5.583	5.342	4.910	4.533	4.203	3.912	3.780	3.656	3.427	3.223	2.799	2.468	2.204	1.990
14	13.004	12.106	10.563	9.295	8.244	7.367	6.628	6.002	5.724	5.468	5.008	4.611	4.265	3.962	3.824	3.695	3.459	3.249	2.814	2.477	2.210	1.993
15	13.865	12.849	11.118	9.712	8.559	7.606	6.811	6.142	5.847	5.575	5.092	4.675	4.315	4.001	3.859	3.726	3.483	3.268	2.825	2.484	2.214	1.995
16	14.718	13.578	11.652	10.106	8.851	7.824	6.974	6.265	5.954	5.669	5.162	4.730	4.357	4.033	3.887	3.751	3.503	3.283	2.834	2.489	2.216	1.997
17	15.562	14.292	12.166	10.477	9.122	8.022	7.120	6.373	6.047	5.749	5.222	4.775	4.391	4.059	3.910	3.771	3.518	3.295	2.840	2.492	2.218	1.998
18	16.398	14.992	12.659	10.828	9.372	8.201	7.250	6.467	6.128	5.818	5.273	4.812	4.419	4.080	3.928	3.786	3.529	3.304	2.844	2.494	2.219	1.999
19	17.226	15.678	13.134	11.158	9.604	8.365	7.366	6.550	6.198	5.877	5.316	4.844	4.442	4.097	3.942	3.799	3.539	3.311	2.848	2.496	2.220	1.999
20	18.046	16.351	13.590	11.470	9.818	8.514	7.469	6.623	6.259	5.929	5.353	4.870	4.460	4.110	3.954	3.808	3.546	3.316	2.850	2.497	2.221	1.999
21	18.857	17.011	14.029	11.764	10.017	8.649	7.562	6.687	6.312	5.973	5.384	4.891	4.476	4.121	3.963	3.816	3.551	3.320	2.852	2.498	2.221	2.000
22	19.660	17.658	14.451	12.042	10.201	8.772	7.645	6.743	6.359	6.011	5.410	4.909	4.488	4.130	3.970	3.822	3.556	3.323	2.853	2.498	2.222	2.000
23	20.456	18.292	14.857	12.303	10.371	8.883	7.718	6.792	6.399	6.044	5.432	4.925	4.499	4.137	3.976	3.827	3.559	3.325	2.854	2.499	2.222	2.000
24	21.243	18.914	15.247	12.550	10.529	8.985	7.784	6.835	6.434	6.073	5.451	4.937	4.507	4.143	3.981	3.831	3.562	3.327	2.855	2.499	2.222	2.000
25	22.023	19.523	15.622	12.783	10.675	9.077	7.843	6.873	6.464	6.097	5.467	4.948	4.514	4.147	3.985	3.834	3.564	3.329	2.856	2.499	2.222	2.000
26	22.795	20.121	15.983	13.003	10.810	9.161	7.896	6.906	6.491	6.118	5.480	4.956	4.520	4.151	3.988	3.837	3.566	3.330	2.856	2.500	2.222	2.000
27	23.560	20.707	16.330	13.211	10.935	9.237	7.943	6.935	6.514	6.136	5.492	4.964	4.524	4.154	3.990	3.839	3.567	3.331	2.856	2.500	2.222	2.000
28	24.316	21.281	16.663	13.406	11.051	9.307	7.984	6.961	6.534	6.152	5.502	4.970	4.528	4.157	3.992	3.840	3.568	3.331	2.857	2.500	2.222	2.000
29	25.066	21.844	16.984	13.591	11.158	9.370	8.022	6.983	6.551	6.166	5.510	4.975	4.531	4.159	3.994	3.841	3.569	3.332	2.857	2.500	2.222	2.000
30	25.808	22.396	17.292	13.765	11.258	9.427	8.055	7.003	6.566	6.177	5.517	4.979	4.534	4.160	3.995	3.842	3.569	3.332	2.857	2.500	2.222	2.000
40	32.835	27.355	19.793	15.046	11.925	9.779	8.244	7.105	6.642	6.234	5.548	4.997	4.544	4.166	3.999	3.846	3.571	3.333	2.857	2.500	2.222	2.000
50	39.196	31.424	21.482	15.762	12.234	9.915	8.304	7.133	6.661	6.246	5.554	4.999	4.545	4.167	4.000	3.846	3.571	3.333	2.857	2.500	2.222	2.000

DISCUSSION QUESTIONS

Q22-1. Why are effective planning and control of capital expenditures important?

Q22-2. Differentiate between the economic and physical life of a project.

Q22-3. Describe the procedure for computing the weighted average cost of capital.
(ICMA adapted)

Q22-4. Explain how each of the following would likely affect a company's weighted average cost of capital:
(a) The issue of a significant amount of bonds payable.
(b) An expansion of the company's operations into activities having a substantially higher degree of risk than the usual operations of the company.
CGA-Canada (adapted)
Reprint with permission

Q22-5. Why would a firm use its weighted average cost of capital as the hurdle rate (minimum rate) for a project investment decision, rather than the specific marginal cost of funds?

Q22-6. Discuss the practical difficulties in estimating the firm's weighted average cost of capital.
CGA-Canada (adapted)
Reprint with permission

Q22-7. (a) Is depreciation deducted for tax purposes likely to differ from book (or financial accounting) depreciation? Explain.
(b) Should book depreciation be considered in estimating the future cash flows from a proposed project? Explain.
(c) Should tax depreciation be considered in estimating the future

cash flows from a proposed project? Explain.

Q22-8. Financial accounting data are not entirely suitable for use in evaluating capital expenditures. Explain.
(AICPA adapted)

Q22-9. Define the payback (or payout) period method.

Q22-10. How do the two average annual return on investment methods differ?

Q22-11. What is the present value concept and why is it important in capital budgeting?

Q22-12. What is the basic difference between the payback method and the present value method?   (AICPA adapted)

Q22-13. What is the difference between the net present value and the discounted cash flow rate of return calculations?

Q22-14. Both the present value method and the discounted cash flow method assume that the earnings produced by a project are reinvested in the company. However, each approach assumes a different rate of return at which earnings are reinvested. Describe the rate of return assumed in each of the two approaches and discuss which of the assumed rates is more realistic.
CGA-Canada (adapted)
Reprint with permission

Q22-15. Discuss benefits to be derived from a follow-up of project results.
(ICMA adapted)

EXERCISES

E22-1. Cost of capital. Wiz Company wishes to compute a weighted average cost of capital for use in evaluating capital expenditure proposals. Earnings, capital structure, and current market prices of the company's securities are:

Earnings:		
	Earnings before interest and income tax	$ 210,000
	Interest expense on bonds	30,000
	Pretax earnings	$ 180,000
	Income tax (assume 45% tax rate)	81,000
	Aftertax earnings	$ 99,000
	Preferred stock dividends	24,000
	Earnings available to common stockholders.	$ 75,000
	Common stock dividends.	30,000
	Increase in retained earnings	$ 45,000
Capital structure:		
	Mortgage bonds, 10%, 10 years.	$ 300,000
	Preferred stock, 12%, $100 par value	200,000
	Common stock, no par, 50,000 shares outstanding	350,000
	Retained earnings (equity of common stockholders)	150,000
		$1,000,000
Market prices of the company's stocks:		
	Preferred stock.	$96
	Common stock	10

Required: Assuming that the current cost and mix of sources of funds are expected to continue over the investment horizon, determine the weighted average cost of capital.

E22-2. Cost of capital. Magnum Tool Company, a manufacturer of diamond drilling, cutting, and grinding tools, has $1,000,000 of its 8% bond issue maturing next month. To meet this debt, an additional $1,000,000 must be raised, and one proposal under consideration is the sale and leaseback of the company's general office building.

The building would be sold to FHR Inc. for $1,000,000 and leased back on a 25-year lease, with annual payments of $110,168, permitting the lessor to recover its investment and earn 10% on the investment. Magnum Tool will pay all maintenance costs, property taxes, and insurance and will reacquire the building at the end of the lease period for a nominal payment.

The current capital structure is:

Capital Component	Amount	Pretax Component Cost
Bonds (including amount to be retired next month)	$5,000,000	8.0%
Preferred stock (market value)	1,000,000	9.0
Common stock and retained earnings (market value)	4,000,000	12.5

Magnum Tool's income tax rate is 40%.

Required: Compute the weighted average cost of capital before and after the bond retirement and the sale-leaseback transaction. (ICMA adapted)

E22-3. Payback and average annual return on investment methods. Poly Products Inc. is considering the purchase of a $40,000 machine, which will be depreciated on the straight-line basis over an 8-year period with no salvage value for both book and tax purposes. The machine is expected to generate net cash inflow before income tax of $12,000 a year. Assume that the income tax rate is 40%.

Required:

    (1) Determine the payback period.
    (2) What is the average annual return on original investment?   (AICPA adapted)

 E22-4. Investment analysis; uniform cash flow. Apernex Company is evaluating a capital budgeting proposal, requiring an initial investment of $30,000. The project will have a 6-year life. The aftertax annual cash inflow due to this investment is $10,000. The desired rate of return is 15%.

Required:

    (1) What is the payback period?
    (2) Compute the net present value of the project.
    (3) What amount would Apernex have had to invest five years ago, at 15% compounded annually, to have $30,000 now?   (AICPA adapted)

 E22-5. Equipment investment analysis; net present value and present value index. Progression Corporation is considering purchasing a new press, requiring an immediate $100,000 cash outlay. The new press is expected to increase annual net aftertax cash receipts by $40,000 for the next three years, after which it will be sold for $30,000, after taxes. The company desires a minimum return of 16% on invested capital.

Required:

    (1) Compute the net present value of the project.
    (2) Compute the net present value index.

E22-6. Effect of depreciation methods on cash flow. Kingsgate Corporation is planning to acquire a machine for one of its projects at a cost of $100,000. The machine has an economic life of eight years, but since it is five-year-class property under MACRS, the entire cost will be recovered for tax purposes in six years. The company's cost of capital rate is 14%, and the income tax rate is 40%.

Required: Determine the present value of the income tax benefits which result from the use of the MACRS recovery percentages provided on page 737, as opposed to the straight-line depreciation alternative. For purposes of computing straight-line depreciation, use a 5-year life with one half of a year's depreciation in the first and sixth years.

 E22-7. Effect of inflation on investment decision. McLoud Company is evaluating a capital budgeting proposal which will require an initial cash investment of $60,000. The project will have a 5-year life. The net aftertax cash inflows from the project, before any adjustment for the effects of inflation, are expected to be as follows:

Year	Unadjusted Estimate of Cash Inflows
1	$20,000
2	18,000
3	16,000
4	10,000
5	10,000

    No salvage is expected at the end of the project. Cash inflows are expected to increase at the anticipated inflation rate of 10% each year. The company's cost of capital rate is 15%.

Required:

    (1) Compute the estimated cash inflow for each year, adjusted for the anticipated effects of inflation.
    (2) Determine the net present value of the cash flows before and after the adjustment for the anticipated effects of inflation.

E22-8. Use of net present value to evaluate asset acquisition. Swift Air Transport Company is considering the acquisition of a new airplane at a cost of $1,000,000. The airplane has an estimated useful life of 15 years, but it qualifies as 7-year property for tax purposes under MACRS. The annual pretax cash inflows from the air freight that will be transported by the new airplane, net of annual operating expenses, is expected to be $120,000 in each of the 15 years the airplane will be used. The company is in a 40% income tax bracket, and its weighted average cost of capital is 15%.

Required: Determine the net present value of the investment in the new airplane. Would you advise management to purchase the airplane? Explain.

 E22-9. Equipment replacement analysis. Kipling Company purchased a special machine one year ago at a cost of $10,000. At that time, the machine was estimated to have a useful life of 7 years and a $500 disposal value. A MACRS tax deduction of $2,000 was taken in the year of acquisition. The annual cash operating cost is approximately $20,100.

A new machine that has just come on the market will do the same job but with an annual cash operating cost of only $16,000. This new machine costs $17,000 and has an estimated life of 6 years with no expected salvage value. The old machine could be used as a trade-in at an allowance of $4,500. The tax basis of the old machine is $8,000.

The new machine qualifies as 5-year property under MACRS, and the income tax rate is 40%. The company's cost of capital is 12%.

Required: Make a recommendation to management, based on the DCF rate of return. (Use the MACRS depreciation rates provided on page 737.)

 E22-10. Net present value and DCF rate of return reinvestment assumption. Aftertax cash flows adjusted for effects of inflation for two mutually exclusive projects (with economic lives of 5 years each) are:

Year	Project A	Project B
0	$(15,000)	$(15,000)
1	5,000	0
2	5,000	0
3	5,000	0
4	5,000	0
5	5,000	35,000

The company's cost of capital is 15%.

Required:

(1) Determine the net present value for each project.
(2) Compute the discounted cash flow rate of return for each project.
(3) Which project should be selected?

PROBLEMS

 P22-1. Make or buy decision requiring capital expenditure analysis. Lyonal Company manufactures several lines of machine products. One unique part, a valve stem, requires specialized tools that need to be replaced. Management has decided that the only alternative to replacing these tools is to acquire the valve stem from an outside source. A supplier is willing to provide the valve stem at a unit sales price of $20 if at least 70,000 units are ordered annually.

Lyonal's average usage of valve stems over the past three years has been 80,000 units each year. Expectations are that this volume will remain constant over the next five years. Cost records indicate that unit manufacturing costs for the last several years have been as follows:

Direct materials	$ 3.80
Direct labor.............	3.70
Variable overhead	1.70
Fixed overhead*.........	4.50
Total unit cost	$13.70

*Depreciation accounts for two thirds of the fixed overhead. The balance is for other fixed overhead costs of the factory that require cash expenditures.

If the specialized tools are purchased, they will cost $2,500,000 and will have a disposal value of $100,000 after their expected economic life of five years. Straight-line depreciation is used for financial accounting purposes, but the most accelerated method available under MACRS is used for tax purposes. The specialized tools are considered three-year property for MACRS purposes. The company has a 40% marginal tax rate, and Lyonal's weighted average cost of capital is 12%.

The sales representative for the manufacturer of the new tools states: "The new tools will allow direct labor and variable overhead to be reduced by $.80 each per unit ($1.60 total per unit)." Data from another manufacturer using identical tools and experiencing similar operating conditions, except that annual production generally averages 110,000 units, confirm the direct labor and variable overhead savings. However, the manufacturer indicates that it experienced an increase in raw materials cost due to the higher quality of materials that had to be used with the new tools. The manufacturer indicated that its costs have been as follows:

Direct materials	$ 4.50
Direct labor.............	3.00
Variable overhead	.80
Fixed overhead.........	5.00
Total unit cost	$13.30

Required:

(1) Prepare a present value cash flow analysis covering the economic life of the new specialized tools to determine whether Lyonal Company should replace the old tools or purchase the valve stem from an outside supplier. Use the MACRS depreciation rates provided on page 737.

(2) Identify additional factors that Lyonal Company should consider before a decision is made to replace the tools or purchase the valve stem from an outside supplier.   (ICMA adapted)

DA **P22-2. Comparison of investment alternatives.** Winsburgh Corporation is considering investing in one of two alternative capital projects. Estimated cash flows relating to the two alternative projects follow:

	Project 1	Project 2
Initial cash investment.................	$120,000	$120,000
Estimated economic life of project	5 years	5 years
Annual aftertax cash inflows:		
Year 1............................	$10,000	$50,000
Year 2............................	20,000	45,000
Year 3............................	30,000	35,000
Year 4............................	60,000	25,000
Year 5............................	90,000	20,000

Required:

(1) Compute the net present value for each of the two alternative projects, assuming that the weighted average cost of capital is 12%.
(2) Compute the discounted cash flow rate of return for each of the two alternative projects.
(3) Considering the results of your computations in requirements (1) and (2), what would you recommend? Explain.

DA **P22-3. Use of present value to value asset.** The City of Grant has been contacted by a downtown bank about purchasing land from the city. The land is adjacent to the bank, and the bank intends to use the property for a parking lot and possibly, at a later date, for expansion. The city is especially interested in working with the bank because of the desirability of maintaining its present downtown location, since the result will enhance the overall health of the downtown business district. Failure to obtain the adjacent property could cause the bank to close its downtown facility. Retention and perhaps expansion of the downtown bank is expected to enhance the city's proceeds from property and sales taxes.

The appraised value of the city's property is $200,000 plus the loss of the continuing use of a water well and storage tank located on the property. The replacement cost of the storage tank is estimated to be $250,000. Loss of the water well means that water must be purchased from the neighboring City of Daniel in addition to what is already being purchased from that city.

The present (19A) cost of producing from the existing well is $32,700 for electricity, $2,500 for labor service, and estimated pump repair and maintenance cost of $20,000 per year for the years 19E through 19H. The annual cost of replacing this lost water supply by additional purchases from the City of Daniel is a fixed demand charge of $46,870 plus a charge of $.2585 per 1,000 for the additional 100,000,000 gallons to be supplied. All costs except for pump repair and maintenance are expected to increase at an annual rate of 8%.

The City of Grant's cost of capital is estimated to be 10%, and it is estimated that the well has a remaining life of 8 years.

Required: Compute an estimated land value that includes the present value of the differential cost of water and identify other considerations that might affect the final price quoted to the bank.

DA **P22-4. Capital expenditure analysis.** Lasko Corporation is considering a process computer for improved production control in its Tin Mill Department. This department receives coils of cold rolled steel from another department of the company. It further reduces the gage of this steel in its own five-stand tandem cold strip mill. The coils of steel, now much thinner in gage, pass through a continuous annealing line, where the strip is heated to 1300 degrees Fahrenheit and allowed to cool slowly in an atmosphere of inert gas. The strip is then cleaned in a pickling line before it moves to the electrolytic tinning line. This last process deposits a thin coating of tin on the continuously moving strip. The coiled tin plate is then shipped to customers in the canning industry.

The Tin Mill Department estimates that the proposed process computer will require an investment of $1,500,000. Resulting aftertax cash savings from reduced costs of labor, materials, utilities, and scrap losses over the useful life of the computer are estimated to be:

Year	Amount
1	$ 300,000
2	500,000
3	450,000
4	400,000
5	350,000
6	300,000
7	250,000
8	200,000
9	200,000
10	200,000
	$3,150,000

Required: With respect to the proposed purchase of a process computer for the Tin Mill Department, compute the following:

(1) The payout period.
(2) The average annual return on original investment and the average annual return on average investment.
(3) The net present value at an assumed 12% cost of capital.
(4) The discounted cash flow rate of return.

P22-5. Comparison of alternative projects. Top management of GWX Corporation is in the process of evaluating two capital expenditure proposals. Because of budget constraints, only one of the two projects can be undertaken during the current year. Forecasts related to the two projects follow:

	Project A	Project B
Cash investment required	$1,000,000	$1,200,000
Estimated economic life	10 years	10 years
Estimated salvage value	none	none
Annual aftertax cash inflows:		
Year 1	$ 50,000	$ 400,000
Year 2	100,000	360,000
Year 3	150,000	320,000
Year 4	200,000	280,000
Year 5	250,000	240,000
Year 6	300,000	200,000
Year 7	350,000	160,000
Year 8	400,000	120,000
Year 9	450,000	80,000
Year 10	500,000	40,000
Total aftertax cash inflows over life of project	$2,750,000	$2,200,000

Required: Compute each of the following for each project:

(1) The payback period.
(2) The net present value, using an assumed 14% cost of capital.
(3) The discounted cash flow rate of return.

P22-6. Feasibility study. Salome Inc. is considering a proposed addition to its Hidden Valley, Colorado ski lift facilities, which will require an investment of $1,000,000 and will have a 6-year useful life with no salvage value. The income tax rate is 40%. The company has sufficient income from other sources to absorb any losses that might be generated from the proposed addition to its facilities in the year in which the loss is incurred. The estimated revenue and expenses over the life of the project, adjusted for the effects of inflation, are:

Estimated Revenues and Expenses
(thousands of dollars)

	Year					
	1	2	3	4	5	6
Revenue	$450	$800	$800	$800	$700	$500
Cash expense	300	330	408	435	435	342
Net pretax cash inflow	$150	$470	$392	$365	$265	$158
Tax depreciation	200	320	192	115	115	58
Taxable income (loss)	$ (50)	$150	$200	$250	$150	$100
Income tax rate	40%	40%	40%	40%	40%	40%
Income tax expense	$ (20)	$ 60	$ 80	$100	$ 60	$ 40

Required: With respect to the proposed addition, compute the following:

(1) The payback period.
(2) The average annual return on original investment, rounded to the nearest 1/10 of 1%.   (Continued)

(3) The average annual return on average investment, rounded to the nearest 1/10 of 1%.

(4) The net present value and the net present value index, rounded to three decimal places, at an assumed 12% cost of capital.

(5) The present value payback period.

(6) The discounted cash flow rate of return.

P22-7. Equipment replacement analysis. Kastlan Corporation is considering the purchase of a replacement machine. The new machine is priced at $64,000. However, the vendor has offered Kastlan a $10,000 trade-in allowance for the old machine. The old machine has a net book value of $4,000 and a tax basis of zero. The new machine will perform essentially the same function as the old machine, except that it will be able to operate at an increased capacity. The following cash flows (which have been adjusted for the anticipated effects of inflation) are predicted over the estimated useful life of the new machine:

Year	Cash Savings Related to Maintenance	Cash Flow from Additional Capacity	Total Increase in Cash Inflow
1	$1,500	$ 6,300	$ 7,800
2	1,200	7,280	8,480
3	900	17,188	18,088
4	600	25,260	25,860
5	300	25,560	25,860
6	0	22,912	22,912
7	0	22,500	22,500

For financial accounting purposes, the new machine is to be depreciated on a straight-line basis over a period of 7 years, with an expected salvage value of $6,000. For tax purposes, however, the machine will be depreciated under MACRS as 5-year-class property. The company's weighted average cost of capital is 12%, and the tax rate is 40%.

Required: Using the MACRS rates provided on page 737, compute each of the following:

(1) Payback period in years.

(2) Average annual return on original investment and average annual return on average investment.

(3) Net present value and the net present value index.

(4) Discounted cash flow rate of return.

P22-8. Investment analysis with inflation adjustment. Bixby Company is considering purchasing new machinery at a cost of $750,000 that will enable it to produce a new product. Both the new machinery and the new product have an estimated life of 10 years. Because of the unique character of the machinery, it is not expected to have any salvage value at the end of its economic life. Estimated cash inflows before considering income taxes and the effects of inflation follow:

Year	Unadjusted Cash Inflows
1	$ 100,000
2	150,000
3	150,000
4	150,000
5	150,000
6	140,000
7	130,000
8	120,000
9	110,000
10	100,000
	$1,300,000

For financial accounting purposes, the new machinery will be depreciated by the straight-line method; however, for income tax purposes, it will be depreciated by the most accelerated method available under

MACRS. The machinery qualifies as 7-year property for income tax purposes, and the company's tax rate is 40%. Top management believes that the annual rate of inflation will be approximately 10% during the 10-year period.

Required: Adjust the cash inflows for the expected effects of inflation (round the price-level index to two decimal places) and compute each of the following:

    (1) Payback period in years.
    (2) Average annual return on original investment and average annual return on average investment.
    (3) Net present value, assuming the company's cost of capital is 15%.
    (4) Discounted cash flow rate of return.

[DA] **P22-9. Purchase vs. leasing.** Wheary Enterprises plans to operate a sightseeing boat along the Charles River in Boston. In negotiating the purchase of a new vessel from Yachts Dynamic Inc., Wheary learned that Yachts Dynamic would lease the boat to them as an alternative to selling it outright. Through such an arrangement, Wheary would not pay the $2,000,000 purchase price but would lease for $320,000 annually. Wheary expects the boat to last for 15 years, when its salvage value would be $200,000. For tax purposes, however, the boat would be 7-year property (i.e., the cost of the boat would be recovered over a period of 8 years, using the MACRS rates for 7-year property provided on page 737).

    The annual net cash inflow, excluding any consideration of lease payments and income tax, is expected to be $600,000. The company's income tax rate is 40% and its cost of capital is 14%.

Required: Make a recommendation to purchase or lease the boat, using the present value method to evaluate each alternative.

[DA] **P22-10. Make, buy, or lease.** Egelston Corporation is a manufacturing concern that produces and sells a wide range of products. The company not only mass produces a number of products and equipment components, but is also capable of producing special-purpose manufacturing equipment to customer specifications.

    The firm is considering adding a new product, with an estimated six-year market life, to one of its product lines. More equipment will be required to produce the new product. There are three alternative ways to acquire the needed equipment: (1) purchase general-purpose equipment, (2) lease general-purpose equipment, or (3) build special-purpose equipment. A fourth alternative, purchase of the special-purpose equipment, has been ruled out because it would be prohibitively expensive.

    The general-purpose equipment can be purchased for $125,000. The equipment has an estimated salvage of $15,000 at the end of its useful life of ten years. After six years, the equipment can be used elsewhere in the plant or be sold for $40,000.

    Alternatively, the general-purpose equipment can be acquired by a six-year lease for $40,000 annual rent. The lessor will assume all responsibility for property taxes, insurance, and maintenance.

    Special-purpose equipment can be constructed by the Contract Equipment Department of Egelston Corporation. While the department is operating at a level which is normal for the time of year, it is below full capacity. The department could produce the equipment without interfering with its regular revenue-producing activities.

    The estimated departmental costs for the construction of the special-purpose equipment are:

Materials and parts.	$ 75,000
Direct labor	60,000
Variable factory overhead (50% of DL)	30,000
Fixed factory overhead (25% of DL)	15,000
Total	$180,000

Corporation general and administrative costs average 20% of the labor cost.

    Engineering and management studies provide the following revenue and cost estimates (excluding lease payments and depreciation) for producing the new product, depending upon the equipment used:

	General-Purpose Equipment		Self-Con-structed Equipment
	Leased	Purchased	
Unit selling price....................	$5.00	$5.00	$5.00
Unit production costs:			
Materials	$1.80	$1.80	$1.70
Variable conversion cost.............	1.65	1.65	1.40
Total unit production cost	$3.45	$3.45	$3.10
Unit contribution margin................	$1.55	$1.55	$1.90
Estimated unit volume	× 40,000	× 40,000	× 40,000
Estimated total contribution margin	$62,000	$62,000	$76,000

	General-Purpose Equipment		Self-Con-structed Equipment
	Leased	Purchased	
Other costs:			
Supervision	$16,000	$16,000	$17,000
Property taxes and insurance..........	0	3,000	5,000
Maintenance	0	3,000	2,000
Total	$16,000	$22,000	$24,000

For tax purposes, the company would depreciate both the general-purpose machine and the special-purpose machine over six years, using the MACRS rates for 5-year property provided on page 737. The salvage value of the special-purpose equipment at the end of six years is estimated to be $30,000.

The company uses an aftertax cost of capital of 14%. Its income tax rate is 40%.

Required:

(1) Calculate the net present value for each of the three alternatives that Egelston Corporation has at its disposal.
(2) Explain which, if any, of the three options Egelston Corporation should select.   (ICMA adapted)

CASES

C22-1. Capital expenditure administration and project evaluation. The management of McAngus Inc. has never used formal planning techniques in the operation of its business. The president of McAngus has expressed interest in the recommendation of its accountants that the company investigate various techniques it could use to manage the business more effectively.

McAngus, a medium-size manufacturer, has grown steadily. It recently acquired another company located approximately 1,000 miles away. The new company manufactures a line of products which complements the present product line. Both manufacturing plants have

significant investments in land, buildings, machinery, and equipment. Each plant is to be operated as a separate division headed by a division manager. Each division manager is to have virtually complete authority for the management of her or his division; i.e., each will be responsible primarily for the profit contribution of her or his division. A complete set of financial statements is to be prepared for each division as well as for the company.

The president and the immediate management team intend to concentrate their efforts on coordinating the activities of the two divisions and investigating and evaluating such things as new markets, new product lines, and new business acquisition possibilities. Because of the cash required for the recent acquisition and the cash needs for desired future expansion, the president is particularly concerned about cash flow and the effective management of cash.

Required: Construct an answer to each of the following requirements to consider known facts about McAngus Inc., as presented in the case. Confine the answer to the accounting techniques and processes involved.

(1) Explain the objectives and describe the process which McAngus can use to plan for and evaluate the long-term commitment of its resources, including cash.

(2) Describe techniques that McAngus can use to help evaluate various alternatives in its long-range plan. Explain the advantages and disadvantages of each.

(AICPA adapted)

C22-2. Ethical considerations in capital budgeting. The Fore Corporation is an integrated food processing company that has operations in over two dozen countries. Fore's corporate headquarters is in Chicago, and the company's executives frequently travel to visit Fore's foreign and domestic facilities.

Fore has a fleet of aircraft that consists of two business jets with international range and six smaller turbine aircraft that are used on shorter flights. Company policy is to assign aircraft to trips on the basis of minimizing cost, but the practice is to assign the aircraft based on the organizational rank of the traveler. Fore offers its aircraft for short-term lease or for charter by other organizations whenever Fore itself does not use the aircraft. Fore surveys the market often in order to keep its lease and charter rates competitive.

W. Earle, Fore's vice-president of finance, has claimed that a third business jet can be justified financially. However, some people in the controller's office have surmised that the real reason for a third business jet was to upgrade the aircraft used by Earle. Presently, the people outranking Earle keep the two business jets busy, requiring Earle to fly in smaller turbine aircraft.

The third business jet would cost $11 million. A capital expenditure of this magnitude requires a formal proposal with projected cash flows and net present value computations using Fore's minimum required rate of return. If Fore's president and the finance committee of the board of directors approve the proposal, it will be submitted to the full board of directors. The board has final approval on capital expenditures exceeding $5 million, and has established a firm policy of rejecting any discretionary proposal that has a negative net present value.

Earle asked R. Arnett, assistant corporate controller, to prepare a proposal on a third business jet. Arnett gathered the following data:

(a) Acquisition cost of the aircraft, including instrumentation and interior furnishing.

(b) Operating cost of the aircraft for company use.

(c) Projected avoidable commercial airfare and other avoidable costs from company use of the plane.

(d) Projected value of executive time saved by using the third business jet.

(e) Projected contribution margin from incremental lease and charter activity.

(f) Estimated resale value of the aircraft.

(g) Estimated income tax effects of the proposal.

When Earle reviewed Arnett's completed proposal and saw the large negative net present value figure, he returned the proposal to Arnett. With a glare, Earle commented, "You must have made an error. The proposal should look better than that."

Feeling some pressure, Arnett went back and checked the computations and found no errors. However, Earle's message was clear. Arnett discarded the realistic projections and estimates and replaced them with figures that had only a remote chance of actually occurring, but that were more favorable to the proposal. For example, first class airfares were used to refigure the avoidable commercial airfare costs, even though company policy was to fly coach, and charter and lease time was increased to 100% of the expected time not used by Fore instead of the 50% actual experience rate. Arnett found revising the proposal to be distressing.

The revised proposal still had a negative net present value. Earle's anger was evident, and Arnett was directed to revise the proposal again, and to start with a $100,000 positive net present value and work backwards to compute supporting estimates and projections.

Required:

(1) Explain whether Arnett's revision of the proposal was in violation of the *Standards of Ethical Conduct for Management Accountants*.

(2) Was Earle in violation of the *Standards of Ethical Conduct for Management Accountants* by telling Arnett how to revise the proposal? Explain.

(3) What elements of the projection and estimation process would be compromised in preparing an analysis for which a preconceived result is sought?

(4) Identify specific internal controls that Fore Corporation could implement to prevent unethical behavior on the part of the vice-president of finance.   (ICMA adapted)

C22-3. Evaluating alternative projects. Quible Industries is comprised of four divisions, each operating in a different industry. The divisions are currently preparing their capital expenditure budgets for the coming year. The Caledonia Division, located in the northeastern U.S., manufactures home appliances that it distributes nationally. The manufacturing and marketing departments of Caledonia have proposed six capital expenditure projects for next year. Detailed information about each project is presented beginning in the next column and in the schedule below. The division manager

must now analyze these investment proposals, and select those projects that will be included in the capital budget to be submitted to Quible Industries for approval. Quible Industries has established a hurdle rate of 12% for capital expenditures for all four divisions. Each of the proposed projects is considered to have the same degree of risk.

Project A. Redesign and modification of an existing product that is currently scheduled to be dropped. The enhanced model would be sold for six more years.

Project B. Expansion of a line of cookware that has been produced on an experimental basis for the past year. The expected life of the cookware line is eight years.

Project C. Reorganization of the plant's distribution center, including the installation of computerized equipment for tracking inventory. This project would benefit both administration and marketing.

Project D. Addition of a new product, a combination bread and meat slicer. In addition to new manufacturing equipment, a significant amount of introductory advertising would be required. If this project is implemented, Project A would not be feasible due to limited capacity.

Project E. Automation of the packaging department that would result in cost savings over the next six years.

	Project A	Project B	Project C	Project D	Project E	Project F
Initial investment	$106,000	$200,000	$140,000	$160,000	$144,000	$130,000
Aftertax cash inflows:						
Year 1	$ 50,000	$ 20,000	$ 36,000	$ 20,000	$ 50,000	$ 40,000
Year 2	50,000	40,000	36,000	30,000	50,000	40,000
Year 3	40,000	50,000	36,000	40,000	50,000	40,000
Year 4	40,000	60,000	36,000	50,000	20,000	40,000
Year 5	30,000	60,000	36,000	60,000	20,000	40,000
Year 6	40,000	60,000		70,000	11,600	40,000
Year 7		40,000		80,000		40,000
Year 8		44,000		66,000		42,000
Total inflows	$250,000	$374,000	$180,000	$416,000	$201,600	$322,000
Payback period	2.2 yrs	4.5 yrs	3.9 yrs	4.3 yrs	2.9 yrs	3.3 yrs
Net present value	$ 69,683	$ 23,733	$ (10,228)	$ 74,374	$ 6,027	$ 69,513
Discounted cash flow rate of return	35%	15%	9%	22%	14%	26%

Project F. Construction of a building wing to house offices presently located in an area that could be used for manufacturing. The change would not add capacity for new lines but would alleviate crowded conditions that currently exist, making it possible to improve the productivity of two existing product lines that have been unable to meet market demand.

Required:

(1) For each of the following quantitative techniques, explain how it is used in evaluating capital expenditure proposals and what it is designed to measure.

   (a) Payback method
   (b) Net present value method
   (c) Discounted cash flow rate of return method

(2) If Caledonia Division has no budget restrictions for capital expenditures and has been told to maximize the value of the company, identify the capital investment projects that should be included in the Division's capital budget to be submitted to Quible Industries. Explain why the projects should be included or excluded.

(3) Assume that Quible Industries has specified that Caledonia Division will be restricted to a maximum of $450,000 for capital expenditures, and that Caledonia should select the projects that maximize the value of the company. Further assume that any budget not spent on the identified projects will be invested at the hurdle rate of 12%. Identify the capital investment projects Caledonia should include in its capital expenditures budget to be submitted to Quible Industries in this situation, and explain the basis for their inclusion.

(ICMA adapted)

C22-4. Follow-up of project results. Recap Corporation made a capital investment of $100,000 in new equipment two years ago. The analysis made at that time indicated that the equipment would save $36,400 in operating ex-

penses per year over a five-year period, or a 24% return on capital before taxes per year based on the discounted cash flow (DCF) rate of return analysis.

The department manager believed that the equipment had lived up to expectations. However, the departmental report showing the overall return on investment (ROI) rate for the first year in which this equipment was used did not reflect as much improvement as had been expected. The department manager asked the accounting section to "break out" the figures related to this investment to find out why it did not contribute more to the department's ROI.

The accounting section was able to identify the equipment and its contribution to the department's operations. The report presented to the department manager at the end of the first year was as follows:

Reduced operating expenses due to new equipment	$ 36,400
Less depreciation (20% of cost)	20,000
Contribution before taxes	$ 16,400
Investment at beginning of year	$100,000
Investment at end of year	80,000
Average investment for the year	90,000
Return on investment ($16,400 ÷ $90,000)	18.2%

The department manager was surprised that the ROI was less than the 24% DCF rate of return, since the new equipment performed as expected.

Required:

(1) Discuss the reasons why the 18.2% return on investment for the new equipment as calculated in the department's report by the accounting section differs from the 24% DCF rate of return calculated at the time the machine was approved for purchase.

(2) Explain how Recap Corporation might restructure the data from the DCF rate of return analysis, so that the expected performance of the new equipment is consistent with the operating reports received by the department manager.

(ICMA adapted)

CHAPTER 23

Decision Making Under Uncertainty

In practice most decisions are based on a single best guess about the future value of each decision variable relevant to the decision problem. Although decision makers recognize that the future is uncertain, formal attempts to incorporate uncertainty into the decision are rarely made. Instead, the problem of uncertainty is usually handled by tempering the decision with business judgment and a "feel" for the uncertainty inherent in the relevant data. As a result, many biased and naive decisions are made.

Probability analysis is one approach to incorporating uncertainty specifically into the decision process. Probability analysis is an application of statistical decision theory that, under conditions of uncertainty, leads to more consistent and reliable decisions than single best guesses. Probabilities based on available information are used to reduce the amount of uncertainty present in the decision problem and improve the quality of management decisions.

■ PROBABILITY ANALYSIS

Technically, a probability is a number between 0 and 1 that represents the likelihood of the occurrence of a particular event. A probability may be thought of as the relative frequency of the occurrence of different recurring events. The probability is operational in the sense that historical events exhibit a frequency pattern, or conceptual in the sense that future events are expected to follow some frequency pattern. Alternatively, a probability may be thought of as the degree of belief about the outcome of a nonrecurring future event, such as the probability that the government will deregulate a particular industry before the end of the year. In either case, the probabilities are no more accurate than the data or subjective estimates upon which they are based. Nevertheless, the specific incorporation of probabilities into the decision process provides a systematic way to evaluate the effect of alternative outcomes on complex decision problems.

In some decision settings, a wealth of reasonably reliable historical data permits the assignment of fairly objective probabilities. As long as the underlying process that generates the decision variable is not expected to change in the future, historical data can be used to model the probability distribution. For example, the actual historical demand for a particular product may be a good predictor of the future demand as long as consumer tastes and preferences, the capacity of consumers to purchase the product, and the price and availability of competitive products do not change. If competitors introduce a new and better product, however, future demand for the old product is likely to decline, which in turn would mean that the frequency distribution of historic demand would not be a very reliable model of the probability distribution of future demand.

To illustrate the use of probabilities in decision making under uncertainty, assume that a company's contribution margin is $10 per unit sold. A study of a 40-month period reveals that sales demand is random; i.e., demand is irregular, with no discernible trend or pattern. Assuming that no change is expected in the underlying process that generates demand for the product (i.e., the action of competitors and the capacity and desire of consumers to purchase the product are not expected to change), experience is a reasonable basis for predicting the future. The relative frequency of the occurrence of each level of sales demand during the sample period can be used as a measure of the probability of the occurrence of each level of sales demand in the future (denoted as $P(x_i)$, where x_i is the ith event, which in this case is level of sales demand). The sum of the probabilities of all possible events must equal one, i.e., $\Sigma P(x_i) = 1$. If the sum of the probabilities of the events were less than one, some event other than those included in the distribution could occur.

Once the probability distribution for demand has been determined, the expected contribution margin from sales of the product (E(X), referred to as the *expected value*) is determined by adding the products of the contribution margin for each possible level of sales (x_i, referred to as the *conditional value*) multiplied by the relative probability of its occurrence ($P(x_i)$). That is, $E(X) = \Sigma(x_i\, P(x_i))$. The computation is illustrated as follows:

(1) Units of Sales per Month	(2) Historical Frequency in Months	(3) $P(x_i)$ Probability	(4) Contribution Margin per Unit	(5) x_i Conditional Value (1) × (4)	(6) E(X) Expected Value (3) × (5)
4,000	8	8/40 = .20	$10	$40,000	$ 8,000
5,000	10	10/40 = .25	10	50,000	12,500
6,000	12	12/40 = .30	10	60,000	18,000
7,000	6	6/40 = .15	10	70,000	10,500
8,000	4	4/40 = .10	10	80,000	8,000
	40	40/40 = 1.00			$57,000

The expected value in this illustration may be thought of as the average contribution margin that the company can expect in the future, based on past experience. The expected value is the mean of the probability distribution. If several alternative projects are being evaluated, the alternative with the largest expected value has the largest expected average contribution margin and, consequently, the largest expected total contribution margin in the long run. However, management may be concerned not only about profitability but also about risk.

The *variance* of a probability distribution (denoted σ^2 and defined as $\sigma^2 = \Sigma(P(x_i)(x_i - E(X))^2)$ and the *standard deviation* (which is the square root of the variance and is denoted σ) are measures of dispersion which are commonly used as measures of risk. Each provides a numerical measure of the scatter of the possible conditional values around the expected value. The greater the dispersion, the greater the likelihood, and consequently the greater the risk, that the actual value (contribution margin in the illustration) will differ materially from the expected value. Computation of the standard deviation is illustrated as follows:

(1) x_i	(2) $(x_i-E(X))$ Difference from Expected Value	(3) $(x_i-E(X))^2$	(4) $P(x_i)$	(5) $P(x_i)(x_i-E(X))^2$
Conditional Value	($57,000)	(2) Squared	Probability	(3) × (4)
$40,000	$–17,000	$289,000,000	.20	$ 57,800,000
50,000	–7,000	49,000,000	.25	12,250,000
60,000	3,000	9,000,000	.30	2,700,000
70,000	13,000	169,000,000	.15	25,350,000
80,000	23,000	529,000,000	.10	52,900,000
Variance				$151,000,000

$$\text{Variance } (\sigma^2) = \$151,000,000$$

$$\text{Standard deviation } (\sigma) = \sqrt{\$151,000,000} = \$12,288$$

If alternative expected values are being compared, such as the expected contribution margins for several different products, the relative riskiness of each alternative cannot be determined by simply comparing standard deviations. Because of the difference in the magnitudes of the expected values, an alternative with a large expected value would be expected to have a larger standard deviation than an alternative with a small expected value. The problem of comparing the relative riskiness of alternatives can be resolved by computing and comparing the *coefficient of variation*, a measure which relates the standard deviation of a probability distribution to its expected value, thereby compensating for differences in the relative size of values involved.

For the illustration above, the coefficient of variation is computed as follows:

$$\frac{\text{Coefficient}}{\text{of variation}} = \frac{\text{Standard deviation } (\sigma)}{\text{Expected value (contribution margin) } E(X)} = \frac{\$12,288}{\$57,000} = .22$$

If another product were analyzed and an expected contribution margin of $100,000 and a standard deviation of $18,000 resulted, the relative risk as measured by the coefficient of variation would be less than for the product illustrated above (.18 (i.e., $18,000 ÷ $100,000) as compared to .22) even though the standard deviation is larger ($18,000 as compared to $12,288).

■ USE OF PROBABILITIES IN STRATEGY ANALYSIS

Probabilities are especially useful in determining the best strategy under conditions of uncertainty. Where several courses of action are available, a payoff table can be constructed to aid in evaluating available alternatives.

For illustrative purposes, assume that the manager of a bakery must decide how many loaves of bread to bake each day. The normal sales price is $1 a loaf. However, the price of bread which is not sold on the day of delivery is reduced to $.30 a loaf. The variable cost of producing and distributing a loaf of bread is $.40. An additional cost of $.10 is incurred in distributing and selling each loaf which is sold at the reduced price. The unit contribution margin is computed as follows:

Regular sales price	$1.00		Reduced sales price			$.30
Less variable cost	.40		Less: Variable cost	$.40		
Unit contribution margin at			Additional distribution			
regular sales price	$ .60		cost	.10	.50	
			Unit loss at reduced price			$.20

Over the past 360 days, the company has experienced the following random sales demand (i.e., there are no cycles or trends in sales demand):

Unit Sales per Day	Number of Days	Probability
10,000	72	.20
11,000	108	.30
12,000	144	.40
13,000	36	.10
	360	1.00

Assuming that sales demand in the future is expected to be the same as in the past, a payoff table can be constructed. For each production level strategy, (1) the contribution margin (conditional value) for each unit sales possibility is computed and (2) the expected contribution margin (expected value) is determined, as follows:

Possible Actions (Quantities to be Produced)	Contribution Margin (Conditional Value) for Possible Sales Quantities				Contribution Margin (Expected Value of Each Strategy)
	10,000	11,000	12,000	13,000	
10,000	$6,000*	$6,000	$6,000	$6,000	$6,000
11,000	5,800**	6,600	6,600	6,600	6,440
12,000	5,600	6,400	7,200	7,200	6,640
13,000	5,400	6,200	7,000	7,800	6,520***
Probability	.20	.30	.40	.10	

*10,000 units at the regular sales price × $.60 = $6,000
**(10,000 units at the regular sales price × $.60) – (1,000 units at the reduced price × $.20 negative contribution margin) = $5,800
***(.20 probability × $5,400) + (.30 probability × $6,200) + (.40 probability × $7,000) + (.10 probability × $7,800) = $6,520

In this situation, the best strategy in the long run would be to produce 12,000 loaves of bread each day, because such a strategy would result in the largest average expected profit.

As in the previous illustration, the standard deviation and the coefficient of variation can be computed for each strategy. For example, the computations for the 12,000-loaf daily production level follow:

(1) x_i	(2) $(x_i - E(X))$ Difference from Expected Value	(3) $(x_i - E(X))^2$	(4) $P(x_i)$	(5) $P(x_i)(x_i - E(X))^2$
Conditional Value	($6,640)	(2) Squared	Probability	(3) × (4)
$5,600	$-1,040	$1,081,600	.20	$216,320
6,400	−240	57,600	.30	17,280
7,200	560	313,600	.40	125,440
7,200	560	313,600	.10	31,360
Variance.				$390,400

$$\text{Standard deviation } (\sigma) = \sqrt{\$390,400} = \$625$$

$$\frac{\text{Coefficient}}{\text{of Variation}} = \frac{\text{Standard deviation } (\sigma)}{\text{Expected contribution margin } (E(X))} = \frac{\$625}{\$6,640} = .09$$

Expected Value of Perfect Information

The opportunity may exist to acquire additional information that will be useful in selecting the best alternative. Information, however, like any good or service, is costly. For example, the baker in the illustration above might conduct a market survey which could improve the prediction of consumer demand. However, a market survey would cost money. Before making such a decision, the cost of the additional information should be weighed against the increase in the expected value that can be obtained by using the information. If the increase in the expected value to be derived from the use of the additional information is greater than the cost, the cost should be incurred. Otherwise, it should not.

In actual practice it is difficult to determine the value of information about a future event until the event has occurred. A market survey would probably result in a better estimate of demand but not a perfectly accurate prediction. On the other hand, it is possible to compute the maximum expected value of additional information by computing the expected value under conditions of certainty and comparing it with the expected value of the best strategy under uncertainty. The expected value under conditions of certainty is the expected value assuming that the probability distribution is an accurate representation of the relative frequency of future demand and that the decision maker knows exactly when each possible event will occur. The maximum increase in the expected value that could be obtained from additional information is the expected value of perfect information and, consequently, the maximum amount one would be willing to pay for additional information.

For the bakery illustration, the expected value of perfect information is the difference between (1) the average contribution margin if the manager knew the sales demand for bread each day with certainty (and consequently produced exactly the amount demanded) and (2) the average expected contribution margin using the best strategy under uncertainty. The expected value of perfect information is determined as follows:

(1) Unit Sales per Day	(2) Contribution Margin per Unit	(3) x_i Contribution Margin (Conditional Value)	(4) $P(x_i)$ Probability	(5) E(X) Contribution Margin (Expected Value)
10,000	$.60	$6,000	.20	$1,200
11,000	.60	6,600	.30	1,980
12,000	.60	7,200	.40	2,880
13,000	.60	7,800	.10	780

Expected value (contribution margin) with perfect certainty $6,840

Less the expected value (contribution margin) using the best
strategy under uncertainty (production of 12,000 loaves per day) . . 6,640

Expected value of perfect information (on a per-day basis) . . . . $ 200

Management could afford to pay up to $200 per day for perfect information because with perfect information the contribution margin would be expected to increase an average of $200 a day. While perfect information is generally not available, this analysis determines the upper limit value of additional information.

■ PROBABILITY REVISION

Probabilities should be revised as new information becomes available. One approach to probability revision is an application of Bayes' theorem. However, before presenting Bayes' theorem, the following additional notation is needed:

(1) Let P(A), P(B), and P(C) be the symbols for the probabilities of the occurrence of events A, B, and C, respectively.

(2) Let P(AB) be the symbol for the probability of the occurrence of both event A and event B, and let P(BC) be the symbol for the probability of the occurrence of both event B and event C.

(3) Let P(A|B) be the symbol for the probability of the occurrence of event A given the occurrence of event B, P(B|A) be the symbol for the probability of the occurrence of event B given the occurrence of event A, and P(B|C) be the probability of the occurrence of event B given the occurrence of event C.

P(AB) and P(BC) are referred to as *joint probabilities*. P(A|B), P(B|A), and P(B|C) are referred to as *conditional probabilities*; i.e., the events enclosed in parentheses are not independent, but instead, are related in some way. If P(A|B) < 1.0 and P(B|A) < 1.0, then A may occur without the occurrence of event B, and B may occur without the occurrence of event A; however, assuming that P(A|B) > 0 and P(B|A) > 0, there is some possibility that both events could occur because there is some logical link between the two events. For example, a company may introduce a new product before the end of the year (event A) without hiring any new employees, and the same company may hire new employees (event B) without introducing a new product, but it is also quite possible that the company may hire new employees in order to have sufficient capacity to be able to produce a new product. In this case, since event A and event B are not independent events, P(AB) = P(B|A)P(A) = P(A|B)P(B); or, in words, the joint probability of A and B (i.e., the occurrence of both events) is equal to the conditional probability of the occurrence of B, given the occurrence of A, multiplied by the probability of the occurrence of A, which is also equal to the conditional probability of the occurrence of A, given the occurrence of B, multiplied by the probability of the occurrence of B.

Now assume that event C is the event that will occur if event A does not occur, i.e., event C is that the company in the example above will not introduce a new product before the end of the year. In this case, event C and event A are mutually exclusive; i.e., the company either will or will not introduce a new product before the end of the year. However, both event C and event B may occur; i.e., the company may hire new employees but not introduce a new product. The relationship between these three events is illustrated in the following Venn diagram:

Venn Diagram

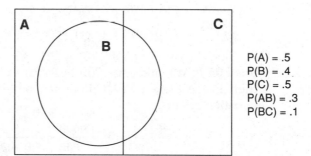

P(A) = .5
P(B) = .4
P(C) = .5
P(AB) = .3
P(BC) = .1

The rectangle labeled A and the rectangle labeled C represent events A and C, respectively, which in this case are of equal size and, therefore, have an equal chance of occurring. Since event A and event C together occupy all of the area in the Venn diagram and do not overlap, one or the other must occur, but not both. Therefore, P(A) + P(C) = .5 + .5 = 1. The circle in the Venn diagram represents P(B), which in this case is .4. The portion of B which overlaps A is the joint probability of the occurrence of both A and B, i.e., P(AB), which is .3. Similarly, the portion of B which overlaps C is the joint probability of the occurrence of B and C, i.e., P(BC), which is .1. Thus, P(B) = P(AB) + P(BC) = .3 + .1 = .4.

Recall from the discussion above that P(AB) = P(A|B)P(B). Since P(AB) and P(B) are both known in this situation, P(A|B), which is the conditional probability of the occurrence of event A given the occurrence of event B, can be determined by dividing both sides of the equation by P(B), which yields:

$$P(A \mid B) = \frac{P(AB)}{P(B)} = \frac{.3}{.4} = .75$$

In terms of the Venn diagram above, this result means that 75 percent of the area occupied by B overlaps the area occupied by A; therefore, if B occurs, there is 75 percent chance that A will also occur. Similarly, since $P(AB) = P(B \mid A)P(A)$, $P(BC) = P(C \mid B)P(B)$, and $P(BC) = P(B \mid C)P(C)$, conditional probabilities $P(B \mid A)$, $P(C \mid B)$, and $P(B \mid C)$ can be determined as follows:

$$P(B \mid A) = \frac{P(AB)}{P(A)} = \frac{.3}{.5} = .6$$

$$P(C \mid B) = \frac{P(BC)}{P(B)} = \frac{.1}{.4} = .25$$

$$P(B \mid C) = \frac{P(BC)}{P(C)} = \frac{.1}{.5} = .2$$

With these values determined, the fact that $P(AB) = P(A \mid B)P(B) = P(B \mid A)P(A)$ and $P(BC) = P(C \mid B)P(B) = P(B \mid C)P(C)$ can be demonstrated as follows:

$P(AB) = .3$	$P(BC) = .1$
$P(A \mid B)P(B) = (.75)(.4) = .3$	$P(C \mid B)P(B) = (.25)(.4) = .1$
$P(B \mid A)P(A) = (.6)(.5) = .3$	$P(B \mid C)P(C) = (.2)(.5) = .1$

Since $P(AB) = P(A \mid B)P(B) = P(B \mid A)P(A)$, then $P(B \mid A)P(A)$ can be substituted for $P(AB)$, and since $P(B) = P(AB) + P(BC) = P(B \mid A)P(A) + P(B \mid C)P(C)$, then $P(B \mid A)P(A) + P(B \mid C)P(C)$ can be substituted for $P(B)$. The following equation results:

$$P(A \mid B) = \frac{P(AB)}{P(B)} = \frac{P(B \mid A)P(A)}{P(B \mid A)P(A) + P(B \mid C)P(C)}$$

Similarly, since $P(B \mid C)P(C) = P(C \mid B)P(B) = P(BC)$, the conditional probability of the occurrence of event C can be derived as follows:

$$P(C \mid B) = \frac{P(BC)}{P(B)} = \frac{P(B \mid C)P(C)}{P(B \mid A)P(A) + P(B \mid C)P(C)}$$

This formulation is Bayes' theorem expressed in its simplest form. Bayes' theorem can be used to revise the original probability estimates for events A and C when new information becomes available (in this case, the occurrence of event B). For this purpose, the term on the left-hand side of the equation (i.e., $P(A \mid B)$ in the first equation or $P(C \mid B)$ in the second equation) is the revised estimate of the probability of the occurrence of the event of concern (i.e., the probability that event A will occur in the first equation or that event C will occur in the second equation now that event B has occurred). This revised probability estimate is referred to as a *posterior probability*. P(A) and

P(C) are the probability estimates of the occurrences of events A and C, respectively, before event B occurred. Since these estimates were made before the new information became available, they are referred to as *prior probabilities*. P(B|A) and P(B|C) are conditional probabilities that express the expected relationship of the new information to events A and C (i.e., the probability that event B would occur and be followed by event A or C). To revise the probabilities of the occurrence of events A and C using Bayes' theorem, each prior probability is multiplied by the conditional probability associated with the related event and, since the sum of the posterior probabilities must equal the sum of the prior probabilities (i.e., P(A) + P(C) = P(A|B) + P(C|B) = 1.0), the product is divided by the sum of the products of all of the prior probabilities multiplied by the conditional probabilities associated with the related event. In the simple two-event world depicted by the equations above, the numerator would be P(B|A)P(A) for the revision of the probability of the occurrence of event A and P(B|C)P(C) for the revision of the probability of the occurrence of event C. Since A and C are the only two events that can occur, the denominator in both cases would be the sum of these two products (i.e., P(B|A)P(A) + P(B|C)P(C)). As a result, the sum of the revised probabilities (i.e., P(A|B) + P(C|B) = 1.0) is equal to the sum of the prior probabilities (i.e., P(A) + P(C) = 1.0).

To illustrate the use of Bayes' theorem in the revision of probabilities, assume that the top management of Kotts Company is planning to introduce a new version of their present product in order to expand its market share. Market surveys indicate that there is a sizeable market for a less expensive version of the product and a smaller, but lucrative, market for a more expensive version. However, rumors are circulating that a competitor will introduce a new version of their product before the end of the year. The introduction of such a product by the competitor would have a material effect on the sales of Kotts Company's products. Based on familiarity with the competitor's previous actions, management assigns the following probabilities to each of the possible events:

	Event	Probability
A	No new product introduced	.5
B	Less expensive product introduced	.2
C	More expensive product introduced	.2
D	Both a less expensive and a more expensive product introduced	.1
		1.0

Given (a) expected market demand for the different products, (b) the expected share of each market given the alternative actions available to Kotts Company and the competitor, and (c) the unit contribution margin of each of Kotts Company's products, a payoff table is constructed on page 778.

Before deciding on a course of action, management finds out that the competitor is hiring engineers (event E). Management believes that there is a .80 probability that the hiring of engineers means that the competitor is planning to manufacture and introduce a more expensive product. This means that there is a .20 probability that the competitor would hire more engineers,

Kotts Company Actions	Events (Actions of Competitor)				
	A No New Product	B Less Expensive Product	C More Expensive Product	D Both Kinds of Products	Expected Value
No new product	$1,000,000	$ 700,000	$ 700,000	$500,000	$ 830,000
Less expensive product	1,300,000	800,000	1,100,000	800,000	1,110,000
More expensive product	1,400,000	1,200,000	800,000	800,000	1,180,000
Both kinds of products	1,500,000	900,000	800,000	700,000	1,160,000
Probability	.50	.20	.20	.10	

even if it had no intention of introducing a new product $(P(E|A) = .20)$, a .20 probability that it would hire more engineers if it were planning to introduce a new less expensive product $(P(E|B) = .20)$, a .80 probability that it would hire more engineers if it were planning to introduce a more expensive product $(P(E|C) = .80)$, and a .80 probability that it would hire more engineers if it were planning to introduce both less and more expensive products $(P(E|D) = .80)$. Based on these newly assessed conditional probabilities, the original probabilities can be revised as follows, using Bayes' theorem:

$$P(A|E) = \frac{P(E|A)P(A)}{P(E|A)P(A) + P(E|B)P(B) + P(E|C)P(C) + P(E|D)P(D)}.$$

$$P(B|E) = \frac{P(E|B)P(B)}{P(E|A)P(A) + P(E|B)P(B) + P(E|C)P(C) + P(E|D)P(D)}.$$

$$P(C|E) = \frac{P(E|C)P(C)}{P(E|A)P(A) + P(E|B)P(B) + P(E|C)P(C) + P(E|D)P(D)}.$$

$$P(D|E) = \frac{P(E|D)P(D)}{P(E|A)P(A) + P(E|B)P(B) + P(E|C)P(C) + P(E|D)P(D)}.$$

	Events (Actions of Competitor)	(1) Prior Probability	(2) Conditional Probability of Hiring Engineers	(3) Prior Probability Times Conditional Probability (1) × (2)	(4) Posterior Probability (3) line item ÷ (3) total
A	No new product	.50	.20	.10	5/19
B	Less expensive product	.20	.20	.04	2/19
C	More expensive product	.20	.80	.16	8/19
D	Both kinds of products	.10	.80	.08	4/19
		1.00		.38	19/19

Notice that the original values in Column (3) correspond to the numerators in the equations that precede the table, and the Column (3) total corresponds to the denominator in each equation. If more information becomes available before the decision is made, the posterior probabilities would become prior probabilities, and the new conditional probabilities (i.e., the probabilities associated with the new information) would be used to compute new posterior probabilities. Also, notice that the conditional probabilities in Column (2) were not totaled. Although each conditional probability must be less than one, the sum of the conditional probabilities need not equal one because they do not represent a collectively exhaustive set of possibilities.

The expected values of the alternative actions being considered by Kotts Company are computed as follows, using the payoff table and the revised probabilities:

Kotts Company Actions	Events (Actions of Competitor)				
	A No New Product	B Less Expensive Product	C More Expensive Product	D Both Kinds of Products	Expected Value
No new product	$1,000,000	$ 700,000	$ 700,000	$500,000	$ 736,842
Less expensive product	1,300,000	800,000	1,100,000	800,000	1,057,895
More expensive product	1,400,000	1,200,000	800,000	800,000	1,000,000
Both kinds of products	1,500,000	900,000	800,000	700,000	973,684
Probability	5/19	2/19	8/19	4/19	

The expected values of the alternatives changed when the probabilities were revised. In this case, the best course of action for Kotts Company also changed from the introduction of a more expensive product to the introduction of a less expensive product.

■ DECISION TREES

Alternatives and their expected results may be portrayed graphically with a decision tree. A decision tree is a graphic representation of the decision points, the alternative actions available to the decision maker, the possible outcomes from each decision alternative along with the related probabilities, and the expected values of each event. A decision tree expedites the evaluation of alternatives by giving the decision maker a visual map of the expected result of each alternative. This kind of analysis is especially useful when sequential decisions are involved.

To illustrate the use of a decision tree in a sequential-decision problem, assume that Wildcat Oil Company is faced with the problem of deciding whether or not to drill a well on a newly acquired lease. Based on statistically available information, the probability of finding oil is .22, and the probability of finding no oil is .78. If oil is found, the company will have a $1,000,000 profit; however, if oil is not found, the company will lose $300,000.

Before deciding whether or not to drill, Wildcat could pay a seismographic service company $50,000 to conduct a seismic test of the proposed site. There is a .2 probability that the seismic test result would be favorable, and a .8 probability that it would not. If the results are favorable, the probability of finding oil would be .7 (with a .3 probability of finding no oil), and if the results are unfavorable, the probability of finding no oil would be .9 (with a .1 probability of finding oil).

In this situation, Wildcat is faced with making two sequential decisions; first, whether or not to purchase a seismic test, and second, whether or not to drill. Based on the data provided, a decision tree can be constructed as shown on page 780.

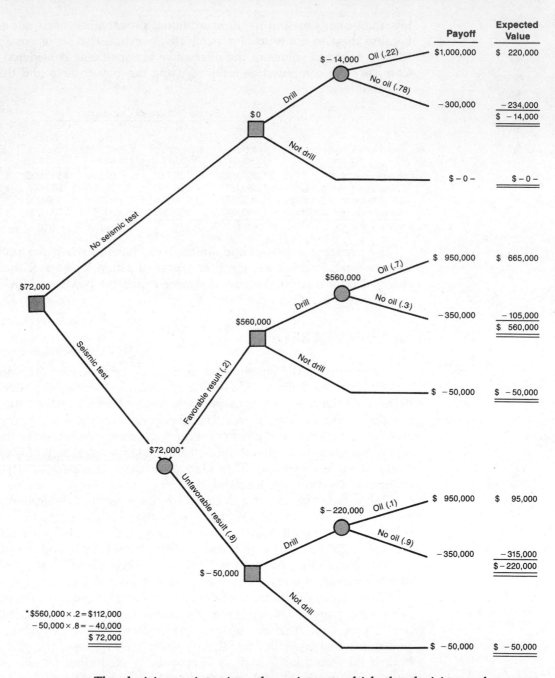

	Payoff	Expected Value

$-14,000 Oil (.22) $1,000,000 $ 220,000

No oil (.78) -300,000 $\underline{-234,000}$ $\underline{\$ -14,000}$

$0 Drill

Not drill $ -0 - $ -0 -

No seismic test

$72,000

Seismic test

$560,000 Oil (.7) $ 950,000 $ 665,000

Drill No oil (.3) -350,000 $\underline{-105,000}$ $\underline{\$ 560,000}$

$560,000

Favorable result (.2)

Not drill $ -50,000 $ -50,000

$72,000*

Unfavorable result (.8)

$-220,000 Oil (.1) $ 950,000 $ 95,000

Drill No oil (.9) -350,000 $\underline{-315,000}$ $\underline{\$ -220,000}$

$ -50,000

Not drill $ -50,000 $ -50,000

*$560,000 × .2 = $112,000
 -50,000 × .8 = $\underline{-40,000}$
              $\underline{\$ 72,000}$

The decision points, i.e., the points at which the decision maker must choose some action, are denoted with squares. The chance points, i.e., the points at which some event related to the previous decision will occur, are denoted with circles. To determine the best choice of action, the expected values for the last alternatives in the sequence are first determined. Then the expected values for the next preceding alternatives are determined, assuming that the best decision alternatives for the subsequent decisions are made. This process is sometimes referred to as "backward induction." The expected value of each action is written above the related chance point, and the expected value of the best choice of action is written above the related decision point.

Notice in Wildcat's decision tree that if a seismic test is not purchased, the expected values of drilling and not drilling are a $14,000 loss and $0 profit or loss, respectively. The best course of action, given that a seismic test is not conducted, is not to drill. On the other hand, if a seismic test is conducted, two possible results may occur. If the test result is favorable, the expected values of drilling and not drilling are a $560,000 profit and a $50,000 loss (the cost of the seismic test), respectively. If the test result is unfavorable, the expected values of drilling and not drilling are a $220,000 loss and a $50,000 loss, respectively. If the test result is favorable, the best course of action is to drill. If the test result is unfavorable, the best course of action is not to drill. If the best courses of action are taken, the expected value of conducting a seismic test is a $72,000 profit. Since the expected value of conducting a seismic test exceeds the expected value of no test, the seismic test should be purchased.

More complex decision trees can be constructed to incorporate additional events and additional sequential decisions. For example, if several different quantities of oil may be found, several different payoffs would be possible. In addition, further testing during the drilling process might decrease the uncertainty about the presence or absence of oil, thereby reducing the potential loss once drilling begins.

■ CONTINUOUS PROBABILITY DISTRIBUTIONS

In the illustrations presented above, the number of possible outcomes was small and the probability distribution was discrete. However, when possible outcomes can take on any value within a defined range, a continuous probability distribution may provide a better description of the nature of the variable and be a better basis for prediction.[1] As a practical matter, continuous probability distributions usually are assumed to have some familiar, well-behaved form such as a beta, gamma, or normal distribution, thereby making it possible to conveniently calculate the distribution parameters of interest, such as the mean or expected value and the standard deviation.

Normal Distribution

The normal distribution is probably the most frequently applied continuous distribution. Although it appears to closely approximate many actual

---

[1]Technically, a variable would be considered continuous if over some interval it could take any one of an infinite number of values. Examples of such variables include time, weight, volume, length, and economic value. Although these items are actually measured in units that are discrete, they are often viewed as continuous because conceptually they can be subdivided into infinitely small units of measure, and practically the number of different discrete values an item may have without such subdivision is large.

business processes, the normal distribution is not appropriate in all cases and should not be used indiscriminately. Its popularity probably stems from the fact that it has certain attractive mathematical properties. First, the normal distribution is symmetric (i.e., the area under the curve to the left of the median, or middle value, is a mirror image of the area to the right of the median), and it has only one mode (i.e., there is only one most frequently occurring event[2]). Since the distribution is symmetric and unimodal, the mode is equal to the median and the mean (or weighted average). As a consequence, the value of the most likely event is the value midway between the two extremes, which is also the mean (and expected value) of the distribution.

Second, although the shape of the distribution may vary depending upon the relative value of the standard deviation, the relationship between the portion of the area under the curve for any given interval from the mean as measured in standard deviations is the same for all normal distributions. In this sense the standard deviation is not only a measure of dispersion of individual observations around the mean, but it is also a measure of distance. Notice in the graphs below that the normal distribution is flatter when the standard deviation is large than when it is small.

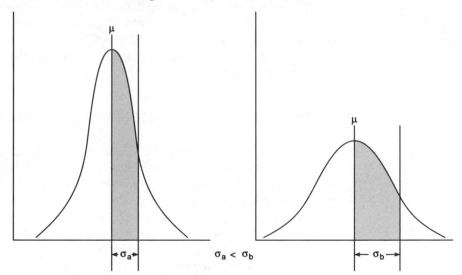

Comparison of Normal Curves with Different Standard Deviations

The total area under each of the two curves above is equal, and the area under each curve between the mean and a distance equal to one standard deviation above the mean is also equal. Since this relationship is the same for

---

[2]Since a continuous variable can take any one of an infinite number of values, the probability of the occurrence of any individual event cannot actually be measured. As a consequence, it is necessary to think of the probability of the occurrence of an event as the probability that an event will have a value that lies within some interval, e.g., the probability that sales will be between $20,000 and $21,000, or if a narrower interval is desired, the probability that sales will be between $20,000 and $20,001. This is the sense in which the "most frequently occurring event" is used here.

all normal curves, the portion of the total area under the curve between the mean of the distribution and any other possible value can be readily determined by dividing the difference between the mean and the value of interest by the standard deviation to obtain a standardized measure (i.e., a measure of the interval between the mean and the value in terms of standard deviations), and then using a table of areas for a standard normal distribution to find the area under the curve for the standardized measure obtained. A partial table for selected areas under the normal curve follows:

$\dfrac{\mu - X}{\sigma}$	Area Under Normal Curve Between μ and X	$\dfrac{\mu - X}{\sigma}$	Area Under Normal Curve Between μ and X	$\dfrac{\mu - X}{\sigma}$	Area Under Normal Curve Between μ and X
.05	.01994	1.05	.35314	2.05	.47982
.10	.03983	1.10	.36433	2.10	.48214
.15	.05962	1.15	.37493	2.15	.48422
.20	.07926	1.20	.38493	2.20	.48610
.25	.09871	1.25	.39435	2.25	.48778
.30	.11791	1.30	.40320	2.30	.48928
.35	.13683	1.35	.41149	2.35	.49064
.40	.15542	1.40	.41924	2.40	.49180
.45	.17364	1.45	.42647	2.45	.49286
.50	.19146	1.50	.43319	2.50	.49379
.55	.20884	1.55	.43943	2.55	.49461
.60	.22575	1.60	.44520	2.60	.49534
.65	.24215	1.65	.45053	2.65	.49598
.70	.25804	1.70	.45543	2.70	.49653
.75	.27337	1.75	.45994	2.75	.49702
.80	.28814	1.80	.46407	2.80	.49744
.85	.30234	1.85	.46784	2.85	.49781
.90	.31594	1.90	.47128	2.90	.49813
.95	.32894	1.95	.47441	2.95	.49841
1.00	.34134	2.00	.47725	3.00	.49865

Definitions of symbols:
μ = mean of the distribution (which is also the expected value of a probability distribution)
X = a value drawn from the distribution
σ = standard deviation of the distribution

To illustrate the use of the table of areas of the normal distribution, assume that Cliff Company is considering introducing a new product. Since the product is new, the mean and standard deviation cannot be computed on the basis of historical data. Nevertheless, assume that based on experience, management believes that the distribution of sales is normal, and its best guess is that 20,000 units will be sold. Since sales are believed to be normally distributed, the most likely single event is the mean (and therefore the expected value) of the distribution, which in this case is 20,000 units. If the standard deviation cannot be estimated directly, an alternative approach would be to have marketing personnel estimate a range of sales in which they have some quantifiable degree of confidence (e.g., 50 percent or 90 percent), and then determine from the table the number of standard deviations required to include an area under the normal curve equal to that degree of confidence. In this case, assume that marketing is 90 percent confident that sales will be between 12,000 and 28,000 units, which means that the 90 percent interval is 16,000 units (28,000 – 12,000 units). Next divide the confidence level by 2, and then from the table above find the number of standard deviations that must be added to or subtracted from the mean to include 45 percent of the area under the curve (.90 ÷ 2 = .45), which in this case is 1.65 standard deviations. Since 1.65 standard deviations must be added to or subtracted from the mean to include 45 percent of the area under the curve, the distance from one side of the 90 percent interval to the other would be 3.3 standard deviations (1.65 × 2). Therefore, the standard deviation would be determined by dividing the number of units in the 90 percent interval by the number of standard deviations required to include 90 percent of the area under the normal curve. The standard deviation in this case is approximately 4,848 units (16,000 units ÷ 3.3 standard deviations).

Further assume that the contribution margin from the sale of one unit of the new product is $2 and that specialized machinery must be rented at a cost of $30,000 in order to manufacture the product. Management would like to know the probability that it will make a profit from selling the new product. In this case, the company would break even if it sells 15,000 units ($30,000 fixed cost ÷ $2 contribution margin per unit) and incur a loss if it sells less than 15,000 units. Therefore, the probability of making a profit will be the area under the normal curve for sales greater than 15,000 units. The distance between the mean of 20,000 units and breakeven sales of 15,000 units is 1.03 standard deviations ((20,000 − 15,000) ÷ 4,848), which means that the area under the curve between breakeven sales and the mean is approximately .35. Since one half of the total area under the normal curve is above the mean, the probability that Cliff Company will make a profit from the new product is .85 (an area of .35 below the mean plus an area of .50 above the mean).

The reliability of the estimated probability of making a profit is highly dependent upon the accuracy of the estimated mean and standard deviation and whether or not the normal curve reasonably approximates the actual distribution of the events of interest. If these estimates are based on historical data rather than subjective estimates, greater reliance can be placed on the results. If historical data are available, the estimated mean and standard deviation are computed from the sample data in the same manner as demonstrated in Chapter 12.

■ MONTE CARLO SIMULATIONS

Many business problems contain variables over which decision makers have little or no control. Such variables may be treated as if they were generated by a stochastic process, i.e., a process that generates events that appear to the decision maker to occur at random. If the decision problem contains many stochastic variables, it becomes complex and difficult (and perhaps in some cases impossible) to evaluate with analytical techniques. In such cases, computer simulation may be a viable alternative. The primary requirement is that the decision problem be one that can be adequately modeled with one or more mathematical equations. Computer simulations that contain stochastic variables are often referred to as *Monte Carlo simulations*.

Monte Carlo simulation utilizes statistical sampling techniques in order to obtain a probabilistic approximation of the outcome of the business system being modeled. The probability distributions of the stochastic variables in the decision problem are simulated in the computer model, using a random number generator. The form of the stochastic processes simulated can be based on historical data or on estimates. The simulation is run numerous times in order to model the output of the business system. Based on the frequency distribution of the simulation results, the decision maker can determine the expected value (i.e., the mean of the simulated probability distribution) and a measure of risk (i.e., the variance and standard deviation) for the decision problem. Monte Carlo simulations are especially useful in planning and evaluating complex new business systems.

■ CONSIDERING UNCERTAINTY IN CAPITAL EXPENDITURE EVALUATION

One way to systematically evaluate the potential effects of uncertainty on proposed capital expenditures is to incorporate probabilistic estimates in the evaluation. Probabilistic estimates are most frequently used with the present value method of capital expenditure evaluation. The net present value is computed in the same way as illustrated in Chapter 22, except that the expected value of the net cash flow in each period, rather than the single most likely net cash flow in each period, is discounted to present value.

As was the case for the short-term decisions discussed above, the variance and the standard deviation are the commonly used measures of risk. For a capital expenditure proposal, the variance and the standard deviation is computed for the net present value of the investment. The relative riskiness of alternative proposals can be evaluated by computing and comparing each alternative's coefficient of variation, which for a capital expenditure proposal is determined by dividing the standard deviation of the net present value by the expected net present value. However, since capital expenditure problems are multiperiod, the variance and the standard deviation of the expected net present value must be computed differently than for single period problems. In a multiperiod problem, the cash flows from different periods must be treated as different random events; i.e., the cash flow possibilities for each period form a separate distribution. As a consequence, the expected net present value for a capital expenditure proposal can be viewed as a random variable drawn from a multivariate distribution. The procedure for computing the variance and the standard deviation for the expected net present value varies, depending upon whether the cash flows in each of the periods are assumed to be independent, perfectly correlated, or partially independent and partially correlated.

If the cash flows in each period are independent (i.e., the magnitudes of the cash flows in subsequent periods are not affected in any way by the magnitudes of cash flows that occur in earlier periods), the variance of the expected net present value is computed by adding the discounted variances of the cash flows in each period.[3] For a two-period project, the variance of the net present value under the assumption that periodic cash flows are independent would be:

$$\text{Variance of NPV} = \sigma_0^2 + \frac{\sigma_1^2}{(1+i)^2} + \frac{\sigma_2^2}{(1+i)^4}$$

where i is the discount rate (the weighted average cost of capital in this case). The standard deviation would be:

$$\text{Standard deviation of NPV} = \sqrt{\sigma_0^2 + \frac{\sigma_1^2}{(1+i)^2} + \frac{\sigma_2^2}{(1+i)^4}}$$

SERVICE ENTITIES   Independent cash flows could occur in practice. For example, independent cash flows could occur when the capital expenditure relates to the production of an established product or service, and the demand for that product is expected to vary in response to temporary changes in consumer tastes and preferences or the capacity to purchase, which are uncorrelated between periods.

If the cash flows are perfectly correlated (i.e., the magnitudes of cash flows in later periods are dependent upon the magnitudes of cash flows in early periods), the variance of the expected net present value is the square of the sum of the discounted periodic standard deviations.[4] For a two-period project, the variance of the expected net present value would be:

$$\text{Variance of NPV} = \left(\sigma_0 + \frac{\sigma_1}{(1+i)} + \frac{\sigma_2}{(1+i)^2}\right)^2$$

$$= \sigma_0^2 + \frac{\sigma_1^2}{(1+i)^2} + \frac{\sigma_2^2}{(1+i)^4} + \frac{2\sigma_0\sigma_1}{(1+i)} + \frac{2\sigma_0\sigma_2}{(1+i)^2} + \frac{2\sigma_1\sigma_2}{(1+i)^3}$$

The standard deviation would be:

$$\text{Standard deviation of NPV} = \sigma_0 + \frac{\sigma_1}{(1+i)} + \frac{\sigma_2}{(1+i)^2}$$

Notice that the variance of the expected net present value under the assumption that the cash flows are perfectly correlated contains interaction terms. As a result, the variance is larger when the cash flows are dependent than when they are independent.

Perfectly correlated cash flows might occur if the capital expenditure relates to the production of a new product or the entrance into a new market. In such a case, consumer acceptance of the product in one period might be expected to have a direct bearing on the level of sales in the following period.

---

[3]See Frederick S. Hillier, "The Derivation of Probabilistic Information for the Evaluation of Risky Investments," *Management Science*, Vol. 9, No. 3, pp. 443-457.

[4]Ibid.

If the cash flows are neither independent nor perfectly correlated, the cash flows may be treated as though they contain a mixture of independent and dependent periodic cash flows.[5] Mathematically, this procedure is fairly simple. In such a case, the expected periodic cash flows could be divided into two components, the independent cash flows and the perfectly correlated cash flows. Separate periodic variances would then be determined for the independent and the dependent cash flows. Once the periodic variances have been determined, a separate overall variance would be computed for the independent and the dependent cash flows in the manner indicated above. The standard deviation of the expected net present value would then be determined by taking the square root of the sum of the overall variance of the independent cash flows and the overall variance of the dependent cash flows.[6]

The difficult problem in practice is to determine how much of each periodic cash flow is independent and how much is dependent. If the distribution of projected cash flows is based on a historical data set, it may be possible to determine statistically the degree of correlation in the cash flows over time. On the other hand, if the expected distribution is not based on a historical data set, the degree of correlation would have to be determined subjectively.

For illustrative purposes, assume that Tipton Company is considering the introduction of a new product called QM-30 which will require the acquisition of specialized equipment at a cost of $120,000. The new equipment will have an estimated useful life of eight years with no expected salvage value. The machine qualifies as 7-year property which means that the following tax depreciation will be available:

Year	Cost	Depreciation Rates	Annual Tax Depreciation
1	$120,000	0.143	$ 17,160
2	120,000	0.245	29,400
3	120,000	0.175	21,000
4	120,000	0.125	15,000
5	120,000	0.089	10,680
6	120,000	0.089	10,680
7	120,000	0.089	10,680
8	120,000	0.045	5,400
		1.000	$120,000

Management's best guess is that it will be able to produce and sell 2,400 units of QM-30 each year. The contribution margin from the sale of QM-30 will be $24 per unit. In order to produce and distribute the new product, the company must incur $15,000 in additional fixed production and marketing costs each year. Although management has no historical data upon which to base its estimate, the aftertax net cash inflows for each year are expected to be normally distributed, which means that management's best guess estimate of

[5]Ibid.
[6]This computation is illustrated in the following section.

the annual cash inflows are also the expected values of the annual cash inflows. The expected value of annual pretax cash inflows net of cash outflows is $42,600 ((2,400 units × $24 contribution margin) − $15,000 annual fixed cost). Assuming the company's effective tax rate is 40 percent, the expected value of annual aftertax cash flows follows:

| (1) | (2) | (3) | (4) | (5) | (6) |
| | Expected Value of Pretax Net | | Expected Value of Taxable | Expected Value of Tax | Expected Value of Aftertax Net |
Year	Cash Flow	Tax Depreciation	Income (2) − (3)	Liability (4) × 40%	Cash Flow (2) − (5)
0	$(120,000)	–	–	–	$(120,000)
1	42,600	$17,160	$25,440	$10,176	32,424
2	42,600	29,400	13,200	5,280	37,320
3	42,600	21,000	21,600	8,640	33,960
4	42,600	15,000	27,600	11,040	31,560
5	42,600	10,680	31,920	12,768	29,832
6	42,600	10,680	31,920	12,768	29,832
7	42,600	10,680	31,920	12,768	29,832
8	42,600	5,400	37,200	14,880	27,720
					$ 132,480

In addition, management believes that the periodic standard deviation of sales will be about 800 units. As a consequence, the aftertax cash flow value of the periodic standard deviation is $11,520 (800 units × $24 contribution margin × (1 − .4 tax rate)).

Assuming that Tipton's weighted average cost of capital is 12 percent, the expected net present value would be determined as follows:

| (1) | (2) | (3) | (4) |
| | Expected Value of Aftertax Net Cash | Present Value | Present Value of Expected Aftertax Net Cash Flow |
Year	(Outflow) Inflow	of $1 at 12%	(2) × (3)
0	$(120,000)	1.000	$(120,000)
1	32,424	.893	28,955
2	37,320	.797	29,744
3	33,960	.712	24,180
4	31,560	.636	20,072
5	29,832	.567	16,915
6	29,832	.507	15,125
7	29,832	.452	13,484
8	27,720	.404	11,199
Expected net present value.			$ 39,674

Independent Cash Flows

If the cash flows in each period are independent, the standard deviation of the expected net present value of $39,674 is computed by taking the square root of the sum of the discounted periodic variances. For the proposed Tipton Company capital investment, the standard deviation under the independent cash flow assumption would be determined as follows:

(1)	(2)	(3)	(4)	(5) Present Value of $1 at 12% Squared	(6) Present Value of Variance
Year	Periodic Standard Deviation	Periodic Variance Col. (2)²	Present Value of $1 at 12%	Col. (4)²	(3) × (5)
0	0	0	1.000	1.000000	0
1	$11,520	$132,710,400	.893	.797449	$105,829,776
2	11,520	132,710,400	.797	.635209	84,298,840
3	11,520	132,710,400	.712	.506944	67,276,741
4	11,520	132,710,400	.636	.404496	53,680,826
5	11,520	132,710,400	.567	.321489	42,664,934
6	11,520	132,710,400	.507	.257049	34,113,076
7	11,520	132,710,400	.452	.204304	27,113,266
8	11,520	132,710,400	.404	.163216	21,660,461
Variance of net present value					$436,637,920

$$\text{Standard deviation of net present value} = \sqrt{\text{Variance of net present value}} = \sqrt{\$436,637,920} = \$20,896$$

Perfectly Correlated Cash Flows

If the cash flows in each of the periods are perfectly correlated with one another, the standard deviation of the expected net present value is determined by summing the discounted standard deviations for each period over the life of the project. For the proposed Tipton Company capital investment, the standard deviation of the expected net present value under the perfectly correlated cash flow assumption would be determined as follows:

(1)	(2)	(3)	(4) Present Value of Standard Deviation
Year	Periodic Standard Deviation	Present Value of $1 at 12%	(2) × (3)
0	0	1.000	0
1	$11,520	.893	$10,287
2	11,520	.797	9,181
3	11,520	.712	8,202
4	11,520	.636	7,327
5	11,520	.567	6,532
6	11,520	.507	5,841
7	11,520	.452	5,207
8	11,520	.404	4,654
Standard deviation of net present value			$57,231

Notice that the standard deviation of the expected net present value when the cash flows are perfectly correlated ($57,231) is substantially larger than when the cash flows are independent ($20,896). This result is consistent with the intuitive notion that the introduction of established products is less risky than the introduction of new products.

Mixed Cash Flows

If the periodic cash flows are neither independent nor perfectly correlated, the cash flows may be treated as though they contain a mixture of independent and dependent periodic cash flows. The expected periodic cash flows are simply divided into two components, the independent cash flows and the perfectly correlated cash flows. A separate expected value and variance is then computed for the independent and the dependent cash flows in the usual way. The standard deviation of the expected net present value is then determined by taking the square root of the sum of the variance of the independent cash flows and the variance of the dependent cash flows. Assume that of the expected annual aftertax net cash inflow for the proposed Tipton Company capital investment, 60 percent is determined to be independent and 40 percent is determined to be perfectly correlated. For simplicity, also assume that 60 percent of the periodic standard deviation of 800 units is determined to be independent and 40 percent perfectly correlated. In this situation, the standard deviation of the expected net present value would be determined as follows:

(1) Year	(2) Expected Independent Aftertax Net Cash Inflow	(3) Expected Dependent Aftertax Net Cash Inflow	(4) Total Expected Aftertax Net Cash Inflow (Outflow) (2) + (3)	(5) Present Value of $1 at 12%	(6) Present Value of Expected Aftertax Net Cash Flow (4) × (5)
0			$(120,000)	1.000	$(120,000)
1	$19,454	$12,970	32,424	.893	28,955
2	22,392	14,928	37,320	.797	29,744
3	20,376	13,584	33,960	.712	24,180
4	18,936	12,624	31,560	.636	20,072
5	17,899	11,933	29,832	.567	16,915
6	17,899	11,933	29,832	.507	15,125
7	17,899	11,933	29,832	.452	13,484
8	16,632	11,088	27,720	.404	11,199

Net present value . . . . $ 39,674

(1) Year	(2) Independent Cash Flow Periodic Standard Deviation	(3) Independent Cash Flow Periodic Variance Col. (2)²	(4) Present Value of $1 at 12%	(5) Present Value of $1 at 12% Squared Col. (4)²	(6) Present Value of Variance (3) × (5)
0	0	0	1.000	1.000000	0
1	$6,912	$47,775,744	.893	.797449	$ 38,098,719
2	6,912	47,775,744	.797	.635209	30,347,583
3	6,912	47,775,744	.712	.506944	24,219,627
4	6,912	47,775,744	.636	.404496	19,325,097
5	6,912	47,775,744	.567	.321489	15,359,376
6	6,912	47,775,744	.507	.257049	12,280,707
7	6,912	47,775,744	.452	.204304	9,760,776
8	6,912	47,775,744	.404	.163216	7,797,766

Variance of net present value for independent cash flows $157,189,651

Year	(1)	(2) Dependent Cash Flow Periodic Standard Deviation	(3) Present Value of $1 at 12%	(4) Present Value of Standard Deviation (2) × (3)
0		0	1.000	0
1		$4,608	.893	$ 4,115
2		4,608	.797	3,673
3		4,608	.712	3,281
4		4,608	.636	2,931
5		4,608	.567	2,613
6		4,608	.507	2,336
7		4,608	.452	2,083
8		4,608	.404	1,862

Standard deviation of net present value for dependent cash flows................ $22,894

$$\text{Variance of net present value for dependent cash flows} = \left(\text{Standard deviation of net present value for dependent cash flows}\right)^2 = (\$22,894)^2 = \$524,135,236$$

Variance of net PV for dependent cash flows $524,135,236
Variance of net PV for independent cash flows   157,189,651
Variance of total net PV of investment $681,324,887

$$\text{Standard deviation of total net present value} = \sqrt{\text{Variance of total net present value}} = \sqrt{\$681,324,887} = \$26,102$$

Evaluating Investment Risk

Once the standard deviation of the expected net present value has been determined, it can be used to evaluate the riskiness of the proposed capital investment. The coefficient of variation, computed by dividing the standard deviation by the expected net present value ($20,894 ÷ $39,674 = .527 for the proposed Tipton Company project under the assumption of independent cash flows), can be compared to the coefficient of variation for similar projects. Alternatives with the smallest coefficient of variation would be the least risky.

Management may wish to know the range of the return, measured in terms of net present value, that is likely to occur at some level of probability. One of the properties of the standard normal distribution is that areas of the normal distribution can be related to deviations from the mean expressed in terms of standard deviations. For example, the area under the normal curve from one standard deviation below the mean to one standard deviation above the mean is about 68 percent of the total area under the curve. The area bounded by two standard deviations above and below the mean is about 95 percent, and for three standard deviations, about 99 percent. Since the sum of more than one normally distributed random variable is itself a normally distributed random variable, the net present value of a multiperiod investment for which the cash flows in each period are expected to be normally distributed can be treated as a normally distributed random variable. Thus, for the proposed Tipton Company capital investment under the assumption of independent cash flows, there is about a 68 percent probability that the net present value will be between $18,780 ($39,674 – $20,894) and $60,568 ($39,674 + $20,894), and there is about a 95 percent probability that the net present value will be between – $2,114 ($39,674 – (2 × $20,894)) and $81,462 ($39,674 + (2 × $20,894)).

Management may wish to know the probability of achieving a net present value greater than zero. If the expected net present value is positive, the probability of actually achieving a net present value greater than zero is equal to the sum of (a) the portion of the area under the normal curve that is above the expected net present value (which is always 50 percent because the expected net present value is the mean, and the distribution is symmetrical) and (b) the portion of the area under the curve between the expected net present value and a net present value of zero. The area (b) can be measured in standard deviations (by dividing the expected net present value by the standard deviation) and then converted to the percentage of the area under the curve, using a table of Z values for the normal distribution, such as the one provided on page 783.

For the proposed Tipton Company capital investment under the assumption of independent normally distributed cash flows, the area under the curve between the expected net present value of $39,674 and a net present value of zero would be 1.8988 standard deviations (($39,674 – 0) ÷ $20,894), which, according to the table of Z values above, is about 47 percent of the total area under the curve. Consequently, the probability that the proposed investment will yield a positive net present value is 97 percent, i.e., 47 percent (the area below the mean but above zero) plus 50 percent (the area above the mean). On the other hand, if the cash flows are expected to be perfectly correlated, the probability that the proposed investment will yield a positive net present value declines to about 76 percent, because the standard deviation of the expected net present value increases from $20,894 to $57,231. The area between the expected net present value of $39,674 and a net present value of zero is .6932 standard deviations (($39,674 – 0) ÷ $57,231), which, according to the table of Z values, is about 26 percent of the area below the mean. The 26 percent of the area below the mean plus the 50 percent above the mean is equal to 76 percent.

The reliability of the estimated range for the net present value and the probability of achieving a positive net present value are highly dependent upon the accuracy of the estimates upon which they are based, i.e., the expected values of the annual cash flows and their estimated standard deviations. If these estimates are based on historical data rather than subjective estimates, greater reliance can be placed on the results.

DISCUSSION QUESTIONS

Q23-1. Why should a manager try to assess the probabilities associated with possible outcomes before making a decision under conditions of uncertainty?

Q23-2. Define expected value.

Q23-3. In what way is the standard deviation of the expected value useful?

Q23-4. What is the coefficient of variation, and how is it used in evaluating alternatives?

Q23-5. Contrast joint probability and conditional probability.

Q23-6. Why would management be interested in the revision of probabilities?

Q23-7. What is a decision tree and how is it used?

Q23-8. What is the difference between a discrete distribution and a continuous distribution?

Q23-9. What are the attractive properties of the normal distribution?

Q23-10. What is the purpose of Monte Carlo simulation?

Q23-11. Even if the cash flows are normally distributed, it is desirable to incorporate probability analysis into capital expenditure evaluation. Why?

Q23-12. In what way does the computation of the variance of multiperiod cash flows differ from the variance of a single period cash flow?

Q23-13. In a capital budgeting context, what is meant by independent periodic cash flows and under what conditions might they be expected to occur?

Q23-14. In a capital budgeting context, what is meant by perfectly correlated periodic cash flows and under what conditions might they be expected to occur?

Q23-15. How might the variance of the net present value of a capital expenditure proposal be computed if the periodic cash flows are neither independent nor perfectly correlated?

EXERCISES

E23-1. **Expected value and coefficient of variation.** Duguid Company is considering a proposal to introduce a new product, XPL. An outside marketing consultant prepared the following probability distribution describing the relative likelihood of monthly sales volume levels and related income (loss) for XPL:

Monthly Sales Volume	Probability	Income (Loss)
3,000	.05	$(35,000)
6,000	.15	5,000
9,000	.40	30,000
12,000	.30	50,000
15,000	.10	70,000

Required:

(1) Compute the expected income or loss (expected value).
(2) Compute the standard deviation and the coefficient of variation.   (AICPA adapted)

E23-2. Expected value and coefficient of variation. In planning its budget for the coming year, Princely Company prepared the following payoff probability distribution describing the relative likelihood of monthly sales volume levels and related contribution margins for Product A:

Monthly Sales Volume	Contribution Margin	Probability
4,000	$ 80,000	.20
6,000	120,000	.25
8,000	160,000	.30
10,000	200,000	.15
12,000	240,000	.10

Required:

(1) What is the expected value of the monthly contribution margin for Product A?

(2) Compute the coefficient of variation for Product A.   (AICPA adapted)

E23-3. Make-or-buy decision under uncertainty. Unimat Company manufactures a thermostat designed for effective climatic control of large buildings. The thermostat requires a specialized thermocoupler, purchased from Cosmic Company at $15 each. For the past two years, an average of 10% of the purchased thermocouplers have not met quality requirements; however, the rejection rate is within the range agreed on in the purchase contract.

Unimat has most of the facilities and equipment needed to produce the components. Additional annual fixed cost of only $32,500 would be required. The Engineering Department has designed a manufacturing system that would hold the defective rate to 4 percent. At an annual demand level of 18,000 units, engineering estimates of the probabilities of several variable manufacturing unit costs, including allowance for defective units, are as follows:

Estimated Per Unit Variable Cost	Probability
$10	.1
12	.3
14	.4
16	.2

Required: Prepare a make-or-buy decision analysis using the probability distribution estimates.

(ICMA adapted)

E23-4. Payoff table. Jessica Company buys and resells a perishable product. A large purchase at the beginning of each month provides a lower per unit cost and assures that Jessica can purchase all the items it wishes. However, unsold units at the end of each month are worthless and must be discarded. If an inadequate quantity is purchased, additional units of acceptable quality are not available.

The units, which Jessica sells for $1.25 each, are purchased at a fixed fee of $50,000 per month plus $.50 each, if at least 100,000 units are ordered and if they are ordered at the beginning of the month.

The needs of Jessica's customers limit the possible sales volumes to only four quantities per month—100,000, 120,000, 140,000, or 180,000 units. However, the total quantity needed for a given month cannot be determined prior to the date Jessica must make its purchases. The sales managers are willing to place a probability estimate on each of the four possible sales volumes each month. They noted that the probabilities for the four sales volumes change from month to month because of the seasonal nature of the customers' businesses. Their probability estimates for December, 19A, sales quantities are 10% for 100,000, 30% for 120,000, 40% for 140,000, and 20% for 180,000.

Required: Prepare a payoff table showing the expected value of each of the four possible strategies of ordering units, assuming that only the four quantities specified are ever sold and that the occurrences are random events. Identify the best strategy.

(ICMA adapted)

DA **E23-5 Payoff table and the expected value of perfect information.** Wurst Inc. operates the concession stands at the State College football stadium. State College has had successful football teams for many years and, as a result, the stadium is virtually always filled. From time to time, Wurst has found that its supply of hot dogs is inadequate, while at other times, there has been a surplus. A review of Wurst's sales records for the past ten seasons reveals the following frequency of hot dogs sold:

Hot Dogs Sold	Number of Games
10,000	5
20,000	10
30,000	20
40,000	15
Total	50

Hot dogs that sell for $.50 each cost Wurst $.30 each. Unsold hot dogs are donated to the local orphanage.

Required:

(1) Prepare a payoff table depicting the expected value of each of the four possible strategies of ordering 10,000, 20,000, 30,000, or 40,000 hot dogs, assuming that the four quantities listed were the only quantities ever sold and that the occurrences were random events.

(2) Compute the dollar value of knowing in advance what the sales level would be at each game (i.e., the expected value of perfect information). (ICMA adapted)

E23-6. Revision of probabilities. Victoria Manufacturing Company plans to introduce a new product known as Quintex. Based on experience and contacts with customers, the vice-president of marketing believes that the demand for Quintex will be between 30,000 and 60,000 units. The following probabilities have been assigned to each possible level of demand:

Demand	Probability
30,000	.10
40,000	.10
50,000	.50
60,000	.30

Before beginning production, the president of the company asked the vice-president of marketing to have the market demand analyzed by an expert system computer program available from a local marketing service company. The program is a market demand analysis model built on the basis of decisions made by several successful experts in the field of market demand analysis. Although the model may overlook some factors unique to the market for Quintex, it captures many important variables and has generally been found to be useful in forecasting product demand. The vice-president complied with the president's request, and the results of the expert system analysis follow:

Demand	Probability
30,000	.20
40,000	.50
50,000	.20
60,000	.10

Required: Using Bayes' theorem, compute the posterior probabilities for the various levels of demand for Quintex, assuming that the demand probabilities generated by the expert system provide new information (i.e., assume the expert system probabilities are conditional probabilities).

E23-7 Decision tree. The manager of Stereo-Fun is trying to decide whether to move his store to the new Market Shopping Mall, or to keep it in its present location. Because of changing economic conditions, the market for stereo equipment may decline, remain the same, or increase, during the coming year. The manager estimates the move to Market Shopping Mall will cost $10,000. In addition, he assesses market conditions and his associated net profits for the next year under both alternatives (excluding the cost of the move) to be as follows:

		Net Profits Expected	
State of Market	Probability	Move to Mall	Do not Move
Decline	.2	$-25,000	$-10,000
Remain the same	.5	50,000	40,000
Increase	.3	100,000	80,000

Required: Construct a decision tree for the manager's problem, and calculate the expected value for each alternative. Should the manager move or not?   CGA-Canada (adapted) Reprint with permission

E23-8. Decision tree. A firm producing stereo amplifiers can manufacture a subassembly or purchase it from another company. Anticipated profits for each alternative, make or buy, and for three different levels of demand for the stereo amplifier follow:

		Expected Net Profits	
State of Market	Probability	Make	Buy
High	.4	$ 50,000	$35,000
Medium	.3	30,000	30,000
Low	.3	-10,000	5,000

Required: Construct a decision tree for the make or buy decision, and calculate the expected value for each alternative. Indicate whether the firm should make or buy.   CGA-Canada (adapted) Reprint with permission

E23-9. Decision tree. A land developer needs to decide which of two parcels of land to bid on for development. The developer assesses the chance of success on bids to be 60% for parcel A and 80% for parcel B. Development of either parcel would take two years, after which time parcel A is expected to generate a profit of $200,000, and parcel B is expected to generate a profit of $100,000. However, if the area where parcel B is located can be rezoned, this parcel could generate a $300,000 profit. Costs of $10,000 would be incurred in preparing and presenting the case for rezoning to the review board. The developer assesses the probability of a successful appeal for rezoning at 50%. An appeal for rezoning would not be undertaken unless parcel B were successfully acquired by bid.

Required: Construct the decision tree for the land developer's problem, and calculate the expected profits for each alternative. On which parcel should the developer place a bid? Should the developer apply for rezoning?
CGA-Canada (adapted) Reprint with permission

E23-10. Break-even analysis. Fargo Inc. is considering the introduction of a new product. Based on past experience, management believes that the distribution of sales is normal. Management's best guess is that the company will be able to sell 50,000 units of the new product in the first year, and management is 50% confident that first-year sales will be between 45,000 and 55,000 units. The contribution margin from the sale of each unit is $5. Special machinery must be rented at an annual cost of $193,750 in order to manufacture the new product.

Required:

(1) Determine the expected standard deviation. (The interval between the mean and X which includes 25% of the area under the normal curve is .667 standard deviations.)
(2) What is the probability that Fargo will make a profit on the sale of the new product? Round the answer to the nearest whole percent.

E23-11. Expected net present value of investment with normally distributed cash flows. Allset Enterprises is considering a capital expenditure proposal that will cost $20,000 and yield an expected aftertax cash inflow of $5,000 each year for 6 years. There is no expected salvage value at the end of the life of the project. The aftertax net cash inflows for each year are expected to be normally distributed with a standard deviation of $800. Allset's weighted average cost of capital is 10%.

Required: Compute the expected net present value of the capital expenditure proposal.

E23-12. Standard deviation of expected net present value when periodic cash flows are normally distributed and independent. Purvis Company is considering a capital proposal that has an expected net present value of $3,000. The periodic cash inflows are normally distributed with a standard deviation of $500 each period. The initial cash outflow has a zero standard deviation. The company's weighted average cost of capital is 12%, and the capital project has an expected life of 8 years. The periodic cash inflows are expected to be independent of one another.

Required: Compute the standard deviation of the expected net present value for the Purvis Company investment.

E23-13. Standard deviation of expected net present value when periodic cash flows are normally distributed and dependent. Ramos Company is considering a capital expenditure for which the periodic cash inflows are expected to be normally distributed and perfectly correlated. The expected net present value of the proposed project is $5,000, and the standard deviation of the cash inflows is $1,000 in each period. The initial cash outflow has a zero standard deviation. The company's weighted average cost of capital is 10%, and the capital project is expected to have a life of 5 years.

Required: Compute the standard deviation of the expected net present value for the Ramos Company investment.

E23-14. Standard deviation of expected net present value when periodic cash flows are neither independent nor perfectly correlated. Vincent Corporation is considering an investment in new machinery with a seven-year estimated useful life and an estimated net present value of $12,000. The cash inflows are expected to be normally distributed; however, 60% of each period's cash inflow is expected to be independent, and the remaining 40% is expected to be perfectly correlated. Cash inflows are expected to be $10,000 each period. The periodic independent cash inflows have a standard deviation of $1,000, and the periodic dependent cash inflows have a standard deviation of $1,500. The initial cash outflow has a standard deviation of zero. The corporation's weighted average cost of capital is 12%.

Required: Compute the standard deviation of the expected net present value for Vincent Corporation.

E23-15. Evaluating capital project risk. Oskervale Company is considering investing in a new plant that will produce a product for which there is an established market. Demand for the product has historically followed a random normal distribution and has been independent from one period to the next. Management has determined that the expected net present value of the investment is $30,000, and the standard deviation of the expected net present value is $25,000.

Required:
   (1) Determine the 95% confidence interval for the net present value, i.e., the range within which the net present value of the proposed investment will fall about 95% of the time.
   (2) Using the table of selected areas under the normal curve on page 783, determine the probability that the net present value of the proposed investment will exceed zero.

PROBLEMS

P23-1. Introduction of new product. Sofak Company is a manufacturer of precision sensing equipment. J. Adams, one of Sofak's project engineers, has developed a prototype of an automatic testing kit that could continually evaluate water quality and chemical content in hot tubs. Adams believes that this kit will permit domestic tub owners to control water quality better at substantially reduced costs and with less time invested. The management of Sofak is convinced that the kit will have strong market acceptance. Furthermore, this new equipment uses the same technology that Sofak employs in the manufacture of some of its other equipment. Therefore, Sofak can use existing facilities to produce the product.

Adams, who is ready to proceed with developing cost and profit plans for the testing kit, asked the Marketing Department to develop a suggested selling price and estimate the sales volume. The Marketing Department contracted with Statico, a marketing research company, to develop price and volume estimates.

Based on an analysis of the market, Statico considered unit prices between $80 and $120. Within this price range, it recommended a price of $100 per kit. The frequency distribution of the unit sales volume that Sofak could expect at this selling price follows:

Annual Unit Sales Volume	Probability
50,000	.25
60,000	.45
70,000	.20
80,000	.10
	1.00

Sofak's Profit Planning Department accumulated cost data that Adams had requested. The new product will require direct materials costing $25 per unit and will require two hours of direct labor to manufacture. Sofak is currently in contract negotiations with its union, making projections of labor costs difficult. The current direct labor cost is $8 per hour. Representatives of management who are negotiating with the union have estimated the possible settlements and related probabilities that follow:

Direct Labor Cost per Hour	Probability
$8.50	.30
8.80	.50
9.00	.20
	1.00

Sofak applies factory overhead to its products using a plant-wide rate of $15 per direct labor hour. This rate was based on a planned activity level of 900,000 direct labor hours which represents 75% of practical capacity. The budgeted factory overhead costs for the current year follow:

	Budgeted Cost	Cost per DLH
Variable overhead:		
Supplies	$ 360,000	$ .40
Materials handling	315,000	.35
Heat, light, and power	1,125,000	1.25
Fixed overhead:		
Supervisory salaries.	1,440,000	1.60
Building depreciation	4,410,000	4.90
Machinery depreciation	3,420,000	3.80
Taxes and insurance	2,430,000	2.70
Total budgeted costs	$13,500,000	$15.00

The introduction of the new product will require some changes in the manufacturing plant. While the plant is below capacity and current facilities can be used, a new production line requiring a new supervisor would have to be opened. The annual cost of the supervisor would be $28,000. In addition, one piece of equipment that Sofak does not own would have to be obtained under an operating lease at an annual cost of $150,000.

Sofak has already paid Statico $132,000 for the marketing study that was mentioned previously. Statico has agreed to conduct the promotion and distribution of the new product for a fee of $6 per unit once Sofak introduces it.

Required:

(1) Determine the annual pretax advantage or disadvantage of introducing the new product using a deterministic approach (i.e., use only the single most likely events in your analysis).
(2) Determine the annual pretax advantage or disadvantage of introducing the new product using an expected value approach (i.e., incorporate the probability distributions in your analysis).
(3) Describe how Sofak could use the data presented to develop a simulation model that could be used for decision making.   (ICMA adapted)

P23-2. Sales probability and contribution margin analysis. Aplet Inc. purchased Avcont Company in 19A during Aplet's expansion period. The subsidiary has been quite profitable until recently. Beginning in 19I, the market share dropped, costs increased primarily due to increased prices of inputs, and the profits turned into losses.

Avcont management wants to take action to reverse the unsatisfactory results the company has been experiencing. One proposal under consideration is to increase the price of Avcont's product. Some members of management believe that the market might accept an 8% increase in price at this time without affecting the expected 10% increase in unit sales volume because no price increases have taken place in this market since 19H. Several other companies are also considering price increases for 19L.

Other members of Aplet management question the feasibility of a price increase because Avcont is operating in an industry that is experiencing declining sales. In addition, the Marketing Department believes that a price increase will have an impact on the expected increase in unit sales volume during 19L. Its estimate of the possible outcomes on unit sales and the related probabilities for the 8% price increase are as follows:

Increase (Decrease) in 19L Unit Sales Volume	Probability
10%	.4
5	.3
0	.2
(5)	.1
	1.0

The subsidiary management is optimistic about the volume of sales for 19L. Recent sales promotion efforts seem to be beneficial, and Avcont expects to increase unit sales 10% during 19L, even though industry volume is expected to decline to 1,100,000 units. However, Avcont management also knows that its variable cost rates will increase 10% (as a percentage of sales dollars) in 19L over 19K levels.

The income statements for 19I and 19J, along with an estimate of the 19K income made in October, 19K, are presented on page 800.

Required:

(1) Determine Avcont's profits for 19L if the 8% price increase takes place and unit sales volume increases 10%.
(2) Will the 8% price increase and 10% volume increase reduce Avcont Company's need for funds from the corporate treasury during 19L? Explain.
(3) Compute Avcont's expected profits for 19L if the probabilistic sales data assembled by the Marketing Department are used.   (Continued)

AVCONT COMPANY
Income Statement for Years Ended December 31
(In Thousands)

	19I	19J	19K (Est.)
Industry unit sales	1,300	1,200	1,200
Avcont unit sales	120	110	110
Sales.	$1,200	$1,100	$1,100
Less variable costs:			
Raw materials.	$ 175	$ 170	$ 175
Labor.	210	215	225
Factory overhead	100	99	100
Marketing	125	115	120
Administrative.	50	50	60
	$ 660	$ 649	$ 680
Contribution margin	$ 540	$ 451	$ 420
Less fixed costs:			
Manufacturing*.	$ 200	$ 210	$ 230
Marketing*	125	140	145
Administration*.	135	145	145
	$ 460	$ 495	$ 520
Profit (loss)	$ 80	$ (44)	$ (100)

*Depreciation and amortization included in fixed costs:

Manufacturing	$60	$70	$70
Marketing	5	6	6
Administration	8	8	9
	$73	$84	$85

(4) A member of the analysis team made the following observation to support the recommendation for a price increase: "Inflationary pressures make it reasonable for a company to forecast increased costs, increased product prices, and increased or at least constant volume because consumers can be expected to accept the product price increases." Comment on the validity of this statement for planning purposes.

(ICMA adapted)

P23-3. Differential cost of quality control system under uncertainty. Home-Heaters Inc. manufactures gas-fired heaters together with circulator pumps and motors. The entire unit circulates hot water through baseboards in the house. Home-Heaters recently developed a compact unit, Model 390Z, that replaces the circulator pump and motor. The unit requires little maintenance and is warranted to operate trouble free for three years. Home-Heaters has established a reputation for high quality products, and the company's management forecasts an annual demand of 1,000,000 units of Model 390Z.

The bill of materials for a unit of Model 390Z requires one precision ball bearing. The diameter of the bearing is 2.75 centimeters, and the engineering specifications do not allow tolerances beyond plus or minus 5%. If the actual bearing size is greater than the specification, the bearing will not fit in the casing. If the bearing is smaller than the specification, the unit will not function efficiently. The bearings used in the Model 390Z are not subjected to quality control inspection prior to assembly of the unit; however, the entire unit is performance tested after final assembly. Based on the pilot production runs, the following information has been gathered.

(a) Cost for a unit of Model 390Z:

Material (including the bearing @ $5).	$ 30
Labor (5 hours @ $8 per hour)	40
Variable overhead (150% of labor cost)	60
Total variable cost	$130

(b) The majority of the rejections experienced during the pilot run were related to the ball bearings.

(c) During assembly, bearings that are too big to fit in the casing are rejected, and new bearings are used. This change in bearings requires six minutes of additional direct labor for each affected unit.

(d) Units rejected during performance testing are reassembled with a new bearing. On average, one additional hour of labor is required for reassembly.

(e) The defective bearings are returned to the supplier for credit.

J. McGill, Home-Heaters' production manager, collected additional data on the rejections during the pilot production runs. McGill's estimate of the probability of rejections for a lot of 1,000 bearings follows:

Rejection During Assembly		Rejection During Performance Testing	
Quantity	Probability	Quantity	Probability
100	.50	20	.40
60	.25	15	.30
30	.15	10	.20
5	.10	5	.10

Required: Determine the maximum amount that Home-Heaters would be willing to spend annually to implement quality control inspection of the bearings before assembly begins.   (ICMA adapted)

P23-4. Differential cost under uncertainty. The administrator for a large midwestern city continually seeks ways to reduce costs without cutting services. The administrator has asked all department heads to review their operations to determine if cost-saving procedures can be implemented.

The Department of Streets is responsible for the proper functioning of the city's computerized traffic control system, including the replacement of the 50,000-bulb units in the traffic lights. The department has kept detailed records regarding the failure rate of the bulb units over the past 18 months. The pattern of bulb failures that has been experienced is as follows:

Failure Occurs Within the Following Quarter of Replacement	Probability
First	.10
Second	.30
Third	.60

The Department of Streets has been replacing the bulb units as they have failed. Using this procedure, the estimated cost to replace the bulb units, exclusive of the cost of the bulb unit, is $5.40 per unit.

The manager of the Department of Streets is considering replacing all of the bulb units at once, such as at the beginning of every quarter, plus replacing bulbs as they fail. The manager estimates that the cost to replace all bulb units at once would be $1.40 per unit, exclusive of the cost of the bulb. The cost to replace each unit as it failed would still be $5.40 per unit.

Each bulb costs $1, regardless of the replacement procedure used.

Required:

(1) Calculate the average quarterly bulb and replacement cost to the Department of Streets if the present policy of replacing the bulb units as they fail is continued.

(2) Calculate the estimated average quarterly bulb and replacement cost if all bulb units are replaced on a regular basis at the beginning of:

(a) Every quarter.

(b) Every second quarter.

(c) Every third quarter.

Show your calculations for all three alternatives.

(3) Why would there be such a large difference between the two estimated replacement costs per unit (replace as failure occurs, $5.40; replace all at once, $1.40)? Explain.   (ICMA adapted)

P23-5. Payoff table and coefficient of variation. The owner of Edward's Clothing Store must decide on the number of men's shirts to order for the coming season. One order must be placed for the entire season. The normal sales price is $12 per shirt; however, unsold shirts at season's end must be sold at half price. The following data are available:

Order Quantity	Unit Sales Price	Unit Cost	Unit Contribution Margin at Regular Price	Unit Loss at Half Price
100	$12.00	$10.00	$2.00	$4.00
200	12.00	9.50	2.50	3.50
300	12.00	9.00	3.00	3.00
400	12.00	8.50	3.50	2.50

Over the past 20 seasons, Edward's has experienced the following sales:

Quantity Sold	Frequency
100	4
200	6
300	8
400	2
	20

The historical sales have occurred at random; i.e., they have exhibited no cycles or trends, and the future is expected to be similar to the past.

Required:

(1) Prepare a payoff table representing the expected contribution margin of each of the four possible strategies of ordering 100, 200, 300, or 400 shirts, assuming that only the four quantities listed are ever sold.
(2) Select the best of the four strategies in (1), based on the expected contribution margin.
(3) Compute the expected value of perfect information in this problem.
(4) Compute the coefficient of variation for each alternative strategy.

P23-6. Probability revision and payoff table. L. J. Gant is a builder who has recently acquired a tract of unimproved real estate upon which new houses will be built. Gant feels that the local housing market is strong enough to absorb all of the houses built on the tract by the end of the year, provided that the size of houses built are those that meet the needs and preferences of the largest number of home buyers. Four different sizes of houses are being considered—1,600, 2,000, 2,400, and 2,800 square-foot houses. However, for economic and marketing reasons, only one size of house will be built on the tract. Based on past experience, Gant assigned the following subjective probabilities to the size of houses most in demand in the local market:

House Size	Probability
1,600	.20
2,000	.50
2,400	.20
2,800	.10

Before beginning construction, Gant read in the paper that an electronics firm announced it was considering locating a research laboratory in the community not far from Gant's planned housing site. If the firm locates a research facility in town, it will significantly increase demand for the 2,400 and 2,800 square-foot houses. Gant believes that there is a 75% probability that the electronics firm will locate its research facility in town and a 25% probability that it will not. The expected payoff for each alternative follows:

Actions House Size To Build	Events (House Size Most in Demand)			
	1,600	2,000	2,400	2,800
1,600 sq. ft.	$200,000	$180,000	$160,000	$140,000
2,000 sq. ft.	160,000	400,000	360,000	320,000
2,400 sq. ft.	120,000	320,000	600,000	540,000
2,800 sq. ft.	80,000	240,000	480,000	800,000

Required:

(1) Compute the posterior probabilities for each of the alternatives related to the proposed housing project.
(2) Compute the expected value of each alternative course of action, and make a recommendation to Gant about which course of action to take.

P23-7. Probability revision. Tekno Institute is an accredited college which offers courses almost exclusively on a correspondence basis. Students pay their tuition fees and each receives a set of lesson materials by mail. These course materials are currently prepared and printed in-house by Tekno.

The following information is available from Tekno's financial records for the year just ended, in which Tekno had a total enrollment of 26,000 students:

	Printing Department	Shipping Department
Salaries	$160,000	$55,000
Employee benefits.	18,200	7,700
Telephone and telegraph	4,000	700
Materials, supplies, and postage	165,100	16,000
Occupancy costs.	10,800	3,400
Administration	7,300	700
Depreciation	25,700	2,500
Total	$391,100	$86,000

Recently, an outside printer presented Tekno with an offer to print Tekno's course lesson materials on a contract basis. The offer stipulated a flat fee of $325,000 for 25,000 sets of lesson materials plus a piecework fee of $15 per set for every set over 25,000. If Tekno decides to accept the offer, the following changes in Tekno's Printing Department would be necessary:

(a) All Printing Department employees would be laid off except for one clerk who would work part-time to monitor communications between Tekno and the printer. The clerk currently works 5 days per week at a salary of $16,000 per year and has agreed to a part-time arrangement of 3 days per week at the same average daily salary rate plus benefits. Since the Printing Department would be eliminated, this clerk would become a member of the Shipping Department. All other Printing Department employees would receive an average of one month's salary as severance pay. In addition, all variable employee benefits of the Printing Department would be eliminated except for the relevant portion associated with the clerk. Variable benefits amount to 10% of salaries. Fixed benefit costs would continue to be incurred, but would be reallocated to other departments in the institute on some reasonable basis.
(b) Telephone and telegraph costs formerly charged to the Printing Department would be reduced to $80 per month.
(c) The Printing Department materials, supplies and postage costs, which are fully variable, would be reduced to $1 per set of lesson materials. This amount would cover the cost of postage.
(d) Occupancy and administration costs of the Printing Department would be eliminated.
(e) The Printing Department's equipment and other fixed assets would be leased to a local business for $33,000 per year.
(f) One set of course lesson materials would be required for each student enrollment. The probability distribution for the anticipated number of student enrollments for next year follows (page 804).

Estimated Enrollment	Probability
25,000	.05
26,000	.15
27,000	.40
28,000	.25
29,000	.15

Required:

(1) On the basis of the information provided, determine whether or not Tekno Institute should accept the outside printer's offer (i.e., compare the fees that would be paid to the outside printer for one year with the savings available from closing the Printing Department for one year).

(2) Assume that before the outside printer is notified, the local newspaper publishes a story indicating that a large manufacturing plant located in Tekno's market area may close. Tekno officials believe that the probability that student enrollments will remain at 26,000 or decline to 25,000 will increase if the plant closes, and that the probability that the plant will close is 90% (a 10% probability that it will remain open). Compute the revised probabilities for student enrollments, and determine whether or not Tekno should accept the outside printer's offer in light of the new information.   (SMAC adapted)

P23-8. Decision tree. Global Credit Corporation (GCC) provides retail and banking institutions throughout the United States and Canada with credit histories of individuals who are seeking various types of financing such as home mortgages, car loans, and retail store credit cards. GCC has branch offices in most major cities in order to provide rapid service to its customers. GCC employs a data base system, and the data base is maintained at the home office in Kansas City for security purposes. Each branch office is equipped with computer terminals that provide direct access to the data base for information retrieval. However, all data entry is completed in Kansas City.

GCC employs a staff of approximately 500 data entry clerks at the home office. The company hires inexperienced personnel and provides a training course immediately upon hiring. Hiring inexperienced personnel allows GCC to realize an average savings in annual salary and related employee benefits of $3,000 per employee. G. Webster, director of human resources, has just completed a review of the employment records of the data entry clerks and has discovered that only 50% of the trainees satisfactorily complete the training course and continue their employment with GCC. The remaining 50% are found lacking in aptitude for the job and are dismissed. While Webster is aware that the turnover rate for this type of position is typically high, this particular problem indicates a failure in the selection process.

Because the full training course for each data entry clerk costs GCC $600 and the retention rate is so poor, Webster is considering using a battery of tests to assist in determining which individuals should be hired and trained. The testing program would cost $200 per applicant to administer. Webster estimates that 75% of the applicants would score at or above the minimum cutoff, i.e., achieve an acceptable score. Those applicants who achieve an acceptable score and are hired would be given an abbreviated training course at a cost of $300. Those applicants who would be hired despite scoring below the cutoff point would still be given the full training course so that there would be no saving in training costs.

After the results of the testing program are known, the Human Resource Department would consider other employee attributes before making a decision. As a result of this additional screening, Webster estimates that 90% of the high-scoring applicants would be hired and sent to the abbreviated training course, and 10% of the low-scoring applicants would be hired and sent to the full training course. The remaining applicants would not be hired.

To assist in the decision regarding the testing program, Webster has assigned probabilities to satisfactory and unsatisfactory training course completion under varying conditions. These probabilities follow:

	Training Course Completion	
	Satisfactory	Unsatisfactory
Test administered, result acceptable	.7	.3
Test administered, result unacceptable	.2	.8
Test not administered	.5	.5

Required: Prepare a decision tree representing GCC's decision problem, including all decision alternatives and possible outcomes with related expected values.   (ICMA adapted)

P23-9. Decision tree. Slick Inc. produces a product called Zap. T. Smoothy, marketing director of Slick Inc., is currently attempting to decide on an appropriate sales price for each unit of Zap for the coming year. Smoothy believes that a higher price would reduce demand for Zap, but that actual final demand would depend on whether the state of the economy next year is weak or strong.

Smoothy's situation is further complicated because next year's materials requirement must be purchased in a single lot of either 200,000 or 240,000 units, and the unit cost of the material will depend upon the size of the lot ordered. The sole supplier of the material will accept no additional orders during the year. Therefore, if Slick Inc. does not purchase enough material to meet actual demand, some orders will be left unfilled. Furthermore, if more material is purchased than is required to fill demand, the excess material will become spoiled and unusable at the end of the year. One unit of material is required for each unit of Zap. Material cost data follow:

Lot Size	Unit Cost
200,000 units	$3.00
240,000 units	2.90

Expected demand for Zap given different states of the economy and different sales prices follow:

	State of The Economy	
Unit Sales Price	Weak	Strong
$5.25	180,000	200,000
5.00	200,000	240,000

Smoothy believes that there is a 60% probability that the economy will be weak and 40% that it will be strong.

Required: Prepare a decision tree representing Slick Inc.'s decision problem, including all decision alternatives and possible outcomes with related expected values.   (SMAC adapted)

P23-10. Decision tree. Strotz Brewery produces and sells nationally a popular premium beer and has enjoyed good profits for many years. In recent years, however, its sales volume has not grown with the general market. This lack of growth is due to the increasing popularity of light beer and the fact that Strotz has not entered this market.

Strotz is now developing its own light beer and is considering potential marketing strategies. Introducing the new light beer nationally would require a large commitment of resources for a full nationwide introduction because Strotz is a late entry into the light beer market. Strotz's advertising agency has helped assess the market risk and has convinced the Strotz management that there are only two reasonable alternative strategies to pursue.

Strategy 1. Perform a test advertising and sales campaign in a limited number of states for a six-month period. Strotz would decide whether or not to introduce the light beer nationally and conduct a nationwide promotional campaign on the basis of the results of the test campaign.

Strategy 2. Conduct a nationwide promotion campaign and make the new light beer available in all fifty states immediately, without conducting any test campaign. The nationwide promotion and distribution campaign would be allowed to run for a full two years before a decision would be made to continue the light beer nationally.

Strotz management believes that, if Strategy 2 is selected, there is only a 50% chance of its being successful. The introduction of light beer nationally will be considered a success if $40 million of revenue is generated, while $30 million of variable cost is being incurred during the two-year period in which the nationwide promotion and distribution campaign is in effect. If the two-year nationwide campaign is unsuccessful, revenue is expected to be $16 million and variable cost will be $12 million. Total fixed cost for the two-year period will amount to $6 million, regardless of the result.

The advertising agency consultants believe that if Strategy 1 is selected, there is a 20% chance that the test will indicate that Strotz should conduct a nationwide promotion and distribution campaign when, in fact, a nationwide campaign would be unsuccessful. In addition, the consultants believe that there is a 20% chance that the test results will indicate Strotz should not conduct a nationwide promotion and distribution when, in fact, a nationwide campaign would be successful. The cost of the test campaign is estimated to be $500,000, and the probability of a successful test is 50%.

Required:

    (1) Prepare a decision tree representing Strotz's decision problem, including all decision alternatives and possible outcomes with related expected values.
    (2) Recommend the best strategy to Strotz management, based on the results indicated by the decision tree analysis.
    (3) Criticize the expected value decision criterion.   (ICMA adapted)

P23-11. Capital expenditure proposal with normally distributed, independent periodic cash flows. Ezell Corporation would like to expand the production of one of its product lines in order to enter into a new geographic market. To provide sufficient capacity, it will be necessary to purchase a new machine at a cost of $200,000. The new machine will have an estimated useful life of 10 years, with no expected salvage value; however, for purposes of income tax depreciation, the machine qualifies as 7-year property. The historical demand for the product is normally distributed. Management believes that future demand will also be normally distributed and independent from one period to another. The expected value of the annual demand for the product produced by the new machine is 4,000 units with a standard deviation of 1,750 units. The contribution margin from the sale of the product is $14 per unit; however, in order to expand production, additional fixed expenditures for marketing and production must be incurred in the total amount of $8,100 per year. Ezell's weighted average cost of capital is 12%, and the company is in the 40% income tax bracket.

Required:

    (1) Determine the expected value of the periodic aftertax net cash flows and the aftertax cash flow value of the periodic standard deviation.
    (2) Determine the expected net present value of the machine.
    (3) Determine the variance and the standard deviation of the expected net present value of the machine.
    (4) Compute the coefficient of variation for the capital expenditure proposal.
    (5) Determine the probability that the net present value from this machine will be greater than zero.

P23-12. Capital expenditure proposal with normally distributed, dependent periodic cash flows. Jaffcon Manufacturing Company is considering purchasing a machine that will cost $180,000. The machine is expected to have a useful life of 8 years, with no expected salvage value; however, for purposes of determining income tax depreciation, the machine qualifies as 7-year property. Management's best guess is that it will be able to sell 5,000 units of the new product each year, with a periodic standard deviation of 2,000 units. Annual sales are believed to be normally distributed; however, since the product is new, sales from year to year are expected to be perfectly correlated. The contribution margin from the sale of one unit is $18. In order to manufacture and distribute the product, annual fixed costs of $10,000 must be incurred. Jaffcon's weighted average cost of capital is 12%, and the company is in the 40% income tax bracket.

Required: With respect to the capital expenditure proposal, compute the following:

    (1) The expected value of the periodic aftertax net cash flows and the aftertax cash flow value of the periodic standard deviation in monetary terms.
    (2) The expected net present value of the capital expenditure proposal.
    (3) The standard deviation of the expected net present value.
    (4) The coefficient of variation.
    (5) The probability that the net present value will exceed zero.

P23-13. Capital expenditure proposal with normally distributed cash flows that are neither independent nor perfectly correlated. Winx Company is considering a capital expenditure proposal that will cost $30,000 but is expected to yield the following aftertax net cash inflows over its 5-year life:

Year	Expected Aftertax Cash Inflow
1	$ 8,000
2	11,000
3	10,000
4	9,000
5	7,000

The cash flows are expected to be normally distributed; however, the cash flows from year to year are not likely to be completely independent of one another. Management believes that for all practical purposes 70% of each year's cash inflows should be treated as independent and 30% as perfectly correlated. The best estimate of the periodic standard deviation of the independent portion of the cash inflows is $1,000, and the periodic standard deviation of the dependent portion is believed to be $500. The company's weighted average cost of capital is 10%.

Required:

(1) Compute the expected net present value of the Winx Company proposal.
(2) Compute the variance and the standard deviation of the expected net present value.
(3) Compute the coefficient of variation for the capital expenditure proposal.
(4) Determine the probability that the net present value will exceed zero.

CHAPTER 24

Marketing Expense and
Profitability Analysis

This chapter presents techniques and procedures that are useful in analyzing and controlling marketing expenses and in analyzing market profitability. *Marketing* is the matching of a company's products with markets for the satisfaction of customers at a reasonable profit for the firm. Marketing managers must decide the (1) product selection, design, color, size, and packaging, (2) prices to be charged, (3) advertising and promotion needed, and (4) physical distribution to be followed. These numerous decisions require organization, planning, and control. Marketing is usually organized by product or brand lines or by territories or districts. The planning and control phases should be based on a well-structured marketing expense and profitability analysis system.

The preparation of budgets and the need for budgeting in planning and controlling the marketing effort of a firm are discussed in Chapter 16. At the end of each month, budget reports that indicate the success or failure of the budgets are issued to responsible managers. However, the problems associated with marketing expenses do not end with these budgetary procedures. Expense control at the departmental level is the important feature of any cost improvement program. Yet, in marketing, the emphasis ordinarily rests on selling rather than on expenditures. To limit marketing expenditures unreasonably might lead to a curtailment of sales activities, which in turn could mean the gradual deterioration or elimination of certain types of sales. On the other hand, indiscriminate and wasteful spending adversely affect the company's profits.

■ SCOPE OF MARKETING EXPENSES

Control and analysis of marketing expenditures complement each other and involve the assignment of marketing expenses to various costing groups such as territories, customers, and products. However, assigned expenses must be controlled through analysis within the jurisdictional function as well, in order to hold each marketing activity to the budgeted level.

This phase of cost accounting calls for the determination of marketing expenses for managerial decisions, thereby making it an integral part of business planning and policy formulation. Management requires meaningful marketing expense information in order to determine and analyze the profitability of (1) a territory or territories; (2) certain classes of customers, such as wholesalers, retailers, institutions, and governmental units; (3) products, product lines, or brands; and (4) promotional efforts by salespersons, telephone, mail, newspapers, magazines, television, or radio.

The scope of today's marketing activities includes not only the fulfilling of existing demands, but also the creation and discovery of new demands for a company's products and services. Industry must concentrate on satisfying customers rather than on merely producing products. This outlook requires the best available working tools for management's use. In many organizations, the marketing activity has always received management's attention, and in some cases even more attention than that rendered to other business operations. In today's economy, the strategic importance and magnitude of marketing activity merit still greater attention to marketing expenses.

■ COMPARISON OF MARKETING AND MANUFACTURING EXPENSES

The control and analysis of marketing expenses present certain complexities. First of all, logistic systems are many and varied. Manufacturers of certain products use basically the same materials and machinery. However, these companies may use vastly different channels of distribution, ranging from a simple, direct distribution to a complex marketing system, with promotional efforts directed to narrow or broad customer groups. Therefore, a meaningful comparison of the marketing expenses of one company with another is almost impossible.

Not only do distribution methods vary, but they are also extremely flexible. A company may find that a change in market conditions necessitates a change in its channels of distribution. Distribution standards must be revised with every change in the method of distribution, so tactics may change several times before the best method is found. Such sweeping changes are not as common in production, however. Once a factory is set up, management is not likely to make substantial changes in its manufacturing techniques until machinery is replaced or new products are introduced. Therefore, standards set for a particular machine or production process seldom require significant revision.

The psychological factors present in selling a product are perhaps the main reasons for differences between manufacturing and marketing costing. Management can control the cost of labor, hours of operation, and number of machines operated; but management cannot control what the customer will do. Various salespersons may have different effects on a customer, who may respond differently to varying appeals. Customer resistance is the enigma in marketing expense analysis. The customer, whose wishes and peculiarities govern the method of doing business, is a controlling rather than a controllable factor.

The attitudes of marketing and manufacturing management also differ. Although factory managers are eager to measure their accomplishments in terms of reduced cost per unit, most sales managers consider sales the yardstick for measuring their efficiency, even though increased sales do not necessarily mean greater profits.

Cause and effect, generally obvious in the factory, are not so readily discernible in the marketing processes. For example, many promotional expenditures are incurred for future results, creating a time lag between cause and effect. Conversely, the effects of manufacturing changes usually are quickly observable, and matching between effort and result can usually be achieved. Furthermore, manufacturing results are more readily quantified than are marketing results. For marketing, it is often not easy to identify quantities or units of activity with the expenditure incurred and results achieved.

Generally accepted accounting practice does not charge Cost of Goods Sold and ending inventories with marketing and administrative expenditures. Nonmanufacturing expenditures (other than acquisitions of long-lived assets such as buildings, furniture, vehicles and other depreciable assets) fall into the category of period expenses, which are charged against revenues in the period in which such expenditures are incurred. Although some marketing expenditures (e.g., advertising, market analysis, and product development) may contribute to the company's ability to earn revenue in future periods, the future value of such expenditures is not objectively measurable. As a consequence, such expenditures are charged to expense in the period in which they are incurred. In contrast, manufacturing expenditures are clearly incurred for the purpose of getting products into a condition to sell. Therefore, such costs are allocated to the products produced during the period and charged against revenue only when such products are sold (or written down under the lower of cost or market rules discussed in Chapter 8).

In the field of marketing, marketing expenditures are commonly referred to as marketing costs, even though such expenditures would be defined as expenses by accountants. In addition, it is more common to speak of marketing cost analysis rather than of marketing cost accounting. A tie-in of marketing costing with the general accounts, although desirable, is often not necessary.

■ MARKETING EXPENSE CONTROL

The control and analysis of marketing expenses should follow methods that are similar to those used for manufacturing costs. The first step in the control of marketing expenses is the classification of natural expenses according to functions or activities. It is essential that each function and its associated expenses be made the responsibility of an individual department head.

Marketing functions are of many types, depending on the nature of the business and its organization, size, and method of operation. Each function should be a homogeneous unit, whose activity can be related to specific items of cost. A function might follow a particular pattern of natural expenses, but most functions will have similar expenses, such as salaries, insurance, property taxes, heat, light, power, and supplies.

Functional classifications of marketing expenses might be structured in the following manner:

1. Selling
2. Advertising
3. Warehousing
4. Packing and shipping
5. Credit and collection
6. General accounting (for marketing)

These functional classifications can be grouped into two broad categories: order-getting expenses and order-filling expenses. Order-getting expenses are the expenses of activities carried on to bring in the sales orders and include selling and advertising. Order-filling expenses are the expenses of warehousing, packing and shipping, credit and collection, and general accounting.

A broad category of marketing administration expenses may also be identified. This category includes the expenses of marketing planning and organization, market research and forecasting, product design and development, and product-line planning.

Direct and Indirect Expenses

Direct expenses are those expenses that can be traced directly to a function or department, such as the salary of a department manager or the depreciation of a delivery truck. Expenses which can be traced to a territory, customer, product, or definite type of sales outlet may also be considered direct expenses. Conversely, indirect expenses are incurred for more than one function or other classification and hence must be allocated. A direct expense may also be allocated when direct identification requires excessive clerical expense.

Marketing expenses may be considered direct, indirect, or a combination of both. For example, marketing expenses may be directly identifiable with functional classifications while being only indirectly identifiable with regard to other classifications, such as territories or products.

Functionally classified marketing expenses which are indirect with respect to other classifications may be allocated to such classifications as territories and products by (1) using a percentage based on actual sales, manufacturing cost, or some other appropriate basis, or (2) creating a standard unit cost for each activity—similar to factory costs. However, the assignment of functional marketing expenses as percentages of actual sales or manufacturing costs, or on some other basis, is of dubious analytical value. The procedure has been used in the past for want of more satisfactory methods. The determination of a functional standard unit costing rate is a more dependable solution. The charging of marketing expense activities on the basis of a costing rate is a logical extension of widely adopted factory standard costing procedures. Furthermore, the availability of such a rate permits quick and decisive analysis.

Actual expenses would be collected in the customary manner and charged to their departmental and natural expense classifications in a subsidiary ledger controlled by a marketing expenses control account in the general ledger.

Selection of Bases for the Allocation of Functional Expenses. The marketing expense allocation process for functional expenses which are indirect as to other classifications poses two basic questions: (1) what bases should be used for the allocation and (2) how far should the allocations be carried out? As a solution to the first, the base used should be the one most closely related to the incurrence of the expense being allocated. The second question occurs because of doubts raised about the usefulness of full allocation of all indirect expenses. The allocation of indirect expenses is arbitrary and may result in misleading expense reports to marketing management. Certain expenses should be omitted from the allocation procedure when they are not measurable in relation to the function or activity. This is especially true when expenses are being allocated for analytical purposes. On the other hand, full marketing cost allocation may be desirable in cost-plus pricing of contracts. With respect to government contracts, CAS 418 calls for the allocation of indirect costs to be based on one of the following, listed in order of preference: (1) a resource consumption measure, (2) an output measure, or (3) a surrogate that is representative of resources consumed.[1]

Factory overhead rates should have a base which most closely expresses the effort connected with the work of the department, such as labor hours, machine hours, or labor cost. A similar procedure for allocating marketing expenses is to divide the total expense of each marketing function by the units of functional service (the base) to obtain the expense per unit. Either an actual rate or a predetermined standard rate may be used, but the latter is preferable for expense control.

The selection of bases or units of measurement requires careful analysis, because the degree to which the final rates represent reasonable expenses is greatly dependent upon the adequacy of the bases selected. Each function must be examined with respect to that factor which most influences the volume of its work. Some examples of allocation bases for different marketing functions are as follows:

Function	Expense Allocation Bases
Selling	Gross sales dollar value of products sold or number of salespersons' calls on customers (based on salespersons' time reports)
Advertising	Quantity of product units sold, relative media circulation, or cost of space directly assignable
Warehousing	Size, weight, or number of products shipped or handled
Packing and shipping	Number of shipping units, weight, or size of units
Credit and collection	Number of customers' orders, transactions, or invoice lines
General accounting	Number of customers' orders, transactions, or invoice lines

---

[1]*Standards, Rules and Regulations, Part 418*, "Allocation of Direct and Indirect Costs" (Washington, D.C.: Cost Accounting Standards Board, 1980).

Determination of Functional Unit Expense. The unit expense of an activity is calculated by dividing the total expense of the function by the total amount of the measurement unit or base selected. A vast amount of information must be collected in order to establish a functional unit expense rate. The tedious assembly of such underlying information is often the reason for the lack of a marketing expense control system.

Fixed and Variable Expenses

Recognition of the fixed-variable expense classification is valuable in controlling marketing expenses and in making decisions dealing with the possible opening or closing of a territory, new methods of packaging goods, servicing different types of outlets, or adding or dropping a product line. Fixed marketing expenses include salaries of executive and administrative sales staffs; salaries of warehousing, advertising, shipping, billing, and collection departments; and rent and depreciation of associated permanent facilities. These fixed expenses also have been called *capacity costs*.

Variable marketing expenses include the expenses of handling, warehousing, and shipping that tend to vary with sales volume. They have been referred to as *volume costs* or as expenses connected with the filling of an order. Another type of variable marketing expense originates in connection with promotional expenses such as salespersons' salaries, travel, and entertainment and some advertising expenses. Management must examine these expenses carefully in the planning stage, since sales volume may have little influence upon their behavior. These expenses are variable because of management decisions. In fact, once agreed to by management, these expenses may be fixed, at least for the budget period under consideration.

Flexible Budget and Standards for Marketing Functions

Sales estimates essentially are the most important figures in any budget. The accuracy and usefulness of most other estimates depend on them. Methods used in determining sales budget estimates are discussed in Chapter 16. Total sales ordinarily are broken down into the various kinds of products to be sold, into monthly or weekly sales and into sales by salespersons, territories, classes of customers, and methods of distribution. In each division, quotas may be useful for determining the desirability of cultivating various outlets and for judging the efficiency of sales methods and policies.

Budgets are prepared to anticipate the amount of functional expenses for the coming period and to provide a basis for comparing and evaluating the actual expenses. Because of the influence of volume and capacity, a comparison of actual expenses with predetermined fixed budget figures does not always give a fair evaluation of the activities of a function. Therefore, the use of flexible budgets for the control of marketing expenses should be considered.

The flexible budget for a distributive function such as billing might take the form shown at the top of page 814.

FLEXIBLE BUDGET FOR BILLING DEPARTMENT

Expenses	Functional Unit—Invoice Line			
	50,000	55,000	60,000	65,000
Clerical salaries	$ 4,000	$ 4,000	$ 4,000	$ 4,000
Supervision	3,000	3,000	3,000	3,000
Depreciation—building.	750	750	750	750
Depreciation—equipment	1,250	1,250	1,250	1,250
Supplies	2,500	2,750	3,000	3,250
Total	$11,500	$11,750	$12,000	$12,250

A standard functional unit expense is then established for each activity or function on the basis of normal capacity. These standard unit expenses will furnish bases for comparisons with actual expenses, and spending and idle capacity variances can be isolated. Using the Billing Department as an example and assuming that 60,000 invoice lines represent normal capacity, the following standard billing rate per invoice line would be computed:

$$\frac{\$12,000}{60,000 \text{ invoice lines}} = \$.20 \text{ per invoice line}$$

Assuming $9,000 fixed expense and $3,000 variable expense, the variable portion of the rate is:

$$\frac{\$3,000}{60,000 \text{ invoice lines}} = \$.05 \text{ per invoice line}$$

The variances for billing expenses can be computed in a manner similar to that discussed in connection with factory overhead (Chapter 13) and consistent with the basic idea of flexible budgeting. If actual sales required 63,000 invoice lines for a month at a total of $12,500, the variances for the Billing Department would be determined as follows:

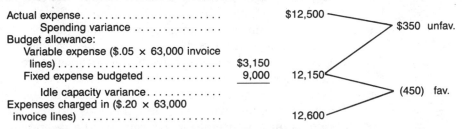

Actual expense........................ $12,500
    Spending variance .... → $350 unfav.
Budget allowance:
    Variable expense ($.05 × 63,000 invoice
      lines)........................... $3,150
    Fixed expense budgeted 9,000   12,150
    Idle capacity variance............. → (450) fav.
Expenses charged in ($.20 × 63,000
  invoice lines) 12,600

The increased volume leads to a favorable idle capacity variance due to overabsorption of fixed expenses. On the other hand, the supervisor overspent the $12,150 budget allowance by $350.

Accountants usually do not carry this type of variance analysis through ledger accounts. The analysis is usually statistical and is presented to management in report form. However, the following journal entries similar to those for factory overhead could be made:

Billing Expense Charged In 12,600
    Applied Billing Expense.................................   12,600

Actual Billing Expense	12,500	
Sundry Credits.......................................		12,500
Applied Billing Expense	12,600	
Billing Expense—Spending Variance	350	
Billing Expense—Idle Capacity Variance		450
Actual Billing Expense.................................		12,500

■ MARKETING PROFITABILITY ANALYSIS

The functional unit expenses are used to analyze expenses and determine the profitability of territories, customers, products, and salespersons. In most cases, a continuous reshuffling or rearranging of expense items is needed to find the required expenses and profits. Marketing expense and profitability analysis has improved over the years with the increasing availability of electronic data processing equipment capable of processing the great amount of quantitative detail so characteristic of these analyses.

Analysis by Territories

Perhaps the simplest analysis of marketing profitability is by territories. When marketing activities are organized on a territorial basis, each identifiable geographical unit can be charged directly with the expenses incurred within its area, thereby minimizing the proration of expenses. Expenses that can be traced directly to a territory are: salespersons' salaries, commissions, and traveling expenses; transportation cost within the delivery area; packing and shipping costs; and advertising specifically identified with the territory. Nontraceable expenses that must be allocated to the territory are: general management, general office, general sales manager, and general accounting. If nontraceable expenses are allocated to the territory, they should be shown separately, so that the territory's contribution to profit and the recovery of common expenses can be readily identified.

When expenses are identified by territories, a comparative income statement can be prepared. This statement, illustrated on page 816, permits control and analysis of expenses as well as the computation of profit margins. When sales or expenses seem to be out of line, management can take corrective action.

Analysis by Customers

Although most marketing expenses can be assigned directly to territories, relatively few of these expenses can be traced directly to customers. Perhaps sales commissions, transportation expenses, and sales discounts can be considered direct, but all other expenses are allocated on the basis of functional unit costing rates.

The large number of customers makes the allocation and analysis of marketing expenses by customers rather cumbersome if not impossible. For this reason, customers are grouped according to certain characteristics to make

INCOME STATEMENT BY TERRITORIES

| | Territory | | |
	East	Central	West
Net sales.	$210,000	$ 80,000	$175,000
Cost of goods sold	160,000	60,000	140,000
Gross profit	$ 50,000	$ 20,000	$ 35,000
Traceable marketing expenses:			
Selling	$ 15,000	$ 8,600	$ 23,900
Warehousing	3,600	1,400	3,100
Packing and shipping	1,500	400	1,900
Advertising	2,000	1,000	500
Credit and collection	800	250	1,200
Total traceable marketing expenses	$ 22,900	$ 11,650	$ 30,600
Contribution to profit and common costs	$ 27,100	$ 8,350	$ 4,400
Allocated indirect costs:			
Institutional advertising	$ 1,400	$ 1,400	$ 1,400
General administration	5,000	5,000	5,000
Total allocated indirect costs	$ 6,400	$ 6,400	$ 6,400
Operating income (loss) per territory	$ 20,700	$ 1,950	$ (2,000)

the analysis meaningful. The grouping may be by (1) territories, (2) amount of average order, (3) customer-volume groups, or (4) kinds of customers.

Analysis of Customers by Territories. This type of analysis reflects territorial cost differences due to the customer's proximity to warehouses, volume of purchases, service requirements, and the kinds of merchandise bought. These factors can make some sales profitable or unprofitable. The analysis proceeds in the same manner outlined for territories, except that the expenses would be broken down by customers or kinds of customers within each territory.

Analysis of Customers by Amount of Average Order. The amount of a customer's order is closely related to profitability. An analysis might indicate that a considerable portion of orders comes from customers who cost the company more in selling to them than the orders are worth in terms of gross profit. Companies have therefore resorted to setting minimum dollar values or minimum quantities for orders as well as price differentials, thereby reducing the number of transactions and increasing profits. Although selective selling has found much favor among many executives, it requires changes in habits and routines.

To present management with a quick view of the situation regarding the amount of the average order in relation to the number of customers, time spent, and total dollar sales, the following chart on page 817 might be helpful.

Analysis by Customer-Volume Groups. An analysis of customers by customer-volume groups is similar to that of the amount-of-average-order analysis. Instead of classifying customers by an order's dollar value, however, the customer-volume group analysis is based on quantity or volume. This type of analysis yields information concerning (1) the profitability of various

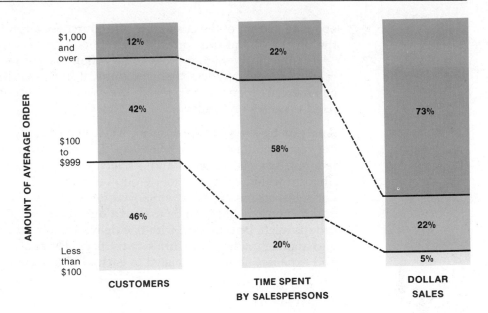

Analysis of Customers by Amount of Average Order

AMOUNT OF AVERAGE ORDER

$1,000 and over — 12% 22% 73%

$100 to $999 — 42% 58% 73%

Less than $100 — 46% 20% 22% / 5%

CUSTOMERS   TIME SPENT BY SALESPERSONS   DOLLAR SALES

customer-volume groups and (2) the establishment of minimum orders and price differentials.

The following analysis indicates that only sales to customers who buy more than 150 units during a week result in a positive contribution margin:

ANALYSIS BY CUSTOMER-VOLUME GROUPS					
Customer-Volume Group (Number of Units Purchased During Week)	Customers (% of Total)	Volume (% of Total)	Gross Contribution Margin per 100 Units	Variable Commercial Expenses per 100 Units	Contribution Margin per 100 Units
Customers unsuccessfully solicited	17.1%	—	—	—	—
1-25	7.6	0.2%	$1.66	$4.01	$(2.35)
26-50	8.3	0.7	1.38	2.55	(1.17)
51-100	12.0	1.9	1.25	1.78	(.53)
101-150	9.3	2.4	1.26	1.32	(.06)
151-200	7.8	2.9	1.14	1.13	.01
201-250	6.4	3.0	1.12	.95	.17
251-500	17.1	13.2	1.06	.75	.31
501-1,000	12.7	18.6	1.02	.49	.53
1,001-10,000	1.7	57.1	.81	.24	.57
Total	100.0%	100.0%			

The variable cost of goods sold is subtracted from sales to compute the gross contribution margin, from which the variable commercial (marketing and administrative) expenses are subtracted to compute the contribution margin. Although the customers buying more than 150 units weekly represent only about 46 percent of the customers, they purchase approximately 95 percent of the units sold and thus provide the profits.

In spite of the higher gross contribution margin received from orders by customers who buy less than 150 units, it is not sufficient to cover variable commercial expenses. As a result, the sales to this group provide nothing for fixed expenses and profit.

Analysis by Kinds of Customers. This type of analysis makes a distinction between manufacturers, wholesalers, retailers, government (local, state, and federal), schools, colleges and universities, and hospitals. Prices might be uniform within each customer group but might vary between groups. Different salespersons are often employed for each category; hence their salaries and related expenses can be assigned directly to the group. Delivery to such groups might be different, with one delivery contracted with outside truckers and another made by the firm's own trucks. For analytical purposes, revenue and expenses should be related to each kind of customer.

Analysis by Products

The effect of the sales of each product or product line is of considerable importance in planning and controlling the marketing effort. The existence of a high sales volume and a companywide profit does not necessarily mean that all is well. Profitable and unprofitable products must be identified in order to plan and control profits effectively.

Just as customers are grouped for purposes of analysis, products sold can be grouped according to product lines or brands possessing common characteristics. A product-line (or brand-line) income statement can be prepared for the evaluation of profitable and unprofitable product lines. The statement on page 819 relates the actual contribution of each product line to total profits and to the recovery of common costs for the year. In this statement, only directly traceable expenses are identified with each product, and expenses are segregated as variable and fixed to demonstrate the contribution margin approach discussed on page 824.

Gross Profit Or Contribution Margin Analysis

If the cost per unit of product is entirely variable as would be the case for wholesalers and retailers, it is useful to compare actual gross profit with planned gross profit and to analyze the sources of the observed difference. Because of the arbitrary nature of allocating fixed factory overhead, it is more useful for manufacturers to analyze the difference in actual and planned contribution margin. The difference may be the result of one or a combination of the following:

1. Changes in sales prices of products.
2. Changes in volume sold.
   a. Changes in the number of physical units sold.

PRODUCT-LINE INCOME STATEMENT
(CONTRIBUTION MARGIN APPROACH)

	Total	Product Line 1	Product Line 2	Product Line 3
Net sales	$3,100,000	$1,540,000	$1,070,000	$490,000
Less variable cost of goods sold	1,927,000	925,000	590,000	412,000
Gross contribution margin	$1,173,000	$ 615,000	$ 480,000	$ 78,000
Less variable marketing expenses:				
Selling	$ 243,300	$ 112,300	$ 89,000	$ 42,000
Warehousing	87,100	48,000	27,500	11,600
Packing and Shipping	66,000	39,000	17,800	9,200
Advertising	38,000	20,000	12,000	6,000
Credit and collection	19,700	12,300	4,200	3,200
General accounting	52,200	23,000	16,800	12,400
Total	$ 506,300	$ 254,600	$ 167,300	$ 84,400
Contribution margin	$ 666,700	$ 360,400	$ 312,700	$ (6,400)
Less fixed expenses:				
Manufacturing	$ 100,000	$ 30,000	$ 52,200	$ 17,800
Marketing	15,000	8,000	6,000	1,000
Administration	5,000	2,000	1,800	1,200
Total	$ 120,000	$ 40,000	$ 60,000	$ 20,000
Margin available for common fixed expenses and operating income	$ 546,700	$ 320,400	$ 252,700	$ (26,400)
Less common fixed expenses	230,000			
Operating income	$ 316,700			

    b. Changes in the types of products sold, often called the *product mix* or *sales mix.*

3. Changes in cost elements, e.g., purchase prices and variable marketing expenses for wholesalers and retailers or materials, labor, variable factory overhead, and variable marketing expenses for manufacturers.

The determination of the various causes for an increase or decrease in gross profit or contribution margin is similar to the computation of standard cost variances, although standard costs or budgets are not required. If standards or budgets are not used, prices and costs of the previous period, or any period selected as the basis for the comparison, serve as the basis for the computation of the variances.

To illustrate the analysis, the following gross profit sections of Spanton Wholesale Supply Company's operating statements are presented:

	Budgeted	Actual	Difference
Sales (net)	$120,000	$140,000	+ $20,000
Cost of goods sold	100,000	110,000	+ 10,000
Gross profit	$ 20,000	$ 30,000	+ $10,000 net increase

In comparison with the budget, actual sales increased $20,000 and costs increased $10,000, resulting in an increase in gross profit of $10,000.

Additional data taken from various records indicate that the sales and the cost of goods sold figures can be broken down as follows:

Product	Quantity	Budgeted Sales Unit Price	Budgeted Sales Amount	Budgeted Cost of Goods Sold Unit Cost	Budgeted Cost of Goods Sold Amount
X	8,000 units	$5.00	$ 40,000	$4.000	$ 32,000
Y	7,000	4.00	28,000	3.500	24,500
Z	20,000	2.60	52,000	2.175	43,500
		Total sales	$120,000	Total cost	$100,000

Product	Quantity	Actual Sales Unit Price	Actual Sales Amount	Actual Cost of Goods Sold Unit Cost	Actual Cost of Goods Sold Amount
X	10,000 units	$6.60	$ 66,000	$4.00	$ 40,000
Y	4,000	3.50	14,000	3.50	14,000
Z	20,000	3.00	60,000	2.80	56,000
		Total sales	$140,000	Total cost	$110,000

In analyzing the gross profit data of Spanton Wholesale Supply Company, the budgeted sales and costs are used as the basis (or standard) for all comparisons. A sales price variance and a sales volume variance are computed first, followed by the computation of a cost price variance and a cost volume variance. The sales volume variance and the cost volume variance are analyzed further as a third step, which results in the computation of a sales mix variance and a final sales volume variance.

The sales price and sales volume variances of Spanton Wholesale Supply Company are computed as follows:

Actual sales.........................		$140,000
Actual sales at budgeted prices:		
X: 10,000 units @ $5.00...........	$50,000	
Y: 4,000 @ 4.00...........	16,000	
Z: 20,000 @ 2.60...........	52,000	118,000
Sales price variance..................		$ 22,000 fav.
Actual sales at budgeted prices.........		$118,000
Total budgeted sales (used as standard)...		120,000
Sales volume variance................		$ 2,000 unfav.

The cost price and cost volume variances are computed as follows:

Actual cost of goods sold		$110,000
Actual sales at budgeted costs:		
X: 10,000 units @ $4.000	$40,000	
Y: 4,000 @ 3.500	14,000	
Z: 20,000 @ 2.175	43,500	97,500
Cost price variance		$ 12,500 unfav.
Actual sales at budgeted costs..............		$ 97,500
Budgeted cost of goods sold (used as standard)...		100,000
Cost volume variance		$ 2,500 fav.

The results of the preceding computations explain the reason for the $10,000 increase in gross profit:

Sales price variance		$22,000 fav.
Volume variances (net) consisting of:		
Cost volume variance.	$2,500 fav.	
Less sales volume variance.	2,000 unfav.	
Net volume variance		500 fav.
		$22,500
Less cost price variance.		12,500 unfav.
Net increase in gross profit.		$10,000

The net $500 favorable volume variance is a composite of the sales volume and cost volume variances. It should be further analyzed to determine the more significant sales mix and final sales volume variances. To accomplish this analysis, one additional figure must be determined—the budgeted average gross profit per unit. The computation is:

$$\frac{\text{Total budgeted gross profit}}{\text{Total budgeted number of units sold}} = \frac{\$20,000}{35,000} = \$.5714 \text{ per unit}$$

The $.5714 average budgeted gross profit per unit sold is multiplied by the actual total number of units sold (34,000 units). The resulting $19,428 is the total gross profit that would have been achieved if all units had been sold at the budgeted average gross profit per unit.

The sales mix and the final sales volume variances can now be calculated:

Actual sales at budgeted prices		$118,000
Actual sales at budgeted costs		97,500
Difference.		$ 20,500
Actual sales at budgeted average gross profit		19,428
Sales mix variance		$ 1,072 fav.
Actual sales at budgeted average gross profit		$ 19,428
Total budgeted sales (used as standard)	$120,000	
Budgeted cost of goods sold (used as standard).	100,000	
Difference.		20,000
Final sales volume variance		$ 572 unfav.
Check: Sales mix variance		$ 1,072 fav.
Final sales volume variance		572 unfav.
Net volume variance		$ 500 fav.

The sales mix variance can be viewed in the following manner:

Product	(1) Actual Sales in Units	Budgeted Sales Units	Budgeted Sales %	(2) Actual Sales (In Budgeted Proportions)*	(3) (1) – (2)	(4) Budgeted Unit Gross Profit**	Sales Mix Variance (3) × (4)
X.	10,000	8,000	22.86	7,772	2,228	$1.000	$2,228 fav.
Y.	4,000	7,000	20.00	6,800	(2,800)	.500	(1,400) unfav.
Z.	20,000	20,000	57.14	19,428	572	.425	243 fav.
Total	34,000	35,000	100.00	34,000	0		
Rounding difference							1
Net sales mix variance							$1,072 fav.

*Total number of units actually sold × budgeted sales % for that product (e.g., 34,000 × 22.86% = 7,772)
**Budgeted sales price per unit – budgeted cost of goods sold per unit (e.g., $5 sales price – $4 cost of goods sold = $1)

With such an analysis, the influence of individual products on the total sales mix variance is specifically measured. The interactive effect of shifts in the mix is also revealed. This detailed information enables management to assess the effects of past as well as future sales mix variations.

The final sales volume variance is the difference in the number of units budgeted and sold, multiplied by the budgeted average gross profit per unit:

Actual sales in units	34,000
Budgeted sales in units.	35,000
Unit sales difference	1,000
Average budgeted gross profit per unit	× $.5714
	$571.40
Rounding difference	.60
Final sales volume variance	$572.00 unfav.

Combining two or more products or product types having different cost or sales prices into a single product category should be avoided. Such aggregation will result in the price variances including a portion of what is actually the mix variance as the mix within such a combination changes.[2]

The variances identified in the preceding computations are summarized as follows:

	Gains	Losses
Gain due to increased sales price	$22,000	
Loss due to increased cost		$12,500
Gain due to shift in sales mix.	1,072	
Loss due to decrease in units sold		572
Total.	$23,072	$13,072
	13,072	
Net increase in gross profit	$10,000	

The gross profit or contribution margin analysis based on budgets and standard costs depicts the weak spots in the period's performance. Management is now able to outline the remedies that should correct the situation.

Because the planned gross profit or contribution margin is the responsibility of the marketing as well as the manufacturing functions, this analysis brings together these two major functional areas of the firm and points to the need for further study by both of them. The marketing function must explain the changes in sales prices and marketing expenses, the shift in the sales mix, and the decrease in units sold, while the production function must account for changes in manufacturing costs.

Analysis by Salespersons

The selling function includes expenses such as salaries, travel, and other expenses connected with the work of sales representatives. In many in-

[2]Robert E. Malcolm, "The Effect of Product Aggregation in Determining Sales Variances," *The Accounting Review*, Vol. LIII, No. 1, pp. 162-169.

stances, salespersons' expenses form a substantial part of the total expense incurred in selling. The control and analysis of these expenses should, therefore, receive management's closest attention. To achieve this control, performance standards and standard costs should be established. These standards are used not only for the control of expenses but also for determining the profitability of sales made by salespersons.

Cost Control. The allocation table on page 812 indicates that selling expenses may be allocated on the basis of the number of calls made. A call or visit by a salesperson usually is made for two reasons: to sell and to promote the merchandise or products. The problem is to determine the cost of doing each of these types of work and to compare the actual expense with the standard allowed for a call.

A salesperson's call often involves several kinds of work: not only calling on the customer, but also helping the merchant with the display in the store. This practice is common in cosmetic, pharmaceutical, and fast-food businesses. Because the salesperson's time is consumed by such activities, a standard time allowed per call is often very difficult to establish. To obtain the necessary statistics for establishing such standards and to make comparisons, the sales representative might be asked to prepare a report providing information regarding the type of calls made as well as the quantity, type, and dollar values of products sold. This information is the basis for much of the analysis discussed previously.

Profitability Analysis. It is possible to analyze sales in relation to profitability. Sales volume alone does not tell the complete story. High volume does not always insure high profit, and the sales mix plays an important part in the final profit. Although a sales representative might wish to follow the line of least resistance, management must strive to sell the merchandise of all product groups, particularly those with the highest profit margins. Since sales territories are often planned for sales according to product groups, it is necessary that anticipated sales be followed up by analyzing the salespersons' efforts. The following table indicates how such an analysis can be made:

SALES, COSTS, AND PROFITS BY INDIVIDUAL SALESPERSONS
FOR APRIL, 19—

(1) Sales-person	(2) Ship-ments	(3) % of Quota	(4) Salary and Commis-sion	(5) Travel Expense	(6) Cost of Handling	(7) Total Cost (4) + (5) + (6)	(8) Gross Profit	(9) Profit (8) − (7)	(10) Profit, % of Sales (9) ÷ (2)	(11) Ship-ments, % of Total*	(12) Potential, % of Total*
A	$26,000	80%	$2,000	$3,000	$2,340	$ 7,340	$ 7,540	$ 200	.8%	6.7%	9.0%
B	26,000	122	1,900	1,800	2,340	6,040	7,800	1,760	6.8	6.7	5.5
C	39,000	100	2,800	2,100	3,500	8,400	11,700	3,300	8.5	10.1	10.5
D	22,000	108	1,800	2,000	1,980	5,780	7,050	1,270	5.8	5.8	5.5
E	21,000	110	1,700	1,700	1,890	5,290	6,720	1,430	6.8	5.4	5.0
F	54,000	125	3,500	3,100	5,700	12,300	14,600	2,300	4.3	14.0	10.0
G	21,000	98	1,600	1,200	1,700	4,500	6,720	2,220	10.6	5.5	5.5
H	46,000	101	3,400	1,000	4,100	8,500	13,800	5,300	11.5	12.0	12.0

*For 8 salespersons out of a total of 15 salespersons.

■ THE CONTRIBUTION MARGIN APPROACH

Generally, the income statement shows a profit figure after all marketing and administrative expenses have been deducted. The total cost and profit approach assigns all the expenses, direct or indirect, fixed or variable, to each segment analyzed. This procedure is commonly used, since management is familiar with it and understands that no profit is realized until all manufacturing and nonmanufacturing expenses have been recovered.

Marketing expense analysis attempts to allocate marketing expenses to territories, customers, products, or salespersons. However, because these marketing expenses contain direct, indirect, fixed, and variable amounts, allocations are often arbitrary, in which case the end results may be misleading. It has been suggested that only the variable manufacturing cost be subtracted from each segment's sales, thus arriving at a figure described as "gross contribution margin." (This approach differs from the conventional income statement wherein *all* manufacturing costs are deducted in arriving at a figure described as "gross profit.") Furthermore, only the variable nonmanufacturing expense would be subtracted from the gross contribution margin of a territory, customer class, product, or salesperson, resulting in the contribution margin for each segment. Fixed expenses would be shown separately and not allocated unless specifically attributable to a segment. When a territory, customer class, or product group contributes nothing to the recovery of fixed expenses, the situation should be examined and remedial steps taken. The product-line income statement on page 819 illustrates this approach. Moreover, nontraceable variable costs, such as variable joint product costs, should be viewed as they relate to the contribution made by the group of products or territories rather than based on arbitrary allocations, e.g., to individual products or territories.

Although sales volume is the ultimate goal of most sales managers, the trend has been toward a greater recognition of contribution margin as the basis for judging the success and profitability of marketing activities in manufacturing businesses. The increased use of standard production costs has aided the analysis of gross profit, as discussed on page 819. Even though a manufacturer might know the production costs, the question remains: "How much can the company afford for marketing expenses?" The problem of determining allowable marketing expenses is intensified because once a sales program gets under way, the majority of expenses become fixed, at least in the short run.

In summary, proponents of the contribution margin approach point out that only specific and direct expenses, whether variable or fixed, should be assigned to territories, customers, product groups, or salespersons, with a clear distinction as to their fixed and variable characteristics. Moreover, for the purpose of identifying expenses with responsible managers, it is desirable to identify whether or not each reported expense is controllable by the manager in charge of the reported activity.

The contribution margin approach has influenced the thinking of the volume-minded sales manager or salesperson who must recognize that profit is more beneficial than volume. The contribution margin is better than sales as an indicator of the amount available for recovery of fixed manufacturing cost, fixed marketing and administrative expenses, and ultimately a desired profit.

■ PRODUCT PRICING

Product pricing is a complex subject and is neither a one-person nor a one-activity job. Theorists and practitioners differ on the appropriateness of various pricing theories. In practice, the solution to a pricing problem becomes a research job that requires the cooperation and coordination of the economist, statistician, market specialist, industrial engineer, and accountant. Since the determination of a sales price requires consideration of many factors, some of which defy measurement or control, prudent and practical judgment is necessary. Accountants can provide executive management and marketing managers with mileposts to be used as guides when traveling the relatively uncharted road toward successful pricing.

Costs generally are considered to be the starting point in a pricing situation, even though a rigid relationship may not be expected to exist. Prices and pricing policy vary in relation to costs and market conditions as well as to the selection of a long- or short-range view. The long-run approach allows changes in products, manufacturing methods, plant capacity, and marketing and distribution methods. It aims to obtain prices which will return all costs and provide an adequate return on the capital invested. A normal or average product cost is the basis used for long-range pricing. A short-range pricing policy looks toward the recovery of at least part of the total cost in order to meet changing needs resulting from fluctuating sales volume, sales mix, and prices. In such cases, the differential cost of a product may serve as a guide for the determination of prices. Variable costs are the principal source of cost differentials which must be computed in such pricing problems (Chapters 20 and 21). In any case, the data used should be current, which may require adjusting historical costs to reflect inflation.

The relationship between costs and prices is one of the most difficult for a manager to determine. Price setting is that field of business in which management truly becomes an art. A sales price, generally thought of as the rate of exchange between two commodities, is determined in many industries in a manner that gives individual companies some degree of control over the price. Even companies that experience a great deal of competition have some measure of control, since products, quality, and/or the services rendered may differ. Although a firm may exercise some control over sales prices, the costs incurred in order to do business are usually more within its control.

Prices may be influenced not only by competition but also by what customers are willing to pay and by governmental regulations and controls. The Robinson-Patman Act (discussed later in this chapter) must be complied with to avoid alleged price discrimination. Even if a company has little or no control over a sales price, it faces the question of whether it can operate profitably at the price that can be charged. Costs must be known and used as building blocks for determining the minimum price required to justify entering or continuing in a given market.

The accountant's assistance to management in the highly important field of pricing products requires knowledge and recognition of inventory costing methods as well as all cost items as they flow through the cost accounting cycle. The development of an appreciation for and an understanding of economic, social, and legal considerations are required. The accountant must be not only an economist but also an investment analyst and must be able to see problems through management's eyes. By doing so, the accountant becomes a vital part of management, with cost accounting as a necessary tool.

Even though price-setting procedures are difficult, several cost-oriented methods are available that will assist in their computation and determination. These methods include (1) profit maximization—relating total revenue to total cost, (2) pricing based on a return on capital employed, (3) conversion cost pricing, (4) the contribution margin and the differential cost approach to pricing, and (5) standard costs for pricing.

Profit Maximization

A key objective of most business enterprises is to obtain a price that contributes the largest amount of profit. Economic theorists describe this as profit maximization. The profit return on each unit sold is not so important as the total profit realized from all units sold. The price that yields the largest total profit is the price to be charged to a consumer.

The following schedule shows the variable cost at $7 per unit, with fixed cost at $300,000 for all ranges of output. The most profitable sales price is $14 per unit, with a contribution margin of $560,000 and a profit of $260,000, after deducting the fixed cost.

Sales Price per Unit	Number of Units To Be Sold	Total Sales Volume	Variable Cost ($7 per Unit)	Fixed Cost	Profit (Loss)
$20	20,000	$ 400,000	$140,000	$300,000	$ (40,000)
18	40,000	720,000	280,000	300,000	140,000
16	60,000	960,000	420,000	300,000	240,000
14	80,000	1,120,000	560,000	300,000	260,000
12	100,000	1,200,000	700,000	300,000	200,000
10	120,000	1,200,000	840,000	300,000	60,000
8	140,000	1,120,000	980,000	300,000	(160,000)

In other situations, the unit variable cost and the total fixed cost may vary according to the total number of units to be sold, thus influencing the most profitable sales price.

Profit maximization is not to be looked upon as the immediate return expected, but rather as a goal to be realized over several months or years. However, during these months and years, sales policies, competition, customer practices, cost changes, and other economic influences might radically alter all previous assumptions. Profit maximization is not necessarily the single objective or even the dominant objective of firms. A recent study found that firms pursue multiple objectives in setting their prices. These include major objectives (such as profits, return on investment, market share, and total sales) and lesser objectives (such as price-earnings ratio, liquidity, employee job security, and industrial relations). While each firm surveyed gave weight to·many of these objectives, certain patterns of dominance were found:

> . . . for firms selling standard products, market share was the dominant pricing policy objective. In contrast, firms handling custom-made products were more concerned with return on investment and (employee) job security. . . . Where firms seemed to be competing on the basis of price and service, sales maximization was the principal pricing objective. Where product innovation was the major source of competition, profits seemed to dominate. . . .[3]

Pricing Based on a Return on Capital Employed

Some companies attempt to develop prices that will yield a predetermined or desired rate of return on capital employed. To illustrate, assume that a single-product company's total cost is $210,000, total capital employed is $200,000, the sales volume is 50,000 units, and the desired rate of return on capital employed is 20 percent. The formula used and the determination of the product's sales price would be:

$$\text{Price} = \frac{\text{Total cost} + (\text{Desired rate of return} \times \text{Total capital employed})}{\text{Sales volume in units}}$$

$$\text{Price} = \frac{\$210,000 + (20\% \times \$200,000)}{50,000 \text{ units}} = \frac{\$250,000}{50,000} = \$5$$

Proof: Sales (50,000 units × $5)	$250,000
Less total cost.	210,000
Profit (20% × $200,000)	$ 40,000

Pricing procedures using capital employed as part of the pricing formula may be complex, however. The illustrations assume no change in capital employed. Actually, as prices and costs change, capital employed may be expected to change. With an increase in capital employed, more cash will be required to serve the business. With higher prices, accounts receivable will be higher, and inventory costs will increase in proportion to increases in factory costs. Decreases would have the reverse effect.

If it is assumed that a firm is in business to maximize its value to the shareholders, then its pricing policy should be based largely on a target rate of return on capital employed. To be effective in its control and analysis, management's pricing decisions should be made after this rate, the standard cost, and the estimated plant capacity have been considered.

---

[3]Lawrence A. Gordon, Robert Cooper, Haim Falk, and Danny Miller, *The Pricing Decision* (New York: National Association of Accountants, 1981; and Hamilton, Ontario: The Society of Management Accountants of Canada, 1980), pp. 9, 15-17.

Conversion Cost Pricing

Conversion cost pricing attempts to direct management's attention to the amount of labor and factory overhead that products require. To illustrate, assume that a company manufactures two products, each selling for $10. The manufacturing cost for each is $9, resulting in a gross profit of $1 per unit, indicating that from a profit point of view it does not matter which product is promoted. However, a breakdown of the costs reveals the following:

Item of Cost	Product A	Product B
Direct materials.............	$ 6	$ 3
Direct labor................	2	4
Factory overhead	1	2
Total manufacturing cost	$ 9	$ 9
Sales price	10	10
Gross profit................	$ 1	$ 1

The cost breakdown indicates that Product A requires only half the labor and factory overhead that is required for Product B. If it were possible to shift all efforts to A, a greater number of units could be produced and sold with the same gross profit per unit. Marketing costs of A versus B also must be considered. Of course, any volume increase might disturb market equilibrium and even cause a decrease in the price because of increased supply.

Contribution Margin Approach to Pricing

In direct costing, the contribution margin figure indicates a product's contribution to the recovery of fixed costs and to profit. The fixed and variable cost classifications permit an evaluation of each product by a comparison of specific contribution margins. While this contribution margin approach might be used for a firm's entire business, it is of even greater value in the analysis of its divisions, plants, products, product lines, customers, and territories. Care must be taken, however, not to confuse contribution with profit, since profit is realized only after all fixed costs are covered.

The differential cost of an order is the variable cost necessary to produce the additional units, plus additional fixed costs (if any) at the new production level. If the cost of additional units is accepted as a basis for pricing them, any price over and above total differential cost would be acceptable. This procedure is, of course, applicable only to the additional units.

To base sales prices on differential cost requires careful scrutiny of all related factors. For example, long-term sales promotion should not be used for a product priced on the basis of differential costs when total cost recovery and a reasonable profit will not result.

Standard Costs for Pricing

If cost estimates used for pricing purposes are prepared on the basis of the standard costs for materials, labor, and factory overhead, the tasks of preparing the estimate and using the data to set the price will be considerably easier. The use of standard costs for pricing purposes makes cost figures more quickly available and reduces clerical detail. Since a standard cost represents the cost that should be attained in an efficiently operated plant at normal capacity, it is essential, once the sales price has been established, that the cost department furnish up-to-the-minute information to all parties to make certain that the cost stays within the rate set by the estimate. Any significant deviation between actual and standard costs should come to light for quick action through the accounting system.

The National Association of Accountants has stated that companies can be divided into four groups with respect to the type of cost figures which they supply to pricing executives. These groups are composed of:

1. Companies which supply executives with standard costs without the application of any adjustments to the standards.
2. Companies in which the standard costs are adjusted by the ratio of actual costs to standard costs as shown by the variance accounts.
3. Companies which use current market prices for materials, and in a few cases for labor, with standard costs for other elements of product cost.
4. Companies which adjust standard costs to reflect the actual costs anticipated during the period for which the prices are to be in effect, including inflation's impact on costs.[4]

When standard costs are used for bid prices, they might be based on estimates previously submitted. However, while some materials parts or labor operations might be identical with those used for another product, executives need the most up-to-date information on all cost components in order to set a profitable price. Companies that must present bids adjust the costs developed from the detailed standards to approximate actual costs expected.

■ EFFECT OF THE ROBINSON-PATMAN ACT ON PRICING AND MARKETING EXPENSES

The Robinson-Patman Act of June, 1936, amended Section 2 of the Clayton Act, which was enacted to prevent large buyers from securing excessive advantages over their smaller competitors by virtue of their size and purchasing power. Since the Clayton Act prohibited discrimination only where it had a serious effect on competition in general, and since it contained no other provisions for the control of price discrimination, the act was amended to ensure competitive equality of the individual enterprise. The following clause (page 830) of the Robinson-Patman Act is of special interest in connection with marketing costs.

---

[4]Research Series, No. 14, "Standard Manufacturing Costs for Pricing and Budgeting," *NAA Bulletin*, Vol. XXX, No. 3, pp. 165-166.

To make it unlawful for any person engaged in commerce to discriminate in price or terms of sale between purchasers of commodities of like grades and quality, to prohibit the payment of brokerage or commissions under certain conditions; to suppress pseudo-advertising allowances; to provide a presumptive measure of damages in certain cases; and to protect the independent merchant, the public whom he serves, and the manufacturer who sells him his goods from exploitation by unfair competitors.

The Robinson-Patman Act intends to preclude price discrimination that decreases competition. The seller has three acceptable defenses for price cuts:

1. They resulted from changing conditions in the market place (discontinued products, distress sales, perishable goods, etc.).
2. They temporarily changed in a good-faith attempt to meet an equally low and lawful price of a competitor.
3. They reflect lower costs that resulted from different methods or quantities of sale or delivery.

The amendment does not imply that price discriminations in the sense of price differentials are entirely prohibited or that a seller is compelled or required to grant any price differential whatever. A vendor may sell to all customers at the same price regardless of differences in the cost of serving them. At the core of the amendment are the provisions that deal with charging different prices to different customers. To meet the third of the defenses for price cuts, differentials granted must not exceed differences in the cost of serving different customers. The cost of serving includes the cost of manufacturing, selling, and delivering, which may differ according to methods of selling and quantities sold. The burden of proof is on both the buyer and the seller and requires a definite justification for the discounts granted and received. It is necessary to prove that no discrimination took place with respect to (1) price differences, (2) discounts, (3) delivery service, (4) allowances for service, (5) advertising appropriations, (6) brokerage or commissions, or (7) consignment policies.

These possibilities for discrimination fall chiefly into the field of marketing expenses. Many interesting problems have arisen because of the nature of these expenses and the numerous variations and combinations in the manner of sale and delivery. As indicated, it is difficult to trace many marketing expenses to particular products. Therefore, it is important for concerns performing distribution functions to accumulate cost statistics regarding their marketing expenses, because the act makes allowances for differences in costs. The act increases the interest in marketing expense analysis and its part in the determination of prices. The cost justification study on page 831 illustrates this point.

A competitor who believes that discrimination exists must file a complaint substantiated by evidence acquired from published price lists or from other persuasive evidence of this kind. The complaint is valid if all of the following violations have been committed:

1. Price discrimination.
2. Discrimination between competitors.
3. Discrimination on products of like grades and quality.

COST JUSTIFICATION STUDY

A producer of heavy bulk chemical, which sells FOB point of manufacture at $25 a ton in minimum quantities of a full rail carload (approximately 40 tons), is offered a contract for 500 to 1,000 carloads a year if it will reduce its FOB shipping point price by 6 percent. The producer does not want to reduce the selling price to other customers, to whom annual shipments range from 10 to 200 carloads. The only source of cost differences is sales solicitation and service expense.

The sales manager estimates (since exact records are not available) that salespersons typically pursue the following call schedule:

Customer Size (in Carloads)	Annual Number of Sales Calls
10–40	12
41–80	24
81–150	36
151 and up	50

The sales manager further estimates that each sales call costs approximately $50-$70 regardless of customer size. After questioning, the manager agrees that study would probably show that calls on large customers (more than 100 carloads) are longer in duration than calls on smaller customers. For study and testing purposes, it was assumed that a call on a small customer costs $60 and a call on a large customer costs $90. The following cost-sales relationship can now be developed:

DIFFERENTIAL COST
LARGE VS. SMALL CUSTOMERS

	Annual Carloads per Customer				
	25	50	100	200	500
Sales value	$25,000	$50,000	$100,000	$200,000	$500,000
Number of sales calls	12	24	36	50	50
Assumed cost per call	$ 60	$ 60	$ 90	$ 90	$ 90
Assumed cost of call per customer	$ 720	$1,440	$3,240	$4,500	$4,500
Assumed cost of call as a percent of sales	2.9%	2.9%	3.2%	2.25%	0.9%

Since the assumed differential costs are less than the 6 percent proposed discount, it appears obvious that a discount of that magnitude is not susceptible to cost justification. Indeed, it is possible that even a one percent discount to a 500-carload customer might be hard to justify since it is probable that more exact costing would narrow the spread in the percentages among the various classes.

Adapted from "Cost Justification of Price Differences" by Herbert G. Whiting, *Management Services*, Vol. 3, No. 4, pp. 31-32. Reprinted with permission of the American Institute of Certified Public Accountants.

4. Discrimination in interstate commerce.
5. Injurious effect on competition.

The most effective method for a firm to answer any such complaint is to have a functional unit cost system for marketing expenses. In fact, no firm should be placed in a situation of having to make a cost study after being cited. Experience has proven that such belated cost justification studies seldom are successful. Therefore, the firm should (1) establish records that show that price differentials are extended only to the extent justified by maximum allowable cost savings and (2) maintain the cost data currently through spot checks conducted periodically to insure that the price differentials are in conformance with current cost conditions.

In justifying price differentials, marginal costing cannot be utilized; i.e., a plant operating at 80 percent capacity and wishing to add an order to increase its capacity to 90 percent cannot restrict its cost considerations to that incremental element of variable cost due to the volume change. The reduced cost per unit resulting from the greater volume must be spread over all units. Thus, the government, in consistently rejecting the marginal approach, endorses instead a method which is often called fully distributed cost analysis and only these fully distributed or average total costs are acceptable for a cost justification defense under the Robinson-Patman Act. The government has held that only identifiable savings, whether manufacturing or marketing, resulting from specific methods or quantities connected with given orders can be properly passed in their entirety to specific customers. For example, if the price difference is related to special manufacturing runs, then cost factors that can be considered include the differences between customer runs, which can cause a difference in unit costs. Typical of such costs are setup costs, skill and number of direct laborers, tool-wear costs, machine downtime, scrap rates, order scheduling, and inspection.

In general, the Robinson-Patman Act seems to work toward greater equity between prices, since pricing schedules appear to be more carefully attuned to differences in costs than they were before the enactment of this particular type of control. The accountant must be prepared to study the subject actively and continuously to help management avoid unintentional price discriminations that might be in violation of the law. The marketing manager must also follow the effect of any pricing policy to determine whether it is profitable and produces the kind of business necessary for the successful operation of the enterprise.

■ ILLUSTRATIVE PROBLEM IN MARKETING COST AND PROFITABILITY ANALYSIS

Ambler Company manufactures and sells a variety of small power tools, dies, drills, files, milling cutters, saws, and other miscellaneous hardware. The company's catalog lists the merchandise under sixteen major classifications. Customers fall into five categories: retail hardware stores, manufacturers, public school systems, municipalities, and public utilities. Territories include New Jersey and Pennsylvania. The company's president believes that in certain areas the cost of marketing the products is too high, that certain customers' orders do not contribute enough to cover fixed expenses and earn a profit, and that certain products are being sold to customers and in territories on an unprofitable basis. Therefore, the president has instructed the controller to review the firm's marketing expenses and to study the steps, methods, and procedures necessary to provide more accurate information about the profitability of territories, products, and customers.

The controller has designed and operated a standard marketing cost system which gives management the desired information for the control and analysis of marketing and administrative expenses. The preparation and assembling of statistical and cost data were carried out in the following sequence:

1. Total marketing expenses were estimated (or budgeted).
2. Six marketing functions (selling, warehousing, packing and shipping, advertising, credit and collection, general accounting) were established.
3. Direct expenses were assigned directly to functions; indirect expenses were allocated to functions via a measurement unit, such as kilowatt-hour, footage, or number of employees.
4. Fixed and variable expenses were determined for each function.
5. Functional unit measurement bases were selected for the purpose of assigning expenses to the segments to be analyzed, i.e., territory or product.
6. Functional unit measurements or bases applicable to a territory or a product were determined.
7. Unit standard manufacturing costs and standard product sales prices were established.
8. Data regarding the types and number of units sold in the territories were prepared.
9. Income statements by (a) territories and (b) product lines in one territory were prepared for management.

Exhibit 1 on page 834 summarizes the results of the study prepared by the controller. Column 1 shows the total budgeted expense per function. Each total is supported by a budget showing the amount for each individual expense of the function. Columns 2 and 3 classify total expenses as variable and fixed. Column 4 indicates the functional unit measurement selected. Column 5 lists the quantity or value of the measurement unit used to determine the functional unit expense rate. Columns 6, 7, and 8 indicate the variable, fixed, and total functional unit expense rates.

Exhibits 2 and 3 list the details necessary for the preparation of Exhibits 1, 4, and 5. To simplify the illustration, nonmanufacturing expenses other than marketing expenses have been excluded.

The product-line income statement for the territory of Pennsylvania (Exhibit 5) indicates that the volume and/or price of Product 1 is not sufficient to result in a profit. In Exhibit 6, this analysis is carried further with the aid of a fixed-variable analysis of manufacturing costs and marketing expenses to determine the contribution made by the product line to the total fixed cost and profit. This exhibit assumes all costs are allocated, both fixed and variable.

Next, the steps required to bring about an improvement in the profitability of this product line should be determined. Functional marketing expense analysis permits this type of analysis, which should eventually lead to a selective selling program supported by product break-even analyses and by cost-volume-profit and differential cost analyses (Chapters 20 and 21).

Exhibit 1
DETERMINATION OF FUNCTIONAL UNIT COSTING RATES

Function	Budgeted Expenses Total (1)	Variable (2)	Fixed (3)	Functional Unit Measurement Base (4)	Quantity (5)	Functional Unit Expense Rates Variable (6)	Fixed (7)	Total (8)
Selling	$ 95,500	$ 38,200	$ 57,300	Gross sales dollar value of product sold	$1,910,000	2%	3%	5%
Warehousing	75,000	45,000	30,000	Weight of units shipped	375,000	$ .12	$ .08	$ .20
Packing and shipping	63,000	37,500	25,500	Quantity of product units sold	150,000	.25	.17	.42
Advertising	54,000		54,000	Quantity of product units sold	150,000		.36	.36
Credit and collection	28,800	18,720	10,080	Number of customers' orders	7,200	2.60	1.40	4.00
General accounting	49,200	21,300	27,900	Number of times product items appear on customers' invoices	15,000	1.42	1.86	3.28
Total functional distribution expense	$365,500	$160,720	$204,780					

Exhibit 2
DATA CONCERNING TRANSACTIONS IN TERRITORIES

Territory	Quantity of Product Sold Product 1	Product 2	Product 3	Number of Times Product Items Appear on Customers' Invoices Product 1	Product 2	Product 3	Number of Customers' Orders Product 1	Product 2	Product 3
Pennsylvania	55,000	30,000	16,000	4,000	2,900	1,000	1,000	1,900	900
New Jersey	25,000	20,000	4,000	2,400	2,800	1,900	1,400	1,100	900

Exhibit 3

DATA CONCERNING PRICE, COST, QUANTITY, WEIGHT, AND TRANSACTIONS OF PRODUCTS

Product Class	Product 1	Product 2	Product 3
Standard product sales price	$10.00	$15.00	$18.00
Unit standard manufacturing cost	8.00	11.00	12.00
Quantity of product units sold	80,000	50,000	20,000
Weight of units shipped (kilograms)	2.25 kg	2.5 kg	3.5 kg
Number of times product items appear on customers' invoices.	6,400	5,700	2,900
Number of customers' orders.	2,400	3,000	1,800

Exhibit 4

INCOME STATEMENT FOR ALL PRODUCT CLASSES IN THE TWO TERRITORIES

	Total	Territory	
		Pennsylvania	New Jersey
Gross sales	$1,910,000	$1,288,000	$622,000
Less cost of goods sold	1,430,000	962,000	468,000
Gross profit	$ 480,000	$ 326,000	$154,000
Less marketing expenses:			
Selling	$ 95,500	$ 64,400	$ 31,100
Warehousing	75,000	50,950	24,050
Packing and shipping	63,000	42,420	20,580
Advertising	54,000	36,360	17,640
Credit and collection	28,800	15,200	13,600
General accounting	49,200	25,912	23,288
Total	$ 365,500	$ 235,242	$130,258
Operating income	$ 114,500	$ 90,758	$ 23,742

Exhibit 5

INCOME STATEMENT BY PRODUCT CLASSES IN THE PENNSYLVANIA TERRITORY

	Total	Product Class		
		Product 1	Product 2	Product 3
Gross sales	$1,288,000	$550,000	$450,000	$288,000
Less cost of goods sold	962,000	440,000	330,000	192,000
Gross profit	$ 326,000	$110,000	$120,000	$ 96,000
Less marketing expenses:				
Selling	$ 64,600	$ 27,500	$ 22,500	$ 14,400
Warehousing	50,950	24,750	15,000	11,200
Packing and shipping	42,420	23,100	12,600	6,720
Advertising	36,360	19,800	10,800	5,760
Credit and collection	15,200	4,000	7,600	3,600
General accounting	25,912	13,120	9,512	3,280
Total	$ 235,242	$112,270	$ 78,012	$ 44,960
Operating income (loss)	$ 90,758	$(2,270)	$ 41,988	$ 51,040

Exhibit 6

INCOME STATEMENT OF PRODUCT CLASS WITH FIXED-VARIABLE ANALYSIS OF MANUFACTURING AND MARKETING COSTS IN THE PENNSYLVANIA TERRITORY

		Product 1
Gross sales		$550,000
Less cost of goods sold (variable unit cost = 60% of $8)		264,000
Gross contribution margin		$286,000
Less variable marketing expenses:		
Selling	$ 11,000	
Warehousing	14,850	
Packing and shipping	13,750	
Credit and collection	2,600	
General accounting	5,680	47,880
Contribution margin		$238,120
Less fixed costs and expenses:		
Manufacturing cost—fixed	$176,000	
Marketing expenses—fixed:		
Selling	16,500	
Warehousing	9,900	
Packing and shipping	9,350	
Advertising	19,800	
Credit and collection	1,400	
General accounting	7,440	240,390
Operating loss—Product Class 1—Pennsylvania		$ (2,270)

DISCUSSION QUESTIONS

Q24-1. What general principles should be observed in planning a system of control for marketing expenses?

Q24-2. How should marketing expenses be classified in order to find the cost of selling jobs or products?

Q24-3. A method still commonly used today in analyzing marketing expenses is to relate them to either the total factory cost or the total sales value. This method is merely a relationship and not a scientific basis. Discuss.

Q24-4. Outline a procedure for determining the marketing expenses for a concern manufacturing two products. This organization uses national advertising and assigns salespersons to definite territories for contact with established dealers and also to secure additional retail outlets.

Q24-5. What are the objectives of profit analysis by sales territories?

Q24-6. What causes changes in the gross profit or contribution margin?

Q24-7. By what methods can a change in the gross profit or contribution margin be analyzed?

Q24-8. Whose task is it to see that the planned gross profit or contribution margin is met?

Q24-9. What difficulties may arise if an attempt is made to set standards for marketing expenses?

Q24-10. Explain briefly the difference between the profit approach and the contribution margin approach in marketing expense analysis.

Q24-11. Discuss the following statement: "Price setting is truly an art."

Q24-12. What accounting-based methods are available that might assist in the determination of a sales price?

Q24-13. Discuss the profit-maximization method of pricing.

Q24-14. Why are standard costs helpful in setting prices?

Q24-15. Why did the Robinson-Patman Act lead to the establishment of marketing expense procedures in business?

EXERCISES

E24-1. Controlling functional activity by using a flexible budget and standards. The flexible budget for the Warehousing Department of Abernathy Supply Company is as follows:

Expense	Functional Unit—Number of Transactions			
	1,000	2,000*	3,000	4,000
Supervision..........	$2,000	$2,000	$2,000	$2,000
Other labor..........	1,000	1,100	1,200	1,300
Depreciation.........	750	750	750	750
Supplies............	250	300	350	400
Insurance...........	250	250	250	250
Rent	200	200	200	200
Total expense........	$4,450	$4,600	$4,750	$4,900

*Normal capacity

During April, the Warehousing Department handled 1,800 transactions. The actual expense was $4,510.

Required: Compute the spending and idle capacity variances for the Warehousing Department.

E24-2. Marketing expense analysis by territories. Red River Hardware Company sells hardware items in New Mexico, Colorado, and Wyoming. Marketing expenses for the past quarter were as follows:

Sales salaries	$58,100		Advertising expense..........	$14,920
Sales commissions	8,460		Warehousing expense	2,940
Travel expense............	2,240		Collection expense...........	900

The company wishes to know the cost of distributing its products in each of the three states. A survey reveals the following information:

(a) Ten salespersons are employed (five in Colorado, three in New Mexico, and two in Wyoming). All are paid at the same base salary.

(b) Sales were as follows:

Salesperson	Colorado	New Mexico	Wyoming
#1............	$54,000	$11,000	$48,000
#2............	32,000	23,000	51,000
#3............	6,000	50,000	
#4............	49,000		
#5............	49,000		

(c) The following commission schedule has been established:

Sales for Each Salesperson	Commission (% of Sales)
For portion under $10,000	0%
For portion $10,000–$50,000	3
For portion over $50,000............	6

(d) Travel expense is allocated 4:3:1 among Colorado, New Mexico, and Wyoming, respectively.

(e) Advertising expense is allocated on the basis of sales.

(f) Warehousing expense is allocated by assigning Colorado and Wyoming $200 and $100, respectively, with the balance distributed in the same ratio as travel expense.

(g) A total of 15,000 remittances were received from customers, of which 3,000 were from Wyoming and 4,500 from New Mexico.

Required: Prepare a marketing expense analysis by territories, detailing each expense category.

E24-3. Income statement by customer classes. Central Manufacturing Company assembles a washing machine that is sold to three classes of customers. The data with respect to these customers are as follows:

Customer Class	Sales	Gross Profit	Number of Sales Calls	Number of Orders	Number of Invoice Lines
Department stores............	$180,000	$ 26,000	240	120	2,100
Retail appliance stores	240,000	80,000	360	580	4,600
Wholesalers.................	300,000	71,000	400	300	3,300
Total	$720,000	$177,000	1,000	1,000	10,000

Actual marketing costs for the year are:

Function	Costs	Measure of Activity
Selling	$65,000	Salespersons' calls
Packing and shipping	12,000	Customers' orders
Advertising.................	20,000	Dollar sales
Credit and collection.........	15,000	Invoice lines
General accounting..........	18,000	Customers' orders

Required: Prepare an income statement by customer classes, with functional distribution of marketing expenses. (When allocating the advertising expense, round to the nearest $100.)

E24-4. Contribution margin analysis. A cost analyst has prepared a monthly contribution margin analysis for Clifton Corporation, comparing actual to budget for the company's two products, Dee and Zee. August budget and actual data follow:

		Sales			Variable Costs		Contribution Margin	
	Units	Unit Price	Amount	Unit Cost	Amount	Per Unit	Amount
Budget:							
Dee	20,000	$9.00	$180,000	$5.00	$100,000	$4.00	$ 80,000
Zee.........	15,000	7.50	112,500	4.00	60,000	3.50	52,500
Total	35,000		$292,500		$160,000		$132,500
Actual:							
Dee	19,000	9.50	$180,500	5.40	$102,600	4.10	$ 77,900
Zee.........	17,000	7.30	124,100	4.20	71,400	3.10	52,700
Total	36,000		$304,600		$174,000		$130,600

Required: Compute the price and volume variances for sales and cost, the sales mix, and final sales volume variances.

E24-5. Gross profit analysis. Spiffy Sporting Goods Shop presents the following data for two types of racquetball gloves, leather and fabric, for 19A and 19B:

	19A			19B		
	Units	Per Unit	Amount	Units	Per Unit	Amount
Sales:						
Leather racquetball gloves	8,000	$8.00	$64,000	12,000	$10.00	$120,000
Fabric racquetball gloves	8,000	4.00	32,000	20,000	6.00	120,000
			$96,000			$240,000
Cost of goods sold:						
Leather racquetball gloves	8,000	$6.00	$48,000	12,000	$ 9.00	$108,000
Fabric racquetball gloves	8,000	3.00	24,000	20,000	5.00	100,000
			$72,000			$208,000
Gross profit	16,000	$1.50	$24,000	32,000	$ 1.00	$ 32,000

Required: Compute the price and volume variances for sales and cost, the sales mix, and final sales volume variances.

E24-6. Salesperson's performance reports. A corporate budget director designed a control scheme in order to compare and evaluate the efforts of the company's three salespersons and the results attained. Specifically, each salesperson is to make five calls per day; the budget provides for $40 per day per salesperson for travel and entertainment expenses; each salesperson was assigned a sales quota of $400 a day. The Budget Department collects the data on actual performance from the daily sales reports and the weekly expense vouchers and then prepares a monthly report. This report includes variances from standard and performance indexes. For the performance index, standard performance equals 100.

The records for November, with 20 working days, show:

Salesperson	Sales Calls	Travel Expenses	Sales
Palmer, K.	70	$1,000	$14,000
Thompson, J.	100	800	8,400
Miller, O.	120	720	6,000

Required: Prepare a monthly report comparing the standard and actual performances of the salespersons, including the performance indexes for (1) sales calls, (2) travel expenses, (3) sales, and (4) sales revenue per call.

 E24-7. Product-line income statement—contribution margin approach. Pralina Products Company has three major product lines—cereals, breakfast bars, and dog food. The income statement on page 840 for the year ended April 30 was prepared by product line, using full cost allocation.

Explanatory data:

(a) Cost of goods sold. The company's inventories of materials and finished products do not vary significantly from year to year. Factory overhead was applied to products at 120% of direct labor dollars. The factory overhead costs for the year were as follows:

Variable indirect labor and supplies.	$ 15,000
Variable employee benefits on factory labor	30,000
Supervisory salaries and related benefits	35,000
Plant occupancy cost	100,000
	$180,000

There was no over- or underapplied factory overhead at year end.

(b) Advertising. The company has been unable to determine any direct causal relationship between the level of sales volume and the level of advertising expenditures. However, because management be-

Pralina Products Company
Income Statement
For the Year Ended April 30, 19--
(In Thousands)

	Cereals	Breakfast Bars	Dog Food	Total
Sales (in pounds).....................................	2,000	500	500	3,000
Revenue from sales..................................	$1,000	$400	$200	$1,600
Cost of goods sold:				
Materials......................................	$ 330	$160	$100	$ 590
Direct labor...................................	90	40	20	150
Factory overhead	108	48	24	180
Total cost of goods sold......................	$ 528	$248	$144	$ 920
Gross profit	$ 472	$152	$ 56	$ 680
Commercial expenses:				
Marketing expenses:				
Advertising	$ 50	$ 30	$ 20	$ 100
Commissions	50	40	20	110
Sales salaries and related benefits	30	20	10	60
Total marketing expense......................	$ 130	$ 90	$ 50	$ 270
General and administrative expenses:				
Licenses	$ 50	$ 20	$ 15	$ 85
Salaries and related benefits...................	60	25	15	100
Total general and administrative expenses	$ 110	$ 45	$ 30	$ 185
Total commercial expense...........................	$ 240	$135	$ 80	$ 455
Operating income	$ 232	$ 17	$ (24)	$ 225

lieves advertising is necessary, an annual advertising program has been implemented for each product line, independent of the others.

(c) Commissions. Sales commissions are paid to the sales force at the rate of 5% on the cereals and 10% on the breakfast bars and dog food.

(d) Licenses. Various licenses are required for each product line, renewed annually for each product line at a fixed amount.

(e) Salaries and related benefits. Sales and general and administrative personnel devote time and effort to all product lines. Their salaries and wages are allocated on the basis of management's estimates of time spent on each product line.

(f) Fixed factory overhead, salaries and related benefits for sales and general and administrative personnel are not traceable to individual product lines on any objective basis.

Required: Prepare a product-line income statement, using the contribution margin approach.   (ICMA adapted)

E24-8. Determining advertising costs. The Kirsty Company produces and sells three products—Economy, Standard, and Deluxe. The following actual results for the current year are based on absorption costing:

	Economy	Standard	Deluxe	Total
Sales in units	2,500	2,000	3,500	8,000
Sales revenue.........................	$50,000	$80,000	$70,000	$200,000
Cost of goods sold	30,000	40,000	50,000	120,000
Gross profit...........................	$20,000	$40,000	$20,000	$ 80,000
Operating expenses:				
Sales commissions...................	$ 5,000	$ 8,000	$ 7,000	$ 20,000
Allocated head office expenses	7,500	12,000	10,500	30,000
Total.............................	$12,500	$20,000	$17,500	$ 50,000
Income from products	$ 7,500	$20,000	$ 2,500	$ 30,000

	Total
Income from products	$ 30,000
Unallocated head office expenses	20,000
Net income before taxes	$ 10,000
Income tax expenses (45%)	4,500
Net income after taxes	$ 5,500

All of the head office expenses are fixed, and 60% of the manufacturing costs are fixed. The company is considering the implementation of an advertising campaign which is expected to increase the sales of Deluxe by 40% and the sales of Standard by 80%; however, the increased sales volume of these two products would cause a 20% decrease in the sales volume of Economy.

Required: Determine the maximum amount that the company could afford to spend on advertising if it wants to achieve a net income after taxes of $22,000. (SMAC adapted)

SS **E24-9. Product pricing.** Mercado Company is considering changing its sales price of Salien, which is presently $15. Increases and decreases of both 10% and 25%, as well as increases in advertising and promotion expenditures, are being considered, with the following estimated results for 19A and 19B:

Price	Estimated Unit Sales 19A	Estimated Unit Sales 19B	Estimated Advertising and Promotion Expenditures 19A	Estimated Advertising and Promotion Expenditures 19B
−25%	190,000	200,000	$200,000	$210,000
−10%	180,000	190,000	250,000	250,000
No change	160,000	170,000	300,000	300,000
+10%	140,000	150,000	400,000	450,000
+25%	130,000	140,000	450,000	550,000

The company has the necessary flexibility in its production capacity to meet these volume levels. The variable manufacturing cost per unit of Salien is estimated to be $7.25 in 19A and $7.80 in 19B.

Required: Determine the recommended sales price. (ICMA adapted)

E24-10. Contribution margin approach to pricing. The Gelotech Company is a large manufacturer of refrigeration units. The firm's product line includes refrigerators for homes, industry, and ships. The firm is composed of three divisions. The Motor Division is responsible for manufacturing the motors for all of the various refrigeration units. In the Shell Division, the refrigerator shells are produced and the motors transferred from the Motor Division are installed. The Marketing Division is responsible for the sale and distribution of the final product.

While a market exists outside the firm for both the motors and shells, the transfer price between divisions is set by executive management. This is done to avoid unnecessary friction, which management feels might impair efficiency and prove wasteful.

Recently the company was asked to submit a bid for 100 refrigeration units for a local shipbuilding firm. The following unit cost estimate has been prepared:

	Motor	Shell	Marketing
Manufacturing materials	$195	$ 180	—
Receiving and handling (60% fixed)	10	25	$ 20
Motor	—	600	—
Refrigeration units	—	—	1,240
Shipping materials	—	—	30
Direct labor	190	220	35
Factory overhead:			
Fixed	55	45	15
Variable	100	80	10
General administrative cost	28	57	67
Transfer price	600	1,240	—

Prior to submitting its bid, Gelotech has learned that its principal competitor has submitted a bid of $1,200 per unit.

Required: Prepare an analysis to determine whether or not Gelotech can match the competitor's bid.

PROBLEMS

P24-1. Standard cost variance analysis; revision of sales prices. Delgado Corporation's actual and standard (for budgeted hours) marketing costs for January are:

	Budget at Standard Cost	Actual
Sales	$750,000	$750,000
Direct marketing costs:		
Selling	$ 12,000	$ 15,000
Shipping salaries	21,000	28,350
Indirect marketing costs:		
Order filling	17,250	21,500
Other costs	2,100	2,500
Total cost	$ 52,350	$ 67,350

Additional data:

(a) The company sells one product at $10 per unit.

(b) The other indirect marketing costs and shipping salaries are allocated on the basis of shipping hours. January shipping hours are:

Budgeted hours	3,500
Standard hours (at January operating level)	4,400
Actual hours	4,500

(c) Order-filling costs are allocated on the basis of sales and are comprised of freight, packing, and warehousing costs. An analysis of the amount of these standard costs by unit order size follows:

Unit-Volume Classification	Order-Filling Standard Costs Classified by Unit Order Size			
	1-15	16-50	Over 50	Total
Freight	$ 1,200	$ 1,440	$ 2,250	$ 4,890
Packing	2,400	3,240	4,500	10,140
Warehousing	600	720	900	2,220
Total	$ 4,200	$ 5,400	$ 7,650	$17,250
Units sold	12,000	18,000	45,000	75,000

Management realizes that the marketing cost per unit decreases with an increase in the size of the order and, hence, wants to revise its unit sales prices upward or downward on the basis of the quantity ordered in proportion to the allocated freight, packing, and warehousing standard costs. Management assumes that the revised unit prices will require no changes in standards for sales volume, the number of units sold in each order-size classification, and the profit per unit sold.

Required:

(1) Compute and analyze variances from standard cost for (a) other indirect marketing costs and (b) shipping salaries. The analysis should compare actual and standard costs at the January standard operating level.

(Continued)

(2) Prepare a schedule computing the standard cost per unit for each order-filling cost in each unit-volume classification. Use the same format as in item (c).

(3) Prepare a schedule computing the revised unit sales prices for each unit-volume classification.

(AICPA adapted)

P24-2. Marketing cost analysis by territories. Starnes Company sells toiletries to retail stores throughout the United States. For planning and control purposes, the company is organized into twelve geographic regions, with two to six territories within each region. One salesperson is assigned to each territory and has exclusive rights to all sales made in that territory. Merchandise is shipped from the manufacturing plant to the twelve regional warehouses, from which the sales in each territory are shipped. National headquarters allocates a specific amount at the beginning of the year for regional advertising.

The net sales for Starnes Company for the six months ended September 30 total $10 million. Costs incurred by national headquarters are:

National administration	$250,000
National advertising.	125,000
National warehousing	175,000
	$550,000

The results of operations for the South Atlantic Region for the six months ended September 30 are:

Starnes Company
Statement of Operations for South Atlantic Region
For the Six Months Ended September 30, 19A

Sales		$900,000
Costs and expenses:		
Advertising fees.	$ 54,700	
Uncollectible accounts expense	3,600	
Cost of goods sold	460,000	
Freight out	22,600	
Insurance.	10,000	
Salaries and employee benefits	81,600	
Sales commissions	36,000	
Supplies.	12,000	
Travel and entertainment.	14,100	
Wages and employee benefits	36,000	
Warehouse depreciation	8,000	
Warehouse operating cost	15,000	753,600
Territory contribution		$146,400

The South Atlantic Region consists of two territories—Green and Purple. The salaries and employee benefits consist of the following items:

Regional vice-president	$24,000
Regional marketing manager.	15,000
Regional warehouse manager.	13,400
Salespersons (one for each territory, with both receiving the same salary base)	15,600
Employee benefits (20%).	13,600
	$81,600

The salespersons receive a base salary plus a 4% commission on all items sold in their territory. Uncollectible accounts expense has averaged .4% of sales in the past. Travel and entertainment costs are incurred by the salespersons in calling upon their customers and are based on a fixed authorized amount. Freight out is a function of the quantity of goods shipped and the distance shipped. Thirty percent of the insurance is expended for protection of the inventory while it is in the regional warehouse, and the remainder is incurred for the protection of the warehouse. Supplies are used in the warehouse for packing the merchandise to be shipped. Wages (a variable cost) relate to the hourly employees who fill orders in the warehouse. The warehouse operating cost account contains such costs as heat, light, and maintenance.

The following cost analyses and statistics by territory for the current period are representative of past experience and of expected future operations:

	Green	Purple	Total
Sales......................	$300,000	$600,000	$900,000
Cost of goods sold*...........	184,000	276,000	460,000
Advertising fees..............	21,800	32,900	54,700
Travel and entertainment........	6,300	7,800	14,100
Freight out..................	9,000	13,600	22,600
Units sold..................	150,000	350,000	500,000
Pounds shipped**.............	210,000	390,000	600,000
Sales travel (miles)............	21,600	38,400	60,000

*Use to allocate inventory insurance to territories.
**Use to allocate supplies and wages and employee benefits to territories.

The executive management of Starnes Company wants the regional vice-presidents to present their operating data in a more meaningful manner. Therefore, management has requested that the regions separate their operating costs into the fixed and variable components of order-getting, order-filling, and administrative. The data are to be presented in the following format:

	Territory Cost		Regional Cost	Total Cost
	Green	Purple		
Order-getting.........				
Order-filling..........				
Administrative........				

Required:

(1) Using management's suggested format, prepare a statement which presents the cost for the region by territory, with the costs separated into variable and fixed categories.
(2) Identify the data that are relevant to making a decision for or against splitting the Purple Territory into two separate territories (Red and Blue). Specify other data needed to aid management in its decision.
(3) Explain the use of standards and flexible budgets for planning and controlling marketing costs, assuming that Starnes Company keeps its records in accordance with the classification required in (1).
(ICMA adapted)

P24-3. Income statements by products and amount-of-order classes. The feasibility of allocating marketing and administrative expenses to products or amount-of-order classes for managerial purposes has been considered by Brentwood Company. It is apparent that some costs can be assigned equitably to these classifications, while others cannot. The company's cost analyst proposed the following bases for apportionment:

	Type of Analysis	
Expense	By Products	By Amount of Order
Sales salaries...............	Not allocated	Sales dollars times number of customers in class
Sales travel.................	Not allocated	Number of customers in class
Sales office.................	Not allocated	Number of customers in class
Sales commissions...........	Direct	Direct
Credit management...........	Sales in dollars	Number of customers in class
Packing and shipping..........	Weight	Weight
Warehousing.................	Weight	Weight
Advertising.................	Not allocated	Not allocated
Bookkeeping and billing........	Sales in dollars	Number of orders
General marketing and administrative...............	Not allocated	Not allocated

From books, records, and other sources, the following data have been compiled:

Amount of Order	Number of Customers	Number of Orders	Cost of Goods Sold	Total Sales	Products Sales		
					X	Y	Z
Under $25	1,000	6,000	$ 59,000	$ 100,000	$ 35,000	$ 40,000	$ 25,000
$26-$100	250	4,000	177,000	300,000	105,000	120,000	75,000
$101-$200	100	4,000	354,000	600,000	210,000	240,000	150,000
Over $200	50	1,000	236,000	400,000	140,000	160,000	100,000
Total	1,400	15,000	$826,000	$1,400,000	$490,000	$560,000	$350,000

Other data:

Product	Weight	Cost of Goods Sold	Units Sold
X	1 kg	$252,000	98,000
Y	3 kg	294,000	70,000
Z	2 kg	280,000	175,000

Marketing and administrative expenses for the year:

Sales salaries	$ 38,250
Sales travel	28,000
Sales office (variable)	15,400
Sales commissions (5%).	70,000
Credit management.	14,000
Packing and shipping	32,900
Warehousing	16,450
Advertising.	150,000
Bookkeeping and billing	42,000
General marketing and administrative	90,000
Total	$497,000

Required:

(1) Prepare a product income statement showing the allocation of marketing and administrative expenses to each product.
(2) Prepare an income statement showing the allocation of marketing and administrative expenses to each order class.

(For both requirements, round all base computations to five decimal places and all allocated amounts to the nearest dollar.)

P24-4. Cost allocations to individual stores; sales expansion decision. Amar Supermarkets Corporation operates a chain of three retail stores in a state that permits municipalities to levy an income tax on businesses operating within their respective boundaries. The tax rate is uniform in all of the municipalities that levy the tax, and does not vary according to taxable income. Regulations provide that the tax is to be computed on income earned within the particular taxing municipality, after reasonable and consistent allocation of the corporation's overhead. Amar's overhead consists of expenses pertaining to the warehouse, central office, advertising, and delivery.

Management has engaged a CPA firm to evaluate two corporation overhead allocation plans that are being considered, so that operating results under both plans can be compared. In addition, management has decided to expand one of the stores in a plan to increase sales by $80,000. The contemplated expansion is expected to increase local fixed operating costs by $8,000 and to require 10 additional deliveries from the warehouse. The CPA firm has been requested to furnish management with a recommendation as to which store should be selected for the prospective expansion.

For the current year ending on December 31, operating results for each store, before taxes and allocation of corporate overhead were as follows:

	Birch	Maple	Spruce	Total
Sales	$500,000	$400,000	$300,000	$1,200,000
Cost of goods sold	280,000	230,000	190,000	700,000
Gross profit	$220,000	$170,000	$110,000	$ 500,000
Local operating expenses:				
Fixed	$ 70,000	$ 60,000	$ 50,000	$ 180,000
Variable	66,000	73,000	31,000	170,000
Total	$136,000	$133,000	$ 81,000	$ 350,000
Income before corporate overhead and taxes	$ 84,000	$ 37,000	$ 29,000	$ 150,000

For the current year, corporate overhead was as follows:

Warehouse and delivery:		
Warehouse depreciation	$10,000	
Warehouse operations	15,000	
Delivery expenses	35,000	$ 60,000
Central office:		
Advertising	$ 8,000	
Salaries	30,000	
Other	2,000	40,000
Total corporate overhead		$100,000

Delivery expenses vary with distances from the warehouse and numbers of deliveries to stores. Delivery statistics for the current year follow:

Store	Miles from Warehouse	Number of Deliveries	Delivery Miles
Birch	100	150	15,000
Maple....	200	50	10,000
Spruce...	25	200	5,000

Required:

(1) Compute each store's income that would be subject to the municipal income tax under the following two plans:
  (a) All corporate overhead allocated on the basis of sales.
  (b) Central office salaries and other central office overhead allocated equally to warehouse operations and to each store first; the resulting warehouse operations costs, warehouse depreciation, and advertising allocated to each store on the basis of sales second; and delivery expenses allocated to each store on the basis of delivery miles last.

(2) Compute each store's increase in relevant expenses, including delivery expenses, before allocation of other corporation overhead and taxes as a result of the contemplated expansion. Determine which of the three stores should be selected for expansion to maximize corporation net income.

(AICPA adapted)

P24-5. Statement of product line contribution margin. Stratford Corporation is a diversified company whose products are marketed both domestically and internationally. The company's major product lines are pharmaceutical products, sports equipment, and household appliances. At the recent meeting of Stratford's board of directors, there was a lengthy discussion on ways to improve overall corporate profits without new acquisitions because the company is already heavily leveraged. The members of the board decided that they required additional financial information about individual corporate operations in order to target areas for improvement.

D. Murphy, Stratford's controller, has been asked to provide additional data that would assist the board in its investigation. Stratford is not a public company and, therefore, has not prepared complete income statements by segment. Murphy regularly has prepared an income statement by product line through contribution margin. However, Murphy now believes that income statements prepared through operating income along both product lines and geographical areas would provide the directors with the required insight into corporate operations.

The following data are available:

	Product Lines			
	Pharma-ceutical	Sports Equipment	Appliances	Total
Production/sales in units	160,000	180,000	160,000	500,000
Average sales price per unit	$8.00	$20.00	$15.00	
Average variable manufacturing cost per unit	4.00	9.50	8.25	
Average variable marketing expense per unit.	2.00	2.50	2.25	
Fixed factory overhead excluding depreciation				$ 500,000
Depreciation of plant and equipment.				400,000
Administrative and marketing expenses				1,160,000

Murphy had several discussions with the division managers for each product line and compiled the following information from these meetings:

(a) The division managers concluded that Murphy should allocate fixed factory overhead on the basis of the ratio of variable costs expended per product line or per geographic area to total variable costs.

(b) Each of the division managers agreed that a reasonable basis for the allocation of depreciation on plant and equipment would be the ratio of units produced per product line or per geographical area to the total number of units produced.

(c) There was little agreement on the allocation of administrative and marketing expenses so Murphy decided to allocate only those expenses that were directly traceable to the segment being delineated; i.e., manufacturing staff salaries to product lines and marketing staff salaries to geographic areas. Murphy used the following data for this allocation.

Manufacturing Staff		Marketing Staff	
Pharmaceutical.	$120,000	U.S.	$ 60,000
Sports equipment	140,000	Canada	100,000
Appliances.	80,000	Europe.	250,000

(d) The division managers were able to provide reliable sales percentages for their product lines by geographic area.

	Percentage of Unit Sales		
	U.S.	Canada	Europe
Pharmaceutical	40%	10%	50%
Sports equipment	40	40	20
Appliances.	20	20	60

Murphy prepared the product line income statement (on page 848) based on the data presented above.

Required:

(1) Prepare a segmented income statement for Stratford Corporation based on the company's geographic areas of sales. The statement should show the operating income for each segment.

(2) As a result of the information disclosed by both segmented income statements (by product line and by geographical area), recommend areas where Stratford Corporation should focus its attention in order to improve corporate profits.
(ICMA adapted)

Stratford Corporation
Statement of Income by Product Lines
For the Fiscal Year Ended April 30, 19A

| | Product Lines | | | | |
	Pharma-ceutical	Sports Equipment	Appliances	Unallocated	Total
Sales in units	160,000	180,000	160,000		
Sales revenue	$1,280,000	$3,600,000	$2,400,000	—	$7,280,000
Variable manufacturing and marketing costs	960,000	2,160,000	1,680,000	—	4,800,000
Contribution margin	$ 320,000	$1,440,000	$ 720,000	—	$2,480,000
Fixed costs:					
Factory overhead	$ 100,000	$ 225,000	$ 175,000	—	$ 500,000
Depreciation	128,000	144,000	128,000	—	400,000
Administrative and marketing expenses	120,000	140,000	80,000	$ 820,000	1,160,000
Total fixed costs	$ 348,000	$ 509,000	$ 383,000	$ 820,000	$2,060,000
Operating income	$ (28,000)	$ 931,000	$ 337,000	$(820,000)	$ 420,000

 P24-6. Contribution margin analysis. Tribal Products Inc. was organized ten years ago by James Littlebear for the purpose of making and selling souvenirs to tourists in Southwestern Arizona. After much experimentation, the product line has been limited to five products: moccasins, strings of beads, rawhide vests, leather belts, and feathered headdresses. All transactions take place in two small buildings located on tribal land.

In 19B, despite an increase in the total number of units sold, the contribution margin of the firm dropped. As a result, Littlebear tentatively blamed the drop in profit on a change in the sales mix.

The accountant has been given the task of analyzing the contribution margin of the past two years, shown as follows, in an attempt to pin down the cause of the loss in profits.

| | | | | 19A | | |
	Product	Quantity	Unit Variable Cost	Total Variable Cost	Unit Sales Price	Total Sales	Contribution Margin
Moccasins	1,000	$2.50	$ 2,500	$5.00	$ 5,000	$ 2,500
Beads	6,000	.20	1,200	.50	3,000	1,800
Vests	1,500	1.75	2,625	3.50	5,250	2,625
Belts	4,000	.45	1,800	1.00	4,000	2,200
Headdresses	500	4.00	2,000	7.50	3,750	1,750
Total	13,000		$10,125		$21,000	$10,875

| | | | | 19B | | |
	Product	Quantity	Unit Variable Cost	Total Variable Cost	Unit Sales Price	Total Sales	Contribution Margin
Moccasins	1,100	$2.60	$2,860	$5.00	$ 5,500	$ 2,640
Beads	6,800	.20	1,360	.50	3,400	2,040
Vests	1,200	1.80	2,160	3.50	4,200	2,040
Belts	4,200	.50	2,100	1.00	4,200	2,100
Headdresses	350	3.80	1,330	7.50	2,625	1,295
Total	13,650		$9,810		$19,925	$10,115

Required: Prepare an analysis of the decline in contribution margin from 19A to 19B (Round the 19A average contribution margin per unit to four decimal places.)

 P24-7. Gross profit analysis. H. Pacer is the general manager for Ace Chemical Supply Company. The following is the company's gross profit data for November, in thousands of dollars:

	Actual	Budget
Sales....................	$14,005	$12,600
Cost of goods sold........	11,323	9,850
Gross profit.............	$ 2,682	$ 2,750

Pacer knew before receiving the statement that sales were above budget for the month and that the effect of recent price increases on most products would be realized this month. Upset upon finding that income results were below budget while sales were more than 10% above budget, Pacer asked the Accounting Department for an explanation. The Accounting Department looked at the detailed budget and found the following data:

Product	Sales in Pounds (In Thousands)	Sales Price per Pound	Cost of Goods Sold per Pound	Gross Profit (In Thousands)
1	2,000	$ .60	$ .60	
2	5,000	.80	.65	$ 750
3	7,000	.20	.12	560
4	4,000	1.50	1.14	1,440
	18,000			$2,750

$2,750 \div 18,000 = \$.1528$ budgeted gross profit per pound

The following gross profit data pertain to November results:

Product	Sales in Pounds (In Thousands)	Sales Price per Pound	Sales in Dollars (In Thousands)	Cost of Goods Sold (In Thousands)	Gross Profit (In Thousands)
1	2,845	$ .735	$ 2,091	$ 1,692	$ 399
2	3,280	1.023	3,355	3,240	115
3	7,340	.195	1,431	991	440
4	4,320	1.650	7,128	5,400	1,728
	17,785		$14,005	$11,323	$2,682

Required: Compute the price and volume variances for sales and cost, the final sales mix, and final sales volume variances.

(Based on a problem in *Management Accounting Campus Report*)

 P24-8. Product pricing. Brazos Corporation produces an electronic component. Product demand is highly elastic within a specified range. At present, 100,000 units are sold at $10 each, and the additional demand expected with price reductions is as follows:

Unit Price	Units of Estimated Demand
$9.75	120,000
9.50	150,000
9.25	190,000
9.00	240,000
8.75	300,000

Present capacity is 125,000 units. Further estimates are that the first capacity increase of 75,000 units will require a $500,000 capital expenditure and, including depreciation, will increase annual fixed costs by $100,000 from the present $250,000 level. Each subsequent addition of 75,000 units of capacity will require further capital investment of $450,000 and will increase annual fixed costs by $75,000. Commercial expenses included in the present $250,000 figure will not change at the higher volumes. The board of directors will not approve additional capital expenditures unless a minimum pretax return of 20% is anticipated.

Other unit costs are estimated as follows:

	Less Than 150,000	150,000 to 200,000*	More Than 200,000*
Direct materials	$4.00	$3.80	$3.60
Direct labor	1.00	1.00	1.10
Variable factory overhead and commercial expenses	1.00	1.00	1.00

*Average costs for total production.

Required: Prepare a profitability statement at the various operating volumes, including the required 20% return on additional investment.

P24-9. Contribution margin approach to pricing. J. Schifflein manufactures custom-made pleasure boats ranging in price from $10,000 to $250,000. For the past thirty years, Schifflein has determined each boat's sales price by estimating the costs of materials, labor, and a prorated portion of overhead and by adding 20% to these estimated costs. For example, a recent price quotation was determined as follows:

Direct materials	$ 5,000
Direct labor	8,000
Overhead	2,000
	$15,000
Plus 20%	3,000
Sales price	$18,000

The overhead figure was determined by estimating the total overhead cost for the year and allocating it at 25% of direct labor.

If a customer rejects the price and business is slack, Schifflein is often willing to reduce the markup to as little as 5% over estimated costs. Thus average markup for the year is estimated at 15%.

Schifflein has just completed a pricing course and believes that the company could use some of the modern techniques taught in the course. The course emphasized the contribution margin approach to pricing, and Schifflein feels that such an approach would be helpful in determining the sales prices of custom-made pleasure boats.

Total overhead (including marketing and administrative expenses for the year) has been estimated at $150,000, of which $90,000 is fixed and the remainder is variable in direct proportion to direct labor.

Required:

(1) (a) Compute the difference in profit for the year if a customer's offer of $15,000 instead of the $18,000 quotation shown above is accepted.
   (b) Determine the minimum sales price Schifflein could have quoted without reducing or increasing profit.
(2) State the advantages that the contribution margin approach to pricing has over the approach used by Schifflein.
(3) Identify the pitfalls, if any, in contribution margin pricing.   (ICMA adapted)

CASES

C24-1. Use of standard rates and selection of cost allocation bases. Cintron Company is a regional office supply chain with 26 independent stores. Each store has been responsible for its own credit and collections. The assistant manager in each store has been assigned the responsibility for credit activities, including the collection of delinquent accounts, because the stores do not need a full-time employee assigned to credit activities. The company has experienced a sharp rise in uncollectibles the last two years. Therefore, corporate management has decided to establish a Collections Department in the home office to be responsible for the collection function company-wide. The home office will hire the necessary full-time personnel. The size of this department will be based upon the historical credit activity of all of the stores.

The new centralized Collections Department was discussed at a recent management meeting. A method to assign the costs of the new department to the stores has been difficult to determine because this type of home office service is somewhat unique. Alternative methods are being reviewed by executive management. The controller favors using a standard rate for charging the costs to the stores. The standard rate would be based on budgeted costs. The vice-president of sales has a strong preference for an actual cost charging system.

In addition, the basis for the collection charges to the stores was discussed. The controller identified the following measures of services (allocation bases) which could be used:

(a) Total dollar sales.
(b) Average number of past-due accounts.
(c) Number of uncollectible accounts written off.
(d) One twenty-sixth of the cost to each of the stores.

The executive vice-president stated that he would like the Accounting Department to prepare a detailed analysis of the two charging methods and the four allocation bases.

Required:

(1) Evaluate the two methods identified—standard rate versus actual cost—in terms of:

  (a) Practicality and ease of use.
  (b) Cost control.

(2) For each allocation base, discuss whether or not it is appropriate to use in this situation, and identify possible behavioral problems.   (ICMA adapted)

C24-2. Marketing profitability analysis of product lines. Travil Corporation has been manufacturing high quality wood furniture for over 50 years. Travil's five product lines are Mediterranean, Modern, Colonial, Victorian, and the recently introduced Country. Business has been very good for Travil recently.

Part of the reason for Travil's recent success has been the ability of S. Grant, chief execu-

tive officer. Grant has assembled a first-rate top management team that has now been together for the past four years. All major decisions are made by this centralized top management team after thorough study and review. Many members of top management were not expecting Grant's suggestion at a regular staff meeting that management should consider dropping the Victorian line—Travil's oldest furniture line.

Grant indicated that Victorian sales had dropped in total and as a percentage of Travil's total sales during the last three years. This conclusion was supported by the following schedule that shows sales percentages by line for the last three years.

Product-Line Sales Percentage

Year	Mediteranean	Modern	Colonial	Victorian	Country	Total
19A	31%	26%	21%	20%	2%	100%
19B	28	28	21	14	9	100
19C	24	26	23	10	17	100

T. Mills, vice-president of sales, commented that the data did not reflect important regional differences in the market. Victorian total sales of $431,000 in 19C were almost entirely in New England and New York. In fact, Victorian sales constituted over one-half of all Travil sales in some of these locations. Mills indicated that more Victorian could be sold if Production could produce it, and that if the Victorian line is dropped, at least two top salespersons would likely be lost to competitors in New England.

However, Mills also conceded that many sales have been lost in other sales regions due to the long lead time on Country. Furthermore, Colonial had obviously benefited from the popularity of Country. In fact, sales in Colonial were dangerously ahead of supply.

B. Jamison, vice-president of production, pointed out that production of all lines was possible in existing facilities. However, Jamison also indentified several problems with the Victorian line. The Victorian line is the least mechanized of Travil's lines, due in part to the high degree of detailed workmanship required. Furthermore, the equipment is old and outdated, requiring increased amounts of maintenance in recent years. The craftsmen needed to maintain the Victorian quality that had become Travil's greatest asset are just not available in the labor market anymore, making it difficult to support increased production. Several of Travil's craftsmen would need special training on their new production assignments if the Victorian line were eliminated. Jamison also indicated that margins on the Victorian line had dwindled due to the relative labor-intensity on that line and the high union wages of the skilled craftsmen. Dropping the Victorian line would also cause $80,000 worth of fabric in inventory to become totally obsolete.

Grant asked R. Turner, chief financial officer, to collect and assimilate the necessary data to aid in the evaluation of whether to keep or drop the Victorian line. As the staff meeting closed, Grant stated, "Eventually we might consider expansion, but currently we must consider our present markets and resources."

Required:

(1) Discuss the type and nature of information that R. Turner should provide to the rest of Travil Corporation's top management team to assist in the decision to keep or drop the Victorian line. Give specific examples of information that Turner should prepare and present.
(2) If the management of Travil Corporation decides to drop the Victorian line for purposes of strengthening the remaining product lines, discuss:

(a) How Travil should communicate this decision to its employees.
(b) The steps that should be taken when operating results become available to review the decision.   (ICMA adapted)

C24-3. Marketing profitability analysis by products and by salespersons. Caprice Company manufactures and sells two products, a small portable office file cabinet that it has made for over 15 years and a home-travel file introduced in 19A. The files are made in Caprice's only manufacturing plant. Budgeted variable production costs per unit of product are as follows:

	Office File	Home-Travel File
Sheet metal	$ 3.50	—
Plastic	—	$3.75
Direct labor (@ $8 per DLH)	4.00	2.00
Variable factory overhead (@ $9 per DLH)	4.50	2.25
	$12.00	$8.00

Variable factory overhead costs vary with direct labor hours. The annual fixed factory overhead costs are budgeted at $120,000. A total of 50% of these costs are directly traceable to the Office File Department, and 22% are traceable to the Home-Travel File Department. The remaining 28% of the costs are not traceable to either department.

Caprice employs two full-time salespersons, Pam Price and Robert Flint. Each salesperson receives an annual salary of $14,000 plus a sales commission of 10% of his or her total gross sales. Travel and entertainment expense is budgeted at $22,000 annually for each salesperson. Price is expected to sell 60% of the budgeted unit sales for each file and Flint the remaining 40%. Caprice's remaining marketing and administrative expenses include fixed administrative costs of $40,000 that cannot be traced to either file, plus the following traceable marketing expenses:

	Office File	Home-Travel File
Packaging expenses per unit	$ 2.00	$ 1.50
Promotion	30,000.00	40,000.00

Data regarding Caprice's budgeted and actual sales for the fiscal year ended May 31, 19D, are presented in the following schedule. There were no changes in the beginning and ending balances of either finished goods or work in process inventories.

	Office File	Home-Travel File
Budgeted sales volume in units	15,000	15,000
Budgeted and actual unit sales price	$29.50	$19.50
Actual unit sales:		
Pam Price	10,000	9,500
Robert Flint	5,000	10,500
Total units	15,000	20,000

Data regarding Caprice's operating expenses for the year ended May 31, 19D, are as follows:

(a) There were no increases or decreases in raw materials inventory for either sheet metal or plastic, and there were no usage variances. However, sheet metal prices were 6% above budget and plastic prices were 4% below budget.

(b) The actual direct labor hours worked and costs incurred were as follows:

	Hours	Amount
Office file	7,500	$ 57,000
Home-travel file	6,000	45,600
	13,500	$102,600

(c) Fixed factory overhead costs attributable to the Office File Department were $8,000 above the budget. All other fixed factory overhead costs were incurred at the same amounts as budgeted, and variable factory overhead costs were incurred at the budgeted hourly rates, except for a $9,000 unfavorable variance in the Home-Travel File Department.

(d) All marketing and administrative expenses were incurred at budgeted rates or amounts, except the following items:

Nontraceable administrative		
expenses		$ 34,000
Promotion:		
Office files	$32,000	
Home-travel files	58,000	90,000
Travel and entertainment:		
Pam Price	$24,000	
Robert Flint	28,000	52,000
		$176,000

Required:

(1) Prepare a segmented income statement of Caprice Company's actual operations for the fiscal year ended May 31, 19D. The report should be prepared in a contribution margin format by product and should reflect total operating income (loss) for the company.

(2) Identify and discuss any additional analyses that could be made from the data presented that would be of value to Caprice Company.

(3) Prepare a performance report for the year ended May 31, 19D, that would be useful in evaluating the performance of Robert Flint. Include variable manufacturing costs at budgeted rates and compute Flint's contribution margin as well as his contribution net of traceable fixed costs. The only fixed costs traceable to individual salespersons are travel and entertainment and salary.

(4) Discuss the effects of Robert Flint's sales mix on Caprice Company's:

(a) Manufacturing operations.
(b) Profits. (ICMA adapted)

C24-4. Sales force motivation and performance. XYZ Recreational Products Company, in an attempt to increase its sales and profits, has decided to change from a straight salary system to a commission-plus-bonus arrangement for compensating its salespersons. XYZ Company manufactures and sells a line of fiberglass canoes and water skis. The company's sales are highly seasonal, with more than 75% of its business occurring between May and September.

The compensation plan under consideration calls for the salespersons to receive monthly a 10% commission on all sales that exceed the monthly sales quotas. If sales do not exceed the monthly quota, the salespersons will receive a 5% commission on the amount sold. The commission would be earned in two installments, one half in the month the order is shipped and one half in the month the customer pays for the product. Sales personnel can earn an additional 2% bonus on all their sales for the year if the quota is attained each month for a 12-month period.

At the beginning of each year, the yearly sales quota for each salesperson is determined by joint agreement between the salesperson and his or her supervisor. The monthly sales quota for each territory is then determined by dividing the annual sales quota by 12.

Required:

(1) List aspects of the new compensation plan that are likely to have a positive effect on employee motivation and performance.

(Continued)

(2) List aspects of the new compensation plan that are likely to have a negative effect on employee motivation and performance.

(CIA adapted)

C24-5. Compensation program for salespersons. Betterview Corporation manufactures a full line of windows and doors, including casement windows, bow windows, and patio doors. The bow windows and patio doors have a significantly higher profit margin per unit than casement windows, as shown in the following schedule:

	Casement Windows	Bow Windows	Patio Doors
Sales price..........	$130	$250	$260
Manufacturing costs:			
Direct materials ...	$ 25	$ 40	$ 50
Direct labor	20	35	30
Variable overhead .	16	28	24
Fixed overhead ...	24	42	36
Total manufacturing cost............	$ 85	$145	$140
Gross profit	$ 45	$105	$120

The company sells almost entirely to general contractors of residential housing. Most of these contractors complete and sell 15 to 50 houses per year. Each contractor builds tract houses that are similar, with some variations in exteriors and rooflines.

When contractors contact Betterview, they are likely to seek bids for all the windows in the houses they plan to build in the next year. At this point, the Betterview salespersons have an opportunity to infuence the window configuration of these houses by suggesting patio doors or bow windows as variations for one or more casement windows for each of the several exteriors and rooflines built by the contractor.

The bow windows and patio doors are approximately twice as wide as the casement windows. A bow window or a patio door usually is substituted for two casement windows. Casement windows are usually ordered in pairs and placed side-by-side in those houses which could be modified to accept bow windows and patio doors.

Joseph Hite, president of Betterview Corporation, is perplexed with the company's profit performance. In a conversation with his sales manager, he declared, "Our total dollar sales volume is growing, but our net income has not increased as it should. Our unit sales of casement windows have increased proportionately more than the sale of bow windows or patio doors. Why aren't our sales representatives pushing our more profitable products?" The sales manager responded with a sense of frustration, "I don't know what else can be done. They have been told which type of windows we want sold, due to the greater profit margin. Furthermore, they have the best compensation plan in the industry, with a $1,000 base monthly salary and commissions of 5% on sales dollars."

Required:
(1) Identify the needs of the salespersons that are being met by the current compensation program.
(2) Explain why Betterview's present compensation program for its salespersons does not support the president's objectives to sell the more profitable units.
(3) Specify alternative compensation programs which may be more appropriate for motivating the salesperson to sell the more profitable units.   (ICMA adapted)

C24-6. Sales compensation plans. Pre-Fab Housing Corporation, a relatively large company in the manufactured housing industry, is known for its aggressive sales promotion campaigns. Pre-Fab's innovative advertising and sales strategies have resulted in generally satisfactory performance in the last few years.

One of Pre-Fab's objectives is to increase sales revenue by at least 10% annually. This objective has been attained. Return on investment is considered good and has increased annually until last year, when net income decreased for the first time in nine years. The latest economic recession could be the cause of the change, but other factors such as sales growth discount this reason.

A significant portion of Pre-Fab's administrative expenses are fixed, but the majority of the manufacturing expenses are variable in nature. The increases in sales prices have been consistent with the 12% increase in manufacturing expenses. Pre-Fab has consistently been able to maintain a companywide manufacturing contribution margin of approximately 40%. However, the manufacturing contribution margin on individual product lines varies from 25 to 55%.

Sales commission expenses increased 30% over the past year. The prefabricated housing industry has always been sales-oriented, and Pre-Fab's management has believed in generously rewarding the efforts of its sales personnel. The sales force compensation plan consists of three segments:

(a) A guaranteed annual salary, which is increased annually at about a 6% rate. The salary is below industry average.
(b) A sales commission of 9% of total sales dollars. This is higher than the industry average.
(c) A year-end bonus of 5% of total sales dollars to each salesperson when their total sales dollars exceed the prior year by at least 12%.

The current compensation plan has resulted in an average annual income of $42,500 per sales employee, compared with an industry annual average of $30,000. However, the compensation plan has been effective in generating increased sales. Further, the Sales Department employees are satisfied with the plan. Management, however, is concerned about the financial implications of the current plan. Management believes that the plan has caused higher selling expenses and a lower net income relative to the sales revenue increase.

At a recent staff meeting, the controller suggested that the sales compensation plan be modified so that sales employees could earn an annual average income of $37,500. The controller believes that such a plan would still be attractive to its sales personnel and, at the same time, allow the company to earn a more satisfactory profit.

The vice-president for sales voiced strong objection to altering the current compensation plan because employee morale and incentive would drop significantly if there were any change. Nevertheless, most of the staff believes that the area of sales compensation merits a review. The president stated that all phases of a company operation can benefit from a periodic review, no matter how successful they have been in the past.

Several compensation plans known to be used by other companies in the manufactured housing industry are:

(a) Straight commission as a percentage of sales.
(b) Straight salary.
(c) Salary plus compensation based on sales to new customers.
(d) Salary plus compensation based on manufacturing contribution margin.

Required:

(1) Discuss the advantages and disadvantages of Pre-Fab's current sales compensation plan with respect to:

(a) The financial aspects of the company.
(b) The behavioral aspects of the sales personnel.

(2) For each of the listed alternative compensation plans, discuss whether or not the plan would be an improvement over the current plan in terms of the financial performance of the company and the behavioral implications for the sales personnel.

(ICMA adapted)

C24-7. Gross profit variances. Handy Home Products Company distributes two home-use power tools to hardware stores, a heavy duty $1/2$" hand drill and a table saw. The tools are purchased from a manufacturer that attaches the Handy Home Products label on the tools. The wholesale selling prices to the hardware stores are $60 each for the drill and $120 each for the table saw.

The budget for the current year and the actual results are presented in the table on page 856. The budget was adopted late in the preceding year and was based on Handy Home Products' estimated share of the market for the two tools.

During the first quarter of the current year, Handy Home Products' industry projections indicated that the total market for these tools would actually be 10% below original management estimates. In an attempt to prevent unit sales from declining as much as industry projections, management developed and implemented a marketing program. Included in the

Handy Home Products Company
Income Statement
For the Year Ended December 31, 19--
(In Thousands)

	Hand Drill		Table Saw		Total			
	Budget	Actual	Budget	Actual	Budget	Actual	Variance	
Sales in units	120	86	80	74	200	160	40	
Revenue	$7,200	$5,074	$9,600	$8,510	$16,800	$13,584	$3,216	unfav.
Cost of goods sold	6,000	4,300	6,400	6,068	12,400	10,368	2,032	fav.
Gross profit	$1,200	$ 774	$3,200	$2,442	$ 4,400	$ 3,216	$1,184	unfav.
Unallocated costs:								
Selling					$ 1,000	$ 1,000	$ 0	
Advertising					1,000	1,060	60	unfav.
Administration					400	406	6	unfav.
Income tax (45%)					900	338	562	fav.
Total					$ 3,300	$ 2,804	$ 496	fav.
Net income					$ 1,100	$ 412	$ 688	unfav.

program were dealer discounts and increased direct advertising. The table saw line was emphasized in this program.

Required:

(1) Analyze the unfavorable gross profit variance of $1,184,000 in terms of sales price variance, cost price variance, sales mix variance, and final sales volume variance.

(2) Discuss the apparent effect of the special marketing program (i.e., dealer discounts and additional advertising) on actual operating results. Provide supporting numerical data where appropriate.

(ICMA adapted)

C24-8. Product pricing. Kolesar Company manufactures office equipment for sale to retail stores. The vice-president of marketing has proposed that Kolesar introduce two new products to its line—an electric stapler and an electric pencil sharpener.

Kolesar's Profit Planning Department has been requested to develop preliminary sales prices for the two new products for review. The Profit Planning Department is to follow the company's standard policy for developing potential sales prices, using as much data as available for each product. Data accumulated

by the Profit Planning Department are shown in the table below.

	Electric Stapler	Electric Pencil Sharpener
Estimated annual demand in units	12,000	10,000
Estimated unit manufacturing costs	$10	$12
Estimated unit marketing and administrative expenses	$4	Not avail.
Assets employed in manufacturing	$180,000	Not avail.

Kolesar plans to employ an average of $2,400,000 assets to support its operations in the current year. The condensed pro forma operating income statement represents Kolesar's planned goals with respect to cost relationships and return on capital employed for the entire company for all of its products.

Kolesar Company
Pro Forma Operating Income Statement
For the Year Ending May 31, 19A
(In Thousands)

Sales revenue	$4,800
Cost of goods sold	2,880
Gross profit	$1,920
Marketing and administrative expenses	1,440
Operating income	$ 480

Required:

(1) Calculate a potential sales price for:

    (a) The electric stapler, using return-on-capital-employed pricing.

    (b) The electric sharpener, using gross-profit-margin pricing.

(2) Could a sales price for the electric pencil sharpener be calculated using return-on-capital-employed pricing? Explain your answer.

(3) Which of the two pricing methods (return on capital employed or gross profit margin) is more appropriate for decision analysis? Explain your answer.

(4) The vice-president of marketing has received from the Profit Planning Department the potential sales prices for the two new products (as calculated in the first requirement). Discuss the additional steps that the vice-president is likely to take in order to set an actual sales price for each of the two products.   (ICMA adapted)

CHAPTER 25

Profit Performance Measurements and Intracompany Transfer Pricing

The establishment of a profit goal based on marketing and manufacturing plans (expressed as budgets and standards), the delegation of authority, the assignment of responsibility to middle and lower management levels, and the creation of decentralized, autonomous divisions of a company lead to the need for measuring the operating and profit performance of all executives. This chapter discusses the return-on-capital-employed concept, a measure used by management in appraising company-wide as well as divisional operating performance. It also discusses intracompany transfer pricing, which plays a significant role in measuring divisional results.

■ THE RATE OF RETURN ON CAPITAL EMPLOYED

Return on capital employed is used here as an internal measure. The term "return on investment" sometimes is used to refer to this notion, but such usage may be confusing because the term also refers to the average annual return on investment method (discussed in Chapter 22), which is a capital expenditure evaluation technique, and to a return or yield on equity capital, which is primarily an investor's guide. The return on equity capital also has some value as an internal measure for financial management.

The Formula

The rate of return on capital employed may be expressed as the product of two factors: the percentage of profit to sales and the capital-employed turnover rate. In equation form, the rate of return is developed as follows:

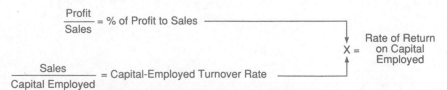

Notice that sales cancels out in the two fractions to yield the rate-of-return-on-capital-employed measure. Although the final measure can be computed directly by dividing profit by capital employed, an evaluation of the full formula that includes profit on sales and turnover of capital employed gives management a better comprehension of the elements leading to the final result. The profit percentage reflects a cost-price relationship affected by the level and mix of sales, the price of products sold, and the success or lack of success in maintaining satisfactory control of costs. The turnover rate reflects the rapidity with which committed assets are employed in the operations.

Because the rate of return on capital employed is the product of two factors, numerous combinations can lead to the same result, illustrated as follows for a 20 percent rate of return:

Percentage of Profit to Sales	Capital-Employed Turnover Rate	Rate of Return on Capital Employed
10%	2.000	20%
8	2.500	20
6	3.333	20
4	5.000	20
2	10.000	20

SERVICE ENTITIES There is no single rate of return on capital employed that is satisfactory for all companies. Manufacturing companies in various industries will have different rates, as will utilities, banking institutions, merchandising firms, and service companies. Management can establish an objective rate by using judgment and experience supported by comparisons with other companies. Every industry has companies with high, medium, and low rates of return. Structure and size of the firm influence the rate considerably. A diversified company might have only a fair return rate when the income and assets of all of its divisions are pooled in the analysis. In such cases, it may be advisable to establish separate objectives for each division as well as for the total company. Methods for divisional analyses are discussed in a later section of this chapter.

The Formula's Underlying Data

None of the factors or elements that produce the final rate can be disregarded, minimized, or overemphasized without impairing the quality of managerial decisions. Complete details of the relationships of the capital-employed ratio to the underlying ratios (percentage of profit to sales and capital-employed turnover rate) are portrayed in the chart on page 860.

A rate of return on capital employed is computed by using figures from the balance sheet and income statement. Probability estimates can be incorporated as a part of the computation.[1] The sales figure commonly used is net sales (i.e., gross sales less sales returns, allowances, and discounts). No gen-

---

[1]William L. Ferrara, "Probabilistic Approaches to Return on Investment and Residual Income," *The Accounting Review,* Vol. LII, No. 3, pp. 597-604.

Relationship of Factors Influencing Rate of Return on Capital Employed

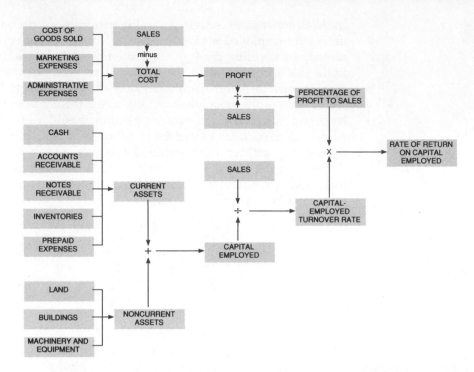

eral agreement exists with respect to the profit and capital-employed figures used in computing the rate. Consistency and uniformity are primary requisites, however, since the return on capital employed generally deals with a complexity of operations and/or a great diversity of divisions. Under such circumstances, it seems wise to avoid additional complexity and to seek clarity in the presentation of operating results without sacrifice of substance.

The income statement generally reports several different levels of profit, such as (1) operating income, which includes cost of goods sold and marketing and administrative expenses but excludes nonoperating income and expenses; (2) income before income tax, which would include the nonoperating income and expense items; and (3) net income, which is the amount that is transferred to retained earnings. Using operating income means that only transactions of an operating nature should be considered. This profit figure is preferred for divisional analyses, since nonoperating items are usually the responsibility of the entire company. The use of income before or after income tax is significant when judging the enterprise as a whole; however, net income is more defensible because taxes deplete company resources, and firm-wide performance should be judged only by the ultimate result. If capital employed is restated to give recognition to inflation accounting, as discussed later in this chapter, then comparability calls for a similar restatement of the effect of inflation accounting on profit.

Capital employed refers to total assets or the sum of current assets and noncurrent assets. In describing capital employed, the word "investment" is intentionally avoided because it is used in connection with capital investment (noncurrent assets) and owner's investment (net worth or equity capital), and its meaning would be confusing.

Many accountants suggest that the amount of capital employed should be averaged over the fiscal period, if possible. Such a procedure tends to equalize unusually high or low year-end asset values or seasonal influences. Also, the sources of funds are not considered in determining the amount of capital employed. Therefore, current and long-term liabilities, which provided the money used in the purchase of assets, are not deducted from the assets. However, some accountants believe that current liabilities should be deducted from current assets to obtain a working capital figure to be used in place of the current assets figure. This is considered theoretically appealing if division managers have control of current liabilities (i.e., if current liabilities are incurred at the division level rather than at the corporate level).

Current Assets. The three most significant items classified as current assets are cash, receivables, and inventories. Problems of valuation are connected with each of these assets.

Cash. Ordinarily, the cash shown on the balance sheet is the amount required for total business operations. Cash funds set aside for pensions, taxes, or future expansion or development programs should be excluded. However, some companies believe that if such items are treated uniformly in relation to total cash or assets, no change of the cash balance sheet figure is warranted. On the other hand, some managers do not accept the stated cash figure but prefer a predetermined percentage of cost of goods sold or annual operating expenses. The reasoning is that the routine transactions of a division require a certain minimum cash balance to be held. Amounts in excess of this minimum are a corporate-level responsibility, not an asset invested in the divisions.

Receivables. Values used for receivables should be either the gross amount or the net amount after deducting the allowance for doubtful accounts. The procedure should be uniform for all receivables allowances.

Inventories. Different inventory costing methods, such as fifo, average, or lifo, give rise to some balance sheet and income statement differences. When return ratios of companies in the same industry are compared, an allowance for such differences should be made. Again, if an allowance account is used for lower of cost or market adjustments, the question arises as to whether the inventory figure used should be net of the allowance. Here, too, uniformity plays a significant role.

Some companies' inventories are costed on a standard cost or direct costing basis. Use of these two bases will, as in the case of lifo, generally depress inventory values on a company's balance sheet. For internal comparison, however, the use of either method on a uniform basis should not influence results. The same reasoning applies to other deviations from normal accounting practices.

Noncurrent Assets. In dealing with noncurrent assets, three alternative valuation methods have been suggested: (1) original cost (original book value),

(2) depreciated cost (original cost less the depreciation allowance, i.e., net book value), and (3) inflation accounting.

Original Cost. Those accountants favoring the original cost basis argue that:

1. Assets of manufacturing companies, unlike those of mining companies, are on a continuing rather than on a depleted and abandoned basis.
2. Gross assets of one plant can be compared better with those of another plant, where depreciation practices or the age of the assets may be different.
3. Accumulated depreciation should not be deducted from the gross asset value of property, since it represents retention of the funds required to keep the stockholders' original investment intact. Actually, noncurrent assets are used to produce a profit during their entire life. Therefore, full cost is considered an investment until the assets are retired from use.

Depreciated Cost. Those accountants who favor the use of the depreciated cost for noncurrent assets state that:

1. While noncurrent assets are conventionally understated at the present time, increasing the original cost should not be attempted since this would only add to the confusion already existing in asset valuation.
2. An investment is something separate and distinct from the media through which it is made. The purchase price of a machine should be regarded as the prepaid cost for the number of years of production expected. Each year this number will decline. The function of depreciation accounting is to maintain the aggregate capital by currently providing substitute assets to replace the aggregate asset consumption (depreciation) of the year.

The several acceptable depreciation methods, such as straight-line or the various accelerated methods, result in balance sheet and income statement differences. When return ratios of companies in the same industry are compared, such differences should be considered.

Inflation Accounting. Those accountants who maintain that noncurrent assets should be included at current cost or at historical cost adjusted to constant dollars argue that such values are more realistic. They believe that a company receiving a certain and apparently satisfactory return based on book values should recognize the situation as being out-of-step with actual conditions. They further assert that some equalization of facility values of different divisions or companies should be provided, especially between those with old plants that were built at relatively low cost and those with new plants that were built at high cost. This method, of course, poses a nontrivial problem of finding proper values.

Closely allied to any discussion of appropriate noncurrent asset values in an inflation accounting context are considerations as to the effect on profits, sales, and capital employed. Sales, costs currently incurred, and current assets might be measured in current dollar values, while the noncurrent assets and their expired cost might lag years behind. When the noncurrent asset effects are translated into current costs or constant dollars, the rate of return on capital employed is more realistic.

Using the Rate of Return on Capital Employed

The return on capital employed is a measure of profitability for the total company as well as for divisions and individual plants and products. While a company's total analysis and comparison with the industry's ratios are significant for executive management, the real purpose of the return-on-capital-employed ratio is for internal profit measurement and control, with trends more meaningful than single ratios. It is not a guide for shareholders or investors who measure profitability or earning power by relating profit to equity capital.

Executive management of many companies has shown a growing acceptance of the rate-of-return-on-capital-employed concept as a tool in planning, in establishing sales prices, and in measuring operational profitability. Return-on-capital-employed information is useful to executives, plant managers, plant engineers, and salespersons. It provides executives with a brief yet comprehensive picture of overall operations, of operations in each division, and of operations for plants and products. The plant manager receives a statement which measures the plant's operating results in a single figure. The product engineer's responsibility is to create products which can be manufactured at minimum cost and sold in profitable quantities without abnormal increases in asset investment. The sales staff realizes that price changes, justified as they may seem, are effective only if they contain a profit increment which yields an adequate return.

The return on capital employed not only acts as a measurement of the cooperative efforts of a company's segments but also shows the extent to which profitable coordination exists. A company's interlocking efforts are most effectively demonstrated by this rate. An appreciation of this concept by all employees will build an organization interested in achieving fair profits and an adequate rate of return.

Budgeting is the principal planning and control technique employed by most companies. Among the multiple phases of budgeting, sales estimating is still considered the most difficult profit-planning task. Assuming that an acceptable sales budget has been established and that production, manufacturing, and commercial expense budgets have been prepared, return-on-capital-employed ratios are useful in evaluating the entire planning procedure.

Management's objectives with respect to the long-range return, as well as the immediate returns for each division, plant, or product, influence and guide budget-building activities. As sales, costs, and assets employed are placed in the perspective of the rate of return on capital employed as envisioned by management, there is a marked change in the attitude of the people responsible for assembling the figures. Segment budgets are compared with predetermined goals. If too low, examination and revision can perhaps achieve the desired result. If an unusually excellent return is calculated, the reasons for it can be investigated. Management can either accept the situation as is or decide on a temporary modification of its planning goal. At any rate, the return on capital employed offers a satisfactory foundation for the construction of both annual and long-range planning budgets. When considering long-range plans regarding addition of new products, dropping of old products, expansion of production facilities, or investing additional capital in research and development, application of the return on capital employed on any future projects has a sobering effect if these projects have been conceived haphazardly or overoptimistically.

A successful technique in planning for profit improvement is to (1) define quantitatively (for sales, profits, and capital employed) the gap which exists between performance at present and that represented by long-term objectives, (2) fix the problems precisely by examining the details of each factor, (3) formulate a specific scheduled program of action for each factor, and (4) translate the planned results of each program in terms of its effect upon income and asset accounts. The application of this technique is shown in the following table:

EFFECT OF PLANNED PROGRAMS FOR PROFIT IMPROVEMENT

	Present		Change by Volume	Change by Cost Reduction	Asset Curtailment	Future	
Assets:							
Inventory	$ 500,000				−$100,000	$ 400,000	
Other current assets	200,000		+$ 20,000			220,000	
Noncurrent assets	300,000			+$80,000		380,000	
Total assets	$1,000,000		+$ 20,000	+$80,000	−$100,000	$1,000,000	
Profit:							
Sales billed	$1,000,000	100.0%	+$200,000			$1,200,000	100.0%
Manufacturing cost	$ 770,000	77.0%	+$140,000	− $88,000		$ 822,000	68.5%
Marketing and administrative expenses	130,000	13.0	+ 10,000	− 2,000		138,000	11.5
Total cost and expense . .	$ 900,000	90.0%	$150,000			$ 960,000	80.0%
Operating profit	$ 100,000	10.0%	+$ 50,000	+$90,000		$ 240,000	20.0%
Return on capital employed:							
% of profit to sales		10.0%					20.0%
Capital-employed turnover rate (times) . . .		1.0					1.2
Return on capital employed (%)		10.0%					24.0%

Divisional Rates of Return

The rate of return on capital employed is commonly used to evaluate divisional performance.[2] Although not always observed in practice, there are

---

[2]Although this discussion refers to divisions, the rate of return on capital employed may be computed for other segments of a business, such as products, territories, etc., following the procedures described for divisions.

two distinctly different uses for the rate-of return-on-capital-employed measure. It may be used to evaluate the profitability of the assets committed to a particular division, or it may be used to evaluate the performance of divisional management.[3] The components of income and the combination of assets used in the computation should depend upon the use of the measure and should exclude arbitrarily allocated common costs.

If the rate of return on capital employed is used to evaluate the profitable use of the assets committed to the division, the measure should include only those items of income and only those assets directly traceable to use by or for the division. It should include only those items that can be avoided if the division is discontinued.[4] An allocation of common costs to divisions would be arbitrary and would consequently distort (and dilute) the economic value of the divisions to the company.

If the rate of return on capital employed is used to evaluate the performance of divisional managers, the measure should include only those items of income and only those assets that are controllable by divisional management.[5] Controllable costs may differ from separable costs. A cost which may be avoidable if a division is eliminated may not be controllable by the division's management. For example, the cost of corporate personnel services may be allocated to divisions on the basis of the number of personnel in each

COST DRIVER

division. Clearly the number of personnel is a cost driver which is directly traceable to divisions (and therefore avoidable when divisions and personnel are eliminated); however, the efficiency of the personnel department (and therefore the cost per employee allocated to the divisions) is not controllable by divisional managers. On the other hand, the number of employees utilized at the divisional level typically is controllable by divisional management, in which case some cost should be allocated to the division. One solution to the problem would be to allocate such costs on the basis of a predetermined rate and to compare actual divisional performance with budgeted performance (see discussion of responsibility accounting and reporting in Chapter 15).

Whether the rate is being used to evaluate the economic value of a division or the performance of division managers, the rate may logically be compared to some target set by management (e.g., the budgeted rate) or to the rate of return for the same division in preceding periods. However, comparing the rate of return on capital employed for one division with that of another division is unsound. Aside from the problem of determining divisional income and assets employed on comparable bases, each division produces different products and operates in different markets. As a consequence, market risk (i.e., variability in demand) is likely to differ for each division, which in turn means that top management should expect divisional returns to differ as well. In order to compensate for risk, divisions operating in highly risky

---

[3]Earl A. Spiller, Jr., "Return on Investment: A Need for Special Purpose Information," *Accounting Horizons*, Vol. 2, No. 2, June 1988, pp. 2-4.

[4]*Ibid.*, p. 2.

[5]*Ibid.*, p. 3.

markets should be required to have larger returns than those in less risky markets. If the rate of return for each division is adjusted for its respective market risk, comparison between or among the divisions may be reasonable (assuming, of course, that income and assets employed are comparably measured). On the other hand, comparing the rate of return on capital employed for one division with another for the purpose of evaluating division managers is almost always unsound. The economic environments of different divisions are generally too disparate to make meaningful comparisons for this purpose.[6] One division may be in a highly competitive market while another is in a protected or monopolistic market. One may be in a declining market while another is in a growth market. It is one thing to evaluate divisional returns for the purpose of trying to decide whether to expand, contract, or discontinue operations, but it is quite another to attribute the differences in divisional rates to the performances of their respective managers. The manager of a division operating in a declining market may be a far more efficient manager than one managing a division in a growth market in spite of the fact that the former's divisional rate of return is lower than that of the latter. If rewards are based on the relative performance of the divisions as measured exclusively by their rates of return, the best managers may become discouraged and either diminish their efforts or quit, while the least efficient managers may be encouraged to continue inefficient behavior. The best managers often are assigned to the weakest divisions where their skills are most needed.

Divisional return-on-capital-employed measures have been criticized as a motivational tool because a division may seek to maximize its rate of return on capital employed rather than absolute profits. Assume that a division which is presently earning a 30 percent rate of return on capital employed is considering a project whose return would be only 25 percent. The divisional management might decline the project because the return on total divisional capital would decrease. Yet, if the acceptance of the project would make the best use of these divisional resources from a total company point of view, then even with a lower rate of return for the division or for the total company, the project should be accepted.

Suboptimum behavior of this sort might be overcome by using *residual income* to measure performance (i.e., a division's income less an amount representing the company's cost of capital employed by the division) instead of or in addition to the rate of return on capital employed. This additional calculation would emphasize marginal profit dollars above the cost of capital, rather than the rate of return on capital employed, thereby motivating divisional management to maximize dollar profit rather than try to achieve a specified profit rate.

Residual income is a counterpart to the return-on-capital-employed computation and is a dollar measure of profitability. The concept is analogous to the net present value obtained when discounting cash flows (Chapter 22). A

---

[6]*Ibid.*, p. 4.

positive residual income indicates earnings in excess of the desired return, while a negative residual income indicates earnings less than the desired return.[7]

Advantages of Using the Return on Capital Employed

In general, the advantages of the use of the rate-of-return-on-capital-employed method are its tendency to:

1. Focus management's attention upon earning the best profit possible on the capital (total assets) available.
2. Serve as a yardstick in measuring management's efficiency and effectiveness for the company as a whole and its divisions.
3. Tie together the many phases of financial planning, sales objectives, cost control, and the profit goal.
4. Afford comparison of managerial results, both internally and externally.
5. Develop a keener sense of responsibility and team effort in divisional managers by enabling them to measure and evaluate their own activities in the light of the results achieved by other managers.
6. Aid in detecting weakness with respect to the use or nonuse of individual assets, particularly in connection with inventories.

Limitations of Using the Return on Capital Employed

The use of the return-on-capital-employed ratio may be subject to some of the following limitations:

1. It may not be reasonable to expect the same return on capital employed from each division if the divisions sell their respective products in markets that differ widely with respect to product development, competition, and consumer demand. Lack of agreement on the optimum rate of return might discourage managers who believe the rate is set at an unfair level.
2. Valuations of assets of different vintages in different divisions might give rise to comparison difficulties and misunderstandings.
3. Proper allocation of common costs and assets requires detailed information about the budgeted and actual use of common facilities. The cost of keeping track of such details may be high.
4. For the sake of making the current period rate of return on capital employed "look good," managers may be influenced to make decisions that are not in the best long-run interests of the firm. This problem is especially likely if managers expect to be in positions for only a short time before being reassigned, thus personally avoiding responsibility for long-run consequences.

---

[7]Ferrara, *op. cit.* p. 599.

5. A single measure of performance, such as return on capital employed, may result in a fixation on improving the components of the one measure to the neglect of needed attention to other desirable activities. Product research and development, managerial development, progressive personnel policies, good employee morale, and good customer and public relations are just as important in earning a greater profit and assuring continuous growth.

Multiple Performance Measurements

Many well-managed companies use multiple performance measurements in order to overcome the limitations of a single measure. An evaluation and reward system should be based on nonfinancial measures of performance as well as financial measures. Multiple performance measures provide central management with a more comprehensive picture of divisional performance by considering a wider range of management responsibilities. In addition to encouraging managers to seek profitability, the implementation of an evaluation and reward structure that includes multiple performance measures provides an incentive to divisional managers to engage in such desirable activities as basic research, new product development, quality improvement, production innovation, employee development, and improvement of market position. In turn, such measures mitigate the problem of trying to evaluate divisional performance on the basis of a single profit measure that may be computed on different bases in each division, and they provide managers with long-run as well as short-run incentives.

QUALITY CONTROL

A multiple performance measurement system may be difficult to implement and administer. Since measurement criteria are not all equally quantifiable, it may be difficult to compare the overall performance of one division with another. It may be difficult for central management to apply the multiple, nonquantifiable criteria on a consistent basis between periods and among divisions. Uncertainty about the weight being placed on the various measures may result in confusion for divisional managers, which in turn may result in diffusion of effort and instability in divisional performance. One company that uses multiple measurements for rating divisional performance describes its method as a quantification of progress against agreed-upon standards. Each year, common standards are adopted by agreement of divisional managers and corporate management. Points are assigned to standards reflecting those areas which require special attention in each division, as determined by management. Performance is measured as follows:

1. Profits for the current year are compared with the profits for the preceding year in absolute dollars, margins, and return on capital employed.
2. Profits are compared with the budget.
3. Cash and capital management measures are employed. Here, the emphasis is on effective management of inventory and receivables.

The claimed advantages of this method are that:

1. Performances of division managers are measured more fairly than they would be from the sole use of a return-on-capital-employed figure.
2. Management can readily see which divisions are performing well and which are not.
3. Lost points serve as "red flags" by directing management to those areas requiring attention, to the reasons for the difficulty, and to the corrective actions taken or needed.
4. The system is flexible, allowing timely shifting of management emphasis when needed.

In this company, management concludes that it is not enough to merely tabulate performance statistics. The results must be effectively communicated, corrective action taken, and good performance rewarded. The system must have the interest and support of division and corporate management.[8] On a more global basis, performance measurements and related compensation plans should (1) reward performance over extended time periods; (2) tie incentive plans to achieving strategic (not financial) goals, such as target market share, productivity levels, product quality and development, and personnel development; and (3) evaluate operating profits before gains from financial transactions; before deductions for approved expenditures on research and development, quality improvements, and preventive maintenance; and before deductions for the incremental amount of accelerated depreciation.[9]

Graphs as Operating Guides

Sound planning and successful operation must point toward the optimum combination of profits, sales, and capital employed. As stated earlier, the combination will necessarily vary depending upon the characteristics of the operation. An industry with products tailor-made to customers' specifications will not have the same profit margins and turnover ratios as industries that mass produce highly competitive consumer goods.

In multiproduct companies, the three basic factors cannot be uniform, due to different types of operations. However, a special type of graph can be of assistance in judging the performance of segments or products in their relationship to a desired overall return on capital employed. Such a graph has the advantage of flexibility in appraising profit performance and offers an approach by which performance can be analyzed for improvement.

The graph on page 870 shows possible combinations of percentage of profit to sales and capital-employed turnover rate which yield a 20 percent return. When individual divisions or products are plotted on the graph, the segment's data might appear to the left or right of the basic curve. If on the

---

[8]Frank J. Tanzola, "Performance Rating for Divisional Control," *Financial Executive*, Vol. XLIII, No. 3, pp. 20-24.

[9]Alfred Rappaport, "Executive Incentives vs. Corporate Growth," *Harvard Business Review*, Vol. 56, No. 4, pp. 85-86.

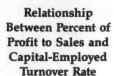

**Relationship
Between Percent of
Profit to Sales and
Capital-Employed
Turnover Rate**

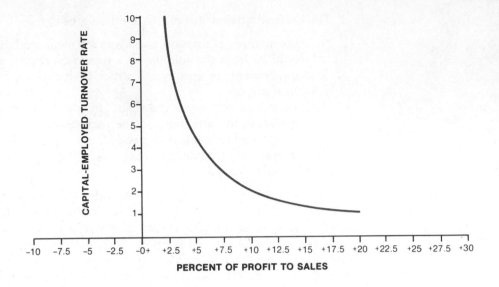

left, the unit has a capital-employed-return performance below that expected for the company as a whole. A segment whose ratios appear to the right of the basic curve has a return in excess of that expected for the entire company. The same interpretation applies when the company's total return is plotted.

■ INTRACOMPANY TRANSFER PRICING

The effectiveness of the return on capital employed as a device for measuring divisional performance depends considerably on the accuracy of allocating the costs and assets associated with the division. In a decentralized multiplant or multiproduct organization, the divisional managers are expected to run portions of the enterprise as semiautonomous businesses. As long as divisions are not entirely independent and separable, goods and services are generally transferred from one unit to another, a situation common to integrated corporations. The finished or semifinished product of one or more divisions or subsidiaries frequently becomes the raw material of one or more other divisions. In addition, some service functions are centralized and might conceivably deal with a number of profit centers. When transfers of goods or services are made, a portion of the revenue of one segment becomes a portion of cost of another, and the price at which transfers are made influences the earnings reported by each profit center. The value of these earnings as a measure of performance depends not only upon the manager's executive abilities but also upon the transfer prices used. The transfer pricing system used can distort any reported profit and make profit a poor guide for evaluating divisional performance. In the end, the cost or price used for the transfer will be used in the calculation of the return on capital employed, due to the very nature of the formula.

Years ago, transfer pricing played only a minor role in cost control. Today, many businesses have become large due to merger, acquisition, or internal growth and have turned to decentralization as a way of managing the increasing diversity of their activities. As a result, the use of transfer pricing has expanded into a complex set of procedures in the administration of the decentralized segments of an enterprise. This complexity and the arbitrary nature of intracompany transfer pricing is one reason for criticism of proposals to report segment or product-line revenues and profits in published financial statements. A steel company may operate a coal mine and sell some of its output on the open market but use the remainder in its own steel mills. The transfer price charged to its own steel mills can control whether the mining division shows a large, small, or zero profit.

External factors may influence the transfer price determination. A company with an overseas plant, where tax rates are low, may keep the transfer price high for materials sent to the domestic facility in order to retain profits abroad. Or a company with warehouses in a state with an inventory tax may keep transfer prices low on goods brought into the state in order to reduce its tax bill.

The existence of multiple management objectives makes it extremely difficult for a company to establish logical and sound intracompany transfer prices. A pricing method can be chosen only after the primary purposes for the use of the information from transfers have been identified. Therefore, a transfer pricing system must satisfy these three fundamental criteria: (1) allow central management to judge as accurately as possible the performance of the divisional profit center in terms of its separate contribution to the total corporate profit, (2) motivate the divisional manager to pursue the division's own profit goal in a manner conducive to the success of the company as a whole, and (3) stimulate the manager's efficiency without losing the division's autonomy as a profit center.[10] The system should also be easy to apply, meet legal and external reporting requirements, and permit each unit of a company to earn a profit commensurate with the functions it performs. As a practical matter, these criteria may be difficult to satisfy, because behavioral considerations are of paramount importance. Accordingly, a transfer price should be a just price to both the selling and buying parties. An advantage gained by one will be a disadvantage to the other and, in the end, may be detrimental to the corporate profit goal.

A profit center manager's interest must remain congruent with the firm's interest. For example, assume that Division X offers its Product A to Division Y at a transfer price of $14, which includes a $2 profit, a $9 variable cost, and a $3 fixed cost that presumably will remain unchanged in total as activity fluctuates. The same product is also available from an outside supplier at $11. Division Y, acting to minimize its costs, will prefer to purchase Product A at the lower external price of $11. However, assuming that from the total firm

---

[10]Joshua Ronen and George McKinney III, "Transfer Pricing for Divisional Autonomy," *Journal of Accounting Research*, Vol. 8, No. 1, pp. 99-112.

point of view, no more profitable use could be made of the Division X facilities used in supplying Product A to Division Y, such a decision would not be congruent with the best short-run interests of the total firm. This incongruence results because the $11 external price is greater than the $9 variable cost which, in this example, is the differential cost, i.e., the incremental cost incurred to produce additional units. Additionally, it should be observed that in the long run full cost must be recovered and a reasonable profit achieved on the facilities that are to be employed.

Five basic methods of pricing intracompany transfers are: (1) transfer pricing based on cost, (2) market-based transfer pricing, (3) cost-plus transfer pricing, (4) negotiated transfer pricing, and (5) arbitrary transfer pricing. No one method of transfer pricing can effectively satisfy all of the requirements in all circumstances, so the best transfer price can be defined only as it is best for a particular purpose in a particular circumstance. Regardless of what transfer price is used, the differential cost of goods transferred from division to division should be determined and used for decision-making purposes.[11]

Transfer Pricing Based on Cost

In a totally centralized firm, executive management basically makes all decisions with respect to the operations of the divisions. This responsibility makes cost control the basis for measuring a manager's performance. A cost-based transfer price is usually sufficient in this situation. A company without any integrated operations might have so little volume of intracompany transfers that it would be too time consuming and costly to price the transfer at other than cost.

The cost figure may be the actual or standard cost, based on direct or absorption costing. The company's cost system should permit the computation of a product's unit cost, even at various stages of production. When service departments are involved in a company's operations, a service charging rate similar to the one described on page 440 should be established in advance of the work performed, so that servicing and benefiting departments or plants know in advance the costs connected with services.

The cost method's primary advantage is simplicity, in that it avoids the necessity to eliminate intracompany profits from inventories in consolidated financial statements and income tax returns. Also, the transferred cost can be used readily to measure production efficiency by comparing actual with budgeted costs. Finally, the method allows simple and adequate end-product costing for profit analysis by product lines.

Considering the disadvantages, a transfer price based on cost is not suited to decentralized companies that need to measure the profitability of autonomous units. Also, producing segments may not be sufficiently conscientious

---

[11]For further study, the nature and scope of several major transfer pricing models categorized as to (1) the economic theory of the firm, (2) mathematical programming approaches, and (3) other analytical approaches, are covered in "Transfer Pricing—A Synthesis," by A. Rashad Abdel-khalik and Edward J. Lusk, *The Accounting Review*, Vol. XLIX, No. 1, pp. 8-23.

in controlling costs that are to be transferred, although the use of standard costs for transfer pricing may alleviate this problem. A transfer price based on cost lacks not only utility for divisional planning, motivating, and evaluating, but also the objectivity required of a good performance standard.

In an analysis of a study of interdivisional transfer pricing, made by the National Industrial Conference Board, Sharav observes that in most cases of vertical transfers (meaning transfers between divisions at different stages of the manufacturing and marketing processes), transfers are priced at cost if the transferring division is viewed as a cost center (where the manager is responsible for cost only). However, if the transferrer is a profit center (where the manager is responsible for cost and revenue), the transfer price may include a profit factor, thus approximating outside market prices. In horizontal transfers (meaning that transferrer and transferee are situated at the same stage of the production and marketing processes), the transfers usually are executed at cost, which may include freight and handling charges. In many cases, companies using cost-based transfer prices choose actual costs which are derived from divisional operating statements and underlying cost records. Standard or budgeted costs are employed when available. Variable costs are used by only a few companies. A modified version of cost is the so-called cost-plus transfer price (as discussed on page 874). It is comprised of cost plus a markup that is meant to provide a return on investment in divisional assets. Much less frequently used, this transfer price may be applied in lieu of the market price.[12]

Another cost-based transfer price that has been advocated is standard variable cost plus the per unit contribution margin given up on the outside sale by the company when a segment sells internally. For profit centers, the result generally approximates market price, while for cost centers, the transfer price is standard variable cost plus the possibility of an assigned portion of fixed cost.[13]

Market-Based Transfer Pricing

The market-based transfer price is usually identical with the one charged to outside customers, although some companies apply a discount to the market price to reflect the economies of intracompany trading. This method is the best profitability and performance measurement because it is objective. It reflects product profitability and division management performance, with divisions operating on a competitive basis. It also aids in planning and generally is required by foreign tariff laws and income tax regulations.

The most serious drawback to this method is the requirement for a well-developed outside competitive market. Unfortunately, a market price is not always determinable for intermediate or unique products. Also, the market-

---

[12]Itzhak Sharav, "Transfer Pricing—Diversity of Goals and Practices," *The Journal of Accountancy,* Vol. 137, No. 4, p. 59.

[13]Ralph L. Benke, Jr. and James Don Edwards, *Transfer Pricing: Techniques and Issues* (New York: National Association of Accountants, 1980).

based price adds an element of profit or loss with each transfer of product. Consequently, the determination of the actual cost of the final product may be difficult, and intracompany profit must be eliminated from inventories in financial statements and consolidated income tax returns.

Statement of Financial Accounting Standards No. 14, "Financial Reporting for Segments of a Business Enterprise," does not specify the transfer pricing method to be used in segment reporting, but it does require disclosure of the method used. The SEC, however, requires disclosure of:

1. When and where intersegment transfers are made at prices substantially higher or lower than the prevailing market price or the price charged to unaffiliated parties for similar products or services.
2. The estimated or approximate amounts (or the percentage of increase or decrease in the amounts) of the revenue and operating profit or loss that the particular segments would have had if the intersegment transfers had been made at the prevailing market price.[14]

Cost-Plus Transfer Pricing

A cost-plus transfer price, i.e., the cost to manufacture plus a normal profit markup, is often used when a market price is not available. In a sense, it is a surrogate for a market price. Although a cost-plus price has the virtue of being easy to compute, it is an imperfect price that can lead to distortions in the relative profitability of the selling and buying divisions. A cost-plus transfer price provides no incentive to the selling division to be efficient. To the contrary, since the profit markup is often a percentage of cost, there is an incentive to inflate cost through arbitrary allocation of common costs and through production inefficiency. In addition, cost-plus transfer pricing has the disadvantage of inflating inventories with intracompany profits that must be eliminated from the financial statements and consolidated income tax returns.

Negotiated Transfer Pricing

Setting the transfer price by negotiation between buying and selling divisions allows unit managers the greatest degree of authority and control over the profit of their units. The managers should consider costs and market conditions and neither negotiating party should have an unfair bargaining position.

A serious problem encountered with this method is that negotiation can not only become time-consuming but can also require frequent reexamination and revision of prices. Negotiated transfer prices often divert the efforts of divisional managers away from activities that are in the best interests of the company to those that benefit the division, and negotiation diverts the efforts of divisional managers away from productive activities. The divisional profit measures may be more of a reflection of the divisional manager's negotiating

---

[14]Robert Mednick, "Companies Slice and Serve Up Their Financial Results Under FASB 14," *Financial Executive*, Vol. XLVII, No. 3, p. 55.

ability than the division's productive efficiency. As a result, evaluations of the relative operating performance of divisions may be distorted when negotiated transfer prices are used. In addition, since the transfer price includes a profit markup, intracompany profits must be eliminated from inventories for financial statements and consolidated income tax returns.

Arbitrary Transfer Pricing

An arbitrary transfer price is simply a price set by central management. The price is generally chosen to achieve tax minimization or some other firmwide objective. Neither the buying division nor the selling division controls the transfer price. The advantage of this method is that a price can be set that will achieve the objectives deemed most important by central management. Since central management is responsible for the overall performance of the company, transfer prices set by central management should result in divisional actions that enhance firmwide performance. The method's disadvantages, however, far outweigh any advantage. It can defeat the most important purpose of decentralizing profit responsibility, i.e., making divisional personnel profit-conscious, and it severely hampers the autonomy and profit incentive of division managers. Again, since arbitrary transfer prices include some markup for profit, intracompany profits must be eliminated from inventories for financial statement and consolidated income tax reporting.

Dual Transfer Pricing

The consuming (buying) and producing (selling) divisions may differ in the purpose a transfer price is to serve. For example, a consuming division may rely on a transfer price in make-or-buy decisions or in determining a final product's sales price based on an awareness of total differential cost. A producing division may use a transfer price to measure its divisional performance and, accordingly, would argue against any price that would not provide a divisional profit. In such circumstances, a company may find it useful to adopt a dual transfer pricing approach in which the:

1. Producing division uses a market-based, cost-plus, negotiated, or arbitrary transfer price in computing its revenue from intracompany sales.
2. Variable costs of the producing division are transferred to the purchasing division, together with an equitable portion of the fixed cost.
3. Total of the divisional profits will be greater than for the company as a whole, and the profit assigned to the producing division would be eliminated in preparing companywide financial statements and for income tax purposes.

Under this system, a producing division would have a profit inducement to expand sales and production, both externally and internally. Yet, the consuming divisions would not be misled. Their costs would be the firm's actual costs and would not include an artificial profit. Variable costs, as well as fixed costs, should be associated with the purchase to ensure that the consuming division is aware of the total cost implications. Of course, the benefits from a dual transfer pricing approach can be achieved only if the underlying cost data are accurate and reliable.

Although the dual transfer pricing method appears to overcome many of the problems inherent in the other transfer pricing methods, it is not commonly used in practice. This lack of use may be due in part to recordkeeping complexity created by the method and in part to the difficulty inherent in evaluating the relative performance of the selling and buying divisions when their profits have been determined on different bases.

DISCUSSION QUESTIONS

Q25-1. How is the return on capital employed computed?

Q25-2. What management activities are measured by each of the factors involved in determining the rate of return on capital employed?

Q25-3. What items are generally included in the term "capital employed"?

Q25-4. State two major objectives that management may have in mind when setting up a system for measuring the return on divisional capital employed.

Q25-5. Identify the basic methods used in pricing intracompany transfers.

Q25-6. A cost-plus transfer price is often used as a surrogate for a market-based transfer price. Explain the primary dis-

advantage of using a cost-plus transfer price relative to using a market-based transfer price.

Q25-7. From an organizational point of view, two approaches to transfer pricing are (a) to let the managers of profit centers bargain with one another and arrive at their own transfer prices (negotiated transfer pricing) and (b) to have the firm's executive management set transfer prices for transactions between the profit centers (arbitrary transfer pricing). State the fundamental advantage and disadvantage of each approach.

CGA-Canada (adapted)
Reprint with permission

Q25-8. Explain the dual transfer pricing approach in intracompany transfer pricing.

EXERCISES

E25-1. Rate of return on capital employed. During the past year, Kaw Waterworks Company had a net income of $160,000. Net sales were $800,000 and total capital employed was $1,600,000.

Required: Compute (1) the capital-employed turnover rate, (2) the percentage of profit to sales, and (3) the rate of return on capital employed.

E25-2. Rate of return on capital employed for regions. Hutton Sales Company has three regions: Eastern, Central, and Western. The cost of assets employed is determined by averaging the December 31, 19A balance of $1,446,000 and the December 31, 19B balance of $1,632,000. The assets are distributed among the Eastern, Central, and Western regions in a ratio of 3:1:2, respectively. The 19B condensed income statement is as follows:

Hutton Sales Company
Income Statement
For the Year Ended December 31, 19B

	Eastern	Central	Western	Total
Sales.....................	$3,078,000	$513,000	$2,308,500	$5,899,500
Cost of goods sold...........	2,016,000	383,000	1,818,500	4,217,500
Gross profit................	$1,062,000	$130,000	$ 490,000	$1,682,000
Commercial expenses	908,100	88,960	443,830	1,440,890
Operating income...........	$ 153,900	$ 41,040	$ 46,170	$ 241,110

Required: For each region and in total, compute:

(1) The capital-employed turnover rate. (Compute answers to one decimal place.)
(2) The percentage of profit to sales. (Compute answers to 1/10 of 1%)
(3) The rate of return on capital employed. (Compute answers to 1/10 of 1%.)

SS **E25-3. Rate of return on capital employed for product lines.** Hayashi Company has three product lines: Recreational, Household, and Hand Tools. The December 31, 19A balance sheet shows total assets of $4,117,000, and the year-end 19B balance sheet totals $5,117,000, with the average of the two balances used to compute the rate of return on capital employed. Asset utilization is allocated one third to Recreational, one sixth to Household, and one half to Hand Tools. The 19B condensed income statement is as follows:

Hayashi Company
Income Statement
For the Year Ended December 31, 19B

	Recreational	Household	Hand Tools	Total
Sales	$3,078,000	$513,000	$2,308,500	$5,899,500
Cost of goods sold	2,016,000	383,000	1,818,500	4,217,500
Gross profit	$1,062,000	$130,000	$ 490,000	$1,682,000
Operating and other expenses	815,760	68,440	420,745	1,304,945
Profit...........................	$ 246,240	$ 61,560	$ 69,255	$ 377,055

Required: For each product line and in total, compute:

(1) The capital-employed turnover rate, computed to one decimal place.
(2) The percentage of profit to sales, computed to 1/10 of 1%.
(3) The rate of return on capital employed, computed to 1/10 of 1%.

E25-4. Transfer pricing. Wallach Iron Mill produces high-grade pig iron in its single blast furnace in Bedford, Pennsylvania. Coal from nearby mines is converted into coke in company-owned ovens, and 80% of the coke produced is used in the blast furnace. The management of the mill is experimenting with divisional profit reporting and control and has established the blast furnace as well as the coke-producing activity as profit centers. Coke used by the blast furnace is charged to that profit center at $6 per ton, which approximates the current market price less costs of marketing (including substantial freight costs). The remaining 20% of the coke produced at a normal annual volume output of 80,000 tons is sold to other mills in the area at $7.50 per ton.

The cost of coal and other variable costs of coke production amount to $4.50 per ton. Fixed costs of the coke division amount to $40,000 a year.

The blast furnace manager, with authority to purchase outside, has found a reliable, independent coke producer who has offered to sell coke at a delivered price of $5 per ton on a long-term contract. The manager of Wallach Iron Mill's coke division claims it cannot match that price and maintain profitable operations.

The manager of the coke division indicates that with an additional expenditure of $60,000 annually for fixed productive and delivery equipment, the division's entire annual normal output could be sold to outside firms at $6 per ton, FOB the Wallach Iron Mill plant. Other marketing expenses will be $.50 per ton. The increased fixed costs would reduce variable production costs by $1.50 per ton.

Required:

(1) Prepare calculations to guide the coke division manager in deciding whether to accept the offer, assuming that Wallach Iron Mill cannot increase its sales of coke to outsiders above the 20% of normal production.
(2) Prepare calculations to aid executive management in deciding whether to make the additional investment and sell the entire coke division's output to outsiders.

E25-5. Transfer pricing. Ace Division of Decker Corporation produces electric motors, 20% of which are sold to Deuce Division of Decker and the remainder to outside customers. Decker treats its divisions as profit centers and allows division managers to choose their sources of sale and supply. Corporate policy requires that all interdivisional sales and purchases be recorded at a transfer price equal to variable cost. Ace Division's estimated sales and standard cost data for the year, based on full capacity of 100,000 units, follow:

	Deuce	Outsiders
Sales	$ 900,000	$ 8,000,000
Variable cost	(900,000)	(3,600,000)
Fixed cost	(300,000)	(1,200,000)
Gross profit	$(300,000)	$ 3,200,000
Unit sales	20,000	80,000

Ace Division has an opportunity to sell to an outside customer the 20,000 units now committed to Deuce Division. The sale price would be $75 per unit during the current year. Deuce Division could purchase its requirements from an outside supplier at a price of $85 per unit.

Required:

(1) Assuming that Ace Division desires to maximize its gross profit, should it take on the new customer and discontinue its sales to Deuce Division? Support your answer by computing the increase or decrease in Ace Division's gross profit.
(2) Assume instead that Decker Corporation permits division managers to negotiate the transfer price. The managers agreed on a tentative transfer price of $75 per unit, to be reduced based on an equal sharing of the additional gross profit to Ace Division resulting from the sale to Deuce of 20,000 motors at $75 per unit. What would be the actual transfer price?   (AICPA adapted)

E25-6. Transfer pricing. The Blade Division of Dana Company produces hardened steel blades. One third of the Blade Division's output is sold to the Lawn Products Division of Dana; the remainder is sold to outside customers. The Blade Division's estimated sales and standard cost data for the year follow:

	Lawn Products	Outsiders
Sales	$ 15,000	$ 40,000
Variable cost	(10,000)	(20,000)
Fixed cost	(3,000)	(6,000)
Gross profit	$ 2,000	$ 14,000
Unit sales	10,000	20,000

The Lawn Products Division has an opportunity to purchase 10,000 identical quality blades from an outside supplier at a cost of $1.25 per unit on a continuing basis. Assume that the Blade Division cannot sell any additional products to outside customers, that the fixed costs cannot be reduced, and that no alternative use of facilities is available.

Required: Should Dana allow its Lawn Products Division to purchase the blades from the outside supplier? Support your answer by computing the increase or decrease in Dana Corporation operating costs.

(AICPA adapted)

PROBLEMS

P25-1. Rate of return on capital employed. Westworth Corporation's management is concerned over its current financial position and return on capital employed. In a request for assistance in analyzing these financial conditions, the controller provides the following statements:

Westworth Corporation
Statement of Working Capital Deficit
December 31, 19A

Current liabilities		$198,625
Less current assets:		
Cash.	$ 5,973	
Accounts receivable (net)	70,952	
Inventory	90,200	167,125
Working capital deficit.		$ 31,500

Westworth Corporation
Income Statement
For the Year Ended December 31, 19A

Sales (90,500 units).	$751,150
Cost of goods sold.	451,000
Gross profit	$300,150
Marketing and general expenses, including $22,980 depreciation	149,920
Income before income tax.	$150,230
Less income tax (50%)	75,115
Net income.	$ 75,115

Noncurrent assets consist of land, a building, and equipment, with a net book value of $350,000 on December 31, 19A.

Sales of 100,000 units are forecast for 19B. Within this relevant range of activity, costs are estimated as follows (excluding income tax):

	Fixed Cost	Variable Cost per Unit
Cost of goods sold.		$4.90
Marketing and general expenses, including $15,450 depreciation	$125,750	1.10
Total	$125,750	$6.00

The income tax rate is expected to be 50%. Past experience indicates that current assets vary in direct proportion to sales dollars. Management feels that in 19B the market will support a sales price of $8.40 at a sales volume of 100,000 units.

Required:

(1) Compute the 19A return-on-capital-employed ratio (after income tax), to 1/10 of 1%.
(2) Compute the 19B rate of return (after income tax) on net book value of total assets to 1/10 of 1%.

(AICPA adapted)

25-2. Profit and rate of return on capital employed using various proposals. Lauren Toy Company manufactures two specialty children's toys marketed under the trade names of Springy and Leapy. During the year, the following costs, revenue, and capital employed by the company in the production of these two items were:

	Springy	Leapy
Sales price per unit.	$ 1.50	$ 1.95
Sales in units.	280,000	150,000
Materials cost per unit	$ .20	$ .30
Labor cost per unit	.50	.75
Variable factory overhead per unit	.15	.20
Variable marketing cost per unit.	.05	.10
Fixed factory overhead	100,000	30,000
Fixed marketing cost.	30,000	15,000
Variable capital employed.	10% of sales	20% of sales
Fixed capital employed	$148,000	$ 91,500

Fixed administrative and other nonallocable fixed costs amounted to $28,000, and nonallocable capital employed was $25,000.

Management, dissatisfied with the return on total capital employed, is considering a number of alternatives to improve this return.

The market for Springy appears to be underdeveloped, and the consensus is that sales can be increased to 325,000 units at the same price with an increase of $9,500 in the fixed advertising cost. An increase in the production of Springy will require use of some equipment previously utilized in the production of Leapy and a transfer of $10,000 of fixed capital and $5,000 of fixed factory overhead to the production of Springy.

For Leapy, it would mean limiting its production to 100,000 units, which could be marketed with the current sales effort at (a) an increase in price of $.15 per unit; (b) without a price increase and with a reduction in current fixed advertising cost of $9,000; or (c) with a $.05 per unit increase in price and a $7,500 reduction in the current fixed advertising cost.

Required:

(1) Compute the income before income tax and the return on capital employed for each product and in total for the year, to 1/10 of 1%.
(2) Compute the income before income tax and the return on capital employed for each product and in total under each alternative, to 1/10 of 1%.

P25-3. Public utility rate based on capital employed. Mauford Water Company is a public utility providing water service to 3,000 customers. As a privately owned public utility, its rates are subject to government regulation. Its rate structure is designed to provide a reasonable rate of return, calculated by expressing net income as a percentage of the company's rate base. The rate base, in turn, is the depreciated cost of the utility plant, averaged between the beginning and end of the year. Operating results for the year were as follows:

Water revenue.		$90,000
Expenses:		
Fixed	$38,668	
Variable	12,852	
Depreciation on utility plant	17,000	68,520
Income before income tax		$21,480
Income tax		4,510
Net income		$16,970

Mauford's directors feel that the present net income is inadequate and are considering applying for higher rates. At present, each customer is charged a flat rate of $30 per annum.

An analysis of metered water consumption data indicates the following ranges of average monthly usage:

Range	Consumption	Number of Customers
A	0-100 cu. ft. (average: 50 cu. ft.)	900
B	101-500 cu. ft. (average: 300 cu. ft.)	1,800
C	over 500 cu. ft. (average: 700 cu. ft.)	300
		3,000

Other data:

Utility plant in service, January 1................	$800,000
Less accumulated depreciation	200,000
Depreciated cost of utility plant, January 1	$600,000
Utility plant addition during the year	$ 81,000

The income tax rate on earnings up to $80,000 is unchanged.

Required:

(1) Calculate the rate base and rate of return for the year, to 1/10 of 1%.
(2) Based on the information:

   (a) Compute the flat rate annual customer charge necessary to provide a 10% rate of return.
   (b) For each of the three consumption ranges, compute the charge per cubic foot of water necessary to provide a 10% rate of return, with the charge for consumption within Range B being double that within Range C, and two thirds of that within Range A; i.e., a customer consuming 150 cu. ft. of water would be billed at the Range A rate for the first 100 cu. ft. and at the lower Range B rate for the additional 50 cu. ft. (Compute answers to nearest 1/10 of a cent.)

CGA-Canada (adapted) Reprint with permission

P25-4. Product pricing and transfer pricing. National Industries is a diversified corporation with separate and distinct operating divisions. Each division's performance is evaluated on the basis of total dollar profits and return on division investment.

The WindAir Division manufactures and sells air conditioner units. The coming year's budgeted income statement, based on a sales volume of 15,000 units, is presented on page 882.

WindAir's division manager believes sales can be increased if the unit sales price is reduced. A market research study conducted by an independent firm at the request of the manager indicates that a 5% reduction in the sales price ($20) would increase sales volume 16%, or 2,400 units. WindAir has sufficient production capacity to manage this increased volume with no increase in fixed cost.

At the present time, WindAir uses a compressor in its units, which it purchases from an outside supplier at a cost of $70 each. The division manager of WindAir has approached the manager of the Compressor Division regarding the sale of compressor units to WindAir. The Compressor Division currently manufactures and sells a unit exclusively to outside firms which is similar to the unit used by WindAir. Specifications for the WindAir compressor are slightly different, which would reduce the Compressor Division's raw materials cost by $1.50 per unit. In addition, the Compressor Division would not incur any variable marketing cost for the units sold to WindAir. The manager of WindAir wants all of the compressors it uses to come from one supplier and has offered to pay the Compressor Division $50 for each unit.

The Compressor Division has the capacity to produce 75,000 units. The coming year's budgeted income statement for the Compressor Division, also shown on page 882, is based on a sales volume of 64,000 units, without considering WindAir's proposal.

WindAir Division
Budgeted Income Statement
For 19A

	Per Unit	Total
Sales revenue	$400	$6,000,000
Manufacturing costs:		
Compressor	$ 70	$1,050,000
Other raw materials	37	555,000
Direct labor.	30	450,000
Variable factory overhead	45	675,000
Fixed factory overhead.	32	480,000
Total manufacturing cost	$214	$3,210,000
Gross profit.	$186	$2,790,000
Commercial expenses:		
Variable marketing	$ 18	$ 270,000
Fixed marketing	19	285,000
Fixed administrative	38	570,000
Total commercial expense . . .	$ 75	$1,125,000
Income before income tax.	$111	$1,665,000

Compressor Division
Budgeted Income Statement
For 19A

	Per Unit	Total
Sales revenue	$100	$6,400,000
Manufacturing costs:		
Raw materials.	$ 12	$ 768,000
Direct labor.	8	512,000
Variable factory overhead	10	640,000
Fixed factory overhead.	11	704,000
Total manufacturing cost	$ 41	$2,624,000
Gross profit.	$ 59	$3,776,000
Commercial expenses:		
Variable marketing	$ 6	$ 384,000
Fixed marketing	4	256,000
Fixed administrative	7	448,000
Total commercial expense . . .	$ 17	$1,088,000
Income before income tax.	$ 42	$2,688,000

Required:

(1) Compute the estimated result if the WindAir Division reduces its sales price by 5%, even if it cannot acquire the compressors internally at $50 each.
(2) Compute the estimated effect on the Compressor Division, from its own viewpoint, if the 17,400 units are supplied to WindAir at $50 each.
(3) Determine whether it would be in the best interests of National Industries for the Compressor Division to supply the 17,400 units to WindAir Division at $50 each.   (ICMA adapted)

P25-5. Transfer pricing. Martin Corporation, a diversified company, recently implemented a decentralization policy under which divisional managers are expected to make their own operating decisions, including whether to do business with other divisions. The performances and year-end bonuses of divisional managers are measured by the return on capital employed of their divisions. Because most divisions have operated at full capacity, it is company policy that all transfers between divisions are to be priced at 120% of standard manufacturing cost (to allow for a "normal" divisional profit margin). This transfer price is not negotiable.

The president of the company is currently faced with a dispute between the general managers of two divisions: the Consumer Products Division and the Engineering Division. The Consumer Products Division makes and sells several household articles, including a home appliance that has, until recently, been one of the company's steadiest sellers. Recently, this division has had marketing difficulties and has reduced its production of the appliance to 56,000 a year from its usual production at capacity. The unused capacity cannot be utilized for other products. The Engineering Division makes a wide variety of items, including a specialized part (Part TX) that is sold to the Consumer Products Division and to a few small outside companies. The latter buy a steady 12% of the Engineering Division's annual production capacity for the part.

The Consumer Products Division uses four of these parts in each home appliance unit and maintains no significant inventory of unused parts but acquires them from the Engineering Division as needed to meet its production requirements. The parts are not available from any other source.

Because the Consumer Products Division has recently reduced its requirement for Part TX, the Engineering Division has been seeking new customers and has received an offer to buy 100,000 units of the part annually, at a price of $5 each, which is less than the $5.40 each paid by the small outside companies but more than the transfer price paid by the Consumer Products Division. The company making the offer is in a market unrelated to that of either the Consumer Products Division or the small outside companies.

Following are data with respect to Part TX and the home appliance involved in the dispute between the two managers:

	Part TX (Engineering Division)	Home Appliance (Consumer Products Division)
Annual production capacity	300,000 units	66,000 units
Unit sales price to outside customers	$5.40	$80.00
Standard manufacturing cost per unit (based on production at full capacity): Division's own costs:		
Variable	$2.00	$37.00
Fixed	1.75	13.00
Transfers from the Engineering Division		18.00
Standard manufacturing cost per unit	$3.75	$68.00

The manager of the Consumer Products Division has requested that the president instruct the manager of the Engineering Division to refuse the offer received, since (1) no other source for Part TX can be found, (2) the marketing problems with the home appliance are expected to be temporary, and (3) the Engineering Division cannot expand its production capacity for Part TX.

Required:

   (1) Determine the action that the manager of the Engineering Division should take as a result of the offer, in order to maximize the results of that division. Include calculations of the offer's effect on the Engineering Division.

   (2) Determine the overall effect on the company, under existing circumstances, if the Engineering Division's manager accepts the offer.

   (3) Identify the factors that the president should consider in deciding whether to intervene in the dispute.

   (4) Revise the transfer pricing policy to assist the divisional managers in making optimal decisions for the company.   (CICA adapted)

P25-6. Transfer pricing. Portco Products is a multi-division furniture manufacturer. The divisions are autonomous segments with each division being responsible for its own sales, costs of operations, working capital management, and equipment acquisition. Each division serves a different market in the furniture industry.

Because the markets and products of the divisions are so different, there have never been any transfers between divisions.

The Commercial Division manufactures equipment and furniture that is purchased by the restaurant industry. The division plans to introduce a new line of counter and chair units which feature a cushioned seat for the counter chairs. J. Kline, the division manager, has discussed the manufacturing of the cushioned seat with R. Fiegel of the Office Division. They both believe a cushioned seat currently made by the Office Division for use on its deluxe office stool could be modified for use on the new counter chair. Consequently, Kline has asked Fiegel for a price for 100 unit lots of the cushioned seat. The following conversation took place about the price to be charged for the cushioned seats.

Fiegel: "We can make the necessary modifications to the cushioned seat easily. The raw materials used in your seat are slightly different and should cost about 10% more than those used in our deluxe office stool. However, the labor time should be the same because the seat fabrication operation basically is the same. I would price the seat at our regular rate—full cost plus 30% markup."

Kline: "That's higher that I expected. I was thinking that a good price would be your variable manufacturing costs. After all, your capacity costs will be incurred regardless of this job."

Fiegel: "I'm currently operating at capacity. By making the cushion seats for you, I'll have to cut my production of deluxe office stools. Of course, I can increase my production of economy office stools. The labor time freed by not having to fabricate the frame or assemble the deluxe stool can be shifted to the frame fabrication and assembly of the economy office stool. Fortunately, I can switch my labor force between these two models of stools without any loss of efficiency. As you know, overtime is not a feasible alternative in our company. I'd like to sell it to you at variable cost, but I have excess demand for both products. I don't mind changing my product mix to the economy model if I get a good return on the seats I make for you. Here are my standard costs for the two stools and a schedule of my factory overhead."

Office Division
Standard Costs and Prices

	Deluxe Office Stool	Economy Office Stool
Raw materials:		
Framing	$ 8.15	$ 9.76
Cushioned seat:		
Padding	2.40	
Vinyl	4.00	
Molded seat (purchased).		6.00
Direct labor:		
Frame fabrication (.5 × $7.50/DLH)	3.75	3.75
Cushion fabrication (.5 × $7.50/DLH)	3.75	
Assembly: (.5 × $7.50/DLH)	3.75	
(.3 × $7.50/DLH)		2.25
Factory overhead: (1.5 DLH × $12.80/DLH).	19.20	
(.8 DLH × $12.80/DLH).		10.24
Total standard cost per unit	$45.00	$32.00
Sales price per unit (30% markup).	$58.50	$41.60

Office Division
Factory Overhead Budget

Overhead Item	Nature of Item	Amount
Supplies.	Variable—at current market prices	$　420,000
Indirect labor	Variable	375,000
Supervision	Fixed	250,000
Power.	Variable with activity—rate fixed	180,000

Overhead Item	Nature of Item	Amount
Heat and light	Fixed—light is fixed regardless of production while heat and air conditioning varies with fuel charges	140,000
Property taxes and insurance. . .	Fixed—rate change is unrelated to production activity	200,000
Depreciation	Fixed	1,700,000
Employee benefits.	20% of supervision, direct and indirect labor.	575,000
	Total factory overhead	$3,840,000
	Capacity in DLH	300,000
	Factory overhead rate per DLH.	$12.80

Kline: "I guess I see your point, but I don't want to price myself out of the market. Maybe we should talk to corporate management to see if they can give us any guidance."

Required:

(1) Kline and Fiegel did ask Portco corporate management for guidance on an appropriate transfer price. Corporate management suggested they consider using a transfer price based upon variable manufacturing cost plus opportunity cost. Calculate a transfer price for the cushioned seat based upon variable manufacturing cost plus opportunity cost.

(2) Which alternative transfer price system, full cost, variable manufacturing cost, or variable manufacturing cost plus opportunity cost, would be better as the underlying concept for an intracompany transfer price policy? Explain your answer. (ICMA adpated)

CASES

C25-1. Rate of return on capital employed. Clarkson Company is a large multi-division firm with several plants in each division. Rate of return on capital employed is used to measure the performance of divisions and plants. The asset base for a division consists of all assets assigned to the division, including its working capital, and an allocated share of corporate assets. The asset base for each plant includes the assets assigned to the plant plus an allocated portion of the division and corporate assets. Only limited control over plant assets is exercised at the plant level.

The plant managers exercise control only over the cost portion of the plant profit budget because the divisions are responsible for sales. Even with respect to costs, plant-level control is limited, because of cost decisions made at higher levels and because the division profit budgets include allocated corporate costs, and plant profit budgets include allocated division and corporate costs.

Recommendations for promotions and salary increases for the executives of the divisions and plants are influenced by how well the ac-

tual rate of return on capital employed compares with the budgeted rate.

The Dexter Plant is a major plant in the Huron Division of Clarkson. During 19A, the property adjacent to the Dexter Plant was purchased by Clarkson. This expenditure was not included in the 19A capital expenditure budget. Corporate management decided to divert funds from a project at another plant since the property appeared to be a better long-term investment. This expenditure was added to the Dexter Plant's capital employed.

Also, during 19A, Clarkson Company experienced depressed sales. In an attempt to achieve budgeted profit, corporate management announced in August that all plants were to cut their annual expenses by 6%. In order to accomplish this expense reduction, the Dexter Plant manager reduced preventive maintenance and postponed needed major repairs. Employees who quit were not replaced unless absolutely necessary. Employee training was postponed whenever possible. The raw materials, supplies, and finished goods inventory were reduced below normal levels.

Required:

(1) Is the Clarkson Company's use of rate of return on capital employed to evaluate the performance of the Dexter Plant appropriate? Explain.

(2) Analyze and explain the Dexter Plant Manager's behavior during 19A.

(ICMA adpated)

C25-2. Rate of return on capital employed as measure of division performance. Torres Corporation is a large, multi-division manufacturing company. Each division is viewed as an investment center and has virtually complete autonomy for product development, marketing, and production.

Performance of division managers is evaluated periodically by senior corporate management. Divisional rate of return on capital employed is the sole criterion used in performance evaluation under current corporate policy. Corporate management believes that rate of return on capital employed is an adequate measure because it incorporates quantitative information from the divisional income statement and balance sheet in the analysis.

Some division managers complain that a single criterion for performance evaluation is insufficient and ineffective. These managers have compiled a list of criteria which they believe should be used in evaluating division managers' performance. The criteria include profitability, market position, productivity, product leadership, personnel development, employee attitudes, public responsibility, and balance between short-range and long-range goals.

Required:

(1) Discuss the shortcomings or possible inconsistencies of using rate of return on capital employed as the sole criterion to evaluate divisional management performance.

(2) Discuss the advantages of using multiple performance measures versus a single performance measure in evaluating divisional management performance.

(3) Describe the problems or disadvantages which can be associated with the implementation of a system of multiple performance measures as suggested to Torres Corporation by its division managers.

(ICMA adapted)

C25-3. Rate of return on capital employed versus residual income. Lawton Industries has manufactured prefabricated houses for over 20 years. The houses are constructed in sections to be assembled on customers' lots.

Lawton expanded into the pre-cut housing market in 19A when it acquired Presser Company, one of its suppliers. In this market, various types of lumber are pre-cut into the appropriate lengths, banded into packages, and shipped to customers' lots for assembly. Lawton decided to maintain Presser's separate identity and, thus, established the Presser Division as a profit center of Lawton.

Lawton uses rate of return on capital employed as a performance measure. All investments in operating assets are expected to earn a minimum return of 15% before income taxes. Presser's return has ranged from 19.3% to 22.1% since it was acquired in 19A. Presser had an investment opportunity in 19F that had an estimated return on assets of 16%. Presser's management decided against the investment because it believed the investment would decrease the division's overall rate of return on capital employed.

The 19F operating statement for Presser Division is presented below. The division's operating assets employed were $12,600,000 at the end of 19F, a 5% increase over the 19E year-end balance.

Presser Division
Lawton Industries
Operating Statement
For the Year Ended December 31, 19F
(In Thousands)

Sales revenue		$24,000
Cost of goods sold		15,800
Gross profit		$ 8,200
Less commercial expenses:		
Administrative	$2,140	
Marketing	3,600	5,740
Income from operations before income tax		$ 2,460

Required:

(1) Calculate the following performance measures for 19F for the Presser Division of Lawton Industries:

(a) Rate of return on capital employed.

(b) Residual income calculated on the basis of the average operating assets employed.

(2) Would the management of Presser Division have been more likely to accept the investment opportunity it had in 19F if residual income were used as a performance measure instead of rate of return on capital employed? Explain.

(3) The Presser Division is a separate profit center within Lawton Industries. Identify the items Presser must control if it is to be evaluated fairly by either the rate of return on capital employed or residual income performance measures.

(ICMA adapted)

C25-4. Divisional performance measures. Peregrine Enterprises is a large, diversified corporation with eight operating divisions. Each division is organized as a profit center with each division manager's remuneration augmented by a bonus based on the extent to which the divisional rate of return on capital employed exceeds 20% before taxes, with a ceiling set at 50% of the base salary. J. Black, president of Peregrine, is disturbed by the recent behavior of some of the company's division managers. The Marine Division operates salvage tugs very successfully, but it has come to Black's attention that the division manager recently turned down the opportunity to acquire a nuclear powered tug at a low price from an insolvent competitor. Similarly, the Airline Division manager has steadfastly refused to replace and update the division's fleet of aircraft despite increasing maintenance costs and harassment from federal safety officials. As the last straw, the Plastics Division manager just ignored the opportunity to bid on a very attractive contract although the plant was operating well below capacity during December.

Black did not like to become involved in the internal decision making of the divisions, but in this instance, it appeared necessary. Recently, at the July planning meeting, Black emphasized to the division managers the need for Peregrine to increase its asset base and grow. Such capital additions served as a hedge against continuous inflation. Accordingly, Black instructed the corporate accountant to put together some of the relevant facts on these rejected investments and respective divisional operating performance. The data assembled follow:

Peregrine Enterprises
Division Operating Performance
For Year Ended December 31, 19X
(In Thousands)

	Marine	Airline	Plastics
Sales revenue	$115,000	$ 35,000	$ 89,000
Cost of goods sold	105,300	32,370	78,880
Gross profit	$ 9,700	$ 2,630	$ 10,120
Less commercial expenses:			
Division selling and administration	$ 1,150	$ 395	$ 190
Corporate headquarters allocation	3,450	1,185	570
Total commercial expense	$ 4,600	$ 1,580	$ 760
Divisional profit (before income tax)	$ 5,100	$ 1,050	$ 9,360
Division current assets	$ 1,430	$ 2,748	$ 6,559
Division fixed assets	30,000	20,000	45,000
Less accumulated depreciation	(12,000)	(18,000)	(16,500)
Corporate headquarters allocation	970	252	941
Divisional capital employed	$ 20,400	$ 5,000	$ 36,000
Divisional return on capital employed	25%	21%	26%
Divisional managers' base salaries	$ 60,000	$ 50,000	$ 70,000
Bonus (10% of base salary for each 1% of return in excess of 20%, limited to 50% of base salary)	30,000	5,000	35,000
Total remuneration paid to division managers	$ 90,000	$ 55,000	$105,000

Financial Data on Recent Investments or Contracts
Turned Down by Divisions
(In Thousands)

	Marine	Airline	Plastics
Capital investments:			
Nuclear powered tug	$10,000		
Fleet replacement		$25,000	
Incremental annual revenue	$10,500	$ 4,500	$10,000
Incremental operating cost	7,680	320	8,868
Incremental gross profit	$ 2,820	$ 4,180	$ 1,132
Less incremental commercial expenses:			
Division marketing and administration . . .	$ 105	$ 45	$ 100
Corporate headquarters allocation	315	135	300
Total	$ 420	$ 180	$ 400
Incremental divisional profit	$ 2,400	$ 4,000	$ 732
Return on capital investment	24%	16%	NA

Required:

(1) Make adjustments that would improve the usefulness of the reported operating figures. Use your adjusted figures to re-calculate the rate of return on capital employed. Also, calculate residual income for all three divisions.

(2) Evaluate the operating performance of each of the three divisions and explain the division managers' decisions to reject the investment and contract opportunities.

(3) Discuss whether or not the Airline Division should be sold. Support your conclusion with both quantitative and qualitative analysis.

(4) Discuss whether or not any changes should be made in the management bonus scheme.

(5) Discuss whether or not any changes should be made in the way the divisional performance measures are com-

puted, i.e., the items included in the measures.   CGA-Canada (adapted)
Reprint with permission

C25-5. Transfer pricing. MBR Inc. consists of three divisions which formerly were three independent manufacturing companies. Bader Corporation and Roach Company merged in 19A and the merged corporation acquired Michael Company in 19B. The name of the corporation was subsequently changed to MBR Inc., and each company became a separate division, retaining the name of the original company.

The three divisions have operated as independent entities, each having its own sales force and production facilities. Each division manager is responsible for sales, cost of operations, acquisition and financing of divisional assets, and working capital management. The corporate management of MBR evaluates the performance of the divisions and division managers on the basis of rate of return on capital employed.

Michael Division has just been awarded a contract for a product which uses a component manufactured by the Roach Division as well as by outside suppliers. Michael used a cost figure of $3.80 for the component manufactured by Roach in preparing its bid for the new product, a figure supplied by Roach in response to Michael's request for the average variable cost of the component. It represents the standard variable manufacturing cost and variable marketing expense.

Roach has an active sales force that is continually soliciting new prospects, and its sales price for the component Michael needs is $6.50. Sales of this component are expected to increase; however, the Roach management has indicated that it could supply Michael with the required quantities at the regular sales price less variable marketing expense. Michael's management has responded by offering to pay standard variable manufacturing cost plus 20%.

The two divisions have been unable to agree on a transfer price. Corporate management has never established a transfer price policy because interdivisional transactions have never occurred. As a compromise, the corporate vice-president of finance has suggested a price equal to the standard full manufacturing cost (i.e., no marketing expense) plus a 15% markup. This price has also been rejected by the two division managers, because each considered it grossly unfair.

The unit cost structure for the Roach component and the three suggested prices are as follows:

Regular sales price.........................	$6.50
Standard variable manufacturing cost.........	$3.20
Standard fixed manufacturing cost	1.20
Variable marketing expense.................	.60
	$5.00
Regular sales price less variable marketing expense ($6.50 – $.60)....................	$5.90
Variable manufacturing cost plus 20% ($3.20 × 1.20)..........................	$3.84
Standard full manufacturing cost plus 15% ($4.40 × 1.15)..........................	$5.06

Required:

(1) State the effect of the three proposed prices on the Roach Division's attitude toward intracompany business.
(2) Evaluate the negotiation method for setting the transfer price.
(3) Specify the extent of desired MBR corporate management involvement in setting the transfer price. (ICMA adapted)

C25-6. Transfer pricing. Defco Division of Gunnco Corporation requests of Omar Division, operating at capacity, a supply of Electrical Fitting #1726 that is not available from any other source. Omar Division sells this part to its regular customers for $7.50 each. Defco, operating at 50% capacity, is willing to pay $5 each for this fitting. Defco will put the fitting into a brake unit which it manufactures on essentially a cost basis for a commercial jet plane manufacturer.

Omar Division produces Electrical Fitting #1726 at a variable cost of $4.25. The cost (and sales price) of the brake unit as it is being built by the Defco Division is:

Purchased parts (outside vendors)	$22.50
Omar Electrical Fitting #1726...............	5.00
Other variable costs	14.00
Fixed factory overhead and administrative expenses................................	8.00
Total	$49.50

Defco believes that the price concession is necessary to obtain the job.

Gunnco uses return on investment and dollar profits in measuring division and division manager performance.

Required:

(1) Recommend whether or not the Omar Division should supply Electrical Fitting #1726 to the Defco Division. (Ignore income tax.)
(2) Discuss whether or not it would be to the short-run economic advantage of the Gunnco Corporation for the Omar Division to supply the Defco Division with Electrical Fitting #1726 at $5 each. (Ignore income tax.)
(3) Discuss the organizational and managerial behavior difficulties inherent in this situation and recommend to Gunnco's president how the problem should be handled. (ICMA adapted)

C25-7. Transfer pricing. Lorax Electric Company manufactures a large variety of systems and individual components for the electronics industry. The firm is organized into several divisions, with division managers given the authority to make virtually all operating decisions. Management control over divisional operations is maintained by a system of divisional profit and return on investment measures which are reviewed regularly by executive management. The executive management of Lorax has been quite pleased with the effectiveness of the system they have been using, and believes that it is responsible for the company's improved profitability over the last few years.

The Devices Division manufactures solid-state devices and is operating at capacity. The Systems Division has asked the Devices Division to supply a large quantity of integrated circuit IC378. The Devices Division currently is selling this component to its regular customers at $40 per hundred.

The Systems Division, which is operating at about 60% of capacity, wants this particular component for a digital clock system. It has an opportunity to supply large quantities of these digital clock systems to Centonic Electric, a major producer of clock radios and other popular electronic home entertainment equipment. This opportunity is the first that any of the Lorax divisions have had to do business with Centonic Electric. Centonic Electric has offered to pay $7.50 per clock system.

The Systems Division prepared an analysis of the probable costs to produce the clock systems. The amount that could be paid to the Devices Division for the integrated circuits, five of which are required for each clock system, was determined by working backward from the sales price. The cost estimates employed by the division reflected the highest per unit cost the Systems Division could incur for each cost component and still leave a sufficient margin so that the division's income statement could show reasonable improvement. The cost estimates are summarized below.

Proposed sales price...............		$7.50
Costs excluding required integrated circuits IC378:		
Components purchased from outside suppliers	$2.75	
Circuit-board etching—labor and variable factory overhead	.40	
Assembly, testing, packaging— labor and variable factory overhead	1.35	
Fixed factory overhead allocations .	1.50	
Profit margin	.50	6.50
Amount which can be paid for integrated circuits IC378 (5 @ $20 per hundred)		$1.00

As a result of this analysis, the Systems Division offered the Devices Division a price of $20 per hundred for the integrated circuit. This bid was refused because the manager of the Devices Division felt that the Systems Division should at least meet the price of $40 per hundred which regular customers pay. When the Systems Division found that it could not obtain a comparable integrated circuit from outside vendors, the situation was brought to an arbitration committee which had been set up to review such problems.

The arbitration committee prepared an analysis which showed that $.15 would cover the variable costs of producing the integrated circuit; $.28 would cover the full cost, including fixed factory overhead; and $.35 would provide a gross margin equal to the average gross margin on all of the products sold by the Devices Division. The manager of the Systems Division reacted by stating, "They could sell us that integrated circuit for $.20 and still earn a positive contribution toward profit. In fact, they should be required to sell at their variable cost—$.15—and not be allowed to take advantage of us."

The manager of Devices countered by arguing that, "It doesn't make sense to sell to the Systems Division at $20 per hundred when we can get $40 per hundred outside on all we can produce. In fact, Systems could pay us up to almost $60 per hundred, and they would still have a positive contribution to profit."

The committee recommended that the price be set at $.35 per unit ($35 per hundred) so that Devices could earn a "fair" gross margin. When this price was rejected by both division managers, the problem was brought to the attention of the vice-president of operations.

Required:

(1) What is the immediate economic effect on Lorax Electric Company as a whole if the Devices Division is required to supply IC378 to the Systems Division at $.35 per unit—the price recommended by the arbitration committee? Explain.

(2) Discuss the advisability of intervention by executive management as a solution to transfer pricing disputes between division managers, such as the one experienced by Lorax Electric Company.

(3) Suppose that Lorax adopted a policy requiring that the price to be paid in all internal transfers be equal to the variable cost per unit of the selling division for that product and that the supplying division must sell if the buying division decides to buy the item. Discuss the consequences of adopting such a policy as a way of avoiding the need for the arbitration committee or for intervention by the vice-president.

(ICMA adapted)

INDEX